Management Accounting

FOURTH EDITION

Leslie G. Eldenburg

Albie Brooks

Judy Oliver

Gillian Vesty

Rodney Dormer

Vijaya Murthy

Nicholas Pawsey

Fourth edition published 2020 by
John Wiley & Sons Australia, Ltd
42 McDougall Street, Milton Qld 4064

Typeset in 10/12pt Times LT Std

Wiley
Terry Burkitt (Director, Publishing and Course Development), Mark Levings (Executive Publisher), Kylie Challenor (Senior Manager, Knowledge & Learning Content Management), Jess Carr (Production Editor), Emily Echlin (Publishing Coordinator), Emily Brain (Production Assistant), Renee Bryon (Copyright & Image Research Supervisor), Delia Sala (Cover Design)

Cover image: © Green Color / Shutterstock.com

Typeset in India by diacriTech

Printed in Singapore by
Markono Print Media Pte Ltd

10 9 8 7 6 5 4 3 2 1

BRIEF CONTENTS

CONTENTS

CHAPTER 8

Process costing systems 237

CHAPTER 9

Absorption and variable costing 269

CHAPTER 10

Flexible budgets, standard costs and variance analysis 296

CHAPTER 17

Strategic management control: a lean perspective 546

CHAPTER 18

Responsibility accounting, performance evaluation and transfer pricing 574

CHAPTER 19

The balanced scorecard and strategy maps 607

ABOUT THE AUTHORS

Albie Brooks

Dr Albie Brooks, BCom, DipEd, MBus, PhD, FCPA, is a Senior Teaching Fellow in the Department of Accounting at the University of Melbourne. His teaching is predominantly in the areas of management accounting and managerial control. Albie's teaching experience includes both undergraduate and post-graduate levels in both domestic and international settings. He has a particular interest in creating and developing student engagement in the study of accounting. His research activities relate to teaching and learning, management accounting and corporate governance issues.

Judy Oliver

Dr Judy Oliver, BBus, MBus, PhD, joined Swinburne University in 2008 as a Senior Lecturer in Accounting. Over the past 24 years, she has also held appointments at Victoria University and the University of Tasmania. Judy teaches first-year accounting and management accounting at both the undergraduate and postgraduate levels. Her research interests are in the areas of management accounting control systems and corporate governance. She has published in journals such as the *Australian Accounting Review, International Journal of Quality & Reliability Management* and the *Journal of Accounting & Organizational Change*.

Gillian Vesty

Dr Gillian Vesty, BBus (Acc), MBus (Res), PhD (Melb), CPA, is a Senior Lecturer in Management Accounting. She coordinates an undergraduate management accounting course at RMIT, teaching in campuses in Australia, Singapore, Indonesia and Vietnam. Having spent 20 years in the healthcare sector, Gillian's research interests include public hospital funding models, performance measurement and capital budgeting. Her more recent research focus has been on sustainability management accounting and, together with Albie Brooks, has been developing computer simulations for enhanced student learning.

Rodney Dormer

Dr Rodney Dormer, CA, B.Com (Auck.), MMgt (Well.), PhD (Well.), teaches management accounting and public sector accounting and management at undergraduate and postgraduate levels at Victoria University of Wellington, New Zealand. He has previously held senior financial and operational management positions in both the private and public sectors. His research interests are focused on how information is used to define and direct organisational performance and how, at times, competing perspectives shape that definition.

Vijaya Murthy

Dr Vijaya Murthy, MCom, MPhil, Grad Dipl, CMA, PhD, is a Senior Lecturer of Accounting in the University of Sydney Business School. Prior to this, Vijaya worked for National Australia Bank in various capacities. She started her career as a Lecturer in Accounting in India teaching both management accounting and financial accounting. Currently, Vijaya specialises in teaching management accounting, and has developed management accounting curriculum and coordinated the management and conduct of the Management Accounting Program at undergraduate level. She also teaches management accounting at the postgraduate level. Vijaya is an active researcher in the management accounting field, specifically in relation to the use of non-financial information by managers and management controls.

Nicholas Pawsey

Dr Nicholas Pawsey is a Senior Lecturer in Accounting. Dr Pawsey joined Charles Sturt University, Albury campus in 2016. He has extensive academic experience having previously held the positions of Academic Coordinator for the La Trobe Business School, Wodonga campus, and Lecturer in Accounting at Charles Sturt University, Bathurst.

His research interests include international accounting convergence, water policy and management, public sector accounting, and accounting education and he has published a number of journal articles, book chapters and conference papers in relation to these topics.

PREFACE

Management Accounting, fourth edition, combines the basic technical issues associated with cost management, management accounting and control with more recent and emerging themes and issues. This provides students of cost and management accounting with a more complete picture of the discipline. The text focuses on helping students to learn through the application of cost and management accounting methods to a variety of organisational settings, and by providing a diverse set of student tasks at the end of each chapter.

Hallmark features of the fourth edition include:
- an introduction to the value chain framework in chapter 1 and the use of this framework as a vehicle to explore a range of management accounting issues
- a focus on management accounting information for decision making
- a student-friendly style with the use of diagrams for illustrative purposes and comprehensive examples within and at the end of chapters
- expanded coverage on job, process and absorption costing
- a chapter focused specifically on sustainability management accounting that is also linked to other chapters in the text.

The authors would like to thank Dr Kenneth Ke from Curtin University for producing the PowerPoints for the new edition, and Dr Jayce Naidoo from Victoria University for updating the test bank.

Chapter focus

Part 1 Management accounting and cost management

Chapter 1 The role of accounting information in management decision making

Chapter 1 provides an overview of organisational decision making and introduces students to the use of management accounting information in decision making. A brief history of management accounting is provided, along with discussion of the emerging Uber-style value networks and key influences on management accounting system designs. Techniques for identifying and using relevant information are reviewed. A model for developing higher quality decisions is introduced. We then provide an introduction to some key terms and detail the value chain as a framework for consideration of a range of management accounting issues.

Chapter 2 Cost concepts, behaviour and estimation

We first review accounting terms that relate to cost behaviour and explain the cost function. At this point we also discuss limitations of the information produced by cost functions and problems with uncertainties and bias in developing cost functions. This focus allows students to consider the quality of information as they learn cost accounting methods. We present and illustrate cost estimation techniques that are used to describe cost behaviour (engineered estimates, analysis at the account level, the two-point method and regression analysis). Scatterplots and regression analysis are introduced as a way to provide additional information about cost behaviour. Linear and nonlinear (for example, learning curve) cost functions are presented.

Chapter 3 A costing framework and cost allocation

In this chapter we first explore the concepts of cost objects, and direct and indirect costs. We then outline a costing framework and use this framework to explore cost allocation issues with a particular focus on service entity settings. We then use the costing framework in a support department setting by exploring the direct, step-down, and reciprocal methods of allocation. Finally, we discuss some of the limitations, or risks, of allocated cost information.

Chapter 4 Cost–volume–profit (CVP) analysis

We first highlight the meaning of cost–volume–profit analysis and its importance in decision making. Then, single and multiple product examples are used to explore the development and use of CVP information, before and after taxes. The margin of safety and operating leverage are introduced and used to analyse risk of operations. Examples show the use of CVP information for both decision-making and monitoring purposes. Examples of spreadsheets with input sections and cell referencing are introduced in the appendix so that students can easily perform sensitivity analysis. Additional information is provided on the use of spreadsheets in performing CVP analysis.

Chapter 5 Planning — budgeting and behaviour

This chapter emphasises the strategic nature of planning and budgeting through a consideration of planning mechanisms to test alternative courses of action (strategic budgeting), planning issues in cost centres and contemporary approaches to budgeting, including the re-invigoration of zero-base budgeting to reign in corporate excesses. Other techniques such as program budgeting and Beyond Budgeting principles are discussed. The dysfunctional and behavioural implications of budgeting are highlighted.

Chapter 6 Operational budgets

Budgeting issues are explored as a tool for both short-term and long-term planning. We outline the role of the master budget and demonstrate the compilation of key components of the master budget. We then describe and illustrate the role of the cash budget, followed by the use of budgets as performance benchmarks through the application of static and flexible budgets.

Chapter 7 Job costing systems

Chapter 7 introduces job costing as it relates to the financial reporting process. The first part of the chapter demonstrates the flow of costs through the manufacturing process and calculates the inventoriable product cost for customised products. Actual versus normal job costing methods are compared, and calculations for over and underapplied overhead are explained. We also include a discussion of the costs of spoilage, rework and scrap in job costing, describing opportunity costs that arise from poor quality. Behavioural implications of the accounting methods used to record spoilage are explored.

Chapter 8 Process costing systems

Chapter 8 presents process costing methods using FIFO and weighted average. We develop a single format that is used to calculate equivalent units for both the FIFO and weighted average methods and help students understand the difference between the two methods. In addition, accounting methods for the spoilage, rework and scrap that arise in mass production are illustrated. Finally, we explore the uses and limitations of process cost information.

Chapter 9 Absorption and variable costing

Absorption and variable income statements are compared and contrasted in this chapter. Factors that affect the choice of fixed overhead allocation rate volume measures (theoretical, practical, normal and budgeted) are explored. The uses and limitations of information produced by these three income statements are discussed. Several examples and problems address the incentives under absorption costing of inventory buildup to improve the current period's income.

Chapter 10 Flexible budgets, standard costs and variance analysis

The development and use of direct and overhead cost standards and variances are presented in this chapter. We explore how standards are established and how variances are calculated and then analysed. The use of standards allows the 'flexing' of the static budget to enable actual performance to be assessed against a budget for the actual level of activity.

Chapter 11 Variance analysis: revenue and cost

This chapter further explores the revenue and cost variances introduced in chapter 8. The variances are further broken down to provide more insight into the variance, whether this is due to market conditions or operating processes. To further explore the variances between actual sales and budgeted sales, the revenue variances are further broken down into market size, market share and product mix variances. The focus on operating activities is seen in the analysis of the direct cost and overhead cost variances into price and efficiency components.

Chapter 12 Activity analysis: costing and management

Activity analysis for costing and management are introduced in this chapter. As a costing tool, comparisons are drawn between activity-based costing (ABC) derived costs and conventionally derived costs. We introduce the ABC cost hierarchy and explore the benefits, cost and limitations of ABC and activity-based management. With a focus on more recent developments in costing, we illustrate time-driven ABC. We use both service-entity and manufacturing settings within the chapter.

Chapter 13 Relevant costs for decision making

Non-routine decisions such as special order, make or buy, keep or drop, product emphasis and maximising constrained resources are covered in the first half of this chapter. As the chapter progresses, we consider the impact of uncertainties and limitations of non-routine operating decisions as well as information quality issues. The second half of the chapter discusses and illustrates issues associated with joint costing using physical volume, sales at the split-off point, net realisable value and constant gross margin NRV methods.

Part 2 Management accounting, extending performance measurement and strategy

Chapter 14 Strategy and control

This chapter introduces and reinforces the links between strategy and the management accounting/control system. We explore management accounting in a 'flat' world, and a number of existing frameworks of strategy and control including those proposed by Otley (1999), Simons's (1995) levers of control framework, Kaplan and Norton's (2008) strategy map framework, Ittner and Larcker's (2001) value-based management framework and Flamholtz's (1996) control system framework. These provide alternative ways of viewing the strategy and control relationship. We conclude the chapter with a discussion of management responsibility and accountability practices.

Chapter 15 Capital budgeting and strategic investment decisions

Net present value analysis, internal rate of return and other capital budgeting techniques (payback and accounting rate of return) are described and compared and contrasted in this chapter. These are explored in the context of a process for addressing capital budgeting decisions. Examples with increasing complexity develop capital budgeting with income taxes. Uncertainties, sensitivity analysis and bias in capital budget information are emphasised in this chapter. The chapter also explores strategic considerations for capital investment decisions which impact traditional models for capital investment decisions. Inflation effects are considered in the appendix using both the real rate and nominal rate methods.

Chapter 16 The strategic management of costs and revenues

Chapter 14 explores a range of issues relating to the strategic management of costs and revenues, including value chain analysis and continual cost improvement, customer profitability analysis, target costing and kaizen costing, life cycle costing, alternative pricing methods and revenue variance analysis. Each of these is explored as tools to achieve longer-term efficiency gains and profitability improvement.

Chapter 17 Strategic management control: a lean perspective

The focus of this chapter is the concept of lean accounting, which is explored in some detail. Other topics explored in the chapter include the theory of constraints, total quality management (TQM) and costs of quality, and issues associated with just-in-time manufacturing (JIT). Overall the focus is on practices that utilise forward-looking techniques to reduce inventories, streamline processes and eliminate waste.

Chapter 18 Responsibility accounting, performance evaluation and transfer pricing

In this chapter, we initially explore issues associated with responsibility accounting and responsibility centre classification. We then explore the use of income-based performance measures and compare use of return-on-investment (ROI), residual income (RI) and economic value added (EVA) as key financial performance measures at the investment centre level. Transfer pricing issues are then addressed through a consideration and comparison of different transfer pricing methods.

Chapter 19 The balanced scorecard and strategy maps

This chapter firstly emphasises the role of strategy maps, particularly to operationalise strategy and as a tool to inform the development of balanced scorecards. The balanced scorecard is then introduced as a method that can be used to combine financial and non-financial performance measures to gauge progress and motivate employees. The strengths and weaknesses of the balanced scorecard are discussed, including uncertainties about the best choice of measures, mistakes in implementation and the effects of bias on performance measure choices.

Chapter 20 Rewards, incentives and risk management

We commence this chapter with a discussion of the relevance of agency theory to reward systems and incentives. We then focus on a range of issues associated with the incentive component of reward systems, including the key components of incentive plans, the advantages and disadvantages of cash and equity as key components of incentive plans, and how compensation is used to motivate performance. We then explore a number of emerging themes with respect to reward systems, including relative performance evaluation, pay-for-performance and the impact of government and regulatory authorities. The chapter concludes with an explanation of risk management and the role of performance measurement and incentives in risk management.

Chapter 21 Sustainability management accounting

Chapter 21 emphasises the relevance of strategic management accounting for a sustainability culture. The emerging and very real global sustainability landscape has increased the scrutiny on organisational, environmental and social practices. In this chapter, examples of how sustainability management accounting can provide managers with strategically relevant information for sustainability performance reporting and management decision making are provided. The aim is to increase student awareness of the global sustainability paradigm and the role that sustainability management accounting can play.

Chapter features

Management Accounting, fourth edition, uses a number of pedagogical features and a common structure in each chapter to enhance teaching and learning. Each chapter contains:
- a brief introduction and set of learning objectives, which also serve as the basis of the chapter summary at the end of each chapter
- the use of illustrative examples within each chapter, with most containing one or more comprehensive examples
- a chapter summary at the end of each chapter
- self-study problems with suggested solution outlines for students to check their progress and understanding
- graded tasks at the end of each chapter, classified into discussion questions, exercises and problems.

MANAGEMENT ACCOUNTING AND COST MANAGEMENT

In part 1 of this text we introduce a range of management accounting/control techniques and practices, with an emphasis on cost-related techniques. The content of the chapters in part 1 comprises the foundation of any management accounting system in an organisation. Following an introduction to the value chain as a framework for management accounting in chapter 1, subsequent chapters explore a range of cost-related techniques. In part 2, we extend our coverage to a range of broader management accounting/control practices.

CHAPTER 1

The role of accounting information in management decision making

LEARNING OBJECTIVES

After studying this chapter, you should be able to:

1.1 recognise the types of decisions managers make for an organisation

1.2 discuss the role of cost and management accounting information in management decision making

1.3 communicate how managers can make higher-quality decisions using accounting information

1.4 describe the value chain framework and its applications in management accounting.

IN BRIEF

Managers use cost and management accounting information to help them make different types of decisions. These include developing organisational strategies, creating operating plans, and monitoring and motivating organisational performance. Higher-quality decisions are achieved by using higher-quality relevant information and decision-making practices. The value chain provides us with a suitable framework from which to explore a range of management decisions as well as a framework for many of the issues raised in the remainder of the text.

1.1 Management decision making

LEARNING OBJECTIVE 1.1 Recognise the types of decisions managers make for an organisation.

People at different levels within an entity continually make many different kinds of decisions. These range from long-term decisions, such as which markets and customers the organisation will pursue, to detailed operational and short-term decisions, such as how to respond to specific customer enquiries on a day-to-day basis. Figure 1.1 presents an overview of the decisions that managers make in organisations. It also suggests the role that information systems have in measuring, monitoring and motivating performance. We will briefly discuss each of the components illustrated in figure 1.1.

| FIGURE 1.1 | Overview of management decision making |

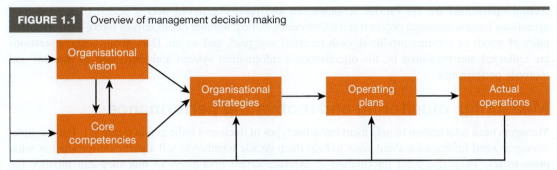

Organisational vision

The most far-reaching decision managers make is to identify and shape the organisation's vision. The **organisational vision** is the core purpose and ideology of the entity, which guides the entity's overall direction and approaches toward its various stakeholder groups. Stakeholder groups include shareholders, owners, employees, customers, suppliers, lenders, local communities and the broader society. Organisational success increases when employees understand the organisational vision and work collectively to achieve it. To clarify and communicate the vision to employees and other stakeholders, managers sometimes divide the vision into one or more written statements. The definitions of these statements vary from entity to entity. In general, a vision statement is a theoretical description of what the organisation should become. A mission statement is a high-level declaration of the organisation's purpose. A core values statement is a summary of the beliefs that define the organisation's culture. Some managers also publish codes of conduct or statements describing the organisation's social or environmental responsibilities. Of course, what is really important is that the beliefs and values underpin managerial action and are 'lived' rather than just being written in documents.

Organisational core competencies

Organisational core competencies are the entity's strengths relative to competitors. The organisational vision and core competencies are closely related. To create value for stakeholders, an organisation must have strengths relative to competitors. The vision should build on existing and achievable strengths. Of course, these core competencies need to be revisited from time to time as both the internal and external environments change.

Organisational strategies

Organisational strategies are the tactics that managers use to take advantage of core competencies while working towards the organisational vision. Although the term **strategies** can mean different things to different people and organisations, it commonly relates to providing direction and guiding long-term decisions. To monitor strategic progress, managers establish and monitor long-term goals such as market leadership or high-quality customer service.

Broad-based organisational strategies are commonly classified as:
• low cost, where the emphasis is on competing on cost
• product differentiation, where the emphasis is on competing on points of difference such as quality of service or product attributes.

The strategy of the organisation is a key influence on the structure and nature of the organisation's information system and, in turn, the management accounting and control system.

Operating plans

Operating plans involve specific short-term decisions that shape the organisation's day-to-day activities such as drawing cash from a bank line of credit, hiring an employee or ordering materials. Operating plans often include specific performance objectives such as budgeted revenues and costs.

Actual operations

Actual operations are the various actions taken and results achieved over a period of time. Actual operations include customer orders received, revenues earned, number of employees hired, costs incurred, units of goods or services produced, cash received and paid, and so on. Data about actual operations are collected and measured by the organisation's information system and then used to monitor and motivate performance.

Measuring, monitoring and motivating performance

Managers need information to help them make the types of decisions indicated in figure 1.1. For example, managers need information about costs to help them decide whether to sell a particular product or what price to set. They also need information to measure actual operations so that they can monitor the success of their decisions and motivate employees to work towards the organisational vision. Decisions are monitored by comparing actual operating results to plans (such as budgets) and to long-term goals. Desirable employee behaviour is often motivated by tying employee performance evaluation and pay to long-term or short-term results. An organisation's information system can be designed to measure and report information used for decision making as well as for monitoring and motivating.

While organisational information systems will commonly have a number of components, with each focusing on specific support (for example, human resources information, technology information, marketing information, production information and accounting-related information), our focus in this text is on the role of cost and management accounting information.

We will revisit a number of these issues in chapter 14, which introduces the second part of the text.

1.2 Cost and management accounting for decision making

LEARNING OBJECTIVE 1.2 Discuss the role of cost and management accounting information in management decision making.

Cost accounting information is used for both management and financial accounting activities. The Institute of Management Accountants (IMA) defines **cost accounting** as 'a technique or method for determining the cost of a project, process, or thing'.[1] Cost accounting is commonly regarded as the precursor to the more recently developed term *management accounting*, which has a somewhat broader perspective.

Cost accounting information often serves as an input into broader management accounting and financial accounting systems. In this way, cost accounting is often viewed as a subset of management accounting in particular, and financial accounting to a limited extent. **Management accounting** is the process of gathering, summarising and reporting financial and non-financial information used internally by managers to make decisions. An example of cost accounting information that is also management accounting information is a breakdown of customer service costs by both product line and average cost per customer service call. **Financial accounting** is the process of preparing and reporting financial information used most frequently by decision makers outside of the entity, such as shareholders and creditors. An example of cost accounting information that is also financial accounting information is the valuation of ending inventory shown on the statement of financial position (also called the balance sheet).

Managers use many types of information to help them make decisions. Information can be gathered formally or informally. Formal methods include point-of-service optical character readers, such as those used when customers purchase merchandise at retail stores. Such systems track inventory levels, geographic distribution of sales, trends, the relationship between prices and sales, and so on. Informal methods are also important for collecting information from inside or outside the organisation.

For example, individuals inside a company often gather product pricing information by reading industry trade journals or examining competitors' websites.

Most organisations have many databases that contain information collected formally or informally from internal or external sources. Access to database information is often restricted to specific individuals. In addition, much valuable information is not readily accessible because it is held in the minds of employees. This information, called *intellectual capital*, is not formally captured by the information system. Thus, it is difficult for decision makers, even within an organisation, to gain access to all of the information they might wish to use. It is easy to argue that managers should obtain more and better information to help them make decisions. However, the benefit must exceed the cost of generating the information.

To facilitate internal decision making (often a role for management accounting) and meet external reporting requirements (a key role of financial accounting), accounting departments within organisations use software to generate a variety of internal and external reports that summarise or highlight information. An **internal report** is a document that presents information for use only inside an organisation. An **external report** is a document that presents information predominantly for use outside an organisation. Figure 1.2 summarises common types of internal and external reports.

FIGURE 1.2 Examples of internal and external reports

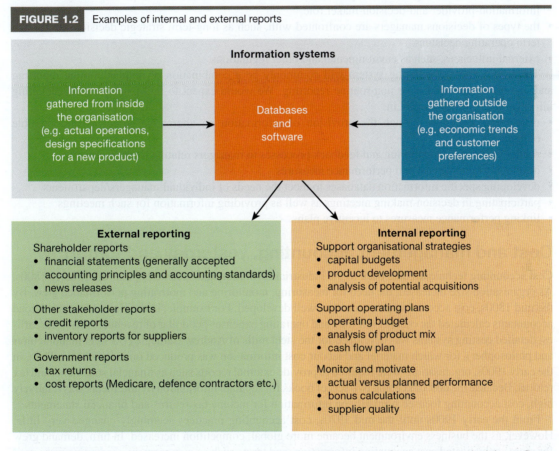

Internal reports are designed to provide information for a variety of management decisions. Some internal reports, such as monthly sales summaries, are issued regularly. Other internal reports, such as the analysis of a potential business acquisition, are generated for one-time use and commonly serve a special purpose.

External reports can be distributed to different constituencies for many purposes. Some external reports, such as income tax returns, are mandatory. Others are discretionary, such as a news release about a joint venture agreement.

Although reports are developed for a specific audience, they may be used for other purposes. For example, internal reports such as quarterly sales data can be shared with people outside the organisation. Similarly, external reports such as financial statements are sometimes used within the organisation. In addition, organisations use reports prepared outside the organisation (for example, by consultants or vendors) for internal decision making. With increasing demands for information both internally and externally, some might argue that the differences between internal and external information are becoming increasing blurred.

Key influences on management accounting system structure

Like any system, the management accounting system requires input, processing and output stages. The management accounting system is likely to be linked to the financial accounting system (as outlined earlier) but will commonly also have its own domain and reporting mechanisms to meet the needs of managers. While any management accounting system will comprise a number of components (such as costing, performance measurement and evaluation, and budgeting), some of the key influences on the nature of the management accounting system might include:

- organisational structure, which relates to such things as the level of centralisation versus decentralisation and how hierarchical or flat the structure is
- the availability of information technology and the use of that technology as part of the information system interface
- organisational strategies, such as the use of a low-cost strategy or differentiation strategy
- culture and organisational vision
- how the management accounting role is viewed within the organisation, which relates to whether management accounting assumes a proactive or reactive role, an information-provider-only role or an information-provider-and-decision-maker role
- the types of decisions managers are confronted with, such as long-term strategic decisions and short-term operating decisions
- external influences, such as environmental and other regulations.

The management accounting system will commonly be a combination of regular, routine reporting and one-off special studies or non-routine reporting. We would expect to find management accounting information performing a role in:

- developing strategies through the provision of information on alternative strategies and possible outcomes
- routine measuring, monitoring and feedback processes to managers relating to operations
- developing suitable cost and performance measures
- developing specific information databases to meet the needs of individual managers/departments
- participating in decision-making meetings as well as providing information for such meetings
- linking performance measures to incentive plans.

Cost and management accounting, yesterday and tomorrow

Cost accounting techniques date back to the industrial revolution and became popular in the early 1800s. As organisation size increased, the need for measuring, monitoring and motivating performance grew. By the mid 1800s, cost accounting practices were well developed. For example, in the United States, railroad accountants calculated the cost per ton-mile and operating expenses per dollar of revenue. One of the earliest detailed costing systems was developed for the steel mills of Andrew Carnegie (US steel manufacturer and philosopher), for which material and labour cost information was produced on a daily basis. Then, in the early 1900s, organisations were required to provide external reports such as financial statements and tax returns. Because the cost of keeping two sets of books for separate information requirements was relatively high, cost accounting focused primarily on information for income tax returns and financial statements.

From the early 1900s until the mid 1970s, cost accounting practices seemingly changed very little. However, as the business environment became more global, competition increased. In turn, demand grew for more sophisticated cost accounting information, and terms such as *management accounting* were used to encapsulate the range of activities now undertaken. Recent technological innovation has enabled cost accountants to develop previously infeasible cost and management accounting systems. Today, cost and accounting information is used for a variety of purposes, including internal decision making, measuring and monitoring performance at all levels of the organisation, and aligning employee and stakeholder goals. Furthermore, managers now use cost accounting information to analyse the profitability of customers and to coordinate transactions with suppliers — extending traditional cost accounting beyond the organisation's boundaries.

As organisations continue to change and adapt to their environment, management accounting will similarly need to adapt to the changing organisational environment. This is critical if management accounting as a function, and management accountants as professionals, are to continue to add value to their organisations. For example, there is an increasing demand for organisations to measure and monitor their environmental performance such as measuring carbon footprints. Management accounting and control has an important role to play within organisations for environmental performance and will be explained in depth in chapter 21. Throughout this text we explore a range of management accounting techniques, tools and practices relevant to organisations. Some of these techniques, tools and practices have been around for a long time (such as standard costing, cost–volume–profit analysis and capital budgeting), while others are more recent developments (such as the balanced scorecard, activity-based costing and sustainability management accounting). Further developments in management accounting tools will undoubtedly surface. Ultimately, the challenge for management accountants and the management accounting function is to ensure that the organisational decision-making needs are appropriately matched with the available management techniques, tools and practices.

The detail and quality of organisational data have improved in recent years. Historically, organisations used one accounting system that focused on conformance to generally accepted accounting principles, which were used for both external and internal reporting. This type of information was not always ideal for management decision making. More recently, enterprise-wide systems such as enterprise resource planning (ERP) and systems applications and products (SAP) systems have better combined financial and management accounting information. However, even with the availability of these ERP and specific-purpose management accounting tools, the organisation of the twenty-first century faces significant risks. The management of these risks is critical. Moreover, even the availability of high-quality information systems does not guarantee success. The global financial crisis of 2008–09, in which we witnessed the collapse or bailout of major banks and corporations around the world, is a reminder of the need to continually develop suitable decision-making systems and for organisations to be vigilant in their application.

Recent information system developments have focused on business intelligence and disruptive technologies and innovation. The internet and business intelligence software provide opportunities for managers to save costs and improve profitability in the following ways:
- integrating systems:
  - throughout an organisation
  - between an organisation and its customers and suppliers
- improving management of:
  - customer relationships
  - supply chains
  - work teams within an organisation
- disruptive purposes:
  - new start-up internet companies with innovative profit offerings
  - disrupting established markets and changing traditional roles for individuals.

We should make some distinction between management accountants as professionals within organisations and the management accounting function. Most organisations will have a management accounting function in one form or another. Even start-up internet companies would draw on a management accounting function. In some organisations, this function might be performed by a variety of differently qualified and trained staff such as accountants (financial or management), costing clerks, engineers, and other staff with management training or experience. In some cases, the label *management accountant* might not even be used, but the management accounting work is still performed as a function. More often, though, the label *management accountant*, or some similar label such as *resource analyst* or *internal management consultant*, might be used. Whatever the terminology adopted, the management accounting function needs to be performed. Much of this text relates to the techniques, tools and practices that commonly comprise the management accounting function.

Relevant information for decision making

A key focus of management accounting is the provision of information for decision making. This requires the ability to distinguish between information that is relevant to a decision and information that is not. **Relevant information** helps the decision maker to evaluate and choose among alternative courses of action. Relevant information concerns the future and varies with the action taken. On the other hand, **irrelevant information** does not vary with the action taken and therefore is not useful for decision making. Although the information may be accurate, it simply does not help the decision maker evaluate the alternatives. Managers are less efficient and make lower-quality decisions when they allow irrelevant information to inappropriately influence their choices.

Whether a given type of information is relevant or irrelevant depends on the decision and other factors. Suppose a student is deciding whether to sign up for a particular university course. If the student has selected a degree program and wishes to graduate as quickly as possible, relevant information includes whether the course counts towards graduation. However, if the student's goal is to take courses in a variety of disciplines to explore possible degree programs, then it might be irrelevant whether the course will help meet graduation requirements.

Throughout the text we will encounter a range of different types of decisions that require the identification of relevant information. For example, the concept of relevant costs is explored in a decision context in chapter 13, while the use of relevant cash flows is explored in chapter 15. Identifying relevant information is a useful skill that requires practice, and we will work on developing this skill throughout this text. We will also encounter different treatments of cost data in decision-making contexts. This is often referred to as *different cost for different purposes*, meaning the decision at hand and the nature of the cost object determine the cost data required and how such data might be used.

1.3 Management accounting information and the quality of decision making

LEARNING OBJECTIVE 1.3 Communicate how managers can make higher-quality decisions using accounting information.

Management accounting information is commonly used in decision making, and this raises two issues: (1) the quality and relevance of the management accounting information; and (2) the quality of the decision-making processes in use within the organisation. Higher-quality decisions result from better information as well as from better decision processes. Organisations often use complex and sophisticated information systems to gather and organise information for decision making. Because of this sophistication, some decision makers are mistakenly confident that the information they use is correct, and they ignore uncertainty. Other decision makers, recognising that uncertainties always cloud decisions, go to the other extreme: instead of relying on imperfect information, they use only their intuition to make important business decisions. Neither of these approaches is optimal. Figure 1.3 summarises the path to higher-quality decisions.

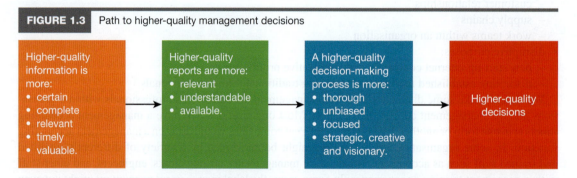

FIGURE 1.3 Path to higher-quality management decisions

Higher-quality information will generally have fewer uncertainties if it is based on viable assumptions. Nonetheless, it is still imperfect and may be in various forms, including financial and non-financial information. It should be complete, timely and directly relevant to the decision. Also, we cannot always operate in the ideal decision-making environment. Managers may confront decisions where information lacks certainty or completeness. In these circumstances, the decision context may be governed by the organisation's attitude to risks. Two issues are worthy of specific mention here.

First, decision-useful information needs to have considered the impact of any opportunity costs on the decision and the associated risks. **Opportunity costs** are the benefits forgone when we choose one alternative over the next best alternative. Although such costs might be more difficult to quantify, they still need to be considered when evaluating alternative courses of action.

Second, the benefits derived from the information collected to support the decision-making process need to exceed the cost of collection. (The evaluation of such costs and benefits is commonly referred to as **cost–benefit analysis**.) This is particularly important when trying to make the information systems more complex, for example, in order to improve the reliability of product cost data. The extra precision derived from the increased complexity needs to warrant the cost of changes to the system.

1.4 Value chain analysis: a framework for management accounting

LEARNING OBJECTIVE 1.4 Describe the value chain framework and its applications in management accounting.

In the mid 1980s, Harvard Professor Michael Porter introduced the idea of the generic **value chain**. A value chain can be described as the key activities engaged in by the organisation or industry. We can view the value chain on two levels: at the industry level, and at the (more common) organisational level.

At the industry level, the value chain comprises the key industry components based on the key activities within the industry. Figure 1.4 shows a sample industry-based value chain for the wine industry. Particular organisations may choose to participate in the entire industry, in only part of the industry (for example, as a vineyard operator such as competitor B), or across most of the value chain (which would make it a vertically integrated entity such as competitor A).

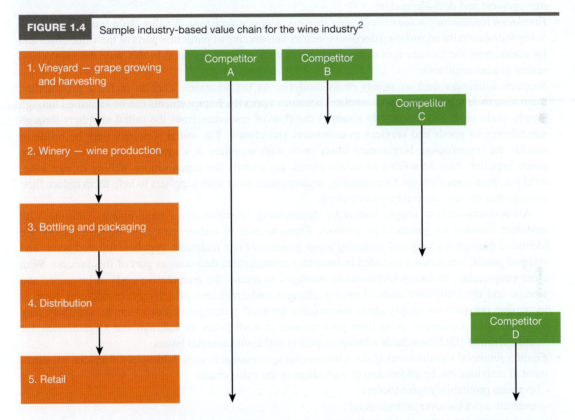

FIGURE 1.4 Sample industry-based value chain for the wine industry[2]

The value chain at the organisational level is the more common view of the value chain. The organisational value chain is usually viewed as a combination of key and support activities. The value chain provides a suitable framework for considering a range of management accounting issues. The value chain:

- *Focuses on activities.* The central feature of the value chain is its focus on *activities and processes* rather than functions or departments. This makes identification of improvements across segments more likely.
- *Encourages a broader organisational view.* This is particularly so for management accounting staff and business unit managers. Management accounting staff are more likely to take a broader perspective if using a value chain framework when considering the consequences of decisions. With production activity as the central focus, we often talk of a consideration of upstream activities such as research and development, design and supply activities; and downstream activities such as warehousing, delivery and customer support.
- *Breaks down more traditional representations of organisational activity.* A value chain framework encourages higher levels of cross-fertilisation and communication between business segments, so that decisions are not confined by the traditional boundaries of functional areas.
- *Externalises thinking by incorporating suppliers and customers.* An organisation's value chain encompasses not only customers and suppliers, but in some cases extends to the customers' customers and the suppliers' suppliers. Analysis of the value chain leads to improved relationships between the

organisation and others in the value chain, creating an extended organisation that can flexibly respond to dynamic and competitive environments. In other words, value chains explicitly recognise that no organisation operates in isolation from suppliers and customers.

- *Reflects value chain relationships in terms of costs.* Costs are transferred in every value-added activity. The end users (consumers) ultimately pay for the profit margins made throughout the value chain. The costs are calculated as cost of sales plus period costs (all other expenses incurred through the value chain).
- *Reinforces other initiatives such as activity-based costing (ABC).* With the focus on activities, a value chain framework provides a sound foundation for exploring activity-based costing (which is covered in chapter 12). ABC uses activities as the foundation of product and service costing. In this sense, activities are the fundamental cost object. We will explore cost objects and cost drivers in the next section. Moreover, a value chain framework complements other recent initiatives such as strategic cost management, which refers to the simultaneous focus on reducing costs and strengthening an organisation's strategic position.[3] This commonly involves taking a longer-term view of cost management and decision making.
- *Provides a foundation for outsourcing and strategic alliance decisions.* A value chain framework serves as the foundation for considering decisions such as outsourcing of particular parts of the value chain and for considering the formation of strategic alliances with, say, a distributor. In this way, the value chain serves as a strategic tool.
- *Supports initiatives such as supply chain analysis.* As organisations work to increase profitability, improving their relationships with suppliers becomes a priority. Improvements can be identified through supply chain analysis. The **supply chain** is the flow of resources from the initial suppliers through the delivery of goods and services to customers and clients. The initial suppliers may be inside or outside the organisation. Negotiating lower costs with suppliers is a straightforward way to reduce costs. Suppliers may be willing to reduce prices, particularly for organisations willing to sign long-term purchase commitments. Occasionally, organisations work with suppliers to help them reduce their costs so that the savings can be passed along.

  Accountants analyse supply chains by determining inventory level requirements, starting with customer demand for products or services. Opportunities to reduce cost and improve quality are identified through tracking and analysing usage patterns of raw materials, supplies, finished goods and shipped goods. Vendors are included in inventory management decisions as part of this process. With close cooperation, inventory levels can be managed to reduce the quantitative costs of insurance and storage and the qualitative costs of quality changes and timeliness of delivery. In addition, there is increasing pressure for supply chain information from all participants. For example, suppliers may be credited by customers as to their performance in such areas as International Organization for Standardization (ISO) Standards relating to quality and environmental issues.
- *Enables financial measurement of downstream and upstream activities.* Ultimately, financial measurement of activities can be undertaken at each stage of the value chain:
  - evaluate profitability (profit/sales)
  - evaluate asset turnover (sales/assets)
  - evaluate returns on assets (income/assets).
- *Categorises activities as value-added and non-value-added.* Value chain analysis involves studying each step in the business process to determine whether some activities can be eliminated because they do not add value. This analysis extends to suppliers and customers, and includes shared planning, inventory, human resources, information technology systems, and even corporate cultures. Eventually, the analysis leads to business decisions for improving value.

Before activities in the value chain can be improved or eliminated, they must be identified and then categorised as value-added or non-value-added. A **value-added activity** is one that is necessary and that the customer/client is prepared to pay for, while a **non-value-added activity** is one that is wasteful (unnecessary) and that the customer/client would not normally be prepared to pay for. Some organisations use four categories, recognising both that it may be possible to improve value-added activities and that time may be needed to eliminate non-value-added activities. Figure 1.5 provides a sample value chain showing the key components.

FIGURE 1.5   Sample organisational value chain for a winery

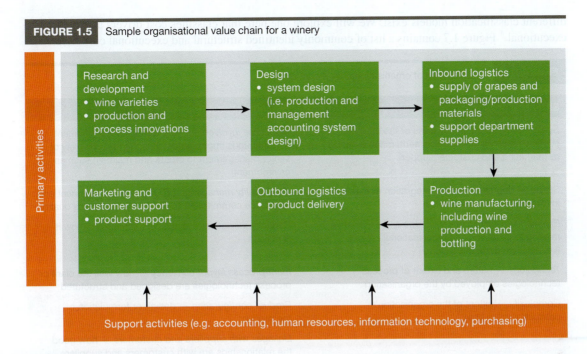

Figure 1.6 presents these four categories with examples of actions that managers could take to improve value. The process of analysing and categorising activities also improves communication, as individuals in each part of the process begin to share their abilities, needs and requirements with others in the value chain.

FIGURE 1.6   Classification of value-added and non-value-added activities

Activity classification	Action to improve value
A necessary activity that cannot be improved upon at this time	None
A necessary activity that could be changed to improve the process	Modify the process to improve value *Example:* Plant layout could be changed so that materials handling activities are reduced.
An unnecessary activity that can eventually be eliminated by changing the process	Eventually eliminate the unnecessary activity *Example:* Eliminate manual recording of employee hours using time cards. A new payroll system is eventually implemented. Plastic identity cards with magnetic strips are swiped through time clocks. The system electronically tracks hours worked and processes wages and salaries.
An unnecessary activity that can quickly be eliminated by changing the process	Immediately eliminate the unnecessary activity *Example:* In team manufacturing, inspection of units completed can be eliminated if each team member inspects each unit before it passes to the next team member.

Cost objects and cost drivers

Throughout this text, a range of new terms and their meanings as they relate to management accounting and decision making will be introduced. Two concepts that are relatively fundamental to much of the text are cost objects and cost drivers. A **cost object** is a thing or activity for which we measure costs. For example, it might be a product or service, a production activity, a customer, a project — or even the entire organisation. A knowledge of the costs of these cost objects can serve a range of different purposes, many of which we will explore throughout the text. **Cost drivers** are the inputs or activities that cause changes in the total cost of a cost object, and they can be defined according to the level within the organisation that is our point of interest. We will explore the role of cost drivers in cost allocation and product/service cost determination later. For now, our attention is on cost drivers at the organisational level. A number of different classification models exist. We will explore one here that classifies cost drivers as structural or executional.[4] Figure 1.7 contains a list of commonly identified structural and executional cost drivers.

FIGURE 1.7 Classification of organisational-level cost drivers[5]

Structural cost drivers	Executional cost drivers
Scale — investment in key parts of the business such as research and development, manufacturing or marketing and customer support	*Workforce involvement* — a workforce commitment to continuous improvement (it is the responsibility of senior management to create and maintain such an environment)
Scope — degree of vertical integration or extent of involvement in the value chain	*Total quality management (TQM)* — a management and workforce commitment to product and process quality
Experience — levels of knowledge and experience relating to initiatives and organisational actions (i.e. have we done this before?)	*Capacity utilisation* — available capacity and how it is utilised
Technology — nature and extent of process technologies employed by the organisation	*Plant/process layout efficiency* — how well the plant or process technologies are designed and structured
Complexity — extent of the organisation's product/ service line	*Product configuration* — design or formulation of the product
	Linkages with suppliers and customers — how good the relationships are with customers and suppliers

Structural cost drivers are those that relate to the underlying economic structure of the organisation. Commonly, the status of each cost driver is determined by decisions taken by senior management, and each is likely to have a significant effect on organisational costs. Executional cost drivers relate to the ability of the organisation to do what it does successfully. For executional cost drivers, more is usually better — for example, the greater the level of workforce involvement, the better.

The value chain and organisational structure

Organisations may be structured in many ways, depending on their strategies and the goods or services supplied. Some companies might be more centralised; others might be structured in a more decentralised way. The larger the company and the more decentralised the company is the greater the organisational complexity (structural cost drivers) and the greater the need for accounting to help manage relationships within (and outside) the organisation (executional costs drivers). Figures 1.8, 1.9 and 1.10 provide examples of the different organisational structures. The first (figure 1.8) is centralised, with the CEO having direct oversight over all the functional value chain activities. The organisation becomes more decentralised when separate business units or divisions are created. Often this is done because the product offerings are associated with different industry value chains and duplication of the functional activities is necessary.

FIGURE 1.8 Centralised organisational structure

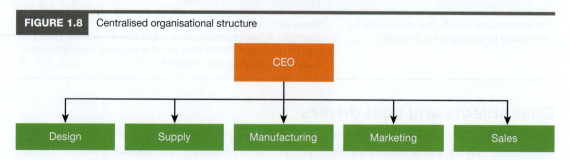

The second diagram (figure 1.9) demonstrates the distinction, with the industrial chemicals division selling to customers who are entirely different from the customers of the pharmaceutical chemicals or the food nutrition divisions. The decentralised structure, while it duplicates functional activities, provides a customer or market focus. Here business unit managers report to the CEO, who is not as close to the operational activities as they would be in a centralised structure. A more radical decentralisation is found in the matrix structure (figure 1.10), where a large international organisation might find the need to segregate geographically as well. Adding another geographical distinction further removes the CEO from daily operations, as they now have geographical managers and industry/product managers reporting on activities. The manager of the European food and nutrition division would have two direct reports, or bosses, which can sometimes be difficult if the industry and geographical goals are not well aligned.

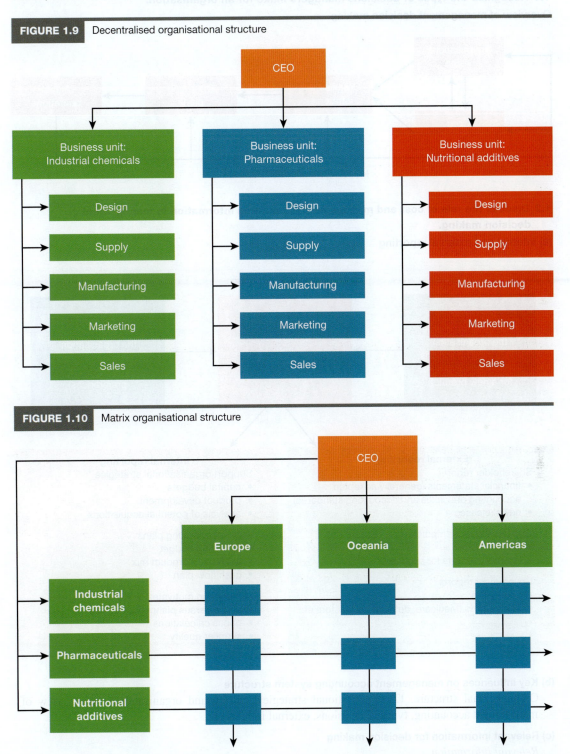

FIGURE 1.9 Decentralised organisational structure

FIGURE 1.10 Matrix organisational structure

The first part of this text focuses on an introduction to a range of management accounting and control tools and practices that commonly form the foundation of any management accounting system within organisations. After obtaining a solid foundation of basic management accounting and control tools in the first part of the text, we extend our understanding of management accounting and control with emphasis on the behavioural aspects of information system design. We do this by reinforcing the role of strategy and the ways in which control system tools are influenced and used. Chapter 14 provides an overview of the second part of this text.

SUMMARY

1.1 Recognise the types of decisions managers make for an organisation.

Overview of management decision making

Measure, monitor and motivate

1.2 Discuss the role of cost and management accounting information in management decision making.

(a) Internal and external reporting

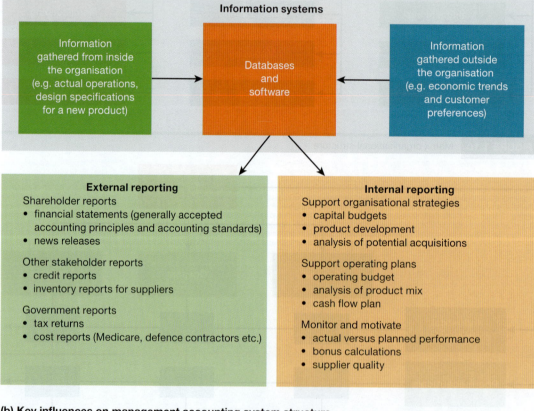

(b) Key influences on management accounting system structure

Organisational structure, IT, organisational strategies, culture and organisational vision, view of management accounting, types of decisions, external influences

(c) Relevant information for decision making

Relevant information

Helps decision makers evaluate and choose among alternative courses of action by:

(i) considering the future

(ii) varying with the action taken.

Includes incremental (avoidable) information (costs or cash flows).

Irrelevant information

- Not useful for decision making
- Includes unavoidable cash flows

1.3 Communicate how managers can make higher-quality decisions using accounting information.

(a) Path to higher-quality management decisions

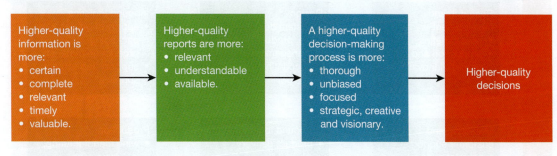

Higher-quality information is more:
- certain
- complete
- relevant
- timely
- valuable.

Higher-quality reports are more:
- relevant
- understandable
- available.

A higher-quality decision-making process is more:
- thorough
- unbiased
- focused
- strategic, creative and visionary.

Higher-quality decisions

(b) Decision-useful information involves a consideration of:
- opportunity costs
- cost–benefit analysis.

1.4 Describe the value chain framework and its applications in management accounting.

A value chain can be described as the key activities engaged in by the organisation or industry.

Sample industry-based value chain for the wine industry

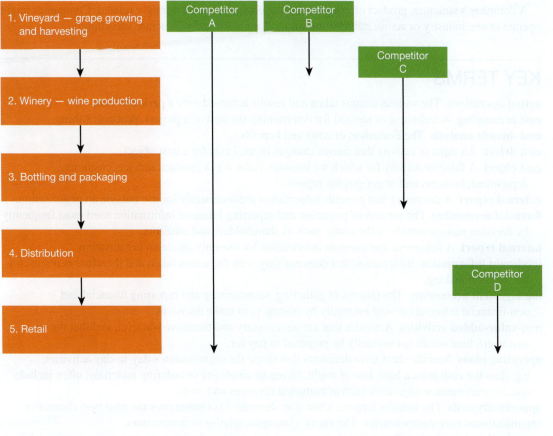

1. Vineyard — grape growing and harvesting

2. Winery — wine production

3. Bottling and packaging

4. Distribution

5. Retail

Competitor A

Competitor B

Competitor C

Competitor D

Sample organisational value chain for a winery

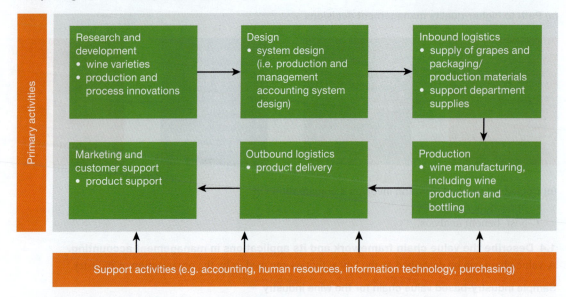

A company's structure, product offerings and value chain design are strongly related. Companies might operate in one industry or across multiple industry value chains and restructure accordingly.

KEY TERMS

actual operations The various actions taken and results achieved over a period of time.

cost accounting A technique or method for determining the cost of a project, process or thing.

cost–benefit analysis The evaluation of costs and benefits.

cost driver An input or activity that causes changes in total cost for a cost object.

cost object A thing or activity for which we measure costs, e.g. a product, service, customer, department, business unit or geographic region.

external report A document that presents information predominantly for use outside an organisation.

financial accounting The process of preparing and reporting financial information used most frequently by decision makers outside of the entity, such as shareholders and creditors.

internal report A document that presents information for use only inside an organisation.

irrelevant information Information that does not vary with the action taken and therefore is not useful for decision making.

management accounting The process of gathering, summarising and reporting financial and non-financial information used internally by managers to make decisions.

non-value-added activities Activities that are unnecessary and therefore wasteful, and that the customer/client would not normally be prepared to pay for.

operating plans Specific short-term decisions that shape the organisation's day-to-day activities, e.g. drawing cash from a bank line of credit, hiring an employee or ordering materials; often include specific performance objectives such as budgeted revenues and costs.

opportunity costs The benefits forgone when one alternative is chosen over the next best alternative.

organisational core competencies The entity's strengths relative to competitors.

organisational strategies The tactics that managers use to take advantage of core competencies while working towards the organisational vision.

organisational vision The core purpose and ideology of the entity, which guides the entity's overall direction and approaches toward its various stakeholder groups.

relevant information Information that helps the decision maker to evaluate and choose among alternative courses of action.

strategies Tactics that relate to providing direction and guiding long-term decisions.

supply chain The flow of resources from the initial suppliers through the delivery of goods and services to customers and clients.

value-added activities Activities that are necessary and increase the worth of an entity's goods or services to customers, and that the customer/client would normally be prepared to pay for.

value chain The key activities engaged in by the organisation or industry.

SELF-STUDY PROBLEMS

SELF-STUDY PROBLEM 1 Organisational value chain

Outline how an organisational value chain helps breakdown traditional organisational boundaries.

SOLUTION TO SELF-STUDY PROBLEM 1

An organisational value chain focuses on the key value-creating activities within an organisation. It is less concerned with the traditional functions of organisational boundaries, instead encouraging a wider perspective to be taken by both operational managers and support areas such as accounting. From a management accounting perspective, that would mean considering the wider implications of a decision rather than just the impact at the local level. The value chain illustrated in figure 1.5 would be adapted to the individual needs and circumstances of a specific organisation.

SELF-STUDY PROBLEM 2 Evaluation of performance across the value chain

New Zealand produces fine quality merino wool garments that are highly sought after by the fashion industry. Merino Designs is a fully integrated company that operates in this industry. It has one particularly popular product in its range, the Merino Jacket.

Merino Designs — The Merino Jacket

Sheep farming

Revenue (wool kg)	$ 25.98		Profit/Sales =	24.6%
Costs: Operating costs	$ 19.59		Sales/Assets =	$0.15
Margin	$ 6.39		ROA	3.6%
Assets	$175.97			

+ $0.32 handling cost

Knitting mills

Revenue	$ 152		Profit/Sales =	8.2%
Costs: Wool	$ 26.30		Sales/Assets =	$0.31
Colour dyeing	$ 22.50		ROA	2.5%
Knitting	$ 36.80	+ $4.25 freight		
Accessories (buttons etc.)	$ 8.60	+ $2.96 tax		
SG&A	$ 45.31			
Margin	$ 12.49			
Assets	$489.97			

Distributor

Revenue	$220.00		Profit/Sales =	11.3%
Costs: Knitted garments	$159.21		Sales/Assets =	$3.87
Operating cost	$ 35.98		ROA	43.7%
Margin	$ 24.81			
Assets	$ 56.86			

Retailer

Revenue	$450.00		Profit/Sales =	6.7%
Costs: Knitted garments	$220.00		Sales/Assets =	$4.56
Operating costs	$199.65		ROA	30.7%
Margin	$ 30.35			
Assets	$ 98.68			

The overall value chain

Revenue	$847.98		Profit/Sales =	8.7%
Profit	$ 74.04		Sales/Assets =	$1.32
Assets	$821.48		ROA	9.0%

Merino Design management would like to understand the performance of this jacket across the varying value chain activities. With reference to the value chain activities and figures shown in the table, provide an overview of the financial performance of the different value chain activities of Merino Designs.

SOLUTION TO SELF-STUDY PROBLEM 2

Merino Designs operates in all areas of the value chain. It farms sheep for wool, has its own woollen knitting mills and distribution department that ships to its Merino Designs stores throughout the world. As can be recognised in the different parts of the value chain, profitability might be higher or lower. Some areas of the value chain are more asset intensive, such as the knitting mills. Each contributes to the overall performance of the organisation. Using this information, managers might decide where activities are value-adding or non-value-adding and could potentially be outsourced. They might use this information to reward the individual managers for good performance.

QUESTIONS

1.1 Explain the value chain and list ways that value chain analysis benefits organisations.	**LO4**
1.2 Why do managers need to measure, monitor and motivate performance?	**LO1, 2, 3**
1.3 List three types of internal reports and explain how each is used. List three types of external reports and explain how each is used.	**LO2**
1.4 What types of information in addition to cost accounting are needed for management decisions?	**LO1**
1.5 Explain relevant information in a decision-making context.	**LO1, 3**
1.6 What is a cost object?	**LO2**
1.7 In your own words, explain the path to higher-quality decisions.	**LO3**
1.8 Outline the meaning of structural cost drivers.	**LO4**
1.9 Identify two key influences on the nature of a management accounting system.	**LO2**

EXERCISES

1.10 Value-added and non-value-added activities   **LO4**

Some activities add value to an organisation, while others do not.

Required

Determine whether each of the following activities is likely to be value-added or non-value-added, and explain your choice.

(a) Inspection activities
(b) Moving materials to workstations
(c) Manufacturing extra inventory to keep employees busy
(d) Packing to fill a customer order
(e) Product design initiatives

1.11 Internal and external reports   **LO1, 2**

Classify the following reports as internal or external.

(a) Operating budget
(b) Credit reports
(c) Financial statements
(d) Capital budget
(e) Tax returns
(f) Analysis of product mix

1.12 Management accounting function   **LO2**

Differentiate between the management accounting function and the management accountant.

1.13 Types of manager decisions   **LO1**

Suppose that the following are activities conducted by Microsoft Corporation.

A. Comparing the timeliness of development steps of a new release of Windows with the timeline that was laid out to guide development.

B. Developing a timeline for the release of new Windows and Microsoft Office products over the next year.

C. Debugging the next version of Windows.

D. Providing technical support to customers who are having problems with Microsoft Office.

E. Estimating cash expenditures for the next year.

F. Comparing budgeted costs to actual costs and discussing major differences with department managers.

G. Deciding whether to construct a new building on the Microsoft site.

Required

Identify whether each activity is most likely part of:

(a) organisational strategies

(b) operating plans

(c) actual operations

(d) measuring, monitoring and motivating.

For each item, explain why.

PROBLEMS

1.14 Industry and organisational value chain   **LO4**

With reference to Merino Designs in self-study problem 2, differentiate between an industry value chain and an organisational value chain.

1.15 Structural cost drivers   **LO4**

(a) With reference to Merino Designs in self-study problem 2, demonstrate the meaning of the structural cost drivers' scope, technology and experience.

(b) Classify Merino Designs' likely strategy as low cost or product differentiation. Explain.

1.16 Relevant information   **LO1, 2, 3**

Suppose you are responsible for ordering a replacement for your office photocopy machine. Part of your job is to decide whether to buy or lease the machine.

Required

(a) Describe something that could be considered relevant information in this decision and explain why it is relevant.

(b) Describe something that could be considered irrelevant information in this decision and explain why it is irrelevant.

(c) Explain why it was important to distinguish between relevant and irrelevant information in this problem.

1.17 Uncertainties; degree of uncertainty   **LO3**

Community Children's Hospital can invest in one of two different projects. The first project is to purchase and operate a hotel that is located two blocks from the hospital. The CEO of the hospital has no experience in operating a hotel, but the hospital does provide rooms for inpatients, and so she is familiar with cleaning requirements and managing housekeeping staff. However, the hospital does little advertising and does not have a large public relations staff. In addition, the hospital and hotel are located in a part of town that is deteriorating.

The other investment opportunity is to replace the heart monitors in the neonatal intensive care unit (critical care for newborns and infants). The new monitors would provide a range of functions, including monitoring the body temperature and blood pressure of infants, as well as monitoring heart functions. Each monitor can be used for up to four infants, with information about each infant forwarded to one computer that is monitored by a special technician. The current monitors are bedside monitors that need to be read every 10 minutes by nursing staff.

Required

(a) Prepare a list of uncertainties that the CEO faces if she buys the hotel.

(b) Prepare a list of uncertainties the CEO faces if she replaces the heart monitors.

(c) Which scenario appears to have a greater degree of uncertainty? Why?

1.18 Cost reduction; value chain analysis   **LO2, 4**

Budget Cupboards produces kitchen and bathroom cupboards that incorporate unusual functions, such as specialty drawers for knives and kitchen tools, and kitchen appliance holders that pop up from under the counter top. Competition in this industry has recently increased. Budget's management wants to cut costs for its basic cupboard models and then cut prices.

Required

(a) The following table lists potential areas for cost reduction. Two potential cost reductions are provided for the first area listed (design phase). For each of the remaining areas, identify two potential ways that Budget Cupboards' management could reduce costs using the structure of the table as shown.

Potential area for cost reduction	Potential cost reductions	
Design phase	Work with suppliers to reduce direct materials costs	Redesign cupboards to use fewer parts
Manufacturing process		
Administration		
Changes in quality or functionality		

(b) Budget does not currently use value chain analysis. Describe several advantages of using value chain analysis.

1.19 Quality of decisions
LO1, 3

Maria and Tracey became good friends while working at the same entity. Two years ago, they both decided to increase their savings so that they could eventually purchase homes. Each began by putting a portion of each month's salary into a savings account. At the end of the first year, they had each accumulated $4000. Because their savings accounts paid a very small interest rate, they decided to invest the savings to earn a higher rate of return. Maria and Tracey both hoped to save enough money to buy homes within five years.

Maria decided to take an investment course offered through the entity. The course taught her about different types of investments and strategies for investing. She then purchased and read an investment book to learn more. Maria learned that some investments are riskier than others, and that investors must balance risk against desired return. Higher risk leads to higher returns on average, but higher risk could also lead to low returns or even loss. She also learned that investment advisers recommend diversifying risky investments. One way to diversify is to invest in mutual funds, which invest in many different organisations. Maria decided that she was willing to assume some risk, but was not comfortable with a high level. She decided to invest her $4000 in a stockmarket mutual fund. She read client reports to learn about different mutual funds, and selected a fund that invests conservatively in fairly stable companies. However, the stockmarket did not do well in the first year. The value of her mutual fund at the end of a year was $4050.

Tracey talked with her boyfriend and other friends about how they invest. Her boyfriend's cousin recommended investing in a start-up company that sells video games. He told her that the games were very popular with teenagers and that the company would probably be acquired, resulting in big gains for investors. This opportunity sounded good to Tracey, so she decided to invest her entire $4000 in the company's shares. After 10 months, she was excited to learn that the company was being acquired. She received shares in the acquiring company in exchange for her original shares. At the end of the year, the market value of her shares was $8200.

Required

Evaluate the quality of the investment decisions made by Maria and Tracey. *Hint:* Refer to figure 1.3.

(a) List the information used by Maria in making her investment decision.

(b) List the information used by Tracey in making her investment decision.

(c) Did Maria appear to use high-quality information? Explain.

(d) Did Tracey appear to use high-quality information? Explain.

(e) Describe Maria's decision-making process. What did she do to explore her options? Did she appear to be biased? What were her priorities? How did she reach a conclusion?

(f) Describe Tracey's decision-making process. What did she do to explore her options? Did she appear to be biased? What were her priorities? How did she reach a conclusion?

(g) Did Maria appear to use a high-quality decision-making process? Explain.

(h) Did Tracey appear to use a high-quality decision-making process? Explain.

(i) Given your analyses of the information and decision-making processes used by Maria and Tracey, which investor made a higher-quality decision? Explain.

1.20 Relevant information; uncertainties; information for decision making
LO1, 2, 3

Janet Baker is deciding where to live during her second year at university. During her first year, she lived in the university residence college. Recently, her friend Rachel asked her to share an off-campus flat for the upcoming school year. Janet likes the idea of living in a flat, but she is concerned about how much it will cost.

To help her decide what to do, Janet collected information about costs. She would pay $400 per month in rent. The minimum lease term on the apartment is six months. Janet estimates that her share of the utility bills will be $75 per month. She also estimates that groceries will cost $200 per month. Janet spent $350 on a new couch over the summer. If she lives in the university residence college, she will put the couch in storage at a cost of $35 per month. Janet expects to spend $7500 on university fees and $450 on books each semester. Room and board on campus would cost Janet $2900 per semester (four months). This amount includes a food plan of 20 meals per week. This cost is non-refundable if the meals are not eaten.

Required

(a) Use *only* the cost information collected by Janet for the following tasks.
  (i) List all of the costs for each option. *Note:* Some costs may be listed under both options.
  (ii) Review your lists and cross out the costs that are irrelevant to Janet's decision. Explain why these costs are irrelevant.
  (iii) Calculate and compare the total relevant costs of each option.
  (iv) Given the cost comparison, which living arrangement is the better choice for Janet? Explain.
(b) Identify uncertainties in the cost information collected by Janet.
  (i) Determine whether each cost is likely to be (1) known for sure, (2) estimated with little uncertainty, or (3) estimated with moderate or high uncertainty.
  (ii) For each cost that is known for sure, explain where Janet would obtain the information.
  (iii) For each cost that must be estimated, explain why the cost cannot be known.
(c) List additional information that might be relevant to Janet's decision (list as many items as you can).
  (i) Costs not identified by Janet
  (ii) Factors other than costs
(d) Explain why conducting a cost comparison is useful to Janet, even if factors other than costs are important to her decision.
(e) Consider your own preferences for this problem. Do you expect Janet's preferences to be the same as yours? How can you control for your biases as you give Janet advice?
(f) Think about what Janet's priorities might be for choosing a housing arrangement. How might different priorities lead to different choices?
(g) Describe how information that Janet gains over this next year might affect her future housing arrangements.
(h) Suppose Janet asks for your advice. Use the information you learned from the preceding analyses to write a memo to Janet with your recommendation and a discussion of its risks. Refer in your memo to the information that would be useful to Janet.

1.21 Relevant information; recommendation   **LO1, 2, 3**

Frank owns a caravan and loves to visit national parks with his family. However, the family only takes two one-week trips in the caravan each year. Frank's wife would rather stay in motels than the caravan. She presented him with the following itemisation of the cost per trip, hoping that he will sell the caravan and use motels instead.

	Cost per trip
Caravan:	
Cost: $20 000	
Usable for 10 seasons, two camping trips per season	$1000
Transportation expense:	
1000 km @ $0.37 per km	370
Includes:	
$0.15 per km for petrol, oil, tyres and maintenance	
$0.22 per km for depreciation and insurance	
Groceries	250
Beverages	100
Cost per trip	$1720
Cost per person ($1720/5 family members)	$ 344

Required

(a) What are the relevant costs for deciding whether the family should go on one more camping trip this year?

(b) What are the relevant costs for deciding whether Frank should sell the caravan? Assume the family will take the same vacations but stay in motels if the caravan is sold.

(c) What factors other than costs might influence the decision to sell the caravan? List as many as you can.

(d) Consider your own preferences for this problem. Do you expect Frank's preferences to be the same as yours? How can you control for your biases and consider this problem from Frank's point of view?

(e) Frank asks you to help him decide what to do. Do you think he should sell the caravan? Why?

1.22 Cost drivers; value chain; strategy; organisational structure   **LO2, 4**

Australian fashion designer Sean Ashby commenced his men's swimwear and clothing business aussieBum in 2001. A keen swimmer and surfer, he was unable to find a good pair of men's cossies and used his life savings of $20 000 to make a series of prototypes, buy materials and commence manufacturing in Australia. Despite rejection from local retailers who did not see the potential for aussieBum to compete with international brands, Ashby has proven critics wrong. He had no choice but to take his business online, with instant exposure to the international market. It now takes thousands of orders a day.

Since the company's inception, Ashby says that aussieBum has 'taken on its own little cult revolution', with celebrities such as Ewan McGregor, Billy Connolly and David Beckham fans of the aussieBum brand. Even Kylie Minogue's male dancers wore aussieBum cossies in the film clip for her song 'Slow'. The marketing thrust behind Ashby's aussieBum is to live the dream — 'the dream to be independent and present our gear in a way that gets noticed. We don't apologise for pushing the boundaries . . . We have a saying at aussieBum — If you doubt yourself, wear something else'.[6]

The company doubled in size every year in its first five years and continued to grow by 20 per cent every quarter. By 2018, aussieBum had an average annual turnover of between $17 million and $20 million, and 90 per cent of its customers were international. The aussieBum brand now takes pride of place in stores such as Selfridges in the UK; Brown Thomas in Ireland; La Maison Stores in Canada; Alpha Male in Melrose Drive, Los Angeles; KaDeWa in Germany; as well as others in Spain, The Netherlands, Sweden, Poland and Russia. As well as direct department store sales, aussieBum's internet retail orders are booming, with aussieBum being distributed to more than 70 countries. It now has over 200 000 consumers ordering direct via its custom built e-commerce site.

Most of the raw materials are sourced from Italy and China. By manufacturing in Australia, aussieBum hopes to promote Australia's culture and relaxed lifestyle as well as eliminate restrictions that might come with outsourcing production to other countries. Moreover, producing locally (through independent manufacturers) provides flexibility and a reduced timeframe in getting new products to market. With a heavy emphasis on innovative product design, aussieBum pays close attention to the design phase of the product process.

Two examples of aussieBum's flexibility and innovative approach to product development and marketing are worthy of note. First, it was able to capitalise on the consumer backlash against competitor Bonds when that company transferred more of its manufacturing offshore. Ashby estimates that aussieBum's sales grew by at least 40 per cent as a result. Second, aussieBum was able to achieve continued growth during the global financial crisis. The company continues to avoid debt and own all its assets outright.[7]

Required

(a) With reference to the information provided, distinguish between structural and executional cost drivers.

(b) Illustrate and describe the industry and organisational value chain in which aussieBum operates.

(c) Classify aussieBum's likely strategy as low cost or product differentiation. Explain.

(d) Classify aussieBum's organisational structure as centralised or decentralised. Explain.

(e) With reference to disruptive innovation, do you consider aussieBum to be a disruptor to the traditional garment industry value chain? Discuss why or why not.

1.23 Value chain   **LO4**

Using figure 1.5 as an example, develop an internal value chain for an airline such as Virgin Australia.

1.24 Value chain in the public sector **LO1, 2, 4**

Traditionally, government organisations have tended to operate in silos, focusing on their own objectives and managing and protecting their own budgets. Recently, however, faced with seemingly intractable economic, social and environmental problems, many government organisations have sought to develop new ways of working. In particular, they have sought to explore how their objectives overlap and depend on other organisations and how they might share information and resources. One example is provided by attempts to reduce crime and enhance public safety in the criminal justice sector.

In New Zealand the Ministry of Justice is the lead agency in the justice sector. The sector includes the New Zealand Police, the Serious Fraud Office, Child Youth and Family, the Department of Corrections and the Crown Law Office.

The organisations in the criminal justice system can be thought of as being involved in a 'pipeline' that begins with crime prevention and the investigation of crime and proceeds all the way through to rehabilitation (see the figure below). Looking at the sector as a pipeline, we can see that policies and actions in any part of the system will affect other parts of the system. By working as a coordinated 'justice sector', changes can be made that result in the best outcomes for the sector as a whole.

Criminal justice pipeline

Within this pipeline, the operations within one agency, Public Prisons, can be further analysed to show the links between its key activities and between the department and other organisations in the sector.

Key activities follow this path:
- offenders are convicted in the courts
- offenders are sentenced and sent to prison
- prisoners undergo an initial assessment
- the serving of the sentence is planned
- prisoner's sentence is managed, including provision of relevant rehabilitation programs
- prisoner's release is planned and managed.[8]

Required

(a) With reference to the information provided, distinguish between the structural and executional cost drivers in this value chain.

(b) Is there an ability for governments to outsource any of these value chain activities?

1.25 Management decision making **LO1, 2**

The Woolworths Group has a goal of having customers put the company first across all their brands. To achieve this the Group has identified five priorities.[9]

1. Building a customer and store-led culture and team.
2. Generating sustainable sales momentum in food.
3. Evolving the drinks business to provide even more value and convenience to customers.
4. Empowering the portfolio businesses to pursue strategies to deliver shareholder value.
5. Becoming a lean retailer through end-to-end process and systems excellence.

Required

(a) Given the strategic priorities, what decisions could management take to influence the structural cost drivers and executional cost drivers?

(b) What type of information would management need in making decisions you have identified in (a)?

ENDNOTES

1. See IMA 1983, *Statement on management accounting no. 2: management accounting terminology*, NAA, Montvale, NJ, 1 June, p. 25.
2. Adapted from Shank, J & Goviindarajan, V 1992, 'Strategic cost management and the value chain', *Journal of Cost Management*, pp. 5–21.
3. See Cooper, R & Slagmulder, R 1999, 'The scope of strategic cost management', in J Edwards (ed.), *Emerging practices in cost management*, Warren, Gorham & Lamont, Boston.
4. This classification model is based on Shank, J & Goviindarajan, V 1992.
5. Adapted from Shank, J & Goviindarajan, V 1992.
6. Information from www.aussieBum.com.
7. AusIndustry 2005, *Aussie cossies kick butt overseas*, AusIndustry success story, Department of Industry, Tourism and Resources, www.ausindustry.gov.au; Australian Trade Commission 2010, 'Case study — aussieBum (NSW)', www.exportawards.gov.au; IBISWorld 2006, *Clothing manufacturing in Australia*, IBISWorld industry report, 11 December; Pascuzzi, C 2006, 'Today aussieBum, tomorrow the world', Mediasearch Music Film & Fashion in Australia, www.mediasearch.com.au; Spicer, R 2006, 'Developing your exports', *Dynamic Business Magazine*, September 2006, www.dynamicexport.com.au; Stephenson, A 2009, 'Bonds anger sees aussieBum sales soar', 2 April, www.news.com.au.
8. Information and diagram adapted from the Ministry of Justice (New Zealand) 2015, 'About the justice sector', www.justice.govt.nz.
9. Information from www.woolworthsgroup.com.au.

ACKNOWLEDGEMENTS

Photo 1A: © Johnny Greig / Getty Images

CHAPTER 2

Cost concepts, behaviour and estimation

LEARNING OBJECTIVES

After studying this chapter, you should be able to:

2.1 demonstrate an understanding of the concept of cost behaviour

2.2 explain the different types of cost behaviour

2.3 describe different cost estimation techniques

2.4 apply estimation techniques to determine the cost function

2.5 apply regression analysis in cost estimation

2.6 reflect on the uses and limitations of cost estimates.

IN BRIEF

Managers need a basic understanding of the entity's costs if they are to react quickly to change and develop successful organisational strategies and operating plans. Managers use cost classifications and cost estimation techniques to understand and predict cost behaviour. They can then identify and estimate costs to assist with decision-making processes.

2.1 Cost behaviour

LEARNING OBJECTIVE 2.1 Demonstrate an understanding of the concept of cost behaviour.

Cost behaviour at the operational level is the variation in costs relative to the variation in an organisation's activities. Accountants need to anticipate changes in costs as decisions are made about activities such as production, merchandise sales and services. These are referred to as cost objects, and we are interested in their cost behaviour. To understand cost behaviour, accountants analyse the effects of changes in their organisations' activities on costs by considering the drivers of those costs. Cost behaviour may be classified on a traditional basis using a fixed and variable cost framework, or take a more contemporary view using an activity analysis cost framework. In this chapter a more traditional view of cost is taken. A further discussion on activity analysis can be found in chapter 12.

The ability to analyse cost behaviour requires knowledge of an organisation's economic environment and operations. Consider an airline. Its costs, such as beverage costs, vary with the number of passengers. Some costs, such as fuel and flight attendant wages, vary with the number of flights. Other costs, such as the leasing of counter space and the salaries of airport management, vary with the number of airports used by the airline, which remains constant in the short term but can change in the long term. Still other costs, such as building costs and corporate headquarters salaries, do not vary with passenger, flight or airport-related volumes. In the next section we will further explore such cost behaviour patterns.

2.2 Variable, fixed and mixed costs

LEARNING OBJECTIVE 2.2 Explain the different types of cost behaviour.

In the management accounting case, we illustrated fixed and variable costs in relation to the coffee industry. In this section, we use the bicycle industry to further explore these concepts. For Mount Dandenong Bikes, a bicycle manufacturer, the cost of tyres varies with the number of bicycles produced. Suppose that each tyre costs $5: the variable cost per bike is $10 and total variable cost increases by $10 for each bike produced. Figure 2.1(a) provides a graph of the variable cost of tyres. Another activity in bike production is mounting the tyres onto wheels. As the number of bikes produced increases, the labour cost to mount tyres onto wheels increases proportionately and is therefore a variable cost. Therefore, total **variable costs** change proportionately with changes in activity levels.

We assume that variable cost per unit remains constant, but sometimes this assumption is not true. Suppose that the managers of Mount Dandenong Bikes are able to negotiate a lower cost for tyres as their purchase quantity increases. For purchases up to 120 tyres, the variable cost per unit is constant at $10 per bike. However, the variable cost per bike drops to $6 for any additional purchases after the first 120 tyres, as illustrated in figure 2.1(b).

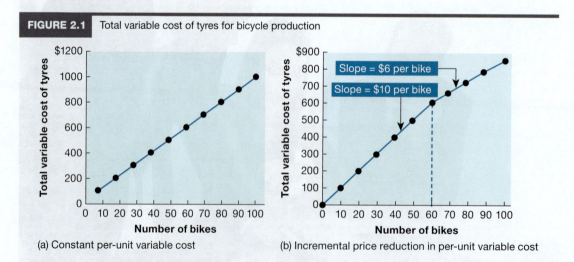

FIGURE 2.1 Total variable cost of tyres for bicycle production

(a) Constant per-unit variable cost

(b) Incremental price reduction in per-unit variable cost

Total **fixed costs** do not vary with small changes in activity levels such as production, sales and services provided. Some fixed costs are easy to classify, such as rent, insurance and property taxes. Figure 2.2(a) illustrates the cost of rent and sales volumes for Mount Dandenong Bikes. Within a specific range of sales ($0 to $30 000), rent cost is $6000. However, if sales are greater than $30 000, more space will be needed and total fixed cost will increase to $8000, as shown in figure 2.2(b). Fixed costs such as rent often increase in a stepwise linear manner.

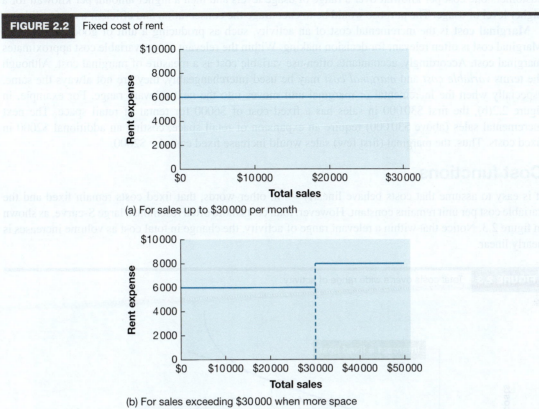

(a) For sales up to $30 000 per month

(b) For sales exceeding $30 000 when more space must be rented

Some fixed costs are more difficult to classify. For example, varying levels of bike production do not significantly change the amount of electricity used, assuming no change in hours of operation. Keep in mind that the dollar amount of a fixed cost is not necessarily 'fixed' at one value. For Mount Dandenong Bikes, the rate for a kilowatt-hour of electricity might change, the cost for heating and cooling depends on weather conditions, and the total electricity bill varies from month to month. Nevertheless, electricity is still considered a fixed cost for bike production because the cost of electricity is not significantly affected by changes in the volumes of operating activity (number of bikes produced).

In reality, many costs are **mixed costs**; they are partly fixed and partly variable. Suppose that Mount Dandenong Bikes incurs a fixed cost of $10 000 to generate a television advertisement, and then a variable cost of $500 each time the advertisement is aired on television. The total television advertising cost is a mixed cost because part is fixed and part varies with the number of times the advertisement is aired on television.

The classification of costs as fixed, variable or mixed is not always straightforward.

Relevant range

A **relevant range** is a span of activity for a given cost object where both total fixed costs and variable costs per unit of activity remain constant. Suppose that an airline begins service to a new destination. The number of flights is estimated, gates and aircraft are leased, and employees are hired. Managers may add or drop a few flights, and the fixed costs and variable costs per flight (fuel and personnel) remain constant. However, if the new route is successful, managers may decide to add a number of new flights, in which case new gates must be leased and new employees hired. The fixed and variable costs for the original destination are no longer valid because the airline is operating within a new relevant range.

Variable cost rates can also change across relevant ranges, as was shown in figure 2.1(b). In that graph, Mount Dandenong Bikes paid $10 per bike for tyres for 0–60 bikes (120 tyres), and $6 per bike after that. Within a particular relevant range of purchases, the variable cost per tyre is constant. However, once purchase volumes move into a different relevant range, a different variable cost per bike applies.

In many cases, the variable cost will be lower at a higher relevant range. But in some cases, especially when resources are limited, a higher variable cost might apply. For example, a utility company may charge customers one cost per kilowatt over a range of usage levels and then a higher amount per kilowatt for a higher level of usage. The purpose would be to encourage the conservation and efficient use of utilities.

Marginal cost is the incremental cost of an activity, such as producing a unit of goods or services. Marginal cost is often relevant for decision making. Within the relevant range, variable cost approximates marginal cost. Accordingly, accountants often use variable cost as a measure of marginal cost. Although the terms *variable cost* and *marginal cost* may be used interchangeably, they are not always the same, especially when the incremental or marginal unit moves into the next relevant range. For example, in figure 2.2(b), the first $30 000 in sales has a fixed cost of $6000 for rental of retail space. The next incremental sales (above $30 000) require an expansion of retail space, costing an additional $2000 in fixed costs. Thus, the marginal (first few) sales would increase fixed costs by $2000.

Cost functions

It is easy to assume that costs behave linearly — in other words, that fixed costs remain fixed and the variable cost per unit remains constant. However, total costs more often resemble a large S-curve, as shown in figure 2.3. Notice that within a relevant range of activity, the change in total cost as volume increases is nearly linear.

FIGURE 2.3 | Total costs over a wide range of activity

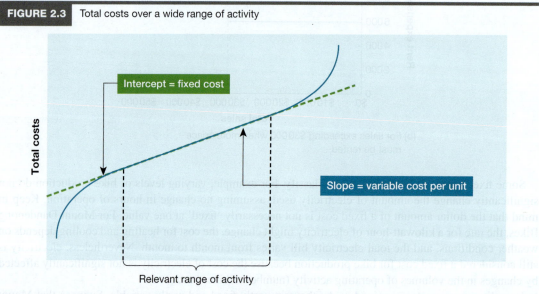

A **cost function** is an algebraic representation of the total cost of a cost object over a relevant range of activity. When we create a cost function, we assume that within a relevant range of activity the total fixed costs remain fixed and the variable cost per unit remains constant. Notice in figure 2.3 that, when volume is very low or very high, the total cost function is non-linear. However, when volume is in the relevant range, the cost function is linear or close to linear.

Given the preceding definitions of fixed and variable costs within the relevant range, we can write the cost function algebraically as:

$$TC = F + V \times Q$$

where TC is total cost,
    F is total fixed cost,
    V is the variable cost per unit of activity, and
    Q is the volume of activity of the cost driver.

When the slope of a variable cost function changes at some point but remains linear after the change, it is called a **piecewise linear cost function**. The variable cost function in figure 2.1(b) is piecewise linear because it involves more than one relevant range. When a fixed cost function changes at some point but remains constant after the change, it is called a **stepwise linear cost function**. The fixed cost function in figure 2.2(b) is stepwise linear because it includes more than one relevant range.

A **cost driver** is some input or activity that causes changes in total cost for a cost object. For an airline when the cost object is the entire organisation, the number of passengers is a cost driver for in-flight beverage costs. The number of flights is a cost driver for fuel and flight attendant wages. The number of airports used by the airline is a cost driver for counter space lease and airport management salaries. Cost drivers are important for a range of management accounting issues and are explored further in other parts of this text.

The same cost object might have different cost drivers in different settings. For example, when electricity is the cost object, in a retail setting the cost driver could be hours the store was open. In a manufacturing setting, the cost driver could be either machine hours or number of units manufactured, assuming that each unit requires the same number of machine hours.

2.3 Cost estimation techniques

LEARNING OBJECTIVE 2.3 Describe different cost estimation techniques.

Although past costs are not directly relevant to decisions, they are often useful in estimating future cost behaviour. For example, past materials and labour costs might be the best estimate of future production costs. Historical costs are generally recorded and coded within the accounting system so that they can be summarised in different ways depending on the cost object of interest. An entity's accounting system might be used to create one or more reports of last year's production costs, material usage and labour hours. The ease with which information can be identified for a particular cost object depends on the design of the accounting system as well as the nature of the information.

Information for some costs cannot be obtained easily from the accounting system. Suppose a manager needs to estimate next year's production costs. They gather information about changes in direct materials costs from their suppliers' price lists or from other vendors' websites.

When estimating a cost function, accountants usually begin with past cost information if it is available. Although past cost information might be accurate and useful, it may at times be unavailable, irrelevant or outdated. Sometimes a combination of information sources is the best choice and the costs obtained will require reclassification into fixed and variable cost components.

As we gather relevant information, we may have a general idea of the cost behaviour. However, we need to select one or more techniques for estimating the dollar amount of fixed and variable costs. The following techniques are used to estimate a cost function:

- engineered estimate of cost
- two-point method
- analysis at the account level
- high-low method
- graphical technique — scatter plots
- regression analysis.

Although each of these methods may be used, the choice is open-ended. No single technique is useful in all circumstances. Although some techniques are generally better than others, the best technique often depends on the circumstances for a particular decision. As we look at each technique, we pay particular attention to its assumptions. Poor management decisions can result if the quality of cost estimates is not considered.

Engineered estimate of cost

One method used to estimate a cost function is the **engineered estimate of cost**. Each activity is analysed according to the amount of labour time, materials and other resources used. Costs are assigned according to these measurements. Suppose Mount Dandenong Bikes begins production of a new model, such as a mountain bike for steep terrain. Engineers and accountants use the new model's design specifications to estimate the cost of direct and indirect materials for a production run of the mountain bikes. In addition, the proposed manufacturing process is analysed to determine the cost effects of any changes from the existing manufacturing processes. The accountants communicate with purchasing department personnel to determine whether the prices of inputs are likely to change. From this information, a total cost function is developed for the production of the mountain bikes for the next period. Although engineers traditionally develop engineered estimates of cost, anyone having sufficient knowledge about activities and costs can develop a cost function using this method.

Analysis at the account level

Another way to create a cost function is to use **analysis at the account level**. Using this technique, we review the pattern of a cost over time in the accounting system and use our knowledge of operations to classify the cost as variable, fixed or mixed. Costs such as managers' salaries are usually fixed; they are often directly associated in the general ledger with a particular department or product. Costs for variable materials used in the production process are usually available in the general ledger or in production records. Costs such as manufacturing overhead are often mixed; they tend to include fixed costs such as insurance and rates for the plant, and variable costs such as indirect supplies used in manufacturing. For costs we identify as mixed, we must use another cost estimation technique such as the two-point method or regression analysis to determine the fixed and variable components. Sometimes we are uncertain about the nature of the cost function. A scatter plot provides helpful information about the relationship between a cost and potential cost driver.

Graphical technique — scatter plots

A **scatter plot** is a graphical technique in which data points for past costs are plotted against a potential cost driver. Scatter plots provide a quick way to learn more about the behaviour of a cost and to determine whether a potential cost driver is viable as Q in the cost function. We visually analyse scatter plots to improve our understanding of a cost's behaviour and to decide whether the cost might be completely fixed, completely variable or mixed.

The following data are from one of Mount Dandenong Bikes' plants. They include weekly costs for packing bikes, together with a possible cost driver, the number of bikes shipped.

Week	Number of bikes shipped	Total packing cost
1	200	$729
2	270	$870
3	250	$820
4	210	$720
5	300	$950
6	175	$700

Figure 2.4(a) shows a scatter plot of these data. Notice that the data points seem to lie in a general upward linear pattern, suggesting that total packing costs increase with the number of bikes shipped. In addition, if we draw a trend line roughly through the middle of the data points as shown in figure 2.4(b) and continue the line to the vertical axis, the intercept appears to be above zero. Thus, the scatter plot suggests that the cost of packing is a mixed cost with an apparent variable component (the slope) and a fixed component (the intercept).

FIGURE 2.4	Scatter plot of total packing costs

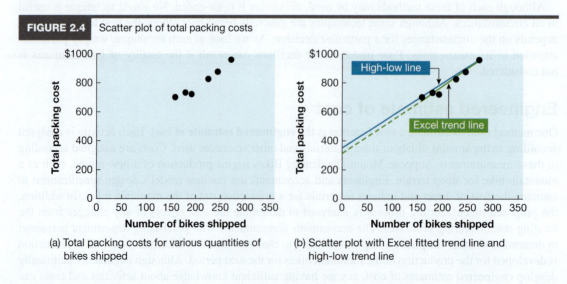

(a) Total packing costs for various quantities of bikes shipped

(b) Scatter plot with Excel fitted trend line and high-low trend line

Two-point method

The **two-point method** uses any two sets of data points for cost and a cost driver to algebraically calculate a mixed cost function. These data points can be drawn from a scatter plot. The line should resemble the general pattern of the data and be drawn using a ruler on a printed scatter plot or using a spreadsheet's line-draw feature. Spreadsheet programs such as Excel create a trend line representing the best fit for the data points.

We create the cost function by selecting and performing calculations with any two points on the line, even if they are not original data points. Variable cost (V) is calculated by computing the slope of the line — the change in cost compared to the change in the cost driver (Q) between the two points. Given V, the fixed cost is calculated by solving for F in the formula $TC = F + V \times Q$ for one of the two data points.

The lower trend line in figure 2.4(b) was originally generated using Excel. Two points on the trend line have values for Q of 240 and 190 bicycles on the horizontal axis. These same points have respective values for TC of $800 and $700 on the vertical axis. Using those two points, we calculate variable cost as follows:

$$\text{Change in cost} \div \text{Change in the cost driver} = (\$800 - \$700) \div (240 - 190)\,\text{bicycles}$$
$$= \$100 \div 50\,\text{bicycles}$$
$$= \$2\,\text{per bicycle}$$

Thus, $V = \$2$ per bicycle. We can now calculate fixed cost using 190 bikes as follows:

$$\$700 = F + 190\,\text{bicycles} \times \$2\,\text{per bicycle}$$
$$F = \$700 - \$380 = \$320$$

The total cost function (per week) for packing bikes is estimated as:

$$TC = \$320 + \$2Q$$

High-low method

The **high-low method** is a specific application of the two-point method using the highest and lowest data points of the cost driver. Although this technique is useful for illustration in classroom settings, it is inappropriate when we want to estimate an organisation's costs as accurately as possible. The problem with this method is that the highest and lowest cost driver observations are often outliers (values that might lie outside the normal range of activities). Therefore, this method frequently distorts the cost function. However, sometimes we have only two or three data points, in which case the high-low method may be our only choice.

The top trend line in figure 2.4(b) uses the highest and lowest observations for number of bicycles packed. Notice that this linear function misses most of the data points. Using the high-low method, we calculate the total cost function for Mount Dandenong Bikes' packing activities as follows:

$$\text{Change in cost} \div \text{Change in the cost driver} = (\$950 - \$700) \div (300 - 175)\,\text{bicycles}$$
$$= \$250 \div 125\,\text{bicycles}$$
$$= \$2\,\text{per bicycle}$$

The variable cost V is $2 per bicycle. Fixed cost is calculated using 175 bikes as follows:

$$\$700 = F + 175\,\text{bicycles} \times \$2\,\text{per bicycle}$$
$$F = \$700 - \$350$$
$$= \$350$$

The total cost function for packing bikes, then, is:

$$TC = \$350 + \$2Q$$

2.4 Estimating the cost function

LEARNING OBJECTIVE 2.4 Apply estimation techniques to determine the cost function.

Figure 2.5 summarises the activities involved in estimating a cost function for a particular cost object. Comprehensive example 1 demonstrates how to create a cost function.

FIGURE 2.5	Estimating relevant costs for a cost object

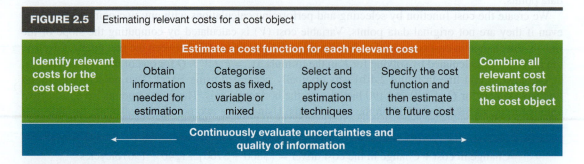

Identify relevant costs for the cost object	Estimate a cost function for each relevant cost				Combine all relevant cost estimates for the cost object
	Obtain information needed for estimation	Categorise costs as fixed, variable or mixed	Select and apply cost estimation techniques	Specify the cost function and then estimate the future cost	

Continuously evaluate uncertainties and quality of information

COMPREHENSIVE EXAMPLE 1

Creating a cost function using the high-low method

Small Animal Clinic is a not-for-profit clinic that provides limited veterinarian services, primarily vaccinations, for the surrounding community. The clinic has been growing each year, and its manager expects this trend to continue. The recent growth has actually been driven by an economic downturn. With rising unemployment, more people are unable to pay regular veterinarian fees. Many have turned to Small Animal Clinic, which charges a lower rate for services. A local foundation has provided Small Animal Clinic a matching grant for its services. For example, if a pet owner pays $30 for an examination and vaccines, the foundation will match the fee with an additional $30. This support has enabled the clinic to keep its rates low.

Identify relevant costs and obtain information needed for estimation

As part of her operating plans, Lucy Brown, the manager of Small Animal Clinic, would like to create a budget of next year's revenues and costs. Lucy estimates that the clinic will provide services for 3800 visits next year. The accountant, Josh Hardy, determined that the cost object is the clinic, and the cost driver for the clinic as a whole is the number of animal visits. Then, from the accounting records, he identified five relevant costs for the clinic: part-time veterinarians, technicians, treatment supplies, rent and administration costs. He performed analysis at the account level to obtain the information needed to estimate future costs. The information for the last three years follows. Because Small Animal Clinic is a not-for-profit entity, its profit is referred to as a *surplus*.

	2017	2018	2019
Animal visits	2 500	3 000	3 500
Veterinary fees	$ 72 500	$ 90 000	$105 000
Foundation matching grant	72 500	90 000	105 000
Total revenue	145 000	180 000	210 000
Expenses			
Part-time veterinarians	24 000	$ 32 800	$ 42 000
Technicians	71 000	78 000	78 049
Treatment supplies	4 000	4 600	5 200
Rent	8 000	8 500	8 750
Administration	38 000	39 600	41 200
Total expenses	145 000	163 500	175 199
Surplus	$ 0	$ 16 500	$ 34 801

Categorise costs, apply cost estimation techniques, and estimate future costs

To create individual cost functions, Josh categorises each cost as fixed, variable or mixed, and identifies potential cost drivers for the variable and mixed costs. He then selects the appropriate cost estimation technique for the mixed costs, develops the cost function, and estimates future costs for each relevant cost.

Part-time veterinarians

Josh studies the payroll records and finds a lot of variation in the cost of veterinarians. Part-time veterinarians are called in as necessary and are paid on an hourly basis. Most of their time is spent with animals, so Josh determines it is a direct cost. Therefore, he thinks that the amount of time the veterinarians spend with each animal might be a cost driver. However, the accounting system does not record the visit time per animal. Instead, records are available for the total number of animal visits. Josh considers other potential cost drivers such as number of veterinarians on call and the hours the clinic is open, but eliminates them because they seem less likely than number of animal visits to have a cause-and-effect relationship with veterinarian wages. Therefore, he categorises veterinarian fees as a variable cost and plans to use the number of animal visits as the cost driver. Josh knows that although veterinarian pay is increased periodically, no increase is planned for next year. Because last year's information is the most current, he uses only last year's data to create the cost function. In 2019 this category included no fixed costs, and the variable cost per animal visit was $12 ($42 000 total cost ÷ 3500 animal visits).

The cost function for veterinarians is:

$$TC = \$0 + \$12 \text{ per animal visit} \times Q \text{ animal visits}$$

Josh can now estimate 2020 costs, with $Q = 3800$ animal visits.

$$TC = \$12 \text{ per animal visit} \times 3800 \text{ animal visits} = \$45\,600$$

Technicians

Josh learns from payroll records that the technical staff are permanent and paid on a salary basis. The technicians clean examination rooms, prepare supplies, fill out paperwork, handle the reception desk and assist the veterinarians with each visit. Because they work on many different tasks, Josh concludes that this cost is indirect and fixed.

Again, Josh uses the most current information in his cost function. A salary increase of 2.5 per cent is expected for 2020. With no variable costs and only the fixed cost of $78 049 for 2019, the updated cost function for technicians is:

$$TC = \left(\$78\,049 \times 1.025\right) + \$0Q = \$80\,000$$

Josh estimates the 2020 cost for technicians to be $80 000.

Treatment supplies

Josh believes that treatment supplies is either a variable or mixed cost. He learns from the technicians that treatment supplies include items that vary depending on the services provided, such as vaccination serum and syringes. He also learns that supplies include items such as lab coats for clinic employees that vary by number of employees rather than visits.

He concludes that the cost of treatment supplies is a mixed cost, and he believes that number of animal visits has a cause-and-effect relationship for the variable portion.

Josh learns that few significant changes occurred in the cost or use of treatment supplies over the past three years. Therefore, he decides to use all three years' data to estimate the cost function. With only three data points, he uses the high-low method to separate the fixed and variable components of treatment supplies. He first identifies the highest and lowest data points for the cost driver, which is number of animal visits. The lowest number of animal visits was in 2017, and the highest number was in 2019. He calculates the variable cost per unit by dividing the change in cost ($5200 − $4000) by the change in volume (3500 − 2500) for these two data points:

$$\left(\$5200 - \$4000\right) \div (3500 - 2500) = \$1200 \div 1000 = \$1.20 \text{ per animal visit}$$

Next, Josh substitutes the variable cost rate into the cost equation for 2019 and solves for the fixed costs:

$$TC = F + V \times Q$$
$$\$5200 = F + \$1.20 \text{ per animal visit} \times 3500 \text{ animal visits}$$
$$\$5200 = F + \$4200$$
$$F = \$1000$$

Josh's cost function for treatment supplies is:

$$TC = \$1000 + \$1.20 \text{ per animal visit} \times Q \text{ animal visits}$$

He can now estimate costs for treatment supplies in 2020, assuming 3800 animal visits.

$$TC = \$1000 + \$1.20 \text{ per animal visit} \times 3800 \text{ animal visits} = \$5560$$

Rent
Josh knows that rent can change annually when the lease is renewed. However, rent changes depend on local rates rather than on the level of operating activity at the clinic. Accordingly, he categorises rent as a fixed cost.

Josh uses the most recent rent amount and sets up his cost function.

$$TC = \$8750 + \$0Q$$
$$TC = \$8750$$

He does not update this figure because he learns that the property manager is not planning to increase rent for 2020. Therefore, his estimate for rent is also $8750.

Administration
Josh learns that administration includes costs to set up files for new animals and office supplies related to the paperwork for each visit. Josh reviews the general ledger entries and finds that the remainder of the administrative cost is for salaries, general office supplies, and telephone, which Josh concludes are fixed costs. Thus, he concludes that administration is a mixed cost, with animal visits as the cost driver for the variable portion.

Josh performs an account analysis of the administrative costs, separating the cost of supplies such as file folders, tabs and the forms required for each visit. From his analysis, he calculates the cost of these supplies as $8000 in 2017, $9600 in 2018 and $11200 in 2019, or about $3.20 per animal visit. He bases his estimate of fixed administrative costs on the most recent year's data. During 2019 total administrative costs were $41200. When he subtracts the variable cost of $11200, this leaves $30000 ($41200 – $11200) as his estimate of the fixed cost. Therefore, his cost function for administration is:

$$TC = \$30\,000 + \$3.20 \text{ per animal visit} \times Q \text{ animal visits}$$

Josh now estimates administration cost for 2020.

$$TC = \$30\,000 + \$3.20 \text{ per animal visit} \times 3800 \text{ animal visits} = \$42\,160$$

Combine all relevant cost estimates
Josh creates the following summary of his cost functions and estimated costs for 2020.

Cost	Category	Fixed cost	Variable cost per visit	2020 Estimated cost for 3800 animal visits
Part-time veterinarians	Variable	$ 0	$12.00	$ 45 600
Technicians	Fixed	80 000	0.00	80 000
Treatment supplies	Mixed	1 000	1.20	5 560
Rent	Fixed	8 750	0.00	8 750
Administration	Mixed	30 000	3.20	42 160
Total		$119 750	$16.40	$182 070

The total cost function for Small Animal Clinic is

$$TC = \$119\,750 + \$16.40 \text{ per animal visit} \times Q \text{ animal visits}$$

Based on Lucy's estimate of 3800 animal visits for next year, Josh estimates that total 2020 costs will be: $119750 + $16.40 per animal visit × 3800 animal visits = $182070.

Estimating profit
Lucy told Josh that she did not expect any major changes from 2019 to 2020 in the types of services provided, the average fees or the matching grant. Although Josh does not know last year's average fees, he calculates it from last year's revenue information (which includes the matching grant):

$$\text{Average revenue in 2019} = \text{Total 2019 revenue} \div \text{Number of animal visits in 2019}$$
$$= \$210\,000 \div 3500 \text{ animal visits}$$
$$= \$60 \text{ per animal visit}$$

Given average revenues of $60 per animal visit, budgeted revenues for next year (including the matching grant) are:

$$\text{Budgeted revenues} = \text{Estimated 2020 animal visits} \times \text{Average revenue rate}$$
$$= 3800 \text{ animal visits} \times \$60 \text{ per animal visit}$$
$$= \$228\,000$$

Using the budgeted revenues and costs as calculated, Josh tells Lucy that he expects Small Animal Clinic to earn a surplus during 2020 of $45 930 ($228 000 – $182 070).

2.5 Regression analysis

LEARNING OBJECTIVE 2.5 Apply regression analysis in cost estimation.

In comprehensive example 1, Josh used the high-low method to estimate the cost function for treatment supplies. This method is often not sufficiently accurate because it uses the two most extreme data points, which could distort the cost function. An alternative estimation technique is regression analysis, a statistical technique that measures the average change in a dependent variable (the cost item being estimated) for every unit change in one or more independent variables (the cost drivers). Regression analysis uses all of the available data points and often improves the accuracy of a cost function.

Simple regression analysis develops a cost function by calculating values for the statistical relationship between total cost and a single cost driver. **Multiple regression analysis** develops a cost function by calculating values for the statistical relationship between total cost and two or more cost drivers.

Simple regression analysis

In figure 2.4 we created a scatter plot for a cost object (packing costs) and a cost driver (number of bikes). We used Excel to generate a trend line and developed a cost function using that data. Simple regression analysis is a statistical method used to find the trend line that minimises the distance from every data point to the line. The slope of the line represents the variable cost per unit, and the intercept of the line with the vertical axis represents the fixed cost. The distance between each observation and the line is called the *error term*. In locating a slope that best fits all of the available data, regression analysis minimises the squared error terms.

Simple regression analysis then estimates the following equation:

$$Y = \alpha + \beta X + \varepsilon$$

where Y is the dependent variable (total cost), α (alpha) is the intercept (fixed cost), β (beta) is the slope coefficient (variable cost per unit), X is the independent variable (the cost driver), and ε (epsilon) is the error term, also called the residual.

We usually use a computer program such as Excel or SAS to perform regression analysis. The ability of computer programs to easily perform regression analyses makes the cost of using this technique low. Thus, the cost of performing regression analysis is not likely to exceed the benefits.

Interpreting simple regression results

Regression analysis provides the best estimate of the cost function in cases with a strong positive linear relationship between the cost and the cost driver. However, the data points we use in a regression rarely fit into an absolutely straight line. Deviations from linearity may occur because the true underlying cost function is not strictly linear. Deviations may also occur because the regression data typically come from past costs and activities that might be mismeasured or include unusual events, shifts in cost behaviour over time or random fluctuations. When interpreting regression results, we need to keep in mind that we are using regression analysis *only* because we do not know the actual cost function and must estimate it. Furthermore, we might not be confident that the cost we are trying to estimate is a mixed cost. We use regression to estimate the cost function and to learn more about how the cost behaves. Figure 2.6 presents the questions that we address when using simple regression to estimate a cost function.

FIGURE 2.6 Questions addressed by simple regression analysis

Question about the cost function	Relevant simple regression statistics
How confident can we be that the actual fixed cost is greater than zero (i.e. that there is a fixed component in the cost function)?	t-statistic and p-value for the alpha coefficient
How confident can we be that the actual variable cost per unit of the cost driver is greater than zero (i.e. that there is a variable component in the cost function)?	t-statistic and p-value for the beta coefficient
Overall, how well does the cost driver explain the behaviour (i.e. the variation) in the cost?	Adjusted R-square, as well as t-statistic and p-value for both coefficients

Figure 2.7 shows the output from regressing Mount Dandenong Bikes' packing costs on the number of bikes packed. For each coefficient (alpha and beta), the regression output includes both a t-statistic and a p-value. We examine the t-statistic calculated for each coefficient to evaluate whether that coefficient is significantly greater than zero. The t-statistic compares the coefficient with its standard error. If the coefficient is small relative to the standard error, we cannot be confident that the coefficient is different from zero. If the t-statistic is significantly large (above 2), we have more confidence that our estimates for fixed and variable costs are different from zero. The p-value gives the statistical significance of the t-statistic, or the probability that the coefficient is not different from zero. Acceptable p-values generally need to be less than 0.10, and preferably less than 0.05.

A low p-value for the alpha coefficient gives us confidence that the fixed cost is significantly different from zero. Similarly, a low p-value for the beta coefficient gives us confidence that the variable cost is significantly different from zero. If a p-value is too high, we conclude that the coefficient should not be used in the cost function. Sometimes only one of the coefficients is statistically greater than zero. In this case, we generally conclude that the cost is not mixed, but instead is variable or fixed (depending on which coefficient is significant).

FIGURE 2.7 Regression analysis results for shipping costs and number of bikes

SUMMARY OUTPUT

Regression statistics

Multiple R	0.982 037 62
R-square	0.964 397 89
Adjusted R-square	0.955 497 36
Standard error	20.930 633 5
Observations	6

	Coefficients	Standard error	t-statistic	p-value
Intercept	314.374 297	47.256 043 8	6.652 573 35	0.002 651 24
X variable 1	2.066 017 23	0.198 478 61	10.409 269	0.000 481 07

Interpreting the output from the Mount Dandenong Bikes example (see figure 2.7), the intercept (fixed cost) is \$314 and the p-value for the t-statistic is 0.002. This result means that the fixed cost has a probability of being zero about 2 in 1000 times. We are quite confident that it is different from zero. The beta coefficient (\$2.07) also has a small p-value (0.0004). Using this information, our total cost function would be TC = \$314 + \$2.07Q, where Q is the number of bikes.

The adjusted R-square statistic reflects an estimate of the percentage of variation in cost that is explained by the cost driver. In the Mount Dandenong Bikes example, the adjusted R-square is 0.95. This result means that the variation in number of bikes packed explains about 95 per cent of the variation in packing cost. An advantage of regression analysis when more than one potential cost driver is involved is that we can compare the adjusted R-squares from several regressions that have different cost drivers for the same cost. The cost driver that provides the highest adjusted R-square explains the largest portion of changes in cost.

We will next illustrate how to use simple regression analysis to estimate a cost function for Small Animal Clinic. The process we will use is summarised in figure 2.8. We will also compare the results for simple regression with the two-point and high-low methods (see comprehensive example 2).

FIGURE 2.8 Using regression analysis to estimate a cost function

1. Consider the behaviour of the cost.	Decide whether the cost is likely to be a good candidate for regression analysis. The best candidates for regression are costs that appear to be mixed.
2. Generate a list of possible cost drivers.	The cost drivers must be economically plausible; changes in the cost driver could potentially affect cost.
3. Gather data.	We need data for both the dependent variable (the cost being estimated) and for one or more independent variables (the cost drivers).
4. Plot the cost for each potential cost driver.	Scatter plots that have a positive slope or a football-shaped pattern indicate a potential linear relationship between the cost and the cost driver. Eliminate any cost drivers that do not figure a positive linear relationship with cost. If no cost drivers remain, the cost should not be estimated using regression analysis.
5. Perform the regression analysis.	For each remaining potential cost driver, perform simple regression analysis with that driver as the independent variable. If necessary, perform a series of multiple regression analyses with different combinations of cost drivers. Use a spreadsheet program such as Excel to perform the regressions.
6. Evaluate the appropriateness of each cost driver.	Use the goodness of fit statistic (adjusted R-square) to select those cost drivers that explain a high proportion of variability in the cost.
7. Evaluate the sign and significance of the cost function's components.	Verify that each coefficient is positive. Use the p-values for the t-statistics to determine whether the intercept coefficient reflecting fixed cost and slope coefficient reflecting variable cost are significantly different from zero.
8. Write the cost function as $TC = F + V \times Q$.	If significantly different from zero, use the intercept coefficient as the estimated fixed cost and the independent variable coefficient as the estimated variable cost.

COMPREHENSIVE EXAMPLE 2

Estimate of cost function using the two-point method and regression analysis

When Josh shows Lucy his revenue and cost estimates, she questions him about the cost of treatment supplies. Believing his estimate to be too high, she asks him to investigate this cost further.

Revised analysis of the treatment supplies cost

When Josh originally estimated the cost function for treatment supplies, he had only three data points — the cost for each of the past three years. With so few data points, he had used the high-low method to estimate the cost function. Using quarterly data, however, would give him more data points, allowing him to use other estimation techniques that would generate a higher-quality cost function.

Josh is also concerned about the accuracy of the data for the number of animal visits, which are tracked manually at the reception desk and sometimes not recorded. He considers using the number of bills recorded in the accounting system to count the number of animal visits, but a single pet owner often brings in more than one pet and yet receives a single bill. He considers whether another cost driver would be more accurate.

▶

Josh knows that the veterinarians use different supplies for each visit because the needs of each pet are different. For example, a puppy may get a series of vaccinations at the same time, whereas an adult dog gets only one or two vaccinations. Yet when he uses number of animal visits as the cost driver, he assumes that the same amount of supplies is used for each visit. Josh knows that the bill for each visit includes charges for supplies. Therefore, the revenue per visit varies with the number and type of supplies used. He determines that revenue might be better correlated with treatment supplies than number of animal visits. He also thinks that the data for revenue per visit are more accurate because they are recorded by the accounting system when bills are created.

Quarterly data

Although Josh believes that revenue may be better correlated with treatment supplies cost than animal visits, he decides to analyse both drivers to learn more about their behaviour. He collects the following quarterly data for his analyses.

Quarter	Treatment supplies cost	Animal visits	Revenues
2017-1	$1 000	500	$18 125
2017-2	920	725	17 400
2017-3	1 120	700	20 300
2017-4	960	575	16 675
2018-1	966	750	18 900
2018-2	1 058	960	20 700
2018-3	1 288	600	24 300
2018-4	1 288	690	26 100
2019-1	1 404	700	28 350
2019-2	1 092	595	23 100
2019-3	1 404	910	29 400
2019-4	1 300	1 295	24 150

Scatter plots

First Josh creates scatter plots of the treatment supplies cost against animal visits and against revenues. When creating the scatter plots, he wants the vertical axes on the two plots to have the same scale so that he can compare them. He visually examines the plots and fits a trend line to each plot. Josh notices that most of the cost points are relatively close to the trend line in the revenue scatter plot shown in figure 2.9(a), whereas many of the data points are further away from the trend line in the animal visit scatter plot in figure 2.9(b). This observation suggests that revenue is likely to provide a more accurate cost function than number of animal visits.

Two-point method

First Josh decides to use the two-point method with revenue as the cost driver. He selects the points when revenues are $20 000 and $25 000, and draws a vertical line from these points on the revenue axis to the trend line, shown in figure 2.9(a). Where each vertical line intersects the trend line, he draws a horizontal line to the cost axis and visually estimates the cost for these points as $1000 and $1233 respectively. Dividing the change in cost ($1233 – $1000) by the change in revenues ($25 000 – $20 000), he estimates a variable cost of $0.047 per dollar of revenue, or 4.7 per cent of revenues. He then uses the data point for cost of $1000 to estimate the fixed cost, using the following formula for the cost function:

$$\$1000 = F + (4.7\% \times \$20\,000)$$
$$F = \$1000 - \$940 = \$60$$

Given these calculations, he estimates the cost function as:

$$TC = \$60 + 4.7\% \times \text{Revenues}$$

Next Josh uses the two-point method with animal visits as the cost driver. He uses the same procedures as previously described to choose two points on the trend line, shown in figure 2.9(b). Given these two points, he estimates the cost function as shown below.

$$TC = \$813 + \$0.42 \times \text{Number of animal visits}$$

Simple regression analysis

Josh is concerned that his calculations using the two-point method may not be as accurate as he would like. He decides to perform simple regression analysis. When number of animal visits is the cost driver as in figure 2.10(a), the adjusted R-square is 0.035, which is very low. But when revenue is the cost driver as in figure 2.10(b), the adjusted R-square is quite high at 0.915, suggesting that changes in revenue explain about 91.5 per cent of the changes in supplies cost. He concludes that revenue is a much better cost driver than animal visits. However, he waits to reach a final conclusion until he analyses the rest of the regression results.

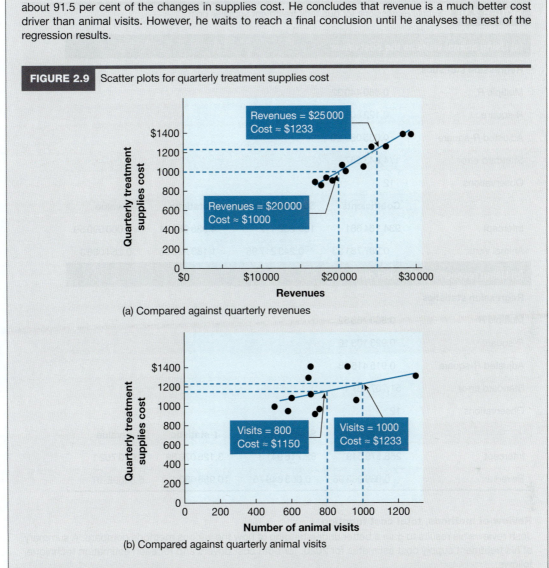

FIGURE 2.9 Scatter plots for quarterly treatment supplies cost

(a) Compared against quarterly revenues

(b) Compared against quarterly animal visits

Focusing on figure 2.10(b), Josh observes that the coefficients for both the intercept (258.7) and independent variable (0.039) are positive, as required to create a cost function. He notices that the p-value for the intercept is 0.01, suggesting only a small probability that the intercept could be zero. The p-value for the coefficient on revenue is even smaller at 0.000 000 68, suggesting a tiny probability that the coefficient could be zero. These results give Josh considerable confidence in the regression results. He creates a new cost function for treatment supplies as follows.

$$TC = \$259 + 4.0\% \times Revenue$$

Revised cost estimate

Josh's earlier estimate of $228 000 for 2020 revenue (refer to comprehensive example 1) includes the matching grant. However, the grant, which accounts for half of all revenues, is not included in the quarterly data used to estimate the new cost function. Therefore, Josh needs to divide estimated revenues in half when using the new cost function: $228 000 ÷ 2 = $114 000. His revised estimate of the treatment supply cost for 2020 is:

$$TC = \$259 + \left(4.0\% \times \$114\,000\right) = \$4819$$

Next, he revises his estimate of total 2020 costs. He previously estimated total costs to be $182 070, including $5560 in treatment supplies. His new estimate for total 2020 costs is $181 329 ($182 070 − $5560 + $4819). Finally, he revises his estimate of the 2020 surplus to account for changes in total costs:

$$Estimated\ surplus = \$228\,000 - \$181\,329 = \$46\,671$$

FIGURE 2.10   Simple regressions for quarterly treatment supplies cost

(a) Using animal visits as the cost driver

Regression statistics

Multiple R	0.350 440 32
R-square	0.122 808 42
Adjusted R-square	0.035 089 26
Standard error	174.643 357
Observations	12

	Coefficients	Standard error	t-statistic	p-value
Intercept	934.164 081	189.252 112	4.936 082 71	0.000 590 59
Animal visits	0.287 781 23	0.243 217 95	1.183 223 65	0.264 086 3

(b) Using revenues as the cost driver

Regression statistics

Multiple R	0.960 783 62
R-square	0.923 105 16
Adjusted R-square	0.915 415 68
Standard error	51.707 487 1
Observations	12

	Coefficients	Standard error	t-statistic	p-value
Intercept	258.579 519	82.716 941 3	3.126 076 89	0.010 762 1
Revenue	0.039 988 96	0.003 649 75	10.956 630 1	6.8389E-07

Review of methods, total cost function

Josh reviews his results to gain a better understanding of how the various methods compare. A summary of his treatment supply cost estimates for 2020, for both cost drivers and for each estimation technique, follows:

		2020 Estimate
Number of animal visits (3800 estimated for 2020):		
High-low method	TC = $1000 + $1.20 per visit × Visits	$5 560
Two-point method	TC = $813 + $0.42 per visit × Visits	$2 409
Simple regression	TC = $934 + $0.29 per visit × Visits	$2 036
Revenues ($114 000 estimated for 2020):		
Two-point method	TC = $60 + 4.7% × Revenues	$5 418
Simple regression	TC = $259 + 4.0% × Revenues	$4 819

Josh is glad that he is no longer using his original estimate based on the high-low method and animal visits as a cost driver. He believes that method would significantly overestimate the treatment costs. He is surprised to learn that the other two methods for animal visits as the cost driver might have significantly underestimated the cost. After comparing the two-point and regression results, he concludes that the two-point method is not very accurate. Overall, he decides that he will probably use regression analysis in the future to help with this type of estimate.

Finally, Josh revises the total cost function for the clinic. Even though revenue from pet owners is now being used as the driver for treatment supplies, other parts of the function still use the number of animal visits as the driver. He subtracts the $1.20 per animal visit that had been attributed to treatment supplies, leaving $15.20 for the other relevant variable costs. He also adjusts total fixed costs of $119 750 by subtracting $741 ($1000 old fixed cost estimate – $259 new fixed cost estimate), leaving $119 009. Thus, the revised cost function is:

$$TC = \$119\,009 + (\$15.20 \times \text{Number of animal visits}) + (4.0\% \times \text{Fee revenue})$$

Josh and Lucy decide to continue budgeting average revenue per animal visit at $60 ($30 in fees plus $30 in matching grant). They can now use this cost function to analyse best-case and worst-case scenarios and will be better prepared for unexpected changes that might occur next year.

2.6 Uses and limitations of cost estimates

LEARNING OBJECTIVE 2.6 Reflect on the uses and limitations of cost estimates.

Uncertainties are a fact of life in the business world. Even the best available information and best decision-making processes may lead to poor outcomes. Nevertheless, managers make better decisions and obtain better average results when they use higher-quality information and decision-making processes. Because of uncertainties about future cost behaviour, we need to evaluate the quality of both our data and the various estimation techniques.

Information quality

One factor that affects the quality of past cost information is whether the accounting system is able to directly trace the costs to individual cost objects. For example, if Mount Dandenong Bikes' accounting system traces the cost of handlebars to each bicycle produced, then past handlebar costs are known with high accuracy. This information, in turn, will improve the quality of future handlebar cost estimates.

If the accounting system cannot trace a relevant cost to a cost object, the cost must instead be allocated. For example, costs such as insurance can be traced to the production facility but cannot be traced to any one bicycle. However, a portion of these costs can be allocated to each bicycle produced. Accounting systems often accumulate indirect costs into overhead cost pools that tend to include a mixture of both fixed and variable costs. Appropriate cost drivers for these cost pools are often difficult to identify. Nevertheless, past accounting data might be the best information available for estimating indirect costs.

Recall from chapter 1 that higher-quality information is more certain, complete, relevant, timely and valuable. Better accounting systems improve the quantity, relevance and timeliness of cost information. However, we may be unable to obtain higher-quality information. For example, in the Small Animal Clinic example, Josh initially lacked sufficient data to use regression analysis to separate mixed costs into fixed and variable components. This circumstance occurs frequently in the business world. Other common reasons why past cost information might be unavailable or unreliable to use include the following.

- The organisation has operated for only a few periods.
- The organisation's operations have changed substantially.
- Inflation, deflation or other economic changes have altered the behaviour of costs.
- The organisation operates in an environment where technologies and costs change rapidly.
- The organisation's accounting system does not currently capture and report the needed information.

Under these circumstances, cost estimates based on past costs are of lower quality than cost estimates from better data. In addition, the quality of information often deteriorates over time. Accordingly, cost functions are most useful for estimating costs over short time periods, such as for the next year.

Average costs

Because financial accounting information is readily available, accountants and managers often want to rely on it for decision making. However, financial accounting measures are usually based on average costs, which are inappropriate for decision making. The **average cost (AC)** is simply computed as total costs (TC) divided by the quantity (Q) of activity or production (AC = TC/Q).

When average costs are used to estimate the cost function ($\text{TC} = 0 + \text{AC} \times Q$), fixed costs are assumed to be variable. Therefore, future costs are either overestimated or underestimated unless future production is exactly the quantity used to calculate average cost per unit. Consequently, we usually avoid using financial statement costs — or any other average costs — for decision making.

Quality of estimation techniques

Figure 2.11 summarises the advantages and disadvantages of each cost behaviour analysis approach introduced in this chapter. None of the methods is best in all circumstances. For example, regression analysis is a higher-quality technique than the two-point or high-low methods for separating mixed costs into fixed and variable components. However, regression cannot be used when too few observations of past costs are available. In addition, most of the methods in figure 2.11 rely on past costs, which might need updating. The engineered estimate of cost method can be used when no past costs are available, and it also provides a benchmark that can be used to monitor the efficiency of costs in the future. Although we know that higher-quality techniques result in higher-quality information, we do not always use higher-quality techniques. Sometimes the cost exceeds the benefit; at other times we do not have adequate information required by a higher-quality technique.

FIGURE 2.11	Advantages and disadvantages of cost behaviour analysis approaches	
Method and description	**Advantages**	**Disadvantages**
Engineered estimate of cost An analysis of labour time, materials and other resources used in each activity. Cost estimates are based on resources used.	• Can use when no past data are available • Provides a benchmark for what future costs should be • Most accurate for estimating costs of repetitive activities • Identifies and measures some non-linear cost functions (e.g. economies of scale and learning curves)	• Difficult to estimate some types of costs, such as overhead • Time consuming • May not identify all costs
Analysis at the account level A review of the pattern in past costs recorded in the accounting system. Knowledge of operations is used to classify cost as variable, fixed or mixed.	• Can be used when only one period of data is available • Best for costs that are fixed or variable • Provides information about types of costs incurred	• Difficult to identify costs that are not strictly fixed or strictly variable • Relies on past costs, which might not represent future costs
Scatter plot A plot of past data points for cost against a potential cost driver. Visual analysis of the plot is used to decide whether the cost might be completely fixed, completely variable or mixed.	• Provides information about cost behaviour in relation to potential cost drivers • Facilitates evaluation of whether a potential cost driver is viable	• Does not compute a cost function • Relies on past costs, which might not represent future costs
Two-point method An algebraic calculation of a linear mixed cost function using any two data points of the cost and cost driver.	• Can be used with as few as two data points • Computationally simple	• Difficult to identify most representative data points for estimating future costs • Ignores all but two data points (inefficient use of data) • Mismeasures the cost function if data points come from more than one relevant range • Relies on past costs, which might not represent future costs

Method and description	Advantages	Disadvantages
High-low method A specific application of the two-point method using the highest and lowest data points of the cost driver.	• Same as two-point method • Does not require judgement for selecting data points	• Same as two-point method • Highest and lowest data points are often atypical, distorting the cost function
Regression analysis A statistical technique that measures the average change in a dependent variable for every unit change in one or more independent variables. Creates a linear cost function where variable cost is the slope of the regression line and fixed cost is the intercept.	• Increases cost function accuracy by using all available data points • Best for a strong positive linear relationship between the cost and cost driver • Easy to perform with available software • Provides statistics for evaluating the quality of results	• Mismeasures the cost function if data points come from more than one relevant range • Inefficient for estimating a strictly fixed or strictly variable cost function • Relies on past costs, which might not represent future costs

Reliance on cost estimates

Concerns we have about the quality of cost information affect our reliance on the results. Managers might delay growth opportunities or alter operating decisions to avoid assuming extra risk in cases where they are less sure about their cost estimates. As managers make decisions, the quality of information affects the alternatives that they consider and the weight they place on various pieces of information.

Data limitations

The results from regression analysis are only as accurate as the data we use. The following need to be checked before data are used in regression analysis.
- The relationship between the cost and cost driver is economically plausible.
- Cost and cost driver data are matched and recorded in the appropriate period.
- Inflation and deflation have been taken into consideration.
- The relevant range reflects similar technologies across the range.
- No clerical errors occurred in the recorded data.
- Any data from periods with unusual events are eliminated.
- The activity levels for which we are predicting cost are within the relevant range; that is, we are not predicting cost for activity levels that are greater (smaller) than the largest (smallest) in our data set.

APPENDIX 2A
Regression analysis — additional topics

MULTIPLE REGRESSION ANALYSIS

Multiple regression is used when more than one cost driver may provide the best estimate of a cost function. We use the same method to estimate the cost function as that illustrated earlier in the chapter. The only difference is that two or more independent variables (cost drivers) are used in the regression analysis.

Choosing cost drivers for multiple regression

Sometimes several cost drivers appear to be correlated with the cost we are estimating; their scatter plots show a possible linear relationship with the cost object. In these cases, we include all of the potential drivers in a multiple regression to determine the significance of each. Then we drop those drivers that have insignificant *t*-statistics. Remember, however, that each potential cost driver must have economic plausibility — a reason to believe that each one might drive the cost we are trying to estimate. Comprehensive example 3 demonstrates how cost drivers are used in multiple regression.

COMPREHENSIVE EXAMPLE 3

Using multiple regression to estimate a cost function

Print Masters Print Shop incurs overhead costs that are related to its printing machines (maintenance, depreciation, insurance etc.) and to the amount of paper printed (ink, storage and handling of paper, packing materials etc.). Figure 2A.1 summarises monthly data for overhead costs, machine hours, and reams of paper used for Print Masters Print Shop.

FIGURE 2A.1 Data for print shop overhead costs and two potential cost drivers

Month	Overhead costs	Machine hours	Reams of paper
1	$68 948	959	828 000
2	87 171	1 227	1 246 000
3	84 448	1 351	874 000
4	89 030	1 480	958 000
5	83 303	952	1 356 000
6	82 660	986	1 332 000
7	78 793	931	1 170 000
8	82 834	1 439	958 000
9	77 829	945	1 238 000
10	72 303	869	978 000
11	78 804	1 171	890 000
12	85 850	1 228	1 162 000
13	70 343	928	892 000
14	85 991	950	1 376 000
15	77 626	1 016	1 160 000
16	70 397	902	928 000
17	77 189	948	1 220 000
18	75 443	1 130	1 064 000
19	79 599	1 335	830 000
20	72 690	1 052	1 034 000
21	76 307	860	1 280 000
22	79 725	1 188	1 096 000

23	80 492	1 254	850 000
24	87 697	1 187	1 390 000
25	76 516	948	936 000
26	83 055	1 015	1 320 000
27	75 021	971	956 000
28	85 210	1 111	1 304 000
29	84 531	1 326	1 238 000
30	78 575	1 017	1 026 000

Scatter plots and simple regression results

A scatter plot is presented for machine hours in figure 2A.2(a) and for reams of paper in figure 2A.2(b). Each plot suggests a potential linear relationship with printing overhead costs because it appears to have an upward slope, although the slope does not appear to be very steep in either plot. Thus, based on the scatter plots, both cost drivers appear to be viable. Simple regression analysis for each potential cost driver confirms this evidence. A summary of the simple regression results is shown following.

As you can see from the summary below the intercepts and slope coefficients for both regressions are highly significant. However, the adjusted R-square is 0.35 for machine hours and 0.22 for reams of paper. Thus, neither driver appears to be an overall good predictor of the variation in printing overhead cost.

	Machine hours	Reams of paper
Intercept coefficient	$58 800	$68 109
t-statistic (*p*-value)	11.43 (<0.0001)	11.63 (<0.0001)
Independent variable coefficient	$19.11	$0.02
t-statistic (*p*-value)	4.09 (0.0003)	3.08 (0.005)
Adjusted *R*-square	0.35	0.22

FIGURE 2A.2 Scatter plot of print shop overhead costs

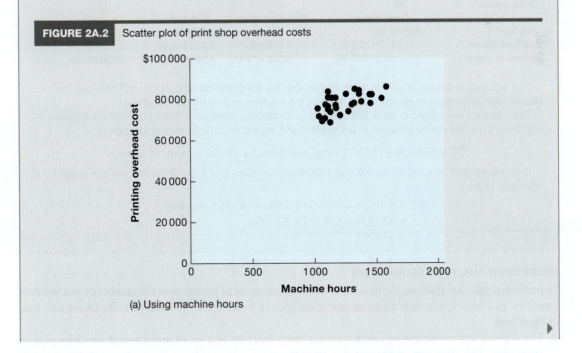

(a) Using machine hours

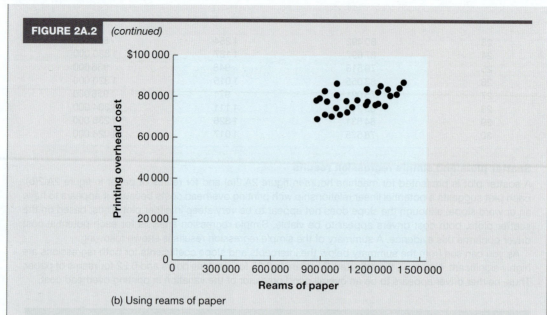

(b) Using reams of paper

Multiple regression analysis

We can perform multiple regression analysis for printing overhead cost using both machine hours and reams of paper as independent variables. We will then see whether any improvement in overall explanatory ability occurs. The following excerpts come from the Excel printout for this regression:

Regression statistics

Multiple R	0.909 216 78			
R-square	0.826 675 15			
Adjusted R-square	0.813 836 27			
Standard error	2 371.267 4			
Observations	30			
	Coefficients	**Standard error**	**t-statistic**	**p-value**
Intercept	30 338.795 1	4 371.832 43	6.939 606 13	1.856E-07
Machine hours	24.371 125 9	2.578 802 04	9.450 560 98	4.7054E-10
Reams of paper	0.020 731 46	0.002 470 49	8.391 635 67	5.2945E-09

The adjusted R-square of 0.81 is much higher than for either individual cost driver. Therefore, the two drivers together appear to explain much more of the variation in printing overhead cost.

The intercept term (fixed cost) is $30 339 and is statistically significant. Both potential cost drivers — machine hours and reams of paper — are positive and significant. The total cost function is:

$$TC = \$30\,339 + (\$24.37 \times \text{machine hours}) + (\$0.02 \times \text{reams of paper})$$

If we expect that next month we will use 1000 machine hours and 1 million reams, we can predict our total cost to be:

$$TC = \$30\,339 + (\$24.37)(1000) + (0.02)(1\,000\,000)$$
$$= \$30\,339 + \$24\,370 + \$20\,000$$
$$= \$74\,709$$

REGRESSION ANALYSIS ASSUMPTIONS

To perform regression analysis, the number of observations must be greater than the number of independent variables. In addition, a number of assumptions are used in linear regression analysis. We investigate four of them here.

1. The dependent variable can be calculated as a linear function of a set of independent variables plus an error term. The error term is the distance from the regression trend line for each actual data point of cost versus cost driver.

2. The error terms have a normal distribution with a mean of zero. The t-statistics are based on the assumption that the errors are normally distributed. If this assumption is incorrect, we cannot know with any confidence whether the coefficients are different from zero.

3. The error terms have a constant variance for all of the observations, and they are not correlated with each other. Constant variance can be a problem with accounting data because costs from one period could be

related to costs in the next period. For example, an accrual that occurs in one period is often reversed in the next period. In addition, variance often increases at higher or lower levels of activity. If error terms are correlated, the standard errors are inaccurate and therefore the t-statistics are not meaningful.

4. Relatively little correlation occurs among the independent variables. If the independent variables are highly correlated (multicollinearity), the coefficients are more likely to be inaccurate and this would create inaccuracies in our estimated cost functions. An example of correlated independent variables could be direct labour hours and machine hours, when labour is used to manage machines.

We test for the linearity assumption by examining a scatter plot to see whether the relationship between cost and the cost driver appears to have a generally linear trend. If this assumption is not met, linear regression analysis is not a useful tool. We test for normal distribution, uniform variance and uncorrelated error terms using scatter plots or other statistics methods. We plot the error terms against the independent variables. If error terms with small (large) values are associated with independent variables of small (large) values, the error terms are correlated with each other and the results from this model will not accurately reflect the underlying cost function. To determine whether independent variables are correlated, we use the correlation functions in a spreadsheet or statistical program. Independent variables that have a high correlation (above about 70 per cent) might cause problems with regression analysis. The correlated variables can be entered in a regression together and then independently to see whether the coefficient and t-statistics are affected by the correlation.

ADDITIONAL REGRESSION ANALYSIS CONSIDERATIONS

We can use regression analysis when we know that the majority of costs are likely to be only fixed or only variable, but in these cases other techniques may be just as accurate and require less data-gathering time. Suppose we want to estimate a cost function for handlebars, which vary with production volume at Mount Dandenong Bikes. Either we ask purchasing to tell us the current per-unit cost and to check for price updates, or we divide the total cost of a recent purchase by the number of units purchased to develop an estimate of that variable cost. Similarly, to estimate a future fixed cost, we base our estimate on the fixed cost from one or more prior periods in the same manner shown for rent in comprehensive example 1.

Stepwise linear fixed costs

We learned earlier that the cost function for some fixed costs is stepwise linear. For example, in figure 2.2(b), the cost function for rent, which increases as more space is needed due to high sales revenues, is shown below.

$$TC = \$6000, \text{ for } Q \leq \$30\,000 \text{ in sales}$$
$$TC = \$8000, \text{ for } Q > \$30\,000 \text{ in sales}$$

| FIGURE 2A.3 | Regression trend line for a stepwise linear fixed cost |

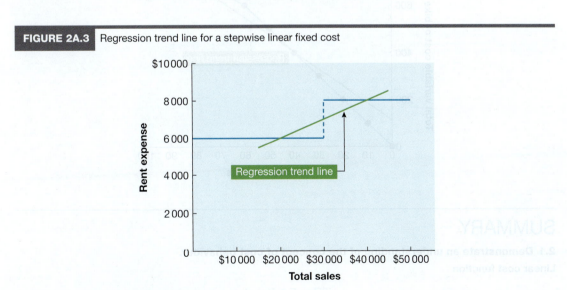

What happens if we apply regression analysis to past cost data from this stepwise linear cost function? Consider the following three possibilities.

1. If all the data points occurred when Q was below $30\,000, then rent will appear to be a fixed cost at $6000.

2. If all the data points occurred when Q was above \$30 000, then rent will appear to be a fixed cost at \$8000.
3. If some data points occurred when Q was below \$30 000 and other data points occurred when Q was above \$30 000, then the regression trend line might be similar to the one shown in figure 2A.3. The simple regression results would appear to have both fixed and variable components. However, the cost estimates from the regression will be accurate only at a few points along the regression trend line.

To develop the most accurate cost function, we must define the cost according to its relevant range and reflect the appropriate limits in the cost function.

Piecewise linear variable costs

We learned earlier that the cost function for some variable costs is piecewise linear; the per-unit cost changes across relevant ranges of activity. For example, in figure 2.1(b), the function for the total cost of bicycle tyres based on a volume purchase discount is:

$$TC = \$10Q, \text{ for } Q \leq \text{bikes manufactured}$$
$$TC = \$600 + \$6(Q - 60), \text{ for } Q > 60 \text{ bikes manufactured}$$

What happens if we apply regression analysis to past cost data from this piecewise linear cost function? Consider the following three possibilities.
1. If all the data points occurred when Q was below 60, then the cost will appear to be variable at \$10 per bike.
2. If all of the data points occurred when Q was above 60, then the cost will appear to be variable at \$6 per bike.
3. If some data points occurred when Q was below 60 and other data points occurred when Q was above 60, then the regression trend line might be similar to the one shown in figure 2A.4. The simple regression results would underestimate per unit variable cost when Q is below 60 and overestimate it when Q is above 60.

Once again, it is important to define the cost according to its relevant range and reflect the appropriate limits in the cost function if we wish to develop the most accurate cost function.

FIGURE 2A.4   Regression trend line for a piecewise linear variable cost

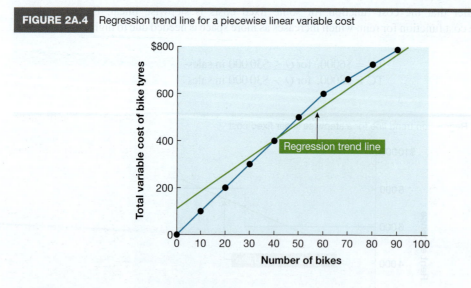

SUMMARY

2.1 Demonstrate an understanding of the concept of cost behaviour.

Linear cost function

$$TC = F + V \times Q$$

TC = Total cost
F = Total fixed cost
V = Variable cost per unit of activity
Q = Volume of activity (cost driver)

Assumptions

Within the relevant range, fixed costs remain fixed and the variable cost per unit remains constant.

2.2 Explain the different types of cost behaviour.

Linear cost functions across more than one relevant range

Stepwise linear: Fixed costs change across relevant ranges.

Piecewise linear: Variable costs change across relevant ranges.

2.3 Describe different cost estimation techniques.

Engineered estimate of cost

Analyse amount of labour time, materials and other resources used in each activity. Estimate costs based on resources used.

Analysis at the account level

Review pattern in past costs recorded in the accounting system.

Use knowledge of operations to classify cost as variable, fixed or mixed.

Two-point method

Algebraically calculate a linear mixed cost function using any two data points of the cost and a cost driver. Preferably use the most representative data points.

High-low method

Apply the two-point method using the highest and lowest data points of the cost driver.

How does a scatter plot assist with categorising a cost?

Plot past data points for cost against a potential cost driver.

Visually analyse plot to decide whether cost might be completely fixed, completely variable or mixed.

2.4 Apply estimation techniques to determine the cost function.

Identify relevant costs for the cost object	Estimate a cost function for each relevant cost				Combine all relevant cost estimates for the cost object
	Obtain information needed for estimation	Categorise costs as fixed, variable or mixed	Select and apply cost estimation techniques	Specify the cost function and then estimate the future cost	
	Continuously evaluate uncertainties and quality of information				

2.5 Apply regression analysis in cost estimation.

Statistically measure the average change in a dependent variable for every unit change in one or more independent variables.

Create a linear cost function where variable cost is the slope of the regression line and fixed cost is the intercept.

Simple regression

Has one independent variable.

Multiple regression (appendix 2A)

Has two or more independent variables.

2.6 Reflect on the uses and limitations of cost estimates.

Examples of reasons to estimate future costs

- Budgeting
- Planning future operations, such as setting employee work schedules, financing activities
- Making specific decisions, such as discontinuing a line of business, renting additional retail store space or hiring new employees

What do managers need to consider when using estimates of future costs?

- Uncertainties
  - Actual future costs are unknown.
  - Reliability of cost estimates is uncertain because of uncertainties about:
    ○ cost behaviour classification
    ○ cost drivers
    ○ changes in cost behaviour over time

- Other considerations
  - Quality of cost information:
    - appropriateness of past costs for estimating future costs
    - accounting system information
    - information from outside the accounting system
  - Quality of estimation techniques
  - Reasonableness of cost function assumptions

KEY TERMS

analysis at the account level A method used to create a cost function by reviewing the pattern of a cost over time in the accounting system and using knowledge of operations to classify the cost as variable, fixed or mixed.

average cost (AC) Computed as total costs (TC) divided by the quantity (Q) of activity or production.

cost behaviour The variation in costs relative to the variation in an organisation's activities at the operational level.

cost driver An input or activity that causes changes in total cost for a cost object.

cost function An algebraic representation of the total cost of a cost object over a relevant range of activity.

engineered estimate of cost A method used to estimate a cost function in which each activity is analysed according to the amount of labour time, materials and other resources used.

fixed costs Costs that do not vary with small changes in activity levels such as production, sales and services provided.

high-low method A specific application of the two-point method using the highest and lowest data points of the cost driver.

marginal cost The incremental cost of an activity, for example, producing a unit of goods or services.

mixed costs Costs that are partly fixed and partly variable.

multiple regression analysis A technique that develops a cost function by calculating values for the statistical relationship between total cost and two or more cost drivers.

piecewise linear cost function A cost function in which the variable cost per unit changes at some point but remains linear after the change.

relevant range A span of activity for a given cost object where both total fixed costs and variable costs per unit of activity remain constant.

scatter plot A graphical technique in which data points for past costs are plotted against a potential cost driver.

simple regression analysis A technique that develops a cost function by calculating values for the statistical relationship between total cost and a single cost driver.

stepwise linear cost function A cost function in which fixed cost changes at some point but remains constant after the change.

two-point method A method that uses any two sets of data points for cost and a cost driver to algebraically calculate a mixed cost function.

variable costs Costs that change proportionately with changes in activity levels.

SELF-STUDY PROBLEMS

SELF-STUDY PROBLEM 1 Cost object; cost function estimation; opportunity cost

A computer manufacturer is deciding whether to produce a large monitor with a thin flat screen. One of the managers suggested that the incremental costs for this line of manufacturing will be primarily variable because the company currently has a lot of idle capacity.

Required

(a) What is the cost object in this decision?

(b) Is the accounting system likely to have the information needed to develop a cost function? Explain.

(c) What might be an appropriate estimation technique for this cost? Explain.

(d) What is the opportunity cost for using this idle capacity? Explain.

SOLUTION TO SELF-STUDY PROBLEM 1

(a) Production of a large monitor with a thin flat screen

(b) If all of the parts for the monitor are currently used in the organisation, all of the information is likely to be contained in the accounting records. But new parts are most likely needed, since the monitor is large and probably involves different technology to achieve thin size. Thus, estimates of costs from suppliers will be needed. In addition, estimates for the amount of labour time will be needed. Although labour cost per hour can be found in the records, the amount of labour time is likely to be different for this monitor than for other monitors. If machines are used in production, an estimation of machine hours is necessary to determine whether maintenance and repair costs will increase.

(c) Estimating the cost of parts and the time involved in production is part of the engineered estimate of cost method.

(d) The opportunity cost of using idle capacity for one product is the contribution of other uses of the capacity. If another product could be manufactured and sold, that product's contribution margin is the opportunity cost. If the capacity can be rented or leased out, the rent or lease payments are the opportunity cost. If there are no other uses for the capacity, the opportunity cost is zero.

SELF-STUDY PROBLEM 2 Cost driver choice using regression

Nursery Supply manufactures wooden planter tubs for small trees. Each wooden planter requires about the same level of effort in labour and machinery. The managers of Nursery Supply want to improve the quality of their budgets. They are considering three alternative cost drivers for overhead: assembly time, labour hours and machine hours. The statistics for regressions using last year's monthly data for each of the three possible cost drivers follow.

Cost driver = Assembly time
Intercept = \$55 000 (t-statistic = 2.44, p-value = 0.08)
Slope = \$21 (t-statistic = 2.85, p-value = 0.05)
Adjusted R-square = 0.31

Cost driver = Labour hours
Intercept = \$20 000 (t-statistic = 2.95, p-value = 0.03)
Slope = \$31 (t-statistic = 3.00, p-value = 0.01)
Adjusted R-square = 0.46

Cost driver = Machinehours
Intercept = \$10 000 (t-statistic = 1.45, p-value = 0.25)
Slope = \$38 (t-statistic = 3.19, p-value = 0.005)
Adjusted R-square = 0.70

Required

(a) Write the cost function for each of the cost drivers.

(b) Explain the meaning of the adjusted R-square for the assembly time analysis.

(c) Explain the meaning of the p-value for the intercept in the machine hours analysis.

(d) Explain the meaning of the p-value for the slope in the labour hours analysis.

(e) Given only the regression results, which cost driver would you choose for overhead costs? Explain.

(f) Why do managers often use models such as a cost function to estimate future costs?

SOLUTION TO SELF-STUDY PROBLEM 2

(a) Each cost function is written using the regression intercept term as the fixed cost and the slope as the variable cost.

Cost driver = Assembly time
TC = \$55 000 + \$21 × assembly time
Cost driver = labour hours
TC = \$20 000 + \$31 × labour hours
Cost driver = Machine hours
TC = \$38 × machine hours

(*Note:* In relation to the cost driver machine hours, because the p-value for its t-statistic is 0.25, the intercept is not statistically different from zero. Therefore, the fixed cost is assumed to be zero.)

(b) The adjusted R-square indicates that variation in assembly time explains about 31 per cent of the variation in overhead. The remaining 69 per cent is unexplained.

(c) The *p*-value for the intercept in the regression of overhead cost against machine hours is 0.25. It means a 25 per cent probability that the intercept (fixed cost) is zero instead of $10 000.

(d) The *p*-value of the slope in the labour hours regression is 0.01, which means a 1 per cent probability that the variable cost for overhead related to labour hours could be zero instead of $31 per labour hour.

(e) First we examine the adjusted *R*-square (see figure 2.8, items 6 and 7). At 70 per cent, machine hours appears to be the best cost driver. However, we also need to evaluate whether its coefficients are reasonable. The slope coefficient is positive and has only a small probability of being zero (*p*-value 0.005), so it is likely to be a reasonable estimate. The intercept coefficient is generally reasonable so long as it is not significantly negative. In this case, the intercept has a high *p*-value (0.25), so we can assume the fixed cost is zero.

(f) Managers cannot know future costs. Nevertheless, they need to estimate future costs to make decisions. A cost function based on past information helps managers estimate future costs; the function can also be updated to incorporate expected cost information so that predictions are as precise as possible. Using a model such as the cost function also helps managers be more methodical in their approach to cost estimation, improving the quality of cost estimates. Higher-quality estimation methods provide higher-quality information for decision making.

QUESTIONS

2.1 'As volume increases, total cost increases and per-unit cost decreases.' What type of linear cost function does this describe? Draw a simple graph of this type of cost function. **LO2**

2.2 A motor vehicle assembly plant closes every August to retool for the next year's model. How should August's cost data be used in estimating the overhead cost function? **LO4**

2.3 You have been asked to provide the managing director with an approximate cost function for the entity's activities, and it must be done by this afternoon. Some members of the board of directors want to understand why performance varies so much across store locations. They have asked for a quick analysis today and want a more detailed analysis next week. Which cost estimation technique(s) should you consider using? Explain. **LO3, 4**

2.4 At two levels of activity within the relevant range, average costs are $192 and $188 respectively. Assuming the cost function is linear, what can be said about the existence of fixed and variable costs? **LO2**

2.5 You are about to start a coffee shop business. What do you understand by 'cost behaviour'? Explain how your accountants could help you in building an understanding of cost behaviour. Identify the likely key costs and classify each as fixed or variable. **LO1, 2**

2.6 Explain how information from a scatter plot helps in categorising a cost as fixed, variable or mixed. **LO3**

2.7 Explain the analysis at the account level approach to developing a cost function. **LO3**

2.8 List two examples of non-linear cost functions and describe a method of developing a cost function for each one. **LO2**

2.9 Why might some have trouble classifying costs as fixed or variable? **LO1, 2**

2.10 The trend line developed using regression analysis provides a more accurate representation of a mixed cost function than the two-point or high-low methods. Explain why. **LO5**

EXERCISES

2.11 Fixed, variable and mixed costs **LO2**

Bridges and Roads is an entity engaged in road construction. Some selected items from its chart of accounts are listed below.

Required

For each account, indicate whether the account represents a fixed, variable or mixed cost for the operation of road construction activity. If mixed, indicate whether it is predominantly fixed or variable. Explain your answers.

(a) Staff wages
(b) Clerical wages
(c) Rent
(d) Licenses

(e) Insurance

(f) Office supplies

(g) Professional dues

(h) Professional subscriptions

(i) Property taxes

(j) Advertising

2.12 Linear, stepwise linear and piecewise linear cost functions **LO2**

(a) Total fixed costs are $10 000 per week and the variable cost per unit is $8. Write the algebraic expression for the cost function and graph it. What are the assumptions of the cost function?

(b) Total fixed costs are $25 000 per week up to 2000 units a week and then jump to $35 000 per week. The variable cost per unit is $8. Write the algebraic expression for the cost function and graph it.

(c) The average cost to produce 10 000 units is $45 and the average cost to produce 12 000 units is $44. Estimate the average cost to produce 15 000 units.

(d) The total cost function for Hot Dog Days, a hot dog cart business, is TC = $5000 + 45% × total revenues. Estimate the total cost for a month when total revenues are $10 000.

2.13 Cost function and assumptions **LO2**

Express Lunch operates a small food van that sells a variety of sandwiches and beverages. Total fixed costs are $20 000 per month. Last month total variable costs were $8000 when total sales were $32 000.

Required

(a) Write out the algebraic expression for the cost function.

(b) What assumptions do we make when we develop this cost function?

2.14 Piecewise linear cost function; regression measurement error **LO3, 5**

The following is the description of a cost: total fixed costs are $50 000 per month and the variable cost per unit is $10 when production is under 1000 units. The variable cost drops to $9 per unit after the first 1000 units are produced.

Required

(a) Write the algebraic expression of the cost function and graph it.

(b) Assume that the cost function just described is a reasonable representation of total costs. If the accountant performed regression analysis on weekly observations of this cost and did not realise that there were two relevant ranges, what problems would arise in the cost function that was produced? In other words, how would the cost function be mismeasured?

2.15 Cost function; opportunity cost; relevant costs **LO2**

Yummy Yoghurt sells yoghurt cones in a variety of natural flavours. Data for a recent month follow:

Revenue		$9 000
Cost of ingredients	$4 500	
Rent	1 000	
Store attendant salary	2 300	
		7 800
Profit		$1 200

Required

(a) Categorise each cost as fixed or variable.

(b) Create a cost function.

2.16 Fixed, variable and mixed costs **LO2**

Spencer and Church is a CPA entity engaged in local practice. Some selected items from its chart of accounts are listed below.

Required

For each account, indicate whether the account represents a fixed, variable or mixed cost for the operations of the local practice office. If mixed, indicate whether it is predominantly fixed or variable. Explain your answers.

(a) Staff wages

(b) Clerical wages

(c) Rent

(d) Licences

(e) Insurance

(f) Office supplies
(g) Professional dues
(h) Professional subscriptions
(i) Property taxes
(j) Advertising

2.17 Cost function using regression; other potential cost drivers   **LO5**

The new cost analyst in your accounting department just received a computer-generated report that contains the results of a simple regression analysis. The analyst was estimating the costs of the marketing department using units sold as the cost driver. Summary results of the report are shown below.

Variable	Coefficient	t-statistic	p-value
Intercept	12.44	1.39	0.25
Units sold	222.35	2.48	0.001
Adjusted R-square = 0.61			

Required

(a) Write an equation for the cost function based on the regression analysis.
(b) What does the adjusted R-square tell you?
(c) What other cost drivers could potentially explain marketing costs? Explain.

PROBLEMS

2.18 Cost function using high-low and regression; quality of cost estimates   **LO4, 5**

Following are sales and administrative cost data for Big Jack Burgers for four months:

	Sales	Administrative costs
September	$ 632 100	$43 333
October	842 500	57 770
November	1 087 900	62 800
December	1 132 100	68 333

Administrative cost is a mixed cost, and sales is a potential cost driver.

Required

(a) Using the high-low method, create a cost function for administrative costs.
(b) In your own words, explain why the high-low method might not be a good method for estimating the cost function.
(c) Create a scatter plot and add a trend line. After examining the plot, use your judgement to determine whether the cost is fixed, variable or mixed.
(d) Perform regression analysis to create a cost function for administrative costs.
(e) Can we know for certain that the cost function from part (d) provides a good estimate for next month's administrative costs? Why?
(f) Discuss whether sales are an economically plausible driver for administration costs for Big Jack Burgers.

2.19 Scatter plot; cost function using regression   **LO3, 5**

The following scatter plot and simple regression results used revenue as a potential cost driver for research and development costs.

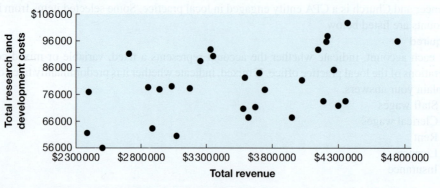

Regression statistics

Multiple *R*	0.462 332 038
R-square	0.213 750 914
Adjusted *R*-square	0.185 670 589
Standard error	10 894.440 62
Observations	30

	Coefficients	Standard error	*t*-statistic	*p*-value
Intercept	50 364.976 82	10 834.062 8	4.648 761 758	7.2426E-05
Revenue	0.008 179 276	0.002 964 572	2.759 007 802	0.010 102 44

Required

(a) Discuss whether the scatter plot suggests that revenue is a cost driver for research and development costs

(b) Using the regression results, write the cost function for research and development costs.

(c) Based on the regression results, discuss whether it would be appropriate to use total revenue as a cost driver for research and development costs.

(d) If you use the cost function from part (b) to estimate next month's research and development costs, what assumptions are you making? Identify at least three assumptions and discuss their reasonableness.

2.20 Cost driver; cost categories; appropriateness of regression; relevant information   LO2

Susan looked at her long-distance telephone bill with dismay. After leaving her job last year to become a self-employed consultant, her long-distance charges had grown considerably. She had not changed long-distance plans for years, partly because she hated taking the time to review the range of service providers and plans. However, the size of her long-distance bill made it clear that it was time to make a change. She had recently seen numerous advertisements by telephone companies offering much lower rates than she was currently paying, but she was sure that at least some of those plans offered low rates only for night and weekend calls.

Susan called her current long-distance service provider and asked how she could obtain a lower rate. She mentioned hearing that a competitor was currently offering long distance at 5c per minute. In responding to the service representative's questions, Susan verified that most of her long-distance calls are weekday and out of state. She also agreed that her activity over the past two months — approximately 500 minutes of long distance per month — was her best estimate for future calling activity. Given this information, the service representative suggested that Susan buy the long-distance service plan with the following features:

 (i) Up to 500 minutes of long distance for a flat fee of $20 per month.

(ii) No refunds would be provided for usage less than 500 minutes per month.

(iii) Any minutes over 500 per month would be billed at 10c per minute.

(iv) No service change fee or cancellation fee would apply.

Required

(a) What is the cost driver for Susan's long-distance telephone costs, assuming that the cost object is her consulting business?

(b) In the proposed service plan, which of the costs are fixed and which are variable? Explain.

(c) Would regression analysis be an appropriate tool for Susan to use in deciding whether to buy the new service plan? Why?

(d) Is the cost of Susan's current long-distance service plan relevant to this decision? Why?

(e) Explain why Susan cannot be certain whether the new service plan will reduce her long-distance costs.

(f) List additional information that might be relevant to Susan in deciding whether to buy the new service plan.

(g) Are Susan's long-distance services most likely a discretionary cost? Explain.

(h) Are Susan's long-distance services most likely a direct or indirect cost, assuming that the cost object is an individual consulting job? Explain.

(i) Describe the pros and cons of the new service plan.

2.21 Cost categories; cost function

LO2, 4, 5

The Leyland Hospital Café has been reporting losses in past months. In July, for example, the loss was $5000.

Revenue		$70 000
Expenses		
Purchases of prepared food	$21 000	
Serving personnel	30 000	
Cashier	5 500	
Administration	10 000	
University surcharge	7 000	
Utilities	1 500	75 000
Loss		$ (5 000)

The café purchases prepared food directly from Hospital Food Services. This charge varies proportionately with the number and kind of meals served. Personnel who are paid by the café serve the food, tend the cash register, wash dishes, wait on and clean tables. The staffing levels in the café rarely change; the existing staff can usually handle daily fluctuations in volume. Administrative costs are primarily the salaries of the lounge manager and her office staff. The university charges the café a surcharge of 10 per cent of its revenue. Utility costs are the costs of cooling, heating and lighting the café during its normal operating hours.

The university's management is considering shutting the café down because it has been operating at a loss.

Required

(a) List the fixed expenses of the café.

(b) List the variable expenses of the café and the most likely cost driver for each expense.

(c) Write out the cost function for running the café.

(d) Estimate the profit or loss for August if the revenues of the café increase to $80 000.

(e) Explain why the original data show a loss but part (d) shows a profit. Be specific.

2.22 Cost behaviour; scatter plot

LO3

Polar Bear Ski Wear is a shop that sells skiwear at a ski resort. Its cost accountant developed the following scatter plot for the cost of electricity for lights, heating and cooling against retail sales revenue.

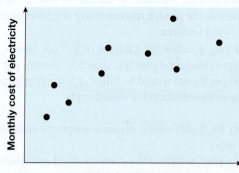

Required

(a) In a business such as retail sales, what usually causes the cost of electricity to vary?

(b) In what time of year would most skiwear be sold at a ski resort?

(c) In the scatter plot, the cost of electricity appears to be related to volume of retail sales. If this shop specialised in selling swimwear, would the scatter plot look different? Explain what would change.

(d) Identify and explain another cost that is similar in nature to the cost of electricity. When you plot the cost against a cost driver, a relationship becomes apparent. However, the cost varies with something other than the cost driver. (Think of other situations where this type of relationship might occur.)

2.23 Cost function using regression; scatter plots; three potential cost drivers LO3, 5

Laura Mills is the controller of Peer Jets International, a manufacturer of small corporate jets. She has undertaken a project to study the behaviour of overhead cost. She has assembled factory overhead data for the last 30 months from the company's manufacturing facility. Laura has asked you to develop a model to predict the level of manufacturing overhead.

The following categories of information are available to Laura. Manufacturing overhead includes all of the overhead costs associated with the manufacturing plant. Labour hours are the number of hours manufacturing employees worked. Machine hours are the total hours that machinery was used for the period. Tons of raw materials are all of the raw materials that were used for that particular month.

Additional data for this problem is available from your instructor.

Required

(a) Create a scatter plot of manufacturing overhead for each of the potential cost drivers.
(b) Would you eliminate any of the potential cost drivers based on the scatter plots? Why?
(c) Explain why you create a scatter plot of the data before you perform regression analysis.
(d) To practise your regression analysis skills, perform a simple regression analysis of manufacturing overhead for each of the three potential cost drivers. Write the cost function from each regression.
(e) Based on the simple regression results, which cost driver does the best job of explaining manufacturing overhead costs? Explain.
(f) Do your regression results support your answer to part (b)? Explain.

2.24 Cost function using multiple regression (appendix 2A) LO5

Refer to the data and requirements of problem 2.23.

Required

(a) Perform multiple regression using all three cost drivers. Compare the adjusted *R*-squares and cost functions for the multiple regression with the results of simple regressions for each potential cost driver.
(b) Which cost drivers do the best job of explaining manufacturing overhead costs? Explain.
(c) Select only the cost drivers that do the best job of explaining manufacturing overhead costs. Perform multiple regression analysis for those cost drivers and write the cost function.
(d) Explain why more than one cost driver is plausible for manufacturing overhead costs.

2.25 Use of prior year costs; quality of information LO6

Software Solutions is a family-owned business that has been in operation for more than 15 years. The board of directors is comprised of mainly family members, plus a few professionals such as an accountant and lawyer. Regina is a staff accountant who has been working on the budget for the last several weeks. The chief financial officer (CFO) needs to present the budget at the next board meeting and wants a preliminary copy in two days. Regina is certain that she will not be able to finish the budget within two days. Several department heads have not turned in their preliminary figures, and two departments have budgeted large increases in fixed costs for replacing computer equipment. Regina knows she should have alerted the CFO about these budgeted increases, but she has not had time.

One of her co-workers knows that Regina is behind and suggests that she use last year's budgets for those departments that have not provided information and also for the departments that increased their budgets by large amounts. The co-worker says that the budget can be straightened out later because the board does not pay attention to the details.

Required

(a) Is this an ethical dilemma for Regina? Why?
(b) Why might it be important for the board of directors to have as much updated information as possible about the budget?
(c) What should Regina do, given that not enough time is available to gather high-quality information? Explain your thinking.

2.26 Scatter plots; cost function using regression; two potential cost drivers LO5

Suppose we need to predict the cost of maintenance for Brush Valley High School for the upcoming school year. From the school district records we gather weekly data about costs and volumes for two potential cost drivers: labour hours used in the maintenance department and number of enrolled students.

		Potential cost drivers	
		Number of maintenance	
Week	**Total maintenance cost**	**hours worked**	**Number of students**
1	$16 690	238	534
2	13 560	194	532
3	13 540	108	534
4	16 060	229	530
5	12 430	101	533
6	20 860	298	537
7	18 420	244	540
8	12 310	98	540
9	13 770	108	541
10	16 990	225	538
11	20 650	289	540
12	14 770	118	539

Required

(a) Identify and explain two potential cost drivers for total maintenance cost, in addition to number of students and maintenance hours worked.

(b) Create a scatter plot, first for maintenance cost against hours worked and then maintenance cost against students.

(c) Would you eliminate either cost driver based on the plots? Explain.

(d) Perform regression analysis using each cost driver. Use your judgement to determine the most appropriate cost driver and write out the cost function for maintenance cost.

(e) Can we know for certain that the cost driver chosen in part (d) is the best cost driver? Why?

2.27 Cost function using account analysis and high-low method **LO3**

The Elder Clinic, a not-for-profit entity, provides limited medical services to low-income elderly patients. The manager's summary report for the past four months of operations is reproduced here.

	March	**April**	**May**	**June**	**Total**
Number of patient visits	849	821	778	842	3290
Patient fees	$ 4 230	$ 4 180	$ 3 875	$ 4 260	$ 16 545
Medical staff salaries	13 254	13 256	13 254	14 115	53 879
Medical supplies used	3 182	3 077	2 934	3 175	12 368
Administrative salaries	3 197	3 198	3 197	3 412	13 004
Rent	1 000	1 000	1 000	1 100	4 100
Utilities	532	378	321	226	1 457
Other expenses	2 854	2 776	2 671	2 828	11 129
Total expenses	24 019	23 685	23 377	24 856	95 937
Operating surplus (loss)	$(19 789)	$(19 505)	$(19 502)	$(20 596)	$(79 392)

The clinic receives an operating subsidy from the city, but unfortunately, the operating loss that has been incurred through June $(79 392) is larger than anticipated. Part of the problem is the salary increase that went into effect in June, which had been overlooked when the budget was submitted to the city last year. To compound the problem, the cold winter months traditionally bring with them an increase in cold-related health problems. Thus, the clinic is likely to experience an increase in patient visits during July.

The clinic's managers are considering an increase in patient fees to reduce losses. However, they are reluctant to raise fees because the patients have low incomes. They will raise fees only if it is necessary.

Required

(a) Use your judgement to classify costs as fixed, variable or mixed. Explain how you classified each item.

(b) Create a cost function for the Elder Clinic. Use the high-low method to estimate the function for any mixed costs.

(c) Use the cost function to estimate July expenses based on a projection of 940 patient visits.

(d) List reasons why management of the Elder Clinic cannot know with certainty what the expenses will be during July. List as many reasons as you can.

(e) Describe the pros and cons of using your cost estimate from part (c) to decide whether to raise patient fees.

(f) The managers need your July cost estimate to help them decide whether to raise patient fees. Use the information you learned from parts (a) to (e) to write a memo to the director of the Elder Clinic presenting your estimate of July costs. Provide the director with appropriate information for understanding your methodology and evaluating the reliability of your cost estimate.

2.28 Cost function judgement and methodology **LO2**

Suppose you have the responsibility of creating a cost function for the costs of an internet service provider's help line.

Required

(a) What is the cost object? Identify where you might obtain information about past costs for the cost object.

(b) Identify at least two potential cost drivers. Explain where you might obtain information about past volumes for each cost driver.

(c) What other information would you like to obtain before estimating the cost function? How might you obtain that information?

(d) Identify the techniques introduced in this chapter that you would be most likely to use in creating the cost function. Explain why.

2.29 Adjusting data for use with regression; outlier **LO5**

Smeyer Industries is a large entity with more than 40 departments, each employing 35 to 100 people. Recent experience suggests that the cost function used to estimate overhead in department IP-14 is no longer appropriate. The current function was developed three years ago. Since then, a number of changes occurred in the facilities and processes used in department IP-14. The changes happened one at a time. Each time a change was made, the cost accountant felt the change was not major enough to justify calculating a new overhead cost function. Now it is clear that the cumulative effect of the changes has been large.

You have been assigned the task to develop a new cost function for overhead in department IP-14. Initial analysis suggests that the number of direct labour hours is an appropriate cost driver. Departmental records are available for nine months. The records reveal the following information.

Month	Actual overhead	Direct labour hours
March	$68 200	8 812
April	71 250	8 538
May	68 150	8 740
June	73 500	9 176
July	38 310	2 123
August	70 790	9 218
September	80 350	8 943
October	68 750	8 821
November	68 200	8 794

An assistant has analysed the data for March through July and made the appropriate adjustments except for the following items (for which the assistant was unsure of the proper treatment).

(i) The semi-annual property tax bill for department IP-14 was paid on 30 June. The entire amount of $3000 was charged to overhead for June.

(ii) The costs to install a new piece of equipment with a life of 10 years in the department were charged to overhead in April. The installation costs were $4300.

(iii) Factory depreciation is allocated to department IP-14 every month. The department's share, $8000, is included in overhead.

(iv) A strike closed the plant for three weeks in July. Several non-union employees were kept on payroll during the strike. Their duties were general housekeeping and 'busy work'. These costs were charged to overhead.

You also have the details for the overhead account for the months of August and September (see following table). You were hired on 1 October and have been keeping the department accounts since then. Therefore, you know that the data for October and November are correct, except for any adjustments needed for the preceding items.

Department IP-14 Overhead control

August	Explanation	Amount
4	Miscellaneous supplies	$10 450
5	Payroll for indirect labour	5 500
15	Power costs: department IP-14	12 250
10	Payroll for indirect labour	6 000
19	Overtime premium	890
24	Factory depreciation	8 000
26	Miscellaneous supplies	27 700
	Total for August	$70 790

September	Explanation	Amount
2	Payroll for indirect labour	$ 6 000
7	Miscellaneous supplies	12 100
15	Power costs: department IP-14	11 100
15	Power costs: department IB-4	10 850
16	Payroll for indirect labour	6 500
16	Overtime premium	950
21	Miscellaneous supplies	19 350
28	Factory depreciation	8 000
30	Payroll for indirect labour	5 500
	Total for September	$80 350

August has 31 days and September has 30 days.

Required

(a) Using the information provided, adjust the monthly cost data to more accurately reflect the overhead costs incurred during each month.

(b) Discuss whether the data for July should be included in the estimate of future costs. Use a scatter plot to help you answer this question.

(c) Develop a cost function by regressing overhead costs in department IP-14 on direct labour hours. Discuss whether your cost function would be reasonable for estimating future overhead costs. Ignore any items you will discuss in part (d).

(d) Identify and discuss any additional adjustments that might be needed to more accurately measure overhead costs for the regression in part (c).

(e) Explain why adjustments probably need to be made to information from accounting records when estimating a cost function.

2.30 Cost function using high-low method   LO4

Wentworth Ltd sold 100 000 1 litre bottles of mineral water last year at $4 per unit and made a profit of $50 000. This year the costs for Wentworth Ltd remained the same, it sold 120 000 units at the same price, and made a profit of $80 000.

Required

(a) Determine the total fixed costs per year and the total variable cost per unit for Wentworth Ltd using the high-low method.

(b) Write an equation for the cost function based on your answer to (a).

2.31 Cost function using high-low method   LO2, 4, 6

Mernda Health Care Centre recently began to offer day surgery procedures. The Centre was not experienced in the costing of such services and, as a temporary measure, the subsidised patient-day charge was set at $100. This charge was similar to other providers in the region. Management decided to review the charge once cost data was available for the first two months of operations. The following data was collected by the accounting department, together with the number of patient days.

Cost category	Month 1 — 2100 patient days	Month 2 — 2250 patient days
Salaries, nurses	$ 6 000	$ 6 000
Aides	1 200	1 200

Laboratory	110 000	117 500
Pharmacy	$ 31 000	$ 32 500
Depreciation	11 800	11 800
Laundry	16 800	18 000
Administration	12 000	12 000
Lease (equipment)	30 000	30 000
Total	$218 800	$229 000

Required

(a) Classify each cost as fixed, variable or mixed, using patient days as the cost driver.

(b) Use the high-low method to separate mixed costs into their fixed and variable components.

(c) The accounting department has estimated that the average patient days per month will be 2000. If the Centre is to be operated as a not-for-profit, how much will it need to charge per patient day?

(d) Suppose the Centre averages 2500 patient days per month. How much would need to be charged per patient day for the Centre to cover costs?

(e) Explain why the per-patient-day charge decreased in (d) above.

(f) Briefly explain the benefit of the classification of costs in the planning for the Centre.

ACKNOWLEDGEMENTS

Photo 2A: © Goodluz / Shutterstock.com
Photo 2B: © Cultura RF / Getty Images
Photo 2C: © zefart / Shutterstock.com

CHAPTER 3

A costing framework and cost allocation

LEARNING OBJECTIVES

After studying this chapter, you should be able to:

3.1 describe the role of cost objects and how they support decision making

3.2 explain and compare direct and indirect costs

3.3 discuss the process of indirect cost allocation

3.4 identify the steps within a costing framework

3.5 apply and evaluate the costing framework in a service entity setting

3.6 apply and evaluate the costing framework in a support department setting

3.7 critically analyse the limitations of cost allocation data.

IN BRIEF

Organisations have a range of different decisions to make using cost data. In this chapter the focus is on the determination of the full cost (or total cost) of a cost object and the issues associated with cost allocation. Managers identify one or more cost objects based on the relevant information they need for a particular decision, for budgeting and planning, or for valuing products or services. To determine the full cost requires the tracing of direct costs and the allocation of indirect costs. The cost data for this purpose may take various forms, including actual costs (found in the general ledger) or data derived from estimates of future cost.

3.1 Cost objects — need for cost information

LEARNING OBJECTIVE 3.1 Describe the role of cost objects and how they support decision making.

It is important for an entity to understand why costs are incurred — to enable the management of costs and to facilitate more informed decision making. Service entities often use cost information to facilitate cost management, productivity measurement and billing. Public sector organisations, such as hospitals and schools, need information in respect of the cost of their activities so that when demand increases they are able to support arguments for increased funding. Consulting firms and other organisations that manage large projects often track job costs in conjunction with their project management systems. Manufacturing entities will need to cost the conversion of raw materials into the finished product. Therefore, it is necessary for an entity to undertake a cost analysis of many aspects of its operations in order to remain competitive and earn a profit or, more simply, to be able to continue to meet the demand for their services.

To undertake a cost analysis, we need to identify the relevant cost object. A **cost object** is anything for which a separate measurement of cost is desired. Examples of cost objects are products, services, customers, departments, business units or geographic regions. You should note that, even though an entity is able to view the costs through these different lenses, the total costs of the entity do not change. Figure 3.1 illustrates some of the many cost objects that cause an entity to incur the costs recorded in the accounting information system.

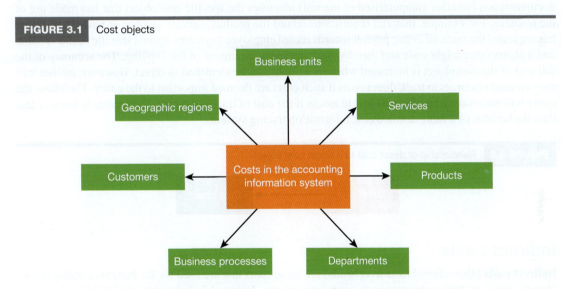

FIGURE 3.1   Cost objects

Entities will use a costing system to collect and report the cost of resources used by particular cost objects. Traditionally, costing systems such as job costing and process costing have focused on the determination of the inventoriable product cost (a cost that complies with accounting standards) for external financial reporting. (Both systems are discussed in more detail in chapter 7.) These systems focus on production costs only and are typically structured on a departmental basis.

However, due to an increasingly competitive business environment coupled with an increase in the level of costs common to many cost objects, entities have had to adopt a new approach to costing systems. They have done this by trying to understand costs incurred at all stages of the value chain: from research and development to design, production, distribution and customer service. As a consequence, costing systems have been developed to support internal management rather than to merely measure the inventoriable product cost (the inventory value of manufactured products). Known as activity-based costing (ABC) systems (see chapter 12), such systems take a more contemporary approach to cost determination by enabling an entity to capture costs both pre- and post-production and to measure the cost of any cost object.

The focus is on aligning costs to activities rather than departments. For example, under a conventional costing system, an entity might assign salary costs to the department that manages accounts payable. However, the salary costs represent employees' efforts in undertaking a variety of activities such as invoice payment, cheque issuing, credit assessment and payment reconciliations against the bank account. A contemporary costing system would assign the salary costs to the activities themselves instead of to the accounts payable department.

We will now discuss how to measure the **full cost** of a cost object and also discuss design issues for costing systems.

3.2 Direct and indirect costs

LEARNING OBJECTIVE 3.2 Explain and compare direct and indirect costs.

The need for cost information will determine the cost object that is the focus for cost collection. The cost information could be needed for a particular decision, for budgeting and planning, or for valuing products or services. When calculating the full cost for any cost object, it is necessary to identify those costs that have a cause-and-effect relationship with the cost object, known as direct costs, and those costs that are common to many cost objects and cannot be easily related to any specific cost object, known as **indirect costs**. The classification of costs as either direct or indirect depends on the particular cost object of interest; the following discussion explores how we distinguish between the two types of costs.

Direct costs

Direct costs are those costs that can be directly linked (attributed) to the cost object. Figure 3.2 shows the relationship between a direct cost and the cost object. To establish this link, an entity needs to implement or make use of an existing tracking system to trace the cost directly to the cost object. Source documentation (whether computerised or manual) identifies the specific cost object that has made use of the resource. For example, material requisitions record the product, service number or business unit that has requested the material items; payroll records record employee payments against specific business units; and a photocopier might code and thereby store the specific purpose of the copying. The accuracy of the full cost of the cost object is increased when more costs can be identified as direct. However, entities will only commit resources to track direct costs if such costs are deemed important to the entity. Therefore, the entity will undertake a **cost/benefit test** to assess if the cost of tracing costs to cost objects is more or less than the benefits of a more detailed cost information tracing system.

FIGURE 3.2	Relationship of direct cost to a single cost object

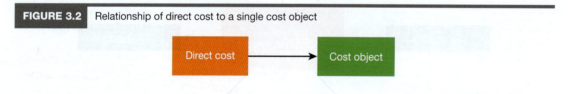

Indirect costs

Indirect costs (also referred to as **overheads**) are those costs that are used for the benefit of multiple cost objects. One cost has a relationship to many cost objects. Figure 3.3 shows the relationship between an indirect cost and the many cost objects that consume the resource. It might be possible to trace such costs directly to an individual cost object, but such an exercise would not pass the cost/benefit test. For example, what would be involved in collecting information about the number of nails used in the construction of a block of apartments or the amount of glue used to laminate several production runs of an office desk?

FIGURE 3.3	Relationship of indirect cost to multiple cost objects

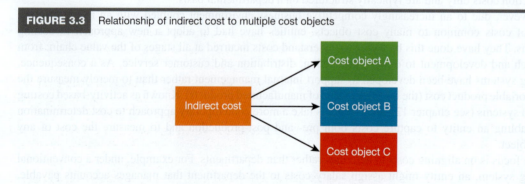

Classifying costs as direct or indirect

As explained above, the classification of a cost as either direct or indirect will depend on the specific cost object that has been identified as the focus for the cost analysis, together with a cost/benefit assessment of tracing the cost. Consider this example of how costs are identified as either direct or indirect for a specific cost object: Fabulous Diamonds is a local indie band that performs regularly at venues around the Asia–Pacific region. You will note the classification of each cost as either direct or indirect in relation to a show held at the Toff of the Town venue in Auckland. Costs incurred by the group during October are:

1. rehearsal room hire to practise for the shows in October (indirect cost)
2. petrol costs incurred to go to rehearsal and the shows in October (no record of kilometres travelled; indirect cost)
3. wages of a sound engineer for each show (direct cost)
4. advertising brochures for the shows during October (indirect cost)
5. interest payment on loan for musical instruments (indirect cost)
6. payments to band members for each show (direct cost)
7. guitar strings — new set needed for each show (direct cost).

The cost object here is the show held at the Toff of the Town venue in October. Only those costs that were incurred directly for this particular show will be classified as direct costs — items 3, 6 and 7. All other costs (items 1, 2, 4 and 5) would be classified as indirect because the expenditure is for the benefit of all shows held in October.

3.3 Process of indirect cost allocation

LEARNING OBJECTIVE 3.3 Discuss the process of indirect cost allocation.

As indirect costs are incurred for the benefit of multiple cost objects, the determination of the full cost for a particular cost object requires the assignment of indirect costs to the many cost objects that receive the benefit of the resources. **Cost allocation** is the process by which indirect costs are assigned to specific cost objects.

Why would an entity allocate indirect costs? The allocation of indirect costs enables the full cost of the cost object to be determined. However, unless required by an external party, such allocation occurs at the discretion of each entity and is done to provide information for internal purposes. Entities are motivated to allocate indirect costs for many reasons:

- to determine the full cost of a specific cost object in order to undertake profitability analysis, provide a basis for pricing decisions, and assist in resource allocation decisions
- to allocate the cost of shared services such as accounts payable, payroll and information technology to organisational units. Cost assignment will remind organisational unit managers of the full economic impact of their decisions
- to encourage the use of central resources. If organisational units are to be charged for the costs of a service (for example, legal services and training services) regardless of whether they use the service or not, then managers will be encouraged to use it
- to control costs by encouraging mutual monitoring. If an organisational unit is to be charged for a shared service, the manager will benchmark the allocated costs against the costs of external providers to ensure that the allocation is within commercial limits
- to comply with external requirements (for example, the determination of inventoriable product costs in line with accounting standards).

Cost drivers

In order to allocate indirect costs, an appropriate cost driver (also known as an allocation base) will need to be identified to establish the link between the indirect cost and the many cost objects that make use of the resource. A **cost driver** provides a measure of activity that explains the cost object's use of the indirect cost. The criteria used to select an appropriate cost driver can include:

- *cause and effect* — choosing the variables that *cause* resources to be consumed (for example, allocating machine costs based on the cost object's use of machine time)
- *benefits received* — identifying the *beneficiaries* of the outputs of the cost object (for example, allocating advertising costs based on the cost object's increase in income)
- *fairness or equity* — selecting the costs that appear *reasonable* and *fair*
- *ability to bear* — allocating costs in proportion to the cost object's *ability to bear them* (for example, allocating indirect costs based on a cost object's level of profit)
- *behavioural* — selecting a cost driver *to modify behaviour* (for example, using direct labour hours to encourage a reduction in the use of labour hours).

An analysis of the above criteria shows that the cause-and-effect cost driver will be the most appropriate to use if the objective is accuracy of the full cost. All other criteria are subjective and may lead to behavioural problems. For example, if you were the manager of the department with the highest revenue, how would you react if you were burdened with the majority of the indirect costs incurred to support all departments? The benefits received by particular cost objects might be difficult to pinpoint; for example, how can an entity identify which particular department benefited from an entity-wide advertising campaign? The ability-to-bear criteria will burden better performing departments, while behavioural criteria are more focused on modifying behaviour than developing the most accurate full cost.

Cost drivers can be classified as either volume drivers or activity drivers. **Volume drivers** use a measure of output to assign the indirect costs; for example, labour hours, machine hours or units of output. It is assumed that indirect costs are consumed by the cost object in relation to its use of the volume driver. However, if indirect costs are caused by factors other than volume, then incorrect allocation may lead to cross-subsidisation between the cost objects. Cost objects that use more of the cost driver will be burdened with a higher proportion of indirect costs. This may lead to the entity making incorrect decisions; for example, by allocating the advertising budget to a product that is actually unprofitable.

The **activity drivers** relate to the attributes of the individual activities that cause the consumption of overhead resources and recognise the amount of the activity used by cost objects. Cross-subsidisation may be eliminated by the use of activity drivers. More discussion about activity drivers can be found in chapter 12.

Determining the allocation rate

Indirect costs are allocated based on the usage of a chosen cost driver. The allocation process involves three steps.
1. *Develop the cost allocation formula.* This requires identifying the indirect costs to be allocated and selecting the cost driver that will link the indirect cost to the cost object.
2. *Calculate the* **indirect cost rate.** This is done by dividing the indirect costs by the total cost driver usage in order to calculate the indirect cost rate per unit of cost driver.
3. *Allocate cost to the cost object.* This is calculated by multiplying the indirect cost rate by the cost object's use of the cost driver.

How does an entity develop the formula to start the allocation process? The structure of the costing system will influence this. The first step is to decide on the number of indirect cost pools; that is, whether there is one or many. A **cost pool** is simply a grouping of individual costs for a particular purpose. Cost pools can be grouped on a departmental basis, an activity basis or on some other criteria. How is this grouping determined? Similar costs will be grouped together on the assumption that the same cost driver explains resource consumption by the cost object, and the number of indirect cost pools will be made via a cost/benefit test. The cost of collecting detailed data will be weighed against the cost of errors in decision making arising from having a less accurate measure of full costs. A cost allocation formula will be developed for each cost pool.

An entity may choose to measure the costs using actual costs or budgeted costs, or even further classify them according to cost behaviour (fixed or variable). This is discussed further in appendix 3A to this chapter. The determination of an actual indirect cost rate (the rate used to assign the cost to the cost object) will not be possible until the end of the financial period, when actual results are known. If the actual indirect cost rate is calculated on a monthly basis, it can vary from month to month due to fluctuations in the cash flow pattern. To overcome this delay in obtaining information and to smooth out fluctuations in cash flows, entities will use budgeted costs to calculate a **predetermined indirect cost rate**. The use of budgeted costs will also provide a benchmark against which actual costs can be measured to assess performance and assist in pricing and budget preparation.

As the number of cost pools increases (that is, costs are further dissected into different categories), the accuracy of the cost information also increases because each new cost pool will have a different cost driver for allocation purposes. However, as the number of cost pools increases, the need to collect information about individual cost drivers also increases. This will lead to an overall increase in the resources needed to undertake the cost assignment.

Once the cost driver has been identified for each cost pool, the total use of the cost driver for the financial period under investigation will need to be determined. Cost driver usage will be based on either the budgeted or actual usage. By dividing the total indirect costs by the total use of the cost driver, a measure of the cost per unit of the cost driver will be calculated. The determination of this unit indirect cost rate will enable the allocation of the indirect costs to the many cost objects that have made use of the resource. Such allocation will be based on each cost object's use of the cost driver and is calculated by multiplying the unit indirect cost rate by the cost object's use of the cost driver.

3.4 A costing framework

LEARNING OBJECTIVE 3.4 Identify the steps within a costing framework.

Identifying the cost pools and related cost drivers enables the full cost for the desired cost object to be determined. Figure 3.4 illustrates the process of determining the full cost (direct cost plus allocated indirect cost) for any cost object.

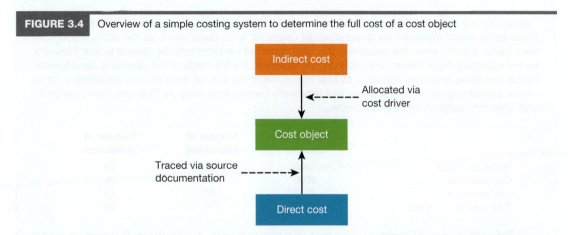

FIGURE 3.4   Overview of a simple costing system to determine the full cost of a cost object

The simple costing system in figure 3.4 depicts the tracing of the direct cost and the allocation of the indirect cost based on the cost object's use of the chosen cost driver. This basic structure is the framework upon which both service and manufacturing entities develop costing systems. The level of sophistication (that is, the number of costs pools and the type of cost drivers) of the costing system will be dependent upon the individual entity's specific cost information needs.

3.5 Applying the costing framework in a service entity setting

LEARNING OBJECTIVE 3.5 Apply and evaluate the costing framework in a service entity setting.

Comprehensive examples 1 and 2 demonstrate the use of a costing system. In comprehensive example 1 the focus is the determination of the full cost of individual operating departments in order to cost insurance policies issued by these departments. In comprehensive example 2 we look at the full cost determination of providing services to clients of a legal firm.

Determination of full cost for operating departments

Partridge Insurance Company has three service departments — finance, personnel and computer services — that provide services to the entity's three operating departments: home insurance, car insurance and life insurance. The following data were recorded for each department for last year. The data details information about departmental costs and the cost drivers identified to allocate the cost of the service departments to the operating departments.

	Cost	Cost driver		
Service departments				
Finance	$ 150 000	Number of invoices	=	5000
Personnel	120 000	Number of employees	=	100
Computer services	300 000	Number of computers	=	60
Operating departments				
Home insurance	500 000			
Car insurance	400 000			
Life insurance	300 000			
Total costs	$1 770 000			

Based on the data, the costs recorded in the general ledger for all departments totalled $1 770 000. These costs would represent the direct costs of operating each department, as the costs would have been traced directly when the documentation was classified for entry into the general ledger. However, for the operating departments, the costs do not represent the full costs of the operating departments. That is, the three operating departments also make use of the service departments' activities, such as invoice processing, personnel services and information technology support. The cost driver usage by each operating department is shown below.

	Number of invoices	Number of employees	Number of computers
Home insurance	1500	50	25
Car insurance	2000	30	25
Life insurance	1500	20	10
Total cost driver usage	5000	100	60

As Partridge Insurance Company uses a cost-plus pricing system, it is necessary to determine the full cost of each operating department to assist in the pricing of insurance premiums for the various policies issued by the entity. This will require the identification not only of the direct costs but also the indirect costs incurred due to the use of resources in the service departments.

Step 1: Overview of cost assignment — identification of cost objects, cost pools and cost drivers

Before commencing any calculations, it is important to understand the costing system that will be used to determine the full cost. The first step is to identify the relevant cost object of interest, the number and type of cost pools, and the cost drivers to assign indirect costs. An overview of the costing system is shown in figure 3.5. The cost objects of interest are the three operating departments: home insurance, car insurance and life insurance. In order to determine the full cost for each of the operating departments, it is necessary to assign the indirect costs, which are the direct costs of each of the three service departments (that is, finance, personnel and computer services). Therefore, we have three indirect cost pools classified on a departmental basis, measuring costs on an actual basis. Figure 3.5 highlights the one-to-one relationship that exists between the direct cost and the cost objects, and the one-to-many relationship between the indirect costs and the cost objects.

The cost drivers identified to allocate the indirect costs are the number of invoices (finance department), the number of employees (personnel department) and the number of computers (computer services department). The actual usage of the cost driver is being used for allocation purposes. Remember that the selection of an appropriate cost driver will be specific to each entity. Other cost drivers might be selected by other entities — perhaps even by different people in the same entity. For example, Partridge Insurance Company could have chosen the time taken to process the invoices rather than using the number of invoices, or the number of keystrokes per person rather than the number of computers, or salary levels rather than the number of employees. The one chosen should reflect the cause and effect link.

The next stage in the allocation process is to calculate the indirect cost rate for each service department cost pool.

Step 2: Determination of the indirect cost rates for each cost pool

In this part of the example there will be three cost allocation formulas — one for each of the three service department cost pools. Each allocation formula will require the determination of the total cost for the accounting period and the total use of the cost driver for each service department. The indirect cost rate can then be calculated and the indirect costs allocated based upon the use of the cost driver by the individual cost objects, which in this example are the operating departments.

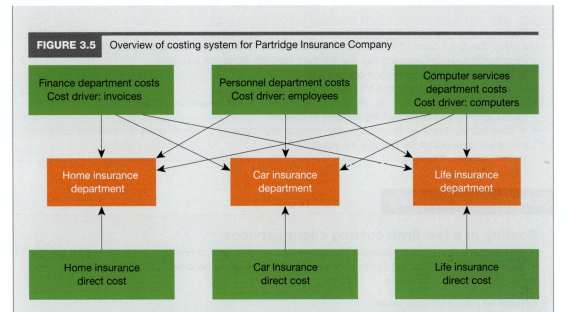

For the finance department the total direct costs are $150 000, with 5000 invoices being processed in the current accounting period. Each invoice paid by the finance department will lead to a $30 charge ($150 000 / 5000 invoices) being assigned to each invoice raised by the operating department to cover the finance department's costs such as finance staff salaries, stationery and telephone costs. Using the same rationale for the personnel department costs and computer services department costs, charges of $1200 per employee and $5000 per computer will be assigned to the operating departments.

Department (Cost pool)	Allocation formula	Indirect cost rate
Finance	$150 000 / 5000 invoices	$ 30 per invoice
Personnel	$120 000 / 100 employees	$1200 per employee
Computer services	$300 000 / 60 computers	$5000 per computer

Step 3: Allocation of indirect costs to the cost objects

Now that the indirect cost rates have been determined, the allocation of the indirect costs can be undertaken by applying the indirect cost rate to the cost object's use of the cost driver. Partridge Insurance Company uses the cost object's actual use of the cost driver to allocate indirect costs. For example, the indirect cost rate for the finance department is $30 per invoice. The home insurance department raises 1500 invoices per year and will be allocated $45 000 (1500 invoices × $30) to cover its share of the costs incurred by the finance department.

	Home insurance	Car insurance	Life insurance
Finance	$45 000	$60 000	$45 000
	(1500 invoices × $30)	*(2000 invoices × $30)*	*(1500 invoices × $30)*
Personnel	$60 000	$36 000	$24 000
	(50 employees × $1200)	*(30 employees × $1200)*	*(20 employees × $1200)*
Computer services	$125 000	$125 000	$50 000
	(25 computers × $5000)	*(25 computers × $5000)*	*(10 computers × $5000)*
Indirect costs allocated	**$230 000**	**$221 000**	**$119 000**

Step 4: Determination of the full cost of each cost object

The full cost for each of the cost objects can now be determined. You will notice that the total cost of $1 770 000 (refer to original information) has now been assigned to the three cost objects — the operating departments.

	Home insurance	Car insurance	Life insurance	Total costs
Indirect costs	$230 000	$221 000	$119 000	$ 570 000
Direct costs	500 000	400 000	300 000	1 200 000
Full cost	**$730 000**	**$621 000**	**$419 000**	**$1 770 000**

This illustration highlights the different lenses that have been used to view the costs — the total cost for the entity, the direct costs of the individual departments and the full cost of each operating department.

Partridge Insurance Company can use the data from the allocation process:

- to determine the full cost of each operating unit
- to review the current premiums on insurance policies
- in strategic management — to make decisions about which insurance policies to offer in the future based upon individual profitability analysis of policies
- in cost management — to pressure the service departments to lower costs if individual business managers believe that the charges are too high.

COMPREHENSIVE EXAMPLE 2

Costing in a law firm: costing client services

Nighthawk Law Company specialises in copyright protection for authors. A client approached the law firm about handling his lawsuit against a large film company that he believes stole the plot from one of his novels for a made-for-TV movie.

Estimated job costs and price

The law partners estimated that the case (the cost object of interest) would require 500 hours of professional labour. Nighthawk's accountant estimated the following direct costs.

Direct professional labour (500 hours)	$ 75 000
Direct support labour	20 000
Fringe benefits for direct labour	15 000
Photocopying	1 000
Telephone calls	1 000
Total direct costs	**$112 000**

Last year, Nighthawk's indirect costs totalled $450 000. The two law partners worked about 5000 professional labour hours. The accountant developed an estimated indirect cost rate of $90 per direct labour hour ($450 000 / 5000). Therefore, the estimated indirect cost for this case is $90 × 500 hours = $45 000 and the total estimated cost is $157 000 ($45 000 + $112 000). The law firm's policy is to mark up full cost by 20 per cent for the estimated price. Using this mark-up, the estimated profit for the case is $31 400 ($157 000 × 20%). Using all of this information, the partners estimate the client's service price as follows.

Direct professional labour (500 hours)	$ 75 000
Direct support labour	20 000
Fringe benefits for direct labour	15 000
Photocopying	1 000
Telephone calls	1 000
Total direct costs	$112 000
Allocated indirect costs ($90 × 500 hours)	45 000
Total costs	157 000
Margin ($157 000 × 20%)	31 400
Total estimated service price	$188 400

Competitor's job costs and price

A competing law firm traces only the direct professional labour hours as a direct cost and considers all other costs to be indirect. These indirect costs are allocated at an estimated rate of $160 per professional labour hour. The accountant for this law firm estimates that this copyright case will cost $75 000 + $80 000 ($160 × 500 hours) = $155 000. The competitor uses the same mark-up rate as Nighthawk Law Company: 20 per cent of estimated total cost, or $31 000 ($155 000 × 20%). The partner in the competitor firm estimates the client's service price as follows.

Direct professional labour (500 hours)	$ 75 000
Allocated indirect costs ($160 × 500 hours)	80 000
Total costs	155 000
Margin ($155 000 × 20%)	31 000
Total estimated service price	$186 000

Monitoring job costs

The prices estimated by the two law firms are close in amount. However, the costs used to estimate the price are also used to monitor costs in each law firm. Nighthawk accounts separately for direct costs such as fringe benefits, photocopying and telephone calls. The competitor includes these costs in the indirect cost pool. Each approach has its pros and cons.

Nighthawk's accounting system incurs additional costs to separately accumulate and assign fringe benefits, photocopying and telephone calls to individual jobs. Each of these costs is accumulated in a separate cost pool. Fringe benefits are allocated to jobs based on information already available about professional and support labour hours or costs. To allocate photocopying costs, the firm needs a system (such as the use of client codes) to record photocopying usage for each job. Telephone costs are traced using telephone logs. The accuracy of records for photocopying and telephone costs depends on the ability and willingness of professional and support staff to maintain good records.

The benefit of separately accumulating and assigning fringe benefits, photocopying and telephone call costs as direct costs is an improved monitoring of costs. The indirect cost pool is considerably smaller and includes fewer different types of costs. As the proportion of costs that can be directly traced to individual jobs increases, the accuracy of the costing system increases. Therefore, systems with lower proportions of indirect costs more accurately capture the flow of resources to individual jobs.

3.6 Applying the costing framework in a support department setting

LEARNING OBJECTIVE 3.6 Apply and evaluate the costing framework in a support department setting.

The costing framework outlined in the previous section enables the calculation of the full cost of a cost object and can be adapted for different purposes and for different settings in order to meet the specific needs of the users of the cost information. The structure used in the costing system is influenced by the choices relating to cost objects, cost pools and cost drivers. We will further explore the costing framework by investigating ways of allocating costs between support departments within an entity.

Operating departments are the departments or divisions within an organisation that commonly manufacture goods or produce services for external customers or clients (for example, the home insurance, car insurance and life insurance departments of Partridge Insurance Company in comprehensive example 1). In a private sector context, they can also be referred to as the revenue-generating departments. Support departments provide internal services to each other and to operating departments (for example, the finance, personnel and computing departments in comprehensive example 1).

As shown in figure 3.6, the process for allocating support department costs to operating departments is a further application of the costing framework discussed earlier in the chapter and demonstrated in comprehensive example 1. This section focuses on alternative ways of allocating the support department costs. The process involves the following steps.

1. Clarify the purpose of the allocation.
2. Identify support and operating department cost pools.
3. Assign costs to cost pools.
4. For each support department cost pool, choose an allocation base.
5. Choose and apply a method for allocating support department costs to other support departments and operating departments.
6. If relevant, allocate support costs from the operating departments to units of goods or services.

Allocation methods

Three allocation methods commonly used to allocate support department costs to operating departments are:
- direct method
- step-down method
- reciprocal method.

A close look at comprehensive example 1 will reveal that we used the direct method to allocate the support department costs. In the following sections we detail the three allocation methods. Each method is formally introduced and illustrated.

FIGURE 3.6   Allocation of support department costs

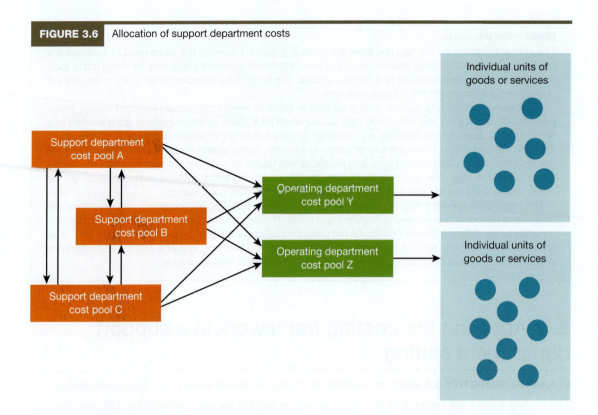

Direct method

The **direct method** allocates the costs of each support department only to the operating departments. Because no costs are allocated among support departments, none of the interactions among support departments are reflected under this method. *Under this method, the cost objects of interest are the operating departments.* In comprehensive example 3 we demonstrate the direct method using Middletown Children's Clinic. Suppose the accountants for the clinic have identified two support departments (housekeeping and administration) and two operating departments (medical and dental). As shown in figure 3.7, the direct method uses each support department's allocation base to allocate the costs for that department to each of the operating departments.

FIGURE 3.7   Direct method

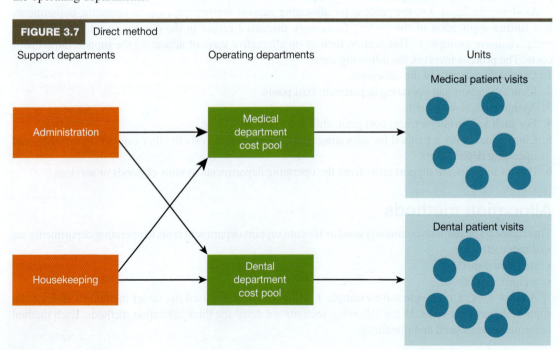

Direct method allocation

Middletown Children's Clinic, a not-for-profit organisation, operates medical and dental clinics for children of low-income families. The organisation receives private donations and government grants to help defray costs. The managers would like to set fees that are as low as possible while also covering costs.

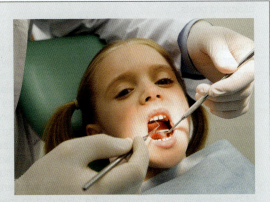

The accounting department at the local college sponsors a work experience program, in which accounting students develop their professional skills and contribute to the community by working as volunteers for not-for-profit organisations. This year, a team of accounting students has been assigned to the clinic. The students have been asked to help allocate all of the clinic's costs to patient visits. The clinic's managers plan to use this information to help set fees. The students will also prepare the annual cost report for the government.

Cost object, cost pools and assigning costs between departments

The clinic provides two different types of services: medical and dental. Because costs probably differ by the type of service provided, the students decide to treat each type of patient visit as a cost object. Therefore, they calculate costs separately for each of the two operating departments and set up a cost pool for each. They learn from an interview with the accountant that the clinic has two support departments: administration and housekeeping. The students set up a cost pool for each of these departments. The accountant helps the students trace the direct costs to each department cost pool. In addition, costs for the entire facility (such as rent and electricity) are gathered into a cost pool and then allocated to all of the departments based on each department's floor space in square metres. The students prepare a summary of the costs assigned to each department as follows.

Cost	Admin.	H/keeping	Medical	Dental	Total
Salaries	$80 000	$40 000	$200 000	$80 000	$400 000
Supplies	15 000	20 000	35 000	10 000	80 000
Facility costs	3 240	360	28 800	3 600	36 000
Total	$98 240	$60 360	$263 800	$93 600	$516 000

Choosing allocation bases

Before the students allocate support department costs, they need to choose allocation bases for the services of the housekeeping and administration departments. One student suggests that floor surface (square metres) is a good base for allocating housekeeping costs. Another student thinks that hours spent in each department would provide a better basis because the departments have different kinds of equipment and different volumes of service. They agree that hours spent is a better choice, but then learn that housekeeping does not keep records of hours by department. Therefore, they return to their alternative choice and use square metres for allocating housekeeping costs as the cost of keeping detailed time sheets would be too high.

For the administration allocation base, the accountant suggests using either the direct costs for each operating department or the number of employees. When the students study the administration department activities, they find that many services relate to employees, such as employee recruiting, training, benefits and payroll. Other services include purchasing and maintenance. They decide that number of employees is more representative than direct costs for the overall activities in administration. Therefore, the students choose the number of employees in each department as the allocation base for administration.

The students gather the following information for the allocation bases.

	Admin.	H/keeping	Medical	Dental	Total
Number of employees	2	2	5	3	12
Square metres	900	100	8 000	1 000	10 000

Having calculated the total costs for each cost pool and chosen an allocation base for each support cost pool, the students are now ready to begin allocating support department costs to operating departments. The accountant tells the students that they can use any reasonable method for allocating support costs to operating departments. The students want to learn more about different methods and their effects on allocated costs.

Direct method calculations

The students begin with the direct method, which is the easiest to perform. They first draw a diagram similar to the one in figure 3.7 to clarify how they will perform calculations. They next calculate the percentage of each support department's costs allocated to each operating department. Costs for housekeeping are allocated based on square metres.

One student observes that the square metres used by administration are not relevant to the direct method because housekeeping costs are not allocated to another support department. Of the 9000 square metres used by the operating departments, the medical clinic uses 8000 square metres, or 89 per cent. Accordingly, 89 per cent of the housekeeping costs will be allocated to medical, and the remaining 11 per cent (1000 square metres / 9000 square metres) will be allocated to dental.

Costs for administration are allocated based on number of employees. The medical clinic employs five of the eight employees who work for operating departments, so 62.5 per cent (5 employees / 8 employees) of the administration costs will be allocated to medical. The remaining 37.5 per cent (3 employees / 8 employees) will be allocated to dental.

The students prepare a report summarising their allocations as shown in figure 3.8. The line for department cost reflects the costs that the students had previously assigned to each department. Of the $60 360 housekeeping cost, 89 per cent ($53 720) is allocated to medical and 11 per cent ($6640) is allocated to dental. Similarly, the administrative cost of $98 240 is allocated 62.5 per cent ($61 400) to medical and 37.5 per cent ($36 840) to dental. The costs allocated from the support departments are added to each operating department's costs. Thus, the total allocated costs (both direct and indirect) are $378 920 for the medical clinic and $137 080 for dental. Notice that the total costs of $516 000 have not been affected by the allocation method. We will use both the step-down method (comprehensive example 4) and reciprocal method (comprehensive example 5) of allocation to contrast how different costing system design can influence the cost determination. You will notice that, in both methods, the cost objects of interest are not only the operating departments but also the support departments.

FIGURE 3.8 Direct method cost allocation report for Middletown Children's Clinic

	Support		Production		
	Admin.	**H/keeping**	**Medical**	**Dental**	**Total**
Allocation bases					
Square metres			8000	1 000	9 000
			89%	11%	100%
Number of employees			5	3	8
			62.5%	37.5%	100%
Costs					
Department cost	$ 98 240	$ 60 360	$263 800	$ 93 600	$516 000
Housekeeping		(60 360)	53 720	6 640	0
Administration	$(98 240)		61 400	36 840	0
Total allocated cost	$ 0	$ 0	$378 920	$137 080	$516 000

Step-down method

The **step-down method** allocates support department costs, one department at a time, to remaining support and operating departments in a cascading manner until all support department costs have been allocated. This method goes beyond the direct method in recognising that support departments provide support not only for the operating departments, but also for other support departments. In this method the cost objects of interest are both support and operating departments. As shown in figure 3.9, the costs for the first support department chosen are allocated to the remaining departments, both support and operating. The process continues, and costs for the remaining support departments are allocated one at a time to the remaining departments until no support department costs remain. For example, in figure 3.9 costs are allocated from administration to housekeeping, but not from housekeeping back to administration.

The step-down method begins by ranking each support department according to the amount of service provided to other support departments. Then support department costs are allocated sequentially, beginning with the support department that provided the most service to other support departments and ending with the support department that provided the least service to other support departments. The ranking can be created using any reasonable criteria. Sometimes a qualitative judgement is made about the degree of services. Alternatively, departments can be ranked using a quantitative measure such as the dollar amount of services provided to other support departments. Calculations for the step-down method are illustrated in comprehensive example 4.

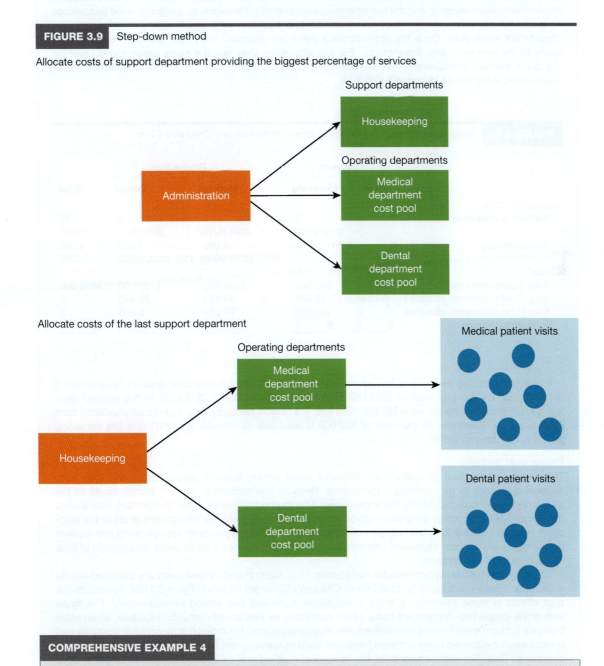

Step-down method

Allocate costs of support department providing the biggest percentage of services

Support departments

Housekeeping

Operating departments

Administration

Medical department cost pool

Dental department cost pool

Allocate costs of the last support department

Operating departments

Medical department cost pool

Medical patient visits

Housekeeping

Dental department cost pool

Dental patient visits

COMPREHENSIVE EXAMPLE 4

Step-down method allocation

After the accounting students allocate Middletown Children's Clinic's costs using the direct method, they recalculate the allocations using the step-down method. The step-down method requires the support departments to be ranked based on the quantity of services provided to other support departments. The students decide to rank administration first because administration probably provides more support to housekeeping than vice versa. For example, administration purchases supplies and provides employee support such as payroll and benefits for the housekeeping department.

The students draw a diagram similar to the one in figure 3.9 to clarify how they will perform calculations. They first allocate administration department costs to all the remaining departments — the other support department (housekeeping) and the two operating departments. Therefore, in determining the percentage of costs for each department, they factor in the two housekeeping employees with the operating department employees. Once the administrative costs are allocated, they next allocate housekeeping costs to the two operating departments. For this allocation, they use the same percentages used for the direct method, because only the two operating departments remain. The students summarise their calculations in the report shown in figure 3.10.

FIGURE 3.10	Step-down method cost allocation report for Middletown Children's Clinic

	Support		Production		
	Admin.	H/keeping	Medical	Dental	Total
Allocation bases					
Number of employees		2	5	3	10
		20% (2/10)	50% (5/10)	30% (3/10)	100%
Square metres			8 000	1 000	9 000
			89% (8000/9000)	11% (1000/9000)	100%
Costs					
Total department cost	$98 240	$60 360	$263 800	$ 93 600	$516 000
Step 1: Administration allocated	(98 240)	19 648	49 120	29 472	0
Step 2: Housekeeping allocated	0	(80 008)	71 207	8 801	0
Total allocated cost	$ 0	$ 0	$384 127	$131 873	$516 000

In the first step, 20 per cent of the administration department's $98 240 cost goes to housekeeping ($19 648), 50 per cent to medical ($49 120) and 30 per cent to dental ($29 472). In the second step, the housekeeping costs are now $80 008 ($60 360 + $19 648) because they include an allocation from administration. Therefore, 89 per cent of $80 008 is allocated to medical ($71 207) and the remaining $8801 is allocated to dental.

Reciprocal method

The **reciprocal method** simultaneously allocates costs among support departments, and then from support departments to operating departments. Because the reciprocal method allows for all of the interactions among departments, it is widely used. This method reflects support department interactions more accurately than either the direct method (which does not address the interactions at all) or the step-down method (which addresses only part of the interactions). Once again both the operating and support departments are the cost objects of interest, but this method provides a more accurate estimate of total costs in support departments.

The reciprocal method is performed in two phases. First, support department costs are allocated among each other. These interactions for Middletown Children's Clinic are shown in figure 3.11(a). To capture the cost effects of these interactions, a set of equations is created and solved simultaneously. The figure shows the simple two-department case, which can easily be performed manually. However, when more than two support departments are involved, the reciprocal method becomes mathematically complex and is more easily performed using software programs such as spreadsheet functions that solve simultaneous equations. Thus, the computations for the reciprocal method are the most complex among the three methods introduced in this section.

After solving the simultaneous equations, the allocated cost for each support department includes costs allocated from the other support departments. Next, this new total cost per support department is allocated to all of the other departments (support and operating) as shown in figure 3.11(b). The reciprocal method is illustrated in comprehensive example 5.

FIGURE 3.11 Reciprocal method

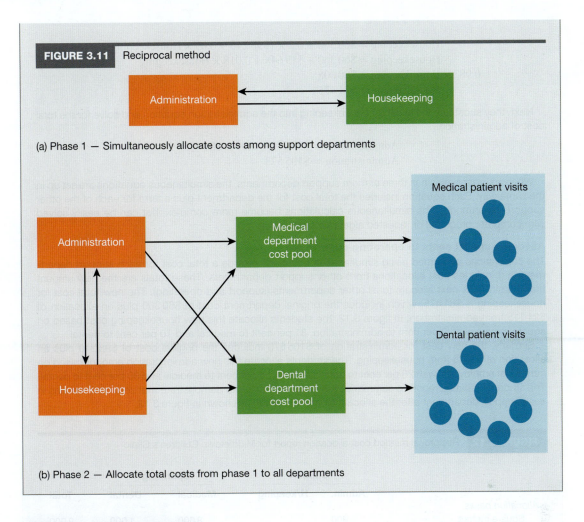

(a) Phase 1 — Simultaneously allocate costs among support departments

(b) Phase 2 — Allocate total costs from phase 1 to all departments

Reciprocal method allocation

After completing the step-down method calculation, the accounting students are ready to apply the reciprocal method to Middletown Children's Clinic's support costs. The students adopt the same allocation bases they used previously, and they draw diagrams similar to the ones in figures 3.11(a) and 3.11(b) to clarify how they will perform calculations.

Allocate support costs among support departments

The students first allocate the support department costs to each other. To simultaneously compute costs between support departments, the students need to set up and solve simultaneous equations. The cost of each support department is written as a sum of directly assigned costs plus costs allocated from the other support department. Administration is allocated based on number of employees. The clinic has 10 employees outside of the administration department, with two of them working in housekeeping. For the purpose of allocating administration costs, housekeeping's portion of employees is 2/10, and

$$\text{Housekeeping} = \$60\,360 + 0.2 \times (\text{Administration})$$

Similarly, housekeeping is allocated based on square metres. Of the 9900 square metres that are not in housekeeping, 900 square metres are in administration. Thus, for the purpose of allocating housekeeping costs, administration's portion of square metres is 900/9900, and

$$\text{Administration} = \$98\,240 + 0.09 \times (\text{Housekeeping})$$

Because only two support departments are involved, only two equations need to be solved simultaneously. The students decide to use the substitution method to solve them. They substitute the administration equation into the housekeeping equation and solve for the total cost of housekeeping:

$$\text{Housekeeping} = \$60\,360 + 0.2 \times \left(\$98\,240 + 0.09 \times \text{Housekeeping} \right)$$
$$\text{Housekeeping} = \$60\,360 + \$19\,648 + 0.018 \times \text{Housekeeping}$$
$$0.982 \times \text{Housekeeping} = \$80\,008$$
$$\text{Housekeeping} = \$81\,475$$

Next, they substitute the result for housekeeping into the administration equation and solve for the total cost of administration:

$$\text{Administration} = \$98\,240 + 0.09 \times \$81\,475$$
$$\text{Administration} = \$105\,573$$

When an organisation has three or more support departments, the simultaneous equations are set up in the same way. Each equation includes the total cost for the department plus a term for each of the other support departments. The simultaneous calculations become more complex, but can be easily solved with computer programs or repeated algebraic substitution.

Allocate support costs to operating departments

The calculations performed using simultaneous equations provide a total cost for each support department that includes cost allocations from other support departments. These totals are the new amount that the students next allocate to all other departments (support and operating). The new total cost for housekeeping is $81 475, which includes the original department cost of $60 360 plus an allocation of $21 115 from administration. In figure 3.12, the students allocate this new housekeeping cost based on square metres, with 9 per cent to administration, 81 per cent to medical and 10 per cent to dental.

Similarly, the new cost for administration of $105 573 includes the original cost of $98 240 plus an allocation of $7333 from housekeeping. The students allocate this new administration amount based on number of employees, with 20 per cent to housekeeping, 50 per cent to medical and 30 per cent to dental. The students create a report to summarise their allocations and to demonstrate that zero cost remains in each support department after the allocations are complete, as shown in figure 3.12.

FIGURE 3.12   Reciprocal method cost allocation report for Middletown Children's Clinic

	Support		Operating		
	Admin.	**H/keeping**	**Medical**	**Dental**	**Total**
Allocation bases					
Square metres	900		8 000	1 000	9 900
	9%		81%	10%	100%
Employees		2	5	3	10
		20%	50%	30%	100%
Costs					
Total department cost	$ 98 240	$60 360	$263 800	$ 93 600	$516 000
Housekeeping	7 333	(81 475)	65 995	8 147	
Administration	(105 573)	21 115	52 786	31 672	
	$ 0	$ 0	$382 581	$133 419	$516 000

Comparing results and choosing an allocation method

When the students finish their calculations for the three allocation methods, they create the following schedule to compare their results.

	Medical	Dental	Total
	$	$	$
Direct method	378 920	137 080	516 000
Step-down method	384 127	131 873	516 000
Reciprocal method	382 581	133 419	516 000

The managers want to know the cost for each patient visit, so the students also calculate the average allocated cost per visit. The accountant tells them that medical usually sees 12 000 patients and dental sees 10 000 patients. Dividing the total allocated costs by these volumes, the total allocated cost per visit under each method is shown in the following table.

	Medical $	Dental $
Direct method	31.58	13.71
Step-down method	32.01	13.19
Reciprocal method	31.88	13.34

The students notice that the fully allocated costs do not vary significantly across methods. They ask their accounting lecturer whether this result is always true. She tells them that the variation depends on the data and number of departments for a given setting. With a larger number of support departments, the differences are usually greater. She also tells them that the step-down and reciprocal methods often yield similar results when only two support departments are involved. She adds that the reciprocal method is the most accurate because it takes into account all interactions.

The students discuss the effort that each method takes. They agree that the direct method requires the least amount of effort and that the reciprocal method requires the most. However, they also agree that they could easily set up a spreadsheet to calculate the clinic's allocations. After concluding that computational difficulty is not a major issue, they recommend the reciprocal method to the clinic.

Comparing the direct, step-down and reciprocal methods

As shown in the Middletown Children's Clinic example, different allocation methods result in different values. Each method has its own pros and cons. The direct method is the easiest to calculate, but computer programs reduce the importance of this issue. An advantage of the direct and step-down methods is that the calculation methods are easier to explain to managers, yet the reciprocal method most accurately considers support department interactions.

3.7 Limitations of cost allocation data

LEARNING OBJECTIVE 3.7 Critically analyse the limitations of cost allocation data.

The process of allocating costs involves many uncertainties, including:
- identifying appropriate cost pools
- deciding whether to establish separate pools for fixed and variable costs
- choosing how to assign costs to cost pools
- identifying the most appropriate allocation bases for each cost pool
- selecting the most appropriate allocation method
- deciding whether the benefits exceed the costs of establishing a more detailed cost allocation system.

Because the process of measuring and allocating costs is uncertain and requires judgement, allocated cost information can be of low quality. The quality of allocated cost information can be improved in many ways. Accountants, managers and operational personnel can work together to identify more appropriate cost pools and allocation bases. Accounting systems can be redesigned to more accurately trace costs to activities and gather better allocation base data. In addition, accountants can adopt allocation methods to more closely match the purpose of the allocation. (In appendix 3A to this chapter, we explore one potential improvement: dual-rate allocations.) Nonetheless, the cost data used to assist in decision making still contains elements of subjectivity due to decisions taken in the costing framework. Therefore, our objective should be to enhance reliability of cost data for decision making while weighing the cost against the benefit of doing so.

Many indirect costs are fixed; they do not change with changes in the allocation base or any other measure of activity. Therefore, allocated indirect costs are not relevant information for most short-term decisions, such as special orders or the use of constrained resources. Nevertheless, managers may mistakenly assume that these allocated costs are variable, particularly when the costing system uses several cost pools and allocation bases. Another problem occurs if the allocation base used to allocate variable indirect costs is not a cost driver, which means it does not accurately reflect the use of variable cost resources.

Managers within an organisation often do not understand how costs are allocated to individual jobs. They may misinterpret cost information and rely on irrelevant information. Accountants must not only produce relevant information for each decision, but also help educate managers about appropriate uses of cost information.

APPENDIX 3A

Single- versus dual-rate allocations

The practice of using only one base to allocate both fixed and variable costs is called **single-rate allocation**. For example, at Middletown Children's Clinic, square metres were used to allocate housekeeping costs. Square metres might be appropriate for allocating housekeeping fixed costs, such as depreciation on any cleaning equipment used, but some housekeeping costs vary with the type of work required in a given area. The time housekeepers spend in each area might be a more appropriate allocation base for the variable costs. Thus, single-rate allocation probably mismeasures resources used. In addition, managers may believe that all support costs are variable, even when they include a large proportion of fixed costs.

Under **dual-rate allocation**, support costs are separated into fixed and variable cost pools, and cost drivers are identified for the variable cost pools to more accurately reflect the flow of resources. Figure 3A.1 presents the dual-rate allocation process under the reciprocal method. Compared to the single-rate allocation, the variable cost allocations reflect a more accurate estimation of the incremental costs of providing support services. Some organisations use variable costs to measure use of a department's services and assign the fixed costs as part of a department's formally adopted budget.

| FIGURE 3A.1 | Dual-rate allocation |

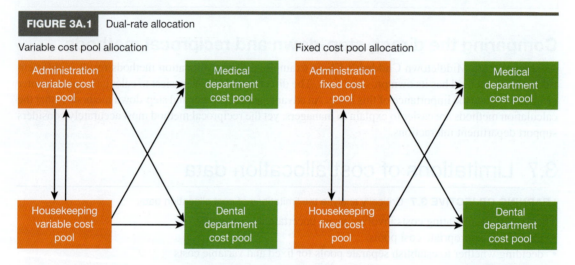

The dual-rate system also has drawbacks. It costs more to develop and maintain. Furthermore, uncertainties about how to classify costs as fixed and variable can introduce additional mismeasurement.

Comprehensive example 6 demonstrates the use of dual rates for Middletown Children's Clinic.

COMPREHENSIVE EXAMPLE 6

Dual rates and reciprocal method with three support departments

After the accounting students allocated administration and housekeeping costs to the operating departments, the accountant asks them whether this information could be used to charge departments for their use of other departments' services. The accountant believes that by charging for support department services, the employees in the user departments would be motivated to manage their use of the support services more cost-consciously (rather than regarding them as 'free'), and some support costs might be reduced. The charges would become part of the current budgeting system in which managers are held responsible for their budgets. Managers receive performance bonuses if costs are maintained at or under budgeted levels.

Charges based on single-rate allocation

The students obtain the total allocated costs for each support department from their previous reciprocal method calculations: $105 573 for administration and $81 475 for housekeeping. Their goal is to calculate a charge representing the use of these services by other departments. Previously, they used number of employees as the allocation base for administration and square metres as the allocation base for housekeeping. They decide to use the allocation bases to calculate a charge for the use of each department's services. For administration services, other departments would be charged a cost per

---

employee. The clinic has 12 employees, two of whom work in administration. The students calculate the charge for administration costs based on the 10 non-administration employees:

$$\$105\,573\ \text{Administration costs}\ /\ 10\,\text{employees} = \$10\,557\ \text{per employee}$$

For housekeeping services, other departments would be charged a cost per square metre. The clinic has 10 000 total square metres, of which 100 are devoted to housekeeping. The students calculate the charge for housekeeping based on the 9900 non-housekeeping square metres:

$$\$81\,475\ \text{Housekeeping costs}\ /\ 9900\,\text{square metres} = \$8.23\ \text{per square metre}$$

The students discuss whether the charges they calculated would be reasonable. They think that the administration charge seems high. They wonder whether other departments should be charged $10 557 for administrative costs for each employee in the department. The charge might encourage managers in the clinic departments to inappropriately reduce the number of employees. For example, the managers might replace an employee with services from a temporary labour agency that would cost the clinic more overall. When the students review the housekeeping charge, they believe that an average annual charge of $8.23 per square metre is reasonable. However, one student asks whether it is reasonable for the housekeeping cost rate for administration to be the same as the cost rate for medical and dental. The clinic areas require special cleaning supplies and greater effort than the administration area. In addition, employees in other departments might feel that they have no control over a fixed charge of $8.23 per square metre. A fixed charge might reduce their motivation to keep work areas clean, increasing the time required by housekeeping.

Analysis of cost behaviour and revision of cost pools

The students had previously learned about dual rates for allocating costs, whereby fixed and variable costs are allocated separately. Some organisations use variable allocations as a charge rate for support services because the variable costs more closely represent the incremental costs that support departments incur to provide services. The students plan to analyse the behaviour of costs in the administration and housekeeping cost pools to determine whether the cost pools should be broken down into separate fixed and variable cost pools. They had previously summarised the costs, as shown below.

Cost	Administration	Housekeeping
Salaries	$80 000	$40 000
Supplies	15 000	20 000
Facility costs	3 240	360
Total	$98 240	$60 360

The students focus first on administration costs. Most of them are for salaries of the manager and the accountant. The manager is responsible for general management of the clinic. The accountant is responsible for accounting and billing functions. The accountant says she spends far more time on billing functions for the operating clinics than on general functions for the whole organisation. The billing functions include receiving information about each patient's charges from the operating departments and then billing patients or their insurance companies, receiving and depositing payments, and following up on denied insurance claims and bad debts. One student points out that the functions of the manager are different from the functions of the accountant. He argues that the costs for these two employees should not be combined in a single cost pool if other departments will be charged for the services. The other students agree that accuracy of the cost allocations will improve if they separate accounting costs from other administration costs, so they decide to establish a separate cost pool called accounting. The accountant helps the students identify the costs that should be assigned to the accounting cost pool, and she summarises the time she usually spends on activities for each department.

When the students study the housekeeping department cost records, they find that housekeeping employees are paid according to an hourly wage, and part of the department's costs vary with time spent working in each area. Therefore, the students think that the variable part of housekeeping costs could be allocated to other departments based on the time spent cleaning each area. However, housekeeping employees do not currently keep track of their time by area. The students discuss this issue with the accountant, who agrees to establish a new record-keeping system for housekeeping employees to keep track of the hours they spend in each department.

Based on their discussions with the accountant and their investigation of the types of costs in each cost pool, the students conclude that costs for all three support departments could be broken down into fixed and variable components. The students and the accountant examine past accounting records and other information to identify fixed and variable costs. The accountant estimates the variable cost of supplies and postage for accounting and billing activities, and the amount of her salary that should be considered a fixed cost of the accounting department. Variable costs in administration include payroll costs that vary by employee, such as fringe benefits, supplies and record keeping for employees. The costs are summarised as follows.

Department	Administration	Accounting	Housekeeping	Total
Variable costs	$11 052	$ 9 210	$30 180	$ 50 442
Fixed costs	50 348	27 630	30 180	108 158
Total cost	$61 400	$36 840	$60 360	$158 600

Charges based on variable cost allocation

The students discuss with the accountant the effects of the new support cost pool on the calculation of charges to other departments. They conclude that other departments should be charged only for variable support costs. Thus, the cost object for each support department is the variable cost of support services provided to other departments.

They next discuss the allocation bases for the variable cost pools. They plan to use the accountant's time to allocate accounting costs. They decide to continue using number of employees for administration. They want to use the time spent in various departments for housekeeping, but they lack recorded information about the amount of time spent in each area. However, the housekeepers estimate that they spend 10 per cent of their time cleaning the administration department, 5 per cent in the accounting area, 55 per cent in the medical clinic and 30 per cent in the dental clinic.

The new variable cost allocation base amounts for all departments are as follows.

	Admin.	Accounting	H/keeping	Medical	Dental	Total
Employees	1		2	5	3	11
Time spent accounting	15%		10%	50%	25%	100%
Time spent cleaning	10%	5%		55%	30%	100%

To apply the reciprocal method, the students must first calculate the total support department variable costs including interactions. They set up simultaneous equations for the interactions among administration, accounting and housekeeping. The equations are:

$$\text{Administration} = \$11\,052 + 15\% \times \text{Accounting} + 10\% \times \text{Housekeeping}$$
$$\text{Accounting} = \$9210 + (1/11) \times \text{Administration} + 5\% \times \text{Housekeeping}$$
$$\text{Housekeeping} = \$30\,180 + (2/11) \times \text{Administration} + 10\% \times \text{Accounting}$$

The students use Excel Solver to find the solutions to this set of simultaneous equations. (Instructions for using Solver are presented in appendix 3B.) The Solver results for each department's total variable cost (including interactions) to be allocated are:

Administration	$16 354
Accounting	$12 416
Housekeeping	$34 395

Given the total allocated variable cost for each support department, the students calculate the support charge per unit of allocation base. The charge for variable administration cost is based on the number of employees:

$$\$16\,354 \div 11 \text{ employees} = \$1486 \text{ per employee}$$

The charge for accounting is based on the time spent by the accountant. The accountant works full time. Allowing four weeks of holidays and eight days of other leave, her estimated work hours per year are:

$$\left[40 \text{ hours per week} \times (52 - 4) \text{ weeks}\right] - (8 \text{ days} \times 8 \text{ hours per day}) = 1856 \text{ hours}$$

Thus, the charge for variable accounting cost is:

$$\$12\,416 \div 1856 \text{ hours} = \$6.69 \text{ (rounded) per hour}$$

The charge for housekeeping is based on time spent cleaning. The cleaning employees work full time, or an estimated 1856 hours per year each. Based on the two housekeeping employees, the estimated total hours are 3712 per year. The charge for variable housekeeping cost is:

$$\$34\,395 \div 3712 \text{ hours} = \$9.27 \text{ (rounded) per hour}$$

The students discuss these rates with the accountant. The administration charge per employee seems low, so department managers would probably not consider these charges in making decisions about employment levels. Many administrative costs are fixed, so the variable portion is small. The accounting charges also seem low, reflecting the high proportion of fixed costs in salary for the accountant. At the same time, charging each department for variable accounting costs helps the department managers recognise that they are using accounting resources.

The housekeeping charges are similar to costs that would be paid if an outside housekeeping service were used, so the managers of the user departments are likely to think that these charges are fair. At the same time, charging the departments for housekeeping based on time spent in each department provides the managers with incentives to keep work areas clean to reduce the number of hours that housekeeping spends in them. The accountant recommends that the fixed costs be assigned to other departments as part of their annual budgets. This way all costs will be allocated, but only variable costs will be charged based on some measure of usage.

Dual-rate allocation

In addition, the accountant reminds the students that they need to allocate costs for the regulatory reports that are filed with the government. For these reports, all support costs must be allocated, not just the variable costs. The students can separately allocate the fixed support costs and then sum the fixed and variable allocations for state reporting.

The students discuss allocation bases for the fixed costs. They use number of employees as the allocation base for administration, time spent for accounting, and square metres for housekeeping. The fixed cost allocation base amounts for all departments are as follows.

	Admin.	Accounting	H/keeping	Medical	Dental	Total
Employees		1	2	5	3	11
Accounting	15%		10%	50%	25%	100%
Square metres	600	300		8000	1000	9900

Once again, the students use Excel Solver to simultaneously allocate the costs among the support departments. (The simultaneous equations and instructions for Excel Solver are found in appendix 3B.)

The students prepare a schedule summarising the variable and fixed cost allocations and calculating the total allocated costs for operating departments, as shown in figure 3A.2. The students discuss how much they enjoyed helping the clinic and gaining experience using three different methods of allocating support department costs, including the use of Solver. They feel the experience was worthwhile. The clinic accountant is glad that the students helped her with this task. She now knows how to use Solver and can revise the allocation scheme over time as the clinic's needs and cost estimates change.

FIGURE 3A.2 Dual-rate support cost allocations for Middletown Children's Clinic

	Support departments			Operating departments		
	Admin.	Accounting	H/keeping	Medical	Dental	Total
Directly assigned costs	$61400	$36840	$60360	$263800	$93600	$516000
Variable cost allocation						
Administration	(16354)	1486	2973	7434	4460	0
Accounting	1862	(12416)	1242	6208	3104	0
Housekeeping	3440	1720	(34395)	18917	10319	0
Fixed cost allocation						
Administration	(58164)	5287	10575	26438	15863	0
Accounting	5138	(34256)	3426	17128	8564	0
Housekeeping	2678	1339	(44181)	35702	4463	0
Total allocated costs	$0	$0	$0	$375627	$140373	$516000

APPENDIX 3B
Using Solver to calculate simultaneous equations for the reciprocal method

Solver, a tool within Excel, can be used to solve simultaneous equations. In this appendix we learn to use Solver for allocating support costs under the reciprocal method.

In comprehensive example 6 (appendix 3A), the accounting students increased the number of support department cost pools from two to three. Therefore, they decided to use Solver to calculate the support department allocations under the reciprocal method. Before using Solver, it is necessary to specify the simultaneous equations. For the Middletown Children's Clinic fixed cost allocation, the simultaneous equations are as follows:

$$\text{Administration} = \$50\,348 + 15\% \times \text{Accounting} + (600/9900) \times \text{Housekeeping}$$
$$\text{Accounting} = \$27\,630 + (1/11) \times \text{Administration} + (300/9900) \times \text{Housekeeping}$$
$$\text{Housekeeping} = \$30\,180 + (2/11) \times \text{Administration} + 10\% \times \text{Accounting}$$

Figures 3B.1 and 3B.2 provide results and formulas using Solver for this set of simultaneous equations. The change cells are given the names Admin, Acct and Housekeep. Solver manipulates these cells to solve the simultaneous equations for each department's cost. The solution includes allocations from the other two support departments. The target function is the sum of the three change cells and is given the following formula:

$$= \text{Admin} + \text{Acct} + \text{Housekeep}$$

Notice in cells B15, B16 and B17 of figure 3B.1 that the simultaneous equations are listed so that they can be entered into Solver as constraints. When adding each constraint in the Solver dialogue box, set the simultaneous equation equal to (by selecting the equal sign in the pull-down menu) the change cell that represents the department for which cost you are solving. For example, the cell with the simultaneous equations for Administration should contain:

$$= B3 + B7 * \text{Acct} + (B8/G8) * \text{Housekeep}$$

FIGURE 3B.1 Fixed cost allocation spreadsheet for using Solver with formulas

	A	B	C	D	E	F	G
1	Middletown Clinic						
2	Departments	Administration	Accounting	Housekeeping	Medical	Dental	Total
3	Costs	50348	27630	30180	263800	93600	=SUM(B3:F3)
4							
5	Allocation Bases						
6	Employees	0	1	2	5	3	=SUM(B6:F6)
7	Accounting time spent	0.15	0	0.1	.5	0.25	=SUM(B7:F7)
8	Square footage	600	300	0	8000	1000	=SUM(B8:F8)
9							
10	Change cells for solver						
11	Admin	Acct	Housekeep				
12	58164.1018577537	34256.4619090369	44180.9374373239				
13							
14	Simultaneous equations						
15	Administration	=B3+B7*Acct+(B8/G8)*Housekeep					
16	Accounting	=C3+(C6/G6)*Admin+(C8/G8)*Housekeep					
17	Housekeeping	=D3+(D6/G6)*Admin+D7*Acct					
18							
19	Target function						
20	=Admin+Acct+Housekeep						
21							
22	Allocation	Administration	Accounting	Housekeeping	Medical	Dental	Total
23	Cost	=B3	=C3	=D3	=E3	=F3	=SUM(B23:F23)
24	Administration Allocation	=-B15	=(C6/$G$6)*$B$15	=(D6/$G$6)*$B$15	=(E6/$G$6)*$B$15	=(F6/$G$6)*$B$15	=SUM(B24:F24)
25	Accounting Allocation	=B7*B16	=-B16	=D7*$B$16	=E7*$B$16	=F7*$B$16	=SUM(B25:F25)
26	Housekeep Allocation	=(B8/$G$8)*$B$17	=(C8/$G$8)*$B$17	=-B17	=(E8/$G$8)*$B$17	=(F8/$G$8)*$B$17	=SUM(B26:F26)
27	Total Allocated Cost	=SUM(B23:B26)	=SUM(C23:C26)	=SUM(D23:D26)	=SUM(E23:E26)	=SUM(F23:F26)	=SUM(G23:G26)

Click Add next to the constraints box. The cell with this formula will be entered on the left-hand side under Cell Reference. Click on the box under Constraint and then highlight the department for the simultaneous equation in the cell reference, in this case Admin.

In the spreadsheet shown in figures 3B.1 and 3B.2, solution values from Solver feed into the bottom part of the spreadsheet that performs the allocation process. You may need to go back and forth between these two spreadsheets to understand how to set up your own spreadsheet for this problem. Notice that the values for costs and allocation bases are at the top of the spreadsheet. If you change any of these values, you will need to run Solver again to determine the new amounts for the three support departments.

FIGURE 3B.2 Fixed cost allocation spreadsheet for using Solver

	A	B	C	D	E	F	G
1	Middletown Clinic						
2	Departments	Administration	Accounting	Housekeeping	Medical	Dental	Total
3	Costs	$50,348	$27,630	$30,180	$263,800	$93,600	$465,558
4							
5	Allocation Bases						
6	Employees	0	1	2	5	3	11
7	Accounting time spent	15%	0%	10%	50%	25%	100%
8	Square footage	600	300	0	8,000	1,000	9,900
9							
10	Change cells for solver						
11		Admin	Acct	Housekeep			
12		$58,164	$34,256	$44,181			
13							
14	Simultaneous equations						
15	Administration	$58,164					
16	Accounting	$34,256					
17	Housekeeping	$44,181					
18							
19	Target function						
20		136601.5012					
21							
22	Allocation	Administration	Accounting	Housekeeping	Medical	Dental	Total
23	Department Cost	$50,348	$27,630	$30,180	$263,800	$93,600	$465,558
24	Administration Allocation	($58,164)	$5,287	$10,575	$26,438	$15,863	$0
25	Accounting Allocation	$5,138	($34,256)	$3,426	$17,128	$8,564	$0
26	Housekeep Allocation	$2,678	$1,339	($44,181)	$35,702	$4,463	$0
27	Total Allocated Cost	$0	$0	$0	$343,068	$122,490	$456,558

SUMMARY

3.1 Describe the role of cost objects and how they support decision making.
The cost object could be anything for which a separate measurement of cost is required. Examples are products, services, departments, business units, processes, customers and activities. Cost objects represent the focus for the costing system.

3.2 Explain and compare direct and indirect costs.

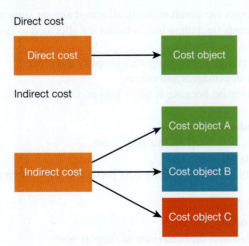

3.3 Discuss the process of indirect cost allocation.

1. Identify the cost object.
2. Determine indirect costs to be allocated to cost objects.
3. Select the appropriate cost driver (either volume or activity) to assign indirect costs.
4. Calculate the indirect cost rate.

3.4 Identify the steps within a costing framework.

Step 1: Overview of cost assignment — identification of cost objects, cost pools and cost drivers
Step 2: Determination of the indirect cost rates for each cost pool
Step 3: Allocation of indirect costs to the cost objects
Step 4: Determination of the full cost of each cost object — tracing of direct costs and allocation of indirect costs

3.5 Apply and evaluate the costing framework in a service entity setting.

Provides an illustration of the application of the costing framework to determine the full cost for:
• individual operating departments in order to cost insurance policies issued by these departments.
• providing services to clients of a legal firm.

3.6 Apply and evaluate the costing framework in a support department setting.

Operating departments

Operating departments are the departments or divisions within an organisation that manufacture goods or produce services for external customers or clients.

Support departments

Support departments provide services internal to the organisation that support the operating departments.

Direct method

Each support department's cost is allocated to only the operating departments.

Pros and cons

• Easiest method computationally, but computers make this factor less important.
• Easy to explain to managers and others.
• Ignores interactions among support departments.

Step-down method

Support department costs are allocated, one department at a time, to remaining support and operating departments in a cascading manner until all support department costs have been allocated.

Pros and cons

• Requires ranking of support departments in terms of services provided to other support departments.
• Moderately easy computations, depending on the number of support departments.
• Moderately easy to explain to managers and others.
• Takes into account some of the interactions among support departments.

Reciprocal method

• First, support department costs are simultaneously allocated among support departments.
• Next, support department costs (including interactions) are allocated to operating departments.

Pros and cons

• Computationally the most complex, but computers simplify the process.
• May be difficult to explain to managers and others.
• Most accurate allocation method because it takes into account all of the interactions among support departments.

Single-rate allocation (appendix 3A)

Uses only one base to allocate both fixed and variable costs.

Dual-rate allocation (appendix 3A)

Accumulates fixed and variable costs in separate cost pools and uses different allocation bases for these cost pools.

Pros and cons

• Reduces mismeasurement of allocations.
• Reduces misunderstandings about the behaviour of support costs.

- Costs more to develop and maintain.
- May introduce additional mismeasurement from problems arising from the need to classify costs as fixed and variable.

3.7 Critically analyse the limitations of cost allocation data.

Uncertainties
- Identifying support and operating cost pools
- Assigning costs to cost pools
- Selecting allocation bases
- Choosing an allocation method
- Measuring the degree of services provided among support departments (step-down and reciprocal methods)

Ways to improve the quality of information
- Use dual-rate allocations
- Redesign accounting system for cost pools and allocation bases
- Make choices regarding estimated versus actual support costs and rates
- Consider perceived fairness

KEY TERMS

activity drivers Factors that relate to the attributes of the individual activities and recognise that things other than volume cause indirect costs to be used by cost objects.

cost allocation The allocation of indirect costs to specific cost objects.

cost/benefit test A comparison of the cost of tracing costs to cost objects against the benefits of a more detailed cost information tracing system.

cost driver An input or activity that causes changes in total cost for a cost object.

cost object A thing or activity for which we measure costs (for example, a product, service, customer, department, business unit or geographic region).

cost pool A group of individual costs that are accumulated for a particular purpose. Cost pools can be grouped on a departmental basis, an activity basis or on some other criteria.

direct cost Cost that can be directly linked to the cost object.

direct method Allocates the costs of each support department only to the operating departments.

dual-rate allocation A method in which support costs are separated into fixed and variable cost pools, and cost drivers are identified for the variable cost pools to more accurately reflect the flow of resources.

full cost The total costs incurred for a cost object.

indirect cost rate The rate used to assign the cost to the cost object.

indirect costs (overheads) Costs that are used for the benefit of multiple cost objects (also referred to as overheads).

predetermined indirect cost rate A method of allocating indirect costs using budgeted rather than actual indirect costs.

reciprocal method An approach that simultaneously allocates costs among support departments, and then from support departments to operating departments.

single-rate allocation The practice of using only one base to allocate both fixed and variable costs.

step-down method A method that allocates support department costs, one department at a time, to remaining support and operating departments in a cascading manner until all support department costs have been allocated.

volume drivers Drivers that use a measure of output to assign the indirect costs (for example, labour hours, machine hours or units of output).

SELF-STUDY PROBLEMS

SELF-STUDY PROBLEM 1 Direct, step-down and reciprocal methods; use of allocation information

Pet Protection is a veterinary clinic that is subsidised by the local humane society. The not-for-profit organisation was set up to encourage low-income pet owners to neuter and vaccinate their pets. The humane society would like to know the cost per animal visit to use in its fundraising campaign literature.

The information for a recent period follows:

Costs before allocation	Support departments		Operating departments		
Direct costs	Maintenance	Administration	Neuter	Vaccinations	Total
Salaries	$25 000	$40 000	$100 000	$ 75 000	$240 000
Supplies	5 000	5 000	15 000	25 000	50 000
Building-related costs	2 400	3 600	12 000	6 000	24 000
Total	$32 400	$48 600	$127 000	$106 000	$314 000
Some possible allocation bases:					
Square metres	200	300	1 000	500	2 000
Employees	1	1	5	3	10

Required

(a) Allocate the support department costs to the operating departments using the following:
  (i) direct method
  (ii) step-down method
  (iii) reciprocal method.
(b) Assume the neuter clinic handles 2400 pet visits and vaccinations handles 5000 pet visits. Calculate the cost per visit for each department under the three methods.
(c) A local TV station has contacted the head veterinarian at Pet Protection. The station will provide free advertising to encourage low-income pet owners to neuter their pets using Pet Protection's services. The veterinarian estimates the cost of a 10 per cent increase in business volume using the total allocated costs developed in part (a) and becomes alarmed at the large total cost. Describe the calculation of total allocated costs and explain why these costs should not be used to estimate future costs.

SOLUTION TO SELF-STUDY PROBLEM 1

(a) Two assumptions are used in making these calculations: (1) the administration costs will be allocated using number of employees and maintenance costs will be allocated using square metres, and (2) the administration support department provides more services to the maintenance support department than the other way around.
  (i) Direct method allocation

	Support departments		Operating departments		
	Maintenance	Administration	Neuter	Vaccinations	Total
Allocation base percentages					
Administration					
Employees			5	3	8
Percentage			62.5%	37.5%	100%
Maintenance					
Square metres			1000	500	1500
Percentage			66.6667%	33.3333%	100%
Departmental costs	$32 400	$48 600	$127 000	$106 000	$314 000
Allocations:					
Administration		(4 860)	30 375	18 225	
Maintenance	(32 400)		21 600	10 800	
Total allocated cost	$ 0	$ 0	$178 975	$135 025	$314 000

  (ii) Step-down method allocation
  For the step-down allocation method, administrative costs are allocated first because they are largest.

	Support departments		Operating departments		
	Maintenance	Administration	Neuter	Vaccinations	Total
Allocation base percentages					
Administration					
Employees	1		5	3	9
Percentage	11.1111%		55.5555%	33.3333%	100%
Maintenance					
Square metres			1000	500	1500
Percentage			66.6667%	33.3333%	100%
Departmental costs	$ 32 400	$ 48 600	$127 000	$106 000	$314 000
Allocations:					
Administration	5 400	(48 600)	27 000	16 200	
Maintenance	(37 800)		25 200	12 600	
Total allocated cost	$ 0	$ 0	$179 200	$134 800	$314 000

(iii) Reciprocal method allocation

The first task in the reciprocal method is to set up and solve simultaneous equations for the interactions among the support departments. The interactions are calculated using the allocation base percentages. When only two support departments are involved, the substitution method can be used to solve the simultaneous equations.

	Support departments		Operating departments		
	Maintenance	Administration	Neuter	Vaccinations	Total
Allocation base percentages					
Administration					
Employees	1		5	3	9
Percentage	11.1111%		55.5556%	33.3333%	100%
Maintenance					
Square metres		300	1000	500	1800
Percentage		16.6667%	55.5556%	27.7777%	100%

Simultaneous equations

The equation for the total costs of each support department is equal to the costs assigned to the departmental cost pool plus an allocation of the costs from the other support department:

$$\text{Maintenance} = \$32\,400 + (1/9) \times \text{Administration}$$
$$\text{Administration} = \$48\,600 + (300/1800) \times \text{Maintenance}$$

The cost for the maintenance department is calculated by substituting the administration equation into the cleaner equation:

$$\text{Maintenance} = \$32\,400 + (1/9) \times (48\,600 + (300/1800) \times \text{Maintenance})$$
$$0.981\,481\,48 \times \text{Maintenance} = \$37\,800$$
$$\text{Maintenance} = \$38\,513$$

The cost for the administration department is calculated by substituting the result for the maintenance cost into the administration equation:

$$\text{Administration} = \$48\,600 + (300/1800) \times \$38\,513$$
$$\text{Administration} = \$55\,019$$

Next, costs are allocated from each support department to the other support departments and to the operating departments. The amounts allocated are based on the computations from the simultaneous equations. The use of simultaneous equations ensures that zero cost remains in each support department after the allocations are complete. In other words, the total cost allocated from maintenance ($38 513) is equal to the costs assigned to the maintenance cost pool ($32 400) plus the costs allocated to maintenance from administration ($6113). Similarly, the total cost allocated from administration ($55 019) is equal to the costs assigned to the administration cost pool ($48 600) plus the costs allocated to administration from maintenance ($6419).

	Support departments		Operating departments		
	Maintenance	Administration	Neuter	Vaccinations	Total
Departmental costs	$32 400	$48 600	$127 000	$106 000	$314 000
Allocations:					
Administration	6 113	(55 019)	30 566	18 340	0
Maintenance	(38 513)	6 419	21 396	10 698	0
Total allocated cost	$ 0	$ 0	$178 962	$135 038	$314 000

(b) The cost per visit is calculated by dividing each operating department's total direct and allocated costs by the number of pet visits per year.

	Neuter	Vaccinations
Direct method	$178 975 / 2400 = $74.57 per visit	$135 025 / 5000 = $27.01 per visit
Step-down method	$179 200 / 2400 = $74.67 per visit	$134 800 / 5000 = $26.96 per visit
Reciprocal method	$178 962 / 2400 = $74.57 per visit	$135 038 / 5000 = $27.01 per visit

(c) The costs per visit are calculated as follows. First, all clinic costs are assigned to departments. Some costs are traced directly to departments (salaries and supplies), and some (building-related costs) are gathered together in a general cost pool and distributed (allocated) among all of the departments. Then, the support department costs (administration and maintenance) are allocated to each other and then to the operating departments (neuter and vaccinations). Many of these costs are fixed and will not change as volumes increase (for example, salaries and building-related costs such as the lease).

Through the allocation process, all of the fixed costs become an average cost per unit. The cost per visit is accurate only at the level of visits used in the denominator. When the veterinarian multiplies the per-visit rate times a larger number of visits, the total cost is overestimated because the per-visit cost is an average cost that includes a portion of fixed cost. These fixed costs do not increase proportionately as volumes increase, but remain constant across a relevant range. To increase the accuracy of future cost estimates, past costs need to be separated into fixed and variable categories, and a cost function needs to be developed. In addition, some of the information used in the cost function should be updated to reflect any anticipated price changes.

SELF-STUDY PROBLEM 2 Costing in the service sector

Consider the following budgeted data for a client case of Bob Crachit's accounting firm. The client wants a fixed price quotation.

Direct professional labour	$20 000
Direct support labour	10 000
Fringe benefits for direct labour	13 000
Photocopying	2 000
Telephone calls	2 000
Computer lines	6 000

Overhead is allocated at the rate of 100 per cent of direct labour cost.

Required

(a) Prepare a schedule of the budgeted total costs for the client. Show subtotals for total direct labour costs and total costs as a basis for mark-up.

(b) Assume that the partner's policy is to quote a fixed fee at 10 per cent above the total costs. What fee would be quoted?

(c) Explain why the listed estimates for costs might not be similar to the actual costs for the job. What factors could affect the accuracy of these estimates? List as many factors as you can.

SOLUTION TO SELF-STUDY PROBLEM 2

(a)

Direct labour costs:		
Professional labour	$20 000	
Support labour	10 000	
Total	30 000	
Other direct costs	$23 000	(fringe benefits + copying + phone + computer*)
Allocated overhead	30 000	(100% of $30 000)
Budgeted costs	$83 000	

*This assumes that computer lines and costs can be traced. If these cannot be traced, then this cost would be assigned to overhead.

(b) Fee = 110% × $83 000 = $91 300

(c) Many factors could affect these costs. Because they are estimations, any relevant factors that were left out of the estimate could influence cost. It is difficult to predict how efficient the resources will be used. It is possible that the professional labour hours required are more or less than estimated, depending on the skills of the professionals and the accuracy with which the amount of work was estimated. If something was overlooked that requires more hours, the estimate will be off. Phone costs and computer costs may be different because rates change, or the job requires more or less telephone or computer work.

Factors that could affect the actual costs: price changes for any of the resources, and unforeseen complications such as computer crashes, problems with communication systems, illness of key professional and support employees, and unforeseen problems in the actual work.

QUESTIONS

3.1 For what purposes do organisations need cost information? **LO1**

3.2 What is a cost object? Give three examples. **LO1**

3.3 How do organisations identify the costs of a cost object? **LO1**

3.4 Explain the difference between a direct cost and an indirect cost. **LO2**

3.5 Discuss the importance of selecting an appropriate cost driver for cost allocation. **LO3**

3.6 Explain the differences and similarities among the direct, step-down and reciprocal methods. **LO4**

3.7 Explain the similarities and differences between support department costs and manufacturing overhead costs. **LO3**

3.8 What should determine the choice of cost allocation method (direct, step-down and reciprocal) discussed in this chapter? **LO4**

3.9 Explain how cost data is sourced in a costing framework. **LO4**

3.10 Outline the key steps in a costing framework. **LO4**

3.11 What factors should be considered when choosing allocation bases? **LO3**

3.12 A product is started in department 1 and completed in department 2. Is department 1 a support department or an operating department? Explain. **LO3**

3.13 Explain the difference between operating departments and support departments. **LO3**

3.14 What are the advantages and disadvantages of using estimated support cost allocation rates? **LO7**

3.15 List at least three possible allocation bases that could be used to allocate accounting department costs to other departments. Give one advantage and one disadvantage of using each allocation base. **LO7**

3.16 Refer to the Partridge Insurance example (comprehensive example 1) in the chapter. Explain how the support departments can be classified as both cost objects and cost pools in the costing system. **LO4**

3.17 During a recent management meeting at Sunset Consulting Services, a team member questioned why the costing system had multiple indirect cost pools given it would be easier just to have one. Provide a brief response to explain why the business has adopted multiple indirect costs pools. **LO3, 5**

EXERCISES

3.18 Direct and indirect costs   **LO2**

Frida's Tax Practice has two departments: tax and audit. The tax department has two product lines: business returns and individual returns. A list of costs and three cost objects from Frida's Tax Practice follow.

Required

For each cost, identify whether it is direct or indirect for each cost object.

	Cost object		
Cost	**Tax department**	**Personal returns**	**Mr Gruper's personal tax return**
(a) Subscription to personal tax law updates publication			
(b) Ink supplies for tax department photocopy machine			
(c) Portion of total rent for tax department office space			
(d) Wages for tax department administrative assistant			
(e) Tax partner's salary			
(f) Charges for long-distance call to Mr Gruper about personal tax return questions			
(g) Tax partner lunch with Mr Gruper (the tax partner has lunch with each client at least once per year)			

3.19 Direct and indirect costs; fixed, variable and mixed costs   **LO2**

Your sister turned her hobby into a small business called Glazed Over. She is a potter and manufactures and sells bowls that can be used for decoration or for birdbaths. She has one employee, who works 40 hours a week no matter how many bowls are made. She has asked your advice in developing a cost function for the bowls so that she can estimate costs for the next period.

Required

The following list of costs comes from your sister's general ledger. Assume the cost object is an individual unit (that is, bowl). Categorise each cost as direct or indirect (D or I), and as fixed, variable or mixed (F, V or M).

(a) Employee wages
(b) Clay used to make bowls
(c) Depreciation on the kilns
(d) Glaze (the finish painted on the bowls)
(e) Brushes for the glaze
(f) Electricity
(g) Business licence
(h) Advertising
(i) Pottery studio maintenance (cost of weekly cleaning service)
(j) Packing materials for the bowls

3.20 Cost driver selection   **LO3**

For each of the following activities undertaken to bake pastries and cakes, identify a suitable cost driver to allocate costs.

(a) Mixing ingredients
(b) Baking pastries and cakes
(c) Decorating cakes
(d) Packing pastries and cakes on trays
(e) Sales
(f) Dispatch to customers

3.21 Direct and indirect costs; and cost driver selection **LO2, 3**

Venture Buses operates throughout the south-eastern suburbs of Melbourne, with its depot located in Cheltenham. Every day, fuel is delivered and stored in tanks located in the depot. This fuel is used by all the buses and administration vehicles. The accountant has been requested to develop a system to assign the cost to the different vehicles in the depot. He has asked your assistance in coming up with a way to identify the fuel costs.

Required

(a) From the perspective of the depot, is the cost of fuel a direct or indirect cost?

(b) From the perspective of the vehicles attached to the depot, can the cost be classified as either direct or indirect? Briefly explain.

(c) What system would be required to have the cost classified as direct?

(d) If the accountant decided to go with an indirect cost classification, how could the cost be allocated?

(e) Identify some factors that would determine which method would be the best for the assignment of fuel costs to the vehicles.

3.22 Calculation of indirect cost rates **LO4**

Wright Medical Centre has identified the following activities and cost drivers for the coming financial year.

Activity	Cost	Cost driver	Total expected use of cost driver
Patient admission	$ 600 000	Number of patients	10 000 patients
Medical consultation	$5 000 000	Time taken for appointment	33 000 hours
X-ray	$1 500 000	Number of X-rays	15 000 X-rays
Prescriptions	$ 700 000	Number of items to be dispensed	200 000 items

Required

Calculate the activity cost rate for each activity.

3.23 Allocation rates **LO6**

DataShow's IT support department budgets its costs at $40 000 per month plus $12 per hour. For November, the following were the estimated and actual hours provided by the IT support department to three operating departments.

	Estimated support hours	Actual support hours
Department A	1600	1500
Department B	1400	1600
Department C	2000	1800
Total	5000	4900

Required

(a) What is the support department's allocation rate if estimated activity is the allocation base?

(b) What is the support department's allocation rate if actual activity is the allocation base?

(c) List one advantage and one disadvantage for each type of allocation rate.

3.24 Allocating support costs to units **LO6**

A local hospital is required to account for the total cost of patient care, including support costs. Patients are assigned all direct costs. Support costs are $240 000 per month plus $90 per patient day. This 120-bed hospital averages 80 per cent occupancy.

Required

(a) Calculate the average daily charge per patient for support costs, assuming 30 days in a month.

(b) Briefly comment on potential problems in using only one indirect cost pool for support costs given that individual patients receive a range of different treatments while an inpatient.

3.25 Direct method using estimated costs, benchmarking **LO6**

Devon Ltd allocates support department costs using the direct method and estimated costs. The support department costs are budgeted at $88 000 for department A, $63 000 for department B and

$40 000 for department C. These costs are allocated using the proportion of total cost the firm would pay to an outside service provider.

	Support			Operating	
	Dept A	Dept B	Dept C	Casting	Machine
Direct costs	$88 000	$63 000	$40 000	—	—
Labour hours				6 000	4 000
Machine hours				2 000	10 000
Costs if support services were purchased outside:					
Department A				$50 000	$60 000
Department B				$40 000	$30 000
Department C				$20 000	$30 000

Required

(a) Allocate budgeted support department costs using the direct method, first using labour hours and then with the outside cost proportions as the allocation bases.

(b) Could Devon Ltd use the cost of purchasing outside as an efficiency benchmark for the cost of both the support departments and the operating departments? List several advantages and disadvantages of this approach.

3.26 Costing for a hospital   LO5

Mercy Hospital uses a costing system for all patients who have surgery. The hospital uses a budgeted overhead rate for allocating overhead to patient stays. In March, the operating room had a budgeted allocation base of 1000 operating hours. The budgeted operating room overhead costs were $66 000.

Patient Dwight Schuller was in the operating room for four hours during March. Other costs related to Schuller's four-hour surgery include:

Patient medicine	$ 250
Cost of nurses	3 500
Cost of supplies	800

Physician cost is not included because physicians bill patients separately from the hospital billing system.

Required

(a) Determine the budgeted (that is, estimated) overhead rate for the operating room.

(b) Determine the total costs of Schuller's four-hour surgery.

3.27 Reciprocal method   LO5

The Brown and Brinkley Brokerage firm is organised into two major sales divisions: institutional clients and retail clients. The firm also has two support departments: research and administration. The research department's costs are allocated to the other departments based on a log of hours spent on tasks for each user. The administration department's costs are allocated based on the number of employees in each department.

Records are available for last period as follows.

	Support departments		Operating departments	
	Research	Administration	Institutional	Retail
Payroll costs	$350 000	$300 000	$400 000	$550 000
Other costs	$230 000	$150 000	$120 000	$240 000
Research hours	100	200	500	300
Number of employees	7	10	8	10

Required

Using the reciprocal method, determine the total cost of operations for each sales division. Use either simultaneous equations or Excel Solver.

3.28 Reciprocal method   **LO6**

Paul's Valley Protection Service has three support departments (S1, S2 and S3) and three operating departments (P1, P2 and P3). The direct costs of each department are $30 000 for S1, $20 000 for S2 and $40 000 for S3. The proportions of service provided by each support department to the others are given in the following table.

	Support departments			Operating departments		
	S1	S2	S3	P1	P2	P3
S1	—	0.4	0.1	0.2	0.2	0.1
S2	0.1	—	0.2	0.2	—	0.5
S3	0.2	0.2	—	0.1	0.4	0.1

Required

Using the reciprocal method, allocate the support department costs to the operating departments.

3.29 Step-down, direct and reciprocal methods; accuracy of allocation   **LO6, 7**

Software Plus Ltd produces flight and driving simulations, and games for personal computers. The company's manager has a complaint about the accounting for support department costs. The manager points to the following table describing the use of various support departments in the company and says, 'According to this table, every department receives services from all the support departments. But I understand that only some of the support departments are bearing costs from the other support departments. Why is that?'

		Percentage use of services				
Support department	Cost	Administration	Maintenance	Information systems	Games manufacturing	Simulation manufacturing
Administration	$40 000	0%	10%	50%	10%	30%
Maintenance	20 000	20	0	10	40	30
Information systems	50 000	35	5	0	40	20

Required

(a) What method has Software Plus Ltd been using to allocate support costs? Explain how you know.

(b) Which method would ignore all interactions among support departments? Explain.

(c) Which method would consider all interactions among support departments? Explain.

(d) Allocate the support department costs to Games and Simulation using the step-down method. Explain how you decided which department's costs to allocate first.

(e) Allocate the support department costs using the direct method.

(f) Allocate the support department costs using the reciprocal method.

(g) In your own words, explain how the step-down method improves upon the direct method.

(h) In your own words, explain how the reciprocal method improves upon the step-down method.

3.30 Direct, step-down and reciprocal methods; assign costs to departments   **LO6**

Cost information for Lake County Library is as follows.

	Support		Operating		
Direct costs	maintenance	Administration	books	Other media	Total
Salaries	$20 000	$40 000	$50 000	$70 000	$180 000
Supplies	5 000	5 000	15 000	25 000	50 000
Allocation base volumes					
Square metres	500	500	1 200	300	2500
Employees	1	1	2	1	5

In addition to directly traceable costs, the library incurred $24 000 for a building lease.

Required

(a) Allocate to departments any costs that have not been traced, and then calculate total costs assigned to each department.

(b) Allocate the support department costs to the operating departments using the direct method.

(c) Allocate the support department costs to the operating departments using the step-down method. Allocate first the costs for the support department having the largest direct costs.

(d) Allocate the support department costs to the operating departments using the reciprocal method. Use either simultaneous equations or Excel Solver.

3.31 Step-down and reciprocal methods; uncertainties; pricing   **LO5**

Kovacik manufactures two types of piggy banks in two different departments: a kangaroo-shaped piggy bank and a platypus-shaped piggy bank. The plant is highly automated and contains only two other departments: (1) engineering and design, and (2) information systems. Kovacik allocates support department costs according to estimated service use. Estimated information for next year is as follows:

	Support		Operating	
	Engineering and design	Information systems	Kangaroo bank	Platypus bank
Direct costs	$2700	$8000	$10 000	$20 000
Services used				
Engineering and design	10%	40%	50%	
Information systems	20%	30%	50%	
Production volume	20%	10%	8000	4000

Total allocated costs are assigned to individual units using the production volume.

Required

(a) Determine the estimated total allocated costs for the operating departments using the step-down method.

(b) Determine the estimated total allocated cost per unit of the kangaroo-shaped piggy bank and the platypus-shaped piggy bank under the step-down method.

(c) Explain why actual total allocated costs will turn out to be different from the estimated total allocated costs.

(d) Determine the estimated total allocated costs for the operating departments using the reciprocal method. Use either simultaneous equations or Excel Solver.

(e) Determine the estimated total allocated cost per unit of the kangaroo-shaped piggy bank and the platypus-shaped piggy bank under the reciprocal method.

PROBLEMS

3.32 Categorisation of support costs   **LO2, 7**

Food on Wheels is a charitable organisation that provides meals for low-income individuals who are unable to leave their homes. To support its services, the organisation solicits contributions from individuals and businesses. Food on Wheels needs to submit financial statements to its major sponsor. The sponsor requires expenses to be assigned to the following cost pools: administrative, fundraising and programs.

The bookkeeper for Food on Wheels is a volunteer who is taking accounting classes at the local community college. He knows that all of the costs to prepare and deliver meals should be assigned to the program. However, he is not sure how to assign some of the costs. In particular, he is concerned about the following two items.

Costs for printing and mailing a monthly newsletter

The newsletter is sent out to donors and clients and asks for donations. It also describes the organisation's activities, provides information for obtaining meal services, and provides recipes for some of the meals that are served. The director of the organisation wants the cost of the newsletter to be classified as a program cost. She maintains that the program information and recipes should be considered educational material. Not-for-profit organisations typically classify educational materials as program expenses.

Director's salary and benefits

The director of Food on Wheels spends much of her time raising funds, meeting with the board of directors and performing other administrative duties. She also manages the cooks and drivers, purchases food and delivery supplies, and schedules the food deliveries. The director has instructed the bookkeeper to allocate her salary and benefit costs as follows: 50 per cent to the program, 25 per cent to fundraising and 25 per cent to administration.

Required

(a) Identify and discuss uncertainties about how each of the following costs should be classified.
  (i) Costs to print and mail the newsletter
  (ii) Director's salary and benefits
(b) Does this situation involve an ethical dilemma for the bookkeeper? Why?
(c) Explain why the director prefers costs to be assigned to program expenses.
(d) Explain how you think sponsors would prefer the costs in part (a) to be assigned.
(e) Suppose you are reviewing cost information for another organisation. Would you expect the organisation's program costs to be biased upward, biased downward, or to be unbiased? Explain.
(f) How would you classify the costs in part (a) if you were the bookkeeper for Food on Wheels? Explain your reasoning.

3.33 Step-down and reciprocal methods; choosing methods; cost pools; uncertainties   **LO3**

Your brother is a physician and has decided to start a home healthcare agency. The state government will reimburse treatment costs for about half of the patients under a new state-sponsored health insurance program for low-income residents. Your brother has asked you to explain the cost report that the state government requires. He tells you that he can use either the step-down or the reciprocal allocation method. He has several choices in allocation bases, but has little choice in the type of cost pools that are allowed.

Required

(a) Explain to your brother the differences in the two allocation methods. Remember that your brother is not familiar with accounting, so use language he will understand.
(b) Your brother wants to know how to choose the best allocation method and bases for his business. List some of the factors your brother should consider as he makes these decisions.
(c) One of the cost pools allowed by the state is a pool for transportation-related costs. Your brother asked colleagues at other home healthcare agencies to list the costs they include in this pool. Each organisation has some costs that are identical, such as depreciation on vehicles, gas and repairs. However, other costs in the pool are different; some agencies include facilities-related costs and others do not. Why would cost pools for the same activity include different types of cost?

3.34 Cost pools and allocation bases   **LO3**

You are an accountant for the Department of Defence. The government is considering a change of rules for the allocation of research and development costs. The government is asking contractors to submit a list of potential cost pools and allocation bases for activities within research and development. The government wants contractors to separate their research and development activities into several smaller cost pools with separate allocation bases.

Your research department performs a variety of different duties, including developing new designs for products, developing and testing new materials for use in these products, designing the manufacturing processes for new products, and redesigning old products and their manufacturing processes. In addition, the research and development department creates commercial uses for new technology that has been developed under government contracts.

Required

(a) List at least four potential research and development activities that could be used as the basis for separate cost pools within the research and development department.
(b) List two or more potential cost allocation bases for each cost pool listed in part (a).
(c) List factors that you might consider in making a choice about the cost pools and the allocation bases.

3.35 Step-down method; choosing allocation order and bases   **LO6**

Space Products manufactures commercial and military satellites. Under its government contracts, the company is permitted to allocate administrative and other costs to its military division. These costs are then reimbursed by the government department. Government guidelines allow administrative costs to be allocated using either the direct costs incurred in the operating divisions or the number of employees as an allocation base. Management information systems (MIS) costs can be allocated either on the basis of direct costs incurred in the operating divisions or on the basis of CPUs (a measure of computer resources used). Data concerning the company's operations appear here.

	Support departments		Operating departments	
	Administrative	**MIS**	**Commercial**	**Military**
Direct costs	$600 000	$200 000	$2 000 000	$4 000 000
Employees	20	10	40	50
CPUs (millions)	20	50	30	70

The MIS department is responsible for computer equipment and systems, and it maintains databases for the entire organisation.

Required

(a) Suppose Space Products uses the step-down method for allocating support department costs. Administrative costs are allocated first on the basis of the number of employees, and then MIS costs are allocated on the basis of CPUs. How much support department cost will be allocated to the military division?

(b) Space Products produced 100 military satellites in the period considered in this problem. Assuming the company uses the allocations calculated in part (a), what is the average cost per military satellite?

(c) Is the average cost that you calculated in part (b) most likely an underestimate, an overestimate or an unbiased estimate of the incremental cost of producing one more military satellite? Explain.

(d) Suppose Space Products uses the direct method of allocating support department costs. What is the maximum amount of support department cost that can be allocated to the military division under the government rules?

(e) Suppose the management of Space Products always calculates its support department cost allocations to maximise the amount of contribution received from the government. Management selects this policy because it allows the company to be more competitive in its commercial markets.

   (i) Discuss possible reasons why the government does not specify a single, unambiguous support cost allocation method.

   (ii) From a taxpayer's point of view, discuss whether you would agree with Space Products' policy.

   (iii) From a competitor's point of view, discuss whether you would agree with Space Products' policy.

3.36 Direct, step-down and reciprocal methods using dual rates and three departments   **LO4, 6**

In comprehensive example 6 (Middletown Children's Clinic), we did not perform direct or step-down methods for the dual-rate costs. Following are the allocation bases for these costs. The support cost data are provided in comprehensive example 6.

	Administration	Accounting	Housekeeping	Medical	Dental	Total
Number of employees	1	1	2	5	3	12
Square metres	600	300	100	8000	1000	10 000
Time spent accounting	15%		10%	50%	25%	100%
Time spent cleaning	10%	5%		55%	30%	100%

Required

(a) Draw a diagram of the direct method for the Middletown Children's Clinic allocations using three support departments.

(b) Allocate the support department costs using dual rates and the direct method.

(c) Draw a diagram of the step-down method using the three support departments.

(d) Allocate the support department costs using dual rates and the step-down method.

(e) Write out the simultaneous equations for the reciprocal allocation.

(f) Set up a spreadsheet that uses Excel Solver to solve the simultaneous equations and then allocates support costs using dual rates and the reciprocal method. Check to see that your solution matches the solution in the text.

3.37 Total cost under alternative allocation bases; special order price   **LO5**

Danish Hospital recently installed an RAP scanner, which is a diagnostic tool used both in suspected cancer cases and for detecting certain birth defects while the foetus is still in the womb. The scanner is leased for $5000 per month, and a full-time operator is paid $3000 per month. Data concerning use of the scanner for a typical month follow.

	Cancer detection	Birth defect detection
Revenue per scan	$600	$400
Direct costs per scan	$100	$50
Minutes required per scan	30	10
Number of scans performed	20	40

The direct costs consist primarily of supplies that are consumed in the scanning process. Currently, less than 20 per cent of the machine's capacity is used.

Required

The following questions will help you analyse the information for this problem.

(a) If the lease cost and the operator salary are allocated on the basis of minutes on the scanner, what is the total cost of a cancer scan?

(b) Suppose the cancer scans are experimental. Rather than charging $600 per scan, the hospital costs are reimbursed under a national contract. The contract will reimburse direct costs as well as an allocated share of the lease cost and operator's salary. As an allocation base, the contract allows either the number of scans or total minutes on the machine. What is the maximum reimbursable cost per cancer scan?

(c) The hospital is bidding on a state contract to supply birth defect scans to low-income pregnant women. The hospital would provide up to 14 scans a month for a fixed fee per scan. Assuming the hospital does not want to lose money on this contract, what is the minimum acceptable fee? Explain how you decided which costs are relevant.

(d) Identify uncertainties about which costs should be included in bidding for the contract described in part (c).

(e) Discuss the pros and cons of using total allocated costs, including administrative overhead, in bidding for the contract described in part (c).

(f) Suppose the hospital is bidding on the contract described in part (c). You have been asked to prepare a report of the hospital's expected costs for the contract. Write a memo to the chief accountant recommending the costs you think should be included in the expected costs. Attach to the memo a schedule showing your computations. As appropriate, refer to the schedule in the memo.

3.38 Step-down method; multiple versus single pool allocations; manager incentives   **LO6**

The Gleason Company, a division of a large international company, has prepared estimated costs for next year that can be traced to each department as follows.

Building and grounds	$ 41 010
Factory administration	78 270
Cafeteria — operating loss	4 920
Machining	104 100
Assembly	146 700
Total	$375 000

Management would like to know the estimated total allocated product cost per unit. These costs will be used as a benchmark for future period operations. The following information is available and can be used as possible allocation bases. The difference between direct labour hours and total labour hours represents hours of supervisory labour or labour hours that are used indirectly for manufacturing. The cost of these hours in machining and assembly is part of manufacturing overhead.

Department	Direct labour hours	Number of employees	Square metres	Total labour hours	Number of purchase orders
Factory administration		2	500		500
Cafeteria	1 000	2	1 000	1 000	4 000
Machining	3 000	4	500	8 000	2 000
Assembly	6 000	5	5 000	10 000	1 000
Total	10 000	13	7 000	19 000	7 500

Required

(a) Allocate the building and grounds costs to all other departments using square metres. Add the allocated costs to direct costs to arrive at the total costs assigned to each department.

(b) Explain whether each remaining department is a support or operating department.

(c) Select a reasonable allocation base for the costs of each support department. Justify your choices.

(d) Compute allocated overhead costs for each operating department. Given the allocation bases you selected in part (b), allocate support department costs to each operating department using the step-down method. Then calculate an overhead rate per direct labour hour for each operating department.

(e) Calculate overhead rates for the operating departments assuming that Gleason uses an average plant-wide factory overhead allocation rate based on direct labour hours. That is, aggregate the support department overhead costs into one cost pool, and use direct labour hours as the allocation base to determine the overhead rate per direct labour hour.

(f) What causes the difference between the rates you calculated in parts (d) and (e)?

(g) Assume that factory administration costs are allocated based on total labour hours, and that the total allocated cost is used to charge other departments for administrative services. List one advantage and one disadvantage of this charge system.

(h) Suppose that you are the manager of the machining department at Gleason. You can outsource some of your department's work. Outsourcing would reduce direct labour hours, and therefore reduce the amount of overhead allocated to your department. What factors should you consider in deciding whether to outsource?

(i) Now suppose that you are the director of finance for Gleason. The manager of the machining department has decided to outsource some tasks. When you analyse the current period results, you notice that while direct labour costs decreased in machining, outsourcing costs are slightly higher this period than the prior period's direct labour costs. When you ask the manager about these costs, he replies that the outsourcing does cost more than using direct labour but, because the amount of overhead for the department decreases, it is more profitable. What happened to the overhead that is no longer allocated to machining? Is the manager's decision beneficial to Gleason Company as a whole? Explain.

3.39 Cost allocation; behavioural issues LO7

In recent years, slow response times and frequent repairs have plagued Jetson Engineering's computer system. The cause was a substantial increase in computer-aided design work that pushed the system beyond its intended capacity. Bob Wilson, the production manager, decided that a new computer should be acquired to absorb some of the additional work. Surprisingly, six months after installing the new computer, he noticed that many of the engineers continued to use the old computer system, even though the new system had excess capacity and several features that simplified programming.

Bob discussed the situation with the supervisors of the entity's six design teams. They explained that the finance director's office allocates the cost of each computer to their work, based on the number of hours they use the computer. One responded, 'Look, the old computer didn't cost much and it's highly utilised — even the accounting department uses that machine. When the cost per hour of use is calculated, it's very low. The new machine, on the other hand, cost a lot of money, and in the first couple of months we didn't use it much because it takes time to learn a new system. I was shocked when I saw how high my charges were for using the new machine. Because the cost is high and use is low, the cost per hour charged to my work was incredible. I'll tell you something: next month we'll probably use the new computer even less. Our job performance doesn't look very good when our jobs cost a fortune to complete because of huge allocations of computer cost.'

'What a mess,' Bob sighed. 'Even though the new computer is bought and paid for and has plenty of capacity, the engineers aren't using it. Don't they realise that most of the computer costs are fixed costs? Using the new computer for 200 hours a month doesn't really cost the company much more than using it for 20 hours a month.'

Required

Recommend a change in the allocation system at Jetson that will change the behaviour of the design teams.

3.40 Comprehensive problem; dual versus single rates; purpose of allocation　　　　　**LO6**

Vines Company is a manufacturer of women's and men's swimsuits. The company uses a dual-rate system to allocate support costs. Last year's support departments' fixed and variable costs are as follows.

	Accounting	Human resources	Maintenance	Total
Variable costs	$18 420	$ 22 104	$ 60 360	$100 884
Fixed costs	55 260	100 696	60 360	216 316
Total cost	$73 680	$122 800	$120 720	$317 200

Allocation base amounts for all of the departments are:

	Accounting	Human resources	Maintenance	Women's	Men's	Total
Employees	2	2	4	10	6	24
Time spent for accounting	15%	10%	20%	30%	25%	100%
Time spent cleaning	5%	10%	15%	30%	40%	100%
Square metres	800	1000	1200	5000	5000	13000
Direct costs	$73 680	$122 800	$120 720	$800 000	$500 000	$1 617 200

Required

(a) Use the following allocation bases for fixed support costs: direct costs for accounting, number of employees for human resources, and square metres for maintenance.
　(i) Allocate fixed support costs using the direct method.
　(ii) Allocate fixed support costs using the step-down method.
　(iii) Allocate fixed support costs using the reciprocal method.

(b) Use the following allocation bases for variable support costs: time spent for accounting, number of employees for human resources, and time spent for maintenance.
　(i) Allocate variable support costs using the direct method.
　(ii) Allocate variable support costs using the step-down method.
　(iii) Allocate variable support costs using the reciprocal method.

(c) Suppose support costs were not broken down into fixed and variable cost pools. What allocation base would you use to allocate the costs for each support department? Explain.

(d) Describe several possible reasons why the managers of Vines Company allocate support costs to operating departments.

(e) Discuss whether a dual-rate support cost allocation system is likely to be better for Vines Company than a single-rate system.

3.41 Costing, service sector　　　　　**LO5**

Hawk and Eagle Co., a law firm, had the following costs last year:

Direct professional labour	$15 000 000
Overhead	21 000 000
Total costs	$36 000 000

The following costs were included in overhead:

Fringe benefits for direct professional labour	$5 000 000
Paralegal costs	2 700 000
Telephone call time with clients (estimated but not tabulated)	600 000
Computer time	1 800 000
Photocopying	900 000
Total overhead	$11 000 000

The firm recently improved its ability to document and trace costs to individual cases. Revised bookkeeping procedures now allow the firm to trace fringe benefit costs for direct professional labour, paralegal costs, telephone charges, computer time and photocopying costs to each case individually. The managing partner needs to decide whether additional costs other than direct professional labour should be traced directly to jobs to allow the firm to better justify billings to clients.

During the last year, more costs were traced to client engagements. Two of the case records showed the following.

	Client cases	
	875	876
Direct professional labour	$20 000	$20 000
Fringe benefits for direct labour	3 000	3 000
Secretarial costs	2 000	6 000
Telephone call time with clients	1 000	2 000
Computer time	2 000	4 000
Photocopying	1 000	2 000
Total costs	$29 000	$37 000

Three methods are being considered for allocating overhead this year:
- Method 1: Allocate overhead based on direct professional labour cost. Calculate the allocation rate using last year's direct professional labour costs of $15 million and overhead costs of $21 million.
- Method 2: Allocate overhead based on direct professional labour cost. Calculate the allocation rate using last year's direct professional labour costs of $15 million and overhead costs of $10 million ($21 million less $11 million in direct costs that are traced this year).
- Method 3: Allocate the $10 million overhead based on total direct costs. Calculate the allocation rate using last year's direct costs (professional labour of $15 million plus other direct costs of $11 million).

Required
(a) Calculate the overhead allocation rate for method 1.
(b) Calculate the overhead allocation rate for method 2.
(c) Calculate the overhead allocation rate for method 3.
(d) Using each of the three rates computed in parts (a), (b) and (c), calculate the total costs of cases 875 and 876.
(e) Explain why the total costs allocated to cases 875 and 876 are not the same under the three methods.
(f) Explain why method 1 would be inappropriate.
(g) Would method 2 or method 3 be better? Explain.
(h) Outline another way to reconfigure the costing system for Hawke and Eagle Co. Discuss your proposed changes.
(i) Explain how job costing in a service business is different from job costing in a manufacturing business.

3.42 Costing, service sector   **LO5**
Refer to question 3.41 above.
Required
(a) Draw a diagram of the costing system currently used by Hawk and Eagle Co.
(b) Draw a diagram to show the proposed changes to the costing system under each of the three methods outlined.
(c) Briefly comment on how the costing system has changed in the systems identified in (b) above.

3.43 Allocating variable and fixed overhead in the service sector

Prime Personal Trainers is a personal training service in Bankstown for people who want to work out at home. Prime offers two different types of services: Set-up and Continuous Improvement. Set-up services consist of several home visits by a personal trainer who specialises in determining the proper equipment for each client and helping the client set up a home gym. Continuous Improvement services provide daily, weekly or biweekly home visits by trainers.

Prime's accountant wants to create a costing system for Set-up services. She decides to use direct labour cost as the allocation base for variable overhead costs, and direct labour hours for fixed overhead cost. To estimate normal capacity, she calculates the average direct labour cost over the last several years. She estimates overhead by updating last year's overhead cost with expected increases in rent, supervisors' salaries and so on. Following are her estimates for the current period.

Direct labour hours (based on 250 normal hours per month)	3 000
Direct labour cost	$ 75 000
Indirect labour cost	25 000
Variable overhead (primarily fringe benefits)	150 000
Fixed overhead (office related costs)	120 000

Inventories consist of exercise equipment and supplies that are used by Prime for new clients. The following information summarises operations during the month of October. A number of new jobs were begun in October, but only two jobs were completed: job 20 and job 22.

Account balances on 1 October:

Equipment and supplies (raw materials)	$5000
Client contracts in process (job 20)	3500
Client contracts in process (job 22)	1500

Purchases of equipment and supplies:

Equipment	$54 000
Supplies	500
Total	$54 500

Equipment and supplies requisitioned for clients:

Job 20	$ 1 000
Job 21	500
Job 22	4 000
Job 23	5 000
Other jobs	40 000
Indirect supplies	500
Total	$51 000

Direct labour hours and cost:

	Hours	Cost
Job 20	10	$ 250
Job 21	18	450
Job 22	15	375
Job 23	6	150
Other clients	180	4500
Total	229	$5725

Labour costs:

Direct labour wages	$ 5 725
Indirect labour wages (160 hours)	1 920
Manager's salary	6 250
Total	$13 895

Office costs:

Rent	$1 000
Utilities	100
Insurance and taxes	900
Miscellaneous	1 000
Total	$3 000

Required

(a) What are the estimated allocation rates for fixed and variable overhead for the current period?

(b) What is the total overhead cost allocated to job 20 in October?

(c) What is the total cost of job 20?

(d) Calculate the amounts of fixed and variable overhead allocated to jobs in October.

(e) Why would the accountant choose to use two cost pools instead of one? Will this method make a difference in client bills when the job includes more equipment and less labour than other jobs?

ACKNOWLEDGEMENTS

Photo 3A: © Shutterstock.com

Photo 3B: © PongMoji / Shutterstock.com

Photo 3C: © Dmitriy Shironosov / iStockphoto

Text 3.35: © John Wiley and Sons Inc

CHAPTER 4

Cost–volume–profit (CVP) analysis

LEARNING OBJECTIVES

After studying this chapter, you should be able to:

4.1 demonstrate an understanding of cost–volume–profit (CVP) analysis and its use in decision making

4.2 define and describe the breakeven point

4.3 apply CVP calculations for a single product

4.4 apply CVP calculations for multiple products

4.5 list the assumptions and limitations that managers should consider when using CVP analysis

4.6 demonstrate an understanding of the use of margin of safety and operating leverage to assess operational risk.

IN BRIEF

Managers need to estimate future revenues, costs and profits to help them plan and monitor operations. They use cost–volume–profit (CVP) analysis to identify the levels of operating activity needed to avoid losses, achieve targeted profits, plan future operations and monitor organisational performance. Managers also need to analyse operational risk as they choose an appropriate cost structure.

4.1 Cost–volume–profit (CVP) analysis

LEARNING OBJECTIVE 4.1 Demonstrate an understanding of cost–volume–profit (CVP) analysis and its use in decision making.

Cost–volume–profit (CVP) analysis is a technique that examines changes in profits in response to changes in sales volumes, costs and prices. Accountants often perform CVP analysis periodically to help plan future levels of operating activity and provide information about:

- which products or services might be best to emphasise
- the volume of sales needed to achieve a targeted level of profit
- the amount of revenue required to avoid losses
- whether to increase fixed costs
- how much to budget for discretionary expenditures
- whether fixed costs expose the organisation to an unacceptable level of risk.

Profit equation and contribution margin

CVP analysis begins with the basic profit equation.

$$\text{Profit} = \text{Total revenue} - \text{Total costs}$$

Separating costs into variable and fixed categories (recall our discussion of fixed and variable costs in chapter 2), we can express profit as:

$$\text{Profit} = \text{Total revenue} - (\text{Total variable costs} + \text{Total fixed costs})$$

or

$$\text{Profit} = (\text{Total revenue} - \text{Total variable costs}) - \text{Total fixed costs}$$

The **contribution margin** is total revenue minus total variable costs. Similarly, the **contribution margin per unit** is the selling price per unit minus the variable cost per unit. Both contribution margin and contribution margin per unit are valuable tools when considering the effects of volume on profit. Contribution margin per unit tells us how much revenue from each unit sold can be applied towards fixed costs. Once enough units have been sold to cover all fixed costs, then the contribution margin per unit from all remaining sales becomes profit.

If we assume that the selling price and variable cost per unit are constant, then total revenue is equal to price times quantity, and total variable cost is variable cost per unit times quantity. We then rewrite the profit equation in terms of the contribution margin per unit.

$$\text{Profit} = [(P - V) \times Q] - F$$

where P = Selling price per unit
V = Variable cost per unit
$(P - V)$ = Contribution margin per unit
Q = Quantity of product sold (units of goods or services)
F = Total fixed costs

4.2 Breakeven point

LEARNING OBJECTIVE 4.2 Define and describe the breakeven point.

Managers often want to know the level of activity required to break even (the point at which total revenue is equal to total costs) as it shows the lower limit of profit when setting prices and determining margins. A CVP analysis can be used to determine the **breakeven point**, or level of operating activity at which revenues cover all fixed and variable costs, resulting in zero profit. We can calculate the breakeven point for any CVP formula by setting profit to zero. Depending on how the formula is set up, we calculate the breakeven point in either number of units or in total revenues.

To determine the breakeven point in number of units, we restate the profit equation as:

$$\text{Fixed costs} \div \text{Contribution margin per unit} = \text{Units to break even}$$

To calculate the breakeven point in sales dollars, we can first calculate the contribution margin ratio. The **contribution margin ratio (CMR)** is the percentage by which the selling price (or revenue) per unit exceeds the variable cost per unit; alternatively, it is the contribution margin as a percentage of revenue.

$$\text{Contribution margin per unit} \div \text{Sales price per unit} = \text{Contribution margin ratio}$$

The CVP equation is adapted to calculate the breakeven point in total revenue by dividing the fixed costs by the contribution margin ratio as follows:

$$\text{Fixed costs} \div \text{Contribution margin ratio} = \text{Total revenue to break even}$$

4.3 CVP analysis for a single product

LEARNING OBJECTIVE 4.3 Apply CVP calculations for a single product.

To illustrate CVP analysis for a single product, let us look at an entity, Mount Dandenong Bikes. Due to the increasing popularity of cross-country cycling, the management of Mount Dandenong Bikes wants to produce a new mountain bike. After discussions with the sales and production teams, management has forecast the following information.

Price per bike	=	$800
Variable cost per bike	=	$300
Fixed costs related to bike production	=	$5 500 000
Targeted pre-tax profit	=	$300 000
Targeted post-tax profit	=	$210 000
Tax rate	=	30%

Calculating breakeven in units and total revenue

The managers of Mount Dandenong Bikes would be interested in using the breakeven data to assess the riskiness of the venture; that is, to calculate (based on sales forecasts) how profitable the bike will be for the entity. The risk can be assessed by comparing the sales forecast to the breakeven sales. Breakeven quantity in units for the mountain bike is calculated as:

$$\text{Breakeven quantity} = \$5\,500\,000 \div \left(\$800 - \$300\right) = 11\,000 \text{ bikes}$$

The breakeven point shows the managers of Mount Dandenong Bikes that the entity needs to sell 11 000 bikes to recover both the fixed and variable costs. For every bike sold, a $500 contribution margin ($800 sales price less $300 variable cost per unit) is generated to contribute towards fixed costs only, as profit is considered to be zero in this scenario. Therefore, the 11 000 bikes will generate a total contribution margin of $5 500 000 (11 000 bikes times $500) which covers the fixed costs. For Mount Dandenong Bikes to generate a profit, sales would need to exceed 11 000 bikes.

The breakeven point can also be calculated to give the total revenue required to cover both fixed and variable costs. To calculate breakeven revenues needed for the mountain bike, we must first calculate the contribution margin ratio (CMR) as follows:

$$\text{CMR} = \left(\$800 - \$300\right) \div \$800 = 0.625$$

A contribution margin ratio of 0.625 means that 62.5 per cent of the revenue from each bike sold contributes first to fixed costs and then to profit after fixed costs are covered. Conversely, 37.5 cents per sales dollar contributes towards variable costs. Dividing the fixed costs by the contribution margin ratio enables the determination of breakeven sales revenue. It can be seen that revenue of $8 800 000 is required to break even:

$$\text{Sales revenue to break even} = \$5\,500\,000 \div 0.625 = \$8\,800\,000$$

Proof:		
	Revenue (11 000 bikes × $800)	$8 800 000
	Variable costs (11 000 bikes × $300)	3 300 000
	Contribution margin	5 500 000
	Fixed costs	5 500 000
	Profit	$ 0

Achieving a targeted pre-tax profit

Although knowledge of the breakeven point is important to measure risk, an entity would want to earn a profit to enable funds to be available for working capital and investment. In the case of Mount Dandenong Bikes, the managers want to earn $300 000 pre-tax profit. In order to achieve this goal, Mount Dandenong Bikes would need to sell more than 11 000 bikes. Any bike sold in excess of the breakeven quantity will generate a $500 contribution margin per bike that goes straight to profit because fixed costs have already been covered at breakeven sales. We determine the quantity of mountain bikes needed to be sold to achieve the targeted profit by incorporating the $300 000 targeted profit into the CVP formula as follows:

$$\text{Quantity} = (\$5\,500\,000 + \$300\,000) \div (\$800 - \$300) = 11\,600 \text{ bikes}$$

Therefore, in order to generate the $300 000 pre-tax profit, Mount Dandenong Bikes will need to sell 11 600 bikes. This is 600 bikes above breakeven sales. Each bike will generate an additional $500 contribution margin, totalling $300 000 (600 bikes × $500).

The contribution margin ratio of 62.5 per cent can also be used to determine the sales revenue of the bikes needed for the targeted profit by using the contribution margin ratio as follows:

$$\text{Sales revenue} = (\$5\,500\,000 + \$300\,000) \div 0.625 = \$9\,280\,000$$

Mount Dandenong Bikes must increase sales by $480 000 (600 bikes times $800) beyond breakeven sales of $8 800 000 to generate the $300 000 pre-tax profit.

Proof:	Revenue (11 600 bikes × $800)	$9 280 000
	Variable costs (11 600 bikes × $300)	3 480 000
	Contribution margin	5 800 000
	Fixed costs	5 500 000
	Pre-tax profit	$ 300 000

With this information the managers of Mount Dandenong Bikes would now go back to their sales team to determine whether this level of sales is achievable. The managers are pleased when the sales team reports back that they have forecasted sales of 12 000 units.

Looking at after-tax profit

Sometimes, profit may be shown as an after-tax amount. In order to undertake the CVP analysis, it is necessary to convert the after-tax amount to a pre-tax amount. If we want to know the amount of pre-tax profit needed to achieve a targeted level of after-tax profit, we solve the following formula for pre-tax profit:

$$\text{Pre-tax profit} = \frac{\text{After-tax profit}}{(1 - \text{Tax rate})}$$

Going back to our example, Mount Dandenong Bikes plans for an after-tax profit of $210 000 and its tax rate is 30 per cent, so

$$\text{Pre-tax profit} = \$210\,000 \div (1 - 0.30) = \$300\,000$$

The entity needs a pre-tax profit of $300 000 to earn an after-tax profit of $210 000.

Cost–volume–profit (CVP) graph

A **cost–volume–profit graph** (or **CVP graph**) shows the relationship between total revenues and total costs; it illustrates how an organisation's profits are expected to change under different volumes of activity. Figure 4.1 presents a CVP graph for the new mountain bike.

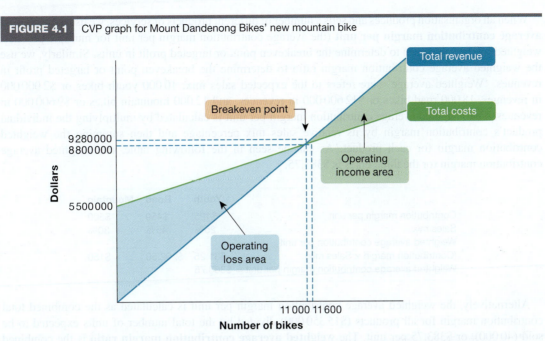

FIGURE 4.1 CVP graph for Mount Dandenong Bikes' new mountain bike

Notice that when no bikes are sold, fixed costs are $5 500 000, resulting in a loss of $5 500 000. As sales volume increases, the loss decreases by the contribution margin for each bike sold. The cost and revenue lines intersect at the breakeven point of 11 000, which means zero loss and zero profit. At this point total revenue and costs equal $8 800 000. Then, as sales increase beyond this breakeven point, we see an increase in profit, growing by the $500 contribution margin pre-tax and $350 contribution margin post-tax for each bike sold. Post-tax profits achieve the targeted level of $210 000 when sales volume reaches 11 600 (600 bikes above breakeven sales times $350 after-tax contribution margin per bike).

4.4 CVP analysis for multiple products

LEARNING OBJECTIVE 4.4 Apply CVP calculations for multiple products.

Many organisations sell a combination of different products or services. The sales mix is the proportion of different products or services that an organisation sells. To use CVP in the case of multiple products or services, we assume a constant sales mix in addition to the other CVP assumptions that are discussed in section 4.5.

Let us resume our example of Mount Dandenong Bikes. In order to broaden its customer base, Mount Dandenong's design team has developed two more new products (a youth bike and a road bike). The increased production will increase the total fixed costs for the entity to $14 700 000. Forecasted sales volumes for each bike are as follows. The sales mix in percentages is calculated from these volumes.

	Youth	Road	Mountain	Total
Forecasted volume (units)	10 000	18 000	12 000	40 000
Expected sales mix (proportion)	25%	45%	30%	100%

Because of increased competition and an economic downturn, the managers of Mount Dandenong Bikes are uncertain about the entity's ability to achieve the forecasted level of sales. They would like to know the minimum amount of sales needed for an after-tax profit of $100 000. The entity's income tax rate is 30 per cent. The expected unit selling prices, variable costs and contribution margins for each product are as follows:

	Youth	Road	Mountain
Price per unit	$200	$700	$800
Variable cost per unit	75	250	300
Contribution margin per unit	$125	$450	$500

When an organisation produces and sells a number of different products or services, we use the **weighted average contribution margin per unit** (the average contribution margin per unit for multiple products weighted by the sales mix) to determine the breakeven point or targeted profit in units. Similarly, we use the weighted average contribution margin ratio to determine the breakeven point or targeted profit in revenues. 'Weighted average' here refers to the expected sales mix: 10 000 youth bikes or $2 000 000 in revenues, 18 000 road bikes or $12 600 000 in revenues, and 12 000 mountain bikes or $9 600 000 in revenues. The weighted average contribution margin per unit is calculated by multiplying the individual product's contribution margin by its relative sales mix percentage and then summing the weighted contribution margin for each product. As can be seen in the following table, the weighted average contribution margin for the three bikes is $383.75.

	Youth	Road	Mountain
Contribution margin per unit	$125	$450	$500
Sales mix	25%	45%	30%
Weighted average contribution per unit (Contribution margin × Sales mix)	$31.25	$202.50	$150
Weighted average contribution margin per unit = $383.75			

Alternatively, the weighted average contribution margin per unit is calculated as the combined total contribution margin for all products ($15 350 000) divided by the total number of units expected to be sold (40 000), or $383.75 per unit. The **weighted average contribution margin ratio** is the combined contribution margin ($15 350 000) divided by combined revenue ($24 200 000), or 63.43 per cent; alternatively, it can be calculated by dividing the contribution margin per unit by the weighted average selling price:

$$\text{Weighted average contribution margin ratio} = \frac{\$383.75}{(\$200 \times 0.25) + (\$700 \times 0.45) + (\$800 \times 0.30)}$$
$$= 63.43\%$$

To achieve a targeted after-tax profit of $100 000, the entity must earn a pre-tax profit of $142 857 [$100 000 ÷ (1 − 0.30)]. To compute the total number of units (bikes) that must be sold to achieve the targeted profit, we divide the fixed costs plus the targeted profit by the weighted average contribution margin per unit:

$$\text{Units needed for target profit} = Q = \frac{F + \text{Profit}}{(P - V)} = \frac{\$14\,700\,000 + \$142\,857}{\$383.75 \text{ per unit}} = 38\,678 \text{ units}$$

Therefore, Mount Dandenong Bikes needs to sell 38 678 units to achieve a targeted after-tax profit of $100 000. To determine the number of units for each product that must be sold, we multiply the total number of units (38 678) by each product's expected sales mix. For example, the entity must sell 38 678 units × 25 per cent, or 9670, youth bikes.

To calculate the amount of revenue needed to achieve the targeted after-tax profit of $100 000, we divide the fixed costs plus the targeted pre-tax profit by the weighted average contribution margin ratio:

$$\text{Revenues} = \frac{F + \text{Profit}}{\text{CMR}} = \frac{\$14\,700\,000 + \$142\,857}{63.43\%} = \$23\,400\,373$$

To determine the revenues for each product that must be sold, we multiply the total revenues ($23 400 373) by each product's expected revenue mix. For example, the entity must achieve $23 400 373 × ($2 000 000 ÷ $24 200 000), or $1 933 914 in revenues from youth bikes. Notice that the required revenue for each product is equal to the required number of units times the expected selling price. For youth bikes, 9670 units × $200 per unit = $1 934 000.

The results of calculations using units and revenues are always identical. However, in some situations per-unit information is not available. In those cases, it is necessary to perform CVP calculations using revenues.

Spreadsheets are often used for CVP computations, particularly when an organisation has multiple products. Spreadsheets simplify the basic computations and can be designed to show how changes in volumes, selling prices, costs or sales mix alter the results. The CVP analysis for Mount Dandenong Bikes products using a spreadsheet is shown in appendix 4A of this chapter.

Discretionary expenditure decision

CVP analysis also helps managers make business decisions such as whether to increase or decrease discretionary expenditures. For example, suppose the managers of Mount Dandenong Bikes want to advertise one of their products more heavily. A distributor pointed out that the road bike price was less than a competitor's price for a model with fewer features. The competitor's brand name is quite well known, but the distributor thinks that she could sell at least 10 per cent more road bikes if Mount Dandenong launched a regional advertising campaign.

The managers of Mount Dandenong estimate that an additional expenditure of $100 000 in advertising will increase road bike sales by 5 per cent, to 18 900 bikes. First, fixed costs would increase by $100 000 to $14 800 000. Second, the expected volume of road bikes sold would increase to 18 900. After-tax profits are expected to increase by $213 500, from $455 000 to $668 500. The change in sales mix affects the weighted average contribution margin; it changes from 383.75 to $385.21.

This can also be calculated by subtracting the $100 000 investment in fixed costs from the additional contribution margin of $405 000 [900 bikes × ($700 − $250)]. The resulting incremental after-tax profit is $213 500 [($405 000 − $100 000)(1 − 0.30)]. Because profits are expected to increase more than costs for this advertising campaign, the managers would be likely to make the additional investment.

4.5 Assumptions and limitations of CVP analysis

LEARNING OBJECTIVE 4.5 List the assumptions and limitations that managers should consider when using CVP analysis.

CVP analysis relies on forecasts of expected revenues and costs. CVP assumptions rule out fluctuations in revenues or costs that might be caused by common business factors such as supplier volume discounts, learning curves, changes in production efficiency or special customer discounts. In addition, many uncertainties may arise about whether CVP assumptions will be violated, such as the following.
- Can volume of operating activity be achieved?
- Will selling prices increase or decrease?
- Will sales mix remain constant?
- Will fixed or variable costs change as operations move into a new relevant range?
- Will costs change due to unforeseen causes?
- Are revenue and cost estimates biased?

All entities are subject to uncertainties, leading to the risk that they will fail to meet expectations.

Even though each organisation is subject to unique business risks, all entities face uncertainties related to the economic environment. Some organisations are subject to more uncertainty than others. For example, uncertainties are greater in industries experiencing rapid technological and market change or intense competition.

4.6 Margin of safety and degree of operating leverage

LEARNING OBJECTIVE 4.6 Demonstrate an understanding of the use of margin of safety and operating leverage to assess operational risk.

In Mount Dandenong Bikes, the managers used CVP information to help learn how much the volume of business could decline before the entity would incur a loss. CVP analysis looking at the sales mix was useful in identifying the specific products to emphasise for increased profitability. Managers are often interested in these types of questions. In addition, information from CVP analysis can be used to help manage operational risk. **Operational risk** relates to the risk of loss resulting from inadequate or failed internal processes, people and systems, or external events.

Margin of safety

The **margin of safety** is the excess of an organisation's expected future sales (in either revenue or units) above the breakeven point. The margin of safety indicates the amount by which sales could drop before profits reach the breakeven point:

Margin of safety in units = Actual or estimated units of activity − Units at breakeven point

$$\text{Margin of safety in revenues} = \text{Actual or estimated revenue} - \text{Revenue at breakeven point}$$

The margin of safety is computed using actual or estimated sales values, depending on the purpose. To evaluate future risk when planning, use estimated sales. To evaluate actual risk when monitoring operations, use actual sales. If the margin of safety is small, managers may put more emphasis on reducing costs and increasing sales to avoid potential losses. A larger margin of safety gives managers more confidence in making plans such as incurring additional fixed costs.

The **margin of safety percentage** is the margin of safety divided by actual or estimated sales, in either units or revenues. This percentage indicates the extent to which sales can decline before profits become zero.

$$\text{Margin of safety percentage in units} = \frac{\text{Margin of safety in units}}{\text{Actual or estimated units}}$$

$$\text{Margin of safety percentage in revenues} = \frac{\text{Margin of safety in revenue}}{\text{Actual or estimated revenue}}$$

When the original budget was created for Mount Dandenong Bikes, the breakeven point was calculated as 11 000 bikes, or $8 800 000 in revenues. However, the managers expect 12 000 mountain bikes to be sold, generating $9 600 000 in revenue. Their margin of safety in units of mountain bikes is 1000 (12 000 − 11 000) and in revenues is $800 000 ($9 600 000 − $8 800 000). Their margin of safety percentage is 8.3 per cent (being 1000 ÷ 12 000, or $800 000 ÷ $9 600 000). In other words, sales volume could drop 8.3 per cent from expected levels before the entity expects to incur a loss.

Degree of operating leverage

Managers decide how to structure the cost function for their organisations. Often, potential trade-offs are made between fixed and variable costs. For example, an entity could purchase a vehicle (a fixed cost) or it could lease a vehicle under a contract that charges a rate per kilometre driven (a variable cost). One of the major disadvantages of fixed costs is that they may be difficult to reduce quickly if activity levels fail to meet expectations, thereby increasing the organisation's risk of incurring losses.

The **degree of operating leverage** is the extent to which the cost function is made up of fixed costs. Organisations with high operating leverage incur more risk of loss when sales decline. Conversely, when operating leverage is high, an increase in sales (once fixed costs are covered) contributes quickly to profit. The formula for operating leverage can be written in terms of either contribution margin or fixed costs, as shown here.

Degree of operating leverage in terms of contribution margin

$$= \frac{\text{Contribution margin}}{\text{Profit}}$$

$$= \frac{\text{Total revenue (TR)} - \text{Total variable costs (TVC)}}{\text{Profit}}$$

$$= \frac{(P - V) \times Q}{\text{Profit}}$$

$$\text{Degree of operating leverage in terms of fixed costs} = \frac{F}{\text{Profit}} + 1$$

Managers use the degree of operating leverage to gauge the risk associated with their cost function and to explicitly calculate the sensitivity of profits to changes in sales (units or revenues):

$$\% \text{ change in profit} = \% \text{ change in sales} \times \text{Degree of operating leverage}$$

For Mount Dandenong Bikes, the variable cost per mountain bike is $300 and the fixed costs are $5 500 000. With budgeted sales of 12 000, the managers expected to earn a pre-tax profit of $500 000 (1000 bikes × $500). The expected degree of operating leverage using the contribution margin formula is then calculated as follows.

$$\text{Degree of operating leverage} = \frac{(\$800 - \$300) \times 12\,000 \text{ bikes}}{\$500\,000} = \frac{\$6\,000\,000}{\$500\,000} = 12$$

We arrive at the same answer of 12 if we use the fixed cost formula:

$$\text{Degree of operating leverage} = \frac{\$5\,500\,000}{\$500\,000} + 1 = 11 + 1 = 12$$

The degree of operating leverage and margin of safety percentage are reciprocals.

$$\text{Margin of safety percentage} = \frac{1}{\text{Degree of operating leverage}}$$

$$\text{Degree of operating leverage} = \frac{1}{\text{Margin of safety percentage}}$$

If the margin of safety percentage is small, then the degree of operating leverage is large. In addition, the margin of safety percentage is smaller as the fixed cost portion of total cost gets larger. As the level of operating activity increases above the breakeven point, the margin of safety increases and the degree of operating leverage decreases. For Mount Dandenong Bikes, the reciprocal of the margin of safety percentage is 12 (1 ÷ 0.0833). The reciprocal of the degree of operating leverage is 0.0833 (1 ÷ 12).

Using the degree of operating leverage to plan and monitor operations

Managers need to consider the degree of operating leverage when they decide whether to incur additional fixed costs, such as building new plants, purchasing new equipment (through depreciation charges) or hiring new employees. They also need to consider the degree of operating leverage for potential new products and services that could increase an organisation's fixed costs relative to variable costs. If additional fixed costs cause the degree of operating leverage to reach what they consider an unacceptably high level, managers often use variable costs — such as temporary labour — rather than additional fixed costs to meet their operating needs.

For example, the managers of Mount Dandenong Bikes have been looking at restructuring their sales team — instead of employing them on a full-time basis, they would subcontract sales staff and pay a commission at $50 per bike sold. This would lead to a reduction in the payroll of $200 000 per annum. The new cost function would be

$$\text{TC} = \left(\$5\,500\,000 - \$200\,000\right) + \left(\$300 + \$50\right)Q = \$5\,300\,000 + \$350Q$$

Fixed costs would reduce by $200 000 to $5 300 000 due to the saving in salary costs, and the variable costs would increase by $50 to $350 due to the sales commission per bike. Due to the change in cost structure, the breakeven point increases considerably to 11 778 (rounded) mountain bikes [$5 300 000 ÷ ($800 − $350) per bike] or $9 422 400. Given planned sales of 12 000 mountain bikes, the pre-tax profit will be $99 900 (222 bikes × $450). Management would not be pleased with this outcome as the pre-tax profit falls from $500 000 to $99 900.

However, is this strategy more favourable at another level of sales? This can be determined by calculating the point of indifference. An **indifference point** is the level of activity at which equal cost or profit occurs across multiple alternatives. To provide the managers of Mount Dandenong Bikes with additional information as they consider changing the cost structure, the management accountant calculates the indifference point. Using the budgeted assumptions, the management accountant sets the two cost functions equal to each other and then solves for Q as follows:

$$\$5\,500\,000 + \$300Q = \$5\,300\,000 + \$350Q$$
$$\$200\,000 = \$50Q$$
$$Q = 4000$$

At the sales level of 4000, each strategy incurs the same level of expenditure of $6 700 000. When sales are fewer than 4000, Mount Dandenong Bikes' profit will be greater using more variable cost. When sales exceed 4000, the entity is better off using more fixed costs. As Mount Dandenong Bikes' breakeven point is considerably higher than this, the strategy to employ the sales personnel on a commission basis would not be in the entity's best interest.

To further reinforce the concepts discussed above, we will now look at comprehensive example 1, which involves the Small Animal Clinic.

CVP analysis

Lucy Brown, Small Animal Clinic manager, and the accountant, Josh Hardy, are completing the operating budget for next year. Lucy estimated that the clinic will experience 3800 animal visits, and Josh estimated the cost function as follows:

$$TC = \$119\,009 + \$16.40Q$$

We can see that estimated total fixed costs are $119 009, with variable costs increasing at the rate of $16.40 per animal visit. Lucy and Josh budgeted revenue per animal visit at $60 ($30 in fees plus $30 in matching grant), giving a contribution margin of $43.60 ($60 − $16.40). Thus, they estimated that the clinic should achieve a surplus of $46 671 [($60)(3800) − $119 009 − ($16.40)(3800)] or [($43.60 × 3800) − $119 009]. The clinic is a not-for-profit entity and pays no income taxes on its surplus.

To complete the planning process for next year, Lucy asks Josh to compute the clinic's breakeven point. As manager of a not-for-profit entity, she is particularly sensitive to financial risk and wants to know how much the clinic's activity levels could drop before a loss would occur.

Compared breakeven to budget

Josh performs the following calculations to compute the breakeven point. With revenue per visit of $60 and variable cost per visit of $16.40, the contribution margin per animal visit is $43.60. Josh solves for Q with profit equal to $0 to find the breakeven point in number of animal visits:

$$Q = \frac{F + \text{Profit}}{(P - V)} = \frac{(\$119\,009 + \$0)}{\$43.60} = 2730 \text{ visits}$$

The breakeven visits for the clinic is therefore 2730. Lucy is pleased to see that the budgeted number of animal visits (3800) is significantly higher than the breakeven number. This result gives her considerable assurance that the clinic is not likely to incur a loss, even if revenues fail to achieve targeted levels or if costs exceed estimated amounts.

Potential investment in new equipment

During the first two months of the year, Lucy learns that the number of animal visits at Small Animal Clinic is running approximately 10 per cent higher than the budget, and costs seem to be under control. Lucy thinks that the clinic might be on track for a high surplus this year.

For the past two years, Lucy has been interested in purchasing equipment costing $200 000 to provide low-cost neutering services. This year PAWS, a local charity, offered to pay for half of the equipment cost, but only after the clinic raises the other half of the funds. Currently the clinic has no excess cash because surpluses from prior years were invested in other projects. Thus, the clinic needs to raise $100 000 to receive the PAWS grant. Lucy asks Josh to calculate the number of animal visits needed to achieve a surplus of $100 000.

Calculating and analysing targeted activity level

Josh calculates the expected quantity needed to achieve $100 000 surplus as follows:

$$Q = \frac{F + \text{Profit}}{P - V} = \frac{\$119\,009 + \$100\,000}{\$60.00 - \$16.40} = \frac{\$219\,009}{\$43.60} = 5024 \text{ animal visits}$$

He then calculates the total dollar amount of revenue needed:

$$\text{Revenues} = \frac{F + \text{Profit}}{(P - V)/P} = \frac{\$119\,009 + \$100\,000}{\$43.60/\$60.00} = \$310\,389$$

Josh tells Lucy that the clinic will need to earn $301 389 in revenues or 5024 visits to achieve a surplus of $100 000. However, can the clinic achieve this level of visits?

The budgeted level of activity (3800 animal visits) is substantially higher than the level of activity needed to break even (2730 animal visits). If animal visits continue to exceed this year's budget by 10 per cent, Josh estimates that animal visits will reach 4180 (3800 × 1.10) by year-end. However, he thinks that it would be very difficult to achieve a targeted surplus of $100 000 (5024 animal visits).

CVP adjusted for change in relevant range

As Josh works on his report, he realises that the clinic's cost function might change if the number of animal visits gets very high. Lucy told him that if animal visits exceed 4000 this year, she will probably hire another technician and need to rent more space and purchase additional equipment. Therefore, Josh's cost function for 5024 visits is wrong. He develops a new cost function assuming that an additional technician, space and equipment will increase fixed costs by about $60 000 per year.

$$TC = (\$119\,009 + \$60\,000) + \$16.40Q = \$179\,009 + \$16.40Q, \text{ for } Q > 4000$$

Thus, Josh's earlier CVP analysis was incorrect when animal visits exceed 4000. The level of activity needed for a targeted surplus of $100 000 needs to be recalculated:

$$(\$179\,009 + \$100\,000) \div \$43.60 = 6400 \text{ for } Q > 4000$$

Josh notices that an activity level of 6400 animal visits is noticeably higher than the 5024 visits he first calculated. He realises how important it is to adjust for the relevant range when performing CVP analyses.

When Josh shows Lucy the new results, they agree that the clinic cannot raise the funds for new equipment by increasing the number of visits to 6400. Lucy may need to cut costs or seek other ways to pay for the neutering equipment. The additional fixed cost would also require the clinic to have a much higher volume of operations to avoid a loss.

Margin of safety

When the original budget was created for the clinic, the breakeven point was calculated as 2730 animal visits, or $163 800 in revenues. However, Lucy and Josh expected 3800 animal visits, for $228 000 in revenue. Their margin of safety in units of animal visits was 1070 (3800 − 2730) and in revenues was $64 200 ($228 000 − $163 800). Their margin of safety percentage was 28.2 per cent (1070 ÷ 3800, or $64 200 ÷ $228 000). In other words, their sales volume could drop 28.2 per cent from expected levels before they expected to incur a loss. Figure 4.2 provides a CVP graph for this information.

Operating leverage

The variable cost per animal visit was $16.40 and the fixed costs were $119 009. With budgeted animal visits of 3800, the managers expected to earn a profit of $46 671.

The expected degree of operating leverage using the contribution margin formula is then calculated as follows:

$$\text{Degree of operating leverage} = \frac{(\$60 - \$16.40) \times 3800 \text{ visits}}{\$46\,671} = \frac{\$165\,680}{\$46\,671} = 3.55$$

FIGURE 4.2 CVP graph and margin of safety for Small Animal Clinic

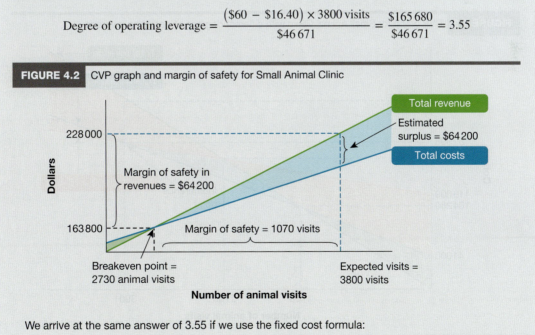

We arrive at the same answer of 3.55 if we use the fixed cost formula:

$$\text{Degree of operating leverage} = \frac{\$119\,009}{\$46\,671} + 1 = 2.55 + 1 = 3.55$$

The reciprocal of the margin of safety percentage is 3.55 (1 ÷ 0.282). The reciprocal of the degree of operating leverage is 0.282 (1 ÷ 3.55).

The technicians at the Small Animal Clinic are paid a salary and work 40-hour weeks. Suppose Lucy could hire part-time technicians at $20 per hour instead of hiring full-time technicians at the current total salaries of $78 009 (for 2 technicians). If each visit requires about an hour of technician time, the new cost function would be TC equals ($119 009 − $78 009) + ($16.40 + $20)Q = $41 000 + $36.40Q. The breakeven point decreases considerably to 1738 animal visits [$41 000 ÷ ($60 − $36.40) per animal visit] or $104 280. Profit at Q = 3800 animal visits is $48 680 [$228 000 − $41 000 − (3800 animal visits × $36.40 per animal visit)]. Operating leverage at 3800 animal visits becomes 1.84 [($41 000 ÷ $48 680) + 1], which is much lower than the 3.55 when technicians are a fixed cost. Although operating leverage improved, the cost for technicians increased from $18.75 per hour [$78 009 ÷ (2 technicians × 2080 hours per technician per year)] to $20 per hour.

The advantage of having technicians as hourly workers is that they can be scheduled only for hours when appointments are also scheduled. When business is slow fewer technician hours are needed, which means less risk of incurring losses if the number of visits drops. Figure 4.3 provides a CVP graph of the two options. Risk decreases considerably when the breakeven point is so much lower. On the other hand, it may be more difficult to hire qualified and dependable technicians unless work hours and pay can be guaranteed.

To provide Lucy with additional information as she considers changing the cost structure, Josh calculates the indifference point. Using the budgeted assumptions, Josh sets the two cost functions equal to each other and then solves for Q as follows:

$$\$41\,000 + \$36.40Q = \$119\,009 + \$16.40Q$$

$$\$20Q = \$78\,009, \text{ so } Q = 3901$$

When visits are fewer than 3901, the clinic profit will be greater using more variable costs. When visits exceed 3901, the clinic is better off using more fixed costs, assuming that the fixed costs remain constant up to 4000 visits. When visits exceed 4000, we know that additional fixed costs will be incurred, and then a new indifference point will need to be calculated.

Notice that the indifference point calculation ignores operational risk. At 3901 animal visits, the clinic is expected to earn the same profit under the two cost-function alternatives. However, the clinic's operational risk is greater for the cost function having higher fixed costs. Therefore, the clinic's manager would not necessarily be indifferent between the two cost functions if 3901 animal visits were expected.

FIGURE 4.3 CVP graph for Small Animal Clinic with different degrees of operating leverage

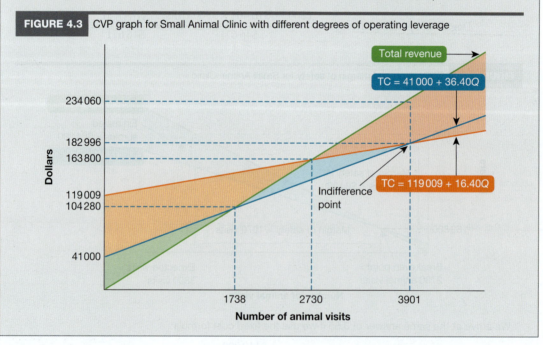

APPENDIX 4A
Performing CVP analysis with the use of a spreadsheet

Spreadsheets are often used for CVP computations, particularly when an organisation has multiple products. Spreadsheets simplify the basic computations and can be designed to show how changes in volumes, selling prices, costs or sales mix alter the results. If the manager wants to use CVP results to plan future operations for individual products, the required revenue for each product needs to be determined. Such computations are performed using the sales mix. The sales mix should be stated as a proportion of units when performing CVP computations in units, and it should be stated as a proportion of revenues when performing CVP computations in revenues. Sales mix computations can become cumbersome if performed manually; it is easiest to use a spreadsheet.

To demonstrate CVP computations using a spreadsheet, we will return to the Mount Dandenong Bikes example, discussed in section 4.4, involving the decision by managers to introduce two new bikes into the product range. We will look at this problem again by using a spreadsheet to assist in our calculations. Figure 4A.1 shows a sample CVP spreadsheet for Mount Dandenong Bikes. Note that all of the input data is placed in an area labelled 'Input section' in the spreadsheet. The calculations are performed outside of this area (formulas for this spreadsheet are shown in figure 4A.2). Spreadsheets designed this way allow users to alter the assumptions in the input section without performing any additional programming.

The spreadsheet in figure 4A.1 first uses the input data to compute expected revenues, costs and income. The revenues and variable costs for each product are computed by multiplying the expected sales volume times the selling price and variable cost per unit shown in the input area. The revenues and variable costs for the three products are then combined to determine total revenues and total variable costs for the entity. After subtracting expected fixed costs and income taxes (30 per cent of pre-tax income), the expected after-tax income is $455 000.

The spreadsheet in figure 4A.1 performs CVP computations using both units and revenues. To achieve a targeted after-tax profit of 100 000, the entity must earn a pre-tax profit of $142 857 [$100 000 ÷ (1 − 0.30)]. To compute the total number of units (bikes) that must be sold to achieve the targeted profit, we divide the fixed costs plus the targeted profit by the weighted average contribution margin per unit:

$$\text{Units needed for target profit} = Q = \frac{F + \text{Profit}}{(P - V)} = \frac{\$14\,700\,000 + \$142\,857}{\$383.75\,\text{per unit}} = 38\,678\,\text{units}$$

Mount Dandenong Bikes therefore needs to sell 38 678 units to achieve a targeted after-tax profit of $100 000. To determine the number of units for each product that must be sold, we multiply the total number of units (38 678) by each product's expected sales mix in units. For example, the entity must sell 38 678 units × (10 000 units ÷ 40 000 units), or 9670 youth bikes.

To calculate the amount of revenue needed to achieve the targeted after-tax profit of $100 000, we divide the fixed costs plus the targeted pre-tax profit by the weighted average contribution margin ratio:

$$\text{Revenues} = \frac{F + \text{Profit}}{\text{CMR}} = \frac{\$14\,700\,000 + \$142\,857}{63.43\%} = \$23\,400\,373$$

The difference between the spreadsheet and this manually calculated amount is due to rounding, as are any differences in the following amounts. To determine the revenues for each product that must be sold, we multiply the total revenues ($23 400 373) by each product's expected sales mix in revenues. For example, the entity must achieve $23 400 373 × ($2 000 000 ÷ $24 200 000), or $1 933 914, in revenues from youth bikes. Note that the required revenue for each product is equal to the required number of units times the expected selling price. For youth bikes, 9670 units × $200 per unit = $1 934 000.

The results of calculations using units and revenues are always identical. Because information in the example was given in units, it would have been easiest to create the spreadsheet using only the computations for CVP in units. However, in some situations per-unit information is not available. In those cases, it is necessary to perform CVP calculations using revenues.

One of the benefits of creating a spreadsheet with a separate input section is that additional CVP analyses can easily be performed by the changing input data. For example, suppose the managers of Mount Dandenong Bikes want to know how many bikes they must sell to break even. We can return to the spreadsheet in figure 4A.1 and change the 'Desired after-tax profit' to zero. The resulting spreadsheet, showing only CVP calculations in units, is presented in figure 4A.3.

	A	B	C	D	E
1					
2	**Input section**	Youth bikes	Road bikes	Mtn. bikes	
3	Expected sales volume-units	10,000	18,000	12,000	
4	Price per unit	$200	$700	$800	
5	Variable cost per unit	$75	$250	$300	
6					
7	Fixed costs	$14,700,000			
8	Desired after-tax profit	$100,000	(enter zero for breakeven)		
9	Income tax rate	30%			
10					
11					
12	**Contribution margin**	Youth bikes	Road bikes	Mtn. bikes	Total bikes
13	Units	10,000	18,000	12,000	40,000
14	Revenue	$2,000,000	$12,600,000	$9,600,000	$24,200,000
15	Variable costs	750,000	4,500,000	3,600,000	8,850,000
16	Contribution margin	$1,250,000	$8,100,000	$6,000,000	$15,350,000
17					
18	Contrib. margin per unit	$125.00	$450.00	$500.00	$383.75
19	Contrib. margin ratio	62.50%	64.29%	62.50%	63.43%
20					
21	Expected sales mix in units	25.00%	45.00%	30.00%	100.00%
22	Expected sales mix in revenues	8.26%	52.07%	39.67%	100.00%
23					
24	**Expected income**				
25	Contribution margin (above)				$15,350,000
26	Fixed costs				14,700,000
27	Pre-tax income				650,000
28	Income taxes				195,000
29	After-tax income				$455,000
30					
31	**Preliminary CVP calculations**				
32	Target pre-tax profit for CVP analysis				$142,857
33	Fixed costs plus target pre-tax profit				$14,842,857
34					
35	**CVP analysis in units**	Youth bikes	Road bikes	Mtn. bikes	Total bikes
36	CVP calculation in units	9,669.614	17,405.305	11,603.537	38,678
37	Revenue	$1,933,923	$12,183,713	$9,282,829	$23,400,465
38	Variable costs	725,221	4,351,326	3,481,061	8,557,608
39	Contribution margin	$1,208,702	$7,832,387	$5,801,768	14,842,857
40	Fixed costs				14,700,000
41	Pre-tax income				142,857
42	Income taxes				42,857
43	After-tax income				$100,000
44					
45	**CVP analysis in revenues**	Youth bikes	Road bikes	Mtn. bikes	Total bikes
46	CVP calculation in revenues	$1,933,923	$12,183,713	$9,282,829	$23,400,465
47	Variable costs	725,221	4,351,326	3,481,061	8,557,608
48	Contribution margin	$1,208,702	$7,832,387	$5,801,768	14,842,857
49	Fixed costs				14,700,000
50	Pre-tax income				142,857
51	Income taxes				42,857
52	After-tax income				$100,000

The managers of Mount Dandenong Bikes could use the CVP spreadsheet to perform several different types of sensitivity analyses. Suppose sales of the mountain bike are falling behind expectations. They could determine the effects of the change in sales mix on results. Every assumption in the data input box is easily changed to update information. Sensitivity analysis helps managers explore the potential impact of variations in data they consider to be particularly important or uncertain.

FIGURE 4A.2 Formulas for Mount Dandenong Bikes spreadsheet

	A	B	C	D	E
1					
2	**Input section**	Youth bikes	Road bikes	Mtn. bikes	
3	Expected sales volume-units	10,000	18,000	12,000	
4	Price per unit	200	700	800	
5	Variable cost per unit	75	250	300	
6					
7	Fixed costs	14,700,000			
8	Desired after-tax profit	100,000	(enter zero for breakeven)		
9	Income tax rate	0.3			
10					
11					
12	**Contribution margin**	Youth bikes	Road bikes	Mtn. bikes	Total bikes
13	Units	=B3	=C3	=D3	=SUM(B3:D3)
14	Revenue	=B3*B4	=C3*C4	=D3*D4	=SUM(B14:D14)
15	Variable costs	=B5*B3	=C5*C3	=D5*D3	=SUM(B15:D15)
16	Contribution margin	=B14-B15	=C14-C15	=D14-D15	=SUM(B16:D16)
17					
18	Contrib. margin per unit	=B16/B13	=C16/C13	=D16/D13	=E16/E13
19	Contrib. margin ratio	=B16/B14	=C16/C14	=D16/D14	=E16/E14
20					
21	Expected sales mix in units	=B3/$E13	=C3/$E13	=D3/$E13	=SUM(B21:D21)
22	Expected sales mix in revenues	=B14/$E14	=C14/$E14	=D14/$E14	=SUM(B22:D22)
23					
24	**Expected income**				
25	Contribution margin (above)				=E16
26	Fixed costs				=B7
27	Pre-tax income				=E16-E26
28	Income taxes				=B9*E27
29	After-tax income				=E27-E28
30					
31	**Preliminary CVP calculations**				
32	Target pre-tax profit for CVP analysis				=B8/(1-B9)
33	Fixed costs plus target pre-tax profit				=B7+E32
34					
35	**CVP analysis in units**	Youth bikes	Road bikes	Mtn. bikes	Total bikes
36	CVP calculation in units	=B21*$E$36	=C21*$E$36	=D21*$E$36	=E33/E18
37	Revenue	=B36*B4	=C36*C4	=D36*D4	=SUM(B37:D37)
38	Variable costs	=B36*B5	=C36*C5	=D36*D5	=SUM(B38:D38)
39	Contribution margin	=B37-B38	=C37-C38	=D37-D38	=E37-E38
40	Fixed costs				=B7
41	Pre-tax income				=E39-E40
42	Income taxes				=E41*B9
43	After-tax income				=E41-E42
44					
45	**CVP analysis in revenues**	Youth bikes	Road bikes	Mtn. bikes	Total bikes
46	CVP calculation in revenues	=$E$46*B22	=$E$46*C22	=$E$46*D22	=E33/E19
47	Variable costs	=B46*B5/B4	=C46*C5/C4	=D46*D5/D4	=SUM(B47:D47)
48	Contribution margin	=B46-B47	=C46-C47	=D46-D47	=E46-E47
49	Fixed costs				=B7
50	Pre-tax income				=E48-E49
51	Income taxes				=B9*E50
52	After-tax income				=E50-E51

FIGURE 4A.3 Spreadsheet results for Mount Dandenong Bikes breakeven analysis

	A	B	C	D	E
31	**Preliminary CVP calculations**				
32	Target pre-tax profit for CVP analysis				$0
33	Fixed costs plus target pre-tax profit				$14,700,000
34					
35	**CVP analysis in units**	Youth bikes	Road bikes	Mtn. bikes	Total bikes
36	CVP calculation in units	9,576.547	17,237.785	11,491.857	38,306
37	Revenue	$1,915,309	$12,066,450	$9,193,485	$23,175,244
38	Variable costs	718,241	4,309,446	3,447,557	8,475,244
39	Contribution margin	$1,197,068	$7,757,003	$5,745,928	14,700,000
40	Fixed costs				14,700,000
41	Pre-tax income				0
42	Income taxes				0
43	After-tax income				$0

SUMMARY

4.1 Demonstrate an understanding of cost–volume–profit (CVP) analysis and its use in decision making.

Cost–volume–profit (CVP) analysis

A technique that examines changes in profits in response to changes in sales volumes, costs and prices.

CVP graph

Shows the relationship between total revenues and total costs; illustrates how an organisation's profits are expected to change under different volumes of activity.

Uses

Describe volume, revenues, costs and profits.
- Values at breakeven or targeted profit:
  - units sold
  - revenues
  - variable, fixed and total costs.
- Sensitivity of results to changes in:
  - levels of activity
  - cost function
  - selling price
  - sales mix.
- Indifference point between alternatives
- Feasibility of planned operations

Assist with plans and decisions such as:
- budgets
- product emphasis
- selling price
- production or activity levels
- employee work schedules
- raw material purchases
- discretionary expenditures such as advertising
- proportions of fixed versus variable costs.

Monitor operations by comparing expected and actual:
- volumes, revenues, costs and profits
- profitability risk.

4.2 Define and describe the breakeven point.

Breakeven point

Level of operating activity at which revenues cover all fixed and variable costs, resulting in zero profit.

Calculation

Set targeted profit equal to zero in the CVP formula.

4.3 Apply CVP calculations for a single product.

CVP formulas

CVP analysis in units needed to attain targeted profit:

$$Q = \frac{F + \text{Profit}}{\text{Contribution margin per unit}} = \frac{F + \text{Profit}}{P - V}$$

CVP analysis in revenues needed to attain targeted profit:

$$\text{Revenues} = \frac{F + \text{Profit}}{\text{Contribution margin ratio}} = \frac{F + \text{Profit}}{(P - V)/P} = \frac{F + \text{Profit}}{(TR - TVC)/TR}$$

Pre-tax profit needed to achieve a given level of after-tax profit:

$$\text{Pre-tax profit} = \frac{\text{After-tax profit}}{(1 - \text{Tax rate})}$$

4.4 Apply CVP calculations for multiple products.

Use CVP formulas for a single product, except for:

$$\text{Weighted average contribution margin per unit} = \frac{\text{Total expected contribution margin}}{\text{Total expected number of units}}$$

$$\text{Weighted average contribution margin ratio} = \frac{\text{Total expected contribution margin}}{\text{Total expected revenue}}$$

4.5 List the assumptions and limitations that managers should consider when using CVP analysis.

CVP assumptions
- Operations within a relevant range of activity
- Linear cost function:
  - fixed costs remain fixed
  - variable cost per unit remains constant.
- Linear revenue function:
  - sales mix remains constant
  - prices remain constant.

Uncertainties
- Actual future volumes, revenues and costs are unknown.
- CVP assumptions might not hold.

In light of assumptions and uncertainties, need to evaluate:
- quality of data used in CVP analyses
- suitability of CVP analysis for the setting
- sensitivity of CVP results to changes in data for important uncertainties.

4.6 Demonstrate an understanding of the use of margin of safety and operating leverage to assess operational risk.

Margin of safety

$$\text{Margin of safety in units} = \text{Actual or estimated units of activity} - \text{Units at breakeven point}$$

$$\text{Margin of safety in revenues} = \text{Actual or estimated revenue} - \text{Revenue at breakeven point}$$

$$\text{Margin of safety percentage} = \frac{\text{Margin of safety in units}}{\text{Actual or estimated units}} = \frac{\text{Margin of safety in revenues}}{\text{Actual or estimated revenues}}$$

Degree of operating leverage

In terms of contribution margin:

$$\text{Degree of operating leverage} = \frac{\text{Contribution margin}}{\text{Profit}} = \frac{\text{TR} - \text{TVC}}{\text{Profit}} = \frac{(P - V) \times Q}{\text{Profit}}$$

In terms of fixed costs:

$$\text{Degree of operating leverage} = \frac{F}{\text{Profit}} + 1$$

Sensitivity of profits to changes in sales (units or revenues):

$$\% \text{ change in profit} = \% \text{ change in sales} \times \text{Degree of operating leverage}$$

Relationship between margin of safety and degree of operating leverage:

$$\text{Margin of safety percentage} = \frac{1}{\text{Degree of operating leverage}}$$

Higher operating leverage (lower margin of safety)

Leads to:
- greater risk of loss
- accelerated profits above the breakeven point.

KEY TERMS

breakeven point Level of operating activity at which revenues cover all fixed and variable costs, resulting in zero profit.

contribution margin Total revenue minus total variable costs.

contribution margin per unit The selling price per unit minus the variable cost per unit.

contribution margin ratio (CMR) Percentage by which the selling price (or revenue) per unit exceeds the variable cost per unit. Alternatively, the contribution margin as a percentage of revenue.

cost–volume–profit (CVP) analysis A technique that examines changes in profits in response to changes in sales volumes, costs and prices. Often used to plan future levels of operating activity and provide information.

cost–volume–profit (CVP) graph Diagram that shows the relationship between total revenues and total costs, illustrating how an organisation's profits are expected to change under different volumes of activity.

degree of operating leverage Extent to which the cost function is made up of fixed costs. Organisations with high operating leverage incur more risk of loss when sales decline.

indifference point Level of activity at which equal cost or profit occurs across multiple alternatives.

margin of safety Excess of an organisation's expected future sales (in either revenue or units) above the breakeven point. Indicates the amount by which sales could drop before profits reach the breakeven point.

margin of safety percentage Margin of safety divided by actual or estimated sales, in either units or revenues. Indicates the extent to which sales can decline before profits become zero.

operational risk The risk of loss resulting from inadequate or failed internal processes, people and systems, or from external events.

weighted average contribution margin per unit Average contribution margin per unit for multiple products weighted by the sales mix.

weighted average contribution margin ratio Combined contribution margin divided by combined revenue. Alternatively, it can be calculated by dividing the contribution margin per unit by the weighted average selling price.

SELF-STUDY PROBLEMS

SELF-STUDY PROBLEM 1 Fixed and variable costs; breakeven units

Sigrid Enterprises operates a single-product entity. Data relating to the product for the current year follows:

Annual volume	32 000 units
Selling price per unit	$50
Variable manufacturing cost per unit	$18
Annual fixed manufacturing costs	$320 000
Variable marketing and distribution costs per unit	$12
Annual fixed non-manufacturing costs	$160 000

Required

(a) Calculate total fixed costs and total variable costs per unit.

(b) Calculate the breakeven units for the current year.

(c) Changes in marketing strategy are planned for next year. This would increase variable marketing and distribution costs by $4 per unit, and reduce fixed non-manufacturing costs by $60 000 per year. Calculate the breakeven units for next year under the new marketing strategy.

SOLUTION TO SELF-STUDY PROBLEM 1

(a)

Total fixed costs	
Annual fixed manufacturing costs	$320 000
Annual fixed non-manufacturing costs	160 000
	$480 000

Total variable costs per unit

Variable manufacturing cost	18
Variable marketing and distribution	12
	$ 30

(b) Breakeven units for the current year

$$= \frac{\$480\,000}{\$50 - \$30}$$

$$= 24\,000 \text{ units}$$

(c) Breakeven units for next year

$$\text{Breakeven units} = \frac{\$420\,000}{(\$50 - \$34)}$$

$$= 26\,250 \text{ units}$$

Therefore, the breakeven units under the new marketing strategy for next year increase by 2250 units.

SELF-STUDY PROBLEM 2 Cost function; targeted profit; margin of safety; operating leverage

Coffee Cart Supreme sells hot and iced coffee beverages, and small snacks. The following is last month's statement of profit or loss.

Revenue		$5000
Cost of beverages and snacks	$2000	
Cost of napkins, straws etc.	500	
Cost to rent cart	500	
Employee wages	1000	4000
Pre-tax profit		1000
Tax		250
After-tax profit		$ 750

Required

(a) What is the total cost function for Coffee Cart Supreme?
(b) What is the tax rate for Coffee Cart Supreme?
(c) Calculate the amount of sales needed to reach a targeted after-tax profit of $1500.
(d) What was Coffee Cart Supreme's degree of operating leverage last month?
(e) What was Coffee Cart Supreme's margin of safety in revenue last month?
(f) What was Coffee Cart Supreme's margin of safety percentage last month?
(g) Suppose next month's actual revenues are $8000 and pre-tax profit is $2000. Would actual costs be higher or lower than expected?
(h) Coffee costs are volatile because worldwide coffee production varies from year to year. Explain how this volatility affects the quality of the cost function for Coffee Cart Supreme.

SOLUTION TO SELF-STUDY PROBLEM 2

(a) To estimate the cost function, we use judgement to classify costs as fixed, variable or mixed. For a typical retail business, rent and wages are likely to be fixed. We estimate fixed costs as the sum of these two costs ($500 + $1000 = $1500). It seems reasonable that the costs of beverages and snacks ($2000) and napkins, straws etc. ($500) would vary with revenues. We use the revenues as the cost driver to estimate variable costs as $2500 ÷ $5000 = 0.50, or 50 per cent of revenues. Thus, the cost function is

$$TC = \$1500 + (50\% \times \text{Revenue})$$

(b) We use income tax expense and pre-tax profit from last month to estimate the tax rate:

$$\text{Tax rate} = \text{Taxes} \div \text{Pre-tax profit} = \$250 \div \$1000 = 25\%$$

(c) We first calculate the amount of pre-tax profit needed to achieve an after-tax profit of $1500.

$$\text{Targeted pre-tax profit} = \$1500 \div (1 - 0.25) = \$2000$$

The contribution margin ratio is

$$(5000 - 2500) \div 5000 = 0.50 \text{ or } 50\%$$

We then perform the CVP calculation for revenues.

$$\text{Revenue} = \left(\$1500 + \$2000\right) \div 0.50 = \$3500 \div 0.50 = \$7000$$

(d) We use the results of our previous computations to calculate the contribution margin, and we then calculate the degree of operating leverage:

$$\text{Contribution margin} = \$5000 - \$2500 = \$2500$$

$$\text{Degree of operating leverage} = \text{Contribution margin} \div \text{Profit}$$

$$\text{Degree of operating leverage} = \$2500 \div \$1000 = 2.50$$

(e) Before calculating the margin of safety, we need to calculate the breakeven point. Note that the margin of safety must be calculated in revenue dollars because we do not have unit or product mix information. The breakeven point is calculated as

$$\$1500 \div 0.50 = \$3000 \text{ in revenues}$$

Current revenues are $5000, so the margin of safety is calculated as

$$\text{Margin of safety} = \$5000 - \$3000 = \$2000$$

(f) We use the formula to calculate margin of safety percentage:

$$\text{Margin of safety percentage} = \$2000 \div \$5000 = 40\%$$

Note that we can check our previous degree of operating leverage computation as follows:

$$\text{Degree of operating leverage} = 1 \div \text{Margin of safety percentage} = 1 \div 0.40 = 2.50$$

(g) The expected and actual costs at $8000 revenue are

$$\begin{aligned} \text{Expected costs} \quad &= \$1500 + \left(50\% \times \$8000\right) = \$5500 \\ \text{Actual costs} \quad &= \$8000 - \$2000 = \$6000 \end{aligned}$$

Actual costs are $500 higher than expected.

(h) When any costs are volatile, predicting them is problematic. Worldwide coffee prices are uncertain for many reasons, such as weather conditions in coffee growing areas, the ability of farmers to increase crops, and coffee demand patterns. In addition, broader factors such as changes in economies and political upheaval influence costs. All of these factors reduce our ability to develop a cost function that accurately predicts future costs, which means that the quality of the cost function is diminished.

SELF-STUDY PROBLEM 3 Sensitivity analysis

Required

(a) Why is it important to be able to change the spreadsheet easily to reflect changes in assumptions?

(b) Suppose that Mount Dandenong Bikes adds a helmet to each youth bike sold. The helmets cost $25 each but incorporate new materials and an innovative design that has reduced injuries and deaths from children's bike accidents. Mount Dandenong Bikes' managers believe that by advertising the new helmet as part of the youth bike package, sales will increase to 13 000. However, an advertising campaign will need to be undertaken to alert parents to the benefits of the new helmet. How much can the entity afford to spend on advertising and still expect to earn the original after-tax profit of $455 000? Assume the selling price remains at $200 per bike package.

(c) Identify CVP input factors that you believe are uncertain for this decision, and use your judgement to determine a new value for each factor. Reflect these changes in the spreadsheet to see how they affect the breakeven point and profitability. Choose a best-case and worst-case scenario to present to the managers of Mount Dandenong Bikes. Make a list of the points you would include in a memo explaining your sensitivity analysis to the managers.

SOLUTION TO SELF-STUDY PROBLEM 3

(a) Accountants and managers will explore changes in more assumptions and vary the values within the spreadsheet more readily if it is easy to do. When these changes are made and the results are analysed, managers better understand how unplanned changes in future operations might affect profitability. This knowledge allows them to more readily evaluate results and adjust operating plans.

(b) Figure 4.4 provides relevant parts of the spreadsheet with the changes.

With increased sales of youth bikes from 10 000 to 13 000 and an increased variable cost from $75 to $100, expected pre-tax profits increase to $700 000. Comparing $700 000 to $650 000, Mount Dandenong Bikes can spend up to $50 000[(490 000 − 455 000) ÷ 0.7] on advertising to maintain its current level of profitability.

FIGURE 4.4 Spreadsheet for Mount Dandenong Bikes youth helmet decision

	A	B	C	D	E
1					
2	**Input section**	Youth bikes	Road bikes	Mtn. bikes	
3	Expected sales volume-units	13,000	18,000	12,000	
4	Price per unit	$200	$700	$800	
5	Variable cost per unit	$100	$250	$300	
6					
7	Fixed costs	$14,700,000			
8	Desired after-tax profit	$100,000	(enter zero for breakeven)		
9	Income tax rate	30%			
10					
11					
12	**Contribution margin**	Youth bikes	Road bikes	Mtn. bikes	Total bikes
13	Units	13,000	18,000	12,000	43,000
14	Revenue	$2,600,000	$12,600,000	$9,600,000	$24,800,000
15	Variable costs	1,300,000	4,500,000	3,600,000	9,400,000
16	Contribution margin	$1,300,000	$8,100,000	$6,000,000	$15,400,000
17					
18	Contrib. margin per unit	$100.00	$450.00	$500.00	$358.14
19	Contrib. margin ratio	50.00%	64.29%	62.50%	62.10%
20					
21	Expected sales mix in units	30.23%	41.86%	27.91%	100.00%
22	Expected sales mix in revenues	10.48%	50.81%	38.71%	100.00%
23					
24	**Expected income**				
25	Contribution margin (above)				$15,400,000
26	Fixed costs				14,700,000
27	Pre-tax income				700,000
28	Income taxes				210,000
29	After-tax income				$490,000

(c) Many different scenarios could occur. No single answer is always correct. Your answer depends on the assumptions that you make. Following are some example assumptions for the best and worst cases. Your most likely case should be between these two values.

One best case is that the new strategy is very popular with customers. More than 13 000 of the bikes are sold. The managers discover that customers are willing to pay a higher price for the bike, so they raise the price. In addition, manufacturing efficiency improves with the greater volume, reducing variable cost per unit. Also, fixed costs are lower than expected because the managers found some costs that could be reduced.

One worst case is that the helmets fail to attract customers. In fact, sales fail to meet original expectations; fewer than 10 000 are sold. Because the entity produced extra bikes expecting an increase in demand, the managers lower the selling price to encourage additional sales. In addition, the entity hired extra workers to meet the expected demand, and other costs such as insurance and electricity are higher than expected. These changes caused both the variable and fixed costs to be higher than originally planned.

Your memo to the managers should:
- explain the assumptions for the best case and worst case scenarios
- explain the reasoning behind the most likely case
- ask managers to consider beforehand how they would respond to the best- and worst-case scenarios
- make suggestions for monitoring the results for the youth bike
- encourage the managers to evaluate the advertising and product results, and make suggestions for improving the operation or dropping the new helmet, if plans are unsuccessful.

QUESTIONS

4.1 If an entity has a mixed cost function, a 10 per cent increase in sales volume should increase income by more than 10 per cent. Explain why. **LO6**

4.2 Explain how to calculate a weighted average contribution margin per unit. **LO3**

4.3 An organisation experiences a 20 per cent increase in pre-tax profits when revenues increase 20 per cent. Assuming linearity, what do you know about the organisation's cost function? **LO6**

4.4 What is the effect on an entity's breakeven point of a lower income tax rate? **LO3, 4**

4.5 To estimate revenues, costs and profits across a range of activity, we usually assume that the cost and revenue functions are linear. What are the specific underlying assumptions for linear cost and revenue functions, and how reasonable are these assumptions? **LO5**

4.6 Explain the relationship between margin of safety percentage and degree of operating leverage. **LO6**

4.7 How do volume discounts from suppliers affect our assumption that the cost function is linear? Explain how we incorporate this type of cost into a CVP analysis. **LO5, 6**

4.8 Explain the term 'sales mix' in your own words. How does sales mix affect the contribution margin? **LO4**

4.9 How are CVP analysis and breakeven analysis related? **LO2**

4.10 Can the margin of safety ever be negative? Explain your answer. **LO6**

4.11 Describe three uses for CVP analysis. **LO1**

4.12 Explain how CVP analysis can be used to make decisions about increases in advertising costs. **LO4**

4.13 Under what circumstances will managers want sensitivity analysis results relating to a CVP analysis? **LO6**

4.14 How do different cost structures affect the breakeven point and operating leverage? **LO3, 4, 6**

4.15 Give an example of how a business can reduce variable costs by increasing fixed costs. **LO6**

4.16 Identify an industry that would have a high level of operating leverage. Briefly comment on your selection. **LO6**

EXERCISES

4.17 CVP single product **LO3**

SmallScale Publishing has just commenced business and will sell only one title, 'New to Business'. Market analysis has indicated that sales for the next 6 months should be 5 000 copies. The accountant has provided information that shows variable costs are $100 per title with fixed costs expected to be $200 000. The book is expected to sell for $150.

Required

(a) Calculate the breakeven number of books to be sold.

(b) Calculate the estimated profit for the first six months.

4.18 CVP multiple products **LO4**

SmallScale Publishing has now been operating for a couple of years. Sales have been growing and management have been excited about business performance. Currently the business sells two very popular books that are gaining international recognition; 'New to Business', and 'How to Make Yourself a Success'. Next year, the estimated total sales are 60 000 books and the breakdown per title together with financial information follows:

	New to Business	How to Make Yourself a Success
Sales (estimated units)	45 000	15 000
Sales price per book	$150	$100
Variable cost per book	$100	$80

Total fixed costs are expected to be $500 000.

Required

(a) Calculate the total number of books to be sold to break even next year. Show the number of books for each title.

(b) Calculate the estimated profit for next year.

4.19 Operating leverage LO6

SmallScale Publishing are considering offering eBooks. Market analysis has been undertaken and the breakdown of sales together with financial information follows. Due to the change in business model, fixed costs are expected to increase to $1 000 000.

	New to Business	How to Make Yourself a Success
Sales (estimated units)	45 000	15 000
Sales price per book	$150	$100
Variable cost per book	$50	$40

Required

(a) Calculate the breakeven in total units.

(b) Compared to your answer in 4.18 above, is the margin of safety higher or lower?

(c) Comment on whether you would recommend the business change to eBooks.

4.20 Cost function; selling price; profit; contribution margin LO3

Find the missing figures for each of the following independent cases.

Selling price/unit	Variable costs/unit	Units sold	Contribution margin (total)	Fixed costs	Profit (loss)
$80	a.	10 000	$200 000	$120 000	b.
$15	$10	c.	$ 25 000	d.	$ 0
$ 4	$ 2	e.	f.	$ 3000	$(1 000)
g.	$75	500	$ 12 500	$ 8 000	h.
$10	i.	1 000	j.	$ 6 000	$(2 000)

4.21 Cost function; selling price; profit; contribution margin LO3

Find the missing figures for each of the following independent cases:

Selling price/unit	Variable costs/unit	Units sold	Contribution margin (total)	Fixed costs	Profit (loss)
$40	$20	60 000	a.	b.	$300 000
$18	c.	10 000	60 000	$ 48 000	d.
e.	$20	50 000	250 000	f.	$ 0
$ 8	$ 6	100 000	g.	$ 50 000	h.
$ 5	i.	500 000	j.	$460 000	$ 40 000

4.22 Targeted profit; not-for-profit breakeven LO3

(a) The variable cost per gift basket is $2, fixed costs are $5000 per month and the selling price of a basket is $7. How many baskets must be produced and sold in a month to earn a pre-tax profit of $1000?

(b) The Community Clinic (a not-for-profit medical clinic) received a lump-sum grant from the City of Sydney of $460 000 this year. The fixed costs of the clinic are expected to be $236 000. The average variable cost per patient visit is expected to be $7.64 and the average fee collected per patient visit is $4.64. What is the breakeven volume in patient visits?

4.23 CVP graph LO3

(a) Create a CVP graph using the information in exercise 4.22, part (a). Explain the information in the graph.

(b) Create a CVP graph using the information in exercise 4.22, part (b). Explain the information in the graph.

4.24 Cost function; breakeven   **LO2**

(a) The average cost per unit was $234 at a volume of 1200 units and $205 at a volume of 1400 units. The profit was $24 000 at the lower volume. Estimate the variable cost per unit.

(b) Sparkle Car Wash Supplier sells a hose washer for $0.25 that it buys from the manufacturer for $0.12. Variable selling costs are $0.02 per hose washer. Breakeven is currently at a sales volume of $10 600 per month. What are the monthly fixed costs associated with the washer?

(c) Monthly fixed costs are $24 000 when volume is at or below 200 units and $36 000 when monthly volume is above 200 units. The variable cost per unit is $200 and the selling price is $300 per unit. What is the breakeven quantity?

4.25 Cost function; breakeven; profit   **LO2**

Ryans Music provides individual music lessons in the homes of clients. The following data are provided with respect to the current year's activity:

Unit selling price[a]	$ 45
Unit labour cost	$ 30
Annual fixed costs	$18 000
Unit sheet music costs	$ 3

[a] Each unit is equal to one half-hour lesson.

Required

(a) Assuming selling prices and costs remain the same calculate the number of lessons that are required to be sold in next year to break even.

(b) If 4000 lessons were to be provided next year, what profit would be achieved?

(c) Next year, Ryans expects the unit labour cost to increase by $2 but, because of local competitive forces, Ryans does not wish to increase the lesson selling price. With some careful management, Ryans hopes to reduce annual fixed costs to $15 000. Calculate the number of music lessons that would need to be performed next year in order to match the current year's profit.

4.26 Contribution margin; contribution margin ratio   **LO3**

Pamcar Industries sells IT equipment, specialising in printers and faxes. The following statement reflects the contribution margin of each activity, and overall profit levels:

	Printers	Faxes	Total
Sales	$3 500 000	$1 600 000	$5 100 000
Less Variable costs	2 300 000	1 120 000	3 420 000
Contribution margin	1 200 000	480 000	1 680 000
Direct fixed costs	400 000	360 000	760 000
Common fixed costs:			
Utilities			36 000
Other administration			162 000
Profit			$ 722 000

Required

(a) Calculate the contribution margin ratios for each of the two areas of activity, and in total.

(b) Using the total contribution margin ratio, calculate the level of sales required to break even.

4.27 Targeted profit   **LO3**

Information for Melong Industries is provided below.

Average selling price per unit	$ 10.00
Average variable costs per unit	
Cost per unit	$ 5.00
Selling costs	1.40
Annual fixed costs	
Selling	$240 000
Administration	380 000
After-tax profit target	$126 000
Tax rate	30%

Required

(a) Calculate the number of units that need to be sold to reach the after-tax profit target.

(b) If the sales units should be 25 per cent less than required to meet the after-tax profit target, what will the after-tax profit actually be?

4.28 Breakeven point; profit; cost function **LO2, 3**

Chloe Enterprises operates a single-product entity. Data relating to the product for the current year are as follows:

Annual volume	32 000 units
Selling price per unit	$60
Variable manufacturing cost per unit	$28
Annual fixed manufacturing costs	$120 000
Variable marketing and distribution costs per unit	$12 = 16
Annual fixed non-manufacturing costs	$360 000 = 280,000

Required

(a) Calculate the breakeven units.

(b) Calculate the profit achieved for the current year.

(c) Changes in marketing strategy are planned for next year. This would increase variable marketing and distribution costs by $4 per unit, and reduce fixed non-manufacturing costs by $80 000 per year. Calculate the units that would need to be sold in the next year to achieve the same profit as the current year.

(d) Would you recommend the change? Explain.

4.29 Breakeven point; profit; cost function **LO2, 4**

Annalise Industries has provided the following information with respect to its current year's activities:

	Product A	Product B	Product C	Product D
Sales mix (200 000 units)	50 000	30 000	100 000	20 000
Selling price	$10	$15	$8	$25
Variable cost/unit	$6	$10	$6	$15
Total fixed costs = $450 000				

Required

(a) Calculate the breakeven point in total units and units per product based on the data.

(b) Calculate the profit (loss) achieved in the current year.

(c) Management is concerned about increasing competition for some of its products, and wants to increase its sales of product D relative to product C. The initiative would increase annual fixed costs by $50 000 and alter the sales mix to 25 per cent (product A), 15 per cent (product B), 40 per cent (product C) and 20 per cent (product D). On the available data, would you recommend the initiative?

4.30 Profit; price for targeted profit **LO3**

The Martell Company has recently established operations in a competitive market. Management has been aggressive in its attempt to establish a market share. The price of the product was set at $5 per unit, well below that of the entity's major competitors. Variable costs were $4.50 per unit, and total fixed costs were $600 000 during the first year.

Required

(a) Assume that the entity was able to sell 1 million units in the first year. What was the pre-tax profit (loss) for the year?

(b) Assume that the variable cost per unit and total fixed costs do not increase in the second year. Management has been successful in establishing its position in the market. What price must be set to achieve a pre-tax profit of $25 000? Assume that sales remain at 1 million units.

4.31 Cost function; breakeven

Data for the most recent three months of operations for the RainBeau Salon are as follows.

	March	April	May
Number of appointments	1 600	1 500	1 900
Hairdresser salaries	$14 000	$14 000	$18 000
Manicurist salaries	12 000	12 000	16 000
Supplies	900	750	950
Utilities	600	480	400
Rent	1 000	1 000	1 000
Miscellaneous	3 500	3 450	3 580
Total costs	$32 000	$31 680	$39 930

A cost-of-living salary increase occurred at the beginning of May.

Required

(a) What is the total cost function for RainBeau Salon?

(b) If the average fee per appointment is $25, estimate the appointments required in June to break even.

4.32 Breakeven; targeted profit; ROI targeted profit

Madden Company projected its income before taxes for next year as shown here. Madden is subject to a 40 per cent income tax rate.

Sales (160 000 units)	$8 000 000
Cost of goods sold	
Variable costs	2 000 000
Fixed costs	3 000 000
Pre-tax profit	$3 000 000

Required

(a) What is Madden's breakeven point in units sold for the next year?

(b) If Madden wants $4.5 million in pre-tax profit, what is the required level of sales in dollars?

4.33 Breakeven; targeted profit; cost changes; selling price

Laraby Company produces a single product. It sold 25 000 units last year with the following results.

Sales	$625 000
Variable costs	375 000
Fixed costs	150 000
Income before taxes	100 000
Income taxes (45%)	45 000
After-tax profit	$ 55 000

In an attempt to improve its product, Laraby's managers are considering replacing a component part that costs $2.50 with a new and better part costing $4.50 per unit during the coming year. A new machine would also be needed to increase plant capacity. The machine would cost $18 000 and have a useful life of six years with no salvage value. The company uses straight-line depreciation on all plant assets.

Required

(a) What was Laraby Company's breakeven point in units last year?

(b) How many units of product would Laraby Company have had to sell in the past year to earn $77 000 in after-tax profit?

(c) If Laraby Company holds the sales price constant and makes the suggested changes, how many units of product must be sold in the coming year to break even?

(d) If Laraby Company holds the sales price constant and makes the suggested changes, how many units of product will the entity have to sell to make the same after-tax profit as last year?

(e) If Laraby Company wishes to maintain the same contribution margin ratio, what selling price per unit of product must it charge next year to cover the increased materials costs?

4.34 Breakeven; single product; profit calculation   **LO2, 3**

Janna Processing is a single-product entity, and provides the summary data shown relating to its product for the current year.

Selling price per unit	$ 50
Variable manufacturing costs	$ 24
Annual fixed manufacturing costs	$500 000
Variable marketing, distribution and administration costs	$ 8
Annual fixed non-manufacturing costs	$256 000
Annual volume	48 000 units

Required

(a) Calculate the breakeven in units and sales dollars.

(b) Calculate the profit earned in the current year.

(c) Janna Processing is considering changes in plant operations and the production process for next year. The changes would result in a reduction of variable costs per unit of $6, and increase fixed manufacturing costs by $265 000. How many units would need to be sold to earn the same profit as the current year? Would you recommend the changes?

4.35 Profit calculation; price to achieve profit target   **LO3**

The management of Kayla Industries has been aggressive in trying to build market share. The price was set at $5 per unit, well below the existing market price. Variable costs were $4.50 per unit, and annual fixed costs in the first year were $600 000.

To encourage sales staff to push sales higher, the management of Kayla Industries is considering placing staff on a remuneration scheme paying a retainer plus 2.5 per cent commission on sales. This will reduce fixed costs by $200 000. Do you consider this to be a good strategy?

4.36 Breakeven; selling price; targeted profit with price and cost changes   **LO3**

All-Day Lolly Company is a wholesale distributor of confectionery. The entity services grocery and convenience stores in the metropolitan area. Small but steady growth in sales has been achieved by the All-Day Lolly Company over the past few years, but confectionery prices also have been increasing. The entity is reformulating its plans for the coming fiscal year. The following data were used to project the current year's after-tax income of $100 400.

Average selling price	$4.00 per box
Average variable costs	
Cost of confectionery	$2.00 per box
Selling costs	0.40 per box
Total	$2.40 per box
Annual fixed costs	
Selling	$160 000
Administrative	280 000
Total	$440 000
Expected annual sales (390 000 boxes) = $1 560 000	
Tax rate = 40%	

Confectionery manufacturers have announced that they will increase prices of their products an average of 15 per cent in the coming year because of increases in raw material (sugar, cocoa, peanuts etc.) and labour costs. All-Day Lolly Company expects that all other costs will remain the same as during the current year.

Required

(a) What is All-Day Lolly Company's breakeven point in boxes of lollies for the current year?

(b) What average selling price per box must All-Day Lolly Company charge to cover the 15 per cent increase in the variable cost of lollies and still maintain the current contribution margin ratio?

(c) What volume of sales in dollars must the All-Day Lolly Company achieve in the coming year to maintain the same after-tax income as projected for the current year if the average selling price of lollies remains at $4 per box and the cost of confectionery increases 15 per cent?

4.37 Breakeven; operating leverage; cost function decision

You are the adviser of a Junior Achievement group in a local high school. You need to help the group make a decision about fees that must be paid to sell gardening tools at the Home and Garden Show. The group sells a set of tools for $20. The manufacturing cost (all variable) is $6 per set. The Home and Garden Show coordinator allows the following three payment options for groups exhibiting and selling at the show:

A. Pay a fixed booth fee of $5600.

B. Pay a fee of $3800 plus 10 per cent of all revenue from tool sets sold at the show.

C. Pay 15 per cent of all revenue from tool sets sold at the show.

Required

(a) Calculate the breakeven number of tool sets for each option.

(b) Which payment plan has the highest degree of operating leverage?

(c) Which payment plan has the lowest risk of loss for the organisation? Explain.

(d) At what level of revenue should the group be indifferent to options A and B?

(e) Which option should Junior Achievement choose, assuming sales are expected to be 1000 sets of tools? Explain.

4.38 Targeted profit; margin of safety; operating leverage **LO6**

The following budget data apply to Newberry's Nutrition:

Sales (100 000 units)	$1 000 000
Costs	
Direct materials	$300 000
Direct labour	200 000
Fixed factory overhead	100 000
Variable factory overhead	150 000
Marketing and administration	160 000
Total costs	910 000
Budgeted pre-tax profit	$ 90 000

Direct labour workers are paid hourly wages and go home when there is no work. The marketing and administration costs include $50 000 that varies proportionately with production volume. Assume that sales and production volumes are equal.

Required

(a) Calculate the number of units that must be sold to achieve a targeted after-tax income of $120 000, assuming the tax rate is 40 per cent.

(b) Calculate the margin of safety in both revenues and units.

(c) Calculate the degree of operating leverage.

4.39 Breakeven; targeted profit; margin of safety; operating leverage **LO6**

Pike Street Fudge makes and sells fudge in a variety of flavours in a shop located in the local public market. Data for a recent week are as follows:

Revenue (2000 kg @ $4.80 per kg)		$9 600
Cost of ingredients	$3 200	
Rent	800	
Wages	4 800	8 800
Pre-tax profit		800
Taxes (20%)		160
After-tax profit		$ 640

All employees work standard shifts, no matter how much fudge is produced or sold.

Required

(a) Calculate the breakeven point in units and in revenue.

(b) Calculate the number of units and the amount of revenues that would be needed for after-tax profit of $3000.

(c) Calculate the margin of safety in units and the margin of safety percentage.

(d) Calculate the degree of operating leverage.

4.40 Breakeven; targeted profit; margin of safety   **LO6**

Vines and Daughter manufactures and sells swimsuits for $40 each. The estimated statement of profit or loss for next year is as follows:

Sales	$2 000 000
Variable costs	1 100 000
Contribution margin	900 000
Fixed costs	765 000
Pre-tax profit	$ 135 000

Required

(a) Calculate the contribution margin per swimsuit and the number of swimsuits that must be sold to break even.
(b) What is the margin of safety in the number of swimsuits?
(c) Suppose the margin of safety was 5000 swimsuits in the current year. Are operations more or less risky next year as compared to this year? Explain.
(d) Calculate the contribution margin ratio and the breakeven point in revenues.
(e) What is the margin of safety in revenues?
(f) Suppose next year's revenue estimate is $200 000 higher. What would be the estimated pre-tax profit?
(g) Assume a tax rate of 30 per cent. How many swimsuits must be sold to earn an after-tax profit of $180 000?

PROBLEMS

4.41 Cost function; breakeven; quality of information; relevant range   **LO2, 3**

Oysters Away picks, shucks and packs oysters and then sells them wholesale to fine restaurants across the state. The statement of profit or loss for last year is as follows.

Revenue (based on sales of 2000 cases of oysters)		$200 000
Expenses:		
Wages for pickers, shuckers and packers	$100 000	
Packing materials	20 000	
Rent and insurance	25 000	
Administrative and selling	45 000	190 000
Pre-tax profit		10 000
Taxes (20%)		2 000
After-tax profit		$ 8 000

Pickers, shuckers and packers are employed on an hourly basis and can be laid off whenever necessary. Salespeople mostly deliver the product and are paid on a salaried basis.

Required

(a) Estimate the cost function for Oysters Away.
(b) What is the breakeven point in cases for Oysters Away?
(c) The manager thinks that the entity will harvest and sell 3000 cases of oysters next year. Estimate the after-tax profit.
(d) Oysters Away harvested and sold 2000 cases in each of the last several years. What does this suggest about the quality of the income information you calculated in part (c)?
(e) Describe reasons why the cost function developed for the relevant range up to 2000 cases might not hold for 2001 to 3000 cases.

4.42 Relevant information; breakeven; targeted profit; price; uncertainties   **LO2, 3**

Francesca would like to lease a coffee cart in Melbourne. The lease is $800 per month, and a city licence to sell food and beverages costs $20 per month. The lessor of the stand has shown Francesca records indicating that gross revenues average $32 per hour. The out-of-pocket costs for ingredients are generally about 40 per cent of gross revenues. Last year Francesca paid 25 per cent of her income in government taxes.

Francesca pays $1000 per month for her apartment. She could store the cart overnight in the apartment's garage, which is currently unused. Real estate developers in Melbourne estimate that about 20 per cent of the cost of a residential building is for the garage.

At present, Francesca is earning $2400 per month as a ski instructor for one of the big ski areas. In the summer she earns about the same income as a kayaking instructor.

Required

(a) List each piece of quantitative information in this problem. For each item, indicate whether it is relevant to Francesca's decision and explain why.

(b) If Francesca leases the cart and works 30 days in a month, how many hours will she have to work each day, on average, to be at least as well off financially as she is in her current job?

(c) If Francesca wants to work only 25 days per month, how much will revenues have to increase for her to work four hours per day and be as financially well off as she is in her current job?

(d) Can Francesca be certain that her revenues will average $32 per hour? Why?

(e) What other information might help Francesca with this decision?

4.43 Sales mix; multiple product breakeven; uncertainties; quality of information   **LO4**

Dreamtime produces two products: regular boomerangs and premium boomerangs. Last month 1200 units of regular and 2400 units of premium boomerangs were produced and sold. Average prices and costs per unit for the month are as follows.

	Regular	Premium
Selling price	$22.15	$45.30
Variable costs	4.31	6.91
Product line fixed costs	8.17	24.92
Corporate fixed costs	5.62	5.62
Operating profit	$ 4.05	$ 7.85

Product line fixed costs can be avoided if the product line is dropped. Corporate fixed costs can be avoided only if the entity goes out of business entirely. You may want to use a spreadsheet to perform calculations.

Required

(a) Assuming the sales mix remains constant, how many units of premium boomerangs will be sold each time a unit of regular boomerangs is sold?

(b) What are the total fixed product line costs for each product?

(c) What are the total corporate fixed costs?

(d) What is the overall corporate breakeven in total revenue and for each product, assuming the sales mix is the same as last month's?

(e) What is the breakeven in revenues for regular boomerangs, ignoring corporate fixed costs?

(f) Why is the breakeven for regular boomerangs different when we calculate the individual product breakeven versus the combined product breakeven?

(g) When managers monitor the profitability of regular boomerangs, are corporate fixed costs relevant? Explain.

(h) CVP analysis assumes that the sales mix will remain constant. Explain why managers generally cannot know for certain what their sales mix will be.

(i) What is the effect of uncertainty about the sales mix on the quality of the information obtained from CVP analyses?

4.44 Cost function; marginal cost; opportunity cost; usefulness of CVP   **LO6**

A neighbour asked for your help preparing a grant for a not-for-profit after-school art program that would benefit primary school children in the neighbourhood. He wants to charge low fees for most children, but also offer some scholarships for low-income children. He needs to have one staff person for every six children to meet state regulations. He can use high school student volunteers for two of these positions, but is concerned about potential absences on their part if he relies on them to meet the state regulations. He would like the program to serve at least 30 children — more, if possible.

He wants you to help him decide on the fees to charge and also to determine how many students could receive scholarships.

Required

(a) Think about the costs involved in an after-school program. Assume that your neighbour can use the local primary school free of charge.

    (i) List costs that will be incurred for the program, and categorise them as fixed, variable or mixed.

    (ii) For each variable cost, choose a potential cost driver. Explain your choice.

(b) Do you think the cost structure would be primarily fixed or primarily variable? Explain. Remember, even though staff work only part time, they will have a regular schedule to meet the state regulations of six children per staff member.

(c) Suppose one of the staff members has only one child to help. What is the marginal cost for three scholarships?

(d) Suppose the program is fully subscribed by fee-paying children. What is the opportunity cost per scholarship?

(e) Will CVP analysis help your neighbour choose a fee that would cover at least 10 scholarships? Explain how you would set up a spreadsheet so that your neighbour could perform sensitivity analysis to make more informed decisions.

4.45 Breakeven; CVP; potential cost structure change; employee reaction   **LO2, 6**

Ersatz manufactures a single product. The following statement of profit or loss shows two different levels of activity, which are assumed to be within Ersatz's relevant range. You may want to use a spreadsheet to perform calculations.

Ersatz Ltd Statement of profit or loss		
	Activity levels	
	1000 units	**1500 units**
Volume		
Sales @ $100 each	$100 000	$150 000
Variable expenses		
Manufacturing @ $40 each	40 000	60 000
Selling @ $10 each	10 000	15 000
Administration @ $6 each	6 000	9 000
Contribution margin	44 000	66 000
Fixed expenses		
Manufacturing	10 000	10 000
Selling	11 000	11 000
Administration	20 000	20 000
Pre-tax profit	$ 3 000	$ 25 000

Required

(a) What is Ersatz's breakeven point in units?

(b) Draw a CVP chart showing the two levels of activity and the breakeven point.

(c) If Ersatz plans to sell 1300 units, what will pre-tax income be?

(d) Your boss asked you to draft an email response to Ersatz's major shareholder, who wants to know why pre-tax profit increases by more than 700 per cent when sales increase by just 50 per cent. Both your boss and the shareholder are busy people and expect short answers.

(e) Management expects that variable costs and selling prices will rise by 3 per cent, but fixed costs will not change. What will the new breakeven point be? Explain the result.

(f) Management wants to change the way that sales representatives are paid. At present, sales representatives are paid $11 000 + $10 per unit. Management will replace this formula with a payment of $20 per unit. At what level of sales will it make no difference in income which cost function is used?

(g) Add the new cost function to the preceding CVP chart.

(h) Which of the two cost functions will minimise selling expenses assuming that sales are above the indifference level calculated in part (f)?

(i) How would sales representatives be likely to respond to the new payment system?

(j) Discuss the pros and cons to the entity of changing the way sales representatives are paid.

4.46 Cost function; breakeven; targeted profit; uncertainties and bias; interpretation   **LO2, 3**

Joe Davies is thinking about starting a company to produce carved wooden clocks. He loves making the clocks. He sees it as an opportunity to be his own boss, making a living doing what he likes best.

Joe paid $300 for the plans for the first clock, and he has already purchased new equipment costing $2000 to manufacture the clocks. He estimates that it will cost $30 in materials (wood, clock mechanism etc.) to make each clock. If he decides to build clocks full time, he will need to rent office and manufacturing space, which he thinks would cost $2500 per month for rent plus another $300 per month for various utility bills. Joe would perform all of the manufacturing and run the office, and he would like to pay himself a salary of $3000 per month so that he would have enough money to live on. Because he does not want to take time away from manufacturing to sell the clocks, he plans to hire two salespeople at a base salary of $1000 each per month plus a commission of $7 per clock.

Joe plans to sell each clock for $225. He believes that he can produce and sell 300 clocks in December for Christmas, but he is not sure what the sales will be during the rest of the year. However, he is fairly sure that the clocks will be popular because he has been selling similar items as a sideline for several years. Overall, he is confident that he can pay all of his business costs, pay himself the monthly salary of $3000 and earn at least $4000 more than that per month. (Ignore income taxes.)

Required

(a) Perform analyses to estimate the number of clocks Joe would need to manufacture and sell each year for his business to be financially successful:
  (i) List all of the costs described and indicate whether each cost is (1) a relevant fixed cost, (2) a relevant variable cost or (3) *not* relevant to Joe's decision.
  (ii) Calculate the contribution margin per unit and the contribution margin ratio.
  (iii) Write down the total cost function for the clocks and calculate the annual breakeven point in units and in revenues.
  (iv) How many clocks would Joe need to sell annually to earn $4000 per month more than his salary?

(b) Identify uncertainties about the CVP calculations:
  (i) Explain why Joe cannot know for sure whether his actual costs will be the same dollar amounts that he estimated. In your explanation, identify as many uncertainties as you can. (*Hint:* For each of the costs Joe identified, think about reasons why the actual cost might be different than the amount he estimated.)
  (ii) Identify possible costs for Joe's business that he has not identified. List as many additional types of cost as you can.
  (iii) Explain why Joe cannot know for sure how many clocks he will sell each year. In your explanation, identify as many uncertainties as you can.

(c) Discuss whether Joe is likely to be biased in his revenue and cost estimates.

(d) Explain how uncertainties and Joe's potential biases might affect interpretation of the breakeven analysis results.

(e) Use the information you learned from the preceding analyses to write a memo to Joe with your recommendations. Attach to the memo a schedule showing relevant information. As appropriate, refer to the schedule in the memo.

4.47 CVP sensitivity analysis; bias; quality of information   **LO6**

Jasmine Krishnan has been taking entrepreneurship courses as part of her business degree. She developed a plan to start a travel agency specialising in semester break trips for students.

She learned how to develop CVP analysis in her cost accounting class. Now she is preparing pro forma (forecasted) statements of profit or loss for a brochure about her plans for the travel agency. She wants to use the information from the CVP as a basis for the statements. Her entrepreneurship professor criticised her business plan because Jasmine included too small an amount for liability insurance. However, when she included the amount suggested by her father's insurance agent, she had to set prices quite high, cut back on the amount she planned as her salary, find lower quality hotels for the students or take some combination of these actions. She thought that hotel quality and prices would affect sales volumes negatively and did not want to risk incurring losses from low revenues during her first few years. She also needed a base level of salary to at least pay for her living expenses.

She decided to ask friends and relatives to invest in her travel agency to ensure she had enough capital for the first few years. Once her reputation was well established, she assumed that higher customer volumes would cover all of her expected costs. She was confident that her planned trips would attract enough students each year to cover most of her costs. From focus groups on campus, she learned which types of trips were most appealing to other students. Now she planned to use sensitivity analysis to solve for volumes that would make the pro forma statements look attractive to investors.

Required

(a) In general, what information do we hope to gain from performing sensitivity analyses? Explain.

(b) Explain how bias might enter into Jasmine's sensitivity analyses.

(c) How might Jasmine's bias affect the quality of the investment brochure information?

(d) Identify a potential ethical problem for Jasmine.

(e) When you consider the wellbeing of Jasmine's family and friends, how would you recommend that Jasmine use sensitivity analysis for her brochure? Explain.

4.48 Small business owners; CVP research on the internet   **LO1, 2**

The internet provides many resources to help small business owners successfully manage their businesses. These resources include information about common techniques used for planning and managing operations.

Required

(a) Why are small business owners often unaware of common business techniques such as CVP analysis?

(b) Why might CVP analysis be even more useful to small business owners than to managers of large entities? (*Hint:* Consider whether information about the margin of safety and size of potential losses might be especially important for people who own small businesses.)

(c) Use an internet search engine to locate websites that provide information about the terms 'breakeven analysis' and 'cost–volume–profit analysis'. Also search for these terms on websites designed explicitly to help small business owners. Summarise what your research tells you about the uses and usefulness of breakeven and CVP analysis.

(d) Suppose you are trying to help a small business owner learn to use breakeven and CVP analysis. Write a memo to the owner explaining what you think the owner should do and include appropriate references to internet resources that would be useful to the owner. Assume that you have already had a brief conversation with the owner about breakeven and CVP analysis, and the owner expressed an interest in learning more. Focus on communicating effectively by avoiding unnecessarily technical language and concentrating on the most important points.

4.49 Not-for-profit breakeven price; budget alternatives   **LO2, 3**

The Elder Clinic, a not-for-profit entity, provides limited medical services to low-income elderly patients. The manager's summary report for the past four months of operations is reproduced here.

	March	April	May	June	Total
Patient visits	849	821	778	842	3 290
Patient fees	$ 4 230	$ 4 180	$ 3 875	$ 4 260	$ 16 545
Medical staff salaries	13 254	13 256	13 254	14 115	53 879
Medical supplies used	3 182	3 077	2 934	3 175	12 368
Administrative salaries	3 197	3 198	3 197	3 412	13 004
Rent	1 000	1 000	1 000	1 100	4 100
Utilities	532	378	321	226	1 457
Other expenses	2 854	2 776	2 671	2 828	11 129
Total expenses	24 019	23 685	23 377	24 856	95 937
Operating surplus (loss)	$(19 789)	$(19 505)	$(19 502)	$(20 596)	$(79 392)

The clinic receives an operating subsidy from the state government, but unfortunately the operating loss incurred through June ($79 392) is larger than anticipated. Part of the problem is the salary increase that went into effect in June, which had been overlooked when the budget was submitted to the state government last year. To compound the problem, the cold winter months traditionally bring with them an increase in cold-weather-related health problems. Thus, the clinic is likely to experience an increase in patient visits during July.

The accountant made the following assumptions in developing the cost function.

- Salaries are fixed, and June values are used.
- Medical supplies vary with patient visits.
- Rent and utilities are fixed, and last period's costs are used.

- Other expenses are mixed and, using regression, fixed cost is $702 and variable cost is $2.53 per patient visit.

  Clinic management is considering an increase in patient fees to reduce losses.

Required

(a) Develop a cost function for this data (refer to chapter 2). Use the cost function you developed to solve for the average patient fee necessary to break even, assuming there are 940 patient visits. Compare this new fee with the average patient fee charged during March through June.

(b) Suppose the clinic raises its patient fees to break even. What problems do you see from the elderly patients' perspective if the fee is raised?

(c) In this setting, would an increase in fees be likely to affect patient volume? What problems do you see from the clinic's perspective if the fee is raised?

(d) Other than raising the fee, what ideas might the clinic consider to balance the budget?

4.50 Cost function; targeted profit; operating leverage; CVP graph; owner goals   **LO3, 6**

Trang Nguyen owns Trang's Stained Glass in Sydney. The business produces and sells three different types of stained glass windows: small, medium and large. Trang has two full-time employees who work regular schedules to cut glass and assemble the windows. She borrowed money from the bank to start the business and pay living expenses. She is concerned that her cash flows might not be high enough either to pay herself or to repay the bank loan. She would like to generate approximately $10 000 in pre-tax profit each month to cover her living expenses and repay the loan.

The following revenue and cost information covers the past four months.

	June	July	August	September
Revenues	$9 050	$10 531	$12 946	$16 116
Raw materials and supplies	1 745	2 433	3 074	4 029
Labour	3 880	4 041	4 246	4 282
Rent	2 000	2 000	2 000	2 200
Miscellaneous	525	701	747	793
Profit	$ 900	$ 1 356	$ 2 879	$ 4 812

Required

(a) Develop a cost function for Trang's Stained Glass.

(b) Determine the level of revenue Trang's Stained Glass must generate to achieve the targeted profit of $10 000 per month.

(c) Calculate Trang's degree of operating leverage for September.

(d) Interpret Trang's degree of operating leverage.

(e) Create a CVP graph showing the breakeven point, targeted profit and margin of safety.

(f) Write a memo to Trang with recommendations about ways she might achieve her goals.

4.51 Building and using a CVP financial model   **LO6**

Toddler Toy Company sells baby dolls, teddy bears and toy cars. The managers established a preliminary budget using the following assumptions. They would now like to evaluate the sensitivity of budgeted results to different sets of assumptions.

Toddler Toy Company
Assumptions for coming year

	Baby dolls	Teddy bears	Toy cars
Volume	200 000	125 000	225 000
Price	$ 3.50	$ 2.75	$ 3.15
Variable costs	2.05	1.75	2.45
Fixed costs	65 000	125 000	35 000
Targeted pre-tax profit = $0			
Investment = $2 million			
Capacity = 1 million units			

Required

(a) Create a spreadsheet that the managers can use for sensitivity analysis. Modify input data in the spreadsheet to answer the following parts of this problem. You may wish to add cell references for percentage changes in prices, volumes and costs.

(b) Assume that the volume of dolls sold increases to 225 000 units with no change in fixed or variable costs. What is the new pre-tax profit? Does the number produced by your financial model appear to be reasonable? (Manually estimate the increase in pre-tax profit if volume increases and fixed costs remain constant. Compare this figure to your spreadsheet result.)

(c) Based on the original assumptions, what is the effect on pre-tax profit if variable costs increase by 5 per cent for each of the three product lines? Assume that nothing else changes.

(d) Return to the original assumptions. Assume that a sales manager proposed a new advertising campaign to boost sales volume. The campaign would cost $30 000 and is estimated to increase the volume of each product as follows.
- Baby doll sales increase by 20 000 units.
- Teddy bear sales increase by 7500 units.
- Toy car sales increase by 30 000 units.

What would be the effect on pre-tax profit if this plan were adopted?

(e) Return to the original assumptions. Now assume that due to competition, Toddler Toys must cut prices on each of its three products by 20 per cent. In addition, a new advertising campaign costing $45 000 must be instituted to counteract bad publicity. Given these assumptions, what is the new breakeven point?

(f) Return to the original assumptions. What would be the pre-tax profit if Toddler Toys increases the price of all three products by 10 per cent and the volume of each product line decreases by 5 per cent?

(g) Given the same assumptions as in part (f), how many units must Toddler Toys sell to earn a targeted pre-tax profit of $100 000? A targeted pre-tax profit of $150 000? A pre-tax return on investment (ROI) of 10 per cent? (*Hint:* To determine the targeted pre-tax profit, multiply 10 per cent by the amount invested.)

(h) Spreadsheets for financial modelling allow sensitivity analysis of revenues, costs and quantities such as estimated product volumes.
(i) Explain why it is not possible to perfectly estimate revenues, costs and quantities.
(ii) Explain how sensitivity analysis can help managers evaluate the pros and cons of alternatives.
(iii) Explain how manager bias might influence estimates of revenues, costs and quantities.

4.52 Building and using a CVP financial model   **LO6**

The following information for Pet Palace, a large retail store that sells pet-related merchandise, was recorded for the first quarter. The store tracks merchandise according to product type. The category 'Other' includes accessories such as dog beds, leashes, kitty litter boxes, bird cages and so on. The entity is considering several different strategies to improve operations for the next quarter.

Input data	Food	Toys	Pets	Other	Total
Revenue	$500 000	$150 000	$75 000	$200 000	$925 000
Variable costs	200 000	50 000	60 000	50 000	360 000
Fixed costs					550 000
Tax rate					25%

Required

(a) Create a spreadsheet that Pet Palace managers can use for sensitivity analysis. Modify information in the data input section and answer the questions in the following parts.

(b) What is Pet Palace's breakeven point? What total revenue is necessary for a targeted after-tax profit of $100 000?

(c) Pet Palace managers are considering their advertising campaign for the next period. They believe they could spend an additional $10 000 on advertising for a product line and increase sales by 10 per cent. One manager wants to increase advertising on pets because that product line is currently the smallest. Another manager believes the advertisements should promote the most profitable products, but he is not sure which products those would be. What is the after-tax profit if pets are promoted? What is the most profitable product? What is the after-tax profit if that product is promoted?

(d) What factors, other than the quantitative results, might influence managers' decisions to increase advertising?

ACKNOWLEDGEMENTS

Photo 4A: © Naluenart Pimu / Shutterstock.com
Photo 4B: © Cultura RF / Getty Images
Figures 4.19, 4.20, 4.24, 4.25, 4.26, 4.27 and 4.28: © John Wiley & Sons, Inc.

CHAPTER 5

Planning — budgeting and behaviour

LEARNING OBJECTIVES

After studying this chapter, you should be able to:

5.1 communicate the role of planning and budgeting for improved profit performance and value creation

5.2 apply the planning and budgeting process to consider the impact of alternative courses of action on profit, assets and cash flow

5.3 identify the various planning and budgeting approaches used in cost centres

5.4 compare traditional and contemporary approaches to budgeting

5.5 reflect on the behavioural implications of budgeting

5.6 critique the Beyond Budgeting approach to management control.

IN BRIEF

This chapter introduces planning and budgeting and their impact on overall strategy, performance measurement and control. Budgets impact on the statement of profit or loss, statement of financial position and cash flows and are used by organisations for multiple reasons. Budgets can be used as a tool for planning and resource allocation to help steer the organisation towards achievement of its goals. The budget itself should not be viewed as the goal. Instead, the budget should be viewed as an outcome of the planning process with the goal of operationalising strategic plans, creating value and shaping the future. As a result of planning and budgeting, information sharing and communication throughout the organisation is top-down, bottom-up and sideways. Before formalising the budget, organisations may test a number of courses of action through the planning processes. Budgets are used to help price business strategies. At times, trade-offs must be made between different courses of action and testing of alternative courses of action will contribute to the organisation's strategic success. Once a course of action is adopted, planning will contribute to the adoption of the final budget to guide the organisation's activities.

Once the strategic plan (budget) is in place it can be used as a tool to evaluate performance. Sometimes multiple budgets can be prepared that identify best, worst and most likely scenarios. Actual results can be compared for deviations from desired performance. Contingencies can be made for worst-case scenarios. Alternatively, budgets can be linked to incentives, with targets and benchmarks set to motivate employees for both short- and long-term activities. This facilitating role of budgeting is explored in more detail in later chapters.

It is important to understand that while budgets play multiple roles, there is also a politics of planning that needs to be considered. Sometimes the political nature of budgets leads to them being viewed as 'fixed contracts' that could result in game playing and empire building. These factors need to be carefully considered.

5.1 The role of planning and budgeting for improved performance and value creation: testing alternative actions

LEARNING OBJECTIVE 5.1 Communicate the role of planning and budgeting for improved profit performance and value creation.

In this chapter, we consider the concept of planning from a strategic perspective to prepare for an understanding of the technical aspects of annual budget preparation and how these budgets might be used for planning and control.

Organisations are continually confronted with resource allocation decisions. Given the significant financial impacts of certain decisions, a deeper understanding of the implications of the planning and budgeting process is required, particularly where there are choices in relation to alternative courses of action. For example, when organisations determine which product or service to emphasise they must also consider the likely financial and non-financial impacts of alternative decisions. The impacts must be considered not only in terms of the organisation's own production or service provision, but also strategically in relation to competitor and market-based responses.

Even planning and budgeting in public sector organisations, such as hospitals, can be substantially impacted by strategic decision making. The provision of healthcare facilities is an important part of long-term government plans, which might be politically motivated. For example, women's and children's hospital facilities might be built to meet population growth. New heart hospitals or upgraded cancer treatment centres might be a result of community lobbying. This kind of analysis falls under the umbrella of what we might term planning and budgeting for strategic success, or strategic budgeting. Once the long-term decision has been made as to the course of action to be pursued, then annual budgets can be put into motion.

5.2 Impact of likely actions on profit, assets and cash flow management

LEARNING OBJECTIVE 5.2 Apply the planning and budgeting process to consider the impact of alternative courses of action on profit, assets and cash flow.

In the planning process, we commonly consider the impact of alternative courses of action on key financial variables. While non-financial considerations are equally important in any final decision, they somehow need to be converted or evaluated in terms of the final financial impacts of **strategic budgeting**.

For each alternative course of action, we need to consider the effect on each of the variables that impact on the financial position of the organisation. Moreover, the links between the key variables in each of the budgeted financial statements are critical. These may be represented in terms of the strategic budgeting cycle, whereby each of the interlinking components demonstrates the relationship between the level of profits generated, the level of cash available to support the strategy, and the extent to which assets generate returns to shareholders and for company growth. This is illustrated in figure 5.1, where we refer to the income cycle (corresponding to the statement of profit or loss), cash cycle (corresponding to the cash flow statement) and assets cycle (corresponding to the statement of financial position and shareholder returns).

Figure 5.2 summarises the key items of interest in strategic planning analysis. You will notice from figures 5.1 and 5.2 that the strategic budgeting emphasis is best considered in the context of organisational strategy.

Sales/revenue estimation

In any planning exercise, the sales or revenue estimation is the key variable. It sets the level of activity and is linked to other key variables such as cash receipts in the cash plan. How sales/revenue is estimated will vary between organisations but will commonly involve a mixture of:
* existing and past history of sales/revenue and product/service mix
* the nature of sales initiatives and impacts, for example, changed product/service offerings, changed mix emphasis, and the likely reaction of competitors
* consideration of the external market through competitor analysis
* review of macroeconomic conditions.

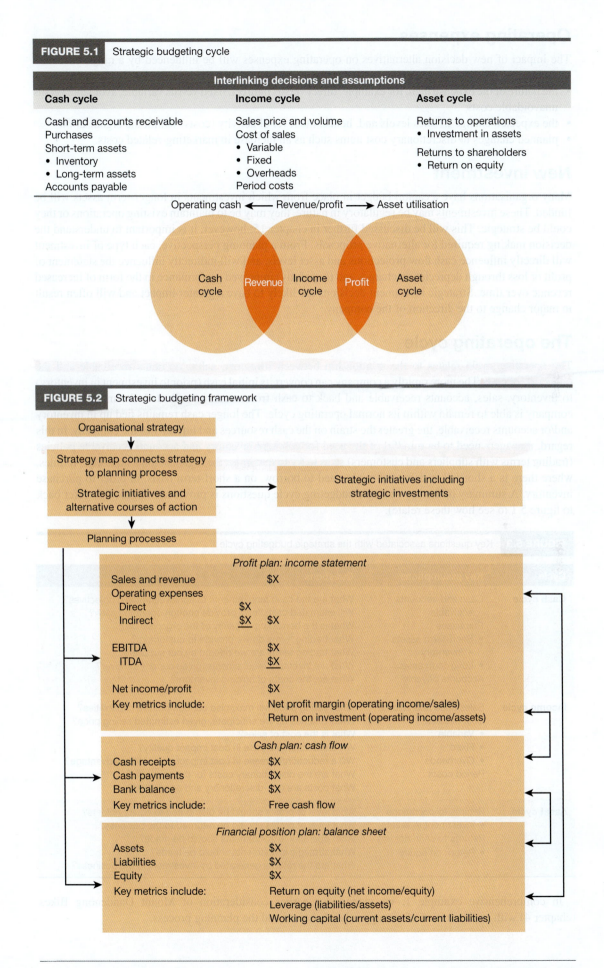

FIGURE 5.1 Strategic budgeting cycle

Interlinking decisions and assumptions

Cash cycle	Income cycle	Asset cycle
Cash and accounts receivable	Sales price and volume	Returns to operations
Purchases	Cost of sales	• Investment in assets
Short-term assets	• Variable	
• Inventory	• Fixed	Returns to shareholders
• Long-term assets	• Overheads	• Return on equity
Accounts payable	Period costs	

Operating cash ← Revenue/profit → Asset utilisation

Cash cycle — Revenue — Income cycle — Profit — Asset cycle

FIGURE 5.2 Strategic budgeting framework

Organisational strategy

Strategy map connects strategy to planning process

Strategic initiatives and alternative courses of action

→ Strategic initiatives including strategic investments

Planning processes

Profit plan: income statement

Sales and revenue		$X
Operating expenses		
Direct	$X	
Indirect	$X	$X
EBITDA		$X
ITDA		$X
Net income/profit		$X
Key metrics include:		Net profit margin (operating income/sales)
		Return on investment (operating income/assets)

Cash plan: cash flow

Cash receipts	$X
Cash payments	$X
Bank balance	$X
Key metrics include:	Free cash flow

Financial position plan: balance sheet

Assets	$X
Liabilities	$X
Equity	$X
Key metrics include:	Return on equity (net income/equity)
	Leverage (liabilities/assets)
	Working capital (current assets/current liabilities)

Operating expenses

The impact of new decision alternatives on operating expenses will be influenced by a range of factors including:

- the nature of the expense item, for example, direct versus indirect, fixed versus variable, avoidable versus unavoidable costs
- the expected change in sales levels and, hence, the level of activity (costs) within the organisation
- planned changes to discretionary cost items such as an increase in marketing-related costs.

New investment

Many organisations have a capital budget in place from which investments in longer-term assets will be funded. These investments may be regulatory in nature, they may be to maintain existing operations or they could be strategic. This will be discussed further in chapter 15; however, it is important to understand the decision making required for alternative proposals. From a planning perspective, each type of investment will directly influence cash flow projections and asset levels, and will indirectly influence the statement of profit or loss through depreciation charges and (hopefully) improved performance in the form of increased revenue over time. Strategic investment decisions are likely to have a greater impact and will often result in major change to the direction of the company.

The operating cycle

The operating cycle relates to the relationship between inventory, sales, accounts receivable and the collection of cash. The more rapidly a company can convert its initial cash (prior to investment in inventory) to inventory, sales, accounts receivable and back to cash from accounts collected, the more liquid the company is able to remain within its normal operating cycle. The longer cash remains tied up in inventory and/or accounts receivable, the greater the strain on the cash resources and liquidity of the company. In this regard, managers need to be mindful of the need for coherent inventory and accounts receivable policies (trading terms with suppliers and customers) so as to try to maximise the organisation's liquidity. At times, where there is a shortfall, a company might need to borrow, on a short-term basis, in order to purchase inventory. A summary of the key strategic budgeting cycle questions is provided in figure 5.3 (refer back to figure 5.1 to see how these relate).

FIGURE 5.3	Key questions associated with the strategic budgeting cycle	
Cycle	**Key assumptions**	**Questions**
Cash cycle	Cash and accounts receivable Purchases • Short-term assets – Inventory • Long-term assets Accounts payable	What are the cash requirements to achieve strategic objectives? Will estimated cash flows provide enough operating cash? What is the borrowing capacity of the organisation? What trading terms do we provide to customers? What trading terms are we offered by our suppliers? What are inventory requirements, given current turnover? What are the costs of holding inventory?
Income cycle	Sales price and volume Cost of sales • Variable • Fixed • Overheads Period costs	What selling price will maximise our competitive capabilities? What volumes do we anticipate, given estimated selling price? What is the cost of sales? Will a reduction/increase in cost impact quality? Will a reduction/increase in cost impact competitive advantage? What are the discretionary costs for the company? What costs are non-discretionary and committed?
Asset cycle	Returns to operations • Investment in assets Returns to shareholders • Return on equity	What level of profits should be distributed to equity holders? What level of profits should be returned to the business? What operational investments should be made? What strategic investments should be made? What are the returns generated by investment in the business?

In comprehensive example 1, we extend our earlier consideration of Mount Dandenong Bikes (chapter 4) with an illustration of strategy-related choices and the planning process.

Mount Dandenong Bikes

Mount Dandenong Bikes is a manufacturer of sturdy mountain bikes for intermediate-level bikers. The budgeted statement of profit or loss (figure 5.4), cash flows (figure 5.5) and financing budget (figure 5.6) are presented to assist decision making, particularly in the consideration of alternative courses of action.

FIGURE 5.4	Budgeted statement of profit or loss for Mount Dandenong Bikes

Statement of profit or loss

Revenues (revenue budget)		$80 000 000
Cost of sales (cost of sales budget)		45 475 000
Gross margin		34 525 000
Operating costs (support department budgets):		
Administration	$16 478 215	
Marketing	9 886 929	
Distribution	4 943 465	
Customer service	1 647 821	
Total operating costs		32 956 430
Operating income		1 568 570
Income taxes ($1 568 570 × 30%)		470 571
Net income		$ 1 097 999

FIGURE 5.5	Summary of cash receipts and disbursements for Mount Dandenong Bikes

Cash flows

	Total
Cash receipts:	
Revenues	$76 666 667
Cash disbursements:	
Direct materials purchases	13 812 500
Direct labour costs	4 014 750
Variable overhead costs:	
Supplies	2 020 000
Indirect labour	3 787 500
Maintenance	1 010 000
Miscellaneous	757 500
Fixed overhead costs:	
Property taxes	1 010 000
Insurance	1 414 000
Plant supervision	5 050 000
Fringe benefits	7 070 000
Miscellaneous	1 616 000
Support department costs	32 956 430
Purchase of equipment	8 000 000
Total disbursements	82 518 680
Excess receipts (disbursements)	$ (5 852 013)

Financing budget

	First	Second	Third	Fourth
			Quarter	
Beginning balance, cash and short-term investments	$ 9 000 000	$ 10 002 158	$ 200 000	$ 200 000
Excess receipts (disbursements)	1 002 158	(11 138 900)	(3 340 900)	7 625 629
Line of credit:				
Borrowings		1 336 742	3 360 951	
Interest on borrowings			(20 051)	(70 465)
Repayments				(4 697 693)
Ending balance, cash and short-term investments	$10 002 158	$ 200 000	$ 200 000	$ 3 057 471

Senior management at Mount Dandenong Bikes has been exploring different options for expanding the business.

- Option 1 is to introduce bike tours through the Dandenong Ranges and surrounding region. The following estimates have been provided by senior management.

Outlay cost for support truck including modifications	$ 62 000
Additional annual revenue	$250 000
Key incremental cost changes are:	
Administration (which is fixed) expected to increase by	$200 000
Marketing costs (mostly fixed) to increase by	$300 000
Labour to conduct each tour and other variable costs	25% of additional annual revenue

- Option 2 is to move into the manufacture of premium brand road bikes. Senior management has made the following estimates.

Additional annual revenue	$1 860 000
Cost of sales is expected to be around 58% overall, which is slightly higher than the mountain bikes only. This is caused by the higher-quality parts and the intense competition in the industry.	
Distribution costs to increase by 10%	
Marketing costs to increase by 5%	
Administration costs to increase by 2%	

For each of these options senior management acknowledges the importance of conducting capital investment analysis (see chapter 15) to evaluate the long-term impact of any investment in long-term assets. They are particularly concerned about the impact of different courses of action on the key financial statements and key broad-based performance metrics of Mount Dandenong Bikes.

Using financial statements prepared in budget form for Mount Dandenong Bikes, we will illustrate the impact of the two options being considered by senior management on profit performance and key metrics. Note that current total asset values equal $14 957 471 and senior management has set targets of 2.5 per cent for profit margin and 12.5 per cent for return on investment (ROI). The statement of profit or loss and key metrics under options 1 and 2 are shown in figures 5.7 and 5.8 respectively.

FIGURE 5.7   Statement of profit or loss and metrics option 1

Statement of profit or loss

	$	$
Revenue		82 500 000
Cost of sales		45 475 000
Gross margin		37 025 000
Operating costs		
Tour labour and extra variable costs	625 000	
Administration	16 678 215	

	$	$
Marketing	10 186 929	
Distribution	4 943 465	
Customer service	1 647 821	34 081 430
Operating income		2 943 570
Income taxes		883 071
Net income after tax		2 060 499
Key metrics		
Profit margin		0.03568
ROI		0.196796
Additional revenue	2 500 000	

FIGURE 5.8 Statement of profit or loss and metrics option 2

Statement of profit or loss		
	$	$
Revenue		81 860 000
Cost of sales		47 478 800
Gross margin		34 381 200
Operating costs		
Administration	16 807 779	
Marketing	10 381 275	
Distribution	5 437 812	
Customer service	1 647 821	34 274 687
Operating income		106 513
Income taxes		31 954
Net income after tax		74 559
Key metrics		
Profit margin		0.001301
ROI		0.007121
Additional revenue	1 860 000	

The objective of this planning exercise is to consider the implications of the alternative actions on key financial parameters; in this case, the statement of profit or loss and two key financial ratios. Of course, other factors would be considered in deciding which (if any) course of action to pursue.

We can see that option 1 is most likely to meet the financial targets relating to the statement of profit or loss. Of course, this option does require a capital investment in the form of a new truck. No such up-front investment is required in option 2. Moreover, this relatively simple analysis would serve as an input into the decision-making process. As such, we would expect additional information — both quantitative and qualitative — to be influential in the decision.

5.3 Planning in cost centres

LEARNING OBJECTIVE 5.3 Identify the various planning and budgeting approaches used in cost centres.

Cost centres are those organisational units where 'cost' is the focus. In cost centres, the manager is deemed responsible, and often evaluated on the management of the costs of the work unit. For example, most support departments like accounting, research and development (R&D) and human resources (HR) are classified as cost centres. In addition, operating units such as production plants might also be classified as cost centres.

Depending on the ease of measuring outputs, or otherwise, cost centres are commonly classified as 'engineered' cost centres or 'discretionary' cost centres (see chapter 18). In *engineered* cost centres, there is a relationship between inputs and outputs that is readily measurable. Therefore, there is a standard against which actual performance can be measured, which forms part of the budgeting process. Any variances against the budgeted measure are identified and managed accordingly. The engineered cost centre environment is more suitable for manufacturing departments where standard products are produced, or for service departments where repetitive activities, such as processing bank loans, are performed. In a production plant, once output is estimated, many of the costs relating to the plant can be estimated (and allocated to products) due to the links between output and the input of resources. However, this is more challenging with *discretionary* cost centres where it is difficult to identify the relationship between inputs and outputs. We will now consider this issue in more detail.

Planning for discretionary cost centres is not always easy, particularly where the organisational production output (service or product) is difficult to link to the individual cost centre. How do we know how much we should spend in areas like HR, advertising, or R&D in instances where activities are future focused and results are based on strategic, long-range plans? For example, in pharmaceutical R&D units (which are commonly classified as discretionary cost centres), the relationship between the input costs of a scientist's innovative research activities and output of new product development and/or total organisational output is often difficult to determine. The scientist's work can result in months or even years of product development, testing and clinical trials before a drug even faces regulatory drug approval for sale. How can organisations overcome this issue in funding resources?

In many countries, including Australia and New Zealand, traditionally governments have funded public hospitals. In Australia, the government has attempted to 'engineer' previously discretionary cost centres by creating a direct relationship between funding for clinical activities performed. However, for many public services or functions this is not possible. Much of the work undertaken by government organisations such as those responsible for environmental conservation or policing is discretionary in nature — difficult to define in advance and directly attribute to outputs delivered or results achieved. In particular, funding provided for the military is mostly associated with ensuring that the *capacity* is maintained to respond as and when necessary.

Another way to assist the planning process is **incremental budgeting**. This involves making some alteration to the expenditure in the cost centre from the previous year, but does little to enhance accountability. That is, adding an adjustment to increase last year's budget as a way of planning for the next period discourages managers from seeking ways to use the organisation's resources more efficiently and effectively. To overcome this, some company policies recommend departments lose authority over unspent budgeted costs and receive lower future funds. However, this policy, in turn, encourages department managers to spend all of their budgeted funds to avoid future cutbacks — planning this year's expenditure based solely on last year's expenditure is likely to result in waste and dysfunctional practices.

5.4 Contemporary approaches to budgeting

LEARNING OBJECTIVE 5.4 Compare traditional and contemporary approaches to budgeting.

There are other approaches to incremental and engineered budgeting, including program budgeting, zero-based budgeting, rolling budgeting, activity-based budgeting and kaizen budgeting. We will now discuss each in turn.

Program budgeting

Program budgeting requires the cost centre to plan its expenditure specifically around the programs or projects conducted by the cost centre. This results in a justification for expenditure on the basis of the programs or projects to be conducted. Program budgeting was originally developed in government departments in the public sector as a means of enhancing expenditure accountability. Instead of focusing on budget line items and using an incremental budgeting approach by adjusting last year's expenditure, program budgeting:
- focuses on expenditure relating to the specific programs of the cost centre
- requires justification for the expenditure for each program, which can be linked to the objectives of the program.

For example, a training department may plan to run a range of different courses over the next 12 months. Each of these is able to be identified as a discrete program and an estimate can be made of the expected expenditure required to conduct each. The expected outcomes from each program can be considered at the planning stage; one of the key issues in discretionary cost centres is that planning and control essentially takes place at the same time during the planning process.

Zero-based budgeting

To reduce problems associated with incremental budgeting, some organisations adopt a planning approach known as **zero-based budgeting**. Under this approach, managers are required to justify proposed budgetary expenditure as if no information about budgets or costs from prior budget cycles was available. This system of building budgets from scratch encourages managers to cut costs and focus on desired outcomes. As a result, there is often reduced wastage, greater performance of value-adding activities and a beneficial focus on quality improvement and associated revenue generation.

Zero-based budgeting (figure 5.9) has largely been used in large non-profit and public sector organisations to carefully manage funding the allocation of funds to the cost centre. Each activity is carefully defined, and costs are questioned and justified by the manager before being allocated. There is no room for budgetary slack and/or waste. One major disadvantage of zero-based budgeting is that it is time consuming, and frequently, the benefits of this approach may not be worth the extra time invested. Until recently, zero-based budgeting was not widely used in for-profit organisations because of these limitations on management time. However, as a result of economic or financial downturns and the need for budgetary overhauls, this approach has been used by investors and venture capitalists to revive for-profit organisations that have grown large and burdensome. Zero-based budgeting has also been used to re-engineer companies in the midst of revolutionary technological change to re-engineer activities and associated costs.

The founders of 3G, an investment company, were one of the early leaders to bring zero-based budgeting back into vogue. The 3G management team have used zero-based budgeting to revamp brands and slash costs in their largest companies such as AB InBev, a beer giant, and Kraft Heinz, a food company. While this approach taken by 3G has previously been admired by co-investor partner, Warren Buffett, the longer term sustainable strategic benefit is questionable. That is, the share price for AB InBev and Kraft has fallen below rivals, who have narrowed the gap by following with similar zero-based accounting techniques. Zero-based budgeting appears to be the new norm for management.[1]

FIGURE 5.9 Application of zero-based budgeting and lean management[2]

3G Capital Partners spend $49 million to purchase and merge Kraft Foods Group Inc. with its already-owned H.J. Heinz Company to create the world's fifth-largest food and beverage company. Having previously implemented zero-based budgeting successfully across all its other companies, the 3G partners used this approach with the Kraft–Heinz merger to slash costs. Kraft managers were asked to focus on every minute detail of the business and justify every routine expense.

As reported by the *Wall Street Journal* the zero-based budgeting accounting technique has led to sweeping cost cuts at 3G's companies, 'from eliminating hundreds of management jobs to jettisoning corporate jets and requiring employees to get permission to make colour photocopies'. 3G's zero-based budgeting approach has prompted other companies in the food and beverage industry to follow suit, 'in part out of fear that they, too, could become targets of activist investors or stronger rivals', as activist investors can see the budgetary slack that has crept into the industry making large companies like Kraft a target for these types of investors. Zero-based budgeting, although an old technique, is growing in popularity, with adopters such as Coca-Cola Co, Mondelez International and Campbell Soup Co. making it 'a symbol of the new reality for U. S. business'. The overall aim of zero-based budgeting is to improve shareholder returns. It also tends to make employees' work more rigorous or even ruthless.

Not just a part of the food and beverage sector, zero-based budgeting is being adopted in other industries in efforts to determine the necessity of each expense item. The pharmaceutical industry, where research and development expenses are high, is a prime example.

Rolling budgeting

The business environment has become increasingly dynamic, requiring quick managerial response to change. A **rolling budget** is prepared monthly or quarterly and reflects planning changes, often through the next 12 to 18 months. Many entities use rolling budgets because they incorporate more current information than either static or flexible budgets. Rolling budgets reflect the most recent results and also incorporate significant changes in business strategy, operating plans and the economy. With current information at hand, the managers can quickly increase or decrease costs and inventory levels during economic upturns or downturns. In turn, production can probably be resumed or expanded quickly when the economy picks up.

As an example, Cisco Systems, a provider of hardware, software and consulting services, uses a budgeting system that combines traditional budgeting with a rolling budget that includes information from an internet-based ordering system. The system provides real-time volume data to update forecasts. As a result, Cisco's managers can make quick changes in operations during downturns. Each year, an annual plan is established based on a combination of top-down management guidance and bottom-up input from operational managers. This budget is then updated quarterly, and any changes are translated into budget targets for future periods.[3]

Activity-based budgeting

Traditional budget models are developed around a few cost drivers that are primarily output based. **Activity-based budgeting** (ABB) uses activity cost pools and their related cost drivers to anticipate the costs for individual activities. A budget is developed for each activity in an entity's activity-based system. For example, assume Mount Dandenong Bikes, discussed in comprehensive example 1, separates its production costs into direct materials, direct labour, and variable and fixed overhead. If the entity was then to switch to ABB it would look at its key product cost drivers, which might include frame assembly, wheel attachment, painting, accessory attachment, inspection and packing. The budget would then be structured based on these activities and allow the identification of resource consumption for each activity.

Kaizen budgeting

Kaizen costing is a system developed in Japan and used for products that tend to have decreasing prices or increasing quality across time, such as home entertainment centres, mobile phones and computers. **Kaizen budgets** set targeted cost reductions across time, anticipating market price reductions across the life of a product. In addition to cost reductions, quality improvements are also targeted. When kaizen budgeting is performed, cost reduction and quality improvement goals are explicitly embedded in the budgets. For example, an entity could budget an increase in the quality of components. If the costs of quality improvements are less than the savings from reduced labour and cycle time, overall costs are reduced.

5.5 The behavioural implications of budgeting

LEARNING OBJECTIVE 5.5 Reflect on the behavioural implications of budgeting.

As highlighted in the previous discussion, budgeting in organisations is not always as straightforward as it seems. It can be a time consuming and problematic process. Dysfunctional behaviour is not only limited to budgeting in discretionary cost centres. Issues of power struggles, blame shifting and game playing frequently occur in all planning processes as managers and employees compete with each other for a share of the organisation's scarce resources. Allocation of resources becomes a primary concern, particularly when power is attributed based on the extent of resources under a manager's control.

When resources are shared among divisions or other organisational groupings, how should the allocation method be decided? Setting priorities often becomes a political activity as managers associate resources under their control with power and status. A political approach to budgeting could be viewed as a personal threat; a game between leaders and would-be-leaders. An overly conservative approach to budgeting could be seen as building in slack to achieve performance targets (and potential bonus payments). An easily achievable budget could be viewed as demotivating, and vice versa. Sometimes senior managers hold back resources when budgeting for their subordinates, aiming to increase subordinate motivation or build in a buffer for unforeseen circumstances.

Budgets become a template for organisational activity. A question for most organisations is how flexible is the template or how flexible should the budget process be? For example, once the budget is set, should it be deviated from? Some managers would argue that it is vital to stick to the planned budget once it has been set. For them, it is like a contract between the manager and employee or the owner and agent. If, for example, an employee's bonus is structured around budget achievement, what would happen if the budget was suddenly changed so the employee could no longer meet or beat the budget? They may end up with a lower bonus or no bonus at all. Is this fair? Frequently changing goalposts could impact on employee morale. It may also have implications for the budgeting process itself: Will employees place as much importance or credibility on the budget and budgeting process if they know it is frequently deviated from?

If, on the other hand, the budget becomes unachievable because of reasons beyond a manager's control, it may also negatively impact on morale. For example, budgets were severely affected during the global financial crisis. Decisions about management rewards linked to budgets in economic downturns can be highly emotive and political topics, particularly when shareholder wealth may have been affected. Yet, in these conditions, management efforts may have increased substantially.

As highlighted, budgets are not always as straightforward as they are made out to be. It is often very hard to extricate budgets from performance evaluation and rewards. Figure 5.10 provides a summary of key budgeting issues faced by contemporary organisations.

| FIGURE 5.10 | Key budgeting issues |

Politics, empire building and game playing
- Budgetary slack — distortion of inputs for establishment of achievable targets
- Budgetary mismanagement — not achieving above budget if only meeting budget is rewarded
- Budget as a weapon — blame shifting to others if budget is not achieved

Ability for the budget to be achieved and/or dynamic
- Lack of flexibility in administration
- Underlying assumptions might vary from actual events

Lack of participation in budgeting process

Excessive reliance on budgets
- Budget achievement does not necessarily mean goal achievement
- Tendency towards meeting budget at any cost with minimal consideration for long-term goals
- Minimal consideration for impacts on other parts of the organisation
- Excessive focus on cost reduction rather than value creation (inputs rather than outcomes)
- A compromise of quality, customer service, profitability and long-run performance

How might organisations address these issues? Some possible solutions include giving priority to planning items associated with strategy achievement. In discretionary cost centres, senior managers should focus on achievement of aggregated outcomes rather than on specific line items or cost constraints. Budgets should be set in ways that avoid an 'if it's not in the budget' mentality. It is also important to foster cooperation rather than competition among employees. That is, senior management should try to link budgets horizontally (to prevent a silo mentality) and involve participation on an organisation-wide basis. The illustrative example in figure 5.11 shows a focus on outcomes that is intended to encourage a more participatory approach to budgeting.

For improved transparency and involvement in budget setting, the process might include joint determination of the budget allocation formula. It might involve allocating resources to a reserve fund for contingency purposes. Alternatively, it might involve using multiple budgets; for example, worst-case, best-case and most-likely case budgetary outcomes could be accounted for. In a transparent planning process, managers ensure their subordinates are aware of the priority on flexibility or for occasional budget revision when necessary. Nevertheless, the tightly entwined links between budget achievement and rewards should not be forgotten. Senior management's budget decisions should not, where possible, demotivate employees or provide them with a constantly moving target.

| FIGURE 5.11 | A participative approach to budgeting[4] |

In New Zealand, the justice sector includes the Attorney–General, the Department of Corrections, the Courts, the Ministry of Justice, the Police and the Serious Fraud Office, which together have a total operating budget of $3.8 billion. That funding is divided into the individual budgets for which each of those agencies is individually responsible. In 2012 they created the Justice Sector Fund (JSF) to enable shared savings across the sector and provide financial flexibility so that savings from one agency can be used to fund another agency's initiatives. By 2017–18, a total of $273 million of savings was reallocated to 66 different initiatives. These included activities to improve public and prisoner safety, and reintegration programs for people released from prison.

The savings will only be allocated to initiatives that contribute to reducing crime and reoffending, and assist the sector to become more modern and cost effective. The challenging goals that the sector was faced with included reducing the overall crime rate by 15 per cent and, more specifically, reducing violent crime by 20 per cent, youth crime by 25 per cent and the rate of reoffending by 25 per cent. In response

▶

to these challenges, the chief executives of the justice sector agencies set up a Sector Leadership Board to drive the initiatives that were required to meet those goals and which could not be managed within the operations and budgets of the individual agencies acting alone.

If the initiatives are shown to be effective, they will be able to obtain long-term funding. This approach to budgeting was made possible by a common vision and set of goals and a willingness among the chief executives to not seek to control and retain funding within individual agency silos.

It has been argued that, in some situations, budgets should be abandoned altogether. The use of rolling budgets as described previously is one move away from traditional budgeting processes. In the following section we consider another alternative, possibly more radical, approach referred to as Beyond Budgeting.

5.6 Beyond Budgeting[5]

LEARNING OBJECTIVE 5.6 Critique the Beyond Budgeting approach to management control.

Beyond Budgeting offers a contemporary management model based on principles that encourage employee empowerment. The core of the Beyond Budgeting movement rests with extreme decentralisation of decision making, with key performance management structured as a form of benchmarking referred to as 'relative' performance evaluation. Annual planning is replaced with adaptive and evolved orientation using rolling forecasts.

One of the most important underlying assumptions of the Beyond Budgeting approach is the assumption that every day is different. With 'different weather tomorrow', the Beyond Budgeting argument is that a fixed budget must be risky, even dangerous, as it is based on assumptions that have not been foreseen. The approach asks, 'How can you foresee something for which you have no experience?' In general, Beyond Budgeting advocates consider traditional 'fixed' contract budgets to be dysfunctional and argue that they should be eliminated. Instead of taking a 'command and control' approach to budgeting they advocate an open and collaboratively dynamic environment whereby employees are motivated towards continuous improvement and are readily equipped with the skills and resources to adapt to changing conditions.

Table 5.1 outlines the principles on which the Beyond Budgeting model is based.[6] In this table, the Beyond Budgeting approach is contrasted with issues associated with traditional budgetary control.

TABLE 5.1   The 12 principles of the Beyond Budgeting model

	Principles	Do this (Beyond Budgeting model)	Not that (budgetary control model)
Leadership-culture principles	Customer focus	Focus everyone on improving customer outcomes	Achieve vertically negotiated targets
	Accountability	Create a network of teams accountable for results	Use centralised hierarchies
	Work environment	Champion success as winning in the marketplace	Take a contractual approach
	Performance	Give teams the freedom and capability to act	Adhere to fixed plans
	Governance	Base governance on clear goals, values and boundaries	Base governance on detailed rules and budgets
	Transparency	Promote open and shared environment	Restrict access to 'need to know'
Management-process principles	Target setting	Set aspirational goals for continuous relative improvement	Use fixed annual targets

Rewards	Reward shared success based on relative performance	Reward based on meeting fixed targets
Planning	Make planning a continuous and inclusive process	Make planning a top-down, annual event
Controls	Base controls on relative performance indicators and trends	Measure variances against a fixed plan
Resources	Make resources available as needed	Use annual budget allocations
Coordination	Coordinate cross company interactions dynamically	Use annual planning cycles

Source: Beyond Budgeting.

Beyond Budgeting in practice: managing without budgets

The most cited exemplar of Beyond Budgeting can be found at Svenska Handelsbanken, a national bank of Sweden.[7] At Handelsbanken, it was shown that a more decentralised model of management control allowed the bank to be successfully managed *without* budgets for several years through varying economic highs and lows. The key to managing successfully without budgets was linked to radical decentralisation and accountability with minimal influence from centralised functions. Transparent accounting and reward systems with relative performance evaluation are extremely important to the Beyond Budgeting movement. Most importantly, managing without budgets relies heavily on high levels of trust among employees with a strong commitment to customer focus.

Radical decentralisation and accountability

Radical decentralisation requires authority to be devolved through the hierarchical layers to lower level branches, teams and individual employees. Radical decentralisation gives individuals autonomy and allows for quick customer response. Small, devolved work teams are expected to contribute to strategic operational planning. They are often given profit responsibility, with the team or branch manager having ultimate responsibility for financial results.

With responsibility comes strategic decision-making power. Decision making might include selecting the best product or service offerings to suit the local region, or which customers to acquire (or eliminate). Local teams are given authority to invest, set prices and offer discounts. They could also be in charge of their own marketing and advertising. The rationale for devolving these frequently centralised services is to allow innovation and creativity and prevent central decisions influencing operational planning.

Where it is not seen as an impediment to customer response and innovation, some centralised functions such as large capital investments are maintained. Support units (legal, financial, HR, information technology and operations) are also maintained. These support units are viewed as the sellers of a service and disciplined to create downward pressure on costs and increased responsiveness. 'Service agreements' negotiated between sellers (support units) and buyers (teams or branches) are based on standard prices (for example, per hour of service utilised). However, to avoid transfer-pricing issues such as dysfunctional game playing, no internal mark-up is included in the price (that is, support units show zero profit with corporate headquarters absorbing any over- or under-allocations).

Employees are held strictly accountable for their performance in executing the team plan. In general, it is expected that each member contributes to profit generation. At the same time, employees are only held accountable for items and costs under their direct/indirect influence. In the Handelsbanken case, there was a strong philosophy based on thrift. Some central activities were forbidden, including centralised memos, instructions or directives. Instead, examples were to be set via coaching. Monthly meetings of regional managers were held for consensus on current issues and the managing director spent two days each year with each region and its branches to challenge their assumptions and operational plans; hear views on the market, customers and competitors; and learn their aims for setting 'stretch' goals.

Accounting and reward systems

Beyond Budgeting proponents argue that the key to instilling accountability originates from the belief that employees enjoy contributing to the organisation; they take pride in their work, are motivated, and innovate to the best of their capabilities. In return for employee dedication, the Beyond Budgeting philosophy points to the need for transparency: organisations should develop and use performance indicators that are widely accepted and trusted by employees.

As shareholder value is argued to be built on happy, autonomous employees, in general, bonuses are not required to motivate the performance of the majority of employees. Instead, employees are paid a salary at a rate considered to be adequate compensation relative to the role they perform. In the Handelsbanken case, the employer contributed generously to an employee pension plan and invited *all* employees to be involved in a performance-based profit-sharing system, which was designed to encourage a team-based, goal-congruent approach to organisational success.

For full transparency, accounting systems must provide consistent and reliable information, which is quickly and easily accessible by all levels of employees throughout the organisation. There must be:

- timely reporting of information
- performance reports that only measure what people can influence
- information reflecting critical performance variables linked to strategy (goal congruence); that is, information on customer acquisitions, customer defections, customer profitability and costs/income
- reporting of trends (to highlight impending problems)
- information about charges from services utilised (that is, no arbitrary allocations).

The accounting systems should provide actual results quickly so that local statements of profit or loss (or statements of comprehensive income) and statements of financial position (also called balance sheets) can be reviewed daily. Only a few simple measures are reported monthly. These could include return on equity (ROE), cost to income ratio, profit per employee and total profitability, rolling averages, customer profitability for medium and large customers, customer satisfaction, transaction volumes, productivity measures, customer acquisitions, customer defections, and level of customer discounts granted.

In the Handelsbanken case, the accounting system information was designed to motivate employees only towards the critical performance variables. Other information such as rolling cash forecasts were prepared, but did not influence the daily decisions of lower level employees. That is, they were prepared only quarterly, were given low visibility, and were used by the CEO and vice-president of finance for only signalling likely quarterly results and cash flow implications, which helped in planning investment and liquidity requirements. The costs of preparing these rolling cash forecasts were minimal (one-quarter of one staff member's salary per year).

Relative performance evaluation

Relative performance data or performance measured *relative* to peer performance (peer may mean an individual, team, branch or an organisation) also forms an important part of the Beyond Budgeting philosophy. Relative performance measurement relies on direct comparison with peers at varying layers throughout the radically decentralised organisation, thereby preventing performance being hidden or distorted by summarised accounting system data.

Employee evaluation is based on the level of the employee's commitment towards customers. Customer intimacy is fostered and made possible by selective recruitment of employees that are considered capable, committed and willing to be involved. The ability of employees to 'fit' in the organisation is an important part of the Beyond Budgeting customer intimacy philosophy. This is reinforced by encouraging employees to be actively involved in setting their own targets or goals and continuously improving based on their capabilities in building strong customer relationships.

In the Handelsbanken case, relative performance evaluation meant that branches, regions and the overall bank were compared to relevant banks using ROE and related measures. Regional comparisons were made with ROE and cost to income. At branch level, a handicapping system was used to foster fair competition among peers. Branch comparisons were made with cost to income, profit per employee and total profit measures. Awards were presented to the best teams to continually motivate employees. We will explore the issue of relative performance evaluation as part of incentive plans in chapter 20.

SUMMARY

5.1 Communicate the role of planning and budgeting for improved profit performance and value creation.

- Likely financial and non-financial impacts of alternative decisions
- Impacts of the organisation's own production or service provision and strategically in relation to competitor and market-based responses
- Planning and budgeting for strategic success, or strategic budgeting
- Once the decision has been made as to the course of action to be pursued, annual budgets can be put into motion

5.2 Apply the planning and budgeting process to consider the impact of alternative courses of action on profit, assets and cash flow.

- Sales/revenue estimation
- Operating expenses
- New investment
- The operating cycle

5.3 Identify the various planning and budgeting approaches used in cost centres.

- Cost centres are organisational units where 'cost' is the focus
- Engineered cost centres, where there is a relationship between inputs and output, there is a standard against which actual performance can be measured
- More challenging with discretionary cost centres, where it is difficult to identify the relationship between inputs and outputs, and so different approaches are necessary
- Incremental budgeting involves making some alteration to the expenditure in the cost or responsibility centre from the previous year

5.4 Compare traditional and contemporary approaches to budgeting.

- Program budgeting
- Zero-based budgeting
- Rolling budgeting
- Activity-based budgeting
- Kaizen budgeting

5.5 Reflect on the behavioural implications of budgeting.

- Politics, empire building and game playing
- Ability for the budget to be achieved and/or dynamic
- Lack of participation in budgeting process
- Excessive reliance on budgets

5.6 Critique the Beyond Budgeting approach to management control.

- Beyond Budgeting in practice: managing without budgets
- Radical decentralisation and accountability
- Accounting and reward systems
- Relative performance evaluation

KEY TERMS

activity-based budgeting A budgeting process that uses activity cost pools and their related cost drivers to anticipate the costs for individual activities. A budget is developed for each activity in an entity's activity-based system.

incremental budgeting A budgeting approach that requires some alteration to the expenditure budget for the cost centre from the previous year.

kaizen budgeting Budgeting that sets targeted cost reductions across time, anticipating market price reductions across the life of a product.

program budgeting Budgeting that requires the cost centre to plan its expenditure specifically around the programs or projects conducted by the cost centre.

rolling budget A budget that is prepared monthly or quarterly and reflects planning changes, often through the next 12 to 18 months. Often reflects the most recent results and incorporates significant changes in business strategy, operating plans and the economy.

strategic budgeting The process of considering alternative courses of action on profit, assets and cash flow management.

zero-based budgeting A budgeting process in which managers justify budget amounts as if no information about budgets or costs from prior budget cycles was available.

SELF-STUDY PROBLEMS

SELF-STUDY PROBLEM 1 Classifying cost centres; allocating resources

Paige's Fashion House is a small, boutique clothing manufacturing and wholesale company. Paige's business has grown over the last few years. She now employs 100 people in design, manufacturing, sales and marketing functions. Up until now, Paige has managed with a central oversight function, which required minimal planning and budgeting. However, now her operations have grown, senior managers are employed to manage each of the functional areas, and Paige realises her budgeting processes need reviewing.

Required

(a) For planning purposes, describe and classify Paige's business functions as to whether they would be discretionary or engineered cost centres.

(b) Briefly explain the difficulties Paige faces in determining resource allocation to these areas.

SOLUTION TO SELF-STUDY PROBLEM 1

(a) Classifying the functional areas as cost centres. Some functions such as design, sales and marketing are more likely to be discretionary cost centres; functions such as manufacturing are more likely to be classified as engineered cost centres, as there is a closer link between inputs and outputs.

(b) Where costs are highly discretionary (for example, for the design function), Paige may have difficulty identifying input/output relationships; she may have to address issues with senior management behaviour such as empire building; building in slack when setting their budget; a compromise of quality if budget focus is on cost containment. The engineered cost centres present less of a problem provided sound input/output relationships have been developed.

SELF-STUDY PROBLEM 2 Planning and budgeting process

Refer to Paige's Fashion House in self-study problem 1.

Required

How might Paige go about establishing a more formal budgeting and planning approach?

SOLUTION TO SELF-STUDY PROBLEM 2

Paige could do a number of things to establish a more formal planning and budgeting system. Some of the key things might include:

- having a clear strategy to guide the planning function
- involving employees at all levels for input
- understanding the profit planning cycle and the importance of revenue estimation in setting the foundation for planning considerations
- considering alternative budgets for discretionary cost centres such as program budgeting, zero-based budgeting, activity-based budgeting
- considering the application of rolling budgets
- even considering a Beyond Budgeting approach if Paige feels this supports the strategy and culture (belief systems) within the organisation.

QUESTIONS

5.1 Outline the meaning of the profit planning or strategic budgeting process. **LO1**

5.2 Explain why it is important that an organisation's budget be linked to strategy. **LO1**

5.3 In the planning or strategic budgeting process, explain how a sales revenue budget can be determined.
LO1, 2

5.4 Distinguish between a discretionary cost centre and an engineered cost centre. **LO3**

5.5 Explain the key concepts of program budgeting. **LO4**

5.6 Explain the key concepts of zero-based budgeting. **LO4**

5.7 Briefly describe the attributes of activity-based and kaizen budgeting. **LO4**

5.8 Explain why the budgeting process might not necessarily be successfully implemented in an organisation. **LO1, 2, 5**

5.9 Outline the key components of Beyond Budgeting. **LO6**

5.10 Why do proponents of the Beyond Budgeting movement recommend abandoning traditional budgets? **LO6**

5.11 What distinguishes zero-based budgeting from other types of budgeting? **LO4**

5.12 Discuss the similarities and differences between annual budgets and rolling budgets. **LO4**

5.13 Classify the following cost centres as more likely to be engineered cost centres or discretionary cost centres. **LO3**
- R&D department
- HR department
- Manufacturing plant

5.14 Explain how program budgeting assists with planning in discretionary cost centres. **LO4**

5.15 Explain how zero-based budgeting assists with planning in discretionary cost centres. **LO4**

EXERCISES

5.16 Budgeting and behavioural implications **LO5**

Jordy is the CEO of a scaffolding construction company. He is about to begin preparing the budget for the coming financial year for the entire organisation. Last year he was disappointed by the animosity he received from his divisional managers. They were not happy with their individual budgeted forecasts. He knew the targets were hard to achieve, but why make them too easy? 'I am not giving away bonuses for nothing,' he thought. Jordy had always prepared the budget himself. He believes that no-one knows the company better that he does. The company was established by Jordy's father more than 30 years ago and Jordy has worked for the company since he left high school.

Required

Advise Jordy on the key requirements for successful budgeting. What changes to the way budgets are currently set would you recommend?

5.17 Strategic budgeting **LO1, 2**

Stevan Donald, the marketing manager for Organic Brewing Company, has projected a 20 per cent increase in sales of hop beers next year.

Required

Comment on how this increase in sales will impact on profit, assets and cash flow.

5.18 Relationships between operational budget and strategic plans **LO2**

At a recent management meeting looking at the entity's achievements against its strategic objectives, an operational manager was heard making the following comment: 'I look after operations on a day-to-day basis. I have the operational budget for the coming year. I don't need to be concerned with the strategic plans. These plans have got nothing to do with my accountabilities.'

Required

Comment on the statement made by the operational manager.

5.19 Principles of Beyond Budgeting **LO6**

Ange Pala, the chief financial officer of a national tourist company, has become increasingly dissatisfied with the current budget process in the organisation. Much of her dissatisfaction relates to the amount of time and resources consumed in the budget process; the relatively poor efforts at estimating costs; and deciding where to focus attention for control purposes. At a recent seminar, Ange was introduced to the concepts of Beyond Budgeting.

Required

Identify three key principles of Beyond Budgeting and outline how they differ from more traditional budgeting principles. (*Hint:* See table 5.1.)

5.20 Profit planning, adjusting strategic plans   **LO2**

Trinity Records is a company that finds and signs a new artist, develops a marketing strategy, records the music, and distributes the music to retailers. Data for the CD division of Trinity Records, which distributes CDs to large retailers, are shown in the following table.

	Budget ('000)	Actual ('000)
Revenue	$16 491	$17 480
Variable production costs	5 892	6 451
Fixed manufacturing costs	1 977	2 032
Variable selling expenses	456	550
Fixed selling expenses	1 275	1 268
Administrative expenses	4 773	5 550
Operating income	$ 2 118	$ 1 629

The budget, set at the beginning of the year, was based upon estimates of sales and costs. Administrative expenses include charges by corporate headquarters for providing strategic guidance. These fixed costs are allocated to divisions using revenue as the allocation base.

Required

Due to a booming economy, the division's unit sales were higher than anticipated, even though the division's share of the CD market fell from 22 per cent to 20 per cent during the year. How will this impact on the future budgeting of the CD division and other divisions of Trinity Records?

5.21 Activity-based budgeting   **LO4**

Discuss how a hospital could use activity-based budgeting to assist with planning for the coming year.

5.22 Zero-based budgeting   **LO4**

The manager of the HR department of Nancy Accountants has been asked to prepare her annual budget on a zero-based budgeting basis.

Required

Outline why this request for a zero-based budget may have been made.

5.23 Activity-based budgeting   **LO4**

Data Processors provides credit card services for the banking industry. It is preparing its budget for 2020 and, as it has been using activity-based costing, it intends to develop an activity-based budget for 2020. The table below provides the actual cost driver rate for 2019, and the expected activity levels for 2020.

Activity (cost driver)	2019 Actual cost driver rate	2020 Expected activity	
		Non-business customers	Business customers
Transaction processing (number of transactions)	$0.40	5 000 000	20 000 000
Statements (number of statements)	4.00	200 000	750 000
New credit cards (number of credit cards)	5.00	100 000	500 000
Billing disputes (number of disputes)	30.00	50 000	100 000

Required

(a) What is the budget for the activities for 2020?

(b) Previously, Data Processors used a traditional line-item budget. What benefits will the organisation gain by converting to the activity-based budget?

(c) How will the activity-based budget assist in reducing costs in the future?

5.24 Kaizen budgets   **LO4**

Continuing from exercise 5.23, the financial controller of Data Processors recently attended an accounting conference which discussed the benefits of adopting kaizen budgeting within an activity-based budget. After meeting with operational managers at Data Processors, it was decided to instil a continuous improvement approach to operations by reducing the cost driver rate by 5 per cent in 2020 and a further 5 per cent in 2021.

Required

(a) Prepare the revised activity-based budget for 2020 and 2021.

(b) Are there potential behavioural consequences of adopting this kaizen approach to budgeting at Data Processors?

5.25 Strategic budgeting, alternative actions — LO2

The Organic Corn Company processes and distributes corn packed in 500-gram plastic bags that are sold to supermarkets for 50 cents each in boxes of 100 bags. The most recent statement of profit or loss and key financial metrics of the Organic Corn Company are provided below.

Statement of profit or loss		
Sales	$800 000	
Cost of sales		$540 000
Gross margin		260 000
Administrative salaries		80 000
Sales commissions		69 000
Advertising		75 000
Bad debts expense		16 000

Management at Organic Corn has been increasingly concerned about the plastic bags being used. It has explored a range of options and is thinking of switching to an alternative packaging option. This will require some significant changes but with only a minimal impact on revenue, at least in the short term. The following estimates have been made with respect to the next 12 months.

- Price increase of 5 cents per 500-gram packet, with volume expected to remain the same in the short term.
- Sales commission expenses are expected to remain the same proportion of sales dollars.
- Administration expenses are expected to increase by 15 per cent.
- Investment in packaging technology will be $125 000: $25 000 in cash, the rest in debt.
- Gross margin expected to be 31 per cent.

Required

(a) Calculate the impact of the new packaging system on annual profit.

(b) Comment on your analysis.

PROBLEMS

5.26 Discretionary cost centres — LO3

Cowmilka is a dairy products producer. Its logistics cost centre has 65 employees and a fleet of 25 milk tankers. It is a cross-functional cost centre with administrative staff (customer service and order processors), mechanics and tanker drivers. Tanker drivers collect milk daily from farmers and deliver it to the various Cowmilka manufacturing plants. There is also a team of 10 human resource (HR) staff that oversee the health and safety training programs for all Cowmilka operations. For example, nearly all Cowmilka's employees are required to possess up-to-date food handling, health and safety qualifications, and pass a short computer-generated health and safety test before entry is allowed onto any of Cowmilka's operational sites.

The board has raised concerns about cost control within the logistics department. In spite of increasing the incremental rate of funding to the logistics cost centre every year, it appears it will, yet again, run into deficit before the end of this financial year.

Required

What advice can you give the board to better control the logistics cost centre's costs?

5.27 Planning and budgeting in support centres — LO3

'I'm really not sure our information systems are as well placed as they could be to help us drive our performance. The industry data and my own observations suggest we need to do better in this regard. I really want to be ready when the market and the economy recovers and make sure we are doing better than the industry with respect to revenue. Also, we need to improve our planning processes and I'm really not too sure how to best plan for our expenditures in areas like R&D.'

Noel McEwen (who has been CEO for three years) was reflecting on recently-released industry information and his own experiences as CEO of Southern District Dairy (SDD). SDD, a privately-owned company, produces a variety of milk, cheese and yoghurt products. Dairy ingredients for production are sourced largely from dairy farms owned by SDD. The company has a strategy of producing high-quality products targeted towards consumers prepared to pay a premium price. Seventy per cent of the company's output is exported to parts of Asia. SDD is structured around three investment centres (business units) supported by four support cost centres (R&D; accounting and finance; HR; and marketing and logistics).

For the support cost centres, budgeted versus actual cost is the key performance metric. The three investment centre units are set the same ROI target of 12 per cent, as Noel believes all should be contributing equally to the company's performance. The budget targets for the support cost centres are usually set on the basis of negotiation with Noel, although the common starting point is always last year's budget. For example, with the R&D cost centre, Noel has linked the annual budget estimate to sales targets. The manager of R&D is then held accountable for managing the department within the annual budget estimate.

Required

(a) What are the possible limitations of the current process for planning and budgeting in the support cost centres of SDD?

(b) Suggest ways in which the planning and budgeting process in the support cost centres of SDD might be improved.

5.28 Strategic budgeting   LO2

Green Building Group specialises in a range of construction services including design services, shop and office fitouts, and recently developed environmental consulting services for architects and local government. Summarised statement of profit or loss and key performance metrics are provided below.

Green Building Group Summarised statement of profit or loss to June 2019				
	Shop fitouts	Design services	Environmental consulting	Total
Revenue	$600 000	$400 000	$60 000	$1 060 000
Gross margin	$150 000	$180 000	$30 000	$ 360 000
Selling, general and administrative expenses	$100 000	$110 000	$15 000	$ 225 000
Operating income	$ 50 000	$ 70 000	$15 000	$ 135 000
Profit margin	8.3%	17.5%	25%	12.7%
Total assets				$1 000 000
Return on assets				13.5%

The CEO of Green Building Group, Sue Smith, is hoping to increase the resources devoted to the environmental consulting services. This is based on the increasing number of queries for this type of work as well as some industry data that suggest 25 per cent growth rates per year over the past few years. Industry experts predict these growth rates to continue. Moreover, the retail business has remained relatively constant over the past three years, while consulting has grown by about 10 per cent per year.

Sue was hoping to use some of the resources currently assigned to retail to the environmental consulting. Moreover, she knew she would have to hire an additional environmental science expert and engage in some targeted marketing of the environmental activity.

Sue is interested to find out the impact of this likely switch in strategic emphasis on the key statement of profit or loss items and metrics for next year.

Required

(a) Based on the information available, make an estimate of revenue across the three areas of activity. Outline your assumptions.

(b) Complete an estimate of the other statement of profit or loss items and key metrics. Outline your assumptions.

(c) What recommendations would you make to Sue?

5.29 Profit planning   LO2, 6

The Dancing Goat is a small coffee operation with ten cafes located around Melbourne. Each has a manager and up to five full-time employees to cover the 7.30 am to 4.30 pm, Monday to Saturday opening hours. Logan, the owner, employs a total of 60 full-time employees and three part-time employees (bookkeeper, roaster and delivery van driver). The company structure is outlined in figure 5.12.

The coffee beans are roasted at the main Sopital Lane cafe and transported daily to the other cafes. Logan makes all decisions in relation to coffee bean purchasing, roasting, retail pricing and product offerings. He also sets up regular coffee training sessions for all employees. Coffee prices are set at a premium ($4.00 per coffee). The cafes offer a deliberately small, but high-quality, gourmet menu (five types of specialty sandwiches made on the premises and unique Dancing Goat-inspired handmade cupcakes supplied by a local gourmet cupcake supplier). The 12 roasted coffee bean blends are also packaged in 250-gram bags, which retail at all the cafes for $12 per bag. Logan visits each of the cafes most days to chat with his managers and ensure operations are running smoothly.

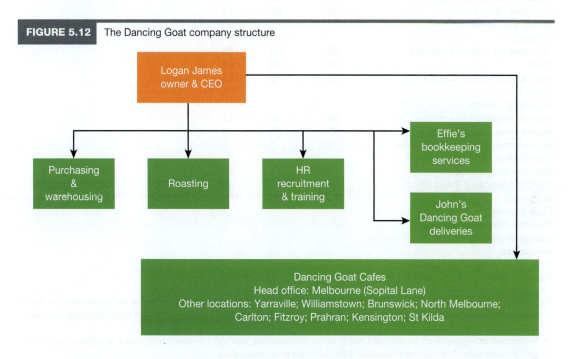

FIGURE 5.12 The Dancing Goat company structure

Logan arranges a meeting with a management accounting consultant to review the partially completed annual summary report (below).

Logan wants advice on how he might improve cash flow. Specifically, Logan wants to know how to increase profit performance and improve working capital. Logan and the consultant discuss the following matters.

- *Inventory:* Logan has recently handed the coffee inventory management over to Max, his Sopital cafe manager. While Max had been earning bonuses for keeping coffee prices down, Logan is concerned about the comments he has received from customers about the quality of their brew. On investigation, Max has been approached by alternative suppliers offering coffee beans at significantly reduced cost. The new suppliers require larger order quantities and, as a result, inventory levels have increased.

- *Accounts receivable:* These are the accounts set up by local community businesses for business-entertaining purposes. Accounts receivable are minimal as they are generally settled, in full, at the end of each month.

- *Accounts payable:* These are probably stretched out as far out as they can be. Nevertheless, Max's new fresh coffee bean suppliers are not offering the payment terms of the previous suppliers set up by Logan. This certainly requires further revision.

Logan wants to emphasise sales of high-margin products rather than the efficiency of operations. He is concerned that an efficiency focus will impact his niche marketing strategy for The Dancing Goat cafes.

Cafe	1 Sopital	2 Y'ville	3 W'town	4	5	6	7	8	9	10	Total
Number of employees	10*	6	6	6	6	6	6	6	6	6	64
Statement of profit or loss											
Sales	600	380	350								
Cost of sales	438	274	248								
Gross margin											
Other expenses											
Utilities/maintenance (coffee machines)	30	18	16								
Depreciation (coffee machines)	3	2	2								
Operating margin	129	86	84								
*Selling and admin expenses**											
Allocated head office expenses	60	38	38								
Rent	50	30	28								
Profit before interest and tax	19	18	18								
Balance sheet											
Identifiable assets											
Cash (average)	25	12	15								
Accounts receivable (average)	25	10	8								
Equipment (coffee machine) — net depreciation	8.5	3	3								
Total identifiable assets	58.5	25	26								
Net asset allocation (head office)	200	80	80								
Net assets	258.5	105	106								
Profit planning											
Free cash flow (net income +/– change in working capital)											
Net income											
Change in net working capital											
Free cash flow											

The Dancing Goat
Financial information for the year ended 31 December 2019

* Employee numbers include Logan as CEO; six full-time and three part-time employees. The head office is situated at the Sopital cafe — the busiest and largest of all the cafes. As such, it generates the highest revenues while also incurring higher rents and head office allocations.

** Selling and admin. expenses are allocated evenly across the remaining nine cafes — these costs include accounting; advertising, staff training and delivery charges (based on daily deliveries to the nine cafes).

(a) The management accounting consultant suggests they review the strategic budgeting or profit planning process at The Dancing Goat. Drawing on relevant aspects of the profit planning process and figure 5.2, describe the discussions they might have in planning for the success of The Dancing Goat.

(b) Assume Logan decides to introduce the Beyond Budgeting model at The Dancing Goat. Outline how the Beyond Budgeting model might work at The Dancing Goat.

5.30 Strategic budgeting, alternative courses of action · LO1, 2, 5

Refer to the Paige's Fashion House case in self-study problem 1.

Paige ensures that members of her staff regularly attend international fashion shows (for design ideas) as well as become involved in Australian fashion shows. While these are costly events to attend, Paige considers it a necessary function of her business as it is important to maintain a high profile as an up-and-coming design group.

The design team always works in advance, designing garments for the following season. A considerable proportion of their time is spent working on the formal collection. The formal garments are recognised in the industry as the *haute couture* range, highly expensive and exotic garments. They bring the 'wow' factor to the fashion parades. Paige often dresses celebrities attending high-profile events, such as the Logies, the Brownlow, DallyM and Allan Border medal presentations, and other Australian sports awards nights, in her latest formal range. The formal range is the signature style from which the other regular streetwear designs (that is, the casual and denim ranges) are created. The streetwear range is the main income earner for Paige's Fashion House. Her design team also designs shoes and bags to match every season's range. These are made for Paige's Fashion House by a high-quality Chinese manufacturing company. The large expense items are the fashion show costs, advertising expenses and the costs of preparing sample garments for fashion parades and celebrity wear. Distribution is generally through a local transport company who deliver small and large orders.

Paige's Fashion House sells its range in about 20 fashion outlets around Australia. Two are very large national department stores and the other 18 are fashion boutiques of varying sizes. Credit terms vary depending on the size of the store. The large department stores manage to stretch payment terms to 120 days, which is tough on cash flows; however, Paige tries to make it up with large deposits on order and 30-day balance payment terms for the smaller boutiques. She tries to extend her own accounts payable as much as she can, but given it is not a large organisation, she has trouble securing credit terms beyond 30 days. The company has to pay a considerable proportion of costs up-front to the bag and shoe manufacturer.

The company needs some inventories of raw materials (fabrics, threads, other) well ahead of time to ensure it can supply once the product range is launched. This is also necessary for the bags and shoes, which are ordered and shipped in advance. Otherwise, finished goods inventory levels are kept relatively small for two reasons. First, much of a new season's range is shipped to stores. Second, unsold inventory is mostly donated or heavily discounted to outlets providing high-quality clothing labels to charities.

The following spreadsheet provides an overview of the new spring collection product range and some key financial information.

Paige's Fashion House — Spring Collection						
Fashion line	Jeans	Casual	Formal	Accessories		Total
				Bags	Shoes	
No. of new lines	8	10	6	4	8	
Statement of profit or loss key items						
Total sales	$320 000	$640 000	$90 000	$216 000	$120 000	$1 386 000
Total cost of sales	224 000	448 000	85 500	172 800	96 000	1 026 300
Gross income	96 000	192 000	4 500	43 200	24 000	359 700
Expenses						
R&D						53 955
Marketing						28 776
Fashion shows						89 925
Cost of sample garments						17 985
Advertising						53 955
Distribution						26 978
General & administration						35 970
Total other expenses						307 544
Net income						52 156
Average sales per line	40 000	64 000	15 000	54 000	15 000	
Average cost of sales per line	28 000	44 800	14 250	43 200	12 000	
Gross margin %						
(target = 30%)	0.3%	0.3%	0.05%	0.2%	0.2%	0.259 523 81%
Expenses % of sales						
(target = 20%)						0.221 892 857
Net income margin						
(target = 10%)						0.037 630 952
Balance sheet items						
Current assets						
Inventory (% of cost of sales)						$ 123 156
Accounts receivable (as a % of sales)						346 500
Current liabilities						
Accounts payable (as a % of cost of sales)						205 260
Shareholders' equity						920 000
Return on shareholders' equity (target = 8%)						0.056 691 848

Required

Paige has asked your assistance on a consulting basis. She is seeking advice as to the direction of her business (strategy) and best course of action in terms of product emphasis going forward. She is pleased with the success of the company to date, but is fully aware of the changing dynamics of the industry. What would you advise? In particular what would you advise with respect to:

(a) a mechanism for assigning expenses to the different product ranges to better assess product profitability

(b) strategic direction and possible courses of action going forward, including impact on key financials (strategic budgeting)

(c) the capacity of the company to meet key financial targets into the future?

5.31 Strategic budgeting   LO1, 2, 5

The Fairyland Children's Centre is a community-based, not-for-profit childcare service. A committee of management oversees its operations, with the elected members being parents of children attending the centre. The centre is licensed to operate with 50 effective full-time places. Due to the preference for part-time care, there are only seven places filled on a full-time basis. From 1 July 2019, a wage increase has been granted to employees. This wage increase could significantly impact the continuing viability of the Fairyland Children's Centre.

The employees have won wage increases of up to $148 per week, which are to be phased in over 18 months as shown below.

1 July 2019	2% increase
31 December 2019	2% increase
1 July 2020	2% increase
31 December 2020	4% increase

The first round of increases is to be paid from 1 July 2019, with the remaining increases to be phased in over the next 18 months. The new wage rates are based on a 38-hour week; however, the Fairyland Children's Centre's Committee of Management varied its employees' conditions of employment some years ago to a 35-hour week. The current wages bill is $600 000 per year.

The wage cost for the Fairyland Children's Centre is influenced by the minimum staffing requirements as set out in regulations issued by the government. The ratio of staff members to children is dependent upon the number of children in particular age groups. This has been one of the factors influencing how the centre has distributed its 50 registered places to each age group, coupled with the space requirements for each age group and the constraints due to the configuration of the rooms in the centre. The places have been divided into four age groups: 6 months to 2 years, 2 years to 3 years, 3 years to 4 years, and 4 years to 5 years. The following table gives a breakdown of the centre's room structure, the number of places allocated to each age group and the minimum staffing requirements for each age group as set in the government's regulations.

Room	Age of children	Number of full-time places per room	Minimum staffing requirement for age group
Babies	6 mths – 2 yrs	9	1 staff per 5 children
Toddlers	2 yrs – 3 yrs	8	1 staff per 5 children
Middle	3 yrs – 4 yrs	10	1 staff per 15 children
Big	4 yrs – 5 yrs	23	1 staff per 15 children

As the minimum staffing requirements must be maintained at all times, additional staff are employed to cover staff absences due to lunch breaks, educational planning sessions, rostered days off, sick leave, annual leave, long service leave, and to maintain ratios at the beginning and end of each day.

As the centre is a not-for-profit concern, any surpluses that are accumulated fund future asset acquisitions or are applied in future years to absorb budget deficits. The centre's financial year runs from 1 January to 31 December. When setting the 2019 budget, the committee was aware that a wage increase was likely to be approved from 1 July but they did not know the exact amount. Therefore, the committee factored an average $25 per week increase per full-time employee (prorated for part-time employees), and $6.50 per day for agency relief staff into the budget. As a result, the 2019 budget incorporated a weekly fee set at $220 and a daily fee at $55 until 30 June, and then $230 per week and

$57 per day from 1 July. A higher daily fee is charged for part-time places due to the additional costs incurred in administration activities associated with health and safety regulations and the likelihood that any vacancies will take longer to fill. In recent years, the centre's director, Tina West, has found it difficult to fill single-day vacancies.

Tina West organised a special meeting of the committee to discuss the impact of the wage increase on the centre. Tina commenced the meeting by giving everyone the background to the wage increase and the details regarding the phasing in of payments and the new classification structure. She explained that managers at local centres in the area are agreeing to pay the full increase immediately rather than in increments as given in the determination. The reason given to justify the full payment now is both to attract and retain staff. In recent years, the ability to recruit qualified staff has been problematic, as many potential employees have sought occupations outside the childcare industry due to the low remuneration. Coupled with this is the centre's current employees' push for the full wage increase to be paid now, or at a minimum to have more than just the first stage payment made from 1 July 2019.

The committee is more than aware of the difficulties in recruiting suitable staff. Over the past two years, several positions have been advertised with few applicants. In fact, the director's position took over three months to fill. In the end, the assistant director at the time was promoted to the director's position, as no external applicants were deemed suitable. Although the committee is pleased that they anticipated the first stage of the wage increase and incorporated it into the 2019 budget, they are still concerned about the overall wage increase on the centre. Committee members expressed concern about paying the future wage increases in advance, and the reaction of parents to a fee hike, especially if this is greater than other childcare centres in the area. The financial viability of the centre could be jeopardised if parents withdraw their children and vacant places cannot be filled quickly.

Required

(a) Draw on the circumstances relating to Fairyland Children's Centre to outline the problems associated with estimating revenue in budget preparation.

(b) Comment on how the estimation of revenue is likely to affect cost planning at Fairyland Children's Centre.

ENDNOTES

1. Kesmodel, D 2015, 'Meet the father of zero-based budgeting', *The Wall Street Journal*, 26 March, www.wsj.com.
2. Kesmodel, D & Gasparro, A 2015, 'Kraft–Heinz deal shows Brazilian buyout firm's cost-cutting recipe', *The Wall Street Journal*, 25 March, www.wsj.com.
3. See Myers, R 2001, 'Budgets on a roll', *Journal of Accountancy*, December, pp. 41–6.
4. Collins, J 2012, 'Justice sector funding pool for better results', New Zealand Government media release, 24 May; www.justice.govt.nz/justice-sector-policy/about-the-justice-sector/.
5. This section draws on work from founders: Hope, J & Fraser, R 2003, 'New ways of setting rewards: the Beyond Budgeting Model', *California Management Review*, vol. 45, no. 4, pp. 104–19; Hope, J & Fraser, R 2003, *Beyond Budgeting: how managers can break free from the annual performance trap*. Boston: Harvard Business School Press; the Beyond Budgeting Transformation Network now known as the BetaCodex Network is a valuable website for Beyond Budgeting resources, www.betacodex.org; the key case study, Lindsay, RM & Libby, T 2007, 'Svenska Handelsbanken: controlling a radically decentralised organisation without budgets', *Issues in Accounting Education*, vol. 22, iss. 4, pp. 625–41.
6. Beyond Codex Network 2008, 'Putting an end to "command and control": 12 principles to defining the 21st century organization', www.betacodex.org.
7. Lindsay & Libby 2007.

ACKNOWLEDGEMENTS

Photo 5A: © racorn / Shutterstock.com
Photo 5B: © Dewald Kirsten / Shutterstock.com
Table 5.1: © Figure 1 from the BBTN White Paper, June 2008, 'Putting an end to "command and control": 12 principles to defining the 21st century organisation'.

CHAPTER 6

Operational budgets

LEARNING OBJECTIVES

After studying this chapter, you should be able to:

6.1 demonstrate an understanding of the role of budgets in developing both short- and long-term plans

6.2 describe the role of the master budget and develop a master budget

6.3 develop a cash budget

6.4 explain the use of budget targets as performance benchmarks

6.5 illustrate how budgets are used to monitor and motivate performance.

IN BRIEF

An entity's long-term strategies are communicated and advanced through short-term and long-term budgets. In addition, budgets provide a mechanism for monitoring an organisation's progress towards its goals. Comparisons of actual to budgeted revenues and costs help managers evaluate performance, leading to improved operations and more accurate planning. Some entities provide employee incentives for meeting or exceeding budget-based benchmarks. Accordingly, budgets are used in planning, monitoring and motivating performance.

6.1 Budgeting — a tool for short- and long-term planning

LEARNING OBJECTIVE 6.1 Demonstrate an understanding of the role of budgets in developing both short- and long-term plans.

University students routinely anticipate both school-related expenditures (such as fees and texts) and living expenses (such as rent and food). Before each semester begins, they may develop financial plans. These plans consider expenses and also potential incoming funds such as scholarships, loans and wages.

At the end of each month or semester, students might compare their actual expenditures to those they had planned. They can then use these comparisons to adjust their plans for future spending or financing. For example, if expenses are outpacing revenues, students have several choices. They can lower their living expenses. They might transfer to a less expensive university, switch from full-time to part-time status or take fewer subjects. They might also increase funds by applying for more scholarships or loans, or by increasing their work hours.

Every organisation faces the same budgetary problems that students face. In the upcoming fiscal period, plans must be developed to anticipate revenues, expenses and cash flows. At the end of the period, actual results are compared to the plan to identify gaps, or variances, from the plan. A **budget** is a formalised financial plan for operations of an entity for a specified future period. This plan helps the organisation coordinate the activities needed to carry out the plan. A budget is an entity's financial roadmap; it reflects management's forecast of the financial effects of an entity's plans for one or more future time periods. Several objectives are met through the use of budgets, as summarised in figure 6.1. Note that appendix 6A contains an article from *Strategic Finance* relating to how organisations might get the best from their budgets and budget processes.

FIGURE 6.1 Budget objectives

- Developing and communicating organisational strategies and goals for the entire entity as well as for each segment, division or department
- Assigning decision rights (authority to spend, and responsibility for decision outcomes)
- Motivating managers to plan in advance
- Coordinating operating activities such as sales and production
- Establishing prices for the internal transfer of goods and services
- Measuring and comparing expected and actual outcomes
- Monitoring actual performance and investigating variances when necessary
- Motivating managers to provide appropriate estimates, meet expectations and use resources efficiently
- Re-evaluating and revising strategies and operating plans as conditions change

In preparing budgets, managers forecast a number of events such as the volume of goods or services they will sell. Using these estimates, plans are developed to determine the resources an organisation needs, including employees, raw materials and supplies, cash and anything else necessary to the future operations.

Budgets also provide a mechanism for defining the responsibilities and financial decision-making authority, or **decision rights**, of individual managers. For example, separate budgets are often developed for each department within an organisation. The manager of each department is then given authority to spend the organisation's resources in accordance with the budget, and is also responsible for meeting budgeted goals.

In chapter 5, we explored a range of budgeting issues, including contemporary approaches to budgeting, behavioural implications of budgeting and the Beyond Budgeting approach to management control. In this chapter, we explore the budget cycle, preparing the master budget, cash budgets, flexible budgets and budget responsibility.

Budget cycle

A **budget cycle** is a series of steps that entities follow to develop and use budgets, as summarised in figure 6.2. Managers typically begin the process by revisiting and possibly revising the organisational vision and core competencies. The rest of this chapter addresses the other steps in the budget cycle. We first learn to translate operating plans into a master budget and then learn how managers monitor actual results, investigate differences between actual and budget, and evaluate and reward performance.

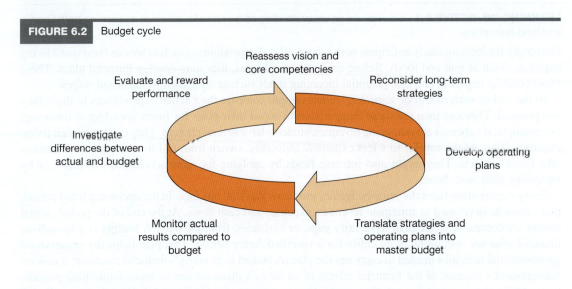

FIGURE 6.2 Budget cycle

6.2 The role of the master budget

LEARNING OBJECTIVE 6.2 Describe the role of the master budget and develop a master budget.

A **master budget** is a comprehensive plan for an upcoming financial period, usually a year. Master budgets reflect an entity's future operating and financing decisions, and are often summarised in a set of **budgeted financial statements**. These statements are forecasts of the future statement of profit or loss (or statement of comprehensive income), the statement of financial position (also called the balance sheet) and cash flows, given an organisation's sales forecasts and expenditure plans for the next period.

Figure 6.3 shows the development of a master budget in a manufacturing organisation. The master budget includes an **operating budget** — management's plan for revenues, production and operating costs. Preparation of the operating budget begins with the organisation's strategies, which in turn lead to a sales forecast and the revenue budget. The volume of production is next forecast using beginning inventory levels, sales forecasts and desired ending inventory levels. The production budget leads to budgets for direct materials, direct labour and manufacturing overhead. These budgets are used to create budgets for ending inventory and cost of sales (also called cost of goods sold). The operating budget also includes budgets for individual support department costs. All of the components of the operating budget are combined with any non-operating items and income taxes in a budgeted statement of profit or loss. Non-operating items might include interest expenses, gains or losses on the sale of fixed assets, or earnings from investments.

The master budget also includes **financial budgets** — or management's plans for capital expenditures, long-term financing and cash flows — leading to a budgeted balance sheet and budgeted statement of cash flows. The cash budget is part of the financial budgets. A **cash budget** reflects the effects of management's plans on cash, and summarises the information that accountants gather about the expected amounts and timing of cash receipts and disbursements. The cash budget is addressed later in the chapter. The capital budget reflects long-term investment. The long-term financing budget, budgeted balance sheet and budgeted statement of cash flows are beyond the scope of this text.

Developing a master budget

Accountants develop a master budget in consultation with top management and every departmental manager within an entity. The master budget is developed using a set of **budget assumptions**, which are plans and predictions about next period's operating activities. Revenues are budgeted assuming a particular forecast of sales volumes and prices, or assuming an estimated percentage change from the prior year. Individual costs are budgeted assuming a fixed amount to be spent — as a percentage of revenues, as a percentage change from the prior year or on some other basis. Accountants assist managers in the process of developing budget assumptions. They may analyse past revenue and cost trends and behaviour, gather information about possible cost changes and obtain estimates from engineers about the effects of planned production changes.

The master budget is usually developed in the sequence shown in figure 6.3 for a manufacturing entity. Given the organisation's strategy, the first step is to forecast sales volumes and revenues. However, some organisations develop the production and support department budgets simultaneously with the revenue budget. Also, some parts of the production and support department budgets might be developed independently of the revenue budget.

FIGURE 6.3   Developing a manufacturer's master budget

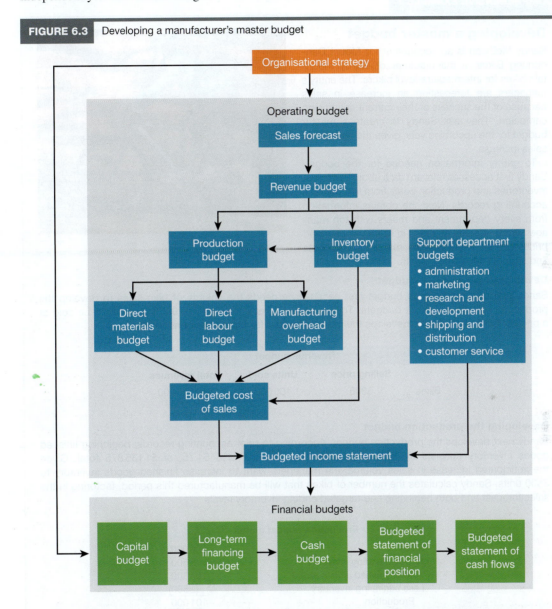

The process of developing a master budget becomes increasingly complex as entities become larger. It is often more complex for international organisations. Communication can be more time consuming because international business segments participate in the budgeting process. Cultural and legal differences influence both internal and external operations and need to be considered. The economies of different countries rarely move in tandem and forecasting sales is more difficult. In addition, currency translations and differences in inflation and deflation rates greatly increase uncertainty in the planning and budgeting process.

In comprehensive example 1, we revisit Mount Dandenong Bikes to show how the accountant develops a master budget by creating individual budgets in the following order:
- revenue budget
- production budget
- direct materials budget

- direct labour budget
- manufacturing overhead budget
- inventory and cost of sales budget
- support department budgets
- budgeted financial statements.

Developing a master budget

Sandy McEwan is an accountant for Mount Dandenong Bikes, a manufacturer of sturdy mountain bikes for intermediate level bikers. The entity's managers are forecasting an increase in sales because of the success of their current advertising campaign. They ask Sandy to create a master budget for the upcoming year, given the forecasted sales increase.

To gather information needed for the budget, Sandy first accesses relevant data about revenues, inventories and production costs from last period's accounting records. Next, he obtains information from every department and meets with top management to identify changes in sales volumes and prices, production processes, manufacturing costs and support department costs.

Developing the revenue budget

Sandy prepares the revenue budget first because he needs the volume of bike sales to develop the production and variable cost budgets. The managers forecasted that 100 000 bikes would be sold at a price of $800 each. Sandy develops the revenue budget for Mount Dandenong Bikes.

Revenue budget			
	Selling price	Units sold	Total revenues
Bikes	$800	100 000	$80 000 000

Developing the production budget

Sandy next develops the production budget. According to prior accounting records, beginning finished goods inventory consists of 2500 bikes at a cost per unit of $454.75, or $1 136 875 total. Given the anticipated increase in sales volume, the managers want to increase finished goods inventory to 3500 units. Sandy calculates the number of bikes that will be manufactured this period, factoring in the sales forecast and both beginning and targeted ending inventory levels.

Production budget (units)	
Sales	100 000
Targeted ending inventory	3 500
Total finished units needed	103 500
Less beginning inventory	(2 500)
Production	101 000

Developing the direct materials budget

Now Sandy can determine the amount of direct materials that must be purchased. The beginning inventory consists of:

Beginning direct material inventories:	
Wheels and tyres	$ 20 000
Components	70 000
Frames	50 000
Total	$140 000

The cost per unit of direct materials is expected to be:

Direct materials (cost per unit):	
Wheels and tyres	$20
Components	70
Frame	50

The managers want ending inventories to be:

Targeted ending direct material inventories:	
Wheels and tyres	$ 25 000
Components	87 500
Frames	62 500
Total	$175 000

Given these assumptions, Sandy prepares the following direct materials budget.

Direct materials budget	
Production of 101 000 bikes:	
Wheels (101 000 × $20)	$ 2 020 000
Components (101 000 × $70)	7 070 000
Frames (101 000 × $50)	5 050 000
Total direct materials used	14 140 000
Targeted ending inventory	175 000
Less beginning inventory	(140 000)
Total purchases	$14 175 000

Developing the direct labour budget

The quantity and cost of direct labour per unit is expected to be:

Direct labour	Hours	Cost per hour
Assembly	1.5	$25
Testing	0.15	15

Sandy prepares the direct labour budget, which forecasts the number of labour hours and the total direct labour costs for producing 101 000 bikes.

Direct labour budget	
Labour hours budget:	
Assembly (101 000 units × 1.5 hours)	151 500 hours
Testing (101 000 units × 0.15 hours)	15 150 hours
Total labour hours	166 650 hours
Labour cost budget:	
Assembly (151 500 × $25)	$3 787 500
Testing (15 150 × $15)	227 250
Total labour cost	$4 014 750

Developing the manufacturing overhead budget

In addition to the direct costs of production, overhead costs need to be included in the budgeting process. Sandy uses information that he collected from last year's operations and updates it with current prices. The cost per unit of variable manufacturing overhead is expected to be as follows:

Variable overhead (cost per unit):	
Supplies	$20.00
Indirect labour	37.50
Maintenance	10.00
Miscellaneous	7.50
Total	$75.00

Sandy expects $20 200 000 to be spent on fixed manufacturing overhead costs.

He calculates the fixed overhead allocation rate by dividing budgeted fixed overhead costs by the budgeted volume of production:

$$\$20\,200\,000 \div 101\,000 \text{ units} = \$200 \text{ per unit}$$

Sandy prepares the manufacturing overhead budget for producing 101 000 bikes.

Manufacturing overhead budget	
Variable manufacturing overhead costs:	
Supplies (101 000 units × $20)	$ 2 020 000
Indirect labour (101 000 units × $37.50)	3 787 500
Maintenance (101 000 units × $10)	1 010 000
Miscellaneous (101 000 units × $7.50)	757 500
Total variable overhead (101 000 units × $75)	$ 7 575 000
Fixed manufacturing overhead costs:	
Depreciation	4 040 000
Property taxes	1 010 000
Insurance	1 414 000
Plant supervision	5 050 000
Fringe benefits	7 070 000
Miscellaneous	1 616 000
Total fixed overhead	20 200 000
Total overhead	$27 775 000
Manufacturing overhead allocation rates (cost per unit):	
Variable	$ 75
Fixed	$ 200

Developing the inventory and cost of sales budgets

To prepare budgeted cost of sales, Sandy needs forecasted costs for ending inventories. Using the fixed and variable production costs, he prepares the ending inventories budget, summarised as follows.

Ending inventories budget		
Direct materials (cost per unit):		
Frame	$ 50.00	
Components	70.00	
Wheels	20.00	
Total direct materials	140.00	
Direct labour:		
Assembly (1.5 hours × $25)	37.50	
Testing (0.15 hours × $15)	2.25	
Total direct labour	39.75	
Manufacturing overhead:		
Variable	75.00	
Fixed	200.00	
Total overhead	275.00	
Total cost per unit	$ 454.75	
Budgeted cost of ending inventory:		
3500 units × $454.75 per unit	$1 591 625.00	

Using information from the preceding budgets, Sandy prepares the cost of sales budget for the forecasted sale of 100 000 units.

Cost of sales budget		
Beginning finished goods		$ 1 136 875
Direct materials used	$14 140 000	
Direct labour	4 014 750	
Manufacturing overhead	27 775 000	
Cost of goods manufactured		45 929 750
Total available		47 066 625
Ending finished goods		(1 591 625)
Cost of sales		$45 475 000

Developing the support department budgets

Having completed the production cost budgets, Sandy next estimates other operating costs, that is, the budgeted costs for all of the support departments. In this illustration, the support costs are all fixed. In other situations, support costs could contain a mixture of fixed and variable costs.

Support department information is gathered from each department manager. The support department budget is summarised as follows.

Support department budget	
Department	**Fixed costs**
Administration	$16 478 215
Marketing	9 886 929
Distribution	4 943 465
Customer service	1 647 821
Total	$32 956 430

Developing the budgeted statement of profit or loss

Finally, Sandy combines the information from all of the individual operating budgets to prepare the budgeted statement of profit or loss. The entity's managers do not anticipate any non-operating statement of profit or loss items, so no additional items must be included in the budgeted statement of profit or loss except for income taxes at the expected rate of 30 per cent.

Budgeted statement of profit or loss		
Revenues (revenue budget)		$80 000 000
Cost of sales (cost of sales budget)		45 475 000
Gross margin		34 525 000
Operating costs (support department budgets):		
Administration	$16 478 215	
Marketing	9 886 929	
Distribution	4 943 465	
Customer service	1 647 821	
Total operating costs		32 956 430
Operating income		1 568 570
Income taxes ($1 568 570 × 30%)		470 571
Net income		$ 1 097 999

Sandy reviews the budgeted statement of profit or loss information with the entity's controller. The budgets are then presented at a meeting with the CEO and the various department heads.

Budgeting in non-manufacturing entities

The individual budgets shown previously in figure 6.3 are for a manufacturing entity. The specific types of budgets that comprise a master budget depend on the nature of an organisation's goods or services and its accounting system. For example, some service entities do not carry inventory; the direct costs of producing services are recognised as a period cost in the statement of profit or loss. Thus, budgets for these organisations generally would not include inventory computations and might not include direct materials. Other service industries, such as retailers, would carry inventory. The categories chosen for individual budgets are based on the categories that managers use to plan and monitor operations.

In the not-for-profit sector, budgets are often a primary source of information about the operations of the entity. Although donors request financial statements, budgets provide much of the operating information used by managers. In governmental entities, budgets must often be legally adopted, placing restrictions on spending authority.

6.3 Developing a cash budget

LEARNING OBJECTIVE 6.3 Develop a cash budget.

The cash budget reflects the effects of management's plans on cash and summarises information that accountants gather about the expected amounts and timing of cash receipts and disbursements. Cash budgets may be prepared quarterly, monthly, weekly or even daily to help management plan the entity's short-term borrowing or investing.

Operating cash receipts and disbursements

Operating cash receipts are estimated from budgeted revenues, taking into account the nature of customer transactions. For example, if sales are made on account, then forecasts must be made for bad debts and for the timing of customer payments. Comprehensive example 2 on Mount Dandenong Bikes includes a simple timing difference for accounts receivables. Several problems at the end of this chapter feature more variation in the timing of receivables and discounts, and the effects of bad debts on the cash budget.

Operating cash disbursements are estimated from the budgets for direct materials, direct labour, manufacturing overhead and support departments. The timing of cash disbursements for these items depends on the payment terms with employees and vendors. For example, the organisation might pay employees on the 15th and last day of each month. Payments to vendors might be made in the month after the purchase of goods or services. Some expenses, such as depreciation, do not require a cash payment.

Other planned cash flows

In addition to operating cash flows, organisations have many other types of cash flows, including:
- purchasing or selling property, plant and equipment
- borrowing or repaying long-term debt
- paying interest on debt
- issuing or redeeming capital stock
- paying dividends to shareholders.

Although the purchase or sale of property, plant and equipment is planned in the capital budget, the cash effects of borrowing and repaying are reflected in annual cash budgets. Similarly, cash flows related to long-term debt and capital stock are planned in the long-term financing budget, but the changes in annual cash flows need to be reflected in the cash budget.

Short-term borrowing or investing

Managers typically use short-term loans or investments to balance the cash budget, taking into account the desired cash balance. Short-term loans may be pre-arranged as a line of credit with a financial institution; the organisation can borrow up to a specified amount as needed to cover cash shortages. Entities often use excess cash to repay short-term debt, with any remainder placed in liquid investments.

The purpose of the cash budget is to ensure adequate levels of cash for day-to-day operations. If an organisation lacks the necessary cash to fund its operations at any given moment, then it is insolvent. Successful new, fast-growing entities, especially franchise companies or companies growing by acquisition, sometimes fail because their assets are not liquid and they cannot pay their employees. To prepare a cash budget, three types of cash transactions are planned:
1. cash receipts
2. cash disbursements
3. short-term borrowings or investments.

Comprehensive example 2 demonstrates the preparation of a cash budget for Mount Dandenong Bikes.

COMPREHENSIVE EXAMPLE 2

Developing a cash budget

The managers tell Sandy that they plan to invest $8 million in new equipment during the second quarter. This expenditure means that the entity may not have enough cash and short-term investments to cover operating cash requirements. Sandy decides to prepare a quarterly cash budget to estimate the entity's borrowing needs.

Cash receipts

To develop the cash receipts portion of the budget, Sandy creates a quarterly schedule showing the timing of cash receipts expected from customers during the year. Because the entity sells merchandise to its customers on account, he needs to forecast the time it will take customers to pay their accounts. He analyses prior accounting records to estimate the sales and collection patterns. He then asks the marketing and credit managers whether they anticipate any changes in sales or collection patterns.

Sandy learns that about half of the entity's $80 million sales occur in the fourth quarter because of holiday sales. Sales are fairly even throughout the other three quarters. Given this information, Sandy forecasts sales revenues as follows:

First quarter (50% × $80 000 000 ÷ 3 quarters)	$13 333 333
Second quarter	13 333 333
Third quarter	13 333 334
Fourth quarter (50% × $80 000 000)	40 000 000
Total budgeted revenue	$80 000 000

Customers usually pay in 30 days and sales are uniform within each quarter, so Sandy forecasts that two-thirds of each quarter's sales will be received in cash during the quarter and one-third in the next quarter. Therefore, first-quarter receipts will include collection of accounts receivable from the prior year. Fourth-quarter revenues from the prior year were expected to be $30 million, so first-quarter receipts should include $10 million (1/3 × $30 000 000). Mount Dandenong sells to the same bicycle dealers every year and has eliminated those who do not pay on time. Therefore, bad debts are usually immaterial; he assumes that all accounts receivable will be collected. The managers do not anticipate any other receipts, such as new long-term borrowings, during the year. Sandy's forecast of cash receipts is presented in figure 6.4. The total estimated amount received from customers ($76 666 667) is less than the budgeted amount of revenues ($80 000 000) because accounts receivable at the end of the year ($40 000 000 = $26 666 667 = $13 333 333) are greater than accounts receivable at the beginning of the year ($10 000 000).

FIGURE 6.4	Cash receipts from customers at Mount Dandenong Bikes

	Quarter				
	First	**Second**	**Third**	**Fourth**	**Total**
Beginning accounts receivable	$10 000 000				$10 000 000
First-quarter sales	8 888 889	$ 4 444 444			13 333 333
Second-quarter sales		8 888 889	$ 4 444 444		13 333 333
Third-quarter sales			8 888 889	$ 4 444 445	13 333 334
Fourth-quarter sales				26 666 667	26 666 667
Total receipts	$18 888 889	$13 333 333	$13 333 333	$31 111 112	$76 666 667

Cash disbursements

Next, Sandy analyses prior accounting records and supplier contracts to identify the normal timing of cash payments to vendors, employees and others. He also asks the production and other department managers whether they anticipate any changes in purchasing or payment patterns.

Sandy forecasts that half of the production will take place during the fourth quarter, to match the pattern of sales. Therefore, half of the direct material purchases will occur during the fourth quarter, with the other half occurring during the first three quarters. Assuming that production is uniform across the first three quarters, Sandy forecasts purchases as follows:

First quarter (50% × $14 175 000 ÷ 3 quarters)	$ 2 362 500
Second quarter	2 362 500
Third quarter	2 362 500
Fourth quarter (50% × $14 175 000)	7 087 500
Total budgeted purchases	$14 175 000

Payments for direct materials are made a month after purchase. As a result, two-thirds of the purchases are paid during each quarter and one-third is paid during the following quarter. Fourth-quarter purchases for the prior year were expected to be $6 million, so payments for these purchases of $2 million (1/3 × $6 000 000) are expected in the first quarter. Sandy uses this information to prepare the quarterly schedule for direct material disbursements in figure 6.5. The total amount paid ($13 812 500) is less than the budgeted amount of direct material purchases ($14 175 000) because accounts payable at the end of the year ($7 087 500 − $4 725 000 = $2 362 500) are greater than accounts payable at the beginning of the year ($2 000 000).

FIGURE 6.5 Disbursements for direct materials purchases at Mount Dandenong Bikes

	First	Second	Third	Fourth	Total
	Quarter				
Beginning accounts payable	$2 000 000				$ 2 000 000
First-quarter purchases	1 575 000	$ 787 500			2 362 500
Second-quarter purchases		1 575 000	$ 787 500		2 362 500
Third-quarter purchases			1 575 000	$ 787 500	2 362 500
Fourth-quarter purchases				4 725 000	4 725 000
Total disbursements	$3 575 000	$2 362 500	$2 362 500	$5 512 500	$13 812 500

Sandy forecasts that the remaining variable costs are incurred in the same pattern as direct material purchases — half over the first three quarters and half during the fourth quarter. He learns that property taxes are due in the second and fourth quarters and insurance payments are due in the first and third quarters. He also knows that depreciation will not be paid because it is a non-cash expense, so he removes it from the list of expenses. Sandy forecasts that the remaining fixed costs are incurred uniformly across the four quarters. He assumes that all costs other than direct material purchases are paid in the quarter in which they are incurred. In addition, he learns from management that the entity will spend $8 million on new equipment during the second quarter. Given these forecasts and assumptions, Sandy completes the cash disbursements section of the cash budget in figure 6.6.

FIGURE 6.6 Summary of cash receipts and disbursements for Mount Dandenong Bikes

	First	Second	Third	Fourth	Total
	Quarter				
Cash receipts:					
Revenues (from figure 6.4)	$18 888 889	$ 13 333 333	$13 333 333	$31 111 112	$76 666 667
Cash disbursements:					
Direct materials purchases (from figure 6.5)	3 575 000	2 362 500	2 362 500	5 512 500	13 812 500
Direct labour costs	669 125	669 125	669 125	2 007 375	4 014 750
Variable overhead costs:					
Supplies	336 666	336 667	336 667	1 010 000	2 020 000
Indirect labour	631 250	631 250	631 250	1 893 750	3 787 500
Maintenance	168 333	168 333	168 334	505 000	1 010 000
Miscellaneous	126 250	126 250	126 250	378 750	757 500
Fixed overhead costs:					
Property taxes		505 000		505 000	1 010 000
Insurance	707 000		707 000		1 414 000
Plant supervision	1 262 500	1 262 500	1 262 500	1 262 500	5 050 000
Fringe benefits	1 767 500	1 767 500	1 767 500	1 767 500	7 070 000
Miscellaneous	404 000	404 000	404 000	404 000	1 616 000
Support department costs	8 239 107	8 239 108	8 239 107	8 239 108	32 956 430
Purchase of equipment		8 000 000			8 000 000
Total disbursements	17 886 731	24 472 233	16 674 233	23 485 483	82 518 680
Excess receipt (disbursements)	$ 1 002 158	$(11 138 900)	$(3 340 900)	$ 7 625 629	$ (5 852 013)

Short-term investments and borrowings

Sandy expects cash and short-term investments at the beginning of the period to total $9 million. The managers wish to maintain a minimum cash balance of $200 000. Any cash deficiencies are financed with the entity's line of credit and require quarterly interest payments at an annual rate of 6 per cent. The entity's policy is to budget zero earnings on short-term investments.

Sandy uses this information to complete the short-term financing portion of the cash budget. He realises that the entity will need to liquidate its short-term investments during the second quarter. It will also have to borrow $1 336 742 in the second quarter and an additional $3 360 951 in the third quarter. These short-term borrowings, totalling $4 697 693 can then be repaid during the fourth quarter when sales increase. Total interest costs on the line of credit are estimated to be $90 516. A summary of the short-term financing budget is shown in figure 6.7.

| FIGURE 6.7 | Short-term financing budget for Mount Dandenong Bikes |

	Quarter			
	First	Second	Third	Fourth
Beginning balance, cash and short-term investments	$ 9 000 000	$10 002 158	$ 200 000	$ 200 000
Excess receipts (disbursements)	1 002 158	(11 138 900)	(3 340 900)	7 625 629
Line of credit:				
Borrowings		1 336 742	3 360 951	
Interest on borrowings			(20 051)	(70 465)
Repayments				(4 697 693)
Ending balance, cash and short-term investments	$10 002 158	$ 200 000	$ 200 000	$ 3 057 471

6.4 Budgets as performance benchmarks

LEARNING OBJECTIVE 6.4 Explain the use of budget targets as performance benchmarks.

Managers and accountants use budgets to monitor operations by comparing actual results to the original budget forecasts. These comparisons serve as benchmarks for performance and help them evaluate whether strategies and operations are meeting expectations. For example, managers learn whether desired sales volumes are achieved or whether costs are under control. In addition, accountants monitor budgets to improve the quality of the budgeting process over time.

Budget variances and uncertainties

Differences between budgeted and actual results are called **budget variances**. If actual revenues are larger than the budget, or actual costs are lower than the budget, the variance is categorised as a **favourable variance**. Conversely, an **unfavourable variance** occurs when actual costs are greater than budgeted or actual revenues are less than budgeted.

Determining the underlying reasons for a variance is sometimes complicated. Suppose an entity experiences a favourable cost variance. This variance might be obtained by efficient use of overhead items. However, it could also occur because managers failed to follow budgeted plans and engaged in less activity than expected.

Because budgets are based on forecasts about the future, it is impossible to prevent variances by exactly achieving budgeted revenues and costs. The degree of forecast uncertainty varies across entities and across time. Some entities have fairly predictable revenues and costs, especially those that purchase and sell under fixed price, long-term contracts. Other organisations have volatile or unpredictable revenues and costs. Budgets are likely to be less accurate — significant variances are more likely to occur — in highly competitive industries, when selling newly developed goods and services, or when subject to fluctuating raw material costs such as petroleum prices.

Static and flexible budgets

The interpretation of budget variances is complicated by deviations from budgeted volume levels. Many costs are variable; they are expected to change proportionately with changes in production levels. Thus, we would expect total variable costs to deviate from budget if sales volumes — and therefore production volumes — deviate from budget. However, a **static budget** is based on forecasts of specific volumes of production or services. All variable costs are calculated for a specific volume of operations. If a static budget is compared to results for a different level of volume, budgeted variable costs are overstated when fewer units or services are produced than budgeted. Similarly, budgeted variable costs are understated if more units or services are produced. These volume effects hide any variances due to operational efficiencies or inefficiencies.

A budget that reflects a range of operations is called a **flexible budget**. Cost–volume–profit (CVP) analysis is a simple version of a flexible budget. Flexible budgets separate fixed and variable costs to more accurately reflect the effects of activity levels on cost. For planning purposes, flexible budgets are used to study the sensitivity of budgeted revenues and costs to different volume levels. A number of software packages for flexible budgeting are available for large entities. For small entities, Excel and other spreadsheets provide similar analysis. These software packages and spreadsheets allow financial modelling of budgets under many different circumstances.

When evaluating actual results at the end of a period, the flexible budget is set at the actual sales or production volume and used as a benchmark for analysing variances. Organisations that use a static budget transform it into a benchmark by adjusting its variable costs to reflect actual volume. However, because fixed costs are not expected to vary with volume, they are not adjusted for any differences between budgeted and actual volumes. Therefore, the flexible budget uses actual volume for variable costs and the budgeted fixed costs. Comprehensive example 3 on Mount Dandenong Bikes illustrates variances for static and flexible budgets.

COMPREHENSIVE EXAMPLE 3

Static versus flexible budget variances

At the end of the budget cycle, Sandy compares actual results for the period to the budget. He plans to create a budget variance report for management.

Static budget variances

Sandy creates the summary in figure 6.8, comparing revenues and costs under the static budget with the actual statement of profit or loss. He uses the budgeted variable costs for this period. Variable costs per bike include:

Direct materials:	
Wheels/tyres	$ 20.00
Components	70.00
Frame	50.00
Total direct materials	140.00
Direct labour	39.75
Variable overhead	75.00
Total cost per bike	$254.75

Sandy includes the budgeted fixed costs for manufacturing overhead ($20 200 000) and the budgeted support department costs ($32 956 430). He calculates variances for sales volume, revenue and each of the cost categories. When Sandy compares the actual results to the budget, he is pleased with the organisation's performance during the period. The overall variance was favourable by nearly $2.7 million, and the revenue variance was positive and large — $10.5 million. However, he is concerned about the large unfavourable cost variances.

As Sandy thinks more about the cost variances, he realises that he would expect to see unfavourable variable production cost variances because the sales volume was higher than planned. Because he used a static budget in his schedule, the cost variances did not reflect the actual volume of sales. Therefore, the schedule gave him poor-quality information for analysing last period's costs.

FIGURE 6.8   Static budget variances at Mount Dandenong Bikes

	Static budget	Actual	Variance	
Bikes sold	100 000	113 500	13 500	Favourable
Revenue	$80 000 000	$90 500 000	$10 500 000	Favourable
Production costs:				
Variable	25 475 000[a]	29 492 408	(4 017 408)	Unfavourable
Fixed overhead	20 200 000	19 400 000	800 000	Favourable

Support department costs	32 956 430	37 565 337	(4 608 907)	Unfavourable
Income	$ 1 368 570[b]	$ 4 042 255		
Total variance			$ 2 673 685	Favourable

[a] Budgeted variable costs × 100 000 = $254.75 × 100 000 = $25 475 000.

[b] Differs from budgeted statement of profit or loss total by $200 000 because some overhead costs are allocated to inventory on the budgeted balance sheet. An increase of 1000 units in inventories was budgeted this period (beginning inventories 2500 and ending inventories 3500). These additional units give rise to a $200 000 (1000 × $200 per unit overhead allocation) increase in income because this amount of fixed overhead is not included on the statement of profit or loss.

Flexible budget variances

Sandy decides to create a new budget variance analysis that reflects the actual volume of sales. He first transforms the static budget into a flexible budget by recalculating budgeted revenues using actual sales volumes (113 500) and budgeted selling price ($800). He then recalculates budgeted variable production costs by multiplying the actual sales volume (113 500) times the budgeted variable cost per unit of $254.75. Because fixed costs are not expected to vary with changes in volume, no adjustments are made to either budgeted fixed production costs or support costs. Finally, Sandy recalculates the variances. Figure 6.9 summarises his revised variance schedule.

FIGURE 6.9	Flexible budget variances at Mount Dandenong Bikes

	Flexible budget	Actual	Variance	
Bikes sold	113 500	113 500		
Revenue	$90 800 000[a]	$90 500 000	$ (300 000)	Unfavourable
Production costs:				
Variable	28 914 125[b]	29 492 408	(578 283)	Unfavourable
Fixed overhead	20 200 000	19 400 000	800 000	Favourable
Support department costs	32 956 430	37 565 337	(4 608 907)	Unfavourable
Income	$ 8 729 445	$ 4 042 255		
Total variance			$(4 687 190)	Unfavourable

[a] Actual quantity sold × budgeted selling price per bike of $800.

[b] Actual quantity sold × this period's budgeted variable cost per unit of $254.75.

Based on the new schedule, Sandy realises that the entity's performance was worse than he previously thought. After accounting for the higher sales volume, the total flexible budget variance is unfavourable by more than $4.6 million. These variances indicate the following:

- The average selling price per bike was lower than the budget.
- The average variable production cost per bike was higher than the budget.
- Total fixed production costs were lower than the budget.
  Total fixed support costs were significantly higher than the budget.

Sandy plans to investigate the reasons for the large unfavourable fixed support cost variance. However, he is unsure whether the other variances are significant enough to justify spending time investigating them. He decides to meet with the controller to discuss how to proceed. This discussion is presented later in the chapter, in comprehensive example 4 on Mount Dandenong Bikes.

6.5 Budgets, incentives and rewards

LEARNING OBJECTIVE 6.5 Illustrate how budgets are used to monitor and motivate performance.

Budgets are used to assign decision rights to individual managers within an organisation. Managers are given authority over resources and then held responsible for meeting budget benchmarks, such as producing units at the budgeted cost per unit. Many entities monitor individual manager performance by comparing actual results to the budget. Bonuses based on meeting or exceeding budget goals help motivate performance. Sometimes broader employee groups receive profit sharing, cash or other bonuses based on achieving or exceeding budgeted income levels. For example, manufacturing plant workers who meet production volume, cost and quality goals could be entitled to share in profits or receive cash bonuses. Sales representatives who meet targeted sales volumes may be rewarded with family trips to resort destinations or awards dinners to celebrate their good performance. These practices raise questions about how information is gathered for budgets and what levels of responsibility should be included.

Budget plans can be developed from the top-down, using information that has been gathered from the bottom-up. In other words, top management provides strategies and suggested organisational targets for the coming period. These strategies and targets are communicated 'top-down' to division and department managers who incorporate them into the budgeted operating plans. Departmental budget requests are then communicated 'bottom-up' to members of top management who are responsible for final budget approval. Although top managers approve the final budget, they rely on the knowledge and experience of individual managers to help them establish reasonable departmental budgets.

Participative budgeting

When managers in the field have more knowledge about future operations than top management, budgets are often developed from the bottom-up. For example, sales representatives at Mount Dandenong Bikes could submit their forecasts for next year to the marketing department. **Participative budgeting** occurs when managers who are responsible for meeting budgets also prepare the initial budget forecasts, setting targets for themselves. Theoretically, participative budgeting motivates employees to meet budget targets because they buy-in to the target-setting process. However, when employees set targets, incentives exist to set them low so that goals can be met easily. In contrast, when top management sets targets, incentives exist to raise targets to induce greater productivity. If targets are either too low or too high — easily met or unachievable — employees have little motivation to improve performance. Therefore, negotiations are often required over a period of time prior to setting the final budget.

Budget manipulation

If performance evaluations and bonuses are based on achieving budgeted results, managers have incentives to manipulate budget requests to meet targets more easily. **Budgetary slack** refers to the practice of intentionally setting revenue budgets too low and cost budgets too high. This practice hampers organisations when more precise information would result in better strategies and operating plans. For example, if sales targets are set too low, an entity could lose sales because it lacks the resources to increase production of goods or services over the short term.

Because uncertainties exist about future revenues and costs, top managers, shareholders and others cannot easily identify and remedy budgets that have been manipulated. However, several methods are used to minimise budgetary slack. For example, independent sources such as consultants or market experts may prepare forecasts. These forecasts are compared to budgeted estimates so that employees providing budget information realise their estimates are being scrutinised. Also, bonuses can be given for accurate forecasts as well as for operating within the budget.

Incentives to manipulate budgets often increase in larger organisations where managers tend to focus only on the resources and performance of their own departments. As a result, they are less likely to consider the entity as a whole and more likely to submit biased budget requests. These requests lead to misallocations of resources among competing departments or projects. To address this problem, some organisations give bonuses based on a combination of department results and overall organisation profitability which reduces incentives to build in slack, while motivating managers to support each other by directing resources towards the best projects.

Budget responsibility

Budgets give managers authority over the use of an organisation's resources. Accordingly, it seems reasonable to hold managers responsible for meeting budget benchmarks. However, when budget variances are used in performance evaluation, a number of challenges arise for managers being evaluated as well as managers conducting the evaluation. Figure 6.10 provides examples of these challenges. Notice that most of these problems relate to holding managers responsible for results when they lack control over factors that affect their variances.

FIGURE 6.10 Challenges in appropriately assigning decision rights

Challenges	Why they arise	Specific examples
Resentment	Department managers held responsible for costs over which they have no control	Allocated support department costs may be high because of poor management in support departments
Isolating the performance of individual managers	Interdependency among divisions and departments	Quality of customer services department affects ability of the sales department to meet future sales targets
Manager turnover	New manager is responsible for old manager's budget decisions	After the production manager is promoted to vice president, the new production manager faces unrealistic budget targets
Employee turnover	Employees are promoted, dismissed or leave	Delays arise in hiring process or a hiring freeze occurs
Uncontrollable external factors	Unanticipated changes in volumes, costs or prices	Oil price and availability changes because of broken pipelines

Budget and variance adjustments to measure performance

Because managers' budgets often include items not under their control, the following adjustments can be made when budgets are used to measure managers' performance.
- Use a flexible budget to determine expected revenues based on budgeted prices and actual volumes.
- Use a flexible budget to determine expected variable costs based on budgeted variable cost rates and actual volumes.
- Remove allocated costs that are not controllable by managers in the departments receiving allocations.
- Update costs for any anticipated price changes in direct materials, direct labour and overhead-related resources.

An example of these adjustments follows.

COMPREHENSIVE EXAMPLE 4

Budget adjustments for performance evaluation

Sandy knows that the sales and production managers receive bonuses if their departmental performances exceed the budget. Before his planned meeting with the controller, Sandy creates a performance schedule for each manager.

Sandy reviews his flexible budget variance schedules (figure 6.9). Because the sales department is responsible for the level of sales as well as prices, he decides that managers should be rewarded for the level of sales above the static budget, but any effects from sales discounts should also be included. Therefore, he prepares the following summary for the sales department.

Sales variances		
Volume variance		
Budgeted sales	100 000	bikes
Actual sales	113 500	
Favourable variance	13 500	bikes
Sales price variance		
Actual sales at budgeted prices	$90 800 000	
Actual sales at actual prices	90 500 000	
Unfavourable variance	$ (300 000)	

The production department sets manufacturing volumes according to information provided by the sales department. Therefore, the production department manager does not have control over production volumes. Sandy decides that the flexible budget variances should reflect costs over which managers have control. The production manager is responsible for the fixed and variable costs in the manufacturing plant, so only those costs are included in his performance evaluation. Sandy finds these details in the flexible budget he had earlier prepared and summarises them for the controller. As he prepares the summary, he checks with the purchasing department to see if any price changes occurred this period. He finds that handlebars' price had increased by $10 per bike, but all other prices remained unchanged. He adds $1 135 000 to the adjusted flexible budget variable production costs to account for the additional $10 cost for each of the 113 500 bikes manufactured. The payroll department had no changes in budgeted labour rates. Sandy also removed the support department costs because these were not under the production manager's control. Sandy's summary is presented in figure 6.11.

FIGURE 6.11   Adjusted production flexible budget variances at Mount Dandenong Bikes

	Flexible budget, adjusted for price changes	Actual	Variance	
Variable production costs	$30 049 125[a]	$29 492 408	$ 556 717	Favourable
Fixed production costs	20 200 000	19 400 000	800 000	Favourable
Total costs	$50 249 125	$48 892 408		
Total variance			$1 356 717	Favourable

[a] Flexible budget at old price ($28 914 125) plus the effects of $10 price increase ($10 × 113 500 bikes), totalling $30 049 125.

Evaluation of department manager performance

Sandy presents these variance summaries to the controller. He tells the controller that the sales manager probably should receive a bonus for an increased level of sales. However, some bikes were sold at a discount, and this fact needs to be investigated further because the discount resulted in $300 000 less in revenues than expected, given actual sales. Sandy believes the production manager should receive a bonus for the total favourable production variance. In addition, he decides that the support department heads should meet to determine the reasons for the large unfavourable variance in their departments.

Turning Budgeting Pain into Budgeting Gain

By John Orlando

It's budget time again. Being a financial executive, you approach the annual process with excitement and a sincere belief that the process will be efficient, positive, and better than last year. Yet when members of your staff ask managers for their departmental budgets, they are met with blank stares, given excuses, or sent a budget whose form is completely unrecognizable from the template you gave the managers at the outset of the budgeting cycle.

Eventually, the dreaded consolidation effort begins, in which any number of accountants spend too many days attempting to fix the department budgets so you can roll them up into the company-wide budget. The spreadsheet is broken in so many places you barely know where to start. Just when you've got the data into somewhat workable form, the CEO tells you the board of directors would like to see "what if" scenarios reflecting the impact of two major business decisions being considered. You find yourself daydreaming about the time when building a budget was actually fun.

Recognize this scenario? As a career CFO, I've lived through it, like you. But the scary part isn't the aggravation that CFOs endure. The scary part is the inaccuracies resulting from this less-than-perfect budget development process that dramatically decrease confidence in the budget, according to a survey conducted by Centage and the Institute of Management & Administration (IOMA).

The CFOs surveyed, who represented companies of all sizes in more than 20 industries, expressed a wide range of confidence levels in their ability to budget for bookings, revenues, expenses, cash flow, and collections/disbursements. CFOs are most confident budgeting expenses. The smaller the company, the more confident they are: 58% of companies with less than $10 million in revenue are "very confident" budgeting cash flow compared to only 29% of those companies with revenue of $500 million or above.

Overall, most finance executives surveyed—about 45%—are only "somewhat confident" in the accuracy of their budgets, and 12% are "not very confident" or "not at all confident" in most budget areas. Yet about 42% are "very to extremely confident" in all areas, particularly in the accuracy of budgeting for their expenses.

The budget process at most companies is broken—an opinion backed up by our survey findings—because of persistent problems that fall into three areas: people, process, and tools. Figure 1 shows how the three are interrelated. For example, a cumbersome Microsoft Excel-based budget template in the hands of department managers who are unfamiliar with spreadsheets is a

March 2009 | STRATEGIC FINANCE

recipe for frustration that leads to alienation from the process. Some CFOs might see the resulting bad attitudes as the root of their budgeting issues, but, in fact, the attitudes are a symptom, not a cause. The root causes lie in the technology and the process.

To improve the budgeting process and build a more accurate budget that inspires confidence, CFOs must address all three problem areas.

People Problems

When CFOs participating in the Centage/IOMA survey were asked to write in their greatest budgeting "pain point," the most common issue by far—regardless of company size—was dealing with department managers. Specific complaints were that managers don't take ownership or hold themselves accountable for their pieces of the budget, don't fully cooperate or participate in budget development, don't understand the process or what's required, don't meet deadlines, pad their budgets, or provide unrealistic numbers.

Robert Cowan, who was CFO of the Professional Convention Management Association (PCMA) at the time of the survey, elaborates on these issues: "The biggest pain points in budgeting and forecasting involve getting buy-in and involvement in the process from all the users and departments. Although management is clear that department heads are responsible for their budgets and any variances, it often seems that too little attention is paid to the budgeting process and…a well-developed budget. Sometimes this is due to other priorities at the time the budget is being created, but oftentimes, it is a direct result of lack of involvement and/or understanding of the purpose of budgeting and why we go through this extensive exercise every year."

Managers' inability to think about budgets strategically frustrates many CFOs, such as the author of this anonymous survey comment. "[Our] biggest budget concerns are getting adequate detail for revenue forecasting—we have multiple product lines, so amounts generated by product line are as important as an overall revenue total. [Also an issue is the] capability of managers to think about the long term and the important metrics that drive their operations; e.g., if they need to increase revenue, what are the drivers, and what items can be leveraged?"

Managers aren't the only ones being called out by CFOs. Survey respondents cited senior executives for their lack of direction on or support of the budget, mak-

Figure 1: The Interrelationship of Budgeting Obstacles
How weaknesses in one area affect the other two areas.

PEOPLE
PROCESS
Don't follow process or meet deadlines
Process not clear to managers

RESULT: Inaccurate budget; lack of confidence in the budget

Confusing, inadequate tools alienate managers
Untrained in spreadsheets, often change the templates
Shortcomings make the process more cumbersome
Built on inadequate tools that undermine the process

TOOLS

ing late changes to key assumptions and targets, not communicating well between parent company and subsidiaries, and micromanaging the numbers. It's a delicate balance: Too much direction, and managers feel the numbers don't belong to them; too little, and the process wanders aimlessly.

Tool Troubles

While CFOs addressed the bulk of their budgeting vitriol toward managers, inadequate technology was a clear second, with 15% of those who submitted a pain point lamenting the shortcomings of their budgeting tools. Four out of five of these replies expressed frustration specifically with budgeting in Excel spreadsheets with comments such as: "Changes are very difficult in Excel, and it is impossible to drill down into data." "[The] process is very manual and FTEs/headcount very difficult to budget and manage. Pulling together all the details in summary and detail reporting is cumbersome."

Other complaints included the time-consuming nature of budgeting in spreadsheets, the frequency of errors, difficulties rolling up numbers, and the inability to create "what if" scenarios. Cowan sums up the concerns with an understatement: "While Excel or other spreadsheet programs are excellent financial tools, they are not necessarily optimized for budgeting."

Given the anti-spreadsheet sentiment pervasive in the

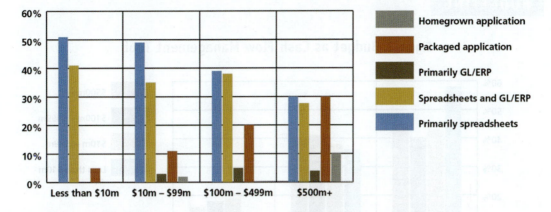

Figure 2: Budgeting Tools by Company Size

Legend:
- Homegrown application
- Packaged application
- Primarily GL/ERP
- Spreadsheets and GL/ERP
- Primarily spreadsheets

financial industry at budgeting time, it's surprising that spreadsheets remain the de facto tool for budgeting, used by an average of 81% of companies either alone or in combination with a general ledger (GL) or enterprise resource planning (ERP) system (see Figure 2).

Three out of four small to medium enterprise (SME) companies (with annual revenue of $100 million to $499 million) budget with spreadsheets alone or in combination with a GL/ERP system. For the small to medium business market ($10 million to $99 million in revenue), 85% of companies build their budgets this way. Although larger companies are more likely to have broken away from spreadsheets and use dedicated budgeting software or applications built in-house, the majority (57%) still use spreadsheets alone or with GL/ERP systems.

If spreadsheets are so troublesome for budgeting, why are they still so prevalent? Evidently, some companies can get by with "hand-grenade budgeting," i.e., almost is close enough. More likely, though, the barriers to change are either a lack of knowledge about other options or inertia.

There's no financial equivalent of a heart attack in the budgeting world—some life-changing event that sends the CFO running for the nearest budgeting software vendor. Instead, some companies eventually realize that their "budgeting cholesterol level" has hit 300 and that they need to change their lifestyle or find themselves in big trouble very soon. In reality, as with physical health, many refuse to acknowledge the early warning signs and take action.

Process Pain

Issues around the budgeting process are a little harder to quantify because a process is wrapped up in people and tools. Theoretically, the process defines how tools should

be used and how people are expected to perform, but in truth what happens is that the limitations of the tools and the inherent weaknesses of human nature bend and reshape your process until you may not recognize it. That's why the end result is never as clear, clean, or accurate as CFOs would like.

Some process issues stem from situations described earlier, such as executives who don't provide enough direction or support on the budgeting process or who feel they can change the budget parameters at will, giving you a moving target as you build the budget. Process issues often emerge at companies with no clear link between the budget and corporate strategy. If one doesn't support the other, your process breaks down at the very top, never mind what shape it will be in by the time it hits the lower ranks.

Suffice to say, if the tools or people aren't working well, chances are the process is broken, too.

Why the Budget Matters

With so many reasons to be dismayed about the budgeting process, it's tempting to give up and accept the status quo. CFOs who want a reason to persevere in their quest for a better budget simply need to be reminded of how much depends on it.

No longer a relatively quick exercise performed once a year, the budget has become a strategic business plan in itself, analyzed and updated regularly throughout the year in the form of monthly forecasts and sliced and diced to allow various views into the company's operations, performance, and future direction. Today's budget is:

A cash flow management tool—Executives at 46% of the companies surveyed view their budgets as "extremely or very important" cash flow management

March 2009 | STRATEGIC FINANCE

Figure 3: Budget as Cash Flow Management Tool

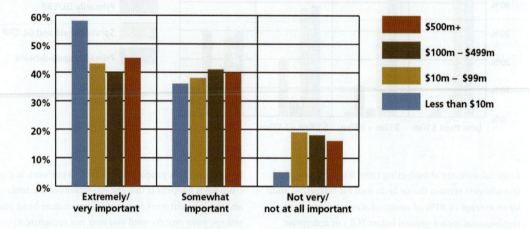

Legend:
- $500m+
- $100m – $499m
- $10m – $99m
- Less than $10m

Categories: Extremely/very important · Somewhat important · Not very/not at all important

tools, and 38% rate them "somewhat important" (see Figure 3 for a breakdown by company size). The budget's cash flow management aspect is most important at companies with annual revenue less than $10 million.

A forecasting tool—More than three-quarters of the executives surveyed reforecast their budgets to help their companies adjust to marketplace fluctuations and changes, and about one-third use rolling forecasts to better manage the business.

A reporting/disclosure mechanism—Almost all companies conduct some regular performance analysis and reporting. About three-quarters of finance executives create full financial reports to meet investor and bank disclosure requirements, and most provide the management team with regular operational/managerial reports. More than 60% also use their financial reports to manage cash flow, reiterating the importance of the budget as a cash flow management tool.

The tool for measuring progress toward key performance indicators (KPI), the most common of which are net income/loss, gross profit, operating expenses as a percentage of sales, and earnings before interest and taxes (EBIT), according to the survey.

A factor in compensation—The overall trend is to link compensation and the achievement of goals such as meeting budget. Even at small companies 55% tie the two, although the trend is most prevalent at larger companies (82% of those with revenue of $500 million and above). The implications of this aren't inconsequential: The majority of companies with up to $500 million in revenue put 10%-20% of compensation in this at-risk category, and 20% or more is most common at the largest companies.

A crystal ball—For CFOs with the right tools, the budget facilitates the creation of "what if" scenarios that show the impact of various business decisions on the numbers. This type of contingency planning is critical for start-ups and other fast-growth companies that need to be prepared to turn on a dime if an initiative doesn't deliver as planned. It also allows CFOs at more traditional companies to weigh various strategic alternatives before settling on a course of action.

Improvement Plan

Now that you're feeling revitalized because you know how important budgets really are, how can you help improve the imperfect budgeting process?

Tackling the weaknesses of spreadsheet budgeting is the easiest challenge, and it's possibly even the most cost-effective one compared to the staff hours required to solve the people aspects of budgeting. A variety of good budgeting applications exist, geared for different sizes of companies and ranging from a few thousand dollars to hundreds of thousands. As Robert Cowan warns, though, "[the] software must be easy to use for those who must use it regularly. Reporting and documentation must be easy, self-contained, and able to be done with minimal assistance from Finance."

Here, again, the tools, people, and process are intertwined. Upgrading your budgeting technology will make your life easier in the obvious ways, such as improved ability to roll up numbers, time savings, and increased accuracy through automation. In addition, by improving your budgeting tools you increase your ability to invest managers in the process and to extract accurate and meaningful data from them. Software that's more sophisticated than spreadsheets often can be easier for novices to use and understand. If it provides a dashboard that managers can adapt for a quick view of their performance, including meeting budget, their interaction with and interest in the budget can grow. This greater ease of use will help adjust management attitudes toward budgeting chores.

But better tools aren't enough. How do you turn the budgeting process from a threat into an opportunity for department managers? How do you get them to accept the need for an accurate, well-thought-out budget; build that budget accordingly; and be supportive of the process? How do you get them to accept accountability?

You can accomplish these objectives by overhauling your budgeting process using seven steps that are drawn from my own experience and backed up by CFO feedback from the survey:

1. Evaluate your process. This is where all CFOs must say mea culpa, for part of the blame for an imperfect budgeting process lies on our shoulders. Is your process as streamlined, simple, and clear as possible? Are assumptions and deadlines clearly defined? If not, make adjustments. Next, assign responsibility. As one CFO commented in the survey, "Leave no area of the P&L (profit and loss statement) without an owner." Finally, work with Human Resources to tie managers' compensation to their P&L. Nothing drives behavior like a well-thought-out compensation plan.

2. Upgrade your technology if you're still using spreadsheets for budgeting, and turn a weakness into a strength.

3. Communicate. The best process in the world can fail without adequate communication. With any employee, first and foremost, always address what your initiative means to them. Most likely, an accurate budget affects them in two ways: It influences the financial health of the company, and it possibly affects their compensation (see number 1). Explain how the budget supports the achievement of corporate strategy and goals and how the company and they prosper if the budget is met.

4. Communicate some more. Explain the process, clearly stating the timetable, assumptions, and responsibilities. Then explain why the budgeting process matters. No one wants to spend time on a process that doesn't matter. Teach them why it does. Sometimes this is handled best by showing the result if the budget is done incorrectly.

5. Train and educate. Conduct training sessions to be sure that all employees with a role in budget development have a basic knowledge of how to build a budget and understand their roles and how to use the tools you provided. As Cowan points out, "Users with a nonfinancial background oftentimes aren't comfortable working with financial figures and don't have the skills to accurately project and cost out what their proposed activities will involve. [Finance] needs to work closely with those departments to obtain and document the budget assumptions and requirements. Often this is not done or not done well, leading to errors in the budget."

6. Collaborate. Be inclusive and collaborative, survey participants told us. "Keep department heads involved; their knowledge of their specific areas of influence is invaluable." Once the training ends and the process begins, check in regularly to provide answers and guidance.

7. Follow through. Budgeting never stops for Finance staff, so why should it for managers? After the annual budget is built, update managers regularly. Your new budgeting tool should make it easy to provide tailored reports for each manager and desktop dashboards where they can follow their performance in many areas, including the budget.

Rolling Up

The difficulty in collecting accurate data from managers who are uninterested or inadequately trained and in consolidating that data using imperfect technology leads to budgets in which CFOs aren't overly confident. As Cowan says, "If the budget inputs are not accurate, then the outputs cannot help but be inaccurate as well."

Yet so much is riding on an accurate budget. Done properly, budgets help CFOs, CEOs, and board members better manage the business and plan for the future. Companies have much to gain by improving their budget process. For starters, it will put the trust back into the numbers they rely on so heavily, and it just might get department managers to understand that their accurate input is vital to the budget's success. **SF**

John Orlando is CFO of Centage Corp. (www.centage.com), a provider of budgeting and forecasting solutions for small to medium-sized businesses that is headquartered in Natick, Mass. You can reach John at (800) 366-5111 or jorlando@centage.com.

This article is based in part on the findings of the *2007 Budgeting Survey: Benchmarks & Issues,* conducted by Centage Corp. and IOMA (Institute of Management & Administration). For a copy of the survey report, visit www.centage.com/pdf/centage_ioma_budgeting_survey.pdf.

SUMMARY

6.1 Demonstrate an understanding of the role of budgets in developing both short- and long-term plans.

Budget objectives

- Developing and communicating organisational strategies and goals for the entire entity as well as for each segment, division or department
- Assigning decision rights (authority to spend, and responsibility for decision outcomes)
- Motivating managers to plan in advance
- Coordinating operating activities such as sales and production
- Establishing prices for the internal transfer of goods and services
- Measuring and comparing expected and actual outcomes
- Monitoring actual performance and investigating variances when necessary
- Motivating managers to provide appropriate estimates, meet expectations and use resources efficiently
- Re-evaluating and revising strategies and operating plans as conditions change

Budget cycle

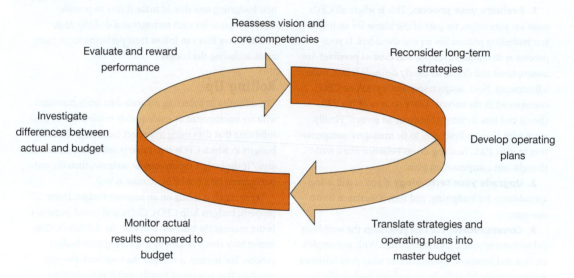

6.2 Describe the role of the master budget and develop a master budget.
Master budget overview

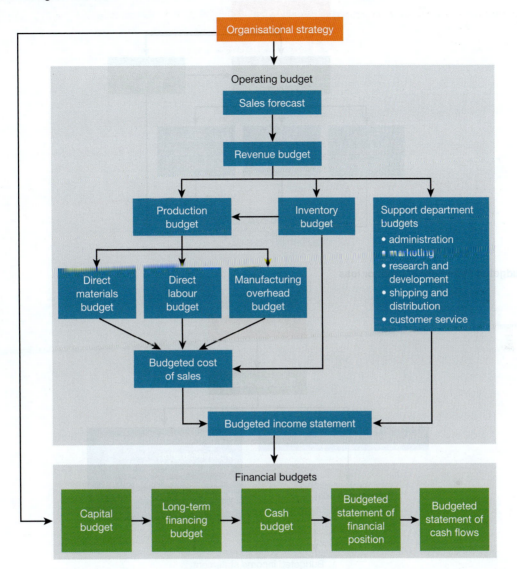

Production and inventory budgets

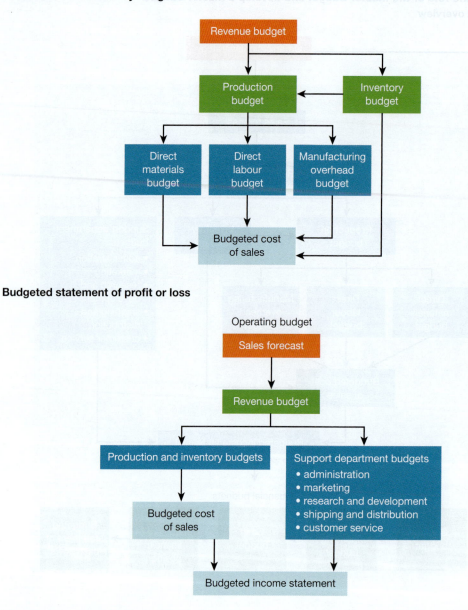

Budgeted statement of profit or loss

6.3 Develop a cash budget.

Operating cash receipts and disbursements

- Forecast timing of cash receipts from customers
- Forecast timing of cash payments for direct materials, direct labour, variable and fixed overhead, and support department costs

Other planned cash flows

- Purchase or sale of property, plant and equipment
- Proceeds or repayments of long-term debt
- Proceeds or redemption of capital stock
- Dividends to shareholders

Balancing the cash budget

- Desired cash balance
- Purchase or liquidation of short-term investments
- Proceeds or repayments of short-term debt
- Interest on short-term debt

6.4 Explain the use of budget targets as performance benchmarks.

Budget variances

- Differences between budgeted and actual results
- May be favourable or unfavourable

Major reasons for variances

- Actual activities do not follow plans
- Budget may be an inappropriate benchmark (that is, budget assumptions may be incorrect)

Static budget variances

- Variances based on the budget for a specific volume of production or services
- Variable cost variances may be misleading
- Useful for measuring performance of individuals/departments responsible for achieving budgeted volume of activity

Flexible budget variances

- Variances based on the budget adjusted for actual sales or production volume
- Variable costs are adjusted for actual volume of activity
- Useful for measuring performance of individuals/departments *not* responsible for achieving budgeted volume of activity

6.5 Illustrate how budgets are used to monitor and motivate performance.

- As benchmarks
- To reward performance

Budget adjustments for performance evaluation

- Use flexible budget to adjust for actual volumes
- Remove costs not under managers' control
- Update costs for anticipated price changes

KEY TERMS

budget A formalised financial plan for operations of an entity for a specified future period.

budget assumptions Plans and predictions about next period's operating activities.

budget cycle A series of steps that entities follow to develop and use budgets.

budget variances Differences between budgeted and actual results.

budgetary slack The practices of intentionally setting revenue budgets too low and cost budgets too high.

budgeted financial statements Forecasts of the future statement of profit or loss, statement of financial position and cash flows, given an organisation's sales forecasts and expenditure plans for the next period.

cash budget Reflects the effects of management's plans on cash, and summarises the information that accountants gather about the expected amounts and timing of cash receipts and disbursements.

decision rights The responsibilities and financial decision-making authority of individual managers.

favourable variance A variance in which actual revenues are larger than the budget, or actual costs are lower than the budget.

financial budgets Management's plans for capital expenditures, long-term financing and cash flows, resulting in a budgeted balance sheet and budgeted statement of cash flows.

flexible budget A budget that reflects a range of operations; fixed and variable costs are separated to more accurately reflect the effects of activity levels on cost.

master budget A comprehensive plan for an upcoming financial period, usually a year. Often summarised in a set of budgeted financial statements.

operating budget Management's plan for revenues, production and operating costs.

participative budgeting A budgeting process in which managers who are responsible for meeting budgets also prepare the initial budget forecasts, setting targets for themselves.

static budget A budget based on forecasts of specific volumes of production or services. All variable costs are calculated for a specific volume of operations.

unfavourable variance A variance in which actual costs are greater than budgeted, or actual revenues are less than budgeted.

SELF-STUDY PROBLEMS

SELF-STUDY PROBLEM 1 Constructing a master budget

Summer Select Patio Furniture is a manufacturer of patio furniture. The patio table department produces table sets. Each table set consists of four chairs, a table and an umbrella. The accountant at Summer Select gathered the following information from all of the departments in the organisation so that she can prepare next year's budget. No change occurred in costs from last period to this period. Support department costs are allocated between two separate production departments. Following is information about costs for the patio table department.

Manufacturing costs			
Direct materials	Chairs	$	75
	Table	$	42
	Umbrella	$	20
Direct labour:			
Hours	Assembly		2
	Packing		0.2
Cost per hour	Assembly	$	20.00
	Packing	$	10.00
Cost per unit	Assembly	$	40.00
	Packing	$	2.00

Inventories		
	Beginning	Targeted ending
Direct materials:		
Chairs	$15 000	$ 20 000
Tables	$10 000	$ 12 000
Umbrellas	$ 5 000	$ 7 000
Finished goods	1000 units at $304 per unit	1200 units

Revenue assumptions		
Selling price	$	500
Table sets sold		50 000

Estimated variable manufacturing overhead costs	
Supplies	$ 422 000
Indirect labour	627 500
Maintenance	80 000
Miscellaneous	125 500
Total	$1 255 000

Estimated fixed manufacturing overhead costs	
Depreciation	$1 004 000
Property taxes	251 000
Insurance	351 400
Plant supervision	1 255 000
Fringe benefits	1 757 000
Miscellaneous	401 600
Total	$5 020 000

Estimated support department costs	
Department	Fixed costs
Administration	$4 819 200
Marketing	2 891 520
Distribution	1 445 760
Customer service	481 920
Total	$9 638 400

Required

Prepare the following budgets: revenue, production, direct materials, direct manufacturing labour, manufacturing overhead, ending inventory, cost of sales and support department costs. Then prepare a budgeted statement of profit or loss, assuming an income tax rate of 35 per cent.

SOLUTION TO SELF-STUDY PROBLEM 1

Revenue budget

The revenue budget calculates forecasted revenues, given forecasted sales volume and price.

	Selling price	Units sold	Total revenues
Table sets	$500	50 000	$25 000 000

Production budget (units)

The production budget calculates the number of units that need to be produced, given current and targeted ending inventory levels and budgeted sales.

	Table sets
Sales	50 000
Targeted ending inventory	1 200
Total finished units needed	51 200
Less beginning inventory	1 000
Production	50 200

Direct materials budget

The direct materials budget calculates the budget for purchases of raw materials, given the beginning and targeted ending inventory levels and budgeted production volume.

Budgeted usage:	
Chairs (50 200 sets × $75 per set)	$3 765 000
Tables (50 200 sets × $42 per set)	2 108 400
Umbrellas (50 200 sets × $20 per set)	1 004 000
Total direct materials used	6 877 400
Add targeted ending inventory	39 000
Deduct beginning inventory	(30 000)
Total purchases	$6 886 400

Direct manufacturing labour budget

The direct manufacturing labour budget calculates the amount of direct labour hours needed for budgeted production and then determines the cost.

Labour hours budget:	
Assembly (50 200 sets × 2 hours)	100 400
Packing (50 200 sets × 0.2 hours)	10 040
Total labour hours	110 440
Labour cost budget:	
Assembly (100 400 hours × $20 per hour)	$2 008 000
Packing (10 040 hours × $10 per hour)	100 400
Total labour cost	$2 108 400

Manufacturing overhead budget

The manufacturing overhead budget summarises the expected fixed and variable overhead costs.

Variable manufacturing overhead costs:	
Supplies	$ 422 000
Indirect labour	627 500
Maintenance	80 000
Miscellaneous	125 500
Total variable overhead	1 255 000
Fixed manufacturing overhead costs:	
Depreciation	1 004 000
Property taxes	251 000

Insurance	351 400
Plant supervision	1 255 000
Fringe benefits	1 757 000
Miscellaneous	401 600
Total fixed overhead	5 020 000
Total overhead	$6 275 000
Manufacturing overhead allocation rates	Cost per set
Variable ($1 255 000 ÷ 50 200 sets)	$ 25
Fixed ($5 020 000 ÷ 50 200 sets)	$ 100

Ending inventories budget

The ending inventories budget determines the unit costs and then forecasts the cost of ending inventory units.

Unit costs (cost per table set):	
Direct materials:	Cost per unit
Chairs	$ 75.00
Table	42.00
Umbrella	20.00
Total direct material	137.00
Direct labour:	
Assembly	40.00
Packaging	2.00
Total direct labour	42.00
Overhead:	
Variable	25.00
Fixed	100.00
Total overhead	125.00
Total unit cost	$304.00

Cost of sales budget

The cost of sales budget calculates the cost of inventory available for sale during the period and the cost of sales.

Beginning finished goods (1000 sets × $304 per set)		$ 304 000
Cost of goods manufactured:		
Direct materials	$6 877 400	
Direct labour	2 108 400	
Manufacturing overhead	6 275 000	
Total cost of goods manufactured		15 260 800
Total goods available for sale		15 564 800
Less ending finished goods (1200 sets × $304 per set)		(364 800)
Cost of sales		$15 200 000

Support department costs budget

The support department costs budget forecasts the total non-manufacturing-related costs for the period.

Department	Fixed costs
Administration	$4 819 200
Marketing	2 891 520
Distribution	1 445 760
Customer service	481 920
Total	$9 638 400

Budgeted statement of profit or loss

Once all of the budget schedules have been prepared, the budgeted statement of profit or loss is created. Revenue is drawn from the revenue budget, and cost of sales from the cost of sales budget. Then the operating costs from the support department costs budget are subtracted to determine operating income.

Revenues	$25 000 000
Cost of sales	15 200 000
Gross margin	9 800 000
Operating costs:	
Administration	$4 819 200
Marketing	2 891 520
Distribution	1 445 760
Customer service	481 920
	9 638 400
Operating income	161 600
Income tax expense ($161 600 × 35%)	56 560
Net income	$ 105 040

SELF-STUDY PROBLEM 2 Comparing actual results to a flexible budget

Suppose that the manager of Summer Select Patio Furniture is evaluated based on budgeted expectations. She is responsible for both sales and production costs. This period the entity produced and sold more units than budgeted, and she expects to get a bonus. Refer to self-study problem 1 for Summer Select Patio Furniture's static budget. The entity's actual results for the period are shown below.

Sales volume	54 000	table sets
Sales revenue	$25 500 000	
Variable production costs	10 980 000	
Fixed production costs	5 000 000	
Fixed support department costs	$ 9 415 300	

Required

(a) Prepare a flexible budget based on actual sales volumes, and then calculate the flexible budget revenue and cost variances.

(b) Review the variances from part (a). For each variance, briefly describe the types of operating or budgeting problems that might have caused these variances.

(c) Compose at least three questions the accountant could ask the manager to better understand how the largest variances arose.

SOLUTION TO SELF-STUDY PROBLEM 2

(a) To create a flexible budget for evaluating the department manager's performance, we modify the static budget to reflect the actual volume of sales, and remove any costs not under the manager's control. It requires a recalculation of budgeted variable costs to reflect actual volume. Because fixed costs remain fixed within a relevant range, we assume that they will not change with the changes in volume. However, we remove the support department costs because they are allocated and not under control of the manager.

	Static budget	Flexible budget	Actual	Variance
Sales volume	50 000	54 000	54 000	
Revenue	$25 000 000	$27 000 000[a]	$25 500 000	$1 500 000 U
Variable production costs	10 200 000[b]	11 016 000[c]	10 980 000	36 000 F
Fixed production costs	5 020 000[d]	5 020 000	5 000 000	20 000 F
Fixed support costs	9 638 400	Not applicable	Not applicable	Not applicable
Forecasted operating income	$ 141 600	$10 964 000	$ 9 520 000	$1 444 000 U

[a] 54 000 × $500.
[b] 50 000 × ($137 + $42 + $25).
[c] 54 000 × ($137 + $42 + $25).
[d] Total budgeted fixed costs.
  F = Favourable/U = Unfavourable

(b) Following are possible explanations for each of the variances; you may think of others.
- The revenue variance is the biggest problem for Summer Select. Instead of selling the furniture for $500 a set, the average revenue was $472.22 ($25 500 000 ÷ 54 000). It is possible that weather or economic factors reduced demand, and so the furniture was discounted during the season. It is also possible that sales volumes were better than expected because of the discounted price. The volume is larger than budgeted, but with the reduced selling price, a large unfavourable revenue variance occurred.
- Variable production costs might be lower than the flexible budget because prices for direct materials, direct labour or variable overhead costs were lower than budget. Or, the use of materials or labour might have been more efficient than in the budget. For example, less scrap might have occurred or employees might have been more productive than anticipated. Other types of variable production costs might also have been lower than budget. For example, machinery might have required fewer repairs than expected. Also, economies of scale may have been introduced, such as fewer set-up costs because production runs were longer, or direct materials costs may have been lower because of volume discounts. However, the favourable variance could possibly signal a reduction in quality, which could create a problem with future sales.
- Fixed production costs were slightly less than expected. The $20 000 variance is a small percentage of the budgeted fixed production costs, so it might be a random variation in cost.
- Fixed support costs might have been lower than the budget for many different reasons: unexpected decreases in the costs of fixed items such as computer software, better purchase prices for office supplies, or outsourcing of services.

    It is important to keep in mind that the variances in part (a) are net amounts. Most likely, each cost category includes some favourable and some unfavourable variances. A relatively small net variance could consist of two or more large offsetting items.
(c) The following list contains possible questions; you may think of others.
  (i) Why were prices discounted, and will the new price carry over to next period?
  (ii) Is the favourable variance in variable production costs due to changes in the quality of materials? How did the savings arise?
  (iii) Were any fixed production costs either much larger or much smaller than expected?

QUESTIONS

6.1 How are budgets related to organisational strategies? **LO1**

6.2 Describe the types of information that managers use to develop budgets. **LO1**

6.3 How are the master budget and flexible budget related? **LO2**

6.4 Explain how the following budgets relate to each other: the revenue budget, the production budget and the direct materials budget. **LO2**

6.5 How can budgeting assist an entity to efficiently use its human resources? **LO4**

6.6 What are the objectives of participative budgeting? **LO5**

6.7 What methods do organisations use to minimise budgetary slack? **LO5**

6.8 What adjustments should be made to static budgets before they are used for management performance evaluation? **LO5**

6.9 What are some of the challenges that organisations face when allocating budget authority and responsibility? **LO5**

6.10 Blowervacs produces and sells leaf blowers. Production levels are high in the summer and beginning of autumn and then taper off through the winter. Sales are high in the autumn and early winter and then taper off in the spring. Explain why preparing a cash budget might be particularly important for Blowervacs. **LO3**

6.11 Discuss the sources of information used to prepare a cash budget for a manufacturing entity. **LO3**

6.12 While preparing the cash budget for next year, the accountant at Mines Ltd. identified a $20 million shortfall. This shortfall was due to a capital expenditure item of the same value. The CEO has identified that the purchase must be made to ensure competitive advantage for the business. Identify several ways that the business could overcome this situation. **LO3**

EXERCISES

6.13 Budgeting for next semester; assumptions; monitoring LO1, 2

Suppose a friend asks you to help her prepare a budget for the next semester.

Required

(a) Assuming you followed a process similar to that presented in this chapter, which budgets would you help her prepare? Explain your choices.

(b) Create a list of information needed to complete the various budgets. Identify which pieces of information need to be estimated.

(c) Create a list of the assumptions your friend will need to make for estimating the necessary information.

(d) How should your friend monitor her budget performance throughout the semester? Write an explanation that your friend, who is not familiar with accounting, will understand.

6.14 Production, direct materials and direct labour budgets LO2

Seer Manufacturing has projected sales of its product for the next six months as follows.

January	40 units
February	90 units
March	100 units
April	80 units
May	30 units
June	70 units

The product sells for $100, variable expenses are $70 per unit and fixed expenses are $1500 per month. The finished product requires three units of raw material and ten hours of direct labour. The entity tries to maintain an ending inventory of finished goods equal to the next two months of sales and an ending inventory of raw materials equal to half of the current month's usage.

Required

(a) Prepare a production budget for February, March and April.

(b) Prepare a forecast of the units of direct materials required for February, March and April.

(c) Prepare a direct labour hours budget for February, March and April.

6.15 Production, labour, materials and sales budgets LO2

Bullen & Company makes and sells upmarket carry bags for laptop computers. John Crane, controller, is responsible for preparing Bullen's master budget and has assembled the following data for next year.

The direct labour rate includes wages, all employee-related benefits and the employer's share of payroll tax. Labour-saving machinery will be fully operational by March. Also, as of 1 March, the entity's enterprise agreement calls for an increase in direct labour wages that is included in the direct labour rate.

Bullen expects to have 10 000 bags in inventory at the beginning of next year, and has a policy of carrying 50 per cent of the following month's projected sales in inventory.

	January	February	March	April
Estimated unit sales	20 000	24 000	16 000	18 000
Sales price per unit	$80	$80	$75	$75
Direct labour hours per unit	4.0	4.0	3.5	3.5
Direct labour hourly rate	$15	$15	$16	$16
Direct materials cost per unit	$10	$10	$10	$10

Required

(a) Prepare the following budgets for Bullen & Company for the first quarter of next year. Be sure to show supporting calculations:

(i) production budget in units

(ii) direct labour budget in hours

(iii) direct materials budget

(iv) sales budget.

(b) Calculate the total budgeted contribution margin for Bullen & Company for the first quarter of next year. Be sure to show supporting calculations.

(c) Discuss at least three behavioural considerations in the profit-planning and budgeting process.

6.16 Flexible budget variances; profit effect of market share decline   LO4

Data for the Stove Division of Appliances Now, which produces and sells a complete line of kitchen stoves, are as follows.

(In thousands)	Budget	Actual
Revenue	$16 491	$17 480
Variable production costs	5 892	6 451
Fixed manufacturing costs	1 977	2 032
Variable selling expenses	456	550
Fixed selling expenses	1 275	1 268
Administrative expenses	4 773	5 550
Operating income	$ 2 118	$ 1 629

The budget, set at the beginning of the year, was based upon estimates of sales and costs. Administrative expenses include charges by corporate headquarters for providing strategic guidance. These fixed costs are allocated to divisions using revenues as the allocation base.

Required

(a) Assume that a different volume of stoves was sold than was budgeted and prepare a flexible budget using the change in revenue to adjust the variable costs. Calculate budget variances.

(b) Due to a booming economy, the division's unit sales were higher than anticipated, even though the division's share of the kitchen stove market fell from 22 per cent to 20 per cent during the year. Using information from the flexible budget, estimate the impact on profits of the decline in market share. (*Hint:* First estimate what the total sales should have been.)

6.17 Direct materials budgeted payments   LO2

Organic Industries intends to start business on 1 January. Production plans for the first four months of operations are as follows.

January	20 000 units
February	50 000 units
March	70 000 units
April	70 000 units

Each unit requires 2 kilograms of material. The entity would like to end each month with enough raw material inventory on hand to cover 25 per cent of the following month's production needs. The material costs $7 per kilogram. The managers anticipate being able to pay for 40 per cent of purchases in the month of purchase. They will receive a 10 per cent discount for these early payments. They anticipate having to defer payment to the next month on 60 per cent of their purchases. No discount will be taken on these late payments. The business starts with no inventories on 1 January.

Required

Determine the budgeted payments for purchases of materials for each of the first three months of operations.

6.18 Preparation of receipts from debtors schedule and cash budget   LO3

Ken Martin, manager of Lonnie Car Repairers, has requested that you prepare a cash budget for the months of December and January. He has provided the following information to assist in this task.

- Projected cash balance at the end of November is $30 000.
- Actual revenue for October and November and projected revenue for December and January are as follows.

	October	November	December	January
Cash sales	$33 000	$ 31 000	$ 42 000	$30 000
Sales on credit	60 000	80 000	100 000	50 000
Total sales	$ 93 000	$111 000	$142 000	$80 000

- Analysis of past records has shown that credit sales are collected over a three-month period, with 50 per cent being collected in the month of the sale, 40 per cent in the next month, and the remainder in the following month. (10%)
- Projected expenditure during December and January is as follows:
  - Selling and administrative expenses are budgeted to be $58 000 each month.
  - A new car-hoist will be purchased for $100 000, with a $20 000 cash payment in December and the balance to be paid in March.
  - Ken wants to maintain a minimum cash balance of $30 000.
  - As more customers will want their vehicles serviced prior to Christmas, the consumables store will need more supplies. Accordingly, an order has been placed for $45 000 of inventory. This will arrive in late November and be paid for in December.

Required

(a) Prepare a schedule showing receipts from customers for the credit sales.

(b) Prepare a cash budget for December and January.

(c) Prepare a report for Ken outlining his cash position over the Christmas period. Give advice regarding any financing requirements or investment opportunities.

6.19 Purchases, cost of sales and cash collection budgets   **LO2**

The Zel Company operates at local flea markets. It has budgeted the following sales for the indicated months.

	June	July	August
Sales on account	$1 500 000	$1 600 000	$1 700 000
Cash sales	200 000	210 000	220 000
Total sales	$1 700 000	$1 810 000	$1 920 000

Zel's success in this specialty market is due in large part to the extension of credit terms and the budgeting techniques implemented by the entity's owner, Barbara Zel. Ms Zel is a recycler; that is, she collects her merchandise daily at neighbourhood garage sales and sells the merchandise weekly at regional flea markets. All merchandise is marked up to sell at its invoice cost (as purchased at garage sales) plus 25 per cent. Stated differently, cost is 80 per cent of selling price. Merchandise inventories at the beginning of each month are 30 per cent of that month's forecasted cost of sales. With respect to sales on account, 40 per cent of receivables are collected in the month of sale, 50 per cent are collected in the month following sale and 10 per cent are never collected.

Required

(a) What is the anticipated cost of sales for June?

(b) What is the beginning inventory for July expected to be?

(c) What are the July purchases expected to be?

(d) What are the forecasted July cash collections?

6.20 Cash budget for revenues and expenses   **LO3**

Maryborough Manufacturing has projected sales in units for four months of operations as follows.

January	$25 000
February	$30 000
March	$32 000
April	$35 000

The product sells for $18 per unit. Twenty-five per cent of the customers are expected to pay in the month of sale and take a 3 per cent discount; 70 per cent are expected to pay in the month following sale. The remaining 5 per cent will never pay.

It takes 2 kilograms of materials to produce a unit of product. The materials cost $0.75 per kilogram. In January no raw materials are in beginning inventories, but managers want to end each month with enough materials for 20 per cent of the next month's production. The entity pays for 60 per cent of its materials purchases in the month of purchase and 40 per cent in the following month.

It takes 0.5 hours of labour to produce each unit. Labour is paid $15 per hour and is paid in the same month as worked. Overhead is estimated to be $2 per unit plus $25 000 per month (including depreciation of $12 000). Overhead costs are paid as incurred.

Maryborough will begin January with no finished goods or work in process inventory. The managers wish to end each month with 25 per cent of the following month's sales in finished goods inventory. They will end each month with no work in process.

Required

Prepare a cash budget listing cash receipts and disbursements for February. The entity will begin February with a cash balance of $80 000.

6.21 Flexible budget and variances; performance measurement; reasons for variances   **LO4**

Play Time Toys is organised into two major divisions: marketing and production. The production division is further divided into three departments: puzzles, dolls and video games. Each production department has its own manager.

The entity's management believes that all costs must be covered by sales of the three product lines. Therefore, a portion of headquarters, marketing and the production division costs are allocated to each product line.

The entity's accountant prepared the following performance report for the manager of the dolls production department.

Performance report dolls production department (Volumes and total dollar amounts are in thousands.)				
	Cost forecasts	**Budget**	**Actual**	**Variance**
Sales volume	1 000	1 000	1 100	100 F
Revenue	$12.00/unit	$12 000	$12 400	$ 400 F
Direct materials	2.00/unit	2 000	2 100	(100) U
Direct labour	1.00/unit	1 000	1 225	(225) U
Variable factory overhead	1.00/unit	1 000	1 100	(100) U
Fixed factory overhead	0.80/unit	800	1 020	(220) U
Production division overhead	0.10/unit	100	105	(5) U
Headquarters	0.20/unit	200	220	(20) U
Marketing	0.50/unit	500	550	(50) U
Operating income	$ 6.40/unit	$ 6 400	$ 6 080	$(320) U

Required

(a) Is Play Time using a static budget or a flexible budget to calculate variances? Explain. Do you agree with this approach? Why?

(b) Develop an appropriate benchmark for evaluating the performance of the dolls production department. Decide whether to include or exclude each cost category, and explain your decisions.

(c) Use the benchmark you created in part (b) to calculate variances.

(d) Review the variances from part (c). Briefly describe the types of operating or budgeting problems that might have caused these variances.

6.22 Prepare cash budget   **LO3**

A college student, Brad Worth, plans to sell atomic alarm clocks with CD players over the internet and by mail order to help pay his expenses during the summer semester. He buys the clocks for $32 and sells them for $50. If payment by cheque accompanies the mail orders (estimated to be 40 per cent of sales), he gives a 10 per cent discount. If customers include a credit card number for either internet or mail order sales (30 per cent of sales), customers receive a 5 per cent discount. The remaining collections are estimated to be:

One month following	15%
Two months following	6%
Three months following	4%
Uncollectable	5%

Sales forecasts are as follows:

September	120 units
October	220 units
November	320 units
December	400 units
January	out of the business

Brad plans to pay his supplier 50 per cent in the month of purchase and 50 per cent in the following month. A 6 per cent discount is granted on payments made in the month of purchase; however, he will not be able to take any discounts on September purchases because of cash flow constraints. All September purchases will be paid for in October.

He has 50 clocks on hand (purchased in August, to be paid for in September) and plans to maintain enough end-of-month inventory to meet 70 per cent of the next month's sales.

Required

(a) Prepare schedules for monthly budgeted cash receipts and cash disbursements for this venture. During which months will Brad need to finance purchases?

(b) Brad planned simply to write off the uncollectables. However, his accounting professor suggested he turn them over to a collection agency. How much could Brad let the collection agency keep so that he would be no worse off?

PROBLEMS

6.23 Preparation of receipts from debtors schedule and cash budget   LO3

Point Piper prepares monthly cash budgets. Provided below is a set of relevant data extracted from existing reports, and the sub-budgets for the months of September and October.

	September	October
Credit sales	$ 314 000	$ 412 000
Direct materials purchases	162 000	216 000
Direct labour	51 400	55 200
Manufacturing overhead	21 600	23 400
Marketing and administration expenses	39 000	39 000
Proceeds from sale of old equipment		8 200
Cash payment for new IT equipment	16 500	

All sales are on credit. Collections from debtors normally have the following pattern: 60 per cent in the month of sale, 30 per cent in the month following the sale, and 10 per cent in the second month following the sale. Fortunately, Point Piper does not have much trouble with bad debts.

Sales in June, July and August were $295 000, $266 000 and $302 000 respectively. Direct material purchases are paid for in the month following the purchase. Purchases in August were $182 000. Manufacturing overhead includes $12 500 for depreciation expense, while the marketing and administration expenses include an amount of $5600 for depreciation expenses. Point Piper expects to be able to repay the principal on a $50 000 loan in October.

Required

(a) Prepare a schedule of receipts from debtors for the two months ending 31 October.

(b) Prepare a cash budget for September and October. The cash balance at 31 August was $12 600.

(c) As part of its longer-term plans, management was hoping to commence a product reinvention program for one of its core products. The project would require an initial cash commitment of $30 000. Management was hoping to fund this from the cash flows of the business. Does this seem feasible?

6.24 Prepare cash budget from financial statements   LO3

The Red Bean Company processes and distributes beans. The beans are packed in 500-gram plastic bags and sold to grocery chains for $0.50 each in boxes of 100 bags. During March, the entity anticipates selling 16 000 boxes (sales in February were 14 000 boxes). Typically, 80 per cent of the entity's customers pay within the month of sale, 18 per cent pay the month after, and 2 per cent of sales are never collected.

The entity buys beans from local farmers. The farmers are paid $0.20 per 500 grams, cash. Most of the processing is done automatically. Consequently, most ($80 000) of the entity's factory overhead is depreciation expense.

The entity advertises heavily. For March, managers expect to publish $75 000 worth of advertisements in popular magazines. This amount is up from February's $60 000. The entity pays for 10 per cent of its advertising in the month the advertisements are run and 90 per cent in the following month. March's budgeted statement of profit or loss and statement of cost of goods manufactured and sold follow. All costs and expenses are paid for as incurred unless specifically indicated otherwise. The entity will begin March with a cash balance of $25 000, and pays a monthly dividend of $15 000 to the owners.

Statement of profit or loss	
Sales	$800 000
Cost of sales	540 000
Gross margin	260 000
Administrative salaries	80 000
Sales commissions	69 000
Advertising	75 000
Bad debts expense	16 000
Operating income	$ 20 000

Statement of cost of goods manufactured and sold	
Beginning balance direct materials	$ 20 000
Direct materials purchases	330 000
Materials available for use	350 000
Ending balance direct materials	30 000
Direct materials used	320 000
Labour costs incurred	90 000
Overhead costs	115 000
Cost of good manufactured	525 000
Beginning finished goods balance	45 000
Goods available for sale	570 000
Ending finished goods balance	30 000
Cost of sales	$540 000

Required

From the information provided, prepare a cash budget for March.

6.25 Time budget; uncertainties; performance evaluation; priorities   **LO5**

Patricia sighed and briefly closed her eyes. She was frustrated with the reconciliation she was working on. She was sure that she was missing something, but could not determine what it was. And she felt the clock ticking, Patricia knew that the time budget for this assignment was only three hours, and she had already worked on it for two hours.

Patricia started with a CPA entity after graduation, three months ago. Her first few assignments had been stressful. She had been a good student in school, and she expected to do well at work too. But she often felt inadequate here, as though she was supposed to know more than she did. Her supervisor, Ron, told her not to worry too much. He said that her job was to learn and that she would be performing well soon. 'All new-hires are slow to begin with,' he told her, 'Just let me know if you have any questions.' However, Patricia felt that she had pestered him with enough questions. Most of the time, the answers to her questions seemed so obvious . . . after Ron had answered them.

She looked at the reconciliation again.

Required

(a) Explain why it might be difficult to establish accurate time budgets for accounting tasks.

(b) Provide possible reasons why Patricia's time on this assignment could exceed the budget.

(c) Explain why Patricia is reluctant to seek Ron's help on this assignment.

(d) Describe how Ron might evaluate Patricia's performance assuming:

  (i) She seeks his help and completes the assignment in four hours.

  (ii) She does not seek his help and completes the assignment in eight hours.

(e) Suppose Patricia does not seek Ron's help and completes the assignment in eight hours.

  (i) What priorities has Patricia used in making this choice?

  (ii) Has Patricia behaved ethically? Why?

(f) What could Patricia learn from this experience that will improve her performance in the future?

(g) Suppose Patricia asked for your advice.

  (i) Use the information you learned from the preceding analyses to write a memo to Patricia with your recommendation. Refer in your memo to the information that would be useful to Patricia.

  (ii) Write one or two paragraphs explaining how you decided what information to include in your memo.

6.26 Performance benchmarks; variances and analysis   **LO5**

Central Coast Public Clinic is a free outpatient clinic for public assistance patients. Among other services, the clinic provides visiting nurses for elderly patients in their homes. A homemaker who cleans and performs other household tasks accompanies each nurse. When the nurses are not visiting clients, they work at the office preparing for visits. When the homemakers complete their visits, they go home.

Each year, the clinic receives a budget allotment from the state government. The government does not allow the clinic to spend more than this allotment. The clinic, in turn, allocates its budget among its various programs. The visiting nurse program was authorised (and spent) $250 396 in 2018 and $279 476 in 2019 as follows.

	2018	2019
Nurses	$135 378	$145 019
Homemakers	60 046	71 500
Medical supplies	18 197	21 402
Cleaning supplies	6 894	9 216
Transportation	9 068	11 144
Clinic general overhead	20 813	21 195
Total expenditures	$250 396	$279 476
Home visits	4 312	5 101
Average cost per home visit	$ 58.07	$ 54.79

The nursing staff received a 5 per cent increase in salary one-third of the way through 2019. The homemakers did not receive an increase in wages in 2018 or in 2019. The prices of medical supplies increased about 2 per cent during 2019 compared to 2018. The prices of cleaning supplies were relatively constant across the two years.

Transportation is provided by the nurses, who are reimbursed $0.20 per kilometre. The clinic's general overhead is allocated to programs on the basis of budgeted program salaries.

Required

(a) In this problem you are not given a budget for 2019. If you want to evaluate the 2019 performance of the clinic, what can you use as the basis of a flexible budget to develop a benchmark?

(b) Prepare a schedule to evaluate the performance of this program in 2019 using the benchmark suggested in part (a).

(c) If you were the general manager of the clinic, what would you like to discuss with the head of the visiting nurse program concerning the 2019 results? Explain.

(d) How many patients should have been served in 2019 for the budget allocation of $279 476 if costs had been under control?

6.27 Comprehensive manufacturing master budget problem   **LO2, 3**

The accountant at Fighting Kites has always prepared a budget that is calculated using only one estimated volume of sales. He has asked you to help him set up a spreadsheet that can be used for sensitivity analysis in the budgeting process. This year it appears that the entity may not meet expectations, which could result in a loss. He is concerned that the entity will incur a loss again next year, and wants to develop a budget that will easily reflect changes in the assumptions. After gathering information about next year's planned operations, he will provide information using a what-if sensitivity analysis.

Part 1 Spreadsheet with input box, revenue and production budgets

Following are the assumptions regarding revenues, direct materials and labour costs, and inventory levels.

Direct materials per kite:		
Nylon	$10	
Ribs	$5	
String	$2	
Direct labour:		
Hours	Assembly	0.5
	Packing	0.1
Cost per hour	Assembly	$30.00
	Packing	$15.00

▶

| Cost per kite | Assembly | $15.00 |
| | Packing | $1.50 |

Inventory information:

Direct materials:	Beginning	Targeted ending
Nylon	$5 000	$7 000
Ribs	$3 000	$3 200
String	$1 000	$1 200
Finished goods (units)	2 000 kites	2 200 kites
Finished goods (cost)	$97 850	

Revenue assumptions:

Selling price	$75
Volume of kite sales	80 000

Required

(a) Create a spreadsheet with a data input box at the top. Into this box put all of the relevant assumption data. This box should be formatted with a border to separate the input data from the cell-referenced data. Set up each schedule with cell references to information in the data input box. Any changes made to information in this box should be reflected through all of the schedules that you set up. As you proceed through parts 2 and 3 of this problem, more information will be given that needs to be located in the assumptions box, such as next year's estimated variable and fixed manufacturing overhead, and support department costs. You will need to leave space in the data input box for this information, or add more rows as you develop the spreadsheet.

(b) Prepare a revenue budget.

(c) Prepare a production budget in units.

(d) Prepare the direct materials usage budget and a direct materials purchases budget.

(e) Prepare a direct labour budget (in hours and cost).

Part 2 Overhead, ending inventory and cost of sales budgets

Refer to the information for part 1. Following are estimated manufacturing overhead costs. Both fixed and variable overhead will be allocated based on the number of kites produced.

Estimated variable manufacturing overhead costs:	
Supplies	$160 250
Indirect labour	200 650
Maintenance	80 200
Miscellaneous	40 100
Total variable overhead costs	$481 200
Estimated fixed manufacturing overhead costs:	
Depreciation	$211 728
Property taxes	28 872
Insurance	67 368
Plant management	240 600
Fringe benefits	336 840
Miscellaneous	76 992
Total fixed overhead costs	$962 400

Required

(f) Prepare a manufacturing overhead budget and determine variable and fixed overhead allocation rates by dividing the budgeted overhead by; budgeted labour hours for the fixed overhead, and units for the variable overhead.

(g) Prepare a schedule that calculates the unit costs of ending inventory in finished goods, and then prepare the ending inventories budget.

(h) Prepare a cost of sales budget.

Part 3 Budgeted statement of profit or loss

Refer to the information for parts 1 and 2. Following is the information that the accountant collected about support department costs.

Support department:	Fixed costs
Administration	$1 034 580
Marketing	620 748
Distribution	310 374
Customer service	103 458
Total support department costs	$2 069 160

Required

(i) Prepare a support department costs budget.

(j) Prepare a budgeted statement of profit or loss. Assume an income tax rate of 25 per cent.

Part 4 Cash budget with bad debts and borrowing

Refer to the information for parts 1, 2 and 3. The entity's managers budget cash flows on a quarterly basis so that they can plan short-term investments and borrowings.

Kite sales are highest during the spring and summer. Sales are fairly even within each quarter, but sales vary across quarters as follows:

January–March	10%
April–June	50%
July–September	30%
October–December	10%

Accounts receivable at the end of the prior year, consisting of sales made during December, totalled $90 000. Payments from customers are usually received as follows:

Pay during the month goods are received	50%
Pay the next month	47%
Bad debts	3%

The managers plan to maintain beginning inventory quantities during January and February, but to increase inventories to the targeted levels by the end of March and maintain those levels throughout the rest of the year.

The entity pays its vendors 10 days after raw materials are received, so approximately two-thirds of all purchases are paid in the month of production and one-third are paid the following month. Accounts payable at the end of the prior year totalled $13 000. Employee wages and other production costs are paid during the month incurred. Property taxes are paid in two equal instalments on 31 March and 30 September, and insurance is paid annually on 30 June. Support costs are paid evenly throughout the year. Estimated income tax payments are made at the end of each quarter based on 25 per cent of total estimated taxes for the year.

In addition to customer receipts, the entity expects to receive $10 000 in proceeds from the sale of equipment during January. It also plans to purchase and pay for new equipment costing $50 000 during January.

The entity finances its short-term operations with a line of credit from the bank, which had a balance of $150 000 at the end of the previous year. The line of credit agreement requires the entity to maintain a minimum cash balance of $100 000 (non-interest-bearing). The entity's line of credit requires quarterly interest payments at an annual rate of 5.5 per cent. (For simplicity, assume that all borrowings and repayments occur on the last day of each quarter.)

Required

(k) Prepare quarterly budgets for cash receipts, cash disbursements and short-term financing.

6.28 Comprehensive restaurant master budget problem   **LO2**

You are the accountant for Wok and Egg Roll Express. Following are assumptions about sales for the coming month. Wok and Egg Roll Express offers three basic meals: noodle bowls, egg rolls and rice bowls. Each meal can be prepared with several different meats or with vegetables only. Costs and prices are similar for all varieties of each meal. Prices for noodles bowls are $4 each, egg rolls are $3 each and rice bowls are $3.50 each. Estimated sales for the next month are 200 noodle bowls, 100 egg roll meals and 500 rice bowls per day.

Part 1 Revenues budget; uncertainties; revenue strategies

Required

(a) Prepare a revenue budget for the next month assuming it is 30 days long.

(b) Discuss factors that affect the budgeted volumes of meals.

(c) Identify possible ways the owner could increase total revenues. Discuss the pros and cons for each of your ideas.

Part 2 Direct materials budget; uncertainties; cost control strategies

The owner of Wok and Egg Roll Express studied the cost of direct materials for each type of meal. He estimates that noodle bowls use about $1 in direct materials, egg rolls use about $0.75 and rice bowls use about $0.90. Food is purchased daily to ensure high quality. Beginning and ending inventory amounts are minimal.

Required

(d) Explain why you would not need to prepare a production budget for Wok and Egg Roll Express.

(e) Prepare a direct materials usage budget and a direct materials purchases budget.

(f) Discuss reasons why actual costs might be different from budgeted costs in part (e).

(g) Suppose the prices of food ingredients increase. Identify possible ways the owner could keep food costs within the budget. Discuss drawbacks for each of your ideas.

Part 3 Direct labour budget; uncertainties; cost control strategies

The owner of Wok and Egg Roll Express employs cooks and cashiers. The cashiers take orders and collect payment, transfer food from the cooks to customers, and clean tables. Cooks are paid $10 per hour, and cashiers are paid $8 per hour. Wok and Egg Roll Express operates four shifts: 10 to 2, 11 to 2, 2 to 10, and 5 to 8. Weekdays and weekends are staffed similarly. Following are the shifts and required workers.

Shift	Cooks	Cashiers
10 am to 2 pm	2	2
11 am to 2 pm	3	3
2 pm to 10 pm	2	2
5 pm to 8 pm	3	3

Required

(h) Prepare a labour budget showing hours and costs for a month. (Assume 30 days per month.)

(i) Discuss reasons why actual labour costs might turn out to be different from budgeted costs in part (h).

(j) Identify possible ways the owner could reduce labour costs. Discuss possible drawbacks for each of your ideas.

Part 4 Overhead budget; uncertainties; cost control strategies

Wok and Egg Roll Express does not separately account for production versus general overhead. Fixed overhead includes production overhead as well as support services and general administration. Variable overhead includes labour-related costs such as payroll taxes and employee benefits. Wok and Egg Roll Express has estimated variable overhead costs as $2.50 per direct labour hour. Following are the estimated fixed overhead costs for one month.

Fixed overhead costs:	
Utilities	$ 1 300
Manager	5 000
Lease	2 000
Miscellaneous	2 500
Total	$10 800

Required

(k) Prepare an overhead costs budget for one month.

(l) Discuss reasons why actual overhead costs might turn out to be different from budgeted costs in part (k).

(m) Identify possible ways the owner could reduce overhead costs. Discuss possible drawbacks for each of your ideas.

Part 5 Budgeted statement of profit or loss; uncertainties; profit strategies

Refer to the information from the preceding budgets. The statement of profit or loss for Wok and Egg Roll Express consists of revenues less direct costs (direct materials and direct labour) to determine the gross margin. Then the overhead costs are deducted to determine operating income.

Required

(n) Prepare a budgeted statement of profit or loss ignoring income taxes.

(o) What are the major uncertainties in Wok and Egg Roll Express' budget? Explain.

(p) Wok and Egg Roll Express' owner would like to increase profits from the store. Suggest several possible ways to accomplish this goal. Explain your reasoning.

6.29 Organisational resources; uncertainties; performance; government budget responsibility   LO1, 5

Required

(a) (i) Explain how the budgeting process helps top managers articulate decisions about the use of resources.

   (ii) Explain how a budget identifies the resources available to individual departments within an organisation.

(b) (i) Explain why the cost of resources such as labour and direct materials is uncertain. Include the effects of market forces in your discussion.

   (ii) Explain how changes in the price of resources such as labour and direct materials might cause managers to change the way those resources are used.

   (iii) Explain how the issues you discussed in parts (i) and (ii) can result in budget variances.

(c) (i) Explain how budgets can be used to measure an organisation's performance.

   (ii) Explain how each of the following budget adjustments improves measurement of variances when evaluating the performance for individual managers within an organisation:
   - using flexible budgets to adjust for actual volumes
   - removing allocated costs
   - updating costs for anticipated price changes.

   (iii) How can the analysis of budget variances lead to continuous improvement in an organisation?

ACKNOWLEDGEMENTS

Photo 6A: © Indypendenz / Shutterstock. com

Photo 6B: © gorillaimages / Shutterstock. com

Text 6.18 and 6.23: © Birt, *Accounting: Business Reporting for Decision Making*, 3rd edn (Milton: John Wiley & Sons).

Appendix 6A: 'Turning budgeting pain into budgeting gain', by John Orlando, *Strategic Finance*, Institute of Management Accountants, March 2009, pp 47–51.

CHAPTER 7

Job costing systems

LEARNING OBJECTIVES

After studying this chapter, you should be able to:

7.1 explain the flow of costs through the manufacturing process

7.2 calculate the inventoriable product cost for customised products

7.3 discuss the issues related to the allocation of overhead to individual jobs

7.4 discuss the issues associated with spoilage, rework and scrap handled in job costing

7.5 critically analyse the uses and limitations of job costing for financial reporting.

IN BRIEF

This chapter will explain how organisations use job costing to assign costs to custom-made products (for example, a super yacht) or services (for example, a legal case). It is also used to assign costs to batches of similar products (for example, loaves of bread), the total cost of which may then be divided by the total volume to identify a unit cost.

Job costing involves tracking direct material and direct labour costs and allocating a relevant proportion of variable and fixed indirect manufacturing costs to custom or distinct products and services. Those full cost figures are used to set prices, monitor profitability and value unsold inventory of finished goods and work in process. In most countries, use of these fully absorbed costs is also required by the accounting standards for inventory valuation.

7.1 The flow of costs through the manufacturing process

LEARNING OBJECTIVE 7.1 Explain the flow of costs through the manufacturing process.

Customised products pose special problems because the nature and levels of costs vary from product to product. Therefore, the accounting systems must be designed to capture costs for individual units or batches of goods as the manufacturing process unfolds.

In this chapter, we focus on measuring and monitoring the product cost of customised goods for financial reporting purposes. Such product costs are known as inventoriable product costs. **Inventoriable product costs** are the direct and indirect costs of producing goods, and include costs incurred in the manufacturing process only. For the production of a catamaran, for example, direct costs include materials such as aluminium, wiring and cabinetry, as well as labour directly involved in the production of an individual catamaran. In addition to direct materials and direct labour costs, product costs also include overhead costs related to production. Production overhead includes costs related to the manufacturing facility, such as depreciation of equipment and insurance costs.

The inventoriable product cost excludes the cost of operating activities that are not directly related to production, such as selling and administration. These **period costs** are expensed directly to the statement of profit or loss in the period in which they occur. Remember that for costs recorded in the general ledger, the entity is required to comply with the rules and regulations governing financial accounting (for example, Australian Accounting Standard AASB 102 *Inventories* and New Zealand Accounting Standard NZ IAS 2 *Inventories*), which exclude the inclusion of non-manufacturing costs as part of the inventoriable product cost.

When a customer with specific product requirements places an order, we call the order a job. For example, a customer order for two car ferries would be considered as two individual jobs by a ship manufacturer, and this is reflected in having two job numbers, say 064 and 065, to separately identify the two vessels. This will allow the management accountant to differentiate the costs between different jobs.

Job costing is the process of assigning costs to custom products with the cost objects being the individual jobs. Direct materials and direct labour are traced to individual jobs, and manufacturing overhead is allocated. Manufacturers that use job costing include aircraft builders, custom motorcycle and motor vehicle manufacturers, and custom design jewellers among others.

When goods are customised, many costs are easily traced to individual products due to source documents such as material requisitions and labour time records. **Source documents** are manual or electronic records created to capture and provide information about transactions or events. For example, the vessels manufactured by a ship manufacturer are customised to suit each customer. Costs of direct materials such as steel or aluminium would be easily traced to an individual vessel as the requisition would clearly indicate which vessel was using the materials. It is also easy to trace the cost of direct labour to construct the vessels from the time reports kept by individual workers. Direct labour and direct materials are also referred to as prime costs. Other production costs, such as the production supervisor's salary or building insurance, are indirect and are therefore allocated as part of overhead to an individual vessel.

One of the purposes of measuring product costs is to provide information for financial reporting. Under the accounting standards (International Financial Reporting Standards (IFRS), published in Australia as the Australian Accounting Standards) product costs must be assigned to inventory. Such costs are classified as *work in process* while the products are in production, and then reclassified as *finished goods* once the production process is complete and the goods are sent to the warehouse. When the products are sold, the cost is transferred to *cost of sales*. This practice allows inventory to be reported at cost on the statement of financial position (also called the balance sheet), and cost of sales to be matched against revenues on the statement of profit or loss (or statement of comprehensive income). Thus, job costing in a manufacturing entity assigns costs first to inventory and then to cost of sales when jobs are completed and sold, as shown in figure 7.1.

To measure the cost of individual jobs, job costing systems typically include a work in process subsidiary ledger. As shown in figure 7.2, direct costs are traced and manufacturing overhead costs are allocated to each job. Total work in process (WIP) is equal to the sum of the accumulated costs for all jobs in the subsidiary ledger. The use of a subsidiary ledger allows the costs of individual jobs to be tracked, and provides the information to move costs for individual jobs through the ledgers as they move through the production process.

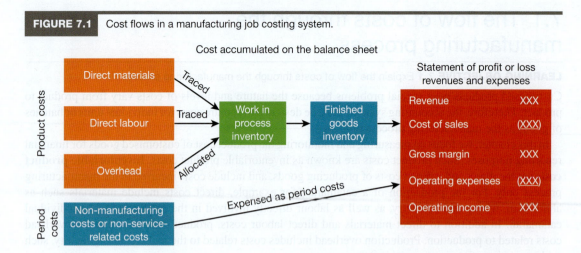

FIGURE 7.1 Cost flows in a manufacturing job costing system.

Cost accumulated on the balance sheet

Job costing is also frequently used in service industry organisations such as hospitals, legal practices, accounting entities and repair shops. However, as there is no requirement under the accounting standards to integrate the system into the financial reporting system, such entities are not the focus of this chapter.

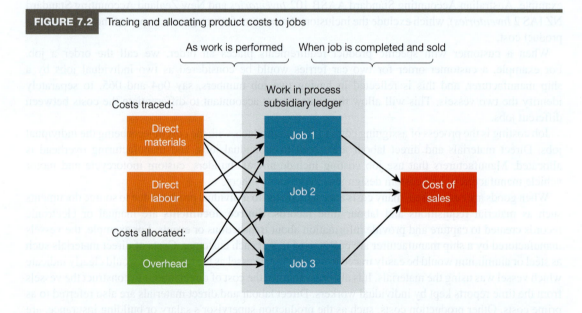

FIGURE 7.2 Tracing and allocating product costs to jobs

7.2 Calculating the inventoriable product cost for customised products

LEARNING OBJECTIVE 7.2 Calculate the inventoriable product cost for customised products.

To understand how an inventoriable product cost is calculated, we will work through an example using an entity that produces aluminium vents for heating and cooling systems, and works with contractors on large commercial jobs. Job costing is an appropriate method as each customer order requires different styles and lengths of vents and joints. Comprehensive example 1 begins our development of the inventoriable product cost for different customer orders for Aluminium Benders by assigning direct costs (material and labour) to individual jobs. We will use one customer order, job 482, to illustrate the process.

Assigning direct costs

An overview of the job costing system used at Aluminium Benders is shown in figure 7.3. It can be seen that Aluminium Benders has two direct cost pools (direct labour and direct materials) and two manufacturing overhead cost pools (machining department costs and assembly department costs).

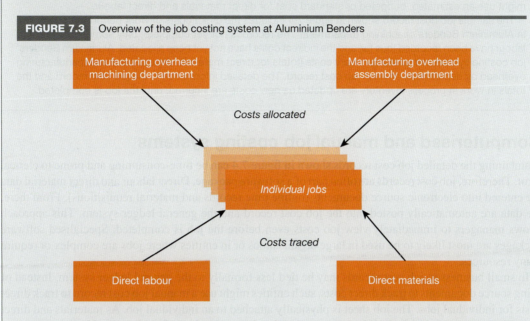

FIGURE 7.3 Overview of the job costing system at Aluminium Benders

Accounting records are used to trace the costs of direct materials and direct labour to each job. The direct labour employees at Aluminium Benders create daily time reports that show the time they spend on individual jobs. The accounting department uses the time reports to calculate employee pay and to trace direct labour hours to individual jobs. As shown in figure 7.4, each report may include several different jobs. (We focus on job 482 for Aluminium Benders' customer Fallon Construction Company.) Similarly, when materials such as sheet metal or metal joints are requisitioned for each job, they are tracked in the accounting system using the materials requisition form shown in figure 7.4.

FIGURE 7.4 Partial job cost record for Aluminium Benders

Machining department materials requisition no. 213

Job number: 482
Date: 13 April 2019

Description	Stock #	Quantity
Sheet metal	4505	16 sheets
Metal joints	3200	30 joints

Authorisation: _____

Machining department labour time report

Employee name: Karen Otto
Employee number: 204
Date: 13 April 2019

Job number	Start time	End time	Hours
482	8:00	12:00	4:00
485	1:00	3:00	2:00
486	3:00	5:00	2:00
Total hours			8:00

Cost per unit from raw materials inventory records

Job cost record for job 482   Customer: Fallon Construction Company
Date started: 13 April 2019

Date Completed: _____

Machining department: direct materials

Date	Part number	Quantity	Cost per unit	Total cost
13/04/19	#4505	16	$20.00	$320.00
13/04/19	#3200	30	$10.00	$300.00
Total				$620.00

Machining department: direct labour

Date	Employee #	Hours used	Hourly rate	Total cost
13/04/19	204	4	$15.00	$60.00
13/04/19	206	6	$14.00	$84.00
Total				$144.00

Hourly rate from payroll records

The cost and activity information gathered from source documents is used to record costs in a subsidiary ledger for each new job. This record is called a **job cost record**, and it contains all of the costs traced and assigned to a specific job. For Aluminium Benders, job 482 for its customer Fallon Construction Company is shown in figure 7.4.

At Aluminium Benders, the cost per unit of direct materials is obtained from the entity's raw materials inventory records. The hourly rate of pay for each employee is obtained from payroll records. Other entities might use an estimated, budgeted or standard cost for direct materials and direct labour.

The sample job cost record shown in figure 7.4 includes the direct costs of work performed on job 482 in Aluminium Benders' machining department. The record is not yet complete; only some materials and labour have been recorded thus far, and the indirect costs have not yet been allocated. Aluminium Benders' job costing system calculates summary costs (totals for direct materials, direct labour and manufacturing overhead by department) on each job cost record. The detailed information in the job cost record and the totals in work in process inventory are updated as new costs are incurred, until the job is completed.

Computerised and manual job costing systems

Maintaining the detailed job cost records shown in figure 7.4 can be time-consuming and prone to clerical error. Therefore, job cost records are often part of a software package. Direct labour and direct material data are entered into electronic source documents (online time records and material requisitions). From there, the data are automatically posted into the job cost record and the general ledger system. This approach allows managers to immediately view job costs even before the job is completed. Specialised software packages are most likely to be used in large organisations or in entities where jobs are complex or require many resources.

In small businesses, job cost records may be tied less formally to the general ledger system. Instead of using source documents to track direct costs, such entities might use a manual job cost record to track direct costs for individual jobs. The job sheet is physically attached to an individual job. As materials and direct labour hours are added to the job, the amounts are recorded on the sheet. Carpenters and home contractors also frequently use this method to monitor direct costs. Amounts from the job cost sheet are recorded in the job cost record in the subsidiary ledger on a periodic basis, when the job is complete, or sometimes as resources are used.

7.3 Allocating manufacturing overhead

LEARNING OBJECTIVE 7.3 Discuss the issues related to the allocation of overhead to individual jobs.

Manufacturing overhead includes all **production costs** except direct materials and direct labour. Allocating manufacturing overhead to individual jobs is a two-stage process. In the first stage, a variety of manufacturing overhead costs are collected in an overhead cost pool. A **cost pool** is a group of individual costs that are accumulated for a particular purpose. In the second stage, costs are allocated from the cost pool to individual jobs. Successful completion of the two stages requires four steps.
1. Identify the relevant cost object.
2. Identify one or more overhead cost pools and allocation bases.
3. For each overhead cost pool, calculate an overhead allocation rate.
4. For each overhead cost pool, allocate costs to the cost object.

1. Identify the relevant cost object

In a job costing system, the cost object is a job. Sometimes a job consists of an individual product, and sometimes it consists of a batch of products. In our example at Aluminium Benders, the cost object of interest is job 482, which is for the manufacture of a large number of aluminium vents required for a specific building by customer Fallon Construction.

2. Identify one or more overhead cost pools and allocation bases

Manufacturing overhead costs are accumulated in one or more cost pools. Some organisations use a single entity-wide or plant-wide cost pool for all fixed and variable overhead costs. Other organisations use separate cost pools for fixed and variable overhead costs. Fixed overhead includes costs such as production management salaries and space rental. Variable overhead includes any cost that varies with activity levels, such as supplies and (sometimes) electricity. If work is performed in separate departments or work areas, separate overhead cost pools may be designated for each department or activity. Accountants use judgement in choosing the number and type of overhead cost pools for a given entity.

The choice of overhead cost pools depends on the organisation of production, the nature of overhead costs and the usefulness of different types of overhead information to management. For example, Aluminium Benders has two production departments: machining and assembly. Each work area might be under the supervision of a different manager who is responsible for controlling costs. The use of separate overhead cost pools for each area would help top management monitor the performance of area managers. Alternatively, a single manager might oversee multiple work areas. Organisations are also more likely to use different overhead cost pools for different types of work activities. For example, machining the aluminium vents and joints is a different type of activity from assembling parts into the finished product. It is appropriate to use different cost pools when the nature or level of overhead costs differs across activities.

For each overhead cost pool, an allocation base is chosen to assign overhead costs to cost objects. An **allocation base** is a measure of activity, preferably an activity that results in the costs being incurred (a cost driver), used to allocate costs to a cost object. If some portion of an overhead cost pool varies with a cost driver, it can be used as the allocation base. For example, the cost of some employee benefits varies with labour hours and labour costs. Indirect costs such as supplies in the machining department may vary with machine use. For cost pools that consist only of variable costs or a mixture of fixed and variable costs, accountants use allocation bases that are likely to affect at least a portion of the costs. For a fixed overhead cost pool, accountants choose an allocation base that is related to activities even though fixed costs are not expected to vary with the allocation base. Manufacturing job costing systems frequently allocate overhead using one of the following bases:

- direct labour hours
- direct labour costs
- machine hours.

Whichever allocation base is selected, it will be necessary for the entity to maintain records of its use.

In our example, the financial controller of Aluminium Benders, Sean Hardy, met with the supervisor of each production department to discuss the best allocation bases to use. After discussions it was determined that, in the machining department, overhead is to be allocated to production jobs using machine hours as the allocation base. In the assembly department, direct labour cost is to be used as the allocation base.

In machining, Sean learns the machines require little direct labour. A large portion of cost in the overhead pool relates to operating the machines, such as depreciation, maintenance and replacement parts. Thus, Sean concludes that machine hours are a reasonable allocation base.

The assembly department has few machines, but labour is used heavily. The labour mix is varied, with both skilled and unskilled workers. Sean agrees that direct labour cost is a reasonable allocation base because some overhead expenses, such as holiday and sick leave pay, vary with labour cost.

However, if Sean had found that the same cost driver/allocation base could be used for both production departments, then only one overhead cost pool would have been used to allocate overhead.

3. For each overhead cost pool, calculate an overhead allocation rate

The **allocation rate** is the dollar amount per unit of allocation base used to allocate overhead to each cost object. (Remember, in a job costing system, each job is a cost object.) If we know the total amount of overhead cost and the total quantity of the allocation base, the **actual overhead allocation rate** is calculated as follows:

$$\text{Actual allocation rate} = \frac{\text{Actual overhead cost}}{\text{Actual quantity of allocation base}}$$

Alternatively, overhead may be allocated using an **estimated allocation rate**. To calculate an estimated rate for the next period, we estimate total overhead costs and the total quantity of the allocation base, and then calculate the rate as follows:

$$\text{Estimated allocation rate} = \frac{\text{Estimated overhead cost}}{\text{Estimated quantity of allocation base}}$$

To understand which allocation rate is more appropriate, it is necessary to understand the differences in the use of actual and normal costing to measure costs in the job costing system.

Actual and normal costing

Under **actual costing**, overhead is allocated using the actual volume of the allocation base times the actual allocation rate. However, managers often need cost information for cost estimation and pricing before total actual cost and resource use information is available at the end of the period. Volumes and costs may also vary between periods because of season factors such as variations in demand or changing temperatures resulting in different power costs. Therefore estimates, calculated at the beginning of each year, are typically used to allocate overhead. When the estimated allocation rate and actual quantity of the allocation base are used to allocate overhead, the method is called normal costing. Information from normal costing systems is used to prepare interim statements of profit or loss, to manage costs and to estimate costs for bids throughout a period. Figure 7.5 compares actual costing and normal costing. Under both methods, actual direct materials and direct labour are traced to each job. Costs can also be measured using standards. We will consider this in later chapters.

FIGURE 7.5	Similarities and differences between actual and normal costing	

	Actual costing	**Normal costing**
Direct costs recorded	Actual cost of direct materials and direct labour	Actual cost of direct materials and direct labour
Overhead cost allocation rate	$\dfrac{\text{Actual overhead cost}}{\text{Actual quantity of allocation base}}$	$\dfrac{\text{Estimated overhead cost}}{\text{Estimated quantity of allocation base}}$
Overhead allocation	Actual allocation rate × Actual quantity of allocation base	Estimated allocation rate × Actual quantity of allocation base

4. For each overhead cost pool, allocate costs to the cost object

Aluminium Benders uses a normal costing method to allocate an estimated overhead rate to each job. Separate overhead cost pools are used for each department, but fixed and variable costs are combined in each pool. The following estimates were developed by Sean for all manufacturing during 2020:

	Machining	**Assembly**
Production overhead	$1 400 000	$2 400 000
Direct labour cost	$ 700 000	$1 000 000
Direct labour hours	35 000	100 000
Machine hours	25 000	10 000

Using normal costing the estimated overhead allocation rate for each department is:

Machining: $1 400 000 ÷ 25 000 machine hours = $56 per machine hour
Assembly: $2 400 000 ÷ $1 000 000 direct labour cost = 240% of direct labour cost
(or $2.40 for every $1 of labour incurred)

The assignment of overhead to individual jobs requires information about each job's use of the allocation base. Sean has created an online system so that the machine operator records the machine hours used for each job. For job 482, three machine hours are recorded for April 2020 and the overhead is allocated based on an estimated allocation rate of $56 per machine hour. This results in an allocation of $168 ($56 by 3 hours) to job 482 in the machining department, as shown in figure 7.6.

Overapplied and underapplied overhead

Under normal costing, periodic adjustments need to be made to reconcile the actual overhead cost with the amount of overhead that has been allocated to jobs. When we determine the overhead allocation rate, we estimate both the cost of overhead (numerator) and the volume of the allocation base (denominator).

At the end of the period, the amounts of overhead in the inventory accounts (work in process, finished goods, cost of sales) are either too little or too much, and so adjustments need to be made. **Overapplied overhead** occurs when actual costs are less than the total amount of overhead allocated to inventory accounts. In contrast, **underapplied overhead** occurs when actual costs are more than the amount of overhead allocated.

FIGURE 7.6 Partial job cost record showing overhead allocation for Aluminium Benders for job 482

Job cost record for job 482   Customer: Fallon Construction Company

Date started: 13 April 2019   Date completed: _____

Machining department: overhead

Date	Allocation base	Hours used	Allocation rate per hour	Allocated overhead
13/4/19	Machine hours	3	$56.00	$168.00
Total				$168.00

To correct for overapplied or underapplied overhead, we first compare the amount of overhead allocated to actual overhead cost:

$$\text{Overapplied (underapplied) overhead} = \text{Allocated overhead} - \text{Actual overhead}$$

This comparison is managed by **overhead cost control accounts**, or overhead clearing accounts. For each cost pool these accounts record both the actual costs incurred during a period (as a debit) and the costs applied to the jobs in work in process (as a credit). Suppose it is the end of the fiscal year at Aluminium Benders and the balances in the accounts represent all transactions for the period. Balances in the overhead cost control accounts for the machining department and assembly department cost pools are shown in figure 7.7. Machining department overhead costs incurred totalled $1 600 000, while costs allocated to jobs totalled $1 120 000 (20 000 machine hours × $56) giving rise to an underapplied overhead of $480 000. Assembly department overhead costs incurred totalled $2 700 000, while costs allocated to jobs totalled $2 880 000 ($1 200 000 direct labour cost × 240%) with an overapplied overhead of $180 000. The combined amount of underapplied overhead is therefore $300 000 (being $480 000 machining underapplied overhead − $180 000 assembly overapplied overhead). The total amount of overhead incurred must then be recorded as a product cost for the period. This is done by an adjusting entry, which is shown later in the chapter.

FIGURE 7.7 Overhead cost control accounts for Aluminium Benders

(a) Before adjustment Machining department overhead cost control account

Total costs incurred	1 600 000	1 120 000	Total costs allocated
Underapplied overhead	480 000		

Assembly department overhead cost control account

Total costs incurred	2 700 000	2 880 000	Total costs allocated
		180 000	Overapplied overhead

(b) After adjustment Machining department overhead cost control account

Total costs incurred	1 600 000	1 120 000	Total costs allocated
		480 000	Adjustment
Balance	0		

Assembly department overhead cost control account

Total costs incurred	2 700 000	2 880 000	Total costs allocated
Adjustment	180 000		
		0	Balance

Comprehensive example 2 shows how indirect costs are allocated and total production costs are calculated.

Allocating indirect costs and calculating total production costs

Sean Hardy, financial controller of Aluminium Benders, wants to be sure that he understands how Aluminium Benders' job costing system allocates overhead, so he recalculates the allocations for job 482. This job was completed this week and shipped to a large office building construction site. The information below was recorded on the job cost record for job 482.

	Machining	Assembly
Direct materials requisitioned	$40 000	$70 000
Direct labour cost	$28 000	$10 000
Direct labour hours	200	1000
Machine hours	100*	500

*Figure 7.6 showed the allocation of three hours used in April.

Using the allocation rates computed previously, Sean recalculates the amount of overhead for job 482 as follows:

Machining: 100 machine hours × $56 per machine hour = $5600
Assembly: $10 000 direct labour cost × 240% of direct labour cost = $24 000

Next, Sean creates a report for management of the total costs for job 482 as follows:

	Machining	Assembly	Total
Direct materials requisitioned	$40 000	$ 70 000	$110 000
Direct labour cost	28 000	10 000	38 000
Overhead allocated	5 600	24 000	29 600
Total cost	$73 600	$104 000	$177 600

Gross profit for job 482 can be calculated by deducting the costs from the revenue generated from the sale. At the end of the period, the $177 600 will be transferred to the cost of sales account.

Recording transactions in the financial accounting system

The general ledger in a manufacturer's job costing system typically includes separate inventory accounts for raw materials, work in process and finished goods, and represents the flow of costs through the production process (refer back to figure 7.1). For Aluminium Benders, the general journal entries (figure 7.8) and the general ledger entries (figure 7.9) are shown to record the costs for job 482, from the issue of raw material to the revenue received from the customer. Notice that the ledger entries are referenced back to the journal entries.

Purchases of raw materials (not illustrated) are recorded in the raw materials inventory account. As direct materials are traced to a job, the cost of the materials is transferred to work in process inventory (entries 1 and 4). Some types of direct materials, such as (indirect) supplies, are not traced to individual jobs when they are used; such costs are transferred into an overhead cost pool. However, this situation is not illustrated. As direct labour employees report their work time, the cost of their wages is debited to the jobs they work on and wages payable is credited for the wages earned (entries 2 and 5).

Many organisations use overhead cost control accounts to monitor the costs for each overhead cost pool. As actual overhead costs are incurred, they are debited to the control account. For example, the assembly department supervisor's salary would be debited to the assembly department overhead cost control and credited to wages payable. Overhead allocated to individual jobs is debited to work in process and credited to the control account (entries 3 and 6).

FIGURE 7.8 Journal entries for job 482

1	Work in process (job 482)	DR	$ 40 000	
	Raw materials inventory	CR		$ 40 000
	To record direct materials requisitioned for job 482 in machining			
2	Work in process (job 482)	DR	$ 28 000	
	Wages payable	CR		$ 28 000
	To record direct labour used for job 482 in machining			
3	Work in process (job 482)	DR	$ 5 600	
	Machining department overhead cost control	CR		$ 5 600
	To record overhead allocated to job 482 in machining			
4	Work in process (job 482)	DR	$ 70 000	
	Raw materials inventory	CR		$ 70 000
	To record direct materials requisitioned for job 482 in assembly			
5	Work in process (job 482)	DR	$ 10 000	
	Wages payable	CR		$ 10 000
	To record direct labour used for job 482 in assembly			
6	Work in process (job 482)	DR	$ 24 000	
	Assembly department overhead cost control	CR		$ 24 000
	To record overhead allocated to job 482 in assembly			
7	Finished goods inventory (job 482)	DR	$177 600	
	Work in process (job 482)	CR		$177 600
	To record completion of job 482			
8	Cost of sales	DR	$177 600	
	Finished goods inventory (job 482)	CR		$177 600
	To record the delivery of job 482			

When a job is complete, the work in process account includes all of the direct material, direct labour and overhead costs that have been assigned to the job. The total cost can then be transferred to finished goods inventory (entry 7). Finally, when revenue for the job is earned, the total cost is transferred from finished goods to cost of sales (entry 8).

Refer back to figure 7.7, which shows the ledger accounts for the individual manufacturing department overhead control accounts. We have already calculated a net underapplied overhead of $300 000 as follows:

	Overapplied or (underapplied) overhead
Machining	$(480 000)
Assembly	180 000
Net underapplied overhead	$(300 000)

Now we must record an adjusting entry so that the total actual amount of overhead incurred is recorded as a product cost for the period. The balance of overapplied or underapplied overhead must be removed through an adjustment at the end of the accounting period. If the amount of the adjustment is material, it is allocated on a pro-rata basis among work in process, finished goods (if any) and cost of sales. If the amount is immaterial, however, it is simply assigned to cost of sales.

FIGURE 7.9 T-accounts for job 482

Raw materials inventory

	$40 000	1
	$70 000	4

Job 482
Work in process inventory

1	$40 000		
2	$28 000		
3	$ 5 600		
4	$70 000		
5	$10 000		
6	$24 000	$177 600	7
	$ 0		

Finished goods inventory

7	$177 600	$177 600	8

Cost of sales

8	$177 600	

Wages payable

		$28 000	2
		$10 000	5

Machining department overhead cost control

		$5 600	3

Assembly department overhead cost control

		$24 000	6

Because the method of adjusting for overapplied or underapplied overhead depends on materiality, we need to decide whether the $300 000 amount for Aluminium Benders is material. One way to evaluate materiality is to calculate the net overapplied or underapplied overhead as a percentage of actual overhead costs. For Aluminium Benders, this calculation is:

$$\$300\,000 \div (\$1\,600\,000 + \$2\,700\,000) = 7\%$$

Many accountants view amounts smaller than 10 per cent to be immaterial. If we decide that the adjustment for Aluminium Benders is immaterial, we adjust the cost of sales total. Because overhead was underapplied, cost of sales would be increased as follows:

Cost of sales	DR	$300 000
Assembly department overhead cost control	DR	$180 000
Machining department overhead cost control	CR	$480 000

If we decide that the adjustment for Aluminium Benders is material, it must be allocated on a pro-rata basis among work in process, finished goods and cost of sales. Suppose the balances in these accounts (representing costs for all jobs) before the adjustment are:

Ending work in process	$ 100 000
Finished goods	20 000
Cost of sales	10 000 000
Total	$10 120 000

The adjustment of $300 000 would be allocated on a pro-rata basis among these accounts based on each account's proportion of the total. The adjusting journal entry is shown below.

Ending work in process		
($100 000 ÷ $10 120 000 × $300 000)	DR	$ 2 964
Finished goods		
($20 000 ÷ $10 120 000 × $300 000)	DR	$ 593
Cost of sales		
($10 000 000 ÷ $10 120 000 × $300 000)	DR	$296 443
Assembly department overhead cost control	DR	$180 000
Machining department overhead cost control	CR	$480 000

The balances before and after the adjustment would be:

	Before adjustment	Adjustment	After adjustment
Ending work in process	$ 100 000	$ 2 964	$ 102 964
Finished goods	20 000	593	20 593
Cost of sales	10 000 000	296 443	10 296 443
Total	$10 120 000	$300 000	$10 420 000

Whether the adjustment is considered material or immaterial, zero balances are left in both overhead cost control accounts after the adjustment, as shown previously in figure 7.7.

7.4 Spoilage, rework and scrap in job costing

LEARNING OBJECTIVE 7.4 Discuss the issues associated with spoilage, rework and scrap handled in job costing.

No matter how carefully goods are manufactured, occasionally some units do not meet quality standards, they are spoiled. **Spoilage** refers to units of product that are unacceptable and are discarded, reworked or sold at a reduced price. Examples of spoilage in job costing include:
- a custom-ordered birdhouse that has an off-centre round hole.
- a bespoke sofa with mismatched pattern.
- custom made mouldings for doors that are too short and cannot be fitted.

Different types of spoiled products are handled in different ways. For example, if the sofa's mismatched pattern is not too noticeable, the sofa could be sold as a factory second. Perhaps the birdhouse can be sold at a discount, but the mouldings probably cannot be sold and must be discarded or reworked.

Spoilage is typically identified through some type of inspection process. Sometimes inspection occurs at the end of the production process immediately before units are moved to finished goods inventory. Other times, inspection occurs at one or more intermediate stages during production. Inspection can also occur at the beginning of the process. For example, denim fabric can be checked for flaws before it is introduced into the production process for manufacturing jeans. Other practices, such as conducting preventive maintenance on equipment rather than waiting for machinery problems to develop, help minimise spoilage.

To calculate the cost of a partially complete spoiled unit, we add up all direct materials and labour costs used and allocate overhead according to the amount of work completed before the unit was removed from production. The way spoilage cost is handled depends on whether the spoilage is considered normal or abnormal.

Normal and abnormal spoilage

Normal spoilage consists of defective units that arise as part of regular operations. Because normal spoilage is considered an ordinary and inherent part of operations, the cost of normal spoilage is included in the costs of all good units produced. The cost of normal spoilage is considered necessary for producing good units. Thus if normal spoilage arises from the requirements of a specific job, the cost of the spoiled units is charged to the job. For example, suppose one of Aluminium Benders' customers wants vents in an irregular shape. If the sheet metal is more difficult to bend into such shapes and materials are consequently spoiled in the machining process, then the cost of the spoilage would be charged to that job.

Normal spoilage also occurs periodically as a regular part of all jobs. For example, suppose that in the machining department at Aluminium Benders the cutting device periodically cuts off centre, no matter how much care is taken by the machine operators. This loss has nothing to do with any specific order; instead, it is a normal part of operations. The cost of normal spoilage common to all jobs is charged to overhead and is allocated with other overhead costs to all jobs.

Abnormal spoilage is spoilage that is not part of everyday operations. It occurs for reasons such as:
- out-of-control manufacturing processes
- unusual machine breakdowns
- unexpected electrical outages that result in a number of spoiled units.

Because abnormal spoilage is considered unusual and is not an inherent part of operations, *the cost of abnormal spoilage is excluded from product costs and is recorded as a separate loss.* Some abnormal spoilage is considered avoidable; that is, if managers monitor processes and maintain machinery appropriately, little spoilage will occur. To highlight these types of problems so that they can be monitored, abnormal spoilage is recorded in a loss from abnormal spoilage account in the general ledger and is not included in the job costing inventory accounts (work in process, finished goods, cost of sales). Comprehensive example 3 demonstrates normal and abnormal spoilage for Aluminium Benders for jobs 512 and 489.

External stakeholders such as shareholders typically do not have access to explicit information about an entity's spoilage rates or costs. Although abnormal spoilage is recorded in a separate loss account in the general ledger, it is typically combined with other financial statement items. Thus, spoilage rarely appears as a line item on published financial statements. Exceptions tend to be large catastrophes, such as damage caused by an earthquake, that are publicly known before financial statements are issued. Therefore, external stakeholders must use indirect ways to analyse the quality of an organisation's production processes. An entity with a high spoilage rate might have a lower than average gross profit margin, higher than average warranty liabilities or a poor reputation for product quality.

COMPREHENSIVE EXAMPLE 3

Assigning spoilage costs

When job 512 was being processed in the machining department, a piece of sheet metal was off centre in the bending machine and two vents were spoiled. This problem occurs periodically, is considered normal spoilage and is recorded as an overhead cost. Because this step comes first in the procedure for making the vents, the only costs incurred were for direct materials ($25). The following journal entry records normal spoilage as an overhead cost, assuming the sheet metal cannot be sold at a discount and its cost has been recorded in work in process inventory.

Overhead cost control (normal spoilage) DR $25		
Work in process inventory (cost of		
spoiled sheet metal) CR $25		

If these costs had been abnormal spoilage, they would have been recorded to a loss from abnormal spoilage account instead of the overhead cost control account.

Job 489 required an especially thin sheet metal to reduce the weight of the vents. When two of the vents were being assembled, they were spoiled because the metal twisted and could not be joined properly. Because the thin metal was a specific requirement for this job, the costs for the spoiled units were recorded as a cost for job 489. Direct materials cost $100 and direct labour cost $150 for the vents up to the time they were spoiled. The metal can be sold to a recycler at a discounted price of $50. The journal entries for the use of direct materials and labour are the same as if the direct materials and labour were not spoiled, because these are additional costs for this specific job. However, the following journal entries record the value of the sheet metal at the time it is spoiled and the subsequent sale of the metal.

Raw material inventory (metal to be sold		
to recycler) DR $50		
Work in process inventory (job 489) CR $50		
Cash DR $50		
Raw material inventory CR $50		

Rework

Rework consists of spoiled units that are repaired and sold as if they were originally produced correctly. For example, electronic equipment that is specially ordered, such as computers or batches of mobile phones, are reworked when defects are discovered during the manufacturing process or through inspection at the end of the process. If the cost of rework is tracked, it is recorded in the same manner as spoilage; normal rework is charged to overhead or to a specific job, and abnormal rework is recorded as a line item loss. Rework costs are often not tracked, however.

Units are sometimes reworked and then sold at a regular price through regular marketing channels. Other times, reworked units remain flawed and must be sold at a reduced price. Costs and benefits are analysed to decide whether to rework a spoiled unit. Suppose a clothing manufacturer discovers several jeans with back pockets sewn on upside down. If the pockets are carefully removed and then sewn on correctly, it might be difficult to tell that there was ever a problem. However, additional cost is added for the labour time to fix the pockets. Furthermore, the pockets might rip more easily because the material has been weakened. The managers need to evaluate whether the costs of reworking the pockets outweigh the benefits.

Scrap

Scrap consists of the bits of direct material left over from normal manufacturing processes. Sometimes it has value and can be sold, and sometimes it is discarded. New technology affects whether something is considered scrap. For example, for many years timber mills burned sawdust, for which they had no alternative uses. As trees became a scarce resource, sawdust became more valuable. With improved glues and new manufacturing processes, products such as specialty logs for fireplaces and chipboard were developed. A process was developed to turn sawdust into pulp for paper mills. Sawdust is no longer scrap but has become an important by-product of milling timber.

Some manufacturers track scrap to measure whether resources are being used efficiently. Scrap is also tracked if it has value and could be stolen. Often it is recorded in physical terms. For example, gold scraps from jewellery manufacture are weighed, the weight is recorded and the scraps are stored in a safe.

From an accounting standpoint, we need to plan for and sometimes guard scrap by setting up control systems. We also need to determine the effect of the value of scrap on inventory costing and the statement of profit or loss. If scrap can be sold, the revenue is recorded either at the time it is produced or at the time it is sold. When the value of scrap is immaterial, it is simply recorded as part of other revenues in the statement of profit or loss.

In job costing, scrap sometimes arises as part of specific jobs. If we can trace it to individual jobs, revenue from the scrap is credited to the specific job in work in process. Scrap revenue reduces the cost of the job with which it is associated. If scrap is common to all jobs, or if it is not worth tracing to individual jobs, the scrap revenue offsets overhead cost for the period. This entry reduces overhead cost for all jobs produced.

If scrap is held for a period of time before it is reused as direct material or sold, we need to estimate its net realisable value so that the value of the scrap can be used to offset overhead costs in the same period in which the overhead costs and associated revenues are recognised. When the price of scrap is volatile, such as gold scraps from jewellery manufacture, estimating its value is more difficult. Some entities develop creative ways to use scrap to benefit employees and others. For example, print shops sometimes bind scrap paper into scratch pads and give them to employees, customers or public schools.

Spoilage opportunity costs

We have learned about methods used to account for the direct costs of spoilage, rework and scrap. Although the direct costs can be significant, managers need to consider several other issues related to the quality of their production processes. One of these is the opportunity costs of spoilage and rework, which can be large. Opportunity costs include:
- forgone profit
- loss of reputation and market share.

An entity forgoes the normal profit from resources that are used to produce spoiled units. Forgone profit is a bigger problem when capacity limits are involved, because the organisation forgoes the profit on resources employed as well as the contribution margin from good units that might have been produced. In addition, some proportion of spoiled units is likely to mistakenly pass inspection. As the number of spoiled units increases, a larger number of spoiled units will inevitably be sold to customers. The sale of these defective units leads to loss of market share because consumers switch brands. The entity eventually loses its reputation for quality products. This leads to further erosion of market share, including customers who never had direct quality problems. These opportunity costs, which are often much greater than the cost of the spoiled units, are not tracked by the accounting system.

7.5 Uses and limitations of job cost information

LEARNING OBJECTIVE 7.5 Critically analyse the uses and limitations of job costing for financial reporting.

Job costing systems measure the cost of products, primarily for customised goods and services. The information from a job costing system can be used for several purposes, including:

- reporting inventory and cost of sales values on financial statements and income tax returns
- developing cost estimates to assist in bidding on potential future jobs
- measuring actual costs to compare to estimated costs
- developing cost estimates for short-term or long-term decisions.

Because a job costing system accumulates and reports costs for individual jobs, the tendency is to mistakenly believe that job costs are measured accurately and that the costs assigned to a job are incremental, that is, would not be incurred if the job were not undertaken. However, job costing systems are subject to uncertainties and require judgement.

Uncertainties in measuring job costs

Little uncertainty tends to surround the direct costs assigned to a job, because those costs are traced to each job. However, judgement is used to decide which direct costs will be traced. Occasionally direct costs are quite small, and the cost of creating a system to track them is greater than the benefit achieved. In these cases, costs that might potentially be traced are instead included with indirect costs in a pool of overhead costs. However, changes in technology sometimes allow accountants to trace costs that were previously too costly to trace. For example, most large photocopiers today include security systems that track the number of copies made to specific account codes. These systems minimise the cost of tracing photocopy costs to individual jobs. Without such a system, the cost of tracking individual copies could be overly expensive. Tracking the use of software and internet services for networked computers or monitoring small supplies such as nails and tape during manufacturing is more difficult. These costs are treated as indirect costs and become part of overhead.

Accountants also choose the type and number of cost pools to use for overhead. For example, overhead costs were pooled at the department level in Aluminium Benders. However, overhead could have been pooled at the plant level. Alternatively, the overhead costs in each department could have been separated into fixed and variable pools. Accountants consider several factors when they choose the number and kind of cost pools to use. From a management control perspective, if costs are tracked to a department or a process, the managers of that department or process can be held responsible for controlling costs. When overhead costs from many departments are pooled, managers and employees within each department have little incentive to control costs. In addition, different departments usually perform different tasks, so their costs may be quite different. If costs are allocated on a department level and these costs more accurately reflect the flow of resources, products can be designed to spend less time in costly departments. When deciding whether to use department or plant-wide cost pools, the benefit gained from gathering information about department costs and the use of department resources by other departments must be worth the cost of tracking them.

Ideally, we would prefer that the overhead allocation process reflect the flow of overhead resources to each product. Thus, an ideal overhead allocation base would be a cost driver. However, fixed overhead is not expected to vary with any allocation base, and it is not always possible to identify or to accurately measure a cost driver for variable overhead. Thus, allocated overhead generally does not accurately measure the overhead resources used by a job.

Uncertainties in estimating future job costs

Managers use job cost estimates to establish a bid for a job, decide whether to accept a job, or make other types of decisions. Managers then monitor operations by comparing actual job costs to the original estimate. Whenever we estimate future events, we face uncertainties about whether the estimates will be accurate. Thus, actual job costs will almost certainly be different from estimated job costs. Managers analyse the differences to evaluate the efficiency of operations and to improve future job cost estimates.

Under normal costing, overhead is allocated to jobs using an estimated overhead allocation rate. The estimated rate is based on estimates of the total overhead cost and the total volume of the allocation base. Actual costs and activity levels are affected by many unforeseen events. These include unanticipated cost inflation or deflation, or an economic downturn that causes business activities to fall short of expectations. Actual costs also differ from expectations because of unexpected improvements or deterioration in production efficiency. Differences between estimates and actual amounts cause overhead to be overapplied or underapplied, and then adjustments are required at the end of an accounting period. However, judgement is necessary in the way that adjustments are made.

SUMMARY

7.1 Explain the flow of costs through the manufacturing process.

Cost flows in manufacturing job costing

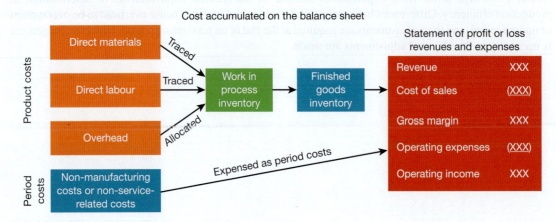

Accounting system

- Source documents (for example, employee time reports and material requisitions)
- Job cost record
- Job cost software

7.2 Calculate the inventoriable product cost for customised products.

- Inventoriable product cost is used for financial reporting and includes manufacturing costs only
- Direct costs (material and labour) are traced with source documentation
- Indirect costs are allocated using an allocation base. It is appropriate to use different cost pools when the nature or level of overhead costs differs across activities

7.3 Discuss the issues related to the allocation of overhead to individual jobs.

Procedures for allocating overhead costs to jobs

1. Identify the relevant cost object — either a single product or a batch of products
2. Identify one or more overhead cost pools and allocation bases. Use different cost pools when the nature or level of overhead costs differs between activities
3. For each overhead cost pool, calculate an overhead allocation rate. The allocation base and resulting overhead allocation rate should reflect an activity that results in the costs being incurred
4. For each overhead cost pool, allocate costs to the cost object

Types of overhead cost pools

- Entity-wide
- Plant-wide
- Separate departments
- Separate activities or processes
- Separate fixed and variable overhead costs

Actual costing

$$\text{Actual allocation rate} \times \text{Actual quantity of allocation base for job}$$

Normal costing

$$\text{Estimated allocation rate} \times \text{Actual quantity of allocation base for job}$$

Adjustment for overapplied or underapplied overhead

$$\text{Overapplied (underapplied) overhead} = \text{Allocated overhead} - \text{Actual overhead}$$

- If material: allocate on a pro-rata basis among work in process, finished goods and cost of sales
- If not material: apply to cost of sales

7.4 Discuss the issues associated with spoilage, rework and scrap handled in job costing.

Type of spoilage, rework or scrap	Accounting treatment
Normal spoilage arising from the requirements of a specific job or process	Charge to the individual job or good units produced
Normal spoilage occurring periodically as a regular part of all jobs	Charge to overhead
Abnormal spoilage	Charge to separate loss account
Opportunity costs of spoilage	Not measured
Rework for defects arising from the requirements of a specific job	Charge to individual job
Rework for defects occurring periodically during normal production	Charge to overhead
Rework for abnormal defects	Charge to separate loss account
Sale of scrap	Record at time of production or at time sold. If not material: record as other income
Scrap traced to individual jobs	Credit to individual job
Scrap common to all jobs or difficult to trace to jobs	Credit to overhead

7.5 Critically analyse the uses and limitations of job costing for financial reporting.

Uses of job cost information

- Assign costs to work in process, finished goods and cost of sales for financial statement and income tax returns.
- Provide information to help managers:
  - monitor operating costs
  - develop costs for future decision making
  - make short-term or long-term decisions.

Allocation of overhead costs

- Required for financial and tax accounting of manufactured goods
- Optional otherwise
- Fixed overhead allocation generally not relevant for short-term decisions

Uncertainties

- Which estimated job costs are relevant for decision making
- Whether and how to trace direct costs
- Choice of overhead cost pools
- Choice of allocation bases
- Estimated overhead allocation rate (under normal costing)
- Method for adjusting overapplied or underapplied overhead (under normal costing)

KEY TERMS

abnormal spoilage Spoilage that is not part of everyday operations.

actual costing A method in which overhead is allocated using the actual volume of the allocation base times the actual allocation rate.

actual overhead allocation rate A method of allocating overhead calculated as follows: Actual allocation rate = Actual overhead cost ÷ Actual quantity of allocation base.

allocation base A measure of activity, preferably a cost driver, used to allocate costs to a cost object.

allocation rate The dollar amount per unit of allocation base used to allocate overhead to each cost object.

cost pool A group of individual costs that are accumulated for a particular purpose. Cost pools can be grouped on a departmental basis, an activity basis or on some other criteria.

estimated allocation rate A method of allocating overhead calculated as follows: Estimated allocation rate = Estimated overhead cost ÷ Estimated quantity of allocation base.

inventoriable product costs The direct and indirect costs of producing goods; include costs incurred in the manufacturing process only.

job cost record A record that contains all of the costs traced and assigned to a specific job.

normal spoilage Defective units that arise as part of regular operations.

overapplied overhead Occurs when actual costs are less than the total amount of overhead allocated to inventory accounts.

overhead cost control accounts Accounts used to record the actual overhead costs incurred during a period and the overhead costs applied to the jobs in work in process.

period costs Non-inventoriable non-manufacturing costs, such as administration costs, incurred with the passage of time.

production costs Costs involved in the production of goods or services.

rework Spoiled units that are repaired and sold as if they were originally produced correctly.

scrap Bits of direct material left over from normal manufacturing processes. Scrap sometimes has value and can be sold, and sometimes it is discarded.

source documents Manual or electronic records created to capture and provide information about transactions or events.

spoilage Units of product that are unacceptable and are discarded, reworked or sold at a reduced price.

underapplied overhead Occurs when actual costs are more than the amount of overhead allocated.

SELF-STUDY PROBLEMS

SELF-STUDY PROBLEM 1 Normal costing with two overhead cost pools

William Felix & Sons uses an estimated overhead rate for allocating production overhead to job orders. The rate is on a machine hour basis for the machining department and on a direct labour cost basis for the finishing department. The entity estimated the following for the current year:

	Machining	Finishing
Production overhead cost	$10 000 000	$8 000 000
Machine hours	200 000	33 000
Direct labour hours	30 000	160 000
Direct labour cost	$900 000	$4 000 000

During January, the cost record for job order no. 806 shows the following:

	Machining	Finishing
Direct materials requisitioned	$14 000	$3 000
Direct labour cost	$600	$1 250
Direct labour hours	30	50
Machine hours	130	10

Total costs and machine hours were as follows for the current year:

	Machining	Finishing
Production overhead incurred	$10 200 000	$7 900 000
Direct labour cost	$950 000	$3 900 000
Machine hours	220 000	32 000

Required

(a) What is the estimated overhead rate that should be used in the:
   (i) machining department?
   (ii) finishing department?
(b) What is the total overhead allocated to job 806?
(c) Assuming that job 806 manufactured 200 units of product, what is the unit cost of job 806?
(d) What is the total amount of overapplied or underapplied overhead in each department at the end of the year?

(e) Provide reasons why William Felix & Sons uses two different overhead application bases. Also discuss why they might use machine hours and labour costs to allocate overhead costs.

SOLUTION TO SELF-STUDY PROBLEM 1

(a) Overhead rates should be calculated using estimated costs and allocation bases:
 (i) Machining: $10 000 000 ÷ 200 000 = $50 per machine hour
 (ii) Finishing: $8 000 000 ÷ $4 000 000 = 200% of direct labour cost

(b) Using the overhead rates from part (a), the total overhead allocated to job 806 should be as follows:

Machining department: $50 × 130 machine hours	$6 500
Finishing department: 200% × $1250 direct labour cost	2 500
Total overhead allocated to job 806	$9 000

(c) To calculate per-unit costs, first calculate the total cost for the batch and then divide by the number of units:

	Machining	Finishing
Direct materials	$14 000	$3 000
Direct labour	600	1 250
Overhead allocated	6 500	2 500
Total	$21 100	$6 750

Total costs: $21 100 + $6750 = $27 850
Cost per unit: $27 850 ÷ 200 units = $139.25 per unit

(d)

Machining department overhead allocated (220 000 × $50)	$11 000 000
Actual overhead in machining	10 200 000
Overapplied overhead	$ 800 000
Finishing department overhead allocated ($3 900 000 × 200%)	$ 7 800 000
Actual overhead in finishing	7 900 000
Underapplied overhead	$ 100 000

(e) William Felix & Sons must believe that the overhead costs in each department are related to different allocation bases. Machining is likely to have more overhead expense for buying, maintaining and using machines. Therefore, machine hours are likely to reflect the activities involved in running machines. In the finishing department, more labour-related costs are incurred. Therefore, it is logical to use labour dollars as an allocation base. Although accountants attempt to pick allocation bases that are related to the activities in a cost centre, the allocations are still arbitrary. Changes in volumes do not result in proportionate changes in costs. A portion of the costs are often fixed and unaffected by changes in the level of the allocation bases. In other words, allocation bases are not necessarily cost drivers. Instead, they are simply measures of activity used to allocate costs logically.

SELF-STUDY PROBLEM 2 Normal and abnormal spoilage

Flockhart Company produces custom-made garden sheds using recycled materials. Currently two jobs are in process: numbers 689 and 690. During production of job 689, lightning hit the factory and caused an electricity surge followed by an outage. Lightning strikes are relatively unusual in the region where the factory is located. At the time of the strike, wood was being sawed to fit job 689. The saw malfunctioned and ruined a large piece of timber that originally cost $175. During production of job 690, two pieces of timber had sawing errors and were scrapped. These pieces of timber originally cost $80 and $75; they could be sold as scrap for $20 and $30. Sawing errors occur for many different jobs on a regular basis.

Required
(a) Consider the spoilage for job 689. Should it be categorised as normal or abnormal spoilage? Explain.
(b) Consider the spoilage for job 690. Should it be categorised as normal or abnormal spoilage? Explain.
(c) Prepare journal entries for the spoilage on both jobs. Assume that the scrap timber has not yet been sold.
(d) Describe the actual and opportunity costs of spoilage.

SOLUTION TO SELF-STUDY PROBLEM 2

(a) The spoilage for job 689 is abnormal spoilage because it occurred from an unusual force of nature. Abnormal spoilage is not part of normal operations and occurs because systems are out of control or an unusual event occurs, such as loss of electricity from an unusual storm. Abnormal spoilage is recorded as a loss for the period.

(b) The spoilage for job 690 is normal spoilage because it arises as a part of ongoing operations. If it occurs because of the requirements of a specific job, it is recorded as a cost for that job. If it occurs as part of operations, it is recorded as an overhead cost.

(c) Journal entry for abnormal spoilage (assuming the requisition of raw material was not recorded as a job cost):

Loss from abnormal spoilage	DR	$175	
Work in process inventory	CR		$175
Abnormal spoilage of timber (job 689 — spoiled timber at cost)			
Overhead cost control	DR	$105	
Raw material inventory (scrap timber)	DR	$ 50	
Work in process inventory	CR		$155
Normal spoilage of timber (job 690 — spoiled timber at cost)			

(d) The actual costs of spoilage include the dollar amounts for direct materials, direct labour and overhead that have been incurred up to the point that the spoiled units are removed from production. The opportunity costs of spoilage include warranty and return costs, and potential loss of reputation and market share. It is difficult to estimate these costs but they can be considerable.

QUESTIONS

7.1 Describe the procedures used in job costing. **LO1**

7.2 Describe an inventoriable product cost. **LO2**

7.3 List three examples of job cost records you would receive if you were building a new home. (*Hint*: Itemised bills made out to you are usually job cost records.) **LO1, 3**

7.4 List several different sources of information used in job costing, and explain why this information is required. **LO1**

7.5 Compare actual and normal cost systems. Discuss the ways in which they are similar and the ways they differ. **LO3**

7.6 Will underapplied and overapplied overhead arise under both actual and normal costing? Explain your answer. **LO3**

7.7 Within the area where you live, work or attend school, name three businesses that would probably use job costing. **LO1**

7.8 Part of a contract between a union and a company guarantees that all manufacturing employees earn five hours of overtime each week. In the company's job costing system, should overtime be treated as a direct or indirect cost? **LO3**

7.9 Exquisite Furniture designs and manufactures custom furniture from exotic materials. Explain why spoilage is sometimes recorded as a cost for a specific job and other times as overhead for this entity. **LO4**

7.10 Explain how manufacturing overhead cost pools and cost allocation are related. **LO3**

7.11 List the most common allocation bases used in job costing and explain under what circumstances each base would be most appropriate. **LO3**

7.12 To what extent do the costs used to value inventories for external financial reporting support internal management decisions on issues such as whether to accept a special, one-off order or whether to outsource part or all of the production process? **LO5**

EXERCISES

7.13 Job costing; determination of manufacturing overhead rates **LO3**

One Glass Brewery estimates the following activity for the coming year:

Expected production	10 000 units
Expected direct labour hours	10 000 hours
Expected manufacturing overhead	$100 000
Manufacturing overhead is allocated on the basis of direct labour hours.	

At the end of the financial period the following information was collected:

Direct labour hours	9000 hours
Manufacturing overhead	$120 000

Required

(a) What was the predetermined manufacturing overhead rate calculated at the beginning of the year?

(b) What was the actual manufacturing overhead rate for the year?

(c) Explain the difference between the rates calculated in (a) and (b) above.

7.14 Job costing overapplied and underapplied overhead; journal entries **LO3**

Shane's Shovels produces small custom-made earthmoving equipment for landscaping companies. Manufacturing overhead is allocated to work in process using an estimated overhead rate. During April, transactions for Shane's Shovels included the following:

Direct materials issued to production	$180 000
Indirect materials issued to production	30 000
Other manufacturing overhead incurred	250 000
Overhead allocated	225 000
Direct labour costs	75 000

Beginning and ending work in process were both zero.

Required

(a) What was the cost of jobs completed in April?

(b) Was manufacturing overhead underapplied or overapplied? By how much?

(c) Write out the journal entries for these transactions, including the adjustment.

7.15 Normal and abnormal spoilage **LO4**

Franklin Fabrication produces custom-made security doors and gates. Currently two jobs are in process: 359 and 360. During production of job 359, the supervisor was on holidays and the employees made several errors in cutting the metal pieces for the two doors in the order. The spoiled metal pieces cost $20 each and had zero scrap value. In addition, an order of five gates that had been manufactured for job 360 required a fine wire mesh that sometimes tore as it was being mounted. Because a similar wire could be used that was much easier to install, the customer had been warned that costs could run over the bid if any difficulty was encountered in installing the wire. One of the gates was spoiled during the process of installing the wire. The cost of the materials and direct labour for the gate was $150. The gate and metal were hauled to the dump and discarded.

Required

(a) Should the spoilage for job 359 be categorised as normal or abnormal spoilage? Explain.

(b) Should the spoilage for job 360 be categorised as normal or abnormal spoilage? Explain.

(c) Prepare spoilage journal entries for both jobs.

7.16 Direct costs and overhead **LO2**

Job 87M had direct material costs of $400 and a total cost of $2100. Overhead is allocated at the rate of 75 per cent of prime cost (direct material and direct labour).

Required

(a) How much direct labour was used?

(b) How much overhead was allocated?

7.17 Analysis of WIP T-account

Jasper Company uses a job costing system. Overhead is allocated based on 120 per cent of direct labour cost. Last month's transactions in the work in process account are shown here:

Work in process

Beginning balance	$ 48 000		
Direct materials	160 000	To finished goods	$442 000
Direct labour	120 000		
Factory overhead	150 000		

Only one job, number 850, was still in process at the end of the month. Job 850 was charged with $9000 in overhead for the month.

Required

(a) What is the ending balance in the WIP account?

(b) How much direct labour cost was used for job 850?

(c) What is the amount of direct materials used for job 850?

7.18 Journal entries

Langley uses a job costing system. At the beginning of June, two orders were in process as follows:

	Order 88	Order 105
Direct materials	$1000	$900
Direct labour	$1200	200
Overhead allocated	1800	300

There was no inventory in finished goods on 1 June. During June, orders numbered 106 to 120 were put into process.

Direct materials requirements amounted to $13 000, direct labour costs for the month were $20 000 and actual manufacturing overhead recorded during the month amounted to $28 000.

The only order in process at the end of June was order 120, and the costs incurred for this order were $1150 of direct materials and $1000 of direct labour. In addition, order 118, which was 100 per cent complete, was still on hand as of 30 June. Total costs for this order were $3300. The entity's overhead allocation rate in June was the same as that used in May and is based on labour cost.

Required

(a) Prepare journal entries (with supporting calculations) to record the cost of goods manufactured, the cost of sales and the closing of the overapplied or underapplied overhead to cost of sales.

(b) Describe the two different approaches to closing overapplied or underapplied overhead at the end of the period. How do you choose an appropriate method?

7.19 Cost of sales schedule

Rebecca Ltd is a manufacturer of machines made to customer specifications. All production costs are accumulated by means of a job order costing system. The following information is available at the beginning of October.

Raw materials inventory, 1 October	$16 200
Work in process, 1 October	5100

A review of the job order cost sheets revealed the composition of the work in process inventory on 1 October as follows:

Direct materials (assuming no indirect materials this month)	$ 1320
Direct labour (300 hours)	3000
Manufacturing overhead allocated	780
	$5100

Activity during October was as follows:

Raw materials costing $20 000 were purchased.
Direct labour for job orders totalled 3300 hours at $10 per hour.
Manufacturing overhead was allocated to production at the rate of $2.60 per direct labour hour.

On 31 October, inventories consisted of the following:

Raw materials inventory	$17 000
Work in process:	
Direct materials	4 320
Direct labour (500 hours)	5 000
Manufacturing overhead allocated	1 300

Required
Prepare a detailed schedule showing the cost of goods manufactured for October.

7.20 Job costing journal entries   **LO2, 3**

Vern's Van Service customises light trucks according to customers' orders. This month the entity worked on five jobs, numbered 207 to 211. Materials requisitions for the month were as follows:

Job	Carpet	Paint	Electronics	Other	Total
207	$ 40	$350	$580	–	$ 970
208	75	200	375	–	650
209	200	400	200	–	800
210	30	150	770	–	950
211	60	–	50	–	110
Indirect	–	–	–	$750	750
Total costs					$4 230

An analysis of the payroll records revealed the following distribution for labour costs:

			Job				
	207	208	209	210	211	Other	Total
Direct labour	$1400	$1200	$800	$1700	$400	–	$5500
Indirect labour	–	–	–	–	–	$2200	2200
Total costs							$7700

Other overhead costs (consisting of rent, depreciation, taxes, insurance, utilities etc.) amounted to $3600. At the beginning of the period, management anticipated that overhead cost would be $6400 and total direct labour would amount to $5000. Overhead is allocated on the basis of direct labour dollars.

Jobs 207 to 210 were finished during the month; job 211 is still in process. Jobs 207 to 209 were picked up and paid for by customers. Job 210 is still on the lot waiting to be picked up.

Required
(a) Prepare the journal entries to reflect the incurrence of materials, labour and overhead costs; the allocation of overhead; and the transfer of units to finished goods and cost of sales.
(b) Close overapplied or underapplied overhead to cost of sales.

7.21 Allocating overhead; overapplied and underapplied overhead; spoilage   **LO3, 4**

The Futons for You Company sells batches of custom-made futons to customers and uses predetermined rates for fixed overhead, based on machine hours. The following data are available for last year:

Budgeted and actual fixed factory overhead cost	$160 000
Budgeted machine hours	100 000
Actual machine hours used	110 000

	Machine hours used
Job 20	11 000
Job 21	16 000
Job 22	14 000
Job 23	9 000

Required

(a) Calculate the estimated overhead allocation rate to be used for the year.

(b) Determine the overhead to be allocated to job 21.

(c) Determine total overapplied or underapplied overhead at the end of the year.

(d) Should cost of sales be increased or decreased at the end of the year? Why?

(e) If the amount of overapplied or underapplied overhead is material, how is it assigned?

(f) Suppose Job 21 required a special fabric cover for the futon pads. This type of fabric dulled the blades of the cutting machine, and a number of fabric covers were unusable. Should this spoilage be recorded for job 21 or for all jobs processed this period? Explain your answer.

7.22 Journal entries for job costing   **LO2**

At the beginning of the accounting period, the accountant for ABC Industries estimated that total overhead would be $80 000. Overhead is allocated to jobs on the basis of direct labour cost. Direct labour was budgeted to cost $200 000 this period. During the period, only three jobs were worked on. The following summarises the direct materials and labour costs for each:

	Job 1231	Job 1232	Job 1233
Direct materials	$45 000	$70 000	$30 000
Direct labour	70 000	90 000	50 000

Job 1231 was finished and sold, job 1232 was finished but is waiting to be sold, and job 1233 is still in process. Actual overhead for the period was $82 000.

Required

Prepare the following journal entries.

(a) Cost recorded during production

(b) Cost of jobs completed

(c) Cost of sales

(d) Allocation of overapplied or underapplied overhead allocated on a pro-rata basis to the ending balances in work in process, finished goods and cost of sales

7.23 Spoilage journal entries   **LO4**

Jones Company manufactures custom doors. When job 186 (a batch of 14 custom doors) was being processed in the machining department, one of the wood panels on a door split. This problem occurs periodically and is considered normal spoilage. Direct materials and labour for the door, to the point of spoilage, were $35. In addition, a storm caused a surge in electricity and a routing machine punctured the wood for job 238. This incident occurred at the beginning of production, so spoilage amounted to only the cost of wood, at $200.

Required

(a) Prepare the journal entries for normal and abnormal spoilage.

(b) Now suppose that the wood from abnormal spoilage can be sold for $25. Record the journal entries for the disposal value.

(c) Jones Company is considering hiring someone to inspect all wood after it arrives at the plant but prior to production. Discuss the pros and cons of hiring an inspector.

PROBLEMS

7.24 Collecting overhead cost information   **LO3**

A family member asked you to review the accounting system used for Hanna's, a custom stained-glass manufacturing business. The owner currently uses a software package to keep track of her bank account but does not produce financial statements. The owner seeks your help in setting up a costing system so that financial statements can be produced on a monthly basis.

Required

(a) What kind of costing system is needed for this setting?

(b) You plan to categorise the banking data for entry into the financial statement records. List the categories you might use for these entries. List only broad categories here (see parts (c), (d) and (e) for more details).

(c) List several costs that might be included in a fixed overhead category.

(d) List several costs that might be included in a variable overhead category.

(e) List several costs that might be included in direct materials.

(f) Write a memo to the owner discussing the alternative choices for the costing system. Include an explanation of the type of information that would need to be captured to support the costing system.

7.25 Cost of rework; control of scrap; accounting for scrap   **LO4**

Dapper Dan Draperies manufactures and installs custom-ordered draperies.

Required

(a) For all drapes, occasionally the sewing equipment malfunctions and the drape must be reworked. Explain how to account for the cost of rework when it is needed.

(b) Explain how to account for the cost of rework when customers choose a fabric that is known to require rework.

(c) Explain why scrap will always arise in this entity.

(d) Dapper Dan can sell scraps to quilting groups or just throw them away. List several factors that could affect this decision.

(e) If Dapper Dan decides to sell scraps, explain the accounting choices for recording the sales value.

7.26 Accounting for scrap   **LO4**

You are helping a friend, Jonah, set up a new accounting system for a small start-up construction entity. He specialises in custom-made energy efficient homes that are built on a cost-plus basis. Cost-plus means that his customers pay a fixed percentage above the sum of direct and overhead costs.

As he goes through the accounts, Jonah asks why you set up a separate account for scrap. He does not believe that scrap should be recorded anywhere in his accounting system because it is worth little, and theft is no problem. He makes weekly trips to a recycling plant where he receives a small sum for the scrap. Most of the time Jonah works on only one house, and the scrap is only for that house. However, once in a while he works on several houses, and the scrap for all of the houses is recycled at once.

Required

(a) Explain the two ways that scrap can be recorded in a job costing system.

(b) Choose the appropriate method for Jonah and explain your choice.

(c) Suppose you are a prospective homeowner. Explain to Jonah why you believe the revenue from scrap associated with your home should be recorded as a reduction in your costs rather than his overall costs.

(d) Write a brief (and diplomatic) paragraph to convince Jonah that he needs to account for the revenues from scrap.

7.27 Job costing; overhead rates   **LO2, 3**

The Eastern Seaboard Company uses an estimated rate for allocating manufacturing overhead to job orders based on machine hours for the machining department, and on a direct labour cost basis for the finishing department.

The company budgeted the following for last year:

	Machining	Finishing
Manufacturing overhead	$5 000 000	$3 000 000
Machine hours	250 000	14 000
Direct labour hours	15 000	16 000
Direct labour cost	$225 000	$2 400 000

During December, the cost record for job 602 shows the following:

	Machining	Finishing
Direct materials requisitioned	$7000	$2000
Direct labour cost	$300	$6750
Direct labour hours	20	300
Machine hours	35	5

Required

(a) What is the estimated overhead allocation rate that should be used in the machining department? In the finishing department?

(b) What is the total overhead allocated to job 602?

(c) Assuming that job 602 consisted of 200 units of product, what is the unit cost for this job?

(d) What factors affect the volume of production in a period? Can we know all of the factors before the period begins? Why?

(e) Explain why the company would use two different overhead allocation bases.

7.28 Plant-wide versus production cost pools   **LO2, 3**

Flexible Manufacturers produces small batches of customised products. The accounting system is set up to allocate plant overhead to each job using the following production cost pools and overhead allocation rates.

Labour-paced assembly	$25 per direct labour hour
Machine-paced assembly	$18 per machine hour
Quality testing	$ 2 per unit

Actual resources used for job 75:

Direct labour hours	3
Machine hours	1.25
Number of units	36

The manufacturing accountant wants to simplify the cost accounting system and use a plant-wide rate. If the preceding costs were grouped into a single cost pool and allocated based on labour hours, the rate would be $35 per direct labour hour.

Required

(a) What cost should be allocated to job 75 using the plant-wide overhead rate?

(b) What cost should be allocated to job 75 using the production cost pool overhead rates?

(c) Why do the allocated amounts in parts (a) and (b) differ?

(d) Which method would you recommend? Explain your choice.

7.29 Effects of robotic equipment on overhead rates   **LO2, 3**

'Our costs are out of control, our accounting system is screwed up, or both!' exclaimed the sales manager. 'We are simply non-competitive on a great many of the jobs we bid on. Just last week we lost a customer when a competitor underbid us by 25 per cent! And I bid the job at cost because the customer has been with us for years but has been complaining about our prices.'

This problem, raised at the weekly management meeting, has been getting worse over the years. The Johnson Tool Company produces parts for specific customer orders. When the entity first became successful, it employed nearly 500 skilled machinists. Over the years the entity has become increasingly automated and now uses a number of different robotic machines. It currently employs only 75 production workers but output has quadrupled.

The problems raised by the sales manager can be seen in the portions of two bid sheets brought to the meeting (shown below). The bids are from the cutting department, but the relative size of these three types of manufacturing costs is similar for other departments.

The cutting department charges overhead to products based on direct labour hours. For the current period, the department expects to use 4000 direct labour hours. Departmental overhead, consisting mostly of depreciation on the robotic equipment, is expected to be $1 480 000.

An employee can typically set up any job on the appropriate equipment in approximately 15 minutes. Once machines are operating, an employee oversees five to eight machines simultaneously. All that is required is to load or unload materials and monitor calibrations. The department's robotic machines will log a total of 25 000 hours of run time in the current period.

For bid 74 683, the entity was substantially underbid by a competitor. The company did get the job for bid 74 687, but the larger jobs are harder to find. Small jobs arise frequently, but the entity is rarely successful in obtaining them.

Cutting department

Bid # 74 683	Machine run time: 3 hours
Materials	
Steel sheeting	$280.25
Direct labour	
Equipment set-up (0.25 hours @ $12.50)	3.13
Equipment tending (1 hour @ $12.50)	12.50
Overhead (1.25 hours @ $370)	462.50
Total costs	$758.38

Cutting department

Bid # 74 687	Machine run time: 11 hours
Materials	
Steel sheeting	$2440.50
Direct labour	
Equipment set-up (0.25 hours @ $12.50)	3.13
Equipment tending (1.25 hours @ $12.50)	15.63
Overhead (1.5 hours @ $370)	555.00
Total costs	$3014.26

Required

(a) Critique the cost allocation method used within the current cost accounting system.

(b) Suggest a better approach for allocating overhead. Allocate costs using your approach and compare the costs of both jobs under the two systems.

(c) Discuss the pros and cons of using job costs to determine the price for a job order.

7.30 Classification of rework costs; uncertainties; critique of rework and scrap policy   **LO4**

Fran Markus is in the cost accounting group at Boats Galore, a large manufacturing company that produces customised boats and yachts. The company sometimes experiences quality problems with its fibreglass raw material, causing flawed areas in boat hulls. The problem is often fixed by reworking the flawed areas. Other times the hull is scrapped because it is too flawed, and a new hull is fabricated. The spoilage policy at Boats Galore is to charge the cost of rework and spoilage to overhead unless it arises because a hull design is particularly complicated. In those cases, the cost is assigned to the job.

Two boats currently under construction require triple the amount of materials and labour time to enhance boat security. The customer wants each hull to be able to withstand the explosion of a small bomb. It is the company's first order with this hull construction. Because of the new design and fibreglass process, the customer has agreed to a cost-plus contract and will pay cost plus a fixed percentage of cost. This contract assures that Boats Galore does not incur a loss from developing the enhanced security hull. This week, the third layer on one of the boat hulls had a flaw in the fibreglass. The area was reworked, after which it met the security requirements.

Fran receives weekly data on labour and materials for each boat under construction. For regular production, workers estimate the time and materials used to rework flawed fibreglass areas, and Fran adds those costs to overhead instead of recording them as a cost of the particular job. Now she needs to decide how to record the cost of rework for the enhanced security hulls. The production people are not sure whether the flaw was due to poor quality fibreglass or to the triple hull design. If Fran adds the cost to the job order, the customer will pay for the labour and supplies as part of the cost-plus price. If she adds the cost to overhead, the cost will be spread across all jobs and only part of it will be allocated to the job having the enhanced security hulls.

Required

(a) Critique the company's accounting policy for rework and scrap.

(b) Describe uncertainties about the accounting treatment for the rework costs on the enhanced security hull job.

(c) Discuss the pros and cons of alternative accounting treatments for the rework costs on this job.

(d) Suppose you are an accounting work-experience student at Boats Galore. Fran asks you to recommend an accounting treatment for the rework costs on the enhanced security hull job.

    (i) Write a memo to Fran with your recommendation. As you write the memo, consider what information Fran will need from you to help her make a final decision.

    (ii) Write one or two paragraphs explaining how you decided what information to include in your memo.

ACKNOWLEDGEMENTS

Photo 7A: © Natee Meepian / Shutterstock.com

CHAPTER 8

Process costing systems

LEARNING OBJECTIVES

After studying this chapter, you should be able to:

8.1 assign costs to mass-produced products

8.2 understand the concept of equivalent units and how they relate to the production process

8.3 calculate product costs using the weighted average and first-in, first-out (FIFO) methods

8.4 create journal entries for process costing

8.5 calculate product costs in a process where there are multiple production departments

8.6 understand the issues associated with spoilage costs in process costing

8.7 identify the uses and limitations of process cost information.

IN BRIEF

Some products are mass produced, making it impractical to trace costs to individual units. Process costing provides a way to overcome this challenge by assigning costs to production departments and then allocating the costs from the department to individual units. The practice of process costing is complicated by the fact that some physical units are likely to be partially complete at the beginning and end of the accounting period. Furthermore, entities typically produce some proportion of defective or spoiled units. To assign costs appropriately to all of the units processed (completed, partially complete or spoiled), accountants must understand both the production process and the various methods for applying process costing.

8.1 Accounting for the cost of mass-produced goods

LEARNING OBJECTIVE 8.1 Assign costs to mass-produced products.

The accounting approach for assigning production costs to mass-produced products is called **process costing**. The purpose of process costing is to assign costs to each unit of a good. However, it is time-consuming and costly to trace costs directly to individual units when products are identical and mass produced. Thus, production costs are traced to cost pools reflecting the production process (usually departments) and then allocated to individual units in a two-stage process. Examples of products for which process costing is used include beverages, food, chemicals, petroleum, plastic products and pharmaceuticals.

In many entities, the production process consists of work performed in a sequence of departments. Thus, costs are assigned to each production department and then allocated to all units that pass through the department. Consider the flow of work and costs for a cherry processor. Fresh cherries are received and washed in the first department. At this point in the process, some of the cherries are sold on the market as fresh cherries. Other cherries will be processed further. In the second department, the cherries are placed in vats and then covered with a syrup solution, brought to a boil and then prepared for canning or drying. Most of the cherries are canned in the second department, but some are transferred to a third department where the syrup is drained before the cherries are dried and packaged.

Notice that each department incurs a variety of costs. Costs in the first department include the purchase price of the cherries, labour, equipment depreciation and maintenance, water, electricity and supplies. It would be impossible to directly measure the cost of water used to clean each kilogram of cherries. However, costs such as water are allocated to each kilogram of cherries by dividing the total cost of water by the total kilograms of cherries processed.

Assigning direct materials and conversion costs

Similar to job costing, costs in a process costing system are assigned to products using a two-stage process. However, in process costing, all costs are first assigned to departments. Costs are then allocated from departments to individual product units, as shown in figure 8.1(a). However, in the cherry processing example, if the cherries are transferred to the next department for further processing, there will be a cost flow between departments. Such costs are referred to as **transferred-in costs**.

In a conventional process costing system, the two categories of product cost are direct materials and conversion costs. **Conversion costs** are direct labour and production overhead costs. Direct labour is grouped with overhead as all units will consume the labour resources in the same pattern, so there is no need to keep detailed records of labour usage as is undertaken with job costing. Direct materials and conversion costs are allocated separately because they are usually incurred at different points in the production process. Figure 8.1(b) shows the cost flow within a department. Some costs, such as indirect materials and indirect labour, are traced to departments through materials and payroll records. However, a number of costs are allocated to departments, such as the cost of rent and insurance for a shared production facility.

Figure 8.2 illustrates how costs are incurred for the cherry production process. In the cleaning department, the direct materials (cherries) are added at the beginning of the process. In the cooking and canning department, some direct materials (water and syrup) are added at the beginning of the process, and others (jars and lids) are added at the end of the process. In the drying department, packaging materials are used at the end of the process. The conversion costs are added throughout processing in all three departments.

8.2 Work in process and equivalent units

LEARNING OBJECTIVE 8.2 Understand the concept of equivalent units and how they relate to the production process.

When the production process covers a span of time, organisations are likely to have partially complete units of goods or services at the beginning and end of an accounting period. The cherry processing example would probably not have beginning or ending work in process (WIP) inventories for the cleaning and cooking and canning departments. The processing in these departments occurs quickly and is complete at the end of a day's operating activity. However, WIP inventory remains in the drying department for several days. Suppose, at the end of an accounting period, cherries in the drying department are in various stages of completion. Some are completely dried and waiting to be packaged. Others were just put into the drying equipment and will need to remain there for several days. We know the number of kilograms the department is currently processing, and we know that we have cherries at many different stages of completion.

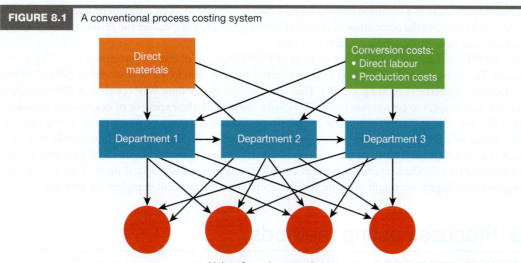

(a) Product cost flows

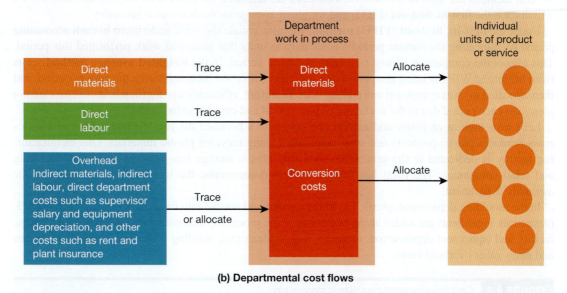

(b) Departmental cost flows

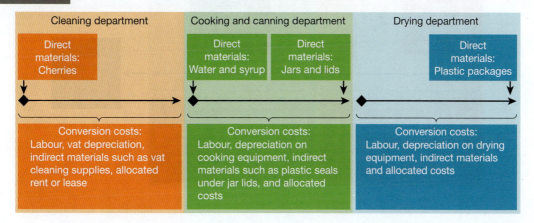

In order to prepare either the interim or final financial statements for the accounting period it is necessary to be able to assign costs to either finished goods or transferred goods and work in process. This is also why individual cost pools are required for allocation purposes as not all units in the process will have incurred the same amount of resources. How can we assign costs to an incomplete unit? This is achieved by converting all units to a common denominator, which is referred to as an **equivalent unit**. For partially complete units, we take the percentage of completion into account, and measure the resources used relative to the resources needed to complete one whole unit.

Suppose WIP in the drying department consists of 1000 kilograms of cherries estimated to be 20 per cent complete. The conversion cost allocated to these cherries is equivalent to the cost needed to fully complete 200 kilograms of cherries (1000 kg × 20%). Thus, we estimate that ending WIP consists of 200 equivalent kilograms with respect to conversion costs. Obviously, we require the expertise of operational personnel to guide the task of identifying the stage of completion of units in the process. An estimate would be made of the amount of completion for the entire volume of cherries in the department. For example, if a large amount of cherries (relative to all of the cherries in the department) has just begun the drying process, we might estimate that the cherries are 20 per cent complete on average. However, if most of the cherries are waiting to be packaged, we might estimate that the cherries are 80 per cent complete on average.

8.3 Process costing methods

LEARNING OBJECTIVE 8.3 Calculate product costs using the weighted average and first-in, first-out (FIFO) methods.

Several methods are used to measure the costs that are allocated for process costing. In this chapter, we will discuss the first-in, first-out (FIFO) and weighted average methods to value inventory.

Under the **first-in, first-out (FIFO) method**, we differentiate the work undertaken in each accounting period by allocating the current period's costs only to units that have had work performed this period. This allows the comparison of unit cost from period to period. In the **weighted average method**, costs from beginning WIP (incurred last period) are averaged with costs incurred during the current period, and then allocated to units completed and ending WIP. Therefore, efficiencies or inefficiencies in costs are not identified each period due to the averaging of past period and current period costs.

Let's now look at an entity and explore the differences between the two methods. Premier Plastics mass-produces plastic products and small appliances using recycled plastic materials. One manufacturing facility is dedicated to the production industrial plastic storage bins used by both manufacturing and retail companies. The plant has two production departments: the moulding department and the assembly department.

In the moulding department, plastic liquid is prepared and poured into moulds. As shown in figure 8.3, plastic mix ingredients are added at the beginning of the process. Conversion costs include direct labour, facility and equipment depreciation, cleaner's wages, electricity, building insurance, supervisor salaries and many other overhead costs.

FIGURE 8.3   Cost flows for producing plastic storage bins

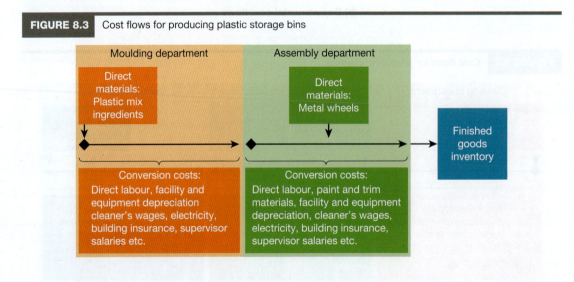

Although the conversion costs are incurred throughout the moulding process, they are not incurred evenly. For example, the machines are periodically shut down for cleaning and maintenance. More labour is required to monitor certain parts of the process, such as when plastic mix ingredients are added. Nevertheless, we simplify the accounting by assuming that conversion costs are incurred evenly throughout the process. When the moulding process is complete, the outer shells are transferred to the assembly department.

In the assembly department, machines remove any rough edges and then smooth the outer and inner surfaces. Next, metal wheels are inserted to the base of each bin. Thus, direct materials are added partway through this process. Finally, details of the cleaning instructions and capacity are painted on each bin. Because the cost for paint and trim for each bin is small, those costs are considered indirect and included in conversion costs. The completed units are transferred to finished goods inventory. As orders are processed, the bins are transferred to the shipping department for packing and delivery.

Premier Plastics commenced operations in March. Nancy Redhouse, the cost accountant for Premier Plastics, wants to help the managers monitor operational costs, so she is considering the best method to use for process cost reports. The moulding department head also wants to use cost information to motivate employees operating the new machines to identify potential process improvements that could further reduce cost or increase quality.

It was first thought that the process cost reports would be prepared using the weighted average method. However, Nancy is concerned that this method might not provide managers with the most current cost information. The FIFO method provides more current cost information due to its focus on the current period's costs only rather than mixing the prior period's cost efficiencies/inefficiencies into the unit cost calculation for the current month. Nancy decides to prepare process cost reports for the first three months using both methods so that she can discuss the results with the managers and obtain feedback for the final decision.

She uses a four-step process to prepare the process cost report under each method.
1. Summarise total costs to account for.
2. Summarise physical and equivalent units.
3. Calculate the cost per equivalent unit.
4. Account for cost of units completed and transferred out and the cost of ending WIP, thereby preparing the process cost reports.

The following calculations focus on process costing for the moulding department over the first three months of production activities. The first month portrays the simplest scenario, with no beginning or ending work in process. During the second month, the computations become slightly more complex with the addition of ending WIP. The third month includes both beginning and ending WIP. For each month, we prepare process cost reports to summarise and compare the results for the FIFO and weighted average methods.

Process cost reports without beginning or ending WIP — first month (March)

During March, 10 000 bins are started by the moulding department of Premier Plastics, completed and transferred to the assembly department. When no work in process is involved, the equivalent unit cost is the average cost per unit for the period, calculated by dividing total cost for direct materials and conversion by the total units produced. Therefore, the cost per equivalent unit is the same under both the FIFO and weighted average methods.

At the end of March, interim financial statements will need to be prepared and it will be necessary to value goods transferred to the assembly department. The valuation process for this month is simplified because all goods started were completed. However, as there are no subsidiary ledgers when using a process costing system, it is necessary to undertake calculations outside the ledger; this is achieved through the preparation of the process cost report. Comprehensive example 1 develops the process cost report for the month of March, comparing the valuation under a FIFO methodology and a weighted average methodology for valuation purposes.

Process cost reports without beginning or ending WIP

Figure 8.4 presents the data and computations for the month of March with no beginning or ending WIP inventory. The cost information was obtained from the moulding department's WIP account in the general ledger and represents all costs incurred and recorded in the account for the month. We can see that for March, the moulding department of Premier Plastics incurred costs of $100 000. The cost of direct materials used during March is $30 000, and conversion costs incurred are $70 000. To prepare the interim financial statements for the end of the month, it will be necessary to assign a cost to the goods transferred to the assembly department only as there is no work in process. Unlike a job costing system, a process costing system does not have a subsidiary ledger that details the costs for individual jobs. Therefore, it is necessary to undertake the cost allocation outside the accounting system. To do this we prepare the process cost report to detail how costs will be allocated to the units of production. Once the costs to be allocated have been identified it is necessary to calculate the physical flow of units to determine how many units need to be accounted for in the process. For March, as all units (10 000) are both started and completed in the same period there is no need to calculate an equivalent unit.

FIGURE 8.4 Moulding department process cost report for March

Moulding department			
Process cost report for the month of March — weighted average and FIFO			
		Equivalent units	
	Totals	**Direct material**	**Conversion costs**
Costs to account for:			
Beginning WIP	—		
Current costs	$100 000	$30 000	$70 000
Total costs to account for	$100 000	$30 000	$70 000
Units to account for:			
Beginning WIP	—		
Started this month	10 000		
Units to account for	10 000		
Finished goods	10 000	10 000	10 000
Ending WIP	—	—	
Units accounted for	10 000	10 000	10 000
Cost per equivalent unit	$ 10.00	$ 3.00[a]	$ 7.00[b]
Assignment of costs to inventory[c]			
Finished goods	$100 000	$30 000	$70 000
Ending WIP	—	—	—
Costs assigned	$100 000	$30 000	$70 000

1. Summarise total costs to account for
2. Summarise physical and equivalent units
3. Calculate cost per equivalent unit
4. Account for costs of units

[a] $30 000 / 10 000 units
[b] $70 000 / 10 000 units
[c] Equivalent unit for each cost category for each item of inventory × cost per equivalent unit (dollars rounded)

This simplifies the calculation of total product cost and is determined by dividing the cost to be allocated by the actual units calculated for each cost pool. For the direct materials, the unit cost is $3 ($30 000 / 10 000 units) and unit conversion cost is $7 ($70 000 / 10 000 units) giving a unit cost of $10 for all completed units. Thus, the cost for the 10 000 units produced is $100 000, which is equal to the total costs to account for. An average cost is calculated for each cost pool because when costs are added at different stages of the process the amount of resources used by each unit is different. By breaking the cost down into separate cost pools we are able to assign costs only to those units that have consumed the resource.

Comparison of weighted average and FIFO for March

Because no beginning WIP is involved, the costs per unit are the same under both the FIFO and weighted average methods. These methods differ only when beginning WIP must be taken into account. Remember that FIFO separates the current month's activity from previous activity, and given there was no beginning WIP, all costs relate to the current period only.

Process cost reports with ending WIP — second month (April)

For the month of April, the moulding department has ending WIP but no beginning WIP. During April, 12 000 units are started, and at the end of the month 10 000 are completed and transferred out to the assembly department, with the remaining 2000 units 30 per cent complete (see comprehensive example 2).

COMPREHENSIVE EXAMPLE 2

Process cost reports with ending WIP in second month

Figure 8.5 presents the data and computations for the month of April. The cost of direct materials used during April is $36 000 and conversion costs are $74 200. Therefore, $110 200 will need to be assigned to inventory at the end of the period. The total work performed during April is equal to those units that were completed and transferred out (10 000 units) and the equivalent units for the 2000 units in ending WIP. To determine the equivalent units for ending WIP, we must consider when the resources are added to the process. Direct materials in the moulding department are added at the beginning of production, so the 2000 units in ending WIP are 100 per cent complete with respect to direct materials, and therefore equivalent units for direct materials equal 2000. The total amount of work performed during April for direct materials is 12 000 equivalent units. However, we assume that conversion costs in the moulding department are incurred evenly throughout production. Therefore, the 2000 physical units in ending WIP are counted as 600 equivalent units (2000 units × 30%) for conversion costs. The total amount of work performed during April for conversion costs is 10 600 equivalent units.

FIGURE 8.5 Moulding department process cost report for April

	Totals	Direct material	Conversion costs
Moulding department Process cost report for the month of April — weighted average and FIFO			
		Equivalent units	
	Totals	**Direct material**	**Conversion costs**
Costs to account for:			
Beginning WIP	—		
Current costs	$110 200	$36 000	$74 200
Total costs to account for	$110 200	$36 000	$74 200
Units to account for:			
Beginning WIP	—		
Started this month	12 000		
Units to account for	10 000		
Finished goods	10 000	10 000	10 000
Ending WIP (30% complete)	2 000	2 000	600[a]
Units accounted for	12 000	12 000	10 600
Cost per equivalent unit	$ 10.00	$ 3.00[b]	$ 7.00[c]
Assignment of costs to inventory [d]			
Finished goods	$100 000	$30 000	$70 000
Ending WIP	10 200	6 000	4 200
Costs assigned	$110 200	$36 000	$74 200

[a] 2000 units × 0.3
[b] $36 000 / 12 000 units
[c] $74 200 / 10 600 units
[d] Equivalent unit for each cost category for each item of inventory × cost per equivalent unit (dollars rounded)

Because Premier Plastics began April with no beginning WIP, the costs per unit are again the same under the FIFO and weighted average methods. However, because we have ending WIP that is partially complete, we now use equivalent units rather than actual units to calculate the per-unit cost.

The inventory valuation process begins by determining the equivalent number of units that will have costs assigned. Remember, at the end of the period the moulding department WIP account will need to be balanced by transferring the cost of completed goods to the assembly department WIP account, with the balance of costs for incomplete units staying in the moulding department WIP account. As the direct materials cost remains $3 per unit and conversion costs are $7 per unit, the total equivalent unit cost remains $10. Thus, the cost allocated to the 10 000 units completed is $100 000 (10 000 units × $10). For ending WIP, the cost of direct materials is $6000 (2000 units × $3) and conversion costs are $4200 (600 units × $7). As the ending WIP is not 100 per cent complete we cannot use the $10 unit cost as this rate assumes resources have been 100 per cent consumed by the product. We can double-check our calculations by verifying that the sum of costs accounted for ($110 200) is equal to the sum of beginning WIP plus the costs incurred during April ($0 + $36 000 + $74 200 = $110 200).

Comparison of weighted average and FIFO for April.

As before, with no beginning WIP, there is no cost difference between the FIFO and weighted average methods. The reason for this is that all costs were incurred in the current period.

Process cost reports with beginning and ending WIP — third month (May)

For May, there is beginning WIP as well as ending WIP. Beginning WIP includes 2000 units (closing WIP for April with an inventory value of $10 200); 9000 units are started, completed and transferred to the assembly department; and another 1000 units are started and 40 per cent complete at the end of the period. The cost of direct materials used during May is $30 500, and conversion costs incurred are $76 680 (see comprehensive example 3). Now that the moulding department has beginning work in process we will need to prepare two process cost reports to accommodate the differences in inventory valuation using the FIFO method or weighted average method. We will begin with the FIFO process cost report.

COMPREHENSIVE EXAMPLE 3

Process cost reports with beginning and ending WIP

FIFO valuation of inventory

For May, we have to account not only for the current costs incurred, but also for the costs assigned to the ending WIP for April. The moulding department's WIP account has total costs of $117 380 recorded, and the breakdown for each cost pool is shown in figure 8.6. The total units to account for during May (12 000) include both beginning WIP (2000 units) and the units started during the month (10 000 units). The total work performed during the month is the sum of work performed to complete beginning WIP units (remaining 70 per cent of conversion activities), the units both started and completed in the current month, and the work performed on units started but not yet completed (estimated to be 40 per cent complete). Because direct materials are added at the beginning of the process, no additional direct materials were needed to complete beginning WIP, meaning the units were 100 per cent complete with respect to direct materials. (If you refer to figure 8.5 you will notice that the 2000 units in ending WIP had 100 per cent of the material costs assigned in March.)

Conversion costs are added throughout the process, so part of the conversion costs for beginning WIP was incurred last period and part was incurred this period. The beginning WIP consisted of 2000 units that were 30 per cent complete, or 600 equivalent units with respect to conversion costs (2000 units × 30%). Conversion work performed during May consisted of completing the beginning WIP equivalent to 1400 [2000 units × (1 − 30%)] units, plus the 9000 units started and completed, plus 400 equivalent units in ending WIP (1000 units × 40%), for a total of 10 800 units.

To determine the equivalent unit cost under FIFO, current period costs are divided by the number of equivalent units for total work performed this period. During May, equivalent unit costs are calculated as shown above: $3.05 for direct materials ($30 500 / 10 000 units) and $7.10 for conversion costs ($76 800 / 10 800 units). These costs are allocated to the work performed to complete beginning WIP

($9940), to the units started and completed ($91 350), and to the equivalent units in ending WIP ($5890). We can double-check our calculations by verifying that the sum of costs accounted for ($9940 + $91 350 + $5890) is equal to the costs incurred this period of $107 180. To determine the costs of goods transferred to the assembly department we must also add the cost incurred for the beginning WIP units during April, which is recorded at $10 200. Therefore, the cost of goods transferred equals $111 490.

FIGURE 8.6   Moulding department process cost report for May — FIFO

Moulding department
Process cost report for the month of May — FIFO

| | | Equivalent units | |
	Totals	Direct material	Conversion costs
Costs to account for:			
Beginning WIP	$ 10 200	$ 6 000	$ 4 200
Current costs	107 180	30 500	76 680
Total costs to account for	$117 380	$36 500	$80 880
Units to account for:			
Beginning WIP (30% complete)	2 000		
Started this month	10 000		
Units to account for	12 000		
Finished goods	11 000		
Beginning WIP — work this month	2 000	—	1 400[a]
Started and completed this month	9 000	9 000	9 000
Ending WIP (40% complete)	1 000	1 000	400[b]
Units accounted for	12 000	10 000	10 800
Cost per equivalent unit	$ 10.15	$ 3.05[c]	$ 7.10[d]
Assignment of costs to inventory[e]			
Finished goods			
Beginning WIP last month	$ 10 200[f]	$ 6 000	$ 4 200
Beginning WIP this month	9 940	—	9 940
Started and completed this month	91 350	$27 450	$63 900
	$111 490		
Ending WIP	5 890	3 050	2 840
Costs assigned	$117 380	$36 500	$80 880

[a] 2000 units × 0.7
[b] 1000 units × 0.4
[c] $30 500 / 10 000 units
[d] $76 680 / 10 800 units
[e] Equivalent unit for each cost category for each item of inventory × cost per equivalent unit (dollars rounded)
[f] Costs from last month

Weighted average inventory valuation

Under the weighted average method, the costs from beginning WIP are averaged with the costs incurred during the period. Average costs, rather than current period costs alone, are then allocated to both the units completed and in ending WIP. As shown in figure 8.7, the weighted average cost per equivalent unit is $3.04 for direct materials ($36 500 / 12 000 units) and $7.09 for conversion costs ($80 880/11 400 units). Because beginning WIP and current period costs are averaged under the weighted average method, average cost per unit is simply allocated to the total units completed and transferred out and to the equivalent units in ending WIP. The equivalent units for each cost pool are then multiplied by the equivalent units to assign costs to inventory.

| FIGURE 8.7 | Moulding department process cost report for May — weighted average |

Moulding department
Process cost report for the month of May — weighted average

		Equivalent units	
	Totals	Direct material	Conversion costs
Costs to account for:			
Beginning WIP	$ 10 200	$ 6 000	$ 4 200
Current costs	107 180	30 500	76 680
Total costs to account for	$117 380	$36 500	$80 880
Units to account for:			
Beginning WIP (30% complete)	2 000		
Started this month	10 000		
Units to account for	12 000		
Finished goods	11 000	11 000	11 000
Ending WIP (40% complete)	1 000	1 000	400[a]
Units accounted for	12 000	12 000	11 400
Cost per equivalent unit	$10.1364	$3.0417[b]	$7.0947[c]
Assignment of costs to inventory[d]			
Finished goods	$111 500	$33 458	$78 042
Ending WIP	5 880	3 042	$ 2 838
Costs assigned	$117 380	$36 500	$80 880

[a] 1000 units $\times$ 0.4
[b] $36 500 / 12 000 units
[c] 80 880 / 11 400 units
[d] Equivalent unit for each cost category for each item of inventory cost $\times$ per equivalent unit (dollars rounded)

Comparison of weighted average and FIFO for May

During May, the per-unit costs differ between FIFO and weighted average. FIFO reflects only the current period costs ($3.05 for direct materials and $7.10 for conversion), while weighted average blends last period's and this period's costs ($3.04 for direct materials and $7.09 for conversion). Most entities experience at least some fluctuation in costs between accounting periods, leading to differences in the per-unit costs calculated under weighted average and FIFO. The costs per unit under weighted average are lower than the FIFO costs, indicating that costs increased in May.

As Nancy reviews her work, she notices that the weighted average method requires fewer calculations. However, she thinks the extra work for FIFO is not a problem because she plans to use a spreadsheet to create future reports. From a management perspective, she thinks that FIFO is probably a better method because it provides more precise information about any changes in per-unit cost between periods. During May, the difference in per-unit cost between weighted average and FIFO was small ($10.1364 versus $10.15). However, she believes it is large enough that managers will prefer the more current data provided by FIFO. When Nancy discusses the two methods with the managers, they agree that the FIFO method provides them with the best information for monitoring monthly costs.

8.4 Journal entries for process costing

LEARNING OBJECTIVE 8.4 Create journal entries for process costing.

At this stage in our example of Premier Plastics we should reflect on the cost recording in the general ledger. In process costing, separate WIP accounts are maintained for each production department. Pools of product costs are accumulated in WIP and are then allocated to the individual units. From the preparation of the process cost reports for March and April we have used two cost pools for costs incurred within a department: direct materials and conversion costs. As units are completed in the first department, their costs are transferred to WIP for the second department. The costs for these transferred-in units are pooled separately from other costs in the second department. Then additional direct materials (if any) and conversion costs are added. At the end of production in the second department, the three categories of cost (transferred-in costs, direct materials and conversion costs) are assigned to units and the costs are transferred out. This process continues for each department until the products are transferred into finished goods.

Journal entries for process costing are similar to those for job costing (see chapter 7). The main difference is that materials, labour and overhead costs are assigned to departments rather than to specific jobs. The costs are then allocated from each department to individual units. First, direct materials move from raw material inventory to the moulding department. Conversion costs are accumulated in the WIP account for each department. The costs for the completed units in the moulding department are transferred to the assembly department WIP account. You will notice that the calculations from our process cost report are necessary to value the units to be transferred to the next department. In the assembly department, additional direct material and conversion costs are added. When assembly work is completed, costs are transferred from the assembly department WIP to finished goods inventory. Figure 8.8 provides the general journal entries for FIFO process costing for the moulding department of Premier Plastics during May.

| FIGURE 8.8 | FIFO process costing — journal entries for the moulding department for May |

1	Moulding department WIP — direct materials	DR	$ 30 500	
	Raw material inventory	CR		$ 30 500
	Direct materials used in the moulding department during May			
2	Moulding department WIP — conversion costs	DR	$ 76 680	
	Cash, accounts payable etc.	CR		$ 76 680
	Conversion costs incurred in the moulding department during May			
3	Assembly department WIP	DR	$111 490	
	Moulding department WIP	CR		$111 490
	Costs transferred to the assembly department for units completed in the moulding department during May			

8.5 Production costs and multiple production departments

LEARNING OBJECTIVE 8.5 Calculate product costs in a process where there are multiple production departments.

As illustrated in figures 8.2 and 8.3, many processes are organised around multiple departments. Process costing for each department is performed separately, but costs for work done in one department are transferred to the next department as units complete processing. Completed units and costs are transferred from department to department until the last production department transfers completed units to finished goods inventory. After the first department, the number of units started consists of units transferred in from the preceding department. In addition, the total costs to account for include a new cost category for costs transferred in. For manufactured products, the cost of direct materials is often a large proportion of the total cost per unit. If the point when direct materials are added is correctly identified, accuracy is increased in the equivalent unit calculations and cost for WIP inventories.

In many processes, direct materials are added at the beginning and WIP is always 100 per cent complete with respect to direct materials. However, direct materials are sometimes added later in the process, as shown in the assembly department in figure 8.3. Direct materials may also be added more than once during the process, as shown for the cooking and canning department in figure 8.2. Alternatively, direct materials are not added in some processes. For example, if cherries were dried and packaged in separate departments, no direct materials would be added during the drying process. Because the process of adding direct materials varies, accountants must analyse the production process itself before performing process costing calculations.

Transferred-in costs and timing of direct materials

Previously we focused on the development of the product costs for the storage units in the moulding department of Premier Plastics. In this section, we follow the ongoing production of the storage units in the assembly department. The finished output from the moulding department is transferred to the assembly department, and the costs assigned to this output are referred to as transferred-in costs in the assembly department. The assembly department smooths and finishes the plastic bins and adds the metal wheels before the units are sent to the warehouse for delivery to customers. The major cost incurred in the assembly department is the metal wheels (direct material) that are added when the bins are about 50 per cent complete; it is assumed that conversion costs are added evenly throughout the assembly process.

After hearing that the managers in the moulding department were pleased with their new FIFO process cost report, the managers in the assembly department asked Nancy to prepare a similar report for their department for June. The following illustrations show both FIFO and weighted average methods to enable the managers in the assembly department to compare the methods.

The procedures to prepare the process cost reports for the assembly department are similar to those performed previously for the moulding department except for the transferred-in costs and timing for the addition of direct materials (see comprehensive example 4).

Transferred-in costs and timing of direct materials

Nancy first refers to the cost flows she previously developed for the assembly department (shown in figure 8.3) and gathers information about June's operations. Nancy determined that beginning WIP inventory (1000 units) was 20 per cent complete and was transferred out to finished goods at the end of the period. Of the 10 000 units transferred in from the moulding department, 8000 units were completed and transferred out to finished goods inventory. The remaining 2000 units in ending WIP inventory were 60 per cent complete. Due to goods being transferred from the moulding department, the process cost reports now have a third cost category; transferred-in costs. All units transferred from the moulding department would be 100 per cent complete as to the transferred-in costs.

Because direct materials are added when units are 50 per cent complete and beginning WIP was only 20 per cent complete, none of the units in beginning WIP included direct materials. Therefore, 100 per cent of the direct materials were added to beginning WIP during June. Ending WIP was 60 per cent complete (past the point where direct material is added to the process), so 100 per cent of the direct materials to those units were added during June.

To calculate the cost per equivalent unit, the costs incurred need to be assigned to each cost pool. This is necessary because costs have been added at different stages of the process, and not all items of inventory may have consumed all costs. After collecting all the data, Nancy prepares the process cost reports. We begin with the FIFO inventory valuation.

FIFO inventory valuation

The process cost report is shown in figure 8.9. The cost of beginning WIP includes the costs transferred in from the moulding department in May plus additional costs incurred in the assembly department during May, which were $2000 conversion costs. You will notice that the 1000 units of beginning WIP has a transferred in cost of $10 150. If you refer to figure 8.6, you will see that the unit cost of completed goods in the moulding department in May was $10.15 per unit.

FIGURE 8.9	Assembly department process cost report for June — FIFO

Assembly department
Process cost report for the month of June — FIFO

			Equivalent units	
	Totals	Transferred in	Direct material	Conversion costs
Costs to account for:				
Beginning WIP	$ 12 150	$ 10 150[a]	—	$ 2 000
Current costs	215 890	95 890[b]	$22 000	98 000
Total costs to account for	$228 040	$106 040	$22 000	$100 000
Units to account for:				
Beginning WIP				
(20% complete)	1 000			
Transferred in from Moulding	10 000			
Units to account for	11 000			
Finished goods	9 000			
Beginning WIP — work this month	1 000	—	1 000	800[c]
Started and completed this month	8 000	8 000	8 000	8 000
Ending WIP (60% complete)	2 000	2 000	2 000	1 200[d]
Units accounted for	11 000	10 000	11 000	10 000
Cost per equivalent unit	$ 21.39	$ 9.589[e]	$ 2.00[f]	$ 9.80[g]

Assignment of costs to inventory[h]
Finished goods

Beginning WIP last month	$ 12 150[i]	$ 10 150	—	$ 2 000
Beginning WIP this month	9 840	—	$ 2 000	7 840
Started and completed this month	171 112	76 712	16 000	78 400
	193 102			
Ending WIP	15 760	19 178	4 000	11 760
Costs assigned	$228 040	$106 040	$22 000	$100 000

[a] 1000 units × $10.15 (refer figure 8.6)
[b] 10 000 units × $9.589 (assumed cost for June in Moulding department).
[c] 1000 units × 0.8
[d] 2000 units × 0.6
[e] $95 890 / 10 000 units
[f] $22 000 / 11 000 units
[g] $98 000 / 10 000 units
[h] Equivalent unit for each cost category for each item of inventory × cost per equivalent unit (dollars rounded)
[i] Costs from last month

During June, 10 000 units were transferred in from the moulding department. The total cost of units transferred in using the FIFO inventory valuation was $95 890, which would be the unit cost of the moulding department for June (note that we have not previously prepared the moulding department's process cost report for June). During June, the assembly department incurred direct material costs of $22 000 and conversion costs of $98 000 to further process the units.

To calculate the FIFO unit cost we only use the current period's costs and divide this by the current period's work which is represented by the equivalent units: 10 000 equivalent units for transferred-in, 11 000 equivalent units for direct material and 10 000 equivalent units for conversion costs. After the calculations we have unit costs of $9.59 for transferred-in, $2.00 for direct material, and $9.80 for conversion costs which can now be used to be value inventory at the end of the accounting period. We can see that units transferred to finished goods have been assigned $193 102 (which includes both current-periods costs plus the costs incurred for the beginning WIP last period), and ending WIP of $15 760.

Weighted average inventory valuation

Figure 8.10 shows the process cost report for June using the weighted average valuation method. The calculations are easier than in the FIFO process cost report as the costs from last period and the current period are added together and an average cost is calculated by dividing the total cost for each cost pool by the equivalent units. There is still a requirement to allocate the total costs of $227 942; however, due to averaging, we now have a finished goods inventory of $192 915 and ending WIP of $35 027.

FIGURE 8.10	Assembly department process cost report for June — weighted average

Assembly department
Process cost report for the month of June — weighted average

		Equivalent units		
	Totals	Transferred in	Direct material	Conversion costs
Costs to account for:				
Beginning WIP	$ 12 136	$ 10 136[a]	—	$ 2 000
Current costs	215 806	95 806[b]	$22 000	98 000
Total costs to account for	$227 942	$105 942	$22 000	$100 000
Units to account for:				
Beginning WIP				
(20% complete)	1 000			
Transferred in from Moulding	10 000			
Units to account for	11 000			

Finished goods	9 000	9 000	9 000	9 000
Ending WIP (60% complete)	2 000	2 000	2 000	1 200[c]
Units accounted for	11 000	11 000	11 000	10 200
Cost per equivalent unit	$ 21.435	$ 9.6311[d]	$ 2.00[e]	$ 9.8039[f]
Assignment of costs to inventory[g]				
Finished goods	$192 915	$ 86 680	$18 000	$ 88 235
Ending WIP	35 027	19 262	4 000	11 765
Costs assigned	$227 942	$105 942	$22 000	$100 000

[a] 1000 units × $10.136 (refer figure 8.7)
[b] 10 000 units × $9.5806 (assumed cost for June in Moulding department)
[c] 2000 units × 0.6
[d] $105 942 / 11 000 units
[e] $22 000 / 11 000 units
[f] $100 000 / 10 200 units
[g] Equivalent unit for each cost category for each item of inventory × cost per equivalent unit (dollars rounded)

Comparison of FIFO and weighted average

Nancy notices that the cost per equivalent unit that is added in the assembly department is similar under both methods, which means that costs during June were similar to May's costs. She asks the managers whether costs in the assembly department fluctuate much from month to month. The managers tell her that a long-term contract with suppliers guarantees prices for at least a one-year period and labour contracts are negotiated annually, so the costs do not fluctuate much from month to month. In addition, volumes do not fluctuate a great deal.

Because costs in the department rarely fluctuate and volumes are reasonably stable, the costs added will be similar under both methods, so either method would be appropriate. However, because the moulding department is now using FIFO, units are transferred in at FIFO cost. To be consistent, Nancy decides that the assembly department should also use FIFO.

8.6 Accounting for spoilage in process costing

LEARNING OBJECTIVE 8.6 Understand the issues associated with spoilage costs in process costing.

Production processes often create **spoilage**, which are units of product that are unacceptable and are either discarded or sold at a reduced price. For example, units in batches of clothing that have flaws in the material or sewing, and several valves in a batch that do not function properly when tested at the end of production. Sometimes spoiled units are reworked (that is, repaired) and sold as if they were originally produced correctly. For example, if the material flaws are not too noticeable, the clothing can be sold as irregular. The costs of spoilage include the resources that are wasted due to spoilage, including the full amount of product costs for units that are discarded and the rework costs for units that are repaired. From an accounting perspective, decisions must be made about how to record the costs of spoilage. Should they be included in the product cost of all good units sold, or should they be recognised as a separate loss? The accounting treatment depends on whether the spoilage is a normal part of the production process.

Recall from chapter 7 that **normal spoilage** consists of defective units that arise as part of regular operations. Because normal spoilage is considered an ordinary and inherent part of operations, the cost of normal spoilage is included in the costs of all good units produced. The cost of normal spoilage is considered necessary for producing good units. For example, if Premier Plastics finds that one out of every 1000 storage units is faulty when inspected at the end of production, then that proportion of spoilage will be treated as normal. If the managers modify operations to reduce product failures, then a new lower rate of spoilage will become normal.

Recall also from chapter 7 that **abnormal spoilage** is spoilage that is not part of everyday operations. Because abnormal spoilage is considered unusual and is not an inherent part of operations, the cost of abnormal spoilage is excluded from product costs and is recorded as a separate loss. Abnormal spoilage occurs because of events such as strikes and natural disasters, or it occurs because operations are out of control. For example, at Premier Plastics an equipment malfunction that ruins a large number of storage units would be considered abnormal spoilage.

To properly account for spoilage in a process costing system, accountants need to identify the point in the production process where spoiled units are removed. Different entities establish different procedures for inspection and removal of spoiled units. Spoilage caused by poor-quality raw materials can sometimes be identified before materials are added to production. Inspection could also occur in the middle of production, at the end of the process in one department, or when processing in all departments is complete. If spoiled units are removed before they are 100 per cent complete, the costs of direct materials and conversion need to be estimated at the point the units are removed from production.

The costs of spoilage are accounted for in a two-step process. First, all product costs are accumulated in the departmental WIP account as usual. The computation of cost per equivalent unit includes all work performed, regardless of whether the units are spoiled. If spoiled units are 100 per cent complete at the time they are removed from production, they are treated the same as any other unit. If they are less than 100 per cent complete, the calculation of equivalent units depends upon their completion percentage, similar to ending WIP. Second, the costs of normal spoilage are allocated to the good units produced, and the costs of abnormal spoilage are written off as a loss for the accounting period. Therefore, the cost of each good unit includes an allocation for the cost of normal spoilage. Comprehensive example 5 illustrates spoilage using the FIFO method.

COMPREHENSIVE EXAMPLE 5

FIFO cost report with normal and abnormal spoilage

While collecting information to prepare the moulding department process cost report for July, Nancy learns that 1000 units were spoiled and discarded. The previous month there was no spoilage. She is puzzled by the high quantity of spoilage during July.

Nancy discusses the spoilage with the moulding department manager. He tells her that 300 units were spoiled because of a problem that occurs three or four times a year with the quality of the plastic raw material. The problem causes a slight discoloration in a number of units. In addition, a new employee accidentally programmed the moulding machine incorrectly, spoiling 700 units during July. All spoilage is discovered when units are turned out of the moulds, at the end of the moulding processing (when they are 100 per cent complete).

After further discussion with the moulding department manager, Nancy learns that approximately 2 per cent of units throughout the year are spoiled because of discoloration. Thus, she decides that for the raw material problem, up to 2 per cent of units produced should be accounted for as normal spoilage. She decides that the spoilage caused by the incorrect equipment setting should be accounted for as abnormal spoilage because in a department with little employee turnover, the manager tells her, this problem rarely occurs.

Nancy finds that during July, 3000 units in beginning WIP were completed, and 9000 units were started and completed. Ending WIP consisted of 1200 units that were 70 per cent complete. Total costs added this period are $28 560 in direct materials and $86 184 in conversion costs.

Before the cost per equivalent unit can be calculated, Nancy had to separate the costs into the two cost pools and then assign the costs to the time period in which they were incurred; that is, either last month and/or the current period. She obtains the beginning WIP cost from the June FIFO cost report: $18 525 ($8400 direct materials and $10 125 conversion costs) and adds the current costs incurred in production. Therefore, the total cost to be assigned is $133 269.

Nancy summarises the work performed in terms of physical and equivalent units. Because spoiled units were identified and removed when they were 100 per cent complete, they represent 1000 equivalent units for both direct materials and conversion costs. Nancy next separates the spoilage between normal and abnormal. She calculates the maximum normal spoilage for July as 240 units (12 000 units completed during July × 2%), which is less than the 300 units spoiled due to discoloration. Therefore, she considers 240 units as normal spoilage. She classifies the remaining 60 discoloured units plus the 700 units spoiled from the incorrect machine setting as abnormal spoilage (total 760 units). Of the 12 000 completed units, only 11 000 were transferred to finished goods due to spoilage. For ease of calculation it is assumed the spoiled units have been taken from the 9000 units started and completed so that only 8000 of these units were transferred to finished goods.

When Nancy prepares the cost report, refer figure 8.11, she calculates the cost of good units started, completed and transferred out. She then adds the cost of normal spoilage to arrive at the total cost transferred to the assembly department ($115 621). Abnormal spoilage is added below this subtotal to reconcile the total cost.

▶

FIGURE 8.11 | Moulding department process cost report for July — FIFO

Moulding department

Process cost report for the month of July — FIFO

		Equivalent units	
	Totals	Direct material	Conversion costs
Costs to account for:			
Beginning WIP	$ 18 525	$ 8 400	$10 125
Current costs	$114 744	$28 560	$86 184
Total costs to account for	$133 269	$36 960	$96 309
Units to account for:			
Beginning WIP (50% complete)	3 000		
Started this month	10 200		
Units to account for	13 200		
Units accounted for:			
Finished goods	11 000		
Beginning WIP — work this month	3 000	0	1 500
Started and completed	8 000	8 000	8 000
Spoilage			
Normal	240	240	240
Abnormal	760	760	760
Ending WIP (70% complete)	1 200	1 200	840
Units accounted for	13 200	10 200	11 340
Cost per equivalent unit	$ 10.40	$ 2.80	$ 7.60
Assignment of costs to inventory			
Finished goods			
Beginning WIP last month	$ 18 525	$ 8 400	$10 125
Beginning WIP this month	11 400	0	11 400
Started and completed this month	83 200	22 400	60 800
Normal spoilage	2 496	672	1 824
	$ 115 621	$31 472	$84 149
Abnormal spoilage	7 904	2 128	5 776
Ending WIP	9 744	3 360	6 384
Costs assigned	$133 269	$36 960	$96 309

Using spoilage cost information

Nancy is concerned about the total costs for spoilage this period. The 1000 spoiled units cost $10 400 ($2496 + $7904). However, she is even more concerned about other problems that arise when spoilage is high. Sometimes inspectors miss some spoiled units, which are then sold as good units. When defective storage units are sold, return costs increase and customers are less satisfied. The storage bins are expensive, and Premier Plastic's reputation suffers when units are less than perfect. Nancy knows that Japanese competitors have zero defect tolerance policies, so their customers rarely receive flawed bins. She decides to meet with the plastics department manager to emphasise the need for lower levels of spoilage.

8.7 Uses and limitations of process costing information

LEARNING OBJECTIVE 8.7 Identify the uses and limitations of process cost information

Process costing systems measure the cost of products, primarily for mass-produced goods. The product costs are used to value inventory and cost of goods sold (also called cost of sales) for external reports such as financial statements and income tax returns. They are also used by managers to monitor operations and develop estimates of future costs for decision making. When managers use process costing information, they need to be aware that it measures the costs of processes, which are then allocated to individual units. Thus, process costing is useful for measuring and monitoring processes. However, process costing is also subject to a number of limitations.

Monitoring process quality and costs

An entity's profitability and long-term success often depend on the ability of managers to control processes and costs. Organisations frequently compete both on product quality and cost. Managers use process cost information to help them evaluate whether production processes are operating as expected. They compare actual process costs to budgets, standard costs or prior periods to identify potential production problems. For example, in Premier Plastics, units were spoiled during July when an employee improperly programmed the moulding equipment. This type of event causes actual costs to be higher than expected. If the managers had not already been aware of this production problem, the calculation of process costs at the end of the month would have alerted them to it.

Managers do not rely on process costing systems alone to monitor quality and cost. They also implement quality control systems, and they separately monitor resource use such as direct materials and direct labour. Quality systems can include inspection to identify spoiled units. Information about normal and abnormal spoilage can then be integrated into the process costing system to help managers measure and monitor the cost of resources wasted due to spoilage.

Process costing information and decision making

Product costs developed in a process costing system are average costs and might not adequately represent relevant costs for many types of decisions such as product pricing, outsourcing, product emphasis or special orders. Sometimes process costing systems can be modified to do a better job of providing managers with estimates of relevant information, such as marginal (or incremental) cost per unit. For example, conversion costs could be divided into fixed and variable cost pools. Managers could then estimate marginal cost using the direct material cost per unit plus the variable conversion cost per unit. Production costing systems often include multiple cost pools representing different activities in the production process. More precise categorisations of cost improve managers' ability It is rarely possible to determine exactly how for decisions.

Uncertainties and mismeasurement of cost flows

It is rarely possible to determine exactly how costs are incurred during process costing. For example, in the moulding department at Premier Plastics, more labour might be used during the beginning of the process when plastic ingredients are added and at the end of the process when units are turned out of the moulds. Equipment and electricity use might be greater during the middle of the processing. However, it is difficult to exactly measure how and when costs such as labour, equipment depreciation, maintenance and utilities are incurred. Accordingly, at least some mismeasurement typically occurs in the allocation of costs in a process costing system.

Also, mismeasurement occurs when accounting for spoilage. Normal spoilage is based on an estimate. Any errors in identifying normal spoilage quantities automatically cause mismeasurement in abnormal spoilage. Therefore, abnormal spoilage costs may be overestimated or underestimated, with an opposite mismeasurement in the cost of good units.

Mismeasurement is likely to be greatest in entities that have little experience producing a product. Over time, greater knowledge is gained about production processes, and the cost allocations become more accurate. However, little benefit may come from developing an accounting system to more accurately allocate process costs. Often, the simple assumptions used throughout this chapter provide sufficiently accurate costs.

Work in process units at different stages of completion

At the end of each period, the percentage of completion for work in process needs to be estimated. Depending on the process, all of the units in work in process inventories might be at different stages of completion. For example, in the assembly department at Premier Plastics, some units of WIP will have the rough edges removed but still be awaiting smoothing. Some will have been smoothed but await the next step within assembly. Others will have the metal wheels added but await final paint and trim work.

When work is at many different stages of completion, estimating the average percentage of completion for ending inventories involves some guesswork. However, these estimates affect the equivalent unit costs for both the current and next period. If the percentage of completion is overestimated in this period, the number of units in the denominator is too large, causing cost per equivalent unit to be too low in this period. Because ending WIP is completed during the next period, an overestimate in this period will cause an underestimate of the work performed in the next period. If ending inventories are a small part of the total costs allocated in this period, inaccurate estimates are less of a problem. But if ending inventories are relatively large, inaccurate estimates could distort process cost reports in this period and the next period.

Hybrid costing systems and operation costing

As manufacturing systems incorporate more technology, entities become more flexible in meeting the diverse needs of their customers. Products that were once mass produced are now customised. Although most of the manufacturing process might be performed identically for all units, at some point individual units are customised. For example, Harley-Davidson customises its motorcycles with special accessories and colours. Flexible manufacturing systems are used in many industries such as computers, cars and bicycles. Customers order these products with specific features. The manufacturing process is a combination of mass-produced components, but during assembly the products are customised. **Hybrid costing** is the accounting approach used to assign product costs by applying a combination of both job and process costing. Often, process costing is used to the point of customisation, after which the direct costs are traced to each specific job.

Operation costing is a particular type of hybrid method used when similar batches of identical products are manufactured. Units in each batch are identical, but the processing of each batch is different and may not include the same steps. For example, consider the production of notebook computers having different configurations. Some batches go through the same processes but differ based on type of memory chip or size of hard drive installed. Some batches go through fewer processes than others. For example, some notebook computers are sold with only one installed battery, while others have both an installed battery and an extra battery.

Operation costing systems track costs using work orders for each batch. These work orders include detailed information about the direct materials required and the steps needed in the manufacturing operation. Direct materials are traced to each batch through the work orders and then allocated to units. In addition, all units within a batch are allocated uniform amounts of overhead. Unlike conventional process costing, operation costing usually includes more than two types of cost pools. The cost pools are designed to match the separate processes that may be allocated to batches of products. This matching of processes and cost pools improves the accuracy of cost assignment to individual products. Managers are better able to focus on the control of physical processes within a given production system because their financial information more accurately matches the flow of resources through specific processes.

APPENDIX 8A
Standard costing use in mass production

A **standard cost** is the cost managers expect to incur for production of goods or services under operating plan assumptions. Under a standard costing system, accounting entries for direct materials, conversion costs and transferred-in costs are recorded at standard (or expected) rather than actual costs. Actual costs are accumulated in a control account, and then costs are allocated to WIP using a standard rate per equivalent unit. At the end of the period, adjustments are made for the differences between actual and standard costs.

Standard costs are used for a variety of reasons. For example, they simplify the process of making accounting entries during the period; actual costs need not be compiled for product costs to be recorded. Standard costs also provide a benchmark against which actual costs can be compared. Managers and operating employees can then be rewarded based on whether the standard costs are achieved or exceeded. These rewards provide motivation for monitoring operations and maintaining higher productivity levels.

Standard costs are allocated to units in a manner similar to FIFO process costing. The difference is that no equivalent cost per unit is calculated. Instead, a standard cost is used to allocate costs to inventory. Comprehensive example 6 revisits the Premier Plastics moulding department in May.

COMPREHENSIVE EXAMPLE 6

Incorporating standard costs into process costing

The standard costs to account for are based on the investigations undertaken by the engineering department. Engineering staff have reviewed the production process and developed standard costs for the bins. The standard costs are direct materials $3 and conversion costs $7. The total costs to account for will be determined by the equivalent units for each cost pool multiplied by the standard cost. This is shown in figure 8A.1.

FIGURE 8A.1	Moulding department process cost report for May — FIFO

Moulding department
Process cost report for the month of May — FIFO (using standard costs)

		Equivalent units	
	Totals	Direct material	Conversion costs
Units to account for:			
Beginning WIP (30% complete)	2 000		
Started this month	10 000		
Units to account for	12 000		
Units accounted for:			
Finished goods	11 000		
Beginning WIP — work this month	2 000	0	1 400
Started and completed this month	9 000	9 000	9 000
Ending WIP (40% complete)	1 000	1 000	400
Units accounted for	12 000	10 000	10 800
Standard cost	$ 10	$ 3	$ 7
Assignment of costs to inventory			
Finished goods			
Beginning WIP last month	$ 10 200		
Beginning WIP this month	$ 9 800	0	$ 9 800
Started and completed this month	$ 90 000	$ 27 000	$ 63 000
Ending WIP	$ 5 800	$ 3 000	$ 2 800
Costs assigned	$ 115 800	$ 30 000	$ 65 600

For May, there is beginning WIP as well as ending WIP. Beginning WIP comprises 2000 units; 9000 units are started, completed and transferred to the assembly department; and another 1000 units are started and 40 per cent complete in ending WIP. As standard costs are used to value inventory, there is no need to calculate a cost per equivalent unit.

▶

Assuming no change from the prior month in the standard costs, the cost of beginning WIP is carried over from the previous month at the cost per equivalent unit. Therefore, beginning WIP includes direct materials cost of $6000 (2000 × $3) and conversion costs of $4200 (600 × $7), for a total of $10 200. During May, standard costs are first allocated to the equivalent units of work performed to complete beginning WIP: $0 for direct materials and $9800 for conversion costs. Next, standard costs of $90 000 ($10 × 9000 units) are allocated to the units started, completed and transferred out. Finally, standard costs of $3000 for direct materials and $2800 for conversion costs are allocated to ending WIP. The total amount of standard cost to account for (beginning WIP plus costs allocated during May) is $115 800.

When standard costs are used as benchmarks, they are compared to actual costs calculated using either weighted average or FIFO. In this example for Premier Plastics, Nancy could compare the standard cost of $10 per unit with the actual weighted average cost per equivalent unit in May of $10.1364 or to the FIFO cost of $10.15. From these comparisons, it appears that actual costs are higher than standard. When actual costs are higher than standard costs, managers investigate the causes and analyse ways to improve operations. If actual costs are lower, the causes may also be analysed so that managers better understand the improvements that have taken place.

SUMMARY

8.1 Assign costs to mass-produced products.

Cost flow in process costing

Steps for preparing a process cost report
1. Summarise total costs to account for.
2. Summarise total physical and equivalent units.
3. Calculate the cost per equivalent unit.
4. Account for cost of units completed and cost of ending WIP.

8.2 Understand the concept of equivalent units and how they relate to the production process.

Equivalent units

Measure of the resources used in partially completed units relative to the resources needed to complete the units.

Equivalent units and pattern of cost flow

Direct materials
• Added at the beginning of the process
• Added during the process
Conversion costs
• Incurred evenly throughout the process
• Incurred unevenly
Identification of spoiled units
• Inspection at the end of the process
• Inspection during the process

8.3 Calculate product costs using the weighted average and first-in, first-out (FIFO) methods.

Weighted average method

Costs from beginning WIP (performed last period) are averaged with costs incurred during the current period and then allocated to units completed and ending WIP.

Calculation of cost per equivalent unit

$$\frac{\text{Beginning WIP} + \text{Current period costs}}{\text{Equivalent units for total work}}$$

First-in, first-out (FIFO) method

The current period's costs are used to allocate cost to work performed this period.

Calculation of cost per equivalent unit

$$\frac{\text{Current period costs}}{\text{Equivalent units for work performed this period}}$$

8.4 Create journal entries for process costing.

Journal entries for process costing are similar to those for job costing.

Process costing differences

Materials, labour and overhead costs are assigned to departments rather than to specific jobs. Costs are then allocated from each department to individual units.

8.5 Calculate product costs in a process where there are multiple production departments.

Transferred-in costs

Costs of processing performed in a previous department.
Transferred-in costs are pooled separately from other costs.

8.6 Understand the issues associated with spoilage costs in process costing.

Normal spoilage

Definition: defective units that arise as part of regular operations.
Accounting: cost of normal spoilage is allocated to good units produced.

Abnormal spoilage

Definition: spoilage that is not part of everyday operations.
Accounting: cost of abnormal spoilage is recorded as a loss for the period.

8.7 Identify the uses and limitations of process cost information.

Uses of process cost information

- Measure costs of mass-produced products.
- Assign costs to inventory and cost of goods sold for financial statements and income tax returns.
- Monitor operations and costs.
- Develop estimates of future costs for decision making.
- Analyse the costs and benefits of quality improvements.
- Identify potential areas for process improvements.

Uncertainties and mismeasurement in process costing

- Actual cost flows might not be known.
  - When are direct materials added?
  - When are conversion costs incurred?
  - How complete are the units in ending work in process?
- What amount of spoilage is normal?
- How achievable are standard costs?

KEY TERMS

abnormal spoilage Spoilage that is not part of everyday operations.

conversion costs Direct labour and production overhead costs.

equivalent unit Conversion of incomplete units of production to a common denominator to enable costs to be assigned.

first-in, first-out (FIFO) method A method in which the current period's costs are used to allocate cost to work performed this period.

hybrid costing The accounting approach used to assign product costs by applying a combination of both job and process costing.

normal spoilage Defective units that arise as part of regular operations.

operation costing A particular type of hybrid method used when similar batches of identical products are manufactured. Units in each batch are identical, but the processing of each batch is different and may not include the same steps.

process costing The accounting approach for assigning production costs to mass-produced products.

spoilage Units of product that are unacceptable and are discarded, reworked or sold at a reduced price.

standard cost The cost managers expect to incur to produce goods or services under operating plan assumptions.

transferred-in costs Costs that are transferred from one department to another department for further processing.

weighted average method A method in which costs from beginning WIP (performed last period) are averaged with costs incurred during the current period, and then allocated to units completed and ending WIP.

SELF-STUDY PROBLEMS

SELF-STUDY PROBLEM 1 Weighted average and FIFO process cost reports

Evergreen Kit Company produces kits for plastic aeroplanes and car models. The company uses process costing to assign costs to its inventory. The company always used the weighted average method but Jussi, the company's new accountant, is thinking about recommending a change to the first-in, first-out (FIFO) method. He plans to prepare inventory cost reports for March using both methods so that he can compare the results.

The company has only one production department. Direct materials are introduced at the beginning of the process, and conversion costs are incurred evenly throughout the manufacturing process. Once each unit is completed, it is transferred to finished goods inventory. Jussi collected the following data for the month of March:

Beginning inventory:	
Work in process (40% complete)	10 000 units
Costs:	
Direct material	$ 8 000
Conversion costs	2 220
Total cost of beginning WIP	$10 220
Units completed and transferred out during March	48 000 units
Units started during March	40 000 units
Ending WIP inventory (50% complete)	2 000 units
Direct material cost used during March	$44 000
Conversion costs incurred during March	$36 000

Required

(a) Using the weighted average method:
  (i) summarise total costs to account for.
  (ii) summarise total physical units and equivalent units.
  (iii) calculate costs per equivalent unit.
  (iv) prepare a process cost report.
(b) Following the same procedures, prepare a process cost report using the FIFO method.
(c) Prepare a table to compare the total costs and cost per equivalent unit under weighted average and FIFO. Provide possible explanations for the difference between FIFO and weighted average costs.

SOLUTION TO SELF-STUDY PROBLEM 1

(a) Weighted average
  (i) Summarise total costs to account for.

		Equivalent units	
	Totals	Direct material	Conversion costs
Costs to account for:			
Beginning WIP (40% complete)	$10 220	$ 8 000	$ 2 220
Current costs	80 000	44 000	36 000
Total costs to account for	$90 220	$52 000	$38 220

  (ii) Summarise total physical units and equivalent units.
    Because direct materials are added at the beginning of the process, all 2000 WIP units are 100 per cent complete with respect to direct materials. However, these 2000 units are only 50 per cent complete with respect to conversion costs, which translates to 1000 equivalent units in ending WIP for conversion costs (50% × 2000).

		Equivalent units	
	Physical units	Direct material	Conversion costs
Units to account for:			
Beginning WIP (40% complete)	10 000		
Units started	40 000		
Units to account for	50 000		
Units accounted for:			
Finished goods	48 000	48 000	48 000
Ending WIP (50% complete)	2 000	2 000	1 000
Units accounted for	50 000	50 000	49 000

(iii) Calculate costs per equivalent unit.

$$\text{Weighted average} = \frac{\text{Beginning WIP} + \text{Current period costs}}{\text{Equivalent units for total work}}$$

Direct materials	$52 000 ÷ 50 000	$1.04
Conversion costs	$38 220 ÷ 49 000	0.78
Total cost per equivalent unit		$1.82

(iv)

Assignment of costs to inventory	Totals	Direct material	Conversion costs
Finished goods	$87 360	$49 920	$37 440
Ending WIP	$ 2 860	$ 2 080	$ 780
Costs assigned	$90 220	$52 000	$38 220

(b) FIFO

Steps 1 and 2 are identical to the schedules presented in part (a). Because the problem did not provide separate beginning WIP costs for weighted average and FIFO, we use the same beginning WIP values for parts (a) and (b).

		Equivalent units	
	Physical units	Direct material	Conversion costs
Units to account for:			
Beginning WIP (40% complete)	10 000		
Started this month	40 000		
Units to account for	50 000		
Units accounted for:			
Finished goods	48 000		
Beginning WIP — work this month	10 000	0	6 000
Started and completed this month	38 000	38 000	38 000
Ending WIP (50% complete)	2 000	2 000	1 000
Units accounted for	50 000	40 000	45 000

Calculate cost per equivalent unit.

$$\frac{\text{Current period costs}}{\text{Equivalent units for work performed this period}}$$

		$44\,000 \div 40\,000$	$1.10
Direct materials		$44\,000 \div 40\,000$	$1.10
Conversion costs		$36\,000 \div 45\,000$	0.80
Total cost per equivalent unit			$1.90

	Totals	Direct material	Conversion costs
Assignment of costs to inventory			
Finished goods	0	0	0
Beginning WIP last month	$10\,220	$ 8\,000	$ 2\,220
Beginning WIP this month	4\,800	0	4\,800
Started and completed this month	$72\,200	$41\,800	$30\,400
	$87\,220	$49\,800	$37\,420
Ending WIP	3\,000	2\,200	800
Costs assigned	$90\,220	$52\,000	$38\,220

(c) Compare weighted average and FIFO

The following table compares total costs and equivalent unit costs under weighted average and FIFO. Remember, the total costs accounted for are equal in this problem only because we used the same beginning WIP costs for both methods.

	Weighted average	FIFO
Costs transferred out	$87\,360	$87\,220
Ending WIP	2\,860	3\,000
Total costs accounted for	$90\,220	$90\,220
Costs per equivalent unit:		
Direct materials	$ 1.04	$ 1.10
Conversion costs	0.78	0.80
Total	$ 1.82	$ 1.90

The weighted average costs include both current period and prior period costs, while the FIFO costs include only current period costs. Because the costs per unit for FIFO are higher than for weighted average, average production costs during March were higher than during the previous month. An increase occurred in both direct materials and conversion costs. These increases might have been caused by inflation in the cost of resources, a decline in production volume, production inefficiencies or other factors.

QUESTIONS

8.1 Describe the differences between mass production and custom production of goods and services. Explain how these differences influence the costing method. **LO1, 2**

8.2 Explain the difference between the weighted average and FIFO methods for process costing. Explain why an entity might choose one method over the other. **LO3**

8.3 Under what conditions will weighted average and FIFO process costing consistently produce similar equivalent unit costs? **LO3**

8.4 Under what conditions could a process complete more units during the period than it started? **LO2**

8.5 'We treat spoiled units as fully completed regardless of when the spoiled units are detected. This method makes unit costing much simpler.' What is wrong with this approach? **LO6**

8.6 In a continuous processing situation (such as an oil refinery), the beginning and ending WIP inventories are frequently the same. How does this simplify determination of equivalent units completed? **LO2, 6**

8.7 Although process costing appears to use precise measurements, it requires several estimates. Discuss where judgement is needed in collecting information for process costing. **LO7**

8.8 Suppose the percent completion of ending WIP is overestimated at the end of year 1. How does this measurement error affect the process costing results in year 1 and year 2? **LO7**

8.9 A department within a processing operation has some finished units physically on hand. Should they be counted as completed units or as ending inventory in the department? Explain. **LO3**

8.10 In processes involving pipeline operations or assembly line operations, if the pipeline or assembly line is always full, then beginning and ending WIP inventories are always 50 per cent complete with regard to conversion costs. Explain. **LO5**

8.11 When units are transferred from one department to another, how are normal spoilage costs recorded? **LO6**

8.12 An entity has one machine through which is drawn a standard type of wire to make nails. With minor adjustments, different sized nails are produced with different sized wire. Would you recommend that the entity employ job or process costing methods? **LO7**

8.13 List two factors that could affect managers' choices for the number of times and points in processing to inspect units. **LO6**

8.14 List three factors that managers might consider in deciding whether to expend resources to reduce spoilage. **LO6**

EXERCISES

8.15 Equivalent units under weighted average and FIFO **LO2, 3**

Francisco's mass-produces folding chairs in Port Sorrell. All direct materials are added at the beginning of production, and conversion costs are incurred evenly throughout production. The following production information is for the month of May:

	Physical units
Beginning WIP (40% complete)	9 000
Started in May	50 000
Completed in May	47 000
Ending WIP (30% complete)	12 000

Required

(a) Calculate the equivalent units used to calculate cost per unit under the weighted average method.

(b) Calculate the equivalent units used to calculate cost per unit under the FIFO method.

8.16 Equivalent unit cost under weighted average and FIFO **LO2, 3**

Fine Fans mass-produces small electric fans in Hawley Beach for home use. All direct materials are added at the beginning of production, and conversion costs are incurred evenly throughout production. The following production information is for the month of October:

	Physical units
Started in October	100 000
Completed in October	94 000
Ending WIP (60% complete)	15 000
Beginning WIP (20% complete)	9 000

	Costs
Beginning work in process costs:	
Direct materials	$ 18 000
Conversion costs	36 000
Costs added this period:	
Direct materials	100 000
Conversion costs	200 000

Required

(a) Calculate the equivalent cost per unit using the weighted average method.

(b) Calculate the equivalent cost per unit using the FIFO method.

8.17 Cost per equivalent unit under weighted average   **LO2, 3**

Fox and Sons is a toy maker that produces Flying Flingbats, a soft foam rubber boomerang. All direct materials are added at the beginning of production, and conversion costs are incurred evenly throughout production. Conversion was 75 per cent complete for the 8000 units in WIP on 1 December and 50 per cent complete for the 6000 units in WIP on 31 December. During the month, 12 000 Flingbats were completed and transferred out as finished goods. Following is a summary of the costs for the period:

	Direct materials	Conversion costs
Work in process, 1 December	$19 200	$ 7 200
Costs added in December	31 200	21 600

Required

Using the weighted average method, prepare a schedule calculating the equivalent unit cost for each cost pool for December.

8.18 Account for costs under weighted average   **LO3**

Refer to the information in exercise 8.17.

Required

Prepare a process cost report under the weighted average method for December.

8.19 Cost per equivalent unit under FIFO   **LO3**

Refer to the information in exercise 8.17.

Required

Using the FIFO method, prepare a schedule calculating the cost per equivalent unit for December.

8.20 Account for costs under FIFO   **LO3**

Refer to the information presented in exercise 8.17.

Required

Prepare a process cost report under the FIFO method for December.

8.21 Costs and journal entries under weighted average and FIFO   **LO4**

Humphrey Manufacturing produces car parts and batteries. All direct materials are added at the beginning of production, and conversion costs are incurred evenly throughout production. The following production information is for the month of April:

Units:
   Work in process, 31 March: 6000 units (40% complete)
   Units started in April: 42 000
   Units completed during April: 40 000
   Work in process 30 April: 8000 units (25% complete)
Costs in beginning WIP:

Direct materials	$ 7 500
Conversion costs	2 125
Total	$ 9 625

Costs added this period:

Direct materials added in April	$ 70 000
Conversion costs added in April	42 500
Total	$112 500

Required

(a) Using the weighted average method, assign costs to production for this period.
(b) Using the FIFO method, assign costs to production for this period.
(c) Write out the journal entries for either the weighted average or FIFO methods.

PROBLEMS

8.22 FIFO process costing; transferred-in costs; direct materials added during process   **LO4**

Benton Industries began the year with 15 000 units in department 3 as beginning WIP. These units were one-third complete, with $40 470 transferred-in costs for prior departments' work and $14 322 for department 3 conversion costs. During the year, 93 000 additional units were transferred into department 3 from department 2 at a cost of $224 130. Department 3 incurred materials costs of $166 840 and conversion costs of $315 228 during the year. Department 3 ended the year with 11 000 units in WIP ending. These units were 40 per cent complete.

Required

Determine the cost of goods completed and the cost of ending WIP in department 3 using FIFO process costing. Assume that conversion costs are incurred evenly and materials are added in department 3 when units are 60 per cent complete.

8.23 Process costing under weighted average; spoilage; journal entries   **LO5**

Victoria's Closet mass-produces luxurious sleepwear for women. Consider the following data for the flannel nightgown department for the month of January. All direct materials are added at the beginning of production in the department, and conversion costs are incurred evenly throughout production. Inspection occurs when production is 100 per cent complete. Normal spoilage is 6600 units for the month.

	Physical units
Beginning WIP (25% complete)	11 000
Started during January	74 000
Total units to account for	85 000
Good units completed and transferred out during current period:	
From beginning work in process	11 000
Started and completed	50 000
Spoiled units	8 000
Ending WIP (75% complete)	16 000
Total units accounted for	85 000

	Costs
Beginning WIP:	
Direct materials	$ 220 000
Conversion costs	30 000
Total beginning WIP	250 000
Costs added during current period:	
Direct materials	1 480 000
Conversion costs	942 000
Costs to account for	$2 672 000

Required

Prepare a process cost report using the weighted average method.

8.24 Process costing under FIFO; spoilage; standard costing   **LO6**

Refer to the information provided in problem 8.23.

Required

(a) Prepare a process cost report using the FIFO method.

(b) Explain how a standard cost report would differ from the FIFO report you just produced.

(c) Under what circumstances would a standard cost report be preferable to a FIFO cost report? Explain your answer.

8.25 Abnormal spoilage; quality savings; opportunity costs   **LO6**

Kim Mills produces material for knitwear. The knit cloth is sold by the bolt. November data for its milling process follow. Beginning WIP was 20 000 units. Good units completed and transferred out during the current period totalled 90 000. Ending WIP was 17 000 units. Inspection occurs at the 100 per cent stage of completion regarding conversion costs, which are incurred evenly throughout the process. Total spoilage is 7000 units. Normal spoilage is 3600 units. Direct materials are added at the beginning of the process.

Required

(a) Calculate abnormal spoilage in units.

(b) Assume that the manufacturing cost of a spoiled unit is $1000. Calculate the amount of potential savings if all spoilage were eliminated, assuming that all other costs would be unaffected.

(c) Discuss the opportunity costs of spoilage and why it might be important to require low defect rates in a manufacturing process.

8.26 Spoilage with inspection point other than 100 per cent   **LO6**

Use the information for Kim Mills from problem 8.25. Now, assume that inspection occurs when units are 40 per cent complete.

Required

(a) Calculate total spoilage for conversion cost calculations.

(b) If normal spoilage is 1800 units instead of 3600, what is abnormal spoilage this period for conversion costs?

(c) List several costs and benefits from moving inspection to an earlier position in the manufacturing process.

8.27 Process costing under weighted average and FIFO; choice of method   **LO4**

Red Dog Products manufactures toys for dogs and cats. The most popular toy is a small ball that dispenses tiny treats and is placed within a larger ball. To get the treats, dogs must roll the balls around until the treats fall out. These balls are mass produced from plastic. Direct materials are introduced at the beginning of the process, and conversion costs are incurred evenly throughout the manufacturing process. Once each unit is completed, it is transferred to finished goods. Data for the month of March are as follows:

Beginning WIP (30% complete):	
Direct material	$ 25 000
Conversion costs	3 000
Total	$ 28 000
Units started during March	80 000 units
Units completed and transferred out during March	88 000 units
Ending WIP inventory (50% complete)	12 000 units
Direct material cost added during March	$220 000
Conversion costs added during March	$ 74 000

Required

(a) Prepare a process cost report using the weighted average method.

(b) Prepare a process cost report using the FIFO method.

(c) What factors might affect the cost accountant's choice of process costing method? Explain.

8.28 Normal and abnormal spoilage; quality improvements   **LO6**

Empire Forge produces small plumbing valves. January data for its valve-making process follow. Beginning WIP was 60 000 units. Good units completed and transferred out during the current period totalled 420 000. Ending WIP was 68 000 units. Inspection occurs at the 100 per cent stage of completion with respect to conversion costs, which are incurred evenly throughout the process. Total spoilage is 36 000 units. Normal spoilage is 12 600 units. Direct materials are added at the beginning of the process.

Required

(a) Calculate abnormal spoilage in units for January.

(b) Calculate the number of units started in January.

(c) Calculate the percentage of units produced that is considered normal spoilage, and calculate the total percentage of units spoiled this period. List several potential business risks when spoilage rates increase dramatically.

(d) Provide arguments for the manager of the valve department about the trade-offs between investing in quality improvements and incurring the costs of undetected spoiled units.

8.29 Process costing under weighted average and FIFO; spoilage   **LO3, 4**

The Rally Company operates under a process cost system using the weighted average method. All direct materials are added at the beginning of production in the department, and conversion costs are incurred evenly throughout production. Inspection occurs when production is 100 per cent completed.

Following are data for July. All unfinished work at the end of July is 25 per cent completed. The beginning inventory is 80 per cent completed.

Beginning inventories	
Direct materials	$ 4 000
Conversion costs	$ 3 200
Costs added during current period	
Direct materials	$36 000
Conversion costs	$32 000
Physical units	
Units in beginning inventory	2 000
Units started this month	18 000
Total units completed and transferred out	14 800
Normal spoilage	1 000
Abnormal spoilage	1 000

Required

(a) Prepare a spreadsheet that uses a data input box and calculates information necessary for a weighted average process cost report and presents the cost report in an easily understood format.

(b) Copy the spreadsheet into a new range or new worksheet. If you use a new worksheet, highlight the tab and rename the worksheet 'FIFO'. Now alter the weighted average calculations so that the spreadsheet uses data from the input box to calculate the information necessary for a FIFO process cost report and presents the cost report in an easily understood format.

(c) Describe factors that would affect an accountant's choice of process costing method, and make a recommendation for a process costing method for Rally. Explain your choice.

8.30 Choice of costing method; process cost report; transferred-in units; spoilage　　　　**LO3, 6**

Toddler Toys produces toy construction vehicles for young children. Plastic pieces are moulded in the plastics department. These pieces are transferred to the assembly department, where direct materials are added after some assembly has been done. For example, plastic pieces of road graders are put together, then the blades and wheel assemblies are added, and finally some details are painted on the sides and back. The direct materials are added in the assembly department when the process is 75 per cent complete. Beginning inventory is 80 per cent complete and ending inventory is 25 per cent complete. Following are data for August.

Beginning inventory costs for the assembly department:	
Transferred in	$ 4 000
Direct materials	2 000
Conversion costs	1 600
Total cost	$ 7 600
Costs incurred in the assembly department during current period:	
Transferred in	$36 000
Direct materials	18 000
Conversion costs	16 000
Total cost	$70 000
Physical units in the assembly department:	
Units in beginning inventory	2 000
Units started this month	18 000
Total units completed and transferred out	14 800
Normal spoilage	1 000 (100% complete)
Abnormal spoilage	1 000 (100% complete)

Required

(a) Choose a process costing method for the assembly department. Explain your choice and describe its pros and cons.

(b) Prepare a cost report using the method you chose in part (a).

8.31 Process costing under weighted average and FIFO; spoilage; rework　　　　**LO4, 6**

The accountant at Cellular Advantage needs to close the books at the end of January using the following information. Direct materials are added at the start of production. Conversion costs are incurred evenly throughout production. Inspection occurs when production is 75 per cent completed.

Normal spoilage is 13 200 units per month.

Physical units	
Work in process, beginning (30% complete)	22 000
Started during the month	148 000
Total units to account for	170 000
Good units completed and transferred out during current period:	
From beginning work in process	22 000
Started and completed	100 000
Total good units completed	122 000
Spoiled units	16 000
Work in process, ending (60% complete)	32 000
Total units accounted for	170 000
Costs	
Beginning inventory:	
Direct materials	$ 440 000
Conversion costs	60 000
Total beginning inventory	500 000
Costs added during current period:	
Direct materials	2 960 000
Conversion costs	1 884 000
Total costs to account for	$5 344 000

Required

(a) Prepare a process cost report using the weighted average method.

(b) Prepare a process cost report using the FIFO method.

(c) Explain why an entity might specify limits for normal spoilage, after which spoilage is considered abnormal.

(d) Reconstruct the work in process and finished goods ledger accounts for this month.

8.32 Two departments; two periods; FIFO and weighted average; estimate accuracy   LO3, 7

Rausher Industries began a new product line this year. Management wants a cost report for the current year and a budget for next year. The product requires processing in two departments. Materials are added at the beginning of the process in department 1. Department 2 finishes the product but adds no direct materials.

During the year work was begun on 12 000 units in department 1, and 9000 of these units were transferred to department 2. The remaining 3000 units were 60 per cent complete with regard to conversion costs in department 1, which incurred $36 000 in material costs and $14 040 in conversion costs.

Department 2 completed and sent 7000 units to the finished goods warehouse. It ended the period with 2000 units 40 per cent complete with regard to department 2's conversion costs, which were $32 760 for the period.

The plan for next year is to begin an additional 15 000 units in department 1. Management expects to finish the year with 5000 units one-half converted in department 1. Department 2 is expected to complete 14 000 units, and its ending inventory is expected to be 70 per cent complete. Materials are expected to be $48 600, and conversion costs for departments 1 and 2 are expected to be $14 545 and $59 075 respectively.

Required

(a) Prepare cost reports for the current year and a budgeted cost report for next year assuming the entity uses the following:
  (i) FIFO process costing
  (ii) weighted average process costing.

(b) The employee responsible for estimating the percentage completion had experience estimating completion percentages for one of Rausher's other product lines. However, she is wondering whether she could improve the accuracy of her estimates. A colleague in another department suggested that she consider using techniques such as timing one unit through each department and identifying points in the production process where units appear to be 25 per cent complete, 50 per cent complete and so on.
  (i) Comment on whether the suggested method is likely to provide an accurate estimate of work in process.
  (ii) List two advantages of improving the accuracy of the estimate. What might be a disadvantage?

8.33 Comparison of actual to standard processing costs; use in bonus decisions **LO7**

Tiffany Campbell is the cost accountant in Computer Components (CC), a small manufacturing entity. CC produces components for one of the large computer manufacturers. Its strategy is to provide highly reliable components at the lowest possible price. To help maintain cost competitiveness, Tiffany produces two process cost reports each month, one based on the FIFO method and the other based on the standard cost method. When the reports are complete, costs from the two systems are compared. If actual costs are under control (that is, within the standard costs) for a particular division, the manager receives a small bonus. If costs have been under control throughout the year, a larger bonus is given at the end of December.

This month Tiffany investigated the results for Kevin Meledrez's division. Actual direct material costs were higher than standard cost, so the equivalent unit cost was higher than the standard. When she spoke to Kevin about the direct material costs in his division, he argued that the standard cost needs to be changed because the current supplier increased the cost of a particular part. Kevin believes that he should not be held responsible for costs that are not under his control; when prices change, the standard should also change.

Tiffany asked Kevin whether he had investigated other vendors who sell the same part to see whether the price change was across the board for all vendors. Kevin says that he has used this vendor for a number of years and is satisfied with the quality and timeliness of delivery. He does not believe that another vendor would provide the same quality and service, so he does not want to consider changing suppliers at this time.

Required

(a) Identify a variety of reasons why actual costs are likely to be different from standard costs for Computer Components.

(b) Discuss whether Kevin would be likely to make the same argument about changing the standard if the supplier's price had decreased.

(c) Describe the pros and cons of changing vendors.

(d) Explain the benefit to the entity of giving managers bonuses based on comparisons of actual to standard costs.

(e) Discuss the advantages and disadvantages of adopting a policy of adjusting the standard cost for changes in vendor prices.

(f) Suppose Tiffany asks for your advice. Use the information you learned from the preceding analyses to write a memo to Tiffany with your recommendation. As you write the memo, consider information that Tiffany needs from you to help her make a final decision.

8.34 Techtra makes electronic components used by other entities in a wide variety of end products **LO5, 6, 7**

Initially Techtra bid for any type of electronic assembly work that became available (mostly subcontract work from other entities experiencing temporary capacity problems). But over the years the entity narrowed its focus. It now produces essentially three products, although minor variations within each product line yield a large number of different models.

Each of the products goes through three separate operating departments: assembly, soldering and testing. When an order is received, it goes to production scheduling. Production scheduling personnel schedule time in each of the three departments. The availability of parts usually determines when a job can be started in the assembly department. If parts are not in stock, they are usually received from suppliers within a week. On the appropriate day, the computerised scheduling program places the job on the assembly department's job list. Simultaneously, an electronic materials requisition goes to the stores department. Materials handling people then deliver the parts to the assembly department. The assembly operation is semiautomatic.

When the department is ready to begin a new job, a worker inserts the appropriate guides into the equipment and adjusts the various settings. Parts are then loaded into the machines, which do the actual assembly. Because a worker keeps several machines running simultaneously, each order is processed using several (sometimes all) of the machines available in the department. Once the units for an order are assembled, an assembly department worker enters its completion in the computerised production system. The system then adds the job to the soldering department's job list. Materials handling personnel load assembled product onto racks and take them to the soldering department.

Soldering processes the jobs on a first-in, first-out basis unless production scheduling asks for priority treatment for a particular job. For each job, the soldering machines must be set up for the appropriate product, but thereafter the operation is totally automatic. Once a job is completed, an entry is made in the production system, which adds it to the testing department's job list. The products are then reloaded onto racks and transported to the testing department.

By the time the products get to the testing department, many of the jobs are near or past their promised delivery date. Thus, the production scheduling system directs the testing department to work on jobs in the order of promised delivery date. Normally the entity expects 3 per cent to 5 per cent of the products to be defective, and plans its lot size for each order accordingly. However, from time to time, an entire order must be scrapped due to faulty assembly or soldering on every unit. When an order is scrapped, it is noted in the production system and a rush replacement order is sent to the assembly department. Completed jobs that pass testing are immediately shipped to customers.

Workers in the assembly, soldering and testing departments each enter information in the production system detailing the amount of time spent working on specific jobs. This information, plus the materials requisitions, is used by the cost accounting system to track the cost of each job. The cost accounting system allocates departmental overhead to each job using overhead allocation rates based on budgeted overhead costs and budgeted hours for each department. General factory overhead — which includes production scheduling, materials handling, property taxes and so on — is charged to each job based on total materials costs. Within each of the three product types, the average cost per unit varies primarily with the size of each job order because of set-up costs. The cost data are used to update the entity's pricing sheets and to determine the efficiency with which each order was produced.

The managers are considering a change in the organisation of the plant. They propose that the plant floor, instead of being arranged in functional departments, could consist of manufacturing 'cells' for each product; that is, they would establish clusters of assembly machines, soldering machines and test equipment. Each cluster would be dedicated to making only one type of product. Under this arrangement, when an order is processed, individual units would proceed one by one through the assembly, soldering and test equipment in the appropriate cell. Most jobs would be completed within a day, but large jobs would sometimes take up to a week. The managers are also considering a change in the way parts are ordered from suppliers. The entity would place orders for each job, requesting delivery of parts on the day production is scheduled to begin.

Required

(a) Describe how the proposed changes would likely affect each of the following.
   (i) Size of work in process and raw materials inventories
  (ii) Material handling and machine set-up costs
 (iii) Cost of defective units
 (iv) Ratio of units produced to units ordered
  (v) Production scheduling costs and machine utilisation rates
 (vi) Average cost per unit of product
(vii) Ability to fulfil a customer's rush order

(b) Assuming the managers adopt the proposed manufacturing changes, answer the following.
  (i) What would be the advantages of adopting a process costing system?
 (ii) The entity would no longer carry significant inventories. How would this change affect the cost accounting?

ACKNOWLEDGEMENTS

Photo 8A: © wavebreakmedia / Shutterstock.com
Photo 8B: © Vorm in Beeld / Shutterstock.com

CHAPTER 9

Absorption and variable costing

IN BRIEF

Accountants use absorption costing for inventory and cost of goods sold (also called cost of sales) when preparing financial statements in accordance with Australian or New Zealand Accounting Standards. Under absorption costing, all manufacturing costs (fixed and variable) are assigned to units manufactured. This accounting method provides useful information by matching manufacturing costs against revenues. As an alternative to absorption costing, variable costing (variable costs only) is used by accountants to provide managers with incremental cost information.

9.1 Different measures of cost for different purposes

LEARNING OBJECTIVE 9.1 Understand the difference between absorption costing and variable costing, and prepare income statements under each method.

No single measure of inventory and cost of goods sold is best for all situations. Financial statement reporting requires average costs, but short-term internal decision making requires only incremental costs. Managers use both variable and fixed cost information for monitoring operations. Meanwhile, the accounting standards provide guidelines on how costs should be measured for reporting to external parties such as investors. With computerised accounting systems, accountants can easily calculate costs in a variety of ways; reports for outside distribution can be different from reports for inside management. As we will learn in this chapter, different types of information are useful in different settings. We will explore absorption costing, which is intended for outside distribution, and variable costing, which is often used for managerial decision making.

Absorption costing and variable costing

Absorption costing

When accountants prepare financial statements according to the accounting standards, they use absorption costing. Under **absorption costing**, all manufacturing costs are recorded on the balance sheet (also called the statement of financial position) as part of the cost of inventory and are then expensed as part of the cost of goods sold when units are sold (figure 9.1). Both fixed and variable manufacturing costs are assumed to have future value to the entity, and are accordingly treated as **product costs**. They include direct materials, direct labour and manufacturing overhead.

FIGURE 9.1 Absorption costing

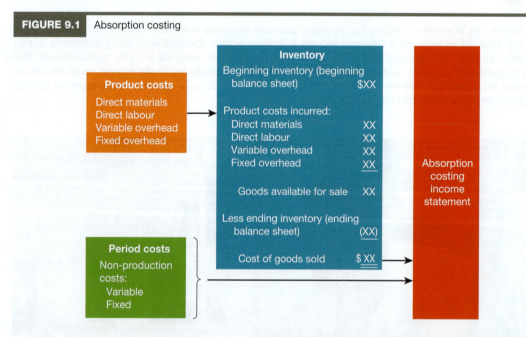

Under absorption costing, direct costs are traced to products and manufacturing overhead is allocated to products. Fixed overhead may be allocated to units using either an actual or budgeted allocation rate. If manufacturing volume is used as the allocation base, fixed overhead cost can be allocated to units using either an actual or an estimated allocation rate as follows:

$$\text{Actual fixed overhead allocation rate} = \frac{\text{Actual fixed overhead cost}}{\text{Actual production volume}}$$

$$\text{Estimated fixed overhead allocation rate} = \frac{\text{Estimated fixed overhead cost}}{\text{Estimated production volume}}$$

When using an estimated fixed overhead allocation rate, several alternative choices are available for the estimated manufacturing volume; we learn about these later in the chapter.

Given the treatment of fixed overhead costs under absorption costing, both manufacturing and sales volumes affect the timing of when fixed overhead is recognised as an expense. If units are produced and sold in this period, overhead costs incurred to produce these units are expensed in this period. If units from the last period are sold, some overhead costs from the last period are expensed in this period. If units produced in this period are not yet sold, the overhead allocated to those units will not be expensed until a future date when the units are sold. The overhead cost associated with those units is included in inventory on the balance sheet.

The absorption costing income statement (figure 9.2) reflects the focus in the accounting standards on distinguishing between manufacturing and non-manufacturing costs. All manufacturing costs are expensed as cost of goods sold (COGS) to match them against revenues when units are sold. For unsold units the manufacturing costs are shown as the asset inventory in the balance sheet. Non-manufacturing costs such as administration, marketing and distribution are treated as period costs. **Period costs** are all costs other than manufacturing costs incurred in the current period. The accounting standards require that period costs be expensed when incurred because these costs are assumed to have no future benefit.

FIGURE 9.2 Absorption costing income statement

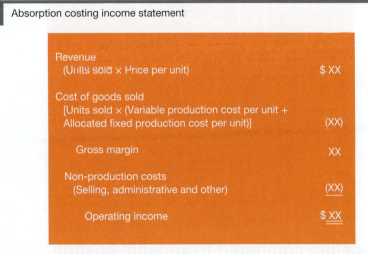

Revenue (Units sold × Price per unit)	$ XX
Cost of goods sold [Units sold × (Variable production cost per unit + Allocated fixed production cost per unit)]	(XX)
Gross margin	XX
Non-production costs (Selling, administrative and other)	(XX)
Operating income	$ XX

Variable costing

Under **variable costing**, all variable costs are matched against revenues and fixed costs are treated as period costs. Therefore, product costs consist of only variable manufacturing costs such as direct materials, direct labour and variable manufacturing overhead (figure 9.3). Inventory on the balance sheet includes only variable manufacturing costs under variable costing.

FIGURE 9.3 Variable costing

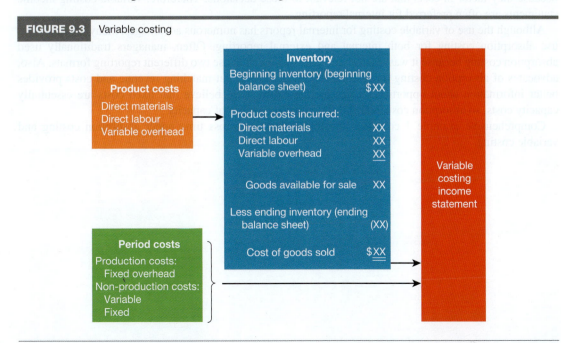

Product costs
Direct materials
Direct labour
Variable overhead

Inventory
Beginning inventory (beginning balance sheet) $XX
Product costs incurred:
  Direct materials XX
  Direct labour XX
  Variable overhead XX
Goods available for sale XX
Less ending inventory (ending balance sheet) (XX)
Cost of goods sold $XX

Period costs
Production costs:
  Fixed overhead
Non-production costs:
  Variable
  Fixed

Variable costing income statement

Expenses in a variable costing income statement are organised differently from an absorption costing income statement. In a variable costing income statement, all costs are separated into variable and fixed categories (figure 9.4); variable manufacturing costs are reported separately from fixed manufacturing costs. Similarly, variable non-manufacturing costs, such as sales commissions, are reported separately from fixed non-manufacturing costs. All variable costs, manufacturing and non-manufacturing, are subtracted from revenues to arrive at the contribution margin. Then all fixed costs, manufacturing and non-manufacturing, are subtracted to determine operating income. This presentation improves the ability of managers to identify cash flows relevant to a product or service for internal decision making.

FIGURE 9.4   Variable costing income statement

Revenue	
(Units sold × Price per unit)	$ XX
Variable costs:	
Production (Units sold × Variable production cost per unit)	(XX)
Non-production (Units sold × Variable non-production cost per unit, such as sales commissions)	(XX)
Contribution margin	XX
Fixed costs:	
Fixed production costs	(XX)
Fixed non-production costs	(XX)
Operating income	$ XX

Absorption costing compared to variable costing

Managers and other employees regularly make decisions about short-term resource allocations within an entity. To do so, they estimate the effects of alternative decisions on cash flows (incremental revenues and costs). Because fixed costs are constant within a relevant range of activity, total fixed costs generally do not change under alternative short-term decisions. Thus, income statements based on absorption costing do not provide managers or other users with the relevant information needed for short-term operating decisions because they factor in costs that are not relevant to those decisions. Therefore, variable costing income statements are often preferred for internal reporting.

Although the use of variable costing for internal reports has numerous advantages, many organisations use absorption costing for both internal and external reporting. Often, managers traditionally used absorption costing because it was expensive and inconvenient to use two different reporting formats. Also, advocates of absorption costing for internal reporting believe that matching revenue and costs provides better information about opportunity costs for the entity. They believe that fixed costs are essentially capacity costs, so absorption costs reflect different products' use of capacity.

Comprehensive example 1 compares income statements across time under absorption costing and variable costing.

Absorption costing and variable costing income statements

Boats Afloat Yacht Company recently started to manufacture recreational yachts. The accountant, Joan Ardmore, prepared the second quarter income statements using absorption costing.

Boats Afloat Yacht Company Second quarter income statement				
	April	May	June	Quarter total
Revenue @ $100 000 per unit	$100 000	$100 000	$300 000	$500 000
Cost of goods sold	100 000	70 000	210 000	380 000
Gross margin	0	30 000	90 000	120 000
Administrative and selling expenses	20 000	20 000	40 000	80 000
Operating income (loss)	$ (20 000)	$ 10 000	$ 50 000	$ 40 000

The sales manager, Stephanie Reynolds, analyses these results and asks Joan to explain why a loss was posted in April but not in May, given that one boat was sold each month. The income statement was prepared using absorption costing, with fixed overhead allocated based on actual costs and actual manufacturing volumes. Joan decides to prepare variable costing income statements for the same period so that she can more easily explain the absorption costing income statement to Stephanie. Joan first reviews the information she gathered and her calculations for the absorption income statement. The selling price per yacht is $100 000, and the entity incurred the following costs.

Variable costs per yacht			
Direct materials			$20 000
Direct labour			$15 000
Variable manufacturing overhead			$ 5 000
Variable selling			$10 000
Fixed costs per month			
Fixed manufacturing overhead			$60 000
Fixed administrative and selling			$10 000
Manufacturing and sales quantities			
	April	May	June
Manufacturing	1	2	2
Sales	1	1	3
Inventory	0	1	0

Absorption costing

When absorption costing is used, all manufacturing overhead (fixed as well as variable) is allocated to inventory. When the entity produces only one product, fixed manufacturing overhead costs can be easily allocated on a pro-rata basis among the actual units produced. The absorption cost per unit is the sum of the variable manufacturing cost per unit plus the actual fixed overhead allocation rate per unit.

Absorption cost per unit			
	April	May	June
Fixed manufacturing overhead	$60 000	$60 000	$60 000
Divided by number of units produced	1	2	2
Actual fixed overhead per unit	$60 000	$30 000	$30 000

Variable manufacturing costs per unit:			
Direct materials	20 000	20 000	20 000
Direct labour	15 000	15 000	15 000
Variable manufacturing overhead	5 000	5 000	5 000
Total variable cost per unit	40 000	40 000	40 000
Total absorption cost per unit	$100 000	$70 000	$70 000

	Absorption cost of goods sold		
	April	May	June
Number of units sold	1	1	3
Absorption cost of unit(s) sold:			
Produced during April	$100 000		
Produced during May		$70 000	$ 70 000
Produced during June			
(2 @ $70 000 each)			140 000
Total cost of goods sold	$100 000	$70 000	$210 000

In April, Boats Afloat produced and sold the same quantity of yachts, resulting in no ending inventory. In May, however, Boats Afloat produced two units and sold only one. Thus, one unit remained in inventory at a cost of $70 000. Then in June, two units were produced and three were sold. June's cost of goods sold reflected sales of three units; two produced in June and one drawn from inventory. Inventory at the end of June was zero.

Variable costing

Joan now separates administrative and selling expenses into variable and fixed categories and prepares variable costing income statements. Notice that under variable costing, the operating income for the months when one boat was sold (April and May) is the same.

	Administrative and selling costs		
	April	May	June
Variable selling cost per unit	$10 000	$10 000	$10 000
Times number of units sold	1	1	3
Total variable selling cost	10 000	10 000	30 000
Fixed administrative and selling expenses	10 000	10 000	10 000
Total administrative and selling expenses	$20 000	$20 000	$40 000

	Variable costing income statements			
	April	May	June	Quarter total
Revenue @ $100 000 per unit	$100 000	$100 000	$300 000	$500 000
Variable manufacturing expenses (for units sold)	40 000	40 000	120 000	200 000
Variable selling expenses	10 000	10 000	30 000	50 000
Contribution margin	50 000	50 000	150 000	250 000
Fixed manufacturing expenses	60 000	60 000	60 000	180 000
Fixed administrative and selling expenses	10 000	10 000	10 000	30 000
Operating income (loss)	$ (20 000)	$ (20 000)	$ 80 000	$ 40 000

Reconciling absorption and variable costing incomes

Notice in comprehensive example 1 that when manufacturing levels are the same as sales levels, income is the same under absorption and variable costing. When manufacturing is greater than sales (refer May's operating income), absorption income is greater than variable income. This is because a portion of the fixed overhead cost ($30 000) has been allocated to a product that is recorded as an asset and therefore has not yet been expensed via cost of goods sold. In turn, when manufacturing is less than sales (refer June's operating income), absorption income is less than variable income. This is because to satisfy the order a product had to be taken from inventory and under the absorption costing method the inventory value includes $30 000 fixed costs incurred in May but not expensed until June. When using variable costing this $30 000 was expensed in May. Therefore, reconciling the two incomes involves calculating the difference in overhead cost that is either added to or subtracted from inventory because sales volumes do not equal manufacturing volumes. Figure 9.5 presents reconciliation calculations that are then illustrated using comprehensive example 2 on Boats Afloat.

FIGURE 9.5	Reconciling absorption and variable costing

Absorption versus variable costing			
	Operating income	Inventory on the balance sheet	Reconciliation calculations
Manufacturing = Sales	Absorption costing income = Variable costing income	No change in inventory quantity on the balance sheet	No reconciliation needed because no difference in income
Manufacturing > Sales	Absorption costing income > Variable costing income	Inventory quantities on the balance sheet increase	Difference in income is equal to: 1. increase in absorption costing inventory minus increase in variable costing inventory 2. fixed overhead allocated during the current period to units added to inventory
Manufacturing < Sales	Absorption costing income < Variable costing income	Inventory quantities on the balance sheet decrease	Difference in income is equal to: 1. decrease in absorption costing inventory minus decrease in variable costing inventory 2. fixed overhead allocated to units in prior period to units removed from inventory

COMPREHENSIVE EXAMPLE 2

Reconciling absorption costing and variable costing income statements

Working from the two income statements, Joan prepares the following reconciliation report. Next, she shows Stephanie the two income statements, explaining the preparation of each one. When Stephanie observes that the quarterly incomes under the two methods are the same, Joan points out that this occurred because the quarter had no beginning or ending inventories. Joan then shows Stephanie the reconciliation report and explains her calculations.

	April	May	June
Difference in income:			
Absorption costing income (loss)	$(20 000)	$ 10 000	$ 50 000
Variable costing income (loss)	(20 000)	(20 000)	80 000
Difference	$ 0	$ 30 000	$(30 000)
Difference in change in inventory:			
Absorption costing:			
Ending inventory	$ 0	$ 70 000	$ 0
Beginning inventory	0	0	70 000
Increase (decrease)	0	70 000	(70 000)
Variable costing:			
Ending inventory	$ 0	$ 40 000	$ 0
Beginning inventory	0	0	40 000
Increase (decrease)	0	40 000	(40 000)
Difference	$ 0	$ 30 000	$(30 000)

The only difference in inventory cost between absorption costing and variable costing is the amount of fixed overhead allocated to inventory under absorption costing. Therefore, the change in inventory difference can be presented by calculating the change in fixed costs included in absorption costing inventory. Ending inventory in May consists of one unit produced during May, when $30 000 in fixed overhead was allocated to each unit. This unit was then sold during June. The difference in operating income between absorption and variable costing is summarised as follows:

	April	May	June
Change in fixed costs included in absorption costing inventory:			
Fixed costs in ending inventory	$ 0	$30 000	$ 0
Fixed costs in beginning inventory	0	0	30 000
Increase (decrease)	$ 0	$30 000	$(30 000)

After examining the two different income statements and the reconciling report, Stephanie decides she wants to receive monthly income statements using both methods. She wants the same financial statement information that is shared with banks and other external stakeholders, in case someone calls and has questions about the entity's financial performance measured in line with the accounting standards. She also wants to use the variable costing income statement to analyse the operating performance of the organisation and its managers.

Stephanie also wants to set up a profit-sharing plan for all employees, rewarding employees when the amounts received from sales cover the costs for the period. She realises that the variable costing income statement provides this information by more accurately measuring substantive economic changes across time.

Incentives to build up inventories

In comprehensive example 2, absorption costing operating income for Boats Afloat is higher than variable costing operating income in periods when the inventory quantities increase. Under absorption costing, part of an entity's fixed overhead cost is recorded as inventory on the balance sheet. As inventory quantity increases, the amount of fixed cost included in inventory increases. Because that portion of fixed cost is not expensed until later, operating income also increases. As a result, managers using absorption costing have incentives to inappropriately build up inventory quantities, especially when sales during the current period decrease. Managers may be motivated by many factors.
- Managers' reputations often increase as a result of increases in reported operating income.
- Managers frequently receive bonus payments based on their ability to meet or exceed targeted operating income levels.
- Managers may be biased in their sales forecasts, preventing them from promptly recognising a decline in sales.

Disincentives to build up inventories

Managers might avoid inventory build-ups for several reasons. If managers become aware of a sales decline, they could be unwilling to use an inventory build-up that, while strengthening short-term earnings, would negatively affect future earnings when those units are either sold or written off. If bonuses are based on variable costing income, managers will not be rewarded for inventory build-ups. Another disincentive is that analysts routinely monitor companies' inventory levels. Excessive inventory levels are often viewed as evidence of poor management or deteriorating sales. In addition, some entities use just-in-time (JIT) inventory management. Under JIT, the potential build-up of inventory is unlikely; so income differences under absorption and variable costing are small.

Uncertainties about desirable inventory levels

The motorcycle manufacturer, Harley-Davidson, is an example of an organisation where managers stated that they intentionally wanted dealers to carry higher inventories to better meet customer demand. Analysts responded that sales were in decline and that dealer inventory increases signalled a forthcoming decline in the company's financial health. Because of uncertainties about factors influencing future sales, it was not possible for investors to determine whether Harley-Davidson's inventories were too high. These uncertainties included the following:

- the extent to which long wait times would cause customers to buy from competitors
- the increase in sales to individuals who would not have waited
- whether an increase in inventories and corresponding decrease in customer wait times would reduce the mystique of the Harley-Davidson brand, causing a decrease in future product demand
- the most desirable manufacturing and inventory levels.

To further complicate matters, outsiders could not know whether the managers were completely candid in explaining their manufacturing policies or whether their manufacturing decisions were biased.

9.2 A closer look at absorption costing using normal costing

LEARNING OBJECTIVE 9.2 Calculate absorption costs using normal costing.

Under absorption costing in comprehensive example 1, fixed production overhead for Boats Afloat was allocated to each yacht based on the actual cost incurred and the actual number of yachts produced each month. An alternative method under absorption costing is to allocate fixed overhead costs using normal costing. Normal costing uses actual direct costs and actual production volumes with an estimated fixed overhead allocation rate.

Suppose the accountant for Boats Afloat calculates an estimated fixed overhead allocation rate based on annual budget data. Assuming that budgeted fixed overhead is $720 000 and annual production is budgeted to be 24 units, the rate used for allocation would be estimated as follows:

$$\text{Estimated fixed overhead allocation rate} = \text{Estimated fixed overhead cost} \div \text{Estimated production volume}$$
$$= \$720\,000 \div 24 \text{ units}$$
$$= \$30\,000 \text{ per unit}$$

The fixed overhead allocation for the month of April would be:

$$\text{Fixed overhead allocation} = \text{Actual units produced} \times \text{Estimated fixed overhead allocation rate}$$
$$= 1 \text{ unit} \times \$30\,000 \text{ per unit}$$
$$= \$30\,000$$

Motivation for normal costing

Using an estimated fixed overhead allocation rate is often preferred to the use of rates based on actual costs for three reasons: denominator, numerator and information timeliness.

1. *Actual production volumes fluctuate (denominator reason).* If overhead is allocated based on actual volume, then the fixed cost per unit could be artificially high or low in different time periods. In the Boats Afloat example, total cost per yacht varied from $70 000 to $100 000 because of differences in fixed production overhead per unit. These differences were caused by variations in production volume across individual months. If production volumes fluctuate randomly or seasonally, then an estimated fixed production overhead rate could be used to avoid distorting costs for individual units.
2. *Fixed production overhead costs fluctuate (numerator reason).* Fixed overhead costs often fluctuate throughout a time period. Suppose an entity is located in a region with cold winters. Utility costs for production facilities might be high during winter months and low during summer months. If fixed overhead is allocated based on actual costs incurred each month, units produced during the winter would be allocated higher overhead costs than units produced during summer months. When an estimated fixed production overhead rate is used, this type of per-unit cost distortion would be avoided.
3. *Actual volume and fixed overhead costs are not known until after accounting for the period is completed (information timeliness).* Normal costing allows managers to assign costs to inventory when the accounting cycle has not been completed. Managers often need to cost inventory during each month or shortly after a month's end. It might not be possible to gather and report complete cost and volume data quickly enough to use actual costs for fixed overhead allocation. So long as normal costs are reasonable estimates, they can be used for faster-paced valuations.

Allocation rate denominator considerations

When calculating an estimated fixed overhead allocation rate, accountants choose the allocation base to use as the denominator. Allocation bases such as direct labour hours, direct labour costs, machine hours or number of units are often used. In this chapter we focus on allocating fixed overhead based on production volumes or different measures of capacity to present the most general case. Capacity is a measure of the constraints within an entity. It can be measured in a number of ways.

Four different levels of capacity could be used as the estimated volume of production under absorption costing. Two of these measures are *supply-based capacity levels*; they measure the amount of capacity that is available for production.

- *Theoretical capacity* is the upper capacity limit; it assumes continuous, uninterrupted production 365 days per year. Theoretical capacity is the maximum volume of goods or services that an entity could hypothetically produce.
- *Practical capacity* is the upper capacity limit that takes into account the organisation's regularly scheduled times for production. Practical capacity excludes potential production that could take place during anticipated and scheduled maintenance downtimes, holidays or other times in which production would normally be interrupted. In other words, practical capacity is theoretical capacity reduced for expected downtimes. Practical capacity is estimated using engineering studies and labour use patterns.

Two additional measures are *demand-based capacity levels*; they measure the amount of capacity needed to meet sales volumes:

- *Normal capacity* is an average use of capacity over time. Normal capacity is the typical volume of goods or services an entity produces to meet customer demand.
- *Budgeted or expected capacity* is the anticipated use of capacity over the next period. Budgeted or expected capacity is based on management's planned operations in which customer demand is forecast.

Volume variance with normal costing

The **volume variance** is the difference between the amount of estimated fixed overhead costs used to calculate the allocation rate and the amount of fixed overhead costs actually allocated to inventory during the period. If allocated volume is greater than estimated volume, then too much fixed overhead is allocated to inventory and the inventory amounts need to be reduced by the variance amount. If allocated volume is less than estimated volume; too little fixed overhead cost is allocated to inventory and inventory values need to be increased by the variance amount. For example, suppose Boats Afloat estimates that fixed overhead costs will be $60 000 per month and fixed overhead is allocated to units using normal capacity of two units per month, or $30 000 per unit. In a month when only one yacht is produced, the volume variance would be:

$$\text{Volume variance} = \text{Expected fixed overhead cost} - \text{Allocated fixed overhead cost}$$
$$= \$60\,000 - \$30\,000$$
$$= \$30\,000$$

In this example, allocated overhead was less than estimated overhead, so inventory accounts on the financial statements need to be increased by $30 000 to ensure that the expense recorded this period is equal to estimated fixed overhead.

When preparing financial statements in accordance with accounting standards, this variance would be closed to cost of goods sold if it was immaterial. If material, it would be allocated on a pro rata basis among cost of goods sold, finished goods and work in process (if any). In this example, the volume variance would be considered material because it is large compared to estimated fixed overhead costs, so cost of goods sold, finished goods and work in process would all be increased. An entity would also need to adjust for fixed overhead spending variances (refer to chapter 11 for further discussion).

Evaluating denominator choices

Because volume variances must be adjusted at the end of an accounting period, the inventory and cost of goods sold values on the financial statements are not affected by the choice of denominator when calculating the estimated fixed overhead allocation rate. Therefore, no income effects need to be considered when choosing the denominator value.

However, managers sometimes use information from the normal costing system for pricing and product emphasis decisions. In addition, the denominator choice often affects budgets. To provide the highest-quality cost information for planning and decision making, inventory values should reflect realistic estimates of the use of resources. The quality of information for decision making and planning decreases when absorption cost information is based on unrealistic capacity levels.

Another factor to consider in choosing the denominator is how the choice affects the management of an organisation's capacity. The largest costs in fixed production overhead are often related to capacity, such as building rent, depreciation, utilities and maintenance. Thus, we can think of the estimated fixed overhead allocation rate as an estimated cost of capacity per unit that could be used to motivate managers to use capacity efficiently. The best choice would allocate a cost to each unit produced, not only to emphasise the need to cover fixed costs but also to provide information about the opportunity cost of unused capacity.

If theoretical capacity is used as the allocation base, the fixed overhead allocation rate is unrealistically small. Therefore, theoretical capacity is rarely used in practice. If normal or budgeted capacity is used, inventory values simply reflect the current use of capacity, which may not be the most efficient use of capacity. In contrast, practical capacity reflects an attainable target for production. When practical capacity is used in the denominator, the fixed overhead allocation rate reflects the cost of supplying capacity. Internal reports can be developed to highlight the capacity available versus the capacity used. These reports focus managers' attention on unused capacity. Thus, the use of practical capacity motivates managers to find new ways to use available capacity. They may be encouraged to increase demand, develop new products, or consider leasing out or eliminating unused capacity.

9.3 Comparison of absorption and variable costing

LEARNING OBJECTIVE 9.3 Identify the uses and limitations of absorption and variable costing income statements.

Figure 9.6 compares the assumptions used in absorption costing and variable costing. These accounting methods differ based on the costs that are considered product costs. Under absorption costing, all manufacturing costs are product costs. Under variable costing, only variable manufacturing costs are product costs. (There is another type of costing called throughput costing where only direct materials costs are product costs.) These methods affect how quickly manufacturing overhead and other costs are expensed on the income statement. Because managers monitor operating income, these methods affect how quickly they are motivated to consider changing manufacturing plans related to these costs.

FIGURE 9.6 Comparison of absorption and variable costing

Absorption costing	Variable costing
In line with accounting standards	Not in line with accounting standards
Useful for external reporting purposes	Useful for performance evaluation and internal decision making
Direct material and direct labour are inventory costs	Direct material and direct labour are inventory costs
Fixed and variable manufacturing overhead allocated to inventory	Fixed manufacturing overhead expensed as a period cost. Variable manufacturing overhead allocated to inventory
Administrative and selling costs (both fixed and variable) expensed as period costs	Administrative and selling costs separated into fixed and variable costs and expensed as period costs
Inventory costs (including per-unit fixed and variable manufacturing costs) not expensed until the units are sold	Inventory costs (only manufacturing variable costs) not expensed until the units are sold

Before technology made it relatively easy to draw many different reports from one database, most entities established an accounting system designed primarily to meet financial and tax accounting requirements. Because absorption costing is required by the accounting standards and income tax rules, it tended to be the only method used. With improved technology, organisations are now able to produce information reports for many different purposes.

Absorption costing income statements focus on matching manufacturing costs to revenues on the income statement. This information is important for external users, such as investors, who monitor the trends in product costs for an entity over time and for comparison with competitors. Variable costing income statements are often used to evaluate the performance of a division or manager, or as a source for information for decision making. Comprehensive example 3 further demonstrates the differences between absorption costing and variable costing approaches.

COMPREHENSIVE EXAMPLE 3

Absorption costing and variable costing

Ski Doodle is a small family-owned business that manufactures snowmobiles. Abel, the co-owner's son, has performed the entity's accounting functions for several years. He always prepares variable costing income statements because the family makes product-related decisions on a regular basis and prefers using incremental costs for those decisions. Recently, the family decided to apply for a loan to expand operations. The bank asked for this month's financial statements and wants them to conform to the accounting standards.

Variable costing

The information for the current period reports along with Ski Doodle's variable costing income statement follow.

Ordinarily, Ski Doodle's prices and costs are:	
Price	$10 000 per snowmobile
Variable manufacturing costs:	
Raw materials	$ 2 000 per snowmobile
Direct labour and variable overhead	$ 2 000 per snowmobile
Fixed manufacturing costs	$60 000 per month
Selling and administrative costs:	
Variable	$ 500 per snowmobile
Fixed	$30 000 per month

Beginning finished goods inventory for the year was zero. Average manufacturing is about 12 snowmobiles per month. Sales are seasonal, so in some months no snowmobiles are produced or sold, while manufacturing and sales are high in other months.

This month beginning inventory was zero, 20 snowmobiles were manufactured and 18 snowmobiles were sold.

Variable costing income statement		
Revenue (18 × $10 000)		$180 000
Variable costs		
Manufacturing (18 × $4000)	$72 000	
Selling (18 × $500)	9 000	81 000
Contribution margin		99 000
Fixed costs		
Manufacturing	$60 000	
Administrative and selling	30 000	90 000
Operating income		$ 9 000

Ending inventory is valued at $8000 (2 units × $4000 variable manufacturing cost per unit).

Absorption costing with actual volume

When Abel develops the absorption costing income statement, he realises that he needs to choose either actual volume or some estimate of volume to calculate the fixed overhead allocation rate. He decides to produce this month's statement both ways to see how they differ from each other and from the variable costing income statement information with which he is familiar.

First Abel produces an absorption costing income statement using actual manufacturing levels. The actual fixed overhead allocation rate is $60 000 ÷ 20 units = $3000 per unit. Accordingly, the absorption cost per unit is $7000 ($4000 variable cost plus $3000 allocated fixed overhead), and COGS is $126 000 (18 units sold × $7000 per unit).

Absorption costing income statement (actual volume)	
Revenue (18 × $10 000)	$180 000
Cost of goods sold (18 × $7000)	126 000
Gross margin	54 000
Administrative and selling [$30 000 + (18 × $500)]	39 000
Operating income	$ 15 000

Ending inventory is valued at $14 000 [2 units × ($4000 + $3000)].

The difference in incomes between variable costing and absorption costing arises because allocated fixed overhead costs increase the value of the absorption costing inventory on the balance sheet. With no beginning inventory, the change in this illustration equals the fixed overhead costs that are included in ending inventory. The two units in ending inventory were each allocated $3000 in fixed overhead. Therefore, total fixed overhead in ending inventory is $6000. Abel prepares a formal reconciliation of the two incomes as follows:

Variable costing income	$ 9 000
Increase in fixed overhead costs in absorption inventory	
($6000 ending − $0 beginning)	6 000
Absorption costing income	$15 000

Another way to reconcile the two incomes is to calculate the difference in the change in inventory cost between the two costing methods:

Increase in absorption costing inventory	
($14 000 ending − $0 beginning)	$14 000
Increase in variable costing inventory	
($8000 ending − $0 beginning)	8 000
Difference	$ 6 000

Absorption costing with normal capacity

Next, Abel allocates fixed overhead using an estimated allocation rate based on a normal capacity level of 12 snowmobiles per month. In this case, the estimated fixed overhead allocation rate is $5000 per unit ($60 000 ÷ 12 units). The cost of each unit produced under absorption costing is now $9000 ($4000 variable cost + $5000 allocated fixed overhead).

Absorption costing income statement (normal capacity)	
Revenue (18 × $10 000)	$180 000
Cost of goods sold (18 × $9000)	162 000
Gross margin	18 000
Administrative and selling [$30 000 + (18 × $500)]	39 000
Operating income (loss)	$ (21 000)

Choice of fixed overhead allocation rate denominator and volume variance adjustment

After he completes the preceding calculations, Abel realises that his choice of denominator level for the fixed overhead allocation rate affects the operating income, which in turn affects the bank's appraisal of Ski Doodle's creditworthiness. Based on his analyses, he thinks the bank will view the entity more favourably if fixed overhead is allocated using the actual manufacturing level. Income for the current period appears higher than when using normal capacity.

Although Abel does accounting for the family business, he is not formally trained as an accountant. Therefore, he is unsure whether his calculations and conclusions are accurate. He suspects that too much overhead has been allocated under the normal capacity version of the absorption costing income statement. He decides to meet with Matt Goodings, the company's CPA.

Matt tells Abel, 'I'm very impressed with what you've done here. I have only one comment about your calculations. When using an estimated volume to allocate fixed costs, there is always a volume variance — the difference between estimated and allocated fixed overhead cost. You estimated a normal capacity of 12 units per month, but said that sales increased more than expected this year. You now expect that manufacturing will average more than 12 units per month. You estimated fixed overhead costs to be $60 000. However, under your estimated normal capacity, $100 000 (20 units × $5000) of fixed overhead costs is allocated to units produced last month. Thus, you have a volume variance of $40 000 — you allocated more overhead to snowmobiles than the estimated cost. Generally accepted accounting principles require you to make an adjustment for this variance in your calculations to ensure that only actual costs are recorded in inventory and cost of goods sold. I'll show you how.' Matt shows Abel the following calculations.

$$\text{Volume variance} = \text{Estimated fixed overhead} - \text{Allocated fixed overhead}$$
$$= \$60\,000 - (20 \text{ units} \times \$5000 \text{ per unit})$$
$$= \$40\,000$$

The volume variance of $40 000 is far more than 10 per cent of the estimated fixed overhead cost of $60 000. Matt concludes that the variance is material and should be allocated on a pro-rata basis among the 20 units produced that are in cost of goods sold and ending inventory. The adjustment is $2000 per unit ($40 000 ÷ 20 units):

Adjustment for the volume variance:	
Cost of goods sold ($2000 × 18 units)	$36 000
Ending inventory ($2000 × 2 units)	4 000
Total volume variance	$40 000

Because more fixed overhead was allocated than estimated, the absorption cost per unit should be reduced by $2000 per unit. Abel recasts the income statement with the volume variance adjustment as follows.

Absorption costing income statement (normal capacity with volume variance adjustment)		
Revenue (18 × $10 000)		$ 180 000
Cost of goods sold:		
Normal costing (18 × $9000)	$(162 000)	
Volume variance (18 × $2000)	36 000	(126 000)
Gross margin		54 000
Administrative and selling [$30 000 + (18 × $500)]		(39 000)
Operating income (loss)		$ 15 000

Abel observes that the operating income using normal capacity with the volume variance adjustment is now identical to the operating income when actual volume was used to allocate fixed overhead. Therefore, the financial statements are not affected by the choice of denominator used for the estimated fixed overhead allocation rate.

SUMMARY

9.1 Understand the difference between absorption costing and variable costing, and prepare income statements under each method.

Absorption costing

Product costs

Direct materials
Direct labour
Variable overhead
Fixed overhead

Period costs

Non-production costs:
Variable
Fixed

Inventory

Beginning inventory (beginning balance sheet)	$ XX
Product costs incurred:	
Direct materials	XX
Direct labour	XX
Variable overhead	XX
Fixed overhead	XX
Goods available for sale	
Less ending inventory (ending balance sheet)	(XX)
Cost of goods sold	$ XX

Income statement

Revenue (Units sold × Price per unit)	$XX
Cost of goods sold [Units sold × (Variable production cost per unit + Allocated fixed production cost per unit)]	(XX)
Gross margin	XX
Non-production costs (Selling, administrative and other)	XX
Operating income	$XX

Variable costing

Product costs

Direct materials
Direct labour
Variable overhead

Period costs

Production cost:
Fixed overhead
Non-production costs:
Variable
Fixed

Inventory

Beginning inventory (beginning balance sheet)	$ XX
Product costs incurred:	
Direct materials	XX
Direct labour	XX
Variable overhead	XX
Goods available for sale	XX
Less ending inventory (ending balance sheet)	(XX)
Cost of goods sold	$ XX

Income statement

Revenue (Units sold × Price per unit)	$XX
Variable costs:	
Production (Units sold × Variable production cost per unit)	(XX)
Non-production (Units sold × Variable non-production cost per unit, such as sales commissions)	(XX)
Contribution margin	XX
Fixed costs:	
Fixed production costs	(XX)
Fixed non-production costs	(XX)
Operating income	$ XX

9.2 Calculate absorption costs using normal costing.

Normal costing

$$\text{Estimated fixed overhead allocation rate} = \frac{\text{Estimated fixed overhead cost}}{\text{Estimated production volume}}$$

Alternative measures of manufacturing volume for normal costing

- Theoretical capacity
- Practical capacity
- Normal capacity
- Budgeted or expected capacity

Volume variance under normal costing

$$\text{Volume variance} = \text{Expected fixed overhead cost} - \text{Allocated fixed overhead cost}$$

If material: allocate on a pro rata basis among all manufacturing during the period (units in work in process, finished goods and cost of goods sold).

If immaterial: allocate to cost of goods sold.

9.3 Identify the uses and limitations of absorption and variable costing income statements.

Absorption costing	Variable costing
In line with accounting standards	Not in line with accounting standards
Useful for external reporting purposes	Useful for performance evaluation and internal decision making
Direct material and direct labour are inventory costs	Direct material and direct labour are inventory costs
Fixed and variable manufacturing overhead allocated to inventory	Fixed manufacturing overhead expensed as a period cost. Variable manufacturing overhead allocated to inventory
Administrative and selling costs (both fixed and variable) expensed as period costs	Administrative and selling costs separated into fixed and variable costs and expensed as period costs
Inventory costs (including per-unit fixed and variable manufacturing costs) not expensed until the units are sold	Inventory costs (only manufacturing variable costs) not expensed until the units are sold

KEY TERMS

absorption costing All manufacturing costs are recorded on the balance sheet (statement of financial position) as part of the cost of inventory and are then expensed as part of the cost of goods sold when units are sold.

period costs All costs, other than manufacturing costs, incurred in the current period.

product costs Manufacturing costs that are assumed to have future value to the entity.

variable costing All variable costs are matched against revenues and fixed costs are treated as period costs.

volume variance The difference between the amount of estimated fixed overhead costs used to calculate the allocation rate and the amount of fixed overhead costs actually allocated to inventory during the period.

SELF-STUDY PROBLEMS

SELF-STUDY PROBLEM 1 Absorption and variable costing

During its second year of operations, Grilling Machines, an entity that manufactures and sells electric tabletop grills, produced 275 000 units and sold 250 000 units at $60 per unit. The beginning inventory balance was 5000 units. No changes in fixed or variable costs occurred in the second year. The managers expected to sell 220 000 units, the same volume of manufacturing as last year. They set that amount as the normal capacity for allocating fixed overhead costs during the second year. For simplicity, assume that the budgeted fixed manufacturing overhead cost equals the actual cost this period. Also, assume that the entity uses the FIFO cost flow assumption. The following costs were incurred during the year.

Variable cost per unit:	$ 15.00
Direct materials	10.00
Direct labour	12.50
Manufacturing overhead	2.50
Selling and administrative	
Total fixed costs:	
Manufacturing overhead	$2 200 000
Selling and administrative	1 375 000

Required

(a) Prepare income statements using absorption costing and variable costing. Provide the details of your calculations in a schedule for each income statement.

(b) Reconcile the difference between operating incomes based on absorption costing and variable costing. Create a schedule to show your work.

(c) Suppose the accountant for Grilling Machines used an actual fixed overhead allocation rate rather than an estimated rate. Using this method, calculate the cost of goods sold and ending inventory under absorption costing. Compare the results to those calculated in part (a).

(d) If the volume variance is not material, how is it closed at the end of the period? Explain the reasoning behind this treatment.

SOLUTION TO SELF-STUDY PROBLEM 1

(a) Calculations for the absorption costing income statement.

Before calculating the product cost per unit, it is necessary to calculate the fixed overhead cost allocation and the volume variance adjustment. The entity's policy is to allocate fixed overhead using normal capacity, which was estimated at 220 000 units.

$$\text{Estimated fixed overhead allocation rate} = \$2\,200\,000 \div 220\,000 \text{ Normal volume of units}$$
$$= \$10 \text{ per unit}$$

At the end of the year, the entity must make an adjustment for its volume variance, which is the difference between total fixed overhead allocated to manufacturing and the original estimate of fixed overhead costs.

Estimated fixed overhead ($10 per unit × 220 000 units)	$2 200 000
Allocated overhead ($10 per unit × 275 000 units)	2 750 000
Volume variance	$ 550 000

The volume variance is considered material because it is greater than 10 per cent of the estimated fixed overhead cost.

$$\$550\,000 \div \$2\,200\,000 = 25\%$$

Material volume variances are adjusted to all units produced. For this problem, 250 000 of the units are in cost of goods sold, and 25 000 units are added to inventory. Because more fixed overhead cost was allocated than estimated, the absorption cost per unit must be reduced by the volume variance.

$$\text{Volume variance per unit produced} = \$550\,000 \times 275\,000 \text{ units}$$
$$= \$2 \text{ per unit}$$

Given the preceding calculations, the absorption product cost per unit is:

Direct materials	$15.00
Direct labour	10.00
Variable overhead	12.50
Fixed overhead allocation rate	10.00
Subtotal before volume variance adjustment	47.50
Volume variance adjustment per unit	(2.00)
Total absorption cost per unit	$45.50

We can now calculate the value of ending inventory: 275 000 units were produced this year and 250 000 were sold, causing inventory to increase by 25 000 units. Beginning inventory was 5000 units, so ending inventory is 30 000 units. Also, recall that the costs in year 1 were the same as the costs in year 2. Because actual volume during year 1 was 220 000 units (rather than 275 000), no volume variance adjustment was needed in year 1. Therefore, beginning inventory was valued at an absorption cost of $47.50 per unit. Under the FIFO cost flow assumption, the beginning inventory was the first units sold and all the units added to inventory are valued at $45.50 per unit.

Units added to inventory (30 000 units × $45.50 per unit)	$1 365 000
Ending inventory	$1 365 000

Because inventory increased during year 2, cost of goods sold under FIFO is calculated taking into consideration that the first units sold were the opening balance of 5000 units and the remaining sales of 245 000 were from the current period's production:

Cost of goods sold	
5000 units × $47.50 per unit	$ 237 500
245 000 units × $45.50 per unit	11 147 500
	$11 385 000

Figure 9.7 shows the two income statements.

FIGURE 9.7	Absorption and variable costing income statements for Grilling Machines

Absorption costing Income statement		Variable costing Income statement	
Revenue ($60 × 250 000)	$ 15 000 000	Revenue ($60 × 250 000)	$15 000 000
Cost of goods sold	(11 385 000)	Variable costs:	
Gross margin	3 615 000	Cost of goods sold	(9 375 000)
Selling and administrative	(2 000 000)	Selling and administrative	(625 000)
Operating income	$ 1 615 000	Contribution margin	5 000 000
		Fixed costs:	
		Fixed manufacturing overhead	(2 200 000)
		Fixed selling and administrative	(1 375 000)
		Operating income	$ 1 425 000
Reconciliation of product costs		**Reconciliation of product costs**	
Beginning inventory	$ 237 500	Beginning inventory	$ 187 500
Product costs incurred:		Product costs incurred:	
Direct materials	4 125 000	Direct materials	4 125 000
Direct labour	2 750 000	Direct labour	2 750 000
Variable overhead	3 437 500	Variable overhead	3 437 500
Fixed overhead allocated	2 750 000	Goods available for sale	10 500 000
Volume variance adjustment	(550 000)	Less ending inventory	(1 125 000)
Goods available for sale	12 750 000	Cost of goods sold	$ 9 375 000
Less ending inventory	(1 365 000)		
Cost of goods sold	$11 385 000		

To prepare the reconciliation of total product costs in figure 9.7, calculate the total amounts for each of the variable manufacturing costs based on actual manufacturing of 275 000 units:

Direct materials (275 000 units produced × $15 per unit)	$ 4 125 000
Direct labour (275 000 units produced × $10 per unit)	$ 2 750 000
Variable overhead (275 000 units produced × $12.50 per unit)	3 437 500
Total variable manufacturing costs	$10 312 500

This reconciliation of product costs provides a double-check on the accuracy of the cost of goods sold and inventory calculations.

Fixed and variable selling and administrative costs are combined on the absorption costing income statement:

Fixed selling and administrative	$1 375 000
Variable selling and administrative (250 000 units sold × $2.50)	625 000
Total selling and administrative	$2 000 000

Calculations for the variable costing income statement

The calculations for the variable costing income statement are similar to those for the absorption costing income statement, except fixed overhead is not allocated as a product cost. Therefore, the variable manufacturing cost per unit used in calculating cost of goods sold and inventory is:

Direct materials	$15.00
Direct labour	10.00
Variable overhead	12.50
Total variable cost per unit	$37.50

Because last year's variable cost per unit is the same as this year's, the units in beginning inventory and the units added to inventory are each valued at $37.50 per unit:

Beginning inventory (5000 units × $37.50 per unit)	$ 187 500
Units added to inventory (25 000 units × $37.50 per unit)	937 500
Ending inventory	$1 125 000

Cost of goods sold is also valued at $37.50 per unit:

Cost of goods sold (250 000 units × $37.50 per unit)	$9 375 000

The reconciliation of product costs shown in figure 9.7 provides a double-check on the accuracy of the cost of goods sold and inventory calculations.

When preparing the income statement, variable selling and administrative costs are separated from fixed selling and administrative costs.

(b) Reconciliation of absorption costing and variable costing income:

Variable costing income	$1 425 000
Increase in fixed overhead costs in absorption inventory[a]	$ 190 000
Absorption costing income	$1 615 000

[a]Units added to inventory × Fixed overhead cost per unit.

[30 000 units × ($10 per unit – $2 per unit)]	$240 000
Less 5000 units × $10	(50 000)
Increase in fixed overhead expenses	$190 000

Under absorption costing, $200 000 of this year's fixed overhead cost is held as ending inventory. Therefore, absorption costing income is $200 000 higher than variable costing income.

The difference in income also could have been calculated using the difference between costing methods in the change in inventory during the year.

Change in absorption costing inventory:

Ending inventory	$1 365 000	
Beginning inventory	237 500	
Change		$1 127 500
Change in variable costing inventory:		
Ending inventory	$1 125 000	
Beginning inventory	187 500	
Change		937 500
Difference between methods		$ 190 000

(c) Using actual fixed overhead costs and actual manufacturing, the fixed overhead allocation rate would have been:

$$\$2\,200\,000 \div 275\,000 \text{ units produced} = \$8 \text{ per unit}$$

This rate is equal to the net amount allocated in part (a) under the normal costing method:

Estimated fixed overhead allocation rate	$10
Volume variance adjustment per unit	(2)
Net fixed overhead allocation	$ 8

This calculation demonstrates that it does not matter which volume measure is used to allocate fixed overhead during the year. Under absorption costing, any material volume variance is adjusted to all units produced, so that actual fixed overhead cost is reflected on the financial statements.

(d) When the volume variance is not material, accountants simplify the adjustment by allocating the entire amount to cost of goods sold. This simplification eliminates the need to revalue units in inventory. Although revaluing the inventory was not difficult for this self-study problem, the computations and accounting entries can become cumbersome when an entity has many products. By definition, an immaterial volume variance would not affect the decisions of people who rely on the financial statements. Therefore, it does not matter how the volume variance is adjusted. It is simpler to allocate the entire amount to cost of goods sold.

QUESTIONS

9.1 Explain the similarities and differences among absorption and variable costing. **LO1**

9.2 Explain how variable costing income statements can be reconciled to absorption costing income statements. **LO3**

9.3 Explain how income could fall even though the unit sales level rises. **LO3**

9.4 The volume of manufacturing in a period has an effect on income calculated using absorption costing but has no effect on income calculated using variable costing. Explain. **LO2, 3**

9.5 The basic issue in variable and absorption costing could be said to be one of timing rather than amount. Explain. **LO1**

9.6 What is the difference between a cost that is variable and variable costing? **LO1**

9.7 Explain how the breakeven point would be affected under both absorption and variable costing. **LO2, 3**

9.8 If inventory physically increases during the period, income under absorption costing will be higher than income using variable costing. Explain. **LO3**

9.9 Why do the accounting standards require absorption costing for financial reporting? **LO1**

9.10 An entity uses variable costing for internal reports. It must convert the variable costing results to absorption costing results for external reports. How can this conversion be accomplished? **LO1**

9.11 How can the use of absorption costing lead managers to make dysfunctional decisions for the entity? **LO3**

EXERCISES

9.12 Absorption and variable income

Famous Desk Company manufactures desks for office use. The variable cost of 100 units in beginning inventory is $80 each. The absorption cost is $146.67 per unit. Following is information about this period's manufacturing.

Selling price	$ 300 per desk
Variable manufacturing cost	$ 80 per desk
Fixed manufacturing costs	$10 000 per month
Variable selling and administrative	$ 30 per desk
Fixed selling and administrative	$ 6 000 per month

Required

(a) Estimate operating income for a month in which 200 desks are manufactured and 220 are sold if the company uses variable costing.

(b) Estimate operating income for a month in which 200 desks are manufactured and 220 are sold if the entity uses absorption costing and allocates fixed manufacturing costs to inventory using a rate based on normal capacity of 150 desks per month.

9.13 Absorption and variable income; reconcile incomes

Rock Crusher Ltd produces two grades of sand (A100 and A300) used in the manufacture of industrial abrasives. The results of operations last year were as follows:

	A100	A300	Total
Manufacturing	4 000 tonnes	6 000 tonnes	10 000 tonnes
Sales	3 000 tonnes	4 000 tonnes	7 000 tonnes
Revenue	$90 000	$150 000	$240 000
Variable manufacturing costs	$20 000	$15 000	$35 000
Variable selling costs	$15 000	$20 000	$35 000

Fixed manufacturing costs were $100 000 and fixed selling and administrative costs were $60 000. The entity held no beginning inventories.

Required

Prepare a spreadsheet that can be used to answer all of the following questions.

(a) If Rock Crusher uses a variable costing system, what was the operating income?

(b) If Rock Crusher uses absorption costing and allocates actual fixed manufacturing costs to inventory on the basis of actual tonnes produced, what was the operating income?

(c) Reconcile and explain the difference between your answers to parts (a) and (b).

9.14 Absorption and variable inventory and income

Plains Irrigation uses absorption costing for its external reports and variable costing for its internal reports. Data concerning inventories appear here:

Valuation basis	September	October	November
Absorption cost	$1346	$2598	$2136
Variable cost	$ 854	$1647	$1329

Required

(a) Why is the value of inventory for Plains Irrigation higher when absorption costing is used than when variable costing is used? Is this result always the case? Why?

(b) What is the relationship between absorption costing and variable costing operating income in October? (State which valuation basis will yield the higher operating income and by how much the two operating incomes will differ.)

9.15 Absorption and variable inventory and income

Asian Iron began last year with no inventories. During the year, 10 500 units were produced of which 9400 were sold. Data concerning last year's operations appear here.

Revenue	$32 900
Variable direct materials costs	2 300
Variable direct labour costs	3 300
Variable manufacturing overhead	2 800
Variable selling	940
Fixed manufacturing overhead	8 250
Fixed selling and administrative costs	14 560

Variable manufacturing costs reflect the variable cost to produce the number of units manufactured. However, variable selling costs are not incurred until the units are sold, so they reflect the cost for the number of units sold. Asian Iron allocates actual manufacturing overhead costs to inventory based on actual units produced.

Required

(a) Calculate the value of ending inventory on the balance sheet under the following methods:
  (i) variable costing
  (ii) absorption costing.

(b) Calculate operating income under each of the following methods:
  (i) variable costing
  (ii) absorption costing.

(c) Estimate the variable costing operating income if 12 110 units were produced and sold in a year.

9.16 Absorption and variable inventory and income; reconcile incomes **LO1, 3**

Wild Bird Feeders produces deluxe bird feeders for distribution to catalogue companies and wild bird stores. The entity uses an absorption costing system for internal reporting purposes but is considering using variable costing. Data regarding Wild Bird's planned and actual operations for last year are presented here.

Beginning finished goods inventory in units		30 000
	Planned activity	**Actual activity**
Sales in units	140 000	125 000
Manufacturing in units	140 000	130 000

The planned per-unit cost figures shown in the schedule were based on the manufacturing and sale of 140 000 units last year. Wild Bird uses an estimated manufacturing overhead rate for allocating manufacturing overhead to its product. Thus, a combined manufacturing overhead rate of $9 per unit was employed for absorption costing purposes last year. Any overapplied or underapplied manufacturing overhead is closed to cost of goods sold at the end of the year.

	Planned costs		**Incurred costs**
	Per unit	**Total**	
Direct materials	$24	$ 3 360 000	$ 3 120 000
Direct labour	18	2 520 000	2 340 000
Variable manufacturing overhead	4	560 000	520 000
Fixed manufacturing overhead	$ 5	$ 700 000	$ 710 000
Variable selling expenses	14	1 960 000	1 750 000
Fixed selling expenses	7	980 000	980 000
Variable administrative expenses	1	140 000	125 000
Fixed administrative expenses	6	840 000	850 000
Total	$79	$11 060 000	$10 395 000

Last year's beginning finished goods inventory for absorption costing purposes was valued at the previous year's planned unit manufacturing cost, which was the same as last year's planned unit manufacturing cost. No work in process inventories was recorded either at the beginning or end of the year. The planned and actual unit selling price was $99 per unit for last year. You may want to use a spreadsheet to perform calculations.

Required

(a) What was the value of Wild Bird's actual ending finished goods inventory on the absorption costing basis?

(b) What last year's actual ending finished goods inventory on the variable costing basis?

(c) What were the manufacturing contribution margin and the total contribution margin under variable costing for Wild Bird's actual results for last year?

(d) Under absorption costing, what were the total fixed costs on the income statement?

   (i) What were the fixed selling and administrative costs?

   (ii) What was the amount of overhead allocated to COGS at standard cost?

   (iii) Do we need to consider sales of units from last period?

   (iv) What was the amount of underapplied or overapplied overhead closed to COGS?

   (v) Sum these amounts for the total fixed costs.

(e) What was the total variable cost expensed last year on the variable costing income statement?

(f) Was absorption costing income higher or lower than variable costing income for the year? Why?

(g) What is the amount of difference in income using absorption costing versus variable costing? How did it arise?

9.17 Absorption and variable income; reconcile incomes **LO1, 3**

The following price and operating cost information applies to Happy Bikers Motorcycle Company.

Price	$10 000	per motorcycle
Variable manufacturing costs:		
Raw materials	$ 2 000	per motorcycle
Direct labour and variable overhead	$ 1 000	per motorcycle
Fixed manufacturing costs	$40 000	per month
Variable selling and administrative	$ 250	per motorcycle
Fixed selling and administrative	$40 000	per month

No beginning balance in finished goods is evident because the beginning inventory account on the balance sheet is zero. Average manufacturing is 10 motorcycles per month. Sales are seasonal, so in some months no motorcycles are produced while in other months manufacturing is high.

During the most recent month, the entity produced 18 motorcycles and sold 15.

Required

(a) Prepare an income statement for the most recent month using the variable costing method.

(b) Prepare an income statement for the most recent month using the absorption costing method and choose a denominator level that represents 'normal' capacity.

(c) Prepare a schedule that reconciles the incomes among the two income statements.

PROBLEMS

9.18 Differences in income; choice of absorption and variable costing **LO1, 3**

King Island Lobster Company is a privately held company that buys lobsters from local fishermen and then delivers them to restaurants in several of Australia's larger cities. The owners use variable costing income statements but one owner's daughter, who just started taking university accounting classes, suggested that absorption income statements meet the requirements of the accounting standards and so should be used.

Required

(a) Explain the difference between absorption and variable income statements.

(b) Provide possible reasons why the company uses variable costing income statements.

(c) Provide possible benefits to the company from using an absorption costing income statement.

(d) What type of statement would you recommend for King Island Lobster Company? Why?

(e) What additional information about King Island Lobster Company would you like to have to improve your recommendation in part (d)?

9.19 Absorption and variable income; normal capacity; choice of denominator **LO1, 3**

Giant Jets is a French company that produces jet aeroplanes for commercial cargo companies. The selling price per jet is €1 000 000. Currently the company uses actual volumes to allocate fixed manufacturing overhead to units. However, Giant Jets' accountant is considering the use of standard costs to produce the absorption income statements. The company anticipates the following.

Variable costs per jet:			
Direct materials			€200 000
Direct labour			150 000
Variable manufacturing overhead			50 000
Variable selling			100 000
Fixed costs per month:			
Fixed manufacturing overhead			€600 000
Fixed administrative and selling			100 000
Sales and manufacturing quantities:			

	Year 1	Year 2	Year 3
Manufacturing	10	6	8
Sales	10	4	10

Required

(a) Prepare income statements using the variable costing method.

(b) Prepare income statements using the absorption costing method. Allocate fixed overhead using actual units produced in the denominator.

(c) In your own words, define 'normal capacity'.

(d) Prepare an income statement using the absorption cost method and choose a denominator level that represents normal capacity. Explain your choice for normal capacity.

(e) Prepare a brief summary that reconciles the incomes among the two income statements for each year.

9.20 Absorption and variable income and inventory; method for manager bonus **LO1, 3**

Fighting Kites produces several different kite kits. Last year, it produced 20 000 kits and sold all but 2000 kits. The kits sell for $30 each. Costs incurred are listed here.

Materials purchased	$ 50 000
Materials used	40 000
Other variable manufacturing costs	60 000
Fixed manufacturing costs	100 000
Variable selling costs	18 000
Fixed selling and administrative costs	100 000

Beginning inventory last year held 2000 kits. Assume that under variable costing, the value of this inventory would have been $10 000. Assume that under absorption costing, the value of this inventory would have been $15 000.

Required

(a) If Fighting Kites uses variable costing, what was its operating income? What was the ending balance in finished goods inventory?

(b) If Fighting Kites uses absorption costing and a denominator level of 25 000, what was its operating income?

(c) If you were asked to make a recommendation for the absorption costing denominator level for next period's operations, what would you suggest? Explain your choice.

(d) If the manager of Fighting Kites is given a bonus based on income, which type of income statement would you recommend to evaluate manager performance? Explain your choice.

9.21 Absorption and variable income and uses; reconcile incomes **LO1, 3**

Security Vehicles converts Hummers into luxury, high-security vehicles by adding a computerised alarm and radar system and various luxury components. The finished vehicles are sold for $100 000 each. Variable manufacturing costs (including the cost of the basic Hummer) are about $60 000 per vehicle. Fixed manufacturing costs are $60 000 per month. The fixed costs for administrative and selling expenses are $20 000 per month plus $5000 per vehicle sold.

At the beginning of last year, Security had no inventories of finished vehicles. In January it produced four vehicles and sold three. In February it produced five and sold six.

Required

(a) What is the operating income for January if Security uses a variable costing system?

(b) What is the operating income for January if Security uses an absorption costing system?

(c) Reconcile the difference between the absorption and variable costing operating incomes in February.

(d) Explain why Security Vehicles might produce both variable and absorption income statements for the same time period.

9.22 Over/underapplied overhead; units versus machine hours as allocation base **LO1, 3**

Northcoast Manufacturing Company, a small manufacturer of parts used in appliances, just completed its first year of operations. The company's controller, Vic Trainor, has been reviewing the actual results for the year and is concerned about the allocation of manufacturing overhead. Trainor uses the following information to assess operations.

- Northcoast's equipment consists of several machines with a combined cost of $2 200 000 and no residual value. Each machine has an output of five units of product per hour and a useful life of 20 000 hours.
- Selected actual data of Northcoast's operations for the year just ended are presented here.

Product manufactured	500 000 units
Machine utilisation	130 000 hours
Direct labour usage	35 000 hours
Labour rate	$15 per hour
Total manufacturing overhead	$1 130 000
Cost of goods sold	$1 720 000
Finished goods inventory (at year-end)	$430 240
Work in process inventory (at year-end)	$0

- Total manufacturing overhead is allocated to each unit using an estimated plant-wide rate.
- The budgeted activity for the year included 20 employees, each working 1800 productive hours per year to produce 540 000 units of product. The machines are highly automated, and each employee can operate two to four machines simultaneously. Normal activity is for each employee to operate three machines. Machine operators are paid $15 per hour.
- Budgeted manufacturing overhead costs for the past year for various levels of activity are shown here.

Units of product	360 000	540 000	720 000
Labour hours	30 000	36 000	42 000
Machine hours	72 000	108 000	144 000
Manufacturing overhead costs:			
Plant supervision	$ 70 000	$ 70 000	$ 70 000
Plant rent	40 000	40 000	40 000
Equipment depreciation	288 000	432 000	576 000
Maintenance	42 000	51 000	60 000
Utilities	144 600	216 600	288 600
Indirect material	90 000	135 000	180 000
Other costs	11 200	16 600	22 000
Total	$685 800	$961 200	$1 236 600

You may want to use a spreadsheet to perform calculations.

Required

(a) Choose the budgeted level of activity (in units) closest to actual activity for the period and determine the dollar amount of total over/underapplied manufacturing overhead. Explain why this amount is material.

(b) Vic Trainor believes that Northcoast Manufacturing Company should be using machine hours to allocate manufacturing overhead. Using the data given, determine the amount of total over/underapplied manufacturing overhead if machine hours had been used as the allocation base.

(c) Explain why machine hours might be a more appropriate allocation base than number of units.

(d) Explain why using units as denominator volume might cause managers to build up inventories under absorption costing in periods when sales were slumping.

9.23 Recommend income format LO1, 3

Your brother started a small business, GameZ, that produces a software game he developed. It is his first year in business, and he kept detailed records. However, his business records consist primarily of entries in his chequebook plus information using a simple method of adding and subtracting cash on a spreadsheet.

Your brother has asked your advice about the kind of financial statements that would be helpful to his business. He would like you to prepare information for two different uses. First, he needs a small bank loan to provide cash during the low season in August. Most of his sales are made in December. He has a steady, low volume of sales for most of the rest of the year. He wants to approach his bank about a line of credit upon which he could draw in August and then pay off in January. In addition, he would like to be able to analyse information from his operations to make decisions about whether to develop a new game, what price to set and how much he could devote to advertising. He also recently hired an assistant to whom he assigned a great deal of responsibility for general operations. He would like to be able to monitor and reward her performance in some way.

Required

Write a memo to your brother in response to his request. Include the following aspects in your memo.

(a) Outline his possible choices for income statement formats.

(b) List the advantages and disadvantages of each format.

(c) Recommend and explain which type of statement should be used for each of his desired purposes.

9.24 Bonuses and manufacturing decisions; profit variances; income statement format   **LO1, 2**

Palm Producers is expecting sales growth, and so it built nearly-identical automated plants in Sandy Beach, Queensland, and in Singapore to produce its new Palm Powerhouse.

Each plant manager is responsible for producing adequate inventories to meet sales orders and for maintaining quality while producing the Palm Powerhouse at the lowest possible cost. Under Palm Producer's decentralised organisation, each plant maintains its own accounting records. Quarterly reports are filed with the corporate controller's office and are then reviewed by corporate management. The following reports were filed for the third and fourth quarter by the two plants.

Sandy Beach plant Income statement for third and fourth quarters (in thousands of dollars)		
	Third quarter	**Fourth quarter**
Revenue	$97 452	$110 951
Cost of goods sold	77 165	74 613
Selling and administration expenses	12 378	12 632
Interest expense	4 312	4 251
Tax expense	1 259	6 809
Net income	$ 2 338	$ 12 646

Sandy Beach plant Statement of financial position for third and fourth quarters (in thousands of dollars)		
	Third quarter	**Fourth quarter**
Assets		
Cash	$ 2346	$ 322
Inventory	12872	30972
Plant (net of depreciation)	152456	148635
Total assets	$167674	$179929
Liabilities and owners' equity (OE)		
Accounts payable	$ 214	$ 1782
Construction bond payable	140385	138426
Owners' equity	27075	39721
Total liabilities & OE	$167674	$179929

Singapore plant		
Income statement for third and fourth quarters		
(converted to A$, in thousands of dollars)		
	Third quarter	Fourth quarter
Revenue	$101 832	$111 085
Cost of goods sold	82 127	87 990
Selling and administration expenses	10 943	10 453
Interest expense	3 854	3 733
Tax expense	1 718	3 118
Net income	$ 3 190	$ 5 791

Singapore plant		
Statement of financial position for third and fourth quarters		
(translated to A$, in thousands of dollars)		
	Third quarter	Fourth quarter
Assets		
Cash	$ 1 564	$ 3 642
Inventory	11 324	13 832
Plant (net of depreciation)	142 342	138 580
Total assets	$155 230	$156 054
Liabilities and owners' equity (OE)		
Accounts payable	$ 347	$ 221
Bond payable	135 762	130 921
Owners' equity	19 121	24 912
Total liabilities & OE	$155 230	$156 054

Required

(a) Suppose each plant manager receives a bonus based on absorption costing operating income that is 5 per cent of operating income. Calculate the bonus for each manager. Explain how this bonus plan might affect the managers' manufacturing decisions.

(b) Examine changes in sales relative to cost of goods sold between the two quarters. What are two possible explanations for Sandy Beach plant's profit increase during the fourth quarter?

(c) Assume that variable costs in this industry are an immaterial part of cost of goods sold. Recast the financial statements using the variable costing approach.

(d) What would you conclude about the relative performances of the two plant managers in the fourth quarter?

(e) Suppose you are the cost accountant for Palm Producers. Write a memo to the CFO recommending the type of income statement that would be best for monitoring divisional performance. Attach to the memo a schedule showing any calculations that might be useful to the CFO. As appropriate, refer to the schedule in the memo.

ACKNOWLEDGEMENTS

Photo 9A: © Roman Samborskyi / Shutterstock.com
Photo 9B: © Alvov / Shutterstock.com
Photo 9C: © Mindscape studio / Shutterstock.com

CHAPTER 10

Flexible budgets, standard costs and variance analysis

LEARNING OBJECTIVES

After studying this chapter, you should be able to:

10.1 understand flexible budgets and the use of sensitivity analysis

10.2 explain how standard costs are established

10.3 communicate how variance information is analysed and used

10.4 apply the principles of flexible budgeting.

IN BRIEF

Budgets provide the roadmap for organisational activities in the coming year. However, when developing and using budgets managers must consider the business risks that might cause organisational performance to deviate from plan. Such deviations will require adjustments to the original profit plan. Management can 'flex the budget' to avoid potential biases that could result due to poor forecasts when the budget was originally developed. Flexing the budget involves recasting the budget to represent actual activity levels. In this way, 'like with like' is considered when assessing actual performance against expectations. For organisations that undertake repetitive processes, the development of standard costs enables a more detailed analysis of variances from budget and allows the budget to be flexed, thereby giving managers improved information for performance assessment when actual volume is different to budgeted volume. Variances are calculated by comparing standard revenues and costs with actual revenues and costs at the actual level of activity. Flexible budgeting allows the volume variance to be isolated so that only price/efficiency variances are used for performance assessment.

10.1 Flexible budgets

LEARNING OBJECTIVE 10.1 Understand flexible budgets and the use of sensitivity analysis.

When managers create operating plans for the upcoming period, they prepare a budget for revenues and costs. In chapter 6, the focus was on the development of the master budget. The master budget is also referred to as a static budget, as it is based on forecasts of *specific volumes* of production or services, together with expectations about employee productivity and other factors that affect revenues and costs. The information in a static budget is therefore biased when compared to actual results for a *different volume* of operations. To overcome differences between budgeted volume and actual volume, managers make use of flexible budget techniques to monitor actual operations and to determine whether operating targets are met. **A flexible budget** is a set of cost relationships that can be used to estimate costs and cash flows for any level of operations within the relevant range. A flexible budget uses the variable cost information from the master budget, but adjusts sales information and variable costs to reflect actual volumes. Because fixed costs are not expected to change, these values are carried over from the static budget.

Flexible budget techniques are also useful in the original planning phase to examine different iterations of the budget before the static budget is locked in. By studying differences between the flexible budget and actual results, managers are able to identify ways to improve future operations and to establish more realistic future budgets. Managers and accountants can easily perform **sensitivity analysis** to estimate the effects of deviations from budget assumptions. Although the master budget may be useful for the initial planning and coordinating activities, it is not useful as a benchmark if activity levels change. Flexing the budget allows the firm to incorporate changed operating conditions to provide a more relevant benchmark to assess actual performance.

10.2 Standard costs

LEARNING OBJECTIVE 10.2 Explain how standard costs are established.

To improve the ability of managers to plan operations and monitor performance, organisations often establish a set of standards for expected costs. A **standard cost** is the cost managers expect to incur to produce goods or services under operating plan assumptions. Key assumptions include:
- volume of production activity
- production processes and efficiency
- prices and quality of inputs.

The use of standard costs is best suited to an entity that has repetitive activities and/or output as it is possible in such an operating environment to establish the expected inputs (standard usage of resources) and costs (standard costs of resources).

As shown in figure 10.1, the total standard cost for a unit of output is the sum of standard costs for the resources used in production. Typical resources include direct materials, direct labour, fixed overhead and variable overhead with standards being established for the cost of each resource. Suppose that Benny's, a wholesale gourmet ice cream manufacturer, uses a standard cost system. Frozen blackberries are one of the direct materials used in Benny's Purple Madness ice cream. The entity's managers determine that one kilogram of frozen blackberries should be included in each bucket of ice cream. They forecast that frozen blackberries this year will cost $1 per kilogram. We can describe the standard cost of frozen blackberries for every bucket of ice cream as $1 per bucket (1 kilogram of blackberries × $1 per kilogram).

Developing standard costs

Standards are set to identify variances and enable the budget variance to be broken down into price and efficiency components. When developing the standard cost, two different types of standards can be used.
1. *Ideal standard* — this standard assumes perfect operating conditions that achieve maximum efficiency. Such standards are forward looking and not historically based. When setting the ideal standard, no allowances are made for process errors or other variations. This can be an unrealistic assumption, as unexpected events (either favourable or unfavourable) can occur. Ideal standards can either motivate employees by encouraging high levels of performance or demotivate employees by setting difficult or even impossible targets. It is important for organisations to be aware of the effect of ideal standards on employees when devising performance evaluation and reward structures. For example, how would you react if you were told you could only pass your management accounting unit by achieving 100/100 on overall assessment.

2. *Currently attainable standard* — this standard assumes 'normal' operating conditions that allow employees to meet the targets set without requiring a 'superhuman' effort. This standard assumes less than 100 per cent efficiency in the process. The standard makes allowances for poor quality inputs, equipment malfunctions and differences in employee skills and experience, all of which may affect the performance outcome.

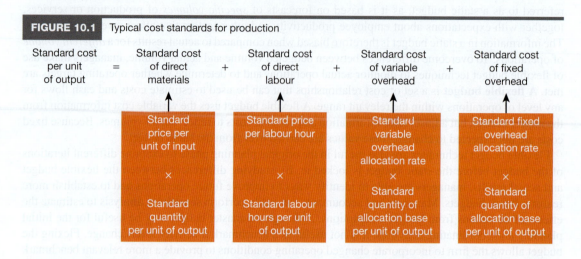

FIGURE 10.1 Typical cost standards for production

The standard an entity should select is the one that will best allow the entity to meet the objectives set for the coming period. In a very competitive environment, an ideal standard may motivate employees to perform at higher levels. As the currently attainable standard has built-in inefficiencies, employees may not be challenged to do better. However, this problem can be overcome by taking a continuous improvement approach by periodically updating standards and introducing stretch targets (say increasing performance by 10 per cent each period) to motivate improved performance.

There are no 'rules' for developing standard costs. Sometimes managers simply use the most recent year's data, while at other times they evaluate and incorporate historical trends. To set a standard for the next period, they update historical data for expected changes in costs or processes. For new products, standards are often set with the assistance of industrial engineers, who estimate quantities and costs for direct materials, direct labour and production overhead. Managers might also seek the periodic assistance of industrial engineers to find ways to improve efficiency, modify output quality or identify cost reduction opportunities for existing products. Production plans include expected efficiency and quality, which means that the normal cost of waste and defects is included in standard costs.

Standard costs are reviewed periodically. Depending on organisational strategy, cost reduction goals may be incorporated into the standards, or quality improvements might require that standards be changed. Standards should serve as achievable targets. Working with current suppliers or investigating alternative suppliers for lower prices could lead to reduced direct materials price standards. As technology improves the productivity of robotic and labour processes, efficiency standards will also change.

Managers use standard costs not only to help plan future costs, but also to monitor and motivate employee performance. To encourage employees to achieve planned productivity, standards are often set at a level that is attainable but without much slack. Sometimes tightening standards can promote productivity improvements. As such, managers should be aware of the behavioural impact of the standards selected when assessing performance.

10.3 Variance analysis

LEARNING OBJECTIVE 10.3 Communicate how variance information is analysed and used.

Variances are calculated for two purposes: bookkeeping and monitoring. Variances calculated for bookkeeping purposes (explored more in chapter 11) do not need to be analysed, but variances used to monitor performance do need to be analysed. **Variance analysis** is the process of calculating variances and then investigating the reasons they occurred. This information is then used to improve future operating plans, as shown in figure 10.2.

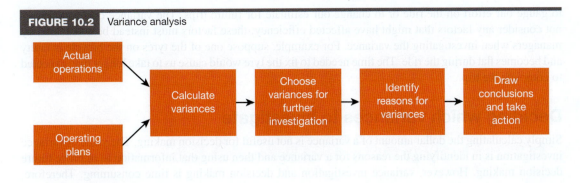

FIGURE 10.2 Variance analysis

A budget variance is a difference between budgeted and actual results.

- A variance is *unfavourable* if actual costs exceeded budgeted costs or if actual revenues fell short of budgeted revenues.
- A variance is *favourable* if actual costs were less than budgeted costs or actual revenues exceeded budgeted revenues.

The budgeted information could be from a static budget, a flexible budget or a budget that has been adjusted to create a better benchmark for performance. Similarly, a **standard cost variance** is a difference between a standard cost and an actual cost. Variance analysis can be used whether or not an organisation uses a standard costing system. The process requires only the ability to compare actual results with some type of benchmark, which might be standard costs, budgeted costs or some other measure of expectations. When entities have a standard cost system in place, the standard costs are used in budgeting to develop flexible budgets. The standard cost variance can be further broken down for analysis into a price variance (which analyses the cost of inputs) and an efficiency variance (which analyses the use of resources).

The different types of variances calculated are:

- static budget compared to actual results = budget variance
- static budget compared to flexible budget = volume variance
- flexible budget compared to actual results = price/efficiency variance

It follows that volume variance + price/efficiency variance = budget variance.

Price variances

A **price variance** is the difference between standard and actual prices paid for resources purchased and used in the production of goods or services. We informally calculate price variances frequently in our daily lives. For example, we may compare the advertised prices of groceries with a standard price (the price we usually pay), and then decide to purchase certain items. Suppose soft drink usually costs $5 for a 12-pack, but is on sale at $2.50. After comparing the sale price to the $5 standard, we may decide to purchase more than the usual amount. Our standard price for two 12-packs of soft drink would have been $10 ($5 per pack × 2 packs), and our actual cost would be $5 ($2.50 per pack × 2 packs). By taking advantage of the sale, we achieve a favourable price variance of $5 ($10 − $5).

This example illustrates several limitations of a price variance. The price variance does not take into account whether sufficient cash flows, storage space or usage requirements justify and accommodate purchasing resources in larger quantities. Perhaps our kitchen lacks sufficient space to store extra groceries if we purchase more than our weekly usage. If we purchase large quantities of perishable foods, they may spoil before they are needed. Also, the price variance does not reflect possible quality differences between resources purchased at higher or lower prices. Suppose the brand of soft drink that is on sale is not the brand we prefer. We may be willing to pay a higher price for our preferred brand. In a business entity, it might be inefficient to use lower-quality direct materials even when they are cheaper.

Efficiency variances

An **efficiency variance** provides information about how economically direct resources such as materials and labour were used. We informally assess our own efficiency frequently in our daily lives. For example, when we plan a bicycle ride on the weekend, we may believe that it will take two hours to ride 30 kilometres. Once we finish the ride, we compare the actual length of time to our estimate. We might use this information to gauge our effort on the ride or to change our estimate for future trips. The variance calculation does not consider any factors that might have affected efficiency; these factors must instead be considered by managers when investigating the variance. For example, suppose one of the tyres on the bicycle is faulty and becomes flat during the ride. The time needed to fix the tyre would cause us to take longer than expected to complete the trip.

Deciding which variances to investigate

Simply calculating the dollar amount of a variance is not useful for decision making. The value of variance investigation is in identifying the reasons for a variance and then using that information to improve future decision making. However, variance investigation and decision making is time consuming. Therefore, managers perform detailed investigation only for variances they consider important. This process is commonly referred to as management by exception.

Importance is decided in two ways. First, the variances that will be calculated and monitored need to be chosen. Managers may decide that a variance is important only if it is larger than a given dollar amount or a given percentage of the budget. Other factors also justify variance investigation. When variance trends are increasing, managers may want to know what causes the trend so that it can be eliminated if possible.

Suppose an unfavourable variance of $3000 occurred last year in the cost of Benny's Purple Madness ice cream — actual cost exceeded standard cost by $3000. Was it caused by an unanticipated increase in the cost of direct materials? Was labour less efficient than expected? If so, did an equipment failure create unexpected employee downtime? Was employee turnover higher than usual, reducing average worker productivity? Did total production levels decline, causing actual fixed overhead cost per unit to be higher than expected? Managers must evaluate these types of questions before deciding what actions to take, if any. Accountants assist in this process, acting as detectives who discover the reasons for cost variances.

Analysing interactions between incentives and variances

Some entities reward employees for meeting or exceeding benchmarks set as standard costs. However, such rewards create a new set of problems. Suppose employees in the cutting department of a clothing manufacturer are rewarded based on how quickly they cut fabric. The cut fabric is then transferred to the sewing department. If employees in the cutting department become less precise as they increase output, the sewing department could face a decrease in efficiency. That decrease could ripple through the rest of the production process. Or, the sewing department might pass along the quality problem into finished goods, contributing further to a long-term quality problem for the entity. If the sewing department is also rewarded based on meeting efficiency standards, employees in that department would be penalised for fixing a problem created by the cutting department. Only when variances are analysed can managers identify whether the incentives are working as expected to promote overall organisational success. Figure 10.3 provides a summary of the general conclusions about variances and related management actions. In the next section we will explore the use of standards in developing a flexible budget to enable the calculation of variances for performance assessment.

FIGURE 10.3	General conclusions about variances and management actions
General conclusion about variance	**General management action**
Operations are out of control.	Take action to correct operations.
Operations are better than expected.	Monitor quality to ensure it is maintained.
Operations are better than expected and quality is maintained.	Modify future operating plans to take advantage of gains.
Benchmark is inappropriate.	Revise benchmark to improve the accuracy of future plans.
Error made is in accounting records.	Take action to correct accounting system.
Variance is random or is not expected to recur.	Do nothing.

10.4 Flexible budgeting in practice

LEARNING OBJECTIVE 10.4 Apply the principles of flexible budgeting.

Benny's is preparing its budget for the coming year. One of Benny's most popular products is Purple Madness ice cream. To assist with the budget for this product, representatives from the production, purchasing and personnel departments of Benny's met to establish the standard cost of the ice cream. After assessing the production process and examining supplier and employee contracts they have identified the following standard inputs and standard costs for the production of one bucket of Purple Madness ice cream.

Production cost/input	Standard cost/input per bucket of Purple Madness ice cream
Direct material — blackberries	1 kilogram per bucket of ice cream
Direct material — blackberries	$1 per kilogram
Direct material — other ingredients	0.5 kilograms per bucket of ice cream
Direct material — other ingredients	$1.50 per kilogram
Direct labour hours — packing	0.1 hour per bucket
Direct labour hours — processing	0.2 hour per bucket
Direct labour cost	$8 per hour
Variable overhead	$2 per direct labour hour
Fixed overhead	$0.40 cents per bucket*

*Based on estimated total annual fixed overhead of $201 600 and estimated output of 504 000 buckets for the year (42 000 buckets per month).

Based on the analysis above, the total standard production cost of one bucket of Purple Madness ice cream is $5.15 per bucket. The calculation of the standard inputs and standard cost per input will allow the management of Benny's to evaluate actual performance as the standards will provide a benchmark against which actual inputs and costs can be compared.

Standard cost of one bucket of Purple Madness ice cream	
Direct material — blackberries (1 kilogram × $1 per kilogram)	$1.00
Other direct material — other ingredients (0.5 kilograms × $1.50)	$0.75
Direct labour — packing (0.1 hour per bucket × $8 per hour)	$0.80
Direct labour — processing (0.2 hour per bucket × $8 per hour)	$1.60
Variable overhead (0.3 × $2.00 per hour)	$0.60
Fixed overhead	$0.40
Total standard cost	$5.15 per bucket

The development of the standard cost allows Benny's accounting staff to prepare the static budget. This budget communicates Benny's performance expectations for the coming year to employees. The static budget highlights that management have budgeted for a sales target of 504 000 ice cream buckets for the year, with the expectation of generating a gross profit of $932 400.

	Static budget
Ice cream buckets	504 000
Revenue	**$3 528 000**
Less cost of sales	
Direct material — blackberries	$ 504 000
Direct material — other ingredients	$ 378 000
Direct labour — packing	$ 403 200
Direct labour — processing	806 400
Variable overhead	$ 302 400
Fixed overhead	$ 201 600
Total production costs	**$2 595 600**
Gross profit	**$ 932 400**

As mentioned earlier, the 'flexing' of the budget is achieved due to the variable costs associated with the activities. To highlight the variable costs, the static budget is shown in a contribution margin format below. This format shows that the Purple Madness ice cream is budgeted to provide a contribution margin of $1 134 000.

	Static budget
Ice cream buckets	504 000
Revenue	**$3 528 000**
Less variable production costs	
Direct material — blackberries	$ 504 000
Direct material — other ingredients	$ 378 000
Direct labour — packing	$ 403 200
Direct labour — processing	$ 806 400
Variable overhead	$ 302 400
Total variable production costs	$2 394 000
Contribution margin	**$1 134 000**
Less fixed production costs	
Fixed overhead	$ 201 600
Gross profit	**$ 932 400**

After the first month of operations, management have requested an analysis of actual performance against budget expectations in order to assess production performance. The accounting staff have collected the relevant revenue and cost data relating to the Purple Madness ice cream from the accounting system and other production records and this is detailed below.

Actual output	40 000 buckets of Purple Madness ice cream
Actual direct material price — blackberries	$1.25 per kilogram
Direct material purchased — blackberries	50 000 kilograms
Direct material used in production — blackberries	39 000 kilograms
Actual direct material price — other ingredients	$1.55 per kilogram
Direct materials purchased — other ingredients	25 000 kilograms
Direct material used in production — other ingredients	21 000 kilograms
Actual direct labour rate per hour	$9.50 per hour
Direct labour hours used — packing	3 950 hours
Direct labour hours used — processing	8 200 hours
Variable overhead	$23 500
Fixed overhead	$20 000

The information above provides details of actual costs for one month during the financial year. Benny's originally budgeted for 42 000 buckets per month (504 000 buckets for 12 months). When compared with actual volume, there is an unfavourable sales volume variance of 2000 buckets. Due to this sales volume variance, the comparison of the static budget against actual data will not provide relevant information for performance assessment as any price or efficiency variance will be affected by the volume difference. In relation to revenue, Purple Madness ice cream was budgeted to sell at $7.00 per bucket; however, the actual sales price was $6.80 per bucket, which will also contribute to an unfavourable revenue variance. An analysis of the static budget against actual results reveals an unfavourable budget variance of $45 925. This variance is *not* appropriate for performance assessment due to the volume difference impacting on the variances.

	Static budget	Actual	Variance	
Ice cream buckets	42 000	40 000	2 000	U
Revenue	**$294 000**	**$272 000**	**$22 000**	**U**
Less cost of sales				
Direct material — blackberries	$ 42 000	$ 48 750	$ 6 750	U
Direct material — other ingredients	$ 31 500	$ 32 550	$ 1 050	U
Direct labour — packing	$ 33 600	$ 37 525	$ 3 925	U
Direct labour — processing	$ 67 200	$ 77 900	$10 700	U
Variable overhead	$ 25 200	$ 23 500	$ 1 700	F
Total variable production costs	$199 500	$220 225	$20 725	U
Contribution margin	**$ 94 500**	**$ 51 775**	**$42 725**	**U**
Less fixed costs				
Fixed overhead	$ 16 800*	$ 20 000	$ 3 200	U
Profit	**$ 77 700**	**$ 31 775**	**$45 925**	**U**

*Monthly amount calculated ($201 600 / 12)
F = Favourable/U = Unfavourable

The preparation of the flexible budget eliminates the variance caused by volume differences in overall activity. The flexible budget is prepared by using actual volume and determining the expected costs for this level of activity based on the standard cost. In other words, if the accounting staff could forecast actual activity with certainty, this is the volume level that the static budget would have been based on at the beginning of the budget period. Following is the flexible budget focusing on the standard costs for the actual production of 40 000 buckets of Purple Madness ice cream for one month during the accounting period. The comparison of the flexible budget and actual results reveal a number of variances:

- an unfavourable sales revenue variance of $8000
- an unfavourable variable production cost variance of $30 225
  giving an overall unfavourable contribution margin variance of $38 225
- an unfavourable fixed production cost variance of $3200
  giving an overall unfavourable profit variance of $41 425.

The variances indicate that the costs incurred were greater than the costs expected based on the standards, and that revenue generated was less than expected based on actual volume.

	Flexible budget	Actual	Variance	
Ice cream buckets	40 000	40 000	—	
Revenue	$280 000	$272 000	$ 8 000	U
Less variable production costs			$ —	
Direct material — blackberries	$ 40 000	$ 48 750	$ 8 759	U
Direct material — other ingredients	$ 30 000	$ 32 550	$ 2 550	U
Direct labour — packing	$ 32 000	$ 37 525	$ 5 525	U
Direct labour — processing	$ 64 000	$ 77 900	$13 900	U
Variable overhead	$ 24 000	$ 23 500	$ 500	F
Total variable production costs	$190 000	$220 225	$30 225	U
Contribution margin	$ 90 000	$ 51 775	$38 225	U
Less fixed production costs			$ —	
Fixed overhead	$ 16 800*	$ 20 000	$ 3 200	U
Profit	$ 73 200	$ 31 775	$41 425	U

*Remember that regardless of the level of activity, budgeted fixed costs will not change.
F = Favourable/U = Unfavourable

By 'flexing' the budget, management are able to compare 'like with like' at the actual sales volume of 40 000 buckets. A more detailed look at the variances between the static budget, flexible budget and actual data is shown on the next page The make-up of the total variance ($45 925) is highlighted by showing that the difference between the static and flexible budget ($4500) is due to the volume difference and the variance between the flexible budget and actual results ($41 425) is due to price and efficiency of the production inputs together with the sales price achieved.

Manager conclusions and actions

Identifying the reasons for variances can be time consuming. However, by using categories in the accounting system to separate variances into component parts, the process becomes easier and the most useful information is produced. As can be seen in the above budget comparison, the unfavourable variance for Benny's Purple Madness ice cream can be separated into the following categories used in its standard costing system: direct materials, direct labour, fixed overhead and variable overhead. This type of breakdown helps managers identify the sources of variances and also highlights possible offsetting of favourable (F) and unfavourable (U) variances between components. The aggregation of favourable and unfavourable variances could hide production problems that need to be investigated. In addition, this breakdown helps managers identify variances that are sufficiently large to justify further investigation.

Once managers identify the reasons for variances, they draw conclusions about what has occurred and consider whether some type of corrective action is needed. Suppose the managers of Benny's find that the unfavourable variance was caused primarily by an unanticipated rise in the cost of ingredients. The managers would next want to know whether the cost increase was temporary or was expected to continue. If the higher cost is expected to continue, they might decide to bring costs back into control by switching to less expensive ingredients. Alternatively, they might decide that their standard cost is no longer appropriate and should be increased to reflect the new cost. If the cost increase was temporary, they might decide that no action should be taken. Sometimes a variance investigation uncovers an error in the accounting records, causing the appearance of a variance when none exists. In this case, managers might take action to correct the accounting system to avoid similar future errors.

	Static budget	Variance Volume		Flexible budget	Variance Price/efficiency		Actual	Total variance	
Ice cream buckets sold	42 000	2000		40 000	0		40 000	0	
Revenue	$294 000	–$14 000		$280 000	–$8 000		$272 000	–$22 000	U
Less variable costs									
Direct material — blackberries (kg)	$ 42 000	–$ 2 000		$ 40 000	$ 8 750		$ 48 750	$ 6 750	U
Direct material — other ingredients (kg)	$ 31 500	–$ 1 500		$ 30 000	$ 2 550		$ 32 550	$ 1 050	U
Direct labour — packing (hours)	$ 33 600	–$ 1 600		$ 32 000	$ 5 525		$ 37 525	$ 3 925	U
Direct labour — processing (hours)	$ 67 200	–$ 3 200		$ 64 000	$13 900		$ 77 900	$10 700	U
Variable overhead	$ 25 200	–$ 1 200		$ 24 000	–$ 500		$ 23 500	–$ 1 700	F
Total variable production costs	$199 500	–$ 9 500		$190 000	–$30 225		$220 225	$20 725	U
Contribution margin	$ 94 500	–$ 4 500		$ 90 000	–$38 225		$ 51 775	–$42 725	U
Less fixed costs									
Fixed overhead*	$ 16 800	$ —		$ 16 800	$ —		$ 20 000	$ 3 200	U
Profit	$ 77 700	–$ 4 500		$ 73 200	–$41 425		$ 31 775	–$45 925	U

*In relation to the fixed overhead variance we are only isolating the spending variance.
F = Favourable/U = Unfavourable

We will explore the variances for Benny's Purple Madness ice cream in more detail and take a closer look at fixed overhead applied to goods and services in chapter 11.

Comprehensive example 1 demonstrates the development of standard costs for a concrete block manufacturer. Comprehensive example 2 continues the example to demonstrate the determination of variances between the budgets (both flexible and static) and actual costs to identify variances. We will revisit this example in chapter 11 to explore the determination and analysis of direct cost variances and overhead variances, and to make cost variance adjustments.

COMPREHENSIVE EXAMPLE 1

Setting standard costs

Concrete Transformation manufactures concrete blocks at its plant in Mildura. When Karen Matthews, the company's new accountant, started work last month, she learned that the entity had never used standard costs. This surprised Karen, as the process used by the entity was repetitive and therefore enables standards to be established for production output. Karen decided to implement a standard cost system to help the managers monitor operating performance.

Karen toured the production facilities with Jordan, the labour supervisor. She learned that workers combine cement mix, sand and water; then they pour the mixture into block forms. The blocks are turned out of the forms and allowed to dry in the sun. Once the blocks are dry, they are stacked on pallets and loaded on trucks for shipment to customers. Workers can be sent home if no work is scheduled; therefore, direct labour cost is variable.

Relevant cash flows and timeline

Because the entity had not previously used standard costs, Karen decided to set next month's standards based on past experience, adjusted for expected changes in activities or costs. To gather information for creating cost standards, Karen first studied the accounting and production records for the past year. Then she reviewed the next month's production schedule, which showed a planned volume of 90 000 blocks. After conducting interviews to learn about next month's production activities and costs, she did not expect any changes from prior costs.

Karen identified the following potential direct costs for producing the blocks: cement mix, sand, water and direct labour. Sand and water are readily available on the entity's land, so it does not incur any costs for them. (In reality, some costs would most likely be incurred for these resources but this example avoids complications by assuming no cost.) Therefore, the only direct materials cost is the cement mix. Based on past accounting and production records, Karen set a standard cost for cement mix of $10 per kilogram. She also estimated that it should take about 1 kilogram of cement mix per block. In addition, Karen set the direct labour cost standard at $10 per hour, and the standard for quantity of labour at 100 blocks per labour hour.

Karen next turned to the production overhead costs and determined that some costs were variable and others were fixed. Variable costs consisted of the cost of supervisors; as the number of direct labour hours increases, the number of supervisor hours also increases. Karen set the variable overhead standard at $2 per labour hour. She then classified all remaining overhead costs as fixed, and estimated next month's spending at $180 000. After considering several allocation bases for the fixed overhead costs, Karen decided that volume of production would be appropriate. With planned production of 90 000 blocks, she set the standard fixed overhead allocation rate at $2 ($180 000 / 90 000 blocks) per block.

Following is a summary of the standards Karen established for the next month:

Direct materials:		
Cost of cement mix	$10	per kg
Quantity of cement mix	1	kg per block
Standard cost per block ($10 per kg × 1 kg per block)	$10	
Direct labour:		
Labour pay rate	$10	per hour

Quantity of direct labour	100	blocks per labour hour
Standard cost per block ($10 per hour × 1 hour per 100 blocks)	$0.10	
Fixed overhead:		
Planned spending	$180 000	
Volume of allocation base (blocks produced)	90 000	blocks
Standard cost per block ($180 000 / 90 000 blocks)	$2	
Variable overhead:		
Spending per labour hour	$2	
Standard cost per block ($2 / 100 blocks)	$0.02	
Total standard cost per block (10 + 0.10 + 2 + 0.02)	$12.12	

Based on these standards and the expected production volume of 90 000 blocks, Karen created the following product cost budget for next month. This would form part of the static budget.

Direct materials (90 000 blocks × $10 per block)	$ 900 000
Direct labour (90 000 blocks × $0.10 per block)	9 000
Fixed overhead	180 000
Variable overhead (90 000 blocks × $0.02 per block)	1 800
Total standard production costs (90 000 blocks × $12.12 per block)	**$1 090 800**

COMPREHENSIVE EXAMPLE 2

Variances and flexing the budget

At the end of the first month of operations after Karen developed the cost standards, she collected the data needed to perform a variance analysis:

- 100 000 cement blocks were produced.
- The entity purchased 130 000 kg of cement mix for $975 000.
- 120 000 kg of cement mix were used.
- Direct labour employees were paid $16 500 and worked 1100 hours.
- Actual fixed overhead costs were $175 000.
- Actual variable overhead costs were $2500.

Karen then prepared a variance report comparing the static production budget (based on 90 000 blocks) and actual production (100 000 blocks).

Production costs Volume	Static budget 90 000 blocks	Actual volume 100 000 blocks	Variance	
Direct materials (90 000 blocks × $10 per block)	$ 900 000	$ 900 000*	$ 0	—
Direct labour (90 000 blocks × $0.10 per block)	9 000	16 500	7 500	U
Fixed overhead	180 000	175 000	5 000	F
Variable overhead (90 000 blocks × $0.02 per block)	1 800	2 500	700	U
Total standard production costs (90 000 blocks × $12.12 per block)	$1 090 800	$1 094 000	$3 200	U

*Based on the actual use of 120 000 kg × $7.50 per kg ($975 000 / 130 000 kg).

The comparison of the static budget and actual volume indicates an unfavourable variance of $3200. However, this budget comparison does not provide relevant information for management as the variances are affected by the difference in production volume. It is not unexpected for costs to be higher in relation to materials and labour when volume is higher. As for the overhead variances, the increased volume allows for more overhead to be applied, thereby giving a favourable variance. Therefore, to provide more relevant information to management it is necessary to 'flex' the static budget to the actual production volume of 100 000 blocks. Karen then prepares a flexible budget to compare with actual results.

Production costs Volume	Flexible budget 100 000	Actual volume 100 000	Variance	
Direct materials (100 000 blocks × $10 per block)	$1 000 000	$ 900 000	$100 000	F
Direct labour (100 000 blocks × $0.10 per block)	10 000	16 500	6 500	U
Fixed overhead	180 000	175 000	5 000	F
Variable overhead (100 000 blocks × $0.02 per block)	2 000	2 500	500	U
Total standard production costs (100 000 blocks × $12.12 per block)	$1 192 000	$1 094 000	$ 98 000	F

Karen examines the total favourable flexible budget variance of $98 000, which certainly gives a different picture compared with the static budget, which reported a $3200 unfavourable variance. To better understand operating performance Karen will need to further breakdown the variances into price and efficiency for each production resource. In some cases, an overall favourable variance means that the organisation has no problems (operations performed better than expected). However, variances reported at the summary level can conceal problems in the operational area. We will explore these variances in more depth in chapter 11 to identify the causes of the variances from a price and efficiency perspective.

To review the above analysis, we construct a table that provides a summary by comparing the static and flexible budgets to highlight the volume variance, and then comparing the flexible budget with actual results to highlight the price/efficiency variances.

	Static budget	Variance Volume	Flexible budget	Variance Price/efficiency	Actual	Total variance	
Production volume	90 000	2 000	100 000	0	100 000	0	
Production costs	$ –			$ –		$ –	
Direct material	$ 900 000	–$100 000	$1 000 000	$100 000	$ 900 000	–$	
Direct labour	$ 9 000	–$ 1 000	$ 10 000	–$ 6 500	$ 16 500	$7 500	U
Variable overhead	$ 1 800	–$ 200	$ 2 000	–$ 500	$ 2 500	$ 700	F
Fixed overhead	$ 180 000	$ –	$ 180 000*	$ 5 000	$ 175 000	$5 000	F
Total production costs	$1 090 800	–$101 200	$1 212 000	$ 98 000	$1 094 000	$3 200	U

*In relation to the fixed overhead variance we are only isolating the spending variance.

SUMMARY

10.1 Understand flexible budgets and the use of sensitivity analysis.

To overcome differences between budgeted volume and actual volume, managers make use of flexible budget techniques. These techniques allow managers to monitor actual operations to determine whether operating targets are met.

A flexible budget is a set of cost relationships that can be used to estimate costs and cash flows for any level of operations.

Sensitivity analysis allows managers to estimate the effects of deviations from budget assumptions.

10.2 Explain how standard costs are established.

A standard cost is the cost managers expect to incur to produce goods or services under operating plan assumptions.

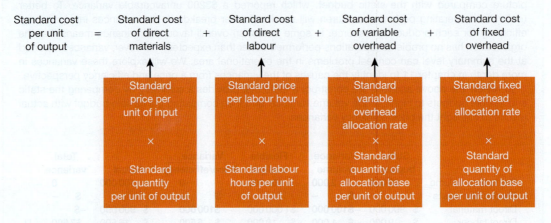

Developing standard costs

Two different types of standards
1. Ideal standard — assumes perfect operating conditions
2. Currently attainable standard — assumes 'normal' operating conditions

Establishing standard costs

Information used
- Historical costs and trends
- Expected changes in costs or processes
- Estimates from industrial engineers

Key assumptions
- Volume of production activity
- Production processes and efficiency, including expected waste and defects
- Prices and quality of inputs

Attainability
- To motivate performance, set standards with little slack

10.3 Communicate how variance information is analysed and used.

A standard cost variance is a difference between a standard cost and an actual cost.

Factors influencing the choice of variances to monitor

- Nature of goods or services
- Cost accounting system used
- Costs that managers consider important
- Cost/benefit trade-off for monitoring individual costs

Factors influencing further investigation of variances

- Size of variance
- Trends in variances

10.4 Apply the principles of flexible budgeting.

Budget calculations

- Establish standard cost
- Calculate the standard cost for actual output (flexible budget)
- Compare the static budget to actual costs to determine volume variance
- Compare the flexible budget to actual costs to determine price/efficiency variances
- Identify variances for each cost category
- Management conclusions and actions

KEY TERMS

efficiency variance Provides information about how economically direct resources such as materials and labour were used.

flexible budget A set of cost relationships that can be used to estimate costs and cash flows for any level of operations within the relevant range.

price variance The difference between standard and actual prices paid for resources purchased and used in the production of goods or services.

sensitivity analysis An analysis of how deviations from budget assumptions will affect outcomes.

standard cost The cost managers expect to incur to produce goods or services under operating plan assumptions.

standard cost variance The difference between a standard cost and an actual cost.

variance analysis The process of calculating variances and then investigating the reasons they occurred.

SELF-STUDY PROBLEMS

SELF-STUDY PROBLEM 1 Flexible budget and variance analysis

Latiefa is the cost accountant at Hallet and Sons, a manufacturer of exquisite glass serving bowls. The materials used for the bowls are inexpensive, but the process is labour intensive. The supervisor decided to use cheaper labour this period to see whether costs could be reduced. Latiefa needs to prepare a report for her supervisor about how effective operations had been during the month of January. She had set the following standards.

		Cost per unit
Direct materials	3 kg @ $2.50	$ 7.50
Direct labour	5 hours @ $15	75.00
Factory overhead:		
Variable	$3 per direct labour hour	15.00
Fixed	$20 per unit	20.00

Variable overhead is allocated by labour hours and fixed overhead is allocated by unit. Estimated production per month is 8000 units (40 000 direct labour hours) with fixed overhead expenditure budgeted at $160 000.

Records for January, based on production of 7800 units, indicated the following:

Direct materials purchased	25 000 kg @ $2.60
Direct materials used	23 100 kg
Direct labour	40 100 hours @ $14.60
Variable overhead	$119 000
Fixed overhead	$180 000

Required

(a) Prepare a flexible budget to enable assessment of the strategy undertaken by management.

(b) Discuss the variances and recommend whether any of them should be investigated further.

SOLUTION TO SELF-STUDY PROBLEM 1

(a) Latiefa could present the following flexible budget to her supervisors.

Production costs Volume	Flexible budget 7 800	Actual volume 7 800	Variance	
Direct material	$ 58 500	$ 60 060	$ 1 560	U
Direct labour	$585 000	$585 460	$ 460	U
Fixed overhead	$160 000	$180 000	$20 000	U
Variable overhead	$117 000	$119 000	$ 2 000	U
Total standard production costs	$920 500	$944 520	$24 020	U

(b) *Discussion of most significant variances*

Because the supervisor hired less-expensive labour this month, it would be expected that the labour variance would be favourable. However, the budget shows a labour variance of $460 unfavourable. It could be that that more hours were required to compensate for less-skilled labour. This variance should be investigated to verify the conjectures.

If less-skilled labour has a negative effect on quality, sales could be lost. Any potential change in the quality of output needs to be investigated.

The fixed overhead spending variance was very large and unfavourable ($20 000). These costs might be out of control and need to be investigated.

Discussion of less-significant variances

Given the unfavourable direct materials price variance, it is possible that the quality purchased this period has improved because less was used than expected. However, a price increase is also a possible explanation. These variances should be investigated to determine whether either or both of the standards should be changed.

We need to determine whether an unfavourable variable overhead spending variance ($2000) was due to additional spending or use of resources.

SELF-STUDY PROBLEM 2 Determining standard costs

The Injector Company is considering purchasing a new machine in its ink cartridge manufacturing facility. This is a replacement machine. The existing machines operate 24/7. Due to the repetitive nature of the manufacturing process the company uses a standard cost accounting system. The accountant is currently reviewing the standard labour cost for the production of the ink cartridges. Based on the current machine output, workers are able to produce 600 cartridges per labour hour; however, the supplier states that the new machine is capable of producing 800 cartridges per labour hour. Injector Company engineers agree that, under ideal conditions, the equipment should be able to generate 800 pieces an hour and they support that rate as a standard. However, production managers point out that the new machine is identical to the machines currently in use and that the current production rate is only 600 pieces per labour hour. Accordingly, production managers advocate the use of 600 as the labour rate standard. The accounting staff believe that the most appropriate standard labour rate would be 700 pieces per labour hour.

Required

Provide a brief report to the management of Injector Company regarding the selection of the most appropriate standard labour rate for the machine. Your report should include:

- the arguments that would be offered by engineering, production and accounting personnel to support their respective proposed standard
- the potential impact on variance analysis.

SOLUTION TO SELF-STUDY PROBLEM 2

The labour rate standard for the new machine is being reviewed and it seems that there are three possible options: 600 (promoted by the production supervisors), 800 (promoted by the supplier and the company engineers) or 700 pieces per labour (promoted by the accounting staff).

The differences are due to the different type of standards being applied by the different parties. The supplier and company engineer are using an ideal standard, assuming the machine is operating at maximum efficiency with no delays caused in the factory. The supplier in particular would want to promote the additional output the new machine could achieve for Injector Company. The company engineers would be looking at the technical specifications, which suggest at maximum capacity 800 pieces per labour hour are possible. The production supervisors are considering current operating conditions and basing the standard on what they consider is attainable at present. The accounting staff may consider that the new machine will lead to improved efficiency and that the output should be able to increase, so the standard they have chosen has stretch goals built in to encourage improved performance.

The selection of the 'wrong' standard will lead to variances that will not be actionable due to the underlying cause being the standard itself rather than any performance issue.

QUESTIONS

10.1	Which type of entities would be suited to the use of a standard cost system?	**LO2**
10.2	Explain the difference between an ideal standard and a currently attainable standard.	**LO2**
10.3	Discuss the different methods that an organisation can use to determine standard costs.	**LO2**
10.4	Discuss the behavioural issues that need to be considered when establishing a standard cost.	**LO2**
10.5	Explain the difference between a static budget and a flexible budget.	**LO1, 3**
10.6	Which item has the same value for both the static budget and the flexible budget?	**LO1, 3**
10.7	Discuss the different types of budget variances that can be calculated.	**LO3**
10.8	Explain how accountants and managers decide which cost variances to monitor.	**LO3**
10.9	List several ways that variances can be used to improve future operations.	**LO1, 2, 3**
10.10	Suppose that utilities are considered a fixed cost for a retail clothing outlet. Why might we expect a variance to occur for the cost of utilities?	**LO3**
10.11	Distinguish between a price variance and an efficiency variance.	**LO2, 3**
10.12	Explain what a favourable variance and an unfavourable variance mean in relation to revenue and costs.	**LO3**
10.13	Why might the role of the accountant be referred to as one of a 'detective' in relation to variance analysis?	**LO3**
10.14	Should management be upset if all variances for the period are unfavourable?	**LO1, 2, 3**
10.15	Should management be excited if all variances for the period are favourable?	**LO1, 2, 3**
10.16	Variance analysis is only useful for organisations using a standard costing system. Discuss.	**LO3**
10.17	Software Galore sells gaming software that is downloaded to the customer's device on purchase. The owner, Fred, was talking with a friend who sang the praises of flexible budgeting in his manufacturing business. Fred was wondering whether a flexible budget would benefit his business decision making. Comment.	**LO1**

EXERCISES

10.18 Selection of appropriate standard cost   **LO2**

Franklin Industries' CEO was talking with the CFO about the appropriate standard cost to use for the new product being launched in the coming year. The CEO argued that standard cost based on ideal performance would enable profits to be maximised through improved efficiency. The CFO argued, however, that the standard cost should be based on attainable performance or recent average historical performance.

Required

Briefly comment on which standard cost is best for Franklin Industries to use in developing the standard cost for the new product.

10.19 Direct costs in flexible budget   **LO2, 4**

Paper Bright Industries uses flexible budgeting to assess budgeted expectations against actual performance. Last month, Paper Bright produced 120 000 units and incurred direct materials cost of $150 000. Its static budget for the year has a direct materials cost of $200 000 for 150 000 units.

Required

(a) Calculate the direct materials cost in the flexible budget.

(b) Calculate the direct materials flexible budget variance.

10.20 Flexible budget and variances   **LO4**

Black Industries has a static budget based on production and sales of 24 000 units. Sales revenue is expected to be $96 000, variable costs $36 000 and fixed costs $32 000. Actual production and sales were 30 000 units with a profit of $50 000.

Required

(a) Calculate the amount of profit in the flexible budget.

(b) Calculate the overall variance between the flexible budget and actual results.

10.21 Flexible budget   **LO1, 4**

Helium Industries manufactures glitter balloons used as party accessories. The balloons are bagged in packages of 100 and sold for $20 per pack. The company incurs fixed manufacturing overhead of $25 000 per year and the fixed overhead is applied based on packs produced. Standard costs are: material $8 per pack, direct labour $5 per pack and variable overhead $3 per pack. The marketing manager believes sales for the coming year will be somewhere between 10 000 and 15 000 packs.

Required

(a) Prepare a flexible budget for sales of 10 000, 12 000 and 15 000. (Allocate fixed overhead based on the sales volume.)

(b) What advantages are there for Helium Industries in using a flexible budget?

10.22 Static and flexible budgets, variances, information quality   **LO4**

The photocopying department in the local polytechnic college has budgeted monthly costs at $40 000 per month plus $7 per student. Normally 800 students are enrolled. During March there were 730 students (which is within the relevant range). At the end of the month, actual fixed costs were $42 000 and variable costs were $3650.

Required

(a) Develop a static budget for photocopying costs based on 800 students.

(b) Calculate the March static budget variance for fixed and variable photocopying costs.

(c) Develop a flexible budget for the actual number of students in March.

(d) Calculate the March flexible budget variance for fixed and variable photocopying costs.

(e) Which variance information — part (b) or (c) — is of higher quality? Explain.

10.23 Calculation of budget variances   **LO3**

The accountant for Moon Industries has taken unexpected leave and has not completed the end-of-period budget analysis. The following incomplete budget analysis was found on her desk.

	Static budget	Variance	Flexible budget	Variance	Actual
	$		$		$
Sales (small)	1 000 000				1 470 000
Sales (large)	1 500 000				1 920 000
Total sales	**2 500 000**				**3 390 000**
Variable costs					
Materials (small)	400 000				690 000
Labour (small)	200 000				330 000
Variable overhead (small)	50 000				74 600
Materials (large)	350 000				510 000
Labour (large)	200 000				270 000

Variable overhead (large)	30 000		35 400
Contribution margin	**1 270 000**		**1 480 000**
Fixed costs			
Manufacturing overhead	120 000		180 000
Selling expenses	50 000		90 000
Admin. expenses	30 000		25 000
Net profit	**1 070 000**		**1 185 000**

Additional information:

Per unit	Large	Small
Selling price	$10 000	$3 000
Variable costs		
Material	4 000	700
Labour	2 000	400
Variable overhead	500	60

Required

(a) Complete the variance analysis report.

(b) Provide a brief report to management of any issues highlighted from your analysis in (a).

10.24 Variances and flexible budgets **LO3**

Sherry North is the supply manager for West Industries, a manufacturer of garden furniture for a major department store in Australia. As part of her bonus plan, Sherry must meet the materials budget that was established at the beginning of the year. As West Industries manufactures three products in large volumes, standard costs are easily established for the factors of production. The reports for the first half of the year indicate that the materials variance is unfavourable. In an attempt to achieve her bonus target, Sherry has been purchasing lower-grade materials at reduced costs from a new supplier. Management have been very pleased with the turnaround in the variance.

Required

What implications do Sherry's actions have for West Industries as a whole (especially in relation to other variances that may be reported in the production area)?

10.25 Static and flexible budgets **LO4**

Plush pet toys are produced in a largely automated factory in standard lots of 100 toys each. A standard cost system is used to control costs and to assign cost to inventory.

	Price standard	Quantity standard
Plush fabric	$ 2 per metre	15 metres per lot
Direct labour	$10 per hour	2 hours per lot

Variable overhead, estimated at $5 per lot, consists of miscellaneous items such as thread, a variety of plastic squeakers, and paints that are applied to create features such as eyes and whiskers. Fixed overhead, estimated at $24 000 per month, consists largely of depreciation on the automated machinery and rent for the building. Variable overhead is allocated based on lots produced. The standard fixed overhead allocation rate is based on the estimated output of 1000 lots per month.

Required

(a) Prepare a production budget for the coming year based on planned production of 12 000 lots.

(b) Compare the budget prepared in (a) with a flexible budget based on actual activity of 15 000 lots.

PROBLEMS

10.26 Developing direct cost standards; cost variances; use of variance analysis **LO1, 2, 3, 4**

The Mighty Morphs produces two popular computer games, Powerful Puffs and Mini-Mite Morphs. Following are the standard costs.

	Powerful Puffs		Mini-Mite Morphs	
	Standard quantity	Standard price	Standard quantity	Standard price
DVDs	1.08 DVD/unit	$0.35/DVD	1.08 DVD/unit	$0.35/DVD
Documentation	1.03 book/unit	$3/book	1.03 book/unit	$5/book
Assembly labour	0.01 hour/unit	$15/hour	0.03 hour/unit	$15/hour

The standards call for more than one disk and documentation book per unit because of normal waste due to faulty DVDs and poor binding.

Actual costs for last week follow.

DVDs purchased (@ $0.39)	$ 780
Number of DVDs used	2025
Number of Powerful Puffs games produced	1000
Powerful Puffs documentation printed (@ $2.95)	$4425
Number of Powerful Puffs documentation used	1005
Number of Mini-Mite Morphs games produced	800
Mini-Mite Morphs documentation printed (@ $4.75)	$4750
Number of Mini-Mite Morphs documentation used	825
Assembly labour cost (55 hours)	$ 795

Management decided that it would require too much effort to keep track of how many DVDs and hours are used for each of the games separately. Accordingly, the DVD materials and labour variances are combined rather than computed separately for each game.

Required

(a) What is the documentation price variance for Mini-Mite Morphs?

(b) What is the efficiency variance for DVDs?

(c) What is the sum of all variances for assembly labour for both games?

(d) Discuss the pros and cons of building waste into the standards.

10.27 Cost variance analysis; use of variance information **LO3**

Baker Street Animal Clinic routinely uses a particular serum in its vaccination program. Veterinary technicians give the injections. The standard dose is 10 cc per injection, and the cost has been $100 per 1000 cc. According to records, 2000 injections were administered last month at a serum cost of $2270. The veterinarian noted that the serum for the injections should have cost $2000 [($0.10 per cc) × (10 cc per injection) × (2000 injections)]. Moreover, she noted some carelessness in handling the serum that could easily lead to unnecessary waste. When this issue was brought to the attention of the technicians, together with the $270 discrepancy in costs, they claimed that the $270 excess costs must be due to the inflated prices charged by the veterinary supply company. Purchasing records reveal that the price for the serum used last month had indeed increased to $105 per 1000 cc.

Required

(a) Provide variance calculations to help you evaluate the technicians' argument.

(b) Discuss whether a significant waste of serum occurred last month. Include quantitative and qualitative information in your discussion.

(c) If you were the manager for the Baker Street Animal Clinic, how would you use the results of your analyses in parts (a) and (b)? Explain.

10.28 Flexible budget and variances; reasons for variances **LO3, 4**

Play Time Toys is organised into two major divisions: marketing and production. The production division is further divided into three departments: puzzles, dolls and video games. Each production department has its own manager. The company's management believes that all costs must be covered by sales of the three product lines. Therefore, a portion of production division costs are allocated to each product line. The company's accountant prepared the following variance report for the dolls production department.

PERFORMANCE REPORT: DOLLS PRODUCTION DEPARTMENT
(Amounts in thousands)

	Budget per unit	Budget	Actual	Variance	
Sales volume		1 000	1 100	100	F
Revenue	$12.00	$12 000	$12 400	$ 400	F
Direct materials	2.00	2 000	2 100	(100)	U
Direct labour	1.00	1 000	1 225	(225)	U
Variable factory overhead	1.00	1 000	1 100	(100)	U
Fixed factory overhead	0.80	800	1 020	(220)	U
Production division overhead	0.10	100	105	(5)	U
Operating income	$ 7.10	$ 7 100	$ 6 850	$(250)	U

F = favourable variance; U = unfavourable variance

Required
(a) Is Play Time Toys using a static budget or a flexible budget to calculate variances? Explain.
(b) Do you agree with this approach? Why or why not?
(c) Develop a flexible budget for the actual sales of 1100 units.
(d) Use the benchmark you created in part (c) to calculate variances.
(e) Review the variances from part (d) and briefly describe what the variances are suggesting regarding performance.

10.29 Flexible budget variance analysis   **LO3, 4**

Cardinal Products hired a new marketing manager early this year. After an informal consumer survey, the marketing manager decided to lower the firm's selling price by 10 per cent and increase television advertising. The operating results at year end were disappointing. The marketing manager prepared the following analysis. He assumed that direct materials and direct labour were variable costs and that advertising was a fixed cost.

	Static budget (100 000 units)	Actual (115 000 units)	Variance
Sales	$600 000	$621 000	$ 21 000
Direct materials	200 000	227 700	(27 700)
Direct labour	125 000	138 000	(13 000)
Variable overhead	50 000	57 000	(7 000)
Fixed overhead	75 000	75 200	(200)
Advertising	20 000	40 000	(20 000)
Operating income	$130 000	$ 83 100	$(46 900)

'As you can see', the marketing manager reported, 'the major problem is due to inefficiencies in production. My plan would have worked if production had kept its costs in line.'

Required
(a) Prepare a flexible budget report.
(b) What is the real source of the disappointing results? Explain.

10.30 Evaluate grading scheme; professional responsibilities   **LO2, 3**

Variance analysis reflects information about actual performance relative to a standard. Variance analysis reports provide managers with information about the performance of employees, from direct labour to supervisors and managers. Grades provide similar information for recruiters who want to hire graduating students. Following is information about Professor Grader's performance measurement system.

Professor Grader is popular; almost all of his students receive A grades. This phenomenon is widely attributed to Professor Grader's superior teaching skills. Grades for this professor's courses are determined as follows.

Item	Points
Mid semester exam	200
Attendance	200
Major assignment	200
Final exam	400

A student needs 700 points for an A, 600 points for a B, 500 for a C and 400 for a D. From the 200 points given for perfect attendance, a student loses 5 points for every class missed (out of 40 class meetings); however, attendance is seldom taken.

If the major assignment paper is 20 pages or longer, 200 points are earned; 10 points are lost for each page less than 20 (thus, a 12-page paper is worth 120 points).

Professor Grader has given the same mid-semester exam for the past 20 years. To reduce the number of exam copies in students' files, Professor Grader does not return the exams; grades are simply reported to individual students. A student group obtained a copy of the exam 15 years ago.

They have chosen not to share the exam with any person who is not a member of the group; thus Professor Grader usually observes that grades on this exam are nearly normally distributed.

The final exam is a take-home exam that the students have two weeks to complete.

Required

(a) Is it possible to develop a perfect system for measuring student performance in a course? Why?

(b) How much variation is likely in student performance for each of the four graded items? Explain.

(c) Describe the weaknesses in Professor Grader's grading system as a performance measurement system.

(d) What are Professor Grader's professional responsibilities to various stakeholders in this situation?

(e) Discuss whether Professor Grader has acted ethically in this situation. Describe the ethical values you use to draw your conclusions.

(f) Is it ethical for students in this situation to access a copy of the prior mid-semester exam or to seek assistance in completing take-home assignments? Does Professor Grader's system affect the students' responsibilities? Describe the ethical values you use to draw your conclusions.

10.31 Evaluating a proposal for measuring performance   **LO2, 3**

Benerux Industries has been in business for 30 years. The entity's major product is a control unit for elevators. The entity has a reputation for manufacturing products of exceptionally high quality, resulting in higher prices for its units than competitors charge. Higher prices, in turn, have meant that the entity has been comfortably profitable. A major reason for the high product quality is a loyal and conscientious workforce. Production employees have been with the entity for an average of 18 years.

Recently the entity hired a cost accountant from the local university. After a few months at Benerux, the new accountant proposed a performance measurement report consisting of two parts. The first part will report the actual number of units started during each month, the target number of units that should have been started and a variance. The second part will calculate an actual cost per good unit completed during each month, the target cost per unit and a variance. The new accountant provided the following additional information concerning the performance report: The first part of the report concentrates on units started because many units are scrapped in the manufacturing process (to maintain high quality). Therefore, the best measure of effort expended is the number of units on which work was begun. The target number of units to be begun in a month is the number of units started in the corresponding month last year plus 5 per cent. In the second part of the report, actual costs per unit will be calculated by dividing total production cost incurred during the month by the number of good units completed during the month.

The target cost per unit is the average cost for manufacturing this kind of product as determined from industry newsletters.

The proposal concluded with the following comments: 'This report should be prepared and distributed quarterly. For maximum benefit, I suggest that a bonus be awarded whenever the number of units started exceeds target and costs are below target. This system will result in substantially improved profits for the entity. It should be implemented immediately.'

Required

(a) Is it possible to develop a perfect system for monitoring and motivating worker performance? Why?

(b) Explain what the managers might learn by monitoring each of the variances in the proposed performance measurement system.

(c) Discuss possible reasons why the entity did not previously use a variance system to monitor and motivate worker performance.

(d) Describe weaknesses in the proposed performance measurement system.

(e) If you were the CFO of Benerux Industries, how would you respond to the new cost accountant's proposal? Discuss whether you agree with the proposal and explain how you would communicate your response.

ACKNOWLEDGEMENTS

Photo 10A: © Getty Images

Photo 10B: © Nejron Photo / Shutterstock.com

CHAPTER 11

Variance analysis: revenue and cost

LEARNING OBJECTIVES

After studying this chapter, you should be able to:

11.1 identify variances for investigation

11.2 understand and calculate relevant profit- and revenue-related variances

11.3 calculate direct cost variances

11.4 understand how direct cost variance information is analysed and used

11.5 calculate variable and fixed overhead variances

11.6 understand how overhead variance information is analysed and used

11.7 close off manufacturing cost variances at the end of the period.

IN BRIEF

Accountants produce information that managers use to monitor operations. The analysis of budget variances is an important part of that information. As we saw in chapter 10, variances are calculated by comparing standard revenues and costs with actual revenues and costs. Through the analysis of these variances, managers are able to assess both market conditions and operating processes that need investigation and identify areas for possible improvement. Variance information helps managers create more accurate plans for future operations and also learn whether planned improvements in operations have been achieved. In addition, variance analysis provides information for evaluating employee performance.

11.1 Identifying variances

LEARNING OBJECTIVE 11.1 Identify variances for investigation.

In chapter 10 we focused on the development of the flexible budget and the use of standard revenues and costs to identify variances between actual activity and budget expectations. We will now explore how such variances can be further broken down and analysed into volume, price and efficiency components to provide more insight into the profitability of Benny's Purple Madness ice cream.

The following are the standard revenue and standard costs developed for one bucket of Purple Madness ice cream. The use of standards assists managers to identify the sources of variances and also highlight possible offsetting of favourable (F) and unfavourable (U) variances between components. The aggregation of favourable and unfavourable variances could hide operational problems that need to be investigated. In addition, this breakdown helps managers identify variances that are sufficiently large to justify further investigation.

Standards for one bucket of Purple Madness ice cream	
Standard revenue	$7.00
Total standard cost	$5.15
Broken down by:	
Direct material	$1.00
Other direct material	$0.75
Direct labour — packing	$0.80
Direct labour — processing	$1.60
Variable overhead	$0.60
Fixed overhead	$0.40

Let's revisit the budget analysis we conducted in chapter 10. The analysis focused on the following budgets:
- static budget (budgeted revenue and costs × budgeted volume)
- flexible budget (budgeted revenue and costs × actual volume)
- actuals (actual revenue and costs × actual volume).

The data relating to each are shown below.

	Static budget	Variance Volume	Flexible budget	Variance Price/Efficiency	Actual	Total variance
Ice cream buckets sold	42 000	2 000	40 000	0	40 000	0
Revenue	$294 000	−$14 000	$280 000	−$ 8 000	$272 000	−$22 000
Less variable costs		$ −		$ −		$ −
Direct material — blackberries (kg)	42 000	− 2 000	40 000	− 8 750	48 750	6 750
Direct material — other ingredients (kg)	31 500	− 1 500	30 000	− 2 550	32 550	1 050
Direct labour — packing (hours)	33 600	− 1 600	32 000	− 5 525	37 525	3 925
Direct labour — processing (hours)	67 200	− 3 200	64 000	−13 900	77 900	10 700
Variable overhead	$ 25 200	−$ 1 200	$ 24 000	$ 500	$ 23 500	−$ 1 700
Total variable production costs	$199 500	−$ 9 500	$190 000	−$30 225	$220 225	$20 725
Contribution margin	$ 94 500	−$ 4 500	$ 90 000	−$38 225	$ 51 775	−$42 725
Less fixed costs		$ −		$ −		$ −
Fixed overhead	$ 16 800	$ −	$ 16 800	−$ 3 200	$ 20 000	−$ 3 200
Profit	$ 77 700	−$ 4 500	$ 73 200	−$41 425	$ 31 775	−$45 925

To gain more knowledge about operations during the period, several variances will be investigated further. An overview of these variances is shown in figure 11.1. We will explore the overall profit variance, followed by more detailed investigations into the revenue variance, and in later sections the focus will be on the breakdown of the price and efficiency variances of production costs — direct material, direct labour, and variable and fixed overhead. The objective of the analysis is to generate meaningful insights into the reasons that actual results differ from budget plans.

FIGURE 11.1   Revenue and cost variance framework

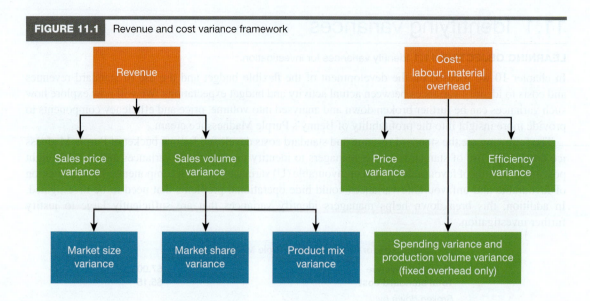

11.2 Profit- and revenue-related variances

LEARNING OBJECTIVE 11.2 Understand and calculate relevant profit- and revenue-related variances.

Profit variance

The budget analysis detailed in section 11.1 highlights that the difference between the planned profit and actual profit ($77 700 − $31 775) is $45 925 unfavourable (U). In addition, looking at the data from a contribution margin perspective there is a planned contribution margin from sales of $2.25 ($94 500 / 42 000 buckets) and an actual contribution margin of $1.294 ($51 775 / 40 000 buckets). Both indicate that actual performance fell short of budget expectations. The variances giving rise to the differences are broken down below in the reconciliation of the planned profit to actual profit. As discussed in chapter 10, the variances are a combination of both volume and price/efficiency variances.

Reconciliation of planned profit and actual profit			
Profit plan (based on static budget)			$77 700
Volume variance			4 500 U
(change in planned total contribution margin difference between static budget and flexible budget)			
Less price/efficiency variances			
(based on difference between flexible budget and actuals)			
Sales price	$ 8 000	U	
Variable production costs	30 225	U	
Fixed production cost	3 200	U	
Total price/efficiency variances			41 425 U
Actual profit			$31 775

Revenue variance

It is common to focus disproportionately on costs relative to revenue. Certainly, cost management is critical and much of this text has a cost management theme. Nevertheless, it is important to reflect on and conduct analysis of the revenue side of organisations. We can focus on revenue drivers in much the same way as we talk about cost drivers. Generic revenue drivers might include:

• competition
• economies of scale
• economies of scope
• capacity/capacity utilisation
• market share
• customer satisfaction

- employee satisfaction
- website traffic growth
- new product/service development
- brand strength
- customer loyalty
- post-sales support.

The particular relevance of these revenue drivers to a specific organisation will depend on the competitive environment. The objective of isolating revenue variances is to generate meaningful insights into the reasons that budgeted revenue and actual revenue might differ. This variance analysis is sometimes referred to as 'competitive effectiveness' due to its analysis of market conditions. When developing standards to assess operating revenue performance, managers will assess market conditions, develop marketing strategies, and establish the type and quality of goods or services they wish to sell.

The revenue variance can be examined from both a volume and price perspective, and a breakdown of total budgeted revenue (as recorded in the static budget) can be seen in the following standard:

$$\text{Total budgeted revenues} = \text{Standard sales price} \times \text{Budgeted volume}$$

The comparison of actual revenues to budgeted revenues allows the identification of the **revenue budget variance**. Revenue variances are caused by a number of different factors, including changes in demand, sales price or discounting practices. In addition, because total revenue is based on the projected sales mix of products, changes in the mix cause changes in revenues. Managers are often concerned about variances between planned and actual revenues. Therefore, accountants produce and analyse several variances that reflect the success of marketing efforts.

Sales price and sales quantity variances

The **sales price variance** reflects the difference between standard and actual selling prices for the volume of units actually sold. The sales price variance is calculated by:

$$\text{Sales price variance} = (\text{Actual price} - \text{Standard price}) \times \text{Actual volume}$$

Sales price variance is favourable if the actual selling price exceeds the standard price, and it is unfavourable if the reverse is true. When an organisation sells more than one product or service, the combined variance is calculated as the sum of the sales price variances for all products and services.

The **sales quantity variance** reflects the difference between the standard and actual quantity of units sold at the standard selling price. The sales quantity variance is calculated by:

$$\text{Sales quantity variance} = (\text{Actual volume} - \text{Budgeted volume}) \times \text{Standard price}$$

Sales quantity variance is favourable when actual sales quantities exceed standard quantities, and it is unfavourable if the reverse is true. When an organisation sells more than one product or service, the combined variance is calculated as the sum of the sales quantity variances for all products and services.

Applying the revenue analysis to Benny's Purple Madness ice cream we are able to identify reasons for the overall revenue variance of $22 000 ($294 000 – $272 000) between the static budget and actual results. The breakdown of the revenue variance is as follows:

$$\text{Sales price variance} = \left(\$6.80 - \$7.00\right) \times 40\,000 \text{ buckets} = \$8000 \text{ unfavourable}$$
$$\text{Sales quantity variance} = (40\,000 - 42\,000) \times \$7 = \$14\,000 \text{ unfavourable}$$

Both variances are unfavourable, as Benny's actual sales volume achieved was lower than budgeted and actual sales price achieved was lower than the standard price.

Sales volume and profit variance

Benny's management would also want to understand how changes in sales volume have impacted on the planned profits. In other words, if Benny's management had prepared the static budget based on actual sales, what would the planned profit have been under that scenario, and how does this compare with the original plan? To isolate the profit variance caused by the sales volume difference, we can compare the static budget with the flexible budget and thereby identify how planned profit is affected by the change in sales volume. The analysis shows that the sales volume difference has caused a $4500 unfavourable overall profit variance. Remember, we can ignore fixed costs — regardless of the level of volume, the total fixed cost will not change at any level of budget volume we investigate — and variable costs per unit of resource remain the same. Because of this, the contribution margin variance is also equal to the overall profit variance. We can calculate three variances that will help us understand why the planned sales volume was different to the actual volume and why there is a profit difference of $4500 unfavourable ($77 700 – $73 200) — and whether this is due to changes in the market size, market share and/or the product mix or some combination thereof.

To assist with the analysis, additional information from the marketing department revealed that the planned market size for the month was 420 000 buckets with actual market size being only 400 000 buckets, with Benny's hoping to achieve a 10 per cent market share. Using this information, we can further analyse the planned profit variance caused by sales volume as follows. You will note that the contribution margin is used to help explain the variance in profit, and when comparing the static and flexible budget this is equal to the contribution margin variance of $4500 unfavourable ($94 500 – $90 000). We can focus on the contribution margin as fixed costs are the same for both levels of activity. We will now seek to understand whether the contribution margin variance was caused by changes in market share, market size or product mix variance (if applicable) or some combination thereof.

1. The **market size variance** provides an indication of the proportion of the sales volume variance that can be attributed to unexpected changes in market size. It is calculated as follows:

$$\text{Market size variance} = \text{Change in market size} \times \text{Budgeted market share}$$
$$\times \text{Planned average contribution margin}$$

2. The **market share variance** provides an indication of the proportion of the sales volume variance that can be attributed to changes in the market share. It is calculated as follows:

$$\text{Market share variance} = \text{Actual market size} \times \text{Change in market share}$$
$$\times \text{Planned average contribution margin}$$

3. The **product mix variance** provides an indication of changes in contribution margin caused by selling a different mix from the planned mix of products. This is only a relevant calculation in circumstances when the products involved are substitute products. In other circumstances this calculation would be of no value. The product mix variance is calculated as follows:

$$\text{Product mix variance} = \text{Change in average standard contribution margin}$$
$$\times \text{Actual unit volume}$$

The detailed calculations for the market size, market share and product mix variances for Purple Madness ice cream are as shown in figure 11.2.

FIGURE 11.2   Market size, market share and product mix variance calculations

Market size variance

Market size variance = Change in market size × Budgeted market share × Planned average
                                    contribution margin
                                = 20 000 buckets × 0.10 × $2.25
                                = $4500 unfavourable

where:

Change in market size = Actual market size – Budgeted market size
                                    = 400 000 – 420 000 = –20 000
Budgeted market share = 10% (Static budget volume / Market size)
Planned average contribution margin = Budgeted contribution margin / Budgeted total volume
                                    = $94 500 / 42 000 buckets
                                    = $2.25

The unfavourable *market size variance* of $4500 suggests that there has been a slowdown in the size of the market.

Market share variance

Market share variance = Actual market size × Change in market share × Planned average
                                    contribution margin
                                = 400 000 × (0.10 – 0.10) × $2.25 = $0

---

where:

Actual market size = 400 000
Change in market share = 0.10 − 0.10 = 0
Planned average contribution margin (calculated above) = $2.25

The analysis shows that there is no *market share variance* this month, as Benny's has still achieved sales equal to 10% of the actual market size — 40 000 buckets is 10 per cent of the market (400 000 × 0.10).

Product mix variance

As the analysis is on *one* product range, the Purple Madness ice cream, there is no product mix variance. Product mix variance will be explored in comprehensive example 1, where we undertake a profit analysis of two other products from Benny's range.

The more detailed breakdown of the $4500 profit variance between the static budget and flexible budget, presented in figure 11.2, would prompt Benny's marketing department to further analyse the market to understand why the market size has contracted and to determine if it is expected to be a short-term or long-term situation. Factors to be considered include general economic conditions, seasonal factors affecting the sale of ice cream and closure of major customers.

COMPREHENSIVE EXAMPLE 1

Benny's

Benny's has a number of different product lines. A budget analysis is presented for two products: French Vanilla and Macadamia Twirl. To assist with further investigation of variances, the marketing department has provided the following data relating to both physical units and financials.

Budgeted market size (litres)	19 633 000	
Budgeted market share	12.00%	
Actual market size (litres)	20 811 000	
Actual market share	11.79%	

	Static budget		Flexible budget			Actual		
	Volume ('000 litres)	$ ('000)	Variance	$ ('000)	Variance	$ ('000)	Volume ('000 litres)	
Sales data								
French Vanilla	2 020	28 076	1 168	29 244	39	29 283	2 104	
Macadamia Twirl	336	8 570	357	8 927	(17)	8 910	350	
Total sales	**2 356**	**36 646**	**1 525**	**38 171**	**22**	**38 193**	**2 454**	
Less variable costs								
Cost ice cream (French Vanilla)								
Dairy ingredients								
(litres)	1 919	16 106	(670)	16 776	92	16 684	1 934	
Other ingredients								
(100 grams)	1 313	6 213	(258)	6 471	104	6 367	1 335	
Labour (hours)	34.01	988	(41)	1 029	(52)	1 081	37.10	

Cost ice cream (Macadamia Twirl)							
Dairy ingredients (litres)	320	2 726	(114)	2 840	165	2 675	318
Other ingredients (100 grams)	241	1 680	(70)	1 750	51	1 699	244
Labour (hours)	30	869	(36)	905	66	839	28.79
Total variable costs		28 582	(1 189)	29 771	426	29 345	
Contribution margin		8 064	336	8 400	448	8 848	
Fixed costs		3 000	0	3 000	500	3 500	
Profit		5 064	336	5 400	52	5 348	

Reconciliation of planned profit and actual profit		
Profit plan (based on static budget)		$5 064 000
Volume variance (comparing flexible and static budget) (change in total contribution margin)		336 000 F
Less price/efficiency variances (comparing flexible budget and actuals)		
Sales price	22 000 F	
Variable costs	426 000 F	
Fixed cost	500 000 U	
Total price/efficiency variances		52 000 U
Actual profit		$5 348 000

Benny's management team wants to understand what contributed to an overall favourable profit variance of $284 000 ($336 000 – $52 000). Can the results be explained by the management team's competitive effectiveness? Has it capitalised on market changes and managed to increase Benny's market share? Has it sold products with a higher contribution margin? Alternatively, can the volume changes be explained by external factors that are possibly outside of management's control? For example, market growth may be reflective of general economic prosperity, or large events held in the region or higher-than-average temperatures may have contributed to a greater demand for ice cream than budgeted. Therefore, to better understand the impact of market conditions on the $336 000 favourable contribution margin variance caused by a change in sales volume, we can break this variance into market size, market share and product mix variances.

Market size variance

The favourable *market size variance* of $483 840 suggests that part of the sales volume growth is related to growth in the size of the market

$$\text{Market size variance} = 1\,178\,000 \text{ litres} \times 0.12 \times \$3.422\,75 = \$483\,840 \text{ F}$$

where:

$$\text{Change in market size} = \text{Actual market size} - \text{Budgeted market size}$$
$$= 20\,811\,000 \text{ litres} - 19\,633\,000 \text{ litres} = 1\,178\,000 \text{ litres}$$
$$\text{Budgeted market share} = 12\%$$
$$\text{Planned average contribution margin} = \text{Budgeted contribution margin} \div \text{Budgeted total volume}$$
$$= \$8\,064\,000 \ / \ 2\,356\,000 \text{ litres}$$
$$= \$3.422\,75$$

Market share variance

The unfavourable *market share variance* of $149 580 suggests that Benny's market share for these products has decreased. While the decline in market share is obvious in the data provided, these calculations help translate this into a financial effect.

$$\text{Market share variance} = 20\,811\,000 \text{ litres} \times 0\,0021 \times \$3.422\,75 = \$149\,580 \text{ U}$$

where:

Actual market size = 20 811 000 litres
Change in market share = 0.12 – 0.1179 = 0.0021
Planned average contribution margin (calculated above) = $3.422 75 ($8 064 000 / 2 356 000 litres)

Product mix variance

The *product mix variance* of $564 suggests a minimal change in the contribution margin, caused by selling slightly more Macadamia Twirl ice cream in proportion to French Vanilla ice cream than planned.

As Macadamia Twirl has a higher contribution margin per unit, the product mix variance is positive.

Product mix variance = ($3.422 98 – $3.422 75) × 2 454 000 litres = $564 F

where:

Planned average contribution margin (calculated above) = $3.422 75
Planned average contribution margin at actual mix = ($8 400 000 / 2 454 000 litres) = $3.422 98
Actual market volume = 2 454 000 litres

Bringing the earlier revenue variances together we can relook at the profit reconciliation to identify the reasons behind the $336 000 favourable profit variance caused by the sales volume variance; for example, sales volume achieved, market impacts, product mix, price and efficiency variances. The analysis of the sales volume variance shows that Benny's had the potential to earn an additional $483 840 profit due to the larger market size. However, as the planned market share was lower than that actually achieved, $149 580 of the potential additional profit was not possible. The impact was softened by Benny's ability to sell more of the Macadamia Twirl, which has a higher contribution margin per unit than the French Vanilla. Therefore, the analysis highlights that attention should be focused on the market size and market share in order to understand how to improve future profitability.

	$('000)	$('000)
Market size variance	483.84	
Market share variance	(149.58)	
Product mix variance	0.56	336

The discussion so far has focused on the analysis of the overall profit variance and the revenue variances. In the sections to follow our attention will shift to the variances relating to production costs to gain a complete picture as to why the expected profit was not achieved by Benny's in relation to Purple Madness ice cream.

11.3 Direct cost variances

LEARNING OBJECTIVE 11.3 Calculate direct cost variances.

To begin the analysis of direct cost variances we need to refer to the standard direct costs that were developed for one bucket of Purple Madness ice cream. The following breakdown of the standard direct costs details the amount of expected resources and the expected price per unit of resource for each bucket.

Standard direct costs of one bucket of Purple Madness ice cream	
Direct material (1 kg × $1 per kg)	$1.00
Other direct material (0.5 kg × $1.50)	$0.75
Direct labour — packing (0.1 hour per bucket × $8 per hour)	$0.80
Direct labour — processing (0.2 hour per bucket × $8 per hour)	$1.60

The standard costs for direct materials and direct labour consist of a standard price times a standard quantity for each of the direct resources used in production. As a result, as shown in figure 11.3, the total variance for direct costs can be broken down into the following two components:
- price variance
- efficiency variance.

FIGURE 11.3   Direct cost variances

Direct material variances

	Actual direct materials purchased at actual price		Actual direct materials purchased at standard price
		Price variance	

Actual direct materials used at standard price		Standard direct materials allowed for actual output at standard price
	Efficiency variance	

Direct labour variances

Actual labour hours used at actual price		Actual labour hours used at standard price		Standard labour hours allowed for actual output at standard price
	Price variance		Efficiency variance	

	Total direct labour variance	

Direct materials price variance

A **direct materials price variance** compares the actual price for the amount of direct materials purchased with the standard price for the direct materials. Direct materials price variances are calculated using the following formula:

$$\text{Direct materials price variance} = (\text{Actual price} - \text{Standard price}) \times \text{Quantity purchased}$$

Benny's purchased 50 000 kilograms of blackberries (one of the direct material inputs to Benny's Purple Madness ice cream) at $1.25 per kilogram. The standard cost is $1 per kilogram. Therefore, the price variance for these berries is:

$$(\$1.25 \text{ per kg} - \$1 \text{ per kg}) \times 50\,000 \text{ kg} = \$12\,500 \text{ U}$$

This variance is unfavourable because the actual price paid for frozen blackberries is higher than the standard price. Similar calculations would be made for the other ingredients used to produce Purple Madness ice cream. As 25 000 kilograms were purchased at $1.55 per kilogram, with the standard cost being $1.50 per kilogram, there is a $1250 unfavourable price variance (25 000 kg × $0.05). In relation to the flexible budget only 39 000 kilograms were actually used in production, so given a $0.25 unfavourable price variance per kilogram, then $9750 (39 000 kg × 0.25) will form part of the flexible budget variance for direct materials.

The direct materials price variance is usually calculated at the time direct materials are purchased. Therefore, direct materials are recorded in raw material inventory at the standard cost rather than actual cost. Two advantages come with this practice. First, it reduces bookkeeping complexity. Because all units of direct material are recorded at the same standard cost in the raw materials inventory account in the general ledger, the actual cost of individual batches of direct material purchases need not be tracked so that the transfer of costs from the raw material account to the work in process account is simplified as all transfers are at standard cost. Second, this approach allows managers to identify the price variance during the period in which the variance occurred — at the time direct materials are purchased. Purchasing department personnel are often held accountable for price variances, so it is more appropriate to measure the variance at the time of purchase rather than at the time the direct materials are used. Depending on how quickly inventory is used, a delay in recognition could prevent managers from rapidly taking any needed action. As noted, however, the direct material price variance relating to the flexible budget compared to actual results will be calculated based on the direct materials used in production.

Direct materials efficiency variance

The **direct materials efficiency variance** compares the actual amount of materials used to the standard amount of materials allowed for the actual level of output. This difference is valued at the standard price. The reason for this is because when material is issued to production it is recorded in the work in process account at standard cost. Also, as the price variance has already been isolated the focus for this variance is efficiency only. The formula follows:

$$\text{Direct materials efficiency variance} = \left(\begin{array}{c} \text{Actual quantity used} \\ \text{for actual output} \end{array} - \begin{array}{c} \text{Standard quantity allowed} \\ \text{for actual output} \end{array} \right) \times \begin{array}{c} \text{Standard} \\ \text{price} \end{array}$$

As Benny's produced 40 000 buckets of Purple Madness ice cream using 39 000 kilograms of blackberries (recall the standard quantity is 1 kilogram per bucket) the efficiency variance is $1000 favourable.

$$[39\,000\,\text{kg} - (1\text{kg per bucket} \times 40\,000\,\text{buckets})] \times \$1 \text{ per kg}$$
$$= (39\,000\,\text{kg} - 40\,000\,\text{kg}) \times \$1 \text{ per kg} = \$1000\,\text{F}$$

This variance is favourable because fewer direct materials were used than called for at standard. Although we call this variance favourable, using fewer blackberries likely affects the quality of Benny's ice cream, so this variance may be investigated. Similar efficiency variance calculations would be performed for the other ingredients. As 21 000 kilograms of other ingredients were actually used in production and the expected usage was 20 000 kilograms (40 000 buckets × 0.5 kg per bucket) then the efficiency variance would be $1500 unfavourable (1000 kg × $1.50 per kg).

Summary of direct material variances

Blackberries

Flexible budget variance	$8750 unfavourable
Explained by:	
Price variance	39 000 kg × ($1.00 – $1.25) = $9750 unfavourable*
Efficiency variance	(39 000 kg – 40 000 kg) × $1.00 = $1000 favourable

Other ingredients

Flexible budget variance	$2550 unfavourable
Explained by:	
Price variance	21 000 kg × ($1.50 – $1.55) = $1050 unfavourable
Efficiency variance	(21 000 kg – 20 000 kg) × $1.50 = $1500 unfavourable

*Remember the price variance based on purchases was $12 500; this $9750 relates to that portion of materials actually issued to production.

Direct labour price variance

A **direct labour price variance** compares the actual price for labour with the standard price. Direct labour price variances are calculated using the following formula:

$$\text{Direct labour price variance} = \left(\begin{array}{c} \text{Actual labour} \\ \text{price per hour} \end{array} - \begin{array}{c} \text{Standard labour} \\ \text{price per hour} \end{array} \right) \times \begin{array}{c} \text{Actual} \\ \text{hours used} \end{array}$$

Benny's paid $9.50 per hour for 3950 hours of work in packing 40 000 buckets of Purple Madness ice cream. The standard labour rate is $8 per hour. The direct labour price variance is calculated as:

$$(\$9.50 \text{ per hour} - \$8 \text{ per hour}) \times 3950 \text{ hours} = \$5925\,\text{U}$$

This variance is unfavourable because Benny's paid more for labour per hour than the standard called for. Likewise for the processing labour, the price variance is equal to the rate difference of $1.50 per hour times labour used of 8200 hours, which gives us a $12 300 unfavourable price variance.

Direct labour efficiency variance

The **direct labour efficiency variance** compares the labour hours worked to produce the actual output to the standard amount of labour hours allowed for the actual output; it values this difference at the standard labour price per hour. Like the direct materials, the direct labour used is recorded in the work in process account at standard cost.

$$\text{Direct labour efficiency variance} = \left(\begin{array}{c} \text{Actual hours for} \\ \text{actual output} \end{array} - \begin{array}{c} \text{Standard hours for} \\ \text{actual output} \end{array} \right) \times \text{Standard price}$$

The standard amount of time to pack 1 bucket of ice cream is 0.1 hour, and 3950 hours were used to pack 40 000 buckets. The direct labour efficiency variance is calculated as:

$$[3950 \text{ hours} - (40000 \text{ buckets} \times 0.1 \text{ hour per bucket})] \times \$8 \text{ per hour}$$
$$= (3950 \text{ hours} - 4000 \text{ hours}) \times \$8 \text{ per hour} = \$400 \text{ F}$$

This variance is favourable because actual hours were less than standard hours. For the processing labour the efficiency variance is the difference between the standard hours allowed (40 000 buckets × 0.2 hour per bucket) less the actual hours of 8200, multiplied by the standard labour rate of $8 which gives us a $1600 unfavourable efficiency variance.

Summary of direct labour variances

Packing labour

Flexible budget variance	$5525 unfavourable
Explained by:	
Price variance	3950 hours × ($8 − $9.50) = $5925 unfavourable
Efficiency variance	(3950 hours − 4000 hours) × $8.00 = $400 favourable

Processing labour

Flexible budget variance	$13 900 unfavourable
Explained by:	
Price variance	8200 hours × ($8 − $9.50) = $12 300 unfavourable
Efficiency variance	(8200 hours − 8000 hours) × $8 = $1600 unfavourable

Journal entries for direct costs and variances

In a standard cost system for a manufacturer, inventory accounting entries are recorded using standard costs. Differences between actual and standard costs are recorded in variance accounts (without the variances being recorded in the general ledger, the debits will not equal the credits). Later in the chapter, we learn to close variance accounts at the end of an accounting period. Figure 11.4 summarises the variances and journal entries used by Benny's for the frozen blackberries direct material and the direct labour for packing 40 000 buckets of Purple Madness ice cream.

Figure 11.4 shows that when 50 000 kilograms of frozen blackberries are purchased, they are recorded in raw material inventory at standard cost ($50 000) and the price variance is recorded ($12 500 U). Then 39 000 kilograms are removed from raw materials inventory at standard cost ($39 000). The direct materials price and efficiency variances account for the difference between actual and standard costs. The labour journal entry is also presented in figure 11.4. The entry for work in process inventory is made at the standard quantity and standard cost. Wages payable is credited for the actual wages owed to employees. The direct labour price and efficiency variances account for the difference between actual and standard costs.

11.4 Analysing direct cost variance information

LEARNING OBJECTIVE 11.4 Understand how direct cost variance information is analysed and used.

Direct cost variances are analysed using the process introduced in chapter 10, figure 10.2. The process begins with calculation of the variances relating to direct material and direct labour. For variances chosen for further investigation, the reasons for the variances are identified. Breaking the variances into price and efficiency components, as illustrated in figure 11.3, helps to identify why actual direct costs differ from standard costs.

Identifying reasons for direct cost variances

In the Benny's example, an unfavourable direct materials price variance and an unfavourable direct labour variance were identified. The combined direct cost variances are unfavourable. Does this result mean that operations are performing worse than expected? What about the favourable direct materials efficiency variance? Is some type of corrective action needed? Before addressing these types of questions, it is necessary to discover the reasons for the direct cost variances.

Figure 11.5 lists examples of circumstances that can cause direct cost variances. Some types of variances are relatively easy to discover. For example, accountants would know whether the entity negotiated a pay increase as well as the amount of the pay increase. To determine whether the pay increase explains an unfavourable direct labour price variance, they could simply compare the amount of the variance with the expected amount of the pay increase. Some types of variances are more difficult to discover. For example, it would not be easy to determine that workers intentionally worked slower than expected. Theft and fraud are hard to discover because the perpetrators deliberately try to hide them. Determining that a standard is incorrect, especially for price variances, may be relatively easy. For other types of variances, however, that process is more difficult because of uncertainties about the reasonableness of standard prices and quantities.

When analysing variances, it is necessary to consider possible trade-offs. A favourable variance in one area might be partially or completely offset by an unfavourable variance in another area. For example, say Benny's managers eliminate monitoring of labour efficiency and focus instead on spoilage rates to increase quality. As a result, labour efficiency could decline and product defect rates improve. However, what if the variance caused by the decline in labour efficiency was larger than the gain from improved quality (that is, lower product defect rates). This may prompt the managers to resume monitoring practices to bring labour efficiency back into control.

FIGURE 11.4 Direct cost variances for Benny's Purple Madness ice cream

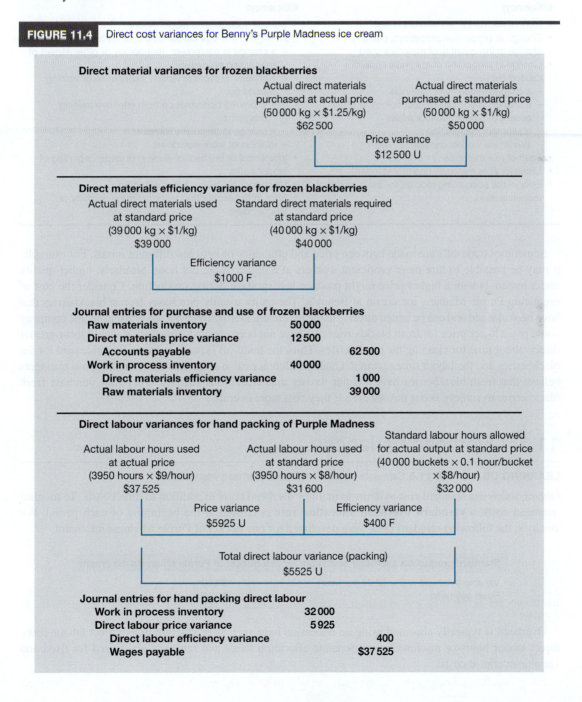

FIGURE 11.5   Examples of reasons for direct cost variances

Direct materials variances	Direct labour variances
Price:	**Price:**
• Change in price paid for materials caused by: – a change in the quality of materials purchased – a change in quantity purchased, leading to a change in purchase discount – a new supplier contract • Unreasonable materials price standard • Error in the accounting records for the actual price of materials	• Change in average wages paid to employees caused by: – a new union contract or enterprise agreement – a change in average experience or training of workers – a change in the government-mandated minimum wage • Unanticipated overtime hours • Unreasonable labour price standard • Error in the accounting records for the actual price of direct labour
Efficiency:	**Efficiency:**

• Normal fluctuation in materials usage
• Change in production processes, causing a change in the quantity of materials used
• Change in proportion of materials spoiled caused by:
 – a change in quality of materials
 – a change in equipment, technology or other aspect of production processes
 – equipment malfunction
 – intentional worker damage
• Theft of raw materials
• Unreasonable materials quantity standard
• Error in the accounting records for the quantity of materials used
	• Normal fluctuation in labour hours
	• Change in average labour time caused by:
	 – a change in equipment, technology or other aspect of production processes
	 – a change in average worker experience or training caused by:
	  ° improved performance from effective training programs
	  ° change in employee turnover
	 – intentional work slowdown
	• Intentional or unintentional over- or under-reporting of labour hours
	• Unreasonable labour hours standard
	• Error in the accounting records for the quantity of labour hours

Sometimes trade-offs are made between price and efficiency or between different inputs. For example, it may be possible to hire more proficient workers at a higher wage per hour. Similarly, higher-quality direct materials with a higher price might produce less spoilage during production. Consider the cost of producing Purple Madness ice cream at Benny's. The entity usually purchases frozen blackberries that have been cleaned and can be added directly to the ice cream. During fresh blackberry season, the company could pay a lower price for fresh blackberries that have not been cleaned. However, it would incur greater direct labour time for cleaning the blackberries. Thus, the trade-off is made between the price paid for the blackberries and the labour time required. Quality differences also affect this decision. Suppose managers believe that fresh blackberries have a better flavour than frozen blackberries. They may purchase fresh blackberries to achieve better flavour even if they cost more overall.

11.5 Overhead variances

LEARNING OBJECTIVE 11.5 Calculate variable and fixed overhead variances.

Organisations use standard cost systems to monitor overhead costs in addition to direct costs. To monitor overhead costs, a **standard overhead allocation rate** is created at the beginning of each period. For Benny's, the following standard rates were developed for one bucket of Purple Madness ice cream.

Standard production overhead cost rates for one bucket of Purple Madness ice cream	
Variable overhead (0.3 × $2.00 per hour)	$0.60
Fixed overhead	$0.40

Overhead is typically allocated using an allocation base such as production units, direct labour costs, direct labour hours or machine hours. Separate allocation bases and rates are often used for fixed and variable overhead costs.

The **standard variable overhead allocation rate** is determined by estimating the variable amount of overhead cost per unit of an allocation base as follows:

$$\text{Standard variable overhead allocation rate} = \frac{\text{Estimated variable overhead cost}}{\text{Estimated volume of an allocation base}}$$

For example, the accountant at Benny's estimated the annual variable overhead costs as $302 400 and the labour hours as 151 200 (0.3 hour per bucket × 504 000 buckets), so the cost function for variable overhead costs is $2 per direct labour hour.

Accountants choose allocation bases for variable overhead that reflect the use of variable resources. Indirect labour costs, such as maintenance wages, might be related to direct labour costs; as the number of employees providing direct labour increases, the number of maintenance worker hours increases. When the proportion of labour-related costs in the variable overhead cost pool is high, direct labour hours or direct labour cost are appropriate allocation bases. Alternatively, other indirect materials cost could be a large proportion of the variable overhead cost pool. In this case, the estimated volume of units would be the most appropriate allocation base. Recall the variable cost behaviour pattern, which is that total costs will vary in proportion to the allocation base.

Although fixed costs do not vary with volume, we need to develop an allocation rate to assign these costs to inventory and cost of sales. Any unit cost calculated will be dependent on the volume in the allocation base. Recall that fixed costs per unit have an inverse relationship to volume. The volume used in the allocation base will be the budgeted volume of the allocation base for the accounting period.

The **standard fixed overhead allocation rate** is determined as follows:

$$\text{Standard fixed overhead allocation rate} = \frac{\text{Estimated fixed overhead cost}}{\text{Estimated volume of an allocation base}}$$

For example, the estimated annual fixed overhead cost for Benny's is $201 600 and the entity allocates fixed overhead based on units produced using a normal volume of 504 000 buckets of ice cream during the year, the standard fixed overhead allocation rate is $201 600 ÷ 504 000 buckets, or $0.40 per bucket. Therefore, standard fixed overhead of $0.40 will be allocated to the cost of each bucket of ice cream.

At the end of the period, variances between standard allocated overhead costs and actual costs are analysed. The **variable overhead budget variance** is the difference between allocated variable overhead cost and actual variable overhead cost. The **fixed overhead budget variance** is the difference between allocated fixed overhead cost and actual fixed overhead cost. As shown in figure 11.6, the overhead variances can be broken down into the following components:

- variable overhead budget variance:
  - spending variance
  - efficiency variance
- fixed overhead budget variance:
  - spending variance
  - production volume variance.

Variable overhead spending variance

The **variable overhead spending variance** is the difference between the actual variable overhead costs for the actual output compared with the total expected variable overhead costs for the actual output. The expected variable overhead costs would be dependent on the actual level of the allocation base, which in the Benny's example is the direct labour hour. We can look at this comparison in more detail to highlight the difference.

Actual variable overhead cost for actual use of allocation base
= Actual use of variable overhead resources
× Actual cost paid for resources consumed

compared to:

Expected variable overhead cost for actual use of allocation base
= Expected use of variable overhead resources
× Expected cost for resources consumed

FIGURE 11.6 Overhead cost variances

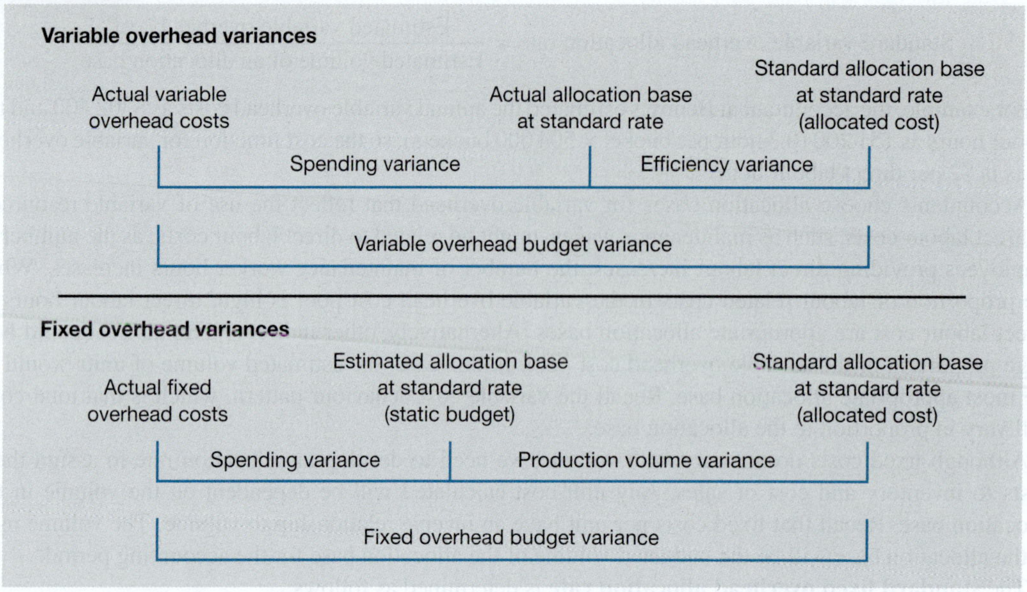

Variable overhead variances

Actual variable overhead costs		Actual allocation base at standard rate		Standard allocation base at standard rate (allocated cost)
	Spending variance		Efficiency variance	
	Variable overhead budget variance			

Fixed overhead variances

Actual fixed overhead costs		Estimated allocation base at standard rate (static budget)		Standard allocation base at standard rate (allocated cost)
	Spending variance		Production volume variance	
	Fixed overhead budget variance			

The above comparison shows that the spending variance could be due to either under/over use of the actual resources or higher/lower cost of the actual resources compared with the standard variable cost allowed for the actual use of the direct labour hours. The variable overhead spending variance helps managers monitor whether the organisation spent the planned amount on overhead. Because variable overhead costs are expected to vary with activity, the calculation for the spending variance takes into account the actual volume of activity. We can see from the breakdown above that the spending variance can be influenced not only by the amount paid for variable overhead resources, but also by the amount used of the resource for the given level of activity of the allocation base.

For Benny's, the allocation base for variable overhead is direct labour hours. The normal annual volume of direct labour hours is 504 000 buckets × 0.3 hour per bucket, or 151 200 hours. The standard variable overhead allocation rate is $2 per direct labour hour or $0.60 per bucket (0.3 hours × $2 per hour). The flexible budget shows that actual variable overhead costs for the month were $23 500 and actual labour hours were 12 150 hours, which gives an actual variable cost rate per direct labour hour of $1.93. The $1.93 is the result of actual use of variable overhead resources times the actual price paid. As this is below the $2 estimated variable cost allocation rate we would expect a favourable spending variance. The variable overhead spending variance is calculated as:

$$\frac{\text{Variable overhead}}{\text{spending variance}} = \frac{\text{Actual variable}}{\text{overhead cost}} - \left(\frac{\text{Standard variable}}{\text{overhead allocation rate}} \times \frac{\text{Actual volume of}}{\text{allocation base}} \right)$$

$$= \$23\,500 - (\$2\,\text{per hour} \times 12\,150\,\text{hours})$$
$$= \$23\,500 - \$24\,300$$
$$= \$800\,\text{F}$$

The variance is favourable because actual variable overhead costs were less than expected, given the actual volume of output. To understand whether this variance is caused by a usage or cost factor, further investigations would need to be undertaken by Benny's managers.

Variable overhead efficiency variance

The difference between the standard amount of variable overhead for the actual volume of the allocation base and the flexible budget for variable overhead cost is called the **variable overhead efficiency variance**. This variance is favourable if the actual volume of the allocation base is less than expected given actual production levels, and it will be unfavourable if the actual volume of the allocation base is more than expected. Therefore, this variance focuses on the volume difference in the allocation base used between the standard and actual. This variance is for bookkeeping purposes (and not for control), as the reason for the variance relates to the use of labour hours and not variable costs. It is calculated as follows:

$$\text{Variable overhead efficiency variance} = \left(\begin{array}{c}\text{Standard volume of}\\\text{allocation base for}\\\text{actual output}\end{array} - \begin{array}{c}\text{Actual}\\\text{volume of}\\\text{allocation base}\end{array}\right) \times \begin{array}{c}\text{Standard}\\\text{variable overhead}\\\text{allocation rate}\end{array}$$

During the month, Benny's produced 40 000 buckets of ice cream. The standard number of direct labour hours for actual production is 12 000 hours (40 000 buckets × 0.3 hour per bucket) and 12 150 actual hours were used. The standard variable overhead allocation rate is $2 per direct labour hour. Therefore, the variable overhead efficiency variance calculation is:

$$(12\,150 \text{ hours} - 12\,000 \text{ hours}) \times \$2 \text{ per hour} = \$300\,U$$

The variance is unfavourable because actual direct labour hours are more than expected, given actual production of 40 000 buckets of ice cream. Therefore, the total variable overhead budget variance is equal to $500 favourable and is the overapplied variable overhead for the accounting period. In a standard costing system, overhead is applied to work in process based on the expected hours, not the actual hours, and the amount applied would be $2 × 12 000 hours ($24 000 as shown in the flexible budget).

Fixed overhead spending variance

The **fixed overhead spending variance** is the difference between actual fixed overhead costs and estimated fixed overhead costs (the static budget amount). Fixed overhead costs are not expected to fluctuate with levels of activity and this is why we did not have a variance between the static budget and the flexible budget. Thus, the spending variance is not affected by the volume of activity; it reflects the amount by which the actual spending on fixed overhead differs from the estimated fixed overhead (the static budget). The spending variance helps managers monitor whether the entity spent the planned amount on overhead. We use the following formula:

Fixed overhead spending variance = Actual fixed overhead costs − Estimated fixed overhead costs

The fixed overhead budget at Benny's was $201 600 which, spread over the 12 months, would be $16 800 per month and actual costs for the month were $20 000. The fixed overhead spending variance is calculated as:

$$\$20\,000 - \$16\,800 = \$3200\,U$$

The variance is unfavourable because more was spent on fixed overhead than was estimated. This variance is also known as the budget variance as it compares actual costs to costs in the entity's annual budget.

Production volume variance

The difference between the standard amount of fixed overhead cost allocated to products and the estimated fixed overhead costs is called the production volume variance. If actual volumes of the allocation base exceed normal (that is, estimated) volumes, fixed overhead will be overapplied and the variance will be favourable. Conversely, if actual volumes of the allocation base are less than normal volumes, fixed overhead will be underapplied and the variance will be unfavourable. The production volume variance is calculated only for fixed overhead. This variance is used for bookkeeping purposes and you will notice that this variance is not included in the budget analysis to understand the difference between planned profit and actual profit. The actual overhead costs need to be allocated to inventory each period. This variance is used to adjust balances at the end of the period so that the total costs recorded in the financial statements are equal to the actual costs incurred. The variance is calculated as follows:

$$\text{Production volume variance} = \left(\begin{array}{c}\text{Standard volume of}\\\text{allocation base for}\\\text{actual output}\end{array} - \begin{array}{c}\text{Estimated}\\\text{volume of}\\\text{allocation base}\end{array}\right) \times \begin{array}{c}\text{Standard}\\\text{fixed overhead}\\\text{allocation rate}\end{array}$$

For Benny's, the estimated monthly fixed overhead was $16 800 and the estimated monthly volume of the allocation base was 42 000 buckets (504 000 buckets ÷ 12 months) (normal production). The standard allocation rate is $201 600 ÷ 504 000 buckets = $0.40 per bucket. Actual production was 40 000 buckets. The production volume variance is calculated as:

$$(40\,000 \text{ buckets} - 42\,000 \text{ buckets}) \times \$0.40 \text{ per bucket} = \$800\,U \text{ (rounded)}$$

Because actual production was less than budgeted production, Benny's fixed overhead is underapplied by $800 due to the volume difference of 2000 buckets ($800 unfavourable) and coupled with the spending variance ($3200 unfavourable) the overall underapplied overhead is $4000. If we recall the formula to calculate the fixed overhead allocation rate, we divided the budgeted fixed overhead ($201 600) by the planned level of output (504 000 buckets), which gave a rate of $0.40 per bucket. Converting this to a monthly rate, we have a formula of $16 800 divided by 42 000 buckets. The fixed overhead variances identify that we underestimated our fixed overhead budget by $3200 and overestimated our production volume by 2000 units. Therefore, if the accountant could estimate with certainty, the predetermined overhead rate for fixed overhead would have been $20 000 / 40 000 buckets giving a rate of $0.50. This also highlights another way to view the $4000 unfavourable fixed overhead variance by taking the difference between the budgeted rate and actual rate ($0.40 – $0.50) and multiplying it by the actual output of 40 000 buckets ($0.10 × 40 000 buckets = $4000).

Summary of overhead variances

Variable overhead

Flexible budget variance	$500 favourable
Explained by:	
Spending variance	$23 500 – (12 150 hours × $2) = $800 favourable
Efficiency variance	(12 150 hours – 12 000 hours) × $2 = $300 unfavourable

Fixed overhead

Budget variance	$3200 unfavourable
Explained by:	
Spending/budget variance	$20 000 – $16 800 = $3200 unfavourable
Fixed overhead applied (bookkeeping purposes only)	
Production volume variance	$800 unfavourable variance

Journal entries for overhead costs and variances

Organisations often use an overhead cost control account to keep track of actual and allocated overhead costs. As actual overhead costs are incurred, they are debited to the account. The account is then credited for the standard amount of overhead costs allocated to inventory. The remaining balance in the overhead cost control account is the total variance. This balance for fixed overhead costs is closed to separate spending and volume variance accounts, while the balance for variable overhead costs is closed to separate spending and efficiency variance accounts. The journal entries for Benny's are shown in figure 11.7 together with a summary of overhead variances.

11.6 Using overhead variance information

LEARNING OBJECTIVE 11.6 Understand how overhead variance information is analysed and used.

The process of analysing overhead variance information is similar to the process for direct cost variances. The analysis begins with calculating and then identifying the reasons for variances. Breaking the variances into spending, volume and efficiency components (illustrated in figure 11.7) helps to identify why actual overhead costs differ from standard costs.

Analysing overhead spending variances

Accountants investigate spending variances to pinpoint the specific fixed and variable overhead costs that differ from expectations. Usually the investigation includes analysing the spending variances for individual overhead costs such as supplies, property taxes, insurance and supervision salaries. Similar to direct costs, many reasons potentially explain why overhead costs differ from expectations. Sometimes unanticipated changes occur in costs. For example, an unfavourable spending variance might arise because an additional supervisor had to be hired when an increase in demand required increased production. Sometimes spending is out of control. For example, the staff may include too many maintenance employees. Once the reasons for variances are identified, managers decide what action to take, as discussed in chapter 10 (see figure 10.3).

FIGURE 11.7   Overhead variances for Benny's

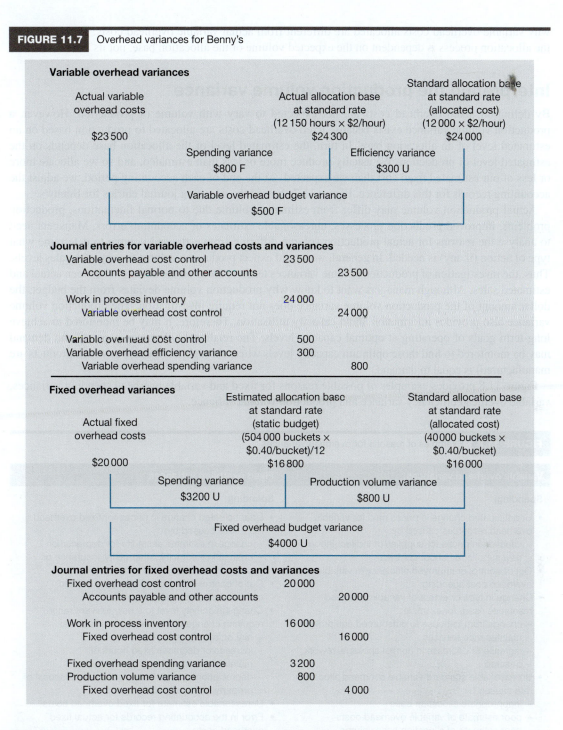

Variable overhead variances

Actual variable overhead costs	Actual allocation base at standard rate (12 150 hours × $2/hour)	Standard allocation base at standard rate (allocated cost) (12 000 × $2/hour)
$23 500	$24 300	$24 000

Spending variance $800 F

Efficiency variance $300 U

Variable overhead budget variance $500 F

Journal entries for variable overhead costs and variances

Variable overhead cost control	23 500	
Accounts payable and other accounts		23 500
Work in process inventory	24 000	
Variable overhead cost control		24 000
Variable overhead cost control	500	
Variable overhead efficiency variance	300	
Variable overhead spending variance		800

Fixed overhead variances

Actual fixed overhead costs	Estimated allocation base at standard rate (static budget) (504 000 buckets × $0.40/bucket)/12	Standard allocation base at standard rate (allocated cost) (40 000 buckets × $0.40/bucket)
$20 000	$16 800	$16 000

Spending variance $3200 U

Production volume variance $800 U

Fixed overhead budget variance $4000 U

Journal entries for fixed overhead costs and variances

Fixed overhead cost control	20 000	
Accounts payable and other accounts		20 000
Work in process inventory	16 000	
Fixed overhead cost control		16 000
Fixed overhead spending variance	3 200	
Production volume variance	800	
Fixed overhead cost control		4 000

Interpreting the variable overhead efficiency variance

Variable overhead costs are allocated to production based on an estimated volume of an allocation base. The allocation base used for variable costs is typically some type of resource input (such as labour hours, labour costs or machine hours) or the volume of output. Because the direct cost efficiency variances already provide information about the efficiency of inputs and outputs, overhead efficiency variances provide no new information.

For example, consider the Benny's illustration. Recall that direct labour hours were used to calculate the standard variable overhead allocation rate. The variable overhead efficiency variance was unfavourable because actual labour hours exceeded standard labour hours. The inefficient use of labour hours was already reflected in the unfavourable direct labour efficiency variance (shown previously in figure 11.4). Thus, the variable overhead efficiency variance provides no new information; for monitoring purposes it is meaningless. However, this variance must be calculated for bookkeeping reasons; it helps to explain why variable overhead costs allocated are different from actual variable overhead costs. That is because the allocation process is dependent on the expected volume of the allocation base, not its actual volume.

Interpreting the production volume variance

By definition, fixed overhead costs are not expected to vary with volume of production. However, a production volume variance exists because fixed overhead costs are allocated to production based on an estimated level of an allocation base. In turn, the estimated level of the allocation base depends on the estimated level of production. We usually produce more or less than estimated, and so we allocate more or less of our estimated fixed cost than we expected. At the end of each accounting period, we adjust the accounting records for this difference. Figure 11.7 showed the adjusting journal entries for Benny's.

Actual production volume may differ from estimated volume due to normal fluctuations, production problems, improved production processes, unreasonable estimates or accounting errors. Managers need to analyse the reasons for actual production volume differing from estimated volume to determine what type of action (if any) is needed. In general, we would expect production volume to vary with sales levels. Thus, the investigation of production volume variances tends to focus on the deviation between actual and estimated sales. Although managers want to know why production volume deviates from the budget, the dollar amount of the production volume variance does not require investigation. The production volume variance also provides information about capacity utilisation. Therefore, it may be monitored to achieve long-term goals of operating at optimal capacity levels. The relationship between capacity and demand may be monitored to find those optimum capacity levels where throughput (the rate at which products are manufactured) is equal to demand.

Figure 11.8 provides examples of possible reasons for fixed and variable overhead spending variances, variable overhead efficiency variance and production volume variance.

FIGURE 11.8 Examples of reasons for overhead variances

Variable overhead variances	Fixed overhead variances
Spending:	**Spending:**
• Unanticipated change in prices paid for variable overhead resources caused by: – variation in prices for supplies or indirect labour – new supplier or labour contract • Out of control or improved efficiency in variable overhead cost spending • Change in type or extent of variable overhead resources used, for example: – change from in-house to outsourced equipment maintenance services – increase or decrease in normal spoilage, rework or scrap • Unreasonable standard variable overhead allocation rate caused by: – inappropriate allocation base – poor estimate of variable overhead costs – poor estimate of allocation base volume • Error in the accounting records for actual variable overhead costs	• Unanticipated change in prices for fixed overhead resources caused by: – change in estimate asset life for depreciation – change in electricity, other utility, insurance or property tax rates • Out of control or improved efficiency in fixed overhead cost spending • Change in activity level to a new relevant range, requiring change in fixed resources such as: – hire or lay off a supervisor – increase or decrease fixed hours of maintenance staff – depreciation change from purchase or disposal of property, plant and equipment • Unreasonable estimate for fixed overhead costs • Error in the accounting records for actual fixed overhead costs
Efficiency:	**Production volume:**
• Fluctuation in efficiency of the allocation base (e.g. labour hours, labour costs, machine hours, units produced)	• Normal fluctuation in volume of allocation base (usually caused by changes in demand) • Improved production processes • Unreasonable estimate of volume of the allocation base • Error in the accounting records for actual output

---

11.7 Cost variance adjustments in the general ledger

LEARNING OBJECTIVE 11.7 Close off manufacturing cost variances at the end of the period.

When all of the production entries and variances are recorded for an accounting period, an additional entry is made to eliminate the variance accounts. Recall from our variance analysis that all costs are recorded in the work in process at standard cost. If the total variance is favourable, fewer resources were used than estimated, and if the total variance is unfavourable, more resources were used than estimated. Normally any difference would be directly charged to the statement of profit or loss (or statement of comprehensive income), thereby adjusting cost of sales.

The type of adjustment made typically depends on whether variances are material, a decision that is a matter of judgement. Amounts are generally viewed as material if their treatment would affect the decisions of people who rely on reported values. If the net amount of variances is deemed immaterial, the adjustment is usually made only to cost of sales. However, the existence of material variances means that the standard costs assigned to product units do not fairly represent the actual cost of the units. Thus, if the net amount of variances is material, an alternative adjustment is to pro rata the variance to work in process, finished goods inventory and cost of sales.

AASB 102 *Inventories* does not allow the variances relating to over/underapplied overhead to be prorated between the cost of sales and inventory for external reporting purposes. All such variances are recognised as an expense. However, a business has the choice to change this for internal reporting purposes particularly if the variances are significant.

Comprehensive example 2 continues our look at Concrete Transformation. Recall that, in chapter 10, we focused on the development of standard costs, and the determination of variances between the budgets (both flexible and static) and actual costs to identify variances. In the following example we delve deeper into understanding these variances and in so doing reinforce our understanding of a standard cost accounting system.

COMPREHENSIVE EXAMPLE 2

Analysing variances

In chapter 10 we were introduced to Karen, the new accountant at Concrete Transformation. One of her first tasks was to develop a standard cost for the concrete blocks manufactured by the business. After many meetings and analysis of both financial and production records, the following standard costs were developed for the resources used in the manufacture of the concrete blocks.

Direct materials:	
Cost of cement mix	$10 per kg
Quantity of cement mix	1 kg per block
Standard cost per block ($10 per kg × 1 kg per block)	$10
Direct labour:	
Labour pay rate	$10 per hour
Quantity of direct labour	100 blocks per labour hour
Standard cost per block ($10 per hour × 1 hour per 100 blocks)	$0.10
Fixed overhead:	
Planned spending	$180 000
Volume of allocation base (blocks produced)	90 000 blocks
Standard cost per block ($180 000 ÷ 90 000 blocks)	$2
Variable overhead:	
Spending per labour hour	$2
Standard cost per block ($2 ÷ 100 blocks)	$0.02

Based on these standards and the expected production volume of 90 000 blocks, Karen created the following budget for next month's production costs.

Direct materials (90 000 blocks × $10 per block)	$ 900 000
Direct labour (90 000 blocks × $0.10 per block)	9 000
Fixed overhead	180 000
Variable overhead (90 000 blocks × $0.02 per block)	1 800
Total standard production costs (90 000 blocks × $12.12 per block)	$1 090 800

At the end of the first month after Karen developed the cost standards, she collected the data needed to perform a direct cost variance analysis:

- 100 000 cement blocks were produced.
- The entity purchased 130 000 kg of cement mix for $975 000.
- 120 000 kg of cement mix were used.
- Direct labour employees were paid $16 500 and worked 1100 hours.
- Actual fixed overhead costs were $175 000.
- Actual variable overhead costs were $2500.

After flexing the budget, Karen identified a $98 000 unfavourable production cost variance, which was broken down by the resources used in production. Karen wants to focus on these individual variances to understand more about the price and efficiency of the resources consumed in production.

	Flexible budget	Variance Price/Efficiency	Actual
Production volume	100 000	0	100 000
Production costs			
Direct materials	$ 1 000 000	$100 000	$ 900 000
Direct labour	$ 10 000	-$ 6 500	$ 16 500
Variable overhead	$ 2 000	-$ 500	$ 2 500
Fixed overhead	$ 180 000*	$ 5 000	$ 175 000
Total production costs	**$1 212 000**	**$ 98 000**	**$1 094 000**

*In relation to the fixed overhead variance we are only isolating the spending variance.

Variances for direct materials and direct labour

Direct materials price variance

Karen first calculates the direct materials price variance. The purchase price last month for the cement mix was $975 000 for 130 000 kilograms, or $7.50 per kilogram. The standard cost is $10 per kilogram. She calculates the direct materials price variance as follows:

$$(\text{Actual price} - \text{Standard price}) \times \text{Quantity purchased}$$
$$= (\$7.50 - \$10) \times 130\,000 \text{ kg}$$
$$= \$325\,000 \text{ F}$$

Because the price per kilogram that Concrete Transformation paid last month is less than expected, the direct materials price variance is favourable. However, in relation to the flexible budget only $300 000 (120 000 kg × $2.50) is relevant as only 120 000 kg of the purchased material was used in production.

Direct labour price variance

Next, Karen calculates the direct labour price variance. During the month, Concrete Transformation paid its employees $16 500 for 1100 hours of work. Thus, the actual price for labour was $15 per hour ($16 500 ÷ 1100 hours). The standard cost is $10 per hour, so $11 000 should have been paid for 1100 hours of work. Therefore, the direct labour price variance is:

$$(\text{Actual labour price per hour} - \text{Standard labour price per hour})$$
$$\times \text{Labour hours used}$$
$$= (\$15 - \$10) \times 1100 \text{ hours}$$
$$= \$5500 \text{ U}$$

Because the entity paid more than the standard labour wage, the direct labour price variance is unfavourable.

Direct materials efficiency variance

After completing the direct cost price variances, Karen calculates the direct cost efficiency variances. Efficiency variances are calculated based on actual production volume (that is, the quantity of concrete blocks produced). During the last month, the entity produced 100 000 blocks using 120 000 kilograms of cement mix. The standard quantity of direct materials is 1 kilogram per block for a total of 100 000 kilograms of cement mix. Karen calculated the direct materials efficiency variance as follows:

$$(\text{Actual quantity for actual output} - \text{Standard quantity for actual output}) \times \text{Standard price}$$
$$= \left[120\,000\,\text{kg} - (1\,\text{kg per block} \times 100\,000\,\text{blocks})\right] \times \$10\,\text{per kg}$$
$$= (120\,000\,\text{kg} - 100\,000\,\text{kg}) \times \$10\,\text{per kg} = \$200\,000\,\text{U}$$

The materials efficiency variance is unfavourable because more materials (20 000 kilograms) than the standard quantity were used.

Direct labour efficiency variance

To calculate the direct labour efficiency variance, Karen first determines the amount of labour that should have been used to produce 100 000 blocks and then compares it to the amount of labour actually used, which was 1100 direct labour hours. The standard quantity of labour is 100 blocks per hour. The direct labour efficiency variance is calculated as follows:

$$(\text{Actual hours for actual output} - \text{Standard hours for actual output}) \times \text{Standard price}$$
$$= \left[1100\,\text{hours} - (100\,000\,\text{blocks} \times 1\,\text{hour per 100 blocks})\right] \times \$10\,\text{per hour}$$
$$= (1100\,\text{hours} - 1000\,\text{hours}) \times \$10\,\text{per hour} = \$1000\,\text{U}$$

Because actual hours exceeded standard hours, the direct labour efficiency variance is unfavourable.

Summary of direct cost variances

After calculating the individual direct cost variances, Karen creates a summary showing all of the variances, as shown in figure 11.9.

Analysing direct cost variance information

Karen examines the total favourable flexible budget variance of $93 500 relating to the direct costs ($300 000 − $200 000 − $5500 − $1000; see figure 11.9). In some cases, an overall favourable variance means that the organisation has no problems — operations performed better than expected. However, Karen is concerned about the large unfavourable efficiency variance for cement mix, and she is puzzled by its large favourable price variance. In addition, the unfavourable direct labour price variance seems high relative to total labour costs. However, Karen decides to focus her attention on only the two largest variances because these explain most of the total direct cost variance.

First, Karen considers the favourable price variance for cement mix. She speaks with Ricardo, who purchases direct materials. He has found a new supplier with better prices. Because he receives a bonus based on reducing the entity's costs, he is looking forward to a sizeable bonus. Karen tentatively thinks that the future standard cost for cement mix should be reduced to reflect the new lower price.

Next, Karen investigates the unfavourable efficiency variance for cement mix. She speaks with Jordan, the labour supervisor. He is very upset about a decrease in the quality of the cement mix from the new supplier; the mix contains inadequate quantities of an ingredient that prevents the blocks from slumping, or losing shape, when they are turned out of the forms. Although 120 000 blocks were produced, 20 000 of them were rejected because of the slumping problem. In addition, more labour hours were needed, leading to overtime payments. These factors explain the unfavourable direct labour price variance. Jordan is concerned that some of the blocks shipped to customers are not the correct shape. Some customers might become dissatisfied and no longer purchase cement blocks from the entity.

Karen plans to recommend to management that the entity pay a higher price (the original standard) for the higher-quality cement mix. Although it appeared that the entity saved money overall last month from the lower-priced mix, most of the savings were offset by unfavourable variances elsewhere caused by the lower quality. Furthermore, she believes that just the risk of lost sales in the future outweighs the cost savings. Karen also plans to work with management to design a better reward system that avoids any further adverse effects that result from the purchasing agent's bonus plan.

Overhead variances

The next stage of analysis for Karen is the overhead costs. At the end of the month, Karen determines that actual fixed overhead costs were $175 000, actual variable overhead costs were $2500, and 1100 actual labour hours were used.

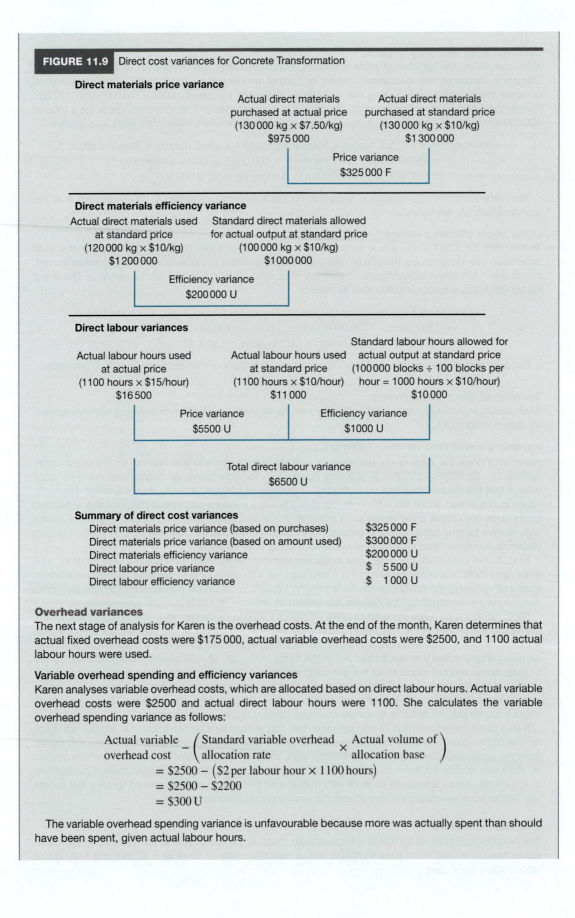

FIGURE 11.9 Direct cost variances for Concrete Transformation

Direct materials price variance

Actual direct materials purchased at actual price (130 000 kg × $7.50/kg) $975 000	Actual direct materials purchased at standard price (130 000 kg × $10/kg) $1 300 000

Price variance
$325 000 F

Direct materials efficiency variance

Actual direct materials used at standard price (120 000 kg × $10/kg) $1 200 000	Standard direct materials allowed for actual output at standard price (100 000 kg × $10/kg) $1 000 000

Efficiency variance
$200 000 U

Direct labour variances

Actual labour hours used at actual price (1100 hours × $15/hour) $16 500	Actual labour hours used at standard price (1100 hours × $10/hour) $11 000	Standard labour hours allowed for actual output at standard price (100 000 blocks ÷ 100 blocks per hour = 1000 hours × $10/hour) $10 000

Price variance
$5500 U

Efficiency variance
$1000 U

Total direct labour variance
$6500 U

Summary of direct cost variances

Direct materials price variance (based on purchases)	$325 000 F
Direct materials price variance (based on amount used)	$300 000 F
Direct materials efficiency variance	$200 000 U
Direct labour price variance	$ 5500 U
Direct labour efficiency variance	$ 1000 U

Overhead variances

The next stage of analysis for Karen is the overhead costs. At the end of the month, Karen determines that actual fixed overhead costs were $175 000, actual variable overhead costs were $2500, and 1100 actual labour hours were used.

Variable overhead spending and efficiency variances

Karen analyses variable overhead costs, which are allocated based on direct labour hours. Actual variable overhead costs were $2500 and actual direct labour hours were 1100. She calculates the variable overhead spending variance as follows:

$$\text{Actual variable overhead cost} - \left(\text{Standard variable overhead allocation rate} \times \text{Actual volume of allocation base} \right)$$
$$= \$2500 - (\$2 \text{ per labour hour} \times 1100 \text{ hours})$$
$$= \$2500 - \$2200$$
$$= \$300 \text{ U}$$

The variable overhead spending variance is unfavourable because more was actually spent than should have been spent, given actual labour hours.

Next, Karen calculates the variable overhead efficiency variance. Based on actual production of 100 000 blocks, the standard volume of the allocation base is 1000 direct labour hours (100 000 blocks × 0.01 hour per block). Given the standard cost of $2 per hour, the variable overhead efficiency variance is calculated as follows:

$$\left(\begin{array}{l}\text{Actual volume of} \\ \text{allocation base}\end{array} - \begin{array}{l}\text{Standard volume of allocation} \\ \text{base for actual output}\end{array}\right) \times \begin{array}{l}\text{Standard variable overhead} \\ \text{allocation rate}\end{array}$$

$$= (1100\,\text{labour hours} - 1000\,\text{labour hours}) \times \$2\,\text{per hour}$$
$$= \$2200 - \$2000$$
$$= \$200\,\text{U}$$

The variance is unfavourable because actual labour hours used in production exceeded the standard number of labour hours (see figure 11.10).

FIGURE 11.10 Variable overhead variances for Concrete Transformation

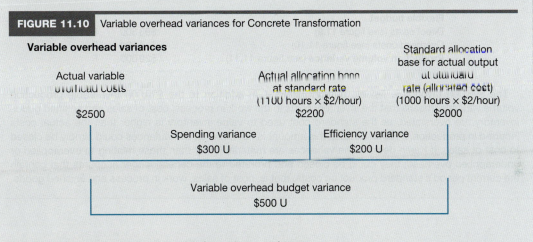

Fixed overhead spending and production volume variances

First, Karen calculates the fixed overhead spending variance as follows:

Actual fixed overhead costs − Estimated fixed overhead costs = $175 000 − $180 000 = $5000 F

The fixed overhead spending variance is favourable because less was spent than expected (see figure 11.11).

FIGURE 11.11 Fixed overhead variances for Concrete Transformation

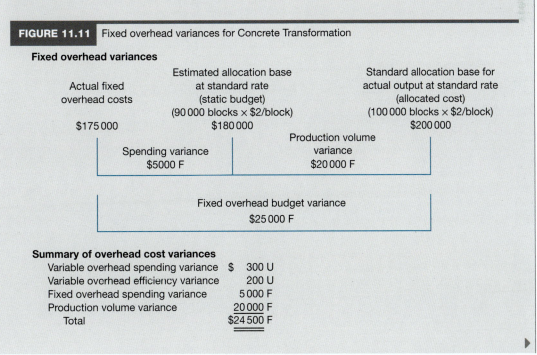

As also illustrated in figure 11.11, Karen calculates the production volume variance as follows:

$$\left(\begin{array}{c}\text{Standard volume of allocation} \\ \text{base for actual output}\end{array} - \begin{array}{c}\text{Estimated volume} \\ \text{of allocation base}\end{array}\right) \times \begin{array}{c}\text{Standard fixed overhead} \\ \text{allocation rate}\end{array}$$

$$= (100\,000 \text{ blocks} - 90\,000 \text{ blocks}) \times \$2 \text{ per block}$$
$$= \$20\,000 \text{ F}$$

Estimated production volume was 90 000 blocks, but 100 000 blocks were actually produced. Therefore, 10 000 more blocks were produced than expected, resulting in a favourable production volume variance; that is, fixed overhead costs were overapplied by $20 000 ($2 per block × 10 000 blocks).

Cost variance adjustments

Consider the production cost variances for Concrete Transformation. The combined variances are as follows:

Flexible budget		
Direct costs (see figure 11.9)	$93 500	F
Overhead costs (see figure 11.10)	$ 4 500	F
Production volume variance (see figure 11.11)	$20 000	F

The $98 000 favourable flexible budget variance, in addition to the $20 000 favourable production volume variance, means that the inventory costs in the work in process, cost of sales and finished goods inventory are overstated, as the standard cost used to value inventory is higher than the actual costs incurred in production. If Karen decides this amount is not material, the variances could simply be closed to cost of sales. If Karen decides the variances are material (other than those relating to overapplied or underapplied overhead) they could be closed and prorated to the general ledger accounts that contain the current period's standard production costs; that is, cost of sales, work in process and finished goods.

SUMMARY

11.1 Identify variances for investigation.

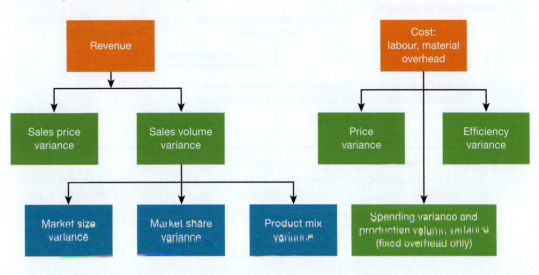

11.2 Understand and calculate relevant profit- and revenue-related variances.

The sales price variance is calculated by:

$$\text{Sales price variance} = (\text{Actual price} - \text{Standard price}) \times \text{Actual volume}$$

The sales quantity variance reflects the difference between the standard and actual quantity of units sold at the standard selling price. The sales quantity variance is calculated by:

$$\text{Sales quantity variance} = (\text{Actual volume} - \text{Budgeted volume}) \times \text{Standard price}$$

The impact of the sales volume variance on profit can be explained as follows.

1. The *market size variance* provides an indication of the proportion of the sales volume variance that can be attributed to unexpected changes in market size. It is calculated as follows:

$$\text{Market size variance} = \text{Change in market size} \times \text{Budgeted market share} \times \text{Planned average contribution margin}$$

2. The *market share variance* provides an indication of the proportion of the sales volume variance that can be attributed to changes in the market share. It is calculated as follows:

$$\text{Market share variance} = \text{Actual market size} \times \text{Change in market share} \times \text{Planned average contribution margin}$$

3. The *product mix variance* provides an indication of changes in contribution margin caused by selling in a different mix from the planned mix of products. This is only a relevant calculation in circumstances when the products involved are substitute products. In other circumstances this calculation would be of no value. The product mix variance is calculated as follows:

$$\text{Product mix variance} = \text{Change in average standard contribution margin} \times \text{Actual unit volume}$$

11.3 Calculate direct cost variances.

Direct cost variances

Direct material variances

	Actual direct materials purchased at actual price	Actual direct materials purchased at standard price
		Price variance

Actual direct materials used at standard price	Standard direct materials allowed for actual output at standard price
Efficiency variance	

Direct labour variances

Actual labour hours used at actual price	Actual labour hours used at standard price	Standard labour hours allowed for actual output at standard price
Price variance	Efficiency variance	

Total direct labour variance

Direct materials price variances are calculated using the following formula:

$$\text{Direct materials price variance} = (\text{Actual price} - \text{Standard price}) \times \text{Quantity purchased}$$

11.4 Understand how direct cost variance information is analysed and used.

- For general process, see chapter 10, figure 10.2
- For examples of reasons for direct cost variances, see figure 11.5

Resource and quality trade-offs reflected in direct cost variances

- Price and efficiency
- Different inputs

11.5 Calculate variable and fixed overhead variances.

Overhead variances

Variable overhead variances

Actual variable overhead costs	Actual allocation base at standard rate	Standard allocation base at standard rate (allocated cost)
Spending variance	Efficiency variance	

Variable overhead budget variance

Fixed overhead variances

Actual fixed overhead costs	Estimated allocation base at standard rate (static budget)	Standard allocation base at standard rate (allocated cost)
Spending variance	Production volume variance	

Fixed overhead budget variance

11.6 Understand how overhead variance information is analysed and used.

- For the general process, see chapter 10, figure 10.2
- For examples of reasons for overhead variances, see figure 11.8

11.7 Close off manufacturing cost variances at the end of the period.

Immaterial variances

Standard costs fairly represent actual costs

- Close to cost of sales

Material variances

Standard costs do not fairly represent actual costs

- Variances other than those relating to over/underapplied overhead — distribute proportionately among:
  - work in process
  - finished goods
  - cost of sales.

Variances relating to over/underapplied overhead

To be written off to cost of sales

KEY TERMS

direct labour efficiency variance The difference between the labour hours worked to produce the actual output and the standard number of labour hours allowed for the actual output. (The difference is valued at the standard labour price per hour.)

direct labour price variance The difference between the actual price for labour and the standard price.

direct materials efficiency variance The difference between the actual amount of materials used and the standard amount of materials allowed for the actual level of output. (The difference is valued at the standard price.)

direct materials price variance The difference between the actual price for the amount of direct materials purchased and the standard price for the direct materials.

fixed overhead budget variance The difference between allocated fixed overhead cost and actual fixed overhead cost.

fixed overhead spending variance The difference between actual fixed overhead costs and estimated fixed overhead costs.

market share variance The proportion of the sales volume variance that can be attributed to changes in market share.

market size variance The proportion of the sales volume variance that can be attributed to changes in market size.

product mix variance The changes in contribution margin caused by selling substitute products or a different mix of products than planned.

revenue budget variance The difference between actual revenues and budgeted revenues.

sales price variance The difference between actual revenues and budgeted revenues for the volume actually sold.

sales quantity variance The difference between actual sales volume and budgeted sales volume for the standard price.

standard fixed overhead allocation rate An allocation rate used to allocate overhead; created at the beginning of each period to monitor overhead costs.

standard overhead allocation rate An allocation rate used to allocate overhead; created at the beginning of each period to monitor overhead costs.

standard variable overhead allocation rate An allocation rate determined by estimating the variable amount of overhead cost per unit of an allocation base.

variable overhead budget variance The difference between allocated variable overhead cost and actual variable overhead cost.

variable overhead efficiency variance The difference between the standard amount of variable overhead for the actual volume of the allocation base and the flexible budget for variable overhead cost.

variable overhead spending variance The difference between the actual variable overhead costs for the actual output and the total expected variable overhead costs for the actual output.

SELF-STUDY PROBLEMS

SELF-STUDY PROBLEM 1 Direct cost and overhead variances, variance analysis

Latiefa is the cost accountant at Hallet and Sons, a manufacturer of exquisite glass serving bowls. The materials used for the bowls are inexpensive but the process is labour intensive. The supervisor decided to use cheaper labour this period to see whether costs could be reduced. Latiefa needs to prepare a report for her supervisor about how effective operations had been during the month of January. She had set the following standards.

		Cost per unit
Direct materials	3 kg @ $2.50	$ 7.50
Direct labour	5 hours @ $15	75.00
Factory overhead:		
Variable	$3 per direct labour hour	15.00
Fixed	$20 per unit	20.00

Variable overhead is allocated by labour hours, and fixed overhead is allocated by unit. Estimated production per month is 8000 units (40 000 direct labour hours) with fixed overhead expenditure budgeted at $160 000.

Records for January based on production of 7800 units indicated the following:

Direct materials purchased	25 000 kg @ $2.60
Direct materials used	23 100 kg
Direct labour	40 100 hours @ $14.60
Variable overhead	$119 000
Fixed overhead	$180 000

The entity's policy is to record direct material price variances at the time materials are purchased.

Required

(a) Prepare a simple, meaningful variance report for direct materials, direct labour, and variable and fixed overhead that Latiefa could present to her supervisor.

(b) Attach to the variance report a discussion of the variances and a recommendation about whether some of them should be investigated further.

SOLUTION TO SELF-STUDY PROBLEM 1

(a) Latiefa could present the following variance report to her supervisor.

	Favourable (F) or unfavourable (U) variance					
	Price/spending		Volume/efficiency		Total	
Direct materials	$ 2500	U	$ 750	F	$ 1750	U
Direct labour	16 040	F	16 500	U	460	U
Total direct cost variance					2 210	U
Variable overhead	1 300	F	3 300	U	2 000	U
Fixed overhead	20 000	U	4 000	U	24 000	U
Total overhead cost variance					26 000	U
Total variance					$ 28 210	U

Calculation check:

Standard costs allocated based on actual production [7800 units × ($7.50 + $75 + $20 + $15)]		$916 500
Less actual costs:		
Direct materials:		
Materials used at standard cost (23 100 kg × $2.50)	$ 57 750	
Unfavourable price variance for material purchases [25 000 kg × ($2.60 − $2.50)]	2 500	
Total direct material cost	60 250	
Direct labour (40 100 hours × $14.60)	585 460	
Variable overhead	119 000	
Fixed overhead	180 000	
Total actual costs		944 710
Total variance		$ 28 210 U

Details of the calculations are shown in figure 11.12.

FIGURE 11.12 Calculations for self-study problem 1

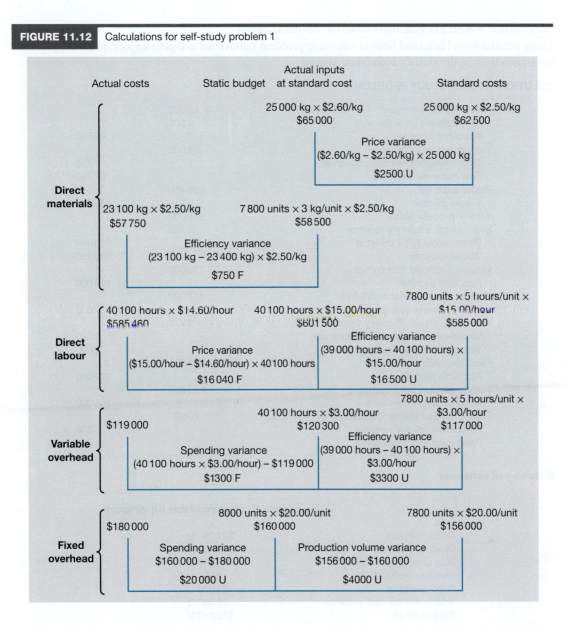

(b) Discussion of most significant variances.
- Because the supervisor hired less-expensive labour this month, it is not surprising that the direct labour price variance is large and favourable ($16 040). However, this positive variance is more than offset by a large unfavourable direct labour efficiency variance ($16 500). It appears that more hours were required to compensate for less-skilled labour. This variance should be investigated to verify the conjectures.
- If less-skilled labour has a negative effect on quality, sales could be lost. Any potential change in the quality of output needs to be investigated.
- The fixed overhead spending variance was very large and unfavourable ($20 000). These costs might be out of control and need to be investigated.
  Discussion of less-significant variances.
- Given the unfavourable direct materials price variance ($2500) and the favourable direct materials efficiency variance ($750), it is possible that the quality purchased this period has improved because less was used than expected. However, a price increase is also a possible explanation. These variances should be investigated to determine whether either or both of the standards should be changed.
- We need to determine whether a favourable variable overhead spending variance ($1300) was due to improvements made in variable overhead costs and whether such improvements can be sustained (that is, whether the standard should be changed).

SELF-STUDY PROBLEM 2 Journal entries for standard costing

Using the data from Hallet and Sons in self-study problem 1 above we will prepare journal entries to record the transactions in the entity's accounting system.

SOLUTION TO SELF-STUDY PROBLEM 2

Raw materials inventory	$ 62 500	
Direct materials price variance	2 500	
Accounts payable		$ 65 000
Work in process material	58 500	
Direct materials efficiency variance		750
Raw materials inventory		57 750
Wages expense	585 460	
Wages payable		585 460
Work in process labour	585 000	
Direct labour efficiency variance	16 500	
Direct labour price variance		16 040
Wages expense		585 460
Variable overhead cost control	119 000	
Accounts payable		119 000
Work in process variable overhead	117 000	
Variable overhead cost control		117 000
Variable overhead efficiency variance	3 300	
Variable overhead spending variance		1 300
Variable overhead cost control		2 000
Fixed overhead cost control	180 000	
Accounts payable		180 000
Work in process fixed overhead	156 000	
Fixed overhead cost control		156 000
Fixed overhead spending variance	20 000	
Production volume variance		4 000
Fixed overhead cost control		16 000

Summary of variances

Cost	Favourable (F) or unfavourable (U) variance
Direct materials	$21 750 U
Direct labour	460 U
Total direct cost variance	2 210 U
Variable overhead	2 000 U
Fixed overhead	24 000 U
Total overhead cost variance	26 000 U
Total variance	$28 210 U

In line with accounting standards, an additional entry is required to eliminate the variance accounts. As the total variance is unfavourable ($28 210) more resources were used than estimated, so the costs in inventory and cost of sales may need to be increased. One method that can be used to assess the materiality of the variances is to compare the combined variance amount to the total amount of actual production costs. The actual production costs were:

Direct material	$ 62 500
Direct labour	585 460
Variable overhead	119 000
Fixed overhead	156 000
Total actual production costs	$922 960

Therefore, the combined variances amount to $28 210 ÷ $922 960, or 3 per cent of actual production costs. If we decide this amount not to be material, the variances could simply be closed to cost of sales; that is, we decrease cost of sales by $28 120. Given that accountants often consider amounts larger than 10 per cent to be material the variance would not be considered important to pro rata among all inventory accounts.

QUESTIONS

11.1 Discuss the three variances that help explain the sales volume variance. **LO2**

11.2 Identify four revenue drivers. **LO2**

11.3 Why is the efficiency variance more useful for control purposes than the price variance? **LO4, 6**

11.4 Explain how accountants and managers decide which cost variances to monitor. **LO1, 4, 6**

11.5 Discuss why the variable overhead spending variance does not just focus on price. **LO5, 6**

11.6 How might the production volume variance encourage excess production? **LO5, 6**

11.7 Discuss the 'bookkeeping' role of standard costing and its performance role. **LO4, 6**

11.8 Explain why variances for direct material and direct labour are separated into price and efficiency variances. **LO4**

11.9 Suppose that utilities are considered a fixed cost for a retail clothing outlet. Why might we expect a variance to occur for the cost of utilities? **LO6**

11.10 Explain why the variance accounts need to be closed at the end of the period. **LO7**

11.11 Fly-a-Kite Company manufactures a variety of kite kits. You have been asked by the production manager to prepare a simple but meaningful variance report for product costs so that she can identify areas in need of improved cost control. List all of the variances you would present in the variance report for production costs and explain why each is useful. **LO1**

11.12 Identify the common variances that are needed to reconcile the accounting records at the end of the period for a manufacturing entity. How are these variances treated at the end of the period if the total variance is immaterial? How are they treated if the total variance is material? **LO1, 4, 5, 7**

11.13 Discuss factors that affect accountants' decisions to investigate the reasons for variances. **LO4, 6**

11.14 Suppose the direct materials price variance is large and favourable, and the direct materials efficiency variance is large and unfavourable. What questions would you be likely to ask when investigating these variances further? **LO5**

11.15 Why are direct materials price variances usually recorded at the time of purchase? **LO3**

11.16 A favourable variance is always good news and an unfavourable variance is always bad news. Discuss. **LO1**

11.17 Briefly explain why actions by the material purchasing manager can cause unfavourable labour efficiency variances for the production manager. **LO4**

11.18 What is the cause of an unfavourable volume variance? **LO5**

11.19 Recently the Victorian Government introduced a solar rebate of $2500 for eligible home owners. How might such an initiative impact on the budget variances for a business that installs solar panels given the rebate was announced halfway through the financial year? **LO2**

EXERCISES

11.20 Revenue variances **LO2**

Sunset Solar installs solar panels throughout Australia. The accountants estimated the market size to be 2 million solar panels with Sunset Solar hoping to achieve 5 per cent market share. The static budget shows that each panel is expected to provide a $2000 contribution margin. At the end of the financial period, the actual sales volume was 90 000 panels. Management were surprised by the low sales volume especially given that analysts had identified that the market size had grown by 2 per cent due to government rebates on solar panel installation.

Required

(a) Calculate the actual market size.

(b) Calculate the actual market share.

(c) Calculate the market size variance.

(d) Calculate the market share variance.

(e) Identify several factors that could have caused the variance identified in (d).

11.21 Direct labour variances **LO3**

Following is information about Pine Furniture's direct labour hours and wages last period.

Actual labour hours at the standard price per hour	1680
Actual labour hours at the actual price per hour	1752
Standard labour hours at the standard price per hour	1750
Standard labour hours at the actual price per hour	1825

Required

(a) Calculate the direct labour efficiency variance.

(b) Calculate the direct labour price variance.

11.22 Direct material variances   LO3

The Neon Manufacturing Company is a joint venture between Australian and Chinese firms with an assembly plant located in Beijing. The company's managers expected to produce 20 000 units of product in March. The standard cost for the materials used for 20 000 units is 173 600 yuan, and the standard cost per unit is 2.80 yuan per kilogram. Actual production in March was 19 100 units. The company purchased and used 57 300 kilograms of materials costing 163 305 yuan.

Required

(a) What was the standard quantity of kilograms per unit?

(b) What was the direct materials efficiency variance for March?

(c) What was the direct materials price variance for March?

11.23 Fixed overhead variances, solve for unknown   LO5

South Clinic charges its patients on the basis of actual direct costs incurred plus fixed costs at the rate of $40 per hour. The fixed cost rate of $40 per hour is based on the assumption of 6000 patient hours monthly, assuming that each patient requires half an hour. During September, 12 400 patients were seen and the following costs were recorded.

Fixed overhead costs allocated to patients	$248 000
Fixed overhead spending variance	$ 24 000 unfavourable

Required

(a) How many patient hours were recorded?

(b) What was the budgeted fixed cost?

(c) What was the production volume variance?

(d) What was the actual fixed overhead?

11.24 Fixed and variable overhead variances   LO5

Glen's Landscaping Supplies uses a standard costing system to allocate overhead costs. The accountant estimated 8500 hours as the volume to develop standard overhead rates. Budgeted costs were $19 125 for fixed overhead and $15 300 for variable overhead. The following results were reported.

Actual hours	8 200
Standard hours	8 300
Actual fixed overhead	$19 000
Actual variable overhead	$14 000

Required

(a) Calculate the spending variances for fixed and variable overhead.

(b) Calculate the overhead allocation rates for fixed and variable overhead.

(c) Calculate the production volume variance for fixed overhead.

(d) Calculate the efficiency variance for variable overhead.

11.25 Direct labour variances and overhead spending variance   LO3, 6

The following data for Kitchen Tile Company relate to the production of 18 000 tiles during the past month. The entity allocates fixed overhead costs at a standard rate of $19 per direct labour hour.

Direct labour:
Standard cost is 6 tiles per hour at $24 per hour
Actual cost per hour was $24.50
Labour efficiency variance was $6720 F
Fixed overhead costs:
  Estimated = $60 000
  Actual = $58 720

Required

(a) How many actual labour hours were worked to produce the 18 000 tiles?

(b) What is the price variance for direct labour?

(c) What is the budget variance for fixed costs?

11.26 Direct materials and labour variances; variances to investigate   **LO3, 4, 7**

The managers of Bathroom Cabinets established the following standards for Model 535:

	Quantity standard	Price standard
Direct materials	0.8 kg per unit	$2 per kg
Direct labour	0.2 hours per unit	$17 per hour

Last month, 15 342 units of Model 535 were produced at a cost of $26 870 for direct materials and $47 000 for direct labour. A total of 13 252 kilograms of direct materials was used. Total direct labour hours amounted to 2730 hours. During the same period, 110 000 kilograms of direct materials were purchased for $273 000. The entity's policy is to record materials price variances at the time materials are purchased.

Required

(a) What is the total standard cost for direct materials and direct labour for the output this period?

(b) What was the direct materials price variance?

(c) What was the direct materials efficiency variance?

(d) What was the direct labour price variance?

(e) What was the direct labour efficiency variance?

(f) Identify any variances that are material (greater than 10 per cent of total direct cost at standard). Discuss whether you would investigate these variances.

11.27 Direct materials and direct labour variances; journal entries   **LO3**

The following information pertains to Nell Company's production of one unit of its manufactured product during the month of June. The entity recognises the materials price variances when materials are purchased.

Standard quantity of materials	5 kg
Standard cost per kilogram	$0.20
Standard direct labour hours	0.4
Standard wage rate per hour	$7.00
Direct materials purchased	100 000 kg
Cost of direct materials purchased per kilogram	$0.17
Direct materials consumed for manufacture of 10 000 units	60 000 kg
Actual direct labour hours required for 10 000 units	3900
Actual direct labour cost per hour	$7.20

Required

(a) Calculate the price and efficiency (quantity) variances for materials and labour.

(b) Record the journal entries for purchase and use of direct materials and the journal entries for direct labour.

11.28 Variable and fixed overhead variances; journal entries   **LO5, 7**

Derf Company allocates overhead on the basis of direct labour hours. Two direct labour hours are required for each unit of product. Planned production for the period was set at 9000 units. Manufacturing overhead is estimated at $135 000 for the period (20 per cent of this cost is fixed). The 17 200 hours worked during the period resulted in the production of 8500 units. Variable manufacturing overhead cost incurred was $108 500 and the fixed manufacturing overhead cost was $28 000.

Required

(a) Determine the variable overhead spending variance.

(b) Determine the variable overhead efficiency (quantity) variance.

(c) Determine the fixed overhead spending (budget) variance.

(d) Determine the production volume (fixed overhead volume or denominator) variance.

(e) Prepare journal entries to close these variances at the end of the period.

11.29 Direct cost and overhead variances; decision to automate **LO3, 4, 5, 6**

Plush pet toys are produced in a largely automated factory in standard lots of 100 toys each. A standard cost system is used to control costs and to assign cost to inventory.

	Price standard	Quantity standard
Plush fabric	$ 2 per metre	15 metres per lot
Direct labour	$10 per hour	2 hours per lot

Variable overhead, estimated at $5 per lot, consists of miscellaneous items such as thread, a variety of plastic squeakers, and paints that are applied to create features such as eyes and whiskers. Fixed overhead, estimated at $24 000 per month, consists largely of depreciation on the automated machinery and rent for the building. Variable overhead is allocated based on lots produced. The standard fixed overhead allocation rate is based on the estimated output of 1000 lots per month.

Actual data for last month follow.

Production	2400 lots
Sales	1600 lots
Plush fabric purchased	30 000 metres
Cost of fabric purchased	$62 000
Fabric used	34 000 metres
Direct labour	4200 hours
Direct labour cost	$39 000
Variable overhead	$12 000
Fixed overhead	$24 920

The entity's policy is to record materials price variances at the time materials are purchased.

Required

(a) Calculate the commonly used direct cost and overhead variances.
(b) Management is considering further automation in the factory. Robot-controlled forklifts could reduce the standard direct labour per lot to 1.5 hours.
   (i) Estimate the savings per lot that would be realised from this additional automation.
   (ii) Assume the entity would be able to generate the savings as calculated. Considering only quantitative factors, calculate the maximum price the managers would be willing to pay for the robot-controlled forklifts. Assume the entity's management requires equipment costs to be recovered in five years, ignoring the time value of money.

11.30 Journal entries for closing variances **LO7**

Following are the variances for Fine Products Manufacturing Company for the month of March. Assume that the price variance for direct materials is calculated at the time of purchase and that the amount of direct materials purchased is equal to the amount of direct materials used, with no beginning or ending inventories for direct materials.

Direct materials price variance	$2000 U
Direct materials efficiency variance	1500 F
Labour price variance	5000 U
Labour efficiency variance	2000 U
Fixed overhead spending variance	200 U
Variable overhead spending variance	1000 F
Variable overhead efficiency variance	1200 U

Fine Products considers anything greater than $5000 as a material variance. Following are end-of-period inventory balances.

Work in process	$ 2000
Finished goods	6000
Cost of sales	24 000

Required

(a) Determine whether the total variance amount is material.
(b) Prepare a journal entry to close the variances at the end of March.

11.31 Revenue variances

The following data represent the flexible budget for Mountain Mist Brewery, a boutique brewery that manufactures and sells boutique ales.

	Static budget		Variance	Flexible budget	Actual		Variance
	Volume (megalitres)	$million	$million	$million	Volume (megalitres)	$million	$million
Sales	52.00	132.17		138.75	54.60	140.10	$7.93 F
Cost of sales	28.45	72.32		75.87	29.87	74.25	$1.93 U
Contribution margin		59.85	3.03	62.88		65.85	$6.00 F
Other costs		9.01				9.28	$0.27 U
Selling and administration costs		15.16				15.58	$0.42 U
EBIT		35.68				40.99	$5.31 F

Note that, overall, the increase in the final price of beer has contributed to the flattening of the Australian beer market. The budgeted market for beer sales in Australia was 1736 megalitres, but the actual market was 1730 megalitres.

Required

(a) Briefly explain the meaning of the $3.03 million contribution margin variance.

(b) Calculate the market share and market size variances for Mountain Mist Brewery.

PROBLEMS

11.32 Revenue variances

Consider the following information for Morgan's Cheese and Butter Division.

	Budgeted volume (kg)	Budgeted sales $	Variance	Flexible budget	Variance	Actual volume (kg)	Actual sales $
Sales data	5 750 000	23 000 000		22 000 000	2 750 000	5 500 000	24 750 000
Cost of sales	4 900 000*	14 700 000		14 060 870	(1 701 630)	4 850 000*	15 762 500
Contribution margin		8 300 000	(360 870)	7 939 130	1 048 370		8 987 500
Operating costs		3 000 000		3 000 000	500 000		3 500 000
Profit		5 300 000	(360 870)	4 939 130	548 370		5 487 500

*The budgeted volumes are recognised here as homogeneous units of expression for heterogeneous units of inputs.

Additional information:

Budgeted market size for cheese and butter	65 000 000 kg
Actual market size for cheese and butter	60 000 000 kg
Budgeted selling price*	$4.00
Budgeted cost of goods sold per kg	$3.00
Actual selling price*	$4.50
Actual cost of sales per kg	$3.25

* The selling price represents the average selling price of combined cheese and butter (per kg).

Required

(a) Calculate the market size and market share variances.

(b) Comment on the meaning of your calculations (for example, how these help Morgan's management evaluate performance).

11.33 Cost–volume–profit pricing and standard cost variances

Fasteners Company has several divisions, and has just built a new plant with a capacity of 20 000 units of a new product. A standard costing system has been introduced to aid in evaluating managers' performance and for establishing a selling price for the new product. Fasteners Company currently faces no competitors in this product market. Managers price the product at standard variable and fixed manufacturing cost, plus a 60 per cent mark-up. Managers hope this price will be maintained for several years.

During the first year of operations, 1000 units per month will be produced. During the second year of operations, production is estimated to be 1500 units per month. In the first month of operations, employees were learning the processes, so direct labour hours were estimated to be 20 per cent greater than the standard hours allowed per unit. In subsequent months, employees were expected to meet the direct labour hours standards.

Experience in other plants and with similar products led managers to believe that variable manufacturing costs would vary in proportion to actual direct labour dollars. For the first several years, only one product will be manufactured in the new plant. Fixed overhead costs of the new plant per year are expected to be $1 920 000 incurred evenly throughout the year.

The standard variable manufacturing cost (after the break-in period) per unit of product has been set as follows:

Direct materials (4 pieces @ $20 per piece)	$ 80
Direct labour (10 hours @ $25 per hour)	250
Variable overhead (50% of direct labour cost)	125
Total	$455

At the end of the first month of operations, the actual costs incurred to make 950 units of product were as follows:

Direct materials (3850 pieces @ $19.80)	$ 76 230
Direct labour (12 000 hours @ $26)	312 000
Variable overhead	160 250
Fixed overhead	172 220

Fasteners Company managers want to compare actual costs to standard costs, in order to analyse and investigate variances and take any corrective action.

Required

(a) What selling price should Fasteners Company set for the new product according to the new pricing policy? Explain.

(b) Using long-term standard costs, calculate all direct labour and manufacturing overhead variances.

(c) Is it reasonable to use long-term standard costs to calculate variances for the first month of operations? Explain.

(d) Revise the variance calculations in part (b), using the expected costs during the first month of operations as the standard costs.

(e) Provide at least two possible explanations for each of the following variances:
  (i) direct labour price variance
  (ii) direct labour efficiency variance
  (iii) variable overhead spending variance
  (iv) fixed overhead spending variance.

(f) The reasons for variances must be identified before conclusions and actions are decided upon. For two of the variance explanations you provided in part (e), explain what action(s) managers would most likely take.

(g) Would it most likely be easier or more difficult to analyse the variances at the new plant compared to Fasteners Company's other plants? Explain.

11.34 Cost variances; variance analysis; employee motivation   **LO3, 4**

Raging Sage Coffee is a franchise that sells cups of coffee from a cart in shopping centres. A computerised standard costing system is provided as a part of the franchise package. A portion of the standard cost data follows.

	Price	Quantity
Coffee beans	$6 per kg	0.04 kg per cup
Clerk/brewer	$10 per hour	0.05 hours per cup

In its first month of operation, the Launceston franchise recorded the following data:

Coffee sold	8260 cups
Coffee beans used	224 kg
Coffee beans purchased	240 kg
Cost of coffee beans purchased	$1800
Clerk/brewers' total hours	600 hours
Clerk/brewers' total wages	$6000

The entity's policy is to record materials price variances at the time materials are purchased.

Required

(a) Are direct labour hours for the cart most likely fixed or variable? Explain.

(b) Given your answer to part (a), should a direct labour efficiency variance be calculated? Why?

(c) Calculate the direct materials price and efficiency variances.

(d) How many cups of coffee did the franchise owners expect to sell this period? Compare this estimate to the amount actually sold.

(e) Provide possible explanations for the drop in sales.

(f) Suppose the clerks/brewers currently receive a bonus based on their ability to control costs as measured using cost variances. Recommend a bonus system that might help the owners contain costs but also increase sales.

11.35 Cost standards; cost variances; improving cost variance information   **LO5, 6**

Sunglass Guys produces two types of wraparound sunglasses on one assembly line. The monthly fixed overhead is estimated at $235 707, and the variable overhead is estimated at $8.15 per Regular Wrap and $12.32 per Deluxe Wrap.

The entity set up a standard costing system and follows the common practice of basing the overhead rate on the total standard direct labour hours required to produce the estimated volume. The company uses only one overhead rate for fixed and variable overhead costs. Data concerning these two products appear here:

	Regular	Deluxe
Estimated monthly volume	4300 units	1400 units
Standard direct labour	0.2 hours per unit	0.3 hours per unit

Last month, actual production volume was 4500 units of the Regular Wraps and 1300 units of the Deluxe Wraps. Actual variable overhead was $54 238 and actual fixed overhead was $237 859. The nine full-time employees who are classified as direct labour worked regular schedules for a total of 1564 hours.

Required

(a) Calculate the standard overhead rate per direct labour hour.

(b) Explain why the entity's overhead cost variances would provide poor information for monitoring and controlling costs.

(c) Using the information available to you in this problem, suggest a method of allocating overhead costs that would provide better variance information. Using this method, calculate relevant variances for monitoring and controlling overhead costs.

(d) For bookkeeping purposes, Sunglass Guys needs to calculate a production volume variance and a variable overhead efficiency variance. Calculate these variances, assuming that overhead costs are allocated using the method in part (c).

(e) Because employees work regular schedules, direct labour costs tend to be fixed. Also, variable overhead consists primarily of indirect materials and facility-level costs (such as building rent, assembly line equipment and utilities). These costs do not differ between Regular Wraps and Deluxe Wraps. Given this information, recommend a better cost allocation base for variable overhead. Explain your choice.

11.36 Activity-based costing; single versus dual rate spending variances; performance evaluation LO5, 6

Data Processors Ltd performs credit card services for banks. The entity uses an activity-based costing (ABC) system. Following is information for the past year:

Activity	Estimated cost	Actual cost	Cost driver
Processing transactions	$2 000 000	$2 200 000	Number of transactions
Issuing monthly statements	1 000 000	1 300 000	Number of statements
Issuing new credit cards	500 000	400 000	Number of new credit cards
Resolving billing disputes	90 000	100 000	Number of disputes
Total	$3 590 000	$4 000 000	

Cost driver	Estimated activity level	Actual activity level
Number of transactions	5 000 000	5 800 000
Number of statements	250 000	270 000
Number of new credit cards	100 000	110 000
Number of disputes	3 000	3 500

Required

(a) Using standard values for costs and activity, calculate an ABC allocation rate for each activity.

(b) Prepare an operating cost statement for Data Processors Ltd that compares the static budget, the flexible budget and actual costs.

(c) Calculate the spending variance for the cost of processing transactions. (*Hint:* Treat this activity the same way you would treat variable overhead costs.)

(d) Suppose the costs for processing transactions include some fixed and some variable costs, as shown:

	Estimated cost	Actual cost
Fixed costs	$1 000 000	$1 300 000
Variable costs	1 000 000	900 000
Total	$2 000 000	$2 200 000

Given this new information, calculate spending variances for the cost of processing transactions.

(e) Discuss possible reasons for the variances calculated in part (d). The CEO and CFO of Data Processors want your opinion about whether and how ABC variance information should be used in departmental manager performance evaluations.

(f) Use the information you learned from the preceding analyses to write a memo to the CEO and CFO presenting your evaluation of (i) whether the use of ABC cost variances in departmental manager performance evaluations would likely improve organisational performance, and (ii) which spending variance — the one from part (c) or part (d) — would provide better information for evaluating the credit card transaction processing manager's ability to control costs. As you write the memo, consider what information the CEO and CFO will need from you to help them make a final decision.

11.37 Cost variance analysis; use of variance information LO7

The Software Development Company produces computer programs on DVDs for home computers. This business is highly automated, causing fixed costs to be very high, but variable costs are minimal. The entity is organised along three product lines: games, business programs and educational programs. The average standard selling prices for each are $16 for games, $55 for business programs and $20 for educational programs. The standard variable cost consists solely of one DVD per program at $2 per DVD, without regard to the type of program. Fixed costs for the period were estimated at $535 000. For the current period, standard sales are 40 000 games, 2000 business programs and 10 000 educational programs. Actual results are as follows.

Sales:		
Games	(35 000 DVDs)	$ 616 000
Business	(4 000 DVDs)	198 000
Educational	(11 000 DVDs)	220 000
Total sales		1 034 000
Variable costs	(50 750 DVDs)	106 575
Fixed costs		533 500
Pre-tax income		$ 393 925

Required

(a) Calculate standard pre-tax income and then reconcile it to actual pre-tax income by calculating the contribution margin sales mix variance, revenue sales quantity variance, sales price variance, materials price and quantity variances, and the fixed cost spending variance.

(b) A new marketing manager was hired during the period. The manager changed prices and redirected sales efforts.

  (i) Discuss whether one or more of the preceding variances are relevant to evaluating the performance of the new marketing manager.

  (ii) What do the variances suggest about the new manager's performance? Explain.

(c) An analysis reveals that the entity will have to pay $1.80 per DVD next period. Prepare next period's master budget. Assume a standard of one disk per program, total unit sales of 55 000, and the actual sales mix and sales prices from this period.

(d) Discuss possible reasons the entity might not meet its budget for next period.

11.38 Direct and overhead cost variance analysis; closing accounts at end of period   **LO7**

Jennifer has just been promoted to manager of the piston division of Car Parts Co. The division, which manufactures pistons for hydraulic drives, uses a standard cost system and calculates the standard cost of a completed piston as $85, as follows:

	Quantity	Price	Cost per piston
Piston shaft	1	$35/piston shaft	$35
Shaft housing	1	$20/housing	20
Direct labour	0.4 hours	$15/hour	6
Variable factory overhead	0.4 hours	$10/hour	4
Fixed factory overhead	0.4 hours	$50/hour	20
Total standard cost			$85

The fixed overhead rate is based on an estimated 1000 units per month. Direct labour is nearly a fixed cost in this division. Selling and administrative costs are $50 000 per month plus $10 per piston sold.

The following information is for production during April:

Number of pistons manufactured	950
Purchase of 1000 piston shafts	$34 950
Number of piston shafts used	954
Purchase of 1000 shaft housings	$20 000
Number of shaft housings used	950
Direct labour costs (397 hours)	$ 6 120
Variable factory overhead costs	$ 3 677
Fixed factory overhead costs	$18 325
Selling and administrative costs	$59 101

The entity's policy is to record materials price variances at the time materials are purchased. You may want to use a spreadsheet to perform calculations.

Required

(a) Prepare a flexible cost budget for the month of April.

(b) Calculate all of the common direct cost variances. (*Note:* There are no variances for shaft housings.)

(c) Calculate all common factory overhead variances.

(d) Calculate a total variance for the selling and administrative costs.

(e) Prepare a complete, yet concise, report that would be useful in evaluating control of production costs for April.

(f) Prepare a report that sums all the variances necessary to prepare the reconciling journal entry at the end of the period. Explain how you would close the total variance; that is, identify the account or accounts that would be affected, and whether expenses in the accounts will be increased or decreased to adjust the records for the total variance.

(g) Suppose you are manager of the piston division and you are reviewing the report prepared in part (e). Use information in the report to identify questions you might have about April's production costs.

11.39 Auditor evaluation of variances for error and fraud; accounting principles for variances   **LO3, 4, 5, 6**

Auditors must plan and perform an audit to obtain reasonable assurance about whether the financial statements are free of material misstatements, which may be caused by either error or fraud. Errors are unintentional misstatements caused by factors such as mistakes in processing accounting data, misinterpretation of facts and confusion about accounting principles. Fraudulent financial reporting and misappropriation of assets are the only two types of financial statement fraud. Fraudulent financial reporting consists of intentional misstatements caused by factors such as manipulation of accounting data, misrepresentation of facts and intentional misapplication of accounting principles. Misappropriation of assets includes stealing assets such as inventory and causing an entity to pay for goods or services that were not received.

Auditors perform a variety of procedures to gather and evaluate information that will help them identify possible material misstatement. One potential audit procedure is to analyse a company's cost variances, which might be caused by error or fraud.

Required

(a) For each of the following variances, describe in detail a possible error that could cause a variance even when no variance actually exists.
   (i) Direct materials price
   (ii) Direct materials efficiency
   (iii) Direct labour price
   (iv) Direct labour efficiency
   (v) Variable overhead spending
   (vi) Variable overhead efficiency
   (vii) Fixed overhead budget
   (viii) Production volume

(b) Suppose a material amount of raw materials inventory theft took place during the past year. Which of the variances in part (a) would most likely reflect this fraud? Explain.

(c) Discuss possible reasons why variance analysis might not uncover the theft described in part (b).

(d) Suppose a production manager fraudulently entered a fictitious employee into the payroll system during the past year. The fictitious employee's salaries are deposited directly into a bank account that is then accessed by the production manager. Which of the variances in part (a) would most likely reflect this fraud? Explain.

(e) During the current year, suppose an accountant accidentally records a large equipment repair as an addition to property, plant, and equipment. Assume that equipment repairs and equipment depreciation are both recorded in variable overhead costs. Which of the variances in part (a) would most likely reflect this accounting error? Discuss how this error would affect the variance during the current year. Discuss how this error would affect the variance during the next year.

(f) Suppose an entity's managers want to report higher earnings on the statement of profit or loss. Describe in detail a possible way that the managers could improve reported earnings by intentionally misapplying accounting principles for variances.

ACKNOWLEDGEMENTS

Photo 11A: © Hero Images / Getty Images
Photo 11B: © Gtranquillity / Shutterstock.com
Photo 11C: © Nejron Photo / Shutterstock.com

CHAPTER 12

Activity analysis: costing and management

LEARNING OBJECTIVES

After studying this chapter, you should be able to:

12.1 reflect on and communicate the differences and similarities between activity-based costing (ABC) and conventional costing

12.2 understand elements of the ABC cost hierarchy

12.3 apply the principles of ABC and conventional costing

12.4 describe the characteristics and use of activity-based management (ABM)

12.5 communicate the benefits, costs and issues related to ABC.

IN BRIEF

Activity-based costing (ABC) is a method that assigns costs to the specific activities performed in a manufacturing or service delivery process. ABC attempts to trace costs to cost objects through an activity lens. The costs of the various activities then become the building blocks used to compile costs for products or other cost objects. Activity-related costs are collected and cost drivers are chosen for each activity cost pool. Direct and indirect costs are then assigned to products or services using these activity-based cost pools and cost drivers. The information derived from ABC can be used with activity-based management (ABM) to improve operations and minimise activities that do not add value to the organisation.

12.1 Activity-based costing (ABC) and conventional costing

LEARNING OBJECTIVE 12.1 Reflect on and communicate the differences and similarities between activity-based costing (ABC) and conventional costing.

A basic costing framework was illustrated in chapter 3. Cost accounting systems have adapted over time to suit changes in:

- operational environments
- technology
- cost structures
- management reporting requirements
- organisational structures, particularly those with a new focus on the value chain.

Traditionally cost accounting systems were focused on product costing for manufacturers. More recently, cost accounting systems have evolved with a focus on activities for cost collection, thereby facilitating applications beyond the manufacturing sector. The activity view of costs has enabled an entity to extend the focus to cost objects other than products, and to take a broader view of allocation bases.

Conventional cost accounting systems

As illustrated in figure 12.1, conventional cost accounting systems trace direct costs and allocate overhead costs to each individual product. Cost allocation is a two-stage process whereby overhead costs are grouped into one or more cost pools in the first stage, and then allocated using an allocation base (such as direct labour cost or hours, machine hours or number of units) in the second stage. Labour has been a common allocation base because it was historically a significant driver of manufacturing costs. As manufacturing becomes less labour-intensive in some industries, labour-related allocation bases are increasingly viewed as arbitrary. It should be noted that labour could still be a suitable allocation base in service industries.

Allocation bases such as machine hours and number of units may also be viewed as arbitrary when they do not reflect a product's use of resources. Any poorly selected allocation base will distort product costs. Some organisations attempt to increase cost allocation relevance by using more than one overhead cost pool.

Even with multiple cost pools, conventional allocation bases rarely reflect the flow of resources to products of different complexity. Suppose that a computer manufacturer uses robotic equipment to assemble custom-ordered computers. Most of the manufacturing overhead costs (for example, depreciation, insurance, general maintenance and software maintenance) are related to the robotic equipment. If the manufacturer lacks an information system that tracks time on the robotic machines or number of new set-ups required, direct labour hours are likely to be used to allocate the fixed overhead related to the machines. However, direct labour might be used only to test and package the machines for shipping, and the times needed for these tasks are the same for every machine produced. As a result, fixed overhead costs are distributed equally among all of the computers regardless of the actual time spent by the robotic machines or the number of new machine set-ups required.

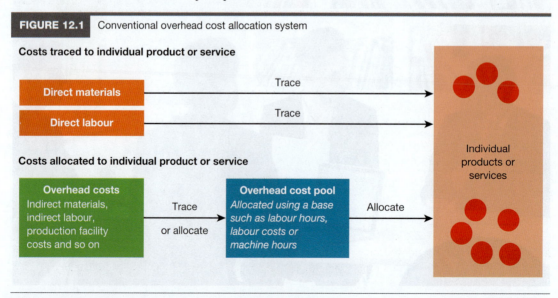

FIGURE 12.1 Conventional overhead cost allocation system

In this setting, the costing system understates the cost of more complex computers that require more assembly time and machine set-ups in the robotic manufacturing process. At the same time, the system overstates the cost of simple computers requiring little robotic assembly time and few changes in set-up. If the information generated by this cost system is used for product decisions, the simple product could be de-emphasised relative to more complex products. Unfortunately, it is highly unlikely that this emphasis reflects the optimal sales mix.

Activity-based costing systems

Activity-based costing (ABC) is a system that assigns overhead costs to the specific activities performed in a manufacturing or service delivery process. It attempts to trace costs more accurately to products or other cost objects. An **activity** is a type of task or function performed in an organisation. The costs of the various activities become the building blocks used to compile total costs for products or other cost objects. The flow of costs in an ABC system is illustrated in figure 12.2.

Note that this figure is an extension of the basic costing framework described in chapter 3 and illustrated in figure 3.4. Examples of the activities performed in a manufacturing setting include materials handling (moving direct materials and supplies from one part of the plant to another), engineering, inspection, customer support and information systems. Examples of activities performed in a service entity such as an insurance firm include policy preparation, development of new insurance products, client support, marketing and information technology.

Under ABC, multiple cost pools are used to reflect the various activities performed in manufacturing a product or providing a service. Accordingly, the costs of overhead resources are first assigned to activity cost pools, and then activity costs are allocated to individual products or services using cost drivers that are chosen to reflect the use of resources. Therefore, ABC focuses on activities as the fundamental characteristic driving cost pool identification and cost driver selection.

FIGURE 12.2	ABC cost allocation system

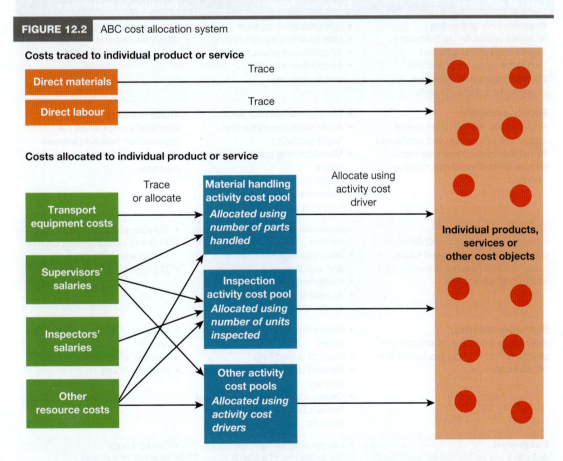

For example, if materials handling is defined as an activity, the cost of buying and maintaining equipment for materials handling (such as forklifts or conveyor belts) is traced directly to an activity cost pool for materials handling. Other costs, such as supervisors' salaries, may be allocated to a number of different activity cost pools, including materials handling. A cost driver such as number of parts handled is used to allocate materials handling costs to individual products. In this example, products that use more parts would be allocated a higher amount of materials handling costs than products that use fewer parts.

12.2 ABC cost hierarchy

LEARNING OBJECTIVE 12.2 Understand elements of the ABC cost hierarchy.

Accountants often use a cost hierarchy (which we introduced in chapter 3) to help them identify activities and then assign costs to those activities. ABC developers identified a number of general categories for the cost hierarchy based on different levels of operation. These categories include the following:

- organisation-sustaining
- facility-sustaining
- customer-sustaining
- product-sustaining
- batch-level
- unit-level.

A general description of each category with examples of costs and cost drivers is provided in figure 12.3. Accountants are not restricted to these categories; other categories can be used to analyse costs when organisations want to focus on different facets of their operations. For example, costs could be categorised by business segment or by strategic emphasis, such as product/service quality or protection of the environment.

FIGURE 12.3 General hierarchy of ABC costs and cost drivers

Level of activities	Examples of costs	Examples of cost drivers
Organisation-sustaining Activities are related to the overall organisation and unaffected by number or types of facilities and customers or by volumes of products, batches or units.	• Administrative salaries • Headquarters housekeeping • Information system salaries • Accountant salaries and equipment	These costs might not be allocated because they do not vary with activity volumes.
Facility-sustaining Activities are related to the overall operations of a facility and unaffected by number of customers served or by quantities of products, batches or units.	• Facility maintenance service • Retail store insurance and heating/cooling • Manufacturing plant manager's salary • Depreciation and liability insurance for individual hospitals in a hospital system	These costs are typically not allocated except when the organisation needs to allocate all product costs for a particular purpose.
Customer-sustaining Activities are related to individual or groups of past, current and future customers and are not driven by total sales volumes and mix.	• Customer sales representative salaries • Technical support salaries and supplies • Customer market research • Special tools for a customer's order	• Number of sales calls • Hours of technical support (not tied to a specific product) • Number of customers
Product-sustaining Activities support the production and distribution of a single product or line of products.	• Production line supervisor salary • Product advertising • Product design engineer salaries • Depreciation of equipment used to manufacture one type of product	• Number of engineering change orders • Number of advertisements • Machine hours
Batch-level Activities are performed for each batch of product and are not related to the number of units in the batch.	• Labour cost for new set-up at the beginning of a batch • Utility costs for heating a kiln for batches of pottery • Shipping costs for batches	• Set-up hours • Number of batches • Weight of orders shipped

---

Unit-level	• Materials handling wages	• Machine hours
Activities produce individual units of goods or services; resource cost is proportional to production volumes or sales volumes.	• Production workers paid based on quantity produced	• Units processed
	• Supplies used to provide services	• Materials quantity processed

Organisation-sustaining activities

Organisation-sustaining activities are tasks or functions undertaken to oversee the entire entity. These activities occur regardless of the number of facilities operated, customers served, products sold, batches processed or units produced. For example, the activities and costs of a corporate head office would be considered organisation-sustaining because they occur regardless of customer, product line, batch or unit volumes. The salaries and office costs of the chief executive officer and chief financial officer would be considered organisation-sustaining costs. In addition, costs such as information technology services are organisation-sustaining costs if they are performed for the entire entity. Because many of these costs are fixed (for example, administrative salaries, depreciation, and rent or lease costs), usually no cause-and-effect relationships exist between organisation-sustaining costs and the activities performed at this level. Therefore, these activity costs are typically assigned to the entire organisation and might not be allocated to specific product lines, batches or units.

Facility-sustaining activities

Facility-sustaining activities are tasks or functions undertaken to provide and manage an area, location or property. These activities occur regardless of the number of customers served, products sold, batches processed or units produced. Therefore, they are assigned to the facility and not allocated to product lines, batches or units. For example, an entity's manufacturing and research facilities incur costs (such as facility manager salary, building depreciation, insurance, security, car parking and telephone services) that do not vary with levels of activity in the facility. These costs would be considered facility-sustaining costs.

Occasionally managers want to know the full costs on a per-unit basis, in which case both organisation- and facility-sustaining costs are allocated. However, identifying causal links between the cost object and cost driver is problematic and can lead to unreliable cost data.

Customer-sustaining activities

Customer-sustaining activities are tasks or functions undertaken to service past, current and future customers. These costs tend to vary with the needs of individual customers or groups of customers. Training aimed at particular customers would probably be considered customer-sustaining costs. Similarly, the commissions and fees paid to sales representatives and agents would be classified as customer-sustaining.

Product-sustaining activities

Product-sustaining activities are tasks or functions undertaken to support the production and distribution of a single product or line of products. These activities are not related to units or batches, but to individual products or product lines. Some of the product-sustaining costs apply to all of the products within a particular division, while other product-sustaining costs relate to only a single product. Thus, numerous ways can be used to define product-sustaining activities at a diverse entity.

Batch-level activities

Batch-level activities are tasks or functions undertaken for a collection of goods or services that are processed as a group. They include costs such as machinery set-up costs. Batch-level costs are related to the number of batches processed, not the number of units in the batch. Thus, batch costs increase as the number of batches increases.

Unit-level activities

Unit-level activities are undertaken to produce individual units manufactured or services produced. Unit-level activities need to be performed for every unit of good or service, and therefore the cost should be proportional to the number of units produced. Unit-level costs commonly include the costs to use and maintain the equipment for filling containers, direct materials costs and (where applicable) direct labour costs.

12.3 Understanding and implementing an ABC model

LEARNING OBJECTIVE 12.3 Apply the principles of ABC and conventional costing.

Overhead costs are gathered into cost pools in the first stage and then allocated to the cost objects (such as product line, batch or units) in the second stage. ABC differs from other allocation methods in that overhead costs are assigned to a larger number of activity-based cost pools, and multiple cost drivers are used as allocation bases. Bear in mind that the total costs are the same irrespective of the method used for allocation. The following procedures are typically followed under the ABC method.[1]

1. Identify the relevant cost object.
2. Identify activities.
3. Assign costs to activity-based cost pools.
4. For each ABC cost pool, choose a cost driver.
5. For each ABC cost pool, calculate a cost driver rate.
6. For each ABC cost pool, allocate activity costs to the cost object.

Each of these procedures is illustrated in comprehensive example 1.

COMPREHENSIVE EXAMPLE 1

ABC model

The Paisley Insurance Company provides a range of insurance products to a variety of residential and commercial customers. The billing department at Paisley provides account enquiry and bill printing services for the two major classes of customers — residential (60 000 accounts) and commercial (10 000 accounts). Until now, the billing department has used what could be labelled a conventional costing system. As illustrated in figure 12.4, all costs in the department are indirect and were allocated to the two classes of customer on the basis of the number of account enquiries.

| FIGURE 12.4 | Billing department — conventional costing system |

Indirect cost pool	$
Labour — supervisors	16 800
Labour — account enquiry	59 200
Labour — billing	33 750
Building occupancy	23 500
Telecommunications	29 260
Technology/computer	89 000
Printing machines	27 500
Paper	3 660
Total indirect costs	282 670
÷ Number of enquiries	11 500
= Cost per enquiry	24.58
Cost allocation	24.58
Cost per residential account	$ 3.69 per account (9000 enquiries × $24.58)/60 000 accounts
Cost per commercial account	$ 6.15 (2500 enquiries × $24.58)/10 000 accounts

Due to increasing competitive forces and an expected increase in demand for Paisley's insurance services, management has questioned the cost data currently available. Moreover, a local service bureau has expressed interest in providing the functions of the billing department, giving Paisley the opportunity to outsource these services at $3.50 per account. Management requested a study to investigate the activities and costs of the billing department and so an ABC study was undertaken.

1. Identify the relevant cost object
The two relevant cost objects of Paisley's billing department are the two types of accounts: residential and commercial.

2. Identify activities

Through a series of interviews with the appropriate staff, four key activities within the billing department were identified: account enquiry, correspondence, account billing and verification. A process map (see figure 12.5) can be developed to show the linkages between activities and resources. In this step there may be less concern about actual dollar amounts and more focus on understanding the processes and activities within the billing department.

FIGURE 12.5 Process map of the billing department's activities

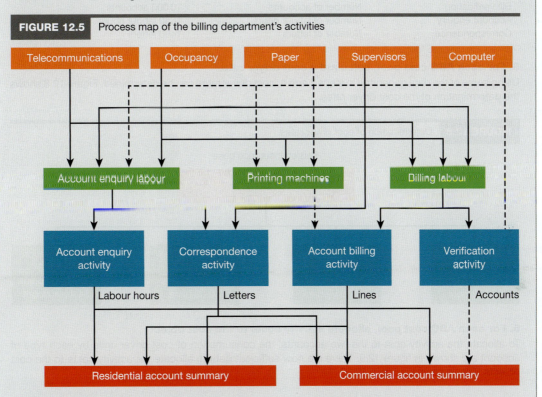

3. Assign costs to activity-based cost pools

Using the process map in figure 12.5 as a guide, the required cost and operational data were collected to enable the costs associated with the activity cost pools to be identified. Sources of data for this exercise include the entity's accounting records, special studies and (sometimes) the best estimates of managers. Figure 12.6 contrasts the cost pools under the conventional and activity-based approaches. Note that the total costs of the billing department are still the same and it is only the cost pool structure that has changed.

FIGURE 12.6 Contrast of conventional and activity-based cost pools

Conventional view		Activity view	
Labour supervisors	$ 16 800	Account enquiry	$102 666
Labour — account enquiry	59 200	Correspondence	17 692
Labour — billing	33 750	Account billing	117 889
Building occupancy	23 500	Verification	44 423
Telecommunications	29 260	Total	$282 670
Computer	89 000		
Printing machines	27 500		
Paper	3 660		
Total	$282 670		

4. For each ABC cost pool, choose a cost driver

Paisley identified cost drivers that were to be used as the allocation base, on the basis of two criteria.
- There had to be a reasonable cause-and-effect relationship between the driver unit and the consumption of resources or the incurrence of supporting activities.
- Data on the cost driver units had to be available at a reasonable cost.
  The cost drivers identified for each activity cost pool are shown in figure 12.7.

FIGURE 12.7 Activity cost pools and activity cost drivers

Activities	Activity cost drivers	Total count of activity cost driver units
Account billing	Number of lines	1 220 000 lines
Bill verification	Number of accounts	10 000 accounts
Account enquiry	Number of labour hours	1650 labour hours
Correspondence	Number of letters	1400 letters

5. For each ABC cost pool, calculate a cost driver rate

Using some of the data generated in steps 3 and 4, cost driver rates can be determined. Figure 12.8 shows the determination of the cost driver rates.

FIGURE 12.8 Determination of cost driver rates

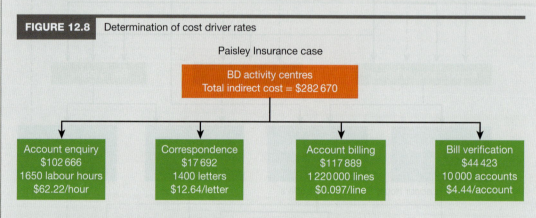

Paisley Insurance case

BD activity centres
Total indirect cost = $282 670

Account enquiry	Correspondence	Account billing	Bill verification
$102 666	$17 692	$117 889	$44 423
1650 labour hours	1400 letters	1 220 000 lines	10 000 accounts
$62.22/hour	$12.64/letter	$0.097/line	$4.44/account

6. For each ABC cost pool, allocate activity costs to the cost object

To allocate the activity cost to the two accounts, the consumption of cost driver units by each type of account are shown in figure 12.9. There are now sufficient data to allocate the activity costs to the cost objects. This is shown in figure 12.10.

FIGURE 12.9 Consumption of cost driver units by each type of account

Residential accounts	
Labour hours	900
Letters	900
Lines	720 000

Commercial accounts	
Labour hours	750
Letters	500
Lines	500 000

FIGURE 12.10 Allocation of activity costs to each cost object

	Residential	Commercial
Account enquiry	$ 55 998[a]	$ 46 665
Correspondence	11 376	6 320
Account billing	69 840	48 500
Bill verification	—	44 423
Totals	$137 214	$145 908
Accounts	60 000	10 000
Cost per account	$ 2.28	$ 14.59

[a] Being $62.22 per hour × 900 hours.

Figure 12.11 contrasts the cost per account under the conventional and activity-based approaches. What is evident is a shift of costs from the residential accounts to the commercial account customers, suggesting the more complex nature of the commercial accounts draws more resources than were allocated under the conventional system.

FIGURE 12.11	Contrast of conventional and activity-based costs for each account[2]		
		Residential	Commercial
Conventional		$3.69	$ 6.15
Activity-based		$2.28	$14.59

12.4 Activity-based management (ABM)

LEARNING OBJECTIVE 12.4 Describe the characteristics and use of activity-based management (ABM).

Activity-based management (ABM) is the process of using ABC information to evaluate the costs and benefits of production and internal support activities, and to identify and implement opportunities for improvements in profitability, efficiency and quality within an entity. ABM relies on accurate ABC information. We will learn about four major uses of ABM:

• managing customer profitability
• managing environmental costs
• managing product and process design
• managing constrained resources.

Managing customer profitability

ABC can be used to identify customer-sustaining activities that cause some customers to be more costly than others. Such activities include providing sales and technical support to specific customers or groups of customers, holding inventory for just-in-time deliveries, and customising orders. Figure 12.12 describes the characteristics of customers having high and low costs.

FIGURE 12.12	Characteristics of customers with high and low service costs

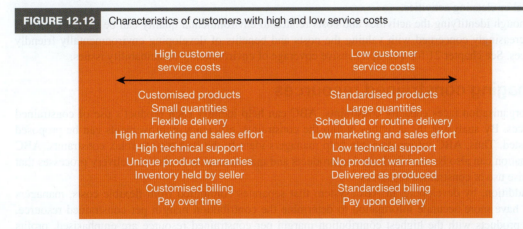

As the costs of serving specific customers are determined, managers can choose different strategies for different types of customers. For example, some customers need very little service but are quite price sensitive. Although margins for these customers are low, these customers are profitable when service costs are also kept low. Customers with high service costs are also profitable when their net margins are high enough to account for the extra service costs. Alternatively, the entity can price its extra services and let customers pick the services they are willing to pay for. We will explore customer profitability further in chapter 16.

Managing product and process design

An advantage of ABC is its focus on activities. As an organisation's activities are analysed more closely, managers improve their understanding of how resources are used. In turn, this analysis enables managers to improve operations and profits. They can focus resources on **value-added activities** (those which the customer/client is normally prepared to pay for), which increase the worth of an entity's goods or services to customers. Conversely, they can reduce or eliminate **non-value-added activities** (often associated with waste such as rework), which are unnecessary and therefore waste resources.

Under ABM, non-value-added activities are identified and eliminated when possible. As ABC systems are implemented, activities can be categorised as:

- required to produce a good or service and cannot be improved at this time
- required but the process could be improved or simplified
- not required to produce a good or service and can eventually be eliminated
- not required and can be eliminated by changing a process or procedure.

Managing environmental costs

Many managers are concerned with the effects of their organisations' manufacturing or operational processes on the environment. In addition, many shareholders are concerned with the 'green' reputation of companies in which they invest. Federal and state regulations may require entities to reduce pollution levels. The direct costs of reducing pollution are often easily tracked, but identifying the costs and benefits of protecting the environment within conventional accounting systems is more difficult. ABC systems can be designed to identify the activities involved in environmental protection and to develop costs for those activities. Analysing overhead activities also helps managers identify opportunities for improved environmental performance.

Suppose a high-quality printing entity used inks that were detrimental to the environment. The cost of ink disposal was traditionally recorded as part of overhead cost. When management developed an ABC system, however, the disposal cost became part of an activity cost pool for the printing process that used these inks. As the activity was analysed, the high cost of disposal became more noticeable. Managers realised that they could invest in an incinerator that used high temperatures to burn the ink so thoroughly that it left little airborne or solid residual. Thus, the ABC process motivated managers to consider alternative methods to reduce the cost of pollution. Once the cost effects of pollution, waste and other environmental activities are identified, managers become more motivated to make investments that improve environmental performance. With these improvements, costs are reduced because organisations no longer incur the costs associated with pollution or waste. In addition, many non-value-added activities are eliminated, such as disposal or cleaning activities.

Although identifying the activities and costs related to environmental quality can be difficult, entities are increasingly concerned with valuing the costs and benefits of developing environmentally friendly practices. See chapter 21 for a comprehensive coverage of environmental sustainability issues.

Managing constrained resources

If an organisation faces capacity constraints, ABC can help identify each product's use of constrained resources. By analysing the activities within the constraints, efficiency improvements can be proposed and tested. Thus, ABC information can help managers identify the best way to relax constraints. ABC information can also be used in designing products and manufacturing or service delivery processes that minimise use of constrained resources.

In addition, by developing an ABC system that separates committed from flexible costs, managers would have more accurate information to determine the contribution margin per constrained resource. When products with the highest contribution margin per constrained resource are emphasised, profits are maximised.

Managing resources supplied and consumed

ABC cost models facilitate the identification of those resources that have been supplied (as reported in the financial statements) and those that have been consumed by the cost object(s). For example, if we consider the correspondence cost pool in comprehensive example 1, we note the following data:

Resources supplied	$17 692
Anticipated activity level	1400 letters
Cost per unit of activity driver	$12.64

If, during the subsequent period, only 1200 letters are consumed by the cost objects, the cost of resources consumed would be $15 168 (1200 letters × $12.64). The difference between the resources supplied

($17 692) and the resources consumed ($15 168) represents unused capacity ($2524). In the longer term, Paisley's costs are going to be reduced only when the resources supplied are reduced, not necessarily when the resources consumed are reduced.

12.5 Benefits, costs and issues related to ABC

LEARNING OBJECTIVE 12.5 Communicate the benefits, costs and issues related to ABC.

Accountants need to consider cost–benefit trade-offs when choosing activities and cost drivers for an ABC system. They must estimate the costs of alternative ABC systems and anticipate the potential benefits from alternative system designs. They also need to recognise that an ABC system might fail to meet expectations.

Benefits of ABC

ABC systems enable managers to focus on measurement at the activity level. Once activities are identified and cost drivers are chosen, employees are more aware of cause-and-effect relationships. This awareness prompts employees to search for ways to improve performance simply because they have more information about the cost effects of an activity. By more carefully analysing activity costs, the importance and materiality of some non-value-added costs becomes more apparent, and motivation to reduce those costs increases. In an ABC system, activities that do not add value to customers are more likely to be identified and eliminated from operations. Examples include holding excess levels of inventories, unnecessary transportation, waste in the set-up process, and inspection inefficiencies.

More than other costing systems, ABC systems measure the flow of resources in an entity. They reduce the arbitrariness in cost measurement by more closely matching cost allocations to the actual use of resources by operating activities. Compared to the allocation bases used in a conventional costing system, the allocation bases used in an ABC system are more likely to be cost drivers and related to costs, rather than just used to allocate cost. One of the key benefits of an ABC system would seem to be its use in special/one-off studies to assist a particular management decision. In such cases it may be unnecessary to embed ABC into the entity's system. For example, in the Paisley Insurance example earlier, ABC was used to produce more up-to-date and reliable cost data associated with residential and commercial account customers of the billing department. Having calculated the relatively more reliable costs and used them in the outsourcing decision, the objective of the ABC system implementation may have been achieved. For example, if university management waned to understand costs of the library services it would identify ABC-related costs by comparing costs for different types of cataloguing services. Embedding ABC into the entity's system would be a separate and perhaps unnecessary decision.

Costs of ABC

Many costs are associated with designing and using an ABC system. They include:
- system design costs such as employee time and consulting fees
- accounting and information system modifications needed to gather and report activity and cost driver information
- employee training to use the ABC system effectively.

Sometimes the cost of developing ABC information is low, especially in cases where the activity cost is readily available and the number of times the activity is performed can be easily tracked. Suppose the activity is inspection of units. The cost consists of the salary and fringe benefits of the inspector, and all units are inspected. Identifying salary costs in an accounting system is easy, and fringe benefits costs can be estimated. The number of units produced should be readily available from production records, and the capacity of the inspection area can be easily estimated. Thus, developing an activity-based cost for inspection may be as simple as dividing the salary-related costs by a chosen measure of unit volume.

Other times, ABC information is more costly to develop. Suppose the activity is the set-up process. This process often includes labour, supplies and other resources. Because cost tracing is one of the components of cost assignment under ABC, it takes time and analysis to identify costs that can be traced and those that should be allocated. In addition, data for the cost driver (such as the number of set-ups) must be tracked.

In general, the costs of an ABC system are higher when more activities — or more complex activities — are involved. It is more difficult to accurately trace costs to activities as their complexity and number increase. In addition, increased employee training is often required. Also, the process of ABC system development bogs down if too much complexity is introduced at one time. However, a failure to sufficiently break down activities might prevent the system from providing useful information.

Accounting researchers have questioned whether the costs of implementing ABC systems were worth the benefits received. They have found that although ABC use was associated with higher quality and improved cycle time, for the average entity no significant association was found between ABC use and return on assets. However, ABC appeared to be related to profitability for firms using advanced manufacturing techniques that combine information technology with more flexible manufacturing practices.[3] Researchers who document successful implementations suggest that important factors include top management support, linkages to strategy, training, non-accounting ownership and performance evaluation.[4] In addition, researchers have found that for small manufacturing entities, simple ABC systems with few activities and cost drivers are best. These systems are inexpensive yet efficient, and easier for managers to understand and implement.[5]

Issues related to ABC

Limitations and uncertainties in ABC implementation

Managers use judgement to decide which activities and cost drivers to include in an ABC system because of uncertainty about the set of activities and drivers that would provide the best information. As the number of activities increases, measurement error also tends to increase because a greater number of allocations are used to assign costs to activity cost pools. In addition, it is not always possible to determine the best cost driver. Information for some cost drivers may be readily available, whereas information for a potentially superior driver might be costly to accumulate. When designing an ABC system, accountants cannot foresee all of the various ways in which the new information could be used in ABM to reduce costs or improve decision making. For example, until activities and costs are evaluated, we may not be able to identify non-value-added activities. Accordingly, the ability to identify the most valuable activities to measure and track is uncertain.

Uncertainties are also part of choosing an appropriate denominator value to determine the allocation rate. The accuracy of estimates used in the denominator affect the allocation of cost. We overstate or understate cost when the denominator estimate is too large or small. Although ABC information is more detailed, measurement errors also increase because of estimates. Thus, the additional detail does not necessarily improve the quality of information.

Accountants also face uncertainties about how an organisation's employees will respond to the design and implementation of an ABC system. In some cases, employees are afraid of major system changes, especially when their jobs might be viewed as non-value-added. As a result, some employees will fail to provide adequate information for designing the system; they might even provide misleading or incorrect information. Moreover, if implementation is poorly executed (such as poor communication and insufficient explanation of objectives), other managers and employees are unlikely to embrace the new costing methodology.

If employees believe that their performance will be evaluated using ABC information, they may provide biased information to show better performance. Once the new system is designed, they may try to undermine implementation and training efforts. Even when employees fully embrace the new ABC system, they might misunderstand it and make inappropriate decisions. Furthermore, if an ABC system is overly complex, even the most enthusiastic employees might not be able to take full advantage of it.

Mismeasurement of costs assigned to ABC activities

As illustrated in figure 12.2, costs must be assigned to each ABC cost pool. Errors may creep into the process of tracing or allocating individual costs, leading to mismeasurement in ABC costs. The allocation process often introduces a degree of measurement error. For example, costs such as supplies and employee benefits might be allocated to a number of activities such as set-up, maintenance and monitoring production. It is impossible to identify the exact amount of cost associated with each activity when we use allocated costs. In addition, errors are sometimes made in assigning costs directly to ABC pools.

In general, the risk of measurement error increases:

- if uncertainties exist about the activity to which costs relate
- when costs are allocated instead of being traced to ABC cost pool
- when the number of ABC cost pools increases.

Comprehensive example 2 focuses on a detailed comparison of conventional job costing and ABC as well as exploring the application of ABC concepts.

Comparison of ABC and conventional job costing

Keener Doors and Windows Company produces two types of wooden doors. Regular doors are high volume and use standard parts and manufacturing processes. Premium doors are lower volume and are considered a customised, specialty item. Managers are considering the pricing policies for both doors because their major competitor recently lowered prices on regular doors. Premium doors have been selling well because they are priced lower than the competitor's specialty doors. The managers are concerned about the effects on profit margins if they reduce the

price of regular doors to match the competition. Although they only consider variable costs in their pricing decisions, they would like to have more information about each product's use of overhead resources.

The cost accountant, Valerie Bradley, suggested that Keener consider implementing an ABC system to better understand the costs for all of the manufacturing activities needed to produce the doors. She believes that the regular doors use fewer overhead resources because all of the regular doors go through routine processes, whereas the premium doors require special processes. Both doors are produced in batches of 100. However, each premium door is processed further to add custom features, such as special routing effects in the wood or special window treatments. Currently, overhead is allocated based on direct labour hours but machines perform much of the work. Valerie believes that labour hours do not reflect the two products' different use of plant overhead resources.

An ABC team is assembled to analyse the manufacturing activities and costs for individual doors in both product lines. The team consists of Valerie, a product designer and several employees from the manufacturing process. They want to compare costs under the current job costing system and a new ABC system. As they consider the task, they realise that ABC allocations typically ignore facility-related costs while job costing allocations include them. For purposes of comparison, they decide to ignore facility-sustaining costs in their calculations for job costing so that the results from both systems are comparable. From the general ledger, Valerie identifies overhead costs of $18 270 000 (not including any facility costs) that were assigned to regular and premium doors last period.

Product costs using job costing

The team recreates the products' job costs using information from the general ledger. Each regular door requires $65 of direct materials and 2.5 hours of direct labour. Each premium door requires $100 of direct materials and 3 hours of direct labour. The job costing system allocates overhead using a factory-wide estimated allocation rate of $32.05 per direct labour hour based on a single cost pool for door production of $18 270 000 and direct labour hours of 570 000 for the year. The following schedule summarises the cost of each type of door:

	Regular doors	Premium doors
Direct materials:		
Regular	$ 65.00	
Premium		$100.00
Direct labour:		
Regular ($20 × 2.5 hours)	50.00	
Premium ($20 × 3 hours)		60.00
Factory overhead:		
Regular ($32.05 × 2.5 hours)	80.13	
Premium ($32.05 × 3 hours)		96.15
Total cost	$195.13	$256.15

The team members notice that the overhead allocation for premium doors is $16.02 (or 20%) greater than for regular doors under the job costing system. However, the shop supervisor believes that premium doors use two to three times more resources than regular doors because of extra processing the premium doors receive on the most expensive equipment.

Product costs using ABC

The managers want to know whether their current pricing policy reflects any differences in resources used by regular doors compared to premium doors. Therefore, the ABC team decides that the relevant cost objects are individual doors and the activities involved in production must be analysed. When the team visits the production area, they ask about the activities performed for each type of door. They learn that the first activity is delivery of materials to workstations. They identify a materials handling cost pool for this activity.

The next steps involve work done in batches, such as the initial cutting, sanding and smoothing of doors. The team learns that two different activities are required: setting up machines for the next batch, and monitoring the machines as batches are processed. Some team members believe that these two activities could be combined into one cost pool allocated on the number of batches run. Valerie asks whether these activities differ between regular doors and premium doors. She learns that the set-up for premium door batches is more complex and takes more time than for regular doors. The batches take the same amount of time, no matter what type of door is produced. Therefore, the team identifies two activity pools — one for set-up costs and one for batch monitoring costs — because the activities in these pools are not homogeneous and cannot be allocated using a single cost driver. After the doors are cut and sanded, they are processed through routing machines. The team discovers that premium doors require more routing machine hours because the designs are more complex. An activity pool for machining is identified. The last activity is inspection. The inspectors explain that premium doors take longer to inspect because of their greater detail. The team identifies inspection as a cost pool.

Now that the cost pools are identified, costs need to be traced or allocated to each pool. Valerie uses annual accounting records and information from employees about supplies used and the amount of time they spend performing different tasks. Materials handling costs are easy to trace because workers perform only materials handling duties, so their wages are traced directly to the cost pool. Equipment depreciation accounts are analysed, and the cost of materials handling equipment is separated. Workers estimate fuel costs and some supply costs because detailed records are not kept for these expenses. Employees who set up and monitor batches estimate the amount of time spent in each activity. The employees performing the machining estimate the time and indirect materials used on each type of door, as do the inspectors.

The team's next step is to select cost drivers. They decide to use number of parts as the cost driver for materials handling because each part is handled separately. The set-up for each batch varies with the complexity of the door design. Regular doors are processed using three simple designs. The machines automatically cut the doors to size and rout simple designs on the doors. Premium door set-up requires more time because the door designs are more complex and usually include windows. The robotic machines cut holes for and insert windows. Set-up for this process is more time intensive. The team decides to use set-up time as the cost driver for this activity. Each batch requires about the same amount of monitoring, so the team selects number of batches as the cost driver for monitoring costs. Premium doors require more machine hours than regular doors because the routing designs are more complex, so machine hours are chosen as the cost driver for machining costs. Each door requires a different amount of time to inspect, so the team selects inspection labour time as the cost driver for inspection.

Before calculating the allocation rates, the team estimates the volume for each cost driver. They have complete records for machine hours and labour hours, but are not sure about information for number of parts because that statistic is not tracked. The materials handling employees estimate the number of parts they handled last year. Records are maintained for the number of batches, so that information is readily available. Employees are asked to estimate time spent in set-up. The number of doors inspected is available, as is total time spent inspecting. However, time per regular versus premium door has not been tracked, so inspectors estimate these figures.

Next, the team gathers information about the amount of each cost driver used by regular and premium doors last month as follows.

	Regular door	Premium door
Number of doors per batch	100	100
Number of batches	1200	900
Number of parts per door	10	20
Machine set-up time	0.5 hours per batch	1 hour per batch
Machine hours per door	1	3
Inspection time per door	0.5 hours	1 hour

Figure 12.13 summarises the steps thus far, showing the activities, related cost drivers, overall costs, estimated volume for each cost driver and estimated allocation rates.

			Cost drivers: estimated volume			
Volume	**Estimated cost**	**Cost driver**	**Regular door**	**Premium door**	**Total**	**Estimated allocation rate**
Number of doors			120 000	90 000	210 000	
Number of batches			1 200	900	2 100	
Activity						
Materials handling	$ 3 000 000	Number of parts	1 200 000	1 800 000	3 000 000	$1 per part
Setting up machines	150 000	Time spent	600	900	1 500	$100 per set-up hour
Monitoring batch operations	420 000	Number of batches	1 200	900	2 100	$200 per batch
Machining doors	11 700 000	Machine hours	120 000	270 000	390 000	$30 per machine hour
Inspecting doors	3 000 000	Time spent	60 000	90 000	150 000	$20 per inspection hour
Total cost	$18 270 000					

Machine set-up time is 0.5 hours per batch for regular doors. At $100 per hour, the cost is $50 per batch. Because each batch consists of 100 doors, the cost per regular door is $0.50. Similarly, the cost per premium door is $1.

The total ABC overhead cost for each type of door is calculated as follows:

	Regular door		**Premium door**	
Materials handling	(10 × $1)	$10.00	(20 × $1)	$ 20.00
Machine set-up	(0.5 × $100 ÷ 100)	0.50	(1 × $100 ÷ 100)	1.00
Monitoring batches	($200 ÷ 100)	2.00	($200 ÷ 100)	2.00
Machine hours	(1 × $30)	30.00	(3 × $30)	90.00
Inspections	(0.5 × $20)	10.00	(1 × $20)	20.00
Total overhead		$52.50		$133.00

Using ABC product cost information

The team believes that the calculations under ABC costing confirm their intuition that the job costing system did not accurately reflect each product's use of resources. Overhead allocated to regular doors was $80.13 under the job costing system but only $52.50 under ABC. For the premium doors, $96.15 in overhead cost was allocated by the job costing system compared to $133.00 under activity-based costing. These results suggest that the old system overstated the cost of regular doors and understated the cost of premium doors. The team believes that the ABC costs are more accurate because they better map the use of resources to each type of product.

When the team presents its results to the company's managers, they decide that the regular door price can be reduced to match competitors' prices and the premium door price can be increased. Valerie reminds the managers that this ABC information contains some allocated fixed costs (such as salaries for supervisors and equipment depreciation), and that these costs probably will not change proportionately with changes in production volumes. Therefore, these ABC costs should be used only as a guide for pricing decisions. After any pricing changes are made, the managers need to monitor sales volumes to determine the effects of price changes on demand and determine whether profitability actually improves.

Using ABM to reduce non-manufacturing costs

The managers at Keener Doors and Windows are pleased with the ABC cost information for door production and ask for additional analysis of marketing and warranty costs for doors. They feel these costs could be reduced if they better understand marketing and warranty activities and their related costs.

Because marketing and warranty service are similar for regular and premium doors, the ABC team concludes that these costs can be analysed using doors as a single product line and windows as the other product line. Thus, they plan to identify activities related to marketing and warranty costs, and then separate the costs for doors from the costs for windows. Product-sustaining marketing costs consist of advertising, marketing department employee costs, sales commissions, and marketing department supplies. The cost of advertising is relatively easy to assign because either doors or windows are featured in advertisements. Marketing department employees estimate the amount of time spent per product line, and any sales commissions are traced to each product line. Miscellaneous supplies are allocated according to employee time spent.

To analyse costs for product-sustaining warranty work, the ABC system needs to separate the costs for warranty work on doors from the warranty work on windows. Depending on the problem, sometimes doors are replaced. In these cases, detailed cost records are kept. Other times the doors are reworked. Tracking the costs of rework is difficult because employees take time from their regular tasks to rework, and they often complete rework tasks during idle times when batches are in process and do not need monitoring. Monthly rework costs rely on employee estimates of time and materials used for rework. The team concludes that the warranty work cost pool probably includes errors in cost measurement. They decide to develop a tracking system for the time and materials used for rework to get better estimates of warranty costs in the future.

The final estimates of the per-door costs for marketing and warranty follow:

| Marketing | $20 per unit |
| Warranty work | $18 per unit |

Applying activity-based management

The team members are surprised that warranty costs are nearly as large as marketing costs. They invite the product design team to meet with customer service representatives to discuss possible product changes to reduce warranty costs. The data for the last period indicate that more than half of the warranty costs — about $10 per door sold — resulted from hinge problems; the whole door must be replaced when a hinge fails. The team immediately begins to solve this problem.

The first suggestion is to reinforce the door around the hinge, but the team learns that this procedure costs $15 per door. One team member researches the newest technology in hinges and finds one that would eliminate 90 per cent of the problem at a cost of $14.50 per door, whereas the current hinges cost $12 per door. After discussing a number of other alternatives, the team recommends the new hinges. Although this increases the cost of each door by $2.50, it is likely that overall warranty costs will be reduced by $9 per door ($10 × 90%). In addition, the team believes that Keener's reputation for high quality has been hurt by the hinge problem, resulting in a loss of market share. Management accepts the team's recommendation and instructs engineering to use the new hinges to improve quality, reduce warranty work and eventually increase market share.

Recent developments in ABC: time-driven ABC[6]

Many entities have either abandoned or decided not to adopt ABC because of complexity, time and cost-related barriers to entry. Time-driven ABC (TDABC) is argued to be more accurate, less costly and less time-consuming than the conventional ABC discussed throughout this chapter. The purpose of this section is to explore time-driven ABC through an extension of comprehensive example 1 presented earlier in this chapter.

The central features of time-driven ABC are:
- a focus on capacity supplied and capacity used
- consideration of the time taken to perform each activity
- the development of a standardised cost per time unit of capacity
- the ability to adjust for flexibility of operations or specialised cost determination.

This means that for time-driven ABC, the resource demands of each cost object are directly estimated — unlike the conventional approach, where the resource costs are assigned to activities and then to the cost object.

In conventional ABC, the cost driver rate is calculated as follows:

$$\text{Total assigned activity cost} \div \text{Total activity quantity}$$

In time-driven ABC, the cost driver rate is calculated as follows:

$$\text{Cost per time unit of capacity} \times \text{Unit times of activity}$$

Comprehensive example 3 draws on comprehensive example 1 to highlight the differences between conventional ABC and time-driven ABC.

Using Paisley to compare conventional ABC and time-driven ABC

The Paisley Insurance Company employs 12 staff in its billing department (BD) operations. The time they spent performing each of the four activities was identified and is highlighted in the following table, along with the conventional ABC results from comprehensive example 1.

Activity	% of time spent	Assigned cost	Activity quantity	Cost driver rate
Account enquiry	35%	$102 666	11 500 account enquiries[a]	$ 8.93/account enquiry
Correspondence	5%	17 692	1400 letters	$12.64/letter
Account billing	40%	117 889	1 220 000 lines	$ 0.097/line
Bill verification	20%	44 423	10 000 accounts	$ 4.44/account
	100%[b]	$282 670		

[a]Recall in comprehensive example 1 that *labour hours* was identified as the suitable activity driver to reflect the cause-and-effect relationship between account enquiry costs and related account enquiry activities. In this case we use an alternative activity driver — *the number of enquiries* — which totalled 11 500 (9000 residential and 2500 commercial). This is more suitable for the time-driven ABC approach as time is the key capacity related variable and so cannot be used in both parts of the following time-driven ABC cost driver equation:

$$\text{Cost per time unit of capacity} \times \text{Unit times of activity}$$

[b]In conventional ABC, employees generally calculate the time spent performing each activity as a percentage of their total time. This assumes that there is no idle or unused capacity. As a result, the estimated cost driver rate will usually be overstated. In time-driven ABC, the time unit of *practical capacity* is calculated to allow for deviations from normal performance (meal breaks, machine downtime, travelling between activities etc.) As a rule-of-thumb, *practical capacity* is determined to be 80 to 85 per cent of *theoretical full capacity*.

The steps taken to determine the time-driven ABC cost driver equation follow.

Step 1: Cost per time unit of capacity at Paisley's billing department = $3.07

The cost per minute of supplying capacity is calculated as $282 670 / 92 160 = $3.07 where $282 670 is the cost of supplying capacity at Paisley (monthly overhead billing department cost) and 92 160 minutes is the total practical capacity provided by 12 full-time employees. Each individual works 8 hours per day; 9600 minutes per month theoretical full capacity; 80% of 9600 = 7680 practical capacity for one worker × 12 workers = 92 160 *total* minutes per month.

Step 2: Unit times of activity

This is the time it takes to carry out one unit of activity for each of the four activities identified at Paisley. Analysis of each activity identified that staff can perform an account enquiry in roughly 2.8 minutes, correspondence in 3.3 minutes, account billing in 0.03 minutes and verification in 1.8 minutes.

In the following table, the quantity of actual activity performed by Paisley in the quarter is shown. The objective of this table is to highlight both the cost driver rate calculated, and the amount of used capacity against the actual capacity available. Note that we have no unused capacity in this situation because we have applied Paisley's actual results for the month of May in this illustration.

Activity (1)	Quantity (2)	Unit time (min) (3)	Total time used (min) (4)	Cost driver rate (3) × $3.07 (5)	Total cost assigned (2) × (5) (6)
Account enquiry	11 500	2.8	32 200	$ 8.60	$ 98 900
Correspondence	1 400	3.3	4 620	10.13	14 182
Account billing	1 220 000	0.03	36 600	0.092	112 240
Bill verification	10 000	1.8	18 000	5.53	55 300
Total used			91 420		280 622
Total supplied			92 160		282 670
Unused capacity			0[a]		$ 0

[a]Difference due to rounding.

For the month of June, Paisley estimated the same quantity of activity as that achieved in May. Because the actual quantities in June (column 2) differ from the estimate, we are able to identify the level of unused capacity

Activity (1)	Quantity (2)	Unit time (min) (3)	Total time used (min) (4)	Cost driver rate (3) × $3.07 (5)	Total cost assigned (2) × (5) (6)
Account enquiry	10 000	2.8	28 000	$ 8.60	$ 86 000
Correspondence	1 400	3.3	4 608	10.13	14 182
Account billing	1 220 000	0.03	36 864	0.092	112 240
Bill verification	8 000	1.8	14 400	5.53	44 240
Total used			83 872		256 662
Total supplied			92 160		282 670
Unused capacity			8 288		$ 26 008[a]

[a]Rounding difference.

Refining the model

When investigating the standard 2.8 minutes taken for an account enquiry, it was found that there were other variables contributing to the complexity of this activity. These included time spent searching client file history; senior manager referrals time; and whether the enquiry was considered a simple, average or complex account enquiry — not whether it was a domestic or commercial enquiry. This means that each variant now becomes a distinct activity, so using time-driven ABC we can adjust the 2.8 minute account enquiry to accommodate the identified variables.

The refinement is not limited to each activity. In fact, the entire four-activity approach to the billing activities of Paisley's billing department can be replaced with a single time equation.

The time-driven ABC process for Paisley is shown in figure 12.14.

FIGURE 12.14 Time-driven ABC process for Paisley Insurance Company

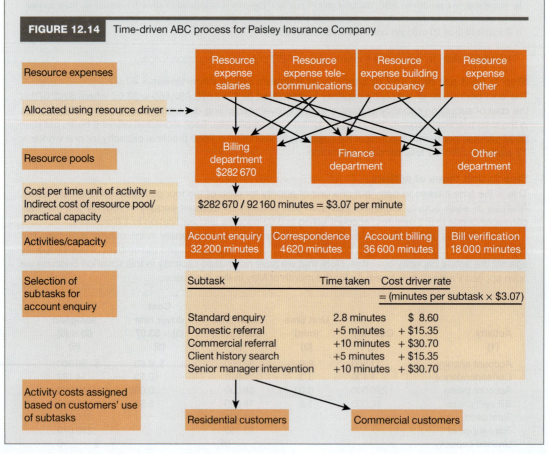

Advantages of time-driven ABC

Time-driven ABC has the following advantages.
1. More informed decision making in relation to the availability and best use of practical capacity:
   * the difference between time available and time required to perform activities is made more obvious
   * idle time can be quantified as input costs minus costs assigned to activities
   * more informed decisions relating to the allocation of staff to activities can be made
   * excess capacity can be eliminated or better managed.
2. Improved computer costing systems capability when using standard rates.[7]
3. Complexity of operations can be incorporated into the time-driven ABC model. For example, standard rates can be:
   * applied in real time to assign individual costs
   * used in quotations to estimate prices for new orders
   * adjusted when existing conditions change:
     – input prices change (salaries and operating expenses)
     – efficiency of the activity changes (learning curves, training programs and re-engineering processes)
     – time units change (new technology and processes).

Limitations of time-driven ABC

Time-driven ABC is relatively new and empirical evidence of benefits is minimal. Like conventional ABC, calculations are still based on subjective and rule-of-thumb estimates. This may result in key cost drivers being based on potentially inaccurate assumptions.

The standardised cost per time unit of capacity might simplify the process. However, it might not necessarily:
* capture the 'value' of time (each minute of costed time is assumed to be equal)
* differentiate the expertise (hence cost) of the employee in performing the activity
* be suitable where overhead costs lack homogeneity.

ABC success rate

While there has been some evidence that ABC's popularity had seemed to be declining, a recent worldwide survey of manufacturing firms,[8] found ABC continued to provide value to managers. Some of the key findings of the survey included:
* ABC helped address the problem of more accurate overhead cost allocation
* ABC resulted in better identification of cause-and-effect relationships providing a better indication of resources consumed
* ABC provide greater support for financial, operational and strategic decisions
* ABC systems are better integrated into budget and planning systems
* ABC systems seem to support product and customer-related decisions.

Only limited evidence is available as to whether the use of ABC results in an improvement in financial performance. One of the problems with collecting this kind of evidence is the challenge of being able to isolate the effect of ABC itself. With so many dynamic things going on inside organisations at any point of time, it is difficult to attribute changes in financial performance to the use of ABC. Nevertheless, there is some evidence to suggest that ABC can produce improved financial performance, particularly when combined with other strategic initiatives such as total quality management and just-in-time production methods.[9]

SUMMARY

12.1 Reflect on and communicate the differences and similarities between activity-based costing (ABC) and conventional costing.

Conventional costing system

Few cost pools allocated using conventional allocation bases

Activity-based costing system (ABC)

Multiple cost pools reflecting activities and cost drivers for allocation bases

Activity

Type of task or function performed in an organisation

Activity identification

- Tracking the use of resources
- Using the cost hierarchy
- Grouping homogeneous costs

Selection of cost drivers

- Cause-and-effect relationship between cost driver and activity costs
- Judgement in choosing and evaluating potential cost drivers

12.2 Understand elements of the ABC cost hierarchy.

Cost hierarchy

- Organisation-sustaining activities
- Facility-sustaining activities
- Customer-sustaining activities
- Product-sustaining activities
- Batch-level activities
- Unit-level activities

12.3 Apply the principles of ABC and conventional costing.

ABC procedures

1. Identify the relevant cost object
2. Identify activities
3. Assign (trace and allocate) costs to activity-based cost pools
4. For each ABC cost pool, choose a cost driver
5. For each ABC cost pool, calculate a cost driver rate
6. For each ABC cost pool, allocate activity costs to the cost object

12.4 Describe the characteristics and use of activity-based management (ABM).

Activity-based management (ABM)

Process of using ABC information to evaluate the costs and benefits of production and internal support activities, and to identify and implement opportunities for improvements in profitability, efficiency and quality within an entity.

Applications of ABM

- Customer profitability
- Product and process design:
  - focus resources on value-added activities
  - reduce or eliminate non-value-added activities
- Environmental costs
- Constrained resources
- Resources supplied and resources consumed

12.5 Communicate the benefits, costs and issues related to ABC.

Benefits

- Increase awareness of cause-and-effect relationships
- Promote performance improvements
- Identify non-value-added activities

- Motivate cost reduction
- Reduce arbitrariness in cost measurement
- Optimise use of constrained resources
- Resources provided versus resources consumed

Costs

- System design and capabilities if expanding activity dictionary
- Accounting system modifications
- Employee training
- Higher costs when:
  - more activities are involved
  - activities are complex
  - ABC system is complex

Issues related to ABC

- Limitations and uncertainties in ABC implementation
- Mismeasurement of costs assigned to ABC activities
- Recent developments in ABC: time-driven ABC (TDABC)

KEY TERMS

activity A type of task or function performed in an organisation.

activity-based costing (ABC) A system that assigns overhead costs to the specific activities performed in a manufacturing or service delivery process. It attempts to trace costs more accurately to products or other cost objects.

activity-based management (ABM) The process of using ABC information to evaluate the costs and benefits of production and internal support activities, and to identify and implement opportunities for improvements in profitability, efficiency and quality within an entity.

batch-level activities Tasks or functions undertaken for a collection of goods or services that are processed as a group.

customer-sustaining activities Tasks or functions undertaken to service past, current and future customers. These costs tend to vary with the needs of individual customers or groups of customers.

facility-sustaining activities Tasks or functions undertaken to provide and manage an area, location or property. They occur regardless of the number of customers served, products sold, batches processed or units produced.

non-value-added activities Activities that are unnecessary and therefore wasteful, and that the customer/client would not normally be prepared to pay for.

organisation-sustaining activities Tasks or functions undertaken to oversee the entire entity. They occur regardless of the number of facilities operated, customers served, products sold, batches processed or units produced.

product-sustaining activities Tasks or functions undertaken to support the production and distribution of a single product or line of products. These activities are not related to units or batches, but to individual products or product lines.

unit-level activities Undertaken to produce individual units manufactured or services produced. Unit-level activities need to be performed for every unit of good or service, and therefore the cost should be proportional to the number of units produced.

value-added activities Activities that are necessary and increase the worth of an entity's goods or services to customers, and that the customer/client would normally be prepared to pay for.

SELF-STUDY PROBLEMS

SELF-STUDY PROBLEM 1 Compute unit ABC costs

The Fallon Company manufactures a variety of handcrafted bed frames. The company's manufacturing activities and related data for the current year follow.

Manufacturing activity	Estimated cost	Cost driver used as allocation base	Estimated volume for cost driver
Materials handling	$ 400 000	Number of parts	800 000 parts
Cutting	1 200 000	Machine hours	40 000 hours
Assembly	3 000 000	Direct labour hours	150 000 hours
Wood staining	1 320 000	Number of frames stained	60 000 frames

Two styles of bed frames were produced in July: a wood frame with fewer parts, and a metal frame that required no staining activities. Direct labour is paid $25 per hour. Their quantities, direct material costs and other data follow:

	Units produced	Direct material	Machine hours	Number of parts	Direct labour hours
Wood frames	5 000	$600 000	5 000	100 000	6 000
Metal frames	1 000	200 000	500	10 000	3 000

Required

(a) Compute the ABC cost allocation rates and then calculate total manufacturing costs and unit costs of the wood and metal frames.

(b) Non-manufacturing activities, such as product design, were analysed and allocated to the wood frame at $10 each and the metal frame at $15 each. Similar analyses were conducted of other non-manufacturing activities, such as distribution, marketing and customer service. The support costs allocated were $50 per wood frame and $80 per metal frame. Calculate the product cost per unit including the non-manufacturing costs.

SOLUTION TO SELF-STUDY PROBLEM 1

(a)

Resource or activity	Wood frames		Metal frames	
Direct materials		$ 600 000		$200 000
Direct labour	6000 × $25	150 000	3000 × $25	75 000
Materials handling	100 000 × $0.50	50 000	10 000 × $0.50	5 000
Cutting	5000 × $30	150 000	500 × $30	15 000
Assembly	6000 × $20	120 000	3000 × $20	60 000
Wood staining	5000 × $22	110 000	0 × $22	0
Total		$1 180 000		$355 000
Per unit	$1 180 000 ÷ 5000	$236 per unit	$355 000 ÷ 1000	$355 per unit

(b) Product cost per unit including manufacturing and non-manufacturing costs:

Wood frame = $236 + $10 + $50 = $296
Metal frame = $355 + $15 + $80 = $450

SELF-STUDY PROBLEM 2 ABC activities and cost drivers; measurement error; usefulness

You have been asked to analyse your sister's preschool operation to determine in what ways she can improve quality and reduce costs. You decide to analyse the activities provided by the preschool and use an ABC system to assign costs to the activities. The following list contains potential activities from which to choose.

* *Learning activities.* At times during the day, children are listening to stories, learning to sing simple songs, following simple directions as part of games or art activities, and playing interactively with special toys developed to enhance eye–hand coordination or understanding of spatial relations.
* *Resting.* The children rest on mats during this activity while one teacher monitors and the other teachers prepare lesson plans.
* *Snack and meal activities.* Snacks and meals are prepared by teachers and one food-service employee. Sometimes the students prepare their own snacks and practise following directions.
* *Free play activities.* While children play inside or outside, a few teachers monitor their progress while others prepare learning activities to be used later.

- *Art and craft activities.* These daily activities promote some of the same skills as the learning activities, but children are encouraged to be more creative.
- *Miscellaneous.* These activities include greeting the children, helping them with their coats, helping them use the restroom, interacting with parents and conferencing with parents.
- *Music activity.* This weekly activity encourages the children's interest in music and dance.
- *Conferencing with parents.* This quarterly activity consists of the head teacher (your sister) meeting with each child's parents for half an hour.

Required

(a) Choose several activities to use for cost pools. Explain your choices.

(b) Choose cost drivers for these pools. Explain your choices.

(c) Identify possible reasons why measurement error might exist in the ABC costs.

(d) How would you estimate the increase in future costs if your sister plans to expand her operations?

SOLUTION TO SELF-STUDY PROBLEM 2

(a) First, consider the activity hierarchy. Some costs can be allocated to the organisation (for example, rent, insurance, licences). Greeting and helping children with coats may be considered part of the organisation-sustaining costs, or they may be viewed as a separate activity cost pool. This reasoning is also true for interacting with parents. However, time greeting and interacting with parents varies on a daily basis but is not necessarily dependent on the number of children or number of classes. Therefore, these activities will most likely be considered part of the facility-sustaining costs.

No product-sustaining costs are evident because the organisation has only one product.

In this entity, we can consider each class a batch when the children are all involved in a similar activity. Resting and free play could be combined into a single batch-level cost pool because no supplies are used in these activities and fewer teachers are interacting with the children. Learning, art and music activities could be combined as a second batch-level cost pool because they require similar numbers of teachers and supplies.

Snacks and meals can be considered a unit-level cost pool that varies with number of children. For this cost pool, flexible and committed costs could be tracked separately. Parent conferences could also be a unit-level cost pool because gathering information about each child and meeting with each child's parents would require about the same amount of time per child.

Notice that the choices of activities are somewhat arbitrary. As an alternative to the preceding set of activities, a separate pool could be established for each activity described in the problem.

(b) The cost driver for resting and play could be measured in time or in days if the same times are used each day. Teacher time might be used as a cost driver for learning activities because most of the teachers are involved in these activities. Number of meals served or number of children could drive the costs of snacks and meals. Number of children would be a likely cost driver for conferencing with parents.

(c) We discuss only two possible types of measurement error in this solution; there are many other possible answers. Measurement error might occur if some of the teachers use unpaid time to prepare activities. These potential costs are not measured. The willingness to spend extra time on preparation varies among teachers. If a new teacher is hired who does not want to spend unpaid time, then labour costs could increase or the quality of the program could decrease.

Another type of measurement error occurs if different groups of children require different levels of monitoring for play time and nap time. For groups that require more time, labour costs could be understated if teachers require more preparation time, or the quality of the program could suffer if no more time is spent in preparation.

(d) Because this organisation relies heavily on labour, the best predictor for expansion costs is to determine the desired ratio of children to teachers. Facility-sustaining cost changes also need to be predicted. Meal and snack costs probably contain both flexible and committed components, taking into consideration the food-service worker who is employed. The cost of raw materials, such as art supplies, would need to be separated from the activity cost pool to predict costs for more children.

QUESTIONS

12.1 Explain how conventional and ABC cost systems differ. **LO1**

12.2 Mannon Company's accountant exclaimed, 'Our cost accounting system allocates overhead based on direct labour hours, but our overhead costs appear to be more related to set-up activities than to the use of direct labour. It seems as though our costing system allocates too much cost to large batches of product and not enough cost to small batches.' Explain what she means. **LO1, 3**

12.3 Describe the ABC cost hierarchies. **LO2**

12.4 The results from allocations using ABC are usually different from the results using conventional cost systems. Explain why these differences arise. **LO1**

12.5 Does it matter if the ABC-generated cost data are somewhat subjective? **LO2**

12.6 Does increasing the number of cost pools always increase the accuracy of allocations under an ABC system? Explain your answer. **LO1, 5**

12.7 Is an ABC system appropriate for every industry and every type or organisation? Explain your answer. **LO5**

12.8 Should ABC be used in service industries? Why? **LO5**

12.9 What makes organisations such as local governments and universities suitable for ABC use? **LO5**

12.10 What use might management make of ABC cost data output in universities, local governments and other such organisations? **LO4**

12.11 Does measurement error increase or decrease when ABC systems are implemented? Explain your answer. **LO3, 5**

12.12 List several costs and several benefits of implementing an ABC system. **LO5**

12.13 Suppose that you are part of a student consulting team working for your university. You need to analyse accounting department activities and set up cost pools for these activities. Explain how you would identify the activities and pools. **LO3**

12.14 Is ABC appropriate for an organisation that sells a wide range of customised products manufactured using flexible manufacturing systems? Why? **LO3, 5**

12.15 Explain the difference between activity-based costing and activity-based management. **LO4, 5**

12.16 Outline the benefits of time-driven ABC. **LO5**

12.17 Using examples, distinguish between value-added and non-value added activities. **LO4**

EXERCISES

12.18 Mapping costs to the cost hierarchy **LO2, 3**

Each of the costs below is incurred by Fairgood & Hernandez, a small CPA firm.

Required

Identify whether each of the following costs most likely relates to an (i) organisation-sustaining activity, (ii) customer-sustaining activity, (iii) product-sustaining activity, (iv) batch-level activity, or (v) unit-level activity. For each item, explain your choice.

(a) Receptionist salary
(b) Financial forecasting software
(c) Photocopy machine rental
(d) Cleaning service
(e) Audit manager salary
(f) Long-distance telephone charges
(g) Meal costs for entertaining clients
(h) Costs of annual employee golf party
(i) Office supplies such as paperclips and paper
(j) Annual subscription for income tax regulations

12.19 Identifying costs using the ABC cost hierarchies **LO2, 3**

MicroBrew is a successful brewery engaged in the development and production of specialty micro brews. It uses an ABC system. During the past year, it has incurred $1 250 000 of product development costs, $850 000 of materials handling costs, $2 500 000 of production line labour costs, $700 000 for production set-up costs, $500 000 in power costs for cooling beer and running equipment and $1 500 000 for manufacturing facility management.

Required

In an ABC cost hierarchy, calculate the total cost that would be classified as:

(a) facility-sustaining
(b) product-sustaining
(c) batch-level
(d) unit-level.

12.20 ABC cost hierarchy   **LO2**

In ABC systems, activities are often separated into a hierarchy of six categories.

Required

In your own words, define and give examples of the following types of activities and costs in an ABC system for a national car rental company.

(a) Unit-level activities and costs
(b) Batch-level activities and costs
(c) Product-sustaining activities and costs
(d) Customer-sustaining activities and costs
(e) Facility-sustaining activities and costs
(f) Organisation-sustaining activities and costs

12.21 Cost pools and cost drivers   **LO3**

Following are lists of potential cost pools and cost drivers.

Cost pool	Cost driver
(a) Machining	(i) Number of employees
(b) Purchasing activities	(ii) Number of parts per unit
(c) Inspection	(iii) Kilograms of laundry processed
(d) Assembly	(iv) Number of invoices
(e) Payroll	(v) Number of batches
(f) A special quick-freezing process for food	(vi) Number of machine hours
(g) Laundry in a hospital	(vii) Number of units

Required

Match each cost driver to the most appropriate cost pool. Use each cost driver only once. Explain your choice.

12.22 ABC costing; ABM   **LO3, 5**

Taylors Cheesecakes supplies cheesecakes to three large supermarket chains. Management has become concerned about the rising costs associated with the processing and dispatch of orders. An activity analysis of the indirect costs identified the following customer-related costs:

Activity cost pool	Cost driver	Estimated indirect costs	Total expected use of cost driver*	Use of cost driver Supermarket customer 1	2	3
Orders processing	Number of orders	$200 000	450	300	100	50
Returns processing	Number of returns	$ 50 000	100	50	25	25
Delivery	Number of deliveries	$100 000	700	400	200	100
Rush orders	Number of rush orders	$ 70 000	50	10	20	20
Sales visits	Number of visits	$ 20 000	100	50	25	25

*Expressed in units of measure of the driver.

Sales are marked up 50% on cost.

Required

(a) Calculate the activity cost rate for each activity.
(b) Assign the activity costs to each of the three customers.
(c) Calculate the contribution for each customer if the sales pattern for each is as follows:
Customer 1 — $300 000; Customer 2 — $150 000; Customer 3 — $200 000.
(d) Advise the management of Taylors Cheesecakes as to whether any changes should be made in its relationships with customers.

12.23 Cost system design — activity analysis   **LO4**

Prahran Daycare (PD) offers childcare services to the local community. For many years it simply offered services for preschoolers. In this environment, managing the costs and services seemed relatively straightforward. In recent years, government subsidies and building programs have enabled PD to offer expanded services. For example, two years ago PD added an after-school care program for older children. It is also planning school holiday programs and a special tours activity.

Until now, the cost system has been relatively simple, with little regard for accumulating costs for the individual services offered. However, the new manager of PD, Noah Day, knows he needs better cost data, both for reliable costing of services and to help him manage the growing costs of PD.

Required

(a) Advise Noah how activity analysis might help with improved cost data.

(b) Advise Noah how he could use activity analysis to help manage the activities.

12.24 Conventional versus ABC costing

LO1, 3, 5

Calder Products manufactures two component parts: AJ40 and AJ60. AJ40 components are being introduced currently, and AJ60 parts have been in production for several years. For the upcoming period, 1000 units of each product are planned for manufacturing. Assume that the only relevant overhead cost is for engineering change orders (any requested changes in product design or the manufacturing process). AJ40 components are expected to require four change orders, and AJ60 only two. Each AJ40 requires 1 machine hour, and each AJ60 requires 1.5 machine hours. The cost of a change order is $300.

Required

(a) Estimate the cost of engineering change orders for AJ40 and AJ60 components if Calder uses a conventional costing method and machine hours as the allocation base.

(b) Now suppose that Calder uses an ABC system and allocates the cost of change orders using the number of change orders as the cost driver. Estimate the cost for change orders for each unit of AJ40 and AJ60.

(c) Calculate the difference in overhead allocated to each product. This figure represents an amount that one product cross-subsidises the other product. Explain what that means.

12.25 ABC costing; ABM

LO1, 3, 5

Applewood Electronics manufactures two large-screen television models: the Monarch, which has been produced since 2010 and sells for $900; and the Regal, a new model introduced in early 2019 that sells for $1140. Applewood's CEO, Harry Hazelwood, suggested that the company should concentrate its marketing resources on the Regal model and begin to phase out the Monarch model.

Applewood currently uses a conventional costing system. The following cost information has been used as a basis for pricing decisions over the past year.

Per-unit data	Monarch	Regal
Direct materials	$208	$584
Direct labour hours	1.5	3.5
Machine hours	8.0	4.0
Units produced	22 000	4 000

Direct labour cost is $12 per hour and the machine usage cost is $18 per hour. Manufacturing overhead costs were estimated at $4 800 000 and were allocated on the basis of machine hours.

Martin Alecks, the new company controller, suggested that an activity-based costing analysis first be run to get a better picture of the true manufacturing cost. The following data were collected:

Activity centre	Cost driver	Traceable costs
Soldering	Number of solder joints	$ 942 000
Shipments	Number of shipments	860 000
Quality control	Number of inspections	1 240 000
Purchase orders	Number of orders	950 400
Machining	Machine hours	57 600
Machine set-ups	Number of set-ups	750 000
Total traceable costs		$4 800 000

	Number of events		
Activity	Monarch	Regal	Total
Soldering	1 185 000	385 000	1 570 000
Shipments	16 200	3 800	20 000
Quality control	56 200	21 300	77 500
Purchase orders	80 100	109 980	190 080
Machining	176 000	16 000	192 000
Machine set-ups	16 000	14 000	30 000

Selling, general and administrative expenses per unit sold are $265 for Monarch and $244.50 for Regal.

Required

(a) Calculate the manufacturing cost per unit for Monarch and Regal under:
  (i) a conventional costing system
  (ii) the ABC system.
(b) Explain the differences in manufacturing cost per unit calculated in part (a).
(c) Calculate the operating profit per unit for Monarch and Regal under:
  (i) a conventional costing system
  (ii) the ABC system.
(d) Should Applewood concentrate its marketing efforts on Monarch or on Regal? Explain how the use of ABC affects your recommendation.

12.26 ABC costing; ABM   LO3

Palmer Company uses an activity-based costing system. It has the following manufacturing activity areas, related drivers used as allocation bases, and cost allocation rates:

Activity	Cost driver	Cost allocation rate
Machine set-up	Number of set-ups	$50.00
Materials handling	Number of parts	0.50
Machining	Machine hours	26.00
Assembly	Direct labour hours	22.00
Inspection	Number of finished units	12.00

During the month, 100 units were produced, requiring two set-ups. Each unit consisted of 19 parts, and used 1.5 direct labour hours and 1.25 machine hours. Direct materials cost $100 per finished unit. All other manufacturing costs are classified as conversion costs. ABC costs for research and marketing costs are $140. All other non-manufacturing ABC costs are $320 per unit.

Required

(a) Calculate the manufacturing cost per unit for the period.
(b) Calculate the total cost (manufacturing and non-manufacturing costs) per unit for the period.

12.27 ABC in job costing; ABM; non-value-added activities   LO3, 5

Kestral Manufacturing identified the following overhead costs and cost drivers for the current period. Kestral produces customised products that move through several different processes. Materials and intermediate products are moved among several different workstations. Custom features are designed by engineers.

Activity	Cost driver	Estimated cost	Estimated activity level
Machine set-up	Number of set-ups	$ 40 000	400
Materials handling	Number of times materials are moved	160 000	16 000
Product design	Design hours	100 000	2 000
Inspection	Number of inspections	260 000	13 000
Total cost		$560 000	

Information for three of the jobs completed during the period follows.

	Job 42	Job 43	Job 44
Direct materials	$10 000	$24 000	$16 000
Direct labour	$ 4 000	$ 4 000	$ 8 000
Units completed	200	100	400
Number of set-ups	2	4	8
Number of times materials are moved	60	20	100
Number of inspections	40	20	60
Number of design hours	20	100	20

Required

(a) If the company uses ABC, how much overhead cost should be assigned to job 42?

(b) If the company uses ABC, calculate the cost per unit for job 43.

(c) Kestral would like to reduce the cost of its overhead activities. Describe non-value-added activities and explain why reducing these specific activities might also reduce cost.

(d) How might Kestral benefit from the use of time-driven ABC?

12.28 Design ABC system; calculate per-unit ABC costs; uncertainties   LO2, 4, 5

Elite Daycare provides two different services, full-time childcare for pre-schoolers, and after-school care for older children. The director would like to estimate an annual cost per child in each of the day-care programs, ignoring any facility-sustaining costs. She is considering expanding the services and wants to know whether full-time or after-school care is more profitable.

The following activities and annual costs apply to the day-care centre. Salaries and wages are $100 000. Full-time children arrive between 8 am and 9 am. Older children arrive about 3 pm. All of the children are gone by 6 pm. Employees estimate that they spend about 20 per cent of their time on meal-related activities, 20 per cent supervising naps or recreation, 10 per cent in greeting or sending children home, and the rest of the time presenting educational experiences to the children. Meals and snacks cost about $20 000. Pre-schoolers receive two snacks and one meal per day, and the older children receive one snack per day. On average, snacks and meals do not differ in cost. Supplies cost $10 000 for the full-time childcare program and $8000 for the after-school program.

Currently, 30 children participate in full-time care and 10 children in after-school care. Because Elite Daycare maintains a waiting list for openings in its programs, the number of children in each program remains steady.

Required

(a) Identify a cost object and then choose a set of activities and cost drivers for Elite Daycare's ABC system. Explain your choices.

(b) Using the activities you chose in part (a), estimate the annual cost per child in each program.

(c) Do uncertainties exist about the proportion of salaries and wages that should be allocated to full-time care versus after-school care? Why?

12.29 ABM; customer profitability   LO4, 5

You are asked for suggestions about increasing profitability for a customer that purchases low-margin products and requires costly services.

Required

(a) In your own words, define activity-based management (ABM).

(b) In your own words, describe high-cost and low-cost customers.

(c) Prepare a brief paragraph suggesting methods to improve profitability for this customer.

12.30 Introductory TDABC   LO5

Chief accountant San Kean Indi at Lewinsky and Dikolli Architects has begun a pilot project exploring the use of time-driven-activity-based-costing (TDABC). Indi became aware of the attributes of TDABC at a recent professional development seminar. Indi has decided to use the administration support function for the pilot.

Relevant information that Indi has managed to collect so far is provided in Table 1.

Lewinsky and Dikolli Architects Table 1:

Total cost of resources supplied in the administrative function	$632 000
Four staff work 8 hours per day for 5 days, 46 weeks per year.	
One staff member works 5 hours per day for 5 days 46 weeks per year.	
Approximately 20% of staff time is spent on other activities other than providing support to the architects	

Required

(a) Why do you think Indi believes TDABC might be applicable for Lewinsky and Dikolli Architects?

(b) Calculate the level of theoretical capacity and practical capacity within the administration support function.

(c) Calculate the cost per time unit of practical capacity.

PROBLEMS

12.31 Setting up an ABC system; uncertainties   LO3, 5

Following is a list of steps that must be performed in setting up an ABC system:
- Identify and sum the costs into activity-based cost pools.
- Choose a cost driver for each activity.
- For each ABC cost pool, allocate overhead costs to the product or service.
- Identify the relevant cost object.
- Identify the activities necessary for production or service delivery.
- For each ABC cost pool, calculate a cost allocation rate.

Required

(a) Number the steps from 1 through 6 to indicate the sequence in which the steps are performed.

(b) For each step, explain whether uncertainties are likely.

(c) Pick the step that you think would require the greatest use of judgement (that is, would include the most uncertainties). Explain your choice.

12.32 ABC cost hierarchy; uncertainties   LO2

In ABC systems, activities are often separated into a hierarchy of categories.

Required

(a) In your own words, explain what is meant by a cost hierarchy in ABC.

(b) Explain why uncertainty is possible in classifying costs within the cost hierarchy.

(c) Explain how categorising costs into a hierarchy helps accountants determine how costs behave.

12.33 ABC versus conventional job costing; uncertainties; advantages and disadvantages   LO1, 5

Vines Ltd produces custom machine parts on a job-order basis. The company has two direct product cost categories: direct materials and direct labour. In the past, indirect manufacturing costs were allocated to products using a single indirect cost pool, allocated based on direct labour hours. The indirect cost rate was $115 per direct labour hour.

The managers of Vines Ltd decided to switch from a manual system to software programs that release materials and signal machines when to begin working. Simultaneously, the company adopted an activity-based costing system. The manufacturing process has been organised into six activities, each with its own supervisor who is responsible for controlling costs. The following list indicates the activities, cost drivers and cost allocation rates.

Activity	Cost driver	Cost per unit of cost driver
Materials handling	Number of parts	$ 0.40
Milling	Machine hours	20.00
Grinding	Number of parts	0.80
Assembly	Hours spent in assembly	5.00
Inspection	Number of units produced	25.00
Shipping	Number of orders shipped	1500.00

The company's information system automatically collects the necessary data for these six activity areas. The data for two recent jobs follow:

	Job order 410	Job order 411
Direct materials cost	$9 700	$59 900
Direct labour cost	$ 750	$11 250
Number of direct labour hours	25	375
Number of parts	500	2 000
Number of machine hours	150	1 050
Number of job orders shipped	1	1
Number of units	10	200
Number of hours in assembly	2	30

Required

(a) Suppose the company had not adopted an ABC system. Calculate the manufacturing cost per unit for job orders 410 and 411 under the old, conventional costing system.

(b) Under the new ABC system, calculate the manufacturing cost per unit for job orders 410 and 411.

(c) Compare the costs per unit for job orders 410 and 411 as calculated. Explain why the cost per unit under the conventional costing system is different from cost per unit under the ABC system.

(d) Explain why uncertainties may arise about the choice of cost drivers for each activity.

(e) Identify and explain to Vines Ltd's managers the possible advantages and disadvantages of adopting the ABC system.

12.34 ABC and costing for processes   **LO1, 3**

Kim Mills produces three different types of fabric using two departments. In department 1, machines weave the cloth. In department 2, the cloth is dyed a variety of colours. Information for the combined use of resources in both departments for the three types of fabric follows.

Bolts are 20 metres each. All fabric is inspected during production. Robotic equipment inspects the fabric for obvious flaws as the bolts are wound up. Each bolt spends about 5 minutes in the inspection process.

	Denim	Lightweight cotton	Heavyweight cotton	Total
Monthly production in units (bolts of fabric)	1000 bolts	4000 bolts	2000 bolts	7000 bolts
Direct materials costs	$8000	$24 000	$20 000	$52 000
Direct labour costs	$660	$1320	$920	$2900
Direct labour hours	33 hours	66 hours	46 hours	145 hours
Machine hours	500 hours	1333.3 hours	1500 hours	3333.3 hours
Number of set-ups for dye colour changes	10 set-ups	30 set-ups	20 set-ups	60 set-ups
Inspection time	83.3 hours	333.3 hours	166.6 hours	583.2 hours

Combined overhead costs for the two departments follow:

Cost to operate and maintain machines	$40 000
Set-up costs	11 000
Inspection costs	6 996
Total	$57 996

Previously, Kim Mills used a costing system that focused on processes. It allocated direct materials to each product separately, but allocated direct labour and conversion costs as if they were incurred equally across the units produced. Under this costing system, the overhead cost for department 1 is $19 332 and for department 2 it is $38 664. Direct labour hours and costs in department 1 are 55 hours at $1100, and the remaining hours are in department 2. Direct materials for department 1 are $6000 for denim, $16 000 for lightweight and $15 000 for heavyweight. The remaining direct materials are added in department 2. No beginning or ending inventory or abnormal spoilage is recorded for Kim Mills during this period.

Required

(a) Set up a spreadsheet to perform the following calculations. Use a data input section and cell referencing.

    (i) Use conventional process costing to allocate the direct materials and conversion costs per department to total bolts produced. Develop a cost per bolt for each type of fabric. (*Hint:* You will need to first calculate the equivalent cost per bolt for conversion costs for each department.)

    (ii) Using activity-based costing, develop a cost per bolt.

(b) Compare the process costing and ABC results. Identify the products with overstated costs and those with understated costs. Explain why the costs are misstated under conventional process costing.

(c) How could managers use the ABC information to improve operations?

12.35 ABC costs; uncertainties; ABM; non-value-added activities LO2, 3, 5

Water Feature Company manufactures kits for fish ponds. The managers recently set up an ABC system to identify and reduce non-value-added activities. The ABC system includes the following cost pools, cost drivers and estimated costs for manufacturing activities.

Activity	Cost driver	Cost allocation rate
Materials handling	Number of parts	$1.00 per part
Forming	Moulding hours	$40.00 per hour
Moulding set-up	Number of batches	$50.00 per batch
Packing and shipping	Weight	$1.30 per kilogram
Inspection	Finished kits	$10.00 per kit
Direct labour	Finished kits	$20.00 per kit
Direct materials	Finished kits	$100.00 per kit

The company manufactures 10 kits per batch. Each kit requires 20 parts and two hours in moulding, and weighs 30 kilograms.

Required

(a) Calculate the total ABC manufacturing cost per batch.

(b) Calculate the total ABC cost per finished kit.

(c) Suppose that Water Feature's managers also want to allocate marketing costs and customer service to each product. Total marketing costs for the period were $15 000 and customer service costs were $25 000. The number of batches produced was 1000. Calculate the total ABC cost per unit and cost per kit, including the costs of marketing and customer services.

(d) Are the activities listed likely to be the only possible set of activities for Water Feature Company? Why?

(e) Describe how the managers and accountants of Water Feature Company might use this new ABC system to identify non-value-added activities.

12.36 Uncertainties; actual versus estimated costs; practical capacity LO3, 5

Data Processors performs credit card services for banks. The company uses an ABC system. The following information applies to the past year:

Activity	Estimated cost	Actual cost	Cost driver
Processing transactions	$2 000 000	$2 200 000	Number of transactions
Issuing monthly statements	1 000 000	1 300 000	Number of statements
Issuing new credit cards	500 000	400 000	Number of new credit cards
Resolving billing disputes	90 000	100 000	Number of disputes
Total	$3 590 000	$4 000 000	

Cost driver	Estimated activity level	Actual activity level
Number of transactions	5 800 000	5 000 000
Number of statements	270 000	250 000
Number of new credit cards	110 000	100 000
Number of disputes	3 500	3 000

Required

(a) Are the activities listed likely to be the only possible set of activities for the ABC system? Why?

(b) Using estimated values for costs and activity, calculate an ABC allocation rate for each activity.

(c) Explain why actual costs and activity levels are likely to be different from estimated amounts.

(d) Is practical capacity likely to be higher or lower than the estimated activity levels? Explain.

12.37 Design ABC cost system; usefulness for ABM LO3, 5

Shearwater Council owns and operates an animal shelter that performs three services: housing and finding homes for stray and unwanted animals, providing healthcare and neutering services for the animals, and pet training services. One facility is dedicated to housing animals waiting to be adopted. A second facility houses veterinarian services. A third facility houses the director, her staff and several dog trainers. This facility also has several large meeting rooms that are frequently used for classes given by the animal trainers. The trainers work with all of the animals to ensure that they are relatively easy to manage. They also provide dog obedience classes for adopting families.

Estimated annual costs for the animal shelter and its services are as follows:

Director and staff salaries	$ 60 000
Animal shelter employees' salaries	100 000
Veterinarians and technicians	150 000
Animal trainers	40 000
Food and supplies	125 000
Building-related costs	200 000

On average, 75 animals per day are housed at the facility, or about 27 375 (75 × 365) animal-days in total. The number of animals housed during the year totalled 4500. In addition, the trainers offer about 125 classes during approximately 30 weeks throughout the year. On average, 10 families attend each class. Last year the veterinarian clinic experienced 5000 animal visits.

One of the director's staff members just graduated from an accounting program and would like to set up an ABC system for the shelter so that the director can better understand the cost for each of the shelter's services. He gathers the following information:

Square metres for each facility:	
Animal shelter	5000 square metres
Director and training	3000 square metres
Veterinarian clinic	2000 square metres
Percentage of trainer time used in classes	50%
Supplies used for veterinarian services	$75 000

Required

(a) Identify cost pools and assign costs to them, considering the three cost objects of interest.

(b) Determine a cost driver for each cost pool and explain your choice.

(c) Calculate the allocation rates for each cost pool and cost driver. Interpret the allocation rate for each cost pool (that is, explain what it means).

12.38 Usefulness of ABC   **LO3, 5**

With reference to Keener Doors in comprehensive example 2, provide answers to each of the following questions regarding the use of ABC information for activity-based management.

(a) Why did the managers ask for additional analysis of marketing and warranty costs?

(b) When managers use ABC information to improve operations, why is it impossible to be certain that the company will achieve benefits?

(c) What benefits of ABM were illustrated? What costs did the company incur to generate these benefits?

(d) In your own words, describe how various quantitative and qualitative factors were weighed in reaching a decision about the hinge problem.

ENDNOTES

1. These procedures can be combined or further separated, so the actual number of procedures in any ABC model may vary.
2. Adapted from Cotton, B 1998, 'Activity-based cost systems', in RS Kaplan & AA Atkinson (eds), *Advanced Management Accounting*, Prentice Hall, New Jersey, pp. 119–22.
3. See Ittner, C, Lanen, W & Larcker, D 2002, 'The association between activity-based costing and manufacturing performance', *Journal of Accounting Research*, June.
4. See Shields, M 1995, 'An empirical analysis of firms' implementation experiences with activity-based costing', *Journal of Management Accounting Research 7*, pp. 148–66; and Foster, G & Swenson, D 1997, 'Measuring the success of activity-based cost management and its determinants', *Journal of Management Accounting Research 7*, pp. 109–41.
5. See Needy, KLS, Nachtmann, H, Roztocki, N, Warner, RC & Bidanda, B 2003, 'Implementing activity-based costing systems in small manufacturing firms: a field study', *Engineering Management Journal*, March, pp. 3–10.
6. Adapted from Kaplan, RS & Anderson, SR 2004, 'Time-driven activity-based costing', *Harvard Business Review*, November, pp. 131–8.
7. Kaplan and Anderson (2004) found that large entities require expansive activity dictionaries to reflect the complex details of their operations. A significant issue is that generic tools such as Excel and even some ABC software packages do not provide the capacity required. For example, at one company an automated ABC costing model took three days to calculate costs for 40 departments, 150 activities, 10 000 orders and 45 000 line items.
8. Stratton, E, Desroches, D, Lawson, R & Hatch, T 2009, 'Activity-based costing: is it still relevant', *Management Accounting Quarterly*, vol. 10, no. 3, pp. 31–40.

9. Cagwin, D & Bouwman, MJ 2002, 'The association between activity-based costing and improvement in financial performance', *Management Accounting Research*, vol. 13, no. 1, pp. 1–39; and Kennedy, T & Affleck–Graves, J 2001, 'The impact of activity-based costing techniques on firm performance', *Journal of Management Accounting Research*, vol. 13, no. 1, pp. 19–45.

ACKNOWLEDGEMENTS

Photo 12A: © fizkes / Shutterstock.com

Photo 12B: © stockphoto mania / Shutterstock.com

Photo 12C: © Nejron Photo / Shutterstock.com

Figure 12.5 and 12.5A: Kaplan, Robert S., Atkinson, Anthony A., *Advanced Management Accounting*, 3rd edn, © 1998. Reprinted by permission of Pearson Education, Inc., New York, New York

Text 12.22 and 12.23: © John Wiley & Sons Australia Ltd

CHAPTER 13

Relevant costs for decision making

LEARNING OBJECTIVES

After studying this chapter, you should be able to:

13.1 describe the process for making non-routine operating decisions

13.2 understand the decision-making process to accept, reject and price special orders

13.3 understand the decision-making process to keep or drop products, segments or whole businesses

13.4 understand the decision-making process to insource or outsource an activity (make or buy)

13.5 explain the decision-making process for product emphasis and constrained resources

13.6 describe the qualitative factors important to non-routine operating decisions

13.7 demonstrate an understanding of joint costing issues.

IN BRIEF

Managers make a variety of non-routine operating decisions that include special orders, outsourcing, keeping or dropping a product line, and constrained resources. Decisions are also made about when to sell joint products and/or whether to process further. Costs are an important part of making these decisions. However, qualitative factors are also important, sometimes overriding cost considerations. Managers weigh a variety of quantitative and qualitative factors in choosing the best course of action.

13.1 Non-routine operating decisions

LEARNING OBJECTIVE 13.1 Describe the process for making non-routine operating decisions.

Many management decisions are unique, making it impossible to create a 'cookbook' to memorise and use. This chapter focuses on non-routine operating decisions. These types of decisions arise when we re-evaluate operations because we want to improve processes, or because resource shortages occur or, a customer wants special treatment. Some examples of non-routine decisions include: whether to commit resources for a special order, whether to use internal resources or to outsource some activities, whether to discontinue a product line or business sub-unit or segment, how to manage limited resources, and whether to sell or process further. Such tactical decisions relate to choosing amongst alternatives with an immediate or limited end in view, typically with the focus on the current financial period and making use of existing capacity.

In contrast, decisions that will impact beyond the current accounting period are more strategic in nature, such as the introduction of new product lines, opening/closing divisions or major infrastructure spending. The objective of such decisions is to enhance the organisation's competitive advantage. Although the identification of relevant revenues and costs is the same as in non-routine decisions, such long-term decisions should consider the time value of money, which is explored in chapter 15.

Most of these decisions require the use of relevant costs/revenues (both qualitative and quantitative) that must (1) arise in the future, and (2) vary with the action taken. Figure 13.1 provides a decision process capable of being used for non-routine operating decisions. Throughout the chapter

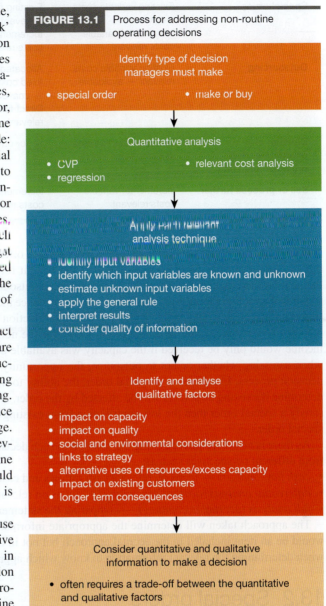

FIGURE 13.1 Process for addressing non-routine operating decisions

Identify type of decision managers must make
- special order
- make or buy

Quantitative analysis
- CVP
- regression
- relevant cost analysis

Apply each relevant analysis technique
- identify input variables
- identify which input variables are known and unknown
- estimate unknown input variables
- apply the general rule
- interpret results
- consider quality of information

Identify and analyse qualitative factors
- impact on capacity
- impact on quality
- social and environmental considerations
- links to strategy
- alternative uses of resources/excess capacity
- impact on existing customers
- longer term consequences

Consider quantitative and qualitative information to make a decision
- often requires a trade-off between the quantitative and qualitative factors

we refer to a general rule for each type of non-routine decision. Bear in mind that this general rule needs to be placed in the context of any specific set of circumstances and that the qualitative factors are considered alongside the quantitative information.

The objective of the quantitative analysis is to identify how the current statement of profit or loss will change as a consequence of the decision faced by management. Costs relevant to the decision can be either fixed or variable, and table 13.1 details how these costs are considered for different decision types. Equally important is the consideration of qualitative factors relating to the decision alternatives. For example, in a special order decision, consideration is given to the impact on existing customers; and in an outsourcing decision, the analysis must consider the ability of the supplier to meet quality standards and delivery timelines. Depending on the circumstances, the qualitative factors may be such that they override any positive financial outcomes from the decision. The final outcome for any decision will also depend on the personal attributes of the decision maker; that is, their level of understanding of the situation and their moral and ethical standards.

TABLE 13.1   Relevant costs in decision making

Decision	Variable costs	Fixed costs	Opportunity costs
Special order	Existing variable costs irrelevant Incremental variable costs relevant	Existing fixed costs irrelevant Incremental (direct) fixed costs relevant	Relevant if current spare capacity not able to satisfy order
Outsourcing	Existing variable costs relevant — avoidable	Allocated (indirect) fixed costs irrelevant — unavoidable Direct fixed costs relevant — avoidable	Relevant if capacity made available from decision leads to additional revenue stream
Deletion of product/service/ organisational unit	Existing variable costs relevant — avoidable	As for outsourcing	As for outsourcing
Sell or process further	Incremental variable costs relevant	Incremental fixed costs relevant	Focus of decision

The need to consider opportunity costs in a decision is often signalled by the current utilisation of the organisation's capacity. An opportunity cost is the benefit forgone when one alternative is chosen over the next best alternative. For example, in relation to an outsourcing decision, the infrastructure no longer required if an activity is outsourced would in the first instance increase the capacity of the organisation. This 'freed up' capacity would enable some alternative production or service delivery which would generate income. The income would be an opportunity cost for the non-outsourcing alternative as this additional income would only be received if the capacity was available due to the outsourcing decision. Therefore, when assessing whether or not to outsource, the opportunity cost would need to be considered in the decision process. In relation to a special order, the ability to fill the request within existing capacity will determine if existing customers will be affected by the order. If current production has to be reassigned to satisfy a special order then the lost contribution from existing sales would be an opportunity cost of the special order.

As there is no set recipe for getting the solution to such decisions it is possible to undertake the analysis from different perspectives such as:
- *cash flow analysis* — focus on relevant cash inflows and cash outflows
- *differential analysis (accrual accounting)* — focus on relevant costs and revenue
- *full analysis (accrual accounting)* — comparing the statement of profit or loss before and after.

The approach taken will determine the appropriate information to be used. For example, depreciation would be an item included in the accrual approach but not in the cash flow approach. So, it is important when determining the relevant information to know which approach is being taken for the analysis.

13.2 Special orders

LEARNING OBJECTIVE 13.2 Understand the decision-making process to accept, reject and price special orders.

Managers need to determine whether to accept a customer's special order, one that is not part of the entity's normal operations. A special order occurs when an existing or new customer places a one-off request for a product or services which may or not be part of the normal operations. The characteristics of a special order may include reduced price, personalisation, non-standard order size or special delivery characteristics. Moreover, the entity may be willing to accept a special order to use idle capacity in order to increase short-term profits or the entity may have a strategic intent to secure business.

General rule for special order decisions

Each non-routine operating decision introduced in this chapter employs a guideline — a general rule — to make a decision. The general rule for special orders is that we want to be as well off after accepting the order as we were before we accepted it. To make this decision, we need to know whether the order replaces regular business. If it does, the price should be at or above the usual price, because the opportunity cost (benefit foregone) of accepting this order is the loss of the usual contribution margin. On the other hand, if idle capacity is available, the special order is acceptable if the organisation at least breaks even. In this case, the minimum acceptable price is equal to the incremental cost of the order. The incremental cost includes most of the variable costs and incremental direct fixed costs. The variable manufacturing costs are usually relevant. However, variable selling costs such as commissions are often irrelevant if the entity requesting the special order places it directly with the manufacturer. Most fixed costs (such as rent and depreciation on plant and equipment) are unavoidable regardless of whether the special order is accepted or not, making them irrelevant. Some fixed costs, such as the lease cost for a piece of equipment needed for the special order, are relevant because they are unique to the special order. Regardless of the above, management may be willing to sell at a loss if the order leads to regular business in the future. The decision is taken from a strategic rather than an operational position.

Comprehensive example 1 on Barkley Basketballs Ltd provides an opportunity to practise making a special order decision.

Special orders

Barkley Basketballs Ltd manufactures high-quality basketballs at its plant which has a production capacity of 60 000 basketballs per month. Current production is 35 000 per month. The manufacturing costs of $24 per basketball are categorised below.

	Variable cost per unit	Fixed cost per unit (at 35 000 per month)	Total cost per unit
Manufacturing costs:			
Direct materials	$12.00	$0.00	$12.00
Direct labour	2.00	0.00	2.00
Manufacturing overhead	0.50	9.50	10.00
Total cost to manufacture	$14.50	$9.50	$24.00
Sales commission	$ 1.00	$0.00	$ 1.00

Jack O'Neil operates not-for-profit basketball camps for disadvantaged youths. Jack asks Billie Walton, CFO at Barkley Basketballs, to sell him 5000 basketballs at $23 per ball, or $115 000 for the entire order.

Billie speaks to the cost accountant and then goes to the production floor to speak to several supervisors to gather information for this decision. She determines that the direct labour cost is variable. Workers are paid an hourly wage and are sent home when there are no balls to manufacture. These workers have no guaranteed salary, but demand is stable so they always work at least half-time, and often 40 hours a week.

Billie asks about the manufacturing overhead and finds that it consists of variable and fixed costs incurred to run the plant where the basketballs are manufactured. Overhead includes insurance, property taxes, depreciation, utilities and various other plant-related costs. She finds that all of the fixed costs are related to a capacity level of 50 000 and will not change if she uses part of the idle capacity of 15 000 units. The supervisor warns her, however, that once production exceeds 40 000 basketballs, bottlenecks occur and the production process will slow down and cause inventory levels to congest the plant, sometimes causing overtime to be paid.

Quantitative analysis

With the 5000 basketballs produced for Jack, total production for the month would be 40 000 basketballs. Bottlenecks and slowdowns do not occur until production exceeds 40 000. Therefore, the special order is within the relevant range of production; the fixed costs should remain fixed. The relevant revenues and costs per basketball are as follows:

Selling price	$23.00
Variable costs (materials, labour and overhead)	$14.50

In deciding whether to accept this special order, fixed costs are irrelevant because they are unavoidable. They will be incurred whether 35 000 or 40 000 basketballs are produced. The variable cost of $1 sales commission per ball is also irrelevant because no sales representatives are involved in this particular transaction. Therefore, the contribution margin for each special order basketball would be $23 – $14.50 equals $8.50. For 5000 basketballs, the total contribution margin would be $42 500.

Qualitative factors

Based on the preceding quantitative analysis, Billie wants to accept the order. However, she first needs to consider the qualitative aspects of the decision. If she sells the basketballs at this lower price, other customers might demand lower prices too, causing Barkley Basketballs to get into a pricing war with itself. However, Jack's entity is not-for-profit; Billie doubts that other customers would object to giving it a discount.

Billie also believes that the company could enhance its reputation if Jack publicises Barkley Basketballs' support of the basketball camps. To evaluate the value of such publicity, she meets with the marketing manager, Mark Jordan. Mark cannot quantify the value, but he suggests that the publicity would definitely help promote the Barkley Basketballs brand name. In addition, the company has funded basketball camps in the past, in keeping with its policy of supporting the community.

Making the decision

After considering all of these factors, Billie discusses the special order with Jack. She offers to lower the price even further than $23. Jack is pleasantly surprised and offers to publicise Barkley Basketballs' generosity. Billie and Jack settle on a price of $20 per ball. The contribution margin of the special order is reduced from $42 500 to $27 500 (5000 balls at $20 – $14.50).

In this situation, Billie is willing to reduce the price of the special order even further for several reasons. In the past, the company donated money to not-for-profit basketball camps, so providing basketballs at a discount fits with management's desire to act in a socially responsible manner. Billie also believes the company will benefit from additional publicity. And the company will still earn a profit from the special order. Although Billie has agreed to a lower price than usual, the special order meets the general rule; ample capacity is available and the price is greater than the relevant costs (variable production costs).

Evaluating the decision process

Later that week, Billie reviews the decision to sell Jack O'Neil basketballs at $20 each. She visits Mark Jordan, who insists that the value of the publicity exceeds the reduction of $15 000 in contribution margin. Billie concludes that the decision to sell the balls at a discount was appropriate.

Note the process used to make this decision. Billie first identified the type of decision (special order). She knew that she needed to know the relevant costs to make this decision. She categorised costs as fixed and variable to help her identify relevant information. Next, she determined which costs were relevant and irrelevant to the special order. In this case, all of the variable production costs and none of the fixed costs or sales commissions were relevant. In manufacturing settings such as this one, where the same product is made repeatedly, manufacturing costs can be estimated with high accuracy. Billie had good reason to be confident in her quantitative analysis. She then weighed the quantitative factors and qualitative factors and decided that, overall, it was best for Barkley Basketballs to offer the special order at a price of $20 per ball.

Billie categorised costs and factors as shown in figure 13.2.

FIGURE 13.2	Relevant costs and qualitative factors for Barkley Basketballs		
	Fixed costs	**Variable costs**	**Qualitative**
Relevant	May increase if $Q > 40\,000$ per month (beyond the relevant range)	Direct material + direct labour + variable overhead = $12 + $2 + $0.50 as long as $Q < 40\,000$ per month	Potential publicity for selling ball at a discount
Irrelevant	Manufacturing overhead	Sales commission per ball (not paid on this special order)	Price concerns of other customers

13.3 Product line and business segment (keep or drop) decisions

LEARNING OBJECTIVE 13.3 Understand the decision-making process to keep or drop products, segments or whole businesses.

When organisations provide multiple products (either goods or services), they periodically review operating results for each product, group of products (product line) or business segment and decide whether to keep or drop the product or segment. If financial statement data are used in these calculations, average costs are often mistakenly included as relevant information. However, managers need to separate relevant and irrelevant cash flows. Therefore, they may need to develop distinct cost functions for each product, product line or segment.

General rule for keep or drop decisions

The general rule is that we discontinue a product, service or business segment when its total contribution margin does not cover avoidable fixed costs (fixed costs that are eliminated if the product is dropped). We first separate costs into fixed and variable. The variable costs are usually relevant. To identify relevant fixed costs, we consider how fixed costs would change if we drop the product, service or segment. Then, we categorise fixed costs as avoidable or unavoidable. To identify and estimate avoidable fixed costs, we analyse the nature of the fixed cost and its relation to the two alternatives (keep or drop). For example, dropping a product might mean that an employee in accounting or marketing could be laid off. The labour costs and fringe benefits for that employee are relevant to the keep or drop decision. They are fixed costs that can be directly associated with the product and are avoidable if the product is dropped. Alternatively, the lease cost for a manufacturing facility that produces a number of products is unavoidable if only one product is dropped. Therefore, the lease cost is irrelevant.

Comprehensive example 2 on Home Aide Services provides an opportunity to practise making a keep or drop decision.

COMPREHENSIVE EXAMPLE 2

Keep or drop

Home Aide Services is a not-for-profit entity that provides a variety of services for people who would prefer to live at home but need assistance. The organisation has several lines of service, including housekeeping, meals, and shopping and transportation services. Lately the organisation has suffered a decline in surplus. The manager, Justin Bean, wants to drop one of the services to increase profitability. Following is the monthly operating statement showing each service activity's contribution to overall surplus.

| | Monthly operating statement by service activity | | | |
	Housekeeping	Meals	Shopping	Total
Revenues	$30 000	$15 000	$10 000	$55 000
Variable costs	15 000	3 000	1 000	19 000
Contribution margin	15 000	12 000	9 000	36 000
Fixed costs	20 000	6 000	5 000	31 000
Surplus (deficit)	$ (5 000)	$ 6 000	$ 4 000	$ 5 000

Quantitative analysis

When Justin tells Elizabeth Klein, the accountant, that housekeeping services should be dropped to save the organisation $5000, Elizabeth says she needs to analyse costs further. The next day she reports to Justin that instead of having an overall surplus of $5000, Home Aide Services would incur a deficit of $2000 if housekeeping was dropped. She presents the following information about the remaining product lines if housekeeping was discontinued.

Adjusted monthly operating statement			
	Meals	**Shopping**	**Total**
Revenues	$15 000	$10 000	$25 000
Variable costs	3 000	1 000	4 000
Contribution margin	12 000	9 000	21 000
Fixed costs	13 000	10 000	23 000
Surplus (deficit)	$ (1 000)	$ (1 000)	$ (2 000)

Justin asks how this could be. Elizabeth explains that when she analysed the costs in more detail, she found that the fixed costs for housekeeping included benefits for the housekeepers. The cost of benefits would be avoided if housekeeping was dropped. These costs are $8000. Total fixed costs are now $23 000 ($31 000 – $8000). These fixed costs are unavoidable and are allocated to the remaining departments. They include the cost of depreciation on cars as well as administrative costs for the entire entity that had been allocated to housekeeping.

Labour costs are a small part of the meal department's total cost. Only $1000 of fixed costs would be avoided if meals were dropped; the employees who prepare meals also help with administrative work. Shopping and transportation includes $4000 in avoidable fixed costs. This amount represents salary and benefits costs for drivers who are available all hours that the service is open.

Monthly operating statement showing service activity contribution to surplus				
	Housekeeping	**Meals**	**Shopping**	**Total**
Revenues	$30 000	$15 000	$10 000	$55 000
Variable costs	15 000	3 000	1 000	19 000
Contribution margin	15 000	12 000	9 000	36 000
Avoidable fixed costs	8 000	1 000	4 000	13 000
Department surplus	$ 7 000	$11 000	$ 5 000	23 000
Unavoidable fixed costs				18 000
Overall surplus				$ 5 000

Elizabeth prepares the following report for Justin.

Relevant benefits and costs	Housekeeping	Meals	Shopping
Revenue forgone	$(30 000)	$(15 000)	$(10 000)
Savings in labour and overhead	23 000	4 000	5 000
Net benefit (cost)	$ (7 000)	$(11 000)	$ (5 000)

With this new information, Justin analyses the costs again. He realises that all of the services are contributing to the unavoidable fixed costs and should be continued.

Qualitative factors

Elizabeth observes that competitors provide all three services. Therefore, dropping housekeeping could affect demand for the other services. Clients might not want to deal with two separate entities when one could provide all the different services they need. Even if housekeeping was just breaking even, it should not be eliminated if dropping it would alienate current customers and cause demand for the other services to decrease. In addition, employee morale could suffer if a number of workers were laid off.

Making the decision

Given this new cost analysis and the qualitative factors, Justin decides to retain all of the current services. However, he decides to investigate alternative ways that the entity could improve its surplus. First, he considers any opportunity costs. If housekeeping was dropped, could Home Aide add nursing or other services instead? Would the surplus added from nursing be higher than housekeeping?

13.4 Insource or outsource (make or buy) decisions

LEARNING OBJECTIVE 13.4 Understand the decision-making process to insource or outsource an activity (make or buy).

Outsourcing, finding outside vendors to supply products and services, has become an increasingly common practice. **Insourcing** is the practice of providing the good or service from internal resources. For manufacturers, outsourcing decisions are often called **make or buy** decisions: Does the entity make the product or provide the service internally, or buy it from an outside supplier? Potential cost savings as well as organisational strategies drive such decisions. Some managers outsource any activity they view as unrelated to the organisation's core competencies.

General rule for make or buy decisions

The general rule for make or buy decisions is to choose the option with the lowest relevant cost. Managers compare the outsourcing costs with the incremental costs for insourcing. Existing fixed costs are relevant only if they can be avoided through outsourcing. The costs for insourcing also include opportunity costs. Sometimes extra space or capacity from outsourcing can be converted to other uses. Another product could be manufactured or the space rented out. The forgone benefits (contribution margin from the new product or rent payments) are an opportunity cost for insourcing.

For example, managers may confront the decision to outsource non-core activities like information technology services, payroll management and cleaning and maintenance activities. Comprehensive example 3 on Wombat Publishers provides an opportunity to practise making an outsourcing decision.

COMPREHENSIVE EXAMPLE 3

Insource or outsource

Wombat Publishers produces the book covers for its hardbound books. Recently, Marliss Book Binders purchased new robotic equipment that cuts, trims and prints book covers in one process. Marliss offered to provide book covers for Wombat at $2 per book. Mark Bonaray, the cost accountant for Wombat Publishers, analyses the cost information for internally producing hardbound book covers as follows:

	Total costs for 100 000 book covers	Cost per unit
Direct materials	$ 75 000	$0.75
Direct labour	50 000	0.50
Manufacturing overhead	100 000	1.00
Supervisor's salary	50 000	0.50
Total cost	$275 000	$2.75

After summarising the costs for producing the book covers in-house, Mark needs to identify costs that are relevant and irrelevant to the decision. First, he gathers more information. He learns from the production manager that the supervisor could be laid off if the book covers are outsourced. As a cost accountant, Mark already knows that manufacturing overhead is an indirect cost. In this case, it is allocated to books based on the number of direct labour hours used in each production process. Overhead costs will be incurred even if the book covers are outsourced. However, after examining past utility bills, Mark estimates that closing off the part of the plant where book covers are produced would save about $30 000, or $0.30 per book cover.

Quantitative analysis

Although outsourcing would save $30 000 of the manufacturing overhead, the remaining $70 000 (or $0.70 per book cover) will be incurred under each alternative and is therefore irrelevant to the decision. The relevant production and outsourcing costs for this decision are as follows.

Relevant costs	Cost per unit Make	Buy	Total cost for 100 000 book covers Make	Buy
Purchase book covers		$2.00		$200 000
Direct materials	$0.75		$ 75 000	
Direct labour	0.50		50 000	
Manufacturing overhead	0.30		30 000	
Supervisor's salary	0.50		50 000	
Total relevant costs	$2.05	$2.00	$205 000	$200 000

Based only on the preceding cost information, Wombat would save $5000 by outsourcing the book covers. However, Mark has not yet considered potential opportunity costs of continuing to produce the book covers in-house. If Wombat Publishers has an alternative use for the space that houses the book cover operations, the contribution margin from the use of that space would be relevant to the decision. For simplicity, we assume that Wombat's management has no alternative use for the space and therefore no opportunity costs to consider for this decision.

Qualitative factors

Another factor Mark considers is the quality of the book covers, which is emphasised in Wombat's book production process. Wombat's sales managers believe that high-quality covers are important to sales. The quality of Marliss's sample covers appears to be high, possibly even higher than Wombat's current level of quality.

Mark is also concerned about the timeliness of delivery. He speaks with Wombat's book cover supervisor, who explains that the department is able to respond to changes in production volumes if given lead time. It has been relatively easy to have Wombat's employees work overtime or to hire part-time employees when a book appears to be a bestseller, causing production levels to rise. When Mark asks Marliss about its ability to manage a very large order caused by unanticipated demand, the sales representative cannot guarantee that such an order could be produced quickly. This concerns Mark, who is aware that when books are bestsellers, large volumes must be produced quickly.

Making the decision

When Mark summarises the relevant information for the decision, he concludes that the savings from outsourcing and the quality differences are relatively small. In addition, he decides that being able to meet demand is worth the additional cost. Based on his analysis, he recommends that the entity continue producing its own book covers.

13.5 Constrained resources

LEARNING OBJECTIVE 13.5 Explain the decision-making process for product emphasis and constrained resources.

When no capacity constraints apply or alternative uses of fixed resources are available, the products with the highest contribution margin per unit are emphasised. Sometimes managers face limits in capacity, materials or labour. When these limits restrict an entity's ability to provide enough products (goods or services) to satisfy demand, the organisation faces a **constraint**. For example, in comprehensive example 3, Wombat Publishers needs cardboard to make book covers. In the case of a shortage of cardboard, the entity faces a shortage of direct materials, or a direct materials constraint. A shortage of labour to run machines or to load books into packing crates would be a labour constraint. Similarly, a shortage of machines to bind the covers onto the books would be a capacity constraint.

When faced with one or more constrained resources, managers have several options. One option is to maximise the contribution margin within the constraint; that is, emphasise the product that contributes the most in light of the constraint. A second option is to incur additional costs to relax the constraint. Two options are available to relax constraints:
1. purchase goods or services from an outside supplier
2. add internal capacity or redesign products and processes to use existing capacity more efficiently.

Managers can also try both options, maximising profit while simultaneously relaxing the constraint.

General rule for choosing the product mix when resources are constrained

When resources are constrained, we need to emphasise products and services that maximise the contribution margin per unit of constrained resource. For example, Fabulous Furniture produces teak tables and chairs for outdoor use. Normally the entity sells about 100 tables and 800 chairs a month. Because of industrial action at the local shipyards, it is unable to purchase enough timber locally to meet current demand.

The sales manager wants to know which product to emphasise — the tables or the chairs — to maximise profits. The accountant calculates the contribution margin per board metre for tables and chairs to make this decision. The contribution margin per table is $400, and the contribution margin per chair is $150. Tables require 4 board metres of teak and chairs require 2 board metres. The contribution margin per board metre for tables is $100 ($400 ÷ 4 board metres), and for chairs is $75 ($150 ÷ 2 board metres). To maximise the contribution margin, the sales manager should emphasise tables and sell as many as possible. If the demand for tables is filled, then the sales manager should emphasise chairs.

General rule for relaxing constraints for one or two products

The general rule for relaxing a short-term constraint for direct materials, direct labour or capacity is that managers would be willing to pay not only what they are already paying, but also some or the entire contribution margin per unit of constrained resource. Their goal would be to acquire added capacity, thereby eliminating the constraint.

In the furniture example, Fabulous Furniture is currently paying $50 per board metre for teak. Once the entity has manufactured as many tables and chairs as possible with the limited supply of teak, it will still experience demand for chairs. Customers will buy elsewhere if they cannot purchase chairs from Fabulous. Fabulous forgoes $75 in contribution margin per board metre on each chair customers would have purchased had teak been available. Consequently, Fabulous can afford to pay what it currently pays ($50) plus up to the entire contribution margin per board metre ($75) to buy more teak. If Fabulous can find a source of teak for $125 ($50 + $75) or less per board metre, it can meet customer demand for chairs.

As the variable cost per unit (including the new cost of materials or labour) approaches the selling price of the product or service, managers become indifferent to purchasing more of the constrained resource for continued production. This general rule is valid under the following assumptions.
- The organisation will forgo sales if the resource constraint is not relaxed.
- Fixed costs are unaffected by short-term decisions made to relax constraints.
- The managers want to maximise profits in the short term.
- Sales of one product do not affect sales of other products.

Capacity constraints are time constraints; that is, we have limited time available for processing products because one or more bottlenecks slow production. Any process, part or machine that limits overall capacity is a **bottleneck**. To maximise use of bottleneck resources, we emphasise products that have the highest contribution margin per bottleneck hour. We calculate the relevant contribution margin in terms of time needed at the bottleneck resource.

For example, suppose Fabulous has only one three-axis milling machine (a computerised piece of equipment that cuts and routs unusual shapes). The milling machine processes all of the tables and chairs, but it can process only four tables per hour or 12 chairs per hour. The contribution margin per machine hour for tables is $1600 (4 ÷ $400) and for chairs is $1800 ($150 ÷ 12). Chairs should be emphasised because they have the highest contribution per hour at the bottleneck resource.

In comprehensive example 4, we revisit Wombat Publishers to practise making a constrained resource decision.

COMPREHENSIVE EXAMPLE 4

Constrained resource

Suppose the managers of Wombat Publishers decide that the entity should continue to make its own book covers. In performing his analysis, Mark assumes ample capacity and materials are available. However, one of Wombat's children's books, *Barry Plotter, Mathematical Wizard*, sells many more copies than expected. This increase in demand leads to a shortage of the special cardboard needed for the book

▶

covers. In turn, Wombat is unable to publish enough books to meet current demand. Customers — both children and their parents — are becoming quite frustrated with Wombat.

Qualitative factors

Mark discusses the cardboard shortage with the sales manager, Dina Wilkinson, who thinks the entity will in all likelihood forgo sales if demand cannot be met in a timely manner. In addition, the sales manager believes Wombat must continue to build positive brand name recognition for the *Barry Plotter* series, so that further books in the series will be well received. Given this information, Mark would like to find some way to produce enough books to meet customer demand.

Quantitative analysis

The books that have already been produced and sold covered all of the entity's fixed costs related to developing, editing and designing the books and their covers. The wholesale price of the books is $10 each. The direct materials ($0.75) and direct labour ($0.50) costs for the covers total $1.25. The remaining variable costs for each book are $1.50 for paper and $1.50 royalty to the author. Therefore, total variable costs per book are $4.25, and the contribution margin per book is $5.75.

At Mark's request, the purchasing agent, Bruce Maxwell, researches alternative cardboard suppliers. Although Bruce locates a supplier, he is concerned because the lowest-cost supplier is demanding a price of $4 per cover for timely delivery.

Making the decision

Mark decides that, in the short run, he is willing to give up some of the contribution margin for this title to build long-term customer satisfaction. Therefore, he is willing to pay as much as the original cost of the cardboard ($0.75 per book) and the original contribution margin ($5.75 per book), or $6.50 per book. He recommends that Bruce purchase additional cardboard at the asking price of $4 per book. The variable costs for this additional printing now include $4 (book cover materials), $0.50 (book cover labour), $1.50 (paper) and $1.50 (royalty), for a total of $7.50 per book. Thus, the contribution margin from each additional book that Wombat produces and sells will be $2.50 ($10 – $7.50). Even though this amount is lower than the original contribution margin of $5.75, Wombat continues to earn at least some contribution margin through its effort to relax the constrained resource of the book cover cardboard.

13.6 Qualitative factors important to non-routine operating decisions

LEARNING OBJECTIVE 13.6 Describe the qualitative factors important to non-routine operating decisions.

Managers make higher-quality decisions when they use higher-quality information and higher-quality decision processes. It is not sufficient for managers to merely *identify* relevant information when making non-routine operating decisions. Figure 13.3 summarises the relevant information commonly used for making non-routine operating decisions, as illustrated in this chapter. Managers must also consider the quality of information, and they must evaluate alternatives objectively and thoroughly.

Three major factors affect the quality of information for non-routine operating decisions: uncertainties, timeliness and analysis technique assumptions.

- *Uncertainties*. Many uncertainties are involved in non-routine operating decisions, as illustrated in the last row of figure 13.3. Uncertainties about future revenues and costs affect all of these decisions. Future revenues and costs can vary depending on changes in the economic environment, customer demand, competition, government regulation, vendor quality, technology and many other factors. However, the degree of uncertainty varies from decision to decision. For example, fewer uncertainties come with a special order from a long-time customer than one from a new customer. Similarly, fewer uncertainties accompany outsourcing with a nearby entity than with an entity on another continent. In addition, decisions having a shorter time horizon, such as a special order that can be completed within one week, are less uncertain than decisions having a longer impact, such as dropping a product.
- *Information timeliness*. Many non-routine operating decisions must be made quickly and rely on up-to-date information. For example, a customer might require a prompt reply to a special order request, or managers may need to change production plans to emphasise different products as circumstances change. Access to timely information is particularly important in industries such as computer manufacturing, where technology, demand and prices change rapidly. Cost information that is only one month old may be irrelevant. Thus, the accessibility and currency of the information system affect the quality of decisions.

- *Analysis technique assumptions.* The reasonableness of assumptions affects the quality of information generated from an analysis technique. For example, regression analysis is useful for estimating costs only within a relevant range of activity. Cost–volume–profit (CVP) analysis assumes that the revenue and cost functions are linear and that operations remain in a relevant range of activity. Although the validity of assumptions cannot be known with certainty, the validity of assumptions in a rapidly changing business environment is more uncertain than in a stable environment.

The general decision rules we learn in this chapter assume that the entity's goal is to maximise short-term profits. This assumption ignores qualitative factors that might be more important than short-term profits for some decisions.

FIGURE 13.3	Summary of information used in non-routine operating decisions

| Information | Type of decision | | | | |
	Special order	Product line and business segment (keep or drop)	Insource or outsource (make or buy)	Product emphasis (under constraints)	Relax constrained resource
General decision rule	Accept if price is greater than or equal to the sum of variable cost, relevant fixed costs and opportunity cost	Drop if contribution margin is less than the sum of relevant fixed costs and opportunity cost	Outsource if buy cost is less than or equal to the sum of variable cost and relevant fixed costs minus opportunity cost	Emphasise product with highest contribution margin (CM) per unit unless resources are constrained, then emphasise product with highest CM per unit of constrained resource	Incur cost to relax constraint if cost is less than or equal to the sum of CM per unit of constrained resource and the current variable cost of the resource
Relevant fixed costs	Only new fixed costs associated with the special order	Only fixed costs that can be avoided if drop	Only fixed costs that can be avoided if buy		Only new fixed costs to relax the constraint
Opportunity cost	Contribution margin of any regular business replaced	Benefits from using released capacity for other purposes	Benefits from using released capacity for other purposes		
Examples of qualitative factors	• Will regular customers expect lower prices? • Will this order lead to improved brand name recognition? • Can we deliver without disrupting current schedules?	• Will dropping one product affect sales of other products? • Will lay-offs affect worker morale?	• Is it easier to ensure high quality via insourcing or outsourcing? • Will delivery be timely? • Are there uncertainties about the supplier's ability to meet contractual obligations? • Is this activity a core competency?	• Does the product emphasis agree with strategic plans? • Are sales of one product likely to affect sales of other products?	• Are there other ways to relax the constraint? • How would brand recognition be affected by delivery delays? • Will the decision affect future supply costs?

		Type of decision			
Information	Special order	Product line and business segment (keep or drop)	Insource or outsource (make or buy)	Product emphasis (under constraints)	Relax constrained resource
Examples of major uncertainties	• How accurate are the cost estimates? • Are we operating in the relevant range? • Will fixed costs increase at higher capacity levels?	• How accurate are the revenue and cost estimates? • How will customers respond to the dropped product?	• How accurate are the cost estimates? • Is our measure of quality appropriate? • How reliable is the vendor or resource supplier?	• How accurate are the contribution margin estimates? • How reliable are the product demand forecasts?	• How accurate are the contribution margin estimates? • How accurate are the constraint use estimates?

Quality of decision process

Three major aspects of the decision-making process affect the quality of non-routine operating decisions: decision-maker bias, sensitivity analysis and prioritisation.

- *Decision-maker bias*. Sometimes decision makers are biased, which reduces their ability to objectively and thoroughly analyse relevant information. Another type of bias involves a preference for either quantitative or qualitative information. Some people tend to rely primarily on quantitative analyses because they are more comfortable with what they view as precise answers. Others, recognising the uncertainties in quantitative analyses, prefer to rely on qualitative factors to make decisions. The best approach is to weigh carefully both quantitative and qualitative factors, taking into account the strengths and weaknesses of information for a particular decision.
- *Sensitivity analysis*. One way to improve decisions in light of low information quality and potential biases is to perform one or more sensitivity analyses. Sensitivity analysis helps managers evaluate how quantitative results would change with changes in various pieces of information. For example, estimates of incremental costs or of cost savings could be increased to evaluate risk. Sometimes the degree of risk in the quantitative estimates for one option might make that option less desirable than another option having less risk.
- *Prioritisation*. Operating plans are designed to help achieve an entity's long-term strategies. In turn, the strategies depend on an entity's vision and core competencies. When addressing any non-routine operating decision, managers should consider whether each option is consistent with the organisation's strategies, vision and core competencies. Entities such as Toyota have established a market position based on high product reliability, making that characteristic an important strategic issue. Some entities, such as Woolworths, place strategic importance on low costs and prices. Samsung Electronics' strategy includes protecting the environment. By considering these types of qualitative issues, managers avoid taking actions that conflict with the entity's long-term interests.

13.7 Joint products and costs

LEARNING OBJECTIVE 13.7 Demonstrate an understanding of joint costing issues.

Some industries simultaneously produce a group of products through a single process. Consider a fish farm where products include fresh fish, frozen fish, frozen fish entrees and fish fertiliser. In the process of making one product, one or more other products or services are created, called **joint products**. As another example, the waste management process of an environmental management firm or a local council can generate revenue from a product, biogas, as well as from the collection of food residuals. Other examples of joint products are readily found in many industries such as oil and gas, chemicals and foods.

Joint products fall into two categories: main product and by-products. A main product has high sales value compared to other joint products. At the fish farm, fresh fish, frozen fish and fish entrees are main products. A by-product has low sales value compared to the other joint products. Fish fertiliser is an example of a by-product. Table 13.2 presents a list of industries that manufacture joint products and gives examples of main products and by-products.

TABLE 13.2	Examples of industries that manufacture joint products			
Industry	Main products	By-products	Example entity
Petroleum (crude oil)	Petrol, diesel, jet fuel	Asphalt	Shell Oil
Copper mining	Copper, silver, lead, zinc	Malachite, azurite	BHP Mining
Cheese production	Fresh cheese, butter	Buttermilk	Bega Cheese
Timber	Timber, veneer, plywood	Bark dust, sawdust	Black Forest Timber
Beef production	Cuts of meat, leather	Dog bones, bonemeal for gardens	Herds

Joint costs are all of the costs incurred to jointly produce a group of goods. These costs are common to all of the joint products and are incurred prior to the split-off point, the point at which individual products are identified. At the fish farm, the split-off point is the point at which the fish are caught and cleaned. The joint costs include the costs to maintain the fish ponds such as labour, fish food, insurance and property taxes, plus all of the costs to clean fish and prepare them for further processing.

Separable costs are the costs incurred after the split-off point. These incremental costs can be easily traced to each specific product. At the fish farm, separable costs are incurred for packaging fresh fish, freezing fish, preparing entrees, and pulverising and emulsifying the waste and bottling it for fertiliser. Figure 13.4 shows the common and separable activities involved in raising fish and lists several of the costs for these activities.

FIGURE 13.4	Raising and processing fish at a fish farm

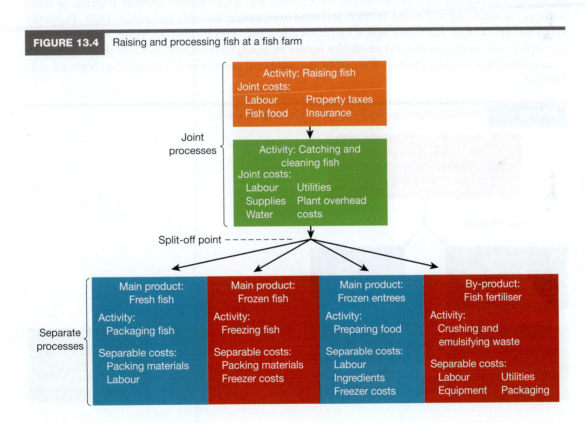

Allocating joint costs

An entity commits to joint costs when managers decide to produce joint products. Joint costs must be allocated to each product for reporting inventory and cost of sales on financial statements, income tax returns and other types of reports. Joint costs must also be allocated for government regulatory reports when entities that sell to both government agencies and commercial organisations seek reimbursement of costs on government-funded projects. Occasionally legal processes scrutinise joint cost allocations, such as when an organisation must support the transfer price used between divisions located in high-tax and low-tax countries. A tax audit by a government or corporate body, or government litigation, may also require joint cost allocation information. In addition, joint costs are sometimes used internally for evaluating division or segment performance.

For the waste management of an environmental management firm or local council, joint costs might be allocated between the collection of food residuals and the production of biogas and biosolids. The allocation of joint costs assists in matching revenues and costs. Therefore, the allocated costs of biogas would be expensed in the accounting period when biogas is sold, and the allocated costs of any unsold biogas would be included in inventory on the statement of financial position (also called the balance sheet). Similarly, the allocated cost of collecting food residuals would be recorded on the statement of profit or loss (or statement of comprehensive income) in the same period in which the revenues are recorded.

Several different methods are used to allocate joint costs to main products. In the following sections we learn about these methods:

- physical output method
- market-based methods:
  - sales value at split-off point
  - net realisable value (NRV)
  - constant gross margin NRV.

To illustrate these methods, we use a sawmill example. Merritt Brothers owns and operates a sawmill in northern Victoria. The entity hires loggers who cut timber and bring it to the mill, where the logs are sawed into timber. In addition, sawdust and woodchips from the sawmill operation are glued and pressed into chipboard.

Figure 13.5 presents the costs and revenues from this operation. The joint costs of cutting trees, debarking logs and sawing logs into timber are $220 per log, which Merritt Brothers commits to when a tree is cut down and sent to the sawmill. Revenue from timber, the main product, is $400. The entity could sell the sawdust and woodchips, a by-product, to a pulp mill for $40. However, Merritt Brothers currently processes the sawdust and woodchips further by gluing and pressing them into chipboard, which is considered another main product. The cost of this additional processing is $46, and the chipboard sells for $146.

| FIGURE 13.5 | Merritt Brothers' revenues and costs for processing one log |

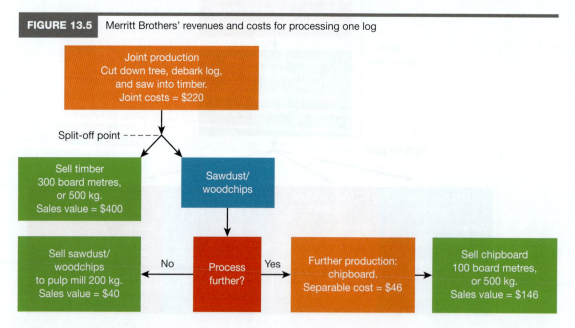

Physical output method

The **physical output method** allocates joint costs using the relative proportion of physical output for each main product. This method is only used when output for all main products can be expressed using the same physical measure, such as metres, kilograms or litres. Each main product is allocated a proportion of joint costs based on that product's physical output divided by the total physical output of all main products.

For Merritt Brothers, either kilograms or board metres could be used as an allocation base. Suppose the entity uses kilograms of final product as the physical volume allocation base. Each log processed results in 500 kilograms of chipboard and 500 kilograms of timber. Thus, the relative weight of chipboard is 500 kilograms/1000 kilograms. The joint costs of $220 are multiplied by this proportion to calculate the amount of joint costs allocated to chipboard:

$$(500\,\text{kg}/1000\,\text{kg}) \times \$220 = \$110$$

A similar set of calculations leads to allocation of $110 of joint costs to timber as follows:

| | Main products | | |
	Chipboard	Timber	Total
Base (kilograms of final product)	500 kg	500 kg	1000 kg
Proportion	500 kg/1000 kg	500 kg/1000 kg	
Allocated joint costs	$110	$110	$220

Suppose Merritt Brothers instead uses the number of board metres of final product as the allocation base. For each log processed, the entity produces 100 board metres of chipboard and 300 board metres of timber. In this case, the amount of joint costs allocated to each main product is calculated as follows:

| | Main products | | |
	Chipboard	Timber	Total
Base (board metres of final product)	100 metres	300 metres	400 metres
Proportion	100 metres/400 metres	100 metres/400 metres	
Allocated joint costs	$55	$165	$220

Sales value at split-off point method

Market-based methods use some proportion of the profit contribution for each main product to determine the joint cost allocation rate. Under the **sales value at split-off point method**, joint costs are allocated based on the relative sales value of main products at the point where joint production ends. For Merritt Brothers, joint production of a log creates timber that can be sold for $400, and sawdust and woodchips that can be sold without further processing for $40. The relative proportions of sales values at the split-off point are used to allocate the joint costs of each main product as follows:

| | Main products | | |
	Chipboard	Timber	Total
Base (sales value at split-off point)	$40	$400	$440
Proportion	$40/$440	$400/$440	
Allocated joint costs	$20	$200	$220

Net realisable value method

The **net realisable value (NRV) method** allocates joint costs using the relative value of main products, taking into account both the additional sales value that is created and costs that are incurred after joint production ends. NRV for each main product is calculated as the final selling price minus separable costs. For Merritt Brothers, timber is not processed further, so its net realisable value is equal to its sales value at the split-off point, or $400. The NRV for chipboard is expected to be $100 ($146 − $46) after further processing. The joint cost allocation calculations are as follows:

| | Main products | | |
	Chipboard	Timber	Total
Base (net realisable value)	$100	$400	$500
Proportion	$100/$500	$400/$500	
Allocated joint costs	$44	$176	$220

Constant gross margin NRV method

The **constant gross margin NRV method** allocates joint costs so that the gross margin percentage for each main product is identical. This method involves two sets of computations. First, the combined gross margin percentage for main products is calculated. Second, joint costs are allocated to each main product to achieve a constant gross margin.

1. *Calculate the combined gross margin percentage.* To calculate the combined gross margin, create an statement of profit or loss for the main products. The gross margin is determined by subtracting the joint and separable costs from the sales. Then the gross margin is divided by sales to determine the gross margin percentage. Continuing with the Merritt Brothers example:

Determine sales:		
Sales:		
Timber		$400
Chipboard		146
Combined sales		546
Determine costs:		
Joint costs	$220	
Separable costs:		
Timber	0	
Chipboard	46	
Combined product costs		266
Combined gross margin		$280
Combined gross margin percentage ($280 ÷ $546)		51.3%

2. *Allocate joint costs to achieve a constant gross margin.* The desired gross margin, based on the preceding calculation, is first subtracted from the sales value to determine the desired amount of total product cost for each main product. Next, separable costs are subtracted from total product costs to determine the amount of joint costs to be allocated to each main product.

	Main products		
	Chipboard	**Timber**	**Total**
Sales	$146	$400	$546
Less gross margin	75	205	280
(51.3% × sales)			
Total product costs	71	195	266
Less separable costs	46	0	46
Allocated joint costs	$ 25	$195	$220

Choosing an appropriate joint cost allocation method

Although each of these joint cost allocation methods is logical, the allocation process itself is arbitrary. We cannot trace joint costs to each product because we always incur all of the joint costs to produce any one product. Therefore, no method for allocating joint costs develops a true cost per product.

Each method of joint cost allocation simply assigns a different proportion of cost to product, and therefore results in a different allocated cost per product. In turn, different allocation methods result in different measures of profitability for each product. Consider the comparison of the gross margin for Merritt Brothers under different allocation methods for each log processed and sold.

Main product	Physical output (weight)	Sales value at split-off point	Net realisable value	Constant gross margin NRV
Timber:				
Sales value	$400	$400	$400	$400
Allocated joint costs	(110)	(200)	(176)	(195)
Separable costs	(0)	(0)	(0)	(0)
Product gross margin	**290**	**200**	**224**	**205**
Chipboard:				
Sales value	$146	$146	$146	$146
Allocated joint costs	(110)	(20)	(44)	(25)
Separable costs	(46)	(46)	(46)	(46)
Product gross margin	**(10)**	**80**	**56**	**75**
Total gross margin	$280	$280	$280	$280

Notice that the total gross margin per log is not affected by the joint cost allocation method. The cost allocation affects only the relative gross margins for the individual products. Accordingly, the joint cost allocation method used by an entity affects the apparent profitability of different products. Sometimes a product can give the appearance that it is sold at a loss, when in fact the entity profits from producing the joint product.

Pros and cons of alternative allocation methods

An allocation method should be chosen to avoid giving the mistaken impression that one or more products are sold at a loss. Under the physical output method, such distortions are likely to occur when the incremental contribution (incremental revenues less incremental costs) of some products is relatively high compared to other products. For example, if Merritt Brothers uses the physical output method using weight as the allocation base, the gross margin for chipboard is negative. If the managers make product-related decisions with this information, they might decide to quit producing chipboard. However, chipboard's incremental revenues exceed its incremental costs. If the entity sold the sawdust and woodchips for $40 (the sales value at split-off point), it would forgo the $100 incremental contribution from producing and selling chipboard ($146 revenue less $46 in separable costs). Thus, if chipboard is dropped, profit drops by $60 per log ($100 – $40). To avoid this problem, market value methods are generally superior to the physical output method.

Nevertheless, the physical volume method is commonly used in some industries because all units are similar in size and have comparable net realisable values. Suppose an entity grows tomatoes and then manufactures different products such as tomato sauce and salsa. The entity incurs joint costs of raising, picking, cleaning and chopping tomatoes. Possible physical output measures include weight, volume or number of same-sized bottles. If the incremental contributions of the different products are similar, a physical output measure would provide approximately the same cost allocation as the other methods. In addition, the physical output method is the easiest to calculate.

If most or all products are sold at the split-off point, then the sales value at split-off point method is generally most appropriate. This method avoids the physical output method problem of negative contribution for some products. As long as the total gross margin at the split-off point is positive, expected revenues always exceed allocated costs under the sales value at split-off point method. However, some products may need further processing before they can be sold and have no value at the split-off point, or the net realisable value of each joint product may change greatly after further processing. In these cases, this method could distort the relative profitability of products. For example, at Merritt Brothers the net realisable value of the chipboard increases from $40 at the split-off point to $100 ($146 – $46) after processing.

The two NRV methods are generally preferred because they are based on the ability of each product to 'pay' for its allocated cost. Using these methods, products appear profitable as long as their revenues are greater than their separable costs. Because the constant gross margin NRV method is more complicated, the NRV method is often chosen. However, the constant gross margin NRV method allocates joint costs so that all joint products appear to have equal profitability. This approach best reflects the inseparability of the joint production process.

Each of these allocation methods is illustrated in comprehensive example 5.

COMPREHENSIVE EXAMPLE 5

Choosing an appropriate joint cost allocation method

Tim Nakamura, an accounting major at the local university, is working part-time as an accountant for Merritt Brothers. When Tim prepares financial statements for the entity, he needs to choose an allocation base for assigning joint costs to products. First, he examines the differences in the allocations and margins for chipboard under the different methods. The following table summarises his findings:

Allocation method	Joint cost allocated to chipboard	Chipboard gross margin
Physical output (using weight)	$110	$(10)
Sales value at split-off point	20	80
Net realisable value	44	56
Constant gross margin NRV	25	75

▶

Tim wants to find the simplest method that most fairly values the contribution of chipboard, since it is the joint product with least value. First, he eliminates the physical output method using weight as the allocation base. Weight distorts the profitability of chipboard because the allocated amount is higher than its revenue. With this allocation method, Merritt appears to lose money on each sale. Tim knows that the sale of chipboard contributes to overall profitability. Next, he eliminates the constant gross margin NRV method because he thinks the calculations would be more difficult to explain to the mill owners and managers. Because the sales value at split-off point method does not reflect the increased value of separately producing chipboard, Tim decides that the NRV method would be the best choice. This method takes into account information about revenues and separable costs for the chipboard.

Processing a joint product beyond the split-off point

Managers often have a choice about whether to sell a product at the split-off point or to process it further. For example, Merritt Brothers can sell the sawdust and woodchip scraps as a product, or it can use the scraps to produce and sell chipboard. When making decisions about whether to process a joint product beyond the split-off point, the joint costs are irrelevant because they are sunk costs. Once managers decide to produce a group of joint products, the joint costs are unavoidable and therefore irrelevant for making product emphasis decisions that identify the final products from a joint process. The product with the highest incremental contribution is the most profitable and should be emphasised. No allocation method is necessary for this type of decision because allocated joint costs represent sunk costs and are not included in the analysis. A decision-making example for Merritt Brothers follows in comprehensive example 6.

COMPREHENSIVE EXAMPLE 6

Joint product decision making

Merritt Brothers currently produces chipboard from its sawdust and woodchip scraps. A local pet store approached Merritt Brothers, wanting to buy sawdust and woodchip scraps. The pet store plans to use the scraps for pet bedding. The pet store is willing to pay $60 for 200 kilograms (the quantity produced from one log) of sawdust and woodchips, which is more than the $40 the entity would receive from a pulp mill. The managers of Merritt Brothers are deciding whether to accept this offer. If they sell sawdust and woodchips to the pet store, they will no longer produce chipboard.

The managers ask Tim to prepare an analysis for this decision. Tim begins his analysis by accessing sales, production and cost records. Using this information, he creates a revenue and cost flowchart (figure 13.6). Tim recalls learning in his cost accounting course that incremental revenues and costs are relevant for decision making. As Tim works on the flowchart, he realises that the revenues from sale of the timber of $400 and the joint costs of $220 are irrelevant to his analysis. Once a tree has been cut down and sawed into timber, these revenues and costs occur whether sawdust and woodchip scrap is sold to the pet store or pulp mill or is converted into chipboard. Accordingly, only the incremental revenues and costs for the scraps and chipboard are relevant.

Using this information, Tim presents Merritt Brothers with the following analysis:

	Sell sawdust and woodchips		Produce chipboard
	To pulp mill	To pet store	
Incremental revenues	$40	$60	$146
Incremental (separable) costs	0	0	46
Incremental contribution	$40	$60	$100

Quantitative and qualitative factors

After Tim explains his analysis to the managers, they decide to continue producing chipboard. They expect to earn $40 ($100 – $60) more profit per log by producing chipboard than from selling scrap to the pet store. In addition, Merritt Brothers prefers this option because it avoids employee lay-offs that would be detrimental to individual employees and to the small town's economy.

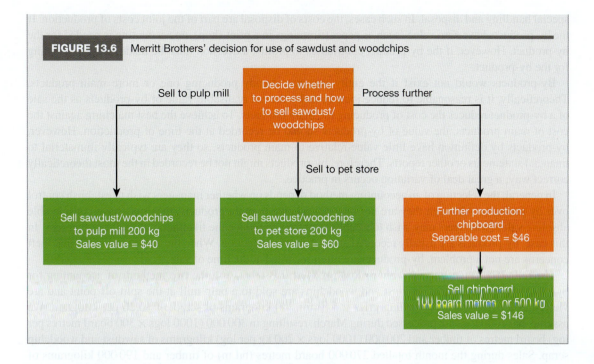

FIGURE 13.6 Merritt Brothers' decision for use of sawdust and woodchips

Decide whether to process and how to sell sawdust/woodchips

Sell to pulp mill

Process further

Sell to pet store

Sell sawdust/woodchips to pulp mill 200 kg
Sales value = $40

Sell sawdust/woodchips to pet store 200 kg
Sales value = $60

Further production: chipboard
Separable cost = $46

Sell chipboard
100 board metres or 500 kg
Sales value = $146

Uncertainty and bias in incremental revenue and cost estimates

Any estimate of future revenues and costs includes uncertainties about achievability. Changes are caused by many factors:

- unforeseen economic trends
- shifts in competition, demand or supply
- changes in technology.

Managers need to consider the risk associated with these uncertainties when making decisions involving joint products. In addition, the degree of uncertainty might vary among alternatives. The overall degree of uncertainty is often greatest for options involving extra processing. For example, the managers of Merritt Brothers decided to continue making chipboard. Their quantitative analysis required estimates of future revenues and costs under different alternatives. Fewer uncertainties overall were probably involved in the option to sell the sawdust and woodchips than for the option to produce chipboard. Thus, the managers might have been less confident in the data used to estimate their incremental profit under the chipboard option.

Joint products and by-products

By definition, by-products have low sales values compared to the other products. In the Merritt Brothers' example, timber is the main product, and scrap (sawdust and woodchips) is the by-product. If scrap is processed further into chipboard, it becomes a main product because the sales value of chipboard is relatively high. Deciding whether a product is a main product or by-product often requires judgement.

Sometimes products that were previously by-products become main products, or vice versa. A by-product can become valuable when new technologies or markets emerge. For example, when Merritt Brothers first began its timber mill, sawdust and woodchips were burned in large pyramid-shaped metal incinerators. As the gluing and pressing processes improved and logs became a scarce natural resource, producing chipboard became technically and economically feasible. Timber scraps are now used in a wide variety of products in addition to chipboard. For example, pulp mills pulverise the scraps and add liquid to make wood pulp that can be further processed into paper goods, cardboard or building materials.

Accounting for by-products

Sometimes by-products of a joint process are disposed of at a net cost, such as when metal scraps are hauled to a recycling centre, or when a joint process results in hazardous material by-products that require special handling and disposal. In such cases, the costs of disposal are part of the joint costs of production. If the by-products have zero value (such as paper trimmings in a print shop), no accounting is needed for the by-product. However, if the by-product contributes to profits, a decision must be made about accounting for the by-product.

By-products would not exist if the entity was not already producing one or more main products. Theoretically, it is reasonable to reduce joint costs by the net realisable value of by-products as the sale of a by-product reduces the cost of producing the main products. To achieve the best matching against the cost of main products, the value of by-products should be recorded at the time of production. However, by-products by definition have little value relative to main products, so they are typically immaterial to financial statements or other reports. Therefore, by-products might not be recorded in the most theoretically correct way; a great deal of variation occurs in practice.

In general, the selection of an accounting method depends on whether managers wish to establish control over by-products. Although they are not material relative to main products, they may have considerable absolute value. Managers may wish to establish controls to reduce the likelihood of theft or other loss. In this case, by-products are usually recorded at the time of production. When the value is so small that theft concerns are not a problem, by-products are often recorded at the time of sale.

The following statements of profit or loss for Merritt Brothers use the two methods of accounting for by-products, assuming that sawdust and woodchips are sold to a pulp mill at the split-off point and are viewed as a by-product. The selling price is $40 for 200 kilograms of scrap, or $0.20 per kilogram. We assume that 1000 logs are processed during March, resulting in 300 000 (1000 logs × 300 board metres per log) board metres of timber and 200 000 (1000 logs × 200 kg per log) kilograms of sawdust and woodchip scrap. Sales during the month totalled 270 000 board metres (bd m) of timber and 190 000 kilograms of scrap. Refer to figure 13.5 for the per-log cost and sales value information.

	Beginning inventory	Production	Sales	Ending inventory
Timber (bd m)	0	300 000	270 000	30 000
Sawdust and woodchips (kg)	0	200 000	190 000	10 000

By-product value recognised at the time of production

When by-product value is recognised at the time of production, the joint costs of the main product are reduced by the net realisable value of the by-product. Later, when the by-product is sold, no gain or loss is recorded. For Merritt Brothers, the net realisable value of the by-product is equal to its sales value at the split-off point ($0.20 per kilogram). This amount is subtracted from the joint cost and reduces the product cost of timber. In turn, this computation reduces the per-unit cost of timber in cost of sales and in ending inventory. You will note that the ending inventory includes timber at cost and by-product at net realisable value. This method allows managers to monitor both the quantity and value of by-products.

Production costs for the main product:	
Joint product costs incurred (1000 logs × $220)	$220 000
Less NRV of by-product (200 000 kg × $0.20)	40 000
Net joint product cost	$180 000
Product cost per log ($180 000 × 1000 logs)	$ 180
Product cost per timber board metre ($180 ÷ 300 bd m)	$ 0.60
Statement of profit or loss:	
Revenue [270 000 bd m × ($400 ÷ 300 bd m)]	$360 000
Cost of sales (270 000 bd m × $0.60)	162 000
Gross margin	$198 000
Ending inventory at 31 March:	
Timber (30 000 bd m $0.60)	$ 18 000
By-product (10 000 kg × $0.20)	2 000
Total inventory	$ 20 000

The journal entries when by-product value is recognised at the time of production are as follows.

Dr Cash	38 000	
Cr Revenue by-product		38 000
Dr Revenue by-product	38 000	
Cr Cost of sales		38 000
Dr By-product inventory	2 000	
Cr Timber inventory		2 000

By-product value recognised at the time of sale

When by-product value is recognised at the time of sale, the value may be recorded as sales revenue, other income, or as a reduction of cost of sales. Because by-products are viewed as immaterial, the choice of accounting treatment is considered unimportant. Until they are sold, by-products are not accounted for in the general ledger. For Merritt Brothers, this practice means that no inventory value is recorded for sawdust and woodchips. In the following example, we assume that the sales value of by-products is reported as part of revenue on the statement of profit or loss.

Income statement:
Revenue:
Timber [270 000 bd m × ($100 ÷ 000 ini 00)] | $000 000
Sawdust (190 000 kg × $0.20) | 38 000
Total revenue | 300 000
Cost of sales [270 000 bd m × ($220 ÷ 300 bd m)] | 198 000[a]
Gross margin | $200 000
Ending inventory at 31 March:
Timber [30 000 bd m × ($220 ÷ 300 bd m)] | $ 22 000[a]

[a] Valued at full joint cost.

The journal entries when by-product value is recognised at the time of sale are as follows.

| Dr Cash | 38 000 | |
| Cr Revenue by-product | | 38 000 |

For the Merritt Brothers example, the difference between gross margins under the two methods is $2000 ($198 000 – $200 000). This amount is offset by the difference in the total values of ending inventory [$20 000 – $22 000 = $(2000)]. In general, the difference between gross margins under the two methods is equal to the difference in the change during the period in the values of total inventory. As long as by-product values are immaterial, the methods have little effect on the statement of profit or loss and statement of financial position.

Joint product costing with a sales mix

In the Merritt Brothers examples, the concepts and calculations for joint product costing were illustrated using simple products. However, in most settings, joint product costing is more complex. In comprehensive example 7 on Premium Pineapple Company, we allocate costs when multiple products and multiple units are involved.

COMPREHENSIVE EXAMPLE 7

Joint product costing with a sales mix

Premium Pineapple Company, located in Taiwan, processes pineapples into pineapple syrup, pineapple juice and canned pineapple. The entity has three product managers — one for each of the three main products. The managers receive bonuses based on the profitability of their individual products. Lately some of the managers have been concerned about the allocations of joint costs and the effect these allocations have on the profitability of each of their product lines.

They approached the accountant, Nancy Wu, about this problem. Nancy explained that several different allocation methods could be used, and that the gross margin of each product would change with each method. The managers wanted Nancy to prepare their usual reports using each of these methods. She agreed to provide the managers with information about product profitability using each of the acceptable joint product cost allocation methods. First she gathered data from the current period.

During the summer, the joint costs of processing pineapples were NT$8 000 000 (NT$ are New Taiwanese dollars). The entity had no beginning or ending inventories for the summer. Production and sales value information for the growing season were:

Product	Cases	Sales value at split-off point (per case)	Separable costs (per case)	Selling price (per case)
Syrup	400 000	NT$16	NT$4	NT$22
Juice	400 000	NT$18	NT$5	NT$25
Canned	800 000	NT$6	NT$3	NT$14

Sales value at split-off for each product varies because the grade and kilograms required for each option vary.

Physical output method
The number of cases is used as the measure of physical output.
1. Determine the number of cases sold by product, and sum them.

Number of cases:	
Syrup	400 000
Juice	400 000
Canned	800 000
Total	1 600 000

2. Use each product's relative proportion of cases to allocate the joint costs.

Allocate joint costs:	
Syrup [(400 000/1 600 000) × NT$8 million]	NT$2 000 000
Juice [(400 000/1 600 000) × NT$8 million]	2 000 000
Canned [(800 000/1 600 000) × NT$8 million]	4 000 000
Total allocated joint costs	NT$8 000 000

Sales value at split-off point method
Each product's proportion of the total sales value at the split-off point is used.
1. Determine each product's total sales value at split-off, and calculate its relative proportion.

Syrup (400 000 × NT$16)	NT$ 6 400 000
Juice (400 000 × NT$18)	7 200 000
Canned (800 000 × NT$6)	4 800 000
Total sales value at split-off point	NT$18 400 000

2. Use each product's relative proportion of sales value at split-off to allocate the joint cost.

Allocate joint costs:	
To syrup [(NT$6.4 million/NT$18.4 million) × NT$8 million]	NT$2 782 609
To juice [(NT$7.2 million/NT$18.4 million) × NT$8 million]	3 130 435
To canned [(NT$4.8 million/NT$18.4 million) × NT$80 million]	2 086 956
Total allocated joint costs	NT$8 000 000

Net realisable value method

The net realisable value (NRV) is the selling price minus separable costs.

1. Determine each product's net realisable value, and sum them.

Syrup [400 000 × (NT$22 – NT$4)]	NT$ 7 200 000
Juice [400 000 × (NT$25 – NT$5)]	8 000 000
Canned [800 000 × (NT$14 – NT$3)]	8 800 000
Total net realisable value	NT$24 000 000

2. Use each product's relative proportion of net realisable value to allocate the joint costs.

Allocate joint costs:	
To syrup [(NT$7.2 million/NT$24.0 million) × NT$8 million]	NT$2 400 000
To juice [(NT$8 million/NT$24 million) × NT$8 million]	2 666 667
To canned [(NT$8.8 million/NT$24 million) × NT$8 million]	2 933 333
Total allocated joint costs	NT$8 000 000

Constant gross margin NRV method

The constant gross margin NRV method uses the gross margin for all products in the joint cost allocation process.

1. Calculate the combined gross margin percentage:

Combined sales	
Syrup (NT$22 × 400 000)	NT$ 8 800 000
Juice (NT$25 × 400 000)	10 000 000
Canned (NT$14 × 800 000)	11 200 000
Total combined sales	30 000 000
Less combined product costs:	
Joint costs	8 000 000
Syrup (NT$4 × 400 000)	1 600 000
Juice (NT$5 × 400 000)	2 000 000
Canned (NT$3 × 800 000)	2 400 000
Total combined product costs	14 000 000
Combined gross margin	NT$16 000 000
Combined gross margin percentage	53.3%
(NT$16.0 mil./NT$30.0 mil.)	

2. Allocate joint costs to achieve a constant gross margin:

	Syrup	Juice	Canned	Total
Sales	NT$8 800 000	NT$10 000 000	NT$11 200 000	NT$30 000 000
Less gross margin (16/30 × sales)	4 693 333	5 333 333	5 973 334	16 000 000
Total product costs	4 106 667	4 666 667	5 226 666	14 000 000
Less separable costs	1 600 000	2 000 000	2 400 000	6 000 000
Allocated joint costs	NT$2 506 667	NT$ 2 666 667	NT$ 2 826 666	NT$ 8 000 000

Comparing methods

Nancy prepared the schedule shown in figure 13.7 so the managers could see the effects of the allocation system on their products' profitability. The syrup and juice managers prefer the physical measure method because it shows the greatest profit for their products. Because his profit was the smallest under this method, the manager of canned pineapple objects wants to use the sales value at split-off point method, where his profits appear higher.

		Allocation method		
	Physical output	**Sales value at split-off point**	**Net realisable value**	**Constant gross margin NRV**
Syrup:				
Sales	NT$ 8 800 000	NT$ 8 800 000	NT$ 8 800 000	NT$ 8 800 000
Separable costs	1 600 000	1 600 000	1 600 000	1 600 000
Incremental contribution	7 200 000	7 200 000	7 200 000	7 200 000
Allocated joint costs	(2 000 000)	(2 782 609)	(2 400 000)	(2 506 667)
Gross margin	5 200 000	4 417 391	4 800 000	4 693 333
Juice:				
Sales	10 000 000	10 000 000	10 000 000	10 000 000
Separable costs	2 000 000	2 000 000	2 000 000	2 000 000
Incremental contribution	8 000 000	8 000 000	8 000 000	8 000 000
Allocated joint costs	(2 000 000)	(3 130 435)	(2 666 667)	(2 666 667)
Gross margin	6 000 000	4 869 565	5 333 333	5 333 333
Canned:				
Sales	11 200 000	11 200 000	11 200 000	11 200 000
Separable costs	2 400 000	2 400 000	2 400 000	2 400 000
Incremental contribution	8 800 000	8 800 000	8 800 000	8 800 000
Allocated joint costs	(4 000 000)	(2 086 956)	(2 933 333)	(2 826 666)
Gross margin	4 800 000	6 713 044	5 866 667	5 973 334
Combined gross margin	NT$16 000 000	NT$16 000 000	NT$16 000 000	NT$16 000 000

When they speak to the director of finance, she addresses the bonus issue from the perspective of responsibility. She points out that the managers are responsible for sales of their product lines and costs of further processing. She suggests that their bonuses should be based on each product's contribution to total profitability before any allocations have been made. In addition, she believes that changes in the contribution over time should be as important as the total contribution, to provide incentives for them to increase sales and contain costs.

Uses and limitations of joint cost information

Joint costs are allocated to individual products primarily to meet requirements for financial accounting, income tax, government regulatory or other external reporting. All product costs must be assigned to inventory and cost of sales. By definition, it is not possible to directly trace joint costs to individual products. Instead, an allocation method must be adopted. Several potential methods may be used, and most of the methods involve estimation of one or more of the following items.

- Physical quantities
- Sales value at the split-off point
- Sales price if processed further
- Separable costs

Whenever estimates are used, the potential arises for bias or other distortions caused by uncertainties.

Because joint costs are assigned to products, the tendency for managers is to use them in making decisions. However, allocated joint costs are irrelevant for most decisions. For example, joint cost allocations should not be used to decide whether to process a joint product beyond the split-off point or in evaluating individual product manager performance. Accountants assist managers by helping them understand whether joint costs are relevant to a particular decision.

SUMMARY

13.1 Describe the process for making non-routine operating decisions.

Decision process

General decision rule

Take the action that maximises current period income (or minimises current period losses).

To apply the general decision rule

Identify and calculate relevant revenues and costs:
- contribution margin per unit
- contribution margin per unit of constrained resource
- fixed costs that differ across alternatives
- opportunity costs.

13.2 Understand the decision-making process to accept, reject and price special orders.

General decision rule

Accept if price is greater than or equal to the sum of variable cost, relevant fixed costs and opportunity cost.

Relevant fixed costs

Include only new fixed costs associated with the special order.

Opportunity cost

Consider the contribution margin of any regular business replaced.

13.3 Understand the decision-making process to keep or drop products, segments or whole businesses.

General decision rule

Drop the product if contribution margin is less than the sum of relevant fixed costs and opportunity cost.

Relevant fixed costs

Include only fixed costs that can be avoided if product is dropped.

Opportunity cost

Benefits from using released capacity for other purposes.

13.4 Understand the decision-making process to insource or outsource an activity (make or buy).

General decision rule

Outsource if the cost to buy is less than or equal to the sum of variable cost and relevant fixed costs minus opportunity cost.

Relevant fixed costs

Include only fixed costs that can be avoided if the decision is to buy.

Opportunity cost

Benefits from using released capacity for other purposes.

13.5 Explain the decision-making process for product emphasis and constrained resources.

Types of constrained resource problems
- Product emphasis
- Product mix when resources are constrained
- Relaxing constraints for two or fewer products
- Relaxing constraints for multiple products and multiple constraints

General decision rule
- Product emphasis: emphasise product with highest contribution margin per unit unless resources are constrained, then emphasise product with highest contribution margin per unit of constrained resource.
- Constrained resource: incur cost to relax constraint if cost is less than or equal to the sum of contribution margin per unit of constrained resource and the current variable cost of the resource.

Relevant fixed costs
- Constrained resource: only new fixed costs to relax the constraint.

13.6 Describe the qualitative factors important to non-routine operating decisions.

Examples of qualitative factors

		Type of decision		
Special order	**Product line and business segment (keep or drop)**	**Insource or outsource (make or buy)**	**Product emphasis (under constraints)**	**Relax constrained resource**
• Will regular customers expect lower prices? • Will this order lead to improved brand name recognition? • Can we deliver without disrupting current schedules?	• Will dropping one product affect sales of other products? • Will lay-offs affect worker morale?	• Is it easier to ensure high quality via insourcing or outsourcing? • Will delivery be timely? • Are there uncertainties about the supplier's ability to meet contractual obligations? • Is this activity a core competency?	• Does the product emphasis agree with strategic plans?	• Are there other ways to relax the constraint? • How would brand recognition be affected by delivery delays? • Will the decision affect future supply costs?

Quality of information

- Uncertainties
- Information timeliness
- Analysis technique assumptions
  - managers would like to maximise short-term profits
  - CVP assumptions (see chapter 4)
  - Additional assumptions for constrained resource decisions:
    ○ The entity will forgo sales if the resource constraint is not relaxed
    ○ Fixed costs are unaffected by short-term decisions made to relax constraints
    ○ Sales of one product do not affect sales of other products

Quality of decision process

- Decision-maker bias
- Sensitivity analysis
- Prioritisation

Examples of uncertainties

		Type of decision		
Special order	**Product line and business segment (keep or drop)**	**Insource or outsource (make or buy)**	**Product emphasis (under constraints)**	**Relax constrained resource**
• How accurate are the cost estimates? • Are we operating in the relevant range? • Will fixed costs increase at higher capacity levels?	• How accurate are the revenue and cost estimates? • How will customers respond to the dropped product?	• How accurate are the cost estimates? • Is our measure of quality appropriate? • How reliable is the vendor or resource supplier?	• How accurate are the contribution margin estimates? • How reliable are the product demand forecasts?	• How accurate are the constraint use estimates? • How accurate are the contribution margin estimates?

13.7 Demonstrate an understanding of joint costing issues.

Joint process

- Jointly produce more than one product
- Joint costs cannot be traced to individual products
- Joint production ends at the split-off point
- Individual products might or might not be processed beyond the split-off point
- Main product has high relative sales value
- By-product has low relative sales value

Joint cost allocation

Physical output method

- Allocate joint costs in proportion to the physical output for each main product
- Examples of physical measures are metres, kilograms or litres
- All main products must be expressed in the same physical measure

Sales value at split-off point method

- Allocate joint costs in proportion to the sales value for each main product at the point where joint production ends
- It is not always possible to measure sales value at the split-off point

Net realisable value (NRV) method

- Allocate joint costs in proportion to the net realisable value for each main product, taking into account the final selling price and separable costs
- Same as the sales value at split-off method if no additional production occurs beyond the split-off point

Constant gross margin (NRV) method

- Allocate joint costs so that the gross margin percentage for all main products is the same
  - First, calculate combined gross margin percentage for all main products
  - Second, calculate joint cost allocation that will result in the same gross margin percentage for all main products, taking into account the final selling price and separable costs

Factors to consider when choosing a joint cost allocation method

Major goal

Avoid distortion of individual main product values

Physical output method

- May inappropriately give impression that a main product is unprofitable, even when it has a positive incremental value
- Appropriate when units of all main products are similar in size and have comparable NRVs

Market-based methods

- Sales value at split-off point method
  - Generally appropriate if most or all products are sold when joint production ends
  - Sales values must exist at the split-off point
- NRV methods generally preferred because allocation is based on the ability of each main product to 'pay' for its allocated cost
- Constant gross margin NRV method best reflects the inseparability of the joint production process

General decision rule and information relevant when deciding whether to process a joint product beyond the split-off point

Process further if the incremental revenue is greater than the incremental cost, including any relevant fixed costs and opportunity costs

Assumptions

- CVP assumptions
- Managers want to maximise profits in the short term
- Sales of one product do not affect sales of other products

Uncertainty and bias in future revenue and separable cost estimates

Consider quantitative and qualitative factors to reach decision

Methods to account for the sale of by-products

Accounting for NRV of by-products

- If net cost, include NRV in joint costs
- If profit, method often considered unimportant because by-product values are immaterial

- Record at time of production:
  - subtract NRV from joint costs
  - by-product inventory carried at NRV
  - establishes control over by-product inventory
- Record at time of sale:
  - sales revenue or other income, or
  - subtract NRV from cost of sales

Joint costing with a sales mix

Effect of sales mix on calculations

The sales mix is incorporated into the calculations for each allocation method.

Uses and limitations of joint cost information

Uses of joint cost information

- Financial statements
- Income tax returns
- Government regulatory reports
- Other external reports

Estimates used in allocation calculations

- Physical quantities
- Sales value at split-off point
- Sales price if processed further
- Separable costs

Improper use of joint cost information

Joint costs are irrelevant for many types of decisions.

KEY TERMS

bottleneck Any process, part or machine that limits overall capacity.

constant gross margin NRV method Allocates joint costs so that the gross margin percentage for each main product is identical.

constraint When limits in capacity, materials or labour restrict an entity's ability to provide enough products (goods or services) to satisfy demand.

insourcing The practice of providing the good or service from internal resources.

joint products In the process of making one product, one or more other products or services are created.

make or buy A decision to make a product or service in-house, or to outsource it to outside vendors.

net realisable value (NRV) method A method that allocates joint costs using the relative value of main products, taking into account both the additional sales value that is created and costs that are incurred after joint production ends.

outsourcing The practice of finding outside vendors to supply products and services.

physical output method Allocates joint costs using the relative proportion of physical output for each main product. Used only when output for all main products can be expressed in the same physical measure, e.g. metres, kilograms or litres.

sales value at split-off point method Allocates joint costs based on the relative sales value of main products at the point where joint production ends.

SELF-STUDY PROBLEMS

SELF-STUDY PROBLEM 1 Make or buy decision

Spa Company produces plunge pools. Currently, the company uses internally manufactured pumps to power water jets. Spa Company has found that 40 per cent of the pumps have failed within their 12-month warranty period, causing huge warranty costs. Because of the company's inability to manufacture high-quality pumps, management is considering buying pumps from a reputable outside supplier who will also bear any related warranty costs.

Spa Company's unit cost of manufacturing pumps is $83.75 per unit, including $17.25 of allocated fixed overhead (primarily depreciation of equipment). Also, the company has spent an average of $22 (labour and parts) repairing each pump returned. Spa Company can purchase pumps for $92.50 per pump.

In the coming year, Spa Company plans to sell 12 800 plunge pools (each pool requires one pump).

Required

(a) Determine whether Spa Company should make or buy the pumps, and the amount of cost savings arising from the best alternative.

(b) What qualitative factors should be considered in the outsourcing decision?

SOLUTION TO SELF-STUDY PROBLEM 1

(a) Quantitative analysis of relevant costs

Cost of manufacturing pump	
Manufacturing	$66.50
Warranty	22.00
Total relevant costs	$88.50
Cost of purchasing pump	
Purchase price	$92.50

The financial analysis indicates that if the pumps are purchased, Spa Company will reduce its profits by $4 per unit ($88.50 – $92.50). When management first looked at this proposal, it might have incorrectly compared the total costs of $105.75 with the purchase price of $92.50. However, as already indicated, this ignores the unavoidable cost of $17.25 (that is, the allocated fixed manufacturing that will be incurred regardless of the decision taken by management)

(b) Qualitative factors

- Warranty returns make customers unhappy and damage the reputation of Spa Company. The above financial analysis has not considered the costs associated with a loss of goodwill. If the contractor was able to supply pumps that were of a higher quality, then the warranty returns would be reduced.
- Regular supply will be important. Spa Company would need to consider whether the contractor could meet delivery schedules.

SELF-STUDY PROBLEM 2 Product emphasis

Power Tool manufactures engines for a broad range of commercial and consumer products. At its plant in Cleveland, it assembles two engines — a rototiller engine and a riding lawnmower engine. Following is information for each product line:

	Rototiller engine	Riding lawnmower engine
Selling price	$800	$1000
Variable costs per unit	560	625
Contribution margin per unit	$240	$ 375
Contribution margin ratio	30%	37.5%

Rototiller engines require 2 machine hours each, and riding lawnmower engines require 5 machine hours each. Only 600 machine hours are available each day for assembling engines. Additional capacity cannot be obtained in the short run. Power Tools only has demand for 200 rototiller engines but can sell as many riding lawnmower engines as it produces.

Required

(a) Which product should Power Tools emphasise? Explain and support your answer with quantitative information.

(b) Using the general decision rule, what premium per machine hour would the managers of Power Tools be willing to pay to increase the number of machine hours available?

SOLUTION TO SELF-STUDY PROBLEM 2

(a) The contribution margin per unit of constrained resource for each engine is as follows (MH = machine hour):

$$\text{Rototiller: } \$240 \div 2\,\text{MH} = \$120 \text{ per MH}$$
$$\text{Lawnmower: } \$375 \div 5\,\text{MH} = \$75 \text{ per MH}$$

For this constrained resource problem, Power Tools should emphasise the product having the highest contribution margin per unit of constrained resource. In this case, the entity should emphasise the rototiller.

(b) If Power Tools can sell more rototillers, it can spend up to $120 per machine hour plus whatever it spends now on variable production costs to increase machine hours. When the demand of rototiller engines has been met, it can spend up to $75 per machine hour plus what it spends now on variable production costs to increase machine hours for the production of lawnmower engines. See figure 13.8.

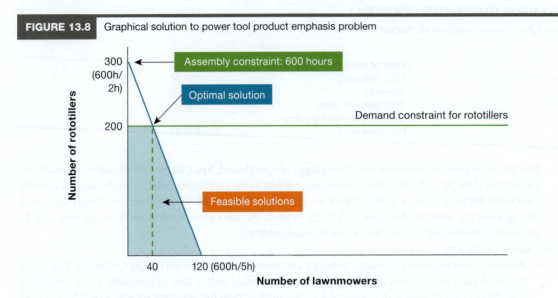

FIGURE 13.8 Graphical solution to power tool product emphasis problem

SELF-STUDY PROBLEM 3 Physical output method; drop a product; special order

Jumping Juice Ltd produces two grades of sparkling apple juice. A diagram of the production process appears in figure 13.9. The process begins when the vat is loaded with apples. The incremental cost of raw materials and processing one load is $250. Each load produces one barrel of premium raw apple juice and two barrels of standard raw apple juice. The variable cost of carbonating and bottling the cider is $200 per barrel for premium cider and $100 per barrel for standard cider. Each barrel of raw juice produces 100 bottles of finished sparkling juice. The fixed costs for one month are: $5000 for the plant, $2000 for handling and bottling premium, and $1000 for handling and bottling standard. Premium cider sells for $5 per bottle and standard cider for $3 per bottle, both wholesale. In a normal month, 100 loads are processed and converted into 20 000 bottles of standard cider and 10 000 bottles of premium cider.

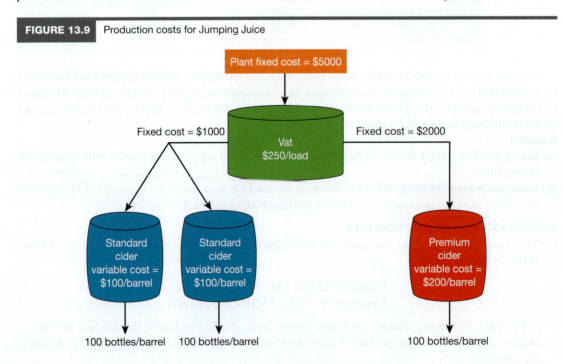

FIGURE 13.9 Production costs for Jumping Juice

Required

(a) In a normal month, what is the total allocated cost (fixed plus variable) per bottle of premium cider if the costs of the manufacturing operation are allocated on the basis of physical output measured by volume?

(b) In a normal month, what is the variable cost per bottle of premium cider if the joint variable costs of the juice entity are allocated on the basis of physical output measured by volume?

(c) Assuming that the $1000 in fixed costs for standard handling and bottling could be avoided, what would be the impact on the profit of the entity in a normal month if the entity discontinued the standard brand and treated all raw cider as premium grade?

(d) Explain to the CEO of the entity why the variable cost per bottle of premium cider you calculated in part (b) should or should not be used in pricing special orders for the premium cider.

SOLUTION TO SELF-STUDY PROBLEM 3

(a) According to the requirements of the problem, the costs of the vat process need to be allocated, which would amount to $30 000 [= $5000 + ($250 × 100)].

	Standard grade	Premium grade
Allocation base:		
Volume	20 000 bottles	10 000 bottles
Relative volume	2/3	1/3
Allocated cost of vat process:		
Standard (2/3 × $30 000)	$20 000	
Premium (1/3 × $30 000)		$10 000
Cost of handling and bottling:		
Standard [$1000 + ($100 × 200)]	$21 000	
Premium [$2000 + ($200 × 100)]		$22 000
Total cost	$41 000	$32 000
Divided by volume	20 000 bottles	10 000 bottles
Cost per bottle	$ 2.05	$ 3.20

(b)

	Standard grade	Premium grade
Allocation base:		
Volume	20 000 bottles	10 000 bottles
Relative volume	2/3	1/3
Allocated variable cost:		
Standard (2/3 × $250 × 100)	$16 667	
Premium (1/3 × $250 × 100)		$ 8 333
Variable cost of handling and bottling:		
Standard ($100 × 200)	$20 000	
Premium ($200 × 100)		$20 000
Total variable cost	$36 667	$28 333
Divided by volume	20 000 bottles	10 000 bottles
Variable cost per bottle	$ 1.83	$ 2.83

Note: While the calculation above would be labelled a variable cost by most accountants, it really is not a variable cost in the usual sense of the word. Of the total 'variable cost per bottle', $1667 (1/3 × 5000) could not be avoided even if no more premium grade cider was produced.

(c)

	As is	Discontinue standard
Production:		
Standard grade	20 000 bottles	
Premium grade	10 000 bottles	10 000 bottles
Revenue		
As is [($3 × 20 000) + ($5 × 10 000)]	$110 000	
Discontinue standard ($5 × 10 000)		$50 000

Factory		
As is [($5000 + ($250 × 100)]	(30 000)	
Discontinue premium		(30 000)
Handling and bottling:		
Standard grade:		
As is [$1000 + ($100 × 200)]	(21 000)	
Discontinue standard		(0)
Premium grade:		
As is [$2000 + ($200 × 100)]	(22 000)	
Discontinue premium		(22 000)
Profit	$ 37 000	$ (2 000)

Profit would decline by about $39 000 if the premium brand was discontinued.

(d) If a special order of premium cider was produced without producing any standard cider, the decision to produce premium would require incurring the fixed and variable vat costs, as well as the fixed and variable costs for premium bottling. The special order would need to pay for all of these costs.

QUESTIONS

13.1 When making a non-routine operating decision, are all future costs relevant? Explain. **LO1**

13.2 Business publications frequently provide subscriptions to students at a substantial discount. Why do you suppose such offers are made? **LO1**

13.3 An organisation is currently operating at capacity. Should it accept a request for a special order based on variable cost plus 40 per cent? Explain. **LO2**

13.4 Refer to the general decision rule for special orders. **LO2**
   (a) Would this same general decision rule apply to a decision to sell afternoon theatre tickets at a discounted price? Explain.
   (b) Identify two other business pricing situations that are similar to the afternoon theatre tickets.

13.5 Describe several methods that can be used to relax constrained resources. **LO5**

13.6 In your own words, distinguish between quantitative and qualitative information. **LO1, 6**

13.7 Grover Nursery is a large nursery in Sydney that has always raised the bedding plants it sells. The managers recently decided to buy bedding plants from a wholesale nursery in another state. **LO4**
   (a) List several quantitative factors that might encourage the managers to buy from another grower.
   (b) List several qualitative factors that might encourage the managers to grow their own plants.

13.8 List two qualitative factors that often need to be considered when making a decision about whether to outsource a product or service. **LO4**

13.9 Explain how managers decide which products in a sales mix to emphasise. **LO5**

13.10 What kind of constraints would arise in an accounting entity during tax season? How could any constraints be relaxed? **LO5**

13.11 List at least three different types of non-routine operating decisions and give an example of each one for a retail clothing factory outlet. **LO1**

13.12 List two qualitative factors that often need to be considered when making a decision about whether to accept a special order. **LO2, 6**

13.13 Give an example of joint products in a service industry and describe the main products and by-products. **LO7**

13.14 A decision about processing a product further should not be influenced by joint cost allocation, but should be based on incremental costs and qualitative factors. Explain. **LO7**

13.15 The allocation of a joint cost among joint products is essentially an arbitrary process. If this statement is true, then why allocate? **LO7**

EXERCISES

13.16 Special order with no spare capacity **LO2, 6**

Crystal Lattice produces exercise mats for use in fitness centres. Production capacity is 20 000 mats per year. Due to a chain of fitness centres closing, Crystal Lattice now has spare capacity of 2000 mats per year. An international hotel chain, Resteasy, has recently contacted Crystal Lattice to place a one-off order for 3000 mats. The hotel chain has recently remodelled a number of its hotels to incorporate fitness centres for guests.

Budgeted costs for 20 000 mats are:
- variable manufacturing costs $800 000
- fixed manufacturing costs $900 000.

Mats normally sell for $100 each, and Resteasy has offered to pay $90 per mat. Resteasy has also requested that each mat be embossed with its company logo. An embossing machine costing $20 000 would therefore need to be purchased by Crystal Lattice. The machine could not be used for other products.

Required

(a) From a financial perspective, should Crystal Lattice accept the special order? Show calculations.

(b) What other factors should be considered before the order is accepted?

13.17 Outsource computations, qualitative factors LO4, 6

Diamond Light Company incurred the following costs to produce 25 000 light switches for floor lamps last year.

Direct materials	$ 50 000
Direct labour	75 000
Variable manufacturing overhead	40 000
Fixed manufacturing overhead	60 000
Total manufacturing costs	$225 000

The Ignition Company has offered to supply the switches for $8 per unit. An analysis of the overhead costs has identified that, if the switches are outsourced, Diamond Light Company would eliminate $10 000 of fixed costs, and could use the released production capacity to generate additional income of $28 000 from producing a different product.

Required

(a) From a financial perspective, should the light switches be outsourced? Show calculations.

(b) What qualitative factors need to be considered in the outsourcing decision?

13.18 Make or buy? LO4

The management of SouthPak Company has asked for your assistance in deciding whether to continue manufacturing a part or to buy it from an outside supplier. The part, called AlphaB, is a component of SouthPak's finished product. An analysis of the accounting records and the production data revealed the following information for last financial year.

1. The production department produced 72 000 units of AlphaB.
2. Each unit of AlphaB requires 20 minutes to produce. Six people in the production department work full-time (4000 hours each per year) producing AlphaB. Each person is paid $12 per hour.
3. The cost of materials per AlphaB unit is $4.
4. Manufacturing costs directly applicable to the production of AlphaB are:

Indirect labour	$15 000
Utilities	3 000
Depreciation	3 600
Rates and insurance	2 000

All of the above costs will be eliminated if AlphaB is purchased.

5. The lowest price for AlphaB from an outside supplier is $8 per unit. Delivery costs will be $0.80 per unit, and a part-time dispatch employee at $17 000 per year will be required.
6. If AlphaB is purchased, the excess space will be used to store SouthPak's finished product. Currently, SouthPak rents storage space at approximately $1.60 per unit stored per year. Approximately 9000 units per year are stored in the rented space.

Required

Should SouthPak make or buy the part? Show all calculations.

13.19 By-product further processing decision LO7

For a given by-product, 100 units can be sold at the split-off point for $8 each, or processed further at a cost of $12 each and sold for $19.

Required

Should the by-product be processed further? Provide calculations and explain your answer.

13.20 Identifying joint products   **LO7**

Required

(a) Which of the following related products would be considered joint products? Explain your choices.

  (i) Sand produced with three levels of fineness

  (ii) Motor vehicles and trucks

  (iii) Milk, yoghurt, butter and cheese

  (iv) Motorcycles and mopeds

  (v) Various lines of clothing manufactured for a discount department store

  (vi) An airline that provides three classes of service: first class, business class and economy class

(b) List two additional product groups that could be considered joint products.

13.21 Identifying joint and separable costs   **LO7**

Outback Cattle Company raises cattle and sells beef products. Following is a list of costs for the operation.

Required

Identify whether each cost is most likely a (J) joint cost or a (S) separable cost. For each item, explain why.

  (i) Veterinary costs for the calves

  (ii) The cost of grinding meat for mince

  (iii) The cost of feed for the cattle

  (iv) The cost of labour to manage the cattle while they grow

  (v) The cost of labour to prepare the cowhide for sale as leather

  (vi) The cost for packaging steaks and roasts

  (vii) The depreciation on the sheds that provide shelter for the cattle

13.22 NRV method, contribution margin and further processing for a service   **LO7**

Deluxe Tours, a tour organiser, leased a cruise liner for a special around-the-world tour. The lease cost is $200 000. Two classes of passengers are booked on the tour: first class and economy class. The total revenue from the 100 first-class passengers is $200 000, and from the 200 economy-class passengers is $200 000. Other costs for the two classes of passengers amount to $30 000 for first class and $30 000 for economy class.

Required

(a) How much of the lease cost would be allocated to first-class passengers if the net realisable value method is used?

(b) What is the contribution margin generated by first-class passengers?

(c) When the cruise liner managers are deciding whether to increase the number of first-class rooms, which joint cost allocation method is best to use? Explain.

13.23 Four joint cost allocation methods with sales mix; further processing decision   **LO7**

Palm Oil Company buys crude coconut and palm nut oil. Refining this oil results in four products at the split-off point: soap grade, cooking grade, light moisturiser and heavy moisturiser. Light moisturiser is fully processed at the split-off point. Soap grade, cooking grade and heavy moisturiser can be individually refined into fine soap, cooking oil and premium moisturiser. In the most recent month (June), the output at the split-off point was:

Soap grade	100 000 litres
Cooking grade	300 000 litres
Light moisturiser	50 000 litres
Heavy moisturiser	50 000 litres

The joint costs of purchasing the crude coconut and palm nut oil and processing it was $100 000. There were no beginning or ending inventories. Sales of light moisturiser in June were $50 000. Total output of soap, cooking oil and heavy moisturiser was further refined and then sold. Data relating to June are as follows.

Product	Separable costs	Sales
Fine soap	$200 000	$300 000
Superior cooking oil	80 000	100 000
Premium moisturiser	90 000	120 000

Palm Oil Company had the option of selling the soap grade, cooking grade and heavy moisturiser at the split-off point. This alternative would have yielded the following sales for the June production:

Soap grade	$50 000
Cooking grade	30 000
Heavy moisturiser	70 000

Required

(a) Allocate the joint cost using each of the following methods:
  (i) sales value at split-off point
  (ii) physical output
  (iii) net realisable value (NRV)
  (iv) constant gross margin NRV.
(b) Could Palm Oil Company have increased its June operating income by making different decisions about further refining the soap grade, cooking grade or heavy moisturiser palm nut oil? Show the effect on the contribution margin of any changes you recommend.

13.24 Make or buy; qualitative factors   LO4, 6

Yoklic Ltd currently manufactures a subassembly for its main product. The costs per unit are as follows:

Direct materials	$ 4
Direct labour	30
Variable overhead	15
Fixed overhead	25
Total	$74

Regina Ltd has contacted Yoklic with an offer to sell it 5000 subassemblies for $55 each.

Required

(a) Should Yoklic make or buy the subassemblies? Create a schedule that shows the total quantitative differences between the two alternatives.
(b) The accountant decided to investigate the fixed costs to see whether any incremental changes would occur if the subassembly was no longer manufactured. The accountant believes that Yoklic will eliminate $50 000 of fixed overhead if it accepts the proposal. Does this new information change the decision? Show your calculations.
(c) What qualitative factors are important for accountants and managers to consider for Yoklic's make or buy decision?

13.25 Constrained resource; qualitative factors   LO5, 6

Johnson and Sons Ltd produces organic orange juice from oranges it grows. Unfortunately, it has been a bad year for oranges because of severe frosts. Johnson has only 10 000 litres of juice. It usually sells 15 000 litres at $3 per litre. The variable costs of raising the oranges are $0.50 per litre. Johnson has loyal customers, but its managers are worried the entity will lose customers if it does not have juice available for sale when people stop by the farm. A neighbour is willing to sell 5000 litres of extra orange juice at $2.95 per litre.

Required

(a) Which type of non-routine operating decision is involved here? What are the managers' decision options?
(b) Using the general decision rule, what is the most per litre Johnson's managers would be willing to pay for additional juice?
(c) Why would Johnson be willing to pay the amount calculated in part (b) for more juice?

(d) Is the quality of the neighbour's juice a concern to Johnson's managers in making this decision? Why?

(e) List another qualitative factor that might affect the managers' decision.

13.26 CVP; single constrained resource **LO5**

Snowbird Snowboards converts regular snowboards to enhance safety capabilities for children. The statement of profit or loss for last year, in which 500 snowboards were produced and sold, appears here.

Revenue		$150 000
Expenses:		
Variable production costs	$60 000	
Fixed production costs	25 000	
Variable selling and administration	10 000	
Fixed selling and administration	35 000	130 000
Income		$ 20 000

Required

(a) What volume of snowboards must be sold to earn pre-tax profits of $30 000?

(b) Snowbird's supplier of snowboards is unable to ship more than 500 boards for the upcoming season. Snowbird has been paying the supplier $85 for each snowboard. (The cost of the snowboards is included in variable production costs.) More expensive snowboards are available from other manufacturers for conversion. If Snowbird's managers expect to sell more than 500 converted snowboards in the upcoming season, what is the most they would be willing to pay outside suppliers for each additional snowboard?

(c) Suppose Snowbird pays the price you calculated in part (b) and sells an additional 200 snowboards. What is the entity's incremental profit on these 200 snowboards?

13.27 Multiple products; multiple resource constraints; sensitivity **LO5**

Mrs Meadows sells two popular brands of biscuits, Chip Dip and Soft Chunk Chocolate Chip. Both biscuits go through the mixing and baking departments, but Chip Dip is also dipped in chocolate in the coating department.

Sales manager Frank Ronan believes that Mrs Meadows can sell all of its daily production of Chip Dip and Soft Chunk. Both biscuits are made in batches of 600 biscuits. The batch times for producing each type of biscuit and the minutes available per day are as follows.

	Mixing	Baking	Dipping
Minutes required per batch			
Chip Dip	20	40	15
Soft Chunk	30	20	0
Minutes available per day	4000	6000	2000

Revenue per batch for Chip Dip is $150 and the variable costs per batch are $100. Fixed costs of $2350 are allocated to Chip Dip. Revenue per batch for Soft Chunk Chocolate Chips is $175 and the variable costs per batch are $135. Allocated fixed costs are $1500.

Required

Set up the target function (contribution margin function) and the constraints for this problem. Enter these constraints and the target function into Excel Solver or another linear programming package and print out a formula sheet and all of the reports.

(a) What is the optimal product mix?

(b) What is the total contribution margin for that product mix?

(c) Following the general decision rule, what would the managers of Mrs Meadows be willing to pay to relax each constraint?

(d) Which constraints are binding?

(e) By how much could the contribution margin for Soft Chunk increase before the optimal product mix changes?

13.28 Keep or drop and constrained resource

The statement of profit or loss for King Salmon Sales, which produces smoked salmon, follows.

Revenue (100 000 kg)	$800 000
Expenses	
Fish	$200 000
Smoking materials	20 000
Packaging materials	30 000
Labour (wages)	300 000
Administration	150 000
Sales commissions	10 000
Total expenses	710 000
Pre-tax income	$ 90 000

Assume that the administrative costs are fixed and that all of the other costs are variable.

Required

(a) Suppose the state government curtails fishing because of low fish counts. As a result, King Salmon Sales can buy only 50 000 kilograms of salmon this year. Assume that the selling price, fixed costs and variable costs remain the same as last year. Using only quantitative information, should King Salmon operate this year? Explain your answer, using calculations. (*Hint:* Before you begin, identify the type of non routine operating decision, the decision options and the relevant information for this decision.)

(b) Assume King Salmon can buy up to 70 000 kilograms of fish at $2 per kilogram and that the remainder of the fixed and variable costs remain the same as last year. Also assume that the selling price remains the same as last year and that the market will purchase at least another 30 000 kilograms of fish. If the managers of King Salmon wish to sell more salmon, what should they be willing to pay to purchase more fish? (*Hint:* This type of decision is different from part (a). Before you begin, identify the type of non-routine decision, the decision options, and the relevant information.)

13.29 Product emphasis and constrained resource

Emily developed an innovative computer game, called Home By Myself (HBM). It was so successful that she quickly followed up with two sequels: Home By Myself II (HBM2) and Home By Myself III (HBM3). The costs of developing the games were $95 000 for HBM, $10 000 for HBM2 and $15 000 for HBM3.

The production process consists of copying the games to blank DVDs using her computer and then packing them with printed instructions in a display box. It takes longer to copy the original game than the sequels. In one hour, Emily can produce (ready for shipping) about 20 copies of HBM, 30 copies of HBM2 or 45 copies of HBM3.

	HBM	HBM2	HBM3
Selling price	$49.00	$29.00	$29.00
Costs			
Blank DVD	1.00	0.50	0.50
Instructions and packaging	4.00	2.00	2.00
Pro-rata development costs[a]	19.00	2.00	3.00
Margin	$25.00	$25.50	$23.50
Daily demand	120 games	120 games	90 games

[a]The pro-rata development costs were determined for each game by dividing the game's development costs by 5000, the estimated minimum total demand for each game.

Required

(a) What is the contribution margin per hour of Emily's time for each game?

(b) In what order should Emily produce the games?

(c) Using the general decision rule for constrained capacity, what is the most Emily should be willing to pay per hour for a worker to duplicate and pack DVDs after her normal working hours? (Assume that the worker would work at the same pace as Emily.)

13.30 Multiple products and resource constraints; sensitivity analysis

Wildlife Foods prepares wild birdseed mixes and sells them to local pet stores, grocery stores and wild bird stores. Two types of mixes have been most successful: Flight Fancy and Multigrain. Flight

Fancy generates a contribution margin of $12 per 100-kilogram bag and Multigrain contributes $9 per 100 kilograms. Because Wildlife Foods has been very thorough in its sterilisation process, the birdseed never germinates and grows. Therefore, it is a top seller and the entity can sell all of the birdseed it produces.

The seed is processed in three stages: mixing, sterilisation and packaging. The time requirements for each batch of 100 bags of Flight Fancy and 10 000 kilograms of Multigrain (which is sold in bulk rather than bags) follow.

	Minutes required			
	Mixing	Sterilisation	Packaging	
Flight Fancy	200	200	100	
Multigrain	100	300	0	(sold in bulk)
Minutes available	6 000	12 000	4 500	

Required

(a) Using a spreadsheet program such as Excel Solver, find the optimal product mix given the current constraints and contribution margins.

(b) Which constraints are binding?

(c) What happens if minutes available for mixing are doubled? Does another constraint become binding? What is the optimal product mix now?

13.31 Special order   LO2

The Cone Head House sells ice cream cones in a variety of flavours. Data for a recent week are as follows.

Revenue (1000 cones @ $1.50)	$1500
Cost of ingredients	530
Rent	300
Store attendant	600
Income	$ 70

The Cone Head's manager received a call from a university student club requesting a bid on 100 cones to be picked up in three days. The cones could be produced in advance by the store attendant during slack periods and then stored in the freezer. Each cone requires a special plastic cover that costs $0.05.

Required

(a) What are the manager's decision options?

(b) What quantitative information is relevant for this decision?

(c) Using the general decision rule, what is the minimum acceptable price per cone for this special order?

(d) Explain why the Cone Head's manager might be willing to sell cones at the price you calculated in part (c).

13.32 Special order; qualitative factors   LO2, 6

Beautiful Biscuits (BB) sells biscuits, brownies and beverages to small local shops. The selling price per brownie is $1.25, the variable cost is $0.75 and the average cost is $1. The principal of a primary school asked BB to provide 10 dozen brownies for its spring picnic. The principal wants to buy the brownies at BB's cost. Unlike regular sales, each special order brownie must be delivered in a plastic container to protect it from dust. The containers cost $0.05 each. The brownies can be prepared ahead of time when workers are not busy.

Required

(a) Under the general decision rule for special orders, what is the minimum price per brownie that BB's management should accept?

(b) If the principal can pay no more than $0.80 per brownie, should BB take the order? Why?

(c) List several qualitative factors that could affect BB's decision if the special order price for brownies is $0.80.

13.33 Outsourcing computations; uncertainties

Saguaro Systems produces and sells speakers and MP3 players. The following information has been collected about the costs related to the systems:

Selling price per unit	$ 70
Production costs per unit	
Direct materials	$ 22
Direct labour	$ 16
Variable overhead	$ 2
Total fixed overhead	$360 000

Saguaro normally produces 25 000 of these systems per year.

The managers have recently received an offer from a Chinese entity to produce these systems for $48 each. The managers estimate that $260 000 of Saguaro's fixed costs could be eliminated if they accept the offer.

Required

(a) Which type of non-routine operating decision is involved here? What are the managers' decision options? What quantitative information is relevant to the decision?

(b) Perform a quantitative analysis for the decision, and present your results in a schedule.

(c) Under the general decision rule for this type of decision, what production level is required for Saguaro's managers to be indifferent?

(d) List as many uncertainties as you can for this decision.

13.34 Special order computations; qualitative factors

Feed Barn packages and distributes three grades of animal feed. The material cost per tonne and estimated annual sales for each of the products are listed.

Product	Material cost	Estimated sales
Super Premium	$10.00	2 000 tonnes
Premium	8.00	3 000 tonnes
Economy	7.00	5 000 tonnes

The fixed cost of operating the machinery used to package all three products is $10 000 per year. In the past, prices have been set by allocating the fixed operating cost to products on the basis of estimated sales in tonnes. The resulting full costs (material costs plus allocated fixed operating cost) are then marked up 100 per cent. Feed Barn has received an offer from a foreign entity for 1000 tonnes of the premium grade feed. Sales to the foreign entity would not affect domestic sales but would require an increase in fixed production costs of $2000.

Required

(a) Which type of non-routine operating decision is involved here? What are the managers' decision options?

(b) What relevant quantitative information is required for this type of decision?

(c) Using only quantitative information, what is the minimum price that the Feed Barn's managers should be willing to accept from the foreign entity?

(d) What types of qualitative factors would the Feed Barn's managers typically consider before agreeing to the sale? Explain.

13.35 Keep or drop; multiple product breakeven; qualitative factors

Horton and Associates produces two products named the Big Winner and the Loser. Last month 1000 units of the Loser and 4000 units of the Big Winner were produced and sold. Average prices and costs for the two products for last month follow:

	Loser	Big Winner
Selling price	$95	$225
Direct materials	40	95
Direct labour	5	25
Variable overhead	5	15
Product line fixed costs	10	40
Corporate fixed costs	25	25
Average margin per unit	$10	$ 25

The production lines for both products are highly automated, so large changes in production cause very little change in total direct labour costs. Workers, who are classified as direct labour, monitor the production line and are permanent employees who regularly work 40 hours per week.

All costs other than corporate fixed costs listed under each product line could be avoided if the product line was dropped. Corporate fixed costs totalled $125 000, and the total sales amounted to 5000 units, producing the average cost per unit of $25. About $10 000 of the corporate fixed costs could be avoided if the Loser was dropped, and about $15 000 of the corporate fixed costs could be avoided if the Big Winner was dropped. The remaining $100 000 could be avoided only by going out of business entirely.

Required

(a) What is the overall corporate breakeven in total sales revenue, assuming the sales mix is the same as last month's?

(b) What is the breakeven sales volume (in units produced and sold) for the Loser? (In other words, what is the sales volume at which Horton should be financially indifferent between dropping and retaining the Loser?)

(c) List at least two qualitative factors that would affect the decision to keep or drop the Loser.

13.36 Product emphasis and keep or drop; product breakeven; relevant information   **LO3, 6**

The statement of profit or loss information for Kallapur and Trombley Cotton Growers follows:

	Premium	Regular	Fancy	Total
Sales units	100 bales	100 bales	100 bales	300 bales
Sales	$2200	$1600	$1800	$5600
Variable costs	1400	1000	1080	3480
Contribution margin	800	600	720	2120
Production line fixed costs[a]	640	725	520	1885
Corporate costs (allocated)[b]	90	80	105	275
Total fixed costs	730	805	625	2160
Operating income (loss)	$ 70	$ (205)	$ 95	$ (40)

[a] If the entity drops the product, these costs are no longer incurred.
[b] None of these corporate costs is expected to change if a product line is dropped.

Required

(a) Using the general decision rule, which product should the entity emphasise? Support your answer with calculations.

(b) Using the general decision rule, should the entity drop Regular (assuming no changes in demand for other products)? Support your answer with calculations. Show how operating income would change if Regular was dropped.

(c) At what point (in bales) would the managers be indifferent to dropping Regular? In other words, what is the breakeven point for Regular?

(d) What other information would you want before you make a decision about whether to drop Regular?

PROBLEMS

13.37 Identifying joint costs; choice of allocation method   **LO7**

Roses to Go is a flower farm that specialises in fragrant roses for florist shops.

Required

(a) List five joint costs that are likely to be incurred by Roses to Go in raising roses.

(b) The roses are sold by the dozen, with no difference in price for any of the bouquets. Which joint cost allocation method would be most appropriate? Explain your choice.

(c) Now assume that Roses to Go raises two different types of roses: fragrant roses and regular roses. The growing requirements for the two types of roses do not differ. However, fragrant roses sell for twice as much as regular roses. Which joint cost allocation method would be most appropriate? Explain your choice.

13.38 Separable and joint costs; NRV; operating income; by-product   **LO7**

Doe Ltd grows, processes, cans and sells three main pineapple products: sliced pineapple, crushed pineapple and pineapple juice. The outside skin, which is removed in the cutting department and processed as animal feed, is treated as a by-product.

Doe Ltd's production process is as follows: Pineapples are first processed in the cutting department. The pineapples are washed and the outside skin is cut away. Then the pineapples are cored and trimmed for slicing. The three main products (sliced, crushed, juice) and the by-product (animal feed) are recognisable after processing in the cutting department. Each product is then transferred to a separate department for final processing.

The trimmed pineapples are forwarded to the slicing department, where they are sliced and canned. Any juice generated during the slicing operation is packed in the cans with the slices. The pieces of pineapple trimmed from the fruit are diced and canned in the crushing department. Again, the juice generated during this operation is packed in the can with the crushed pineapple. The core and surplus pineapple generated from the cutting department are pulverised into a liquid in the juicing department. An evaporation loss equal to 8 per cent of the weight of the good output produced in this department occurs as the juices are heated. The outside skin is chopped into animal feed in the feed department.

Doe Ltd uses the net realisable value method to assign costs of the joint process to its main products. The by-product is inventoried at its net realisable value. The NRV of the by-product reduces the joint costs of the main products.

A total of 270 000 kilograms entered the cutting department in May. The schedule shows the costs incurred in each department, the proportion by weight transferred to the four final processing departments, and the selling price of each product.

		May processing data and costs	
Department	**Costs incurred**	**Proportion of product by weight transferred to departments**	**Selling price per kg of final product**
Cutting	$60 000	—	None
Slicing	4 700	35%	$0.60
Crushing	10 580	28	0.55
Juicing	3 250	27	0.30
Animal feed	700	10	0.10
Total	$79 230	100%	

Required

(a) How many kilograms of pineapple result as output for pineapple slices, crushed pineapple, pineapple juice and animal feed?

(b) What is the net realisable value of each of the main products?

(c) What amount of the cost of the cutting department (joint costs) is assigned to each of the main products and the by-product using Doe Ltd's allocation method?

(d) What is the gross margin for each of the three main products?

(e) How valuable is the gross margin information for evaluating the profitability of each main product?

(f) If no market exists for the outside skin as animal feed and, instead, it must be disposed of at a cost of $800, what effect will this cost have on the costs allocated to the main products?

13.39 Special order capacity constraint; relevant information; qualitative factors   **LO2, 6**

Rightway Printers, a book printing shop, is operating at 95 per cent capacity. The entity has been offered a special order for book printing at $8.50 per book; the order requires 10 per cent of capacity. No other use for the remaining 5 per cent idle capacity can be found. The average cost per book is $8 and the contribution margin per book for regular sales is $1.50.

Required

(a) Which type of non-routine operating decision is involved here? What are the managers' decision options?

(b) What information is relevant for this decision? Does the problem give you all of the information the managers need to make a decision? What other information is needed?

(c) Using the general decision rule, what premium are the managers willing to pay (per book) to relax the constrained capacity, assuming no qualitative factors are relevant?

(d) Explain how capacity affects the quantitative analysis for this decision.

(e) What qualitative factors could affect this decision?

13.40 Make or buy; qualitative factors

Vernom Ltd produces and sells to wholesalers a highly successful line of summer lotion and insect repellents. Vernom has decided to diversify to stabilise sales throughout the year. A natural area for the entity to consider is the production of winter lotions and creams to prevent dry and chapped skin.

After considerable research, a winter products line has been developed. However, because of the conservative nature of the entity's managers, Vernom's CEO has decided to introduce only one of the new products for this coming winter. If the product is a success, further expansion will be initiated in future years.

The product selected is a lip balm to be sold in a lipstick-type tube. The product will be sold to wholesalers in boxes of 24 tubes for $8 per box. Because of available capacity, no additional fixed charges will be incurred to produce the product. However, a $200 000 fixed charge will be assigned to allocate a fair share of the entity's fixed costs to the new product. The remaining overhead costs are variable.

Using estimated sales and production of 100 000 boxes of lip balm as the standard volume, the accounting department has developed the following costs per box of 24 tubes.

Direct labour	$ 4
Direct materials	6
Total overhead	3
Total	$13

Vernom approached a cosmetics manufacturer to discuss the possibility of purchasing the tubes for the new product. The purchase price of the empty tubes from the cosmetics manufacturer would be $1.80 per 24 tubes. If Vernom accepts the purchase proposal, it is estimated that direct labour and variable overhead costs would be reduced by 10 per cent and direct materials costs would be reduced by 20 per cent.

Required

(a) Should Vernom Ltd make or buy the tubes? Show calculations to support your answer.
(b) What would be the maximum purchase price acceptable to Vernom for the tubes? Explain.
(c) Instead of sales of 100 000 boxes, revised estimates show sales volume at 125 000 boxes. At this new volume, additional equipment at an annual rental of $20 000 must be acquired to manufacture the tubes. However, this incremental cost would be the only additional fixed cost required, even if sales increased to 300 000 boxes. (The 300 000 level is the goal for the third year of production.) Under these circumstances, should Vernom make or buy the tubes? Show calculations to support your answer.
(d) The entity has the option of making and buying at the same time. What is your answer to part (c) if this alternative is considered? Show calculations to support your answer.
(e) What qualitative factors should Vernom managers consider in determining whether they should make or buy the lipstick tubes?

13.41 Special order; qualitative factors; uncertainties; sensitivity

Jazzy Cases manufactures several different styles of jewellery cases. Management estimates that during the first quarter of this year the entity will operate at about 80 per cent of normal capacity. Two special orders have been received, and management is making a decision about whether to accept either or both orders.

The first order is from Penny-Wise Department Stores. The manager would like to market a jewellery case similar to one of Jazzy's current models. Penny-Wise wants its own label on the cases and is willing to pay $5.75 per case for 20 000 cases to be shipped by 1 April. The cost data for Jazzy's case, which is similar to the requested case, follow:

Selling price per unit	$9.00
Cost per unit	
Raw materials	$2.50
Direct labour (0.25 hours × $12)	3.00
Overhead (0.25 machine hours × $4)	1.00
Total cost per unit	$6.50

According to the specifications supplied by Penny-Wise, the special order case requires less expensive raw materials. Therefore, the raw materials for the special order will cost $2.25 per case. Management believes that the remaining costs, labour time and machine time will remain the same as for Jazzy's case.

The second order is from the Star-Mart Company. Its managers want 8000 cases for $7.50 per case. These jewellery cases, to be marketed under the Star-Mart label, would also need to be shipped by 1 April. However, these cases are somewhat different from any cases currently manufactured by Jazzy. Following are the estimated unit costs:

Cost per unit	
Raw materials	$3.25
Direct labour (0.25 hours × $12)	3.00
Overhead (0.5 machine hours × $4)	2.00
Total cost per unit	$8.25

In addition to these per-unit costs, Jazzy would incur $1500 in set-up costs and would need to purchase $2500 in special equipment to manufacture these cases. Currently, Jazzy would have no other use for the equipment once this order was filled.

Jazzy's capacity constraint is total machine hours available. The plant capacity under normal operations is 90 000 machine hours per year, or 7500 hours per month. Fixed manufacturing overhead costs are allocated to production on the basis of machine hours at $4 per hour and are budgeted at $360 000 per year.

Jazzy can work on the special orders throughout the entire first quarter, in addition to performing its normal production. Jazzy's managers do not expect any repeat sales to be generated from either special order.

Required

(a) What is the excess capacity of machine hours available in the first quarter? Explain how machine hour capacity affects the special order decision.

(b) Ignore the Star-Mart order. Using the general decision rule, what is the minimum acceptable price for the Penny-Wise order?

(c) Ignore the Penny-Wise order. What is the contribution margin per case for the Star-Mart order? What would be the total expected profit (loss) incurred by accepting this order?

(d) Using only quantitative information, decide which special orders Jazzy should accept.

(e) What qualitative factors are likely to be important to this decision?

(f) Identify and explain uncertainties that affect Jazzy's decision.

(g) What might happen to costs if Jazzy's production exceeds 95 per cent of its capacity? Discuss how increased use of capacity from a special order might affect the entity's costs. (*Hint:* Think about whether bottlenecks could arise and how they might affect costs.)

(h) Suppose you are the cost accountant for Jazzy.

   (i) Write a memo to Jazzy's management recommending whether the entity should accept each of the special orders. Attach to the memo a schedule showing your computations. As appropriate, refer to the schedule in the memo.

   (ii) Write one or two paragraphs explaining how you decided what information to include in your memo.

13.42 Special order computations and decision   **LO2, 6**

George Jackson operates a small machine shop. He manufactures one standard product available from many other similar businesses, and he also manufactures custom-ordered products. His accountant prepared the following annual statement of profit or loss.

	Custom sales	Standard sales	Total
Sales	$50 000	$25 000	$75 000
Costs			
Materials	10 000	8 000	18 000
Labour	20 000	9 000	29 000
Depreciation	6 300	3 600	9 900
Power	700	400	1 100

Rent	6 000	1 000	7 000
Heat and light	600	100	700
Other	400	900	1 300
Total costs	44 000	23 000	67 000
Income	$ 6 000	$ 2 000	$ 8 000

The depreciation charges are for machines used in the respective product lines. The power charge is apportioned on an estimate of power consumed. The rent is for the building space, which has been leased for 10 years at $7000 per year. The rent and the heat and lights are apportioned to the product lines based on the amount of floor space occupied. All other costs are current expenses identified with the product line causing them.

A valued custom-parts customer has asked Jackson if he would manufacture 5000 special units for her. Jackson is working at capacity and would have to give up some other business to take this order. He cannot renege on custom orders already agreed to, but he would have to reduce the output of his standard product by about one-half for a year while producing the specially requested customer part. The customer is willing to pay $7 for each part. The material cost will be about $2 per unit and the labour will be $3.60 per unit. Jackson will have to spend $2000 for a special device that will be discarded when the job is done.

Required

(a) Calculate and present the following costs related to the 5000-unit custom order.
  (i) The incremental cost of the order
  (ii) The full cost of the order (incremental plus allocated fixed costs such as depreciation, rent etc.)
  (iii) The opportunity cost of taking the order
  (iv) The sunk costs related to the order
(b) Should Jackson take the order? Explain your answer.

13.43 Foreign versus domestic production and comparative advantage   **LO6**

Scott Mills was originally a producer of fabrics, but several years ago intense foreign competition led management to restructure the entity as a vertically integrated cotton garment manufacturer. Scott purchased spinning organisations that produce raw yarn and fabricators that produce the final garment. The entity has both domestic and international operations.

The domestic spinning and knitting operations are highly automated and use the latest technology. The domestic operations are able to produce cotton fabric for $1.52 per kilogram. The domestic fabricating operations are located exclusively in rural areas. Their locations keep average labour costs to $16.40 per hour (including fringe benefits). The cost to ship products to the entity's distribution centre is $0.10 per kilogram.

The entity's foreign subsidiary is a fabricating operation located in the Maldives, a group of islands near India. The average wage rate there is $0.70 per hour. The subsidiary purchases cotton fabric locally for $1.60 per kilogram. The finished products are shipped to Scott Mills' distribution centre in New South Wales at a cost of $1.80 per kilogram. Both the domestic and foreign subsidiary use the same amount of fabric per product. Scott Mills has been producing three products for the private label market: sweatshirts, dress shirts and lightweight jackets. In the past the entity processed a new order at whichever fabricating plant had the next available capacity. However, projections for the next few years indicate that orders will far exceed capacity. Management wants each plant to specialise in one of the products.

The plants are constrained by the amount of sewing time available in each. The domestic plant has 8000 hours of sewing machine time available per week, while the foreign subsidiary has 10 000 hours available per week. The domestic plant's variable overhead is charged to products at $4 per machine hour, while the subsidiary's variable overhead averages $1 per machine hour.

The windcheaters require 1 kilogram of cotton fabric to produce, the dress shirts use 400 grams of fabric and the jackets require 1 kilogram of fabric. The domestic plant has special-purpose equipment that allows workers to sew a sweatshirt in 6 minutes, a shirt in 15 minutes and a jacket in one hour. The foreign plant's equipment constrains production to five sweatshirts per hour, three dress shirts per hour or two jackets per hour. The wholesale prices are $8.76 each for the sweatshirts, $7.50 for the dress shirts and $37 for the jackets.

Required

(a) Using only quantitative information, should the entity close its domestic operations and expand the foreign subsidiary?

(b) Assuming that wages in the domestic operations remain constant, at what level of wages in the foreign subsidiary would the managers be indifferent between producing sweatshirts at one location versus the other?

(c) Discuss qualitative factors, including ethical issues, that might influence the decision in part (a).

(d) Discuss whether production quality is likely to be a bigger concern for products produced at the foreign subsidiary versus products produced in the domestic operation.

(e) If demand for each product exceeds capacity, in which product should each plant specialise?

(f) Management insists on manufacturing all three products to maintain good customer relations. If demand for each product exceeds capacity, management would prefer to specialise according to your answer to part (e). At which plant should management produce the third product?

13.44 Outsource; relevant costs; qualitative factors; uncertainties; biases   LO4, 6

Falco Services processes mortgage loan applications. The cost of home appraisals is included in its service fee, but Falco uses an outside appraisal service. The cost of appraisals has been increasing rapidly over the last several years, reaching $180 per appraisal last year. Falco's CFO asked one of the accountants to estimate the cost of doing the appraisals in-house. Several of Falco's mortgage brokers worked previously as real estate agents and have performed informal appraisals; however, none have professional appraisal experience. The accountant's son-in-law owns the entity that currently performs most of the appraisals.

The accountant prepares a report for the CFO that includes the following estimates for 1000 appraisals. Appraisers would have to be hired, but no additional computer equipment, space or supervision would be needed. The report states that the total costs for 1000 appraisals would be $195 000 or $195 per appraisal. The current appraisal price is $180, so the report recommends that Falco continue to outsource the appraisal services.

Costs:	
Supplies and paper	$ 5 000
Professional labour	100 000
Overhead	90 000
Total costs	$195 000
Cost per appraisal	$ 195

Professional labour is the cost to hire two appraisers. Overhead consists of fixed overhead, which is allocated at 50 per cent of the cost of professional labour, and variable overhead (mostly fringe benefits), which is 40 per cent of the cost of professional labour. Falco's CFO has to decide whether to continue to use the appraisal service or to hire appraisers and provide the service in-house.

Required

(a) Which type of non-routine operating decision is involved here? What are the managers' decision options?

(b) What is the expected total incremental cost for 1000 appraisals?

(c) Which costs in the accountant's report are not relevant? Prepare a revised report that includes only relevant costs.

(d) Using the general decision rule, should Falco outsource appraisal services or provide this service itself?

(e) List uncertainties about Falco's ability to begin a new appraisal service at or below the cost calculated. List as many uncertainties as you can.

(f) List possible qualitative factors that Falco's CFO should consider in making this decision. List as many as you can.

(g) Explain why the accountant might have been biased, and explain what effects that might have on the cost report.

(h) What are the costs to Falco of relying on the accountant's report for this decision? What are the costs to the accountant of admitting that she might be biased in preparing information for this decision?

13.45 Keep or drop uncertainties; relevant information; qualitative factors **LO3, 6**

Gourmet Fast Foods produces and sells many products in each of its 35 different product lines. Occasionally, a product or an entire product line is dropped because it ceases to be profitable. The entity does not have a formalised program for reviewing its products on a regular basis to identify products that should be eliminated.

At a recent meeting of Gourmet's top management, the head of operations stated that several products or possibly an entire product line were currently unprofitable. After considerable discussion, management decided that Gourmet should establish a formalised product discontinuance program. The purpose of the program would be to review the entity's individual products and product lines on a regular and ongoing basis to identify problem areas.

The CFO proposed that a person be assigned to the program on a full-time basis. This person would work closely with the marketing and accounting departments to determine the factors that indicate when a product's importance is declining, and to gather the information that would be required to evaluate whether a product or product line should be discontinued.

Required

(a) Explain why the managers of Gourmet Fast Foods cannot know for sure when a product or product line should be discontinued.

(b) What factors might indicate the diminishing importance of a product or product line? List as many factors as you can.

(c) If you were assigned to this position, what information would you want from the accounting system?

(d) If you were assigned to this position, would you want any information other than that produced by the accounting system? If so, what type of information would be useful, and where would you be likely to obtain it?

(e) List several benefits of assigning an employee full-time responsibility for a product discontinuance program.

(f) If you were assigned to this position, describe the steps you would take as you analyse a given product.

13.46 Outsource computations; qualitative factors; cost of quality **LO4,6**

Mills and Vines just received a bid from a supplier for 6000 motors per year used in the manufacture of electric lawnmowers. The supplier offered to sell the motors for $88 each. Mills and Vines' estimated costs of producing the motor are as follows.

Direct materials	$40
Direct labour	20
Variable overhead	20
Fixed overhead	64

Prior to making a decision, the entity's CEO commissioned a special study to see whether any decreases were possible in fixed overhead costs. The entity would avoid two set-ups, which would reduce total spending by $10 000 per set-up. One inspector would be laid off at a savings of $28 000. A person in materials handling could also be laid off at a savings of $20 000. Engineering work would be reduced by 500 hours at $15 per hour. Although the work decreases by 500 hours, the engineer assigned to the motor line also spends time on other products.

Required

(a) Ignore the information from the special study. Using the general decision rule, determine whether the motor should be produced internally or purchased from the supplier.

(b) Repeat the analysis, using the information from the special study.

(c) Identify and discuss any qualitative factors that would affect the decision, including strategic implications.

(d) After reviewing the special study, the controller made the following remark: 'This study ignores the additional activity demands that purchasing the motor would cause. For example, although the part would no longer be inspected on the production floor, we will need to inspect the incoming parts in the receiving area. Will we actually save any inspection costs?' Discuss whether you agree with the controller. Identify and explain other costs that might increase if the part is outsourced.

13.47 Product emphasis with constrained resource; cost function; uncertainties   **LO5,6**

Riteway currently produces and sells five different products. Total demand for the products exceeds the entity's capacity to produce all of them. The constraint on production is the time available on a special machine. Data on the products and time required on the special machine are summarised in the following chart.

| | Product | | | | |
	A	B	C	D	E
Selling price	$12	$15	$18	$24	$32
Variable manufacturing cost	$8	$9	$11	$12	$18
Variable marketing cost	$1	$1	$3	$2	$6
Machine hours needed per unit	0.2	0.3	0.25	0.5	0.4
Maximum unit demand per period	10 000	7 500	20 000	1 500	2 000

The entity has only 5500 hours of time available on the special machine per period. Fixed costs are $110 000 per period.

Required

(a) How many units of each product should the entity produce and sell to maximise income?

(b) On further analysis, it was determined that, while fixed costs do not vary as production volumes change, they do vary based on the number of different product lines. If only two types of products are produced, these costs are $60 000, but if all five types of products are produced, these costs will be $135 000. Using the two-point method, determine a linear cost function for the cost of product lines.

(c) Describe possible business reasons for the cost behaviour described in part (b).

(d) Using the results from part (a) and the cost function you developed for part (b), prepare an statement of profit or loss for the entity by product line and by total products.

(e) Review the results in part (d). Prepare a new product line statement of profit or loss that reflects any changes that should be made in the production plans to maximise income.

(f) Identify reasons why the managers cannot be certain that they have accurately estimated the following for each product: selling price, variable costs, machine hours needed per unit and maximum unit demand per period.

(g) Discuss how the uncertainties in part (f) might affect the managers' production decisions.

13.48 Comprehensive problem   **LO3, 6**

Elder Services is a not-for-profit entity that has three departments in three separate locations, in addition to the headquarters. The entity provides services for elderly clients who are still living at home. One department provides meals, one department provides cleaning services and one department provides healthcare services. Elder Services relies on client fees and a small grant from the state government to provide services. Following are the results from last year's operations.

Departments	Meals	Cleaning	Health	Total
Visits	$10 000	$ 10 000	$ 10 000	$ 30 000
Revenues	50 000	100 000	150 000	300 000
Variable cost (labour and supplies)	30 000	50 000	120 000	200 000
Fixed overhead costs	4 000	8 000	10 000	22 000
Transportation				
($4000 fixed + $5000 variable)	9 000		9 000	
($10 000 fixed + $2000 variable)		12 000	12 000	
$5000 variable[a]			5 000	5 000
Headquarter costs allocated				
(based on revenues)	10 000	20 000	30 000	60 000
Total expenses	53 000	90 000	165 000	308 000
Surplus (deficit)	$ (3 000)	$ 10 000	$ (15 000)	$ (8 000)

[a]Nurses use their own cars.

In the past, the government provided small grants each year to cover losses for Elder Services. However, due to an economic downturn and decreased tax funds in the current year, the government will not be able to provide any support next year. In light of these changes, the managers of Elder Services are trying to decide how to balance the budget.

Required

(a) What is the contribution margin per visit for each department?

Consider the next three situations independently.

(b) To eliminate losses, the director of Elder Services would like to close the department that provides health services for clients. Assume no alternative uses are planned for the health services building and no change would occur in headquarters costs. Estimate the surplus (or deficit) if the health services department is closed.

(c) What would the estimated total surplus (deficit) be if cleaning services increase by 2000 clients, assuming no changes in fixed costs?

(d) What would the estimated total surplus (deficit) be if Elder Services closes the meals division and that space is leased to another entity for $2000 per month?

Suppose you are hired to help Elder Services' managers decide what to do about the lack of funding from the government this year. Ignore parts (b), (c) and (d) and answer the following questions as part of your analysis.

(e) Which type of non-routine operating decision does Elder Services need to make? What are the managers' decision options?

(f) Perform quantitative analyses to help you decide whether one or more of the options listed in parts (b), (c) and (d) would be beneficial to the finances of Elder Services.

(g) Now assume that the options in parts (b), (c) and (d) above are available. List uncertainties about Elder Services' ability to achieve the quantitative results for each option: (b), (c) and (d). List as many uncertainties as you can.

(h) List qualitative factors that the managers of Elder Services need to consider in making this decision. List as many factors as you can.

(i) As a consultant to Elder Services, how might you go about acquiring qualitative information?

(j) Suppose you decide to interview Elder Services employees to help you gather qualitative information. Identify possible reasons that information you obtain from employees might be biased. List as many reasons as you can.

(k) Describe possible trade-offs the managers of Elder Services might need to make in deciding what to do.

ACKNOWLEDGEMENTS

Photo 13A and 13B: © Robert Kneschke / Shutterstock.com
Photo 13C: © brillenstimmer / Shutterstock.com

PART 2

MANAGEMENT ACCOUNTING, EXTENDING PERFORMANCE MEASUREMENT AND STRATEGY

In part 2 of this text we focus on the connection between strategy and managerial control systems. We commence with an exploration of the links between strategy and control in chapter 14, which lays the foundation for the remaining chapters. Some of the issues explored in subsequent chapters include strategic capital expenditure, strategic management of costs and revenue including a consideration of lean accounting concepts, strategy maps and the balanced scorecard, rewards, incentives and risk management, and sustainability accounting.

CHAPTER 14

Strategy and control

LEARNING OBJECTIVES

After studying this chapter, you should be able to:

14.1 understand the changing management accounting and control environment

14.2 distinguish between strategy and control

14.3 communicate the key components of the important strategic management accounting frameworks

14.4 reflect on the importance of, and techniques associated with, management responsibility and accountability practices.

IN BRIEF

Management accounting is not only a technical and practical craft, it is also involved in radical social, environmental and technical change. This chapter introduces the important aspects that we cover in the rest of this book. The emphasis is on strategy and management accounting and control in a networked world where organisational boundaries and traditional accounting controls have become less relevant.

14.1 Management accounting and control in a 'flat world'[1]

LEARNING OBJECTIVE 14.1 Understand the changing management accounting and control environment.

Management accounting has undergone several transformations over the years. Prior to the 1980s, accounting for internal control did not have a strategic component. Instead, cost accounting techniques such as product costing, standard costing, inventory valuation and overhead allocation were the focus for the management accountant. Managerial accounting decisions focused on capital budgeting, make versus buy decisions, or other responsibility types of accounting. Many of these techniques are covered in the first part of this book. These introductory management accounting topics emphasise the *technical aspects* of management accounting. This type of accounting takes a prescriptive, backward-looking focus to management accounting and control.

From about the 1980s onwards, management accounting broadened to include strategic management accounting control concepts — largely influenced by the 'strategy' work of Simmonds[2] and Porter[3]. Rather than a backward focus, strategic management accounting looks to the future and is practical or pragmatic in nature. Instead of a single, discipline-focused function, a broader cross-discipline approach was required for management accountants, so they could better understand and implement strategic management accounting controls throughout the entire organisation. During the 1980s, the strategic focus started to decline. There were concerns that the financial reporting function was dominating decision making and did not at all facilitate the management accounting function (refer to *Relevance Lost* by Johnson and Kaplan). According to Johnson and Kaplan,[4] at a time of rapid technological change and global competition, a renewed emphasis on strategic management accounting was required. Better resource utilisation would be achieved if management accounting was separated from the financial reporting function. Since this seminal work, contemporary management accounting has continued with a stronger strategic emphasis and is in some ways quite separate from financial reporting.

Management accounting has a social, technical and economic focus. These factors have implicated management accounting in *radical* change. For example, management accounting is seen as a useful vehicle in which to implement economic theory and issues relating to social and environmental change. Issues such as intellectual capital and other intangible assets are now being included in management accounting and control systems. Likewise, environmental economics and issues of global warming are requiring corporate externalities be internalised in management accounting and control tools. For example, how might we best incorporate mandated reporting of environmental and sustainability issues in our internal information systems, and how might this influence decision making? Management accounting is rearranging traditional organisational boundaries and is implicated in 'network orchestration' that extends to management control of global supply chains. Network orchestration is about designing and managing global networks, controlling them through techniques such as empowerment, and creating value through integration.

Friedman discusses 'Globalisation 1.0' (the rounding of the old flat world), 'Globalisation 2.0' (the rise of the multinational) and, from the 2000s onwards, 'Globalisation 3.0'; that is, the emergence of the 'Flat World'. Friedman's 'Flatteners' involve accelerating the connecting of the unconnected through technological advancements and include the 'rise of the personal computer, development of the internet, workflow software, outsourcing, offshoring, uploading, supply chaining, insourcing, in-forming'.

Alongside these developments has been the growth in the generation and use of big data sets. These data sets provide opportunities for the management accounting role in organisations to make sense of the data; and organise it into information sets to be useful for decision making. For example, one early use of large data sets has been with respect to customer analysis and customer profitability with the objective of providing higher quality information with respect to customers and customer groups.

Management accounting and control tools are still being developed. In some ways the links to corporate reporting are becoming more entwined as an enterprise-wide accounting focus has extended to include both financial and non-financial conformance–performance indicators. The links need to be better managed and understood.

Finally, Shank reinforces the need for management accounting to continue to evolve. He states 'if we stop teaching students how to become "strategic accountants", the CFOs of the future will rely on accounting decision models distanced from business reality; businesses will fail'. Given these concerns and the radical changes already observed in management accounting, the second part of this book is dedicated to emphasising the importance of strategic management accounting techniques.

Some of the key trends in management accounting[5] and control have been identified as including:

- increasing focus on customer and distribution channel profitability along with performance management tools
- a shift towards more predictive accounting and business data analytics
- the need for an enhanced understanding of the behavioural influences of cost and performance management.

These reinforce the need for management accounting and control to continually evolve by adapting to the changing needs of organisations.

14.2 Introduction to strategy and control

LEARNING OBJECTIVE 14.2 Distinguish between strategy and control.

The terms *strategy* and *control* have been given a variety of definitions in a range of discipline areas for both teaching and research purposes. Our intention is to provide suitable definitions as the terms relate to management accounting and control and the second part of this text.

When organisations put in place suitable management accounting and control system tools, there needs to be some form of guidance. This guidance commonly comes in the form of the organisation's strategy. There is little else to use as a guide. In retrospect, organisations can always look back and conclude errors were made and decisions were not optimal. However, this is not known at the time the decision is taken. So, an organisation's strategy provides some guidance — a benchmark to use to increase confidence in the decision(s) being made. This reinforces the importance that an organisation has a clear strategy or future direction to guide managerial control system design and influence managerial action. While various definitions of strategy exist, we commonly view strategy in business to mean *future direction*, which enables focusing of the organisation's resources and decision making around a common theme.

A number of frameworks exist that define strategy in more detail. Here, we will focus on the prolific works of Porter[6] to define strategy. In this framework, strategy is seen as operating at two levels.

1. The *organisational or corporate level*. At this level, the organisation makes decisions about what industries or types of businesses it chooses to be in. For example, when Google purchased YouTube for $1.65 billion, it made a decision to be in the video-sharing business/industry.
2. The *business-unit level*. At this level, the organisation seeks out competitive advantage at the business-unit level within the industries it has chosen to compete in.

Usually, we would expect organisations to use competitive analysis tools such as:

- SWOT (strengths, weaknesses, opportunities and threats) analysis, which is an assessment of an organisation's internal strengths and weaknesses and an evaluation of an organisation's external opportunities and threats. This should also include a consideration of intangible considerations including intellectual capital, networks and strategic alliances
- Porter's competitive forces model, which can be used to assess an organisation's competitiveness within its industry and market. This model is illustrated in figure 14.1.

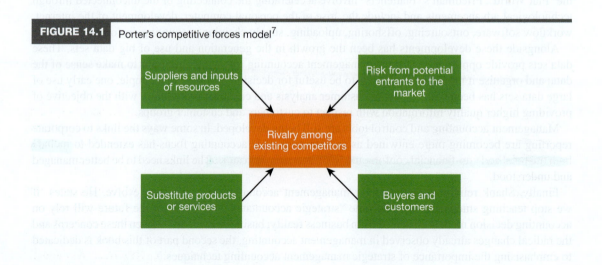

FIGURE 14.1 Porter's competitive forces model[7]

As we discussed in chapter 1, we can apply Porter's generic classification of strategy as being either:

1. a *cost leadership strategy*, where the organisation or business unit primarily focuses on holding a cost leadership position in the industry (for example, in Australia, Tigerair Australia and Jetstar compete in the low-cost airline segment of the industry)
2. a *product differentiation strategy*, where the organisation or business unit primarily focuses on features such as quality, service and innovation as a competitive advantage.

The demands of the contemporary business environment mean that strategy for many organisations is an evolving concept rather than a static one. With increasing speed of technological innovations and organisations moving between and across industries, strategy is continually being challenged, adapted and modified. For example, Nokia, originally a mobile phone company, is now focused on telecommunications infrastructure and computer software; Amazon, originally an online bookseller, now has huge investments in data warehousing and cloud computing; and Microsoft, for a long time focused purely on PC software, is now a significant player in telecommunications and cloud computing. It is important to note the role of management accounting and control in making these strategic decisions and then in the monitoring of performance against the strategy.

Like strategy, the term *control* can be defined differently and applied in different contexts. For our purposes control is commonly used as a short-form term for managerial control and/or managerial control system tools. The ultimate objective of control in this context is to influence the decisions and behaviour of managers within organisations. The broader aspect of management control might encompass:[8]

- planning what should be done, including strategy and future direction
- coordinating the activities of the organisation
- communicating information for decision making
- evaluating information
- determining courses of action, which might be to remain on the current path or result in new opportunities and a new path/strategy or direction.

Underlying these activities is the concept of managerial control systems performing the dual role of:

1. *decision influencing*, which suggests control system tools can be structured to directly influence behaviour and decisions. For example, budget targets and incentive plans perform the role of trying to direct managerial attention and behaviour along a desired path
2. *decision facilitating*, which suggests a key role of managerial control system tools is to provide relevant and timely information to support decision making. For example, cost system data support pricing decisions, reliable discounted cash flow analysis supports some capital budgeting decisions, and reliable customer feedback data supports a customer-intimacy strategy.

We can illustrate the potential link between strategy and management control system tools as shown in figure 14.2.

FIGURE 14.2   Organisational strategy and managerial control system tools

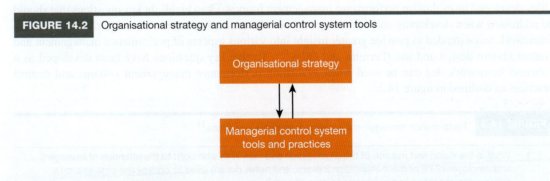

It is a common view that organisational strategy should inform the nature and use of the control system tools used within the organisation. However, there is also a view that control system tools may inform strategy. For example, in dynamic environments the use of suitable performance measures and feedback mechanisms may result in early detection of industry and environmental changes that may be sufficient to warrant a review of current strategies.

It is also important to highlight the role of *formal* and *informal* controls. Much of this book is about the more formal controls put in place as part of a managerial control system. However, in some organisations, it is not the formal controls that exert the most influence over behaviour and decision making; as we discuss later in this chapter in relation to Simons' levers of control, some organisations have strong cultures or belief systems that may be classified as informal. Belief systems may be formalised through documentation, but commonly this documentation does not exist and the culture and belief systems may be seen as informal, but quite visible as they are *lived* within the organisation.

Other informal controls include:

- informal cultural practices, usually based on the significant influence of the owner/founder (particularly when the organisation is small)
- key practices, such as observation and employee engagement, that permeate the 'routines' of the organisation
- hiring practices that are structured in such a way to seek new employees most likely to suit the existing culture of the organisation
- informal meetings, social work settings and one-on-one consultations between senior managers and subordinate managers.

14.3 Frameworks for strategy and control

LEARNING OBJECTIVE 14.3 Communicate the key components of the important strategic management accounting frameworks.

A number of different management accounting frameworks have been designed to capture the dynamics of the relationship between strategy and control. Each might be viewed as a different 'lens' from which to view the connections between strategy and management accounting and control constructs. These frameworks provide a suitable set of connections between key constructs, which we will develop and explore further in the subsequent chapters of the text. Our intention is not to provide an exhaustive list of all existing frameworks. Rather, we focus on five key frameworks that have been influential in informing teaching and research in management accounting and control. These are:

1. Ferreira and Otley's performance management systems framework
2. Simons' levers of control framework
3. Kaplan and Norton's strategy map framework
4. Ittner and Larcker's value-based management framework
5. Flamholtz's control system framework.

Each of these provides a different perspective on the relationship between strategy and control and the impact of strategy and control on the structure of control system design within organisations. Each will now be discussed.

Ferreira and Otley's performance management systems framework

Otley developed an evaluative performance management framework to highlight key questions that should be addressed when developing and evaluating a system for managing organisational performance.[9] This framework was extended to provide greater insight into various aspects of performance management and control system design and use (Ferreira and Otley[10]). Twelve key questions have been developed as a coherent framework that can be used when evaluating performance management systems and control practices as outlined in figure 14.3.

FIGURE 14.3	Performance management systems framework questions[11]

1	What is the vision and mission of the organisation and how is this brought to the attention of managers and employees? What mechanisms, processes, and networks are used to convey the organisation's overarching purposes and objectives to its members?
2	What are the key factors that are believed to be central to the organisation's overall future success and how are they brought to the attention of managers and employees?
3	What is the organisation structure and what impact does it have on the design and use of performance management systems (PMS)? How does it influence and how is it influenced by the strategic management process?
4	What strategies and plans has the organisation adopted and what are the processes and activities that it has decided will be required for it to ensure its success? How are strategies and plans adapted, generated and communicated to managers and employees?

5   What are the organisation's key performance measures deriving from its objectives, key success factors, and strategies and plans? How are these specified and communicated and what role do they play in performance evaluation? Are there significant omissions?

6   What level of performance does the organisation need to achieve for each of its key performance measures (identified in the previous question), how does it go about setting appropriate performance targets for them, and how challenging are those performance targets?

7   What processes, if any, does the organisation follow for evaluating individual, group, and organisational performance? Are performance evaluations primarily objective, subjective or mixed and how important are formal and informal information and controls in these processes?

8   What rewards — financial and/or non-financial — will managers and other employees gain by achieving performance targets or other assessed aspects of performance (or, conversely, what penalties will they suffer by failing to achieve them)?

9   What specific information flows — feedback and feedforward —, systems and networks has the organisation in place to support the operation of its PMS?

10   What type of use is made of information and of the various control mechanisms in place? Can these uses be characterised in terms of various typologies in the literature? How do controls and their uses differ at different hierarchical levels?

11   How have the PMS altered in the light of the change dynamics of the organisation and its environment? Have the changes in PMS design or use been made in a proactive or reactive manner?

12   How strong and coherent are the links between the components of PMS and the ways in which they are used (as denoted by the previous 11 questions)?

These 12 framework questions relate closely to the central issues faced by contemporary organisations and management accountants in relation to making their strategy operational. In following Ferreira and Otley's evaluative advice when examining an organisation's approach to performance measurement, valuable insights can be gleaned. It is important to see and understand areas where management control systems are in alignment (or vice versa) with organisational strategy. This framework provides insight into areas that can inform evaluators of potential conflicts and the likelihood of dysfunctional behaviour. The 12 questions are schematically presented in figure 14.4.

FIGURE 14.4   Performance management systems framework[12]

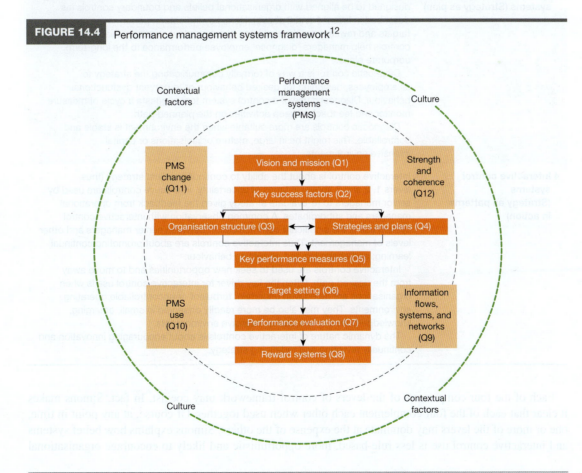

Performance management systems framework developments to Otley's original 1999 contribution have been significantly influenced by Simons' levers of control framework. We discuss the levers of controls in more detail in the following section.

Simons' levers of control framework[13]

In a series of articles[14], Simons articulated his framework which is focused on two key aspects: (1) key *influences* on the nature of the control systems and control system tools (belief systems and boundary systems); and (2) key ways in which the control system tools might be *used* (diagnostic and interactive). These are briefly outlined in table 14.1.

TABLE 14.1   Simons' levers of control summary

Levers of control (The 4Ps of strategy)	Explanation
1 Belief control systems (Strategy as perspective)	Belief systems tell a story of 'what we believe in' or 'what we stand for'. We would expect the culture, mission and values of the organisation to be expressed through the belief system. Belief systems can be formalised in mission statements or informally expressed in management styles.
2 Boundary control systems (Strategy as position)	Boundary systems are about the competitive strategies adopted (cost leadership or differentiation for creating a sustainable advantage), the structural choices made (to delineate territories in which a company or business might seek to be unique) and the rules that direct or channel behaviour. Belief systems can be formalised in policies and work-unit designs. While they can be informally controlled by the CEO or manager oversight function, in large, growing organisations this can become a management challenge. Thus the need for formalised rules, procedures and policies to direct behaviour. Boundary systems help communicate the acceptable level of risk that can be taken by subordinates.
3 Diagnostic control systems (Strategy as plan)	Diagnostic controls are the management accounting and control systems designed to be aligned with organisational beliefs and boundary controls (as described in levers 1 and 2 above). Here, key indicators, performance measures, targets and rewards are developed to direct employee actions. Diagnostic controls help managers 'diagnose' employee performance to the long-term corporate plans. Diagnostic control is a way of formally communicating the strategy to all employees, designing for desired behaviour or to prevent dysfunctional behaviour. Diagnostic use of a control system tool suggests a cycle of measure, monitor and feedback to keep activities on the planned path. Diagnostic controls are more suitable when the environment is stable and controllable. This might be in large, mature organisations or capital intensive environments.
4 Interactive control systems (Strategy as patterns in action)	Interactive control is about the ability to continually adjust strategy (thus, levers 1, 2 and 3 above) in times of uncertainty. Interactive controls are used by senior managers to re-evaluate strategy given the feedback from operational managers and subordinates. A common observation with interactive control system use is the significant communication between senior managers and other levels of management. Thus interactive controls are about promoting continual learning; and observing and correcting behaviour. Interactive controls are used to seek new opportunities and to move away from the desired path. Often the key driver for interactive control use is when organisations are faced with uncertain, turbulent or uncontrollable operating environments. They may also be more readily observed in small, emerging, knowledge-based or low capital intensive environments. The dynamic nature of interactive controls is about encouraging innovation and continually revisiting and redefining strategy.

Each of the four components of the levers of control framework may coexist. In fact, Simons makes it clear that each of the four complement each other when used together. Of course, at any point in time, one or more of the levers may dominate at the expense of the others. Simons explains how belief systems and interactive control use is less rule-based, more opportunistic and likely to encourage organisational learning and innovation. Boundary systems and diagnostic control on the other hand are viewed as being more rule-based and predictable, with a focus on constraint.

Kaplan and Norton's strategy map framework[15]

Kaplan and Norton have significantly influenced the nature of performance measurement systems in organisations, particularly through their work on strategy maps and balanced scorecards (see chapter 19). Our focus here is on their framework demonstrating the links and steps between strategy formulation and the operations of the organisation. This framework is illustrated in figure 14.5.

FIGURE 14.5   Translating strategy into operational plans[16]

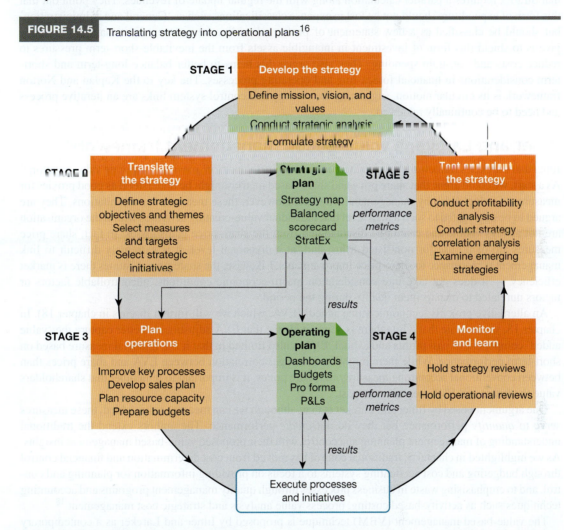

You will be familiar with some of the terms in figure 14.5 from the first part of this text (for example, Stage 3 'Plan operations' links with the budget preparation activities discussed in chapter 6). The strategic themes implicated in stages 1 to 5 of the framework are the focus of the second part of this text (for example, balanced scorecards and profitability analysis). Within the five-step circle are links to the operational tools that are developed and used by the organisation. For example, the strategy map is the starting point for all balanced scorecard projects.

According to Kaplan and Norton, a strategy map describes the process of value creation through a series of cause-and-effect linkages between objectives in the four balanced scorecard perspectives. These perspectives (financial, customer, internal business process, learning and growth), detailed in chapter 19, are about making visible goals relating to financial and customer objectives, value-chain operations and the way an organisation might learn and grow. The strategy map illustrates how a corporate strategy can be sliced into individual, organisation-specific themes, each with its own cause-and-effect relationships. The strategic themes provide a common structure for the varying divisions within the organisation to develop their own maps within the overall organisational picture. They help provide a governance structure that assigns accountability for management actions.

Under the balanced scorecard is 'StratEx' (strategic expenditure). Kaplan and Norton suggest this generally involves investment in intangible assets or assets that require a different form of analysis than for tangible assets (such as property, plant and equipment where discounted cash flow models are most commonly used). StratEx often involves discretionary spending (such as research and development, advertising, promotion, training, customer databases and strategic initiatives) and does not always bear a tight causal relationship with sales and operating levels. Amounts are often difficult to quantify and are frequently determined using a rule-of-thumb (for example, 5 per cent of sales or industry benchmarks).

Because this expenditure requires a judgement call by experience executives, Kaplan and Norton argue that StratEx requires a parallel calculation along with the regular update of revenues. They point out that this form of expenditure should not be lost in expense classifications such as 'General and Administration' but should be classified as a new statement of profit or loss line item. One of the main reasons they give is to shield this form of investment in intangible assets from the inevitable short-term pressures to reduce costs and constrain spending. They also argue this helps to better balance long-term and short-term considerations in financial forecasting and operating processes. The key to the Kaplan and Norton framework is its circular motion, suggesting the strategy and control system links are an iterative process and need to be continually reviewed.

Ittner and Larcker's value-based management framework

Ittner and Larcker's framework[17] poses the question 'How do investors measure corporate value creation?' As a start, we could argue that share price and share-based metrics might be understood as good proxies for measures of value added by management activities. However, these measures have limitations. They are argued to be aggregated to such a high level that individual value-creating activities within the organisation are not always visible and cannot be disentangled from the share price gains/losses. In fact, share price measures are of no use for non-listed firms, and, at a divisional level, it is extremely difficult to link management performance to share-price improvements. Likewise, the share price assumes there is market efficiency — it does not take into consideration macro-economic conditions, uncontrollable factors or factors unrelated to management quality during the period.

An alternative proxy is 'economic value added' (EVA, which we will further discuss in chapter 18). In chapter 18, we indicate that while there is some evidence that EVA adjustments better capture the 'value added' component of past profits and capital, EVA is also limited in that it is a financial measure based on short-term performance. While there might be a stronger correlation between EVA and share prices than between conventional accounting measures and share prices, it is important to remember that shareholders value the future and EVA measures the past.

One argument posed by Ittner and Larcker is that, although we can measure value added, these measures serve to *quantify* performance but they do not *create* performance. The authors extend the traditional understanding of management planning and control with their proposed value-based management insights. As we highlighted in chapter 5, traditional control has moved from cost determination and financial control through budgeting and cost accounting systems to a focus on providing information for planning and control, and to emphasising waste in business processes through quality management programs and accounting techniques such as activity-based costing, process value analysis and strategic cost management.[18]

The value-based management (VBM) technique is proposed by Ittner and Larcker as a contemporary step towards improving management decision making by aligning overall aspirations, decision analysis and management processes and focusing on the drivers of shareholder value. For them, the value-based management framework is about integrating the emerging practices in accounting performance measurement and control into one comprehensive system for performance. This approach focuses on defining organisational strategies around shareholder value creation and implementing information systems to assist value creation while focusing on the underlying 'drivers' of value. It is also about aligning management processes and performance measurement system design to link incentive compensation plans with value creation. This is shown in figure 14.6.

VBM is a discipline that focuses on the holistic management of the organisation. It emphasises the creation of value as defined by the organisation's stakeholders. That is, through *economic value creation* as recognised by markets and owners, *customer value* achieved by delivering the desired goods or services to customers on time and at competitive prices, and *employee value* recognised by employees as substantive and meaningful jobs with commensurate compensation. The entire value chain (see chapter 1) is acknowledged in value-based management including *supplier value* through building strong relationships and ensuring suppliers are managed well and paid on time. The final aspect of VBM is *societal value.* That is, recognising and mitigating both societal and environmental impacts created in the organisation's daily activities.

FIGURE 14.6 Ittner and Larcker's value-based management framework[19]

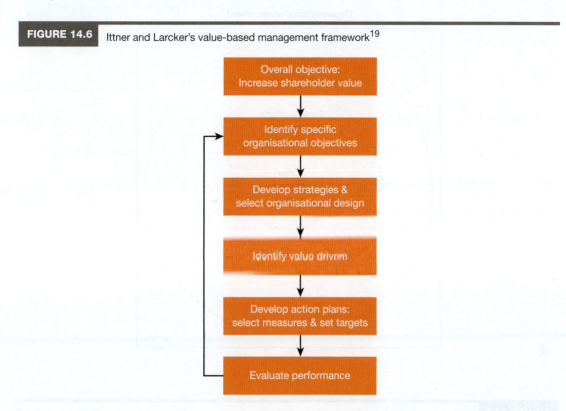

The VBM framework remains consistent with economic models of managerial accounting practice but also incorporates other financial and non-financial accounting developments. The contemporary approaches to management accounting are highlighted throughout the remainder of this chapter. Issues such as budgeting for strategic management purposes, management accounting systems and risk management control, and sustainability accounting are just some of the contemporary topics covered in the second part of this book. These contemporary approaches aim to better manage corporate responsibility and accountability.

Flamholtz's control system framework[20]

Flamholtz views the management accounting and control system within what he refers to as the *organisational control system*. This organisational control system is depicted in figure 14.7.

The organisational control system exists within an organisational environment and contains three key components.

1. *The core control system.* The core control system contains most elements of what we might more readily consider when we think of the management accounting and control system: planning, operations, measurements, feedback, and evaluation and rewards. These parts of the core control system (referred to as *the framework*) are represented in figure 14.8. In effect, if we were to hover over any reasonably sized organisation, we would be able to observe aspects of the core control system in operation. Moreover, these parts operate more or less in a loop and are closely connected.
2. *Organisational structure.* Flamholtz explains that structure can itself function as a form of control as decisions around structure influence the behaviours of organisational members. The organisational structure specifies the reporting hierarchy and the degree of decision autonomy, as evidenced through the degree of decentralisation.
3. *Organisational culture.* Organisational culture can mean many different things. Within his framework, Flamholtz refers to 'culture' to mean the organisational members' values, beliefs and social norms that permeate the organisation. As a consequence, organisational culture may be a control in itself. Moreover, how strong the culture is may influence the type of more formal controls needed within an organisation.

FIGURE 14.7 Schematic representation of an organisational control system[21]

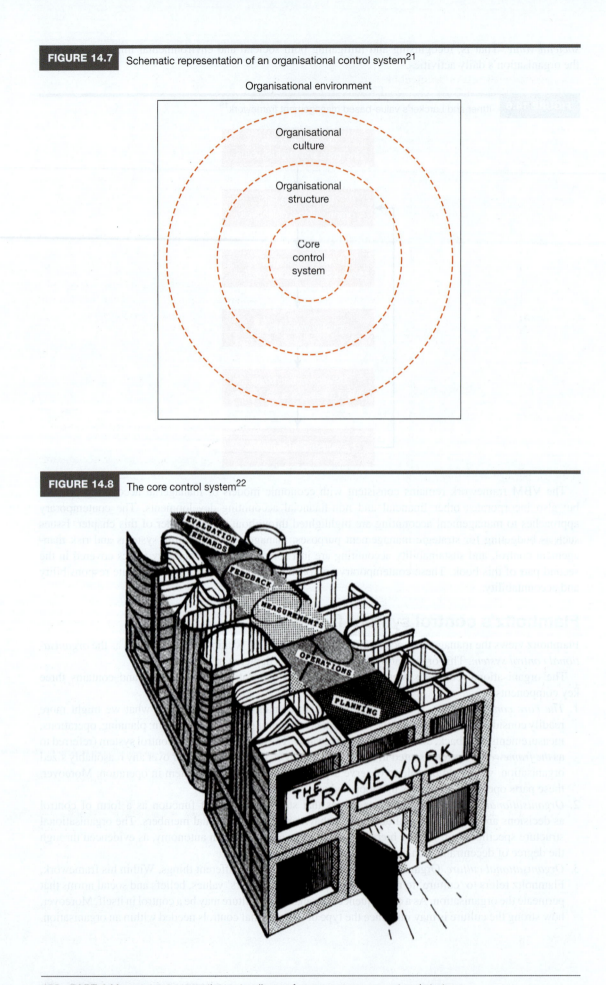

Organisational environment

Organisational
culture

Organisational
structure

Core
control
system

FIGURE 14.8 The core control system[22]

EVALUATION

REWARDS

FEEDBACK

MEASUREMENTS

OPERATIONS

PLANNING

THE FRAMEWORK

Flamholtz identifies four key functions of 'control'.
1. Motivate decisions consistent with organisational goals and objectives.
2. Integrate the efforts of different parts of the organisation.
3. Provide information about the operations, people and processes.
4. Facilitate the implementation of strategic plans.

14.4 Management responsibility and accountability practices

LEARNING OBJECTIVE 14.4 Reflect on the importance of, and techniques associated with, management responsibility and accountability practices.

Responsibility accounting is the process of assigning authority and responsibility to managers of sub-units in the organisation and then measuring and evaluating their performance. Under responsibility accounting, managers are generally held responsible (accountable) only for factors over which they have control. Sometimes this is not the case and managers must rely on good network relationships, particularly when accountability is shared. For example, the assignment of costs from head office may fall outside the control of a manager but may still form part of the manager's performance, and transfer pricing policies (see chapter 18) may result in managers needing to consider other units within the organisation as well as their own.

As organisations grow in size, senior managers have an increasingly difficult time maintaining control and influencing decision making. On the positive side, many organisations benefit from the wide range of expertise among employees. However, as decision making becomes dispersed, mechanisms must be established for measuring, monitoring and motivating decisions throughout the organisation. Responsibility accounting assists by assessing the performance of individual managers and business units against targets and thereby identifying any variances that can then be investigated.

An important principle behind responsibility accounting is that an individual should be held accountable only for performance measures (that is, costs, revenues, quality, production output, market share) over which they have control. In contrast, a business unit's performance should be assessed based on all performance measures attributable to that unit. The determination of where decision-making responsibility sits within an organisation will be dependent on a number of factors — organisational structure (and whether it is centralised or decentralised), the type of knowledge required for decision making, the culture and belief systems of the organisation, and how technology is used.

Of interest for the management control of different organisational structures is the links between organisational structure and management accountability.[23] Figure 14.9 explains these relationships in more detail.

Figure 14.9 demonstrates that the span of attention of a manager relates to those things that the manager is likely to focus on; that is, the manager's *field of view*. Three key issues will drive the nature of the span of attention. Work-unit design is related in part to organisational structure. For example, whether the manager is responsible for a cost centre, profit centre or investment centre (see chapter 18), and the kind of organisational structure in place, such as whether the organisation is structured as functions or divisions.

Span of control relates to the functions and people under the manager's control; that is, where the manager's responsibilities lie. Span of accountability relates to the performance measures for which the manager will be held accountable. Obviously, this will also be influenced by work-unit design. For example, a manager in charge of a cost centre is most likely to have financial measures of performance related to some element of cost performance. When structuring suitable managerial control system tools to guide managerial behaviour and decision making, issues associated with managers' span of attention are an important consideration.

In an article about the problems of organisational structure, Kleinbaum and Tushman[24] argued that organisational structures often encourage 'silos' and as a consequence make collaboration and innovation difficult to achieve. Interestingly, in achieving a suitable and relevant (for example, linked to strategy) structure, organisations may inadvertently create the kind of thinking they are trying to avoid. As outlined above, this all has consequences for managerial attention; if the structure only encourages a focus on the specific work-unit when collaboration across work-units is also important, then the repercussions may be significant. For example, as Kleinbaum and Tushman wonder: how did Time Warner not develop an innovation like iTunes when it had work units that focused on music (Warner Music) and the internet (AOL)? So, what can be done about this problem? One way to try to foster collaboration within rigid organisational structures is to use informal networks within an organisation. This can be achieved by individual managers moving between organisational units, fostering collaboration and innovation. These managers are referred to as *idea brokers*. Of course, if work-unit collaboration is not particularly important, then 'silos' might be fine.

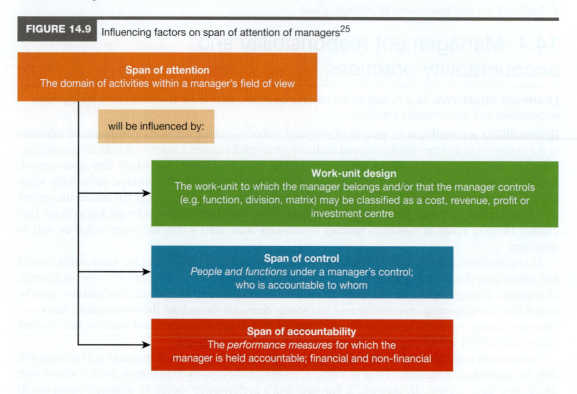

FIGURE 14.9 Influencing factors on span of attention of managers[25]

Strategy, control and remaining chapters

We explore issues associated with strategy and control in the remaining chapters in this part of the book. In chapter 15 we focus on the process of making strategic investment decisions, and how this requires consideration of a range of information types.

For senior managers, accountability often comprises the entire value chain and includes external as well as internal value chain players. In chapters 16 and 17 we explain how techniques such as value chain and supply chain analysis, lean-thinking, just-in-time (JIT) production and managing quality costs assist in management responsibility and accountability. The link between costs and prices has become increasingly important with global competition. In a flattening world, managers and accountants must simultaneously manage both across the entire value chain and within the value chain. Successful organisations continuously improve their cost efficiency, charge competitive prices and focus on long-term organisational strategies. Over the long term, profitable organisations continuously seek ways to become more efficient, reduce costs and improve interactions with suppliers and customers.

Performance evaluation is an essential component of effective management responsibility and accountability practices. Management responsibility differs throughout the organisation, depending on the level of control. Responsibility centres, as explained in chapter 18, are sub-units (segments, divisions, departments) in which managers are accountable for specific types of operating activities. Four common types of responsibility centres are cost centres, revenue centres, profit centres and investment centres. Performance can be evaluated in varying ways and might include financial performance measures such as costs, revenues, profits, return on investment (ROI), EVA or share-based performance measures. As highlighted previously, on their own these measures have limitations.

The balanced scorecard (chapter 19) introduces non-financial performance measurement concepts and helps contribute to accountability and value-based management of organisations. Effective management responsibility and accountability is a part of good management practices. However, when managers are incentivised and highly rewarded for risk taking, dysfunctional behaviour can occur. As highlighted in chapter 20, incentives, rewards and the management of risk are important themes of the twenty-first century. This is particularly so given the severity of many high-profile corporate collapses and global financial crisis. Risk management frameworks address the mitigation of business risk. A significant part of risk management is the appropriate design and implementation of internal control systems to mitigate risk. However, it is important for the management accountant to understand that these systems should be structured to manage, *not* eliminate, risk. Successful companies need to carefully balance management control and risk taking.

Risk management includes issues of social responsibility and environmental concerns. Sustainability management accounting, as explained in chapter 21, is an emerging area for accountants to develop tools that will assist in operationalising actions to enhance organisations' environmental, social and ethical performance. As illustrated in chapter 21, management responsibility and accountability has moved beyond organisational boundaries to include the global society and nature.

SUMMARY

14.1 Understand the changing management accounting and control environment.

- Transformation of management accounting in an environment of increased globalisation
- An increased focus on social, technical and economic factors
- Management accounting and control tools are still evolving

14.2 Distinguish between strategy and control.

Strategy normally relates to a future direction enabling a focus of organisational resources and decision making around a common theme. Strategy may be viewed at:

- the corporate level, and/or
- business unit level

and might include SWOT analysis and/or the use of Porter's competitive forces model.

Control may relate to managerial control and/or managerial control system tools. Management control often encompasses:

- planning what should be done, including strategy and future direction
- coordinating the activities of the organisation
- communication information for decision making
- evaluating information
- determining courses of action, which might include remaining on the current path or might result in new opportunities and a new path/strategy or direction.

Management control may have a decision-influencing and/or decision-facilitating role. Moreover, there is a need to consider both the use of formal and informal controls.

Organisational strategy and managerial control system tools are directly linked.

14.3 Communicate the key components of the important strategic management accounting frameworks.

- Ferreira and Otley's performance management systems framework
- Simons' levers of control framework
- Kaplan and Norton's strategy map framework
- Ittner and Larcker's value-based management framework
- Flamholtz's control system framework

14.4 Reflect on the importance of, and techniques associated with, management responsibility and accountability practices.

Responsibility accounting is the process of assigning authority and responsibility to managers of sub-units and then measuring and evaluating their performance. The span of attention of a manager is influenced by the:

- work-unit design
- span of control
- span of accountability.

KEY TERM

responsibility accounting Process of assigning authority and responsibility to managers of sub-units, and then measuring and evaluating their performance.

SELF-STUDY PROBLEM

SELF-STUDY PROBLEM

Starbucks has become a worldwide phenomenon in coffee. However, over the past few years, Starbucks appears to have stumbled with respect to strategy. For example, lower customer satisfaction suggested the company had moved too far away from its customised coffee experience to one that seemed more focused on efficiencies. Starbucks was also forced to close most of its Australian stores after failing to win over the Australian market.

Required

Using Porter's five forces model, comment on the issues that would have confronted Starbucks senior management with respect to the company's experience in the Australian market.

SOLUTION TO SELF-STUDY PROBLEM

1. *Threat of new entry.* In Australia, the coffee business is very fragmented. Coffee chains such as Gloria Jean's and Starbucks are not as strong as the coffee chains in the United States. There are many small independent operators successfully competing against these companies in Australia. The barriers to entry are low.

2. *Power of suppliers.* Being able to source quality coffee beans and achieve consistent coffee bean supply are important issues for Starbucks. As coffee is a traded commodity, suppliers can be powerful in low supply/high demand situations. Nevertheless, Starbucks is a powerful international player with many stores around the globe. Suppliers would be keen to maintain the volume supply if the price they were receiving from Starbucks is competitive. Moreover, Starbucks presence in the coffee supply chain is significant.

3. *Power of buyers.* Starbucks would have price-sensitive customers. As highlighted previously, there are plenty of local coffee shops for customers to choose from.

4. *Threat of substitutes.* Starbucks, like all coffee stores, has plenty of competitors with substitute products. For example, juice bars (Boost Juice), and other hot beverages competitors such as hot chocolate producers (Max Brenner) or local convenience stores selling soft drinks or water (7-Eleven).

5. *Rivalry among existing competitors.* Strong price competition, no switching costs, industry shrinking or growing (varies), overcapacity (in some areas), important market, introduction of advertising campaigns (coffee cards), service improvements (stock variety to entice customers), aiming to make and be known for 'good quality' coffee (barista talent) all contribute to a dynamic industry, with a range of factors driving success.

QUESTIONS

14.1 Define strategy and differentiate between corporate-level strategy and business-unit level strategy. **LO2**

14.2 Briefly explain the link(s) between strategy and managerial control systems. **LO1, 2**

14.3 What role does management accounting and control information play in developing new strategic directions? **LO3**

14.4 What role does management accounting and control information pay in monitoring the success of the new strategic direction taken by an entity? **LO3**

14.5 Distinguish between diagnostic and interactive use of specific control system tools. **LO3**

14.6 Using examples, explain the meaning of informal controls. **LO2**

14.7 Differentiate between belief systems and boundary systems. **LO3**

14.8 Outline the meaning of responsibility accounting. **LO4**

14.9 Explain the meaning of span of control, span of accountability and span of attention. **LO4**

14.10 What factors would force an organisation such as an airline to review its strategic direction? **LO4**

EXERCISES

14.11 Strategy and control **LO1, 3**

In their 2014 annual report, airline Virgin Australia commented on the strategic direction of the company.[26]

After completing the Game Change Program, the Group commenced Virgin Vision 2017, a strategy to maximise the Group's potential by extracting value from the business. Over the next three years, the Virgin Australia Group focused on:

- capitalising on growth business opportunities
- driving yield enhancement
- implementing a new cost program
- optimising the balance sheet
- setting a new standard in customer experience
- developing people to their full potential.

Required

(a) Using the four components of Simons' levers of control framework, comment briefly on how the management accounting and control system could be used to monitor the performance in achieving the strategic objectives.

(b) Draw on Porter's five forces to explain the competitive issues for Virgin Australia management.

(c) Access the most recent annual report of Virgin Australia. Identify some of the key performance measures used by the airline (and reported externally) to monitor its performance.

14.12 Managerial accountability; span of attention   LO4

Maddy is the divisional manager of the internet technologies division of IT World Ltd. The following information is currently available with respect to her role.

- The internet technologies division is classified as a profit centre.
- Maddy reports to the CEO.
- The internet technologies division is responsible for software development, webpage construction, and IT services and consulting.
- Maddy has four unit-level managers within her division, each in charge of functional profit centres.
- IT World Ltd uses a division-focused set of performance measures. Maddy's primary performance measure relates to the operating profit of the internet technologies division. She is also evaluated on the basis of client satisfaction ratings and employee satisfaction scores.

Required

(a) Comment on the key factors influencing Maddy's span of attention. Consider the influence of work-unit design, span of control and span of accountability.

(b) Assume that IT World Ltd's senior management has decided to alter the performance measures to reflect organisational performance only. How might this influence Maddy's span of attention?

14.13 Levers of control   LO3

Marissa Nafsik founded Mana Consulting (MANA) in 2010. The company has grown from a one-person operation to a rather diverse consulting company specialising in management consulting, technology consulting, particularly with respect to internet technologies, and, more recently, a forensic accounting service. MANA now employs 45 professional staff and 10 administrative staff.

In the early days, Marissa was able to manage the company by meeting with staff on a one-on-one basis, holding lots of social gatherings and developing a strong culture of friendliness and hard work. The work seemed to get done with minimal formal monitoring of staff. Marissa was also very careful about who she hired, as it was important to her that new employees would adapt quickly to the company's culture.

Of course, as the company has grown, Marissa has found it increasingly difficult to use her personal touch like in the early days. As the company grew, she thought it best to document the kind of culture she wanted to preserve. Each employee was provided a copy of the MANA WAY as she called it. Still, as the company continued to grow, Marissa felt she was losing control. She found it more difficult to spend time with her staff and found herself constantly in her office planning, tendering for new consulting work, speaking with clients about work programs and the like.

Moreover, since the forensic accounting business has started to take off, she has restructured the company into three divisions with a consulting manager for each division. She thought her best option for influencing the managers' performance was to set some key targets relating to revenue within each division as well as to costs. She also set some expectations about client and employee satisfaction.

What was worrying her now was whether she needed to rethink her negative attitude towards incentives and bonuses. She sat back in her chair and reflected. She was proud of what she had created but, in some ways, longed for the early days.

Required

(a) Using Simons' levers of control, analyse the case — identify and provide evidence of the existence of each of Simons' levers of control.

(b) Do you have any suggestions for how Marissa should proceed?

PROBLEMS

14.14 Managerial control systems; levers of control[27]　　　　　　　　　　　　　　LO3

Unilever is a large Dutch–British consumer product manufacturer with sites around the world including Australia and New Zealand. Unilever's product range comprises well-known consumer product brands including *personal hygiene* products — Dove, Pond's, Vaseline, Sunsilk, Lynx, Rexona; *laundry detergents* — Radiant, Surf, Lux; and *food and nutrition* products — Bertolli (olive oil), Amora (salad dressings), Lipton (tea), Streets (ice cream, with Magnum their number 1 brand) and Knorr (Unilever's number 1 brand worldwide for flavourings and gravy).

Recently, Unilever's management has re-evaluated its strategic direction, and has reorganised some of its business units and reduced its workforce. It also launched six global strategic initiatives, one of them relating to *'business simplification'*.

In response to the global strategic initiative, Jean-Lin Toulemonde (Unilever Australasia chairman) launched a 'radical business simplification program at Unilever, designed to eliminate unnecessary work, make people more effective, and lift the company's business performance'. Jean-Lin has a strong belief in business that 'simple is often best' and has looked to simplify things wherever possible.

> If you ask yourself whether you can imagine an organisation that is successful, responsive, fun to work at, full of motivated people and that is also very bureaucratic, the answer is clear: you can't. The good news is your people can't either! Bureaucratic procedures develop slowly but inexorably. I use the analogy of the street signs you see on Sydney streets — no doubt each of those sign placements made sense at one time, but the aggregate effect now is often chaos. Businesses need a periodic spring-cleaning, if they are to keep working effectively.

> Jean-Lin considered that part of that complexity came from the nature of the business.

> Unilever operate in many markets, with many product categories and many brands. In that type of environment it's easy to end up trying to do too many things, rather than doing fewer things better. It's easy to become over-stretched, from both a process and resources point of view, and end up wasting opportunities.

He explained how the senior management team called for a more focused approach to fit with Unilever's overall strategy 'which is essentially about fewer, but bigger brands, and fewer, but more important activities'. He explained how they also identified problems with the Unilever organisational structure. They looked hard at the value-chain processes within Unilever to see where they could simplify them.

They also evaluated their performance measurement control systems (PMCS). Jean-Lin argued that 'if you measure everything that moves in your business, you may simply be complicating your business. We had a concept of "loose versus tight" controls — let things happen in the business, don't try to control everything, and trust our people to deliver the results. You don't need a lot of additional measures and KPIs [key performance indicators] — you simply need to measure whether you are achieving your original objectives'.

He thought the biggest concern for divisional managers related to the delegation of control. He explained the questions coming from this layer of senior management was 'are you really prepared to give me responsibility and resources to simplify the way I operate, and will you punish me if I make mistakes?' Once we convinced people we were serious, and that mistakes would not be treated unreasonably, then people became enthusiastic and prepared to take risks.

Required

(a) Jean-Lin has provided a brief insight of management control at Unilever. Drawing on this insight, evaluate the role of performance measurement and control at Unilever. Use Simons' levers of control to help guide your response.

(b) How can performance measurement and control systems help with the implementation of Unilever's organisational strategy?

14.15 Strategy and control　　　　　　　　　　　　　　　　　　　　　　　　　　LO2, 4

Informal networks (such as the use of idea brokers and specific management groups) are one way of overcoming a lack of collaboration and innovation.

Required

Drawing on any of the five strategy and control frameworks outlined in the chapter, explain how organisations could use managerial control systems to help overcome a lack of collaboration and innovation.

ENDNOTES

1. This discussion is based on the work of Friedman, T 2005, *The world is flat*, Farrar, Straus & Giroux, New York; Fung, V, Fung, W & Wind, Y 2008, *Competing in a flat world: building enterprises for a flat world*, Wharton School Publishing, Pearson Education, New Jersey; Shank, JK 2006, 'Strategic cost management: upsizing, downsizing, and rightsizing', *Contemporary Issues in Management Accounting*, March, pp. 355–79; Wickramasinge, D & Allawatage, C 2007, *Management accounting change: approaches and perspectives*, Routledge, London and New York.
2. Simmonds, K 1981, 'Strategic management accounting', *Management Accounting* (UK), vol. 59, iss. 4, pp. 26–9.
3. Porter, M 1980, *Competitive strategy*, New York: Free Press.
4. Johnson, HT & Kaplan, RS 1987, *Relevance lost: the rise and fall of management accounting*, Harvard Business School Press, Boston, Massachusetts.
5. Cokins, G 2013, Top 7 trends in management accounting, Parts 1 and 2, *Strategic Finance*, December 2013, January 2014. Institute of Management Accountants, US.
6. These works include Porter (1980); Porter, M 1985, *Competitive advantage: creating and sustaining superior performance*, New York: Free Press; Porter, M 2008, 'The five forces that shape competitive strategy', *Harvard Business Review*, January, pp. 78–92.
7. From Porter, M 2008.
8. Adapted from Anthony, R & Govindarajan, VJ 2004, *Management control systems* 11e, McGraw Hill.
9. Much of this discussion is based on the work of Otley, D 1999, 'Performance management: a framework for management control systems research', *Management Accounting Research*, vol. 10, pp. 363–82 and Berry, AJ, Coad, AF, Harris, DT & Stringer, C 2009, 'Emerging themes in management control: a review of recent literature', *The British Accounting Review*, vol. 41, iss. 1, pp. 2–20.
10. Ferreira, A & Otley, D 2009, 'The design and use of performance management systems: an extended framework for analysis', *Management Accounting Research*, vol. 20, pp. 263–82.
11. Ferreira and Otley 2009.
12. Ferreira and Otley 2009, p. 268.
13. Much of this section is based on the work of Simons including Simons, R 1994, 'How new top managers use control systems as levers of strategic renewal', *Strategic Management Journal*, vol. 15, pp. 169–89; Simons, R 1995, *Levers of control*, Harvard Business School Press. Also see Simons, R 2000, *Performance measurement and control systems for implementing strategy*, Prentice-Hall.
14. Nixon, W & Burns, J 2005, 'Introduction: management control in the 21st century', *Management Accounting Research*, vol. 16, pp. 260–68.
15. Based on the work of Kaplan, R & Norton, D 2008, *Strategy maps: converting intangible assets to tangible outcomes*, Harvard Business School Press.
16. Kaplan and Norton 2008.
17. Ittner, CD & Larcker, DF 2001, 'Assessing empirical research in managerial accounting: a value-based management perspective', *Journal of Accounting and Economics*, vol. 32, iss. 1–3, pp. 349–410.
18. Ittner and Larcker 2001, pp. 2–4.
19. Ittner and Larcker 2001.
20. Flamholtz, E 1996, 'Effective organizational control: A framework, applications and implications', *European Management Journal*, vol. 14, no. 6, December, pp. 596–611.
21. Adapted from Flamholtz, E 1996, 'Effective organizational control: A framework, applications and implications', *European Management Journal*, vol. 14, no. 6, December, p. 599.
22. Flamholtz, E 1996, 'Effective organizational control: A framework, applications and implications', *European Management Journal*, vol. 14, no. 6, December, p. 596.
23. This section draws on the work of Simons R 2000, *Performance measurement and control systems for implementing strategy*, Prentice-Hall.
24. Kleinbaum, A & Tushman, M 2008, 'Informal networks key to thinking outside silo', *Australian Business Intelligence*, 4 August.
25. This draws on the work of Simons 2000, pp. 50–3.
26. Virgin Australia 2014, *Annual report 2014*, p. 7.
27. Toulemonde, JL 2010, 'Simple is best: business simplification at Unilever', *CEO Forum*, www.ceoforum.com.au.

ACKNOWLEDGEMENTS

Photo 14A: © Kzenon / Shutterstock.com

Figure 14.1: © Porter, ME 1998, *On Competition*. Boston: Harvard Business School Press, 1998.

Figure 14.3 and 14.4: © Ferreira and Otley 2009. 'The design and use of performance management systems: An extended framework for analysis', *Management Accounting Research*, vol. 20, iss. 4, pp. 263–282.

Figure 14.5: © Kaplan and Norton 2008. *The Execution Premium: Linking Strategy to Operations for Competitive Advantage*. Boston: Harvard Business School Press.

Figure 14.6 and 14.7: © Ittner, CD and Larcker, DF 2001, 'Assessing empirical research in managerial accounting: a value-based management perspective', *Journal of Accounting and Economics*, vol. 32, iss. 1–3, pp. 349–410.

Figure 14.8: © The core control system, first-page figure from Flamholtz, E 1996, 'Effcctive organizational control: a framework, applications, and implications', *European Management Journal*, vol. 14, no. 6, December, p. 596.

CHAPTER 15

Capital budgeting and strategic investment decisions

LEARNING OBJECTIVES

After studying this chapter, you should be able to:

15.1 communicate the process of capital investment decisions

15.2 recognise and apply the relevant cash flows in capital investment decisions

15.3 perform and interpret net present value (NPV) analysis

15.4 understand the uncertainties of NPV analysis

15.5 reflect on alternative methods (internal rate of return, payback, accrual accounting rate of return) used for capital investment decisions

15.6 discuss additional issues to be considered for strategic investment decisions

15.7 communicate how income taxes affect capital investment decision cash flows

15.8 understand how real and nominal methods are used to address inflation in an NPV analysis.

IN BRIEF

Managers periodically make decisions about long-term investments for new projects or replacement of old assets. These decisions focus on creating long-term value consistent with organisational strategies. The outcomes from these decisions are generally more uncertain than shorter-term decisions because we forecast further into the future. In addition, the time value of money becomes important. However, there are also long-term investments that might be classified as strategic investments. In these circumstances, standard evaluation models may not be sufficient.

15.1 Capital investment decisions

LEARNING OBJECTIVE 15.1 Communicate the process of capital investment decisions.

Compared to operating decisions that primarily affect short-term activities, investment decisions have long-term effects. As we learned in chapters 1 and 14, managers develop strategies from the entity's vision and core competencies. These strategies are aimed at the organisation's overall purpose, which usually includes long-term profitability.

Capital budgeting

Capital budgeting is a process that managers use when they choose among investment opportunities that have cash flows occurring over a number of years. These opportunities commonly fall into three categories.

1. *Operational capital investment decisions* affect only part of an entity's operations, have easily predictable lives and represent relatively small capital outlays for an entity. These investments commonly relate to the replacement of existing assets such as machinery or equipment to maintain or enhance capacity or efficiency.
2. *Investment decisions to comply with regulatory, safety, health and environmental requirements* are acquisitions that cannot be deferred or rejected without incurring potentially huge penalties in the future such as the threat of action by regulatory authorities.
3. *Strategic capital investment decisions* affect all or a considerable part of an entity's operations, have uncertain lives and require large investments. These investments are more likely to impact the strategy of the organisation. By their very nature, they are more difficult to evaluate. The evaluation of these kinds of investments will be explored a little later.

For the moment, the capital budgeting tools explored below are applicable to operational capital budgeting decisions and investments to comply with regulatory requirements.

The objective of capital budgeting is to increase the long-term value of the organisation. Figure 15.1 summarises the steps in the capital budgeting process. The process is similar to that for non-routine operating decisions (chapter 13). The major difference is that capital budgeting decisions affect cash flows in future years. Therefore, the **time value of money**, which refers to the idea that a dollar received today is worth more than a dollar received in the future, is an important factor. Because of its importance, we will learn analysis techniques that allow managers to account for the time value of money when evaluating capital budget decisions.

Decision alternatives

Entities identify new projects, products and services through a variety of methods. Individuals, teams and whole departments are responsible for identifying future investment opportunities. Organisational strategies are reflected in long-term decisions about products, services and acquisitions of new business segments. For example, organisations that maintain reputations for low-cost, high-quality products want to invest in new technology to improve quality while reducing cost.

FIGURE 15.1	Process for addressing capital budgeting decisions

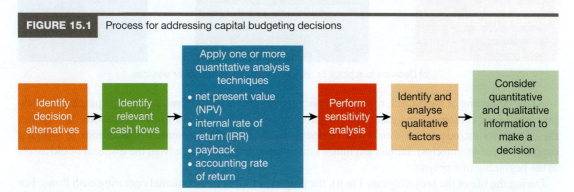

When deciding whether to accept or reject proposals, managers analyse capital budgeting projects as if they were stand-alone projects. However, they may face capital constraints so that accepting one project would eliminate another. In these cases, alternative investments are commonly analysed simultaneously so that they can be compared.

15.2 Relevant cash flows

LEARNING OBJECTIVE 15.2 Recognise and apply the relevant cash flows in capital investment decisions.

The process of identifying relevant cash flows for capital investment decisions is similar to the process for any other type of decision. Relevant cash flows must arise in the future, and differ among decision alternatives (possible courses of action).

Figure 15.2 presents timelines and lists of common types of cash flows for two different types of capital investment decisions: new product or process development, and asset replacement decisions. Cash flows must be estimated for all future periods affected by the potential investment. We usually begin by creating a timeline to help us think about the nature and timing of relevant cash flows.

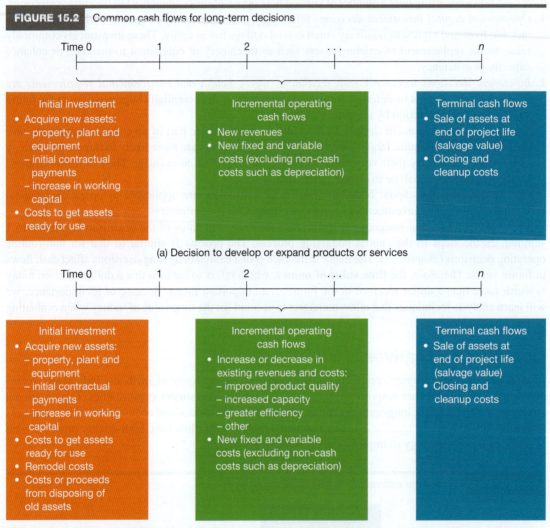

FIGURE 15.2 Common cash flows for long-term decisions

At the beginning of the project, time 0, the entity faces initial cash outflows such as the purchase of new property, plant, equipment and other costs required to get assets ready for use in operations. Sometimes these outflows include initial contractual payments (such as signing bonuses) or additions to working capital (such as inventories). Initial cash inflows or outflows may also come from the disposal of old assets at the beginning of a project.

During the life of the project (years 1 to n), the project has annual incremental operating cash flows. For a new or expanded product or service, these cash flows may include new revenues as well as new fixed and variable costs. When replacing or reorganising assets, revenues and costs may increase or decrease because of improved product quality, increased capacity or greater efficiency.

Any terminal cash flows appear at the end of the project's life (year n). Terminal cash flows typically include proceeds from the sale of assets at the end of the project (the salvage value). However, assets such as equipment may be obsolete and have zero salvage value. Some projects require terminal cash outflows, such as the costs to reinstate the quality of land (called land reclamation) at the end of a mining operation.

In this chapter, we learn the four quantitative analysis techniques listed in figure 15.1 for analysing potential investment projects. The first two methods — net present value (NPV) and internal rate of return (IRR) — explicitly take into account the time value of money, making them preferred methods. However, many managers still use the other, less-preferred methods — payback and accrual accounting rate of return. Therefore, we introduce all of these methods and present the advantages and disadvantages of each.

15.3 Net present value (NPV) method

LEARNING OBJECTIVE 15.3 Perform and interpret net present value (NPV) analysis.

In business, we need to value a project today but the associated cash flows occur in the future. Therefore, we discount the future dollars to determine their value in today's dollars. In appendix 15A of this chapter you will find tables with factors that you multiply by cash flows to determine either a **future value** (the amount received in the future for a given number of years at a given interest rate) for a given investment today, or a **present value** (the value in today's dollars of a sum received in the future).

Suppose you want to buy a $20 000 sports car two years from now. Assume you can invest money today and earn a rate of return of 10 per cent per year. How much would you have to invest today so that in two years you will have $20 000? In other words, what present value is needed to create a future value of $20 000 at an annual interest rate of 10 per cent? To calculate the present value, we multiply the future value ($20 000) by the present value factor for 10 per cent and two time periods. Using table 15A.1 for present value of $1, locate the 10% column and go down to the row representing 2 periods. The factor is 0.826. Multiply this factor by the future value of $20 000. You need $16 520 today to have enough money to buy the car in two years.

Present value of a series of cash flows

Managers are often involved in evaluating projects with different time horizons. One project might end in 5 years and another in 10 years. The future values of such projects are not strictly comparable, because a dollar received 5 years from now is not worth the same as a dollar received 10 years from now. For this and other reasons, the cash flows for projects are generally converted to their present values. The projects can then be compared on a common basis.

The **net present value method (NPV)** determines whether an organisation would be better off investing in a project based on the net amount of discounted cash flows for the project. The net present value of a project is calculated as:

$$NPV = \sum_{t=0}^{n} \frac{\text{Expected cash flow}_t}{(1 + r)^t}$$

where t = time period (years)

n = life of the project

r = discount rate (an annual percentage rate expressed in decimal form)

The expected cash flows include the initial investment, incremental operating cash flows and terminal cash flows. If the NPV is positive, the project is generally considered acceptable because it is expected to increase the entity's value. If investment resources are limited, invest in the project(s) having the highest NPV. Following is an example of the NPV method.

Suppose Gordon wants to convert 30 000 square metres of a building he owns into a café space that will attract local university students. The initial investment is $1 400 000. Gordon expects to rent the café space for $1 per square metre per month, and to pay a management company fees representing 15 per cent of rents. He forecasts that property taxes and insurance will be about $30 000 per year.

Therefore, the incremental cash flows are $276 000 = [$1 per m^2 × 30 000 m^2 × 12 months) × (1 − 0.15)] − $30 000.

Gordon expects to be able to sell the café business at the end of 10 years for $400 000. (We will ignore income taxes for these calculations.) Gordon's discount rate is 14 per cent. The timeline and cash flows for this project are shown in figure 15.3.

FIGURE 15.3   Timeline and cash flows for Gordon's café business

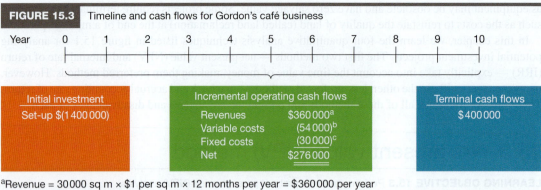

^aRevenue = 30 000 sq m × $1 per sq m × 12 months per year = $360 000 per year
^bManagement fee = $360 000 × 15% = $54 000
^cProperty tax and insurance

The total discounted cash flow after the initial investment is the sum of individual present values, as follows.

Period	Interest rate	Present value factor (PVF)	Cash flow	Discounted cash flow
1	14%	0.877	$276 000	$ 242 052
2	14	0.769	276 000	212 244
3	14	0.675	276 000	186 300
4	14	0.592	276 000	163 392
5	14	0.519	276 000	143 244
6	14	0.456	276 000	125 856
7	14	0.400	276 000	110 400
8	14	0.351	276 000	96 876
9	14	0.308	276 000	85 008
10	14	0.270	276 000	74 520
terminal value	14	0.270	400 000	108 000
		Total discounted cash flows		$1 547 892

Notice that the incremental operating cash flows during years 1 to 10 are identical. In other words, Gordon expects to receive an annuity of $276 000 per year for 10 years, and in year 10 he also receives the terminal cash flow value of $400 000.

In the case of an annual annuity (that is, equal net cash flows each year), we can simplify the present value calculation using the present value of an ordinary annuity (PVFA) of $1 factor from table 15A.2 in appendix 15A.

$$PV = \$276\,000 \times (PVFA\ 10\ years,\ 14\%) + \$400\,000 \times (PVF\ 10\ years,\ 14\%)$$
$$= \$276\,000 \times 5.216 + \$400\,000 \times 0.270$$
$$= \$1\,439\,616 + \$108\,000$$
$$= \$1\,547\,616$$

Notice that we should obtain the same present value for the project cash flows regardless of the method we use (the difference between $1 547 892 and $1 547 616 is due to rounding). However, if we are performing these calculations manually, we can often save time by using the annuity table.

Net present value of a project

Once we calculate the present value of a series of cash flows for Gordon's project, we can compare the net present value to the investment amount because both amounts are now valued in today's dollars. We use the following formula to calculate NPV for Gordon's project:

$$NPV = \text{Initial investment cash outflow} + PV\ \text{of cash inflows}$$
$$= -\$1\,400\,000 + \$1\,574\,616$$
$$= \$174\,616$$

At the end of 10 years, we estimate that Gordon will have realised $174 616 in today's dollars. Because this NPV amount is greater than zero, the general rule is that Gordon would want to invest in this project.

If Gordon was considering more than one investment, he could calculate the profitability index for each project. The **profitability index** is the ratio of the present value of the cash inflows to the present value of the investment cash outflows. The decision rule for a solitary investment is that the investment should be undertaken if the index is equal to or greater than 1. For example, Gordon's profitability index would be:

$$\text{Profitability index} = \frac{\text{Present value of cash inflows}}{\text{Present value of investment cash outflows}} = \frac{\$1\,574\,616}{\$1\,400\,000} = 1.125$$

If Gordon was comparing a number of different projects and could not undertake all of them, he would consider both today's dollar amount and the profitability index. The profitability index and the NPV method always accept and reject the same project, but the index allows managers to rank projects according to their profitability. It provides a simple way to identify which projects are expected to earn a higher return.

Identifying a reasonable discount rate

A discount rate, r, must be selected to apply the NPV formula. The **discount rate** is the interest rate that is used across time to reduce the value of future dollars to today's dollars. Many decision makers simply set the discount rate at the entity's **weighted average cost of capital**, which is the weighted average rate for the costs of the various sources of financing such as debt and equity. However, this method ignores variations in risk among projects. If a project involves little risk, then a lower discount rate might be appropriate. Conversely, a higher discount rate is appropriate for projects having higher risk.

Judgement is required to incorporate an estimate of project risk. One way to think about project risk is to consider the return on other investment opportunities that appear to be of similar risk. For example, the share market has returned, on average, about 11 per cent across time. We can think about how the risk of a particular project compares with the risk of investing long term in the share market. If the project seems more (less) risky than investing in the market, a discount rate greater (less) than 11 per cent might be appropriate.

15.4 Uncertainties and sensitivity analysis

LEARNING OBJECTIVE 15.4 Understand the uncertainties of NPV analysis.

When we perform NPV analysis, the general rule is to accept the project if NPV is greater than zero. Many assumptions are built into this general rule. For example, we assume that we know the:
- cost of initial investment
- timing and dollar amounts of incremental revenues and costs
- terminal cash flow values
- project life
- appropriate discount rate.

However, we cannot know any of these factors with absolute certainty. Also, uncertainties grow with the number of years being forecast; a 15-year project has more uncertainties than one completed in five years.

Cash flow uncertainties

The preceding illustration for Gordon's café business decision includes little uncertainty about the initial investment cash flows. Gordon knows for certain the set-up cost of his building and the market value of the space. He also negotiates a final bid with a building contractor for converting the space into café areas. Some uncertainty may be involved in the cost of renovation. As long as the specific nature of the renovations are known and can be completed fairly quickly before costs change, the cost estimate from the contractor should be reasonably close to the final cost. However, renovation costs of Gordon's building could rise dramatically if contractors discover unforeseen problems, such as asbestos that must be removed.

We always encounter uncertainty when estimating future revenues, costs and terminal cash flow values. However, our ability to accurately estimate cash flows decreases as we forecast further into the future. Long timeframes reduce our ability to anticipate customer tastes, changes in technology, productivity, competition, availability of resources and changes in regulation. For example, certain entities (such as healthcare providers that provide services covered by Medicare) rely heavily on reimbursement from the government.

Changes in reimbursement rates or changes in the basis of reimbursement greatly affect the expected revenues of these organisations. As another example, unexpected spikes in petrol and diesel prices affect transportation entities and the organisations that use them, such as freight distributors and grocery stores.

Estimating cash flows for projects involving new products or services is more difficult than for projects involving changes or expansions of existing products and services. Revenues must sometimes be based on a market that does not currently exist. It is nearly impossible to anticipate all potential costs. Substantial errors are likely in these types of predictions.

Project life and discount rate uncertainties

The expected life of a project is also uncertain. Difficulties in estimating the life of a project are often related to difficulties in estimating revenues and costs. Managers are likely to continue a project if it is profitable. The reverse is true if the project is unprofitable. Managers may also change how they define an organisation's core competencies. Such changes increase or decrease the strategic importance of a project, leading to an extension or cancellation of the project.

Several factors affect the discount rate for NPV analysis including interest rates, inflation and the riskiness of the project. However, none of these factors are known, and the length of time for capital projects increases the uncertainty.

Estimation bias

Because of the many uncertainties involved, managers use considerable judgement in making capital project estimates. However, those responsible for forming the estimates are often the ones who originated the idea for the project. Intentionally or not, these managers are likely to form estimates that favour adoption of the project. In addition, they are more likely to fail to identify all possible project costs than to anticipate costs that will not occur — another estimation bias that favours project adoption.

Sensitivity analysis

Sensitivity analysis helps managers evaluate how their NPV results would change with variations in the input data. Spreadsheets enable the discount rate, cash flows and any other underlying assumptions to be easily varied to consider alternate outcomes. Decision makers can then consider the results of alternative scenarios under different sets of assumptions (see comprehensive example 1). For example, what is the change in NPV if we reduce our revenue estimates by 10 per cent? What if we increase the discount rate by 1 per cent? What if the terminal cash flow value is zero? The sensitivity of results to variations in assumptions helps managers evaluate the risk of investments.

COMPREHENSIVE EXAMPLE 1

Net present value and sensitivity analysis

Gordon has a basement space in his building that would be a suitable food storage area for one of the cafés because it has no windows. One of Gordon's potential tenants offered to rent the space from Gordon for $60 000 per year, with an increase of $2000 after three years. However, Gordon would like to open a health club to serve the tenants in his building, people living in the neighbourhood as well as staff and students who attend the nearby university.

Relevant cash flows and timeline

Gordon hires a consultant to gather information about the project and to recommend a plan of action. The fee for this service is $5000. The following list includes the relevant information the consulting entity estimates for the project.

1. The cost of renovation and new equipment that will be purchased is $650 000. The terminal cash flow value is estimated at $100 000 after five years.
2. Promotion costs to advertise the club will be $120 000 for the first year and $50 000 per year thereafter.

3. The revenues for the health club are estimated to be $300 000 in the first year, $400 000 in the second, and $500 000 in the third, fourth and fifth years.
4. The operating costs for the health club are estimated to be $200 000 for the first year and $130 000 for each of the following years.

Gordon sets up a timeline, shown in figure 15.4. Notice that he ignores sunk costs (the fee paid to the consulting entity) and includes opportunity costs (forgone rent).

FIGURE 15.4   Timeline and cash flows for Gordon's health club project

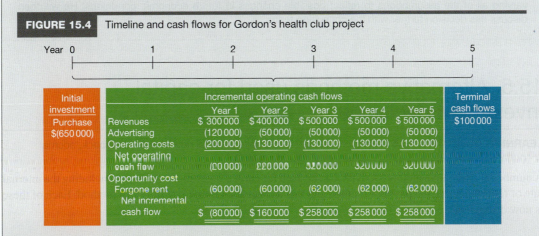

NPV analysis

Gordon sets up a spreadsheet as shown in figure 15.5. He organises the spreadsheet with an input section so that any of the assumptions made for the NPV analysis can be easily varied in performing a sensitivity analysis, and uses a 10 per cent discount rate. He includes a cell reference (B13) for changes in revenues. Based on these NPV calculations, Gordon expects to realise $1851 in today's dollars, over and above the investment amount of $650 000, if he invests in the health club.

FIGURE 15.5   NPV calculations for Gordon's health club

	A	B	C	D	E
1	Gordon's Health Club Project				
2	Assumptions				
3	Discount rate	10%		Teminal value	$100,000
4	Initial investment	$650,000			
5	Cash flows				
6	Period	Revenues	Operating costs	Advertising	Forgone rent
7	1	$300,000	$200,000	$120,000	$60,000
8	2	$400,000	$130,000	$50,000	$50,000
9	3	$500,000	$130,000	$50,000	$62,000
10	4	$500,000	$130,000	$50,000	$62,000
11	5	$500,000	$130,000	$50,000	$62,000
12	Change to assumptions for sensitivity analysis:				
13	Change revenues	0%			
14					
15					
16	PV calculations				
17		Net cash flows	Discounted		
18	1	($80,000)	($72,727)		
19	2	$160,000	$132,231		
20	3	$258,000	$193,839		
21	4	$258,000	$176,217		
22	5	$258,000	$160,198		
23	Total discounted operating CF		$589,759		
24	Terminal value				
25	5	$100,000	$62,092		
26					
27	NPV				
28	Operating CF	$589,759			
29	Terminal value	$62,092			
30	Less				
31	Investment	($650,000)			
32	NPV	$1,851			

Examples of Excel formulas:
   Net cash flow in cell B18: = (1 + $B$13)*B7 − (C7 + D7 + E7)
   Discounted cash flow in cell C18: = −PV($B$3, A18,, B18)

When Gordon reviews his spreadsheet calculations with the consultants, they indicate some uncertainty about the assumptions. The consulting team is concerned that the revenue estimates might be too high. The building is located in an older part of town, and people might not want to walk in the neighbourhood at night to get to the club. They suggest that Gordon reduce the revenues by 5 per cent for sensitivity analysis. He enters –5% in the appropriate input cell. With this drop in revenues, he would incur a $79 696 loss over the five-year life of the project. Gordon decides to develop a series of spreadsheets varying all of the assumptions to reflect possible changes in future economic conditions. He will then discuss this decision further with the consulting team.

15.5 Alternative methods used for capital investment decisions

LEARNING OBJECTIVE 15.5 Reflect on alternative methods (internal rate of return, payback, accrual accounting rate of return) used for capital investment decisions.

A number of alternative methods to NPV can be used for capital investment decisions, including the internal rate of return method, the payback method and the accrual accounting rate of return method. Each of these is now discussed.

Internal rate of return

The **internal rate of return (IRR)** method determines the discount rate necessary for the present value of the discounted cash flows to be equal to the investment. Therefore, the IRR represents the investment's 'own' rate of return as opposed to the NPV, which is determined by the cash flows being benchmarked against a set return. In other words, the method solves for the discount rate at which a project's NPV equals zero. The calculation of IRR is similar to NPV analysis in that it is based on discounted cash flows. In the NPV analysis, we assumed a discount rate and solved for the NPV. In the case of IRR, we search for the discount rate that results in an NPV of zero. This discount rate is the internal rate of return.

IRR calculations

Earlier in the chapter, Gordon analysed a decision to invest in a café space targeted towards students. Suppose he is now trying to decide whether to install coin-operated vending machines outside the café. He knows that students eat a lot of snack foods, but the closest 24-hour convenience store is eight blocks away. Gordon thinks that the students will purchase beverages and food from vending machines if he installs them. The equipment will cost $5000 and have a useful life of five years. He expects to net $1500 in annual cash flows from operating the machines (revenues minus food and maintenance costs). The equipment will have no terminal cash flow value at the end of five years. Gordon thinks it could be a good investment but he would like to know what his expected rate of return would be. The cash flows for this project are shown in figure 15.6.

| FIGURE 15.6 | Timeline and cash flows for Gordon's coin-operated equipment project |

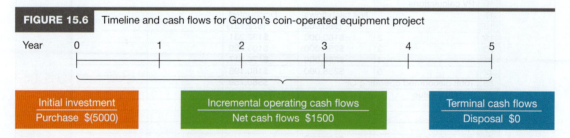

Gordon wants to find the discount rate at which the NPV equals zero. Recall that the NPV is calculated by subtracting the initial investment from the NPV of cash inflows. Because the cash inflows are uniform across time, Gordon can use the present value of an ordinary annuity of $1 table (see table 15A.2 in appendix 15A). Then, the IRR is the interest rate ($X\%$) at which:

$$\text{Initial investment} = \text{NPV of cash inflows}$$
$$\$5000 = \$1500 \times (\text{PVFA 5 years}, X\%)$$

Solving for the present value of an annuity factor:

$$(\text{PVFA 5 years}, X\%) = \$5000 \div \$1500 = 3.333$$

Gordon uses the table to locate the interest rate ($X\%$) at which the present value of an annuity factor is approximately equal to 3.333 for a time period of five years. Finding the row for five time periods, he sees that the factor for 15 per cent is 3.352. This factor is very close to 3.333, so he concludes that the IRR is close to 15 per cent. This return is higher than the discount rate he used to calculate the NPV of the cafe project, and this project is probably less risky, so Gordon decides it is a worthwhile investment.

The approach using the present value of an ordinary annuity of $1 table can be applied only when the cash flows from a project are uniform over time. For uneven cash inflows, such as for Gordon's cafe project, a trial-and-error approach may be used along with the present value table. We first try a discount rate and calculate the NPV of the project using that discount rate. If the NPV is greater than zero, we try a larger discount rate; if it is less than zero, we decrease the discount rate.

We can easily calculate a more precise IRR using a spreadsheet. Using Excel's IRR function (see figure 15.7), Gordon learns that the IRR for his coin-operated machine project is 15.24 per cent. When he calculates the NPV using the IRR as the discount rate, the NPV is zero.

FIGURE 15.7	IRR for Gordon's coin-operated equipment project

	A	B
1	Net cash flows:	
2	Time 0	($5,000)
3	Year 1	$1,500
4	Year 2	$1,500
5	Year 3	$1,500
6	Year 4	$1,500
7	Year 5	$1,500
8		
9	IRR	15.24%
10	NPV	$0

Excel formula to calculate internal rate of return in cell B9: = IRR(B2:B7)
Excel formula to calculate net present value in cell B10: = B2 + NPV(B9, B3:B7)

Comparison of NPV and IRR methods

Certainly, without spreadsheets, the NPV method is computationally simpler than the internal rate of return method. Determining IRR can be time-consuming, particularly for projects returning uneven cash flows. The use of a spreadsheet reduces the effort considerably. However, if several projects are being analysed, their NPVs can be summed to determine the NPV for that group or portfolio of projects, whereas IRR can be neither summed nor averaged.

An important difference between the two methods is that the IRR method assumes cash inflows can be reinvested to earn the same return that the project would generate. However, it may be difficult for an entity to identify other opportunities that could achieve the same rate when IRR is high. In contrast, the NPV method assumes that cash inflows can be reinvested and earn the discount rate — a more realistic assumption. If the discount rate is set equal to the organisation's cost of capital, then alternative uses of cash would include paying off creditors or buying back shares. For the preceding reasons, the NPV method is preferable.

Both methods are used widely in business. One reason for the continued use of IRR is that many people find it intuitively easier to understand than NPV. In addition, managers may want to compare the IRR on prior projects to current project return rates as they consider new investment. For example, Gordon could compare the IRR for the health club with any new projects and decide whether to accept a project with a lower IRR.

Payback method

The **payback method** measures the amount of time required to recover the initial investment. Assuming that cash flows from the project are constant over future years, the payback period can be calculated by dividing the initial investment cash flow by the annual incremental operating cash flows. Consider Gordon's decision to install vending machines in the café space.

$$\text{Number of years to pay back the investment} = \frac{\text{Initial investment}}{\text{Annual incremental operating cash flow}} = \frac{\$5000}{\$1500} = 3.33$$

Thus, the payback period for this example is 3.33 years. If incremental annual cash flows are uneven, then the payback period can be found by calculating the cumulative incremental operating cash flows until the initial investment amount has been fully covered. The number of years needed to cover the initial investment is the payback period.

Future cash flows can be discounted to reflect the opportunity cost of using funds for other projects; this is referred to as **discounted payback**. A key disadvantage of payback is that it does not value the cash flows that are received after the investment has been recovered. However, the payback method is used extensively as a screening tool, and sometimes used with NPV or IRR when meaningful estimates of relevant cash flows are lacking because the project or product is so new that it provides no historical data for reference. Longer payback periods reflect higher risk; therefore, projects with shorter payback periods are preferable because cash is not committed over long periods.

Accrual accounting rate of return method

The **accrual accounting rate of return** is the expected increase in average annual operating income as a percentage of the initial increase in required investment. In Gordon's vending machine decision, the net increase in income needs to be adjusted so that it reflects accrual accounting income. For financial statements, suppose that Gordon uses straight-line depreciation. With a five-year life and no terminal cash flow value, annual financial statement depreciation is $1000 per year ($5000 / 5 years). Assuming depreciation is the only difference between cash flows and financial statement income, accrual accounting income is $500 ($1500 − $1000). The accrual accounting rate of return of 10 per cent is the expected incremental accounting income from the project divided by the initial investment ($500 / $5000).

This method presents several problems. First, it ignores the time value of money. In addition, depreciation is deducted from the numerator but the full investment amount is the denominator, so the investment amount is essentially double counted. This method is frequently used to evaluate division or department performance because the financial information is readily available, but it is not an appropriate method for evaluating long-term investment decisions.

15.6 Strategic considerations for investment decisions

LEARNING OBJECTIVE 15.6 Discuss additional issues to be considered for strategic investment decisions.

Strategic investments are investments that affect all or a considerable part of an entity's operations, have uncertain lives and require large investments. These investments will more than likely impact the strategy of the organisation. By their very nature, they are more difficult to evaluate. Traditional tools such as net present value are often considered insufficient *on their own* to evaluate these kinds of investments. Managers often need to consider qualitative factors as well as quantitative analyses (such as NPV analysis) when making a strategic investment decision. In this section, we learn about a variety of factors that might be considered when evaluating strategic investment decisions.

First, we need to consider why more traditional evaluation tools are insufficient when used on their own to evaluate strategic investments, including that strategic decisions are commonly large financial investments, the financial benefits may take some time to flow, and many of the benefits may be difficult to quantify.

These additional considerations in strategic capital investments are as follows.

The type of information required in decision making

An issue frequently downplayed by accountants is the important role of non-financial information in decision making. As highlighted in figure 15.8, the non-financial information may present as quantitative information in a physical format (that is, number of tonnes of carbon emissions, number of hospital patients requiring blood tests, litres of waste) or qualitative information in narrative form, sometimes based on opinions or judgements (that is, if we do not reduce carbon emissions our reputation will be damaged, if we invest in the more-costly alternative we will reduce waste). Some of this information can then be converted to cash flows in a stepped process by estimating or applying monetary values to this data. Equally important is the recognition that some of the estimates might be too subjective and such information is best kept in narrative format. This does not mean that qualitative information is less important than quantitative. As will be highlighted below, sometimes this information is more powerful in the decision process.

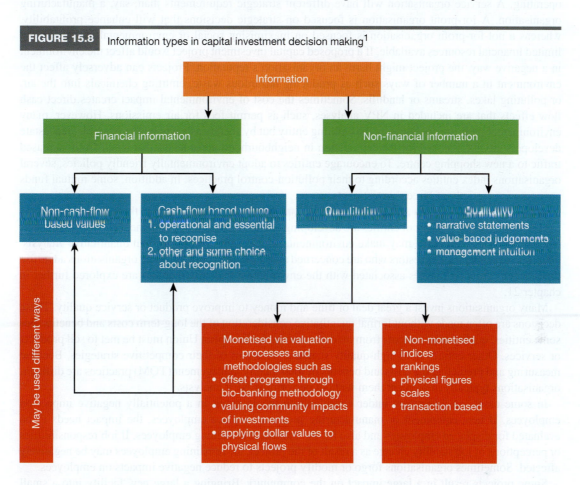

FIGURE 15.8 Information types in capital investment decision making[1]

Moving baseline concept

One of the issues often ignored in capital budgeting decisions is a concept commonly referred to as the *moving baseline*. The moving baseline concept challenges conventional comparisons, which are usually between what might be (the financial effect of adopting the project) and the status quo (things remaining as they are). The moving baseline suggests that if the project is not adopted, the 'status quo' may not remain; that is, performance may deteriorate. This may be as a result of, for example, a competitor making an acquisition if the entity passes up the opportunity. A consideration of the moving baseline commonly results in increasing the attraction of the proposed project. In effect, investments may need to be made, simply to maintain current operating performance, that is, avoid a performance decline.

Project champion

Some organisations will place an emphasis on which manager is proposing the project and their previous track record. This concept is hard to capture in any financial analysis but may be an important additional consideration in deciding whether to proceed with a proposal.

Cost of reversing the decision

This concept relates to how an organisation might deal with a situation where the decision to invest needs to be reversed and the implications of doing this. The implications might be financial (such as penalties built into contracts), but also include damage to the organisation's reputation.

Reputation, risks, environment, quality and community

Strategic decision making requires a consideration of the broader environment in which the company is operating. A service organisation will have different strategic requirements than, say, a manufacturing organisation. A for-profit organisation is focused on strategic decisions that will enhance profitability, whereas a not-for-profit organisation is focused on maximising social or environmental goals with the limited financial resources available. If a proposed capital investment project would affect the environment in a negative way, the project might harm an organisation's reputation. Projects can adversely affect the environment in a number of ways such as producing hazardous waste, emitting chemicals into the air, or polluting lakes, streams or landfills. Sometimes the cost of environmental impact creates direct cash flow effects that are included in NPV analyses, such as permit fees for air emissions. However, many environmental costs are not borne by the emitting entity but by society as a whole. For example, real estate developers are not assessed for the degradation in neighbourhood noise levels that result from increased traffic to a new shopping centre. To encourage entities to adopt environmentally friendly policies, several organisations index entities according to their pollution-control practices. In addition, some mutual funds are comprised strictly of 'green' investments.

Because reputation effects are difficult to value, managers typically incorporate these concerns qualitatively. An increasing number of entities are developing environmental policy statements to help guide their strategic decisions, and they may make environmental investments without formal quantitative analysis. To attract customers and investors who are concerned about the environment, some organisations advertise their 'green' practices. Issues associated with the environment and sustainability are explored further in chapter 21.

Many organisations invest a great deal of time and money to improve product or service quality. These decisions are often made without formal quantitative consideration of the long-term costs and benefits. For some entities, quality requirements from markets such as the European Union must be met to sell products or services. Other entities hold high-quality standards as a part of their competitive strategies. Because measuring and predicting the costs and benefits of total quality management (TQM) practices are difficult, organisations typically implement them without performing NPV analysis.

In some cases, an investment under consideration would result in a potentially negative impact on employees. If new equipment or manufacturing processes replace employees, the impact needs to be evaluated for displaced employees and also for the morale of remaining employees. If job responsibilities or perceptions of job stability change as a result of the project, the remaining employees may be negatively affected. Sometimes organisations forgo or modify projects to reduce negative impacts on employees.

Some projects result in a large impact on the community. Bringing a large new facility into a small community can change the dynamics of the entire community. Closing a plant or service upon which a community relies can result in a negative reputation for an organisation. A negative corporate image can have far-reaching effects on the entity as a whole, including loss of market share and morale problems with employees and management.

As indicated in figure 15.8, the qualitative factors are vitally important in the decision-making process. How these more qualitative factors are incorporated into the investment decision model will vary from firm to firm. For example, some firms may choose to try and quantify some of these qualitative factors through the use of ratings and indices, resulting in the calculation of an overall index. Others may choose to simply leave them as qualitative factors to be considered alongside the more formal quantitative analysis such as NPV. The resource allocation process follows a series of iterative processes from strategic information requirements through to thorough evaluation of the proposal(s) using all information sources. If there are competing proposals the outputs are evaluated and ranked for debate by senior management before the decision is made.

Before the decision process can be commenced, it is useful to categorise the capital investment as not all investments involve complex decision making. Some investments, although costly, might be relatively straightforward in evaluation. Some might be mandatory (non-discretionary) and link to a company's survival while others might be more discretionary in nature. Non-discretionary investments might be made for regulatory reasons, such as the requirement to purchase occupational health and safety equipment. Firefighting equipment is an example of an expensive regulatory capital outlay. The information required for this decision would rely more on purchase cost data (that is, the most cost-effective decision alternative that fits the purpose). Non-discretionary investments are also made for strategic reasons and relate to survival in a competitive environment.

For example, if one of Apple's competitors, such as Samsung, does not invest in new technology to keep pace with the changing mobile phone industry, it might be argued that it would not remain viable in this highly competitive and dynamic environment. In this situation, owners and managers of Samsung would claim that investment in new technology is non-discretionary for this company.

Capital investment appraisal in this situation requires a complex approach to management decision making, often drawing on a wide range of information sources. Discretionary capital investment decisions are more operational in nature and are necessary for the day-to-day running of the business. This type of decision (for example, new factory machinery or an upgrade in computers and software) again might require large cash outlays but largely relies on information that details operational cash flows over the life of the investment. These decisions are classified as discretionary because organisations might prefer to delay upgrading their equipment. The machinery might still be operational and useful for a company even if it is fully depreciated. Traditionally, information provided by DCF and NPV is suitable to evaluate these investment types.

In comprehensive example 2, we provide an illustration of the three categories of capital investments and discuss how each might be evaluated.

COMPREHENSIVE EXAMPLE 2

Cowmilka

Cowmilka is an Australian dairy cooperative run jointly by more than 1000 Australian farmers and 900 employees. The farmers and employees are all committed professionals with a passion for dairy. This is formalised in the company's vision and belief statements and communicated widely to all employees so that these are 'lived' and not just writing on dust-covered wall charts. Cowmilka pays its farmer members the highest possible price for their milk and has developed a strategy based on growth, efficiency and innovation. It is a widely shared belief that value is created by:

- growth in exports and value-added products
- efficiency in production and logistics
- innovation in product development and processes.

Cowmilka's strategy focuses on innovation and quality products and service levels. Individual segments pursue their specific strategies within this context. At present, there is little re-evaluation of the strategic intent of the company. A relatively high proportion of Cowmilka's milk production is exported every year. Globally, the dairy market is dynamic and current milk demand outstrips supply. However, in Australia the volumes have significantly reduced over the last few years as the ongoing drought has reduced milk yields.

Further, the butter market has come under threat as consumers have begun switching to vegetable-based products because of increasing dairy prices. Butter prices have increased by 100 per cent over the last year to $8.00 per kilogram. As a result of the drought and market price fluctuations it has been difficult for Cowmilka to fully realise its budgeted growth in volume over the last couple of years.

Cowmilka has four core divisions, managed as profit centres and structured around the following product groups:

- milk products
- cheese and butter
- yoghurt
- ice cream.

Each division is functionally structured with specialisations in research and development (R&D), marketing and customer sales. The four divisions are evaluated on the basis of profit performance against predetermined targets agreed to through discussions with senior management. Nonetheless, senior management has the final say. Focus is placed on identifying reasons for negative deviations from target performance. Cowmilka also has a centralised logistics division, which, among other things, coordinates milk distribution. This division is evaluated on the basis of cost performance.

The raw ingredient, milk, is shared among the divisions and is transported from the farms to the closest manufacturing plant. Cowmilka has six manufacturing plants located in the dairy belts of Australia, one of which is entirely dedicated to ice cream manufacture. The other five production sites jointly process cheese, butter, yoghurt and/or milk products according to production schedules set by the other three profit centre managers. The profit centre managers meet weekly to discuss production planning and milk allocations. They are required to accurately forecast customer orders to optimise plant efficiency. The manufacturing plants are managed as cost centres and each plant manager is held accountable for production output. Wastage is expected to be close to zero and poor forecasting results in high production run set-up/change-over costs. The plants operate 24 hours a day, seven days a week with capacity to produce around 680 million litres of milk per year. Quality control is essential.

A special board meeting has been called to consider several strategic planning and control issues, including three capital investment proposals. These are outlined as follows.

Agenda item 1: Capital investment proposals review

Proposal 1: The logistics manager requires investment in three new milk tankers to replace an ageing fleet of tankers to improve fleet efficiency. Currently, the fleet has high maintenance costs and an unacceptable number of tanker breakdowns.
Total cost: $324 000

Proposal 2: The manufacturing manager is required to purchase waste and water management equipment for each of the six production sites to meet new health and safety regulations. New legislation requires that this equipment be installed before the end of the following financial year.
Total cost: $350 000

Proposal 3: To achieve Cowmilka's desired goals of growth and a stronger international position the manager of the cheese and butter division, Colin Way, is proposing to acquire a small New Zealand company called Fintona Buttergold. Cowmilka's cheese and butter division is pursuing a cost leadership position selling prepackaged cheese and butter into supermarkets on contract agreements. The supermarkets sell the cheese and butter as their home-brand products. Colin is keen to diversify his division's product range and argues that growth into niche markets would add value to their existing range. Colin prepared the following information for the board and attached a spreadsheet of calculations which projected reasonable returns for the next few years.

'Fintona Buttergold is a specialised butter plant with state-of-the-art butter manufacturing capabilities. It is known for its butter, which is sold in small packages and 250 millilitre cartons for restaurants and gourmet supplies. It is a highly regarded competitor in the New Zealand market, and has loyal customers and a friendly sales team managed by a strong leader (the current owner of the firm, who may not stay with the company after it is sold). It has recently begun marketing its products internationally and sales forecasts indicate that sales will continue to grow and production will be at capacity.'
Total cost: $3 500 000

Each of the three potential investments is quite different and a different approach is used in the evaluation process. Let's consider each proposal in turn.

Proposal 1

This is a proposal to replace old delivery trucks. Consequently, it relates to the maintenance of existing capacity and traditional capital budgeting tools should be sufficient to evaluate this proposal. The calculation of net present value (NPV), IRR and payback should provide sufficient financial data to support the decision-making process.

Proposal 2

This proposal relates to the acquisition of waste and water management equipment, which is required under environmental regulations. In this case, managers could use the low-cost alternative if the investment is relatively straightforward and inexpensive; or discounted cash flows if the investment is more complex and expensive.

Proposal 3

This proposal requires a far more strategic investment than proposals 1 and 2. This investment will result in a change of strategy for Cowmilka with a greater focus on differentiation and high-quality products, rather than the low-cost strategy currently pursued. The size of the investment is also significantly greater than under the other two proposals. Calculations such as NPV may not be sufficient on their own to evaluate the proposal. Other considerations in the decision-making process might include:
- whether the change in strategy is well timed
- the impact of not investing. That is, if Cowmilka does not invest in Fintona, there may be a fair chance that another firm will. The decision not to acquire Fintona may, over time, have a negative impact on Cowmilka's financial performance. So, not investing does not guarantee that the status quo will remain for Cowmilka
- the track record of the managers making each proposal. In this case, the track record and past performance of Colin Way would be considered an important consideration in the decision. Also, the nature of the analysis undertaken by Colin would be scrutinised to ensure it is of the highest quality
- costs of reversing the investment. In this case, reversing the decision to purchase Fintona will mean reselling the business.

Of course, each of these factors is more qualitative than quantitative. This makes them a little more difficult to incorporate into the investment decision than pure financial analyses. Nevertheless, while the quantitative analysis will be critical to the decision, the more qualitative factors are best considered along with the financial analysis represented by NPV, IRR and payback calculations.

Making and monitoring investment decisions

Managers consider a number of factors when making the final decision about a proposed capital budgeting project. The results of any quantitative analyses as well as the qualitative issues already discussed are taken into account. Accountants often prepare analyses of projects that align with organisations' strategic plans. Managers use these analyses to examine financial outcomes under a number of different scenarios. They often have a better grasp than accountants of certain business factors, such as competitors' product development and prices. In addition, managers may use their own informal estimates to determine an NPV.

A summary of the overall strategic decision-making process is provided in figure 15.9. This highlights the different times when financial and non-financial information is required. In the early phases of the decision process, the information is less refined. As the decision becomes a reality, some of the qualitative information is quantified and part of cash flows. With larger more strategic projects, there will be regulatory and operational aspects embedded within the broader project. Further expenditure might be the result of the decision-making processes. For example, a mining company might be required to invest in occupational health and safety, or in reputation-enhancing investments to appease the local community for the noise and pollution generated by its proposed mining venture.

FIGURE 15.9	Strategic decision-making process[2]

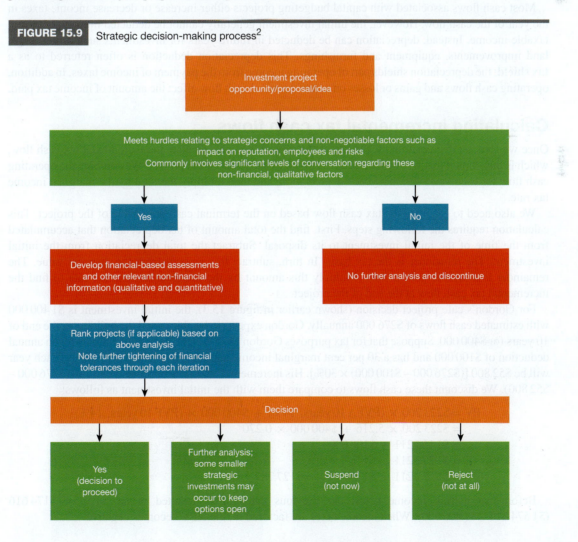

After a project has been accepted, accountants and managers monitor its progress and compare actual performance to the capital budget expectations. Some projects are relatively simple to implement and require little monitoring (for example, the replacement of equipment in a coin-operated laundry). Other projects are more complex, such as Gordon's new line of business through the health club. More complex projects that take longer to implement need more monitoring to reduce the probability of budget overruns.

Because these projects are long-lived, outcomes are almost always different from expectations. A **post-investment audit** provides feedback about whether operations are meeting expectations. When results are below expectations, processes are investigated and improvements can be implemented. In addition, the process of re-evaluating past decisions usually improves future decision making. The more we learn about factors that affect the accuracy of our forecasts and investigate unanticipated problems or benefits, the better we can predict these occurrences in future projects.

15.7 Income taxes and the net present value method

LEARNING OBJECTIVE 15.7 Communicate how income taxes affect capital investment decision cash flows.

Income taxes affect an organisation's cash flows and, in turn, capital budgeting decisions. Because individual states and countries have different income tax rules, the specific tax effects on a proposed project depend on the tax jurisdictions of the organisation and the project. Taxes become even more complex as an entity grows and expands internationally. In addition, income tax laws change periodically, and capital budgeting requires current knowledge of tax laws. Before developing NPV analyses in a complex entity, accountants consult tax experts so that their analyses reflect the cash flows that would actually take place. Importantly, the tax effects of an investment decision may be a key driver of a decision to proceed with an investment.

Most cash flows associated with capital budgeting projects either increase or decrease income taxes in the year of the cash flow. However, the initial investment generally cannot be deducted immediately from taxable income. Instead, depreciation can be deducted in future years for investments such as buildings, land improvements, equipment and furnishings. This depreciation deduction is often referred to as a **tax shield**; the depreciation shields part of operating income from the payment of income taxes. In addition, operating cash flows and gains or losses on assets' terminal cash flow affect the amount of income tax paid.

Calculating incremental tax cash flows

Once we forecast depreciation for the life of the project, we can calculate the incremental tax cash flow, which is the amount that will be paid or saved on taxes each year of the project. We combine the operating cash flow for each year with that year's depreciation, and then multiply the total by the marginal income tax rate.

We also need to calculate the tax cash flow based on the terminal cash flow value of the project. This calculation requires the following steps. First, find the total amount of tax depreciation that accumulated from the time of the initial investment to its disposal. Subtract the total depreciation from the initial investment. The remainder is the tax basis. In turn, subtract this amount from the disposal value. The remainder is a taxable gain or loss. Multiply this amount by the marginal income tax rate to find the incremental tax cash flow at the end of the project.

For Gordon's cafe project decision (shown earlier in figure 15.3), the initial investment is $1 400 000 with estimated cash flows of $276 000 annually. Gordon expects to be able to sell the building at the end of 10 years for $400 000. Suppose that for tax purposes Gordon uses straight-line depreciation with an annual deduction of $100 000 and has a 30 per cent marginal income tax rate. His income tax expense each year will be $52 800 [($276 000 − $100 000) × 30%]. His incremental cash flow becomes $223 200 ($276 000 − $52 800). We discount these cash flows to compare them with the initial investment as follows:

$$PV = \$223\,200 \times (PVFA\ 10\,years,\ 14\%) + \$400\,000 \times (PVF\ 10\,years,\ 14\%)$$
$$= \$223\,200 \times 5.216 + \$400\,000 \times 0.270$$
$$= \$1\,164\,211 + \$108\,000$$
$$= \$1\,272\,211$$
$$NPV = \$1\,272\,211 - \$1\,400\,000 = \$127\,789$$

Before considering income taxes, our previous calculations resulted in an NPV of $174 616 ($1 574 616 − $1 400 000). When income taxes are factored in, the NPV becomes negative.

15.8 Inflation and the net present value method

LEARNING OBJECTIVE 15.8 Understand how real and nominal methods are used to address inflation in an NPV analysis.

The NPV calculations in the chapter did not take into account the fact that many revenues and costs tend to inflate or deflate over time. When these changes occur, it is inappropriate to use today's revenue and cost values when forecasting future cash flows, particularly for projects spanning many years. Sometimes costs such as transportation fuel increase rapidly. Wages or supplies might increase at a slower rate over time. Still other costs, such as new technology, might actually decrease over time. Cash flows from projects in other countries sometimes have different inflation rates from those in Australia. Managers need to incorporate these types of expected differences in their NPV analyses.

Inflation is the decline in the general purchasing power of the monetary unit, meaning that more monetary units (such as dollars) are needed to purchase goods or services. **Deflation** is the opposite, or an increase in the general purchasing power of the monetary unit. Because either can distort an NPV analysis, cash flows should be adjusted for anticipated levels of inflation or deflation.

Real and nominal methods for NPV analysis

Two types of interest rates need to be considered when analysing inflation, as shown in figure 15.10. The first type, the **real rate of interest**, is the rate of return required on investments when no inflation is a factor. It is calculated as the sum of the risk-free rate and a risk premium. The **risk-free rate** is the 'pure' rate of interest paid on short-term government bonds (without considering inflation). The risk premium is an element above the risk-free rate that entities demand for undertaking risks. The second type, the **nominal rate of interest**, is the rate of return required on investments when inflation is present. It is calculated by increasing the real rate of interest by the expected rate of inflation.

FIGURE 15.10 Real and nominal interest rates

Real rate of interest = Risk-free rate + Risk premium

Nominal rate of interest = $(1 + \text{Real rate}) \times (1 + \text{Inflation rate}) - 1$

Cash flows and the discount rate should be measured using a consistent approach. In the **real method**, cash inflows and outflows are forecast in real dollars (no inflation) and discounted using a real rate. The examples we have used so far used real cash flows.

In the **nominal method**, cash inflows and outflows are forecast in nominal dollars (inflated) and discounted using a nominal discount rate. Real cash flows can be converted to nominal cash flows using the following formula:

$$\text{Nominal cash flow} = \text{Real cash flow} \times (1 + i)^t$$

where i = rate of inflation

t = number of time periods in the future

Suppose Gordon hires an accountant at $35 000 per year to help with his new businesses. If the accountant's salary is valued in a NPV analysis using the real method over a five-year period, the cash flows will be uniform across time. But if the salary inflates at 2 per cent per year, the cash flows will increase across time. Figure 15.11 compares the real and nominal cash flows.

FIGURE 15.11 Real versus nominal cash flows

Period	Real cash flows	Nominal cash flows
1	$35 000	$35 000 \times 1.02^1 = $35 700
2	$35 000	$35 000 \times 1.02^2 = $36 414
3	$35 000	$35 000 \times 1.02^3 = $37 142
4	$35 000	$35 000 \times 1.02^4 = $37 885
5	$35 000	$35 000 \times 1.02^5 = $38 643

In some cases, the depreciation expense that can be deducted on an income tax return does not change over time. However, under inflation, the real amount of annual depreciation tax savings decreases over time. Nominal cash flows can be converted to real cash flows as follows:

$$\text{Real cash flow} = \frac{\text{Nominal cash flow}}{(1+i)^t}$$

Internal consistency in NPV analysis

If cash inflows and outflows are valued in real terms and then discounted using a nominal rate, or vice versa, the approach is internally inconsistent. Because nominal rates include inflation, they tend to be higher than real rates. Discounting real cash flows using a nominal rate creates a bias against the adoption of many worthwhile capital investment projects because the discounted present value of cash inflows is understated. Discounting nominal cash flows using a real rate overstates discounted cash flows and creates a bias toward accepting projects that may have a negative NPV.

When we expect relevant cash flows to be influenced by inflation or deflation, we must select a method (real or nominal) and then use that method consistently for all calculations. We perform the NPV analysis as before. The only differences are:

- cash flows must be adjusted so that they are internally consistent with the method used
- only a real discount rate should be used under the real method, and only a nominal discount rate should be used under the nominal method.

Figure 15.12 summarises the types of adjustments to cash flows that are required under the real and nominal methods.

| FIGURE 15.12 | Cash flow adjustments required under the real and nominal methods |

Cash flow	Adjustments for real method	Adjustments for nominal method
Initial investment	No adjustment	No adjustment
Depreciation tax shield	Adjust from a nominal to a real amount for each year (deflate)	No adjustment
Remaining cash flow: • Incremental operating cash flows • Income taxes on incremental cash flows • Terminal cash flows • Income taxes on terminal gain or loss	If original cash flow estimates include inflation, then the cash flows must be adjusted from nominal to real amounts for each year; the tax cash flows must then be recalculated	If original cash flow estimates do not include inflation, then the cash flows must be adjusted from real to nominal amounts for each year; the tax cash flows must then be recalculated

Adjustment formulas: Nominal cash flow = Real cash flow $\times (1+i)^t$

$$\text{Real cash flow} = \frac{\text{Nominal cash flow}}{(1+i)^t}$$

where i = rate of inflation
t = number of time periods in the future

APPENDIX 15A
Present and future value tables

TABLE 15A.1 Present value of $1

Periods	4%	5%	6%	7%	8%	9%	10%	11%	12%	13%	14%	15%	16%	17%	18%
1	0.962	0.952	0.943	0.935	0.926	0.917	0.909	0.901	0.893	0.885	0.877	0.870	0.862	0.855	0.847
2	0.925	0.907	0.890	0.873	0.857	0.842	0.826	0.812	0.797	0.783	0.769	0.756	0.743	0.731	0.718
3	0.889	0.864	0.840	0.816	0.794	0.772	0.751	0.731	0.712	0.693	0.675	0.658	0.641	0.624	0.609
4	0.855	0.823	0.792	0.763	0.735	0.708	0.683	0.659	0.636	0.613	0.592	0.572	0.552	0.534	0.516
5	0.822	0.784	0.747	0.713	0.681	0.650	0.621	0.593	0.567	0.543	0.519	0.497	0.476	0.456	0.437
6	0.790	0.746	0.705	0.666	0.630	0.596	0.564	0.535	0.507	0.480	0.456	0.432	0.410	0.390	0.370
7	0.760	0.711	0.665	0.623	0.583	0.547	0.513	0.482	0.452	0.425	0.400	0.376	0.354	0.333	0.314
8	0.731	0.677	0.627	0.582	0.540	0.502	0.467	0.434	0.404	0.376	0.351	0.327	0.305	0.285	0.266
9	0.703	0.645	0.592	0.544	0.500	0.460	0.424	0.391	0.361	0.333	0.308	0.284	0.263	0.243	0.225
10	0.676	0.614	0.558	0.508	0.463	0.422	0.386	0.352	0.322	0.295	0.270	0.247	0.227	0.208	0.191
11	0.650	0.585	0.527	0.475	0.429	0.388	0.350	0.317	0.287	0.261	0.237	0.215	0.195	0.178	0.162
12	0.625	0.557	0.497	0.444	0.397	0.356	0.319	0.286	0.257	0.231	0.208	0.187	0.168	0.152	0.137
13	0.601	0.530	0.469	0.415	0.368	0.326	0.290	0.258	0.229	0.204	0.182	0.163	0.145	0.130	0.116
14	0.577	0.505	0.442	0.388	0.340	0.299	0.263	0.232	0.205	0.181	0.160	0.141	0.125	0.111	0.099
15	0.555	0.481	0.417	0.362	0.315	0.275	0.239	0.209	0.183	0.160	0.140	0.123	0.108	0.095	0.084
16	0.534	0.458	0.394	0.339	0.292	0.252	0.218	0.188	0.163	0.141	0.123	0.107	0.093	0.081	0.071
17	0.513	0.436	0.371	0.317	0.270	0.231	0.198	0.170	0.146	0.125	0.108	0.093	0.080	0.069	0.060
18	0.494	0.416	0.350	0.296	0.250	0.212	0.180	0.153	0.130	0.111	0.095	0.081	0.069	0.059	0.051
19	0.475	0.396	0.331	0.277	0.232	0.194	0.164	0.138	0.116	0.098	0.083	0.070	0.060	0.051	0.043

(continued)

TABLE 15A.1 (continued)

Periods	4%	5%	6%	7%	8%	9%	10%	11%	12%	13%	14%	15%	16%	17%	18%
20	0.456	0.377	0.312	0.258	0.215	0.178	0.149	0.124	0.104	0.087	0.073	0.061	0.051	0.043	0.037
21	0.439	0.359	0.294	0.242	0.199	0.164	0.135	0.112	0.093	0.077	0.064	0.053	0.044	0.037	0.031
22	0.422	0.342	0.278	0.226	0.184	0.150	0.123	0.101	0.083	0.068	0.056	0.046	0.038	0.032	0.026
23	0.406	0.326	0.262	0.211	0.170	0.138	0.112	0.091	0.074	0.060	0.049	0.040	0.033	0.027	0.022
24	0.390	0.310	0.247	0.197	0.158	0.126	0.102	0.082	0.066	0.053	0.043	0.035	0.028	0.023	0.019
25	0.375	0.295	0.233	0.184	0.146	0.116	0.092	0.074	0.059	0.047	0.038	0.030	0.024	0.020	0.016
26	0.361	0.281	0.220	0.172	0.135	0.106	0.084	0.066	0.053	0.042	0.033	0.026	0.021	0.017	0.014
27	0.347	0.268	0.207	0.161	0.125	0.098	0.076	0.060	0.047	0.037	0.029	0.023	0.018	0.014	0.011
28	0.333	0.255	0.196	0.150	0.116	0.090	0.069	0.054	0.042	0.033	0.026	0.020	0.016	0.012	0.010
29	0.321	0.243	0.185	0.141	0.107	0.082	0.063	0.048	0.037	0.029	0.022	0.017	0.014	0.011	0.008
30	0.308	0.231	0.174	0.131	0.099	0.075	0.057	0.044	0.033	0.026	0.020	0.015	0.012	0.009	0.007

TABLE 15A.2 Present value of an ordinary annuity of $1

Periods	4%	5%	6%	7%	8%	9%	10%	11%	12%	13%	14%	15%	16%	17%	18%
1	0.962	0.952	0.943	0.935	0.926	0.917	0.909	0.901	0.893	0.885	0.877	0.870	0.862	0.855	0.847
2	1.886	1.859	1.833	1.808	1.783	1.759	1.736	1.713	1.690	1.668	1.647	1.626	1.605	1.585	1.566
3	2.775	2.723	2.673	2.624	2.577	2.531	2.487	2.444	2.402	2.361	2.322	2.283	2.246	2.210	2.174
4	3.630	3.546	3.465	3.387	3.312	3.240	3.170	3.102	3.037	2.974	2.914	2.855	2.798	2.743	2.690
5	4.452	4.329	4.212	4.100	3.993	3.890	3.791	3.696	3.605	3.517	3.433	3.352	3.274	3.199	3.127
6	5.242	5.076	4.917	4.767	4.623	4.486	4.355	4.231	4.111	3.998	3.889	3.784	3.685	3.589	3.498
7	6.002	5.786	5.582	5.389	5.206	5.033	4.868	4.712	4.564	4.423	4.288	4.160	4.039	3.922	3.812
8	6.733	6.463	6.210	5.971	5.747	5.535	5.335	5.146	4.968	4.799	4.639	4.487	4.344	4.207	4.078
9	7.435	7.108	6.802	6.515	6.247	5.995	5.759	5.537	5.328	5.132	4.946	4.772	4.607	4.451	4.303
10	8.111	7.722	7.360	7.024	6.710	6.418	6.145	5.889	5.650	5.426	5.216	5.019	4.833	4.659	4.494
11	8.760	8.306	7.887	7.499	7.139	6.805	6.495	6.207	5.938	5.687	5.453	5.234	5.029	4.836	4.656
12	9.385	8.863	8.384	7.943	7.536	7.161	6.814	6.492	6.194	5.918	5.660	5.421	5.197	4.988	4.793
13	9.986	9.394	8.853	8.358	7.904	7.487	7.103	6.750	6.424	6.122	5.842	5.583	5.342	5.118	4.910
14	10.563	9.899	9.295	8.745	8.244	7.786	7.367	6.982	6.628	6.302	6.002	5.724	5.468	5.229	5.008
15	11.118	10.380	9.712	9.108	8.559	8.061	7.606	7.191	6.811	6.462	6.142	5.847	5.575	5.324	5.092
16	11.652	10.838	10.106	9.447	8.851	8.313	7.824	7.379	6.974	6.604	6.265	5.954	5.668	5.405	5.162
17	12.166	11.274	10.477	9.763	9.122	8.544	8.022	7.549	7.120	6.729	6.373	6.047	5.749	5.475	5.222
18	12.659	11.690	10.828	10.059	9.372	8.756	8.201	7.702	7.250	6.840	6.467	6.128	5.818	5.534	5.273
19	13.134	12.085	11.158	10.336	9.604	8.950	8.365	7.839	7.366	6.938	6.550	6.198	5.877	5.584	5.316

(continued)

TABLE 15A.2 (continued)

Periods	4%	5%	6%	7%	8%	9%	10%	11%	12%	13%	14%	15%	16%	17%	18%
20	13.590	12.462	11.470	10.594	9.818	9.129	8.514	7.963	7.469	7.025	6.623	6.259	5.929	5.628	5.353
21	14.029	12.821	11.764	10.836	10.017	9.292	8.649	8.075	7.562	7.102	6.687	6.312	5.973	5.665	5.384
22	14.451	13.163	12.042	11.061	10.201	9.442	8.772	8.176	7.645	7.170	6.743	6.359	6.011	5.696	5.410
23	14.857	13.489	12.303	11.272	10.371	9.580	8.883	8.266	7.718	7.230	6.792	6.399	6.044	5.723	5.432
24	15.247	13.799	12.550	11.469	10.529	9.707	8.985	8.348	7.784	7.283	6.835	6.434	6.073	5.746	5.451
25	15.622	14.094	12.783	11.654	10.675	9.823	9.077	8.422	7.843	7.330	6.873	6.464	6.097	5.766	5.467
26	15.983	14.375	13.003	11.826	10.810	9.929	9.161	8.488	7.896	7.372	6.906	6.491	6.118	5.783	5.480
27	16.330	14.643	13.211	11.987	10.935	10.027	9.237	8.548	7.943	7.409	6.935	6.514	6.136	5.798	5.492
28	16.663	14.898	13.406	12.137	11.051	10.116	9.307	8.602	7.984	7.441	6.961	6.534	6.152	5.810	5.502
29	16.984	15.141	13.591	12.278	11.158	10.198	9.370	8.650	8.022	7.470	6.983	6.551	6.166	5.820	5.510
30	17.292	15.372	13.765	12.409	11.258	10.274	9.427	8.694	8.055	7.496	7.003	6.566	6.177	5.829	5.517

Periods	4%	5%	6%	7%	8%	9%	10%	11%	12%	13%	14%	15%	16%	17%	18%
1	1.040	1.050	1.060	1.070	1.080	1.090	1.100	1.110	1.120	1.130	1.140	1.150	1.160	1.170	1.180
2	1.082	1.103	1.124	1.145	1.166	1.188	1.210	1.232	1.254	1.277	1.300	1.323	1.346	1.369	1.392
3	1.125	1.158	1.191	1.225	1.260	1.295	1.331	1.368	1.405	1.443	1.482	1.521	1.561	1.602	1.643
4	1.170	1.216	1.262	1.311	1.360	1.412	1.464	1.518	1.574	1.630	1.689	1.749	1.811	1.874	1.939
5	1.217	1.276	1.338	1.403	1.469	1.539	1.611	1.685	1.762	1.842	1.925	2.011	2.100	2.192	2.288
6	1.265	1.340	1.419	1.501	1.587	1.677	1.772	1.870	1.974	2.082	2.195	2.313	2.436	2.565	2.700
7	1.316	1.407	1.504	1.606	1.714	1.828	1.949	2.076	2.211	2.353	2.502	2.660	2.826	3.001	3.185
8	1.369	1.477	1.594	1.718	1.851	1.993	2.144	2.305	2.476	2.658	2.853	3.059	3.278	3.511	3.759
9	1.423	1.551	1.689	1.838	1.999	2.172	2.358	2.558	2.773	3.004	3.252	3.518	3.803	4.108	4.435
10	1.480	1.629	1.791	1.967	2.159	2.367	2.594	2.839	3.106	3.395	3.707	4.046	4.411	4.807	5.234
11	1.539	1.710	1.898	2.105	2.332	2.580	2.853	3.152	3.479	3.836	4.226	4.652	5.117	5.624	6.176
12	1.601	1.796	2.012	2.252	2.518	2.813	3.138	3.498	3.896	4.335	4.818	5.350	5.936	6.580	7.288
13	1.665	1.886	2.133	2.410	2.720	3.066	3.452	3.883	4.363	4.898	5.492	6.153	6.886	7.699	8.599
14	1.732	1.980	2.261	2.579	2.937	3.342	3.797	4.310	4.887	5.535	6.261	7.076	7.988	9.007	10.147
15	1.801	2.079	2.397	2.759	3.172	3.642	4.177	4.785	5.474	6.254	7.138	8.137	9.266	10.539	11.974
16	1.873	2.183	2.540	2.952	3.426	3.970	4.595	5.311	6.130	7.067	8.137	9.358	10.748	12.330	14.129
17	1.948	2.292	2.693	3.159	3.700	4.328	5.054	5.895	6.866	7.986	9.276	10.761	12.468	14.426	16.672
18	2.026	2.407	2.854	3.380	3.996	4.717	5.560	6.544	7.690	9.024	10.575	12.375	14.463	16.879	19.673
19	2.107	2.527	3.026	3.617	4.316	5.142	6.116	7.263	8.613	10.197	12.056	13.232	16.777	19.748	23.214

(continued)

TABLE 15A.3 *(continued)*

Periods	4%	5%	6%	7%	8%	9%	10%	11%	12%	13%	14%	15%	16%	17%	18%
20	2.191	2.653	3.207	3.870	4.661	5.604	6.727	8.062	9.646	11.523	13.743	16.367	19.461	23.106	27.393
21	2.279	2.786	3.400	4.141	5.034	6.109	7.400	8.949	10.804	13.021	15.668	18.822	22.574	27.034	32.324
22	2.370	2.925	3.604	4.430	5.437	6.659	8.140	9.934	12.100	14.714	17.861	21.645	26.186	31.629	38.142
23	2.465	3.072	3.820	4.741	5.871	7.258	8.954	11.026	13.552	16.627	20.362	24.891	30.376	37.006	45.008
24	2.563	3.225	4.049	5.072	6.341	7.911	9.850	12.239	15.179	18.788	23.212	28.625	35.236	43.297	53.109
25	2.666	3.386	4.292	5.427	6.848	8.623	10.835	13.585	17.000	21.231	26.462	32.919	40.874	50.658	62.669
26	2.772	3.556	4.549	5.807	7.396	9.399	11.918	15.080	19.040	23.991	30.167	37.857	47.414	59.270	73.949
27	2.883	3.733	4.822	6.214	7.988	10.245	13.110	16.739	21.325	27.109	34.390	43.535	55.000	69.345	87.260
28	2.999	3.920	5.112	6.649	8.627	11.167	14.421	18.580	23.884	30.633	39.204	50.066	63.800	81.134	102.967
29	3.119	4.116	5.418	7.114	9.317	12.172	15.863	20.624	26.750	34.616	44.693	57.575	74.009	94.927	121.501
30	3.243	4.322	5.743	7.612	10.063	13.268	17.449	22.892	29.960	39.116	50.950	66.212	85.850	111.065	143.371

TABLE 15A.4 Future value of an ordinary annuity of $1

Periods	4%	5%	6%	7%	8%	9%	10%	11%	12%	13%	14%	15%	16%	17%	18%
1	1.000	1.000	1.000	1.000	1.000	1.000	1.000	1.000	1.000	1.000	1.000	1.000	1.000	1.000	1.000
2	2.040	2.050	2.060	2.070	2.080	2.090	2.100	2.110	2.120	2.130	2.140	2.150	2.160	2.170	2.180
3	3.122	3.153	3.184	3.215	3.246	3.278	3.310	3.342	3.374	3.407	3.440	3.473	3.506	3.539	3.572
4	4.246	4.310	4.375	4.440	4.506	4.573	4.641	4.710	4.779	4.850	4.921	4.993	5.066	5.141	5.215
5	5.416	5.526	5.637	5.751	5.867	5.985	6.105	6.228	6.353	6.480	6.610	6.742	6.877	7.014	7.154
6	6.633	6.802	6.975	7.153	7.336	7.523	7.716	7.913	8.115	8.323	8.536	8.754	8.977	9.207	9.442
7	7.898	8.142	8.394	8.654	8.923	9.200	9.487	9.783	10.089	10.405	10.730	11.067	11.414	11.772	12.142
8	9.214	9.549	9.897	10.260	10.637	11.028	11.436	11.859	12.300	12.757	13.233	13.727	14.240	14.773	15.327
9	10.583	11.027	11.491	11.978	12.488	13.021	13.579	14.164	14.776	15.416	16.085	16.786	17.519	18.285	19.086
10	12.006	12.578	13.181	13.816	14.487	15.193	15.937	16.722	17.549	18.420	19.337	20.304	21.321	22.393	23.521
11	13.486	14.207	14.972	15.784	16.645	17.560	18.531	19.561	20.655	21.814	23.045	24.349	25.733	27.200	28.755
12	15.026	15.917	16.870	17.888	18.977	20.141	21.384	22.713	24.133	25.650	27.271	29.002	30.850	32.824	34.931
13	16.627	17.713	18.882	20.141	21.495	22.953	24.523	26.212	28.029	29.985	32.089	34.352	36.786	39.404	42.219
14	18.292	19.599	21.015	22.550	24.215	26.019	27.975	30.095	32.393	34.883	37.581	40.505	43.672	47.103	50.818
15	20.024	21.579	23.276	25.129	27.152	29.361	31.772	34.405	37.280	40.417	43.842	47.580	51.660	56.110	60.965
16	21.825	23.657	25.673	27.888	30.324	33.003	35.950	39.190	42.753	46.672	50.980	55.717	60.925	66.649	72.939
17	23.698	25.840	28.213	30.840	33.750	36.974	40.545	44.501	48.884	53.739	59.118	65.075	71.763	78.979	87.068
18	25.645	28.132	30.906	33.999	37.450	41.301	45.599	50.396	55.750	61.725	68.394	75.836	84.141	93.406	103.740
19	27.671	30.539	33.760	37.379	41.446	46.018	51.159	56.939	63.440	70.749	78.969	88.212	98.603	110.285	123.414

(continued)

TABLE 15A.4 (continued)

Periods	4%	5%	6%	7%	8%	9%	10%	11%	12%	13%	14%	15%	16%	17%	18%
20	29.778	33.066	36.786	40.995	45.762	51.160	57.275	64.203	72.052	80.947	91.025	102.444	115.380	130.033	146.628
21	31.969	35.719	39.993	44.865	50.423	56.765	64.002	72.265	81.699	92.470	104.768	118.810	134.841	153.139	174.021
22	34.248	38.505	43.392	49.006	55.457	62.873	71.403	81.214	92.503	105.491	120.436	137.632	157.415	180.172	206.345
23	36.618	41.430	46.996	53.436	60.893	69.532	79.543	91.148	104.603	120.205	138.297	159.276	183.601	211.801	244.487
24	39.083	44.502	50.816	58.177	66.765	76.790	88.497	102.174	118.155	136.831	158.659	184.168	213.978	248.808	289.494
25	41.646	47.727	54.865	63.249	73.106	84.701	98.347	114.413	133.334	155.620	181.871	212.793	249.214	292.105	342.603
26	44.312	51.113	59.156	68.676	79.954	93.324	109.182	127.999	150.334	176.850	208.333	245.712	290.088	342.763	405.272
27	47.084	54.669	63.706	74.484	87.351	102.723	121.100	143.079	169.374	200.841	238.499	283.569	337.502	402.032	479.221
28	49.968	58.403	68.528	80.698	95.339	112.968	134.210	159.817	190.699	227.950	272.889	327.104	392.503	471.378	566.481
29	52.966	62.323	73.640	87.347	103.966	124.135	148.631	178.397	214.583	258.583	312.094	377.170	456.303	552.512	669.447
30	56.085	66.439	79.058	94.461	113.283	136.308	164.494	199.021	241.333	293.199	356.787	434.745	530.312	647.439	790.948

SUMMARY

15.1 Communicate the process of capital investment decisions.

Capital budgeting process

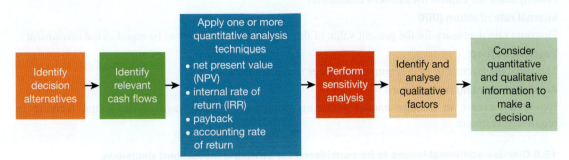

Types of long-term investment decisions

- Operational
- Compliance
- Strategic

15.2 Recognise and apply the relevant cash flows in capital investment decisions.

Common types of relevant cash flows

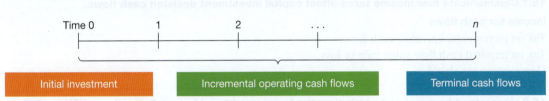

15.3 Perform and interpret net present value (NPV) analysis.

Calculation of net present value

$$NPV = \sum_{t=0}^{n} \frac{\text{Expected cash flow}_t}{(1 + r)^t}$$

Potential discount rates

- Weighted average cost of capital
- Rate reflecting project risk

General decision rules

- Projects with a positive NPV are generally acceptable
- If investment resources are limited, invest in the project(s) having the highest NPV
- If profitability index is greater than 1, accept project
- Projects can be ranked on a profitability index

15.4 Understand the uncertainties of NPV analysis.

Major assumptions and uncertainties

- Cost of initial investment
- Timing and dollar amounts of incremental revenues and costs
- Terminal cash flow values
- Project life
- Appropriate discount rate
- Marginal income tax rate
- Depreciation rules for income taxes

Potential manager bias
Sensitivity analysis
Evaluate how NPV results change with variations in assumptions.

15.5 Reflect on alternative methods (internal rate of return, payback, accrual accounting rate of return) used for capital investment decisions.
Internal rate of return (IRR)
Discount rate necessary for the present value of the discounted cash flows to be equal to the investment
Payback method
Measures the amount of time required to recover the initial investment
Accrual accounting rate of return
Expected increase in average annual operating income as a percentage of the initial increase in required investment

15.6 Discuss additional issues to be considered for strategic investment decisions.
Qualitative issues
Moving baseline concept
Track record of project champion
Cost of reversing the decision
Reputation, risks, environment, quality and community
Post-investment audit
Improve implementation, results and accuracy of future capital budgets

15.7 Communicate how income taxes affect capital investment decision cash flows.
Income tax cash flows
Tax on incremental operating cash flows
Tax on terminal cash flow value gain or loss
Depreciation tax shield

15.8 Understand how real and nominal methods are used to address inflation in an NPV analysis.
Real method
Discount real cash flows at the real rate of interest

$$\text{Real rate of interest} = \text{Risk-free rate} + \text{Risk premium}$$

Nominal method
Discount nominal cash flows at the nominal rate of interest

$$\text{Nominal rate of interest} = (1 + \text{Real rate}) \times (1 + \text{Inflation rate}) - 1$$

Internal consistency in NPV analysis
Cash flows and interest rate must be calculated using the same method (real or nominal)
Cannot use real method if different cash flows are subject to different rates of inflation (or deflation)

KEY TERMS

accrual accounting rate of return The expected increase in average annual operating income as a percentage of the initial increase in required investment.

capital budgeting A budgeting process in which managers choose among investment opportunities that have cash flows occurring over a number of years.

deflation An increase in the general purchasing power of the monetary unit; the opposite of inflation.

discount rate The interest rate that is used across time to reduce the value of future dollars to today's dollars.

discounted payback Future cash flows that have been discounted to reflect the opportunity cost of using funds for other projects.

future value The amount received in the future for a given number of years at a given interest rate, for a given investment today.

inflation The decline in the general purchasing power of the monetary unit, meaning that more monetary units (such as dollars) are needed to purchase goods or services.

internal rate of return (IRR) A method that determines the discount rate necessary for the present value of the discounted cash flows to be equal to the investment.

net present value method (NPV) A method that determines whether an organisation would be better off investing in a project based on the net amount of discounted cash flows for the project.

nominal method A method in which cash inflows and outflows are forecast in nominal dollars (inflated) and discounted using a nominal discount rate.

nominal rate of interest The rate of return required on investments when inflation is present. Calculated by increasing the real rate of interest by the expected rate of inflation.

payback method Measures the amount of time required to recover the initial investment.

post-investment audit Provides feedback about whether operations are meeting expectations.

present value The value in today's dollars of a sum received in the future.

profitability index The ratio of the present value of the cash inflows to the present value of the investment cash outflows.

real method An approach for calculating discounted cash flows in which cash inflows and outflows are forecast in real dollars (no inflation) and discounted using a real rate.

real rate of interest The rate of return required on investments when no inflation is a factor. Calculated as the sum of the risk-free rate and a risk premium.

risk-free rate The 'pure' rate of interest paid on short-term government bonds without considering inflation.

tax shield A depreciation deduction in future years for investments such as buildings, land improvements, equipment and furnishings. The depreciation shields part of operating income from the payment of income taxes.

time value of money The idea that a dollar received today is worth more than a dollar received in the future.

weighted average cost of capital The weighted average rate for the costs of the various sources of financing such as debt and stock.

SELF-STUDY PROBLEMS

Newberry and Mills Company is considering the purchase of new robotic manufacturing equipment. The purchase price is $85 000. The cost for shipping the machine to the plant is $2000. Another $3000 will be spent to remodel the area in which the machine is to be installed. The purchase price includes installation costs. The entity has already spent $1500 in travel costs and employee time on the search for this equipment. The machine is expected to save $30 000 a year in labour and insurance expenses over the next four years, and is expected to be obsolete in four years. Newberry and Mills uses a 10 per cent discount rate as the required rate of return on capital budgeting projects. Ignore income taxes.

Required
(a) Calculate the net present value.
(b) Calculate the profitability index.
(c) Calculate the internal rate of return.
(d) Calculate the payback period.
(e) List factors that you would vary to perform sensitivity analysis and explain why you would vary them.

SOLUTION TO SELF-STUDY PROBLEM 1
(a) First, we summarise the cash flows across time. Notice that the $1500 in travel and employee costs is a sunk cost and does not affect the NPV calculation. Also, no terminal cash flows occur for this project.

Time 0	Years 1–4
Investment	$30 000 savings
$85 000 purchase	
2 000 shipping	
3 000 remodel	
$90 000	

Because cash flows are equal across time, we can treat the incremental cash flows in years 1 to 4 as an annuity to calculate NPV:

$$NPV = -\$90\,000 + \$30\,000 \times (PVFA\ 4\ years,\ 10\%)$$
$$= -\$90\,000 + \$30\,000 \times 3.170 = -\$90\,000 + \$95\,100$$
$$= \$5100$$

(b) Profitability index = $95 100 / $90 000 = 1.057
(c) IRR (calculated using the IRR function in an Excel spreadsheet) = 12.59%
(d) Payback = $90 000 / $30 000 = 3 years
(e) Factors that could be varied for sensitivity analysis include all of the assumptions such as the initial investment amount, the labour and insurance savings, and the discount rate. Because we cannot know future economic conditions, and we cannot know whether technology developments will improve models more rapidly than we expect, we need to perform sensitivity analysis for all of the assumptions we make. Even the initial investment could change if remodelling is more substantial than expected.

SELF-STUDY PROBLEM 2 NPV; IRR; payback with inflation and income taxes

Kestrel and Sons drills residential and commercial wells. The entity is in the process of analysing the purchase of a new drill that would cost $80 000 and have an expected useful life of six years. Several employees have spent $5000 in travel expenses to locate the best drill. Operating the drill would increase revenue by $60 000 per year, but cost an additional $39 000 for labour, maintenance and other related costs. The managers estimate the salvage value of the drill to be $8000. Kestrel's marginal income tax rate is 25 per cent. Government regulations require that each well be registered and that the location of the well meets certain health requirements, such as being at least 100 metres away from septic and sewage systems. An ongoing controversy over the last 15 years centres around whether individual homeowners should be allowed to drill wells but, so far, no regulation has been proposed.

Required

(a) Using a five-year depreciation period, an inflation rate of 4 per cent, a risk-free rate of 5 per cent and a risk premium of 8 per cent, calculate the NPV for the purchase of the drill using the nominal method.
(b) Calculate the IRR.
(c) Calculate the payback period using nominal cash flows.
(d) What regulatory issues would Kestrel consider as qualitative factors?
(e) How would the issues you identified in part (d) affect your assessment of the project risk?

SOLUTION TO SELF-STUDY PROBLEM 2

(a) Figure 15.13 provides a spreadsheet with the NPV calculation using the nominal method for Kestrel and Sons. This spreadsheet demonstrates a format different from that shown in the chapter examples.
(b) Figure 15.14 provides a spreadsheet with the IRR calculation for Kestrel and Sons.
(c) Because the net cash flows in this problem are not uniform (that is, they are not identical) across time, the payback period must be calculated by manually determining the years it takes to recover the investment. Payback does not include the time value of money, so we analyse the cash flows before they are discounted.

	Net nominal cash flow	Balance to recover
Time 0		$80 000
Year 1	$16 380 + $4 000 = $20 380	$80 000 – $20 380 = $59 620
Year 2	$17 035 + $6 400 = $23 435	$59 620 – $23 435 = $36 185
Year 3	$17 717 + $3 840 = $21 557	$36 185 – $21 557 = $14 628
Year 4	$18 425 + $2 304 = $20 729	$14 628 – $14 628 = 0

The initial investment is expected to be fully recovered in more than three years, but less than four. We can estimate the proportion of the fourth year needed to complete the payback as:

$$\$14\,628 \div \$20\,729 = 0.7 \text{ of year } 4$$

Thus, the payback period is estimated as 3.7 years.

(d) Kestrel would have to consider the possible upcoming change in regulation making it impossible for homeowners to drill wells. The percentage of wells drilled that are residential would decrease greatly. If this percentage is high, Kestrel may not be able to bring in the predicted revenue.

(e) The risk premium should probably be increased if residential drilling is a large (say, greater than about 30 per cent) proportion of Kestrel's business. Sensitivity analysis can be done around the discount rate by varying the risk premium to determine the risk rate that brings the NPV to zero.

FIGURE 15.13 NPV calculation for self-study problem 2(a)

	A	B	C	D	E
1	Cash flows:				
2	Increase in revenue	$60,000	Discount rate information:		
3	Increase in labour	($39,000)	Risk-free	5.00%	
4	Total	$21,000	Project risk	8.00%	
5	Terminal value	$8,000	Inflation	4.00%	
6	Investment:				
7	Purchase equipment	($80,000)	Tax rate	25.00%	
8					
9	Nominal discount rate	17.52%			
10					
11	Incremental cash flows:				
12	Period	Incremental CF	Inflated	Less tax	Discounted
13	1	$21,000	$21,840	$16,380	$13,938
14	2	$21,000	$22,714	$17,035	$12,335
15	3	$21,000	$23,622	$17,717	$10,916
16	4	$21,000	$24,567	$18,425	$9,660
17	5	$21,000	$25,550	$19,162	$8,548
18	6	$21,000	$26,572	$19,929	$7,565
19	Total PV of incremental cash flow				$62,961
20					
21	Depreciation tax savings:				
22	Period	MACRS	Depreciation	Tax savings	Discounted
23	1	20.00%	$16,000	$4,000	$3,404
24	2	32.00%	$25,600	$6,400	$4,634
25	3	19.20%	$15,360	$3,840	$2,366
26	4	11.52%	$9,216	$2,304	$1,208
27	5	11.52%	$9,216	$2,304	$1,028
28	6	5.76%	$4,608	$1,152	$437
29	Total PV of tax savings				$13,077
30					
31		Today's dollars	Inflated	After tax	Discounted
32	Terminal value	$8,000	$10,123	$7,592	$2,882
33					
34	Net present value:				
35	Incremental CF	$62,961			
36	Tax savings	$13,077			
37	Terminal value	$2,882			
38	Less investment	($80,000)			
39	NPV	($1,080)			

Examples of Excel formulas:

Nominal discount rate in cell B9: = (1 + D3 + D4)*(1 + D5) − 1

Inflated incremental cash flow in cell C15: = −FV($D$5, A15,, B15)

After-tax incremental cash flow in cell D15: = C15*(1 − $D$7)

Present value of incremental cash flow in cell E15: = −PV($B$9, A15,, D15)

FIGURE 15.14 IRR calculation for self-study problem 2(b)

	A	B	C	D	E	F
41	Combined cash flows:					
42	Period	Investment	Incremental CF	Tax savings	Terminal	Total
43	0	($80,000)				($80,000)
44	1		$16,380	$4,000		$20,380
45	2		$17,035	$6,400		$23,435
46	3		$17,717	$3,840		$21,557
47	4		$18,425	$2,304		$20,729
48	5		$19,162	$2,304		$21,466
49	6		$19,929	$1,152	$10,123	$31,203
50						
51	Internal rate of return	17.46%				

Excel formula to calculate internal rate of return in cell B51: = IRR(F43:F49)

QUESTIONS

15.1 State the three categories of capital investments and briefly explain the best capital investment evaluation tools suitable for each. **LO1, 6**

15.2 Describe the pros and cons of each of the capital budgeting methods learned in this chapter: **LO5**
(a) net present value
(b) internal rate of return
(c) payback
(d) accrual accounting rate of return.

15.3 A community health clinic operates as a not-for-profit entity. Typical capital expenditure decisions involve acquiring equipment that will perform medical tests beyond those currently possible at the clinic (hence, adding revenues) and/or perform tests more efficiently than currently (hence, decreasing expenses). To evaluate such expenditures, the clinic uses a discount rate equal to the return on its investment trust portfolio. Briefly explain why it does this. **LO1, 4**

15.4 Suppose an entity has five different capital budgeting projects from which to choose, but has constrained funds and cannot implement all of the projects. Explain why comparing the projects' NPVs is better than comparing their IRRs. **LO1, 5**

15.5 Due to a newly released safety regulation, Red Rock Chocolates will have to replace the fire safety equipment throughout its production facilities. How should Red Rock management assess this asset replacement? **LO2**

15.6 At recent management meeting the following statement was made by the Chief Operating Officer: 'this project is strategic for the firm and therefore non-discretionary'. Briefly comment on this statement. **LO6**

15.7 Forecasting the terminal cash flow value of equipment 20 years from now is difficult to do accurately, but errors in estimation probably have a small effect on the NPV. Explain. **LO2, 3, 4**

15.8 When projects have longer lives, it is more difficult to accurately estimate the cash flows and discount rates over the life of the project. Explain why this statement is true. **LO1, 6**

15.9 The present value of a given cash flow gets smaller as the number of periods gets larger, regardless of whether cash flow is discounted with a real rate or nominal rate. Explain why this relationship happens and what it means from an economic perspective. **LO8**

15.10 Two methods can be used to incorporate the effects of inflation or deflation into an NPV analysis. In your own words, explain how a nominal discount rate is different from a real discount rate. Why are analyses using the nominal approach potentially more accurate than those using the real approach? **LO8**

15.11 How might inflation influence a decision to acquire an asset now rather than later? **LO8**

15.12 If an entity has unlimited funds, what criterion should be used to determine which projects to invest in? **LO1, 4, 6**

15.13 An international entity requires a rate of return of 15 per cent domestically and in developed countries, but 25 per cent in less-developed countries. Does this requirement mean that the entity is exploiting the less-developed countries? **LO1, 4**

15.14 When we covered cost–volume–profit (CVP) analysis in chapter 4, we calculated the amount of pre-tax profit needed to achieve a given level of after-tax profit. We could calculate a pre-tax rate of return given an after-tax rate of return. Why would it be inappropriate to use a pre-tax discount rate in capital budgeting? (For example, if an entity requires an after-tax return of 10 per cent and has a marginal income tax rate of 50 per cent, why not use a 20 per cent pre-tax rate of return and ignore the separate income tax calculations?) **LO7**

EXERCISES

15.15 Capital budgeting process **LO1**

Put the following six steps for capital budgeting in the most likely order, numbering the first activity as number 1, the second as 2 and so on.
- Perform sensitivity analysis
- Identify decision alternatives
- Analyse qualitative factors
- Identify relevant cash flows

- Apply the relevant quantitative analysis technique
- Consider quantitative and qualitative information to make a decision

15.16 Time value of money
LO2

(a) What is the present value of $8000 received in seven years at 8 per cent interest?

(b) Bonnie Lee buys a savings bond for $125. The bond pays 6 per cent and matures in 10 years. What amount will Bonnie receive when she redeems the bond?

(c) Erik Peterson needs to have $10 000 at the end of five years to purchase a second car. His investment returns 6 per cent. How much does he need to invest now?

(d) Conan Bardwell will receive $1000 in six years from an investment that returns 12 per cent. How much did he invest?

15.17 Present value and future value calculations
LO2, 3

Diamond Ltd agreed to sell some used equipment to one of its employees. Alternative financing arrangements for the sale have been discussed, and the present and future values of each alternative have been determined.

Required

(a) Diamond offered to accept a $1000 down payment and set up a note receivable that calls for four $1000 payments at the end of each of the next four years. What is the NPV of this note if it is discounted at 6 per cent?

(b) The employee agrees to the down payment but would like the note for $4000 to be payable in full at the end of the fourth year. Because of the increased risk associated with the terms of this note, Diamond would apply an 8 per cent discount rate. What is the true selling price of the equipment?

(c) Suppose the employee borrows the $5000 at 8 per cent interest for four years from a bank so that he can pay Diamond the full price of the equipment immediately. Also, suppose that Diamond could invest the $5000 for three years at 7 per cent. What is the selling price of the equipment? What would be the future value of Diamond's investment?

15.18 NPV analysis
LO3

Government supervisors in a remote area of Queensland are considering the purchase of a small used plane to save on travel costs. The plane will cost $400 000 and can be sold in five years for 20 per cent of the original cost.

Required

If 10 per cent is the required rate of return, what minimum annual savings in transportation costs are needed for this plane to be a good investment? Ignore income taxes.

15.19 NPV calculations with taxes
LO3

Overnight Laundry is considering the purchase of a new pressing machine that would cost $96 000 and produce incremental operating cash flows of $25 000 annually for 10 years. The machine has a terminal cash flow value of $6000 and is depreciated for income tax purposes using straight-line depreciation over a 10-year life. Overnight Laundry's marginal tax rate is 33.3 per cent. The entity uses a discount rate of 18 per cent.

Required

What is the NPV of the project?

15.20 NPV and IRR calculations
LO3, 5

Axel Ltd is planning to buy a new machine with the expectation that this investment should earn a rate of return of at least 15 per cent. This machine, which costs $150 000, would yield an estimated net cash flow of $30 000 a year for 10 years.

Required

(a) What is the NPV for this proposal?

(b) What is the IRR for this proposal?

15.21 Equipment replacement; NPV; IRR; payback
LO3, 5

Garfield Construction is considering replacing an old machine that is currently being used. The old machine is fully depreciated, but it can be used for another five years, at which time it would have no terminal cash flow value. Garfield can sell the old machine for $60 000 on the date that the new machine is purchased.

If the purchase occurs, the new machine will be acquired for a cash payment of $1 million. Because of the increased efficiency of the new machine, estimated annual cash savings of $300 000 would be generated during its useful life of five years. The new machine is not expected to have any terminal cash flow value.

Required

(a) Garfield requires investments to earn a 12 per cent return. What is the NPV for replacing the old machine with the new machine?

(b) What is the IRR to replace the old machine?

(c) What is the payback period for the new machine?

15.22 NPV, IRR, ARR and payback methods
LO3, 5

Amaro Hospital, a not-for-profit entity that is not subject to income taxes, is considering the purchase of new equipment costing $20 000 to achieve cash savings of $5000 per year in operating costs. The estimated useful life is 10 years, with no salvage value. Amaro's minimum expected return is 14 per cent.

Required

(a) What is the NPV of this investment?

(b) What is the IRR?

(c) What is the accrual accounting rate of return based on the initial investment?

(d) What is the payback period?

15.23 Strategic investment decisions
LO4, 6

FreshTucker Limited allows divisional managers to make capital investment decisions up to $10 million. However, divisional managers are required to send to head office details of each decision taken, including their justifications. The manager of the hospitality and conference facilities division, Ceila Wang, has been trying to improve this process within her division. At present, department managers within the division are required to provide a detailed NPV analysis of their investment proposals. Because of the nature of her division, Ceila wonders whether the right long-term projects are treated fairly within this decision model. She feels that some of the investment opportunities proposed by department managers are more strategic and a lot of potential projects do not seem to be meeting the positive NPV requirement.

Required

(a) Identify reasons why the projects are not meeting a positive NPV requirement.

(b) What type of qualitative factors would be relevant to the projects?

15.24 Strategic investment decisions
LO4, 6

Refer question 15.23 above. Outline how Ceila might improve the investment decision-making model within the hospitality and conference facilities division to cater for strategic investments.

15.25 Relevant cash flows; NPV analysis with taxes and inflation
LO3, 7, 8

Clearwater Bottling Company sells bottled spring water for $12 per case, with variable costs of $7 per case. The company has been selling 200 000 cases per year, and expects to continue at that rate unless it accepts a special order from Blue Danube Restaurant. Blue Danube has offered to buy 20 000 cases per year at $9 per case. Clearwater must agree to make the sales for a five-year period. Blue Danube will not take fewer than 20 000 cases but is willing to take more.

Clearwater's current capacity is 210 000 cases per year. Capacity could be increased to 260 000 per year if new equipment costing $100 000 were purchased. The equipment would have a useful life of five years and no salvage value. Maintenance on the new equipment would increase fixed costs by $20 000 each year. Variable costs per unit would be unchanged. Clearwater has a marginal income tax rate of 25 per cent. Inflation is estimated to be 4 per cent over each of the next five years. The risk-free rate is estimated to be 5 per cent. Clearwater can earn a rate of 12 per cent if it invests in an alternative investment having similar risk.

Required

(a) Create a timeline showing the relevant cash flows for this problem.

(b) Ignoring inflation, using straight-line depreciation over five years and using a 12 per cent discount rate, determine the NPV if 20 000 cases are sold.

(c) Ignoring inflation, using straight-line depreciation over five years and using a 12 per cent discount rate, determine the number of cases Blue Danube would need to purchase to bring the NPV to zero.

15.26 NPV and payback with taxes
LO3, 7

Equipment with a cost of $60 000 will, if acquired, generate annual savings of $30 000 for six years, at which time it will have no further use or value. The entity has a marginal tax rate of 40 per cent and requires a 10 per cent rate of return. It uses straight-line depreciation. Ignore inflation.

Required

(a) What is the after-tax cash flow for each year?

(b) What is the NPV of this investment?

(c) What is the payback period?

15.27 IRR **LO5**

Ferris Industries has $50 000 available to invest in new equipment. Management is considering four different equipment investments, each of which requires $50 000. The expected after-tax cash flow for each project has been estimated as follows:

	Year					
	1	**2**	**3**	**4**	**5**	**6**
Project 1	$10 000	$12 000	$14 000	$16 000	$16 000	$16 000
Project 2	40 000	5 000	(3 000)	40 000	5 000	1 000
Project 3	18 000	(16 000)	50 000	50 000	3 000	3 000
Project 4	30 000	—	—	30 000	30 000	30 000

Required

(a) Rank the projects in terms of desirability using the internal rate of return for each project as the criterion. Use Excel or a similar spreadsheet to calculate the IRRs

(b) What other factors should be considered in making the decision of which investment to choose?

15.28 Alternative technologies and capital budgeting with taxes **LO4, 7**

Lymbo Company must install safety devices throughout its plant or it will lose its insurance coverage. Two alternatives are acceptable to the insurer. The first costs $100 000 to install and $20 000 to maintain annually. The second costs $150 000 to install and $10 000 to maintain annually. Each has a five-year income tax life and a 15-year useful life. Lymbo's discount rate is 12 per cent, its marginal tax rate is 30 per cent and it uses straight-line depreciation.

Required

(a) Which system should be installed? Why?

(b) If Lymbo was a not-for-profit entity that does not pay income taxes on its operations, which system would be installed?

15.29 Business expansion; NPV, taxes **LO3, 7**

MacArthur's is a fast food company planning to invest in a restaurant expansion that entails the refurbishment and opening of four new stores across the country. The cost of this investment is $4 800 000. It is to be depreciated (straight-line basis) over a period of 10 years with no residual value. The discount rate is 8 per cent. The company tax rate is 30 per cent. The other relevant cash flow information relating to this project is presented in the following table.

Year	Net cash inflow
1	$ 999 400
2	$1 599 400
3	$2 399 400
4	$3 999 400
5	$4 799 400
6	$5 999 400
7	$5 199 400
8	$4 799 400
9	$2 399 400
10	$ 799 400

Rather than building the new stores, the MacArthur's management team have also considered expanding offshore. However, the management accountant is concerned about the riskiness of this business and that not all factors have been included in the calculation. There is difficulty in capturing some qualitative non-financial factors and estimating other longer-term cash flows.

Required

(a) Calculate the NPV for the proposed investment.

(b) Following on from the calculations in part (a), should MacArthur's make the investment in the four new stores?

(c) What would you advise on preparing for the offshore decision? Discussion should include reference to the financial and non-financial factors that may influence this decision and suggestions to improve the decision model.

15.30 Business expansion; NPV, taxes   **LO2, 3, 4, 7**

Diggers is a coal mining company. Diggers has planned to invest in replacement equipment. Its existing equipment has come to the end of its useful life and will be scrapped with no resale value. The cost of the new replacement investment is $2 500 000. It is to be depreciated (straight-line basis) over a period of 10 years with no residual value. The discount rate is 8 per cent. The company tax rate is 30 per cent. The other relevant cash flow information relating to this project is presented in the following table.

Year	Net cash inflow
1	$ 500 000
2	$ 800 000
3	$1 200 000
4	$2 000 000
5	$2 400 000
6	$3 000 000
7	$2 600 000
8	$2 400 000
9	$1 200 000
10	$ 400 000

The management team have also considered moving to clean coal technology to help improve the image of the company around issues of sustainability and stakeholders' environmental concerns. While the net present value (NPV) of the alternative clean coal technology option has been calculated as $2 million, the management accountant is concerned that not all factors have been included in the calculation. There is difficulty in capturing some qualitative non-financial factors and estimating other longer-term cash flows.

Required

(a) Calculate the NPV for the proposed investment.

(b) In your opinion, which investment should the coal mining company make (replacement or clean coal technology)? Discussion should include reference to the financial and non-financial factors that may influence this decision and suggestions to improve the decision model.

PROBLEMS

15.31 Real interest rates; uncertainties; effects of time   **LO8**

Managers often use the real interest rate to help them decide whether to take on a new project.

Required

(a) What two factors are included in the real interest rate?

(b) What economic factors could affect the two aspects you identified in part (a)? List as many factors as you can.

(c) Discuss how certain you can be that interest rates will remain constant over the life of a project.

(d) Does the time length of a project affect your answer to part (c)? Why?

15.32 IRR; developing a discount rate; evaluating risk   **LO5, 6**

The local homeless shelter received a large donation from a wealthy benefactor and asked you to review its decision-making process for the proposed investment choice. The shelter's financial adviser suggested using the IRR to evaluate three different projects:

• a hotel that offers rooms based on the renter's ability to pay

• an apartment complex for elderly who receive rent subsidisation from a federal government agency

• a small cardboard-box manufacturing entity that will serve as a job training facility for homeless clients.

Required

(a) In your own words, describe the advantages and disadvantages of using IRR for this decision.

(b) This not-for-profit entity uses an IRR hurdle rate of 15 per cent for most projects. Is it a good idea for an organisation to use the same hurdle rate for most projects? Why?

(c) List information that might help you develop a hurdle rate for each project.

(d) Which alternative do you believe is most financially risky for the homeless shelter? Explain your thinking.

15.33 Timeline; maximum payment for zero NPV; qualitative factors; uncertainties   **LO3, 4, 7**

The Mavericks are a professional football team with a long tradition of winning. However, over the last three years, the team has not won a major championship, and attendance at games has dropped considerably. A large football manufacturer is the team's major corporate sponsor. Cliff Walker, president of the football company, is also the president of the Mavericks. Cliff proposes that the team purchase the services of a star player, Jackson Howard. Jackson would create great excitement for Maverick fans and sponsors.

Jackson's agent notifies Cliff that terms for the superstar's signing with the Mavericks are a signing bonus of $8 million payable now and a house in a Sydney beachside suburb at a cost of $5 million. The annual salary and cost of living adjustments are under negotiation.

Cliff's initial reaction is one of shock. However, he decides to examine the cash inflows expected if Jackson is signed for a four-year contract. Net gate receipts would most likely increase by $2 million a year, corporate sponsorships would increase $2.5 million per year, television royalties would increase $0.5 million per year and merchandise income (net of costs) would increase $1 million per year. Cliff believes that a 12 per cent discount rate is appropriate for this investment. The Mavericks' marginal tax rate is 20 per cent. The signing bonus can be amortised (depreciated) over the four-year period for income tax purposes, providing an annual tax deduction of $2 million.

Required

(a) Create a timeline showing the relevant cash flows for this problem.

(b) Assuming that he is not willing to lose money on the contract, what is the maximum amount per year that Cliff would be willing to pay Jackson? You will need to set up a spreadsheet for this calculation and, through trial and error, find an amount that brings the NPV to zero, or use an algebraic approach and annuity factors.

(c) Identify possible additional factors that Cliff should consider when deciding whether to sign Jackson to the four-year contract. List as many factors as you can.

(d) For each of the relevant cash flows in this problem, discuss why Cliff cannot be certain about the dollar amount of the cash flow.

15.34 Qualitative factors in investment decisions   **LO1, 4, 6**

Energy plays an important role in improving people's lifestyles. In Australia, our energy consumption is growing and is forecasted to increase by 50 per cent over the next 15 years. The available power resources in Australia (currently 80 per cent coal-fuelled) will not cope with the increasing demands. Further investment opportunities are required for long-term power supply, and options are currently being investigated by governments. Due to Australia's high greenhouse gas emissions from the current coal-fired power plants, some have advocated for nuclear energy as the optimal 'clean' power alternative. Australia exports up to 10 000 tonnes of uranium per year (enough to supply more than twice its annual electricity needs), but has not yet used uranium to fuel its own energy industry. The adoption of nuclear power generation could reduce greenhouse gas emissions by one-fifth, and supply electricity to a third of the country. Any decision to invest in nuclear power is deemed politically sensitive. Nuclear power generation would require adopting world's best practice to prevent unsafe reactor designs and minimise environmental risks.

An Australian study found that accurate capital budgeting and subsequent cost control is a major factor in determining the successful provision of environmentally clean and cheap electricity in Australia. The report detailed the history of costing issues faced by nuclear power plant investors around the world. The most significant implementation problems relate to design flaws and licensing delays (for example, the Shoreham plant in Long Island, New York State, cost $5 billion to build and was never allowed to operate). Subsequent operational costing issues highlighted in the report were as a result of inadequate operator training and non-uniform designs that prevented the achievement of economies of scale in output volume.

The study provided a breakdown of the history of costs relating to nuclear power plant employment. In general, the costs consist of the:

- construction costs of building a plant with 1 GW capacity (approximately $1000 per kW)
- operating costs of running the plant and generating energy (approximately 1.3 cents per kW-hour)
- cost of waste disposal from the plant (approximately 0.2 cents per kW-hour)
- cost of decommissioning the plant (approximately 10 per cent of construction costs).

According to the report, construction costs are difficult to quantify but estimates provided have been based on worldwide examples. Construction timeframes were estimated to be around three years to completion and commencement of operations. Part of the operating cost estimates includes the raw material (uranium ore) costs, which are approximately 0.05 cents per kW-hour. The costs provided were based on a 40-year plant lifetime with discount interest rates of around 5 per cent. If the proposed capital budgeting scenario lives up to its promises, the study concludes that nuclear power will provide cheaper electricity than any fossil-fuel-based generating facility in Australia. While the investment analysis might suggest nuclear power is a financially worthwhile investment for Australia, it is important to note that the final decision to invest in a project such as this one will depend on many other qualitative factors, including stakeholder acceptance.[3]

Required

(a) Identify the key qualitative factors that would need to be considered in any investment decision relating to nuclear power.
(b) How might these qualitative factors be incorporated into a decision model?

15.35 Capital budgeting methods; sensitivity analysis; spreadsheet development; uncertainties   LO6
Your brother, Jack, was laid off from his job with a large and famous software company. He would like to sell his shares in the company and use the proceeds to start a restaurant. The shares are currently valued at $500 000. He received a job offer from a competitor that will pay $90 000 per year plus benefits. He asked you to help him decide the best course of action.

Required

(a) What are the alternatives that Jack faces?
(b) Choose the most appropriate analysis technique and explain your choice.
(c) If your brother chooses to open a restaurant, what are his opportunity costs?
(d) List the steps you would take to develop a spreadsheet that your brother could manipulate to help with the quantitative aspects of this decision. Assume that you have time only to set up a template and that your brother will fill in the specific information. However, you need to tell him the general categories of information he will need to gather.
(e) List uncertainties about whether taking the job offer would turn out well for your brother. List as many uncertainties as you can.
(f) List uncertainties about whether opening a restaurant would turn out well for your brother. List as many uncertainties as you can.
(g) Explain why it is possible for your brother to make a good decision even though he cannot know for sure how well his alternatives would work out.

15.36 Choice of method; uncertainties; addressing company policy   LO1, 4, 6
Paradise Resorts, a Hong Kong company that owns and operates holiday resorts, has hired you to analyse its investment opportunities in Australia. The entity's managers have always used the payback method and have asked you to prepare an analysis comparing three different resorts: one on the Gold Coast, another on the Sunshine Coast and a third holiday resort in the Northern Territory.

Required

(a) List four methods that could be used to analyse this long-term decision. Describe each method in your own words.
(b) In your own words, describe the advantages and disadvantages of each method you identified in part (a).
(c) Explain why it is not possible to perfectly predict a project's cash flows.
(d) In using quantitative results for decision making, would you place equal reliance on the results of all four analysis techniques? Explain.
(e) Discuss how the managers of the Hong Kong company might respond to your advice if you recommend an analysis method other than the payback method.
(f) Write a brief memo to the CEO of the company recommending your choice of analysis method, and explaining the most important issues for the CEO to consider when choosing an analysis method.

15.37 Timeline; relevant costs; NPV; payback; uncertainties   **LO2, 3, 5, 6**

Irrigation Supply is negotiating with a major hardware chain to supply heavy-duty sprinkler heads at $18 000 each year for five years. Irrigation Supply would need to retool at a cost of $20 000 to fill this order. Incremental costs associated with the order (in addition to the retooling costs) would be $12 000 per year. In addition, existing fixed overhead costs would be reallocated among Irrigation Supply's products, which would result in a $1000 overhead charge against the special order. For income taxes, the retooling costs would be depreciated using the straight-line method with no terminal cash flow value, ignoring the half-year convention. Irrigation Supply's marginal income tax rate is 25 per cent. Assume that all cash flows (except the initial retooling costs) occur at year-end. The entity's discount rate is 16 per cent.

Required

(a) Create a timeline showing the relevant cash flows for this problem.

(b) What is the NPV of the special order?

(c) What is the payback period for this project?

(d) For this problem, what do you learn from the NPV analysis and what do you learn from the payback period?

(e) The managers of the hardware store (the customers in this problem) believe that demand will ensure their ability to purchase sprinkler heads from Irrigation Supply. Explain why the hardware chain's managers cannot be certain about the future demand for sprinkler heads.

(f) Discuss how uncertainties for the hardware store could lead to uncertainties for Irrigation Supply.

15.38 Government infrastructure investment   **LO4, 6**

As part of community town planning, an industrial estate was proposed for development on the outskirts of a growing township which was a two-hour commute from the Melbourne CBD. The estate required water and sewerage facilities to be provided. At this stage, the land featured native vegetation including a few big old gum trees, an old cave with Indigenous Australian artefacts, an old building near the cave and a local waterhole frequented by native wildlife.

As part of the estate development, the following factors were considered by the Council Water Board:

1. financial NPV
2. environmental impacts:
   - land clearing
   - discharges to the environment (liquid waste into sewerage drains; carbon dioxide emissions to air; noise pollution)
   - water requirements
3. social impacts:
   - Indigenous heritage
   - European heritage
   - community acceptance

The following two developments were submitted to the Council's Water Board.

Project 1		Project 2	
Financial NPV	−$8 000 000	Financial NPV	−$4 000 000
Environmental impacts		Environmental impacts	
Land clearing: 5 hectares (biodiversity impacted; loss of animal and plant species) Discharges: Additional facility cost to provide greywater use to water sports oval		Land clearing: 7 hectares (biodiversity impacted; loss of animal and plant species) Discharges: Treated water discharged directly to stream	
Water requirements: Pumping station (noise buffer included in NPV costs); additional electricity for pumping		Water requirements: Gravity fed water, as using land where Indigenous cave artefacts are (no noise buffer required)	

(continued)

(continued)

Project 1 Social impacts	Project 2 Social impacts
Indigenous heritage: Cave site avoided in proposal European heritage: NIA	Indigenous heritage: Cave site used in proposal European heritage: Old building near cave site will be demolished
Community acceptance: Consultations suggest this option is acceptable	Community acceptance: Several complaints have been received

Required

(a) Which project should be accepted?

(b) Discuss the ramifications of each option.

15.39 NPV with and without inflation; tax effects   **LO7, 8**

Xi Phan, CEO of the Furniture Supply Group, is considering an investment to upgrade his current computer-aided design equipment. The new equipment would cost $110 000, have a five-year useful life and a zero terminal cash flow value. The new equipment would generate annual cash operating savings of $36 000. The entity's required rate of return is 18 per cent each year.

Required

(a) Calculate the NPV of the project. Assume a 25 per cent marginal tax rate and straight-line depreciation, ignoring the half-year convention.

(b) Phan is wondering whether the method in part (a) provides a correct analysis of the effects of inflation. The 18 per cent required rate of return incorporates an element attributable to anticipated inflation. For purposes of his analysis, Phan assumes that the existing rate of inflation, 5 per cent annually, will persist over the next five years. Recalculate the NPV, adjusting the cash flows as appropriate for the 5 per cent inflation rate.

(c) Compare the quantitative results for parts (a) and (b). In general, how does inflation affect capital budgeting quantitative results?

(d) Explain why managers cannot predict future inflation rates with total accuracy.

(e) In your own words, explain how failure to consider the effects of inflation might bias managers' capital budgeting decisions.

15.40 NPV with taxes and inflation; uncertainties; sensitivity analyses and interpretation   **LO6, 7, 8**

Kelly Black is manager of the customer service division of a retail computer store, Quik Computers. Kelly would like to buy computer diagnostic equipment that costs $10 000. The equipment will last five years. Kelly estimates that the incremental operating cash savings from using the equipment will be $3000 annually, measured at current prices. For income tax purposes, she will depreciate the equipment using the straight-line method and ignoring the half-year convention. Kelly requires a 10 per cent real rate of return. The annual inflation rate is 5 per cent, and the marginal income tax rate is 30 per cent.

Required

(a) Create a spreadsheet schedule showing the NPV calculations for the equipment.

(b) Identify factors in your calculations that are uncertain, and explain why the factors are uncertain.

(c) Explain how changes in technology might influence the risk involved in this project.

(d) Decide which of the factors you identified in part (b) would likely have a significant impact on the NPV calculation. Use your spreadsheet to vary each of these factors, performing sensitivity analyses.

(e) Use the quantitative results and your judgement to interpret your sensitivity analyses. Which factors seem to have the largest and smallest effects on the NPV results?

(f) Describe the pros and cons of investing in the equipment.

(g) Suppose you are the cost accountant for Quik Computers. Use the information you learned from the preceding analyses to write a memo to Kelly with your recommendation about whether to accept or reject this project. Refer in your memo to one or more attachments of spreadsheet schedules that would be useful to Kelly. In your memo, address the most important factors that Kelly should consider in making the decision.

15.41 NPV with taxes and inflation; qualitative factors; sensitivity analysis   **LO6, 7**

Wildcat Welders manufactures new and repairs old irrigation sprinkler systems in Western Australia. The entity has been plagued with industrial accidents involving its old welding technology. A new (safer) welding robot has been developed that will reduce labour costs, workers compensation costs and direct materials costs. The investment would be $10 million. The annual cash savings would be $7 million but it would cost $2 million a year to operate the machine.

The robots have an eight-year useful life with a terminal cash flow value of $1 million. The robots qualify for a government depreciation schedule that allows for faster depreciation of some capital assets. The schedule is as follows:

Year	1	2	3	4	5	6	7	8
Depreciation rate	14.29%	24.49%	17.49%	12.49%	8.93%	8.92%	8.93%	4.46%

Inflation is estimated to be 5 per cent per year. The risk-free rate is estimated to be 4 per cent, and the entity's managers require a minimum risk premium of 6 per cent. Wildcat's marginal income tax rate is 25 per cent.

Required

(a) Develop a spreadsheet to calculate the NPV of this project, using the nominal rate method. Be sure to include a data input box at the top of the spreadsheet to allow for sensitivity analysis.
(b) Identify a qualitative factor that could potentially override a negative NPV in making the decision to buy this equipment. Explain.
(c) Alter the risk premium to perform sensitivity analyses, and answer the following questions:
   (i) Explain how you decided which values of the risk premium were reasonable to investigate.
   (ii) Describe how changing the risk premium affects the NPV for this project.
   (iii) The new equipment would most likely lower Wildcat's risk of future lawsuits because of the reduced accident rate. Explain how this factor affects your assessment of the appropriateness of the risk premium.
(d) Because Wildcat is uncertain about whether the annual cash savings from the equipment would be $7 million, alter the cash savings to perform sensitivity analyses and answer the following questions:
   (i) Explain how you decided which values of the cash savings were reasonable to investigate.
   (ii) Describe how changing the cash savings affects the NPV for this project.
   (iii) Identify the level of cash savings that results in a NPV of zero.
(e) Suppose that current inflation is 2 per cent. Given this information, how reasonable is the inflation rate used by Wildcat? Perform sensitivity analysis around the inflation rate by changing the rate and observing the effects of the change on NPV. Explain how you made your choices.

15.42 Strategic investment decisions   **LO6**

The Nutrition Division of Regal Foods focuses on health-related products. Historically, the Nutrition Division has been an excellent contributor to group performance, with annual growth rates of up to 12 per cent for the period 2006 to 2012, and revenues exceeding $2 billion. However, divisional manager Bruce Buncle has found growth increasingly difficult to maintain. An increasingly crowded market for health and nutritional products seems to be the main driver of these difficulties. As a consequence, debt levels of the division seem to be rising. However, Buncle is conscious that he needs to develop new products and markets in line with company objectives.

Regal currently uses a common capital investment evaluation process for all investment projects in excess of $10 million. A summary of key criteria includes the following.

• Projects must generate a positive NPV over the life of the project.
• A minimum annual return on investment (ROI) of 10 per cent must be achievable within two years of the project commencing.
• Project proposals must be presented in standard format with supporting calculations.

Buncle cites the following example to illustrate his frustrations with the current process.

Buncle and his management team have been considering a range of investment opportunities and have been contemplating a major investment in the bottled water industry. While the industry has its challenges (for example, environmental opposition to the use of plastic bottles, tightening environmental regulations and the expectation of reduced carbon emissions), Buncle and his management team see a lot of potential with such a strategic move. However, where significant capital expenditure is required, Buncle finds the company investment decision-making processes frustrating.

The management team within the Nutrition Division has identified a new spring water source in a regional area — Hepburn Shire. The division plans to build a new water bottling plant to take advantage of the springs. The local authorities are happy to support the project. In fact, the local authorities are willing to forgo local taxes and provide subsidies to ensure the plant is built. The region has experienced relatively high levels of unemployment in recent years and the new plant will generate some 100 local new jobs. While there is some local opposition to the new facility on environmental grounds, Buncle considers these to be manageable. While he knows the project's financial benefit looks not all that favourable, he believes the investment is a good strategic move for his division (particularly with the synergies expected with other parts of the division) and aligns with the company's growth strategy. A summary of the project's details is provided in the table.

Bottled water project at Hepburn Shire — summary data

Life	10 years
Cost	$28.2 million
NPV	($0.6 million)
Average ROI over 10 years	12%
ROI in year 1	6%
Average ROI over first three years	8%

Buncle has raised his frustrations with senior management, arguing that projects such as his bottled water project are never going to meet the strict and somewhat narrow criteria currently used by Regal. He has been asked to come up with an alternative model for evaluating these types of strategic investments. He hopes to use the bottled water project to demonstrate his suggested model.

Buncle has come to you for some advice on the development of a new model.

Required

(a) Outline the key components of your proposed model for evaluating strategic investments at Regal Foods.

(b) Use the bottled water project of the Nutrition Division to illustrate the benefits of your model. On the basis of your analysis, would you recommend the investment be undertaken?

ENDNOTES

1. Vesty, G, Brooks, A & Oliver, J 2015, 'Contemporary capital investment appraisal from a management accounting and integrated thinking perspective: case study evidence', *Sustainability and capital investment case studies*, CPA Australia, cpaaustralia.com.au.
2. ibid.
3. Information from World Nuclear Association 2010, www.world-nuclear.org; Australian Bureau of Agriculture and Resource Economics (ABARE) 2003, *Australian energy; national and state projections to 2019–20*, report for the Ministerial Council on Energy, June; *The Economist* 2006, 'Nuclear power: the ghostly flickers of a new dawn', 23 November, p. 77; Howard, J (Prime Minister) 2006, transcript of address to the Committee for Economic Development of Australia, Sydney Convention and Exhibition Centre, 18 July, www.pm.gov.au; *Nuclear power education*, www.nuclearinfo.net.

ACKNOWLEDGEMENTS

Photo 15A: © fizkes / Shutterstock.com
Photo 15B: © Bojan Milinkov / Shutterstock.com
Photo 15C: © Olaf Speier / Shutterstock.com
Figure 15.8 and 15.9: © CPA Australia

CHAPTER 16

The strategic management of costs and revenues

LEARNING OBJECTIVES

After studying this chapter you should be able to:

16.1 explain the value chain activities that provide for continuous cost improvement

16.2 explain the concept of customer profitability analysis and suggest qualitative factors for inclusion in a strategic customer analysis model

16.3 understand target costing principles and techniques

16.4 communicate the concept of kaizen costing and explain how it compares to target costing

16.5 describe the characteristics of life cycle costing

16.6 evaluate pricing methods and describe how cost-based prices and market-based prices are managed.

IN BRIEF

Managers and accountants make decisions about long-term organisational strategies as well as short-term operating plans. These strategies and plans include mutually dependent decisions about how to control costs and price products. Both this chapter and the next specifically explore these issues. In this chapter, we focus on value chain analysis for cost improvement, customer profitability, kaizen costing, life cycle costing, target costing principles and pricing considerations. Managers increasingly adopt these practices to help them improve efficiency and achieve profitability goals.

16.1 Value chain activities for continuous cost improvement

LEARNING OBJECTIVE 16.1 Explain the value chain activities that provide for continuous cost improvement.

The link between costs and prices has become increasingly important with global competition. Managers and accountants must simultaneously manage both. Successful entities continuously improve their cost efficiency, charge competitive prices and focus on long-term organisational strategies. Over the long term, profitable organisations continuously seek ways to become more efficient, reduce costs and improve interactions with suppliers and customers. A variety of methods — such as value chain and supply chain analysis, just-in-time (JIT) production and managing quality costs — are available for analysing and improving the systems used to produce and deliver goods and services. We begin this chapter by learning several specific methods used to manage costs, and then we explore pricing methods.

Value chain and supply chain analysis

As discussed in chapter 1, analysis of the value chain can lead to improved relationships between the entity and others in the value chain, creating an extended organisation that can respond flexibly to dynamic and competitive environments. The analysis of value-added or non-value-added activities within the entity and in relation to suppliers and customers can lead to business decisions that either eliminate non-value-added activities or improve value. This can also serve as a source of competitive advantage as organisations aim to manage their value chain better than their competitors. Value chain analysis can also lead to improved communication, as individuals in each part of the process begin to share their abilities, needs and requirements with others in the value chain. For example, in response to budget cuts the University of California was able to reduce annual operating expenses by more than US$75 million by undertaking a comprehensive study of the cost and quality of administrative activities. One area of saving was found in eliminating duplicated activities across faculties and instead creating a shared service centre. In Europe, Volkswagen has an ambitious plan to cut costs by 5 billion euros to strengthen its competitive edge against rivals such as Toyota. It is aiming to achieve the savings by ceasing production of unprofitable models and reducing expensive equipment.

Value chain analysis also encourages managers to consider whether they should outsource some of their value-added activities; for example, if outsourcing is less costly than performing the activity internally or if it is not a core competency of the organisation. For example, Microsoft's managers probably decided to outsource Xbox manufacturing because the production of hardware components is not one of Microsoft's core competencies. Ultimately, the decision of whether to outsource an activity depends on both quantitative and qualitative factors.

As organisations work to increase profitability, improving their relationships with suppliers becomes a priority. Improvements can be identified through supply chain analysis. As discussed in chapter 1, the **supply chain** is the flow of resources from the initial suppliers through the delivery of goods and services to customers and clients. The initial suppliers may be inside or outside the entity. Negotiating lower costs with suppliers is a straightforward way to reduce costs. Suppliers may be willing to reduce prices, particularly for organisations willing to sign long-term purchase commitments. Occasionally, entities work with suppliers to help them reduce their costs so that the savings can be passed along.

Accountants analyse supply chains by determining inventory level requirements, starting with customer demand for products or services. Opportunities to reduce cost and improve quality and response are identified through tracking and analysing use patterns of raw materials, supplies, finished goods and shipped goods. Vendors are included in inventory management decisions as part of this process. With close cooperation, inventory levels can be managed to reduce the quantitative costs of insurance and storage and the qualitative costs of quality changes and timeliness of delivery.

Technology and internet capabilities increasingly provide suppliers with access to their customers' inventory level information. Suppliers use this information to time deliveries so that their customers maintain desired inventory levels. Suppliers also use this information to improve their own production planning. Providing internet access to product or service information can be risky, however. Organisations need adequate security measures such as firewalls to protect sensitive information that might have competitive value. An example of the use of technology to improve production planning can be seen locally with Woolworths' Mercury Two Program, a $1 billion supply chain overhaul. Mercury Two is focused on identifying customer buying patterns so that Woolworths will not only be able to know what customers have bought, but also anticipate what customers will buy. Based on such demand predictions, Woolworths will then work with suppliers so that they can adapt their systems to meet the customer demand predictions. With the growth of online shopping for groceries, Woolworths has identified that customers will want delivery options that best suit them. This opens up many possibilities for the delivery process, such as collection at a store, railway station or any outlet run by Woolworths. The availability of different delivery options will make the distribution system more complex and Woolworths will need to address how to make the supply chain efficient. Woolworths hopes to achieve cost savings and revenue growth by rethinking the supply chain, and making use of big data to understand and meet customers' needs and wants.

Beyond issues of cost, quality, response time and information access, environmental and social considerations are also critical aspects of supply chain analysis. Sustainable supply chain management requires firms to consider a range of issues including:

- the environmental and social performance and credentials of potential and current suppliers
- the source of raw materials: water-efficient farming practices, avoidance of harmful chemicals, reuse and use of recycled materials
- manufacturing and human rights, and environmental protection, worker safety and conditions; compliance with environmental standards and legislation; production of recyclable or biodegradable products; minimisation of energy use, water use and emissions
- distribution: use of modern and efficient clean modes of transportation; intelligent transport decisions; local sourcing; carbon offsetting
- retailing: promotion of customer recycling-practices; provision of product sustainability information.

Companies committed to managing the environmental impacts of their supply chains can commit to green supply chain management (GSCM) principles (figure 16.1). These principles recognise the importance of green purchasing; green manufacturing and materials management; green distribution and marketing; and reverse logistics. Reverse logistics involves closing the supply chain loop by remanufacturing and recycling materials into products with market value.

Interest in such closed-loop supply chains has intensified given growing awareness of the notion of a circular economy. The circular economy movement strives to establish restorative economic systems which are 'not just concerned with the reduction of the use of the environment as a sink for residuals, but rather with the creation of self-sustaining production systems in which materials are used over and over again'.[1]

One particularly noteworthy commitment of a large firm to closed-loop supply chain management was the pledge by Apple to one day be able to manufacture iPhone and other products from recycled materials alone. This will be achieved through initiatives designed to encourage customers to return old products and investment in in-house disassembly processes. This has included the development of a new machine known as Liam that currently dismantles more than 2 million phones per year. Significant further work, however, is required to boost this number of dismantled phones to match annual iPhone sales volumes.[2]

From a social perspective, much of the interest in sustainable supply chain management has been triggered by major industrial disasters in which, for instance, employees working in unsafe factories have suffered serious injury or death. One such example was the Bangladesh Rana Plaza disaster in which more than 1000 garment workers were killed when the factory they were working in collapsed. This incident resulted in a global outcry and pressure was placed on large fashion brands to do more to eliminate the possibility of such incidents ever happening again in their supply chains. Doing so is a significant challenge given the complexity of global supply chains. It is not uncommon for a large multinational company to have many thousands of first-tier suppliers and an overall supply chain that extends more than 15 layers.[3]

Beyond the denial of worker safety within global supply chains, given estimates of more than 20 million people forced to work as labourers worldwide, the issue of modern slavery has been at the forefront of public attention. Following the passing of the *Modern Slavery Act*, large organisations (with greater than A$100 million in consolidated revenue) are now required to report annually on the modern slavery risks within their operations and supply chains; the actions they are taking to mitigate these risks; and the effectiveness of these actions. These statements will be approved by the organisations' board of directors (or equivalent) and made publicly available through a central Australian government register.[4]

FIGURE 16.1 Green supply chain management[5]

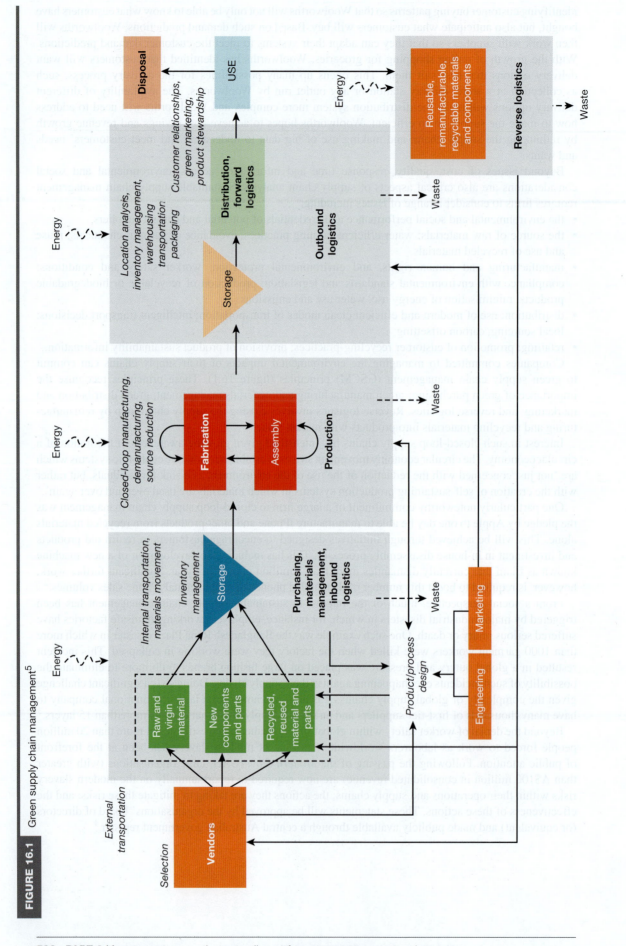

16.2 Customer profitability

LEARNING OBJECTIVE 16.2 Explain the concept of customer profitability analysis and suggest qualitative factors for inclusion in a strategic customer analysis model.

In chapter 12, we introduced the concepts of managing customer profitability. We did this as part of activity-based management. Recall that comprehensive examples 1 and 3 in chapter 12 focused on the Paisley Insurance Company. The billing department at Paisley effectively focused on two types of customers: residential and commercial. From these examples we were able to identify the cost of servicing each type of customer and the use of activity analysis was able to provide a more reliable estimate of this cost than a non-activity-based analysis.

The broader issue, of course, is how useful customer profitability data can be in understanding resource consumption and sources of profitability. Focusing on the customer or client as the cost object may reveal useful insights for improving organisational performance. For many organisations, a relatively small number of customers or clients will generate most of the profitability, while little contributions to profitability are sourced from a larger number of customers/clients. Of course, this does not mean that the less profitable customers/clients should be dropped, as there are often good reasons to maintain these customers/clients. What is important is for organisations to be able to differentiate between the more profitable and the less profitable customers/clients.

To conduct customer profitability analysis we need to be able to identify the resources consumed and the associated costs of servicing the customers/clients. The customers or customer groupings become the cost object for the purposes of cost assignment. We need to identify the revenue from each customer (or customer group) and the resources and costs of servicing each customer (or customer group). We may conduct this analysis at various forms of aggregation. For example, depending on the objective of the exercise, an organisation might have a choice between calculating the profitability of every customer (which may be hundreds) or focusing on particular customer groupings. In Paisley Insurance's situation in chapter 12, the focus was on two customer groupings: residential and commercial customers.

So, what makes some customers more profitable than others? First, we need them to be buying profitable products and/or services. In this way there is a strong connection between product and customer profitability. Second, some customers demand significantly more resources (costs) in the sales/service delivery process. For example, less profitable customers are more likely to place lots of small orders requiring more shipments, require significant customisation and lots of on-site visits, demand discounts, and pay late. Of course, on their own, each of these activities may not be too detrimental, particularly if the organisation is able to set prices accordingly. However, this is not always the case and the bargaining power may not reside with the organisation.

Figure 16.2 provides an overview of some of the characteristics of higher resource (cost) consuming and lower resource (cost) consuming customers. Note that this is only an issue for an organisation when it cannot charge higher prices to compensate for the additional costs.

FIGURE 16.2   Resource consumption and customers

Higher resource consuming customers tend to:
- demand additional support services
- place non-routine orders/requests
- require customised features in product/service delivery
- exceed credit terms available
- make poor use of technology in ordering and service delivery process
- require more frequent deliveries due to order size
- frequently return goods for credit
- delay payments requiring follow-up by administration.

Lower resource consuming customers tend to:
- make better use of technology in ordering and service-delivery process
- be consistent with ordering routines
- not require customised features within given price range
- not require additional support beyond original agreement
- make payments within credit terms.

Comprehensive example 1 introduces the Dublin Shirt Company, which will be extended later in the chapter and also in chapter 17. In this example, we illustrate the calculation of customer profitability data relating to three types of customers.

The Dublin Shirt Company[6]

Introduction

The Dublin Shirt Company was established in Ireland by its American parent. It is a wholly owned subsidiary. The Republic of Ireland was an attractive location due to the abundant supply of cheap, well-educated and English-speaking labour. In addition, it had the lowest corporate tax rate in the European Union and a regulatory regime that was unambiguously pro-business. The company manufactures polo-type sports shirts for the growing worldwide sports shirt market.

The company is located in a small provincial town on the outskirts of Dublin and has annual sales of just under €16 million and an investment base (that is, net assets) of some €3 million. For the most recent financial year, the company budgeted for and generated a small loss. A small profit was budgeted for and reported for the previous year. The CEO of the US parent has already issued warnings about the continued operation of the company in Ireland due to its precarious financial position. Obtaining a significant amount of interest-free, short-term loans from its parent company recently averted a cash flow crisis. If nothing else, everyone knew that making losses in a low-tax regime was bad tax management for the group! (The average return on sales is about 4 per cent for similar companies in Ireland). The company has a modern knitting plant and is currently operating at 70 per cent capacity. There are approximately 100 employees, and most of these are female machine operatives who are paid on an hourly basis. The weekly payroll calculations consume a great deal of resources since they are done manually. Because of the high investment in capital equipment in previous years, together with the loss reported for the current year, no provision for taxation needs to be made.

Manufacturing

The Dublin Shirt Company manufactures all of its shirts. The basic product produced by the company is a white sports shirt (in different sizes). Shirts are made in three men's sizes: medium, large and extra large. The company does not manufacture small-sized shirts as it considers this size to be suitable only for children and it believes this market segment to be rather small. The normal production cycle for an order of white shirts is five days.

Depending on the client requirements, a shirt may be customised to order. The customisation service includes dyeing, stamping/printing and/or embroidery processes. All three processes are not necessarily required for each shirt. For example, some shirts may be dyed then embroidered; others may be dyed and stamped or printed. Some shirts do not require dyeing but may be printed, stamped or embroidered.

Nearly two-thirds of the shirts are dyed in various colours. This increases the production cost and extends the production cycle of an order by about three days. In addition, a characteristic feature of the 'sports shirt' is the promotional text and/or logo that is added to each shirt. The promotional text and/or logo can be either printed on or machine embroidered. In the majority of cases, the text is usually printed and this is referred to as the printing process. The technical term used is that of 'stamping' whereby the appropriate text/logo is added to each sports shirt using a special printing machine. Recently, the firm has had some difficulty with the 'staying power' of the material printed on these shirts. Customers have complained that the ink eventually cracks and peels off. A small but increasing number of shirts (about 15 per cent) have the text or logo of the sports event embroidered rather than 'stamped'. This embroidery work adds enormously to the appeal of the product. The company tries to produce each order well in advance of dispatch so that there will always be a certain amount of finished goods in stock at the end of each financial period.

Customers

The company's sales are all on credit and are predominantly made to England and the United States — countries that are outside the euro zone. (To avoid foreign exchange fluctuations, the company invoices all its sales in euro.) Typically, customers take about 60 days to pay their account. Currently, the company has 986 active customers. These customers differ primarily in the volume and type of their purchase order, so management classifies each customer in one of three groups — priority (8), team (154) and shop (824). Priority customers are typically the large, international sports events that generate a great deal of TV coverage. Typical examples are the British Open, Wimbledon and Super Bowl. Shop customers are single shop operations (such as pro shops at golf courses), and team customers are typically associated with specific teams or clubs. It is company policy to conduct a full credit check on new customers to avoid the potential of bad debts. As a result, the amount of bad debts incurred has been insignificant in recent times. The low amount of bad debts is also partly due to the speed with which invoices are issued to customers, together with a regular and frequent follow-up of all unpaid invoices. Figure 16.3 gives product and customer classification statistics for the past financial year.

FIGURE 16.3	Product and customer statistics

| | Sales in units by customer category | | | |
Shirt size:	Priority	Team	Shop	Total
Extra large	272 500	166 000	105 500	544 000
Large	366 000	186 000	103 000	655 000
Medium	360 000	190 000	960 000	1 510 000
Total units sold	998 500	542 000	1 168 500	2 709 000
Sales revenue (€)	€6 029 700	€3 284 300	€6 566 900	€15 880 900
No. of units dyed	750 000	400 000	550 000	1 700 000
No. of units stamped	698 500	472 000	1 138 500	2 309 000
No. of units embroidered	300 000	70 000	30 000	400 000
No. of orders received	2 330	11 450	57 909	71 689
No. of shipments made	1 470	9 230	49 286	59 986

The company has a different marketing approach to customers in each of its three categories. A small group of in-house salespeople sell directly to buyers in the priority customer category. Independent salespeople, paid on a commission-only basis, call on the licensing agent of customers classified in the team category. Advertisements placed in regional magazines and newspapers target customers primarily in the 'shop' customer segment, who telephone or post in their orders. Not surprisingly, a significant cost for all categories is the provision of sample shirts to potential clients.

Information and performance

In an attempt to start some sort of strategic planning exercise within the Irish plant, senior managers recently identified its main competitive strengths and weaknesses. Management believes that the critical strength of the company is in the quality of the product, and that the weakness in recent years has been in customer service, particularly in meeting scheduled deliveries. Production costs are accumulated as outlined in figure 16.4.

FIGURE 16.4	Production and cost accumulation process

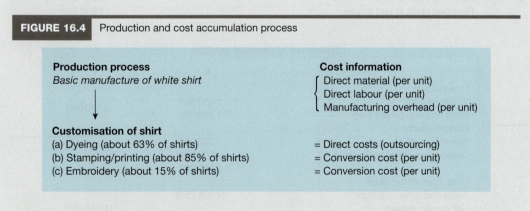

Costs are accumulated separately for the basic manufacturing process (that is, the manufacture of white shirts), and also for the customisation process. The former process accumulates costs as direct materials, direct labour or manufacturing overhead. In this process, production overheads are absorbed on the basis of direct labour cost and this approach has been in use for a number of years. Costs associated with customising shirts are accumulated separately under the heading of direct costs (for dyeing) and conversion costs for stamping/printing or for embroidery. Figure 16.5 shows the firm's unit costs and sales prices for various items for the most recent year.

FIGURE 16.5 Cost and revenue data

Basic manufacture	Quantity	Average sales price	Direct material	Direct labour	Manufacturing overhead
Extra large	544 000	€6.60	€0.60	€0.40	€0.24
Large	655 000	€6.20	€0.55	€0.35	€0.21
Medium	1 510 000	€5.45	€0.39	€0.30	€0.18
Total	2 709 000				

Customising	Quantity	Direct cost (unit)	Conversion cost (unit)	Total cost
Dyeing	1 700 000	€1.40	N/A	€2 380 000
Stamping	2 309 000	N/A	€0.40	€ 923 600
Embroidery	400 000	N/A	€1.30	€ 520 000
				€3 823 600

The typical monthly management-reporting package consists of a summarised statement of profit or loss and summarised statement of financial position (figure 16.6), together with a detailed schedule of aged accounts receivable. The statement of profit or loss shows the reported loss for the recent financial year.

Statement of profit or loss

	Units	€
Sales: Extra large	544 000	3 590 400
Large	655 000	4 061 000
Medium	1 510 000	8 229 500
	2 709 000	15 880 900
Less: Cost of goods manufactured	€	
Basic manufacturing costs	2 715 310	
Customising	3 823 600	6 538 910
Gross profit		9 341 990
Less: Non-manufacturing overheads		
Selling and distribution expenses	5 761 600	
Administration expenses	3 584 450	9 346 050
Loss for year		(4 060)
Retained profit brought forward		1 537 810
Retained profit at end of year		1 533 750

Statement of financial position

	€	€
Fixed assets		
Buildings (net)	2 450 000	4 190 000
Plant and equipment (net)	1 740 000	
Current assets		
Stock (inventory)	550 000	
Debtors (accounts receivable)	2 600 000	
	3 150 000	
Less: Current liabilities		
Trade and other creditors	(4 406 250)	
Net current assets		(1 256 250)
Total assets less current liabilities		2 933 750
Financed by		
Ordinary share capital		1 400 000
Retained profits		1 533 750
Shareholders' equity		2 933 750

To restore profitability to the company, management would first like to ascertain the profitability of the customers in its three customer categories — priority, team and shop. At the moment, management has no basis for assessing customer profitability. Yet, it is intuitive that some customers generate high profits while others do not generate enough revenues to cover the expenses to support them. The basic problem here is that different customers demand different levels of support. Management is aware that the use of activity-based costing information would enable a type of customer profitability analysis to be applied. Management have recently obtained data on how the selling, distribution and administrative expenses could be incorporated into a customer profitability analysis by identifying cost pools and cost drivers for various customer-related activities (see figure 16.7).

FIGURE 16.7 The assignment of selling, distribution and administrative costs to customer-related activities

| | Percentage distribution to: | |
Customer-related activities	Selling and distribution	Administration
Accounts maintenance	Nil	70%
Sales commission	5%	Nil
Shipping activities (i.e. deliveries)	50%	10%
Sales visits	15%	Nil
Tracking misplaced/lost items	20%	20%
Marketing/promotion	10%	Nil
	100%	100%

Customer-related activity	Assumed cost driver
Accounts maintenance	Number of orders received
Sales commission	Direct allocation to team customers only
Shipping activities (i.e. deliveries)	Number of shipments (deliveries) made
Sales visits	Direct allocation to priority customers only
Tracking misplaced/lost items	Number of units sold
Marketing/promotion	Management estimate*

*Decided as 20 per cent to 'team' customers and 80 per cent to 'shop' customers

Our main purpose in this illustration is to show the calculation of the profitability of each of the customer groups of the Dublin Shirt Company. That is, the priority, team and shop customers. This is shown in figure 16.8.

FIGURE 16.8 Customer profitability analysis

Selling, distribution and administration costs assigned to activity cost pools			
	Selling and distribution	Administration	Total
	€	€	€
Accounts maintenance		2 509 225	2 509 115
Sales commission	288 080		288 080
Shipping	2 880 800	358 445	3 239 245
Sales visits	864 240		864 240
Tracking	1 152 320	716 890	1 869 210
Marketing/promotion	576 160		576 160
Total	5 761 600	3 584 560	

Activity cost pool activity driver rates (using data from above and figure 16.3)			
Cost pool	Amount €	Driver unit	Cost per activity driver unit
Accounts maintenance	2 509 115	71 689 orders	€35 per order
Sales commission	288 080	To team customers	All to team
Shipping	3 239 245	59 986 ship	€54 per ship
Sales visits	864 240	To priority customers	All to priority
Tracking	1 869 210	2 709 000 units	€0.69 per unit
Marketing/promotion	576 160	20% team, 80% shop	Team = 115 232 Shop = 460 928

Customer profitability analysis				
	Priority	**Team**	**Shop**	**Total**
	€	**€**	**€**	**€**
Revenue	6 029 700	3 284 300	6 566 900	
Basic management costs	1 057 360	577 600	1 080 350	
Gross profit	4 972 340	2 706 700	5 486 550	
Customised costs	1 719 400	839 800	1 264 400	
Adjusted gross profit	3 252 940	1 866 900	4 222 150	
Non-manufacturing overhead costs				
Accounts maintenance	81 550*	400 750	2 026 815	
Sales commission	—	288 080	—	
Shipping	79 380	498 420	2 661 444	
Sales visits	864 240	—	—	
Tracking	688 965	373 980	806 265	
Marketing/promotion	—	115 232	460 928	
Total non-manufacturing overhead	1 714 135	1 676 462	5 955 452	
Profit	1 538 805	190 438	(1 733 302)	(4 059)

* €35 per order × 2330 orders (from figure 16.3)

What conclusions can we draw from this analysis? Shop customers are unprofitable even though they generate the most revenue. This is predominantly caused by the demand for indirect resources by shop customers. The non-manufacturing overhead assigned to shop customers (based on resources consumed) is substantially higher than for priority or team customers. Dublin Shirt now has sufficient initial data to develop ways to improve the profitability of shop customers. Through a focus on the activities associated with the non-manufacturing overhead, Dublin Shirt can work with individual customers to change the costly behaviour. For example, much of the additional resource (cost) consumption by shop customers is a function of Dublin Shirt trying to work with so many smaller customers with relatively high demands. For example, sales units to shop customers (824 customers) is only marginally higher in total than for priority customers (8 customers) (€1 168 500 versus €998 500). We should, however, note that this analysis is only a first-order analysis. Prior to any major decision regarding individual customers, more detailed and comprehensive analysis should be undertaken.

Of course, while the customer profitability analysis illustrated in comprehensive example 1 is a useful starting point for understanding customers, it is not comprehensive; in fact, it is quite narrow in terms of the issues considered. This is particularly so when we take a strategic view of customers. What we can say is the quantitative customer profitability analysis (as per comprehensive example 1) is one input into what should be a more comprehensive model for evaluating and managing customers. For example, the following may be considered.

- The nature of the contractual arrangements with individual customers and potential for related sales. For example, current sales to a customer may be small but this customer may be a subsidiary or have links to a larger potential or existing customer. For Dublin Shirt, a shop customer may have links to a team or priority customer (either current or potential).
- The life cycle stage of each customer. For example, it does not make sense to treat a new customer with future upside potential the same as a long-term customer in decline.
- Threats to the market. For example, the business is exposed to higher risk factors if entry barriers to the market are low and/or where competition is high.
- The status of customer relationships. For example, Dublin Shirt may have a far stronger connection to some customers that goes beyond simply the sales transaction. This might be based on a long record of meeting customer expectations, or as a result of the work of sales staff.
- Bargaining power. The business may have significantly stronger bargaining power with some customers relative to others. This will affect actions able to be taken in relation to individual customers.

16.3 Building desired profit into decisions

LEARNING OBJECTIVE 16.3 Understand target costing principles and techniques.

Accountants use estimates of revenues and costs to provide information for a range of operating decisions. In the short term, the general rule is to sell goods or services so long as estimated revenues exceed estimated variable costs (that is, so long as a profit is expected). However, in the long term, organisations need to earn a reasonable return on investment. We will now discuss the following techniques used to plan for long-term profitability:

- target costing
- Kaizen costing
- life-cycle costing

Although these methods alone do not result in increased profitability, they help accountants become more deliberate about profit planning. When costs appear to be too high, these methods also encourage accountants and managers to identify and implement cost management techniques.

Target costing

When launching a new product, managers traditionally determine the cost of the product and then use the cost to help them set a price that would achieve a desired profit margin. Managers use this information to evaluate the feasibility of the new product.

An alternative decision-making approach is *target costing*, which uses market-based prices to determine whether products and services can be delivered at costs low enough for an acceptable profit. In a target-costing approach, competitors' products are *reverse engineered* (taken apart and put back together again) to better understand the manufacturing process and the product design. In turn, the product and manufacturing process are redesigned so that the product meets a pre-specified target cost. Organisations can then sell products at competitive prices and still earn profits.

For example, in the late 1970s and early 1980s Komatsu, a heavy equipment company, used target costing to develop products similar in quality and functionality to those of Caterpillar. Komatsu was able to set its prices lower than Caterpillar. Prior to the mid 1980s, Caterpillar was financially stable. But in the late 1980s, the company struggled against a weak global economy and the competition from Komatsu, losing $1 billion over a three-year period. Mark Thompson, a business analysis manager with Caterpillar's wheel-loader and excavator division, recalled, 'We had to do something drastic. The viability of the company depended on it.'[7] Caterpillar's managers turned to target costing, the same method that enabled Komatsu to become so competitive. Caterpillar accountants and analysts studied publicly available financial statements to identify Komatsu's costs. They learned that Caterpillar's production costs were 30 per cent higher than Komatsu's.

Next, Caterpillar's engineers purchased, tore apart, and reverse engineered Komatsu's products to determine the processes and designs Komatsu used in manufacturing. Caterpillar managers then invested $1.8 billion in plant modernisation. They eliminated non-value-added processes, examined their procedures to purchase raw materials and supplies, moved to a just-in-time inventory system and reduced the number of parts used in Caterpillar products. Using target costing techniques, Caterpillar produced record-setting profits at the time, although it was later adversely affected by a downturn in the heavy equipment industry.[8]

Target costing process

As highlighted in the Caterpillar example, target costing helps organisations improve production processes and profits. **Target costing** is the process of researching consumer markets to estimate an appropriate market price, then subtracting the desired return to determine a maximum allowable cost. This target cost is the maximum cost at which the entity can produce a good or service to generate the desired profit margin. The entity then determines whether the good or service can be designed and produced to meet the target cost. This step involves managing both product design and manufacturing phases. If expected costs exceed the target, managers will choose not to provide a good or service. To date, target costing has been used primarily for products that have already been manufactured by other organisations, but it is increasingly being used for new goods and services.

The key value of target costing is that it focuses managers' attention on the design phase where most cost savings potentially occur because 70 per cent to 80 per cent of product costs are typically committed at this point. Costs that occur both when the manufacturing process is set up and during manufacturing are locked in during the design phase. For example, new equipment is chosen and direct materials are specified that will be used in production. Although the actual costs occur over a product's life cycle, the decisions made in the planning phase have the greatest influence over those costs. Under target costing, the decision to produce a good or service depends on expected costs developed in the design phase. The steps in a target costing design cycle are summarised in figure 16.9. The description of each step follows.

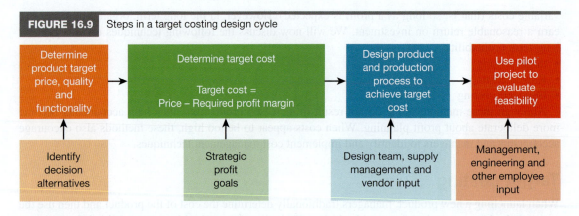

FIGURE 16.9 Steps in a target costing design cycle

Determine product target price, quality and functionality	Determine target cost Target cost = Price − Required profit margin	Design product and production process to achieve target cost	Use pilot project to evaluate feasibility
Identify decision alternatives	Strategic profit goals	Design team, supply management and vendor input	Management, engineering and other employee input

Determine the product target price, quality and functionality

Accountants and managers use studies such as consumer surveys, focus groups and market research of competitors' prices to determine a competitive price for a specific product. Researchers collect information about consumer preferences, including trade-offs customers are willing to make between price, quality and functionality for a product or service. A competitive price *for a given level of product quality and functionality* can then be estimated. In industries where customers are willing to pay higher prices for higher quality or more functionality, managers strategically differentiate their products and establish market positions. The same is true when customers are willing to give up a certain amount of quality or functionality to obtain lower prices.

The automobile industry provides a good example of product differentiation. Some manufacturers emphasise a low price for lower levels of quality and functionality. Other manufacturers emphasise quality and are able to charge higher prices. Some manufacturers emphasise functionality such as all-wheel-drive capability or trucks with four-door cabs. Increases in functionality are usually accompanied by increases in product prices. When cars are being designed, the marketing department analyses consumer preferences to determine the optimal levels of quality and functionality for a particular price.

Customers in some industries are unwilling to pay for higher quality or functionality. In Caterpillar's industry (heavy machinery), the products are used in construction. Purchasing decisions tend to revolve around price and only one quality factor: reliability. Extra functions such as air-conditioned cabs are unlikely to increase a product's marketability.

Determine the target cost

After a competitive price is determined for specific levels of product quality and functionality, the required profit margin is subtracted from the price to arrive at the target cost:

$$\text{Target cost} = \text{Price} - \text{Required profit margin}$$

The required profit margin is usually a function of the organisation's long-term strategic goals. Managers who use this method assume that producers cannot set the price but instead must take the market's price. Accordingly, the production decision focuses on the entity's ability to produce goods or services at the specified target cost.

Design the product and production process to achieve the target cost

A product design team is assembled from personnel in product engineering, marketing and accounting. This team designs the product at the specified levels of quality and functionality and then develops the manufacturing process. During the design phase, the team focuses on reducing the complexity of the product and manufacturing process to meet the target cost. If the team is unable to meet the target cost, the design process is reiterated with negotiations on possible trade-offs between price, quality and functionality. If the product still cannot be manufactured at the target cost after several iterations, production plans are dropped.

A similar process takes place in service industries. Teams — including professional, marketing and accounting personnel — design the type of service to be provided as well as the service delivery modes. The next step is taken only if the target cost is achieved in the design phase.

Use a pilot project to evaluate feasibility

Once the production process has been designed so that the cost to manufacture a product is at or below the target cost, a pilot project replicates a small version of the production line to determine the feasibility of the product and process design and cost. If the pilot project is successful, full production begins. If it is unsuccessful, the team returns to the design phase. Similar pilot projects are used in service entities to evaluate feasibility.

Factors that affect the success of target costing

Target costing performs best when:
- product development and design phases are long and complex
- the production process is complex
- the market is willing to pay for differences in quality or function
- the manufacturer can push some cost reductions onto suppliers and subcontractors
- the manufacturer can influence the design of subparts.

Target costing is inappropriate in industries with simple production processes, such as food products and beverages, which are typically unable to differentiate their products based on quality and functionality. In the food industry, advertising campaigns and brand name recognition influence price the most.

Comprehensive example 2 describes the target costing process for Mount Dandenong Bikes.

COMPREHENSIVE EXAMPLE 2

Target costing

Mount Dandenong Bikes is a manufacturer of high-quality mountain bikes that compete with products from companies such as Trek and Bianchi. One of Mount Dandenong Bikes' employees developed a new braking system that allows bikers to descend steep slopes using a consistent braking pattern that pumps both front and back brakes at regular preset intervals, depending on the brake setting that the biker chooses. The marketing department surveyed current customers and found they would be willing to pay more for this option. Because the company's brand name is not yet well established,

prices for its bikes need to be kept below those of its major competitors. The owner, Michelle Miles, wants the company to launch a line of bikes with the new braking system. Her accountant recommends that the company use target costing to develop the new product to ensure that the design is feasible.

Determine product target price, quality and functionality

After conducting customer surveys and a number of focus groups, Mount Dandenong Bikes' marketing staff identify five features that are highly important to prospective customers: the weight of the bike, the bike's ability to withstand hard riding in difficult terrains for long periods of time, appearance, ease of handling, and riding comfort over rough terrain. Depending on the brand name of the bike and its components, the market price for competing models with these features ranges between $800 and $1200. The model with the highest market share in that price range is priced at $949. From the survey and focus group information gathered, Michelle believes that a bike with the new braking system and the same levels of quality and functionality as the competitors' models should be priced at $950 to achieve a 25 per cent market share. She decides to call the new model the Mountain Braker.

Determine target cost

Michelle sets a minimum profit margin of 10 per cent on new products. Given this information, Michelle's accountant sets the new product's target cost as follows:

Price	$950
Less profit margin	95
Target cost	$855

Design product and production process to achieve target cost

Michelle establishes a team to handle the product and manufacturing process design. The team consists of one person from each of the following areas: marketing, engineering, purchasing, accounting and administration.

First, the team identifies an initial cost for the Mountain Braker. The engineer alters the basic bike design to incorporate the new braking system. The cost estimate of $905 is higher than the target cost of $855, so the team considers ways to reduce the cost. The team assembles information about current costs and necessary cost reductions, assuming sales of 50 000 bikes. They identify areas with the most potential for cost reduction, and then establish the following estimates for these reductions.

Cost category	Current cost per bike	Target cost	Cost reduction needed
New brake development	$ 50	$ 50	$ 0
Manufacturing	710	680	30
Total manufacturing costs	760	730	30
Selling and distribution	55	50	5
Warranty and support	35	30	5
Administration	55	45	10
Total cost	$905	$855	$50

Product design changes

The team decides to use value chain analysis to seek opportunities for cost reduction. They focus on the product design phase of the value chain. The engineer analyses the current design, searching for steps in the manufacturing process and components that can be eliminated. The accountant provides cost information for prospective changes. The marketing person provides information about customer reactions to proposed changes.

- *Reflectors.* The team suggests eliminating the reflectors mounted on the spokes. Because the Mountain Braker would be used primarily in very rough terrain, any reflectors are likely to break. Furthermore, the relatively few riders who use the bike on roads do not rely on reflectors but use battery-operated headlights and taillights instead. The accountant estimates that $15 per bike can be saved by eliminating the reflectors and the process of mounting them. After sending emails to prospective customers, the marketing team member confirms that eliminating reflectors will not affect consumer demand for the product or expected price.
- *Bike seats.* When the engineer suggests a cheaper bike seat that is easier to mount, the marketing representative organises a focus group with prospective customers to determine the effect on sales. Feedback from the focus group indicates that the price would have to be reduced if a lower-quality seat is installed, so this idea is dropped.

Supplier negotiations

The team next focuses on the direct materials purchasing function in their value chain analysis. They investigate cost reductions from current suppliers and search for similar-quality components at reduced prices from new suppliers. Purchasing personnel meet with all of the components suppliers to negotiate cost reductions.

- *Handlebars.* The handlebars supplier suggests a new product with comparable quality to the current handlebars but with a cost reduction of $10 per bike. Marketing determines that the new handlebars would not affect customers' perceptions of quality.
- *Tyres.* Purchasing works with the company that supplies tyres. Buying tyres in larger lots can save the supplier delivery and storage costs, and the company currently has storage space available. The new purchase agreement reduces costs by $5 per bike.
- *Tyre tubes.* Purchasing finds a new tyre tube vendor that can supply tubes at a cost reduction of $5 per bike.

Combined, the changes recommended by the team are expected to reduce manufacturing costs by $35 ($15 + $10 + $5 + $5), rather than the needed $30. Thus, the target cost for manufacturing costs is met. The team now focuses on the remaining costs that need to be reduced.

Non-manufacturing costs

The target costing team meets with the marketing department and the director of finance to identify reductions in selling and distribution, warranty and support, and administration costs.

- *Selling and distribution.* Marketing is concerned that reducing commissions or advertising will affect total sales and potential market share gains for Mount Dandenong Bikes. Marketing wants no cost reduction on advertising or commissions for this new product. The successful introduction of the new braking system relies in part on individual sales representatives highlighting the feature and in part on an advertisement campaign featuring the braking system. However, the shipping company has agreed to a reduction in shipping costs of $5 per bike because volumes have been increasing rapidly — it is cheaper for the shipping company to ship large lots.
- *Warranty and support.* Management is concerned that reducing customer warranty and support costs — both areas in which Mount Dandenong Bikes currently has a strong reputation — would be

risky with a new product. If the entity reduces these costs and then is unable to provide its current level of service, a loss of reputation could result. Fortunately, manufacturing costs were reduced by $5 more than originally planned. Therefore, the team decides not to reduce warranty and support costs at this time.

- *Administration*. Some administrative functions, such as payroll, have recently been outsourced. It appears that the administrative cost reduction of $10 per bike will be easily met.

Total planned cost reduction

The following summary shows the cost reduction estimates achieved by the design team.

Cost category	Reduction needed (revised)	Reduction achieved
New brake development	$ 0	$ 0
Manufacturing:	35	
Reflectors		15
Handlebars		10
Tyres		5
Tubes		5
Selling and distribution (reduced shipping charges)	5	5
Warranty and support (no reduction necessary)	0	0
Administration (outsourcing services)	10	10
Total	$50	$50

Pilot project to evaluate feasibility

Once the team reconfigures the bike, a pilot manufacturing line is set up and 100 bikes are produced. The first 50 bikes cost $780 to produce but, as the manufacturing line employees learned how to install the new braking system more quickly, the last 50 bikes cost $730 as projected.

The managers decide to begin full production of the new product. This decision turns out well for the entity; the bike sells faster and in larger numbers than anticipated.

16.4 Kaizen costing

LEARNING OBJECTIVE 16.4 Communicate the concept of kaizen costing and explain how it compares to target costing.

Kaizen costing is continuous improvement in product cost, quality and functionality. It is similar to target costing in that cost targets (goals) are set based on price predictions. However, kaizen costing occurs after the product has been designed and the first production cycle is complete. Market prices tend to decrease over many products' life cycles. Under kaizen costing, accountants forecast declining prices and establish cost-reduction goals to maintain a desired level of profit margin. Therefore, the objectives of kaizen costing include not only continuous improvement but also continuous cost reduction.

Because kaizen costing relies on sales forecasts, the kaizen plan is similar to a budget, except that kaizen costing provides for explicit cost reductions. Figure 16.10 summarises the kaizen planning process for revenues and costs.

In manufacturing entities, estimated variable costs are the sum of estimates for direct material and direct labour costs, plus variable manufacturing overhead. Accountants and managers develop plans to estimate reductions for these variable costs. Estimated reductions in fixed costs are developed from human resource plans for fixed labour and service department personnel, combined with facility investment plans and the fixed expense plans (design, maintenance, advertising, sales promotions, and general and administrative expenses). These estimated costs are based on the prior period's actual costs, adjusted for any anticipated price changes.

In service entities, the estimated variable costs are developed from projections of supplies and direct labour that vary with the amount of services provided, variable overhead and any variable merchandising costs in retail industries. The estimated fixed costs are developed in the same manner used for manufacturing organisations.

After the targeted cost reduction goals are set, each department is assigned responsibility for specific cost reduction amounts. These goals are met in several ways. One option is to use value chain analysis to redesign the production or service process to increase overall productivity and efficiency. Meetings may be held with manufacturing or service personnel to brainstorm ideas for cost reduction. To encourage idea generation, some entities even share any initial gains in cost reduction with the employees who suggest the cost-reducing changes. Another option is to use supply chain analysis, working with suppliers and issuing target cost reductions for intermediate manufacturing parts or service supplies. Some companies work with suppliers to develop new product and process designs needed to achieve cost reductions. Employee suggestion schemes may also be used to capture ideas from the workers who have the knowledge, skills and experience of the production process.

| FIGURE 16.10 | Kaizen planning process for revenues and costs |

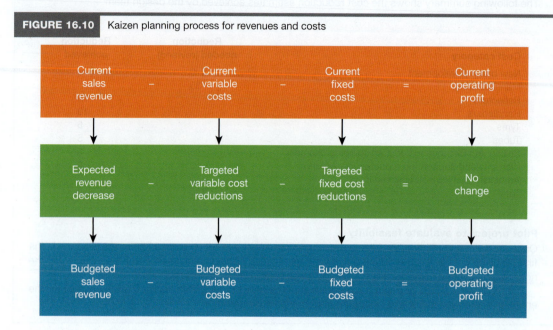

Comprehensive example 3 continues the Mount Dandenong Bikes example and applies kaizen costing to analyse a price and cost reduction of one of their products.

COMPREHENSIVE EXAMPLE 3

Kaizen costing

Mount Dandenong Bikes has now been producing Mountain Brakers for two years, and sales are beginning to drop because competitors are producing similar braking systems. The marketing manager believes that if the company wants sales and market share to increase, prices will have to decrease. The accountant recommends that the company use kaizen costing to reduce the price and cost of the Mountain Braker.

Cost reductions

The marketing manager estimates that the bike's price should be reduced by 10 per cent to be competitive with other manufacturers. Therefore, costs also need to be reduced by 10 per cent to maintain the same percentage margin, although the dollar value of the margin will decrease. The bike's current price is $950 with a cost of $855. The new price will be $855, and the corresponding cost reduction needed is $85.50. The current margin is $95, and the new margin will be $85.50. The following summary assumes that reductions will be made proportionately across all cost categories.

Cost category	Current cost per bike	Needed cost reduction (10% goal)
New brake development	$ 50	$ 5.00
Manufacturing	675	67.50
Selling and distribution	50	5.00
Warranty and support	35	3.50
Administration	45	4.50
Total	$855	$85.50

The same team that developed the Mountain Braker at target cost in the design phase meets again to suggest further cost reduction plans. After careful analysis, they find no way to reduce costs for the new braking system at this time. Therefore, the $5 needed cost reduction for the brakes will have to come from another process or component.

Process design changes

Using value chain analysis, the team reviews the manufacturing processes and the bike design, searching for non-value-added activities or components that can be eliminated. A new gear system has been developed by one of the vendors that eliminates two steps in the manufacturing process. As a result, the engineer estimates that one labourer could be moved to another bike production line to replace a retiring worker, reducing total labour costs. This reduction amounts to $10 per bike.

Supply chain analysis

The Mount Dandenong Bikes team meets with suppliers to determine whether cost reductions or product improvements are possible from the components used in manufacturing. The wheel and spoke vendor has improved the quality of its product and dropped the price, saving $13 per bike. A new bike frame that is just as solid as the current frame has been developed from an innovative new alloy and will save $35.

At the end of the last quarter, the supplier of tubes and tyres asked for a small price increase. The purchasing department surveys vendor websites for tubes and tyres. After contacting several different vendors, a price reduction is negotiated with a new supplier of tyres. An additional vendor is added to supply tubes at a reduced price. These two cost savings amount to $10 per bike.

Overall, the team is able to achieve total cost reduction for manufacturing of $68 ($10 + $13 + $35 + $10). This amount is $0.50 more than is needed from manufacturing, but leaves a $4.50 required reduction because the cost of brakes could not be reduced.

Non-manufacturing costs

The team now turns its attention to achieving the remaining cost reductions. The marketing representative points out that several top mountain bike race competitors currently using the new bike generate sales efficiently. Relying on their efforts costs less than the current advertising campaign. Therefore, the team decides to reduce advertising costs by $5 per bike, which meets the selling and distribution cost target. Warranty and support costs are significantly lower than anticipated, primarily because the new braking system is so reliable. A reduction of $8 is easily attainable at this time. This amount is $4.50 ahead of target, making up for the lack of cost reduction from the brakes.

The team member from administration mentions that a new information system was installed last quarter. The department dropped some non-value-added activities, such as manual entry of production data. One staff member resigned and will not be replaced. The savings will be at least the needed $4.50 per bike. The overall cost reduction targets and estimates are as follows:

Cost category	Kaizen cost reduction	Actual cost reduction
New brake development	$ 5.00	$ 0.00
Manufacturing:	67.50	10.00
Process change	5.00	13.00
Wheel and spoke system	3.50	35.00
Frame		10.00
Tyres and tubes		5.00
Selling and distribution		8.00
Warranty and support		
Administration (outsourcing services)	4.50	4.50
Total	$85.50	$85.50

Continuous monitoring of costs

The team reports back to the accounting department that the overall cost reduction targets can be met. Once the changes have been made, the marketing department decides to cut costs even further. However, a problem arises with the braking system. To maintain the current quality, Mount Dandenong Bikes will have to pay $4 more for components because several vendors raised their prices. With these two changes, Mount Dandenong Bikes is still below the kaizen cost reduction target.

Using target and kaizen costing over time

Target and kaizen costing are used together in entities facing declining prices across time. Figure 16.11 provides a generic timeline showing the use of these two methods across a product's life cycle. Some organisations may lower margins before dropping the product, but at some point the product is discontinued because cost is equal to price and no further cost reductions are possible.

FIGURE 16.11 Target and kaizen costing over time for a product

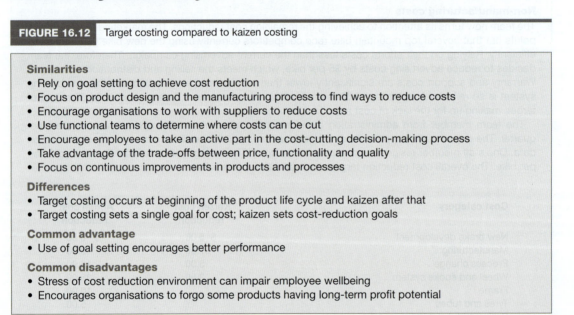

Figure 16.12 compares target costing and kaizen costing, listing their similarities and differences, and common advantages and disadvantages.

FIGURE 16.12 Target costing compared to kaizen costing

Similarities
- Rely on goal setting to achieve cost reduction
- Focus on product design and the manufacturing process to find ways to reduce costs
- Encourage organisations to work with suppliers to reduce costs
- Use functional teams to determine where costs can be cut
- Encourage employees to take an active part in the cost-cutting decision-making process
- Take advantage of the trade-offs between price, functionality and quality
- Focus on continuous improvements in products and processes

Differences
- Target costing occurs at beginning of the product life cycle and kaizen after that
- Target costing sets a single goal for cost; kaizen sets cost-reduction goals

Common advantage
- Use of goal setting encourages better performance

Common disadvantages
- Stress of cost reduction environment can impair employee wellbeing
- Encourages organisations to forgo some products having long-term profit potential

16.5 Life cycle costing

LEARNING OBJECTIVE 16.5 Describe the characteristics of life cycle costing.

Life cycle costing is a decision-making method that considers changes in price and costs over the entire life cycle of a good or service, from the time the product is introduced through a number of years.

Some products have high up-front costs, such as research and development; other products may incur large costs when the product is abandoned, such as environmental clean-up costs. Sometimes products cannot achieve high revenues at the beginning of their life, but generate increasing revenues over the product's life cycle. Under target costing, such products might be rejected even though they have good long-term potential. Under life cycle costing, managers consider the profitability of the product over a number of years. If forecasts predict that sales over time will cover all product costs and eventually add to profits, a life cycle budget is developed for both manufacturing and environmental costs so that decision makers can evaluate their decision and identify possible areas for cost reductions across time.

Life cycle costing is used when the initial product is produced and sold at a loss, but accountants and managers anticipate that a combination of continued sales volumes and cost reductions over time will lead to profits in the long term. It is also used to identify products that may not be profitable when the costs of decommissioning the operation are included as part of total product costs, for example, environmental clean-up costs when mines are shut down. In addition, life cycle costing is used to focus managers' attention on the high development or decommissioning costs during the product and manufacturing design phase to encourage them to manage all of these costs as they develop new products.

An example of a product decision that considered the product's life cycle is Microsoft Xbox. Microsoft's managers decided to sell Xbox at a loss, but they expected continuing sales of games to eventually create profits for the entire product line. In addition, Microsoft probably anticipates manufacturing cost reductions for the Xbox over time. Another example of life cycle costing is the manufacture of printers and ink cartridges. Printers are often sold at a loss, but the revenue streams from ink cartridges more than make up for these initial losses.

Because life cycle costing takes into account cash flows that occur over multiple time periods, the net present value method is usually used to analyse product profitability.

16.6 Price management: pricing methods

LEARNING OBJECTIVE 16.6 Evaluate pricing methods and describe how cost-based prices and market-based prices are managed.

Determining appropriate prices for an organisation's products or services is an important activity because pricing decisions have both short- and long-term consequences. Price often influences customer decisions. A failure, however, to charge customers sufficient prices for products and services can have disastrous impacts on a firm's performance. For example, Microsoft reduced the prices of its Xbox to remain competitive with the Sony PlayStation. The example indicates that, even in markets with few competitors, prices are often based on competitor's prices, not just production costs.

Cost-based pricing

Cost-based prices are determined by adding a mark-up to some calculation of the product's cost. To apply this method, both a cost base and a mark-up rate are selected.

$$\text{Cost based price} = \text{Cost Base} + \text{Mark-up}$$

As we have explored throughout this book, the cost base of an item can be calculated in several ways. Some organisations use variable cost as the base, whereas others use an average cost based on absorption costing that includes both variable and fixed costs. If cost-based prices are used, it is important that the cost base is accurately measured as any cost inaccuracies will flow through to the price paid by customers. In this regard, the use of activity based costing can be beneficial given the ability to accurately allocate overhead costs.

Organisations frequently rely on mark-ups they have used for many years. Such mark-ups often originate from general industry practice and may be found in trade journals. For example, clothing retailers typically price using a 100 per cent mark-up on their variable costs. If a retailer pays $10 per blouse to the wholesaler, the variable cost per blouse is $10, and the blouse would be priced at $20. Mark-up percentages are also chosen so that the organisation earns a target rate of return on investment. Given differences in calculation methods and cost structures, cost-based prices vary a great deal across organisations.

$$\text{Mark-up} = (\text{Selling Price} - \text{Cost Base})/\text{Cost Base}$$

Cost based pricing can be used in many contexts including tender bid pricing. Government departments, for instance, frequently award contracts for different capital projects and service activities based on a competitive tender process. External entities bidding to win such tender contacts typically base the price of their bid on the budgeted cost of the project. Depending on the circumstances, this will include any material and labour costs needed to meet the requirements of the contract. Corporate overhead or administration charges, based on a predetermined charge-out rate, are also typically included.

Various strategic factors influence the mark-up for tender bids. In some instances (for example, to secure new long-term partner or demonstrate capacity to deliver a high quality service), a firm may be willing to include a smaller mark-up. In other situations (for example, when there is uncertainty regarding possible cost forecasts), a firm might include a larger mark-up. There can also be legal issues involved in pricing competitive tender bids. One such area relates to the Australian Competitive Neutrality principles which seek to ensure that government and private businesses are able to compete on an equal footing. Competitive neutrality compels government businesses entities to commit to full cost-recovery to ensure that they are not able to obtain an advantage relative to their private sector counterparts.[9]

As an example, Bombardier Jets is a small company that customises Lear jets for wealthy clients. At present, the company's managers are negotiating with three potential customers for next year's sales. The company's accountants summarised cost information for each plane as follows.

	Potential customer			
(In thousands)	Rock star	CEO	Sports figure	Total
Avoidable costs				
Basic jet plane	$ 800	$ 800	$ 800	$2400
Production	200	1200	600	2000
Selling costs	100	200	100	400
Total avoidable costs	$1100	$2200	$1500	$4800
Unavoidable costs				
Production				$3000
Administration				600
Total unavoidable costs				$3600

The unavoidable costs are the overhead costs to customise the jets, such as facility costs (rent or depreciation etc.) and equipment-related costs. These costs are primarily fixed.

The company has a policy of calculating price by applying a 50 per cent mark-up on cost. Two potential cost-based pricing schemes follow.

Alternative A. Under this alternative, unavoidable costs are allocated to the three contracts equally ($3600 ÷ 3 jets = $1200 per jet). Then a mark-up of 50 per cent is added to total costs as follows.

	Potential customer			
(In thousands)	Rock star	CEO	Sports figure	Total
Total avoidable costs	$1 100	$2 200	$1 500	$ 4 800
Allocated unavoidable costs	$1 200	$1 200	$1 200	$ 3 600
Total costs	$1 925	$3 400	$2 700	$ 8 400
Price (150% of total cost)	$3 450	$5 100	$4 050	$12 600

Alternative B. Under this alternative, unavoidable costs are allocated to each contract based on its proportion of avoidable costs. For example, the rock star's allocated cost is ($1100 ÷ $4800) × $3600 = $825. A mark-up of 50 per cent is then added to total costs to arrive at the price as follows.

	Potential customer			
(In thousands)	Rock star	CEO	Sports figure	Total
Total avoidable costs	$1 100	$2 200	$1 500	$ 4 800
Allocated unavoidable costs	$ 825	$1 650	$1 125	$3 600
Total costs	$1 925	$3 850	$2 625	$ 8 400
Price (150% of total cost)	$2 887	$5 775	$3 938	$12 600

Which alternative would you recommend? Would you want any additional information before making this decision? As illustrated by these two price alternatives, determining product cost is not straightforward. Decision makers always face uncertainty in determining an appropriate cost base. The price differences under alternatives A and B are caused by arbitrary allocations for overhead costs that cannot be attributed directly to the product. Should such allocations influence prices? To avoid this problem, some entities use only avoidable costs in their price calculations. However, they also face uncertainty in determining an appropriate mark-up percentage. Why is the mark-up 50 per cent and not 20 per cent, 30 per cent or some other amount? What should the mark-up be if only avoidable costs are included in the calculation? Most importantly, what are customers willing to pay?

Market-based pricing

High quality and brand name for an entity such as Bombardier Jets are likely to be as important, if not more important, than price. Accordingly, a cost-based pricing scheme might not maximise profits. As the company's managers make pricing decisions, they need to understand competitors' prices; however, they should also consider each buyer's ability and willingness to pay for the product. To maximise profits, Bombardier Jets should charge the highest price possible, but not such a high price that the customer buys from a competitor or decides not to buy a jet.

Market-based prices are determined using some measure of customer demand. Under market-based pricing, managers strive to identify what customers are willing to pay (WTP) for a good or service. As illustrated in figure 16.13, market prices are influenced by the degree of product differentiation and competition.

| FIGURE 16.13 | Market prices, product differentiation and degree of competition |

A significant amount of marketing research has been devoted to understand the drivers of consumers' WTP. Some studies have, for example, considered the willingness of consumers to pay for groceries from national brands, relative to a retailer's own private labels.[10] Others have explored how the WTP of some customer segments can be influenced by organic production and certification[11]; genetic modification[12] and sustainability factors.[13]

At one extreme, organisations face many competitors and cannot differentiate their products. In this case, the market price is the commodity price that customers would pay to any organisation offering the good or service. For example, farmers typically sell agricultural products at a quoted market price. The same is true for mining companies selling gold or silver. In such cases, managers estimate prices by referring to published rates.

At the other extreme are monopolies selling unique goods or services and having no competition. Monopolies such as residential water services are often owned or regulated by the government. In these cases, the entity is not allowed to establish a free market price but must charge the regulated price.

Rate of return regulation is often used in these contexts. This involves permitting regulated entities to charge cost-reflective prices which enable them to cover operating costs, depreciation costs and also generate a return on their asset base. Such practices have been controversial at times given the possibility that they may encourage regulated firms to be inefficient and over-invest in, or 'gold-plate', infrastructure assets. In response, some regulators have sought to encourage regulated entities to more thoroughly engage with their customers to ensure that their operations are more in line with customer expectations. Other regulators have adopted price-cap regulation. This involves approved prices for regulated entities being based on inflation and adjusted for an efficiency saving.[14]

Occasionally short-term monopolies arise. For example, the only pub in town with beer after a heat wave can theoretically charge as much as the market will bear until competitors receive beer deliveries. Most goods and services fall between these two extremes. Organisations can typically differentiate their product in the market because features and brand names are important. However, these organisations are subject to competition, which must be considered when setting prices. To set prices, they estimate consumer demand for product characteristics such as quality and functionality.

Price elasticity and demand

Organisations with differentiated products can formally or informally incorporate consumer demand into their pricing policies. For example, contractors who build expensive houses often negotiate prices with individual buyers. The negotiations continue throughout the construction period when unforeseen costs arise or when the home buyer makes choices such as carpeting and wall coverings that are more expensive than anticipated. A more formal way to incorporate demand into prices is through the price elasticity of demand.

As prices increase, demand usually falls. This sensitivity of sales to price increases is called the **price elasticity of demand**. Cigarettes are an example of a product where changes in price have a substantial effect on sales; that is, demand is elastic. In contrast, customised planes such as Bombardier Jets are a product with relatively inelastic demand. Price changes have little effect on demand, and factors such as quality and the ability to customise are more important (within limits) than price.

To develop a price that maximises profit, we follow the steps shown in figure 16.14. The first step is to calculate the price elasticity of demand. To perform this calculation, data must be available to calculate the percentage change in quantity that occurs for a percentage change in price. The second step is to determine the profit-maximising price, a calculation that is based on the strong assumption that changes in volume result *only* from changes in price. This assumption is never completely true, however, so the mark-up amount needs to be interpreted with caution. It only provides guidance about pricing decisions.

FIGURE 16.14   Computing the profit-maximising price

Step 1: Calculate the price elasticity of demand.

$$\text{Elasticity} = \frac{\ln(1 + \% \text{ change in quantity sold})}{\ln(1 + \% \text{ change in price})}$$

where ln is the mathematical function for natural logarithm

Step 2: Calculate the profit-maximising price.[a]

$$\text{Profit-maximising price} = \left[\frac{\text{Elasticity}}{(\text{Elasticity} + 1)}\right] \times \text{Variable cost}$$

[a] The profit-maximising mark up formula is

$$\left[\frac{\text{Elasticity}}{(\text{Elasticity} + 1)} - 1\right]$$

We add 1 to the mark-up before we multiply by variable cost to determine the profit-maximising price.

These calculations are based on information about prices, sales volumes and variable costs. Two factors affect the profit-maximising price: (1) changes in the product's demand sensitivity to price, and (2) changes in variable costs. Information about fixed costs is irrelevant. Comprehensive example 4 shows how these calculations help an entity set prices.

COMPREHENSIVE EXAMPLE 4

Using price elasticity to calculate product prices

French Perfumery produces two perfumes: Breezy and Exotique. Breezy is a well-known inexpensive perfume, and its customers are sensitive to price. Several competitors market similar products, and close substitutes are available at discount chemists and department stores. Exotique is a customised perfume sold only in small boutique stores where few substitutes are available and where customers are less sensitive to price. French's accountant, Mimi, needs to develop pricing guidelines for management. She performs the following analysis.

Profit-maximising prices for Breezy and Exotique
Mimi calculates the variable cost of Breezy as $2 per mL and $10 per mL for Exotique. Based on information from historical accounting records, she believes that every 10 per cent increase in price for Breezy results in a decrease in sales of 20 per cent because customers for this product are so price

---

sensitive. She calculates the price elasticity for Breezy as −2.34 [ln(1 − 0.2) ÷ ln(1 + 0.1)]. In turn, she uses the elasticity to calculate a profit-maximising price of $3.50 {[−2.34 ÷ (−2.34 + 1)] × $2}.

Mimi estimates that for every 10 per cent increase in price, sales of Exotique would decrease only 12 per cent. She calculates price elasticity of demand for Exotique as −1.34 [ln(1 − 0.12) ÷ ln(1 + 0.1)]. The profit-maximising price is then $39.40 {[−1.34 ÷ (−1.34 + 1)] × $10}. According to these calculations, the mark-up for Breezy is 75 per cent and the mark-up for Exotique is 294 per cent. Exotique's demand is less sensitive to price changes than Breezy's, so Mimi knows that Exotique's demand is more inelastic. Products or services with inelastic demand have higher optimal mark-ups than products or services with more elastic demand.

Market price guidelines

When Mimi presents her calculations to managers, she cautions them about this information. Although the calculations seem precise, they should be interpreted only as guidelines for price setting, not absolute determinants of price. She warns them that similar to other decisions, the managers need to consider uncertainties when making pricing decisions. For example, measurement error may occur in collecting information about how price changes affect sales. She explains to the managers that these formulas are extremely sensitive to errors, and small changes in assumptions create a large effect on the calculations. Also, price elasticity can vary over time due to changes in competitor prices and customer preferences. Managers need to anticipate and monitor for changes in product demand.

Mimi also explains the following assumptions underlying her calculations:

- the price elasticity of demand is constant
- the variable cost is constant
- the product price has no effect on other product costs or sales.

The managers know that these assumptions may not always hold, so they decide to make small incremental changes to prices and then track profitability to determine the profit-maximising price.

Accountants use historical information to estimate the effects of price changes on sales volume. Some organisations might rely on price elasticity information published by their industries. Other organisations use optical scanners to capture historical price and volume data. The quality of this type of information improves as sales volumes increase. Companies can rapidly gather data and monitor relationships between price and volume. They can also analyse how sales behave for groups of products. For example, supermarkets often sell some products as 'loss leaders', lowering the price on a specific product to bring customers into the store. In these cases, managers assume that increases in sales of other products will more than make up for the forgone profit from the loss leader.

The quality of product demand estimates using historical data depends in part on sales volumes. Large retailers collect large amounts of sales data and conduct price experiments to learn more about how volumes respond to price changes. Entities with lower sales volumes also collect sales and price data, but they are likely to face more error in their estimates of product demand.

Other market-based pricing methods

As noted earlier, Microsoft Xbox is an example where companies sometimes use competitors' prices to establish their own market prices. For common products in retail settings, competitors' prices are easily observed. However, it may be difficult to learn about competitors' prices when fewer transactions occur or are made in non-retail settings.

For example, market prices for items that were previously difficult to value can be gathered from auction websites such as eBay, GraysOnline, Yahoo! and Amazon. Access to market prices is made possible with new forms of organisation and internet technology. Given the large range of products and prices that are readily available, these sites increase the consistency of prices, even for objects such as antiques. Because increasing numbers of organisations include product and service price information on their websites, the internet also makes it easier for managers to monitor competitors' prices.

The internet is likely to cause prices to become more elastic because close substitutes are more easily found and priced. The internet also increases the global reach of many companies. Together, the internet and global competition have forced an increasingly large number of organisations to use market-based pricing.

Cost-based versus market-based pricing

A major drawback of cost-based pricing is that it ignores customer demand. Prices are likely to be higher or lower than what customers are willing to pay for goods or services. For example, Motorola based the price of its global cellular phones on costs, rather than surveying the market for a competitive price. This decision resulted first in prices for the phone and calling rates that were higher than customers would pay, and eventually contributed to the bankruptcy of the entire project. In other situations, cost-based prices are too low and organisations forgo potential profits.

With cost-based prices, sales volumes inappropriately influence the price, causing a downward demand spiral known as the **death spiral**. If production decreases because demand has decreased, then the average product cost increases and the price based on that average cost increases. When the product has an elastic demand curve, price increases cause sales to decline even more. This decline, in turn, causes average cost to increase even further, producing more price increases and more sales deterioration. This pattern persists until the product is discontinued because it cannot cover its costs.

Despite these disadvantages, cost-based pricing is a commonly used method.[15] Surveys of manufacturers consistently report that they prefer to mark up an average cost that includes a portion of fixed cost, using a mark-up system based on desired return.[16] This preference might reflect the fact that it was difficult in the past for an entity's information systems to gather the data needed to calculate profit-maximising sales prices. The major benefit of using cost-based pricing is its simplicity. Prices are calculated from readily available cost data.

Using market-based prices to estimate revenues, managers make better decisions about sales volumes or whether to sell goods or services, leading to more success in organisational strategies. The disadvantage is that estimating market demand and prices is often difficult. However, more sophisticated information systems make it easier for managers to estimate demand, marginal costs and revenues, leading to an increasing trend in the use of market-based pricing.

Other influences on price

Regardless of the general technique used, a number of other factors influence prices for individual organisations or in specific circumstances.

Some industries charge different prices at different times to reduce capacity constraints, a practice called **peak load pricing**. For example, some cinemas charge less for movies shown early in the day. Telephone companies often charge less for calls made at night or on the weekend. In the airline industry, a variety of prices are offered to customers based on factors such as advanced ticket purchase, whether the customer is travelling for business or leisure, and whether the customer wants preferential seating and other services. During economic downturns, even organisations with set prices may negotiate with customers.

Price skimming occurs when a higher price is charged for a product or service when it is first introduced. The term refers to the practice of skimming the cream off the market. When new technology is introduced, such as notepads that transcribe handwriting to word processing, high prices are charged to cover the initial research and development. Prices are then reduced as competitors enter the market.

Penetration pricing is the practice of setting low prices when new products are introduced to increase market share. This practice describes Microsoft's willingness to reduce the price of Xbox to match its competition. Penetration pricing is legal if its intent is to reduce customer uncertainty about product or service value. However, if the purpose is to eliminate competition, then it could be considered predatory pricing, which is illegal in Australia.

Sometimes managers take advantage of unusual circumstances to increase prices. **Price gouging** is the practice of charging a price viewed by consumers as too high. If managers can convince consumers that prices are based on costs, they avoid being labelled as price gougers.

Transfer prices are the prices charged for transactions that take place within an entity. Prices are set for the use of support departments such as human resources and accounting. In a manufacturing setting, intermediate products are often transferred to other departments where further assembly takes place before the final product is sold to external markets. These intermediate products need to be priced so that appropriate decisions can be made about the value of selling products internally or externally. Transfer price policies also have incentive and tax effects (covered in chapter 18).

Pricing in not-for-profit entities

Not-for-profit entities are concerned with many objectives other than profit maximisation. Their pricing methods tend to be more complex than those used by for-profit entities. Grants, donations and interest from endowed funds often help defray the cost of products and services. Because of these sources of funds, not-for-profits do not always expect to recover all of their costs from prices or fees they charge.

Some not-for-profit organisations charge a fee based on the client's income. This fee is called a sliding scale fee; as client income decreases, the fee decreases. Clients who can afford to pay more are charged more. Other not-for-profits charge high prices to everyone, but then provide charity services for low-income clients or discount the charges to selected clients. For example, hospitals might set prices for services high enough that revenues from insured patients cover the costs of providing services to uninsured patients. In addition, Medicare often pays for only a portion of the costs incurred by Medicare patients. Therefore, hospital managers attempt to use pricing policies to shift some of these costs to other patients. The result is that charity care and treatment of Medicare patients tend to inflate hospital prices for other patients.

Some not-for-profit entities use price-setting policies to achieve organisational goals. For example, many universities discount tuition or offer grants and scholarships to students with high entrance scores. Their goal is to improve the quality of incoming students. A stronger student body enhances these schools' reputations and may in turn increase the number of applicants.

Government regulations, ethics and pricing

Organisations are not free to establish any price they wish; some pricing practices are illegal. In Australia, illegal practices include price discrimination, predatory pricing, collusive pricing and dumping. Courts often use costs to determine whether an entity has violated laws.

Price discrimination is the practice of setting different prices for different customers. Although not-for-profit organisations charge prices according to ability to pay, Australian regulations forbid for-profit organisations from charging some customers higher prices for the same product if the intent is to lessen or prevent competition for customers. Entities can use cost differences as a defence against price discrimination charges.

It is also illegal for organisations to practise **predatory pricing**, which is the deliberate act of setting prices low to drive competitors out of the market and then raising prices. However, low prices are not considered predatory if they can be justified by cost differences.

Many governments also forbid **collusive pricing**, which occurs when two or more organisations conspire to set prices above a competitive price. Consumer welfare is harmed by such practices. In Australia, the Australian Competition and Consumer Commission (ACCC) has previously investigated allegations of petrol price fixing among rival petrol suppliers. They argue that sometimes the selling or buying prices can be set at the same level so that the price fluctuations are matched by equivalent fluctuation by competing businesses. Although this may seem like collusive behaviour, legitimate commercial reasons may include highly visible prices displayed by competitors (for example, on petrol price boards) allowing competitors to quickly adjust their prices to match price movements.[17]

Under Australian law, **dumping** occurs when a foreign-based entity sells products in Australia at prices below the market value in the country where the product is produced, and the price could harm an Australian industry. The Australian Government imposes an anti-dumping tariff. The tariff is set so that the new price will be equivalent to the prices charged by Australian entities. These rules have been applied in a number of industries. Other countries enact similar laws to protect home country manufacturers from unfair competition from foreign businesses. In 2014 an Australian photovoltaic (solar power) module manufacturer initiated an anti-dumping claim over the importation of Chinese photovoltaic products. The claim made was that the importer was selling solar products below cost.[18]

There are a number of examples that illustrate how pricing decisions can raise ethical considerations. In some circumstances, pricing products at low prices can be construed as unethical given the role of lower prices in promoting consumption of potentially harmful items like tobacco and alcohol. In regard to these items, governments use excise taxes to act as price signals to constrain demand. In other contexts, pharmaceuticals for example, high prices can be viewed as unethical given the potential perception of profit gouging by powerful multinational companies. The defence of high pharmaceutical prices, however, is the importance of allowing firms to recover the significant cost of research and development (R&D) and to encourage investment in new and more effective treatments. Again, regulation plays a role through government subsidies (for example, the Australian Pharmaceuticals Benefits Scheme) and permission for generic brands to enter the market.

SUMMARY

16.1 Explain the value chain activities that provide for continuous cost improvement.

Continuously improve costs over the long term by:
- enhancing efficiency
- reducing costs
- improving interactions with suppliers and customers
- identifying and eliminating non-value-added activities
- minimising rework, scrap and waste
- reducing production cycle time
- negotiating lower prices with suppliers.

16.2 Explain the concept of customer profitability analysis and suggest qualitative factors for inclusion in a strategic customer analysis model.

Customer profitability analysis may contain a quantitative component that requires the identification of resources consumed and costs by individual customers or groups of customers. Moreover, a qualitative assessment may also be conducted as input to a strategic assessment of an organisation's customers.

Higher resource consuming customers tend to:
- demand additional support services
- place non-routine orders/requests
- require customised features in product/service delivery
- exceed credit terms available
- make poor use of technology in ordering and service delivery process
- require more frequent deliveries due to order size
- frequently return goods for credit
- delay payments requiring follow-up by administration.

Lower resource consuming customers tend to:
- make better use of technology in ordering and service-delivery process
- be consistent with ordering routines
- not require customised features within given price range
- not require additional support beyond original agreement
- make payments within credit terms.

16.3 Understand target costing principles and techniques.

Decision-making method that considers prices as given and then determines whether products and services can be provided at costs low enough for an acceptable profit.

Target costing design cycle

16.4 Communicate the concept of kaizen costing and explain how it compares to target costing.

Kaizen costing

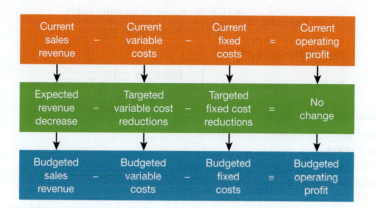

Comparison of kaizen and target costing

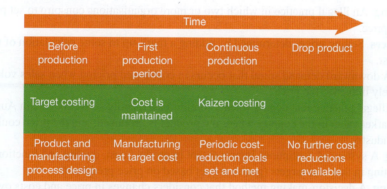

16.5 Describe the characteristics of life cycle costing.

Life cycle costing

Consider changes in price and costs over the entire life cycle of a good or service, from the time the product is introduced through a number of years.

- Allow initial losses or large decommissioning costs.
- Expect a combination of sales volume increases and cost reductions over time.

16.6 Evaluate pricing methods and describe how cost-based prices and market-based prices are managed.

Must choose:

- measure of cost (variable, fixed and variable etc.)
- mark-up percentage.

Establishment of market-based prices

Factors affecting market prices

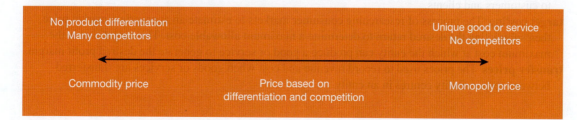

Computations for profit-maximising price

Step 1: Calculate the price elasticity of demand.

$$\text{Elasticity} = \frac{\ln\left(1 + \% \text{ change in quantity sold}\right)}{\ln\left(1 + \% \text{ change in price}\right)}$$

Step 2: Calculate the profit-maximising price.

$$\text{Profit-maximising price} = \left[\frac{\text{Elasticity}}{(\text{Elasticity} + 1)}\right] \times \text{Variable cost}$$

Other market-based pricing methods

Match competitors' prices using information from:
- competitor retail stores
- competitor websites
- internet auction sites.

KEY TERMS

collusive pricing An illegal practice in which two or more organisations conspire to set prices above a competitive price.

cost-based prices Selling prices determined by adding a mark-up to some calculation of the product's cost.

death spiral A downward demand spiral that occurs in cost-based pricing when sales volumes inappropriately influence the price.

dumping An illegal practice that occurs when a foreign-based entity sells products in Australia at prices below the market value in the country where the product is produced, and the price could harm an Australian industry.

kaizen costing A system of continuous improvement in product cost, quality and functionality. Similar to target costing in that cost targets (goals) are set based on price predictions.

life cycle costing A decision-making method that considers changes in price and costs over the entire life cycle of a good or service, from the time the product is introduced through a number of years.

market-based prices Selling prices determined using some measure of customer demand; managers strive to identify what customers are willing to pay for a good or service.

peak load pricing The practice of charging different prices at different times to reduce capacity constraints.

penetration pricing The practice of setting low prices when new products are introduced to increase market share.

predatory pricing An illegal practice of deliberately setting prices low to drive competitors out of the market and then raising prices. Low prices are not considered predatory if they can be justified by cost differences.

price discrimination An illegal practice of setting different prices for different customers.

price elasticity of demand The sensitivity of sales to price increases.

price gouging The practice of charging a price viewed by consumers as too high.

price skimming The practice of charging a higher price for a product or service when it is first introduced.

supply chain The flow of resources from the initial suppliers through the delivery of goods and services to customers and clients.

target costing The process of researching consumer markets to estimate an appropriate market price, then subtracting the desired return to determine a maximum allowable cost. This target cost is the maximum cost at which the entity can produce a good or service to generate the desired profit margin.

transfer prices The prices used to record revenue and cost when goods or services are transferred between responsibility centres in an entity.

SELF-STUDY PROBLEMS

SELF-STUDY PROBLEM 1 Target and kaizen costing

You have recently been hired as an accountant for a start-up entity in the computer peripherals industry. The owners have developed and are manufacturing several wireless devices, such as a small electronic notebook, to enhance user mobility. They want to become more competitive in this market and also develop several other products. They have asked you for ideas about ways to control costs and determine whether proposed new products will be profitable.

Required

Write a memo to the owners describing how they could use target costing and kaizen costing.

SOLUTION TO SELF-STUDY PROBLEM 1

Many possible approaches may be taken to write a memo on these topics. The body of one possible memo follows. Note that the memo is written to inform and help the managers of the entity make a decision.

> You asked for my recommendations about ways to control costs and to determine whether proposed new products will be profitable. In this memo I briefly describe two techniques — target costing and kaizen costing — that could be implemented to achieve these goals.
>
> *Target costing.* Target costing helps determine whether a proposed new product will be profitable. This technique involves the following steps.
> - Estimate the market price of the proposed product.
> - Given the market price, determine what the cost must be to achieve our desired profitability.
> - Estimate the costs of producing the product. If the estimated cost exceeds the target cost, search for ways to reduce costs.
> - Drop the product idea if it is not feasible to achieve the target cost.
> - For potentially-feasible new products, conduct pilot production projects to further evaluate estimated costs.
>
> The biggest advantage of target costing is that it would help us focus on ways to design products and manufacturing processes to meet our profitability goals. If costs are too high, we will be forced to look for ways to reduce them, which might also lead us to make changes to the proposed features of a new product.
>
> The target costing process would also help us involve everyone in the organisation in making product decisions and setting cost goals. This involvement would encourage employees to 'buy in' to the target costs, which will help us achieve them.
>
> *Kaizen costing.* Kaizen costing helps control costs over the life of a product, taking into account the fact that selling prices decline over some product's life. The process for kaizen costing is similar to the process described for target costing. We would estimate the future selling prices of our existing products and determine the cost we need to achieve for our desired profit.
>
> Kaizen costing would help us make decisions about products we wish to continue. If we cannot find ways to reduce costs to achieve desired profitability, then we should consider dropping it.
>
> *Risks.* I believe that both of these methods would help us meet our goals. However, you should be aware of three major risks:
> - Both methods involve a great deal of estimation for prices and costs. The rapid change in our industry presents a high risk of errors in our estimates that might prevent us from achieving our profitability goals.
> - Teams of personnel from marketing, engineering, production and accounting would be needed for implementation. It will be critical for everyone to work toward common goals rather than to focus only on their own work areas. Thus, the team members should be chosen carefully and would need to understand that the teams have high priority.
> - These techniques might discourage us from adopting new products or continuing existing products that have long-term value. The teams need to consider long-term as well as short-term factors in making final recommendations.

SELF-STUDY PROBLEM 2 Cost-based and market-based prices; minimum acceptable price

Torquay Produce Suppliers packages and distributes three grades of animal feed. The material cost per tonne and estimated annual sales for each of the products are listed here:

Product	Material cost	Estimated sales
Super Premium	$16	1000 tonnes
Premium	$12	1500 tonnes
Economy	$10	2500 tonnes

The fixed cost of operating the machinery used to package all three products is $20 000 per year. In the past, prices have been set by allocating the fixed overhead to products on the basis of estimated sales in tonnes. The resulting total costs (material costs plus allocated fixed overhead) are then marked up by 100 per cent.

Required

(a) Determine the price per tonne for each grade of feed using the method described for setting prices.

(b) Does the price in part (a) take into account how much customers are willing to pay for the product? Explain.

(c) Suppose a 10 per cent increase in price would result in about a 40 per cent decrease in the amount of the economy grade feed sold. Estimate the price that would maximise profits on the economy grade feed.

(d) Explain how the price for economy grade feed calculated in part (c) should be used.

(e) Suppose a Geelong distributor would like to buy 200 tonnes of economy grade feed and has offered to pay $2400 for the special order.

    (i) What is the relevant cost to Torquay Produce Suppliers for this order?

    (ii) Considering only quantitative factors, what is the minimum acceptable price per tonne?

SOLUTION TO SELF-STUDY PROBLEM 2

(a)

	Economy	Premium	Super Premium
Materials cost	$10	$12	$16
Allocated fixed overhead			
$20 000 ÷ 5000 = $4 per tonne	4	4	4
Total cost	14	16	20
Mark-up (100% of total cost)	14	16	20
Price	$28	$32	$40

(b) No. A cost-based price *assumes* that customers are willing to pay a set mark-up above cost. However, a price based on cost might be higher or lower than customers are willing to pay.

(c) The price for economy grade feed can be computed in two steps:

$$\text{Elasticity of demand} = \ln(1 - 0.40) - \ln(1 + 0.10) = -5.36$$
$$\text{Profit-maximising price} = [-5.36 - (-5.36 + 1)] \times \$10 = \$12.30$$

(d) The price in part (c) is only a guideline for pricing. The elasticity formulas are sensitive to error, so the profit-maximising prices are used only as guidelines. Torquay Produce Suppliers could reduce the price of economy grade feed slowly and see how volumes and profits change.

(e) (i) The relevant cost of filling the special order is the variable cost, which in this problem is the cost of materials: $10 per tonne × 200 tonnes = $2000.

    (ii) Under the general quantitative decision rule for special orders, the minimum acceptable price is the variable cost. The minimum acceptable price would be $10 per tonne.

QUESTIONS

16.1 How might customer profitability analysis be used to improve organisational performance? **LO2**

16.2 Explain the similarities and differences among target costing, kaizen costing and life cycle costing. **LO3, 4, 5**

16.3 Identify three products for which target costing and kaizen costing could be used. Identify three products for which target costing and kaizen costing would be inappropriate. **LO3, 4**

16.4 Explain the target costing cycle, and discuss the decision criteria used to determine whether a product will be manufactured using a target costing approach. **LO3**

16.5 How can the principles of target costing assist with the decision to invest or continue to invest in the game console market? **LO3**

16.6 In competitive markets such as the game console industry, how might management respond to techniques such as life cycle costing? **LO5**

16.7 Explain cost-based pricing and give an example that shows how prices would be determined using this method. **LO6**

16.8 Explain market-based pricing and explain where managers and accountants can find information that would help them set prices using this type of approach. **LO6**

16.9 Supply chain analysis focuses particularly on one aspect of value chain analysis. Explain how supply chain analysis is performed and how it relates to value chain analysis. **LO1**

16.10 List some common advantages and disadvantages for target and kaizen costing. **LO3, 4**

16.11 If fixed costs are included in the marked-up costs used in setting cost-based prices, a problem may occur when demand declines. Describe this problem. **LO6**

16.12 Explain why not-for-profit entities do not always set prices so that their operating costs are recovered. **LO6**

EXERCISES

16.13 Customer profitability analysis   LO2

Hector Gonzales runs the Floral Art Company, which supplies floral arrangements to three large supermarket chains throughout Australia. Management has become concerned about the rising costs associated with the processing and dispatch of orders. An activity analysis of the indirect costs identified the following customer-related costs.

Activity cost pool	Cost driver	Estimated indirect costs	Total expected use of cost driver*	Use of cost driver Supermarket customer		
				1	2	3
Orders processing	Number of orders	$200 000	450	300	100	50
Returns processing	Number of returns	$ 50 000	100	50	25	25
Delivery	Number of deliveries	$100 000	700	400	200	100
Rush orders	Number of rush orders	$ 70 000	50	10	20	20
Sales visits	Number of visits	$ 20 000	100	50	25	25

* Expressed in units of measure of the driver.
Sales are marked up 50 per cent on cost.

Required
(a) Calculate the activity cost rate for each activity
(b) Assign the activity costs to each of the three customers.
(c) Calculate the contribution for each customer if the sales pattern for each is as follows: Customer 1 — $350 000; Customer 2 — $160 000; Customer 3 — $210 000.
(d) Advise the management of the Floral Art Company as to whether any changes should be made in its relationships with customers. Advise Hector as to how he should go about executing these changes.

16.14 Market-based price (elasticity formula)   LO6

Duncans sells doughnuts. Data for a recent week are as follows.

Revenue (1000 doughnuts @ $1.75 each)		$1750
Cost of ingredients	$640	
Rent	500	
Store attendant	600	1740
Pre-tax profit		$ 10

The manager estimates that, if Duncans increased the price of doughnuts from $1.75 to $1.93 each, weekly volume would be cut to 850 doughnuts due to competition from other nearby cake shops.

Required

Estimate the profit-maximising price per doughnut.

16.15 Customer profitability analysis; strategic considerations LO2

Cougar Toys is a toy wholesaler supplying to a range of different customers. With concerns about sources of profitability from these different customers, Cougar has embarked on a relatively simple customer analysis exercise. In the first instance, customers have been classified as large, medium or small based essentially on sales volume. The results of this analysis are provided in the following table.

	Sales in units by customer category			
	Large	Medium	Small	Total
Sales revenue	$2 500 000	$1 600 300	$1 400 900	$5 501 200
Cost of sales	1 500 000	880 165	770 495	3 150 660
Gross profit	1 000 000	720 135	630 405	2 350 540
Order filling costs	Assigned on the basis of number of orders			420 000
Distribution-related costs	Assigned on the basis of number of deliveries			835 000
Marketing/promotion/sales	Assigned on sales dollars			935 000
Administration-related costs	Assigned on number of deliveries			460 600
Total expenses				$2 650 600
Profit (loss)				$ 300 060
Cost driver				
No. of orders received	35	45	80	160
No. of deliveries made	50	63	110	223

Required

(a) Using the activity analysis data, calculate the profitability of each of the customer groups.

(b) Management is concerned about the consolidation taking place in the industry. They know that going forward, customer relations and the strategic management of customers will be critical. Identify a number of the critical strategic factors that management might want to monitor in addition to the financial profitability analysis.

16.16 Target costing LO3

Search online for two organisations that have used target costing.

Required

Briefly comment on what you find in relation to this practice.

16.17 Life cycle costing LO5

Search online for two organisations that have used life cycle costing.

Required

Briefly comment on what you find in relation to this practice.

16.18 Market-based prices (elasticity formula) LO6

Arnie's Flowers is a small Mt Macedon florist shop. Arnie sells flowers for bouquets, and she also prepares and delivers flower arrangements.

Required

(a) Arnie is trying to decide how much to charge for a new type of rose that wholesales for $0.40 per bud. he ran a special on a similar rose last month and discovered that a 20 per cent discount on the usual price increased sales by about 35 per cent. What would you suggest as a starting price for the rose? Explain.

(b) Arnie has been wondering whether he has been charging the right prices on some of her specialty bouquets. She has been using a mark-up for all specialty items of 200 per cent (that is, he charges three times wholesale cost). Arnie estimates that a 10 per cent increase in price on such items would decrease her unit sales by about 12 per cent. Perform calculations to estimate a profit-maximising mark-up. Based on your calculation, do you think he should increase or decrease her mark-up? Explain.

16.19 Target costing LO3

Suppose that Hyundai used target costing to decide whether to produce a new vehicle, such as a Hybrid SUV Vehicle.

Required

(a) Describe the steps Hyundai's design team would have taken.

(b) Explain why managers cannot easily predict demand for a new product such as the Hybrid SUV Vehicle.

16.20 Customer profitability — qualitative factors   LO2

Refer to Paisley Insurance in comprehensive example 1 in chapter 12. In this example, an ABC and non-ABC version of the costs of servicing each type of account customer — residential and commercial — was determined.

Required

State some important qualitative and/or strategic factors that would warrant consideration alongside the quantified cost data.

16.21 Market-based price (elasticity formula); uncertainties; other pricing factors   LO6

Chocolate Creations is a shop located at Docklands in Melbourne. It makes and sells specialty chocolates in a variety of flavours. Revenue and cost data for a recent week are as follows.

Revenue (1500 kg @ $6 per kg)		$9000
Cost of ingredients	$2400	
Rent	800	
Wages	3200	6400
Pre-tax profit		$2600

All employees work standard shifts, regardless of how many chocolates are produced or sold. Henrietta, the shop's manager, estimates that, if she decreased the price of chocolates by $0.60 per kg to a new price of $5.40 per kg, weekly volume would increase by 20 per cent.

Required

(a) Calculate the price elasticity of demand.

(b) Calculate the profit-maximising price.

(c) Based on the profit-maximising price, does it appear that Henrietta should drop the price of the chocolates? Why?

(d) List possible relevant factors that could influence Henrietta's price decision. List as many factors as you can.

16.22 Market-based (elasticity formula) and cost-based prices; special order decision   LO6

Oysters Away shucks and packs oysters and sells them wholesale to fine restaurants across the country. The statement of profit or loss for last year follows:

Revenue (2000 cases)		$200 000
Expenses:		
Wages for pickers, shuckers and packers	$100 000	
Packing materials	20 000	
Rent and insurance	25 000	
Administration and selling	45 000	
		190 000
Pre-tax profit		$ 10 000

Pickers, shuckers, and packers are employed on an hourly basis and can be laid off whenever necessary. Salespeople merely deliver the product, and so are paid on a salaried basis.

Linda Hanson, manager of Oysters Away, believes that a price increase of 10 per cent would result in a 15 per cent decrease in sales.

The King Krab Restaurant is providing dinner for a meeting of the Pickers, Shuckers and Packers Union in Melbourne. King Krab offered to pay Oysters Away $65 a case for 300 cases of oysters. This sale would not affect Oysters Away's regular sales.

Required

(a) Ignoring the King Krab offer, estimate the profit-maximising price for Oysters Away.

(b) Assuming Linda is not willing to lose money on the King Krab order, what is the minimum price that she should accept for the special order?

(c) What other relevant factors might Linda consider before she makes a decision about the King Krab order? List as many factors as you can.

16.23 Kaizen costing

Blade Runner produces regular scooters and motorised scooters. Blade Runner scooters are considered the most reliable in the marketplace. Demand has been volatile, with huge increases in demand during the holiday season. In the past, the entity filled demand by anticipating demand increases and manufacturing inventories ahead of time.

Recently, competition in the motorised scooter line has escalated, and Blade Runner needs to reduce prices and therefore cut costs. The motorised scooter's current cost is $150. To be competitive, the marketing department says the price should be 10 per cent lower than the current price. Management currently achieves a pre-tax return of 10 per cent on sales of the scooters and wants to continue this rate of return.

The following per-unit costs for motorised scooters are based on production of 700 000 per year.

Direct materials (variable)	$ 45
Direct labour (variable)	15
Machining costs (fixed depreciation and maintenance)	10
Inspection costs (variable)	10
Engineering costs (fixed)	20
Marketing costs (fixed)	25
Administrative costs (fixed)	25
Total cost	$150

Required
(a) Calculate the price recommended by the marketing department.
(b) Given the price you calculated in part (a), calculate the new contribution margin and the target cost.
(c) Calculate the planned cost reduction for each cost category, assuming proportional cost reduction across categories.

16.24 Kaizen costing; proposed cost reductions; uncertainties
LO4

Refer to the information in exercise 16.23. The following cost reduction suggestions were made by the kaizen costing team.

- *Direct materials* — suppliers agreed to cost reductions of $4.50 for direct materials.
- *Direct labour* — an engineer suggested that the scooters could be manufactured more quickly if production batches were cut in half. The engineer believes that a labour savings of $1.50 per scooter could be attained.
- *Machining costs* — the team has been unable to identify ways to reduce machining costs in the manufacturing process, but suggests that some of the machining tasks could be outsourced to suppliers so that some parts are pre-assembled, reducing the need for machine hours. This outsourcing would increase the cost of direct materials by $0.50 per unit but cut machining costs by $1.30 per unit. The supplier has been very reliable, but does not currently have the machining expertise and would have to purchase equipment and hire several workers to fill these orders.
- *Marketing* — marketing has agreed to combine advertising campaigns for both products and believes they will save $2.50 per unit without losing sales.
- *Administration and engineering* — no cost containment appears possible in administration because a new enterprise resource program was recently acquired. However, the head of engineering believes that her costs can be cut by $4 per unit. She believes that some employees are no longer needed because part of the new program was designed especially to provide information for product and manufacturing process design that had been manually collated in the past.

Required
(a) Calculate the new cost per category. Compare the total cost with the kaizen cost. Determine whether further cost-containment efforts need to be made.
(b) In your own words, describe the next step in the kaizen process.
(c) List qualitative factors that might be relevant to Blade Runner's managers as they decide on any product or process changes. List as many factors as you can.
(d) For each of the planned cost reductions, discuss uncertainties about whether the entity will achieve the planned cost reduction.

PROBLEMS

16.25 Cost-based and market-based pricing; elasticity; uncertainties; economy effects　　　**LO6**

John Gold has owned and operated the Heritage Jewellery store for a number of years. He uses the standard mark-up of 300 per cent (known as a 'triple key' in this industry) and uses an average cost that includes an allocation of overhead as the cost base. Lately, jewellery sales at the store have faltered as the country faces a recession. John's son is taking a cost accounting course and suggests that his father should use a pricing formula based on the price elasticity of demand.

Required

(a) In your own words, provide a plausible explanation for John's current use of cost-based pricing.

(b) Explain elasticity to John in simple terms.

(c) In your own words, explain how price changes affect demand for products that are highly elastic.

(d) Explain why John's price elasticity of demand cannot be predicted with certainty.

(e) List possible reasons why a product's price elasticity of demand would change. List as many reasons as you can.

(f) Explain how changes in the economy affect prices. Give examples from the current business environment.

16.26 Customer analysis, non-quantifiable factors　　　**LO2**

Tania Wells owns and operates Gym Gear R Us, a growing internet business that specialises in the sale of gym wear for men, women and children. Tania designs her products but has them manufactured offshore. Since starting the business three years ago, she has been able to build the company to the point where it is now generating annual sales in excess of $1 million. Tania's long-term plans include reaching a sales target of $3 million within the next three years. She is clear about a number of things that are critical to the business:

• product quality and a variety of product offerings
• quick order-turnaround times and speed of delivery to customers.

Even though there are many individual customers, Tania wants to develop a customer development model that will identify the key issues associated with building stronger customer relationships.

Required

Identify some of the key components suitable for inclusion in a customer development model for Gym Gear R Us.

16.27 Cost reduction; value chain analysis　　　**LO1**

Budget Cupboards produces kitchen and bathroom cupboards that incorporate unusual functions such as specialty drawers for knives and kitchen tools, and kitchen appliance holders that pop up from under the countertop. Competition in this industry has recently increased. Budget's management wants to cut costs for its basic cupboard models and then cut prices.

Required

(a) The following table lists potential areas for cost reduction. Two potential cost reductions are provided for the first area listed (design phase). For each of the remaining areas, identify two potential ways that Budget Cupboard's management could reduce costs.

Potential area for cost reduction	Potential cost reductions	
	(i)	(ii)
Example: Design phase	Work with suppliers to reduce direct materials costs	Redesign cupboards to use fewer parts
Manufacturing process		
Administration		
Changes in quality or functionality		

(b) Budget Cupboards does not currently use value chain analysis. Describe several advantages of using these methods when price competition increases.

16.28 Target and kaizen costing; uncertainties; manager incentives　　　**LO3, 4**

Suppose you are having a conversation with Sandy, another student in this course. Sandy is confused about the differences and similarities between target costing and kaizen costing.

Another student, Kevin, overhears your conversation with Sandy and insists that neither of these methods is beneficial. Kevin argues that some entities run into financial problems using these methods because their managers manipulated the cost estimates to appear however they wanted. If the managers wanted to launch a new product or keep an old one, they made sure their cost estimates supported their decision.

Required

(a) In your own words, explain how target costing and kaizen costing are the same and how they are different.

(b) Compare the information needed to apply the target costing and kaizen costing methods.

    (i) List the types of relevant information needed for each method.

    (ii) List the uncertainties in the relevant information for each method.

(c) Discuss ways in which managers might be able to create biased estimates under a target or kaizen costing system.

(d) Kevin argues that the types of issues you described in part (c) mean that target and kaizen costing are not beneficial. Discuss the validity of this argument.

16.29 Cost-based and market-based pricing; collusion   **LO6**

Burton Turner and Short Whittum live in a small town in northern Queensland. They both own petrol stations, and provide fuel and engine repair services for the area. The town is somewhat isolated and, during the wet season, it is sometimes difficult to travel to other towns across the often-flooded river. While having coffee one morning, Turner and Whittum discuss the prices they charge for fuel and for repair services. They decide that it would be a good policy if they both set the same prices, because then customers would choose between the two businesses based on the quality of service and the brand name of the petrol.

Required

(a) What pricing alternatives are available to Turner and Whittum for setting prices? List as many alternatives as you can.

(b) Is this an open-ended problem? Why?

(c) Explore this problem from different perspectives:

    (i) Turner and Whittum

    (ii) customers

    (iii) government officials.

(d) Compare and contrast the legal and ethical issues in this situation. How are they the same? How are they different?

(e) Ignoring possible legal issues, is the proposed pricing policy of Turner and Whittum ethical? Why?

(f) Suppose you are a government official, and you receive an anonymous phone call telling you that Turner and Whittum are charging the same prices for fuel and repair services. How would you monitor the two entities to determine whether their actions are illegal?

16.30 Target costing; relevant information — The Dublin Shirt Company[19]   **LO3**

Consider the Dublin Shirt Company in comprehensive example 1 and the additional material provided below.

Two recent developments that may have an impact on the company should be noted. First, in the present climate, the Dublin Shirt Company can only afford to reduce its prices if it can cut costs. The sales director suggests that the company can lower its quality inspection costs by reducing inspections, which will improve on-time delivery rates. This proposal is to be discussed at the next board meeting.

Second, last week, the sales director proposed that the company should enter the American market for women's sports shirts, where comparable shirts sell for the equivalent of €9.75. This is considered to be an excellent selling price, given the small size of the shirt. Overall production costs would be similar to medium-sized shirts and normal selling, distribution and administration costs would amount to €3 per unit. Each shirt would require dyeing and also normal embroidery. A marketing consultant has obtained information about specific features required for the female wearer. Working in conjunction with the firm's cost accountant, he has presented information on these features and approximate cost as follows.

Feature required by female wearer	Cost (per unit) to add	Importance ranking (5 = most important)
Hanger (on inside of collar)	€0.02	2
Hanger (on outside of shoulder)	€0.04	3
Patch (breast) pocket	€0.10	3
Embroidery on single sleeve	€0.25	5
Double stitching (on V-neck etc.)	€0.08	4

It is anticipated that the Dublin Shirt Company will sell these products through an agent, with whom they have never dealt but who would like to place an order for 100 000 shirts this year. The company recognises that this (new) market will require additional selling costs in the United States, equivalent to €1 per shirt. The Dublin Shirt Company requires a contribution of €2 per unit but the goods are to be invoiced in US dollars unlike current sales that are invoiced in euro.

Required

(a) What is the target manufacturing cost for these shirts? Indicate what features, if any, should be added to the shirts already produced, in keeping with your target cost calculations.

(b) Identify the strategic and international business factors that the management of the Dublin Shirt Company should consider in making this decision.

16.31 Cost-based pricing; death spiral; uncertainties; customer reaction   LO6

Suppose the owner of Haywood Ceramics needs to raise prices to stay in business, but is concerned that raising prices would result in a death spiral. To avoid a decline in sales, the owner is considering sending letters to her customers explaining why the price increase is necessary. The letter would inform customers about the cost increases that necessitated the price increase, explain what the entity is doing to keep costs as low as possible, and allow customers to place orders for a given time period at the current price.

Required

(a) Describe the death spiral in your own words.

(b) Explain why the owner cannot be sure how customers will respond to a price increase.

(c) Suppose the owner decides to send letters to her customers. From a customer's point of view, discuss possible pros and cons of this strategy.

(d) Would you recommend that the owner send letters to her customers? Why?

16.32 Market-based pricing; relevant information   LO6

Frosty Treats, a boutique ice cream shop, has asked your advice in setting pricing policies. Frosty Treats manager has collected information about prices and sales over the last four years.

Required

(a) Explain how you would use the prices and sales information to suggest a possible pricing strategy.

(b) What other information would you gather before you complete your recommendation? List as many types of information as you can.

16.33 Market-based pricing; customer preferences   LO6

Transrapid is developing a new magnetically levitated train to run between major cities in Germany at a speed of 500 kilometres per hour. Engineers developed a system with trains departing every 10 minutes. Suppose Transrapid asked you to research customer preferences and to recommend a pricing policy. It costs considerably more to have trains depart as frequently as 10 minutes apart, so a cost-based pricing schedule will result in ticket prices that are considerably higher than alternative modes of transportation.

Required

(a) In addition to customer preferences, what information would you like to gather before recommending a pricing policy? Explain why each item you list is relevant.

(b) Explain why it is important to understand customer preferences before building the system.

(c) Is the need to consider customer preferences different for this organisation than for another type of entity? Why?

16.34 Market-based price (elasticity formula); uncertainties　　　　　　**LO6**

Hanson & Daughters produces a premium label apple juice to wholesalers at a current price of $7 per 5-litre container. Costs for a recent month, in which 100 000 5-litre containers were produced and sold, are shown below:

	Variable	Fixed
Materials	$10 000	$ 0
Labour	20 000	40 000
Factory overhead	10 000	80 000
Selling and administration	10 000	100 000
Total	$50 000	$220 000

Hanson & Daughters' customers are loyal. Recently, a 10 per cent increase in wholesale price resulted in only a 10 per cent decrease in litres sold.

Required

(a) Calculate the price elasticity of demand.

(b) Calculate the profit-maximising price.

(c) Explain why the management of Hanson & Daughters cannot be certain that another 10 per cent price increase would cause only another 10 per cent decrease in litres sold.

(d) Provide possible reasons why so many customers were willing to continue purchasing the apple juice when prices increased by 10 per cent. List as many reasons as you can.

(e) Describe the assumptions underlying the profit-maximising price you calculated in part (b). How realistic are these assumptions for Hanson & Daughters? What might occur if these assumptions are not met for Hanson & Daughters?

(f) What would you recommend to Hanson & Daughters concerning its price for apple juice? Explain your reasoning.

16.35 Cost reduction and market-based prices at a university　　　　　**LO1, 3, 4, 6**

Bainbridge University offers an MBA degree that is widely respected around the world. The tuition for the program has always covered the costs of the program until a recent recession increased the sensitivity of students to the cost of tuition. The business school managers decided to freeze the tuition cost for the past few years. The director of the MBA program asked a cost accounting class to act as consultants for the program and to make recommendations on possible ways to reduce costs or to increase tuition. You are part of a student team assigned to this project.

Required

(a) Is this problem open-ended? Why?

(b) List relevant types of analyses that your team might perform.

(c) Describe the steps you will take as you analyse the program, including the types of information you would like to use.

(d) Explain how you would decide on an appropriate level of tuition.

16.36 Life cycle costing　　　　　　　　　　　　　　　　　　　　　　　**LO5**

Fancy Fleece developed a new outdoor wear fleece fabric that is both wind and water resistant, but retains a soft and fuzzy feel. The research and development process was more expensive than Fancy's managers anticipated, and the materials in the fabric are also more expensive than anticipated. The managers believe that if Fancy prices the fleece to cover total costs, no one will buy it.

The marketing department held several focus groups with manufacturers who produce and sell winter jackets and pants to determine an appropriate price. The marketing department also surveyed customers who recently purchased fleece jackets to determine the amount of premium they would be willing to pay for a jacket that is both wind and water resistant. The marketing department concluded that the new fleece fabric would sell at a price that covers variable costs, but does not cover the total costs of production and development. You have been asked to help the managers decide whether to produce the fleece and how to price it if they do produce it.

Required

(a) What kind(s) of analysis would you perform for this decision?

(b) Explain whether it would generally be better for Fancy Fleece to use cost-based or market-based pricing.

(c) Identify uncertainties about how much it will cost to produce the fleece. List as many uncertainties as you can.

(d) Explain why the managers of Fancy Fleece cannot be certain that they would be able to sell the polar fleece to cover variable costs.

16.37 Profit effect of price change LO6

The accountants at French Perfumery decided to increase the price of a scent called Breezy by 10 per cent, from $6 per bottle to $6.60. French's accountants expect the 10 per cent price increase to reduce unit sales by 20 per cent. Current sales are 200 000 bottles, and total variable costs are $800 000.

Required

(a) Estimate the pre-tax profit effect of the price change, assuming no effect on the variable cost rate, on total fixed costs or on sales of other products. (*Hint:* Calculate the contribution margin at the old and new prices and volumes.)

(b) How certain can the accountant be that volume will decline 20 per cent if the selling price increases to $6.60? What effect does this uncertainty have on the managers' decision to increase the selling price?

16.38 For-profit versus not-for-profit pricing; setting a market price LO6

Suppose the Tasmanian government decided to preserve some beautiful caves in the southwestern part of the state. To defray the cost of preservation, the Tasmanian state tourism managers decided to open the caves to guided tours. To prepare the caves for visitors, vapour locks were built so that the moisture content of the caves would remain stable. The Tasmanian government spent $10 million on the facilities. Now the managers need to decide on a price for the tours.

Required

(a) Describe how pricing policies in not-for-profit entities are different from pricing policies in for-profit entities.

(b) Use the internet or other sources to identify current prices for other similar attractions.

(c) What additional information would you gather to evaluate the price?

(d) Do you believe that the volume of tours is likely to be sensitive to the price charged for tours? Why?

(e) The managers of the park department need your price recommendation. Use the information you learned from the preceding analyses to write a memo to the park department recommending a price for the tour. Provide appropriate information for park department managers to understand your methodology and evaluate the risks associated with your price recommendation.

16.39 Cost-based pricing in a not-for-profit entity LO6

Cairns Legal Services is part of a larger not-for-profit entity (Capricorn Resource Centre) that provides free legal and job placement services and houses a food bank for qualified clients. Last year's costs for 5000 visits to legal services are presented here.

Lawyer's salary	$ 90 000
Part-time secretary	12 000
Miscellaneous supplies	6 000
Paralegals' salaries	70 000
Administrative costs[a]	34 000
Rent[b]	10 000
Total	$222 000

[a] A portion of the administrative costs of the Cairns Council. These costs have been allocated to programs based upon the salary costs of the program.
[b] A portion of the rent for the Capricorn Resource Centre. Total rent is allocated on the basis of the space occupied by each program.

Expected grants for the next year from the federal government and the Cairns Council have been reduced due to an economic downturn. The organisation's executive director is considering dropping legal services. Eliminating the legal services program will result in a savings of about $4000 in administrative costs. The space vacated by legal services could be used by the food bank, which is presently renting quarters in another building for $8000 a year.

The director decided that individuals receiving legal services from the resource centre are to pay for their services, with exceptions based upon need determined on a case-by-case basis. It is not clear what the director means when he says that clients are to pay for their services.

Required

(a) If the director means that each person using legal services should pay for his or her own avoidable costs, what minimum fee should be charged on average for a legal service visit?

(b) If the director means that all of the people using legal services should collectively pay for the avoidable costs of the legal services program, what minimum fee should be charged on average for a visit?

(c) If the executive director wants the fee to cover the total costs of the Cairns Legal Services including avoidable and allocated costs, what minimum fee should be charged for a visit?

(d) Suppose the centre begins charging the price you calculated in part (b). What problems might arise if these fees are implemented? Consider whether the price change would affect the client's behaviour, and then how that behaviour change might affect Cairns Legal Services.

(e) Suppose the centre begins charging the price you calculated in part (c). Considering that the price is based on allocated costs, explain why this price might be viewed as arbitrary.

(f) Discuss why a Capricorn director might issue an edict about having clients pay for their services, but not provide guidance about what the edict means.

ENDNOTES

1. Genovese, A, Acquaye, AA, Figueroa & Koh, SL 2017, Sustainable supply chain management and the transition towards a circular economy: Evidence and some applications. *Omega, 66*, 344–357.

2. Bradshaw, T 2017, Apple makes 'closed loop' recycling pledge. *Financial Times*. 20 April. Retrieved from: https://www.ft.com/content/885a89a0-1da3-3f43-9ff9-8bb5c4c4db64.

3. Aston, A 2013, Can new supply chain approaches prevent another Rana Plaza? *The Guardian*. 14 Sep. Retrieved from: https://www.theguardian.com/sustainable-business/supply-chain-development-tactics.

4. Redmond, P 2018, At last, Australia has a Modern Slavery Act. Here's what you'll need to know. *The Conversation*. 3 December. Retrieved from: https://theconversation.com/at-last-australia-has-a-modern-slavery-act-heres-what-youll-need-to-know-107885.

5. Hervani, AA, Helms, MM & Sarkis, J 2005, Performance measurement for green supply chain management. *Benchmarking: An international journal, 12*(4), 330–353.

6. Adapted from Clarke, P in association with Jaras, P & Bremer, W 2002, *Cases from management accounting practice: case 3 Dublin Shirt Company*, Institute of Management Accountants.

7. Kroll, K 1997, 'On target', *Industry Week*, 9 June, pp. 14–22.

8. 'Quarterly financial results,' news release, January 2004, available at www.caterpillar.com, click on 'Investor Information'; and Kahn, M 2004, 'Consumer non-cyclicals may cycle higher,' *Barron's Online*, 9 February.

9. Merrett, A 2014, Government Inc: time to revisit competitive neutrality. *The Conversation*. 14 July. Retrieved from: https://theconversation.com/government-inc-time-to-revisit-competitive-neutrality-28962.

10. Steenkamp, JBE, Van Heerde, HJ & Geyskens, I 2010, What makes consumers willing to pay a price premium for national brands over private labels? *Journal of Marketing Research, 47*(6), 1011–1024.

11. Van Doorn, J & Verhoef, PC 2011, Willingness to pay for organic products: Differences between virtue and vice foods. *International Journal of Research in Marketing, 28*(3), 167–180.

12. Burton, M, Rigby, D, Young, T & James, S 2001, Consumer attitudes to genetically modified organisms in food in the UK. *European Review of Agricultural Economics, 28*(4), 479–498.

13. Van Loo, EJ, Caputo, V, Nayga Jr, RM, Seo, HS, Zhang, B & Verbeke, W 2015, Sustainability labels on coffee: Consumer preferences, willingness-to-pay and visual attention to attributes. *Ecological Economics, 118*, 215–225.

14. Pawsey, N, Nayeem, T & Huang, X 2018, Use of Facebook to engage water customers: A comprehensive study of current UK and Australian practices and trends. *Journal of Environmental Management, 228*, 517–528.

15. *Survey of American manufacturers* 1992, Grant Thornton, New York; and Mochtar, K & Arditi, D 2001, 'Pricing strategy in the US construction industry,' *Construction Management and Economics*, July, pp. 405–15.

16. Shim, E & Sudit, E 1995, 'How manufacturers price products,' *Management Accounting*, February.

17. Australian Competition and Consumer Commission 2001, 'ACCC calls for stronger criminal sanctions including jail sentences for price-fixing offences under Trade Practices Act', media release MR 131/01, 8 June, www.accc.gov.au.

18. Morris, N 2015, 'What do solar anti-dumping tariffs mean for Australia?', *Business Spectator*, 11 March, www.businessspectator.com.au.

19. Clarke, P 2002, op. cit. (7).

ACKNOWLEDGEMENTS

Photo 16A: © monkeybusinessimages / Getty Images

Photo 16B: © Clara / Shutterstock.com

Photo 16C: © inigocia / Shutterstock.com

Photo 16D: © mlasaimages / Shutterstock.com

Figure 16.1: © Hervani, AA, Helms, MM, & Sarkis, J 2005, 'Performance measurement for green supply chain management'. *Benchmarking: An international journal*, *12*(4), 330–353.

Extract 16A and 16B: © Text Extracts from pp.1–5 from the 'Dublin Shirt Company Case Study' by Peter Clarke, from *Cases from management accounting practice*, Institute of Management Accountants, 2002.

CHAPTER 17

Strategic management control: a lean perspective

LEARNING OBJECTIVES

After studying this chapter, you should be able to:

17.1 reflect on and communicate the lean thinking philosophy

17.2 describe the theory of constraints (TOC) and throughput costing

17.3 explain the concept of just-in-time (JIT) manufacturing

17.4 understand and apply the concepts of total quality management (TQM) and the cost of quality.

IN BRIEF

In chapter 16 we learned about the target costing approach, a technique that requires not only a forecast of the expected revenues of a product but the proactive management of costs during the design and development stages. In this chapter, we explore a philosophy that fits well with the target costing approach — a concept known as 'lean thinking' originating from Womack, Jones and Roos' 1991 seminal text *The machine that changed the world*. This chapter aims to highlight the principles of lean thinking and its focus on forward-looking techniques to reduce inventories, streamline processes and eliminate waste, while ensuring the production and delivery of quality products and maintaining a customer-focused approach. This lean approach also requires an alternative to traditional historical, backward-looking cost accounting approaches where decisions are based on past transactions gathered from the general ledger system.

17.1 Lean thinking philosophy

LEARNING OBJECTIVE 17.1 Reflect on and communicate the lean thinking philosophy.

Lean thinking is about the elimination of all sources of organisational waste and taking a completely customer-focused approach to maximise customer value. Lean initiatives are based on the belief that only a small fraction of the total time and effort in an organisation adds value for the end customer and a large amount of employee effort actually adds no value at all from a customer perspective. All the non-value activities and costs associated with overproduction, non-essential inventory, material movement, transportation (both staff and product) and inappropriate processing are regarded as waste. Waste removal has to be pursued throughout the whole value chain from suppliers to customers (and sometimes beyond).

The term 'lean production' was first described by Womack, Jones and Roos in their 1991 seminal text *The machine that changed the world*. The lean philosophy is generally attributable to Toyota when its approach to production was observed by researchers (including Womack) during the 1980s. Toyota's production system is based on two concepts: 'jidoka', meaning that when a problem occurs production stops, thus preventing defective products; and 'just-in-time', which ensures each process produces only what is needed by the next process in a continuous flow. Lean production is a synergy of approaches resulting in seamless production flows at a customer-demanded pace with minimal waste. It is an integrated business system of superior technology that draws on a wide variety of concepts including just-in-time (JIT) manufacturing, total quality management (TQM) and the theory of constraints (TOC).

A lean approach is not only applicable to manufacturing organisations. In Australia, two examples of the adoption of a lean approach by service organisations can be seen with the REA Group (digital advertising) and Metro Trains (public transport). The REA Group applied the JIT production theory of the automotive industry to software development, matching the approach with the customer-focused, agile model of programming in the information technology industry. Metro Trains applied the theory through visualisation of problems and breaking down barriers between the shop floor and management.[1]

The lean approach has also been widely applied within the healthcare sector. Lean interventions within this sector involve a commitment to improve the quality of healthcare, the elimination of activities which do not add value for the patient and the streamlining of value adding activities.[2] The results of the application of lean approaches within the healthcare sector have often been less than effective. However, there have also been successful cases in which lean thinking delivered improved quality and cost savings; for example, at the Virginia Mason Medical Centre in Seattle, Washington, US.[3] As summarised in figure 17.1, the success of the lean approach in this organisation was largely dependent on the use of lean 'as part of a comprehensive management system in concert with institutional culture change and new leadership approaches to all aspects of healthcare delivery'.[4]

FIGURE 17.1 Key strategies for effective lean management in healthcare[5]

Key strategy	Implementation
Unrelenting focus on the patient	All activities are evaluated by whether or not they add value from the patient's perspective, a unifying shared vision
Uniform improvement method	A common language and approach used by all
A strategic plan that serves as the organisation's compass	Strategic plan is highly visible, presented at the start of all improvement and management meetings, with the relevance of that meeting to the strategic plan clearly defined
Integration of daily management and quality improvement	The same teams and the same tools for daily management and quality improvement. In effect, all management is quality improvement, which is critical to sustain gains
Leadership present on the 'shop floor', understanding and supporting teams	Leaders can best know what is going on in the organisation, and can best coach and support teams when physically present where the work is occurring
Daily leader routines that are transparent and predictable	Leading by example requires standard work by leaders, and transparency promotes bidirectional accountability for managers and staff

(continued)

FIGURE 17.1 *(continued)*

Key strategy	Implementation
Respect for people	All staff are empowered to contribute to improvement, and all are valued for their contribution to the institution
Physician, leadership and board compacts	Reciprocal agreements between the institution and physicians, leaders and board members defining the responsibilities and expectations for all parties
A visual environment so one easily sees operational conditions	Work is made open and visible so that any problems become apparent and can be addressed in real time. Production dashboards are publicly displayed
Long-term thinking	Constancy of purpose among leadership, ensuring continuity independent of specific individuals
Alignment	Alignment from the board of directors to frontline staff. All must understand the unwavering commitment to the patient focus and the Virginia Mason Production System (VMPS) method

Womack and Jones[6] developed a model to illustrate lean thinking and this is presented in figure 17.2. In the figure, step 1 is about identifying value in every product-manufacturing or service-related activity. It is essential in this preliminary stage that 'value' is defined through the eyes of the customer. Step 2 is about identifying all the value-adding activities involved in producing each product or service. It is essential at this design stage that all non-value-adding activities, regarded as waste, are identified and eliminated. Step 3 is about sequencing organisational flow so the product or service moves smoothly towards the customer. It is about ensuring employees are correctly trained to perform the tasks required. It is about continually identifying bottlenecks, inventory build-up and unsatisfactory lead times and ensuring all parts of the organisation operate as part of a continuous flow through the value chain. Step 4 is about implementing a pull system based on customer demand. It is about signalling the upstream link in the supply chain that one more component of value is required by the customer. The pull system ensures production remains in sync with customer demand. Step 5 is about learning and growth within the organisation. It is about ensuring that each time the process is repeated, it is improved in the ongoing pursuit of perfection.

FIGURE 17.2 The lean thinking model[7]

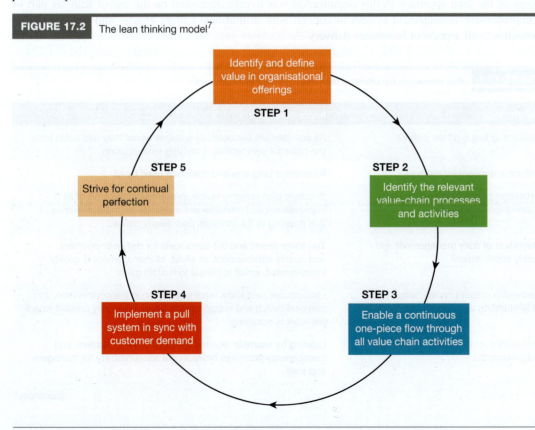

Changes in business processes require changes to the accounting practices that provide the relevant information for decision making. Alternative approaches are needed to the traditional historical, backward-looking cost accounting approaches, where decisions are based on past transactions gathered from the general ledger system. Hence, a lean accounting approach is crucial to lean thinking and requires a refocus on accounting practices, control and performance measurement that involves 'cradle-to-grave' analysis. Lean accounting requires a departure from traditional forms of accounting and strives for value creation through:

- reduced transaction processing steps
- eliminating standard costs in favour of actual costs
- eliminating cost allocations
- refocusing performance measurement systems to emphasise social controls such as training
- decentralising business units to autonomous work cells.

Figure 17.3 highlights empirical evidence of practices associated with the lean accounting philosophy.

FIGURE 17.3	Description of variables prior to and following the implementation of lean accounting (specifically for manufacturing)[8]	
Variables	**Before lean**	**After lean**
Strategic manufacturing technology	**Batch-and-queue manufacturing** • Produced to forecast • Separate functional areas • Ad hoc teams to increase quality • Employees are single tasked	**Lean manufacturing** • One piece flow • Produces to customer order • Manages bottlenecks to optimise flows • Produces in teams • Quality built into process
Organisational structure	**Vertical structure** • Vertical reporting • Functional (departmental) responsibility centres • Employees are single tasked	**Cell structure** • Flatter with cell- and value-stream teams • Multi-functional members • Employees responsible for entire production process (multiple machines and tasks)
Accounting practices	**Output controls** • Traditional variance measures • Traditional manufacturing variances • Low margin exception reports • Facility measures included traditional accounting measures • Accounting group tracks performance measures • Information provided to managers and supervisors	**Output controls** • Non-traditional operational measures • Operational measures • No variance analysis • Posted throughout facility and shop floor • Generated from the bottom-up on a frequent basis
	Behavioural controls • Absent • Technical process documents located in supervisor and engineering offices	**Behavioural controls** • Standard operating procedures (SOPs) • SOPs visible in cell and includes pictures of each part of the process • Yellow floor markings indicate flow of material and finished goods
	Social controls • Absent • Empowerment: supervisors and managers only • Peer pressure: none (individual contributors) • Visualisation: none; paper reports only to manager and supervisor • Training: single process only	**Social controls** • Heavy reliance • Empowerment: formation of cells and teams; self-selection of cell team members; vacation and work schedules • Peer pressure: cell members pressure one another to perform; cell members pressure one another to gain additional training and skills; posted responsibility for action items • Visualisation: yellow marking on floor indicating layout of machines, tools and inventory; cell and value stream metric boards; flip charts • Training: skills matrix; intranet training

As highlighted by figure 17.3, under a lean accounting approach, accounting activities are developed to streamline transactional processing and remove all non-value-adding activities. For accountants to become lean accountants they must reduce reliance on variance analysis and focus on real-time operational decisions through actual cost data. An important principle of lean accounting is the use of actual costs instead of standards. That is, accounting data should not motivate managers to focus on achieving economies of scale through making product based on stock availability, or concentrating on batch sizes or volume variances. Instead, data should be aligned with achieving a one-piece flow and making product to order based on customer demand. A final significant feature of lean accounting is the rejection of full absorption costing. The lean belief is that cost allocations only distort effective decision making. For example, the absorption costing statement of profit or loss treats direct materials, direct labour and both fixed and variable overheads as product costs, and selling, general and administration costs as period costs. Any excess inventory built up will increase income as it includes deferred fixed overhead. Reducing inventories will decrease income and the previously deferred fixed overhead is required to be expensed. As a result of the distorted absorption income, efforts to reduce inventory levels are penalised and the lean thinking philosophy is compromised.

Lean accounting activities in a lean thinking organisation might include the following.

- Purchase orders are converted to annual blanket purchase orders in order to reduce transaction processing.
- Accounts payable are processed in accordance with lean 'pull' principles so suppliers are paid when appropriate.
- Invoices are no longer required. Suppliers are paid from the packing slip according to terms on the blanket purchase order. This system may be electronically developed.
- Labour is considered a period cost and treated as more fixed than variable.
- Rather than full absorption costing to value inventory, a material-only cost system is used. Overhead may be allocated at the product family level but not in any great detail.
- Rather than assigning standard costs and calculating variances, a value-stream costing system is used, which only allocates facility charge by square footage or otherwise actual costs for the week.
- Bills of materials are replaced by standard operating procedures and actual unit costs.
- A perpetual inventory is not needed for inventory tracking due to low inventory levels. Instead, throughput costing is used.
- Responsibility reporting is value-stream oriented. A value stream statement of profit or loss is used to calculate unit product costs, absorb only used resources, and drive improvement by highlighting the effects of inventory reduction.
- Purchasing is driven by visual signalling systems while production is driven by customer orders.[9]

In conclusion, the lean approach is argued to provide for continuous improvement made possible by increasing profits and investment in people and projects. Increased profitability is achieved by moving away from traditional cost-cutting approaches and cutting the *workload* and not the workforce. As a result, productivity is increased and so is the satisfaction of both employees and customers. Lean thinking is customer driven. It is about generating a cycle of increasing profitability providing for continual investment.

17.2 Theory of constraints

LEARNING OBJECTIVE 17.2 Describe the theory of constraints (TOC) and throughput costing.

The **theory of constraints (TOC)** centres on identifying bottlenecks or other process constraints. The TOC is an important part of the lean thinking philosophy (refer to step 3 of the lean thinking model as outlined in figure 17.2). In this section, we focus in more detail on the value-creating steps required within an organisation to ensure a smooth product flow to the customer. According to the TOC, an entity is viewed as a system with the main goal of making more money now as well as in the future. The system comprises a set of elements, or a chain of linkages with interdependent relationships.

The TOC concentrates on the weakest link in the chain (the constraint) that limits the system from achieving higher performance. According to Goldratt, every business system has at least one constraint.[10] The sources of constraints can be diverse (figure 17.4). The constraint may be on the *supply side*, where insufficient capacity or capabilities exist in the process. For example, insufficient time available at the constraining factor may lead to physical manufacturing or service-related issues. A supply-side constraint may also be caused by a technical, policy or financial limitation. In service entities, the constraining factor may be related to intangible assets such as the necessary knowledge and skills held by individuals required for the successful completion of various projects. The source of a constraint might also exist on the *demand side*, where there may be insufficient demand caused by pricing, customer budgets or competition that leads to idle capacity.

FIGURE 17.4	The sources and potential causes of constraints

Source of constraint	Potential cause
Supply side	Technical limitations Physical limitations Financial limitations
Demand side	Customer budgets Competition

In viewing a company as a system, there are constraint and non-constraint resources. According to the TOC, there is no point in maximising the use of non-constraint resources. Attempts to achieve local efficiencies should be directed only on constraint resources. Goldratt proposed a five-step focusing process for managing constraints to achieve higher performance and continuous system improvement.

1. *Identify* the constraint(s) in the system.
2. Decide how to *exploit* the constraint(s). That is, how to make the best possible use of the constraint given the existing limitations.
3. *Subordinate* everything else to the constraint. That is, avoid over-utilisation of non-constraint resources and rigorously focus on what the constraint needs.
4. *Elevate* the constraint(s). That is, offload some demand or expand capability. Take steps to minimise idle time at the constraint and consider issues such as inventory levels (JIT versus safety stock) or quality costs.
5. If in the previous steps a constraint has been broken, *go back* to step 1, but do not allow inertia to cause a system constraint.

This five-step process should continuously increase *throughput* while concurrently decreasing *inventory* and *operating expenses*.

An approach to maximise flow through the constraint is known as the drum-buffer-rope concept. The 'buffer' is the activity of maintaining only a small amount of work in process; the 'drum' relates to the activity associated with inserting materials into the constraint only when needed. The need or demand for materials is calculated according to specified lead times. This is the role of the 'rope' activity. In this way all resources are coordinated to keep the constraint busy without a build-up of work.

Throughput costing

Developed in the 1980s as part of the theory of constraints, **throughput costing** is a modified form of variable costing that treats direct labour and variable overhead as period expenses and measures the impact of bottlenecks and constraints on an organisation's goal achievement. Throughput costing has become popular for internal reporting purposes as some managers realised that product costs under both absorption and variable costing are excessive because they include more than direct materials.

In many entities, conversion costs such as direct labour and overhead do not vary proportionately with volume of manufacturing. Under throughput costing, inventory is valued using only direct material costs (figure 17.5). All other costs are treated as period costs.

The throughput contribution is defined as revenue less direct material costs for the units sold. Accountants and managers in companies using TOC methods believe that throughput costing helps them make better short-term decisions because costs other than direct materials tend to be relatively fixed in the short run. For example, direct labour may be a fixed cost if workers are guaranteed a work schedule such as a 40-hour week. When direct labour is fixed and little or no variable overhead cost is involved, the variable statement of profit or loss is similar to the throughput costing statement of profit or loss. Therefore, throughput costing focuses managers' attention on three key measures: throughput (revenue generated), inventory (investment in what is to be sold) and operating expenses (costs incurred to convert inventory to throughput). This approach encourages managers to increase throughput and decrease the cost of inventory and operating expenses. Figure 17.6 shows a statement of profit or loss format for throughput costing.

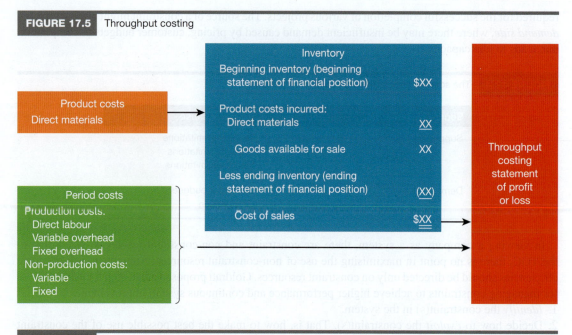

FIGURE 17.5 Throughput costing

FIGURE 17.6 Throughput costing statement of profit or loss

Advantages of throughput costing

Throughput costing can be thought of as an extreme version of variable costing. Only direct material costs are assigned to inventory and cost of sales. When costs such as direct labour and manufacturing overhead are categorised and treated as operating costs rather than product costs (inventory), managers' attitudes about these costs tend to change. They are encouraged to reduce operating costs when needed, such as when sales decline. Under throughput costing, managers are more likely to consider reducing costs such as direct labour. Conversely, under absorption costing, many manufacturing costs are initially categorised as assets (inventory) until goods are sold. As a result, managers may perceive less need to reduce direct labour and overhead cost. Compared to absorption and variable costing, throughput costing also reduces the incentives for managers to build up inventory to inappropriate levels.

Figure 17.7 summarises the key features of throughput costing. In throughput costing, costs are not allocated to products. Nor does throughput costing involve calculating the cost of products, on the basis that the goal is to focus management attention on increasing the efficiency of the constraint. Complicated accounting allocations based on erroneous assumptions only confuse decision making. Linked with target costing under the umbrella of lean thinking, the TOC commences with customer demand for a product at the price willing to be paid by the customer. This is highlighted in comprehensive example 1.

FIGURE 17.7   Key features of throughput costing

- Not in accordance with accounting standards
- Useful for short-term capacity decision making, focuses manager's attention on reducing labour and overhead costs because they are considered operating costs instead of product costs (inventory)
- Only direct materials are inventory costs
- Direct labour, fixed and variable overhead, and all other costs expensed as operational expense, a period cost
- Administrative and selling costs expensed as operational expense, a period cost
- Inventory costs (only direct materials) not expensed until the units are sold

TOC performance measurement

There are two significant key performance measures used in TOC.

- *Profit (NP)* defined by total throughput minus operating expenses:

$$NP = T - OE$$

- *Return on investment (ROI)* defined as throughput minus operating expenses divided by investment:

$$ROI = (T - OE) - I$$

The components of these measures are explained below.

Throughput (T)

Throughput is the rate at which the system generates cash through sales. Throughput is only represented by 'fresh money' from outside sales and *not* internal accounting-generated income. Throughput of a product refers to its selling price minus its totally variable cost:

$$Tu = P - TVC$$

where Tu = Throughput per unit of product
    P = Price per unit of product
    TVC = Totally variable cost

TVC is not to be confused with the cost accounting measure. TVC generally relates to 'totally variable' costs only, such as raw materials. All other costs (that is, labour, rent, utilities) are generally classified as operating expenses (OE).

Investment (I)

Investment is all the cash the system invests in purchasing items it intends to sell. It is also called 'inventory' but is not represented as added value to the product as in traditional 'work in process' and 'finished goods'. The measurement (I) does not include accounting profits generated by the cost allocation process, as added value to products is considered an internal distortion. The concern is with the company as an entire system and the only time value is added to the system is when a product is sold. With this methodology it is not possible to increase short-term profits by increasing work in process or finished goods inventory (that is, by delaying the recognition of some expenses that will decrease profits in future periods).

Operating expenses (OE)

Operating expenses are all the cash the system spends in turning investment into throughput. Operating expenses may include such things as direct labour, rent and energy costs. However, operating expenses should *not* be classified or thought of as fixed costs. These measures are also highlighted in comprehensive example 1.

Benefits and limitations of the theory of constraints and throughput costing

TOC analysis is a useful management tool to improve a business system as a whole. The TOC enables managers to optimise constraints while balancing the flow of production with demand. Any product-mix changes generated by TOC should result in immediate cash flow effects. Accountants and managers in companies using the TOC believe that throughput costing helps them make better short-term decisions. This is because virtually all costs (other than direct materials) tend to be relatively fixed in the short term.

However, TOC analysis could focus management attention too much on short-term results to the detriment of long-term strategic goals. As a result of short-term decision making, labour and overhead costs might be unnecessarily reduced because these costs are considered to be operating costs instead of product costs. The TOC will highlight these costs without indicating whether they are appropriate for the level of operations. Likewise, if costs are too high, the TOC will not show how to bring them under control.

When applying TOC analysis, managers should be aware of the mutually dependent relationship between their short-term operating decisions and their longer-term strategic objectives. Combined use of the TOC, activity-based management (ABM) and activity-based costing (ABC) may provide better longer-term measures of success within each area of the organisation.[11]

Managers can use a wide range of tools to analyse production and delivery systems, with the goal of improving cost and quality. Accountants help managers by bringing these tools to their attention and providing the analysis.

COMPREHENSIVE EXAMPLE 1

Theory of constraints example[12]

A manufacturing company offering five colour products determines that the maximum profit (NP) from manufacturing and selling these five products is US$123 400 (ROI 26.92%), given the current capacity of the constraint or bottleneck is 70 000 minutes. This is illustrated in figures 17.8 and 17.9. In this situation, the company assumes it will produce and sell in rank of its most profitable products until there is no remaining capacity. While it would be ideal to manufacture products in this way, a sales mix to accommodate customer and strategic marketing demands must be prepared rather than using order to throughput margins. When there is an internal constraint, the company should work out the most important customers to supply and *not* produce more than the demand quantity. The adjusted set of figures (column H onwards in figure 17.9) reveals the customer and market demand driven TOC profit as US$36 000 (ROI 7.85%).

These calculations allow the company to make certain strategic decisions about product mix and customer demand. They also encourage TOC firms to seek ways to elevate their constraint. In figures 17.10 and 17.11, the company has decided to employ a new worker at US$1000 a month. It also changed a process that impacts both the TVC of a raw material of product Yellow and the time this product spends on the constraint. The TVC increases by US$5 (now US$35) with time on the throughput changing from 4 minutes to 3 minutes. Yellow now becomes the second-most profitable product. According to this freed up capacity, the company can now establish a new marketing and customer demand driven product mix. As can be seen, this process of developing TOC tables enables a series of what-if analyses to be performed by the company.

FIGURE 17.8	Operating expenses (initial)

Item	US$
Wages	550 000
Sales and marketing	250 000
Rent	55 000
Transport	18 000
Financial expenses	11 000
Depreciation	10 000
Others	20 000
Total	**914 000**

FIGURE 17.9 Database of products

					Capacity of constraint = 70 000 minutes				Demand/capacity of constraint = 154%					
A	B	C	D (B – C)	E	F (D/E)	G	H	I	J		K		L	
Product	Price	TVC	Throughput per unit	Time on constraint	Throughput/ time on constraint	Demand (forecast)	Max. thr. mix	Sales mix	Accum. utilis. of constraint %		Total throughput per product		Total throughput per product	
Red	125	51	74	4	18.50	5 000	5 000	5 000	28.6	28.6	370 000	370 000	370 000	370 000
Blue	237	83	154	10	15.40	1 500	1 500	400	50	34.3	231 000	61 600	231 000	61 600
Yellow	82	30	52	4	13.00	7 200	7 200	7 200	91.1	75.4	374 400	374 400	374 400	374 400
Green	155	75	80	8	10.00	1 500	775	150	100	77.1	62 000	12 000	62 000	12 000
Orange	60	27	33	4	8.25	8 000	0	4 000	100	100	0	132 000	0	132 000
												Total throughput	1 037 400	950 000
												OE	914 000	914 000
												Profit	123 400	36 000
												Inventory	5 500 000	5 500 000
												ROI (annual)	26.92%	7.85%

FIGURE 17.10 Operating expenses (to elevate constraint)

Item	US$
Wages	551 000
Sales and marketing	250 000
Rent	55 000
Transport	18 000
Interest	11 000
Depreciation	10 000
Others	20 000
Total	**915 000**

FIGURE 17.11 Database of products (after constraint changes)

							Capacity of constraint = 70 000 minutes				Demand/capacity of constraint = 143.7%		
A	B	C	D (B − C)	E	F (D/E)	G		H	I	J		K		L
Product	Price	TVC	Throughput per unit	Time on constraint	Throughput/time on constraint	Demand (forecast)		Max. thr. mix	Sales mix	Accum. utilis. of constraint %		Total throughput per product		Demand (forecast)
Red	125	51	74	4	18.50	5 000		5 000	5 000	28.6	28.6	5 000	5 000	5 000	28.6
Yellow	82	35	47	3	15.67	7 200		7 200	7 200	59.4	59.4	7 200	7 200	7 200	59.4
Blue	237	83	154	10	15.40	1 500		1 500	400	80.9	65.1	1 500	1 500	400	80.9
Green	155	75	80	8	10.00	1 500		1 675	1 050	100	77.1	1 500	1 675	1 050	100
Orange	60	27	33	4	8.25	8 000		0	4 000	100	100	8 000	0	4 000	100
											Total throughput		1 073 400	986 000
											OE		915 000	915 000
											Profit		158 400	71 000
											Inventory		5 500 000	5 500 000
											ROI (annual)		34.56%	15.49%

17.3 Just-in-time (JIT) production

LEARNING OBJECTIVE 17.3 Explain the concept of just-in-time (JIT) manufacturing.

Cost of sales represents the major cost for manufacturing and retail firms. Accordingly, there can be significant scope to obtain savings through lean manufacturing and the efficient management of raw materials, work-in-process and finished goods inventories. Service firms can also gain significant savings through the efficient management of supplies.

As presented in figure 17.12, when making inventory purchase decisions, manufacturers and retailers must balance the pros and cons of either:

1. smaller orders and inventory levels which minimise inventory holding costs, or
2. larger orders and inventory levels which minimise the number of required orders and ordering costs.

FIGURE 17.12	Pros and cons of large versus small inventory levels	
Inventory practice	**Pros**	**Cons**
Large quantities of inventory are ordered in bulk and large quantities of inventories are held in stock	• Fewer orders will need to be placed • Selling in bulk will likely be preferable to suppliers • Minimise risk that inventories are not available for sale/use when required • Large purchases of inventory can enable firm's to hedge against possible inventory price rises driven by inventory supply/demand forces or foreign currency movements	• Cash is tied up in inventory • Inventory holding costs are increased • Inventory may perish, be damaged or become obsolete before sale/use
Small quantities of inventory are ordered and only a small quantity of inventories is held in stock	• Cash is freed up • Inventory holding costs are minimised • The risk that inventory may perish, be damaged or become obsolete before sale/use is mitigated	• Orders will need to be placed more frequently • Selling in smaller quantities will likely be undesirable to suppliers • Exposure to risk that inventories are not available for sale/use when required • Reduced ability to use large purchases of inventory to hedge against possible inventory price rises driven by inventory supply/demand forces or foreign currency movements

The **economic order quantity (EOQ)** is attributed as being the first quantitative formula for the determination of the ideal inventory purchase quantity which keeps overall holding and ordering costs to a minimum. Whilst the EOQ model is relatively simple and practical to apply, many of the model's assumptions (i.e. stable demand and costs) are unrealistic in most contexts.[13]

$$\text{EOQ} = \sqrt{(2 \times \text{Annual usage} \times \text{Cost per order} / \text{Annual carrying cost per unit})}$$

For example, a manufacturer of electric vehicles requires 20 000 lithium batteries per annum to meet production requirements. These batteries are ordered from an external supplier and the cost to place each order is $75.00. The annual carrying cost associated with holding each battery is $25.00. In this example, the EOQ model would suggest that the optimal order quantity is 347 (rounded to the next whole unit):

$$347 = \sqrt{(2 \times 20\,000 \times 75.00/25.00)}$$

Given growing competitive pressures and the problematic nature of some of the EOQ assumptions, many leading firms have moved towards **just-in-time (JIT) production and inventory control systems**, whereby materials are purchased and units are produced at the time customers demand them. JIT is considered a *demand-pull system* (refer to step 4 in figure 17.2) because products and their parts are manufactured just as they are needed for each step in the manufacturing process.

In JIT inventory control systems, organisations work with suppliers so that goods or materials are delivered just as they are needed for production or for sale. Suppliers make frequent deliveries of small lots of goods directly to the production floor or to sales areas in merchandising entities.

In JIT manufacturing systems, the production process is often broken into steps that are performed in *manufacturing cells*. A cell is an area where all of the equipment and labour is grouped for a particular part of the manufacturing process. Parts and supplies arrive just in time to be used for each specific manufacturing task. When one cell finishes its set of tasks, the product is either complete or moves to the next cell where more work is performed. Production is continuous; as soon as team members finish their production tasks on one unit, another unit is begun. The product moves through all of the cells until the manufacturing process is complete. The manufacturing sequence is organised not only to minimise handling and storage but also to minimise defect rates.

Successful implementation of JIT systems requires that entities:
- find high-quality suppliers
- choose a manageable number of suppliers
- locate suppliers with short transit times for materials being delivered
- develop efficient and reliable materials handling processes
- develop management commitment to the JIT process.

JIT systems reduce costs by maximising the use of space, reducing defect rates and increasing manufacturing flexibility. Each team member is responsible for product inspection so that defects are identified quickly and quality problems can be remedied immediately. When manufacturers produce a number of different product models under a JIT system, changeover to the next model occurs almost immediately. This approach enhances manufacturing flexibility. Experts in operations management believe that the JIT approach may be one of the most significant developments in management innovation in the last century.[14]

The JIT approach was developed by Toyota in the late 1970s and its philosophy has informed the company's production processes since. Figure 17.13 shows a conceptual diagram of the kanban system (a production control method) adopted by Toyota. The kanban works as a communication device that tells which parts have been used in a process from a preceding process. At the core of its production system Toyota has the philosophy of completely eliminating all waste, with the objective of 'making the vehicles ordered by customers in the quickest and most efficient way, in order to deliver the vehicles as quickly as possible'.[15]

| **FIGURE 17.13** | Conceptual diagram of the kanban system[16] |

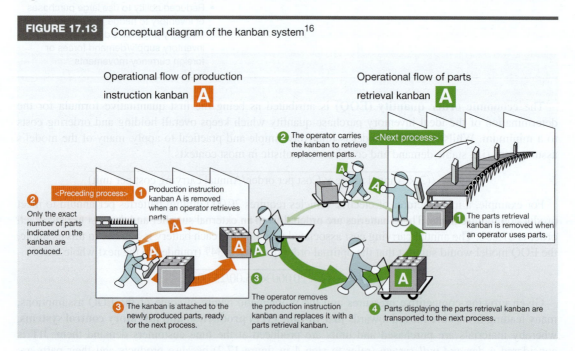

Referring to figure 17.13, it is evident that if parts are unavailable then production stops. This is one drawback of the JIT systems: production halts when suppliers are unable to deliver supplies as needed. Sometimes unforeseen events interrupt the delivery schedule. For example, the Australian company Tristar brought the automotive industry to its knees when its 350 workers went on strike for four days in protest against changes to existing work entitlements. At that time Tristar was the major supplier of power-assisted rack and pinion steering gears, ball joints, lower control arms, steering linkage components and other suspension components to four car manufacturers in Australia — Ford, Holden, Toyota and Mitsubishi. As these manufacturers work to JIT supply systems, they had only a single day's worth of components on hand and were forced to lay off thousands of workers. Toyota was the only company initially unaffected because it was manufacturing left-hand drive vehicles using components from Japan. The estimated cost of this five-day stoppage was reported to be $230 million in lost revenue with $100 million in exports disrupted. In all, 25 per cent of the Australian economy was affected in some way by this dispute.[17]

17.4 Total quality management (TQM): managing quality

LEARNING OBJECTIVE 17.4 Understand and apply the concepts of total quality management (TQM) and the cost of quality.

Some organisations position themselves as high-quality producers and work towards continuous improvement in quality, while other entities seek only to match the quality of their competitors. Part of organisational strategy is the choice of product quality levels. For example, Sony has a reputation for high quality. Its potential customers might demand superior quality products and be willing to pay a premium price for a quality game console, such as the latest generation PlayStation. To improve quality, many organisations adopt a variety of advanced business practices such as total quality management (TQM).

Total quality management (TQM) is an important part of the lean approach and promotes an organisation-wide philosophy and problem-solving methodology to focus on systematically and continuously improving the quality of products, processes and services. Key elements of TQM include a strong customer focus, extensive employee participation and development, a well-defined and well-executed approach to process management and a strong emphasis on design quality.[18] TQM requires that an entity communicates and maintains the quality standard throughout the entire value chain.[19] As part of TQM, processes are put in place to ensure that defects and waste are eliminated from operations.

W Edwards Deming was an American statistician who profoundly influenced the quality revolution and the invention of TQM. He spent time in Japan teaching 'statistical process control' and was awarded a medal by the Japanese Emperor in 1960 for his services to the Japanese manufacturing industry. Over time his work became known and admired around the world and in the 1980s contributed greatly to lean thinking and manufacturing. For companies to improve quality while reducing costs, Deming promoted 14 principles of management. He argued the key is to practise continual improvement while thinking of the company as a system and not separate steps. His 14 points are shown in figure 17.14.

FIGURE 17.14	Deming's 14 principles of management[20]

1	Create constancy of purpose toward improvement of product and service, with the aim to become competitive and to stay in business, and to provide jobs.
2	Adopt the new philosophy. We are in a new economic age. Western management must awaken to the challenge, must learn their responsibilities, and take on leadership for change.
3	Cease dependence on inspection to achieve quality. Eliminate the need for inspection on a mass basis by building quality into the product in the first place.
4	End the practice of awarding business on the basis of price tag. Instead, minimise total cost. Move towards a single supplier for any one item, on a long-term relationship of loyalty and trust.
5	Improve constantly and forever the system of production and service, to improve quality and productivity, and thus constantly decrease costs.
6	Institute training on the job.
7	Institute leadership. The aim of supervision should be to help people and machines and gadgets to do a better job. Supervision of management is in need of an overhaul, as well as supervision of production workers.
8	Drive out fear, so that everyone may work effectively for the company.

(continued)

FIGURE 17.14 *(continued)*

9		Break down barriers between departments. People in research, design, sales, and production must work as a team to foresee problems of production and in use that may be encountered with the product or service.
10		Eliminate slogans, exhortations, and targets for the workforce asking for zero defects and new levels of productivity. Such exhortations only create adversarial relationships, as the bulk of the causes of low quality and low productivity belong to the system and thus lie beyond the power of the workforce.
11	(a)	Eliminate work standards (quotas) on the factory floor. Substitute leadership.
	(b)	Eliminate management by objective. Eliminate management by numbers, numerical goals. Substitute leadership.
12	(a)	Remove barriers that rob the hourly paid worker of his right to pride in workmanship. The responsibility of supervisors must be changed from sheer numbers to quality.
	(b)	Remove barriers that rob people in management and engineering of their right to pride in workmanship. This means, inter alia, abolishment of the annual or merit rating and management by objective.
13		Institute a vigorous program of education and self-improvement.
14		Put everybody in the company to work to accomplish the transformation. The transformation is everybody's job.

Deming argued against the use and reliance of inspections in relation to quality work. For organisations to adopt a TQM philosophy and 'live by' Deming's principles it is necessary for an entity to understand its current situation in relation to quality. In order to take corrective action, management needs to understand activities in the value chain and identify costs that are due to poor quality. By focusing on the costs of quality, quality problems can be converted into the language of management — money. Identifying the potential profit improvements from a quality focus will encourage continuous improvement initiatives, which will in turn focus on lean operations. The next section and comprehensive example 2 consider the value chain approach to quality management and detail four categories of quality management activities. It is important to note that Deming's TQM approach calls for quality to be built into processes along the value chain from the outset.

Value chain approach to quality management

In this section we focus on value chain quality efforts that strive to reduce spoilage, rework and related opportunity costs.

Activity analysis along the value chain can be used to determine the costs of quality and to help refine quality strategies. Figure 17.15 defines four categories of quality activities — prevention, appraisal, internal and external — and provides examples of activities performed within each category. These actions are taken to minimise the opportunity costs that arise when customers have problems with defective units or low-quality services. When quality failures occur, reputations suffer and market share is lost. These losses are difficult to value, and are therefore often ignored when accountants and managers consider the costs and benefits of maintaining high-quality processes.

Sometimes the costs of quality failures are extremely high, such as the loss of reputation and market share that occurs when a great deal of publicity is generated about defective goods or processes. In 1995, the reputation and profitability of South Australian smallgoods factory operator Garibaldi suffered when an *E. coli* bacterial contamination occurred that resulted in the death of a four-year-old child.[21] Firestone and Ford lost market share and experienced lower sharemarket prices when news was released about an increased rollover and fatality rate in Ford Explorers that was also associated with Firestone tyres. One of Firestone's plants, in which a strike had occurred and inexperienced workers had been hired to replace the striking employees, has been implicated as a source of defective tyres.[22] The cost of quality failures such as these catastrophes is nearly impossible to value, yet is extremely important to consider in measuring the costs and benefits of proposed quality improvement initiatives.

In this value chain approach to quality, management decisions are required about the trade-offs of investing in different categories of quality activities. Following Deming's philosophy, organisations should only invest in prevention activities. With quality management inherent in this lean approach to TQM, competitors are forced to maintain equally high levels of quality. In comprehensive example 2, value chain activity analysis and activity management practices are used to reduce cost and improve quality.

FIGURE 17.15 Quality-related activities

Definition	Examples
Prevention activities Activities performed to ensure defect-free production	• Design and process engineering • Routine equipment maintenance • Inspection of incoming raw materials • Quality training and meetings
Appraisal activities Activities performed to identify defective units	• Inspection of products • Inspection of manufacturing process • Monitoring of service delivery process • Testing
Internal activities Activities undertaken in the production or rework of failed units	• Producing spoiled units • Reworking spoiled units • Repairing machine and equipment • Re-engineering and redesigning
External activities Activities undertaken after the product has been sold to remedy problems caused by defects and failed units	• Product recalls (replace both good and defective units) • Warranty repair work • Replacing defective units • Liability lawsuits

COMPREHENSIVE EXAMPLE 2

Activity analysis and the cost of quality

Swiss Watch is a watch manufacturer in Switzerland with a reputation for producing high-quality watches. Lately, however, a competitor has advertised both quality improvements and price reductions in its line of watches. Pierre Borgeaud, the head of cost accounting at Swiss Watch, conducted a study to determine whether costs could be reduced. His initial focus was on activities related to quality. Although the managers want to maintain high quality, they also want to reduce costs and therefore prices. The study categorised quality costs into four activities: prevention, appraisal, internal and external.

Estimating the costs of quality

Using information gathered from the general ledger, last year's quality activity costs were estimated as shown (amounts in Swiss Francs).

Prevention costs (inspecting materials from suppliers)	SFr 10 000
Appraisal costs (inspection)	20 000
Internal costs (spoiled units)	5 000
External costs (warranty)	8 000
Total costs of quality	SFr 43 000

When Pierre reviewed these costs, he believed that they were too low. He decided to seek more information than provided by the general ledger accounts. He spoke with employees both individually and in their work teams and found that informal inspections occurred frequently. He asked employees to estimate time spent on quality-related activities. He learned that when defect rates begin to increase, employees respond by spending more time on quality-related activities. He estimated that it cost an additional SFr 50 000 last year in prevention costs for the informal inspections that occurred when defect rates increased. In addition, employees would spend time analysing and correcting the process to improve quality. He estimated this cost to be about SFr 2000 and categorised the cost as prevention-related. He also discovered additional internal costs of SFr 6000 incurred for rework that had not been included in the original estimates. Finally, he discovered an additional SFr 7000 in external service costs for handling returns. He summarised his revised estimate of the costs of quality as follows:

	First estimate	Additional costs	Total costs
Prevention costs	SFr 10 000	SFr 50 000	SFr 62 000
		+ SFr 2 000	
Appraisal costs	20 000		20 000
Internal costs	5 000	6 000	11 000
External costs	8 000	7 000	15 000
Total costs of quality	SFr 43 000	SFr 65 000	SFr 108 000

Using quality cost information to better manage operations

Pierre reported his revised cost estimate to managers, who shared the information with a team of production employees. The team members were surprised at the high cost, and they discussed ways to reduce it. The team believed that the entity could reduce quality costs by identifying and removing defective units earlier in the production process. Therefore, they recommended tracking the number of defective units discovered by employees on the line versus those units found by the inspectors.

Production employees also recommend analysing the types of defects discovered by inspectors to help the employees identify and correct potential problems earlier in the production process. The team believed that some of the inspectors could be assigned to other activities, decreasing the overall costs of quality. In addition, the team recommended tracking the types of warranty problems that occur to identify changes in the design or manufacturing process that would minimise the cost of warranty work and simultaneously improve customer satisfaction.

In conclusion, the lean approach requires quality to be perfected at the source. While we have learned about the varying quality activities and the potential for trade-offs between them, in a lean organisation, ambitious goals for quality are set and employees are multi-skilled to ensure optimum quality is strived for and maintained throughout the entire value chain. For lean organisations, there is no trade-off made in quality costs. The lean philosophy believes the activities associated with quality appraisal — in particular, internal and external quality costs — are 'waste' and considered to be a failure in the application of lean thinking. When waste is eliminated, quality should improve. Quality should be inherent in every aspect of the value stream as a continuous one-piece flow. Perfection in quality is crucial and is continually strived for.

SUMMARY

17.1 Reflect on and communicate the lean thinking philosophy.

The lean thinking model

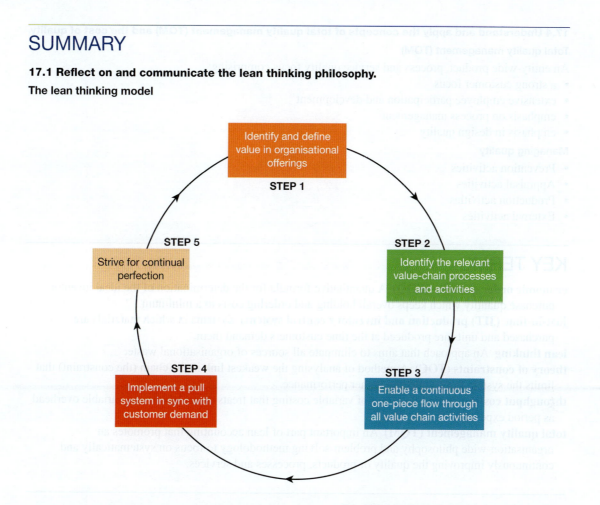

17.2 Describe the theory of constraints (TOC) and throughput costing.

Theory of constraints (TOC)

Entity is viewed as a system.

- Main goal to make money now and in the future
- Comprises a set of elements (a chain of linkages) with interdependent relationships
- TOC concentrates on the weakest link in the chain
- Source of constraint can be the *supply* or *demand* side of the value chain
- *Throughput costing* is a part of the TOC. It is a modified form of variable costing that measures the impact of bottlenecks and constraints on an organisation's goal achievement

  Five steps of the TOC.

1. Identify the system's constraint(s)
2. Decide how to exploit the system's constraint(s)
3. Subordinate everything else to the above constraint(s)
4. Elevate the system's constraint(s)
5. If in the previous steps a constraint has been broken, go back to step 1, but do not allow inertia to cause a system constraint

17.3 Explain the concept of just-in-time (JIT) manufacturing.

Just-in-time (JIT) manufacturing

When making inventory purchase decisions, manufacturers and retailers must balance the pros and cons of either:

1. smaller orders and inventory levels which minimise inventory holding costs, or
2. larger orders and inventory levels which minimise the number of required orders and ordering costs.

   In just-in-time inventory control systems, materials are purchased and units are produced as customers demand them.

17.4 Understand and apply the concepts of total quality management (TQM) and the cost of quality.

Total quality management (TQM)

An entity-wide product, process and service quality focus comprising:
- a strong customer focus
- extensive employee participation and development
- emphasis on process management
- emphasis in design quality.

Managing quality
- Prevention activities
- Appraisal activities
- Production activities
- External activities

KEY TERMS

economic order quantity (EOQ) A quantitative formula for the determination of the ideal inventory purchase quantity which keeps overall holding and ordering costs to a minimum.

just-in-time (JIT) production and inventory control systems Systems in which materials are purchased and units are produced at the time customers demand them.

lean thinking An approach that aims to eliminate all sources of organisational waste.

theory of constraints (TOC) A method of analysing the weakest link in the chain (the constraint) that limits the system from achieving higher performance.

throughput costing A modified form of variable costing that treats direct labour and variable overhead as period expenses.

total quality management (TQM) An important part of lean accounting that promotes an organisation-wide philosophy and problem-solving methodology to focus on systematically and continuously improving the quality of products, processes and services.

SELF-STUDY PROBLEMS

SELF-STUDY PROBLEM 1 The Dublin Shirt Company — the Theory of Constraints[23]

As introduced in chapter 16, the Dublin Shirt Company was established in Ireland by its American parent. It is a wholly owned subsidiary and manufactures polo-type sports shirts for the growing worldwide sports shirt market, which includes supply of shirts for major sporting events such as the British Open, Ryder Cup, Super Bowl and Wimbledon. The Dublin Shirt Company markets its products through regional magazines and newspaper advertisements. It also employs a small group of in-house salespeople, as well as using independent salespersons on a commission-only basis.

The company has a modern knitting plant with approximately 100 employees. Shirts are made in three men's sizes: medium, large and extra large (XL). The normal production cycle for an order of white shirts is five days. The company tries to produce each order well in advance of dispatch so that there will always be a certain amount of finished goods in stock at the end of each financial period. Depending on the client requirements, the shirt may be customised to order. The customisation service includes dyeing, stamping/printing and/or embroidery processes. All three processes are not necessarily required for each shirt. For example, nearly two-thirds of the shirts are dyed in various colours, which increases the production cost and extends the production cycle of an order by about three days. Once the shirts are dyed they are then embroidered or dyed and stamped or printed. The remaining non-dyed white shirts may be printed, stamped or embroidered. One characteristic feature of the 'sports shirt' is the promotional text and/or logo that can be printed or machine embroidered onto each shirt. The printing (or 'stamping') process is done with a special printing machine, but recently there have been issues with the 'staying power' of the material printed on these shirts. Customers have complained that the ink eventually cracks and peels off. A small but increasing number of shirts (about 15 per cent) now have the text or logo of the sports event embroidered rather than 'stamped'. This embroidery work adds enormously to the appeal of the product.

In strategic planning, Dublin Shirt management developed an overall mission 'to provide a reasonable return to shareholders by providing high-quality products to customers, delivered on time and at the lowest cost'. It was agreed Dublin Shirt's main competitive strength is in the quality of the product. Their weakness, however, is in customer service, particularly in meeting scheduled delivery times. This is impacting on sales and it is currently operating at 70 per cent capacity. In the present climate, Dublin Shirt can only afford to reduce its prices if it can cut costs. The sales director suggests that the company could lower its quality inspection costs by reducing inspections, which will improve on-time delivery rates. This proposal is to be discussed at the next board meeting.

Required

The management of the Dublin Shirt Company has hired your consultancy firm to advise on the current situation and potential future developments. You are to prepare a presentation for the company's board of directors, including coverage of the following point: The managing director thinks that theory of constraints (TOC) might be a worthwhile approach to managing capacity at the Dublin Shirt Company. Do you agree with this proposal?

SOLUTION TO SELF-STUDY PROBLEM 1

Students may elect to agree or disagree with the views of the managing director. Those who would disagree might recommend the use of activity-based costing (ABC) as a long-term alternative to the TOC. ABC is useful to highlight and manage unused capacity if the practical volume of the cost driver is used to calculate the activity rates. ABC traces costs to products based on the way each product uses resources, which is suggested to be based on product complexity rather than volume. ABC proponents prefer to use non-volume drivers to allocate batch and product-level costs (refer to chapter 12).

Students who elect to agree with the views of the managing director would argue that the TOC would be a worthwhile proposition for the management of capacity, albeit a short-term approach within a lean thinking philosophy. The TOC focuses on the constraint, if internal, by maximising profit and prioritising production based on throughput per unit at the constraint. In the Dublin Shirt Company's case, the source of the constraint is possibly on the demand side as the case highlights the company is operating at 70 per cent capacity. Decisions would be made about how this external constraint might be alleviated. For example, if the constraint is due to competitor pricing or customer budgets, The Dublin Shirt Company should subordinate all available resources to product promotion and marketing to entice new and existing customers. At the same time, continual review of corporate strategy is necessary to manage issues at the Dublin Shirt Company, including those factors that will bring about an increase in demand for its products.

SELF-STUDY PROBLEM 2 The Dublin Shirt Company — lean accounting

More recently, the Dublin Shirt Company investigated ways in which it could cut costs. The sales director suggests that the company can lower its quality inspection costs by reducing the number of inspections. By drawing on cost reduction initiatives, based on the principles of lean accounting, prepare a response that considers the sales director's proposal?

SOLUTION TO SELF-STUDY PROBLEM 2

Lean accounting is a forward-looking accounting approach that is based on the belief that only a small fraction of employee time and effort is spent on customer value-creating activities. The philosophy behind lean accounting is to eliminate waste in processes. Waste is highly correlated with quality management in lean organisations. For example, rework of defective products is considered as 'waste'. The manufacture and distribution of shirts at the Dublin Shirt Company would be considered as a 'one piece flow', producing to customer orders. Given the team-based approach in a lean organisation, quality is reinforced by value-stream teams, which consist of multi-functional members who have (or acquire) the skills necessary to ensure optimal quality is maintained and built into the processes. Employees are given responsibility for their quality output, which is maintained by strong social controls such as cell member pressure and continuous learning.

QUESTIONS

17.1 What is the lean thinking philosophy? Outline the five steps in the lean thinking model. **LO1**

17.2 Describe the behavioural and social controls in a lean manufacturing environment. How would they be different to in traditional (non-lean) organisations? **LO1**

17.3 What is a just-in-time manufacturing system? Why would organisations choose to adopt it? **LO3**

17.4 Outline the five steps in the theory of constraints. In many examples of the TOC in practice, idle capacity is generated. Why? Can this be a good thing? **LO2**

17.5 Explain how the TOC fits within the lean thinking philosophy. **LO1, 2**

17.6 Describe the four types of quality-related activities. **LO4**

17.7 Should the lean thinking firm be concerned about the costs of quality activities? Explain by drawing on Deming's 14 principles of management. **LO1, 4**

17.8 What is throughput costing? How is it linked to lean accounting? **LO2**

17.9 Explain why a lean organisation would refuse to implement an absorption costing system. **LO2**

17.10 Proponents of the TOC suggest that it is problematic to make decisions based entirely on resource consumption (that is, the ABC system) because there is no guarantee that the spending to supply resources will fully align with the levels of resources that might be demanded in the near future. Explain this comment. **LO2**

17.11 Based on your understanding of the TOC, explain why conventional standard costed work in process inventories might hide problems, obscure interdependencies and make it difficult to identify the real constraint in a system. Why might this conventional method lead companies to build excessive work in process inventories? **LO2**

17.12 Briefly comment on how a lean approach will impact on accounting practices? **LO1**

EXERCISES

17.13 Categorising quality activities **LO4**

Following is a list of quality-related activities.

(a) Inspecting units when they are 100 per cent complete to remove defective units.

(b) Designing a process with as few parts as possible to reduce the chance of defects.

(c) Warranty costs for defective products returned to the factory for rework.

(d) Reworking spoiled units before they leave the factory.

(e) Costs to defend the entity against lawsuits for damages caused by defective products.

(f) Tracking number of defects for each manufacturing team and posting daily defect rates on a plant-wide bulletin board.

(g) Redesigning a manufacturing process to lower the rate of defects.

Required

Mark each activity according to whether it pertains to prevention (P), appraisal (A), internal (I) or external (E) costs.

17.14 Lean approach **LO1**

Elimination of waste to maximise customer value is at the core of the lean approach.

Required

Search online to find two organisations that have adopted a lean approach to operations. Identify the objective that led to the adoption of lean thinking and any changes that have been made to business processes as a result of the lean approach.

17.15 Lean thinking in an internet-based sales organisation **LO1**

Paige Maddern owns and operates Paige Nightwear (PN), an internet-based company specialising in high-quality nightwear for men and women. From the outset, Paige has kept a number of key principles in mind which guide most of the business decisions and operations of PN including:

1. All products are to be manufactured locally by small manufacturers that satisfy strict quality control procedures and a quality audit conducted by PN.

2. The use of high-level electronic intelligence systems which support:
   • real-time tracking of all orders throughout the complete order-filling process
   • an objective of all orders shipped within 24 hours of receipt of an order
   • real-time reporting of orders, sales and cost data, including product profitability
   • electronic links to manufacturing suppliers, enabling production to be triggered by sales order data
   • customer follow-up procedures which ensure a constant flow of customer feedback regarding the products as well as delivery processes.

Paige has always believed that, as an internet-based company, it is important to make use of a range of technologies to maintain customer loyalty and customer growth. It was not going to be enough to just have good-quality products.

Required

(a) How do electronic links to manufacturing suppliers, enabling production to be triggered by sales order data, help reduce waste?

(b) Given PN's operating environment and the key principles Paige uses to guide her company, what kind of accounting practices would you expect and not expect to observe with respect to output controls (refer to figure 17.3).

17.16 Lean accounting[24] **LO1**

Synergy Clothing (Synergy) began operations as a clothing manufacturer in the 1940s. It has grown from a small firm into a multi-divisional diversified clothing company with three key divisions: Fashion, which focuses on shirts and jeans; Uniforms which focuses on corporate and uniform wear; and Sportswear, which focuses on sports clothing with a specialty in custom sports uniforms. Until recently, the company had been owned by the same family. The grandson of the founder, Tim Peseta, still occupies a senior management position, although significant changes have occurred since the company was listed on the stock exchange in 2003. Since becoming a public company, a number of key structural and control system changes have been made by the new management team led by CEO Noel Oliver.

One of the first actions Noel took was to bring in a consulting firm to make an assessment of the whole organisation with a particular emphasis on the Fashion division. Noel had concerns that there was significant waste in the Fashion division but he needed real evidence that this was the case.

The consultant's report was comprehensive and addressed the issues of particular interest to Noel. Provided below is an excerpt from the report that relates to some of the thoughts of the consultant relating to the fashion division (FD):

1. Customers and market
   - The FD was trying to supply product to any customer (retail outlet), irrespective of size of order, with little consideration for the costs associated with doing so. The consultant described this as trying to 'deliver a purple polka dot shirt on a Sunday afternoon'.
   - The tendency for the FD to have a product for every part of the market without much regard for the innovative product technologies that had made the FD's brand strong in the past.
   - The focus on producing 50 ranges per season, much of which it would seem was *made to stock*, and remained as finished goods inventory awaiting an order.

2. Operations and staffing
   - There appeared to be insufficient resources dedicated to the design activity with the entire activity staffed by the equivalent of two staff.
   - Excessive inventory levels both in terms of raw materials (cloth, where purchasing seemed to occur in an unplanned way predominantly by Tim Peseta on annual international buying trips) and finished goods (shirts, estimated at 290 000 items).
   - Production volumes were governed by an economic order quantity model, which appeared to contribute to the excessive inventory levels, while the production process utilised manual, semi-automated and fully-automated procedures.

Notwithstanding Tim's tight control over the FD's operations, morale on the shop floor appeared high, with many long-term employees (one machinist having been with the firm for 42 years).

Required

(a) Identify which of the above issues raised by the consultant could be addressed using the principles of lean accounting.

(b) Using lean accounting principles, what solutions would you provide for the issues you have identified in part (a)?

17.17 The TOC at Paisley Insurance Company **LO2**

As introduced in chapter 12, Paisley Insurance Company provides a range of insurance products to residential and commercial customers. Figure 17.16 shows the process map of Paisley's billing department activities.

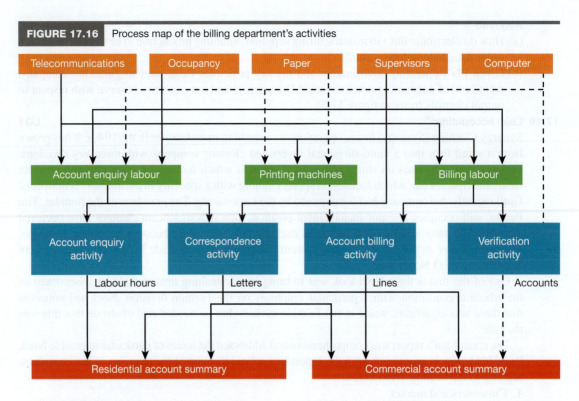

FIGURE 17.16 Process map of the billing department's activities

The following four key activities and available hours are identified as key activities within the billing department.

Activity	Number of hours available per week
Account enquiry activity	134
Correspondence activity	19
Account billing activity	153
Verification activity	75

A recent concern for Paisley's managers relates to the growing number of customer complaints associated with poor-quality billing activities. On further investigation, several sources of bottlenecks have been observed at all stages of the billing department's processes. For example, account enquiries often require detailed individual advice from Paisley's insurance sales department. Supervisors for the correspondence activity have specialised skills and sometimes hold-ups in supervisory activities have resulted in accounts not being processed correctly or sent out on time. Bottlenecks in account billing have also occurred with unanticipated breakdowns of their ageing printing machines. Likewise, the verification activity is also performed by specialised employees. Currently, there is a shortage of labour for this activity, particularly while the senior manager is on maternity leave. At varying times, these bottlenecks have contributed to delays in sending bills out (hence, delayed payment to Paisley), as well as billing errors and growing customer complaints.

Required

(a) Drawing on your knowledge of the TOC, explain how this system might be useful for Paisley Insurance Company.

(b) As part of a wider concept of lean thinking, explain how a lean approach might help Paisley Insurance Company improve the quality of the billing department activities.

17.18 Throughput costing   **LO2**

During its second year of operations, Grilling Raine Computing, an entity that manufactures and sells laptop stands, produced 275 000 units and sold 250 000 units at $60 per unit. The beginning inventory balance was 5000 units. No changes in fixed or variable costs occurred in the second year. The managers expected to sell 220 000 units, the same volume of manufacturing as last year. They set that amount as the normal capacity for allocating fixed overhead costs during the second year. For simplicity, assume that the budgeted fixed manufacturing overhead cost equals the actual cost this period. Also assume that the entity uses the first-in, first-out (FIFO) cost flow assumption.

The following costs were incurred during the year:

Variable cost per unit:		
Direct materials	$	15.00
Direct labour		10.00
Manufacturing overhead		12.50
Selling and administrative		2.50
Total fixed costs:		
Manufacturing overhead		$2 200 000
Selling and administrative		1 375 000

Required

Prepare a statement of profit or loss using throughput costing.

17.19 JIT production   LO3

Big Bertram uses the just-in-time method to manufacture golf clubs. The manufacturing schedule for the clubs is developed as customers place orders. Each club is made within a cell where five workers have production stations. The raw materials are delivered to the cell as needed. Each worker in the cell performs one step in the manufacturing process and then inspects the club before giving it to the next person. When a club is finished, it is set on a finished goods rack, which is sent to the packaging department at regular intervals.

Required

(a) What do we call a manufacturing system such as the one used by Big Bertram?

(b) Describe the general advantages of this type of system.

(c) The supplier that manufactures the weights that are inserted in each club head would like to monitor Big Bertram's inventory levels through the internet so that its new software can release deliveries at appropriate times. List qualitative factors that might affect Big Bertram's decision about this proposal.

17.20 Quality costs using ABC versus traditional costing   LO4

New-Rage Cosmetics uses a traditional cost accounting system to allocate quality control costs uniformly to all products at a rate of 14.5 per cent of direct labour cost. Monthly direct labour cost for Satin Sheen make-up is $27 500. In an attempt to more equitably distribute quality control costs, New-Rage is considering activity-based costing. The following monthly data have been gathered for Satin Sheen make-up.

> Incoming material inspection:
> Cost driver — type of material
> Cost allocation rate — $11.50 per type of material
> Quantity — 12 types of material
> In-process inspection:
> Cost driver — number of units
> Cost allocation rate — $0.14 per unit
> Quantity — 17 500 units
> Product certification:
> Cost driver — per order
> Cost allocation rate — $77 per order
> Quantity — 25 orders

Required

(a) Calculate the amount of quality control cost assigned to each order of Satin Sheen make-up using:
    (i) activity-based costing (*Hint:* Total all the ABC costs for one month and divide by the number of orders.)
    (ii) traditional cost accounting.

(b) Explain the difference in quality control costs assigned under the two methods.

17.21 Quality costs   LO4

Suppose that the director of a lost dogs' home is concerned about an increase in number of adopted dogs returned to the home because of behaviour problems. When dogs are returned, the home incurs extra animal intake and adoption costs, in addition to extra costs for board, room and more training for the dogs. In addition, the director is concerned that adopting families may not want another dog because of their unhappy experience. The director views this as a quality problem and wants to improve quality in adoption services and reduce costs at the same time.

Required

(a) List the four types of quality activities presented in the chapter. What type of quality problem is the lost dogs' home experiencing? Explain your answer.

(b) Will an ABC system help managers determine costs for their quality activities? Explain.

(c) List one new cost pool and cost driver that could be used to improve the director's ability to analyse quality.

17.22 JIT manufacturing   **LO3**

Livermore Components is a supplier of drive shafts to the motor vehicle industry. Currently it supplies two of the large car manufacturers in Australia and is also highly ranked in a tender bid to supply drive shafts to a Malaysian car manufacturer. Much of the value chain in the Australian industry is structured on the basis of JIT principles. It has been this way for some time and most of the industry participants compete on this basis. Suppliers to the large car companies (including Livermore) understand they lack bargaining power but most of them find a way to successfully participate.

The dilemma facing Livermore's management is the offshore contract in Malaysia. If Livermore was to become the successful tenderer, the Malaysian manufacturer would also require component delivery on a JIT basis.

Required

Using your understanding of JIT principles, outline the ramifications for Livermore if successful in the tender process.

17.23 TOC   **LO2**

A senior nurse manager working in an endoscopy clinic in the northern suburbs of Melbourne is contemplating issues that have surfaced with the purchase of a new endoscope (colonoscope) used to investigate intestinal problems. This valuable medical equipment now enables the clinic to process its patients more quickly through the operating theatre; however, there now appears to be bottlenecks elsewhere.

Typically, patients begin to arrive at the clinic at 7.30 am. The operating list commences at 8.00 am. There is one administration staff, one surgeon, one anaesthetist, one theatre nurse, one anaesthetic nurse, one recovery room nurse and one recovery lounge nurse. The surgical procedures undertaken are either gastroscopy or colonoscopy.

On a typical morning, the patient is first checked in by the administration personnel (15 minutes). They are then required to change into a theatre gown before an anaesthetic nurse assessment to ensure they are prepared and physically ready for surgery (30 minutes). The surgeon and anaesthetist find time between procedures to check the patient has signed the operating consent form and understands the procedure about to be undertaken (2–5 minutes). The patient is taken to theatre from the waiting lounge area (by the anaesthetist and anaesthetic nurse). The preparation and administration of initial anaesthetic takes 10–15 minutes. The endoscopy procedure takes anywhere between 10 minutes and 40 minutes depending on the procedure (colonoscopy or gastroscopy) and the complexity of the patient's condition (total average theatre time 20–55 minutes). The endoscopes are prepared by the theatre nurse for the surgeon. The theatre nurse also assists the surgeon during the procedure. Cleaning, sterilisation and preparation takes 40 minutes for either type of endoscope.

Once the procedure is complete, the patient is then taken to the recovery area by the anaesthetist and nurse where 30 minutes of recovery-room nursing observation is administered: 1:1 (patient:nurse) care is provided (5–10 minutes), and then 3:1 (patient:nurse) care is provided (20 25 minutes). The patient is then moved to the recovery lounge where they are observed by the recovery lounge nurse as they rest on a recliner and are provided with refreshments until they are ready to be dressed and discharged (approximately 60 minutes). The patient is generally discharged about 4.5 hours after arriving at the clinic. The surgeon and anaesthetist only operate morning or afternoon shifts (morning: 8.00 am to 12 midday; afternoon: 2.00 pm to 6.00 pm). Sometimes the lists run overtime, but by no more than one hour.

Required

The senior nurse manager needs to evaluate the maximum number of patient bookings for a typical day and the nursing staff requirements. How might the TOC help with this evaluation?

PROBLEMS

17.24 Lean accounting and quality   LO1, 4

Lance Novak recently acquired Chiefs Loft, a restaurant in an inner-city suburb of Brisbane. Past records show the restaurant has generally experienced quite good customer numbers. While conducting his due diligence and from the first few weeks in the restaurant, a number of issues/concerns have emerged which Lance believes warrant swift action. These concerns include the following.

- While the customer numbers have been as expected, other than by observation there is little data maintained on repeat customers.
- The process for taking orders is still completed manually and there appears to be duplication and double-handling of paper and documentation.
- A number of different suppliers are used, even for similar products. It seems the previous owners would play one supplier off against the other to get better prices.
- The 'production' process in the kitchen from taking the order to delivering the meal to the customer seems cumbersome with unnecessary delays.
- The accounting data seems too late to be of much use in managing the restaurant from day to day.

Lance's brother works in the strategic consulting area and has offered to have a look at the restaurant and make recommendations to improve operations and performance at Chiefs Loft.

Required

Drawing on your understanding of lean accounting and TQM, prepare a report on the recommendations you think Lance's brother is likely to make.

17.25 Cost reduction; JIT; value chain analysis   LO3

Budget Cupboards produces kitchen and bathroom cupboards that incorporate unusual functions (such as specialty drawers for knives and kitchen tools, and kitchen appliance holders that pop up from under the countertop). Competition in this industry has recently increased. Budget's management wants to cut costs for its basic cupboard models and then cut prices.

Required

(a) The following table lists potential areas for cost reduction. Two potential cost reductions are provided for the first area listed (design phase). For each of the remaining areas, identify two potential ways that Budget Cupboard's management could reduce costs.

Potential area for cost reduction	Potential cost reductions	
	(i)	**(ii)**
Example: Design phase	Work with suppliers to reduce direct materials costs	Redesign cupboards to use fewer parts
Manufacturing process		
Administration		
Changes in quality or functionality		

(b) Budget Cupboards does not currently use JIT production. Describe several advantages of using these methods when price competition increases.

17.26 Inventory management system; data accuracy; internal controls; estimating benefits   LO3

Automotive parts company Mopar implemented a new inventory management system costing $1.5 million. Mopar distributed parts from three central and 11 regional warehouses to hundreds of parts dealers. The entity filled orders for approximately 1 million line items per week from an inventory of 280 000 parts for Chrysler, Dodge and Jeep brand vehicles.

Mopar implemented the new system to improve its management of inventory levels. The entity previously maintained inventories based on forecasted demand, but often ran out of some parts and carried inventory levels that were too high for other parts. When a customer ordered a part that was out of stock at a particular warehouse, the entity incurred extra costs to search for the part at other warehouses. If the part was not found, Mopar placed a rush order to have it shipped directly to the customer from one of its 3000 suppliers. When inventory of a part was too high, valuable warehouse space was wasted and the entity incurred unnecessary inventory carrying costs. To reduce these types of problems, the entity had manually tracked data for 100 of the highest-cost and best-selling parts. The managers used measures such as how often a part was out of stock to adjust inventory purchases.

The new inventory system included a database that would track parts at all warehouses as well as suppliers, customers and forecast levels. The system helped managers identify $3.5 million in overstocked inventory. They expected an additional $10 million in annual savings from reduced backorders and rush orders.[25]

Required

(a) Is Mopar's new inventory system likely to completely eliminate out-of-stock occurrences? Why?

(b) Discuss whether it would be beneficial for Mopar to institute a JIT inventory management system.

(c) Benefits from Mopar's new system depend on the accuracy of data in its inventory database. Identify possible reasons why the data may be inaccurate.

(d) Describe possible internal controls that could prevent or detect and correct inaccuracies in Mopar's inventory database.

(e) Mopar's managers expected to achieve $10 million in annual savings from reduced backorders and rush orders. Suppose you are asked to develop an estimate of these savings. How might you go about making the estimate? What types of data would you use? What types of assumptions would you need to make?

ENDNOTES

1. 'How learning 'lean' management can lift the bottom line', *The Australian*, 26 August 2014, www.theaustralian.com.au.

2. Andersen, H, Røvik, KA & Ingebrigtsen, T 2014, Lean thinking in hospitals: is there a cure for the absence of evidence? A systematic review of reviews. *BMJ open, 4*(1), e003873.

3. Kaplan, GS, Patterson, SH, Ching, JM & Blackmore, CC 2014. Why Lean doesn't work for everyone. *BMJ Qual Saf*, bmjqs-2014.

4. ibid.

5. Adapted from Kaplan et al. 2014.

6. Womack, JP & Jones, DT 2003, *Lean thinking: banish waste and create wealth in your corporation, revised and updated*, Simon & Schuster, New York, NY.

7. This figure was adapted from the lean thinking model created by Womack & Jones 2003.

8. Adapted from Kennedy, FA & Widener, SK 2008, 'A control framework: insights from evidence on lean accounting', *Management Accounting Research*, vol. 19, iss. 4, December. In this case study of EBS Limited, a subsidiary of Tri-Metal Inc., the researchers either observed the practices, discussed the practices in interviews with EBS employees or found evidence in photos and archive records.

9. Kennedy, FA & Brewer, PC 2005, 'Lean accounting: what's it all about?', *Strategic Finance*, Institute of Management Accountants, November, pp. 27–34.

10. Goldratt, EM 1990, *The haystack syndrome, sifting information out of the data ocean*, Croton-on-Hudson, North River Press, New York.

11. Gupta, M, Baxendale, S & McMamara, K 1997, 'Integrating TOC and ABCM in a health care company', *Journal of Cost Management*, August, pp. 23–33.

12. Corbett, T 1999, 'Making better decisions case study', *CMA Management*, November, pp. 33–37.

13. Bahl, HC, Ritzman, LP & Gupta, JN 1987, OR practice—Determining lot sizes and resource requirements: A review. *Operations Research, 35* (3), pp. 329–345.

14. Schonberger, RJ 1996, *World class manufacturing: the next decade,* The Free Press, New York.

15. Toyota 2015, 'Toyota production system', www.toyota-global.com.

16. Reproduced from Toyota 2015, 'Just-in-time — philosophy of complete elimination of waste', www.toyota-global.com.

17. Frost, S 2001, 'Australian auto workers halt A$17 billion industry' *Asian Labour Update*, iss. 40, July–September.

18. As defined by the US Department of Commerce in 1994.

19. See Ittner, C & Larcker, D 1995, 'Total quality management and the choice of information and reward systems', *Journal of Accounting Research*, vol. 33, pp. 1–34.

20. Deming, Dr W Edwards 1982 & 1986, *Out of the crisis: quality, productivity and competitive position*, Cambridge University Press, Cambridge. www.ifm.eng.cam.ac.uk.

21. South Australian State Government Minister for Health 1995, media release, 1 February, Adelaide.

22. See Merrick, A 2000, 'Bridgestone tire issue clouds labor negotiations', *Wall Street Journal* (eastern edn), 1 September, p. A4.

23. Clarke, P in association with Juras, P. Bremer, W 2002, *Cases from management accounting practice: case 3 Dublin Shirt Company*, Institute of Management Accountants.

24. This problem has been adapted from Brooks, A & Vesty, G 2008, 'Double two', *Accounting Perspectives*, 7, 3, pp. 257–170.

25. Information from Mopar's website at www.mopar.com; Xenakis, J 2000, 'How to slash inventory costs,' *CFO.com*, 13 December.

ACKNOWLEDGEMENTS

Photo 17A: © Monkey Business Images / Shutterstock.com

Photo 17B: © Rikard Stadler / Shutterstock.com

Figure 17.13: © Toyota

Figure 17.14: Deming, W. Edwards, *Out of the crisis*, pp. 23–24, © 2000 Massachusetts Institute of Technology, by permission of The MIT Press.

Figure 17.8–17.11: © CPA Canada

CHAPTER 18

Responsibility accounting, performance evaluation and transfer pricing

LEARNING OBJECTIVES

After studying this chapter, you should be able to:

18.1 explain how decision-making responsibility and authority relate to performance evaluation

18.2 identify appropriate responsibility centres and explain how responsibility centres are used to measure, monitor and motivate performance

18.3 calculate and outline the uses and limitations of return on investment, residual income and economic value added for monitoring performance

18.4 communicate alternative prices used for transferring goods and services within an entity

18.5 calculate transfer prices and outline the issues associated with transfer pricing.

IN BRIEF

The operations of organisations involve managers with different levels of responsibility and authority making decisions and guiding operations. Problems can arise as the interests of managers of different departments may conflict. In the case of corporations, conflicts can further arise between the interests of the owners' or shareholders' and managers. In other contexts, including government entities and non-government-organisations (NGOs), conflicts could exist between funding agencies and managers.

Accounting information plays an important role in managing these potential conflicts and promoting accountability. Accounting information is used to measure performance, monitor and motivate managers and employees and ensure alignment of interests. As discussed by Henderson[1], the power of measuring and evaluating the performance within organisations has long been recognised given the old cliché: 'what gets measured gets done'. When something is measured, we are able to begin to evaluate whether we have achieved what we set out to do. The right measures must be selected though and performance measurement must work in conjunction with other activities used to achieve strategic outcomes. Simply measuring profit will not increase it!

Before managers or employees can be held accountable for the results of their decisions and actions, their rights and responsibilities need to be defined. Then return on investment, residual income, economic value added or other measures can be used to gauge and reward performance. In large entities, resources may be transferred internally from one department to another. When prices for these transfers are set appropriately, goal congruence is strengthened and may increase the value of the organisation. However, transfer prices can encourage suboptimal decisions that may be beneficial at the divisional level, but not at the organisational level.

18.1 Decision-making authority and responsibility

LEARNING OBJECTIVE 18.1 Explain how decision-making responsibility and authority relate to performance evaluation.

As entities grow in size, top managers have an increasingly difficult time maintaining control over decision making. On the positive side, many entities benefit from the wide range of expertise among employees. However, as decision making is dispersed, mechanisms must be established for measuring, monitoring and motivating decisions throughout the organisation. Responsibility accounting assists by assessing the performance of individual managers and business units against the performance targets that have been set, thereby identifying any variances between actual and planned performance that can then be investigated. However, an important principle behind responsibility accounting is that an individual should only be held accountable for decisions and costs over which they have control. In contrast, if a business unit's performance is being assessed then all costs (and revenue where applicable) attributable to that unit should be included in the analysis.

The determination of where decision-making responsibility sits within the organisation will be dependent on a number of factors — organisational structure, whether centralised or decentralised decision making, type of knowledge required for decision making, and technology to support globalisation. We will now briefly discuss each of these factors.

Centralised and decentralised entities

When managers make choices about locating decision-making authority, they are also making choices about organisational structure. When decision making is *centralised*, the right to make or authorise decisions lies within top levels of management. When decision making is *decentralised*, the rights and responsibilities for decision making permeate all levels of the organisation. Where the decision making is located is often referred to as decision rights.

In the current dynamic business environment, many factors influence organisational structures, and changes in these structures are made over time. The type of knowledge needed for successful operations influences the location of authority and responsibility. In small entities, top managers are sufficiently knowledgeable about operations, but as the entity grows, it becomes more difficult and costly to transfer knowledge about customer needs to top management and then back down to operational personnel. Changes to organisational structure reflect the different knowledge needs. Organisations are regularly altering their structure to try to better reflect decision making and accountabilities.

Advantages and disadvantages for each type of organisational form are listed in figure 18.1. Whether decision making within an entity should be centralised or decentralised is not always a straightforward decision. Organisations often begin with centralised decision making, then adopt a decentralised structure as they grow large. However, some large entities find that a centralised approach is best because it leads to greater alignment of decisions with the organisational vision and strategies.

For example, when Soichiro Honda founded Honda Motor Company in 1948, he personally made most of the product-related decisions, while his partner made the finance and marketing decisions. The entity was much larger in 1973 when Honda retired. A new decision-making process involving 30 senior executives was adopted. Research and design engineers were given more control over new model development. With this process, it was difficult for the entity to respond to a more dynamic consumer market, and Honda began to lose market share. In the early 1990s, however, a new CEO re-established centralised decision making. Although employees resisted the change, decision making rested in the hands of a few powerful executives. This strategy produced the desired results and helped improve Honda's market share.

During the time that Honda centralised decision making, many other organisations — Fiat, General Electric and Motorola among them — decentralised theirs. With increased technology and access to information, the timeliness of decision making becomes a competitive strategy. To increase the speed of decisions, entities are increasingly giving decision-making authority to employees who have the most knowledge about the organisation's production processes and customer characteristics. Leaner organisations with fewer middle managers more easily move decision authority up and down the hierarchy. In dynamic industries where competition is high, remaining agile may be critical. For example, Google has had to restructure its European operations in part to facilitate better decision making at the local level.

Blockchain technology is another key example of the potential power of decentralisation. In simple terms, blockchain is a method of recording and validating transactions which avoids the need for a central ledger or recording system. Instead, blockchain is based on a distributed public ledger in which each participant within a peer-to-peer network maintains a record of all transactions. A chain of blocks is created as new information is added to previous blocks. The involvement of a wide number of participants, each contributing to establish consensus regarding the ledger's contents, increases confidence in the reliability of the data. Such an approach can improve efficiencies given the avoidance of the need for trusted third-party validation through, for example, banks, auditors, government or lawyers. This fundamental change in accounting technology, from a system of trust based on a central or intermediary party to one involving a distributed approach to consensus, could transform the ways in which transactions are recorded in modern economies. The blockchain approach has enabled Bitcoin and other cryptocurrencies to flourish given the resolution of the 'double-spending' problem.[2] Other examples of the potential uses blockchain technologies has included its proposed use to record share trade data by the Australian Securities Exchange from 2020.[3]

| FIGURE 18.1 | Advantages and disadvantages of centralised and decentralised entities |

Centralised entities		Decentralised entities	
Advantages	**Disadvantages**	**Advantages**	**Disadvantages**
• Less monitoring of decisions • Decisions are intended to benefit the overall entity • If decision makers have complete information, timely and efficient decisions are made • Good for stable operations and economic conditions	• More monitoring of employee effort because employees may be less motivated • Decision makers may not have complete information, resulting in poorer quality decisions • When knowledge from sub-units is required, the decision-making process slows down • Not appropriate for dynamic processes and volatile economic conditions	• Timely decision making; appropriate for dynamic processes and unstable economic conditions • Decisions are made by individuals having the most knowledge and expertise • Upper management has time to focus on organisational strategies • Decision-making authority combined with reward systems provide more motivation to exert optimal effort at the sub-unit level	• Decisions may meet objectives of the decision maker's sub-unit, but not meet organisational goals • Decisions may not be coordinated among sub-units, resulting in less-effective decision making for the organisation as a whole • Decision makers may not understand or agree with organisational strategies • Lack of coordination among sub-units may lead to duplication of products, services and effort

Decentralisation has been further promoted as a possible method of tackling key sustainability concerns relating to water and energy supply services. Conventionally, in most developed nations, water supply services are dependent on centralised water collection and storage (large dams and reservoirs) and distribution through centralised water mains networks. Decentralised water systems, by comparison, involving household or apartment level water storage and reuse systems are becoming increasingly economically feasible. These decentralised water solutions may help to relieve the pressure placed on water systems by climate change and population growth. There has also been a trend towards decentralisation within the energy sector as an increasing number of households move away from a reliance on the central harvesting of fossil-fuel based energy and adopt on-site renewable sources (like solar or wind). Decentralised energy production can reduce carbon dioxide pollution and may reduce the need for costly electricity grid upgrades.

General versus specific knowledge

Knowledge is an important resource within entities. The type of knowledge needed to make high-quality decisions affects the location of authority within organisations. **General knowledge**, such as information about volume of sales or product prices when organisations sell few products, is usually easy to transfer from one person to the next. Decisions based on general knowledge are likely to be centralised, made primarily by the CEO and other top managers. Transferring the general knowledge needed for decision making to an entity's headquarters is relatively easy and therefore not very costly. Examples of centralised organisations include small businesses where the owner makes most of the operating decisions and relies on a few employees to carry out those decisions. Large businesses that produce few products, such as steel companies, are often centralised.

Some decisions require **specific knowledge**; that is, detailed information about particular processes, customers or products — information that is costly to transfer within the entity. Examples of specific knowledge are the technical details of the manufacturing or service delivery processes, and information gained over time from working with individual customers. When decision makers need specific knowledge, they must either have the knowledge themselves or seek ways to obtain it.

In this regard, the importance of **knowledge management (KM)** processes designed to enable organisations to 'find, select, organise, disseminate, and transfer important information and expertise' are widely accepted.[4] These processes recognise the value of knowledge as an asset or strategic resource. Contemporary leadership approaches to KM acknowledge employees both for their knowledge and also their intellectual qualities, and doing so can promote innovation.[5]

Technology and globalisation

Technology has enhanced global communications and reduced the costs of business transactions so that entities can more easily locate units in other countries. Accordingly, organisations have become increasingly multinational. When entities expand to other countries, managers within each country are likely to have specific knowledge of cultural and customer preferences. Decisions made at the unit level are likely to be more timely and of higher quality because local decision makers best understand how to gather information relevant to operations in that country. A major development in technology as it relates to information and communication is the role of 'big data' in organisations. Technology now facilitates the ability for organisations to develop and/or access large data sets. While this is still an evolving issue for accounting, big data is likely to have a significant impact on how information is generated, organised and made useful for decision making. In an accounting sense, big data may be viewed as data sets that simply cannot be accommodated within the existing software systems, necessitating the development of new information systems to accommodate the data.

18.2 Responsibility accounting

LEARNING OBJECTIVE 18.2 Identify appropriate responsibility centres and explain how responsibility centres are used to measure, monitor and motivate performance.

Accounting information is used in both centralised and decentralised entities to measure, monitor and reward performance. In centralised entities, information produced by the accounting system for decision making is used primarily by top managers who are held responsible for both their effort and the quality of their decisions. Employees carry out tasks that result from these decisions and are held responsible for their effort and compliance with top-down decisions. Therefore, individual and team efforts require close monitoring to determine their contributions toward success. Managers use variance and productivity reports to gauge employee (individual and team) efforts.

In decentralised entities, decision making occurs throughout management levels and in the field. Employees in lower levels are held responsible for their efforts and the quality of their decisions. Therefore, accounting systems are used to provide decision-making information for all levels, from management to front-line employees. Broader accounting measures related to overall financial performance are then used to measure and monitor performance.

Responsibility accounting is the process of assigning authority and responsibility to managers of sub-units, and then measuring and evaluating their performance. Under responsibility accounting, managers are held responsible only for factors over which they have control. **Responsibility centres** are sub-units (segments, divisions, departments) in which managers are accountable for specific types of operating activities. Four common types of responsibility centres are cost centres, revenue centres, profit centres and investment centres. Figure 18.2 provides specific examples of each responsibility centre and examples of performance measures that are likely to be used in these centres. It is important to note that regardless of the type of responsibility centre, the performance measure(s) selected to evaluate performance need to reflect the organisational goals and strategic directions of the entity and the responsibility centre. Performance measures influence behaviour and decision making. Poorly selected performance measures may encourage poor decision making by managers of responsibility centres.

FIGURE 18.2	Examples of responsibility centres and performance measures

Responsibility centres	Examples	Performance measures used
Cost centres	• Manufacturing departments • Service production departments, such as road maintenance for a city • Support departments, such as accounting and billing departments in a hospital • Discretionary cost centres, such as marketing and research and development (R&D)	• Cost budgets and variances • Comparisons to benchmark cost per unit or service • Efficiency measures (days to close, number of new products) • Industry benchmarks (e.g. R&D as a percentage of sales)
Revenue centres	• Travel agencies • Sales departments for manufacturers	• Revenue budgets and variances • Growth in revenues • Customer satisfaction
Profit centres	• Retail sales outlets for clothing, books or restaurants • Corporate divisions and departments responsible for revenues and costs	• Revenue and cost budgets and variances • Accounting earnings such as operating income or earnings before or after taxes
Investment centres	• Corporate divisions and business segments responsible for investment decisions	• Return on investment (ROI) • Residual income • Economic value added (EVA)

Cost centres

In **cost centres**, managers are held responsible only for the costs under their control. Some cost centres provide support services that are relatively easy to monitor because their outputs are measurable. Cost centres are also used for sub-units that produce goods or services eventually sold by others. Managers in these cost centres are responsible for producing their goods or services efficiently.

Cost centre managers are expected either to minimise costs for a certain level of output or to maximise output for a certain level of cost. Cost centre performance is measured and monitored several ways. Some organisations rely on cost budgets and variances. Measures of other factors such as quality and timeliness of delivery are also relevant. For example, manufacturing a product may be done in a cost-effective way; however, if it does not meet quality standards, customers will react, which will lead to a decrease in sales revenue.

As discussed in chapter 5, cost centres can be classified as either engineered (standard) cost centres or discretionary cost centres. The difference relates to whether or not outputs can be measured. Engineered cost centres are able to measure inputs and outputs. Therefore, there is a standard against which actual performance can be measured and any variances identified. This type of cost centre suits manufacturing departments that produce a standard product and service departments performing repetitive activities, for example, processing of loans in a bank. Discretionary cost centres are more suited to business units where it is difficult to identify the relationship between inputs and outputs. Examples of such centres include advertising and marketing units. In relation to an advertising unit, it is difficult to identify whether a particular advertising campaign is responsible for increased sales, and so it is more difficult to link the costs to the organisation's output. In this type of environment, cost control is achieved by measuring actual expenditure against budget and using budgeting tools like program budgeting, zero-based budgeting and activity-based budgeting (which were discussed in more detail in chapter 5).

Revenue centres

In **revenue centres**, managers are held responsible for the revenues under their control. Revenue centres frequently sell products from manufacturing sub-units. Managers are expected to maximise sales. If the manager in a revenue centre is responsible for setting prices, gross revenues can be used as a performance measure. If corporate headquarters rather than the manager sets prices, then managers' performance can be evaluated using a combination of sales volumes measured in units and sales mix. Many organisations treat their sales departments as revenue centres and reward employees based on sales generated. In not-for-profit entities, fundraising activities might be treated as a revenue centre.

Profit centres

Managers in **profit centres** are held responsible for both revenues and costs under their control. Profit centres produce and sell goods or services, and may include one or several cost centres. Profit centre managers are responsible for decisions about inputs, product mix, pricing, and the volume of goods or services produced. Because profit centres include both revenues and costs, performance is typically measured using some combination of revenue and cost measures. Not-for-profit entities tend to use revenue and cost budgets and variances as performance measures, although some focus managers' attention on operating margins when performance is poor. For-profit entities use some measure of profits such as accounting earnings.

Investment centres

Managers of **investment centres** are held responsible for the revenues, costs and investments under their control. Investments include any assets related to the investment centre, such as fixed assets, inventory, intangible assets and accounts receivable. Investment centres resemble profit centres, where profitability is related to the assets used to generate the profits.

Because investment centres include revenues, costs and investment, performance measures need to address all of these factors. We will shortly learn about three commonly used measures: return on investment (ROI), residual income and economic value added (EVA).

Responsibility centres and suboptimal decision making

Top managers use judgement to decide the best types of responsibility centres for the entity. The choices depend on the size of the organisation, the nature of operations and the organisational structure. Ideally, responsibility centres should reduce agency costs (discussed later, in chapter 20) by holding managers responsible for decisions over which they have authority. For example, accounting departments are often viewed as cost centres because their managers have authority primarily for the expenditure of resources. Similarly, business segments are generally treated as investment centres because segment managers have authority over revenues, costs and investment.

Nevertheless, responsibility centre accounting sometimes leads to suboptimal decision making. Too often managers make decisions that are in the best interests of their own responsibility centres, but suboptimal for the entity as a whole. Each type of responsibility centre has a specific set of agency problems. Managers in cost centres focus on minimising costs and maximising efficiency, which can lead to declines in quality and delivery timeliness. In turn, sales could drop and the overall entity suffers. Similarly, revenue centre managers, who are typically rewarded for increasing revenues, may fail to consider product contribution margins and inappropriately emphasise less-profitable products. These managers have incentives to offer discounts and generous payment terms that reduce overall profitability. In profit centres, managers are encouraged to stress short-run profits by cutting costs — such as maintenance, advertising and R&D — that benefit long-term performance. Similarly, in investment centres, managers may reduce investment to increase short-term results. Or, they may invest in projects that are more or less risky than is appropriate for the entity. To address these agency problems, appropriate performance measures and reward systems need to be implemented. The impact of using different financial performance measures on management decision making will be illustrated the following section using investment centres.

18.3 Income-based performance evaluation

LEARNING OBJECTIVE 18.3 Calculate and outline the uses and limitations of return on investment, residual income and economic value added for monitoring performance.

Investment centres are common in large decentralised organisations, and provide a useful vehicle to demonstrate the behaviour-influencing focus of alternative performance measures. Because managers are responsible for costs and revenues, as well as for investments, the measures used for monitoring and motivating purposes typically include the return and the size of investment. Three financial measures commonly used to evaluate investment centre performance are:

- return on investment
- residual income
- economic value added.

Before moving to the behavioural effect of these performance measures, we should note that each is more than adequate in providing feedback on the performance of individual work units. While each is calculated differently, they provide important summary-type financial information about work-unit and organisational performance.

Return on investment

Return on investment (ROI) is the ratio of operating income to average operating assets. Operating income is calculated as earnings before interest and taxes (EBIT). Operating assets include all assets used in the production of goods or services, such as cash, accounts receivable, inventory, and plant and equipment. Non-operating assets (such as investments in other entities, or property and equipment currently rented to other entities) may be excluded from this calculation. When evaluating the entire entity's performance, all assets would be included because owners want to evaluate their return based on the entire investment. But when evaluating the performance of a sub-unit, judgement is used to determine which assets should be included. Any assets included should be under the control of the managers being evaluated. The average of beginning and ending operating assets is calculated for this component for two main reasons. First, the measure is intended to capture operations over a period of time, not just at the end of the time period. Second, the measure could be manipulated by temporarily decreasing investment at the time performance is measured.

ROI is used to evaluate investment centre performance. It can be compared across sub-units within a single organisation, among a group of entities within an industry, and within a single organisation across time. In addition, ROI can be decomposed into two components that provide additional information about performance. ROI is decomposed by multiplying both the numerator and denominator by revenue and then rearranging terms:

$$\text{ROI} = \text{Operating income} \div \text{Average operating assets}$$
$$= (\text{Operating income} \div \text{Average operating assets}) \times (\text{Revenue} \div \text{Revenue})$$
$$= (\text{Revenue} \div \text{Average operating assets}) \times (\text{Operating income} \div \text{Revenue})$$

Because revenue divided by average operating assets represents investment turnover, and operating income divided by revenue represents the return on sales, we can now rewrite the ROI formula as:

$$\text{ROI} = \text{Investment turnover} \times \text{Return on sales}$$

The decomposition of ROI into investment turnover and return on sales is often referred to as *DuPont analysis*. The method originated at the global science company DuPont Company in the early 1900s so that results from a wider range of business activities could be compared. Investment turnover is a measure of the sales generated by each dollar invested in operating assets. Return on sales measures managers' abilities to control the operating expenses related to sales during a period. This decomposition focuses attention on the role that assets play in generating revenues and the role that increased revenues and decreased costs play in generating profits. Improvement in ROI occurs when sales increase and costs do not increase proportionately (some cost is fixed), when costs are reduced for a given level of sales, or when investment decreases for a given level of income. In this manner, ROI provides managers guidance about factors that improve performance (see comprehensive example 1).

COMPREHENSIVE EXAMPLE 1

Return on investment

Computer Wizards is an Australian company that produces and sells computer monitors nationally and internationally. Jason Black is responsible for the New Zealand operations and Cecilia Earnhart manages the Australian division. Following is information about two divisions.

	New Zealand division*	Australian division
Average operating assets	$2 000 000	$200 000
Operating income	$ 500 000	$ 60 000

* All New Zealand information has been converted to Australian dollars.

The top managers of Computer Wizards measure the performance of its divisions using ROI. Following are the calculations for each division.

$$\text{New Zealand ROI} = \$500\,000 \div \$2\,000\,000 = 25\%$$
$$\text{Australian ROI} = \$60\,000 \div \$200\,000 = 30\%$$

Jason was recently hired from outside the company to improve operations in the New Zealand division. One of his objectives is to achieve an ROI at least as high as the Australian division. Given the New Zealand division's sales of $5 000 000, Jason decomposes the ROI as follows.

$$\text{Return on sales} = \$500\,000 \div \$5\,000\,000 = 10\%$$
$$\text{Investment turnover} = \$5\,000\,000 \div \$2\,000\,000 = 2.5 \text{ times}$$
$$\text{ROI} = 10\% \times 2.5 = 25\%$$

This decomposition highlights three general ways he can increase ROI: increase sales, decrease costs or decrease investment in operating assets. Jason decides to investigate these alternatives.

Increasing ROI

One alternative is to focus primarily on increased sales. The New Zealand division currently has idle capacity, and Jason would like to emphasise a new group of products. He believes that current capacity can support an increase in sales of $600 000 without requiring additional investment. The increased sales would increase operating income by $116 000. The expected return on sales would then be:

$$\$616\,000 \div \$5\,600\,000 = 11\%$$

and investment turnover would be:

$$\$5\,600\,000 \div \$2\,000\,000 = 2.8 \text{ times}$$

leading to an improved ROI slightly higher than that of the Australian division:

$$\$616\,000 \div \$2\,000\,000 = 30.8\% = 11\% \times 2.8$$

Alternatively, Jason could focus on reducing expenses. He believes that manufacturing costs could be reduced by as much as $100 000. He would implement this plan using kaizen costing; that is, by organising a team with members from marketing, accounting and engineering to analyse production activities and identify non-value-added activities that could be eliminated. Also, the products and manufacturing processes could be redesigned to reduce the number of parts or processes. If the team is successful and expenses are reduced by $100 000, operating income would be $600 000 instead of $500 000. This plan alone could increase return on sales to:

$$\$600\,000 \div \$5\,000\,000 = 12\%$$

and ROI would equal that of the Australian division:

$$12\% \times 2.5 = 30\%$$

Jason considers one more approach to increase ROI. He can reduce the New Zealand division's investment in operating assets. He knows that internal processes are inefficient; inventory and work in process are built up throughout different manufacturing areas. He would like to implement cellular production and just-in-time inventory practices. These modifications would allow the division to sell a small building currently in use. He believes that these actions would reduce operating assets to $1 667 000. The investment turnover would then be:

$$\$5\,000\,000 \div \$1\,667\,000 = 3 \text{ times}$$

and ROI would be:

$$10\% \times 3 = 30\%$$

Jason knows that increasing sales, reducing costs and changing production processes are all worthy long-term goals, but it will take a year or more to see the results of any of these plans. He would prefer to increase ROI within a shorter timeframe. Recently a competitor made an offer to sell the New Zealand division a component that is currently manufactured in-house. If Jason purchases the component, operating earnings would decrease, but he could easily sell the small building because most of it houses the production facility for the component. Investment turnover would still be three times, but return on sales would drop to 9 per cent ($450 000 ÷ $5 000 000) and thereby increase ROI to 27 per cent.

Choosing a plan of action

Jason decides to discuss his options with Renee Forsyth, the CFO for Computer Wizards. All of the plans he is considering require a great deal of time and effort. He believes that the strategies are sound but is uncertain whether his expectations can be met. An increase in sales depends in part on the continuing upswing of the economy. Cost reductions take time and concentrated effort on the part of employees. Changing the manufacturing process could take several years because a new floor plan would have to be laid out, teams would have to be established and work would be disrupted while implementing the new lines. Furthermore, the employees might need several months to work efficiently under the new system. The easiest choice is to outsource, and Jason knows that outsourcing would improve his ROI in the short run. However, he believes that focusing on in-house manufacturing cost reductions would be a better strategy for Computer Wizards in the long run. The company's use of ROI to measure performance discourages this type of strategy, so Jason wonders whether a different performance measure could be adopted that would better reward behaviour to benefit the overall entity.

Advantages and disadvantages of ROI

A division's ROI is easily compared with internal and external benchmarks and with other divisions' returns on investment. Holding managers responsible for some level of ROI reduces the tendency of managers to overinvest in projects. Another advantage of ROI is that its components motivate managers to increase sales, decrease costs and minimise asset investments.

However, ROI also discourages managers from investing in projects that reduce the division's ROI, even though they might improve the ROI for the overall entity or have only a short-term negative effect on a division's ROI, and over the long term would increase divisional ROI. As divisional ROI is often a key component of any incentive plan for divisional managers, then managerial decision making will be further sharpened by the impact on the personal rewards of the manager.

Suppose Jason had an opportunity to invest $1 750 000 in a project that would generate sales of $2 500 000 and a return on sales of 10 per cent (same as the original assumptions), or $250 000 operating income per year. The division's ROI including this investment would be:

$$\text{Investment turnover} = \$7\,500\,000 \div 3\,750\,000 = 2\,\text{times}$$

$$\text{ROI} = 10\% \times 2 = 20\%$$

Even though the investment reduces the division's ROI, Computer Wizards forgoes $250 000 if the project is not undertaken. If the level of risk and the return are comparable to projects from other divisions, Computer Wizards would prefer the benefits from this investment. When such favourable investments are not undertaken by the divisional manager because of the impact on short-term ROI (and hence may reduce the bonus of the manager) such decisions are often referred to as being dysfunctional.

Another disadvantage of ROI is that it does not incorporate measures of risk. Managers may increase ROI by investing in riskier projects, which often have higher returns than less-risky projects. If they are rewarded solely for increasing ROI, managers may undertake risky projects without considering the added risk to the entity. This problem arises more often when managers' time horizons are short; for example, when they are planning to retire or change jobs. In such cases, managers often prefer immediate improvements in performance measures.

Furthermore, when managers with short-time horizons evaluate projects based on ROI, they might inappropriately cut costs that provide long-term benefit for the entity. For example, they might cut R&D, maintenance or employee training; or forgo an investment project because of its short-term impact on divisional ROI. This form of decision-making would also be classified as dysfunctional.

ROI is typically calculated using financial accounting assets and income. Under financial accounting rules, assets are recorded at their original cost, and some intangible assets (such as brand name) are not recognised. These rules cause the investment in assets to be understated, particularly when the value of assets (such as property) has increased or when an entity has significant intangible assets. Understatements in assets cause ROI and investment turnover to be overstated. In addition, financial accounting rules measure revenues and costs in ways that can distort ROI. For example, overhead or support department costs might be allocated to a division using a method that does not reflect the division's use of resources. If the division's costs are understated or overstated, ROI will be distorted.

Despite these limitations organisations continue to use ROI to assist with the evaluation of divisional performance. Research conducted by Lillis[6] in an Australian setting identified four key factors which, if present, may overcome some of the limitations of ROI, particularly with respect to the tendency to forgo suitable investment opportunities due to a short-term negative impact on current ROI. These four factors, which seem to foster a more organisational-level culture, are:
1. long-range strategic planning
2. the effective use of multiple measures in combination
3. familiarity of central management with divisional operations
4. management service histories.

So, in settings where the use of ROI might be expected to facilitate dysfunctional decision making, but does not, we may find the existence of one or more of the above factors.

Residual income

Because of the disadvantages of ROI just described, some organisations prefer to use residual income to measure performance of sub units. **Residual income (RI)** measures the dollar amount of profits in excess of a required rate of return (commonly referred to as a capital charge). It is calculated as follows:

$$\text{Residual income} = \text{Operating income} - \text{Required rate of return} \times \text{Average operating assets}$$

Many entities set a minimum return expectation for operations and new investments. Residual income takes this expectation into consideration; it is the difference between actual operating income and the required income, given the entity's investment in operating assets and its required rate of return. The size of investment affects residual income less than ROI because it is used only to value the dollar amount of expected return, not as a denominator. Compared to ROI, residual income is less influenced by changes in investment. For a divisional manager evaluating the impact of an investment proposal on the division, with RI the benchmark is in effect the company's required rate of return. For a higher performing division this is likely to be below the current ROI for the division, removing the dysfunctional tendencies sometimes promoted by the sole use of ROI. Comprehensive example 2 demonstrates the calculation of residual income.

COMPREHENSIVE EXAMPLE 2

Residual income

Jason consults with Renee, and they decide to investigate other performance measures. The first option they consider is residual income. The required rate of return for the company is 10 per cent. Given the investment in operating assets, the required dollar amount of return for each division is as follows:

	New Zealand	Australia
Average operating assets	$2 000 000	$200 000
Required rate of return	10%	10%
Required return	$ 200 000	$ 20 000

Residual income is calculated as follows:

	New Zealand	Australia
Operating income	$500 000	$60 000
Required return (capital charge)	200 000	20 000
Residual income	$300 000	$40 000

Renee explains that the New Zealand division provides Computer Wizards with $300 000 in income above and beyond the required return. However, as they discuss the value of residual income as a performance measure, Jason suggests that it has some of the same problems as ROI because it is still based on operating income. In addition, Renee cannot compare results in the New Zealand division to Australia's because of the size difference in the two divisions. Therefore, they decide to consider other alternatives.

Advantages and disadvantages of residual income

The use of residual income does not penalise investment in projects with lower returns than current project returns. Suppose the New Zealand division invests $1 750 000 in new assets that generate annual sales of $2 500 000 and operating income of 10 per cent ($250 000). If this project is undertaken, the New Zealand division residual income will be:

Operating income ($500 000 + $250 000)	$750 000
Required return [($2 000 000 + $1 750 000) × 10%]	375 000
Residual income	$375 000

Because the project is expected to increase residual income by $75 000 ($375 000 – $300 000), managers would be motivated to invest in it. In general, when residual income is used as a performance measure, managers are willing to invest in any projects with returns equal to or greater than the required rate of return. With the use of RI, the current ROI of the division is not an influencing factor on decision making.

However, residual income has its own problems. Because it is an absolute dollar value, larger sub-units are more likely to have larger residual incomes. For Computer Wizards, the New Zealand division's residual income is much greater than that of the Australian division. As a result, managers find it difficult to compare performance across units.

A disadvantage it shares with ROI is that residual income increases as investment and costs decrease (holding sales constant). Therefore, managers may cut costs such as R&D, maintenance or employee training that likely have long-term benefits for the entity.

Another problem with residual income occurs if senior managers from each sub-unit estimate their own required rate of return; they have incentives to set a required rate of return that is too low. In turn, a low required rate of return encourages managers to invest in less-profitable projects. They may also invest in less-risky projects and forgo riskier projects that would be profitable for the overall entity. Because operating income is measured using financial accounting information, residual income suffers from the same earnings-related problems as ROI.

Economic value added

Economic value added (EVA®) is a type of residual income that incorporates a number of adjustments to reduce the disadvantages produced by residual income.[7] The basic EVA calculation follows.

$$EVA = \text{Adjusted after-tax operating income}$$
$$- \left[\text{Weighted average cost of capital} \times (\text{Adjusted total assets} - \text{Current liabilities}) \right]$$

The weighted average cost of capital (WACC) is calculated by analysing all sources of invested funds, including both debt and equity financing (valued as the opportunity cost to investors). It is the after-tax cost of all long-term financing for the entity or division. With EVA, each division can use its actual cost of capital, taking into consideration the industry and risk characteristics.

The adjustments made to develop the EVA calculation include substituting after-tax operating income for EBIT, which is consistent with using the (after-tax) weighted average cost of capital and also gives managers incentives to reduce taxes. Analysts and consultants recommend that organisations choose among 160 other adjustments to provide managers with incentives specific to the entity. One purpose of adjusting financial accounting income and assets is to minimise suboptimal decision making.

Measures used for internal purposes need not follow **accounting standards**, which are a set of accounting methods and disclosures used to prepare financial statements for external parties. Instead, the measures are created to reflect economic costs and benefits over time. For example, research costs, which must be recognised immediately as an expense under Australian or New Zealand Accounting Standards, are often capitalised for EVA calculations. This adjustment encourages managers to invest in R&D projects that have long-term value for the entity. The calculation of EVA is demonstrated in comprehensive example 3.

COMPREHENSIVE EXAMPLE 3

Economic value added

Jason and Renee next consider the use of EVA at Computer Wizards, and calculate EVA for each division. Jason develops the following information.

	New Zealand	Australia
Total assets	$2 000 000	$200 000
Operating income	$ 500 000	$ 60 000
Weighted average cost of capital	7.2%	10%
Current liabilities	$ 20 000	$ 5 000
After-tax operating income	$ 300 000	$ 40 000
Tax rate	40%	33.3%

Jason and Renee first calculate EVA without any adjustments beyond income taxes:

$$\text{EVA} = \text{Adjusted after-tax operating income} \\ - \left[\text{Weighted average cost of capital} \times (\text{Total assets} - \text{Current liabilities}) \right]$$

EVA New Zealand:
After-tax operating income $300 000
WACC × (Total assets − Current liabilities)
[7.2% × ($2 000 000 − $20 000)] 142 560
$157 440

EVA Australia:
After-tax operating income $ 40 000
WACC × (Total assets − Current liabilities)
[10% × ($200 000 − $5000)] 19 500
$ 20 500

Because EVA incorporates income taxes, incentive is provided to minimise taxes paid. In addition, the weighted average cost of capital is a more realistic capital charge than managers' subjective choices of required rates of return. The Australian division operates in a riskier business environment than the New Zealand division, which is reflected in its higher WACC.

Advantages and disadvantages of EVA

Several advantages of EVA result from the various adjustments made to personalise the measure to each entity. These adjustments provide specific incentives that align the goals of managers with owners. However, some disadvantages need to be considered as well. For example, the appropriateness of the specific cost of capital for a division or entity is a matter of judgement, as is the level of risk that has been incorporated. The adjustments are also a matter of judgement. We do not know how to perfectly measure economic revenues, costs or assets, and a variety of acceptable ways provide different incentives. Because EVA is so complex, consulting entities often must be used to determine the appropriate adjustments. This process can be expensive and time consuming. Moreover, because of this complexity, it might be argued that EVA is more suitable at higher levels in an organisation than at lower levels. A comparison of ROI, residual income and EVA is provided in comprehensive example 4.

COMPREHENSIVE EXAMPLE 4

Comparison of ROI, residual income and EVA

After completing these computations, Jason and Renee decide to examine the rankings of the two divisions using these three measures. Under ROI, the Australian division (30 per cent) appears to perform better than the New Zealand division (25 per cent). But under residual income and EVA, the New Zealand division outperforms the Australian division. They recognise that size has an effect on both residual income and EVA. Renee decides to use both ROI and EVA as performance measures. Jason suggests that Renee also consider the use of non-financial performance measures. He believes that increasing customer satisfaction should increase financial performance because repeat and new customers will increase revenues. Renee agrees that by focusing on customer satisfaction, any potential customer-related problems are likely to be discovered sooner, and agrees to give the measure further consideration.

Income-based performance evaluation in the public sector

As a result of public-sector management reforms, the performance of government-controlled entities is often monitored through a range of financial metrics. For example, return-on-asset ratios are commonly used to evaluate the performance of government-controlled water businesses. However the use of these ratios can be problematic given the use of fair-value measurement. Upward revaluations to water infrastructure assets can impact the reliability of between-period comparisons of the return-on-asset performance given the impact on depreciation charges and asset carrying values.[8] The relevance of return-on-asset measures for many government entities is questionable.

Consider, for example, hospitals whose underlying objective is to deliver high-quality healthcare services and patient care. In the interests of patient outcomes, it is important that managers make effective investments in new technologies and assets which expand their capacity. These investments enable their organisations to offer new and higher quality patient services. Accordingly, asset replacement ratios are often used to evaluate the performance of hospitals. These ratios compare the rate of capital investment in new assets against the rate of depreciation and/or amortisation. If a hospital consistently has asset replacement ratios of less than one, it can suggest that insufficient funds are being invested to maintain hospital assets.

Figure 18.3 provides an example of the use of asset replacement ratios by the Victorian Auditor-General's Office (VAGO) to evaluate the performance of hospitals in different jurisdictions within the state of Victoria.[9] While the average across the sector has been consistently above 1.0, there is a variance in the rate of asset replacement between rural, metropolitan and regional hospitals. The commentary provided by VAGO (2017) notes that the results for regional hospitals were distorted by the significant funds allocated to the Bendigo Health Care Group in 2016–17.

| FIGURE 18.3 | Physical asset replacement indicator for the public hospital sector, 2012–13 to 2016–17[10] |

Hospitals	2012–13	2013–14	2014–15	2015–16	2016–17	Average
Metropolitan average	1.05	1.35	1.51	2.95	0.82	1.54
Regional average	1.25	1.35	1.42	1.16	5.10	2.06
Rural average	1.46	1.21	1.03	0.63	0.81	1.03
Small rural average	0.76	1.00	1.57	0.78	0.66	0.95
Financial year average	1.09	1.32	1.48	2.33	1.74	1.59

18.4 Transfer pricing

LEARNING OBJECTIVE 18.4 Communicate alternative prices used for transferring goods and services within an entity.

In decentralised organisations, it is common for different business units to rely on other units within the entity for goods or services. A **transfer price** is the price used to record the revenues and costs of such transfers of goods or services between responsibility centres within an entity. The primary reasons for placing a transfer price on the cost of internally transferred goods and services include the following.

- Ensuring that internally transferred goods and services are used efficiently. Placing a price on internally received goods and services acts as a price signal to the receiving department. If these goods and services are not used efficiently, the receiving department's performance will be negatively affected.
- Enabling the performance of departments within a decentralised organisation to be evaluated reliably. The full costs of departments should include the value of any internally transferred goods and services.
- Promoting decision making by individual departmental managers that is consistent with the interests of the overall organisation.

The reliance on other internal business units for goods and services can often be more cost-effective than relying on external suppliers. Measurement of an appropriate transfer price for internally transferred goods and services can be difficult and may create conflict between departments. While internal transfer prices have no impact on the organisation's overall profit because no external parties have been involved in the transaction, they can still impact an individual department's apparent financial performance. Naturally, the manager of the selling department will want to maximise the transfer price to maximise their department's profit. The manager of the receiving department, on the other hand, will want to minimise the transfer price. As we will see, if transfer prices are set incorrectly, there may be situations in which departmental managers are making decisions that are good for their own department but detrimental to the organisation as a whole.

Transfer prices and conflicts among managers

When compensation is tied to the financial performance of sub-units, managers tend to overlook their contribution to the entire organisation and focus instead on how decisions affect their sub-unit's financial performance. Conflicts arise among managers, leading to suboptimal operating decisions.

Suppose Porcelain & More, a bathroom fixtures manufacturer, operates with three profit centres: taps, sinks and bathtubs. The tap department supplies mixer taps to the sinks and bathtubs departments. The sinks and bathtubs departments install the mixer taps before selling their finished products to external customers. The taps department can also sell the mixer taps to external customers for $20 per unit.

When taps are sold by the tap department to external customers, this department receives credit in its operating income for the entire contribution margin. How should the mixer taps be priced when they are transferred internally to the sink and bathtub departments? The manager of the taps department would like to recognise the same revenue that is recorded for external sales. However, managers from the sink and bathtub departments would like to record in their books only the variable cost for the mixer taps that are internally transferred. They have legitimate claims, because their departments are responsible for selling the completed sinks and bathtubs. The managers from the three departments are in conflict with each other. All of them would prefer to show high departmental profits and therefore would prefer to recognise most of the contribution for each product sold.

The following example illustrates what the contribution margins of the different departments of Porcelain & More would be if different transfer prices are used. For simplicity, the example assumes that all of the output of the taps department (40 000 mixer taps) is transferred internally to meet the requirements of sinks and bathtubs departments who each sell 20 000 completed products to external customers. Beyond the cost of the transferred taps, the sinks and bathtubs departments also incur their own variable costs to complete their department's production processes.

	Taps	Sinks	Bathtubs
Units produced/sold	40 000	20 000	20 000
Market price	$20	$75	$150
Variable cost	$10	$30	$ 75

First, let's assume that transfer price for tap sales to the sinks and bathtubs departments is set at the market price of $20 per unit. Notice how, from the perspective of the organisation as a whole, the revenue to the taps department ($800 000) is cancelled out as this revenue becomes part of the cost of the sinks ($400 000) and bathtubs ($400 000) departments. Such revenues from internal transactions are not recognised by the organisation as a whole because no external parties were involved in the transactions. *Example 1:* All output of taps department transferred to sinks and bathtubs departments at market price ($20)

	Taps		Sinks		Bathtubs		Total
Total revenue	$800 000	(40 000 × $20 transfer price)	$1 500 000	(20 000 × $75 external market price)	$3 000 000	(20 000 × $150 external market price)	
Variable costs	−$400 000	(40 000 × $10)	−$ 600 000	(20 000 × $30)	−$1 500 000	(20 000 × $75)	
Cost of transferred taps			−$ 400 000	(20 000 × $20 transfer price)	−$ 400 000	(20 000 × $20 transfer price)	
Contribution margin	$400 000		$ 500 000		$1 100 000		$2 000 000

Second, let's assume that the transfer price for tap sales between the taps department and sinks and bathtubs departments is set at the variable cost of $10 per unit. Again, notice how: 1. from the perspective of the organisation as a whole, the revenue to the taps department ($400 000) is cancelled out as this revenue becomes part of the cost of the sinks ($200 000) and bathtubs ($200 000) departments; and 2. regardless of the transfer price, the total contribution margin of the firm is the same (i.e. $2 000 000). While the overall result for the organisation is the same regardless of the transfer price, the contribution margins of the individual departments are significantly different. This will be a source of conflict between the departments of Porcelain & More.

Example 2: All output of taps department transferred to sinks and bathtubs departments at variable cost ($10)

	Taps		Sinks		Bathtubs		Total
Total revenue	(40 000 × $10 $400 000 transfer price)		$1 500 000	(20 000 × $75 external market price)	$3 000 000	(20 000 × $150 external market price)	
Variable costs	−$400 000	(40 000 × $10)	−$ 600 000	(20 000 × $30)	−$1 500 000	(20 000 × $75)	
Cost of transferred taps			−$ 200 000	(20 000 × $10 transfer price)	−$ 200 000	(20 000 × $10 transfer price)	
Contribution margin	$0		$ 700 000		$1 300 000		$2 000 000

Now let's assume that the sinks and bathtubs departments have been approached by an external supplier with an offer to supply the mixer taps for a discounted price of $18 per unit. If the internal transfer price of mixer taps had been set at the market price ($20), the managers of the sinks and bathtubs departments might be tempted to take up this offer. As illustrated below, the contribution margins of the sinks department would be each be $40 000 higher than compared to example 1 when the transfer price was set at the market price. However, the firm would be $320 000 worse off (i.e. $2 000 000 less $1 680 000 or $8 × 40 000). From the perspective of the firm, it is much more cost effective if the taps department manufacturers the mixer taps for $10 per unit than if an external supplier is paid $18 per unit. Again, this illustrates potential transfer pricing tensions between the interests of individual departments and the firm as a whole.

Example 3: Taps department produces zero mixer taps and sinks and bathtubs departments source all mixer taps from an external supplier for $18 per unit

	Taps	Sinks		Bathtubs		Total
Total revenue	$0	$1 500 000	(20 000 × $75 external market price)	$3 000 000	(20 000 × $150 external market price)	
Variable costs	$0	$ 600 000	(20 000 × $30)	$1 500 000	(20 000 × $75)	
Cost of externally acquired taps		−$ 360 000	(20 000 × $18 external price)	−$ 360 000	(20 000 × $18 external price)	
Contribution margin	$0	$ 540 000		$1 140 000		$1 680 000

Setting an appropriate transfer price

The measurement of appropriate internal transfer prices has been subject to much debate over many years. During this time, general rules, based on economic considerations have been established. The general rule to measure the minimum transfer price is:

Minimum transfer price = variable cost to produce/sell + any contribution margin forgone from the transfer

As the following illustrations highlight, whether or not there is any contribution margin forgone or opportunity cost from the transfer, depends on whether the selling division potentially has: 1. external customers for their products and services, and 2. spare capacity. These examples draw from the previous data concerning the operations of the Porcelain & More and their taps, sinks and bathtubs departments. Recall the taps department manufactures mixing taps for use by the sinks and bathtubs departments. The variable cost to produce these taps is $10 per unit. The mixer taps can also be sold to external customers for $20 per unit.

Example 1: taps department has no spare capacity and an external market for mixer taps exists

If the taps department has no spare capacity and mixer taps are required to be supplied to either the sinks or bathtubs departments, the taps department will forgo the contribution margin from sales to external customers. The taps department does not have capacity to meet both internal and external sales. The lost contribution margin from sales to external customers will be $10 given the selling price ($20) less the variable cost to produce the mixer taps ($10). If we add this forgone contribution margin to the variable cost ($10), which is the general rule in this circumstance, this will produce a minimum transfer price of $20. Note that this price is equal to the market price. This price ensures that the taps department is not penalised for having to give up sales to external parties if they are required to supply mixer taps to other internal departments. The general rule will not result in a price that is above the market price. If the transfer price was above the market price, the buying department would be inclined to use external suppliers.[11]

$$\text{Minimum transfer price} = \$10 + (\$20 - \$10) = \$20$$

Example 2: taps department has spare capacity and an external market for mixer taps exists

If the taps department has spare capacity and mixer taps are required to be supplied to either the sinks or bathtubs departments, the taps department will not need to give up any contribution margin from sales to external customers. The taps department has capacity to meet both internal and external sales. As a result, there will no opportunity cost or forgone contribution margin if internal transfers of mixer taps occur and the minimum transfer price will be equal to the variable cost to produce the mixer taps ($10). This price ensures that the taps department is able to recoup the variable cost of production. The taps department would be unlikely to be willing to sell mixer taps for anything less than the variable cost of production.

$$\text{Minimum transfer price} = \$10 + \$0 = \$10$$

While there are some merits to the use of the general transfer rule, it is problematic given that the price will vary depending on the supplying unit's capacity. Most managers prefer stable transfer prices across time. In addition, selling managers may regard a price equal to variable cost as unfair when excess capacity exists, because the purchasing department receives credit for the entire contribution margin for products that are essentially manufactured by both departments. Therefore, other transfer price polices are typically used.

The following methods are often used for setting transfer price policies in manufacturing and service organisations:

- market based
- cost based
- activity based
- dual rate
- negotiated.

Market-based transfer prices

The use of current prices in competitive markets is the simplest method of determining transfer prices. **Market-based transfer prices** are based on competitors' prices or on the supply-and-demand relationship. The use of market-based pricing has the added benefit of ensuring that the savings from manufacturing components internally are recognised by the supplying department. Doing so can help to promote capital investment decisions by the supplying department that are consistent with the long-term interests of the firm. As a variant, the selling unit might offer a discount on the market price to internal customers.

However, it is important to recognise that market-based transfer prices are most appropriate under a restrictive set of conditions. These conditions include the presence of a highly competitive market for the intermediate product so that the selling department can sell as much as it wants to outside customers and the purchasing department can buy as much as it wants from outside suppliers, all without affecting the price. These conditions are rarely met. When those conditions are met, the market price provides an objective value for intermediate products. The problem with market-based transfer prices is that information about underlying costs is not revealed.

Cost-based transfer prices

Cost-based transfer prices are based on the cost of the good or service transferred. Cost can be computed in different ways, ranging from variable costs to fully allocated costs. If a product has no external market because it is a subcomponent of another product, some type of cost-based transfer price is commonly used.

Suppose that the fixtures department of Porcelain & More usually produces about 40 000 sets of fixtures and incurs about $200 000 in manufacturing overhead cost during an accounting period. The average fixed cost per unit would be $5 ($200 000 ÷ 40 000 units). Under a full production cost transfer price policy, Porcelain & More could set a transfer price of $15 ($10 variable cost + $5 fixed cost). This transfer price allows each department to split the contribution margin that arises when fixtures are sold as part of sink and tub kits.

Cost-based transfer prices present several disadvantages. When products have an external market and departments are profit centres, the transfer price affects decisions about transferring internally or purchasing externally. This situation can lead to suboptimal decisions, such as the purchase of units from external providers shown in the earlier Porcelain & More example. In addition, when transfer prices include allocated fixed costs, managers in selling departments do not have as much incentive to reduce fixed costs. They can pass the responsibility for allocated fixed costs to another department through the transfer pricing policy.

Activity-based transfer prices

A variation of cost-based transfer prices is the use of **activity-based transfer prices**. Here, the purchasing unit is charged for the unit-level, batch-level and possibly some product-level costs for products transferred, plus an annual fixed fee that is a portion of the facility-level costs. Suppose the tubs department at Porcelain & More plans to buy enough fixtures internally so that it uses 20 per cent of the fixture department's capacity. Under activity-based transfer pricing, the tubs department could pay for the unit and batch costs of each fixture and also pay 20 per cent of the fixtures department facility-level costs. By making this lump sum payment, the tubs department essentially reserves some of the fixture department's capacity for units it will purchase internally.

An advantage of activity-based transfer pricing is that the purchasing department has an incentive to accurately project the number of units it will purchase internally. This accuracy enhances an entity's planning abilities. Suppose managers in the fixtures department believe that external sales will be forgone by selling 20 per cent of their fixtures to the tub department. Because they receive a fixed price from the tub department, they know ahead of time that they need to increase capacity to accommodate external sales. They can more easily plan for these changes.

However, because of uncertainty in demand, organisations may sometimes need to reallocate capacity to attain the highest contribution. In a changing business environment, departments should be allowed to subcontract with each other so that the departments with the best opportunities are using most of the capacity.

Dual-rate transfer prices

Dual-rate transfer prices allow the selling department to be credited for the market price, and the purchasing department to be charged the variable cost. When financial statements are consolidated at the end of the accounting period, adjustments are made so that overall organisational profit is accurately reported. This method provides appropriate information and incentives when the selling department has excess capacity. Also, it is most similar to a policy that uses an opportunity cost for the transfer price. A disadvantage of the method is that it overstates profitability at the sub-unit level, and managers may believe that the entity as a whole is more profitable than it actually is.

Negotiated transfer prices

Negotiated transfer prices are based on an agreement reached between the managers of the selling and purchasing departments. This method ensures that both managers have full information about costs and market prices, and that the transfer price provides appropriate incentives. A disadvantage of this method is that it usually requires more time because both managers prefer more contribution margin. Managers' time is valuable to the organisation for other responsibilities, and negotiation time may not be a high priority for the organisation as a whole. The strength of the negotiating skills of the managers may also affect the negotiated price. Comprehensive example 5 demonstrates the application of negotiated transfer prices.

Negotiated transfer prices

The New Zealand division of Computer Wizards produces computer monitors. These monitors are sold on the open market for $110 each or the Australian division uses them as part of a complete computer package. When the monitor is transferred internally, the entire computer package gives the entity a contribution margin of $415 each. The entity currently uses market price plus shipping as a transfer price. Jason is happy with this transfer price, but Cecelia has asked Renee to consider changing the policy, because her division shows lower earnings than it should. She would prefer to purchase monitors from Jason, but often purchases less expensive and lower quality monitors from an external vendor to improve her division's earnings.

The New Zealand division can produce 10 000 monitors per month and usually operates at 70 per cent capacity. The following data pertain to production at this level.

	Average cost
Direct materials	$25
Direct labour	15
Supplies	5
Total variable cost per monitor	45
Allocated fixed costs	50
Total average cost per monitor	$95

If a monitor is sold on the open market, the customer pays the shipping cost. The cost of shipping each monitor from New Zealand to Australia is about $10.

The New Zealand division is currently operating at 50 per cent of its capacity, substantially below normal. Jason would like to sell more monitors internally to help cover fixed costs. Both managers contact Renee, who tells them to negotiate a policy that is fair to both divisions. Jason would like to set a transfer price that is below the market price but above the variable cost, so that some of the fixed costs are covered by internal transfers. Cecelia would prefer to pay only the variable cost plus the shipping charge because the New Zealand division's fixed costs will not change if production increases, and workers would be idle part of the time without the internal transfers.

After negotiating for several weeks, the two managers go back to Renee for help. Renee has laid out the following information based on a selling price for the computer package of $950.

	Average cost
Direct materials	$240
Direct labour	75
Supplies	175
Total variable cost per monitor	490
Cost of monitor	110
Allocated fixed costs	$200
Total average cost per computer package	$800

Renee explains that, from Computer Wizard's perspective, the contribution margin on monitors sold externally is $65 ($110 − $45). When the monitor is transferred internally, the relevant cost to Computer Wizards is $45, the variable cost. The relevant contribution margin for the computer package is $415 ($950 − $490 − $45). When Cecelia purchases a monitor externally for $110, the contribution margin is $350 ($950 − $490 − $110). Therefore, corporate headquarters would prefer internal transfers over purchases from outside vendors.

Renee suggests that Cecelia pay Jason a flat amount to help cover fixed costs and also pay the variable cost for each monitor transferred. Jason agrees to this policy as long as the division operates with excess capacity. However, he points out that when the division lacks enough capacity to fill both external and internal orders, he will sell externally and forgo internal transfers to increase profits for the New Zealand division.

Renee calculates the difference in the entity-wide contribution margin when transferring monitors internally versus purchasing them externally at $65 ($415 − $350). This difference happens to be the same as the contribution margin for the New Zealand division when monitors are sold externally. Therefore, Jason and Cecelia are indifferent to whether sales take place internally or externally *when the New Zealand division is at capacity*. Meanwhile, both managers agree that developing a transfer price policy that suits not only both divisions but also the overall entity is more difficult than it first appeared.

18.5 Additional transfer price considerations

LEARNING OBJECTIVE 18.5 Calculate transfer prices and outline the issues associated with transfer pricing.

The preceding section addressed the incentives of managers for transfer prices between operating units. The following additional factors affect the choice of transfer prices.

International income taxes

In the case of multinational companies, transfers of goods and services occur between subsidiaries located in different countries around the world. The prices used for such transfers can be controversial given the ability for such organisations to manage their tax exposure through strategic transfer price decisions. An organisation with subsidiaries located in high-tax and low-tax countries could potentially charge a high transfer price in the low-tax countries so that most of the contribution margin arises where taxes are lowest (figure 18.4). To restrict entities' abilities to shift income in this manner, income tax regulations typically stipulate the use of market-based transfer prices. While global organisations rarely find themselves in breach of the law, this issue of taxation is attracting increased attention by authorities and governments around the world. To illustrate, Apple has used a transfer pricing method that enabled the firm to allocate profits internally and minimise its effective tax rate.[12] The details of international tax regulation are complex and beyond the scope of this text.

FIGURE 18.4	Apple's use of transfer pricing to allocate profits internally and minimise the effective tax rate

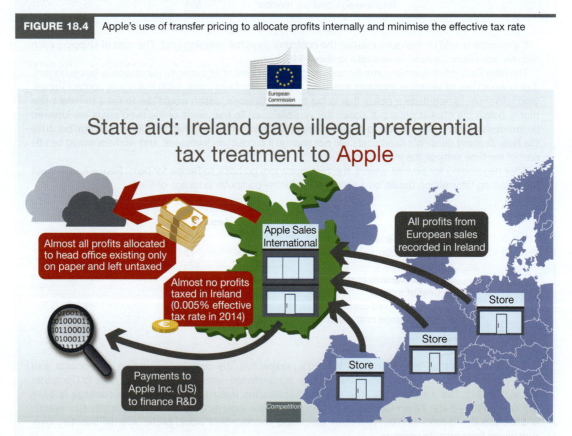

Transfer prices for support services

Many organisations set transfer prices for support services (also known as shared services). Their objective is to motivate efficient use and cost-effective production of internal support services such as accounting, printing, human resources and purchasing. When support departments provide services without charge to user departments, the user departments tend to use the support services inefficiently. In turn, inefficient use tends to encourage support departments to grow unnecessarily large. Transfer prices can encourage more efficient use of support services.

Transfer prices are often based on fully allocated costs and therefore include allocations of fixed support department costs and allocations from other support departments. As a result, the transfer prices can be high. High transfer prices can encourage user departments to outsource the support services. As we learned in the Porcelain & More example, outsourcing is not always beneficial to the entity as a whole. Outsourcing can cause internal services to be duplicated, resulting in excess capacity and inefficient use of resources.

Setting transfer prices for internal services

Because top managers prefer to have support services used efficiently, they want to set transfer prices that motivate this behaviour. The best transfer price policy is an opportunity cost approach. Each department is charged an amount that reflects the value of any opportunities forgone by not using the service for its next best alternative use.

Suppose that Computer Wizards' production and assembly equipment needs routine maintenance to prevent downtime during regular hours of operation. The maintenance department schedules its repair and maintenance time during lunch hours and at the end of each production shift. Currently, the maintenance department is operating close to capacity. Other departments need to schedule non-routine tasks, such as painting walls and repairing damaged flooring, well in advance. If a department wants maintenance personnel to hang pictures in an office, the value of the opportunity forgone might be the cost of hiring a contractor to provide routine maintenance on equipment or to paint walls. However, if the maintenance department has extra capacity and workers are idle part of the time, the opportunity cost of hanging pictures would be zero.

Implementing a transfer price policy based on opportunity costs is problematic because opportunities change over time with changes in demand and capacity. In addition, finding and valuing alternative uses for some services can be difficult. Therefore, organisations use transfer price policies for internal services similar to those used for transferring goods. Cost-based transfer prices range from variable costs to fully allocated costs. Market-based transfer prices are set at amounts that would be paid if the service were outsourced.

Some entities establish a price per job for each task, keep prices low on jobs they want to have performed internally, and set prices high on jobs that are considered unnecessary or inappropriate. Suppose the managers of Computer Wizards believe that the maintenance personnel should not be hanging pictures. They could set the transfer price for hanging pictures high enough to discourage other departments from asking the maintenance department to perform this service.

Transfer of corporate overhead costs

Another type of transfer price occurs when corporate overhead costs are allocated to other responsibility centres. Managerial performance rewards based on accounting profits can stimulate much discussion between corporate headquarters and profit centre managers about whether allocating overhead costs is appropriate, and whether the allocation plan and allocation bases are appropriate. Under responsibility accounting, managers should be held accountable only for costs that they control. Because they have little or no control over corporate costs, they should not be held responsible for those costs in performance evaluations.

Many organisations do allocate corporate headquarters costs. Sometimes these are considered a corporate tax and are allocated based on revenues or profitability. In this manner, sub-units operating under optimal circumstances absorb more overhead than sub-units with poor results because of economic or industry conditions that are not under managers' control.

SUMMARY

18.1 Explain how decision-making responsibility and authority relate to performance evaluation.

Centralised and decentralised entities

Centralised entities		Decentralised entities	
Advantages	**Disadvantages**	**Advantages**	**Disadvantages**
• Less monitoring of decisions • Decisions intended to benefit the overall entity • With complete information, timely and efficient decisions are made • Good for stable operations and economic conditions	• More monitoring, employees may be less motivated • Without complete information, poorer quality decisions • When knowledge from sub-units is required, slows decision-making • Not appropriate for dynamic processes and volatile economic conditions	• Timely decision making; appropriate for dynamic processes and unstable economic conditions • Decisions made by individuals having the most knowledge and expertise • Upper management can focus on organisational strategies • Decision-making authority and reward systems provide motivation at the sub-unit level	• Decisions may not meet organisational goals • Decisions may not be coordinated among sub-units • Decision makers may not understand or agree with organisational strategies • Lack of coordination may lead to duplication of products, services and effort

General versus specific knowledge

Decision authority is related to the type of knowledge within an entity.

18.2 Identify appropriate responsibility centres and explain how responsibility centres are used to measure, monitor and motivate performance.

Types of responsibility centres

- Cost centres
  - Discretionary cost centres
- Revenue centres
- Profit centres
- Investment centres

18.3 Calculate and outline the uses and limitations of return on investment, residual income and economic value added for monitoring performance.

Return on investment (ROI)

$$ROI = \frac{\text{Operating income}}{\text{Average operating assets}}$$

DuPont analysis

$$ROI = \left(\frac{\text{Revenue}}{\text{Average operating assets}} \right) \times \left(\frac{\text{Operating income}}{\text{Revenue}} \right)$$

$$ROI = \text{Investment turnover} \times \text{Return on sales}$$

Residual income

$$\text{Residual income} = \text{Operating income} - (\text{Required rate of return} \times \text{Average operating assets})$$

Economic value added (EVA)

$$EVA = \text{Adjusted after-tax operating income} \\ - \left[\text{Weighted average cost of capital} \times (\text{Total assets} - \text{Current liabilities}) \right]$$

Advantages and disadvantages

ROI is easier to compare across sub-units, but motivates suboptimal decisions, both in long-term investment and short-term cost cutting.

Residual income provides more appropriate investment incentives than ROI but is not comparable across sub-units.

EVA minimises suboptimal decision-making incentives but is complex to calculate and not comparable across sub-units.

18.4 Communicate alternative prices used for transferring goods and services within an entity.

Ideal transfer price

- Opportunity cost

Alternatives

- Cost-based transfer price
- Activity-based transfer price
- Market-based transfer price
- Dual-rate transfer price
- Negotiated transfer price

18.5 Calculate transfer prices and outline the issues associated with transfer pricing.

Uses

- Assign cost to goods and services transferred internally for financial reporting and income taxes
- Motivate efficient use of support services
- Allocate corporate overhead costs

Incentive issues

- Conflicts among managers
- Suboptimal decision making
- Managers should not be held responsible for costs over which they have no control
- International income taxes

KEY TERMS

accounting standards A set of accounting methods and disclosures typically used to prepare financial statements for external parties.

activity-based transfer prices A transfer pricing method in which the purchasing unit is charged for the unit-level, batch-level and possibly some product-level costs for products transferred, plus an annual fixed fee that is a portion of the facility-level costs.

cost-based transfer prices Transfer prices based on the cost of the good or service transferred. Cost can be computed in different ways, ranging from variable costs to fully allocated costs.

cost centres Responsibility centres in which managers are responsible only for the costs under their control.

dual-rate transfer prices Transfer prices in which the selling department is credited for the market price, and the purchasing department is charged the variable cost.

economic value added (EVA®) A type of residual income that incorporates a number of adjustments to reduce the disadvantages produced by using unadjusted residual income.

general knowledge Information about volume of sales or product prices when organisations sell few products; such information is usually easy to transfer from one person to the next.

investment centres Responsibility centres in which managers are responsible for the revenues, costs and investments under their control.

knowledge management (KM) Processes designed to enable organisations to find, manage and transfer important information and expertise.

market-based transfer prices Transfer prices based on competitors' prices or on the supply-and-demand relationship.

negotiated transfer prices Transfer prices based on an agreement reached between the managers of the selling and purchasing departments.

profit centres Responsibility centres in which managers are responsible for both revenues and costs under their control.

residual income (RI) Measures the dollar amount of profits in excess of a required rate of return.

responsibility accounting The process of assigning authority and responsibility to managers of sub-units, and then measuring and evaluating their performance.

responsibility centres Sub-units (segments, divisions or departments) in which managers are accountable for specific types of operating activities. Four common types of responsibility centres are cost centres, revenue centres, profit centres and investment centres.

return on investment (ROI) The ratio of operating income to average operating assets.

revenue centres Responsibility centres in which managers are responsible for the revenues under their control.

specific knowledge Detailed information about particular processes, customers or products; such information is costly to transfer within the entity.

transfer price The price used to record revenue and cost when goods or services are transferred between responsibility centres in an entity.

SELF-STUDY PROBLEMS

SELF-STUDY PROBLEM 1 ROI; residual income; EVA

Outdoor Express is a large manufacturer of recreational equipment. Performance of the camping division is measured as an investment centre because the managers make all the decisions about investments in operating equipment and space. Following is financial information for the camping division:

Average operating assets	$2 000 000
Current liabilities	500 000
Operating income	300 000

Camping division's required rate of return is 12 per cent, but Outdoor Express's weighted average cost of capital is 9 per cent, and the tax rate is 30 per cent.

Required

(a) Calculate return on investment for the camping division.
(b) Calculate residual income for the camping division.
(c) Calculate EVA for the camping division.
(d) Briefly discuss the advantages and disadvantages of each method.

SOLUTION TO SELF-STUDY PROBLEM 1

(a) $\text{ROI} = \dfrac{\text{Net operating income}}{\text{Average operating assets}} = \dfrac{\$300\,000}{\$2\,000\,000} = 15\%$

(b) Residual income = Net operating income − (Required rate of return × Investment)
$$= \$300\,000 - (12\% \times \$2\,000\,000) = \$300\,000 - \$240\,000 = \$60\,000$$

(c) EVA = After-tax operating income − [Weighted average cost of capital
× (Total assets − Current liabilities)]
$$= [\$300\,000 \times (1 - 0.30)] - [9\% \times (\$2\,000\,000 - \$500\,000)]$$
$$= \$210\,000 - \$135\,000 = \$75\,000$$

(d) ROI and residual income motivate managers to reduce costs and investment, whereas EVA provides incentives to invest as long as the return is equal to or greater than the required rate of return. In addition, ROI and residual income do not include taxes, so no incentive is provided for managers to minimise taxes. EVA can be adjusted for intangibles such as leases and R&D spending. Therefore, it can be designed to minimise managers' abilities to artificially improve the performance measure.

SELF-STUDY PROBLEM 2 Transfer price; excess versus full capacity; outsourcing

The Perth division of Aeronautic Controls (AC) produces a digital thermometer. The thermometer can be sold on the open market for $180 each, or it can be used by the Brisbane division in the production of a temperature control gauge that has a unit contribution margin of $140 (given that the digital thermometer is transferred at variable cost plus shipping).

The Perth division is currently operating at 70 per cent of its capacity of 2000 digital thermometers per month. Following are average costs per unit at this level of capacity:

	Average cost
Direct materials	$ 50
Variable supplies	10
Fixed costs	100
Total average cost per thermometer	$160

If a digital thermometer is sold on the open market, the customer pays the shipping cost. The cost of shipping a digital thermometer from Perth to Brisbane is $15.

Required

(a) What is the best transfer price for AC overall if a digital thermometer is transferred to Brisbane and the Perth division is operating at 70 per cent of capacity?

(b) What is the best transfer price for AC overall if a digital thermometer is transferred to Brisbane, but the Perth division is operating at full capacity and the digital thermometer could have been sold on the open market?

(c) With respect to your responses to parts (a) and (b) above, briefly outline the relevance of 'capacity' in transfer pricing situations.

SOLUTION TO SELF-STUDY PROBLEM 2

(a) When the Perth division has excess capacity (30 per cent in this case), the transfer price should be the variable cost of $75 (direct materials of $50 plus supplies of $10 and shipping of $15).

(b) If the Perth division could sell all of its thermometers on the open market, the transfer price should be the market price of $180 plus $15 shipping = $195.

(c) The extent of capacity in the selling division is relevant when deciding an ideal outcome with respect to transfer pricing. Capacity introduces the concept of opportunity cost into transfer pricing.

As determined in (a) above, when the Perth division has excess capacity the ideal transfer price is the variable cost of $75 (including shipping). However, when the Perth division is at full capacity (with an option to sell outside), the ideal transfer price would be $195. This ensures the Perth division is not disadvantaged (through loss of contribution margin) by internal sales.

In reality, organisations do not have the luxury of considering the ideal price for each individual transaction. They will develop a transfer pricing policy which includes a transfer pricing method (and rules about sourcing autonomy) that will hopefully produce an ideal outcome as often as possible.

The Brisbane division might find an external vendor that could produce the digital thermometer at a cost less than the transfer price, but that would decrease AC's overall contribution margin. In addition, the Brisbane division could forgo special orders that would have a positive contribution margin for AC if the division uses the internal transfer price to determine whether to accept the order.

QUESTIONS

18.1 Explain the differences between general and specific knowledge. Give an example of an industry where knowledge is quite general and an example of an industry that requires specific knowledge. **LO1**

18.2 Explain why organisational form may vary if specific knowledge versus general knowledge is needed for decision making. **LO1**

18.3 Identify the four different types of responsibility centres and explain the general objectives of each. **LO2**

18.4 A national company, Fast Print, decided to expand into several developing countries. The company has been managed under a centralised organisational form, but is considering changing to a decentralised form. List the advantages and disadvantages of making this change. **LO2**

18.5 Explain how return on investment (ROI) is calculated and how it can be decomposed into two financial measures. **LO3**

18.6 Explain how and why the use of ROI for performance evaluation can cause managers to make decisions that could be harmful to an entity in the long run. **LO3**

18.7 Explain how residual income is calculated, and define required rate of return in your own words. **LO3**

18.8 Explain why the use of residual income for performance evaluation provides better incentives in some ways than ROI, but still causes managers to make some decisions that could be harmful to an entity in the long run. **LO3**

18.9 Explain how EVA differs from residual income. **LO3**

18.10 An organisation's plant in Queensland manufactures a product that is shipped to a branch in Tasmania for sale. Does it make any difference which branch (each is a profit centre) is charged for the cost of transportation? Explain. **LO2, 4**

18.11 Suppose transfer prices are set at market prices and a manager who previously purchased internally begins to purchase externally. Explain what it means to say that the outsourcing decision might have been suboptimal. **LO4**

18.12 Describe as many different methods for setting transfer prices as you can. **LO4**

18.13 Cost allocation has no impact on the transfer price set. Discuss. **LO4**

18.14 'Transfer pricing is a waste of an entity's resources; it all gets eliminated on consolidation.' Discuss. **LO4**

18.15 Why do you consider that taxation authorities require an international transfer price to be set based on an arm's length transaction? **LO4**

18.16 At a recent management meeting at Skyward Industries, the Transport Division manager was heard to say 'this transfer pricing is a waste of time — at the end of the year all the internal transactions are eliminated on consolidation in the financial reports'. Comment on this statement. **LO4**

EXERCISES

18.17 Residual income; ROI; EVA **LO3**

The following selected data pertain to Garfield Landscaping for last year.

Sales	$2 000 000
Variable costs	$1 200 000
Traceable fixed costs	$ 200 000
Average invested capital (assets)	$3 000 000
Current liabilities	$ 200 000
Required rate of return	15%
Marginal tax rate	36%
Weighted average cost of capital	12%

Required

(a) Calculate the residual income.
(b) Calculate the return on investment.
(c) Calculate the economic value added.

18.18 ROI; residual income; breakeven point; contribution margin **LO3**

Mirror Industries laminating division, BrightShine, incurred the following costs and expenses in the last period.

	Variable	Fixed
Direct materials	$200 000	
Direct labour	150 000	
Factory overhead	70 000	$42 000
General, selling and administrative	30 000	48 000
Totals	$450 000	$90 000

During the period, BrightShine produced 300 000 units of laminated board, which were sold for $2 each. Mirror's investment in BrightShine was $500 000 and $700 000 at the beginning and ending of the year respectively. BrightShine's weighted average cost of capital is 15 per cent.

Required

(a) Determine BrightShine's return on investment for the year.

(b) Calculate BrightShine's residual income (loss) for the year.

(c) How many laminated boards did BrightShine have to sell during the year to break even?

(d) What was BrightShine's contribution margin for the year?

18.19 EVA for segments   **LO3**

Following is information for the Fulcrum Company's three business segments located in Europe.

	Segment A	Segment B	Segment C
Pre-tax operating income	$ 8 000 000	$ 4 000 000	$ 6 000 000
Current assets	8 000 000	6 000 000	8 000 000
Long-term assets	32 000 000	26 000 000	16 000 000
Current liabilities	4 000 000	2 000 000	3 000 000

Fulcrum's applicable tax rate for the segments is 30 per cent, and its weighted average cost of capital for each segment is 10 per cent.

Required

Determine the segment with the highest EVA.

18.20 ROI, EVA, residual income   **LO3**

Senior management at Harriot Industries, an Italian-based fashion house and cosmetics company, have been engaged in a debate around the best key financial measure relevant to evaluating the performance of senior executives and divisional managers. Currently, the performance of senior managers and divisional managers is based on return on investment (ROI), which forms the basis of the bonus payments, provided ROI increases are achieved each year.

The main source of tension seems to be that some of the accounting staff are pushing for the use of economic value added (EVA) or, at the very least, residual income (RI) to be used at both the senior executive and divisional levels.

You have been asked to contribute some views. On a recent visit to the head office of Harriot Industries you were able to access details on a printout from a digital whiteboard that represented a discussion about performance measures and a potential investment project in the Logistics Division. Some of this material is provided below.

Investment project: Logistics Division

Project outlay	$4 500 000
NPV	$1 200 000
Average ROI in first two years	10%
Average ROI over project life	12%
Current ROI of Logistics Division	16% p.a.
Current cost of capital and hurdle rate	9%

Required

Using the information provided in the table, demonstrate (perhaps including calculations) the key arguments that might be put forward to support the view that the sole use of return on investment (ROI) may be *inappropriate*, particularly at the divisional level.

18.21 ROI; residual income; explaining the better measure   **LO3**

The following financial data are for the evaluation of performance for Sandy Point Construction:

Average operating assets	$500 000
Net operating income	$65 000
Minimum required rate of return	10%

Sandy Point Construction currently uses return on investment to evaluate investment centre managers. An accounting student from the local university suggested to the controller that residual income could be a better performance measure.

Required

(a) Calculate ROI for Sandy Point Construction.

(b) Calculate residual income for Sandy Point Construction.

(c) Write a brief memo to the controller explaining why residual income is a better performance measure.

18.22 Lease versus buy decision; ROI; residual income; EVA; manager incentives   **LO3**

Refer to the information in problem 18.21. The manager of Sandy Point Construction is considering a new project. She can buy or lease equipment that will allow the quicker construction and erection of frames on-site. The purchase price of the equipment is $150 000 or the cost to lease is $2000 per month. She estimates the return (incremental revenues minus incremental expenses, including lease cost) to be $40 000 per year. She knows that purchasing the equipment will increase the value of average operating assets. If she leases the equipment, expenses will increase, but not assets. In other words, the lease will be accounted for as an operating lease. Although it is more cost effective to purchase the equipment, she has decided to lease it.

Required

(a) Calculate the new ROI if the equipment is (i) purchased, or (ii) leased.

(b) Calculate the new residual income if the equipment is (i) purchased, or (ii) leased.

(c) One of the adjustments that can be made using EVA is to treat all operating lease costs as if they were purchases — in other words, to capitalise the lease. If Sandy Point Construction used EVA with this adjustment, how might the manager's incentives and behaviour change? Explain.

18.23 ROI; transfer prices; taxes; employee motivation   **LO3, 5**

Fowler Electronics produces colour plasma screens in its Bien Hoa plant in Vietnam. The screens are then shipped to the entity's plant in Sturt, South Australia, where they are incorporated into finished televisions. Although the Bien Hoa plant never sells plasma screens to any other assembler, the market for them is competitive. The market price is $750 per screen.

Variable costs to manufacture the screens are $350. Fixed costs at the Bien Hoa plant are $2 000 000 per period. The plant typically manufactures and ships 10 000 screens per period to the Sturt plant. Taxes in Vietnam amount to 30 per cent of pre-tax income. The Bien Hoa plant has total assets of $20 000 000.

The Sturt plant incurs variable costs to complete the televisions of $110 per set (in addition to the cost of the screens). The Sturt plant's fixed costs amount to $4 000 000 per period. The 10 000 sets produced each period are sold for an average of $2500 each. For Sturt, the tax rate is 45 per cent of pre-tax income. The Sturt plant has total assets of $30 000 000.

Required

(a) Determine the return on investment for each plant if the screens are transferred at variable cost.

(b) Determine the return on investment for each plant if the screens are transferred at market price.

(c) To reduce taxes, will Fowler prefer a transfer price based on cost or market price? Explain.

(d) Will the top managers in each plant prefer to use cost or market price as the transfer price? Explain.

(e) How would you resolve potential conflict over the transfer price policy?

18.24 Transfer price; sale to outside versus inside customer   **LO4, 5**

The Enviro division of Solar Sun produces solar panels, 20 per cent of which are sold to the Energy Plus division of Solar Sun and the remainder to outside customers. Solar Sun treats its divisions as profit centres and allows division managers to choose their sources of sale and supply. Corporate policy requires that all interdivisional sales and purchases be recorded at variable cost as the transfer price. Enviro division's estimated sales and standard cost data for 2019, based on its full capacity of 100 000 units are as follows:

	Energy Plus	Outsiders
Sales	$ 900 000	$8 000 000
Variable costs	(900 000)	(3 600 000)
Fixed costs	(300 000)	(1 200 000)
Gross margin	$(300 000)	$3 200 000
Unit sales	20 000	80 000

Enviro has an opportunity to sell the 20 000 units to an outside customer at a price of $75 per unit on a continuing basis. Energy Plus can purchase its requirements from an outside supplier for $85 per unit.

Required

Assuming that Enviro division desires to maximise its gross margin, should Enviro accept the new customer and drop its sales to Energy Plus for 2019? Why?

18.25 Choice of transfer price   **LO4, 5**

The following information relates to a new computer chip that Hand Held has developed for its new mobile phone:

Chip division		
Market price of finished chip to outsiders	$	24
Variable cost per unit		12
Contribution margin	$	12
Total contribution for 30 000 units	$360 000	
Mobile phone division		
Market price of finished products	$	128
Variable costs:		
From chip division		12
Other direct materials		50
Mobile phone division		
Assembly		38
Packaging		20
Contribution margin	$	8
Total contribution for 20 000 units	$160 000	

The variable costs of the mobile phone division will be incurred whether it buys from the chip division or from an outside supplier.

Required

(a) What is the highest price that the managers of the mobile phone division would want to pay the chip division for the chip? Explain.
(b) If the chip division is working at full capacity and cannot produce additional units, what transfer price for the chip would be best for the entity as a whole? Explain.
(c) If the chip division is not operating at capacity and has no prospect of reaching capacity, what is the lowest price its managers would typically be willing to sell chips to the mobile phone division?

18.26 Transfer pricing   **LO4, 5**

Georgina Chan is the chief financial officer of Colorado Pty Ltd, which has three interdependent divisions where, on average, about 30 per cent of the output of one division is transferred to one of the other divisions. She is currently dealing with a dispute within the accounting office about the best way to treat transfer pricing within the company. The chief executive officer has advised that any change to the policy should not compromise what is best for the company overall.

Senior accountant Andy Chan says 'as we are a highly decentralised firm, the only way to go is to use market price as the key method and allow sourcing autonomy'.

Meanwhile, graduate accountant Roger Singh says 'I disagree. If we go with full cost plus a 15 per cent mark-up and no sourcing autonomy, that would be best'.

Required

State one advantage and one disadvantage of each proposed policy and advise which policy you think would serve the company best. Briefly explain.

PROBLEMS

18.27 Transfer price; incentives for internal services   **LO4, 5**

Avra Valley Services has two divisions, Computer Services and Management Advisory Services. Both divisions work for external customers and, in addition, work for each other. Fees earned by Computer Services from external customers were $400 000 in 2019. Fees earned by Management Advisory Services from external customers were $700 000 in 2019. Computer Services worked

3000 hours for Management Advisory Services in 2019, and Management Advisory Services worked 1200 hours for Computer Services. The total costs of external services performed by Computer Services were $220 000, and for Management Advisory Services costs were $480 000.

Required

(a) Determine the operating income for each division and for the entity as a whole if the transfer price from Computer Services to Management Advisory Services is $50 per hour, and the transfer price from Management Advisory Services to Computer Services is $60 per hour.

(b) The manager of Computer Services has found another entity willing to provide the same services as Management Advisory Services at $50 per hour. All of the employees in both units are guaranteed 40-hour working weeks. Currently, Management Advisory Services has idle capacity because of an economic downturn. Calculate the change in operating income for the entity as a whole if Computer Services uses outsourced services instead of using Management Advisory Services.

(c) Recommend a transfer price policy that would provide incentives to use the internal services. Explain your recommendation.

(d) Discuss possible qualitative factors that might affect the attractiveness of the outsourcing option.

18.28 Choice of transfer price; fairness to managers   **LO4, 5**

Prem International has two large subsidiaries: Oil and Chemical. Oil is an oil-refining entity, and its main product is petrol. Chemical produces and sells a variety of chemical products. Chemical owns a polystyrene processing plant next to Oil's refinery. The polystyrene plant was built at the same time that Oil built a benzene plant at the refinery. Benzene is the raw material needed by Chemical to produce polystyrene. Chemical's managers believe they can sell 100 million kilograms of polystyrene per year, which is less than full capacity. Following are Chemical's expected revenues and costs for the polystyrene plant (volume is measured in weight because weight is not affected by temperature):

	Per kg
Selling price	$0.30
Costs: Benzene (to be purchased from Oil)	$?
Variable production costs	0.03
Fixed production costs	0.05

Oil can operate at full capacity and sell all of the petrol it produces. Following are Oil's expected revenues and costs for the production of petrol:

	Per kg
Selling price	$0.16
Costs: Crude oil	$0.06
Variable production costs	0.02
Fixed production costs	0.07

For every kilogram of benzene that Oil produces, it will forgo selling a kilogram of petrol. However, 100 million kilograms per year would be only a small portion of total volume at the refinery. Following are Oil's expected revenues and costs for the production of benzene (these costs include the costs of refining the crude oil):

	Per kg
Selling price (to Chemical)	$?
Costs: Crude oil	$0.06
Variable production costs	0.04
Fixed production costs	0.09

Required

(a) On an entity-wide basis, should Prem International produce polystyrene this year? Why?

(b) Using the usual quantitative rules for short-term decisions, what is the maximum price that Chemical's managers would be willing to pay for benzene?

(c) Would Chemical's managers be willing to pay the maximum transfer price calculated in part (b)? Why?

(d) Using the usual quantitative rules for short-term decisions, what is the minimum price that Oil's managers would be willing to receive for benzene?

(e) Would Oil's managers be willing to receive the minimum transfer price calculated in part (d)? Why?

(f) What transfer price might be fair to the managers of both subsidiaries? Explain.

18.29 **Transfer price; entity versus division profit; idle capacity**   **LO4, 5**

The furniture division of International Woodworking purchases timber and makes tables, chairs and other wood furniture. Most of the timber is purchased from the Port Angeles Mill, also a division of International Woodworking. The furniture division and the Port Angeles Mill are profit centres. The furniture division manager proposed a new Danish-designed chair that will sell for $150. The manager wants to purchase the timber from the Port Angeles Mill. Production of 800 chairs is planned using capacity in the furniture division that is currently idle. The furniture division can purchase the timber for each chair from an outside supplier for $60. International Woodworking has a policy that internal transfers are priced at variable cost plus allocated fixed costs. Assume the following costs for the production of one chair:

Port Angeles Mill		Furniture division	
Variable cost	$40	Variable costs:	
Allocated fixed cost	30	Timber: Port Angeles Mill	$ 70
Fully absorbed cost	$70	Furniture division variable costs:	
		Manufacturing	75
		Selling	10
		Total variable cost	$155

Required

(a) Assume that the Port Angeles Mill has idle capacity and would incur no additional fixed costs to produce the required timber. Would the furniture division manager buy the timber for the chair from the Port Angeles Mill, given the existing transfer price policy? Why?

(b) Calculate the contribution margin for the entity as a whole if the manager decides to buy from the Port Angeles Mill and is able to sell 800 chairs.

(c) What transfer price policy would you recommend if the Port Angeles Mill always has idle (excess) capacity? Explain why this transfer price policy provides incentives for the managers to act in the best interests of the entity as a whole.

(d) Explain how the idle capacity affects the recommendation in part (c).

18.30 **ROI; residual income; EVA; effect on investment decision; performance evaluation**   **LO3**

Strong Welding Equipment Company produces and sells welding equipment nationally and internationally. Following is information about two divisions and amounts are shown in US dollars.

	Brazil	US
Invested capital (total assets)	$4 000 000	$400 000
Net operating income	$1 000 000	$120 000
Required rate of return	10%	10%
Weighted average cost of capital	9%	9%
Current liabilities	$ 80 000	$ 10 000
After-tax income	$ 600 000	$ 80 000

Required

(a) Calculate each division's ROI.

(b) Calculate each division's residual income.

(c) Calculate each division's EVA.

(d) Suppose the Brazilian division had an opportunity to invest $3 500 000 in a project that would generate sales of $5 000 000 and return on sales of 10 per cent, or $500 000. Would the division manager be likely to undertake this project if he or she is evaluated using ROI? Explain.

(e) Recommend a performance evaluation measure that would increase the managers' incentives to make decisions that would be in the best interests of the owners.

18.31 Choosing type of responsibility centre; support cost allocation; ROI   **LO2, 3**

The ATCO Company purchased the Dexter Company three years ago. Prior to the acquisition, Dexter manufactured and sold plastic products to a wide variety of customers. Since becoming a division of ATCO, Dexter only manufactures plastic components for products made by ATCO's Macon division. Macon sells its products to hardware wholesalers.

ATCO's corporate management gives the Dexter division management a considerable amount of authority in running the division's operation. However, corporate management retains the authority for decisions regarding capital investments, price setting of all products, and the quantity of each product to be produced by the Dexter division.

ATCO has a formal performance evaluation program for the management of all of its divisions. The performance evaluation program relies heavily on each division's return on investment. The accompanying statement of profit or loss of the Dexter division provides the basis for the evaluation of Dexter's divisional management.

The corporate accounting staff prepare all of the divisions' financial statements. The corporate general services costs are allocated on the basis of sales dollars, and the computer department's actual costs are apportioned among the divisions on the basis of use. The net division investment includes division fixed assets at net book value (cost less depreciation), division inventory, and corporate working capital apportioned to the division on the basis of sales dollars.

Dexter division of ATCO Company		
Statement of profit or loss		
for the year ended 31 October (in thousands of dollars)		
Sales		$4 000
Costs and expenses:		
Direct materials	$ 500	
Direct labour	1 100	
Factory overhead	1 300	
Total	2 900	
Less: Increase in inventory	350	
Cost of sales		2 550
Engineering and research		120
Shipping and receiving		240
Division administration:		
Manager's office	210	
Cost accounting	40	
Personnel	82	
Total division administration		332
Corporate headquarters costs:		
Computer	48	
General services	230	
Total corporate headquarter costs		278
Total costs and expenses		3 520
Divisional operating income		$ 480
Net plant investment		$1 600
Return on investment		30%

Required

(a) Discuss the financial reporting and performance evaluation program of ATCO Company as it relates to the responsibilities of the Dexter division.

(b) Based upon your response to part (a), recommend appropriate revisions of the financial information and reports used to evaluate the performance of Dexter's divisional management. If you conclude that revisions are not necessary, explain why they are not needed.

18.32 Transfer pricing   **LO4, 5**

Sunshop Books is a multi-divisional book company that listed on the stock exchange about three years ago. Like many in the industry, Sunshop started out in the 1980s as a single-site suburban bookstore. Company CEO Lewis Negus has been in the role for three years, having joined the company around the time of its stock exchange listing. It was expected that the listing would provide much needed capital to enable the company to compete in what was becoming a rapidly changing and dynamic environment due to:

- continual merger and acquisition activity
- developments in technology such as e-readers and e-books as well as in the development of digital applications
- the financial difficulties experienced by industry participants particularly in the retail sector. The company is currently structured around three main divisions as follows.
- *Publishing:* This division publishes educational textbooks, adult fiction and non-fiction books, and children's books. Sunshop has a strong reputation for producing educational texts for the school and university markets.
- *Retail:* This division grew out of the original shop. Sunshop owns a number of specialist bookshops itself; with a focus on developing close links with customers. Of course, the retail shops also served as an outlet for many of the books published by the Publishing division. As well as owning its own shops, Sunshop had also taken an ownership stake in a number of specialist retail bookstore chains.
- *Technologies-based division:* This division focuses on technological applications and works closely with the Publishing division in particular. This includes developing technological content to support the hardcopy textbooks produced by the Publishing division. For example, a recent project included the development of smart-card technology containing interactive software that enables students to self-test on content in the specific chapters of an auditing text.

Each divisional manager is evaluated on the basis of return on investment along with a mix of other measures. Bonuses are paid on the basis of ROI performance alone.

Transfer pricing issues

While senior management valued divisional manager autonomy and decision making, they felt the organisational interests should normally prevail. To this end, the key components of the company's transfer pricing policy were:

- all transfers would occur at full costs plus a mark-up of 10 per cent
- there would be no sourcing autonomy; transacting internally would be the first priority
- divisions would be permitted to use any spare capacity to meet external demand.

The manager of the Technologies-based division — Carly Taylor — has raised concerns about the policy. Carly is proud of the innovation and creativity that the technological developments the division has been able to generate, particularly in the last two years. This has resulted in an increase in demand for their services from external customers including other book publishers and educational institutions. Carly argues that her divisional ROI would be higher if she had more autonomy to service outside customers. She says 'full costs plus 10 per cent just does not give us enough of a return . . . we could be earning twice the profit on outside work'.

Required

(a) Evaluate the current transfer pricing system (including consideration of the strengths and limitations).
(b) What changes would you make to help address the limitations you identified? How would these changes be an improvement on the current system?

ENDNOTES

1. Henderson, R 2015, What gets measured gets done. Or does it? Forbes. 8 June. https://www.forbes.com/sites/ellevate/2015/06/08/what-gets-measured-gets-done-or-does-it/#5f00d01c13c8.
2. Davidson, S, De Filippi, P & Potts, J 2018, Blockchains and the economic institutions of capitalism. *Journal of Institutional Economics*, p. 1–20.
3. Eyers, J 2018, ASX blockchain to go live at end of 2020. *Financial Review*. 27 April. https://www.afr.com/technology/asx-blockchain-to-go-live-at-end-of-2020-20180427-h0zcgx.
4. Gupta, B, Iyer, LS & Aronson, JE 2000. Knowledge management: practices and challenges. *Industrial management & data systems, 100*(1), pp. 17–21.
5. Inkinen, H 2016, Review of empirical research on knowledge management practices and firm performance. *Journal of knowledge management, 20*(2), pp. 230–257.
6. Lillis, A 1992, 'Sources of influence on capital expenditure decisions: a contextual study of accounting performance measurement', *Management Accounting Research*, 3, pp. 213–27.
7. EVA is a registered trademark of Stern Stewart & Co. More information can be found at www.sternstewart.com.

8. Pawsey, N & Crase L 2013, The mystique of water pricing and accounting. *Economic Papers: A journal of applied economics and policy, 32*(3), pp. 328–339.
9. VAGO (2017). Results of 2016-17 Audits: Public Hospitals. https://www.audit.vic.gov.au/report/results-2016-17-audits-public-hospitals?section=32664.
10. ibid.
11. Adams, L & Drtina, R 2008, Transfer pricing for aligning divisional and corporate decisions. *Business Horizons, 51*(5), pp. 411–417.
12. Sadiq, K 2016, European Commission warns multinationals as Apple order to pay €13 billion in tax. *The Conversation.* 31 August. https://theconversation.com/european-commission-warns-multinationals-as-apple-ordered-to-pay-13-billion-in-tax-64657.

ACKNOWLEDGEMENTS

Photo 18A: © Daxiao Productions / Shutterstock.com
Photo 18B: © Tino Mager / Shutterstock.com
Figure 18.3: © Victorian Auditor-Generals Office
Figure 18.4: © European Union, 1995–2018

CHAPTER 19

The balanced scorecard and strategy maps

LEARNING OBJECTIVES

After studying this chapter, you should be able to:

19.1 understand how financial and non-financial measures are used to evaluate organisational performance

19.2 communicate the role of strategy maps in the balanced scorecard process

19.3 evaluate and develop a balanced scorecard

19.4 explain how a balanced scorecard is implemented

19.5 identify and communicate the strengths and weaknesses of the balanced scorecard.

IN BRIEF

Successful entities adopt a strategic decision-making process to ensure that strategies and operating activities are aligned with the organisation's vision and core competencies. They also engage in continuous improvement by monitoring and learning from the results of their strategies and operations. Accountants develop and utilise performance measurement systems which track a variety of financial and non-financial measures to monitor results. A commonly-used performance measurement system design is the balanced scorecard. The balanced scorecard is an integrated, formal approach for identifying and measuring an entity's performance from four perspectives: financial, customer, internal business process, and learning and growth. However, a balanced scorecard is more than just a performance measurement tool. It is also used as a means of communicating an organisation's strategies, key priorities and critical success factors throughout the organisation. To this end, the more recently developed strategy map serves as an important tool in informing the development of balanced scorecard measures. Strategy maps provide an important link between organisational strategy and balanced scorecards.

19.1 Measuring organisational performance

LEARNING OBJECTIVE 19.1 Understand how financial and non-financial measures are used to evaluate organisational performance.

We explored the concept of strategy in chapter 14. As part of the discussion, we outlined how successful organisations have a clear understanding of their future direction in terms of what industries or types of businesses they intend to be in and how they will seek out a competitive advantage. Whatever the organisational strategy might be, it should be reflected in the management control system tools in place in the organisation. Performance measurement systems play a significant role in supporting management control. Such systems define the strategic objectives and provide feedback on performance through the measurement of a range of key performance indicators. This articulation of a clear link between strategic objectives and performance measurement helps to ensure that the focus is on the goals of an entity. Performance measurement systems can cover many aspects, from the organisation as a whole, individual departments or divisions, or even individual employees.[1] Given the selection of suitable performance measures, in dynamic business environments performance measurement systems can detect changes in a firm's operations or environment and stimulate a rethink of current strategies. A well designed performance system can both appraise the assumptions of a firm's strategy and also evaluate the validity of the strategy.

Traditional, financially based performance measurement systems drew from backward-looking costing and accounting systems. Such traditional approaches have been heavily criticised as impairing competitiveness given their focus on the short term and failure to adopt a strategic focus and recognise the external environment. These criticisms have resulted in the development of modern performance measurement which adopts a balanced or multi-dimensional view of performance. Modern performance measurement systems incorporate both financial and non-financial measures and both lead and lag indicators. Social media and other big data sources are creating opportunities to enhance performance measurement systems. As sustainability becomes a prominent focus of many organisations, the inclusion of social and environmental performance measures within performance measurement systems is becoming common.

Financial and non-financial measures

Chapter 18 introduced a range of commonly used financial measures based on dollars or ratios of dollars for different responsibility centres. We explored, for example, how revenue growth could be used to review the performance of revenue centre. In regards to investment centres, by comparison, financial measures including ROI, RI or EVA can be relevant. Such financial measures are commonly obtained from the financial accounting system, which is designed to report financial measures for the overall organisation, divisions, product lines and departments. Financial measures also compare budget to actual results.

Non-financial measures provide performance information that cannot be measured in dollars. Defect rates, throughput time and employee retention are among the non-financial measures used to reflect performance that promotes long-term financial success. One important issue relating to non-financial measures is that they still need to be quantified in some way. For example, customer satisfaction is not a measure in itself but an important dimension we might like to measure. Many entities do this by developing a customer satisfaction index based on formal feedback mechanisms from customers. The use of the net-promoter-score (NPS)[2] is a common example of an approach to measure customer satisfaction. The measurement of a firm's NPS involves asking customers — on a scale from 0 to 10 — how likely they would recommend the firm to a friend or colleague. Customers are rated as shown in figure 19.1:

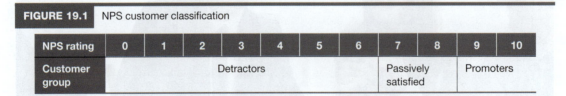

FIGURE 19.1	NPS customer classification										
NPS rating	0	1	2	3	4	5	6	7	8	9	10
Customer group	Detractors							Passively satisfied		Promoters	

A firm's final NPS is calculated by deducting the percentage of detractors from the percentage of promoters. As a benchmark, firms often strive for a NPS of more than 75%. The benefit of the use of the NPS is that in most industries, the leading firms tend to be those with the highest number of promoters.[3]

As summarised in Figure 19.2, the inclusion of non-financial measures within a performance measurement system has many benefits. Chief among these benefits is that non-financial measures tend to be more accessible to non-management employees and others with limited accounting acumen. Non-financial measures can further enable managers to locate the underlying causes of problems in a timely fashion. For example, consider a firm which has recorded a significant direct materials efficiency variance. This financial measure identifies that the firm has a significant issue that warrants further investigation. This measure on its own, however, does not reveal the underlying cause of the problem and many employees won't understand how direct material variances are calculated. If, however, we supplement this financial information with relevant non-financial measures (for example, the rate of product defects and the quantity of materials returned to suppliers), we are likely to be better able to pinpoint the problem.

Notwithstanding the potential benefits associated with the use of non-financial measures, there are a number of possible disadvantages of their use. Some non-financial measures can be quite subjective. Consider, for example, how customer or employee satisfaction can be dependent on customer or employee attitudes as expressed through surveys. Many factors can influence such attitudes and these other factors will need to be allowed for if such surveys are to be used for management decision making. Finally, there is the issue of measure selection. In some instances, different financial measures may produce disparate results and it can sometimes be difficult to establish a clear relationship between non-financial and financial measures. Consider, for example, how a positive direct material price variance that was achieved through the selection of a low-cost supplier could be in conflict with non-financial performance relating to the number of product returns or customer complaints.

FIGURE 19.2 Benefits and disadvantages of non-financial measures[4]

Benefits of non-financial measures	Disadvantages of non-financial measures
More user-friendly and relevant to non-management employees	Subjective in nature
More likely to lead to longer term performance gains, as they tend to be linked more readily to the organisation's goals	Including too many measures can impede understanding and be costly to collect, so there is a need to limit the number of measures
Tend to diminish the likelihood of myopic management decision making, as they usually promote more long-term thinking	Inappropriate measures can be chosen
Can identify problems in a more timely fashion, and locate the entity's problems and benefits	There is no proven cause and effect link between non-financial measures and economic success
Can be easily structured to suit an organisation's goals	Various measures give conflicting results
Can be benchmarked easily	

Lead and lag indicators

Non-financial measures are commonly classified as *lead indicators*. Lead indicators are the drivers of performance and enable us to anticipate a firm's future performance.[5] Given this, lead indicators act as early warning signs that something may not be working within an organisation. To illustrate this, consider how a maintenance department could measure a machine's noise and vibration levels and obtain a lead insight into possible future issues with the operation of the machine.[6]

If the operations to which the lead indicators refer are managed well, this will lead to enhanced performance in the reported financial measures, which are commonly classified as *lag indicators*. Lag indicators summarise the outcomes of a firm's past performance. A firm's net profit or gross profit ratios are commonly referred to examples of lag indicators which identify the outcomes of a firm's strategy in delivering strong profitability in the past period. In a cause-and-effect manner, such lag financial indicators will be driven by lead indicators relating to, for example, customer satisfaction, product quality and production efficiency.

Performance measures: other considerations

Beyond considerations of whether the selected performance measures are financial or non-financial and whether they are lag or lead indicators, various other considerations are relevant. Neely et al.[7] commented that the design of a performance measure, 'involves much more than simply specifying a robust formula' and proposed a comprehensive list of characteristics which enable managers to evaluate their choice of measures (figure 19.3).

FIGURE 19.3	Characteristics of effective performance measures[8]

Performance measures should:

1. be derived from strategy	12. be consistent (in that they maintain their significance as time goes by)
2. be simple to understand	13. provide fast feedback
3. provide timely and accurate feedback	14. have an explicit purpose
4. be based on quantities that can be influenced, or controlled, by the user alone or in co-operation with others	15. be based on an explicitly defined formula and source of data
5. reflect the 'business process' — i.e. both the supplier and customer should be involved in the definition of the measure	16. employ ratios rather than absolute numbers
6. relate to specific goals (targets)	17. use data which are automatically collected as part of a process, whenever possible
7. be relevant	18. be reported in a simple consistent format
8. be part of a closed management loop	19. be based on trends rather than snapshots
9. be clearly defined	20. provide information
10. have visual impact	21. be precise and exact about what is being measured
11. focus on improvement	22. be objective and not based on opinion

Performance measurement system alternatives

Effective performance measurement systems:
1. recognise the importance of ensuring that the performance measures used to monitor success in organisations are clearly linked to strategy
2. include a range of financial and non-financial indicators
3. recognise the relationship between lead and lag indicators.

As presented in Figure 19.4, a range of innovative performance measurement models or frameworks have been developed. While many models have emerged, our focus in this chapter is the balanced scorecard. The balanced scorecard is arguably the most influential performance measurement model and it has been used by many organisations globally. Balanced scorecards have been described as one of the most significant management accounting innovations and a large number of research studies have explored their use in decision making, adoption and implementation, and their impact on organisational performance.[9]

FIGURE 19.4	Performance measurement system designs[10]

Model/framework	Measures/indicators/criteria	Reference
Sink and Tuttle	Efficiency, Effectiveness, Quality, Productivity, Quality of work life and innovation, Profitability/budget ability, Excellence, survival and growth	Sink and Tuttle (1989)
PM (performance measurement) matrix	Cost factors, Non-cost factors, External factors, Internal factors	Keegan et al. (1989)
Results and determinants matrix	Financial performance, Competitiveness, Quality, Flexibility, Resource utilization, Innovation	Fitzgerald et al. (1991)

PM questionnaire	Strategies, actions and measures are assessed, Extent to which they are supportive, Data analysis as per management position or function, Range of response and level of disagreement	Dixon et al. (1990)
Brown's framework	Input measures, Process measures, Output measures, Outcome measures	Brown (1996)
SMART pyramid (Performance pyramid)	Quality, Delivery, Process time, Cost, Customer satisfaction, Flexibility, Productivity, Marketing measures, Financial measures	Developed by Wang Laboratories. Lynch and Cross (1991)
Balanced Scorecard (BSC)	Financial, Customer, Internal processes, Learning and growth	Kaplan and Norton (1992)
Consistent PM system	Derived from strategy, continuous improvement, fast and accurate feedback, explicit purpose, relevance	Flapper et al. (1996)
Framework for small business PM	Flexibility, Timeliness, Quality, Finance, Customer satisfaction, Human factors	Laitinen (1996)
Cambridge PM process	Quality, Flexibility, Timeliness, Finance, Customer satisfaction, Human factors	Neely et al. (1997)
Integrated dynamic PM system	Timeliness, Finance, Customer satisfaction, Human factors, Quality, Flexibility	Ghalayini et al. (1997)
Integrated PM framework	Quality, Flexibility, Timeliness, Finance, Customer satisfaction	Medori and Steeple (2000)
Integrated PM system	Finance, Customer satisfaction, Human factors, Quality, Flexibility, Timeliness	Bititci (1994)
Dynamic PM systems	External and internal monitoring system, Review system, Internal deployment system, IT platform needs	Bititci et al. (2000)
Integrated measurement model	Customer satisfaction, Human factors, Quality, Flexibility, Timeliness, Finance	Oliver and Palmer (1998)
Comparative Business Scorecard	Stakeholder value, Delight the stakeholder, Organizational learning, Process excellence	Kanji (1998)
Skandia Navigator	Financial focus, Customer focus, Human focus, Process focus, Renewal and development focus	Edvinsson and Malone (1997); Sveiby (1997)
Balanced IT Scorecard (BITS)	Financial perspective, Customer satisfaction, Internal processes, Infrastructure and innovation, People perspective	ESI (1998) as mentioned in Abran and Buglione (2003)
BSC of Advanced Information. Services Inc (AISBSC)	Financial perspective, Customer perspective Processes, People, Infrastructure and innovation	Abran and Buglione (2003)
Intangible Asset-monitor (IAM)	Internal structure: Growth, Renewal, Efficiency, Stability, Risk (Concept models, Computers, Administrative systems); External structure: Customer, Supplier, Brand names, Trademark and image; Individual competence: Skills, Education, Experience, Values, Social skill	Sveiby (1997)
QUEST	Quality, Economic, Social and Technical factors	Abran and Buglione (2003)
European Foundation for Quality Management (EFQM)	Leadership, Enablers: people management, policy and strategy, resources; Processes, Results: people and customer satisfaction, impact on society; and Business results	www.efqm.org/ as mentioned in Wongrassamee et al. (2003)

Introduction to balanced scorecards and strategy maps

We will explore the specifics of balanced scorecards and strategy maps in subsequent sections. For the moment, we need to establish the importance of the links between strategy, strategy maps and balanced scorecards in measuring performance. We know from chapter 14 that strategy sets the future direction of the organisation. Strategy maps take the organisation's strategy, develop strategic themes linked to that strategy, and develop strategic objectives within each of the four perspectives commonly used in the balanced scorecard. The balanced scorecard details the specific performance metrics that reflect the strategic objectives. Figure 19.5 illustrates these relationships.

FIGURE 19.5 Strategy, strategy maps and the balanced scorecard

Next we explore strategy maps and the balanced scorecard in more detail.

19.2 Strategy maps

LEARNING OBJECTIVE 19.2 Communicate the role of strategy maps in the balanced scorecard process.

Strategy maps came to prominence in 2004 when Kaplan and Norton published their book *Strategy maps*, which focused on linking organisational strategy to the measures developed for the balanced scorecard. As illustrated in figure 19.5, in some ways strategy maps became the link between strategy and the balanced scorecard. In Kaplan and Norton's own words:

> A strategy map provides a visual representation of the strategy. It provides a single-page view of how objectives in the four perspectives integrate and combine to guide the strategy. It illustrates the cause-and-effect relationships that link desired outcomes in the customer and financial perspectives to outstanding performance in critical internal processes — operations, management, customer management; and in innovation and regulatory/social processes.[11]

The focus of the strategy map should be to:
- provide a link between the organisation's strategy and the balanced scorecard
- (where appropriate) convey the key strategic themes developed from the organisation's strategy
- convey the organisation's strategic objectives in the four balanced scorecard perspectives.

These strategic objectives should reflect hypothesised cause-and-effect relationships represented by a series of 'if' and 'then' statements. For example, the strategic objectives developed for the learning and growth perspective (say, 'if' we improve employee skills) should produce outcomes in the internal business process perspective (say, 'then' we will reduce lead times) and the customer perspective (say, 'then' we will improve customer satisfaction). In evaluating the final balanced scorecard, it is good to check that the hypothesised cause-and-effect linkages are correctly put into action through carefully selected measures. When reviewing the final measures, if the cause-and-effect relationships are hard to identify, the wrong measures have most likely been put in place. In this way, the strategy map is a good check on the usefulness and appropriateness of the balanced scorecard measures. While some research questions claims about the cause-and-effect links in balanced scorecards (see, for example, Norreklit[12]), we can, at a minimum, use strategy maps to be confident about the *links* between the strategic objectives and the measures in the balanced scorecard.

The strategy map for the State Library of Queensland in figure 19.6 provides one example of what a strategy map could look like for a not-for-profit entity. Organisations are likely to adapt the strategy map to meet their specific needs, so not all strategy maps will look the same or even similar. For example, from figure 19.6 we can see that the State Library of Queensland has developed strategies around its specific organisation outcomes.

FIGURE 19.6   State Library of Queensland's strategy map[13]

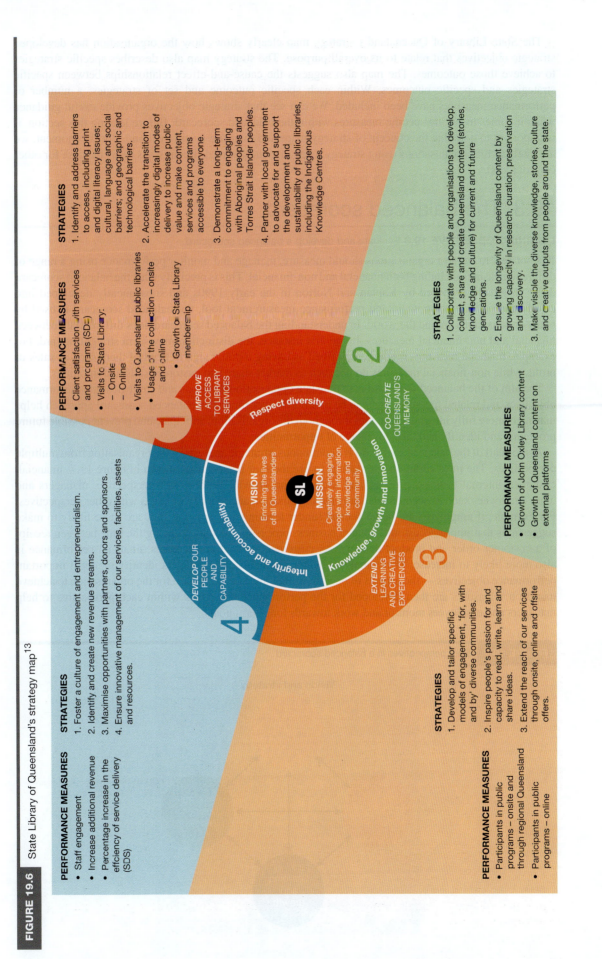

PERFORMANCE MEASURES
- Staff engagement
- Increase additional revenue
- Percentage increase in the efficiency of service delivery (SDS)

STRATEGIES
1. Foster a culture of engagement and entrepreneurialism.
2. Identify and create new revenue streams.
3. Maximise opportunities with partners, donors and sponsors.
4. Ensure innovative management of our services, facilities, assets and resources.

PERFORMANCE MEASURES
- Client satisfaction with services and programs (SDS)
- Visits to State Library:
  – Onsite
  – Online
- Visits to Queensland public libraries
- Usage of the collection – onsite and online
  • Growth of State Library membership

STRATEGIES
1. Identify and address barriers to access, including print and digital literacy issues; cultural, language and social barriers; and geographic and technological barriers.
2. Accelerate the transition to increasingly digital modes of delivery to increase public value and make content, services and programs accessible to everyone.
3. Demonstrate a long-term commitment to engaging with Aboriginal peoples and Torres Strait Islander peoples.
4. Partner with local government to advocate for and support the development and sustainability of public libraries, including the Indigenous Knowledge Centres.

STRATEGIES
1. Collaborate with people and organisations to develop, collect, share and create Queensland content (stories, knowledge and culture) for current and future generations.
2. Ensure the longevity of Queensland content by growing capacity in research, curation, preservation and discovery.
3. Make visible the diverse knowledge, stories, culture and creative outputs from people around the state.

PERFORMANCE MEASURES
- Growth of John Oxley Library content
- Growth of Queensland content on external platforms

PERFORMANCE MEASURES
- Participants in public programs – onsite and through regional Queensland
- Participants in public programs – online

STRATEGIES
1. Develop and tailor specific models of engagement, 'for, with and by' diverse communities.
2. Inspire people's passion for and capacity to read, write, learn and share ideas.
3. Extend the reach of our services through onsite, online and offsite offers.

The State Library of Queensland's strategy map clearly shows how the organisation has developed strategic objectives that relate to its overall purpose. The strategy map also describes specific strategies to achieve those outcomes. The map also suggests the cause-and-effect relationships between specific strategies and specific outcomes. Within each specific outcome and set of strategies, a number of performance measures have been included. We can see that strategic objectives provide useful guidance when it comes to setting specific measures within the balanced scorecard. Before leaving this section, it is important to note that the concept of strategy maps and their use is still evolving. For the moment, we are likely to find organisations using strategy maps in a number of different ways (as is the case for other control tools).

19.3 The balanced scorecard

LEARNING OBJECTIVE 19.3 Evaluate and develop a balanced scorecard.

It is not new to suggest organisations should measure, manage and monitor performance using a range of different measures including both financial and non-financial. This is precisely what the balanced scorecard does. Originally proposed by Kaplan and Norton in the early 1990s and subsequently developed into a fully comprehensive strategic and performance measurement tool, the balanced scorecard is used by many organisations around the world. In understanding the balanced scorecard, let's differentiate between financial and non-financial measures. In the first instance, the distinction may seem straightforward. For example, financial measures might be described as having a dollar sign in front of them such as sales or profit, while non-financial measures do not such as market share and customer-satisfaction ratings.

The aim of the balanced scorecard is to translate organisational visions and strategies into performance objectives and related measures that can be monitored over time. The balanced scorecard approach helps managers more fully integrate strategies throughout the organisation, anticipate and prevent possible future problems, and identify and take advantage of opportunities.

At the heart of the balanced scorecard is a continuous, strategic analysis of the organisation from multiple perspectives. The most common approach is to use the four perspectives shown in figure 19.7: financial, customer, internal business process, and learning and growth. Within each perspective, managers and other employees such as accountants study the organisation and identify linkages with other perspectives. For example, if employees are better trained (under learning and growth), they are more likely to make suggestions that improve customer-related business processes, such as reducing the time between receipt of a customer order and product delivery. As customer satisfaction increases, financial performance is also more likely to increase. These analyses help accountants and managers identify the most important performance objectives — the aspects of operations that must be successful for the organisation to achieve its vision. Measures are then developed for the performance objectives within each perspective to help managers and employees monitor and work towards long-term goals.

FIGURE 19.7	Four perspectives in a balanced scorecard

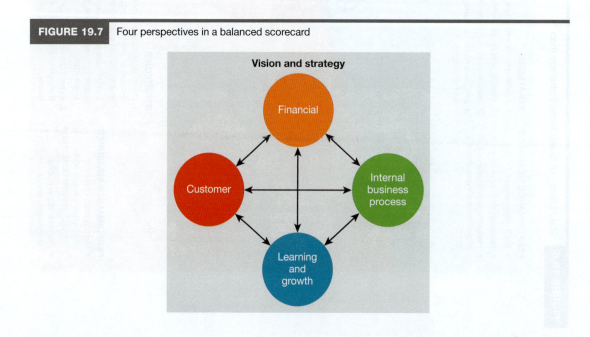

A balanced scorecard may be used at various levels within an organisation. Commonly we see three main levels. First, an organisational-level balanced scorecard such as a balanced scorecard prepared at the corporate level. A balanced scorecard at this level would capture corporate-level metrics. Second, balanced scorecards may be prepared at the divisional or segment level within an organisation. Finally, balanced scorecards are being increasingly used at the individual level. In this case, scorecards are structured to reflect the environment under the control of individual managers and executives. We are also seeing these individual scorecards used as a key input to the structure of incentive plans. This link to incentive plans will be explored further in chapter 20. Where the same organisation uses scorecards at all three levels (that is, corporate, divisional and individual), we would expect to observe some common threads across the levels such as the reinforcement of strategy, with the measures likely to become increasingly specific and local as we move from the corporate to the individual.

Financial perspective and related measures

When accountants and managers analyse their entities from a **financial perspective**, they identify desired financial results, given the organisation's vision. For-profit entities usually have goals of providing owners with some level of return on investment. Not-for-profit entities typically have financial goals of maintaining a certain level of financial liquidity and stability, accumulating sufficient resources for some long-term purpose, or gaining maximum efficiency from resources. Financial goals and objectives encourage managers to evaluate the effectiveness of their strategies and operating plans based on the economic wellbeing of the organisation. They also help employees relate the activities they perform to the entity's financial outcomes.

Financial perspective measures are designed to determine an organisation's progress towards desired financial results. In for-profit entities, these measures are usually related to profitability, growth and owner value. Common measures include operating income, return on investment, residual income and economic value-added. In not-for-profit entities, financial measures often include operating income, cost per service provided, and variances from budgets.

Customer perspective and related measures

When accountants and managers analyse the entity from a **customer perspective**, they are concerned with identifying the customers that they want, and developing strategies to get and keep them. The analysis includes identifying the targeted customers, markets and products that are most consistent with the organisation's vision and core competencies. Entities that better meet customer needs — creating value for customers — are also more likely to generate desired financial results. Thus, this link connects the financial and customer perspectives. In assessing customer needs, managers consider their organisational strategies, and examine the nature of products or services compared to consumer views about trade-offs among price, quality and functionality.

The customer's perspective is usually evaluated using outcome measures such as market share and customer satisfaction. The performance measures used in for-profit and not-for-profit entities are often similar. These measures include customer retention and profitability, new customer acquisition, and market share in a targeted market segment or geographical region. Customers are often surveyed to gather information on their perceptions about and interactions with the entity. Market surveys and focus groups are also used to measure image and reputation.

Internal business process perspective and related measures

When accountants and managers analyse the organisation from an **internal business process perspective**, they are concerned with the methods and practices used inside the entity to produce and deliver goods and services. One goal of this analysis is to improve processes that will increase customer satisfaction. Another goal is to improve the efficiency of operations, which contributes directly to the organisation's financial results. Internal business processes can be analysed using a value chain approach. A value chain is the sequence of business processes through which value is added to goods and services. Analysis of the value chain leads to the identification of processes that are critical to the organisation's success. Often, customer-related processes are emphasised in balanced scorecards because these processes have the greatest impact on customer satisfaction and financial success. Figure 19.8 presents a generic customer-oriented value chain including three principal internal business processes: the innovation cycle, the operations cycle and the post-sales service cycle.

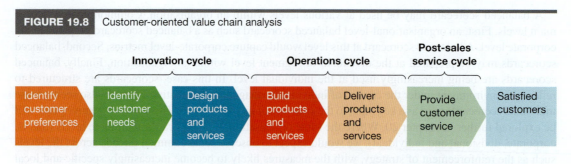

FIGURE 19.8 Customer-oriented value chain analysis

An alternative to the value chain approach is an operational audit conducted by internal auditors. An operational audit is an objective and systematic examination of evidence to provide an independent assessment of the performance of an entity, program, activity or function. Operational audits provide information to improve accountability and to facilitate decision making.

Innovation cycle and related measures

The first step in the value chain, the **innovation cycle**, is concerned with processes to identify customer needs and to design goods and services that meet those needs. Many entities mistakenly focus their efforts primarily on more efficient production of existing products. Yet goods and services must meet customer needs. The balanced scorecard encourages managers to establish internal processes that identify customer preferences for quality, functionality and price, and also predict the potential market size. Organisations often use market and customer research to identify and nurture new markets, new customers and new needs of current customers. Managers brainstorm completely new products, and also develop new opportunities and markets for existing products.

The innovation process also ensures that proposed goods and services are produced efficiently, given the organisation's core competencies. For example, entities use target costing and kaizen costing to reduce product prices and improve quality.

Operations cycle and related measures

The second step in the value chain, the **operations cycle**, is concerned with production and delivery of goods or services that are identified and designed in the innovation cycle. The operations cycle addresses the short-term wellbeing of the entity. It begins with the systems used to accept and process customer orders, and is complete with delivery of the good or service. Quality, efficiency, consistency and on-time delivery are emphasised in this part of the value chain.

Historically, many entities focused on the operations process. Cost containment goals and cost monitoring methods were often in place at the commencement of operations. Traditional **financial measures** such as standard costs, budgets and variances were often used to monitor operational performance. This focus sometimes led to suboptimal behaviour. For example, efficiency measures create incentives to build inventories so that labour and machines are kept busy. Quality is sacrificed to increase efficiency. Excessive inventory levels and poor quality are costly to organisations over time. As a result, traditional measures of operations may be only a small part of a balanced scorecard approach.

Over the last several decades, entities have increasingly competed on quality and timely delivery, in addition to price. For example, Dell Computers advertises the quality and reliability of its systems as well as its ability to deliver computers within days of an order. Measurements of quality, cycle time and cost are developed to monitor and enhance performance in these areas. With the growth of internet sales, competition on price and product customisation has intensified. For example, price information about computers and peripherals is widely available on the internet, both by manufacturers such as Dell and Apple and by retail sellers. To be competitive, organisations must improve their operations processes to meet or beat their competitors' prices, quality and reliability.

Entities that specialise in custom products often measure the accuracy with which orders are completed and speed of delivery. The specific operating characteristics identified and monitored as performance objectives depend on the organisation's vision, core competencies and strategies. Managers choose performance measures to monitor organisational progress, rewarding positive trends in areas that lead to customer satisfaction and financial success.

Post-sales service cycle and related measures

The final step in the value chain, the **post-sales service cycle**, considers the service provided to customers after product delivery. Post-sales services include providing warranty work, handling returns, correcting defects and collecting and processing payments. In addition, when products are highly sophisticated, entities often train the employees who will be using them. Another aspect of the post-sales service cycle is the safe disposal of hazardous wastes and by-products.

For some organisations, post-sales service is part of a product differentiation strategy. Hospitals have recently focused on the billing and collection processes of post-sales service. By emphasising accurate coding on patient bills, hospitals have fewer claims denied by insurers and increase their operating revenues. To achieve greater accuracy in coding, many hospitals provide in-depth employee training and hire better-educated employees in their billing and collections departments.

Performance measures for customer-related post-sales service could include aspects of the billing and collections cycle, such as the dollar amount of bad debts and days in accounts receivable. In addition, costs for warranty work and rework can be measured, or the number of defective products returned or reworked can be tracked. Measures for waste and by-product disposal could include number of kilograms of waste and clean-up costs.

Learning and growth perspective and related measures

When accountants and managers analyse an entity from a **learning and growth perspective**, they are concerned with achieving future success by discovering new and better strategies. They also want to improve customer satisfaction and internal business processes, ensure that employees have sufficient knowledge and expertise, and check that internal processes support existing strategies. The learning and growth perspective is naturally linked to the internal business process perspective. As managers focus on improving internal business processes, they also identify opportunities for enhancing the capabilities of employees, information systems and operating procedures.

Three key areas of interest[14] have emerged in the learning and growth perspective:

- human capital and employee development, which relates to the skill set, knowledge and capacities of employees
- information capital, which relates to the information technology and associated infrastructure to support the organisation's strategy
- organisation capital, which relates to culture, leadership, alignment of goals, incentives and strategy, and teamwork.

When an organisation has each of the three components aligned with its strategy, Kaplan and Norton argue the organisation possesses a high degree of organisation readiness, which essentially means the organisation is adaptable, able to execute strategy and is ready for change.

Employee learning and growth measures include satisfaction, retention, training and skill development. These measures are tailored for the type of organisation and industry. To assist in decision making, information systems must produce timely, reliable and accurate information about customers, competitors and operations. Measures of information timeliness and accuracy include number of days to close (the amount of time that elapses before financial statements are available to managers) and errors per report. Over time, company policies become outdated. Periodically, these policies need to be analysed to determine whether they are current or should be changed in response to new knowledge or technologies. A performance measure could be the number of times that policies and procedures are reviewed over a five-year period. To monitor learning and growth measures, current performance of operations is usually used as a baseline and improvements are evaluated over time.

Clearly, any balanced scorecard developed must be structured to meet the needs of the entity to which it relates. Figures 19.9 (a) and (b) demonstrate the different types of balanced scorecards that might evolve to meet organisational needs. In chapter 21, we explore the balanced scorecard further, particularly as it relates to issues of sustainability management accounting.

Comprehensive example 1 discusses developing balanced scorecard measures for Mountain Mist Brewery.

FIGURE 19.9 Sample balanced scorecards

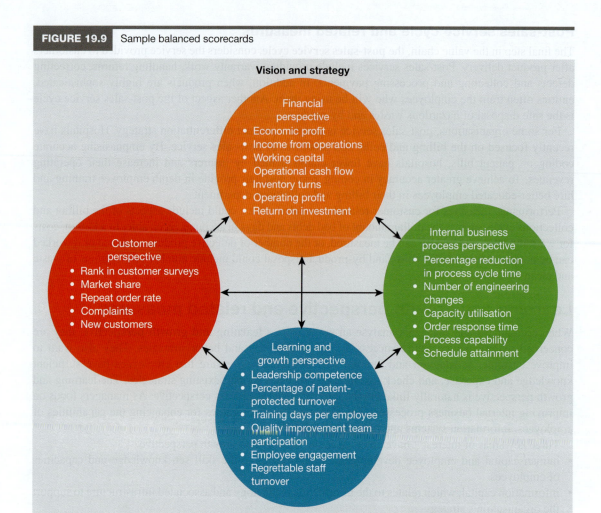

(a) Sample balanced scorecard measures applicable in a manufacturing setting[15]

	Actual %	Target
Customer perspective		
Community/consumer satisfaction	92	90% or better
Medical practitioner satisfaction	71	80% or better
Pharmacist satisfaction	90	90% or better
Internal business processes perspective		
Processing time performance	93	90% or better
Claim processing accuracy	93	99%
Medicare transactions online	49	N/A
General practices online	86	N/A
Growth and development perspective		
Staff satisfaction	66	85% or better
Staff training completion rate	86	95%
Voluntary staff turnover	10	5%

(b) Sample balanced scorecard measures applicable in a medical insurance setting[16]

Preparing a balanced scorecard set of measures — Mountain Mist Brewery

In the early 1980s, Bernard Hancock built a small brewery on his 150-acre property in the Macedon Ranges. The brewery, named Mountain Mist Brewery, was designed with ales in mind and Bernard introduced a number of cutting-edge and innovative technologies to make the well-known, popular pale ale Misty Hop and others such as Hazy Heidi, Mountain Maid and Sunny Sherpa. The brewery's highest selling pale ale (Misty Hop) is widely recognised as a high-quality boutique beer and is sold, along with the brewery's other ales, to clubs and restaurants around Australia. All Mountain Mist Brewery ales are distributed in kegs (large containers) and 12-bottle cartons through its Victorian and national wholesalers. The brewery has continued to expand capacity on its site to meet growing consumer demands.

In 2015, total revenue in the Australian beer industry was $4 billion. The Australian industry is dominated by two key players, Carlton and United Breweries and Lion Nathan National Foods, which account for 86 per cent of industry revenue. The industry is becoming less concentrated though, with drinkers switching to premium imports and the range of craft beers provided by small breweries. A number of micro-breweries are successfully servicing small regional areas, including Mountain Mist Brewery in Victoria with 3 per cent of industry revenue.[17]

Mountain Mist Brewery's capacity is currently running at 52 megalitres of beer per annum. Bernard strives to leverage economies of scale, with investment in high-tech brewing equipment and automated packaging machines. Bernard believes the quality of his product is the most significant influence on customer satisfaction, increased sales and the corporate profile. Bernard claims the main selling feature of his Mountain Mist ales is the use of specialty hop flowers, sourced from Tasmania and brewed according to his innovative brewing processes. The other major ingredient, malt, is sourced from barley grown in northern parts of Victoria. The pale malt for Misty Hop is made according to strict Mountain Mist specifications. Bernard claims that the natural spring water taken directly from the spring on the Mountain Mist Brewery site offers superior tasting quality that will match, or better, the quality of any pale ale around the world.

Bernard's key objectives and strategic intent for Mountain Mist Brewery are:

1. to grow profitably with incremental investment into selected markets to become one of the top six breweries in Australia
2. to continuously improve perceived consumer quality by improving taste, freshness, package integrity and package appearance
3. to enhance distributor service with better lead times, accurate order fills and lower product damage
4. to continuously lower company costs per litre of beer so Mountain Mist can maintain resources for long-term productivity and success, while ensuring that product quality is not compromised by cost-cutting initiatives
5. to continuously improve business performance through engaging and developing employees to ensure that all employees understand the critical importance of quality in all processes and their contribution to the success of the organisation.

While Australian boutique beers such as Misty Hop are becoming more prominent in the market, overall volume growth for the entire industry is flat. The industry has also been faced with declining levels of consumption as well as increased competition from other beverages such as wine and spirits.

Bernard wants to construct a suitable organisational-level balanced scorecard incorporating measures that reflect Mountain Mists' key objectives and strategic intent.

Provided below are sample measures suitable for each balanced scorecard perspective.

Financial perspective

Strategic objective	Measure
Reduce the cost per litre of beer produced	Cost per litre of beer
Achieve profitable growth particularly in new markets	Revenue growth in new markets Profit achieved in new markets
Grow profitably through incremental investment	Return on investment

Customer perspective

Strategic objective	Measure
Improve customer/consumer satisfaction	Customer satisfaction index
Become one of top six brewers in the country	Market share
Increase the number of distribution (customer) outlets	Number of new outlets achieved per year

Internal business process perspective

Strategic objective	Measure
Improve distribution performance	Distribution lead times
Increase order-fill rates and accuracy	Order-fill accuracy
Increase productivity	Manufacturing cycle times Cost per unit (keg or bottle)
Enhance customer relationships	Percentage of sales in new outlets

Innovation and growth perspective

Strategic objective	Measure
Increase employee development	Staff training hours/participation for: • customer relationship management • quality management
Develop satisfaction of employees	Employee satisfaction index Employee turnover rate
Increase management/employee participation in financial planning (organisation-wide understanding)	Participation rate of managers in budgeting and planning processes
Attract and retain quality personnel	Rating of new employees' technical capabilities
Develop IT infrastructure to support knowledge sharing	Number of highly engaged employees (intranet participation)

Role of social media performance measures

An increasing amount of data is now available to firms as more and more individuals utilise the Internet and social media platforms to buy products and services and engage with organisations. More data is also increasingly available through the Internet of Things (IoT) processes, whereby an increasing number of smart devices are connected to the Internet and capture data through sensors. It has been suggested that in the future, 'anything that can be connected, will be connected'.[18] Such Internet and social media data can have the characteristics of 'Big Data'. That is, high volume, high velocity, and higher variety of different forms of data.[19]

There are a number of ways in which Internet and social media data can be used as a performance measure. One common example is in relation to online reviews. The influence of word of mouth product recommendations on consumer purchase decisions has long been recognised.[20] Nowadays, consumer word of mouth information is available in electronic form as consumers rate and comment on products and services on social media sites, company and third-party websites, blogs and forums. From a performance measurement perspective, firms can use the average online ratings, online ratings variance and/or the volume of online ratings of products and services as possible relevant performance measures. A range of studies have confirmed such measures as being relevant in helping firms to predict future sales.[21]

Beyond online ratings measures, various other performance measures are likely to be relevant for different social media applications. As presented in figure 19.10, such social media performance measures can enable firms to better understand the extent to which consumers are aware of a firm's brand and are engaged in the brand. A range of social media data capture and analysis tools are available. Many automated tools are available, for instance, to evaluate the valence or polarity (i.e. negative, neutral, positive) of individual tweets, Facebook and other online comments. Such tools: 1) draw from large databases of words that have been classified accordingly to their polarity, and 2) automatically classify individual comments as either being positive, neutral or negative based on the words used. Comments which include a large number of positive words (i.e. adore, applaud, best) compared to negative words (i.e. hate, abusive, appalled) are classified as positive. Once captured and analysed from a customer satisfaction perspective, firms can monitor the average weekly sentiment of relevant tweets and Facebook comments.

FIGURE 19.10	Social media performance measurement examples[22]	
Social media application	**Brand awareness measures**	**Brand engagement measures**
Blogs	• number of unique visits • number of return visits • number of times bookmarked • search ranking	• number of members • number of RSS feed subscribers • number of comments • amount of user-generated content • average length of time on site • number of responses to polls, contests, surveys
Twitter	• number of tweets about the brand • valence of tweets +/− • number of followers	• number of followers • number of @replies
Forums and discussion boards (e.g. Google Groups)	• number of page views • number of visits • valence of posted content +/−	• number of relevant topics/threads • number of individual replies • number of sign-ups
Social networks (e.g. Facebook, LinkedIn)	• number of members/fans • number of installs of applications • number of impressions • number of bookmarks • number of reviews/ratings and valence +/−	• number of comments • number of active users • number of 'likes' on friends' feeds • number of user-generated items (photos, threads, replies) • usage metrics of applications/widgets • impressions-to-interactions ratio, rate of activity (how often members personalise profiles, bios, links, etc.)
Video and photosharing (e.g. Flickr, YouTube, Instagram)	• number of views of video/photo • valence of video/photo ratings +/−	• number of replies • number of page views • number of comments • number of subscribers

Using the balanced scorecard diagnostically or interactively (levers of control)

As detailed in chapter 14, control system tools like the balanced scorecard may be used by organisations in different ways. Two common uses relate to Simons' levers of control: diagnostic use and interactive use.

When a control system tool is used diagnostically, the focus is on the achievement of pre-set targets. These targets relate to measures linked to organisational strategy. In some ways, diagnostic use is all about *measure, monitor and feedback*. That is, measure the performance around key performance metrics, monitor performance outcomes against pre-set targets and provide feedback to managers to focus on achieving target performance in the next period. The objective is to focus on the intended strategy and measures in place. The assumption is that the intended strategy is the right one, so alternative strategies are not explored via the control system tool (in this case, the balanced scorecard).

When a control system tool is used interactively, the focus is directed at using the tool to review strategy to help deal with the organisation's strategic uncertainties. Measures are in place and targets are set in much the same way as when the tool is used diagnostically. However, instead of using feedback on the performance metrics to stay on track as intended, the feedback process may result in a review of the intended strategy. This may be largely driven by the uncertainties faced by an organisation such as changes in the regulatory environment or an intense competitive environment. Control system tools such as the balanced scorecard can be useful in addressing uncertainty. For example, carefully selected measures provide feedback about uncertainties and *early warning signals* to indicate issues with the current strategic path.

Belief systems, boundary systems and the balanced scorecard

Balanced scorecards provide the opportunity for an organisation to articulate its strategy and mission. We would expect to find the fundamental core values and beliefs of the organisation that underpin its strategy in metric selection and in the targets set. Moreover, the process used to develop the scorecard is likely to reflect the belief system of the organisation. For example, an organisation with open communication and a culture of group consultation is likely to use a collaborative and consultative style of balanced scorecard implementation.

With respect to boundary systems, through the measures used and targets set, balanced scorecards are able to articulate the expected behaviour from managers and employees. This is particularly so when balanced scorecards are used on an individual basis. Appropriate metric selection is important, otherwise the wrong kind of behaviour and poor decision making would be encouraged.

19.4 Steps in implementing a balanced scorecard

LEARNING OBJECTIVE 19.4 Explain how a balanced scorecard is implemented.

The process of implementing a balanced scorecard is summarised in figure 19.11. These general steps are customised for each entity. Note that these steps focus on the technical aspects of implementation. A range of behavioural aspects will also influence the success or otherwise of the implementation. These include:

- top management support
- achieving a management buy-in
- use of multiple champions
- adequate communication throughout the implementation process
- use of implementation feedback protocols
- organisation-wide participation.

FIGURE 19.11   Steps in implementing a balanced scorecard

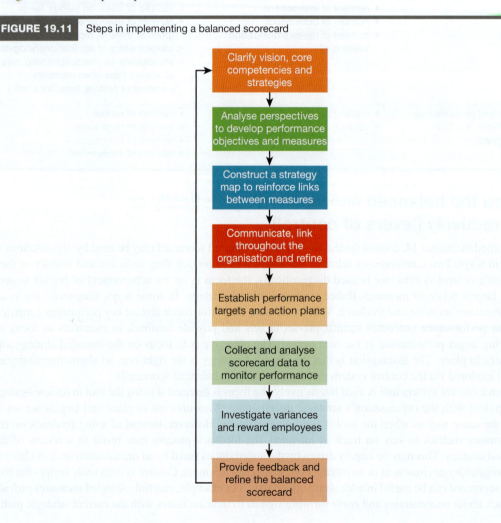

Clarify vision, core competencies and strategies

Clarifying the entity's vision, core competencies and strategies is central to the balanced scorecard approach. The vision provides an overall direction for the organisation. The core competencies and strategies provide guidance for achieving the organisational vision over the long term. To clarify the vision, statements are developed at the organisational level and for divisions, product lines or departments. This process leads to discussion and consensus, which further clarify an entity's purpose. Similarly, the process of clarifying core competencies and strategies helps others understand how to achieve the organisation's vision.

Analyse perspectives to develop performance objectives and measures

The next step is to analyse the organisation from the four perspectives. This step translates the organisation's vision and strategies into a set of performance objectives within each perspective. The analyses identify what the organisation must do well to attain its vision, focusing on the linkages between perspectives. The performance objectives should be limited to factors that achieve the organisation's vision and strategies.

The four perspectives introduced earlier are most commonly used for balanced scorecards. However, different entities define their perspectives differently. These perspectives differ by ownership type (for-profit versus not-for-profit), by industry, by organisation and by subunit within organisations.

For each performance objective, one or more measures are identified to monitor the organisation's progress. Corrective action is then taken, as needed. The measures are financial and non-financial, covering both quantitative and qualitative data. Accountants are often more comfortable with quantitative measures, such as the average time to complete a customer's order or the number of new customers obtained. However, qualitative data, such as the results of customer and employee satisfaction surveys, are useful for some performance objectives.

Input measures capture activity or effort whereas outcome measures capture results. Balanced scorecards focus on these types of expected links. Overall, balanced scorecards usually contain a range of measures, with four to seven performance measures used for each of the perspectives.

Construct a strategy map to reinforce links between measures

As outlined previously, the use of strategy maps in a balanced scorecard framework is a more recent development. Organisations are able to confirm the usefulness of their measures through construction of a one-page diagrammatic representation of the links between the measures in each of the perspectives. This can occur at a relatively broad level like the strategy map of the State Library of Queensland presented earlier in figure 19.6, or it might be more specific, showing links between most of the measures.

Communicate, link throughout the organisation and refine

The balanced scorecard is usually presented as a top-down plan. High-level executives define the vision, core competencies and strategies of the organisation, then communicate them to divisions and departments. Yet success of the balanced scorecard approach depends on the efforts of individuals throughout the entity. To succeed, the balanced scorecard must be communicated both up and down the organisation. Links must be developed between organisational, divisional, departmental and individual objectives. Aligning goals increases the likelihood that all employees work together.

Sometimes the results of multiple units are formally combined with the results of another unit. For example, the results of individual departments might be combined into the results of a division. Part of this balanced scorecard combines data for all offices within the physical plant department. For instance, the safety office is responsible for all lost time from work-related injuries and for ensuring that all physical plant employees receive peer review safety training. Similarly, the human resources office is responsible for hiring employees within a desired timeframe.

Sometimes a common set of balanced scorecard measures is used across departments. These measures are common because some of the performance objectives are the same. Common measures help ensure consensus throughout the entity, minimising the need to develop separate systems for data collection. Measures that differ across offices relate to operating activities that are unique to individual offices, departments or divisions.

Organisation-wide implementation of a balanced scorecard requires significant amounts of communication and time. The process often begins with pilot projects then expands across the entity as experience is gained and more sectors of the entity participate in the process. Refinements are often made to the original balanced scorecard after organisations have implemented it at the lowest levels.

Establish performance targets and action plans

It is not sufficient for an entity to create a balanced scorecard to measure progress towards its long-term vision and strategies. The organisation must also establish specific performance targets and related action plans, all of which are usually tied directly to each performance objective in the balanced scorecard. Performance targets are set for three- to five-year periods with interim milestones, increasing the organisation's focus on long-term results. Some entities formally reward individuals or groups of employees for attaining performance targets. The action plans give employees specific guidance about their efforts towards targets.

When the balanced scorecard is used to compensate employees, different weights may be placed on various measures in employee bonus packages. For example, if customer satisfaction ratings are inadequate, bonuses are made more dependent on improved satisfaction ratings. However, finding the optimal weighting among measures is difficult. If too much weight is put on customer satisfaction and not enough on financial measures, employees may spend a great deal of time in activities that increase satisfaction but do not improve profits.

Collect and analyse scorecard data to monitor performance

Balanced scorecard measures are captured periodically — monthly, quarterly, annually or other time-frames. Scorecard data are collected and analysed for different measures using different timeframes. Before calculations and comparisons to targets can be performed, systems for data collection must be established. In some cases, accounting systems are developed to capture relevant data. Non-financial measurement instruments may need to be developed. Survey instruments are either acquired or developed. Methods then need to be established for collecting samples and summarising results. Trends in balanced scorecard measures are analysed.

Investigate variances and reward employees

Actual results are compared to performance targets to determine whether the results are better or worse than desired. Then significant variances are analysed to identify their causes, leading to modifications in future plans. If the balanced scorecard is also used for employee compensation, rewards are computed and distributed.

Provide feedback and refine the balanced scorecard

An important part of the balanced scorecard method is the feedback loop that uses results and experience to refine the process. Managers use their analysis of balanced scorecard results to evaluate the success of their strategies and operating plans. This evaluation leads to revisions in organisations' visions, core competencies, strategies and operating plans. The effectiveness of the balanced scorecard is also gauged. Accountants and managers modify the set of measures to adapt to changes in the entity and to provide better information over time. Some measures may be dropped or changed, and new measures may be added.

Comprehensive example 2 demonstrates the implementation of a balanced scorecard in a hospital setting.

COMPREHENSIVE EXAMPLE 2

Implementing a balanced scorecard

Two hospitals in a large regional area have emergency departments, but neither department is financially sustainable. Because the region needs at least one emergency department, the state and local governments met with hospital officials to determine the best course of action. Both hospitals had spent considerable time reviewing their visions, core competencies and current business strategies. They agree that only the teaching hospital should continue operating an emergency department. The teaching hospital's mission is to provide high-quality patient care and a learning centre for medical students. The teaching hospital needs an emergency department so that medical students can prepare more thoroughly for careers as GPs and specialists.

Top managers at the teaching hospital decide to institute a balanced scorecard. They focus first on service in the emergency department, because many more patients will be admitted when the other hospital closes its emergency department. These managers believe that new measures of efficiency could help ease the transition.

The managers are also concerned about the current financial losses incurred by the emergency department. Clinical processes in the emergency department need to be cost effective and high quality to maintain the hospital's reputation.

Clarify vision, core competencies and strategies

A team of hospital administrators and emergency department employees meet to discuss the balanced scorecard implementation. The team decides that the hospital's vision, core competencies and strategies also apply in the emergency department. The hospital and emergency department's patient care goals are to provide high-quality care in a timely manner and at a low cost for all patients. The hospital and emergency department's teaching goals are to provide a high-quality education for medical students, focusing on technological developments and innovative patient care treatment.

Analyse perspectives to develop performance objectives and measures

The team decides that the standard four perspectives (financial, customer, internal business process, and learning and growth) are appropriate for analysing the emergency department's strategies and operations.

From a financial perspective, the hospital needs to at least break even to guarantee ongoing operations. The controller analyses historical records for the department and finds that it has always operated at a loss. Until last year, research grants and government subsidies were usually enough so that the department broke even. The financial perspective is important because the department needs financial resources to continuously update the equipment and technology needed to provide high-quality patient care. After discussing performance measures, three are chosen that are identical to those used by the hospital as a whole. Two of the measures are profit margin ratios, which address the emergency department's ability to control costs relative to revenues. The operating margin ratio includes only operating costs and revenues, while the excess income margin ratio includes non–operating revenue in the form of donations and grants, which typically supply the needed funds for expansion or new technology. The third measure addresses reimbursement levels for the emergency department.

Next, the team analyses the customer perspective. The hospital outsources patient satisfaction surveying, and it monitors average satisfaction by department to focus on patients' perceived quality of care. However, the survey results are only available quarterly. The department wants measures that predict patient satisfaction and that can be monitored daily. With timely feedback, problems will be identified and corrected quickly, before too many patients are unhappy with some aspect of service. The team decides that most patients would care about the average time they wait to be seen by a doctor. In addition, several quality-of-care measures could be monitored, such as the error rate in medication delivery, time waiting before admission to wards and time for specialist referral. The final list is included in figure 19.12.

The team then analyses the internal business process perspective. The hospital's long-term goals include managing patient care and clinical processes efficiently to maintain high quality and contain costs. The team decides that four aspects of internal business processes are critical to the emergency department's success. It then focuses on identifying measures for those four aspects.

For innovation processes, the team would like to motivate improvements in routine care such as delivering medications, arranging X-rays and blood tests, and cleaning and restocking cubicles for quick patient turnaround. Process improvements include innovative ways to streamline daily routines and to increase patient comfort. The number of process improvements in routine care will be tracked.

Clinical processes involve the technical aspects of care giving, such as setting up monitoring equipment and then using the information provided. The team decides to focus on the time taken for a patient to be discharged as a performance measure for clinical processes. In addition to focusing on the decision to discharge patients at an appropriate time, tracking this measure will also encourage nurses to focus on the discharge process. The team believes that time spent on discharge instructions is linked to full patient recovery. For example, patients are sometimes readmitted because they become dehydrated at home. Some medications require patients to drink extra amounts of water; if this requirement is not carefully explained during the discharge instruction process, patients do not recover as quickly and may require readmission.

Financial perspective
- Operating margin ratio[a]
- Excess income margin ratio[b]
- Average ratio of reimbursements to costs (categorised by diagnosis)

Internal business process perspective
Innovation of processes
- Number of process improvements in care to increase patient comfort
Clinical processes
- Time taken for discharge
Cost containment
- Average cost per patient by diagnosis type
Post-treatment service
- Time spent on discharge instructions

Customer perspective
- Doctor response time
- Medication errors
- Patient satisfaction survey results for quality of treatment care
- Time waiting before admission to ward
- Time for specialist referral

Learning and growth perspective
- Number of new treatment processes developed
- Number of hours per employee in training time

Calculations:
[a]Ratio of operating income to operating revenue
[b]Ratio of operating plus non-operating income to operating plus non-operating revenues

The team considers several possible ways to measure cost containment, but decides to focus initially on a general measure of cost — the average cost per patient by diagnosis type. This measure can be monitored as frequently as desired, allowing emergency department managers to quickly identify any adverse trends in cost. It also provides a way for managers to monitor cost effects when new procedures are implemented.

The emergency department's managers consider post-treatment service (when needed) to be very important. Service after a patient leaves the centre contributes to the quality of the patient's care. The team decides to measure this aspect using the time spent on discharge instructions. With more time spent on discharge instructions, patients should receive better home care, reducing the probability that they will be readmitted. The team considers measuring the number of telephone calls made and emails sent with follow-up questions about patient home care, but decides that it is more important to focus on instructions before the patient goes home.

Finally, the team focuses on the learning and growth perspective. To maintain and improve the emergency department's reputation for innovative patient treatment, the team decides to track the number of new treatment processes developed. Because new technologies and care-giving practices are developed continually, the hospital provides a variety of medical education classes for nurses and other department staff. To encourage employees to take advantage of these classes, the team chooses number of hours of training per employee as a performance measure.

Communicate, link throughout the organisation and refine

Once the team develops a tentative balanced scorecard for the emergency department, the plan is presented to top hospital administrators and to employees in the department. The administrators consider whether the emergency department objectives align with the overall hospital mission, strategies and objectives. They believe that this scorecard appropriately addresses the hospital mission and praises the team. Employees and medical students also feel that the scorecard helps them understand how the emergency department's objectives should be carried out.

Establish performance targets and action plans

The balanced scorecard team believes that the measures in figure 19.12 are appropriate for analysis. They ask the accounting department to collect information about last year's operations so they will have baseline information for comparison with future results. The team recommends that management and employees review the trends each month. After three months, the usefulness of this list of performance measures will be reassessed and the balanced scorecard can be changed accordingly.

Figure 19.13 summarises the information developed by the accounting department for last year's operations. The hospital's accounting system tracks patient charges for supplies and services by department; however, reimbursement is tracked at the hospital level because different payers pay different portions of charges, and some patients do not pay due to full reimbursement from their medical insurance provider. Therefore, the patient revenue is assigned to the emergency department based on its average mix of care for Medicare, privately insured and other patients. As a result, revenue is measured with error, and the information may not be of quality high enough for a performance measure.

FIGURE 19.13   Balanced scorecard data for the teaching hospital's emergency department

Overall department financial information:	
Patient revenue	$5 040 000
Operating costs (cost of patient care)	0 300 000
Non-operating revenues	1 500 000
Non-operating costs	$ 300 000
Information on emergency department operations	
Number of patients seen in emergency	252
Time to be seen by doctor (200 patients)	2 000
Time waiting before admission to ward (200 patients)	4 000
Time for specialist referral (200 patients)	4 000
Number of medication errors	10
Patient satisfaction survey results for quality of treatment care	
Number surveyed	130
Average satisfaction rating (1 to 5 = very satisfied)	3.8
Other patient-related data	
Total patient days	2 142
Time taken for discharge (200 patients)	4 000
Minutes spent on discharge instructions	5 040
Employee-related information	
Total time spent in training (hours)	875
Number of employees	35
Process improvement	
Number of process improvements in care	3
Number of process improvements in treatment	2

The cost data about patient care in the emergency department is quite accurate, although patient costs include fixed cost allocations. Any change in the allocation bases or methods reduces comparability of patient cost information over time. Patient survey information is gathered by the quality and utilisation department. Although the team would like daily information about customer satisfaction measures, surveys about patient satisfaction with services provided are given randomly to 20 per cent of the emergency department's patients during the first three days of each month. The survey response information is forwarded to the accounting department on the third day. The accounting department does not have time to track this measure more frequently. Employees estimate their time in training each month. Because they do not always fill out the reports, they are contacted by accounting each month to update any missing estimates. Time spent on discharge instructions for each patient will be reported by discharge nurses using a new form developed by the accounting department. Once a month, accountants will meet with physicians and nurses to determine the number and type of improvements and innovations in treatment and care-giving processes.

The balanced scorecard team uses the information in figure 19.13 to calculate last year's performance as shown in figure 19.14. Team members review this information and then meet with personnel at the other hospital to collect information about its emergency department. They then determine appropriate benchmarks and action plans for the emergency department during the transition period.

Because measures for the combined emergency departments are likely to be different from the current centre, a transition period will be needed to determine appropriate benchmarks. During the transition time, emergency department staff hired from the other hospital will be introduced to the scorecard. Within several months, targets can be set for every performance measure, and monitoring will begin. Information from the scorecard will be evaluated to determine areas in need of improvement. In addition, the current balanced scorecard will be re-evaluated and changed as appropriate.

Financial perspective performance measures

Operating margin ratio:

$$\frac{\text{Operating margin}}{\text{Patient revenue}} = \frac{\$5\,040\,000 - \$6\,300\,000}{\$5\,040\,000} \qquad (25)\%$$

Excess income margin ratio:

$$\frac{\text{Operating plus non-operating income}}{\text{Operating plus non-operating revenue}} = \frac{\$(60\,000)}{\$6\,540\,000} \qquad (1)\%$$

Ratio of reimbursement to cost:

$$\frac{\text{Patient revenue}}{\text{Operating margin}} = \frac{\$5\,040\,000}{\$6\,300\,000} \qquad 0.8$$

Customer perspective performance measures

Average time to be seen by doctor (minutes)	10
Time taken for admission to ward (minutes)	20
Time for specialist referral (minutes)	20
Medication errors	10
Average satisfaction with quality of treatment care	3.8

Internal business process perspective

Innovation of processes

Number of process improvements in routine care	3

Clinical processes

Time taken for discharge	20

Cost containment

Average cost per patient (Operating costs / No. of admissions)	$25 000

Post-treatment service

Time spent on discharge instructions (minutes)	20

Learning and growth perspective

Number of new treatment processes developed	2
Average training hours per employee	25

19.5 Strengths and weaknesses of the balanced scorecard

LEARNING OBJECTIVE 19.5 Identify and communicate the strengths and weaknesses of the balanced scorecard.

Similar to other accounting techniques, the balanced scorecard has both strengths and weaknesses.

Strengths

Entities are under increasing pressure to meet customer needs, use resources efficiently, compete effectively under changing conditions, employ new technologies and operating methods, and provide a good return to shareholders. These demands require more effective implementation of vision and strategies. The proponents of the balanced scorecard method argue that it improves performance by helping organisations integrate their visions and strategies into operations more completely. Many of the advantages of this approach, already described, are summarised in figure 19.15.

Weaknesses

Any method designed to help entities improve management decision making involves weaknesses because the process of management decision making is inherently uncertain. No perfect solutions have yet been discovered. Major weaknesses of the balanced scorecard are summarised in figure 19.15. First, the balanced scorecard faces questions about its costs and benefits. Considerable time and effort are needed to develop and use the balanced scorecard. Outside consultants are often employed, and the time involved for key managers can be considerable.

FIGURE 19.15 Strengths and weaknesses of a balanced scorecard

Strengths	Weaknesses
Communication and linkages • Encourages clarification and updating of vision and strategies • Provides a tool to communicate strategy throughout the organisation • Improves communication and consensus throughout the entity • Links short-term and long-term performance objectives to the vision and strategies	Implementation is expensive and time-consuming Uncertainties • Appropriateness of vision and strategies • Accuracy of identified core competencies • Best set of performance objectives and measures • Reliability of scorecard data • Reasonableness of targets • Doubt about links among perspectives
Guidance for improvements • Enables periodic performance reviews of progress towards vision and strategies • May lead to improved financial performance • Helps managers use operational data for decision making	Mistakes in implementation • Ambiguous or generally defined objectives • Information systems not integrated • Insufficient resources • Lack of senior management support • Focusing on inappropriate objectives
Motivation • Aligns unit and individual goals with the organisational vision and strategies • Motivates employee effort • Reduces optimisation of sub-units at the expense of the entity as a whole • Promotes action towards achieving strategies	Biases • Manager selection of familiar or easily attainable objectives and measures • Resistance from units and individuals • Process viewed as a temporary fad May result in excessive number of performance measures particularly at the individual level May be inappropriate as the basis for compensation Vision may not adequately capture core values including relations with regulators, approach towards the environment etc.

Uncertainties

Uncertainty is part of any balanced scorecard. The underlying assumptions are that the vision and core competencies have been properly identified and that implementation of the organisation's strategies leads to success. However, the best choices for a vision and set of strategies are ambiguous; managers might incorrectly identify the entity's strengths relative to competitors. Furthermore, the process of identifying appropriate performance objectives and measures is not straightforward. The balanced scorecard methodology requires managers to identify the most important aspects of operations, yet they cannot be known with certainty. Once performance objectives are selected, additional uncertainty about the best set of measures arises. Some measures are more reliable than others, although less-reliable measures can at times address a more relevant aspect of operations.

Uncertainties about choices of information for a balanced scorecard challenge managers and accountants. For example, potential customer satisfaction measures include market share, number of return customers, number of new customers, and ratings on satisfaction surveys. Although the number of return customers and number of new customers can be measured with a high degree of accuracy, this information may not be as relevant for gauging customer satisfaction as other measures. Market share may or may not be reliable, depending on the accuracy of information about total industry sales. Many factors influence the reliability of survey ratings, including the survey design, methods for collecting samples and the types of customers surveyed. To decide on the best measure, managers and accountants need to weigh the quality and relevance of information across potential measures.

Another uncertainty is the best choice for performance targets, including how quickly an entity should be able to achieve its performance objectives. Low targets may fail to motivate sufficient effort. High targets discourage performance when employees perceive them as unrealistic.

The balanced scorecard also assumes specific linkages among the four perspectives. In particular, it assumes that improved performance in internal business processes and in learning and growth lead to improved customer-related measures. In turn, improved customer-related measures are assumed to lead to improved financial performance. These assumptions, however, might not hold because of uncertainties about the measures and about the interrelationships among aspects of an organisation's activities. Researchers found cause-and-effect relationships only between the customer perspective measures and financial performance measures. Although research studies do not prove the absence of links, they raise doubts about the linkage that managers and accountants need to consider.

Mistakes in implementation

Analysts and consultants point out a number of areas where mistakes are often made in balanced scorecard implementations, leading to poor results. Sometimes performance objectives are ambiguous or defined too generally, reducing the balanced scorecard's effectiveness in communicating the actions needed to achieve the entity's vision and strategies. Sometimes the organisation's information systems are not designed adequately to capture information needed. The balanced scorecard can be expensive to implement, and may face inadequate resources for designing, implementing, communicating, following through on results and refining the methodology over time. Although senior managers are generally involved in the initial adoption of a balanced scorecard, they may give the process inadequate support.

Another mistake relates to the selection of inappropriate objectives and related measures. Author Jim Collins argues that many entities focus on the wrong financial measures. His research suggests that managers of the best-performing companies often succeed because they adopt more insightful measures to monitor their businesses. For example, Gillette shifted its focus from profit per division to profit per customer. This shift helped Gillette recognise the importance of repeatable purchases of high-margin products such as Mach3 razor cartridges. Companies where managers failed to adopt similarly insightful measures were not as successful.[23]

Biases

Several types of biases reduce the effectiveness of a balanced scorecard. Recent research suggests that managers select performance measures with which they are most familiar — measures that may not induce behaviour that leads to financial success.[24] In addition, managers have incentives to choose performance objectives and measures that highlight areas that are strengths instead of areas that need improvement. Any organisational change is likely to encounter resistance. For example, employees may view the balanced scorecard as a temporary management whim that does not deserve their attention. These types of resistance can prevent the entity-wide commitment and effort required for balanced scorecard success.

Other factors

Some questions surround whether or how the balanced scorecard should be used to compensate employees. Because of the uncertainties already discussed, many employees perceive balanced scorecard measures to be unfair for use in compensation calculations. An issue regarding the use of the balanced scorecard in compensating managers is how to adequately 'weight' the measures. Some organisations develop a balanced scorecard index, reflecting the balanced scorecard performance and linking it to compensation (see chapter 20 for an in-depth discussion of compensation and reward systems). In addition, weights or other formulaic approaches for using balanced scorecard results lead to game-playing and sub-optimisation, contrary to the purpose of a balanced scorecard.

Another criticism of the balanced scorecard approach is that it does not adequately capture core values, including relations with regulators or approaches towards the environment. An entity's core values are theoretically embedded in its vision and strategies. However, current literature on the balanced scorecard places little emphasis on values.

Moreover, something that is often overlooked is whether we are in danger of 'over-measuring' performance and as a consequence placing too much pressure on managers and operational employees. Perhaps, the 'balance' in balanced scorecards reminds us not to overdo it.

How valuable is the balanced scorecard?

Given these perceived weaknesses in the balanced scorecard, some people are inclined to dismiss this methodology; they want greater certainty about benefits. However, any method that managers use to help them develop and implement business strategies is subject to significant uncertainty. We learned in chapter 1 about the path to higher-quality management decisions, presented again in figure 19.16. Higher-quality decisions occur from use of:

- higher-quality information
- higher-quality reports
- higher-quality decision-making processes.

FIGURE 19.16 Path to higher-quality management decisions

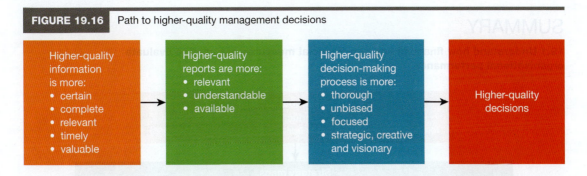

The best questions to ask about the balanced scorecard methodology are whether it helps managers and employees throughout the entity make higher-quality decisions, and whether the benefits from improved decision making exceed the costs of implementing and maintaining a balanced scorecard. Is the information in a balanced scorecard of higher quality than the information managers previously used? Are balanced scorecard reports more relevant, understandable and available on a timely basis? Does use of the balanced scorecard encourage managers and other employees to be more thorough, less biased, more focused, and more strategic, creative and visionary? Proponents of the balanced scorecard methodology argue that the answer to each of these questions is 'yes.' They also point out that the balanced scorecard should not be viewed as a static formulaic approach. Instead, it must be re-evaluated and refined periodically to provide better information for monitoring and motivating performance. Periodic re-evaluation allows managers to eliminate or alter measures that do not fit well and to identify potential new measures that offset unintended negative effects. As the entity learns, it can do a better job of designing and using a balanced scorecard. Organisations that fail to engage in continuous improvement are less likely to achieve high-quality results.

SUMMARY

19.1 Understand how financial and non-financial measures are used to evaluate organisational performance.

Organisational strategy
For example, low cost, product differentiation, blue ocean (organisational specifics may build on these generic strategies)

Strategy maps
Articulate organisational strategy through strategic themes and strategic objectives within the four perspectives of the balanced scorecard

Balanced scorecard
Uses the strategic objectives developed in the strategy map to communicate performance metrics within each of the four perspectives of financial, customer, internal business process, and learning and growth

19.2 Communicate the role of strategy maps in the balanced scorecard process.

A strategy map provides a visual representation of the strategy with a single-page view of how objectives in the four balanced scorecard perspectives (financial, customer, internal business process, and learning and growth) integrate and combine to guide the strategy. It illustrates the cause-and-effect relationships that link desired outcomes in the customer and financial perspectives to outstanding performance in critical internal processes — operations, management, customer management, innovation and regulatory/social processes.

The focus of a strategy map should be to:
- provide a link between the organisation's strategy and the balanced scorecard
- (where appropriate) convey the key strategic themes developed from the organisation's strategy
- convey the organisation's strategic objectives in the four balanced scorecard perspectives.

19.3 Evaluate and develop a balanced scorecard.

Balanced scorecard

Formal method to incorporate both financial and non-financial performance measures into organisational management systems. Translates organisational vision and strategies into performance objectives and related performance measures that can be monitored over time.

Four perspectives

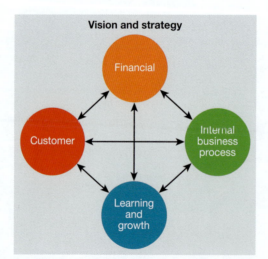

Identifying internal processes critical for success

- Innovation cycle
- Operations cycle
- Post-sales service cycle

The balanced scorecard and the levers of control

Using the balanced scorecard diagnostically or interactively relates essentially to the primary use and purpose of the scorecard. When used diagnostically, the focus is on the achievement of pre-set targets. In some ways, diagnostic use is all about *measure, monitor and feedback*. When used interactively, the focus is directed at using the tool to review strategy to help deal with the organisation's strategic uncertainties.

Belief systems, boundary systems and the balanced scorecard

The balanced scorecard may reinforce the belief system and through the metrics used direct managerial attention in the form of a boundary system.

19.4 Explain how a balanced scorecard is implemented.

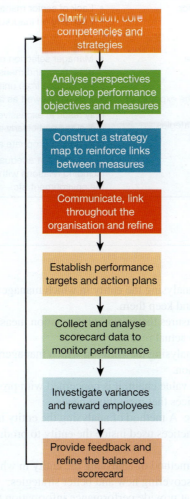

19.5 Identify and communicate the strengths and weaknesses of the balanced scorecard.

Strengths	Weaknesses
Communication and linkages • Encourages clarification and updating of vision and strategies • Provides a tool to communicate strategy throughout the organisation • Improves communication and consensus throughout the entity • Links short-term and long-term performance objectives to the vision and strategies	Implementation is expensive and time-consuming Uncertainties • Appropriateness of vision and strategies • Accuracy of identified core competencies • Best set of performance objectives and measures • Reliability of scorecard data • Reasonableness of targets • Doubt about links among perspectives
Guidance for improvements • Enables periodic performance reviews of progress towards vision and strategies • May lead to improved financial performance • Helps managers use operational data for decision making	Mistakes in implementation • Ambiguous or generally defined objectives • Information systems not integrated • Insufficient resources • Lack of senior management support • Focusing on inappropriate objectives
Motivation • Aligns unit and individual goals with the organisational vision and strategies • Motivates employee effort • Reduces optimisation of sub-units at the expense of the entity as a whole • Promotes action towards achieving strategies	Biases • Manager selection of familiar or easily attainable objectives and measures • Resistance from units and individuals • Process viewed as a temporary fad May result in excessive number of performance measures particularly at the individual level May be inappropriate as the basis for compensation Vision may not adequately capture core values including relations with regulators, approach towards the environment etc.

KEY TERMS

customer perspective A method of analysing the entity in which managers identify the customers they want and develop strategies to get and keep them.

financial measures Performance measures that provide information measured in dollars or ratios of dollars, and also compare budget to actual results.

financial perspective A method of analysing the entity in which managers identify desired financial results, given the organisation's vision.

innovation cycle The first step in the value chain, it is concerned with processes to identify customer needs and to design goods and services that meet those needs.

internal business process perspective A method of analysing the entity in which managers are concerned with the methods and practices used inside the entity to produce and deliver goods and services.

learning and growth perspective A method of analysing the entity in which managers are concerned with achieving future success by discovering new and better strategies.

non-financial measures Measures that provide performance information that cannot be measured in dollars, e.g. defect rates, throughput time and employee retention.

operations cycle The second step in the value chain, it is concerned with the production and delivery of goods or services that are identified and designed in the innovation cycle.

post-sales service cycle The final step in the value chain, it considers the service provided to customers after product delivery, e.g. providing warranty work, handling returns, correcting defects and collecting and processing payments.

SELF-STUDY PROBLEMS

SELF-STUDY PROBLEM 1 Balanced scorecard implementation; pros and cons

Mount Dandenong Bikes wants to implement a balanced scorecard. Its mission statement reads, 'We build high-quality, reliable bikes at competitive prices'. The entity's competitive strategy is to continuously improve the functionality, reliability and quality of its bikes while holding prices at levels similar to competitors. The entity operates three sub-units organised around the product lines for the three types of mountain bikes it currently produces. A fourth bike line in development includes a finished design, with engineers currently working on the plans for the manufacturing process. Mount Dandenong Bikes sells directly to bike shops and operates an internet site that allows bike shops to place orders for customised products.

Required

(a) Describe the implementation cycle for the balanced scorecard at Mount Dandenong Bikes.

(b) Describe the four perspectives of the balanced scorecard, and list one or more performance objectives for each perspective that are likely to be important for Mount Dandenong Bikes.

(c) Pick one performance objective for each perspective in part (b) and identify two or more potential measures. Explain how each measure would link to improved financial performance.

(d) Describe the pros and cons of implementing a balanced scorecard for Mount Dandenong Bikes.

SOLUTION TO SELF-STUDY PROBLEM 1

(a) Steps for implementing a balanced scorecard (from figure 19.11) for Mount Dandenong Bikes:

1. *Clarify vision, core competencies and strategies.* Mount Dandenong Bikes already developed its mission statement. The entity's managers should also consider writing a vision statement and core values statement. In addition, the managers need to clarify Mount Dandenong Bikes' core competencies. Even though the entity already specified its strategies, the managers should review them and revise them as necessary.

2. *Analyse perspectives to develop performance objectives and measures.* The managers need to analyse the entity's vision and strategies from each of the four perspectives for the balanced scorecard: financial, customer, internal business process, and learning and growth. Within each perspective, they need to identify performance objectives and related measures. To identify performance objectives, the managers must determine the critical actions that the organisation must take to achieve its strategies. They need to define what they mean by high quality from a customer's perspective. They also need to analyse competitors' prices and quality to determine the amount of cost containment and levels of quality needed.

3. *Construct a strategy map to reinforce links between measures.* The managers will use the perspectives and related measures identified in step 2 to illustrate the links between each of the measures. This will be shown diagrammatically in a strategy map, which also serves as a useful vehicle to test the adequacy of the measures. If cause-and-effect links cannot be demonstrated, then a reassessment of the measures will be necessary.

4. *Communicate, link throughout the organisation and refine.* The managers will develop a communication plan and obtain assistance from personnel throughout the organisation in clarifying and refining the decisions made in steps 1 and 2. The managers would then decide whether the different sub-units should develop their own balanced scorecards. The final set of performance objectives and measures must be communicated effectively to align employee efforts with the entity's objectives.

5. *Establish performance targets and action plans.* Through discussions among management and employees at different levels in the entity and analysis of previous results, performance targets and action plans are developed for each performance objective. The managers must also decide whether to use the balanced scorecard data for employee compensation. For employees whose compensation depends on the results, managers need to prioritise the objectives that relate to that employee's performance and establish a weighting scheme for linking rewards to performance. For example, production line employees could receive bonuses when production quantity and quality reach target levels.

6. *Collect and analyse scorecard data to monitor performance.* The managers need to ensure that information systems are in place to collect and report scorecard data. Trends can be noted. As data are collected, actual results can be compared to targets.

7. *Investigate variances and reward employees.* The managers need to analyse reasons for variance from targets. They also need to consider what the results mean for future strategies, operating plans and performance objectives.

8. *Provide feedback and refine the balanced scorecard.* The managers need to establish a feedback loop so that the information they learn is used to make adjustments as they go through the balanced scorecard process in the future. It means a re-evaluation of the process, beginning at step 1, as necessary.

(b) Four perspectives and possible performance objectives:

- The *financial perspective* analyses the economic consequences of Mount Dandenong Bikes' operations and decisions. A possible performance objective is a profitability level that is in the top quartile within the industry.
- The *customer perspective* analyses the role of customers in Mount Dandenong Bikes' success. Possible performance objectives are:
  - provision of goods and services that satisfy customers so that they remain loyal
  - an increase in the size of the loyal customer base.
- The *internal business process perspective* analyses the role of the entity's internal methods and practices in Mount Dandenong Bikes' success. Possible performance objectives are:
  - continuous improvements in functionality and quality that are important to customers (innovation cycle)
  - production of each bike as cost effectively as possible in a timely manner (operations cycle)
  - reliable products, with few returns and little warranty work (operations and post-sales service cycle)
  - customer satisfaction with interactions that occur after purchase (post-sales service cycle).
- The *learning and growth perspective* analyses the role of continuous improvement efforts in Mount Dandenong Bikes' success. Possible performance objectives are:
  - productive and well-trained employees
  - systems that support operations in a cost-effective manner.

(c)

Performance objective	Measures and links to financial performance
Financial perspective A profitability level in top quartile within the industry	• Operating margin. A higher operating margin leads to higher profits, which is a common indicator of financial success. • Economic value-added. EVA takes into account the level of profits as well as the cost of capital. • Average price per bike. The average price feeds into both operating margin and EVA. As prices go up, if costs and volumes are held constant, operating margins and EVA should increase.
Customer perspective Provision of goods and services that satisfy customers so that they remain loyal	• Customer satisfaction ratings (with emphasis on quality and price satisfaction). If customer satisfaction ratings are high, Mount Dandenong Bikes is likely to keep its current customers and add new ones, which would lead to higher market share, higher sales volumes, better operating margins and higher EVA. • Market share. Higher market share would lead to higher sales volumes, better operating margins and higher EVA. • Number of return customers and number of new customers. If the number of return and new customers increases, then sales volumes should also increase, leading to better operating margins and higher EVA.
Internal business process perspective Reliable products with few returns and little warranty work	• Number of bikes returned. If return rates and warranty work are low, customers are more satisfied and sales increase, leading to higher profits. In addition, Mount Dandenong Bikes spends less on post-sales service, which also increases profits. • Dollar value of warranty work. Same as above.
Learning and growth perspective Productive and well-trained employees	• Employee retention. Satisfied and well-trained employees are less likely to leave the entity. They also will monitor quality and efficiency of the production lines and make suggestions for improvements, leading to better cost-efficiency and higher-quality products, in turn leading to higher profits. More satisfied employees are also more likely to have positive interactions with customers, leading to improved sales and higher profitability. • Employee hours of training. Better training improves performance of work and interactions with customers, leading to higher sales and lower costs, increasing profits.

(d) *Pros:* Mount Dandenong Bikes begins the process of clarifying and updating its vision. Communication improves throughout the organisation as the vision and strategies are refined. Long-term and short-term performance objectives are linked to the vision and strategies. This linkage enables employees to understand their contribution to the overall entity and aligns employee goals with those of Mount Dandenong Bikes. Individual employees use their scorecards to guide their efforts towards reaching Mount Dandenong Bikes' goals and objectives. Mount Dandenong Bikes managers will periodically review their vision and core competencies, and their progress towards achieving them. Managers also have better information for decision making. These actions should lead to improved financial performance.

Cons: Implementing a balanced scorecard is expensive and time-consuming. If Mount Dandenong Bikes is already operating efficiently, the benefits from implementing the scoreboard may not be as large as the costs. If the vision or understanding of core competencies is inappropriate or inadequate, goals and objectives in the balanced scorecard may not relate to improved financial performance. If targets are unreasonably high or low, employees have no motivation to meet them. If the objectives are not well thought-out and communicated clearly, employees may not understand the objectives or how they relate to overall organisational performance. Measures could be chosen for which no data are available, or the data available are measured incorrectly or with error. Managers may choose performance measures that represent their strengths, rather than making unbiased choices.

QUESTIONS

19.1 Explain the differences between financial and non-financial performance measures and give two examples of each. **LO1**

19.2 Differentiate between a lag indicator and a lead indicator. Provide two examples of each. **LO1**

19.3 What is strategic decision making? What role does it play in the balanced scorecard? **LO4**

19.4 Outline the purpose of strategy maps. **LO2**

19.5 Identify the four generic perspectives of the balanced scorecard and explain how they are related. **LO3**

19.6 Describe the implementation process for the balanced scorecard. **LO4**

19.7 How might a balanced scorecard be used? **LO4**

19.8 What potential problems could arise if the balanced scorecard was developed without a strategy map being available? **LO2**

19.9 Allied Trucking moves produce from farms to markets. Its managers decided to implement a balanced scorecard around the entity's vision statement: 'We aim to be the industry leader in cost-effective and timely delivery of produce.' Provide two potential performance measures for each of the four perspectives for the balanced scorecard for Allied Trucking. **LO3**

19.10 Suppose that a travel agency decided it would no longer compensate employees with sales commissions, but instead pay a salary with a bonus for high customer satisfaction ratings. What problems would you foresee from the agency's financial perspective? **LO5**

19.11 (a) Pick two public companies, go to their websites and identify their major strategies. **LO2**

(b) Pick one of the companies from part (a) and go to the website of a competitor in the same industry. (For example, if you chose Coles, you might go to the website of Woolworths.) Now compare the strategies of both companies and list any similarities and differences.

19.12 Explain why demand might increase for relevant and useful information in the future. What professional skills will help you meet that need? **LO1, 3**

EXERCISES

19.13 Balanced scorecard measures for financial perspective **LO3**

Following is financial information for the last period for Curry House, a regional entity with a number of fast-food stores:

Revenue from operations	$10 450 200
Operating costs	$ 9 927 690
After-tax profits	$ 391 883
Cost of capital	12%
Required rate of return	15%
Average assets	$ 4 180 080

Required

Describe and calculate several measures that could be used for the financial perspective.

19.14 Financial and non-financial measures LO1

Managers increasingly use a mixture of financial and non-financial measures for organisational performance.

Required

In the following list of performance measures, identify those that are financial (F) and those that are non-financial (N).

(a) Customer satisfaction ratings

(b) Market share

(c) Operating margin

(d) Return on sales

(e) Annual average purchase amount per customer

(f) Defect rate

(g) Normal spoilage

(h) Labour efficiency variance

(i) Number of new products developed annually

(j) Revenues from new products introduced this year

19.15 Balanced scorecard measures for customer perspective LO3

Leyland College is in the process of developing a balanced scorecard. The administrators decided that their customers are parents and future employers of their students. They believe the students are their products.

Required

Discuss whether each of the following potential measures would be useful for the customer perspective in the balanced scorecard.

(a) Parent ratings of satisfaction with the high school curriculum

(b) Graduation rate

(c) Percentage of students employed during the summer after graduation

(d) Employer satisfaction ratings for Leyland College graduates

(e) Monthly earnings of graduates

(f) Number of graduates attending classes beyond high school

(g) Cost per student per year

(h) Number of classes per student per semester

(i) Average number of college credit hours completed per teacher

19.16 Learning and growth perspective LO3

Markman Ltd, a large pharmaceutical company, is concerned about the ability of its research and development department to develop profitable new prescription drugs. Once a drug has been developed and patented, it takes 9 to 12 years to meet all of the regulatory requirements. The company can then market the drug for about 11.5 years, on average, before the patent expires. Then competitors produce generic drugs. Employees currently participate in profit-sharing plans, but the company wants to give additional bonuses to improve performance. Markman decided to implement a balanced scorecard approach.

Required

(a) Explain why monitoring and rewarding non-financial performance might be particularly important for Markman.

(b) List one objective for Markman's learning and growth perspective.

(c) List two performance measures for the objective you picked in part (b).

19.17 Balanced scorecard measures for four perspectives LO3

Part of the process for developing a balanced scorecard is to identify one or more measures for each perspective.

Required

Categorise each of the following potential balanced scorecard measures according to the following perspectives:

F   Financial
C   Customer
I   Internal business process
L   Learning and growth

The measures are:

(a) Percentage of customer orders delivered on time
(b) Ratio of research and development cost to number of new products developed
(c) Economic value added (EVA)
(d) Number of hours of employee training
(e) Direct labour price variance
(f) Market share
(g) Percentage of customer orders delivered without error
(h) Days in accounts receivables
(i) Throughput time
(j) Direct materials efficiency variance
(k) Asset turnover
(l) Employee retention rate
(m) Percentage of bad debts collected
(n) Customer satisfaction ratings
(o) Number of degrees and certificates held per employee or department
(p) Percentage of purchase orders that are error free

19.18 Strategic plans; balanced scorecard measures for not-for-profit entity   **LO2, 3**

You have been invited by a classmate to help found a new not-for-profit entity named Students Care. The organisation's purpose is to provide scholarship money for children in Africa who have become orphans because of the AIDS epidemic. The organisation will operate only on campus, and the target donors are students. Suppose a wealthy businesswoman has offered to coordinate distribution of the scholarship funds to needy students, but wants to see a business plan for the organisation that describes the organisational vision and lists the core competencies, strategies and operating plans.

Required

(a) Explain what each item on the businesswoman's list means. For each item, provide a possible example for Students Care.
(b) Consider the perspective of internal business processes. Your classmate wants to measure the number of hours per week that volunteers spend collecting donations but you believe it should be dollars collected per volunteer hour spent in collection, measured on a weekly basis. Give one advantage and one disadvantage for each measure.
(c) You have had difficulty determining a measure of learning and growth, but a campus association recently organised a series of short workshops on improving student fundraising activities, as well as other aspects of governing student entities. Discuss the advantages and disadvantages of using the number of Students Care volunteers attending workshops as a measure for this perspective.
(d) Outline how the use of a strategy map might have been useful in the balanced scorecard process.

19.19 Balanced scorecard perspectives, performance objectives and measures   **LO1,3**

Perspectives, performance objectives and potential performance measures for the balanced scorecard at Holiday Resorts are as follows.

Perspectives.
  i. Financial
 ii. Customer
iii. Internal business
 iv. Learning and growth

Performance objectives:
A. Reduce housekeeping costs
B. Improve the quality of, and results from, advertising campaigns
C. Decrease vacancy rate during the off-season
D. Increase number of return customers

E. Increase overall profits

F. Increase the use of internet-based reservations

G. Retain high-quality employees

H. Increase the number of activities available to customers

I. Improve the quality of stay for holiday makers

J. Provide employee training in quality customer service

K. Reduce error rate in reservations

Potential performance measures:

1. Operating margin
2. Customer complaint rate
3. Survey customers at check-in about how they first heard about the resorts
4. Housekeeping cost per room
5. Number of employee hours spent in training
6. Error rate in reservation process
7. Percentage of reservations made using the website
8. Customer surveys about satisfaction and quality
9. Employee turnover rates
10. Number of activities per resort that are available to customers
11. Percentage and number of return customers
12. Number of hours of employee training offered
13. Vacancy rates
14. Customer focus groups inquiring about quality and potential success of advertising
15. Number of suggestions that improve quality of service

Required

(a) For each perspective (i–iv), identify at least one appropriate performance objective (A–K).

(b) For each performance objective (A–K), identify at least one appropriate performance measure (1–15).

(c) Explain the links between the measures.

19.20 Balanced scorecard at individual level; strategy map; boundary systems   **LO2, 4**

Required

(a) How might organisations such as Qantas and Virgin Australia use a strategy map in the process of developing their scorecards?

(b) Explain how the airlines might be able to use the balanced scorecard as a form of boundary system.

19.21 Balanced scorecard perspectives: internal business process, innovation and growth   **LO3,4**

The Galaxy Hotel Group owns and operates a number of mid-level boutique hotels mostly in regional Australia. Galaxy is structured around regions with a regional general manager usually given the responsibility of working closely with the managers of the hotels within their region. Commonly, a regional general manager is responsible for around six to eight hotels. Within Australia, Galaxy has six regional general managers who report to the CEO, Angelo Vellma. Galaxy's strategy has focused on meeting the needs of business and holiday travellers seeking 3 to 3.5 star accommodation for relatively short stays that are affordable but comfortable. One thing Galaxy enforces is its objective of having the same high-level service at each hotel.

The CFO of Galaxy, Caitlin Zhang, has raised the idea of introducing a balanced scorecard. At this stage it has only been discussed at board level, but most of the board members are in favour of its implementation. As Zhang points out, 'it will focus the attention of employees on our key priorities as well as provide the opportunity to reinforce our strategy throughout the company'. Zhang's first draft balanced scorecard developed for use at the individual hotel level is provided below. To date, Zhang has constructed the first draft alone, without consulting others.

Perspective	Objective	Measures
Financial	Maximise revenue	Revenue per available room
Customer	Improve customer orientation	Guest customer cards — overall satisfaction score Team member survey — overall satisfaction score from a comprehensive survey of hotel staff Mystery shopper results — average of scores from random visits

Internal business process	Improve operational effectiveness	Earnings before interest, taxes, depreciation and amortisation (EBITDA) Month-end reporting cycle time
Reputation/quality management	Meet all quality and star-rating benchmarks	Standards compliance (a measure based on a hotel's compliance with quality standards)

Another board member, Patrick Ryan, wonders about using the balanced scorecard a little differently. 'Perhaps we could use the scorecard to facilitate discussion with our regional managers and individual hotel managers. Not all are the same and they obviously face different challenges. The scorecard could be used by senior management to meet with regional managers and discuss the performance of hotels in the region, and perhaps re-work part of the scorecard and set different priorities as the regions work to meet local challenges.'

Required

(a) Angelo Vellma is a little concerned about the draft scorecard. He had recently attended a seminar on balanced scorecards and is worried about the lack of measures relating to what he thinks are important issues at the individual hotel level. He is particularly concerned at the lack of an internal business process perspective and a learning and growth perspective in the scorecard. Identify two measures relevant at the individual hotel level at Galaxy for the internal business process perspective and the learning and growth perspective. Provide a brief justification for each measure.

(b) Comment on the implementation process of the balanced scorecard at Galaxy to date.

19.22 Future direction of accounting information LO1

Think about the type of work you will perform in your future career.

Required

(a) Give examples of the types of financial and non-financial information you will probably use in your work.

(b) List several methods you could use to produce information that will help predict future operations for your employer or for clients.

(c) What types of continuous learning do you foresee in your career?

(d) Explain why you may need to use creative or innovative ideas in your career.

PROBLEMS

19.23 Balanced scorecard; strategy map and implementation LO2, 5

Terence Smythe, a veterinarian, decided to join a small group of vets, so that he no longer has to be on call every night. Practice members share the responsibility of emergencies with other members of the group. In the past, Terence differentiated his practice by specialising in the treatment of large farm animals. None of the other vets specialise in large farm animals but all of them treat some farm animals. Terence's son just finished an accounting degree and recommended that the vets group consider implementing a balanced scorecard as they develop the policies and practices for the new group.

Required

(a) Explain what each of the four perspectives of the balanced scorecard mean in the context of a vets group.

(b) Recommend several methods the group could use to assess a performance objective of customer satisfaction.

(c) Recommend two measures for each of the four perspectives for the vets group. Explain your recommendations.

(d) Construct a strategy map to reflect the links between the measures selected. Briefly discuss the links.

19.24 Balanced scorecard measures **LO1, 3, 4**

Curry House owns a number of stores that sell fast food. As part of its compensation packages, Curry House provides employees with bonuses based on customer satisfaction surveys. Recent analysis of the data shows a positive correlation between survey ratings and sales; that is, as customer satisfaction increases, sales increase. However, at a certain point in this trend, sales plateau even though the ratings continue to increase. In addition, increasing customer satisfaction causes costs to also increase because more time is spent with each customer, and more employees are on hand to help with food preparation and cashiering to reduce the time that customers wait for their food to be prepared. Other factors that appear to affect customer satisfaction are the general cleanliness of the store and the attitudes of the cashiers as they provide customer service. A factor that strongly affects sales at each store is its health rating from the local council. These ratings are published in the local daily newspaper. When a store has a low rating, sales at that outlet drop off until publication of an improved rating occurs. The owner wants to add one or more financial performance measures to the bonus package so that employees will earn more money when customer satisfaction increases at the same time that financial performance is also increasing.

Required

(a) Describe advantages and disadvantages of using a combination of performance measures reflecting the customer and financial perspectives.

(b) Management would like to add other customer-related measures and is considering replacing survey satisfaction with some other measure. List one potential measure and list at least one advantage and one disadvantage for it.

(c) List one additional performance measure that could be included in the compensation package. Explain what it is and what it would contribute.

(d) Explain how the scorecard measures (particularly the customer perspective) are being used in part as a boundary system.

19.25 Balanced scorecard; financial and non-financial measures **LO1, 3, 4**

Dyggur Equipment manufactures and sells heavy equipment used in construction and mining. Customers are contractors who want reliable equipment at a low cost. The entity's strategy is to provide reliable products at a price lower than its competitors. Management wants to emphasise quick delivery and quick turnaround when equipment needs repair or service so that contractors are not without their equipment often or for long. Dyggur is considering the performance measures shown below for use in its balanced scorecard.

Required

(a) Categorise each of the following potential balanced scorecard measures as:

F   Financial

C   Customer

I   Internal business process

L   Innovation and growth

The measures are:

(a) Manufacturing cycle time per product

(b) Market share

(c) Average ratings on customer satisfaction surveys

(d) Average cost per unit

(e) Economic value added

(f) Percentage of receivables collected

(g) Dollar value of warranty work

(h) Time between order and delivery

(i) Time it takes to repair returned equipment

(j) Number of focus groups for new products

(k) Number of new uses for current products

(l) Number of times new technology is applied to current products

(m) Number of product change suggestions from sales

(n) Number of engineering change orders to improve manufacturing cycle

(o) Revenue growth

(p) Employee training hours

(q) Number of quality improvement suggestions from employees

(r) Number of new customers

(s) Number of repeat customers

(t) Employee turnover rate

(u) Defect rates for manufacturing production

(v) Percentage of error-free rates in:

(i) purchasing

(ii) billing

(iii) customer record keeping

(b) Explain how Dyggur would use the scorecard solely as a diagnostic tool.

19.26 Strategy; balanced scorecard measures and process   **LO1, 4**

Refer to the information in problem 19.25. Dyggur Equipment wants to offer weekend servicing of heavy equipment. None of its competitors offer this service, and management believes this service will bring in new business and help retain current customers.

Required

(a) List several advantages and disadvantages of this strategy.

(b) List one financial and two non-financial performance measures that could be used to monitor the success of this plan.

(c) Suppose the managers decide to launch this new service. At the end of the first year of operating weekend service, performance is evaluated by gathering and analysing measures such as those identified in part (b). How can this information be used to improve performance for the next period?

(d) Given that Dyggur management are now exploring new strategies, outline how senior management could use the balanced scorecard interactively.

19.27 Mission statement; strategy; balanced scorecard implementation   **LO1, 2**

Squeezers Juice and Tea Company manufactures organic juices and chai teas that are sold at wholefoods stores. Several of its products have been featured in movies because the company's products are popular with celebrities. The owners and employees value organic products and innovative combinations of juices and teas with outstanding taste. Several employees have found sources of unusual ingredients from organic farmers around the world. The ingredients are more expensive than those used by other juice manufacturers. Although Squeezers cannot set unrealistically high prices, it focuses on high quality. Demand for the entity's products is stable even though it sets the highest prices for juices in its market.

Recently, the costs of several unusual ingredients increased because of weather conditions. The owner is concerned that increasing prices any further could reduce demand. She has taken a business workshop and learned about the balanced scorecard. She wants to incorporate a balanced scorecard at Squeezers.

Required

(a) Draft a potential mission statement for Squeezers. Explain how you decided what should be included in the statement and how it should be worded.

(b) Explain the entity's business strategy and core competencies.

(c) Identify several performance objectives for each of the four perspectives.

(d) Select two performance objectives for each of the four perspectives, and identify a potential performance measure for each. Explain your choices.

(e) Describe possible methods to collect the data needed for each of the performance measures in part (d). For example, what existing information might be available? What new record keeping might be required? Would the company need to develop surveys?

19.28 Participative strategic planning process and benefits; manager behaviour   **LO1, 2**

(This problem assumes knowledge from management classes.) Quantum Computers produces and sells laptop computers. The entity is currently deciding whether to continue concentrating on the laptop computer market or to expand by entering the highly competitive computer desktop workstation market.

Most of the management staff has been with Quantum for a long time. Michael Mitchem, Quantum's president, wants his management staff to assist him in Quantum's strategic planning process. Mitchem has scheduled a three-day offsite meeting for the management staff to join together for the entity's strategic planning process.

Required

(a) What functional areas should be discussed during the strategic planning process?

(b) Identify at least six factors to be considered in a thorough strategic planning process that will move a company such as Quantum to another level of product development.

(c) Identify at least three benefits that Quantum can derive from a participatory strategic planning process.

(d) Discuss the expected behaviour of the managers at Quantum who participate in the three-day offsite strategic planning meeting.

19.29 **Balanced scorecard; strengths and weaknesses** LO1, 3, 5

Brewster House is a not-for-profit shelter for the homeless. Lately funding has decreased, but the demand for overnight shelter has increased. In cold weather, clients are turned away because the shelter is full. The director believes that the current capacity could be used more efficiently. No one has taken time to analyse the physical layout of the shelter and current use of space. Several rooms are used for storage that could probably be used for temporary housing. The stored boxes need to be sorted and moved. Volunteers currently assign beds and manage overnight housing, because the director is busy with fundraising. Volunteers work just a few shifts each week, so no one has taken responsibility for coordinating improvements in the services offered. The director is considering whether to implement a balanced scorecard to focus the attention of all volunteers on areas that need improvement.

Brewster receives funds from several sources, including a set annual budget from the local council and direct donations from supporters. The director develops a budget each year based on expected funding but she cannot precisely predict donations. The budget is used primarily to justify funding requests submitted to the council.

The director has asked a group of accounting students from the local university to evaluate operations and recommend whether the entity should develop a balanced scorecard. She cannot give bonuses based on the measures, but she wonders whether developing and monitoring performance measures would encourage the volunteers to increase the use of capacity. She also wonders whether some information from the balanced scorecard could be used to show donors the effectiveness of operations.

Required

(a) Describe several potential costs and benefits of the balanced scorecard for this organisation.

(b) Describe one potential measure for each scorecard perspective appropriate for Brewster House. Explain how information for each measure will be collected.

(c) Prepare a memo to the director that recommends whether Brewster House should adopt a balanced scorecard. In writing the memo, consider what information the director needs from you to help her make a decision.

19.30 **Strategy, balanced scorecard for organisation and employee** LO3, 4

Mark Hopper owns Dane Champions, a dog kennel that raises champion Great Danes for showing and breeding. His vision is to be the best-known breeder of Great Danes globally. His strategy is to breed and sell dogs from outstanding lineage from the standpoint of both physical health and good-natured temperaments. Following is information about operations over the last year.

Number of breedings	10
Number of puppies	45
Number of puppies sold	40
Number of puppies returned	2
Revenue from puppies	$ 24 000
Kennel operating costs (not including Mark's salary)	$ 35 000
Travel expenditures	$ 55 000
Number of trips to dog shows	20
Winnings from dog shows	$110 000
Number of championships	17
Number of dogs shown	4
Puppy owners' average satisfaction rating on a scale of 1 to 5, with 5 as most satisfied	4.5
Training time to prepare puppies for new homes (total hours)	14
Training time to prepare dogs for shows (hours per week per dog)	2

Required

(a) Is the entity's strategy one of cost leadership or product differentiation? Explain.

(b) (i) Prepare a simple balanced scorecard with one performance measure for each of the four perspectives for Dane Champions using only the data presented. Explain your choices.

   (ii) Explain how these measures are linked.

(c) Kennel operating costs include the cost of a local high school student who cleans out the kennels every afternoon after school. Mark is considering whether to set up an individual scorecard for the student. He only pays minimum wage, and although the student is fairly slow, the kennels are kept reasonably clean. Mark wonders whether the student would resent being monitored more closely. Describe one reason for using a scorecard with the student and one reason against using it.

19.31 Balanced scorecard variances   LO3, 4

A large supermarket has used a balanced scorecard for several years. The store's vision is to provide customers with low-cost goods and a high-quality shopping experience. The entity's strategy has been to focus on reducing waiting time for help on the floor and at the checkout counter. Information for the last two years follows.

	2019	2020
Average sale (Total revenue/Total invoices)	$15	$12
Average variable cost per sale	$7	$7
Average customer wait time at counter (minutes)	1.5	1.5
Average customer wait time for help on sales floor (minutes)	3	2
Shipping cost per order	$18	$15
Total returns	$57 000	$60 000
Total revenue	$800 000	$748 000
Total labour cost	$200 000	$220 000
Utilities cost (electricity and phone)	$2 100	$2 400
Number of items out of stock	120	180
Employee turnover	2	3

Required

(a) Classify each performance measure according to one of the four balanced scorecard perspectives.

(b) Analyse the change in each performance measure from 2019 to 2020. Give one possible reason for the change.

(c) Which performance measures need further investigation? Explain.

(d) What do the balanced scorecard results suggest about the success of the entity's strategy to reduce waiting time? Explain.

(e) When an organisation focuses on one strategy, problems sometimes arise in other areas. Do the balanced scorecard results provide evidence of possible deterioration in any operational areas? Explain.

19.32 Evaluate balanced scorecard design   LO4, 5

Frieda's Fizz brews specialty soft drinks, including ginger beer and other flavours. Its vision is 'To proudly produce and sell extraordinarily smooth, rich and delicious soft drinks to satisfy kids of all ages'. The entity has a reputation for high quality and unique flavour, enabling it to sell soft drinks at a premium price to gourmet grocery stores in the local area. The entity's managers plan to expand the business to other geographic regions, but they want to ensure that they maintain high quality as the entity grows. They have decided to implement a balanced scorecard, and they have chosen the following balanced scorecard measures.

Financial perspective:

1. Breakdown of manufacturing cost per case: ingredients, direct labour, packaging materials and overhead

2. Operating profit per case

3. Return on investment
   Customer perspective

4. Number of customer complaints relating to taste, freshness, package integrity, appearance and foreign objects

5. Quality index (an internal measure of manufacturing quality, including microbiology and chemistry)
6. Percentage sales growth

Internal business process perspective:

7. Ratio of plant production hours to total available time
8. Throughput (number of cases packaged)
9. Waste and scrap as a percentage of total production cost

Learning and growth perspective:

10. Number of work-related injuries
11. Number of training hours per employee
12. Number of community volunteer hours per employee

Required

(a) Explain why uncertainties exist about the best balanced scorecard measures for Frieda's Fizz. (Do not discuss any of the measures already listed. Instead, focus on why any set of measures might not provide ideal information and on why the managers cannot know with certainty which set of measures is best.)

(b) For the balanced scorecard perspective:
 (i) Describe the strengths and weaknesses of the measures chosen for that category.
 (ii) Reach a conclusion about the reasonableness of the set of balanced scorecard measures for that category.

(c) What are the pros and cons of implementing a balanced scorecard?

(d) How valuable do you think the balanced scorecard will be in helping the managers of Frieda's Fizz meet its vision? Explain.

(e) The managers of Frieda's Fizz want your evaluation of their proposed balanced scorecard. Use the information you learned from the preceding analyses to write a memo to the managers presenting your evaluation of:
 (i) whether they should adopt a balanced scorecard
 (ii) the proposed balanced scorecard design.

19.33 Strategies and balanced scorecard measures for a country   **LO1**

Brian Henshall, Foundation Emeritus Professor of Management at the University of Auckland, suggests a number of potential performance measures that could be used to monitor performance for the country of New Zealand. Henshall recommends that measures be published monthly to gauge progress. He also argues that a discussion of potential performance measures would help citizens define what they want. Ultimately, the measures could be used to monitor the performance of elected officials. Following are some of Henshall's suggestions.[25]

Tangible wealth:

• gross domestic product (GDP), percentage change as a measure of growth
• the ratio of government wealth creation to business wealth creation, as a measure of government economic performance
• GDP per person employed and per total number of people in New Zealand, as efficiency measures
• New Zealand dollar exchange rate (percentage change for last quarter or last year), as a measure of economic stability
• ratio of bankrupt firms to all trading entities, as a measure of business stability

Environmental intangible wealth:

• a pollution index that measures degradation of the environment from pollution
• a ratio of protected land relative to total government-owned land
• a ratio of alternative energy resources relative to total energy produced

Physical and social infrastructure:

• educational expense as a percentage of GDP
• healthcare expense as a percentage of GDP
• accidents index
• serious crimes index

Demographics:

• changes in population growth, year to year
• growth in education levels
• a demographic index that monitors innovations by diversity of peoples
• unemployment rates

Required

(a) Suppose government officials developed an objective to increase the number of university graduates because they believe increased education will lead to increased GDP. Brainstorm and identify several ideas for action plans to carry out this strategy.

(b) Pick one of your ideas from part (a) and discuss its pros and cons.

(c) Brainstorm ideas for action plans to increase the number of high school graduates.

(d) Pick one of your ideas from part (c) and discuss its pros and cons.

ENDNOTES

1. Birt, J, Chalmers, K, Maloney, S, Brooks, A, Byrne, S & Oliver, J 2017, *Accounting: Business reporting for decision making*. 6th Edn. John Wiley & Sons Australia, Ltd.
2. Reichheld, FF 2003, The one number you need to grow. *Harvard business review, 81*(12), pp. 46–55.
3. ibid.
4. Adapted from Birt et al. 2017, p. 587.
5. Norreklit, H 2000, 'The balance on the balanced scorecard — a critical analysis of some of its assumptions', *Management Accounting Research*, vol. 11, pp. 65–88.
6. Parida, A & Chattopadhyay, G 2007, Development of a multi-criteria hierarchical framework for maintenance performance measurement (MPM). *Journal of Quality in Maintenance Engineering, 13*(3), pp. 245–246.
7. Neely, A, Richards, H, Mills, J, Platts, K & Bourne, M 1997, Designing performance measures: a structured approach. *International Journal of Operations & Production Management, 17*(11), p. 1131.
8. Adapted from Neely et al. 1997, p. 1137.
9. Hoque, Z 2014, 20 years of studies on the balanced scorecard: trends, accomplishments, gaps and opportunities for future research. *The British Accounting Review, 46*(1), pp. 33–59.
10. Adapted from Parida, A & Chattopadhyay, G 2007.
11. Kaplan, R & Norton, D 2004, 'How strategy maps frame an organisation's objectives', *Strategic Finance*, March/April, p. 45.
12. Norreklit, H 2000.
13. State Library of Queensland 2014, *Strategic plan 2014–18*, www.slq.qld.gov.au.
14. As identified by Kaplan and Norton in Kaplan, R & Norton, D, 2004, 'How strategy maps from an organization's objectives', *Strategy and Leadership*, vol. 32, 5, pp. 10–17.
15. Copyright 2002, *Strategic Finance*, published by the Institute of Management Accountants (IMA) 2002, Montvale, NJ, www.imanet.org. Adapted with permission.
16. Adapted from Medicare Australia Health Insurance Commission 2003, *Annual report 2002–03*, p. 10.
17. Craft Beer Industry Association 2015, 'Brewers', www.australiancraftbeer.org.au; and IBISWorld 2015, 'Beer manufacturing in Australia: market research report', August, www.ibisworld.com.au.
18. Morgan, J 2014, A simple explanation of 'the internet of things'. Forbes. May 13. Retrieved from: https://www.forbes.com/sites/jacobmorgan/2014/05/13/simple-explanation-internet-things-that-anyone-can-understand/#51c261d11d09.
19. O'Leary, DE 2013, Big Data', The 'Internet of Things' and The 'Internet of Signs'. *Intelligent Systems in Accounting, Finance and Management, 20*(1), pp. 53–65.
20. Chu, SC & Kim, Y 2011, Determinants of consumer engagement in electronic word-of-mouth (eWOM) in social networking sites. *International Journal of Advertising, 30*(1), pp. 47–75.
21. Cui, G, Lui, HK & Guo, X 2012, The effect of online consumer reviews on new product sales. *International Journal of Electronic Commerce, 17*(1), pp. 39–58.
22. Adapted from Hoffman, DL & Fodor, M 2010, Can you measure the ROI of your social media marketing? *MIT Sloan Management Review, 52*(1), p. 44.
23. Collins, J 2001, *Good to great: why some companies make the leap … and others don't*, HarperBusiness, New York, pp. 106–07.
24. Lipe, M & Salterio, S 2000, 'The balanced scorecard: judgmental effects of common and unique performance measures', *The Accounting Review*, July, pp. 283–96.
25. Henshall, BD 2002, 'Kiwi Scorecard,' *New Zealand Management*, July 2002, pp. 15 ff.

ACKNOWLEDGEMENTS

Photo 19A: © Pressmaster / Shutterstock.com

Photo 19B: © Monkey Business Images / Shutterstock.com

Figure 19.9a: © Copyright 2002, 'Strategic Finance', published by the Institute of Management Accountants IMA 2002, Montvale, NJ, www.imanet.org.

Figure 19.9b: © Health Insurance Commission

Figure 19.6: © State Library of Queensland

Rewards, incentives and risk management

After studying this chapter, you should be able to:

20.1 explain agency theory and the link between agency costs and reward system design

20.2 communicate the key components of reward systems

20.3 explain the advantages and disadvantages of cash and equity as key components of incentive plans

20.4 demonstrate an understanding of different reward system structures

20.5 demonstrate an understanding of current themes and trends in reward systems

20.6 identify and communicate the attributes of different types of risk and how they might be managed.

IN BRIEF

Reward systems (sometimes referred to as compensation plans or remuneration plans) and associated incentive payments for executives and senior managers are sometimes considered controversial in contemporary society. The controversy relates to allegations of disconnect between organisational performance and the incentives and rewards paid to executives. In particular, debates over excessive rewards at times of economic downturn have required both corporate regulators and companies to pay increasing attention to the role and scope of incentives in both encouraging and rewarding executives in their varying decision-making roles. More recently, governments and regulatory authorities have called for increased regulation and greater corporate disclosure of performance linked to executive incentive payments. In addition, there is now a greater emphasis on the role of strategic management accounting techniques and how they might overcome issues associated with incentives that encourage decisions with a short-term focus and promote a silo mentality within organisations. Moreover, the management of risk is becoming an increasing area of concern for boards, executives and regulators. While incentive plans are important in the process of managing risk, other internal controls are important tools in managerial control systems. Understanding the link between strategic performance measurement, reward system alternatives and risk can be beneficial for boards when structuring incentive plans for executives and senior managers and developing suitable risk management controls.

20.1 Agency theory and rewards

LEARNING OBJECTIVE 20.1 Explain agency theory and the link between agency costs and reward system design.

Agency theory is an analytical framework that examines potential conflicts between owners and managers, and between managers and employees. Within agency theory, the two types of information consumers are principals and agents. **Principals** hire agents to make decisions for them and to act on their behalf; **agents** in turn are people who act on behalf of others — the principals. As shown in figure 20.1, the shareholders of a company are principals, and the CEO is their agent. In not-for-profit entities, stakeholders such as donors own the entity and hire the CEO. As the top manager of an entity owned by shareholders or other stakeholders, the CEO makes decisions, plans strategies and protects the interests of the owners. At the same time, the CEO is a principal, and the lower-level managers and employees are agents for both the CEO and in turn the owners.

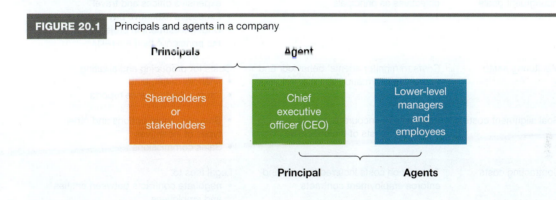

FIGURE 20.1 Principals and agents in a company

Agency costs

Problems arise when the goals of principals are not completely shared by their agents. For example, employees may exert insufficient effort, or managers may waste organisational resources. The costs that arise when agents fail to act in the interest of principals are **agency costs**. Figure 20.2 shows several types of agency costs, including direct costs that occur when agents do not work in the principals' best interests, as well as costs incurred to monitor and motivate agent performance.

Figure 20.2 provides some insight into the links between agency theory, reward systems and managerial control. Reward systems and incentive plans try to align the interests of shareholders and managers. The challenge from a managerial control system perspective is to do this in a way that encourages better individual and organisational performance than if incentives did not exist.

When entities are small, principals minimise agency costs by personally overseeing agent behaviour and performance. However, as organisations grow larger, agent behaviour is more difficult to observe, and agency costs tend to increase. To reduce agency costs, entities establish accounting systems to monitor and influence agent behaviour. For example, public companies publish audited financial statements, and employees are often paid bonuses for achieving profit goals.

Thus, accounting information is used not only to measure and monitor an organisation's activities, but also to measure, monitor and motivate the performance of agents. This would form part of the management control system of the entity.

It is impossible to completely eliminate agency costs because agent behaviour and decision making cannot be perfectly observed or measured. Poor results might be caused by poor agent performance or by circumstances outside of the agent's control. Similarly, favourable results cannot be attributed to the agent's performance alone. For example, the sales generated by a salesperson are partly a function of the effort and skills of the salesperson and partly a function of the price and quality of the product, economic conditions, competition, customer tastes and so on.

One way to reduce agency costs is to give specific decision-making authority to agents and then hold them responsible for the results of their decisions. This idea lies behind the corporate form of business organisation. Shareholders give managers authority to decide how company resources are used. Then shareholders hold the managers responsible for creating shareholder value. Similarly, the authority for decisions can be dispersed throughout an organisation. To reduce agency costs, individual employees are held responsible for their decisions, and limits are placed on their decision-making authority. For example, the maître d' in a restaurant is responsible for seating people, and has the authority to choose where customers sit. However, the maître d' has no responsibility for the menu items; the chef has the authority to purchase food and to choose the items to be offered on the menu.

FIGURE 20.2	Agency costs	
General agency cost	**Explanation**	**Specific examples**
Losses from poor decisions	Agents may not expend the effort needed to gather appropriate information and make good decisions	• Purchasing poor-quality raw materials • Investing in an unprofitable project • Not prioritising projects by attributes that would benefit the entity
Losses from incongruent goals	Agents do not value the same goals and objectives as principals	• Consumption of perquisites such as expensive offices and travel • Excessive executive pay • Underinvestment in projects that are in the principal's best interests
Monitoring costs	Costs to monitor agents' behaviour and to provide information about agent effort	Costs for producing and auditing: • financial statements • internal performance reports
Goal alignment costs	Payments to encourage agents to act in the best interests of the principals	• Bonuses, share options and other types of incentives • Sales commissions
Contracting costs	Transaction costs incurred to write and enforce employment contracts	Legal fees to: • negotiate contracts between entities and employees • sue employees when they do not meet contractual obligations

Rewards

Rewards and incentives paid to executives and managers tend to create controversy, particularly in the financial press. This controversy usually surrounds perceived excessive payments (for example, annual payments or severance payments upon CEO termination or end of tenure) to executives and managers. A considerable amount of emotion surrounds executive remuneration. Nevertheless, when the pay to CEOs seems excessive relative to company performance, shareholders and other stakeholders have the right to question the policies of the board of directors of the company. However, we need to remember that reward systems and pay are about more than just the CEO's remuneration. Organisations have remuneration arrangements with the directors of the board, senior executives, divisional and unit managers, line managers and employees. In this sense, structuring pay systems linked to individual or group performance becomes more complex than determining the pay arrangements for the CEO alone.

20.2 The structure of reward systems

LEARNING OBJECTIVE 20.2 Communicate the key components of reward systems.

Reward systems may be structured in a variety of ways. At the two extremes, all pay might be fixed (as is the case for many employees) or all pay might be variable (or at risk) depending on the achievement of pre-set targets and incentives, as is the case for some sales-type roles. Most of our attention in this chapter relates to executives and managers at senior, divisional and unit levels in an organisation. In most cases, reward systems at these levels are a combination of fixed and variable components.

In the first place, an interesting question is why incentives (bonuses or rewards) are included in the remuneration structure of executives and managers. It is often maintained that incentives have a positive effect on performance. Consequently, we see incentives used in reward systems for CEOs, senior executives and managers of divisions and units, as well as for roles where incentives have generally always existed (for example, sales roles). Some argue that incentives should be used more broadly throughout all roles in an organisation. The incentives commonly used in remuneration structures can be described as *extrinsic rewards*. Extrinsic rewards are *external* incentives that a manager receives for meeting pre-set levels of performance, including bonuses in the form of cash or equity, or other external rewards such as holidays. On the other hand, *intrinsic rewards* relate to personal satisfaction gained from doing a job/ task well.

Some researchers and consultants such as Deming, Kohn and Pink argue that extrinsic rewards do little in the long term to foster superior performance. For example, several decades ago, W Edwards Deming, a quality management guru, argued strongly against the use of extrinsic rewards in his 14 principles of management (outlined in chapter 17). In particular, principles 11 and 12 of his 14 principles state:[1]

11. (a) Eliminate work standards (quotas) on the factory floor. Substitute leadership.
    (b) Eliminate management by objective. Eliminate management by numbers, numerical goals. Substitute leadership.
12. (a) Remove barriers that rob the hourly paid worker of his right to pride in workmanship. The responsibility of supervisors must be changed from sheer numbers to quality.
    (b) Remove barriers that rob people in management and engineering of their right to pride in workmanship. This means, inter alia, abolishment of the annual or merit rating and management by objective.

He also suggested it best to pay people well and then help them forget about pay. Likewise, Kohn in a *Harvard Business Review* paper[2] argued strongly against the use of extrinsic rewards such as incentives. More recently Pink[3] questioned the incentive effect of many of our reward structures. A counterargument[4] is that while incentives may be badly used by some organisations, if properly managed they can be powerful tools in attracting and retaining talented people and boosting productivity. The debate about whether extrinsic rewards in the form of incentives produce superior performance (or at least better performance compared to no incentives) will continue. The fact remains that organisations are likely to continue to use incentives as part of reward system structures. From the perspective of managerial control system design, the challenge is identifying a suitable structure and components to influence managerial behaviour and decision making in a manner that adds value to the organisation over time.

Where incentives are to be included in reward systems, key considerations include the following.
- Who incentives apply to (senior executives, divisional and unit managers, line managers, others). For example, a company might use incentives only at the executive level or it might use a broad incentive based on organisational performance for all employees (including executives and managers).
- Whether performance is measured at the individual, divisional/unit and/or corporate levels or some combination thereof. Moreover, if a combination of performance is used, what weightings will apply? For example, it is common to find that senior executive levels will have a higher weighting towards corporate performance than, say, line managers.
- What performance measures will be used.
- Whether a distinction between short-term and longer-term incentives will be made and, if so, what proportion of total rewards should relate to short-term performance versus long-term performance.

20.3 Forms of incentives

LEARNING OBJECTIVE 20.3 Explain the advantages and disadvantages of cash and equity as key components of incentive plans.

Broadly speaking, incentives are commonly paid in either cash or equity. Or course, each has its own advantages. For example, payments in cash:
- might be preferred by a risk-averse executive or manager
- do not dilute the company's equity holdings.

Cash payments reduce the overall cash available in the company for alternative uses and as they are immediate they do not encourage a longer-term view of performance by recipients.

Equity payments, on the other hand:
- encourage a longer-term view of performance by recipients on the premise that improved company performance over time is likely to impact favourably on the share price of the company and therefore translate to higher incentive payments in the future
- may help to overcome the agency problem by aligning the interests of shareholders and managers

- involve no cash outflow for the company (unless loans are provided to executives to acquire the equity as is the case in some schemes).
Equity rewards also have their downside, including:
- the dilution of shareholder value as a result of an increase in the number of issued shares
- the possible temptation for managers to engage in accounting misstatement or fraud to meet market expectations and maintain share prices.

Types of equity incentives

Equity incentives commonly take one of two forms — shares or share options — although other forms are also available.

Shares as incentives

When shares are provided directly to executives and managers for meeting expected performance targets, the executive or manager immediately increases their shareholding in the company. This, of course, is the link to overcoming the agency problem as the executive/manager's interests are aligned with other shareholders.

Share options as incentives

Share options are an instrument that gives the holder the right but not the obligation to convert the options to shares at sometime in the future, according to a predetermined price.[5] The options can be exercised (converted to shares) provided the performance benchmarks are met. One of the advantages of share options is that the shares are not immediately attainable, yet the effect of the executive or manager having an equity interest in the company still exists. A further advantage is that as there is a time lag between when the options are granted and when they are able to be exercised, encouraging a longer-term view. There has been a growth in the use of share options as a component of executive reward systems over the last 10 to 15 years. Nonetheless, according to Denis et al.,[6] share option detractors argue that options may promote excessive risk taking, their usefulness as an incentive is limited due to limited downside risk and, like shares, they may encourage accounting manipulation to maintain option and share values.

20.4 Structuring reward systems containing incentives

LEARNING OBJECTIVE 20.4 Demonstrate an understanding of different reward system structures.

A common criticism of executive incentives is that they tend to focus on short-term results at the expense of results over the longer term. Of course, a relevant issue is what constitutes the short term and what constitutes the long term. In accounting, it is common to define the short term as relating to a one-year period. The interesting question, then, is what constitutes the long term? As two years seems inadequate as a longer-term view, it is common to think of a three- to five-year time horizon as the long term. Perhaps, two to three years might constitute a medium-term perspective.

There have been attempts to focus the attention of executives on the long-term performance of the organisation. This can be achieved in a number of ways, although equity-based rewards have been common vehicles. Whether compensation is partly structured to focus on the long term depends on two key factors.
1. *The time horizon relating to the target measure.* For example, if a reward is contingent on meeting a return on investment (ROI) target or an earnings per share target based on a one-year performance, the focus is more short term. On the other hand, if the same measures are based on a three- or five-year average, there is more focus on longer-term outcomes in the use of the measure.
2. *The 'lasting' nature of the reward itself.* For example, compared to cash, equity-based rewards such as shares and share options are viewed as having a more lasting effect in that as long as the executive/manager continues to hold the equity (shares or share options) they are more likely to take actions that will (where possible) have a positive impact on the share price in the long term.

To encourage managers to focus on the long term, many companies have increased the use of equity-based compensation. Share options, in particular, became popular during the 1980s and 1990s.

Compensation tied to the value of equity was viewed as a way to encourage managers and other employees to focus on increasing the long-term value of the company and addressing the agency problem discussed previously. It was assumed that giving executives the opportunity to become substantial shareholders in the company would motivate them to act in the best interests of that company. Organisations around the globe have followed this practice of incorporating significant levels of equity-based rewards into compensation contracts.

In structuring a reward system containing incentives, decisions need to be made about:
- the measures to be used
- the time period to which performance will relate
- the targets to be met to receive the incentive
- the form of incentives to be used.

Figure 20.3 shows examples of measures, targets and rewards.

FIGURE 20.3	Performance measures and examples of targets and rewards

Financial measure	Example of benchmark or target	Example of reward
ROI	A set percentage	Cash bonus or equity-related reward
Economic value added (EVA)	Dollar target or percentage change	Cash bonus or equity-related reward
Operating income or growth in income	Dollar target or percentage growth target	Cash bonus or profit sharing
Cost savings	Cost reduction of a set percentage (e.g. 5 per cent)	Gain sharing — employees receive a percentage of the savings
Revenue growth	A set percentage	Cash bonus plus paid family vacation to award ceremony at resort destination
Market share	A set percentage	Cash bonus as part of a set of measures
Employee engagement	A specified rating	Cash bonus as part of a set of measures

Compensation contracts often include a base salary and bonuses. In the largest Australian companies, bonuses typically make up 40 per cent or more of the total compensation for top executives. Bonuses may be a combination of cash, shares, share options and deferred compensation (salary or bonuses paid in the future, often after retirement). As mentioned previously, CEO compensation attracts controversial press coverage, particularly when CEOs achieve pay increases at a time of declining or stagnant company performance.

We explore two common forms of incentive structures in the two comprehensive examples that follow. First, in comprehensive example 1, we explore the change in compensation from a more case-based system to one including equity-type rewards and a more comprehensive set of performance measures. Second, in comprehensive example 2, we explore the operation of a compensation system based on a shared bonus pool.

COMPREHENSIVE EXAMPLE 1

Evaluation of incentive plan alternatives

The importance of the upcoming annual management meeting of Goldman, Mason and Vernon (GMV) is playing on the minds of the two most senior board members: Sharon Goldman (daughter of founder Bill Goldman) and Bruce Clayton. The business model of GMV had worked well for the last 20 years, but increasing uncertainty in financial and product markets combined with a worldwide reduction in activity has resulted in the board considering a number of changes within the  organisation to ensure its continued success. The most contentious of these changes, a new incentive compensation plan, is to be debated by senior managers at the next senior management meeting.

The company

GMV operates as a listed private-equity company. It was established in 1991 by Bill Goldman as a company making rather small strategic acquisitions. Bill had seen the company grow to what it is today, the only listed private-equity firm in Australia and New Zealand. GMV looks to make strategic acquisitions of unrelated companies where it is considered significant operational improvements can be made. Each of the acquired entities operates as a separate autonomous business unit of GMV, although there are a number of key elements common across each entity, such as the budgeting, planning and incentive systems used.

At present, GMV has six key business units. Each of the business units is led by a business unit manager. Each business unit manager reports to the CEO, who in turn reports to the board. The business units are highly decentralised, with business unit managers responsible for a range of functions including product or service development, manufacturing (where applicable) and marketing strategies. Innovation and limited risk taking are encouraged within an environment of open mindedness. These concepts are captured in GMVs fundamental beliefs and values statement, which includes a description of beliefs relating to decentralisation, growth, communication, education, incentives and goals, and innovation.

The incentive system

Until recently, the reward system in place at GMV was relatively simple. All senior managers (eight managers), business unit managers (six managers) and the top six managers in each business unit (36 managers) shared in a common bonus pool. The bonus pool was determined on the following basis.

$$\$\,100\,000 + 10\% \text{ of increases in combined divisional operating profits}$$

The bonus pool was shared 15 per cent to senior management, 50 per cent to business unit managers and 35 per cent to managers within the business units. The bonus payment was in the form of cash.

The good points about this plan include:

- the shared bonus pool treats 'everyone' the same
- using 10 per cent of combined divisional profit promotes goal congruence, although the business units are unrelated; that is, there are no interdependencies
- the cash form reflects the risk-averse nature of many of the managers

The not-so-good points about this plan include that it:

- seems to focus only on annual performance
- does not isolate and reward business unit performance
- focuses only on divisional profits and therefore just one performance measure
- rewards only in the form of cash.

The proposal for a new incentive plan has been prepared by the CFO, Sam Dementiava. Briefly, Sam's proposal includes:

1. senior managers being rewarded on the basis of organisational economic value added (EVA). If annual targets (as set by a board subcommittee) for EVA are met, each of the senior managers will be eligible to receive a specified parcel of shares in the company.
2. incentives for business unit managers based on:
   (i) corporate wide EVA (25 per cent)
   (ii) business unit EVA (25 per cent)
   (iii) a mix of non-financial measures relevant to each business unit as agreed with the CEO (50 per cent). Where targets are met, business unit managers will receive their incentive in the form of company shares.
3. incentives for senior managers within business units being rewarded solely on the basis of business unit EVA. Incentives will be paid in cash.

The good points about this plan are that it:

- isolates business unit and managerial performance, so it may be more likely to match span of control with span of accountability, particularly at the business unit level
- contains a mix of measures: EVA at corporate and business unit levels, non-financial measures at business unit level
- has some mix of incentives across the company for each manager; that is, cash and shares, but managers only receive one or the other form of incentive.

However, the downsides include:

- business unit EVA may not reflect operational managers' span of control within their business units
- there is some dominance of EVA as the key performance measure
- it still appears to be based on annual performance only, suggesting a focus on short-term performance.

Sharon and Bruce know the board has some serious deliberations ahead. They are aware that incentive plans generally have attracted negative publicity. They are determined to have the board make the right decisions with respect to GMV's incentive plan. The important issue for us to note from Sharon and Bruce's dilemma is that any form of incentive plan will have positive and negative points.

Distribution of cash bonus pools

In some organisations, the main variable component of pay comes in the form of a cash bonus, shared among eligible managers and employees from a common bonus pool. Distributions of cash bonus pools are used in organisations such as financial services (for example, banks) and professional services firms (for example, architects, accountants and consultants). A number of key questions/decisions about the operation of such bonus plans are necessary:

1. How will the size of bonus pool be determined?
2. Who will be eligible to participate in the bonus pool distribution?
3. How will the bonus pool be distributed to the eligible staff members?

   Ben Lorney is a lead partner in Reed Design Services (RDS), an architectural and structural engineering firm. Partners and senior managers share in an annual bonus pool. The key characteristics of the bonus system are provided below.

Eligible partners and managers	16
Size of the bonus pool	$300 000 + 20% of profits in excess of $2.5 million
Distribution of bonus pool	Based on bonus units earned on the basis of achieving target billable hours:
	• No bonus units if target billable hours not reached
	• Two bonus units if target billable hours reached
	• Four bonus units if target billable hours exceeded by 5%
	• Six bonus units if target billable hours exceeded by 10%
	• Eight bonus units if target billable hours exceeded by more than 10%
	Maximum bonus units per partner/manager = 8

This year, the profit of RDS was $3.2 million. Information from the internal database shows the billable hours against target for each of the partners/managers.

Threshold	Number of partners/managers
Did not reach target billable hours	4
Reached target billable hours	6
Exceeded target billable hours by 5%	2
Exceeded target billable hours by 10%	2
Exceeded target billable hours by more than 10%	2

Size of the bonus pool

$$\text{Bonus pool} = \$300\,000 + \left(20\% \times \$700\,000\right)$$
$$= \$440\,000$$

The total number of bonus units and the value of each bonus unit

Threshold	Number of partners/managers	Number of bonus units earned (each)	Total number of bonus units
Did not reach target billable hours	4	0	0
Reached target billable hours	6	2	12
Exceeded target billable hours by 5%	2	4	8
Exceeded target billable hours by 10%	2	6	12
Exceeded target billable hours by more than 10%	2	8	16
Total number of bonus units			48

Value of each bonus unit = $440 000/48 bonus units = $9167

The value of the bonus for each partner/manager

The value of the bonus for each partner/manager is shown below in the right-hand column.

Threshold	Number of partners/ managers	Number of bonus units earned (each)	Total number of bonus units	Value of bonus for each partner/manager
Did not reach target billable hours	4	0	0	0
Reached target billable hours	6	2	12	$18 334
Exceeded target billable hours by 5%	2	4	8	$36 668
Exceeded target billable hours by 10%	2	6	12	$55 002
Exceeded target billable hours by more than 10%	2	8	16	$73 336

20.5 Emerging themes in reward systems

LEARNING OBJECTIVE 20.5 Demonstrate an understanding of current themes and trends in reward systems.

Current themes in reward systems include relative performance evaluation, pay-for-performance issues and regulation and government intervention. Each of these is now discussed.

Relative performance evaluation

Relative performance evaluation (RPE) in incentive systems is about the comparison of company performance, using suitable measures, against the performance of a peer group. The peer group may be based on, for example, industry or size. In the case of industry, the Australian Securities Exchange (ASX) classifications would most likely be used. In the case of size, it would be likely for larger companies to use the ASX 100.

As reported by Albuquerque[7], evidence as to whether RPE in CEO incentive systems is successful is mixed. Even so, anecdotal evidence seems to suggest that companies in Australia are using RPE, perhaps for a number of reasons. First, by using external benchmarks, the board of directors is able to discharge its accountability, as CEOs are rewarded based on performance relative to other companies. Second, as pointed out by Albuquerque, RPE provides insurance against external shocks and is likely to be a more informative measure of CEO actions.

Pay-for-performance issues

Pay-for-performance issues relate to whether sufficient benefits (such as improved organisational performance) are derived from linking executive pay to executive performance. The research results relating to pay-for-performance issues are relatively mixed and inconclusive. Of course, this is often the driver of much of the media attention relating to CEO pay; for example, how can CEO pay be increasing when company performance is decreasing? There are explanations for this. First, there is often a time lag between the measurement of performance and receipt of the reward. For example, in the case of a longer-term incentive, which might be based over a three- or five-year period, one year of reduced performance will not, of itself, mean longer-term targets are not met. So, while performance in any one year may appear to be poor, the CEO may still be eligible for the incentive. Second, poor metric selection can mean that a CEO is meeting the targets set, yet these targets may not relate to measures of performance commonly used. Stapledon[8] makes a number of other suggestions to explain the relatively weak link between CEO pay and company performance, including the following.

- A relatively small proportion of the total remuneration is 'at-risk'.
- A lack of performance hurdles or the performance hurdles used not reflecting share price or dividends.
- The use of relative performance evaluation as outlined previously may result in the CEO being able to obtain at least part of the incentive even when performance may be average. This is partly caused by the use of a sliding scale of performance to be eligible for some portion of the incentive.

- External benchmarking (set by external remuneration consultants) often results in CEO pay being similar across companies.

To improve the pay-for-performance link, Jensen and Murphy in their landmark remuneration report[9] recommended designing incentive plans so that the pay-for-performance link is linear and using *bonus banks* that allow bonuses to be negative as well as positive. The point about bonus banks suggests that incentive plans need to have more downside potential; however, in practice, many plans have unlimited upside but very limited downside potential. Singapore's Temasek Holdings is one example of a company that has used bonus banks. Here, everyone has a wealth-added bonus bank.[10] When wealth-added (a form of EVA measure) goes up, money goes into the bonus bank; when wealth added goes down, money comes out of the bonus bank. The bonus bank is used to pay deferred bonuses, which may take upwards of three years to vest.

Regulation and government intervention

Much of Australia's regulatory requirements with respect to reward systems focus on senior executives and board members and are found in the *Corporations Act 2001* as amended by the *Corporations Amendment (Improving Accountability on Director and Executive Remuneration) Act 2011*. These requirements are supplemented by the ASX Listing Rules and the ASX Corporate Governance Council's *Corporate governance principles and recommendations*, 3rd edition. Most of the regulatory requirements relate to disclosure in the annual report of public companies with the objective of improving the nature and quality of information provided to shareholders and other stakeholders.

While the global financial crisis was triggered by a range of factors, significant attention has been focused on the reward and compensation arrangements of senior executives, particularly of those companies and institutions that required financial assistance from governments in order to survive. In Australia, the government commissioned an investigation by the Productivity Commission. The commission made two key findings, one related to remuneration structures and one to women being under-represented on boards. The commission's report made it clear that while remuneration structures are company and context specific and a matter for company boards to determine, there are a number of dimensions that should be addressed by all companies in the process of informing shareholders regarding remuneration policies and practices. A number of these would be regarded as sound managerial control practices and are linked to issues raised in this and previous chapters. The key finding in relation to remuneration is detailed in figure 20.4.

FIGURE 20.4	Finding 2 of the Productivity Commission[11]

Remuneration structures are company and context-specific and a matter for boards to resolve rather than being amenable to prescriptive direction. That said, some key dimensions often warrant being explained clearly to shareholders and, where appropriate, could usefully be addressed in companies' treatment of their remuneration policies in the remuneration report:

- how the remuneration policy aligns with the company's strategic directions, its desired risk profile and with shareholder interests
- how the mix of base pay and incentives relates to the remuneration policy
- how comparator groups for benchmarking executive remuneration and setting performance hurdles and metrics were selected, and how such benchmarks have been applied
- how incentive pay arrangements were subjected to sensitivity analysis to determine the impact of unexpected changes (for example, in the share price), and how any deferral principles and forfeiture conditions would operate
- whether any 'incentive-compatible' constraints or caps apply to guard against extreme outcomes from formula-based contractual obligations
- whether alternatives to incentives linked to complex hurdles have been considered (for example, short-term incentives delivered as equity subject to holding locks)
- whether employment contracts have been designed to the degree allowable by law, to inoculate against the possibility of having to 'buy out' poorly-performing executives in order to avoid litigation
- whether post-remuneration evaluations have been conducted to assess outcomes, their relationship to the remuneration policy and the integrity of any initial sensitivity analysis.

In addition, the commission made 17 recommendations covering a range of other issues, including the role and structure of company remuneration committees, advice on reducing the complexities in remuneration reports in annual reports, the role and reporting of the role of expert advisers to company remuneration committees, and advice on dealing with shareholder dissent regarding a company's remuneration report.

One of the key components of the *Corporations Amendment (Improving Accountability on Director and Executive Remuneration) Act 2011* was to introduce what is referred to as the 'two-strikes policy'. This policy was designed to provide shareholders a greater say on executive compensation. Essentially, if 25 per cent of the shareholder votes oppose the proposed remuneration report two years in a row (in the second year, the board must specifically respond to the original 'no' vote), then shareholders may be given the option of requiring a vote on board positions.

Connecting the incentive to performance metrics

In chapter 19, we explored performance metrics and balanced scorecards. Identifying suitable and relevant performance metrics within organisational settings is a challenging task. Once we then start attaching incentives or bonuses to the achievement of targets for these performance metrics, it becomes even more vital that we are using the most suitable metrics available. The Banking Royal Commission conducted in Australia in 2018 found evidence of banks and financial institutions using poorly-applied performance measures with incentives attached, resulting in poor management, employee behaviour and decision making. For example, the sole use of 'sales' of banking products to customers is likely to promote employee focus only on sales, with little regard for the longer-term consequences for both the customer and the bank.

The message here is that organisations face challenges to first, identify the most suitable set of performance measures and then second, if incentives are going to be used, attach an appropriate incentive structure to the performance metrics. This process should continually be under review to ensure unintended behavioural consequences are avoided.

20.6 Risk management

LEARNING OBJECTIVE 20.6 Identify and communicate the attributes of different types of risk and how they might be managed.

Risk management has become a very important theme of the twenty-first century, particularly given the severity of many high-profile corporate collapses. Earlier risk management frameworks developed by the accounting professional bodies have recognised the benefits provided by internal controls. However, since a series of high-profile corporation collapses (including Enron and WorldCom) and the global financial crisis of 2008, risk management frameworks have continued to be adapted and formalised to address the mitigation of business risk. As we have highlighted so far in this chapter, rewards for successful risk taking can be high. A significant part of risk management is the appropriate design and implementation of internal control systems to mitigate risk. It is important that the management accountant understands that these systems should be structured to manage but not *eliminate* risk. That is, successful companies need to carefully balance management control and risk taking.

Risk management and compliance

In Australia, there is a prescriptive requirement for directors of companies to report on the governance structures and internal controls used to mitigate business risk within their organisation. See, for example, *AS/NZS ISO 31000: 2009 Risk Management — Principles and Guidelines*, published by Standards Australia in November 2009, which is promoted as the leading resource available to Australian directors, senior executives and others responsible for managing organisation risk and achieving objectives.[12]

In addition, executives of listed companies are expected to follow the *Corporate governance principles and recommendations*, 3rd edition, published by the ASX's Corporate Governance Council, in particular, principle 7 Recognise and manage risks. Risk management also features in other recommendations such as principle 1 (the roles and responsibilities of the company board to ensure the entity has an appropriate risk management framework and setting the 'risk appetite' for management to work within), principle 4 (that the CEO and CFO endorse the entity's financial statements with opinions formed on the basis of a sound system of risk management) and principle 8 (ensuring the remuneration of senior executives encourages them to pursue short-term *and* long-term success without taking undue risks). The ASX Corporate Governance Council recommends that senior managers also review the guidance provided by the Australian and New Zealand Risk Management Standard as well as well-known global risk management frameworks.

The integrated approach to risk management

Two key risk management frameworks, designed to promote an enterprise-wide view to governance and risk management include the Committee of Sponsoring Organizations of the Treadway Commission (COSO) *Enterprise risk management — integrated framework* and the International Federation of Accountant's (IFAC) *Enterprise governance framework*. This emergent enterprise-wide approach to risk management is important for all accountants, including management accountants, to understand how they might play an active role in designing meaningful enterprise-wide systems of governance and risk management that will continue into the future.

COSO Enterprise risk management — integrated framework

Otherwise known as 'Enterprise risk management (ERM)', this framework offers a significant addition to risk management approaches. It advocates integrating risk management (from a corporate governance perspective) with strategic risk management (from an internal business governance perspective) on the premise that both external and internal risks can prevent an organisation from achieving its strategic objectives. The framework defines enterprise risk management as:[13]

> A process, effected by an entity's board of directors, management and other personnel, applied in strategy setting and across the enterprise, designed to identify potential events that may affect the entity, and manage risk to be within its risk appetite, to provide reasonable assurance regarding the achievement of entity objectives.

The enterprise-wide approach the COSO framework promotes is set in four categories:
1. *strategic* — high-level goals, aligned with and supporting the mission
2. *operations* — effective and efficient use of resources with reduced surprises and losses
3. *reporting* — reliability of reporting
4. *compliance* — with applicable laws and regulations.

In this context, the role of the management accounting function is to assist in designing systems of enterprise-wide communication that encourage the alignment of risk appetite and strategy. Systems of capital allocation taking an enterprise-wide approach will also enhance understanding of overall capital needs and allow for improved deployment of capital throughout the organisation.

IFAC Enterprise governance framework

A further important integrated framework of enterprise governance was designed in 2004 by IFAC in conjunction with the Chartered Institute of Management Accountants (CIMA). As highlighted in figure 20.5, this framework sees enterprise governance as a balance between the dimensions *conformance* (board structures and roles, executive remuneration, and compliance with regulation) and *performance* (strategy and value creation in relation to appetite for risk and understanding the key decision-influencing drivers of performance). Reconciliation of conformance with performance comes from understanding and actively managing risks as well as integrating risk management in the internal control systems and decision-making processes at all levels of the organisation. The framework draws on the Information Systems Audit and Control Foundation's (ISACA) definition of enterprise governance:[14]

> The set of responsibilities and practices exercised by the board and executive management with the goal of providing strategic direction, ensuring that objectives are achieved, ascertaining that risks are managed appropriately and verifying that the organization's resources are used responsibly.

FIGURE 20.5 The Enterprise governance framework[15]

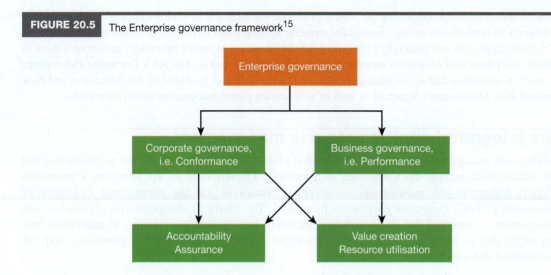

FIGURE 20.5 The Enterprise governance framework[15]

Risk management principles — summary

In summary, the risk management principles recommended by the varying risk management frameworks and the ASX Corporate Governance Council's principle 7 include the following key recommendations that should be widely understood and embedded in day-to-day organisational activities.

1. *Risk oversight* or the implementation and continual review of the effectiveness of the organisation's risk management system. This responsibility is to be a core function of the board and delegated 'risk management committee'. It is important that the tone is set from the top with strong cultural and ethical practices essential to the implementation of sound internal control.

2. *Risk management system* including the development and regular monitoring and reporting of a risk profile for every business unit within the organisation. This should include the identification and management of key risks, the assessment of control design and operation and the evaluation of key risk indicators.

3. *Risk profile and risk classification framework.* While the range of risks can be broad they must be relevant to the company and include both financial and non-financial activities. They can be classified in a variety of ways but might include classifications such as the following.[16]

  (i) Strategic risks associated with market-related activity and competitive dynamics, including threats from competitors and changes in technology such as technological innovations.

 (ii) Financial risks, such as the level of exposure to creditors and potential for a shortfall in liquidity.

(iii) Legal and regulatory risks, for example, the exposure to and ability to comply with applicable and impending laws and regulations in Australia and overseas.

(iv) Operational risks, including anything that might damage the ability of an organisation to provide product or service offerings to customers. Operational risks are influenced by the extent of formalised (and constantly maintained) procedures and protocols, the ability of employees and service providers to understand and follow prescribed organisational procedures, evidence of systems that provide timely, complete and accurate transaction recording and reporting, the ability of an organisation to safeguard its assets (including information), and the ability to respond to crises and support business operations under adverse operating circumstances.

These classifications are not independent and would need to be adapted to specific organisational settings and for changing circumstances. For example, we would expect to see cyber security threats as a key component of the risk classification framework of many organisations. For example, figure 20.6 presents the seven-part risk classification framework of the Lego Group.

FIGURE 20.6 The risk classification framework of the Lego Group[17]

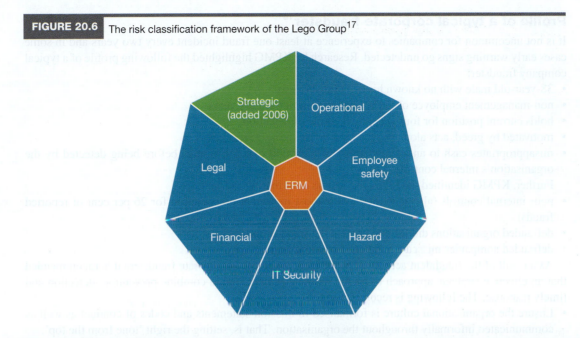

Incentives, rewards and risk management

As indicated previously, the rewards for risk taking can be high. Extreme examples of excessive risk taking can be found in rogue trading scandals, which provide useful insights into control and risk management practices, or the lack of these. The following examples illustrate how poor *structural safeguards* (that is, clearly defined lines of authority and accountability) and *system safeguards* (that is, accurate and timely reporting and secure databases) can expose an organisation to fraudulent activities. Likewise, the risk exposure for organisations increases when poor structural and system safeguards are mixed with a lack of employee proficiency or a lack of understanding of company codes of conduct and desired behaviour.

The following examples provide important insights for management accounting control system development and highlight the importance and necessity for management accountants to be involved in improving risk management practices.[18]

- Daiwa Bank (Toshihide Iguchi). Iguchi's fraudulent activity ran from 1984 to 1995 during which time he accumulated US$1.1 billion in unauthorised trading losses. The Daiwa Bank was heavily fined and ordered to cease operations in the United States.
- Barings Bank (Nick Leeson). Leeson's trading losses amounted to more than US$1 billion from 1992 to 1995. The losses were hidden in an 'error account'. Barings was eventually declared bankrupt and sold to the ING Group. Leeson later admitted in an interview that, 'Barings would never have collapsed without the incompetence of others who should have known what was going on but either failed to detect it, didn't properly investigate, or turned a blind eye'.
- Allied Irish Bank (John Rusnak). Rusnak successfully hid trading losses by using fictitious options contracts from 1997 to 2002 when routine checks finally uncovered the US$7.5 billion of firm capital he lost by secretly betting that the yen would rise against the dollar.
- Kidder, Peabody & Co. (Joseph Jett). Jett exploited a weakness in Kidder's trading and accounting systems that allowed him to recognise false profits up to US$350 million in order to mask US$100 million in losses. After the scandal, Kidder was sold to the Paine Webber Group. It was revealed that Jett received US$11 million in bonuses over two years based on his bogus profits, and his supervisor earned US$28 million in bonus and other compensation during that period.
- Société Générale (Jérôme Kerviel). Kerviel accumulated more than US$7 billion in losses with so-called directional bets on 'plain vanilla' futures transactions concealed with fictitious transactions in the opposite direction that supposedly cancelled out the risk. He used the lack of internal controls to evade scrutiny.

Profile of a typical corporate fraudster[19]

It is not uncommon for companies to experience at least one fraud incident every two years and in some cases early warning signs go undetected. Research by KPMG highlighted the following profile of a typical company fraudster:

- 38-year-old male with no known history of dishonesty
- non-management employee of the victim organisation for six years
- holds current position for four years by the time of detection
- motivated by greed, acts alone
- misappropriates cash to an average value of $262 000 over 11 months before being detected by the organisation's internal controls.

  Further, KPMG identified the following factors contributing to fraud:
- poor internal controls (also identified as the most important precondition for 26 per cent of reported frauds)
- defrauded organisations did little to prevent the fraud occurring
- defrauded companies missed a number of warning signs.

As a result of the fraudulent activity of rogue traders and other corporate fraudsters it is recommended that an effective strategic approach to fraud risk management should combine prevention, detection and timely response. The following is recommended.[20]

- Ensure the organisational culture is formalised in mission statements and codes of conduct as well as communicated informally throughout the organisation. That is, setting the right 'tone from the top'.
- Ensure senior managers understand their organisation's products. This includes control systems to align company and employee interests such as appropriate personnel selection and fit with organisational culture, performance reviews and understanding job performance, and continuous skill training.
- Establish strong business line supervisory controls, including daily reviews of trades, reviews of exception reports, procedures for creating, monitoring and enforcing position and trading limits with intraday monitoring.
- Require more (not less) scrutiny of successful traders. This involves providing opportunities for job rotation and team work and not ignoring unusual/exceptional performance as in the Kidder and Barings cases.
- Ensure incentive systems do not encourage excessive risk taking, including monitoring employee compliance with policies, laws and regulations and their overall performance, measuring performance relative to the organisation's stated goals and quality of earnings, being aware of competitors' compensation practices for similar roles, and understanding the inherent risk in and caused by relevant trading activity.
- Encourage employees to take holidays, which allows for job rotation and performance to be open to scrutiny by others.
- Encourage risk managers to challenge traders' valuations via routine, independent, consistent and rigorous valuation practices.
- Ensure operations, risk management and compliance reporting lines are separate from the business lines, including segregation of duties of the front and back offices, and operations and risk reporting to different senior managers.
- Ensure dual or matrix reporting lines are clear. This prevents unclear accountability and control and is also important when company growth or expansion occurs (that is, through acquisitions and mergers).
- Recognise that strong back-office controls are as essential as front-office controls. A strong accounting control system provides support and helps with an enterprise-wide view of operations.

Effective risk management architecture

The previous discussion suggests that effective risk management architecture is critical and should be subject to active oversight by the board. For the management accounting function, risk management should embody well-conceived risk identification measures and reporting systems.

There should be strong systems of:

- *Communication*, including systems in place that allow for timely and active reporting and communication among senior management, business lines and risk management functions, codes of conduct that communicate required risk-taking behaviour of employees, mission statements that specify the organisation's values and strategic goals.

- *Performance measurement* — senior managers and boards should be able to rely on a larger (not narrower) range of risk measures and ensure they are based on solid underlying assumptions and measurement processes in their risk evaluation of subordinates. Incentives linked to performance measurement should be monitored, particularly in environments where there is extreme pressure to achieve performance targets and high rewards for risk taking with a single financial measure of performance.
- *Enterprise-wide control* — a well-defined risk management architecture ensures information is developed *across* the organisation to be used in continuous adjustments of business strategy, risk management practices and exposures. Safeguards should be in place so that direct lines of authority and responsibility arc understood by all and ensure the protection of databases and confidential company information. Structural safeguards are particularly important when organisations are in growth stages (expanding rapidly). Job rotation, and team work and assignments mitigate the risk of fraudulent or inappropriate behaviour by individuals. Finally, organisations should undertake regular employee assessment and training to ensure their employees can operate proficiently in their respective roles.

SUMMARY

20.1 Explain agency theory and the link between agency costs and reward system design.

Principals and agents

Principals hire agents to make decisions for them and to act on their behalf.

Agency costs

Costs that arise when agents fail to act in the interest of principals:
- losses from poor decisions
- losses from incongruent goals
- monitoring costs
- goal alignment costs
- contracting costs.

Reducing agency costs

To measure, monitor and motivate performance.
- Assign responsibility for decision making
- Link decision-making authority to performance measurement
- Use income-based measures to assess performance
- Motivate performance with compensation schemes

20.2 Communicate the key components of reward systems.

- All pay fixed
- All pay variable
- Incentives — extrinsic versus intrinsic rewards

20.3 Explain the advantages and disadvantages of cash and equity as key components of incentive plans.

Forms of incentives

- Cash
- Equity

Types of equity incentives

- Shares
- Share options

20.4 Demonstrate an understanding of different reward system structures.

- Depends on time horizon relating to target measure and the nature of the reward itself
- Decide on measures, time period, targets and form of incentives
- Evaluate different reward system structures
- Analyse a shared bonus pool system

20.5 Demonstrate an understanding of current themes and trends in reward systems.

- Relative performance evaluation
- Pay-for-performance issues
- Regulation and government intervention

20.6 Identify and communicate the attributes of different types of risk and how they might be managed.

- Risk management and compliance
- The integrated approach to risk management
- COSO Enterprise risk management framework — integrated framework
- IFAC Enterprise governance framework
- Risk management principles — summary
- Incentives, rewards and risk management
- Effective risk management architecture

KEY TERMS

agency costs The costs that arise when agents fail to act in the interest of principals.
agency theory An analytical framework that examines potential conflicts between principals and agents.
agents People who act on behalf of others — the principals.
principals People or entities who hire agents to make decisions for them and act on their behalf.

SELF-STUDY PROBLEM

SELF-STUDY PROBLEM Cowmilka

Cowmilka is an Australian dairy cooperative run jointly by more than 1000 Australian farmers and 900 employees. It is situated in Victoria, where more than 60 per cent of all Australian dairy farming is located. The Cowmilka Cooperative was formalised in 1928, and Cowmilka now processes approximately 650 million litres of milk each year. Collectively, Cowmilka has grown to become a well-known, medium-sized cooperative with a total herd of around 200 000 dairy cattle and annual exports amounting to 70 000 tonnes of manufactured dairy products (milk products, cheese and butter). The farmers and Cowmilka's employees are all committed professionals with a passion for dairy. This is formalised in the company's vision (see below) and belief statements which are communicated widely to all employees and stakeholders (farmers, customers, creditors, and the local community) through regular newsletters, emails and intranet correspondence. The cooperative also has a well-maintained website.

> Cowmilka's vision is to be a leading Australian cooperative. We strive to offer quality products and embrace change through innovation. Most importantly, we value our people, customers and community. We build for the future.

Cowmilka's senior managers meet regularly for formal strategy meetings. They are also encouraged by the CEO to maintain informal discussions with their operational staff and undertake regular plant tours as part of their management control activities. As a joint initiative, Cowmilka Cooperative has developed a strategy based on growth, efficiency and innovation. It is a widely shared belief that Cowmilka value is created by:

- growth in exports and value-added products
- efficiency in production and logistics
- innovation in product development and processes.

Dairy farming is a water-intensive industry and requires irrigated pastures for plentiful milk supply. While the global dairy market is dynamic with milk demand currently outstripping supply, in Australia milk volumes have been affected by ongoing drought. As a result, many farms now rely on purchased feed and irrigation, which has significantly impacted on the cost of inputs in relation to output prices. As a result of the drought and market price fluctuations, it has been difficult for Cowmilka to fully realise its budgeted growth in volumes over the last couple of years.

In addition, the butter market has come under threat as consumers have started switching to vegetable-based products (margarines). While this trend was turned around somewhat in the 1990s with innovations in butter blends (that is, spreadable butter), in the long run there remains a gradual decline in butter consumption, arguably due to consumer health concerns, taste changes and increasing dairy prices. Butter is now viewed by retailers to be a luxury commodity.

The Cheese and Butter division, managed by Curtis Way, is under pressure by Cowmilka's CEO, Murray Gray, to review its existing operations and consider opportunities that might be more closely aligned with the overall Cowmilka strategy identified above. The Cheese and Butter division pursues a cost leadership position, supplying packaged cheddar (block cheese and shredded cheese) into supermarkets on contract agreements. The supermarkets 'market' the Cowmilka products under their home-brand labels.

One option Curtis presents is the acquisition of a small New Zealand cheese company called Fintona Buttergold. Curtis believes this acquisition will allow the division to expand its existing product range into the previously untapped niche feta cheese market. Feta cheese is made from 70 per cent sheep's milk and 30 per cent goats' milk, so it is quite a different proposition for Cowmilka, which has not previously considered diversifying from its traditional cows' milk product range. Curtis is excited by the opportunity presented by the acquisition. According to industry analysts, the specialty fresh cheese market (of which feta is the significant product) is the market most likely to allow manufacturers to add value and improve market share.

Fintona Buttergold is a specialised cheese plant with state-of-the-art manufacturing capabilities. It is known for its feta cheese, Fintona Feta, which is sold to specialty gourmet suppliers. Fintona Cheese is a highly regarded competitor in the New Zealand market, with loyal customers and a friendly sales team managed by a strong leader, the current owner. Curtis has managed to negotiate a price of $30 million with the current owner. The price requires the current owner to stay on and run the Fintona operations for a period of at least 12 months. The owner indicates he may not stay with the company after completion of this contract period. Curtis is hoping that one of Fintona's senior managers or someone from the Australian Cowmilka operations may be in a position to take over control at this time. In addition to strong local sales, Fintona has recently begun marketing its Fintona Feta internationally and sales forecasts indicate that sales will continue to grow and production will reach capacity. Curtis's calculations project reasonable returns from the Fintona Cheese operations for the next few years.

Required

(a) Cowmilka's CEO and the Cheese and Butter divisional manager have had some preliminary discussions regarding the position of Fintona Buttergold's owner 12 months after the acquisition. Identify some of the key considerations in structuring a suitable reward system plan for a new manager for the Fintona Division.

(b) Your team is charged with preparing a report outlining the risk profile of Cowmilka. Prepare notes on the range of risks relevant to Cowmilka.

SOLUTION TO SELF-STUDY PROBLEM

(a) The reward system plan would need to be well structured to attract and retain a suitability qualified manager. A key issue is that Cowmilka is a cooperative, not a publicly listed company. This places some restrictions on the components of the plan. For example, issuing equity (shares and/or share options) as part of the incentives is not possible, so Gray and Way will most likely develop incentives that are cash based. Moreover, in this circumstance, the fixed component of the plan might be larger than might otherwise be the case. This may help initially with attracting a suitable manager. To this extent, standard practice within the industry may come to bear on the final structure of the plan.

The incentive component may be in three parts. First, there would need to be an incentive linked to the performance of the Fintona division, which may be best measured by ROI, EVA, divisional profit or some combination of a set of balanced scorecard measures. This would comprise a major part of the reward plan and could be annual or based on a three-year average. Second, there may be an incentive for organisational performance using measures such as ROI or EVA. This might comprise a smaller part of the incentive and could be based on annual performance or a three-year average. Third, it might be desirable to use a form of individual evaluation based on, for example, a survey of subordinates or a balanced set of measures.

The measures used should reflect the organisational and divisional strategies and drive superior performance through goal-congruent decision making. As mentioned, because of the nature of the organisation, most of the rewards are likely to be in the form of cash, though it may be possible in conjunction with the manager to use other forms of reward.

(b) The range of risks relevant to Cowmilka can be classified as strategic risks, financial risks, legal and regulatory risks and operational risks, and include both financial and non-financial activities.

- *Strategic risks.* These might include the threat of drought on the supply of milk products, consumers' move away from butter products, the threats from direct competitors (international and local) and substitutes (such as margarines, oils and soy-based products), and the potential for the reduction in milk supply to influence product delivery to customers, which might damage Cowmilka's reputation in the long run. The issues associated with the Cheese and Butter division's current cost leadership strategy, which appears to be at odds with the value-creation strategy of the firm, should also be highlighted.

   However, it is important to also draw attention to Cowmilka's strong focus on formalising its mission and belief statements, and maintaining informal discussions with the factory floor. These are important in continual monitoring and evaluation of the strategic direction of the cooperative. It would appear that Cowmilka might be well aware of the risks to its strategic goals, which is possibly why the CEO has asked Curtis to consider further opportunities that might be more closely aligned with the overall Cowmilka strategy. There are also risks associated with the proposed acquisition. For example, the risks of rapid growth, of potential disconnect between the strategies of Cowmilka and Fintona, and of blurred lines of accountability with the merger.

- *Financial risks.* Issues might include potential reductions in cash flow due to declining supply and the risk of financing associated with the acquisition.
- *Legal and regulatory risks.* Given this industry's intense use of water and fuel for transport, Cowmilka may have some exposure to impending legislative requirements associated with water saving and carbon emissions targets.
- *Operational risks.* A significant risk for Cowmilka relating to milk production is of mistakes being made, given the nature of the food industry, which must comply with strict hygiene practices. Security of production is very important to prevent contamination (deliberate or unintentional) which could lead to the demise of Cowmilka, particularly if it becomes involved in any major product recall. While little information is provided on the accounting systems or formal procedures and protocols, students might assume that Cowmilka has strong policies and procedures in place for all employees to follow. The managers provide a strong oversight function and appear capable of safeguarding assets as well. As responding to adverse operating circumstances. There is evidence of active 'enterprise-wide' involvement and regular communication between the different lines of business. A possible recommendation is that Cowmilka use a broad range of financial and non-financial performance measures in its performance measurement systems, encourage teamwork, and perform employment profiling and regular skill updates to mitigate the risk of fraudulent activity or inappropriate behaviour by individuals.

QUESTIONS

20.1 Explain agency theory and how it relates to reward systems. **LO1**

20.2 Explain the difference between shares and share options. **LO2**

20.3 What are the arguments for reward systems at the executive level to contain a longer-term component? **LO3**

20.4 Discuss why an incentive package might include individual, divisional and corporate-level performance targets. **LO4**

20.5 Describe the advantages and disadvantages of equity rewards. **LO3**

20.6 How can target measures be used to promote either short-term or long-term performance? **LO4**

20.7 Describe agency costs and give several examples of them. **LO1**

20.8 What is the role of rewards and incentives for executives in reducing agency costs? **LO1**

20.9 The use of RPE systems for the evaluation of individual managers has been abandoned by many organisations. Microsoft is one example. Given this, can we conclude that RPE is no good? **LO4**

20.10 Identify why RPE would be used at the company level. **LO4**

20.11 'Executives should only be compensated based upon the achievement of targets. They should not receive a fixed salary component.' Discuss. **LO4, 5**

20.12 Describe two disclosures required by the Corporations Act with respect to executive remuneration. **LO4, 5**

20.13 Should a remuneration plan include a cash bonus or share options? Under which circumstances would either be appropriate? **LO3, 4**

20.14 What are the advantages and disadvantages of having an individual's remuneration linked to performance outcomes? **LO4, 5**

20.15 What role do the ASX Corporate Governance Council's *Corporate governance principles and recommendations* and the Corporations Act play in executive remuneration? **LO5**

20.16 Why would a company restrict when a senior executive can exercise their share options? **LO2, 3, 5**

20.17 Explain why boards of directors will often employ independent remuneration consultants to assist in developing and assessing compensation plans. **LO5**

EXERCISES

20.18 Structuring a compensation plan **LO2, 4**

Describe the factors that need to be considered when structuring a compensation plan for executives.

20.19 Balanced scorecard; incentives **LO2, 3**

Many organisations use a balanced scorecard set of measures to determine the short-term incentive for senior managers and executives.

Required

Outline any potential difficulties associated with using a set of balanced scorecard measures to determine the short-term incentive.

20.20 Relative performance evaluation.   **LO2, 3, 5**

Relative performance evaluation at the company level often results in using a market index like the ASX100 as the peer group.

Required

Outline the potential advantages and disadvantages of this practice.

20.21 Behavioural effect of share options   **LO3**

Assume you are a senior manager at a publicly listed company. Under the company's longer-term incentive plan you have recently received a parcel of share options. These share options can only be exercised (converted to shares) after three years.

Required

How might this incentive affect your behaviour and decision making?

20.22 Assessing rewards based on accounting profit   **LO2, 4**

Stevan is the divisional manager with the Liberty Property Development Group. His performance report shows a positive divisional margin but a loss for the year. Stevan has complained to the CEO about the common costs that have been charged to his division, and questions the method of charging. If they were not charged or were allocated in a different way, he would have a favourable profit figure and would be awarded his bonus.

Required

Should Stevan's bonus be awarded based on the profit or loss figure? Why?

20.23 Risk profiling   **LO6**

You are required to offer advice to a small but growing community bank. Describe the steps you would take to prepare a risk profile for this organisation.

20.24 Developing a reward system and reward targets   **LO2, 3, 4**

You are a remuneration consultant. The board of a large multinational bank has asked you to draft a proposal for a new reward system for senior executives. Currently all senior executives are paid a fixed salary.

Your investigations at the entity reveal its mission is to be 'the number one provider of quality banking services in the southern hemisphere'. You note that the entity has planned for 10 per cent profit growth over the next five years with a corresponding growth in share price. The entity has identified customer satisfaction, product quality and product innovation as the key indicators of success.

The directors are concerned as company profits have been declining. They consider a revised remuneration scheme may motivate senior executives to grow profits and the share price.

Required

Prepare a report to the board outlining a new remuneration plan for the executives of the entity.

20.25 Reward systems for different levels of employees   **LO2, 4**

Freshwater is an entity that processes and distributes bottled water throughout Australia and New Zealand. You have been employed as a remuneration consultant to develop a new reward system for the entity.

Required

Explain how you would develop an incentive plan for the CEO, the divisional manager of the process division, and the sales manager who arranges customer sales. How are the reward systems similar? How are the reward systems different?

20.26 Assessing reward systems   **LO2, 3, 5**

You are a remuneration consultant employed by a listed company to assess the CEO's reward plan. The board is concerned that the CEO is overpaid in absolute terms and also when compared to other CEOs of major corporations.

Required

How might you determine whether or not the reward plan is appropriate?

20.27 Remuneration disclosure   **LO5**

The ASX *Corporate governance principles and recommendations* set out rules to deal with enhanced management performance and effectiveness and requires disclosure of the process for performance evaluation of the board, its committees and individual directors and key executives. However, the outcomes of individual evaluations are not required to be disclosed.

Required

Why do you think such a recommendation is included in the guidelines?

20.28 Actions to mitigate risk   LO6

Ben, an employee of Joseph's, appears to be extremely enthusiastic about his back-office accounting role. He has been with Joseph's company for about four years and has performed well in his position. Ben is very keen to progress in the company and Joseph has recently decided to offer him a posting at a small international operation in Asia. While the role is to remain in the back office, the position will not require efforts on a full-time basis. Instead, Joseph decides to provide Ben with an opportunity to manage the currently vacant front-office trading role. While the operation is small and Ben has limited trading skills, Joseph is sure Ben will be able to manage both roles and hopefully learn about, and at the same time develop, the trading arm of this international operation. Joseph decides to award Ben an uncapped bonus on profits earned for the group on top of his negotiated annual base salary.

Required

Prepare a report advising Joseph on the risk management ramifications of his decisions. What actions should Joseph take to mitigate any perceived risk?

20.29 Shared bonus pools   LO4

Becky Tan is the CFO at Frosters Systems, a diversified company with eight different business units (divisions). Becky has been asked by the CEO to develop a shared bonus pool system.

Required

What key decisions will Becky have to make to set up the shared bonus system?

20.30 Risk classification framework   LO6

Harley–Davidson, Inc. has found itself having to confront a number of risk-related issues. These have mainly related to:

 (i) the need to increase the number of recalls due to faults
(ii) surging costs of making the repairs to faulty motorbikes
(iii) increasing pressure on market share.

Required

Classify each of the three events above according to the risk classification framework (strategic, operational, legal and regulatory, and financial).

20.31 Shared bonus pool   LO4

Sarah Tesar is the lead partner of a medium-sized accounting firm. The eight partners share in an annual bonus pool. The characteristics of the bonus pool system include:

• The bonus pool size each year is calculated as 40 per cent of annual profit.
• The bonus pool is allocated on the basis of bonus units awarded according to the partners' performance against target fees generated from new clients. This is meant to reinforce the firm's strategy of growth through new client acquisition. If the fees target is met, one bonus unit is awarded; if the fees target is exceeded by 10 per cent, two bonus units are awarded; if the fees target is exceeded by 20 per cent, four bonus units are awarded; and if the fees target is exceeded by more than 20 per cent, six bonus units are awarded.

This year the annual profit was $2.2 million and the partner performance according to their fees from new client target was as follows: three partners achieved 10 per cent above target; three other partners achieved 20 per cent above target; and two partners exceeded the target by more than 20 per cent.

Required

(a) Calculate:
    (i) the value of the bonus pool to be shared
    (ii) the value of one bonus unit
    (iii) the value of the bonus each manager would receive for the year.

   One of the partners, Russell Morris, has sought a meeting with Sarah to discuss the shared bonus pool system. He wrote in an email to Sarah 'I spend a lot of my time providing our in-house training programs . . . I can't be out chasing new clients at the same time! Why do we only have one measure for the bonus system?'

(b) How important is the selection of the bonus allocation formula and the measure(s) to be used?

(c) In the light of Russell's email, would you advise Sarah to make any changes to the current system? Explain.

20.32 Executive remuneration: two-strikes policy LO4, 5

Investigate which companies have experienced either one-strike or two-strikes on their remuneration reports in the last year or two. Summarise your results and collect the specifics of one example.

PROBLEMS

20.33 Developing a reward system LO2, 4

Synergy Ltd's incentive plan is based on a shared bonus pool. Return on investment (ROI) is used as the main performance metric and is calculated as:

$$\text{Operating profit before tax} \div \text{Assets at gross book value}$$

Receipt of the incentive is dependent on the achievement of annual ROI targets. These targets were set in consultation with division managers. Moreover, the senior management team is rewarded on the basis of organisational ROI. The amount of bonus received by managers is determined as follows. The bonus pool is determined as:

$$\$100\,000 + 10\% \text{ of increases in annual combined ROI}$$

The bonus pool is shared 15 per cent to senior management (shared equally among 10 managers on the basis of organisational ROI), 50 per cent to divisional managers (shared among three managers according to divisional ROI) and 35 per cent to managers within the divisions (shared among 12 managers according to divisional ROI). The bonus payment is in the form of cash. While some members of the management team have expressed concerns about the use of ROI as the key performance metric, the CEO is intent on keeping things simple and believes that ROI is a good summary measure on which to base senior management and divisional manager rewards.

One of the senior managers, Sonia Lee, has become persistent in her objections to the current bonus scheme. She feels the scheme needs to reflect shareholder interests with suitable measures at each level of the company that reflect managers' span of control and the right mix of incentives.

Required

You have been asked to advise the board of Synergy Ltd on a possible new incentive plan that addresses the concerns of Sonia Lee. Prepare a report outlining the detail of your incentive plan. Make sure you explain how your plan addresses Sonia's concerns.

20.34 Risk management LO6

The Dancing Goat is the name Logan Jones chose for his café. The origins of the name came from a 1600s fable of a young goat herder watching his goats dance after they ate red coffee beans. Logan wanted his customers to have the same pleasant 'dancing' experience when they drank his specialty coffee blends. In his Sopital Lane café in Melbourne, Logan has a central roasting room in which he roasts fresh coffee beans from around the world. He offers 12 blends of coffee and delights customers with the atmosphere of his classy, European-style café with couches and low tables. The Dancing Goat has become very successful and Logan began to expand his operations to several locations around Melbourne. He roasts the coffee at the main Sopital Lane café and transports it daily to the other cafés.

Logan now has 10 cafés located around Melbourne. They offer a deliberately small, but high-quality gourmet menu. Logan is well liked by his staff and they all understand his requirement for friendly service, a pleasant atmosphere and excellent coffee. Every new staff member learns to make coffee to Logan's strict specifications and wears The Dancing Goat uniform with pride. Logan is particularly pleased when returning customers at each of the cafés praise his friendly, well-trained staff. Nevertheless, after several years of successful operations, the profitability of the Dancing Goat has begun to decline. Logan has decided to revisit The Dancing Goat's 'branding' strategy. He recently read the following article relating to the Starbucks decision to 'unbrand':[21]

> The idea is that the [Starbucks] chain will turn some of its premises into individually branded neighbourhood coffee shops, to find out whether it will do better by adopting a facade that's more like an old-fashioned neighbourhood coffee shop. In its home-town of Seattle, an outlet called 15th Avenue Coffee and Tea will be the test-bed for this new non-brand, selling beer and wine as well as high-end brew.

Logan is particularly interested in Starbucks' test-bed 15th Avenue Coffee and Tea store, which courted coffee connoisseurs with the same elaborate coffee brewing machines that Logan decided to purchase for The Dancing Goat cafés. Although Logan is a little dubious about the potential success of the Starbucks' approach in his operations, he is aware that several café managers are dissatisfied and keen to make significant changes. Logan ponders 'Why not let one of the cafés loose for a couple of years to trial a similar unbranding approach?' Logan could set simple performance targets based on profitable growth and pay uncapped incentives. He will allow the manager to determine what would best suit the local clientele without too much interference from Logan. After all, Logan knows the manager of the trial café he has selected is not scared to take risks. Logan will be satisfied as long as the profitability of this café remains at an acceptable level.

Required

Given your understanding of risk management, briefly provide advice to Logan on:
(a) The risk profile and level of risk exposure for The Dancing Goat of the new approach.
(b) How Logan might reduce this level of risk exposure.

20.35 Reward plan structure   LO2, 4

Whistlestop Adventure has grown from a one-man operation into a large, soon-to-be-listed, adventure clothing and equipment company. For much of its four-year history, Whistlestop has used one company-wide incentive plan that all employees and managers participated in. The plan is based on equal sharing of a bonus pool determined on the basis of 10 per cent of all profits earned over $2 million. As the company has grown, the benchmark profit figure has changed, but otherwise the plan has remained substantially the same. The company founder explained that the plan was structured this way to encourage an organisational and team view, an objective that has permeated the company's activities since its beginning.

With the impending stock exchange listing, the newly constituted remuneration committee has been working on the development of new incentive plan for executives and managers. The brief from the board includes the requirement to 'develop an incentive plan in line with the company's strategy of revenue growth through high-quality products and customer service, and align the interests of the new executive team with shareholders'.

Required

(a) If you were a member of the remuneration committee of Whistlestop, how would you suggest the incentive plan be structured to meet the requirements set by the board?
(b) What are the dangers for Whistlestop in moving away from the current incentive plan to a new one? How could these dangers be overcome?

20.36 Evaluating a reward system   LO2, 4

You are on the board of a computer software company that has three distinct divisions: home networks, small business systems and ERP systems. In a bid to encourage higher performance, it has been proposed that the company would benefit from creating a reward system with a profit-sharing component for divisional managers. At present, divisional managers are paid a fixed salary. The proposal is for the company to pool 5 per cent of the company's profits each month and pay this amount at the end of the year based on divisional managers' performance against targets. The targets will be set in the preliminary performance review at the beginning of the year. Targets will cover both divisional and company-wide performance. It is thought that this approach will encourage a commitment to the organisation and encourage individuals to strive for better results. There will be a vote for the current proposal at the next board meeting.

Required

(a) Discuss the advantages and disadvantages of the proposal.
(b) Outline an alternative reward system.

20.37 Behavioural issues associated with reward systems   LO3, 4, 5

Fitness Forever International sells personal exercise equipment both within Australia and internationally. One division of Fitness Forever produces a product called Absaway, which is a specialised piece of equipment that focuses on exercising the abdominal region. The Absaway is manufactured with both internally sourced and purchased-in components.

The divisional performance report shows that the division made sales of 20 000 units at a price of $100 each. The variable costs were $60 per unit. Fixed costs were $200 000.

Fitness Forever calculates managers' bonuses based on profit. The manager of the Absaway division wants to maximise his bonus. To ensure that the divisional margin is reported at its highest possible level, the manager has been producing more units of the Absaway than required based on sales forecasts. Producing more units has the effect of increasing the ending inventory which, in the statement of profit or loss, reduces the cost of sales. This, in turn increases the divisional margin. The extra production of Absaway units has to be stored, thus increasing the need for warehouse space.

Required

(a) Comment on the strategy of the manager to produce more units of product than are needed in order boost divisional profits. Is it in the best interest of Fitness Forever?

(b) You have been asked to comment on the current reward system at the next board meeting and make recommendations about any changes you think are necessary. What will you say?

20.38 Assessing a remuneration plan LO2, 3, 4

Hailey's Hair Products has two criteria upon which its reward system is based: (1) rewarding executives for performance and (2) adding to shareholder value.

At present, the remuneration package for executives consists of a base salary, annual bonus and stock options. The base salary is considered critical to attract the 'best' people to positions with the bonus and stock options encouraging performance that leads to increases in the share price. Base salaries are set at competitive levels to attract and retain the 'best' people. The bonus is payable if executives meet the annual performance targets set by the board at the beginning of the year. The stock options are not able to be exercised until five years after being granted. A recent initiative has meant that executives are able to substitute the bonus payment for stock options (but still with the five-year restriction).

The board's remuneration committee is made up entirely of independent directors and makes use of outside advisers to ensure that recommendations are fair to all shareholders.

Required

Evaluate the remuneration plan for executives.

20.39 Risk classification LO6

Regal Foods is a multi divisional company operating in a range of locations around the globe. Its product-based divisions are: Ice Cream and Associated Dairy Products, Confectionery, Nutrition, and Prepared Food. Regal has total sales in excess of $10 billion. The CEO, Ruby Day, recently undertook a company review which identified the following strategies and objectives:

- optimising product performance through strong research and development, product innovation and market share growth
- enhancing financial performance through financial discipline and targeted capital expenditure.

Divisional managers have traditionally been allowed significant autonomy in line with the decentralised divisional structure. CFO Paul Falkenberg has recently introduced relative performance evaluation (RPE) at the divisional level to promote competitiveness, with the objective of growing the company.

Ice Cream and Associated Dairy Products Division

The Ice Cream and Associated Dairy Products Division focuses on such products as ice cream, yoghurt, milk and cheeses. The current divisional manager is Alette Rennie, who has been in the position for the past three years. In that time, Alette has achieved average annual divisional revenue growth of 6 per cent. However, there are concerns about some of the exposures the division has. For example, in a recent email to the CFO and CEO, Alette expressed concerns about some of the division's exposures to the agricultural industry, the increasing global competition in dairy products, and the lack of bargaining power of the company in the local milk price wars.

Nutrition Division

The Nutrition Division focuses on health-related products. Historically, the Nutrition Division has been an excellent contributor to group performance, with annual growth rates of up to 12 per cent for the period 2006 to 2012, and revenues exceeding $2 billion. However, divisional manager Bruce Buncle has found it increasingly difficult to maintain growth. An increasingly crowded market for health and nutritional products seems to be the main driver of these difficulties. As a consequence, debt levels of the division seem to be rising. However, Buncle is conscious that he needs to develop new products and markets in line with company objectives.

Buncle and his management team have been considering a range of investment opportunities and have decided on a major investment in the bottled water industry. While the industry has its challenges (for example, environmental opposition to the use of plastic bottles, tightening environmental regulations and the expectation of reduced carbon emissions), Buncle and his management team see a lot of potential with such a strategic move. However, where significant capital expenditure is required, Buncle finds the company investment decision-making processes frustrating.

The management team within the Nutrition Division has identified a new spring water source in a regional area. The local authorities are in favour of the springs being used to supply the Nutrition Division with spring water for a new water bottling plant to be built in the region. In fact, the local authorities are willing to forgo local taxes and provide subsidies to Regal to ensure the plant is built. The region has experienced relatively high levels of unemployment in recent years and the new plant will generate some 100 local new jobs. While there is some local opposition to the new facility on environmental grounds, Buncle considers these to be manageable. While he knows the project's financial benefit is mainly after the third year, he knows that the investment is a good strategic move for his division.

Required

Using the risk classification framework (strategic, operational, legal and regulatory, and financial) identify the key risks to which Regal and its divisions are exposed.

20.40 Incentives and risk management LO2, 3, 4, 6

Part A

In the early 1980s, Bernard Hancock built a small brewery on his 150-acre property in the Macedon Ranges. The brewery, named Mountain Mist Brewery, was designed with ales in mind and Bernard introduced a number of cutting-edge and innovative technologies to make the well-known, popular pale ale Misty Hop and others such as Hazy Heidi, Mountain Maid and Sunny Sherpa. The brewery's highest selling pale ale (Misty Hop) is widely recognised as a high-quality boutique beer and is sold, along with the brewery's other ales, to clubs and restaurants around Australia. All Mountain Mist Brewery ales are distributed in kegs (large containers) and 12-bottle cartons through its Victorian and national wholesalers. The brewery has continued to expand capacity on its site to meet growing consumer demands.

Bernard's vision for Mountain Mist Brewery is to:

- grow profitably with incremental investment into selected markets to become one of the top six breweries in Australia
- continuously improve perceived consumer quality by improving taste, freshness, package integrity and package appearance
- enhance distributor service with better lead times, accurate order fills and lower product damage
- continuously lower company costs per litre of beer so Mountain Mist can maintain resources for long-term productivity and success
- continuously improve business performance through engaging and developing employees.

Given recent sound performance, Bernard is pleased he had made the decision to expand Mountain Mist's production interstate. This decision was made in line with Bernard's key objective to be one of the top six national competitors. Mountain Mist currently holds seventh position. With its nearest competitor, Little Creatures, expanding into the eastern market from its Western Australian base, Bernard wants to ensure Mountain Mist will not only maintain market share but grow in size to take Little Creatures' sixth position. Bernard wants to improve Mountain Mist's brand presence in the western region, as well as reduce the transportation costs of moving beer across Australia. A local presence in Western Australia would also help reduce reliance on national retail distribution channels.

A production site has been selected. A production manager from the Macedon Ranges site has been given the role of overseeing the operational set-up and staying on to manage the new operation. Others, such as microbiologists from the Mountain Mist laboratory, have also been offered the opportunity to move interstate. Thus, Bernard is moving some expertise from the Macedon Ranges and employing more staff at both sites to meet the new staffing requirements. As well as wanting a smooth manufacturing set-up, Bernard argues that it is vital for the Mountain Mist beer to be 100 per cent comparable between manufacturing sites. For Bernard, there are many issues still to contend with in relation to sourcing raw materials.

Bernard also needs to employ a manager to oversee the sales side of the Western Australia venture. He has offered the role of Western Australia Sales Manager to Matt Jerome. Matt is in his late 20s and had been working for Mountain Mist for about four years in the administration area as an accounts clerk. He has recently spent time on the administrative side of the new Western Australian operations. Bernard is pleased with Matt's work and knows he is keen to move from administration and account keeping into managing sales at the new facility. While he has not had any previous sales experience, Bernard is keen to offer Matt this personal development opportunity.

Matt's salary comprised a base salary and an incentive based on sales performance. While Mountain Mist had the corporate balanced scorecard (described earlier), they did not link scorecard results to their sales managers' incentive plans. Bernard was concerned that the balanced scorecard measures would not drive the innovation and risk he required of his sales team. For example, Bernard wanted his sales team to continue to have the flexibility to make last minute changes if their customers required. He thought if they were influenced by rigid balanced scorecard performance measures, they might, in fact, be demotivated. He was also worried that they would work to the measure rather than profit maximisation through meeting customers' unique, changeable and often immediate needs. Thus, Matt was able to earn a bonus based on the sales generated in the Western Australian region. Matt was also given the autonomy to hire his own sales and administration staff to help manage this new sales division. In addition, Bernard left Matt responsible for overseeing both sales and bookkeeping roles. After all, Matt had excelled at his administrative role in the past.

Bernard has contemplated varying remuneration options for Matt. Although Matt will have assets under his control, Bernard decides to reward Matt based on the following incentive structure:

- base salary — $120 000 per annum
- individual bonus — based on the Western Australian division's EBIT (capped at $50 000 per annum)
- corporate bonus — based on Mountain Mist's corporate performance (2 per cent share of 'above budget' corporate profit pool)
- other — 50 per cent of private health insurance cost, relocation expenses for Matt's family.

Matt has moved his family from the Macedon Ranges to Western Australia and begun to promote Mountain Mist Brewery. The aim is to have manufacturing operations and sales in place for summer.

Required

(a) Discuss the benefits and limitations of Matt's incentive scheme proposed by Bernard.

(b) It is mentioned in the case that Matt has assets under his control. What performance measurement alternatives could Bernard have used? How might they improve (or otherwise) on the scheme proposed by Bernard?

Part B

Once the Western Australian operation has settled and sales are going well, Bernard considers further expansion opportunities. Given the mature life cycle status of the brewery industry, declining consumption, strong competition from leading producers and competition from substitute products, Bernard wants to expand his business in other value-adding ways. He calls on his management team for ideas. One potential idea worth pursuing comes from Damien Poulsen, a long-term employee.

Damien Poulsen has been Bernard's one and only production manager in charge of Mountain Mist's spring water. Bernard has great respect for Damien's work ethic and long-standing commitment to Mountain Mist. Damien is also a qualified microbiologist and employs a team of experts to extract and process the Mountain Mist spring water for the brewing department. A large portion of the Spring Water department's (SWD) activities relates to the quality control (QC) function for Mountain Mist Brewery. Their main requirement is to ensure the spring water continually meets Mountain Mist's strict specifications. The mix of sulphates, calcium, phosphorous and magnesium must be correct as excessive amounts of any ingredient can result in poor tasting ales. It can also lead to residue forming on the ale containers.

As the spring water from Mountain Mist's Macedon Ranges spring provides beautifully tasting spring water (free of excessive mineral content) and more than enough spring water for the beer manufacture, Damien Poulsen suggested to Bernard that they expand production into bottled water sales. He points out that spring water is the fastest growing beverage type in Australia and Mountain Mist would be foolish not to take advantage of the opportunity to participate in this market. Australians spent more than $500 million on bottled water last year, a 1.6 per cent increase on the previous year. The current key competitors in the bottled water market include Coca-Cola Amatil Limited (42 per cent), P&N Beverages Australia Pty Ltd (22 per cent) and others (36 per cent). These key competitors own prominent brands including Mount Franklin, Peats Ridge and Cool Ridge. Damien suggests to Bernard that a niche marketing opportunity exists and that they should compete with the higher-priced sparkling and still water brands, which include European imports such as San Pellegrino and Perrier.[22]

Damien is also aware of exploiting the growing market sensitivities towards increased water consumption. For instance, climate change has increased demand for bottled water (because of the extended hot summers). However, the demand remains high throughout the cooler seasons of the year for other sports and health-related reasons. The factors that significantly contribute to increasing demand for bottled water include general health awareness and greater knowledge of the benefits of adequate water consumption, concerns about the microbiological condition and taste of tap water in some regions, and the fact that many consumers are beginning to acknowledge bottled water as a healthy alternative to high-sugar soft drinks.

In Damien's proposal, he outlines the cost structure required for the bottled spring water proposal. He builds his figures from the industry data. He bases his figures on the average retail price for one-litre of bottled water ($2.53). Damien outlines the purchases that are most significant to this industry. They include containers, labels and other packaging materials. He explains how the costs for water extraction, such as pumping equipment, have been included in the depreciation cost (but mentions that these costs are currently paid for in full by the brewery). Water costs are relatively minor. That is, they pay the Macedon Ranges Shire Council fees for ground water extraction; however, the fees are insignificant.

In the proposal, Damien also mentions that he could draw on existing labour for the production processes, but will need a small number of additional staff to handle the clerical, sales and marketing functions. The total labour costs are equivalent to 14.7 per cent of revenue. In this machine-intensive industry, approximately 53 per cent of total labour is required for managerial, clerical, sales, marketing and other functions. The remaining 47 per cent of total labour is involved in the bottled water production.

Damien includes asset acquisitions and associated depreciation costs in his proposal. To begin, he includes full depreciation costs on existing equipment required for the filtration, UV sterilisation and zonation processes that remove undesirable compounds and organic elements from the spring water. Damien also includes the purchase of new assets such as computers and automated bottle production lines in his depreciation costs. In addition, he includes the purchase and depreciation on two trucks required to transport the bottled water to distributors from the Mountain Mist source. In Damien's list of acquisitions required, he makes mention of new legislative requirements associated with environmental emissions. With this impending legislation, Damien allocates funds to the newly implemented carbon pollution reduction scheme (CPRS) that will measure, monitor and report on the Mountain Mist carbon emissions. To meet the legislative requirements, Damien needs to allocate a percentage of staff resources (15 per cent of one full-time employee's wages) and equipment to correctly measure their carbon emissions. He notes that this additional cost will be incurred regardless of the decision to invest in the bottled spring water project.

Damien also includes accounting, auditing, repair, maintenance, market research and advertising as components of 'other' costs. Marketing is a significant cost to the bottled water industry given the need to differentiate a largely homogeneous product. He explains that, in Europe, for water to be designated 'natural' it must be bottled at the spring. This could be an important marketing feature for Mountain Mist bottled spring water, even though Australia does not have such a labelling requirement. He mentions how competitor water that has been transported in holding tanks to bottlers can risk contamination. As such, water that is not bottled on site may require chlorination which in turn affects the taste. Mountain Mist water, as it is bottled onsite, can truly offer the 'natural' European equivalent marketing feature. Damien explains how they would pitch this style of marketing in the up-market hospitality channel representing pubs, restaurants, cafés, cinemas and arenas. They will also focus on marketing to supermarkets and convenience stores as sales through these major outlets comprise 67 per cent of total bottled water sales, but, in this setting, they will not compete on price. He points out that while price is important (that is, they will compete with house brands and generics), the image, particularly from the large brands, remains the most important factor in establishing market share. The niche market could bear additional costs for perceived additional quality and image created by the brewery arm.

The main thrust of Damien's argument is for Mountain Mist to exploit its economies of scope by expanding its beverage offerings. He explains that while materials and packaging are the main cost pressures, he hopes to achieve up to 60 per cent gross profit margin on the Mountain Mist private-label bottle water sales. He argues that he can reduce many of the costs. For example, input costs will be reduced as Mountain Mist has the spring water onsite. Rent is not applicable as

Mountain Mist owns the Macedon Ranges facilities. In addition, wages, much of the depreciation and other costs can be allocated to the brewing division as it is currently paying for them anyway.

As Bernard evaluates Damien's $30 million bottled water proposal, he also considers the key success factors in the bottled water manufacturing industry.[23]

- Control of distribution arrangements — arrangement of distribution ensures timely delivery, low costs and maximised product reach.
- Economies of scope — economies of scope refer to the efficiencies in distribution, marketing and administration when a firm produces a wide range of beverage brands.
- Having a good reputation — first movers have an advantage in this industry in that they can establish strong reputations, which means new competitors need to spend heavily on marketing to catch up.
- Market research and understanding — market research into consumer profiles, attitudes and preferences are important for informing both brand promotion and bottle and label design.
- Marketing of differentiated products — product innovation and differentiation (including packaging) contributes significantly to selling the industry's products.
- Economies of scale — scale economies are very important to a low-value product since high volumes must be produced and sold to achieve reasonable profits.
- Establishment of brand names — strong brand names contribute to the appeal of bottled water as an accessory, as well as building a product's reputation of quality. This allows bottlers to both win market share within particular consumer segments, and to charge premium prices.
- Attractive product presentation — the design of the bottle is of importance in winning market share and justifying higher pricing in this competitive industry.
- Effective product promotion — use of in-store merchandising can have a strong influence on consumer choice.

This all sounds quite interesting to Bernard, but he does wonder at the effect of the carbon pollution reduction scheme and the more recent negative publicity bottled water is receiving. This negative publicity surrounds the view that bottled water is not environmentally friendly as it requires significant greenhouse gas emissions and plastic bottles commonly end up in landfill.

Bernard wonders at the viability of Damien's $30 million proposal.

Required

(a) Advise Bernard on the types of strategic risks you might associate with Mountain Mist. In your discussion, include the risks associated with the expansion of Mountain Mist's brewing to Western Australia and into the spring water market. You may also wish to discuss the beverage industry in general.

(b) What do you consider the level of risk exposure for Mountain Mist? Justify your answer using the risk profile discussion in this chapter.

(c) What suggestions do you have for Bernard to overcome these risks?

20.41 Remuneration plan   **LO2, 4, 5**

Matahari Ltd manufactures and installs renewable energy systems. It has four divisions in Australia: Wind, Thermal Solar, Photo Voltaic (PV) and Installation. The company was listed on the Australian Securities Exchange in 2013.

The CEO, William Smith, believes that divisional managers should be given a high degree of autonomy and held accountable for the performance of their divisions. He believes that if the divisions prosper then the company and its shareholders will prosper.

Before the beginning of each financial year, William reviews performance and then sets a return-on-investment (ROI) target for each division for the coming year. ROI is defined as the operating profit as a percentage of the book-value of the assets employed. Targets are set in consultation with the respective divisional manager with due regard to the prevailing market conditions. William makes sure that the ROI target is challenging but achievable. Over the past ten years, the ROI targets have tended to increase slightly each year. Key personnel within each division are awarded a performance bonus, if and only if, the ROI of that division exceeds the target.

For the past seven years, Matahari has been using a bonus and incentive scheme to motivate and reward key personnel. The scheme is based on the distribution of a bonus pool. The size of the bonus pool is 10 per cent of Matahari's residual income for the year and is capped at $1.5 million per year. The bonus pool is distributed to divisions on the basis of the ROI achieved by each division.

If a division does not reach its target, it does not receive a bonus. If a division achieves its target, it receives a bonus score equal to the division's actual ROI less the division's target ROI, up to a maximum of 5.00 points. The bonus pool is then distributed according to each division's score relative to the total bonus score. The bonus awarded to a division is then distributed to key personnel as determined by the divisional manager.

William is disappointed that Chloe Lee, the manager of the PV Division, has not taken the opportunity to increase her division's production capacity. The shareholders are supportive and would be happy to finance the expansion. William recalls that divisional managers have been reluctant to submit investment proposals on several occasions in the past.

William has also found himself starting to think more about the suitability of the bonus system and underlying performance measures. A member of William's business network has suggested that Matahari would benefit from the adoption of a balanced scorecard. William gets nervous when people start talking about non-financial measures; he thinks his focus on a small number of key financial measures has worked well to date and aligns with shareholder interests.

Required

(a) For the year ended 30 June 2019, Matahari's residual income was $13 939 000. The target and actual ROI's for each division are given in the table below. Calculate the bonus awarded to each division by completing the table below.

Division	Target ROI	Actual ROI	Bonus score	Bonus awarded ($'000) (to the nearest thousand)
Wind	11.0%	12.5%	1.2	
Thermal Solar	9.5%	10.0%	0.5	
PV	12.8%	14.0%		
Installations	12.0%	11.5%		
Bonus pool				

(b) State two key strengths of the existing bonus plan.

(c) Identify one key weakness of the existing bonus plan and suggest a change that would alleviate the weakness.

ENDNOTES

1. Deming, WE 1982 & 1986, *Out of the crisis: quality, productivity and competitive position*, Cambridge University Press, Cambridge, www.ifm.eng.cam.ac.uk/dstools/process/Deming.html.
2. Kohn, A 1993, 'Why incentive plans cannot work', *Harvard Business Review*, September–October, pp. 54–63.
3. Pink, DH 2009, *Drive: the surprising truth about what motivates us*, Riverhead Hardcover.
4. *The Economist* 2010, 'Driven to distraction', 14 January, www.economist.com.
5. In some schemes, the predetermined price may be zero. These schemes are often referred to as performance rights.
6. See Denis, D, Hanouna, P & Sarin, A 2006, 'Is there a dark side to incentive compensation?', *Journal of Corporate Finance*, 12, 467–88.
7. Albuquerque, A 2009, 'Peer firms in relative performance evaluation', *Journal of Accounting and Economics*, 48, pp. 69–89.
8. Stapledon, G 2006, *The pay for performance dilemma*, Working Paper, SSRN database.
9. Jensen, M & Murphy, K 2004, *Remuneration: where we've been, how we got to here, what are the problems and how to fix them*, Finance Working Paper no: 44/2004, ECGI Working Paper Series in Finance.
10. Stein, P 2009, 'Singapore firm shows Wall Street how to share gains and pains with shareholders', *The Australian*, 26 January, p. 22.
11. Australian Productivity Commission 2009, *Report: executive remuneration in Australia*, no. 49, 19 December, Commonwealth of Australia.
12. Refer to Standards Australia at www.standards.org.au.
13. Committee of Sponsoring Organizations of the Treadway Commission 2004, *Enterprise risk management — integrated framework*, September, www.coso.org.
14. International Federation of Accountants 2004, *Enterprise governance: getting the balance right*, February, www.ifac.org, p. 4.
15. International Federation of Accountants 2004.
16. As an example, the Australian Securities Exchange uses this risk profile classification in its risk management policies, www.asx.com.au.
17. Frigo, M & Læssøe, H 2012, 'Strategic risk management at the Lego Group', *Strategic Finance*, February, p. 29.
18. Adapted from Wilmer Cutler Pickering Hale & Dorr LLP 2008, Securities briefing series, *Rogue traders: lies, losses, and lessons Learned*, March, pp. 2–10.
19. *Lawyers Weekly* 2009, 'Face of corporate fraud unmasked', 11 March, www.lawyersweekly.com.au.
20. Adapted from Wilmer Cutler Pickering Hale & Dorr LLP 2008.
21. Higgins, J 2009, 'Will Starbucks 'unbranding' start a chain reaction?', *BNET UK*, 6 August, www.blogs.bnet.co.uk.
22. *IBISWorld* 2009 and 2010, *IBISWorld industry report: bottled water manufacturing in Australia: C2186*, 17 March 2009/21 January 2010, www.ibisworld.com.au.
23. *IBISWorld* 2009 and 2010.

ACKNOWLEDGEMENTS

Photo 20A: © Pressmaster / Shutterstock.com

Photo 20B: © Rawpixel.com / Shutterstock.com

Photo 20C: © Suwannar Kawila / EyeEm / Getty Images

Figure 20.5: © International Federation of Accountants. Exhibit A5, file name: 20190225-TRAN-Australia-Wiley-RC-NF-ExA5-fig Enterprise Governance-final

Figure 20.6: © The risk classification framework of the Lego Group Figure 2 from p. 29 of Frigo M & Laessoe H 2012, 'Strategic risk management at the Lego Group', *Strategic Finance*, February, pp. 27–35.

Extract 20A: © IBIS World

Extract 20B: © Productivity Commission 2009, *Executive remuneration in Australia*, Report no. 49, Final Inquiry Report, Melbourne.

CHAPTER 21

Sustainability management accounting

LEARNING OBJECTIVES

After studying this chapter, you should be able to:

21.1 discuss how the concepts of sustainability and sustainability management apply to corporate practice

21.2 recognise why it is essential for management accountants to take an integrated thinking approach to sustainability

21.3 outline the scope and benefits resulting from sustainability management accounting practices

21.4 demonstrate an understanding of key sustainability management accounting tools

21.5 communicate the issues faced by managers when trying to implement sustainability change processes within their entities.

IN BRIEF

The relationship between management accounting control systems and organisational goals and culture is a key consideration for managers wishing to pursue sustainability management practices in their individual businesses. Sustainability management is a process undertaken by entities striving for a simultaneous improvement of their *economic, environmental* and *social* goals. Sustainability management accounting is the tool used by organisations to achieve their sustainability management goals. Sustainability management decision making is optimised when supported by management accounting tools that are aligned with sustainability management strategies.

21.1 Sustainability and management accounting

LEARNING OBJECTIVE 21.1 Discuss how the concepts of sustainability and sustainability management apply to corporate practice.

As we have outlined throughout this text, management (or cost) accounting constitutes the central tool for internal decision making and primarily focuses on satisfying the information needs of internal management. As you will recall, the generally accepted management accounting practices are *not* regulated as they are in financial accounting. Thus, managers will adopt the specific management accounting practices and associated tools that will satisfy their individual organisational goals and culture.

The growing awareness of, and concern for, social and environmental welfare issues has changed the ways in which companies account for their social and environmental practices. While many organisations have implemented specific environmental or social management systems for external reporting purposes (to providers of capital as well as other stakeholders), the issue for management accountants is how to integrate these systems within management control practices. For a sustainability culture and related practices to develop within entities, sustainability management strategies should be aligned with sustainability management accounting systems.

Sustainability and United Nations Sustainable Development Goals

In 1983, the United Nations set up the World Commission on Environment and Development (WCED) to promote quality of life for the present *and future* generations. At a broad level, the UN defines *sustainability* as 'development that meets the needs of the present without compromising the ability of future generations to meet their own needs'.[1] The key aims associated with sustainability and sustainable development are to ensure society:

- lives within environmental resource limits
- achieves social justice
- fosters economic and social progress.

These overarching aims have been further divided into 17 interconnected Sustainable Development Goals[2] which together address our global challenges. Each goal has associated targets which are to be achieved by 2030. The 17 goals are outlined in figure 21.1.

| FIGURE 21.1 | United Nations Sustainable Development Goals |

Sustainable Development Goals	Fact	Targets
1: No Poverty	783 million people live below the poverty line.	50 per cent reduction.
2: Zero Hunger	One in nine people in the world today (815 million) are undernourished.	End hunger.
3: Good Health and Wellbeing	More than 5 million children die before their fifth birthday each year.	Reduce global maternal mortality ratio to less than 70 per 100 000 live births.
4: Quality Education	57 million primary age children remain out of school.	Ensure that all girls and boys complete free, equitable and quality primary and secondary education.
5: Gender Equality	750 million women and girls were married before the age of 18 and at least 200 million women and girls in 30 countries have undergone FGM.	End all forms of discrimination against all women and girls everywhere.
6: Clean Water and Sanitation	three in ten people lack access to safely managed drinking water services and six in ten people lack access to safely managed sanitation facilities.	Achieve universal and equitable access to safe and affordable drinking water for all.

7: Affordable and Clean Energy	13 per cent of the global population still lacks access to modern electricity.	Ensure universal access to affordable, reliable and modern energy services.
8: Decent Work and Economic Growth	The global unemployment rate in 2017 was 5.6 per cent, down from 6.4 per cent in 2000.	Sustain per capita economic growth in accordance with national circumstances and, in particular, at least 7 per cent gross domestic product growth per annum in the least developed countries.
9: Industry, Innovation and Infrastructure	Basic infrastructure like roads, information and communication technologies, sanitation, electrical power and water remains scarce in many developing countries.	Develop quality, reliable, sustainable and resilient infrastructure, including regional and trans-border infrastructure, to support economic development and human well-being, with a focus on affordable and equitable access for all.
10: Reduced Inequalities	In 2016, over 64.4 per cent of products exported by the least developed countries to world markets faced zero tariffs, an increase of 20 per cent since 2010.	Progressively achieve and sustain income growth of the bottom 40 per cent of the population at a rate higher than the national average
11: Sustainable Cities and Communities	Half of humanity — 3.5 billion people — lives in cities today and 5 billion people are projected to live in cities by 2030.	Ensure access for all to adequate, safe and affordable housing and basic services, and upgrade slums.
12: Responsible Production and Consumption	Should the global population reach 9.6 billion by 2050, the equivalent of almost three planets could be required to provide the natural resources needed to sustain current lifestyles	Implement the ten-year framework of programmes on sustainable consumption and production, all countries taking action, with developed countries taking the lead, taking into account the development and capabilities of developing countries. Achieve the sustainable management and efficient use of natural resources.
13: Climate Action	As of April 2018, 175 parties had ratified the Paris Agreement and 168 parties had communicated their first nationally-determined contributions to the UN framework convention on Climate Change Secretariat.	Strengthen resilience and adaptive capacity to climate-related hazards and natural disasters in all countries. Integrate climate change measures into national policies, strategies and planning.
14: Life Below Water	Oceans cover three quarters of the Earth's surface, contain 97 per cent of the Earth's water, and represent 99 per cent of the living space on the planet by volume. Over 3 billion people depend on marine and coastal biodiversity for their livelihoods.	By 2025, prevent and significantly reduce marine pollution of all kinds, in particular from land-based activities, including marine debris and nutrient pollution.
15: Life on Land	Around 1.6 billion people depend on forests for their livelihood, including 70 million indigenous people. Forests are home to more than 80 per cent of all terrestrial species of animals, plants and insects.	By 2020, ensure the conservation, restoration and sustainable use of terrestrial and inland freshwater ecosystems and their services, in particular forests, wetlands, mountains and drylands, in line with obligations under international agreements. By 2020, promote the implementation of sustainable management of all types of forests, halt deforestation, restore degraded forests and substantially increase afforestation and reforestation globally By 2030, combat desertification, restore degraded land and soil, including land affected by desertification, drought and floods, and strive to achieve a land degradation-neutral world.

Sustainable Development Goals	Fact	Targets
16: Peace, Justice and Strong Institutions	Promote peaceful and inclusive societies for sustainable development, provide access to justice for all and build effective, accountable and inclusive institutions at all levels.	Significantly reduce all forms of violence and related death rates everywhere. End abuse, exploitation, trafficking and all forms of violence against and torture of children.
17: Partnerships for the Goals	**Finance:** Total government revenue as a proportion of GDP, by source. Number of countries that adopt and implement investment promotion regimes for least developed countries. **Technology:** Number of science and/or technology cooperation agreements and programmes between countries, by type of cooperation. Fixed Internet broadband subscriptions per 100 inhabitants. **Capacity Building:** Dollar value of financial and technical assistance (including through North–South, South–South and triangular cooperation) committed to developing countries. **Trade:** Worldwide weighted tariff-average. Developing countries' and least-developed countries' share of global exports. **Systemic Issues:** Number of countries with mechanisms in place to enhance policy coherence of sustainable development. Number of countries reporting progress in multi-stakeholder development effectiveness monitoring frameworks that support the achievement of the sustainable development goals. Number of countries that have national statistical legislation that complies with the Fundamental Principles of Official Statistics.	

*Adapted from https://sustainabledevelopment.un.org only a selection of targets provided. For more comprehensive view, visit the United Nations website.

As you will learn in this chapter, management accounting can support the achievement of these goals in several ways including support with: financial and non-financial performance measurement and evaluation; allocation of capital and financial resources to projects and initiatives that link with the Sustainable Development Goals; and, identifying, monitoring and management of associated risk factors that have the potential to impact corporate reputation and risk management.

Important to the Sustainable Development Goals is managing the impact of climate change. The impact of climate change on global economies is high on most countries' political agendas. For example, in the United Kingdom, the Stern Review, one of the most comprehensive reviews ever carried out on the economics of climate change, estimated that the risks of unabated climate change could be equivalent to 20 per cent of global GDP.[3] In Australia, Ross Garnaut prepared a Climate Change Review for the Australian government to address the extent of Australia's role in global mitigation of climate change. Efforts to control pollution and negate the social and environmental impacts associated with climate change have resulted in new carbon accounting approaches. Australia is a member of the International Carbon Action Partnership (ICAP), an international government forum which brings together government policy makers to discuss emission trading research and practice.[4] These are highlighted in comprehensive example 1.

COMPREHENSIVE EXAMPLE 1

Greenhouse gases

Governments and other stakeholders are increasingly focused on greenhouse gas pollution which has the potential to cause major global climate change. Greenhouse gases consist of water vapour, carbon dioxide (CO_2), methane, nitrous oxide and chlorofluorocarbons (CFCs). Excess greenhouse gas emissions are created by:

- human activities such as burning fossil fuels (coal, petroleum and natural gas) to provide energy for industrial processes transportation, agriculture, heating and lighting; clearing land and burning forests
- farming and intensive agriculture practices
- decomposing waste in landfill rubbish tips
- industrial atmospheric pollutants.

This human action has increased atmospheric CO_2 levels by 30 per cent, thereby trapping radiation and contributing to a changing climate (or global warming). The concentration of CO_2 is rising at a faster rate than can be absorbed by the plants, soils and oceans of the world, causing an increase in the frequency of extreme weather events such as floods, droughts and cyclones; rises in sea levels; changing rainfall patterns; and decreasing sea ice and melting glaciers.

For the last few years and despite continued political debates over global emission targets there has been an understanding that greenhouse gas emissions need to be significantly reduced to mitigate the impact of climate change. In 2015, it was generally understood that global greenhouse gases need to be cut by at least 50 per cent below 1990 levels by 2050 to prevent global temperatures increasing by more than 2 degrees Celsius. In 2018, the United Nations (UN) revised its warnings and suggested that urgent and unprecedented changes were needed to keep climate change to a maximum of 1.5 degrees Celsius. Rising temperatures contribute significantly to the risk of drought, floods, extreme heat and poverty for hundreds of millions of people. Under the United Nations Framework Convention on Climate Change and the Kyoto Protocol, it is argued that for these substantive decreases in greenhouse gas emissions, there must be global commitment to:

- reduce energy demand
- increase energy efficiency
- reduce use of fossil fuels
- increase use of renewable energy sources
- reduce deforestation
- continue research and development of sustainable technologies
- negotiate a comprehensive global climate deal to which all nations will commit.

Achieving the above requires actions; for example, stricter regulation by governments or the implementation of market devices.

Three economic approaches to controlling greenhouse gas emissions that have been widely debated and adopted by many countries around the world are: (1) taxation, (2) cap-and-trade and (3) cost containment. The difference between the first two is in the price versus quantity of emissions. For example, government taxes will fix the price of emissions at the tax rate but not the quantity emitted. Alternatively, the cap-and-trade system is a market-based approach that will fix the allowable quantity of emissions circulating in the marketplace, but the market price of emissions remains uncertain. The ICAP forum promotes cap-and-trade as an effective climate policy response. It has been argued that both approaches offer extreme examples. The mid-way 'cost containment' approach is also being debated by environmental economists and climate change policymakers.[5] Rather than the 'right to emit' being supplied with infinite elasticity at a fixed price (tax) or with zero elasticity at a fixed supply (the cap), the cost containment approach works with the idea of a 'safety valve' in which a cap-and-trade system is coupled with a price ceiling at which additional allowances can be purchased (in excess of the cap). So long as the allowance price is below the safety-valve price, this hybrid system acts like cap-and-trade systems with emissions fixed but the price left to adjust. When the safety-valve price is reached, however, this system behaves like a tax, fixing the price but leaving emissions to adjust.[6]

Since the United Nations Climate Change 2015 Paris Agreement there are 21 global emissions trading schemes (ETS) across 28 jurisdictions at different levels of government. Economies with an ETS produce more than 50 per cent of the global GDP and are home to a third of the global population. Altogether, approximately 15 per cent of global emissions are now covered by a domestic ETS including many European countries and, more recently, the Chinese ETS.[7] While the United States, in general, does not participate in emissions trading, there are state-level schemes that have been launched, including one in California. At this stage, the Australian Government has not committed to relaunch Australia's abandoned emissions trading scheme.

Organisations operating in an emissions trading geographical zone are required to purchase permits if they will emit pollution. The cost to purchase permits, in a dynamic market, is argued to be high enough to motivate organisations to innovate and reduce pollution across their varying value-chain inputs, processes and outputs. It is also anticipated that alternative energy demand will lead to global investment in renewable energy worth billions of dollars within a decade.[8]

The World Bank indicates that the total value of the global carbon market in 2018 is around $82 billion (combining 26 carbon taxes and 25 emissions trading schemes worldwide). This has been a 56 per cent increase from the 2017 value of $52 billion. Given that the global market for carbon trading is set to be one of the largest global futures trading schemes, the potential requirement for carbon trading accounting by organisations will become an important aspect of management accounting control systems. Carbon trading provides challenges and opportunities for organisations. Carbon credits created as part of the market for carbon trading represent a new class of asset. Industries that are heavy emitters of CO_2 will be faced with potential financial liabilities for continuing to emit the gas, or possible rewards for reducing emissions, so carbon trading has the potential to motivate behavioural and cultural responses within organisations as well as create an avenue for organisational learning. The amount and type of energy consumed will become a larger focus for entities. For example, alternative renewable energy resources such as that provided by solar power, wind farms or possibly even nuclear power[9] provide additional opportunities for governments and organisations to reduce greenhouse gas emissions and enhance profits through carbon credits.

Politico-economic views and societal pressures are increasingly reflected in changing organisational practices. Achieving sustainability outcomes is a complex process that requires substantive change across the globe. For organisations to encompass the notion of sustainability within their business practices, several key sustainability management factors need to be considered. For example, a change in corporate culture requires critical thinking, reflection and education that focuses on long-term organisational learning and widespread knowledge acquisition. Change is more likely to be achieved by the work of multi-disciplinary, cross-departmental teams rather than individual champions promoting sustainability. Thus, participation and collaboration from multiple stakeholders throughout the value chain, from the suppliers to the organisational employees through to the customers, is a key factor for successful sustainability management outcomes.

Sustainability management

Sustainability management is the measuring, monitoring and integrated control of the materially important capital inputs to ensure sustainable corporate profits in the value creation process. It is a process undertaken by entities striving for a simultaneous improvement of their *economic, environmental* and *social* goals. It is unique to every entity and depends on the industry in which the organisation operates (for example; mining, industrial, service or government). Desired sustainable outcomes should be reflected in the corporate mission, the image the organisation wishes to project to stakeholders and the strategic goals the organisation wants to accomplish. For most organisations, sustainability management is a continuous cycle as highlighted in figure 21.2.

FIGURE 21.2	Sustainability management cycle

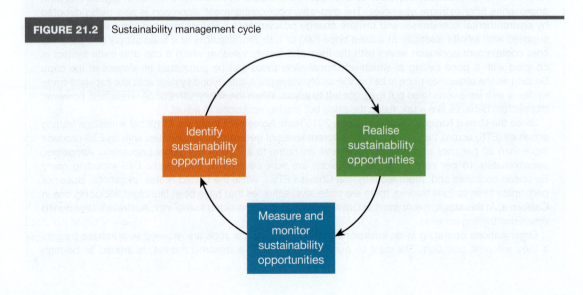

The cycle commences with the identification of sustainability opportunities, followed by the process of realising the sustainability opportunities, which are measured and monitored as part of an entity's management control system. This cycle allows for management to reflect on the actions taken and to develop and direct future sustainability practices. Sustainability opportunities are continuously enabled through technological advances, knowledge acquisition and changes to societal expectations.

Sustainability opportunities can focus on minimising costs by improving current use of resources, or they might present as innovative ways of bringing fresh revenue into the entity. Sometimes, the requirement for sustainability can take a contingency perspective, where sustainability management opportunities emerge through the requirement to comply with tightening legislative requirements and other external factors such as political and societal pressure.

In response to the United Nations Sustainable Development Goals and the growing pressures for corporations to acknowledge their social responsibility, The Prince of Wales' Accounting for Sustainability (A4S) Project, provides sustainability management support to practitioner bodies and corporate executives.[10] Through the work of A4S and the further establishment of its Accounting Bodies Network, accounting approaches to sustainability management are being translated to practice.

The International Integrated Reporting Council (IIRC) is a key player, whose role is to foster an integrated approach to corporate reporting. The IIRC recommends that accountants focus on value creation from multiple capital inputs (financial, manufactured, intellectual, human, social and relationship, and natural capital) and provide an Integrated Report (<IR>) that outlines the management of the value creation (preservation, diminution) process over time.[11] The work by the IIRC has extended the triple bottom line consideration of improving all three economic, social and environmental dimensions in unison, which in turn has extended the A4S ideals of *integrated thinking* as an important part of sustainability management.

Sustainability management is the measuring, monitoring and integrated control of the materially important capital inputs — the financial, manufactured, intellectual, human, social and relationship, and natural capital dimensions. These dimensions are often in conflict, and the role of sustainability management is to work toward sustainable corporate profits in the value creation process. Integrated thinking is the ability of senior managers to actively consider the relationship between an organisation's operations and capital. Integrated thinking approaches validate management's contributions to performance reporting and strategic management control.

As was highlighted in comprehensive example 1, the process of sustainability management can also be part of political and governmental intervention. At the corporate level, sustainability management is part of a process that contributes strategically to the achievement of a company's mission while recognising both private and societal impacts.[12] The **private impacts** are those that are internal or have a direct impact on the organisational value chain. **Societal impacts** were often considered 'externalities', or those costs and benefits that are not generally accounted for in an entity's conventional accounting system.

However, with the push to meet sustainable development goals and reduce the impact of climate change, the carbon pollution that is emitted indirectly from the consumption of energy and directly from the production process, is no longer considered a negative externality. Other negative externalities include the potential for dirty production processes that affect the health of surrounding residents and contribute to global warming. An example of a positive externality is an improvement in the health and productivity of people in a locality or region because of investment by businesses. Increasingly, companies are required to consider these as risk and reputation factors and include them in their day-to-day management accounting and reporting practices.

The measuring and monitoring of greenhouse gas emissions offer organisations the potential to realise sustainability opportunities, as highlighted in the following section and comprehensive example 2.

Managing natural capital with carbon footprint accounting

A **carbon footprint** is defined as 'a measure of the CO_2 equivalent emissions attributable to an activity, commonly used at an individual, household, organisation or product level'.[13] The International Organization for Standardization's standard *ISO 14040:2006 Environmental Management — Life Cycle Assessment* offers stringent guidelines for life cycle assessment of corporate activities and is an important standard for organisations electing to become involved in their own carbon footprint accounting. A 'cradle-to-grave' analysis of corporate inputs and outputs is a necessary part of categorising corporate emissions. Calculating a carbon footprint for an entity requires the scope of the carbon emissions be understood and classified according to direct, indirect and embodied emissions.

- *Scope 1:* Direct emissions are those generated from within the organisation (for example, direct electricity generation, emissions from industrial processes, fuel usage for transporting inputs such as fuel consumption by airlines, direct fugitive emissions or onsite waste).
- *Scope 2:* Indirect emissions are generated from purchased electricity. For example, emissions can be measured by recording electricity consumption.
- *Scope 3:* Embodied emissions are emissions embedded in purchased materials or outsourced activities. For example, emissions found in waste disposal, business travel and fuel usage for transporting outputs. A company cannot avoid disclosing emissions by electing to outsource. These emissions are required to be accounted for.

Australia's National Greenhouse Accounts track annual emissions from 1990 and are used to meet Australia's reporting commitments to the United Nations Framework Convention on Climate Change (UNFCCC), track progress against Australia's emission reduction commitments, and inform policy makers and the public.[14] In addition, the *National Greenhouse and Energy Reporting Act 2007* (NGER Act) requires large companies (those emitting more than 25 000 tonnes of CO_2 equivalent, or consuming more than 25 000 megawatt hours of electricity or 2.5 million litres of fuel in a financial year) to report their greenhouse gas emissions annually. Bound by legislation, accounting for greenhouse gas emissions from corporations and other land-based activities requires accuracy in measurement. The ability to calculate removals of greenhouse gases from the land (sinks) requires extensive knowledge of the growth and life cycles of forests and agricultural crops, climate, soils, land cover change and land management. For a comprehensive analysis of impacts on natural capital, the National Greenhouse Accounts draw on many resources, including ecosystem modelling referred to as the Full Carbon Accounting Model (FullCAM).[15]

Once a baseline carbon footprint has been determined, a company can monitor and manage the key emissions of concern. A carbon footprint can be reduced by operating efficiencies and changes in practices. For example, an emissions monitoring plan can be tailored to include organisation-wide, divisional, departmental or individual performance management and control. Depending on a company's sustainability philosophy and core activities, it might also elect to become carbon neutral. **Carbon neutrality** commonly refers to 'a situation where the net emissions associated with a product or an organisation's activities are equal to zero through the acquisition and retirement of carbon offsets that meet additionality criteria'.[16] This means that a company's carbon footprint can also be managed by purchasing approved abatements.

COMPREHENSIVE EXAMPLE 2

Alcoa's sustainability management

Alcoa Corporation is a world leader in light metal technologies and has operated in Australia for 55 years, employing around 4275 people. Alcoa World Alumina and Chemicals (AWAC) is a joint venture between Alumina and Alcoa, set up in 1995 to focus on mining activities. Alumina owns 40 per cent and Alcoa Corporation owns 60 per cent. The Australian operation is the world's largest integrated bauxite mining, alumina refining and aluminium smelting system. Approximately 36 million tonnes of bauxite, 9 million tonnes of alumina and 300 000 tonnes of aluminium are produced every year. This represents

around 45 per cent of Australia's alumina, 13 per cent of Australia's aluminium and approximately 7 per cent of total world production. Alcoa is one of Australia's leading exporters, contributing around $5 billion in exports per year.[17]

As a significant global industrial resource corporation, Alcoa's energy-intensive operations have not been immune to the climate change spotlight. The smelting of aluminium is a very energy-intensive process with more than 80 per cent of the industry's greenhouse gas emissions resulting from consumption of brown-coal-generated electricity. These emissions are considered to be indirect, or Scope 2 emissions, resulting from the generation of purchased energy. The other 20 per cent are direct, or Scope 1, emissions resulting from owned or controlled sources. Within the aluminium industry, 1.4 tonnes of CO_2 equivalent (CO_2-e) emissions are generated per tonne of aluminium produced. This equates to nearly 7 per cent of Australia's total CO_2-e emissions.[18] AWAC's total CO_2-e emissions have been declining since the baseline measures in 2005. In 2017, AWAC CO_2-e emissions were 11 317 033 tonnes (made up of 7 575 617 tonnes of direct (Scope 1) emissions and 3 741 416 tonnes of indirect (Scope 2) emissions. In 2017, AWAC reported an additional 34 468 831 tonnes of indirect embodied emissions (Scope 3). Australia's national inventory total CO_2-e emissions is 533 700 000 tonnes.[19]

In light of the controversy surrounding global warming and Alcoa's high greenhouse gas emissions, Alcoa must also be seen to be proactive in responding to calls to improve corporate sustainability. This can be observed in company activities such as sustainability reporting, specific public relations campaigns and new product and process innovations. Alcoa has a sustainability mission that considers human, social and financial capital: 'At Alcoa, we use our values to build financial success, environmental excellence, and social responsibility in partnership with all stakeholders'. In identifying and realising sustainability opportunities, Alcoa promotes its 'green products' for use in food packaging, smart buildings, electronics and road, air and space transportation.

The company's innovative developments have been so successful that it is restructuring into two separate entities: a 'technology-driven value-add company' and a 'globally competitive upstream company', where the latter focuses on its core mining activity, under the umbrella of AWAC, the joint venture between Alumina and Alcoa. In measuring and monitoring sustainability, Alcoa reports in full accordance with the Global Reporting Initiative (GRI) guidelines and measures its sustainability impact using life cycle assessment (LCA) techniques (discussed later in this chapter). Alcoa also aims to reduce its carbon footprint by the efficient use of resources and control of emissions, waste and land use. This means that certain inputs are recognised as materially important to Alcoa and included in its internal performance measurement processes and corporate disclosures. For example, Alcoa's sustainability performance measurement systems include the measurement and management of: greenhouse gas emissions, energy, health and safety, economic performance, environmental footprint (emissions and waste), local communities and biodiversity. Two key priorities relate to mining rehabilitation and bauxite residue management. They manage environmental uses using environmental management systems certified by ISO14001:2004 and refinery quality management systems certified by ISO9001: 2008. Among the measures are specific targets that relate to:

- *natural capital:* total direct and indirect CO_2-e emissions, water usage, landfill waste, land rehabilitation, and recycling or re-use of their bauxite residue, aluminium can recycling, and biodiversity development plans including the monitoring of plant species richness
- *human capital:* zero fatalities, incident rate, and representation of women and minorities at executive level
- *social and relationship capital:* number of manufacturing locations implementing the Alcoa Community Framework, representation of employee volunteers, and investments in community programs.

The concepts introduced in this comprehensive example will be further highlighted later in the chapter.

Sustainability management accounting

The 'sustainability accounting package' includes the application of management accounting techniques that suit a holistic sustainability management framework. Sustainability management will produce the most benefits when it becomes an integrated organisational practice, which means senior managers should not only think about sustainability in an integrated way (integrated thinking) but extend their focus toward specific accounting tools. The sustainability accounting package should be viewed in unison and integrated with other social and environmental guidelines and best practices, promoted by organisations such as the United Nations and the International Organization for Standardization.[20]

Senior managers use management accounting techniques to support the work of financial accountants, whose focus is on reporting environmental liability costs to external parties such as shareholders and financial institutions. They will also draw on information from sustainability audits and assurance services, designed to monitor, verify and improve the quality and context of information provided for management information as well as corporate disclosures. In some countries, audited environmental or sustainable reporting is a mandatory process. In Australia, however, these services are generally voluntary and unregulated — but are increasingly being used by organisations to promote their image and reporting credibility with their stakeholders.[21] The information required for external financial reporting purposes is far narrower than that required for internal management accounting purposes. As highlighted in figure 21.3, there is a vast array of information that flows internally, but it is condensed to fit external regulatory requirements or management disclosure choices.

For management accountants, the focus is on internal reporting for sustainability management purposes. Sustainability management accounting uses techniques similar to the conventional and contemporary management accounting techniques covered in the earlier chapters of this text, but does so through a sustainability lens. In figure 21.3, sustainability management accounting is noted as the management accounting arm of the wider sustainability or environmental accounting package.[22] **Sustainability management accounting** is the tool that is used to attain the organisation's (or specific business unit's) sustainability goals. It is an important part of the business model that simultaneously integrates the organisation's use of financial, manufactured, intellectual, human, social and relationship, and natural capital performance with strategic management.

Ideally, management accountants working in environments that encourage sustainability accounting should have a thorough understanding of the drivers (reputation, regulation, revenue enhancement, cost control etc.) behind a sustainability culture as well as the relationship between external reporting and internal management practices. It is desirable that management accountants should be able to apply internal sustainability management accounting control practices to the information being disclosed in external reports and likewise match the information being disclosed externally to internal management accounting control systems. The sustainability management accountant's role is to provide information for both sustainability decision making and financial sustainability reporting. This helps to ensure a balanced conformance–performance approach is taken for sustainability enterprise governance.[23]

FIGURE 21.3 The context of sustainability accounting as part of sustainability management[24]

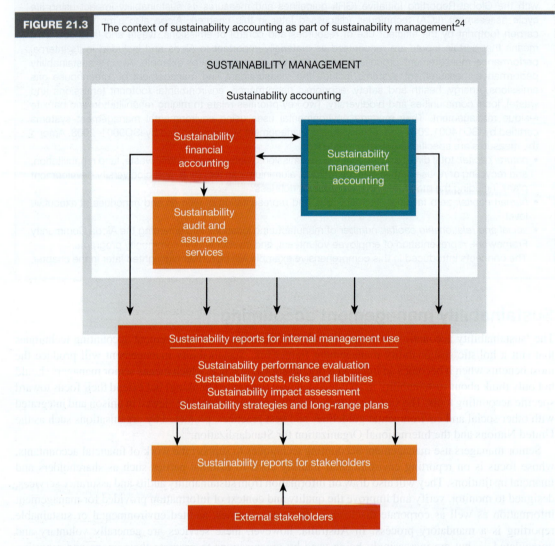

Sustainability accounting and reporting is about highlighting a company's sustainability philosophy and activities to its stakeholders. For example, rather than emphasise energy efficiency, sustainability reports are meant to reveal corporate inputs and outputs produced from 'clean' and/or 'dirty' energy production and associated outcomes on the use of multiple types of capital in value creation activities. That is, using resources such as uranium, water, wind, solar, natural gas or brown coal fired power has a sustainability market value. Organisations such as supermarkets use sustainability reports to highlight activities such as banning food products implicated in global deforestation or promoting recyclable green bags for groceries as an alternative to environmentally hazardous plastic bags. Governments are promoting energy-saving products by offering rebates and concessions.

Particular products are sought after by consumers because they have an environmentally friendly image and/or are supplied by an entity that is recognised for its sustainability and philanthropic efforts. Greater emphasis on people and the communities in which organisations operate are important in sustainability reporting, with large organisations such as Alcoa, BHP Billiton, National Australia Bank, Fonterra and Santos looking to promote their image through corporate disclosures and by investment in sustainability management practices.[25]

Increasingly, companies are faced with significant economic considerations that might relate to their current and future sustainability management practices. Legislative requirements for corporate reports and disclosures relating to their social and environmental practices are increasing. In general, there is growing societal pressure for companies to enact sustainability management practices. However, potential investors are often sceptical about the extent to which organisations might legitimise their activities with sustainability disclosures, suspecting them of using disclosure merely as a form of 'impression management'.[26]

There is a view among certain ethical investors that the voluntary nature of disclosure can increase the potential for reporting bias. This scepticism is compounded by non-uniform information that makes it difficult for stakeholders to compare businesses, hence the push for Integrated Reporting <IR>. Other initiatives to improve the reliability of reports include GRI, Integrated Reporting, ISO standards that relate to sustainability measurement and the Dow Jones Sustainability Index (DJSI). These external compliance tools influence (and are influenced by) the internal dynamics of management control systems and organisational teams and structures. It is believed that management compliance with these reporting initiatives will enhance a company's access to capital and will increase shareholder value. Other factors that account for the reasons why companies report their corporate social performance are highlighted in figure 21.4.

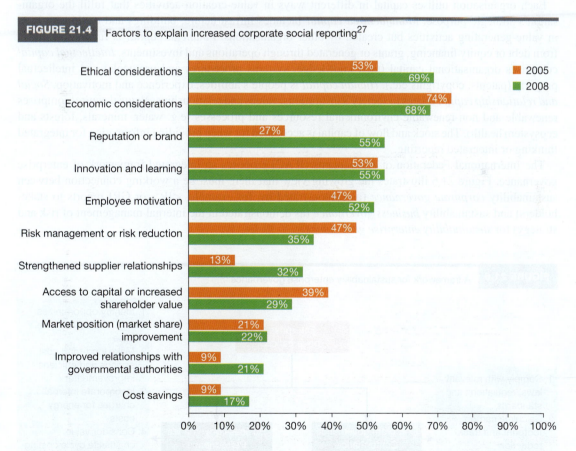

FIGURE 21.4 Factors to explain increased corporate social reporting[27]

It is important to understand how management accounting tools assist in the translation of corporate sustainability disclosures to internal management practices.[28] Thus, the conversion of external reports to internal sustainability management practices and control systems (and vice versa) is a developing domain for future management accountants and management accounting researchers.

21.2 Sustainability, ethics and integrated thinking

LEARNING OBJECTIVE 21.2 Recognise why it is essential for management accountants to take an integrated thinking approach to sustainability.

When viewing sustainability activities through a company's business model, the flow of capital inputs, processes and outputs to capital outcomes can be measured and monitored. If understood in terms of their value creation, preservation or diminution over time, more holistic and systematic decisions about strategies and resource allocation can be made. This approach is termed integrated thinking and is where senior management have the capacity to take a systems thinking approach to sustainability management.

The IIRC argues that accountants and senior managers need to recognise that the corporate business model is at the core of the organisation. The business model draws on various types of capital (financial, manufactured, intellectual, human, social and relationship, and natural) as *inputs* and, through its business *activities*, converts them to *outputs* (products, services, by-products and waste). This leads to *outcomes* in terms of effects on capital (see figure 21.5).[29]

FIGURE 21.5   Integrated thinking and organisational value creation

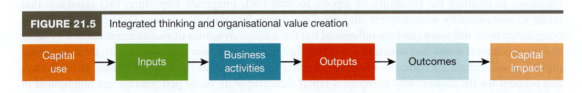

Each organisation utilises capital in different ways in value-creation activities that fulfil the organisation's strategic purpose. *Manufactured capital* includes infrastructure, buildings and equipment used in value-generating activities but created by other organisations. *Financial capital* is funding available from debt or equity financing, grants or generated through operations and investments. *Intellectual capital* comprises organisational capital (tacit knowledge, systems procedures and protocols) and intellectual property (patents, copyrights etc.). *Human capital* is people's abilities, experience and motivation. *Social and relationship capital* relates to society's institutions, values and relationships. *Natural capital* comprises renewable and non-renewable environmental resources and processes (e.g. water, minerals, forests and ecosystem health). The stock and flow of capital is accounted for when providing information for integrated thinking or integrated reporting.

The International Federation of Accountants (IFAC) proposes an integrated framework of enterprise governance. Figure 21.6 illustrates the growing view that there must be a working connection between sustainability *corporate governance* (as demonstrated by, for example, <IR> or GRI reports to stakeholders) and sustainability *business governance* (as demonstrated in the internal management of risk and strategy) for *sustainability enterprise governance*.

FIGURE 21.6   A framework for sustainability enterprise governance[30]

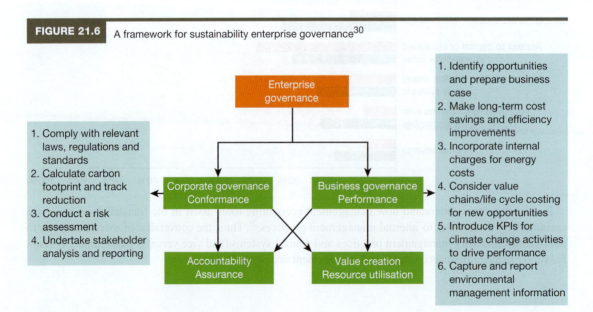

The links to *conformance* and corporate governance are through the adherence to codes, standards and formal internal corporate governance controls.

The links to *performance* and business governance are through:

- the strategy (which strategy is chosen and how clear it is)
- how strategy is executed
- the entity's ability to respond to changes, including changing market conditions
- the entity's ability to successfully undertake mergers and acquisitions.

The following key themes (with the negative potential consequences/attributes in parentheses) are important for enterprise governance.

- Organisational culture and the 'tone at the top' (failure to uphold high ethical standards)
- The CEO (dominant, charismatic and unchallenged)
- The board of directors (weak, poor oversight)
- Internal controls (not enough balance in earnings growth, individual initiative, and the CFO's focus on 'goal kicking' versus 'goal keeping')[31]

The conformance–performance accounting connection requires a greater collaboration between the financial and management accounting functions and other organisational stakeholders, such as risk management experts or engineers involved in sustainability activities at both operational and strategic decision-making levels of the organisation.

In organisational culture, the 'tone at the top' and ethics play important roles in sustainability management and are strategically relevant to overall organisational performance. Responsible and ethical behaviour is essential for not only senior management but every employee within an entity. The unethical behaviour of a few accountants and managers can greatly affect investor beliefs and the value of the share market. When investors lose faith in information produced by organisations, they are less likely to invest in those organisations and market downturns occur. These events happen because accountants and managers fail to use ethical decision making.

The steps in ethical decision making are presented in figure 21.7.

FIGURE 21.7 Steps in ethical decision making

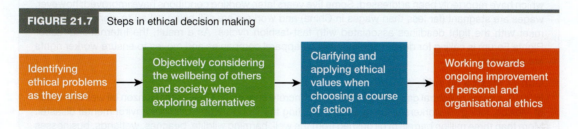

When following these steps in developing management control systems — particularly performance evaluation systems — the constructs relating to ethics and ethical decision making are often difficult for managers to classify, quantify, measure and monitor. One of the main reasons is the social and cultural diversity of individual entities.[32] Ethical issues also form an important part of strategic risk management. All managers must continually assess the level of strategic risk and monitor both internal and external environments for information that could destabilise their planned sustainability strategy. Risk can emerge in the form of breakdowns in internal processes (that is, operational risk), in the devaluing of a company's assets due to financial, intellectual or physical damage (asset impairment risk) or in a loss of competitive capabilities because of supplier, competitor or regulatory effects (competitive risk). These three different forms of strategic risk can lead to a reduced reputation for the company (reputation risk).[33]

Comprehensive example 3 illustrates the social issues faced by large companies such as VW, BHP Billiton, Rana Plaza, BP and Santos. Both direct and indirect stakeholders of these organisations are affected by management actions. What do you think some of the stakeholder social issues and claims might be? What are the identifiable risks? How might an entity protect itself from these risks? The comprehensive example also highlights the risks and liabilities that can arise for larger companies that have co-ownership, even minority interests. Just because investments are not directly under parent company control does not mean that sustainability responsibilities and liabilities are waived. The scope and benefits relating to sustainability management accounting are discussed in greater detail in the next section.

Ethics and social responsibility

VW emissions scandal

About 11 million Volkswagen (VW) and VW-manufactured cars with diesel engines have been fitted with a 'defeat device' that detects when the car's emissions performance is being tested and 'cheats' by changing the performance to improve results. The result was that engines could emit up to 40 times more nitrogen oxide pollutants than what is permitted in the US and yet still pass the tests. VW has subsequently recalled millions of cars worldwide, setting aside €4.8 billion for the cost of the recall, resulting in the company posting a quarterly loss of €2.5 billion in October 2015.[34]

BHP Billiton and Samarco mine dam disaster, Brazil

In November 2015, a dam owned by BHP Billiton and Vale SA's Samarco mine in Brazil collapsed. Sixty million cubic metres of mud flattened villages and contaminated 400 kilometres of riverways. Several workers and nearby residents were killed and hundreds more lost their homes to the mud flows. BHP's share price fell to ten-year lows as investors considered the consequences of the Brazil disaster. The companies may face fines and lawsuits. Costs have been estimated to be at least $850 million in insurance claims on top of $1.4 billion in clean-up.[35]

Bangladesh Rana Plaza building collapse

In 2013, a building in which five garment factories supplying global brands were housed collapsed, killing 1135 people. Thousands more were injured. The day before the building collapsed, garment workers noted cracks in the walls but were told to return to work the next morning.

A total of 38 people were formally charged with murder and three were charged with helping the building owner, Sohel Rana, flee across the border to India. Rana was arrested after a four-day manhunt and is the principal accused in this tragic event. The incident prompted sweeping changes in the industry. Initially, this resulted in many garment factories being closed with a loss of exports and jobs while hazards and poor factory conditions were rectified and eliminated. An independent group of inspectors was appointed as part of the Accord on Fire and Building Safety in Bangladesh, which was established and agreed by more than 200 apparel companies from 20 countries. The inspectors found thousands of hazards, which have reportedly been addressed. Some five years later, working conditions have improved; however, wages are stagnant (far less than wages in China) and workers are still being asked to work overtime to meet with the tight deadlines associated with fast-fashion cycles. As a result, the International Labor Rights Forum is calling for deeper commitment by apparel companies and moves to ensure worker rights are protected.

Gulf of Mexico oil spill

In 2010, a surge of natural gas blasted through a concrete core of the Deepwater Horizon oil well in the Gulf of Mexico, killing 11 workers, injuring 17 and creating the world's worst offshore environmental disaster. More than three million barrels of oil gushed from the well, harming wildlife, beaches, wetlands, businesses and livelihoods. Contractor Halliburton had recently installed the concrete core in the rig, owned by Transocean and leased to BP. In extensive legal debates, liability was assigned to BP (67 per cent), Transocean (30 per cent) and Halliburton (3 per cent). In 2012, BP agreed to pay US$4.5 billion and US$7.8 billion to settle the criminal and class action cases, respectively. Separate criminal charges were made against three BP employees. In 2015, BP agreed to pay US$18.7 billion to settle civil claims.[36]

Santos pays for clean-up operation

The town of Sigaorjo in East Java, Indonesia, was swamped by a wall of mud erupting from a natural gas well. Some 15 000 villagers were displaced. The catastrophe also forced the permanent relocation of the cross-Java toll road, a rail link, a gas pipeline and other infrastructure. The clean-up and rebuilding costs were estimated at up to $1 billion. Blame for the mudflow was initially attributed to incorrect drilling practices at an exploration well owned by Lapindo Brantas, in which Santos has an 18 per cent ownership stake. Given the enormity of the disaster, though, geologists have argued that it was more likely to be an 'act of God' — the result of a mud volcano. The mud continues to flow out of the ground at 200 000 cubic metres a day, and experts say that the flow may continue for a further 30 years. The lengthy legal process left Santos unable to inform the market of its total exposure to liability. The fine was eventually agreed at $32 million (based on 18 per cent ownership). In the meantime, more than $1 billion was wiped off Santos's market capitalisation.[37]

These incidents highlight the importance of management accounting controls to help measure and monitor sustainability risk for the longer term and restore stakeholders' belief in the corporate commitment to health, safety, environmental responsibility and sustainable development.

21.3 Scope and benefits of sustainability management accounting

LEARNING OBJECTIVE 21.3 Outline the scope and benefits resulting from sustainability management accounting practices.

Traditional and contemporary management accounting techniques can be used in sustainability management control practices to:
- plan and direct management attention to sustainability issues
- inform sustainability management decisions
- control and motivate behaviour towards sustainable outcomes.

Sustainability management accounting is a two-way process of reporting information for decision making.

1. It can generate information about how the use of resources with sustainability-related impacts can affect the financial performance of the entity.
2. It can be used to consider how organisational operations might affect environmental and social performance.

For organisations to develop a sustainability culture with knowledge of sustainability management accounting applications, the scope of sustainability management accounting practice should be communicated to all employees. Once the sustainability boundaries are defined, specific management accounting tools can be developed to optimise management decisions.

Sustainability scope considerations

The *scope* of sustainability management accounting undertaken by organisations relates to the process of integrated thinking and identifying and measuring costs and revenues associated with sustainability management. This is done by identifying the easiest internal costs and revenues through to the more difficult costs and revenues. The greatest difficulty is often associated with societal costs and revenues, or those that are external to the entity — the 'externalities', previously considered beyond the scope of sustainability accounting because they do not directly affect the statement of financial position (also called the balance sheet). However, for strategic management purposes, externalities should not be ignored.

Efforts by governments and lobby groups are increasingly aimed at creating new legislative and reporting requirements to make organisations more liable for their externalities. This requires that the previously-ignored costs (and revenues) be included in the financial statements and performance reports of the entity that created the externality. Thus, an astute business manager would insist that all information relating to the identification and measurement of externalities — whether they are currently in existence or potentially created through incorrect or non-sustainable management decisions — be included in the reports.

Accounting can help to internalise previously ignored externalities by identifying, measuring and managing risks, for example:
- providing apparel retailers with the control systems that will monitor work place conditions of their outsourced manufacturing sites in under-developed countries
- allocating capital and resources to the reduction of greenhouse gas emissions.

If carbon credits are vehicles of income or liabilities for entities, then carbon accounting has the potential to dramatically alter decision-making processes relating to the allocation of entity resources. Because carbon accounting involves measuring production efficiencies in relation to greenhouse gas emissions, the management accountant will be required to track and report monthly/annual emission targets as if they were potential revenue or liabilities for the organisation. The process of carbon accounting will therefore affect processes along the entire value chain including:
- the choice of raw materials and suppliers
- design or re-engineering requirements
- type of energy used in production processes
- methods of waste management adopted
- in-house or outsourced production
- packaging and transportation options
- the image and culture represented to suppliers, staff, and potential and existing customers.

Figure 21.8 outlines the scope for sustainability management accounting practices in organisations. The scope (in ascending order of difficulty) begins with the easier-to-measure factors at level 1 through to the more difficult societal impacts at level 5. The sum of levels 1 to 4 is generally referred to as 'private costs'. That is, the costs that directly affect entities' reported profits. Note that while level 5 externalities might previously have been ignored by organisations, sustainability management is optimised when all current (or potential future) externalities are identified and internalised and (where possible) included in sustainability management accounting control systems. This is discussed further in comprehensive example 4.

FIGURE 21.8	Scope for sustainability management accounting practices[38]

	Scope	Description
Private costs	**Level 1**	**Conventional costs** Includes the costs of direct raw materials, utilities, labour, supplies, structures, capital equipment and related depreciation
	Level 2	**Hidden costs** Includes upfront environmental costs such as search costs relating to finding environmentally conscious suppliers, initial design costs of environmentally preferable products, regulatory costs that are often obscured in overhead costs, and future decommissioning or remediation costs
	Level 3	**Contingent costs** Defined in probabilistic terms and includes fines for breaching environmental requirements, clean-up costs, lawsuits relating to unsound products or service provision
	Level 4	**Image and relationship costs** Are difficult to determine and would seldom be separately identified within an accounting system. However, they could be expected to have some influence on the value of some intangible assets such as goodwill, brand names and so forth.
Societal costs	**Level 5**	**Societal costs** Are often referred to as externalities, and represent costs that an entity imposes upon others as a result of its operations but which the entity typically ignores. These costs include environmental damage caused by the organisation for which it is not held accountable, or adverse health effects caused by organisation-generated emissions for which the organisation is not held responsible. It is difficult and sometimes controversial to put a cost on these effects and, with the exception of a few organisations worldwide, most entities ignore such costs when calculating profits. However, physical measures can be developed and related key performance indicators (KPIs) can be used to assess performance.

Management decisions benefiting from sustainability management accounting

Several types of management decisions benefit from sustainability management accounting information. They are listed in figure 21.9.

FIGURE 21.9	Types of management decisions benefiting from sustainability management accounting information[39]

Product design	Risk management	Cost allocation
Process design	Sustainability compliance strategies	Product retention and mix
Facility siting	Capital investments	Product pricing
Purchasing	Cost control	Performance evaluations
Operational	Waste management	

Specific management accounting tools may assist with decision making as a result of identifying and measuring revenues and the direct and indirect costs associated with sustainability management practices. Cost accounting techniques may be used to measure sustainability cost flows. The extent to which the level 1 to 5 costs are included in decision making reveals the extent of full cost accounting adopted in decision-making practices. Capital budgeting projects relating to long-term sustainability management might be used as a vehicle to communicate sustainability strategies throughout the entity, as well as to promote wider-level discussions on the opportunity costs related to sustainability projects. Product costing and pricing techniques that encourage sustainability-related overhead costs to be directly allocated to department and products could enhance management decisions.

Strategic sustainability practices for the improved use of resources might include industry- or entity-wide strategic tools (such as value chain analysis) to identify the value-adding opportunities throughout the entire value chain. The flow of raw materials along the value chain can be evaluated for compliance with the entity's sustainability standards. Likewise, the sustainability costs related to waste from general production processes (solids, effluent, emissions) or material losses (scrap, rejects, dumping of dead and excess stock) should be accounted for in materials flow analysis.

Sustainability management accounting will also inform make or buy decisions. Life cycle assessment is useful in encompassing all organisational functions relating to sustainability opportunities over an extended period of time. Of growing importance is the need to determine the opportunity costs and risk assessment of forgoing sustainability opportunities and investment. For example, the choice of energy resources and the potential impact on carbon emissions is a growing concern for global entities, and needs to be considered in calculations for internal decision-making purposes.

The balanced scorecard (discussed in chapter 19) is considered a useful tool for sustainability performance evaluation as well as a strategy communication tool — particularly once it is adapted to become a sustainability balanced scorecard. As mentioned earlier, a growing number of Australian companies are using management accounting tools such as the balanced scorecard as a combination tool for corporate sustainability disclosure and internal management control.

COMPREHENSIVE EXAMPLE 4

Government infrastructure investment — New Zealand

As part of community town planning, an industrial estate was proposed for development on the outskirts of a growing township. The estate required water and sewerage facilities. At this stage the land was vacant but included some vegetation — a few big old native trees (cabbage trees, five finger or puahou, totara, southern beech as well as some old kauri pines), an old cave with indigenous cave painting and other artefacts, an old building near the cave and local waterhole for wild animals. As part of the estate development the council water board considered the following factors:

1. financial net present value (NPV)
2. environmental impacts
   - land clearing
   - discharges to the environment (liquid waste into sewerage drains, CO_2 emissions to air, and noise pollution)
   - water requirements
3. social impacts
   - indigenous heritage
   - European heritage
   - community acceptance.

The following table presents two development proposals that were submitted to the council's water board from the operational teams. The first row presents a financial figure relating to operational cash flows (discounted over 30 years to today's value). This figure represents the outlay cost and costs to operate the water and sewerage on an annual basis (electricity for pumping, maintenance etc.). The second two rows represent the environmental and social impacts in the form of qualitative data. There were heated debates among the managers when deciding what project should be accepted as there were ramifications associated with each project.

▶

Project 1		Project 2	
Financial NPV	–$8 000 000	Financial NPV	–$4 000 000

Environmental impacts:
Land clearing: 4 hectares (biodiversity impacted, loss of animal and plant species)
Discharges: additional facility cost to provide grey water to water sports oval
Water requirements: pumping station (noise buffer included in NPV costs), additional electricity for pumping

Environmental impacts:
Land clearing: 7 hectares (biodiversity impacted, loss of animal and plant species)
Discharges: treated water discharged directly to stream
Water requirements: gravity-fed water, as using land where indigenous cave artefacts are (no noise buffer required)

Social impacts:
Indigenous heritage: cave site avoided in proposal
European heritage: N/A

Community acceptance: consultations suggest this option is acceptable

Social impacts:
Indigenous heritage: cave site used in proposal
European heritage: old building near cave site will be demolished

Community acceptance: several complaints have been received

While the financial NPV would indicate project 2 should be accepted (even though it has a negative NPV, it is $4 000 000 cheaper), the qualitative data suggest project 1 is the right one to choose. The answer depends on the scope that the evaluator wants to take. The data presented represent all five levels (as highlighted in figure 21.8). Notably, there are issues associated with the NPV calculation, as it does not include any financial data relating to environmental and social costs. Some of the board members wanted dollar values on the other aspects to help justify their decision (for example, a price for community willingness to pay for project 1 versus project 2). They called for a full cost accounting approach to recognise all costs and benefits of the analysis. Others did not mind that the data were in a qualitative format as they recognised some of the potential expenses that they might/might not incur if one option was taken over the other. The operational management team then tried to quantify a large amount of the costs and benefits so they could compare these with the NPV and the traditionally accepted cash flows. However, at the next meeting, there was a strong debate over the assumptions that were made to come up with the figures. They all agreed that they were quite subjective. Nevertheless, and in spite of all the debating and attempts at full cost accounting, the council finally decided to follow the more expensive project due to the sustainability-related impacts and negative community backlash which would tarnish their image.

It should be recognised from comprehensive example 4 that it is not always easy to accurately work out the level 4 and level 5 costs. In this case the decision was made without a full cost accounting approach and qualitative data actually reinforced the decision (also see chapter 15). Frequently companies are faced with decisions such as these, which need a thorough investigation of the potentially costly ramifications if they ignore level 4 and level 5 costs.

21.4 Sustainability management accounting tools

LEARNING OBJECTIVE 21.4 Demonstrate an understanding of key sustainability management accounting tools.

We will now look at some of the more widely used tools in sustainability management practices. The scope and strategies relating to sustainability are typically reflected in operational routines and practices, and are managed and communicated within the management accounting control framework. For improved decision making, sustainability-related income and sustainability-related costs in particular are traced to sustainability-related pools. The drivers of sustainability income and costs can be managed using a holistic value chain approach and life cycle analysis. The process of capital budgeting for sustainability can be better managed when sustainability costs, income and associated drivers are readily identifiable by managers with detailed sustainability knowledge.

Sustainability value chain analysis

In chapter 1 we introduced the usefulness of value chain analysis to analyse a company's strategic position. In a similar way the value chain is also useful in sustainability accounting to understand both positive and negative impacts of corporate sustainability activities on society (see figure 21.10).

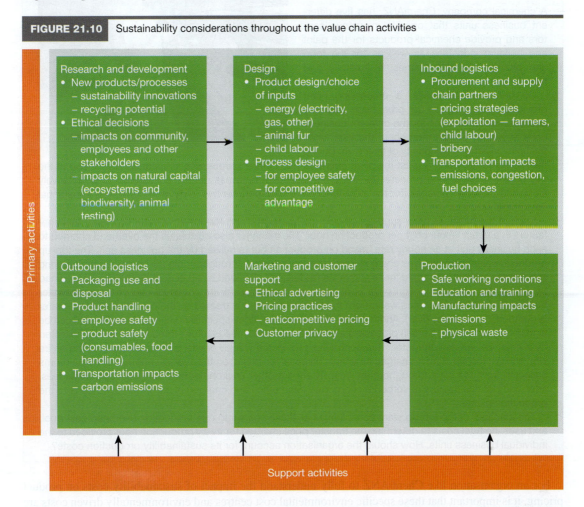

FIGURE 21.10 Sustainability considerations throughout the value chain activities

This value chain analysis approach to sustainability management also promotes an all-encompassing, organisation-wide approach to sustainability accounting as illustrated previously in the sustainability enterprise governance framework (see figure 21.6).

Sustainability cost allocation and full cost accounting

In many organisations, sustainability costs tend not to be treated as separate costs within the accounting system. They are generally treated as overheads, without their own related cost driver(s), and allocated equally to the cost objects. In some circumstances, sustainability costs might also be accounted for as period costs. As highlighted thus far, the identification and classification of sustainability boundaries, costs and cost objects requires organisation-wide involvement. The tracking and tracing of sustainability costs, and the determination of cost pools and related cost drivers, is crucial for sustainability management accounting purposes. Before sustainability costs can be allocated to the cost object, consensus among the key managers is vital. For example, the cost object might be individual business units, production departments, cost centres, production lines, specific equipment, or the individual job, product or service. Input from department managers is important, particularly where the performance of that unit or manager is based on sustainability cost consumption. Most importantly, the extent of full cost accounting or *fuller* cost accounting undertaken depends on the scope (level 1 to level 5; see figure 21.8) included in the analysis. In comprehensive example 5, a common situation is presented where even the level 1 and 2 sustainability costs can be lost in incorrect or general overhead cost pools.

Sustainability costs and product prices

A chemical company, ChemiANZ, has five different business units that operate in various sectors and provide chemical products for the paint and building industries as well as for the food and pharmaceutical industries in Australia and New Zealand.

On one production site, a processing plant provides additional top-up production capacity and associated services for the different business units at various stages throughout the year when the units have no idle capacity of their own. During the months of July and August the plant operated two different processes simultaneously for two of the five business units. One process (for the pharmaceutical business unit) is considered to be relatively clean and the other process (for the industrial chemical department) is 'dirty' and consumes substantial environmental costs.

Each of the business units supplies its own raw materials, and the top-up production plant manager factors in a direct labour cost per production hour. The manager also calculates the overhead charged to each business unit at an hourly rate based on production hours utilised by the business unit. The top-up production plant also receives charges from other cost centres throughout the 25-hectare manufacturing site. For example, it is charged for its annual use of facilities provided by other cost centres that are owned by ChemiANZ. The production plant is charged an annual fee for its continual use of the wastewater treatment plant (contaminated water from the production plant is treated by the plant before clean water is pumped into a nearby river). Another cost department provides specialised energy supplies that can be high in CO_2 emissions. Certain processes emit solid waste that needs to be stored in drums and collected by a chemical waste contractor. This contractor provides a weekly waste pick-up service for the entire site, and the top-up plant is charged an annual disposal fee based on the average number of waste drums collected from the plant throughout the year. There are other environmental costs relating to legal fees, fines and permits that are absorbed by corporate head office and charged in corporate overheads to the production plant.

The manager of the top-up plant consolidates all these costs into one production overhead cost pool, and uses the total costs to determine the transfer price charged for every production hour provided to the individual business units. How should the organisation account for its sustainability production costs?

For an organisation like ChemiANZ to fully understand the impact of sustainability costs on product pricing, it is important that these specific environmental cost centres and environmentally driven costs are differentiated from the other traditional overhead basket of costs. The final determination of product cost will depend on how the environmental costs are allocated. In figure 21.11, the problem of environmental costs being allocated equally among processes and products is highlighted. Accounting for sustainability, in figure 21.11 and comprehensive example 5, might require the isolation and tracking of sustainability costs to the cost object (that is, the 'dirty' production process). This will enable the cross-subsidised 'dirty' products to be sold at a higher price that reflects the environmental harm caused by their production. Alternatively, it allows the more environmentally friendly product the opportunity to maintain market share at a less expensive price. In this situation, it could be difficult to make comparisons between two entirely different products in different sectors. Nevertheless, by isolating the environmental costs, managers are provided with greater insights into alternative or improved sustainability production processes.

FIGURE 21.11	Sustainability costs and overhead cost allocation[40]	'Clean' process A	'Dirty' process B
Revenues		$200	$200
Production costs		100	100
Environmental costs		0	50
Recalculated profit		100	50
If environmental costs are overhead		25	25
Then the book profit is		$ 75	$ 75
Which is incorrect by		−25%	+33%

Activity-based costing (ABC) enhances the understanding of business processes associated with each product by allocating sustainability costs on the basis of the activities that caused the cost. As discussed in chapter 12, activity-based costing aims to direct the indirect costs more accurately to the cost object. Activity-based costing will reveal where sustainability value is added and where it is lost. Thus, in sustainability management accounting, activity analysis can help to improve the economic consequences of sustainability management by preventing the distortion of product or service provision as well as providing more accurate information for investment decisions.

In the ChemiANZ example, certain sustainability allocation bases might provide greater insight for costing in the top-up processing plant. For example, what if the water treatment plant installed a meter on every input line and charged on volume of emissions or waste treated per line. Likewise, it might be more appropriate to monitor toxicity levels rather than volume. Certain processes might emit large volumes of relatively clean water compared to others with far greater toxicity levels but lower volume output. As all water must enter the river at safe levels, dirtier production output waste will absorb higher treatment costs and potentially greater business risks relating to spills and litigation. Alternatively, the relative costs of treating different kinds of waste emissions might also be a more suitable allocation base for the water treatment plant. Every situation requires individual assessment for the correct choice of allocation base. While attention is given to environmental factors, this approach is also useful for evaluating social costs, including occupational health and safety, training and overheads that contribute to enhancing corporate image and reputation.

Sustainability life cycle costing

Life cycle analysis is a technique that evaluates all the activities involved in the design, development, production, sale, transportation and disposal of a product or service (see figure 21.12). The life cycle of a product or a service is often referred to as 'cradle-to-grave'.

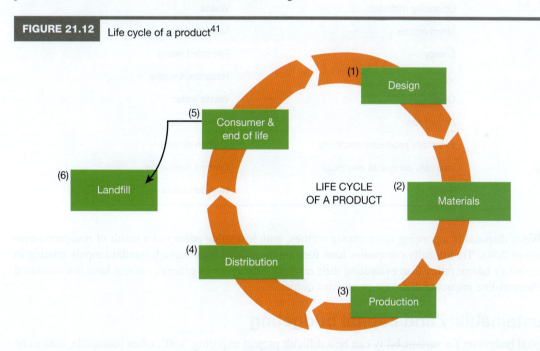

FIGURE 21.12 Life cycle of a product[41]

Life cycle costing involves summing the costs of these activities throughout the internal and industry value chains — whether they are part of an entity's activities or not. Life cycle analysis is integral to sustainability management, and is about making more informed decisions in relation to the inputs and outputs generated through organisational activities.

Activity analysis can provide information relating to the life cycle costs of value chain activities pertaining to:
- the products manufactured (decisions may be made to drop or outsource)
- the preferred sustainability suppliers
- re-engineering the design of product or service

- re-engineering operating processes to accommodate changes in
  - energy sources
  - waste disposal
  - packaging and recycling.

When taking a life cycle approach, both private and societal sustainability activities and costs can be included.

A sustainable operation is based on the principle that 'what goes in must come out'. In most cases, *non-productive output* occurs as a result of operations. The non-productive output (different forms of waste) must be stored or disposed of — resulting in additional sustainability costs for the entity. Figure 21.13 provides an example of a general input–output chart of accounts that could form the basis for sustainability reporting and decision making. The items are measured in physical units of mass or energy. If the general input–output chart of accounts is used by senior managers for sustainability decision-making purposes, they can provide valuable insights for managing life cycles and evaluating the impact of resource efficiencies (or inefficiencies) on the bottom line. These insights might not be revealed with traditional cost management tools.

FIGURE 21.13	General input–output chart of accounts[42]

Input in kg/kWh	Output in kg
Raw materials	Product
Auxiliary materials	Main product
Packaging	By-products
Operating materials	Waste
Merchandise	Municipal waste
Energy	Recycled waste
Gas	Hazardous waste
Coal	Waste water
Other fuels	Heavy metals
Externally produced electricity	Carbon dioxide
Internally produced electricity	Carbon monoxide
Water	Nitrogen oxide

Waste disposal is a growing issue among entities, with lost value arising as a result of non-productive resource flows. Traditionally companies have focused on cost savings through standard inputs relating to materials or labour rather than evaluating their resource efficiency. In general, entities have not measured the bottom-line impact of their non-productive output.

Sustainability and capital budgeting

Capital budgeting for sustainability can be a difficult project requiring 'soft', often intangible, data to be evaluated in conjunction with quantitative data that is based on the best possible estimates of future costs and liabilities. Recall that capital budgeting involves economic variables relating to:
- initial investment costs
- discounted operating costs and earnings
- profit generated
- net present value, return on investment and payback.

In general terms, if the investment is more profitable than gaining interest on a bank deposit, then the project is considered to be worthwhile.

All capital budgeting projects relating to sustainability should consider the conventional costs associated with the project *but* also the contingent and image-related costs that represent the true profitability and riskiness of the project. Sustainability capital budgeting should reflect the varying scope, levels and categories highlighted in figure 21.8. The sustainability categories decision makers should consider include:

- conventional costs (raw materials, utilities, labour)
- administration costs (monitoring, reporting and training)
- contingency costs (potential clean-up, accidents, compensations, fine)
- image benefits and costs (often referred to as 'intangible' costs, or goodwill)
- external costs (potentially internalised at a later stage through regulations, taxes, fees, fines or other non-budgeted expenses).

Figure 21.14 provides an outline of a sustainability capital budgeting calculation sheet recommended by the United Nations Division for Sustainable Development. The UN suggests that this calculation sheet be used to highlight the sustainable costs and benefits of a single project. It can also be used as a basis for direct comparisons between alternative projects. When inputting data into the format provided in figure 21.14, it is important to recognise that, as with most capital budgeting projects, the inputs and outputs for the initial years should be reasonably quantifiable, measured and reflecting true position. However, the later years of the capital budgeting calculations often require 'guesstimates', which should be sufficient.

The main aim of this calculation process is to highlight costs and not ignore potential savings from sustainability projects. Furthermore, sustainability capital budgeting contributes to ensuring that the so-called soft or intangible factors at least are recognised and become some sort of rough estimates. The benefits of sustainability are highlighted in the following savings potential:

- benefits from reducing waste emissions and disposal costs — carbon emission credits, internal and external disposal costs, related equipment, transport, insurance and liability, production permits and sustainability reporting costs
- reduction in worker health costs, reduced risks of accidents and worker absenteeism because of dangerous materials and reduced motivation, external stakeholder liabilities and contingencies
- savings in energy, water, materials, packaging and scrap
- potential earnings from emerging/new by-products
- improved relations with authorities, which may shorten waiting times for permits and regulated procedures
- savings in remediation costs, which can be extremely high in non-renewable energy production facilities.[43]

Recognising and quantifying sustainability costs and benefits is invaluable for organisations in two ways. First, it is essential for calculating the profitability of existing sustainability investments. Second, it is essential for understanding the potentially hidden or contingent costs relating to long-term operations and future projections. In addition to savings, positive outcomes relating to improved employee morale; shareholder, community and customer satisfaction; and image and relationship enhancement can also flow to the entity.

Capital budgeting for sustainability should be done with maximum knowledge, specialist input and appropriate timelines to ensure that all possible quantitative and qualitative factors are included in the model. Tangible cash flows relating to the impact of changes in input prices and other matters, such as those relating to the regulatory environment (that is, future fees, fines and penalties) must be taken into account. It is also essential that the less tangible aspects are included in the management accounting information.

Different sustainability scenarios should be raised, costed and made available to decision makers. For optimum sustainable decisions, various capital investment scenarios must be evaluated. For example, the alternative scenarios presented for a company that uses significant electricity such as Alcoa could range from capital investment to improve traditional coal-powered operations through to adopting other sustainable and renewable power sources based on solar, wind or water-generated power.

FIGURE 21.14 Sustainability capital budgeting sheet[44]

Calculation sheet Environmental/social cost/expenditure categories	Initial investment	Year 1	Year 2	Year 3	Year 4	Future liability	Soft factors
1. Waste and emission treatment							
1.1 Depreciation for related equipment							
1.2 Maintenance, operating materials, services							
1.3 Personnel							
1.4 Fees, taxes, charges							
1.5 Fines and penalties							
1.6 Insurance and environmental liabilities							
1.7 Provisions for clean-up costs, remediation							
2. Prevention and environmental management							
2.1 External services for environmental management							
2.2 Personnel for general environmental management activities							
2.3 Research and development							
2.4 Extra expenditure for integrated technologies							
2.5 Other environmental management costs							
3. Material purchase value of non-product output							
3.1 Raw materials							
3.2 Packaging							
3.3 Auxiliary materials							
3.4 Operating materials							
3.5 Energy							
3.6 Water							
4. Processing costs of non-product output							
Σ Environmental expenditure							
5. Environmental revenues							
5.1 Subsidiaries, awards							
5.2 Other earnings							
Σ Environmental revenues							
6. Soft factors							
6.1 Increased turnover, customer satisfaction, new markets, differentiation from competitors, improved customer relationships							
6.2 Improved corporate image							
6.3 Improved contacts with authorities and agencies, reduced legal compliance costs							
6.4 Reduced risks for accidents, liabilities and contaminated land							
6.5 Increased creditworthiness, better ratings by investment companies							
6.6 Better community relations							
6.7 Increased employee motivation and morale, less worker illness and absenteeism							
Σ Total benefit							

Sustainability balanced scorecard

The balanced scorecard is a performance measurement system that links key performance measures with business strategy in four main ways: financial, customer, internal processes, and innovation and learning (refer to chapter 19). The key to balanced scorecard success is the focus on the cause-and-effect relationships between the performance measures that ultimately lead to successful operations as measured by shareholder wealth (the score) in the financial perspective. The balanced scorecard was originally intended to be the *shareholder* scorecard.[45] Kaplan and Norton did not consider it to be a *stakeholder* scorecard despite introducing key measures relating to staff and customers. Over time, the balanced scorecard has been adapted for use in the not-for-profit and public sectors where financial outcomes are not necessarily the goals. It has also begun to be popular with organisations as a tool for monitoring sustainability.

A sustainability balanced scorecard can be developed in three ways.[46]

1. The environmental and social aspects can be integrated within the four standard perspectives.
2. An additional 'sustainability' perspective can be added.
3. A separate sustainability balanced scorecard can be developed.

If the sustainability measures are captured within the existing scorecard, this ensures that cause and effect relationships are developed between the measures and perspectives so that sustainability becomes entwined within the entity's overall vision and strategic objectives. Sustainability actions can thereby be captured in organisational 'innovation and learning' perspectives and become integral to the value chain activities ('internal processes') undertaken by the organisation. Successful sustainability practices will be rewarded by the 'customer' who purchases the entity's products or services. Sustainability success should then be reflected in the 'financial' perspective. This should demonstrate that the social, environmental and financial dimensions are managed in unison. One concern with this first style of integrated scorecard is that for 'successful' sustainability operations, entities might focus solely on their private measures (financial success) to the exclusion of societal measures. Depending on how the measures are integrated into the balanced scorecard, there is a risk that the organisation might ignore the externalities to focus on the bottom line.

The second development relates to an additional sustainability perspective being added. This reinforces the fact that sustainability is central to the organisation's mission and strategies. An additional quadrant also provides scope for approximately four to six more key sustainability measures to be included in the balanced scorecard (a traditional scorecard has about 22 to 24 measures in total). The importance placed on achieving these measures will depend on the weighting given to these measures in comparison to the others. A problem that has been previously identified with balanced scorecard use is that too much emphasis tends to be placed on the financial quadrant in comparison to others.[47] This is a risk with the sustainability measures, particularly when including an additional quadrant and related measures. In this situation, the weighting of measures has the potential to be diluted in comparison to the financial measures and so receive less attention by managers and subordinates who are being evaluated.

A separately 'derived' sustainability balanced scorecard is considered to be the most useful of the three approaches.[48] First, it enables sustainability teams or departments to more closely monitor the social, environmental and financial dimensions. Second, it does not consist of individual sustainability measures that are 'tacked onto' existing operational measures. All measures on this scorecard have been derived from operations where sustainability is the fundamental building block. For optimal outcomes, the individually derived sustainability balanced scorecard should not be viewed independently from other performance measurement systems but considered as an *extension* of the other alternatives.[49] In this way, the derived scorecard should be developed in conjunction with an existing balanced scorecard to ensure that the sustainability measures are given strategic relevance and position in the management accounting framework. Thus, the difference between the first two scorecard alternatives and the derived balanced scorecard is that the derived scorecard measures emerge from a core balanced scorecard in which sustainability becomes the fundamental driver.

The scope of sustainability accounting encourages the inclusion of items previously treated as externalities or societal costs. A further extension to the 'derived' sustainability balanced scorecard can be made by adding an additional 'societal' perspective.[50] This means that the purpose of the derived scorecard can both fulfil the private interests of the firm and shareholder, and also draw managers' attention to the strategically relevant societal interest to be captured in the additional perspective. Figure 21.15 presents an overview of the process of formulating a sustainability balanced scorecard. It considers the issues covered throughout this chapter — sustainability accounting, reporting principles, and the balanced scorecard as an integration framework.

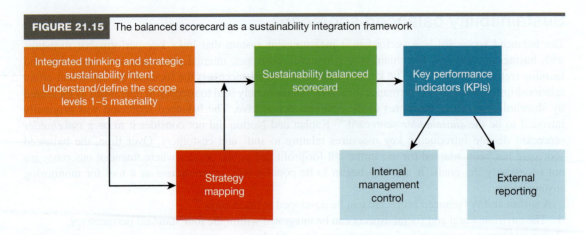

The measures should be tailored to the specific business unit and fit with the entity's corporate vision and strategies. The environmental measures might relate to emissions, waste, materials, energy or other factors that can directly affect the environment. The social aspects relate to any factor/exposure of a business unit, and the additional societal (or non-market) perspective measures might relate to freedom of action, legitimacy or legality.[51] Success in fully realising opportunities for cost savings or revenue generation through sustainability accounting requires that both technical and human factors work together.

21.5 Sustainability management accounting — issues relating to successful integration

LEARNING OBJECTIVE 21.5 Communicate the issues faced by managers when trying to implement sustainability change processes within their entities.

It has been found that integrating sustainability within the organisation and into everyday practices can be achieved by a broad systems thinking approach. Successful organisations achieve this through recognising the importance of:

1. adopting a clear, shared vision for the future
2. building teams, not just champions
3. using critical thinking and reflection
4. going beyond stakeholder engagement
5. adopting a systematic approach
6. moving beyond expecting a linear path to change.

These insights are a strategic tool for managers to use when proactively implementing sustainability management practices within their organisations.[52]

It is important to recognise accounting as both a technical and a social practice. Several key technical and behavioural/social issues must be considered.[53] The technical issues, as highlighted in figure 21.16, relate to strategic development being supported by appropriate management accounting systems. A broad view of sustainability costs and benefits is necessary to capture associated externalities. Costing systems should enable sustainability costs and benefits to be directly allocated to the associated operations of the entity rather than being accumulated within overhead accounts, treated as period costs or allocated to wrong revenue or costing categories.

If suitable management accounting tools are in place with appropriate feedback mechanisms, the behavioural issues relating to performance evaluation and rewards (discussed in chapter 20) should be minimised. To optimise organisational change towards sustainability, other factors such as top management support and the adoption of a team-based approach in preference to a single sustainability 'champion' to promote sustainability throughout the organisation should be considered. For example, by using a multidisciplinary team (or cross-departmental teams), sustainability management ownership is created across the entity and the potential for change to corporate culture is increased.

For management accountants, an opportunity to play a key role in the sustainability management change process — as a change agent (where high consideration is given to many non-financial factors) — may be provided. A note of caution: if 'accounting' is viewed as a purely technical or financial function by other organisational members, then a change in the way accounting is viewed within the entity might be required. It is essential that there is adequate communication between all business units and support departments.

FIGURE 21.16 Sustainability management accounting: technical and behavioural issues

Technical issues	Behavioural/social issues
• Defining sustainability costs • Suitable objectives in line with sustainability strategies • Identification of suitable social and environmental measures for performance evaluation • Setting challenging but achievable targets • Positioning of sustainability performance within the organisational performance measurement system • Able to demonstrate sustainability links to operations via strategy map • Issues associated with regularity of reporting, timeliness of feedback and format of reports • Use of a pilot test • Use of external consultant or not	• Senior management support • Multiple advocates • Creating ownership of the project of participants • Not conducting other initiatives that could conflict with sustainability management protocols • Perceptions of management accounting within the company • Suitable communication and feedback mechanisms

Progress towards sustainability may also be thwarted if other initiatives conflict with sustainability management practices. For example, if an entity is undergoing a downsizing program, then issues relating to the social setting and employee morale must be managed if the remaining employees are to support the sustainability program. In such situations, it is essential for managers to recognise that sustainability management practices that are economically sound should continue to be practised in times of crisis and not only when operations are successful.[54]

Comprehensive example 6 discusses ten elements required to successfully embed sustainability within organisational practices.

COMPREHENSIVE EXAMPLE 6

Mondelēz Australia's strategy map

The Prince's Accounting for Sustainability (A4S) Project identified ten elements (see figure 21.17) required to successfully embed sustainability within organisational practices. These are essential to integrated thinking.

FIGURE 21.17 Integrated thinking: ten elements required to successfully embed sustainability[55]

1. Board and senior management commitment
2. Understanding and analysing the key sustainability drivers for the organisation
3. Integrating the key sustainability drivers into the organisation's strategy
4. Ensuring that sustainability is the responsibility of everyone in the organisation and not just of a specific department
5. Breaking down sustainability targets and objectives for the organisation as a whole into targets and objectives which are meaningful for individual subsidiaries, divisions and departments
6. Processes that enable sustainability issues to be taken into account clearly and consistently in day-to-day decision making
7. Extensive and effective sustainability training
8. Including sustainability targets and objectives in performance appraisal
9. Champions to promote sustainability and celebrate success
10. Monitoring and reporting sustainability performance in an integrated way

These factors were used to examine Mondelēz Australia, previously recognised for its Kraft Foods and Cadbury chocolate labels. The walls of Mondelēz Australia's head office are lined with posters of iconic brands, such as Vegemite, which first went on sale in 1923 in Australia, and Cadbury Dairy Milk Chocolate, which has had a presence in Australia since 1881. In drawing on the ten A4S factors, the strategy map (figure 21.18) enables the reader to follow the corporate sustainability intent and key goal to specific strategies that result in the development of key performance indicators and initiatives that, in turn, help to demonstrate strategy in practice.

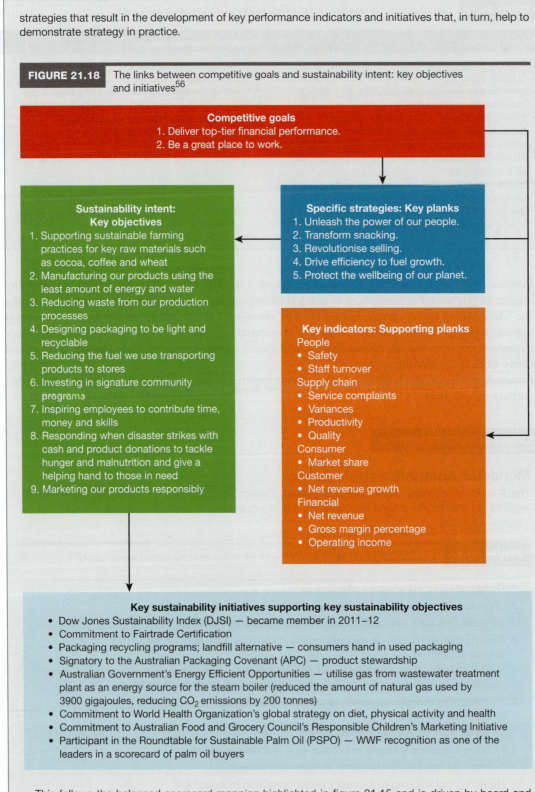

FIGURE 21.18 The links between competitive goals and sustainability intent: key objectives and initiatives[56]

Competitive goals
1. Deliver top-tier financial performance.
2. Be a great place to work.

Sustainability intent: Key objectives
1. Supporting sustainable farming practices for key raw materials such as cocoa, coffee and wheat
2. Manufacturing our products using the least amount of energy and water
3. Reducing waste from our production processes
4. Designing packaging to be light and recyclable
5. Reducing the fuel we use transporting products to stores
6. Investing in signature community programs
7. Inspiring employees to contribute time, money and skills
8. Responding when disaster strikes with cash and product donations to tackle hunger and malnutrition and give a helping hand to those in need
9. Marketing our products responsibly

Specific strategies: Key planks
1. Unleash the power of our people.
2. Transform snacking.
3. Revolutionise selling.
4. Drive efficiency to fuel growth.
5. Protect the wellbeing of our planet.

Key indicators: Supporting planks
People
• Safety
• Staff turnover
Supply chain
• Service complaints
• Variances
• Productivity
• Quality
Consumer
• Market share
Customer
• Net revenue growth
Financial
• Net revenue
• Gross margin percentage
• Operating income

Key sustainability initiatives supporting key sustainability objectives
• Dow Jones Sustainability Index (DJSI) — became member in 2011–12
• Commitment to Fairtrade Certification
• Packaging recycling programs; landfill alternative — consumers hand in used packaging
• Signatory to the Australian Packaging Covenant (APC) — product stewardship
• Australian Government's Energy Efficient Opportunities — utilise gas from wastewater treatment plant as an energy source for the steam boiler (reduced the amount of natural gas used by 3900 gigajoules, reducing CO_2 emissions by 200 tonnes)
• Commitment to World Health Organization's global strategy on diet, physical activity and health
• Commitment to Australian Food and Grocery Council's Responsible Children's Marketing Initiative
• Participant in the Roundtable for Sustainable Palm Oil (PSPO) — WWF recognition as one of the leaders in a scorecard of palm oil buyers

This follows the balanced scorecard mapping highlighted in figure 21.15 and is driven by board and senior management commitment.

SUMMARY

21.1 Discuss how the concepts of sustainability and sustainability management apply to corporate practice.

Sustainability

The development that meets the needs of the present without compromising the ability of future generations to meet their own needs.

Sustainability management

The process of measuring, monitoring and simultaneous control of the economic, environmental and social dimensions of an entity.

21.2 Recognise why it is essential for management accountants to take an integrated thinking approach to sustainability.

Accountants and senior managers need to recognise that the corporate business model is at the core of the organisation. The corporate business model:
- draws on various types of capital as inputs:
- financial
  - manufactured
  - intellectual
  - human
  - social and relationship
  - natural
- uses business activities to convert capital inputs to outputs:
  - products
  - services
  - by-products
- waste
- leading to outcomes in terms of effects on capital.

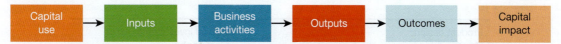

- Management accounting plays an important role in integrated thinking and value creation, reservation and diminution over time.
- There is a growing view that there must be a working connection between sustainability corporate governance and sustainability business governance for sustainability enterprise governance.
- The conformance–performance accounting connection requires a greater collaboration between the financial and management accounting functions and other organisational stakeholders.

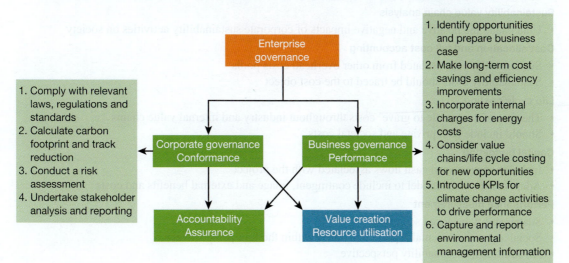

Ethics as part of the internal management decision-making process

Identifying ethical problems as they arise	→	Objectively considering the wellbeing of others and society when exploring alternatives	→	Clarifying and applying ethical values when choosing a course of action	→	Working towards ongoing improvement of personal and organisational ethics

Ethical issues and strategic risk management

Types of risk:
- Operational risk
- Asset impairment risk
- Competitive risk
- Reputation risk

21.3 Outline the scope and benefits resulting from sustainability management accounting practices.

Scope

The scope of sustainability management accounting relates to the process of integrated thinking and identifying and measuring costs and revenues associated with sustainability management.

• Conventional costs • Hidden costs • Contingent costs • Image and relationship costs	Private
• Societal costs	Societal

Benefits

Product design	Capital investments
Process design	Cost control
Facility siting	Waste management
Purchasing	Cost allocation
Operational	Product retention and mix
Risk management	Product pricing
Sustainability compliance strategies	Performance evaluations

21.4 Demonstrate an understanding of key sustainability management accounting tools.

Sustainability value chain analysis
- Understand the positive and negative impacts of corporate sustainability activities on society

Cost allocation and full cost accounting
- Sustainability costs isolated from other overhead costs pools
- Sustainability costs should be traced to the cost object

Life cycle costing
- The sum of the 'cradle to grave' costs throughout industry and internal value chains
- Should include both private and societal costs

Capital budgeting
- Includes conventional cash flows associated with the project
- Adapt conventional model to include contingent, image and external benefits and costs

Performance measurement
- Sustainability balanced scorecard
- Social and environmental aspects integrated within the four perspectives
- An additional sustainability perspective
- A separate sustainability balanced scorecard

21.5 Communicate the issues faced by managers when trying to implement sustainability change processes within their entities.

Technical issues	Behavioural issues
• Defining sustainability costs • Suitable objectives in line with sustainability strategies • Identification of suitable social and environmental measures for performance evaluation • Setting challenging but achievable targets • Positioning of sustainability performance within the organisational performance measurement system • Able to demonstrate sustainability links to operations via strategy map • Issues associated with regularity of reporting, timeliness of feedback and format of reports • Use of a pilot test • Use of external consultant or not	• Senior management support • Multiple advocates • Creating ownership of the project of participants • Not conducting other initiatives that could conflict with sustainability management protocols • Perceptions of management accounting within the company • Suitable communication and feedback mechanisms

KEY TERMS

carbon footprint A measure of the carbon dioxide equivalent emissions attributable to an activity, commonly used at an individual, household, organisation or product level.

carbon neutrality A situation where the net emissions associated with a product or an organisation's activities are equal to zero through the acquisition and retirement of carbon offsets that meet additionality criteria.

life cycle analysis A technique that evaluates all the activities involved in the design, development, production, sale, transportation and disposal of a product or service. The life cycle of a product or a service is often referred to as 'cradle to grave'.

life cycle costing A decision-making method that considers changes in price and costs over the entire life cycle of a good or service, from the time the product is introduced through a number of years.

private impacts Effects that are internal or have a direct impact on the organisational value chain.

societal impacts 'Externalities', or those costs and benefits that are not generally accounted for in an entity's conventional accounting system.

sustainability management The measuring, monitoring and integrated control of the materially important capital inputs (financial, manufactured, intellectual, human, social and relationship, and natural) to ensure sustainable corporate profits in the value creation process.

sustainability management accounting The tool used to attain the organisation's (or specific business unit's) sustainability goals. It is an important part of the business model that simultaneously integrates the organisation's use of financial, manufactured, intellectual, human and social and relationship and natural capital performance with strategic management.

SELF-STUDY PROBLEMS

SELF-STUDY PROBLEM 1 Corporate Reputation Index

The title of most reputable company in Australia is determined by consumer surveys based on the following seven drivers of reputation: products and services, innovation, workplace, citizenship, governance, leadership, and financial performance.[57]

The top ten companies in 2015 were:

1. Toyota Motor Corporation
2. Samsung
3. JB Hi-Fi
4. Nestlé Australia
5. Air New Zealand
6. Australia Post

7. Bendigo and Adelaide Bank
8. ALDI Australia
9. Qantas Airways
10. Mazda Australia

Interestingly, Toyota received this number one position despite announcing that it would end its manufacturing operations, and consolidate the business by the end of 2017.

Required

To demonstrate strategic sustainability intent, a diverse range of management accounting tools are required along the entire value chain. What steps would a company such as Toyota undertake to achieve these results?

SOLUTION TO SELF-STUDY PROBLEM 1

The steps Toyota would need to undertake are first to identify the sustainability opportunities at an organisational as well as societal level. This might lead to initial strategies relating to revenue, cost flow determination and capital budgeting relating to the potential sustainability opportunity. Second, realisation of the identified opportunities would be based on management decisions being made at different stages throughout both organisational and industry value chains. Third, Toyota's suite of sustainability management accounting tools should be able to measure and monitor the outcomes of its operations and their success in aligning the economic, environmental and social dimensions with its business strategy. Toyota's results demonstrate the leadership capacity to build a strong reputation and maintain trust among all stakeholders, including employees, even after delivering bad news.

SELF-STUDY PROBLEM 2 Sustainability balanced scorecard

ChemiANZ owns a petrochemical plant that refines and produces paints and resins for the building industry. The plant uses a large amount of water in its production processes. The water is treated in an onsite water treatment plant before clean water is emitted into the adjoining river system. The heavy metal waste is stored in drums and collected by contractors on a weekly basis. The petrochemical plant has had previous environmental issues with the Environmental Protection Agency (EPA) regarding toxic spills in the adjoining river and complaints about its excessive greenhouse gas emissions. ChemiANZ is a subsidiary company of ChemiWide Ltd, a large multinational group based in Denmark. Senior managers from ChemiWide Ltd were concerned about their sustainability rating with shareholders and called a meeting with the Australian managers to discuss opportunities for improving their image and stakeholder relationships.

Required

Outline some of the quantitative and qualitative factors about its sustainability performance that ChemiWide Ltd might discuss in its meeting. How could a sustainability balanced scorecard be used by ChemiANZ?

SOLUTION TO SELF-STUDY PROBLEM 2

ChemiWide Ltd could use a number of strategies to guide its discussion at the meeting. The GRI core environmental and social indicators provide a useful framework for evaluating sustainability performance by providing a range of indicators against which the entity could benchmark its performance.

ChemiANZ could develop a balanced scorecard based around key measures from the GRI. For example, measures that relate to activities within a chemical industry might include staff awareness and training, energy consumption (amount and type), waste (greenhouse gas emissions, other waste), number/type of workplace accidents, water consumption/treatment and environmental litigation costs.

QUESTIONS

21.1 What is the link between sustainability strategies and management accounting? **LO1**

21.2 Define the terms 'sustainability', 'sustainability management' and 'sustainability management accounting'. **LO1**

21.3 Is sustainability achievable in all entities regardless of their operating activities? **LO1**

21.4 Why should the economic, environmental and cultural dimensions be managed in unison? **LO1, 2**

21.5 Will organisational efforts towards sustainability result in reduced organisational profits? **LO1, 2**

21.6 Outline the relationship between the scope (levels) of costs and full cost accounting. **LO3**

21.7 What types of management decisions can benefit through using sustainability cost information? **LO3, 4**

21.8 Discuss the importance of ethical decision making in a sustainability management accounting framework. **LO2**

21.9 What are the potential benefits from developing an input–output chart of accounts? **LO4**

21.10 What key measures should be included in a sustainability balanced scorecard? **LO4**

21.11 What are some of the sustainability-related considerations that managers should acknowledge when evaluating their organisation's value chain? **LO4**

21.12 What are some of the factors that managers should consider when implementing sustainability practices in their organisations? **LO5**

21.13 Briefly comment on how legislation and societal expectations could influence the scope of sustainability management practice within organisations. **LO1, 5**

EXERCISES

21.14 Sustainability threats and opportunities **LO1, 2, 3, 4, 5**

The World Coal Institute claims that coal provides 26.5 per cent of global primary energy needs and generates 41.5 per cent of the world's electricity. Coal is one of the cheapest forms of fuel available on the planet. However, burning fuel produces CO_2, which contributes to excessive greenhouse gas emissions and global warming. Rather than change energy sources, Clean Coal Technologies (CCTs) have been promoted as a means of reducing emissions, reducing waste as well as increasing the efficiency (or amount of energy) gained from coal.[58]

Required

Referring to the information in this exercise and drawing on comprehensive example 2, discuss some of the sustainability management threats and opportunities for the future of Australian coal producers.

21.15 Carbon trading **LO1, 4**

(a) Explain how carbon trading might reduce greenhouse gas emissions.

(b) How might the existence of carbon trading schemes affect the management accounting system within organisations?

21.16 Balanced scorecard indicators **LO4**

Comment on how the inclusion of environmental and social indicators in a balanced scorecard might contribute to an organisation's profitability.

21.17 Contingent costs **LO4**

List some costs that could be considered to be 'contingent' sustainability-related costs for the mining industry.

21.18 Externalities and sustainability **LO1, 3**

Using Bank Australia as an example, list some of the positive externalities that might be achieved as a result of its operations. What are some of the negative externalities that could result from the banking operational activities?

21.19 Sustainability cost classification **LO3, 4**

Using the following table, classify each sustainability cost according to its appropriate category (levels 1–5).

Category level 1–5	Sustainability cost
Contingent costs	Clean-up costs from a chemical accident
Conventional costs	Community relations program
Image and relationship costs	Costs associated with prolonged licensing permits
Potentially hidden costs	Costs associated with stricter monitoring
Societal costs	Decommissioning of site
	Disposal of waste
	Environmental labelling
	Feasibility studies
	Future compliance costs
	Goodwill/impairment related costs
	Habitat and wetland protection

(continued)

(continued)

Category level 1–5	Sustainability cost
	Landscaping around site
	New capital equipment costs
	Personal injury
	Petroleum
	Raw materials
	Remediation costs
	Site studies
	Staff training
	Sustainability legal expenses
	Sustainability reports

21.20 Sustainability disclosures; management accounting tools   **LO1, 4**

Search the newspapers/internet to find examples of Australian companies disclosing their sustainability practices using management accounting information or tools such as the balanced scorecard. Provide a report on your findings.

21.21 Carbon footprint accounting   **LO1**

Consider the carbon footprint of an airline such as Qantas. Could an airline ever become carbon neutral or positive? Explain. What about a botanical garden? Discuss.

PROBLEMS

21.22 Sustainable management practices   **LO4, 5**

In an Environment Victoria audit, it was found that Australian supermarkets could save $41.6 million annually if 'green bags' were universally adopted.[59] This audit was conducted at Leo's Fine Foods in Kew, Victoria. It was conducted as a timed experiment; that is, clocking a checkout operator on the time taken to fill reusable green or single-use plastic shopping bags. The results are highlighted in the table below.

	Average time (seconds)		
No. of items	Single-use bags	Reusable bags	Difference
4	5.35	5.30	−0.05
8	14.23	13.15	−1.08
16	31.98	32.75	+0.77
32	73.73	79.28	+5.55
48	124.97	114.22	−10.75

The results show little difference in transaction times for single-use bags compared with reusable bags. As a result of this experiment, Henty strongly suggests that governments introduce a levy on single-use plastic bags to encourage further use of green bags.[60]

Required

(a) If you were designing or conducting this experimental process, what concerns might you have about the results being considered representative of the true situation being investigated?

(b) What other sustainable management practices might supermarkets employ to decrease waste?

21.23 Environmental decision making — Environment Aotearoa and 'dirty dairying' in New Zealand   **LO1, 2**

In October 2015, Statistics New Zealand published the first comprehensive and independent report on the state of the country's environment. This provided information on five 'domains' — air, atmosphere and climate, fresh water, land, and marine. The report was the first in a three-yearly cycle that reports on one domain every six months and provides a combined, comprehensive picture once every three years.

At the time of its release the Minister for Statistics, Craig Foss, stated:

> This is the first comprehensive report on New Zealand's environment produced by Statistics New Zealand. It puts into practice the maxim that you manage what you measure. Robust, independent financial reporting has helped achieve significant improvements in New Zealand's financial management and our ambition is to achieve the same for the environment.[61]

Similarly, the Minister for the Environment, Nick Smith, explained:

> New Zealand's environment is so important to our quality of life, our successful exporting industries and our nation's brand that we need robust, independent reporting. It enables us to know where we match up, what areas need more attention, and helps us figure out what we need to do about problem areas.[62]

As the country's population increases, its economy develops and lifestyles change, pressures on its natural resources grow. For example, there have been longstanding issues associated with dairy farming polluting rivers, referred to as 'dirty dairying', with at least 151 prosecutions over a four-year period from July 2008 to June 2012 involving 300 charges for unlawful discharges of dairy effluent.[63] Regular and independent monitoring of the state of those resources is a first and vital step towards stopping, and hopefully reversing, further degradation.

Required

(a) With the use of online data, search for evidence that the dairy industry in New Zealand is working to prevent 'dirty dairying'.

(b) Is it possible for you to know the conditions under which the products you purchase are produced? Why?

(c) Is it possible for managers of a dairy cooperative, such as Fonterra, to know with certainty that their outsource partners comply with agreed-upon working conditions? Why?

21.24 Performance evaluation and sustainability balanced scorecard LO2, 4

Refer to comprehensive example 3 and search online for more details about these disasters. Could a performance measurement system be useful in mitigating disasters such as these? Is there any way management accounting could provide useful early warning signals for senior management operating in large decentralised organisations such as these?

21.25 Performance evaluation and sustainability balanced scorecard LO4, 5

Brewster House is a not-for-profit shelter for the homeless. Lately, funding has decreased but the demand for overnight shelter has increased. In cold weather, clients are turned away because the shelter is full. The director believes that the current capacity could be used more efficiently. No one has taken time to analyse the physical layout of the shelter and current use of space. Several rooms are used for storage that could probably be used for temporary housing. The stored boxes need to be sorted and moved. Volunteers currently assign beds and manage overnight housing, because the director is busy with fundraising. Volunteers work just a few shifts each week, so no one has taken responsibility for coordinating improvements in the services offered. The director is considering whether to implement a balanced scorecard to focus the attention of all volunteers on areas that need improvement.

Brewster receives funds from several sources, including a set annual budget from the local council and direct donations from supporters. The director develops a budget each year based on expected funding but she cannot precisely predict donations. The budget is used primarily to justify funding requests submitted to the council.

The director has asked a group of accounting students from the local university to evaluate operations and recommend whether the entity should develop a balanced scorecard. She cannot give bonuses based on the measures, but she wonders whether developing and monitoring performance measures would encourage the volunteers to increase the use of capacity. She also wonders whether some information from the balanced scorecard could be used to show donors the effectiveness of the operations in achieving social goals.

Required

(a) Describe how the balanced scorecard could be developed to help demonstrate the social sustainability goals.

(b) Provide details of sustainability-related measures for each scorecard perspective you have designed for Brewster House.

(c) What issues would Brewster House management have to overcome to ensure a change in practice?

21.26 Sustainability; outsourcing; monitoring measures   LO5

To reduce costs and focus on core competencies, many entities are increasingly outsourcing manufacturing activities to vendors in countries having low labour costs such as China, India, Thailand, Indonesia and Mexico. Certain activists claim that this practice is socially irresponsible. They claim that numerous factory problems in low-cost countries include excessive work hours, poverty wages, toxic gas releases and harassment of union organisers.[64] The problems were exacerbated after the collapse of a garment factory in Bangladesh resulting in 1137 deaths and 2500 injuries. As a result, 41 people, including the building's owner, were charged with murder or culpable homicide. Such conditions have prompted individuals and organisations to reconsider their purchasing habits and policies.

However, some people argued that boycotts against certain companies cause more harm than good; workers who were already poor often lost their jobs, and unionisation efforts and other improvements were hindered.[65] They suggest it is difficult for companies to adequately monitor working conditions at outsource locations. Workers were often afraid to talk to inspectors, and they sometimes provided inaccurate information. For example, they sometimes erroneously said that they were not paid overtime because they did not understand how their pay was calculated. In the Bangladesh case, it was found that the owner and managers of the garment factory had forced the workers to enter the building on the day of the accident despite major cracks appearing on the building a day earlier.[66]

Required

(a) Describe whether and how sustainability management practices (that is, business practices related to human rights, labour standards and the environment) affect your decisions as a consumer.

(b) Is it possible for you to know the conditions under which the products you purchase are produced? Why?

(c) Is it possible for managers of companies that retail the final products to know with certainty that their outsource partners comply with agreed-upon working conditions? Why?

(d) Would the inclusion of compliance monitoring costs in its purchasing decision process help?

(e) Identify and explain four measures that a company could use to monitor worker conditions in outsource factories. For each measure, describe how the company might collect reliable data.

(f) How should entities weigh corporate social responsibility and profits when deciding whether or how to outsource manufacturing? Describe the values you use in drawing your conclusions.

21.27 Ethical decision making — promoting inappropriate uses of ABC   LO2, 4

When activity-based costing was first developed, consultants sometimes promoted it for inappropriate uses. Many consulting services focused on using ABC information for short-term decisions, such as pricing and product emphasis. Yet in the early stages of ABC and activity-based management development, both flexible and committed costs were included in ABC cost pools and were not tracked separately. As a result, ABC unit costs included both fixed and variable costs, even when the fixed costs were irrelevant for decision making. ABC promoters suggested that all costs were variable in the long run, and they ignored criticism of their methods.

If ABC cost rates include fixed costs, their unquestioned use in setting prices is detrimental to operations. If demand falls then production volumes might fall too, causing costs per unit to increase followed by increases in prices. This type of pricing policy can lead to a death spiral, in which prices increase inappropriately as volumes decline.

After ABC was developed, it was quickly added to cost accounting curriculums at many different universities. However, a few academics were highly critical of ABC and eventually provided evidence that overhead costs included a large portion of fixed costs, even in the long run.[67] As research evidence accumulated, ABC consultants advised entities not to allocate facility-level costs and to categorise costs within each activity cost pool as flexible and committed. Then total costs could be used to analyse processes and improve operations, but flexible cost information could be retrieved for decision making.

Currently, 'incremental ABC cost analysis' services are being promoted. These services are sometimes called predictive accounting. Because consulting services can be expensive and judging the outcome of new ideas difficult, managers need to incorporate healthy scepticism when considering the potential costs and benefits of products and services promoted by consultants.[68]

Required

What ethical problems might arise for managers when considering the use of consultants to develop ABC techniques for sustainability opportunities? Your answers should relate to the promotion of ABC for pricing, other short-term decisions, and incremental ABC or predictive accounting relating to sustainability opportunities. You should also consider the potential for consultant bias and whether the technique will benefit the client, particularly when the consulting service might have uncertain outcomes.

21.28 Sustainability and job costing in a service sector   **LO1, 4**

Green and Greener Co., a law firm specialising in environmental litigation, had the following costs last year:

Direct professional labour	$15 000 000
Overhead	21 000 000
Total costs	$36 000 000

The following costs were included in overhead:

Fringe benefits for direct professional labour	$ 5 000 000
Paralegal costs	2 700 000
Telephone call time with clients (estimated but not tabulated)	600 000
Computer time	1 800 000
Photocopying	900 000
Total overhead	$11 000 000

The entity recently improved its ability to document and trace costs to individual cases. Revised bookkeeping procedures now allow it to trace fringe benefit costs for direct professional labour, paralegal costs, telephone charges, computer time and photocopying costs to each case individually. The managing partner needs to decide whether more costs other than just direct professional labour should be traced directly to jobs to allow the entity to better justify billings to clients.

During the last year, more costs were traced to client engagements. Two of the case records showed the following:

	Client cases	
	875	876
Direct professional labour	$20 000	$20 000
Fringe benefits for direct labour	3 000	3 000
Secretarial costs	2 000	6 000
Computer time	2 000	4 000
Photocopying	1 000	2 000
Total costs	$29 000	$37 000

Three methods are being considered for allocating overhead this year:

- Method 1: Allocate overhead based on direct professional labour cost. Calculate the allocation rate using last year's direct professional labour costs of $15 million and overhead costs of $21 million.
- Method 2: Allocate overhead based on direct professional labour cost. Calculate the allocation rate using last year's direct professional labour costs of $15 million and overhead costs of $10 million ($21 million less $11 million in direct costs that are traced this year).
- Method 3: Allocate the $10 million overhead based on total direct costs. Calculate the allocation rate using last year's direct costs (professional labour of $15 million plus other direct costs of $11 million).

Required

(a) Calculate the overhead allocation rate for method 1.
(b) Calculate the overhead allocation rate for method 2.
(c) Calculate the overhead allocation rate for method 3.
(d) Using each of the three rates calculated in parts (a), (b) and (c), calculate the total costs of cases 875 and 876.
(e) Explain why the total costs allocated to cases 875 and 876 are not the same under the three methods.

(f) Explain why method 1 would be inappropriate.

(g) Would method 2 or method 3 be better? Explain.

(h) Explain how professional service entities (like law firms) might engage in sustainability practices.

21.29 Ethical decision making — inappropriate allocation of underapplied overhead[69]   **LO2, 3, 4**

The Australian government has contracted with alternative energy industry organisations to develop new energy technologies. These contracts are sometimes based on cost. Because these organisations are also developing technologies for non-government entities, incentives exist to shift overhead costs to the government so that commercial operations become more competitive. Because cost allocations are private information, research provides only indirect evidence that this cost shifting occurs. The following vignette is fictional, but it illustrates potential ethical problems that arise when governments use cost-based contracts for product development.

Deep Water Hydro is a hydroelectricity energy company that focuses on innovative research and development solutions for alternative energy supply for both commercial and government agencies. Because one of its commercial contracts fell through last year, the entity had fewer jobs than anticipated. Consequently, the company's overhead costs were underapplied at the end of the year, so an adjustment was made to increase cost of sales.

Deep Water's policy is to allocate production overhead as a percentage of direct labour costs for each contract. One of the government contracts completed last year was to develop a hydro-electricity generator that would supply energy from seawater entering Port Philip Bay in Melbourne. The job contract was based on cost-plus-fixed-fee for a total cost of $245 million. The hydroelectricity project was Deep Water's only government contract last year. Commercial business completed was $105 million, so cost of sales totalled $350 million.

Disagreement about underapplied overhead adjustment

The government official in charge of the contract complained to the federal contract auditor that Deep Water's underapplied overhead should not have been closed to cost of sales. Instead, he argued that it should have been allocated on a pro rata basis among the contracts in progress, finished goods and cost of sales. The auditor asked to see the cost accounting records and financial statements for the period.

The $350 million in cost of sales included $245 million for the government contract. When the underapplied overhead ($100 million) was closed to cost of sales, the government portion of underapplied overhead was $70 million [$100 × ($245 ÷ $350)]. Because the contract specified that the government would pay costs plus a fixed amount, the overhead adjustment effectively increased the revenue under the contract by $70 million.

Following is an analysis of the direct costs and cost allocations (in millions).

	Contracts in progress	Finished goods inventory	Cost of sales	Total work on jobs this period
Direct materials used	$250	$50	$100	$400
Direct labour	92	8	50	150
Overhead allocated	184	16	100	300
Total before adjustment	526	74	250	850
Add:				
Underapplied overhead	0	0	100	100
Total after adjustment	$526	$74	$350	$950

Actual direct labour costs were $150 million, and the pre-adjustment allocated overhead was $300 million. Therefore, the original allocation rate was 200 per cent ($300 ÷ $150) of direct labour cost. Total actual overhead turned out to be $400 million (the $300 million plus the $100 million underapplied). If Deep Water accountants could have perfectly estimated overhead at $400 million and direct labour cost at $150 million, they would have used 267 per cent ($400 ÷ $150) as the allocation rate.

The underapplied overhead amount was material ($100 million out of $400 million, or 25 per cent). Therefore, the government auditor decided that it should have been allocated on a pro rata basis among the three accounts that reflected work done this period: contracts in progress, finished goods and cost of sales. Had this method been used, the adjustment would have been allocated as follows:

	(millions)
Contracts in progress ($526 million ÷ $850 million) × $100 million	$ 61.9
Finished goods ($74 million ÷ $850 million) × $100 million	8.7
Cost of sales ($250 million ÷ $850 million) × $100 million	29.4
Total adjustment	$100.0

The government's share of the cost of sales adjustment would be ($245 ÷ $350) × $29.4 million equals $20.6 million. When the auditor compared this to the original adjustment of $70 million, she knew the government had been overcharged.

Alternative methods for allocating overapplied or underapplied overhead

The auditor offered Deep Water three alternatives for allocating the overhead adjustment. Under governmental contracts, underapplied overhead could be allocated based on direct materials cost, direct labour cost or total direct costs. If Deep Water uses direct materials, cost of sales is increased by $25 million, of which the government portion is $17.5 million. If direct labour cost is used, cost of sales is increased by $33.3 million, of which the government portion is $23.3 million. If total direct cost is used, cost of sales is increased by $27.3 million, of which the government portion is $20.1 million.

The government and Deep Water must now negotiate to determine the most appropriate proration method.

Required

(a) Is allocating proportionately more cost to government contracts an ethical problem for Deep Water? Why?

(b) When the government pays more than commercial customers pay for work done, does this situation pose a business problem, a social problem or both? Explain.

(c) Discuss the preferences of various stakeholders for this problem, including:
- managers
- shareholders
- commercial customers
- governmental customers
- competitors
- Australian taxpayers.

(d) Is it fair for the government to pay more for products and services than commercial customers pay? Is it fair for taxes to subsidise the overhead costs for a private business?

(e) How can an entity monitor whether its accounting practices are ethical?

21.30 Ethical decision making; timely reporting of sustainability budget problems   **LO2, 5**

A dilemma that individuals face is whether to be truthful when it appears that a project is over budget. Being over budget typically means that actual costs exceed budgeted costs or that a planned timeline will not be met. People often delay reporting an over-budget condition either because they believe they can catch up later or because they wish to delay negative repercussions. Unfortunately, information delays prevent managers from responding rapidly and decisively to delays in project timing and cost overruns, leading to additional dissatisfaction and inefficiencies.

Suppose an energy company establishes a budget of professional hours for a particular sustainability audit job. The hours are broken down by audit area, with one area being the valuation of 'clean energy' inventory and cost of sales. During the last year, the audit client adopted new procedures for assigning product costs to individual units. The audit budget includes extra hours for the estimated time needed to document and assess the reasonableness of the new method.

Many factors could cause this part of the audit to be over budget. Consider the following two scenarios.

1. The client failed to establish appropriate records needed to easily audit the new method, and this part of the audit will require more than the budgeted time to complete.

2. The auditor assigned to this part of the audit is inexperienced and is unable to complete the work in the budgeted time.

Regardless of the reason for the overage, managers in charge of the audit need to be notified as soon as possible so that they can consider possible ways to realign staff and complete the total job on time. In addition, in the first scenario the audit entity might be able to bill the client for the extra work involved if the audit contract includes a provision for such price adjustments.

However, this scenario would most likely require the client to be notified promptly, while the work is still being performed. In the second scenario, the overage may result in a poor performance evaluation, especially if the auditor has similar problems in other audit areas. Yet the overage might be considered reasonable in light of the auditor's inexperience. Even so, the auditor should be able to accomplish the following:

- develop alternative estimates of time and resource requirements for a project
- effectively facilitate and control the project process and take corrective action as needed.

Therefore, the auditor must quickly recognise an impending overage and formulate appropriate strategies for completing the task as efficiently as possible. The auditor also needs to keep her supervisor apprised of the situation and seek help, when needed.

Required

(a) Have you ever failed to meet a deadline on a group project? If so, what were the reasons for the delay? When and how did you report the delay to your team members? Has someone you know failed to meet a deadline? Does a failure to meet an agreed-upon deadline create an ethical problem? Why?

(b) Explore the responsibilities, expectations, assumptions, incentives and consequences for this problem from different perspectives, including:
- the team member who is late
- other team members
- the team's client.

(c) Draft a policy statement that you could adopt with future team members to handle project delays. How might this policy lead to improved team performance?

(d) Think about your future career. How can you work towards developing your professional responsibility as a member of a work team?

21.31 Ethical decision making — wasted soup   **LO2**

While she was watching operations at a food processing plant, a consultant noticed a large amount of soup on the floor under a filling machine. An operator washed this soup away each day. When asked about the loss of soup, the production manager replied that no losses occurred. In this manager's view, no problem existed because the production line operating costs were below budgeted costs. Later, a productivity team analysed the amount of soup wasted over a given time period. The team estimated the cost of the leak to be $750 000 a year. To correct the problem, the plant installed a set of valves costing $50 000. The new valves eliminated the loss of soup.

Instead of measuring performance against expected budget levels, managers could compare actual profits to ideal profits that could be earned if operations were to run at their true potential. By focusing on the gap between ideal and actual profits, managers are encouraged to identify lost profit potential and to reconsider critical processes. Once gaps are identified, managers rank them according to their value to the organisation and correct them in priority order.

Required

(a) Is it an ethical problem when employees observe inefficiencies in the workplace, such as the loss of soup in this case? Why?

(b) Why is it common for employees to do nothing when they observe inefficiencies? Compare the responsibility of operation workers to the responsibility of the operating manager with respect to identifying and correcting inefficiencies. In what ways are the responsibilities the same? In what ways are they different?

(c) Is it ethical for employees to ignore inefficiencies? Why? What values did you use to arrive at the conclusion?

(d) People do not always seek to achieve their best performance. For example, students sometimes apply minimum effort to achieve a targeted grade. What does it mean for individuals to seek continuous improvement?

21.32 Environmental accounting reports; ABC and ABM for environmental costs   **LO1, 2, 3, 4**

Many countries provide motivation for entities to produce environmental accounting reports. For example, 17 countries — United Kingdom, Denmark, Netherlands, Belgium, France and Germany among others — participate in the European Sustainability Reporting Awards program. In Japan, the Global Environmental Forum and the National Association for the Promotion of Environmental Conservation have given Environmental Report Awards since 1997. In addition, Tokyo Keizai and the Green Reporting Forum have given a Green Reporting Award since 1998. These awards encourage organisations to take responsibility for environmental conditions that affect the wellbeing of society as a whole. Visy Industries in Australia has also been recognised by similar Australian sustainability awards programs.

You are required to conduct research about corporate environmental disclosures. Choose one company located in Japan and a competitor located in Australia. Go to each company's website and search for information about its environmental policies and procedures. Also conduct research to find governmental guidelines for environmental accounting. Go to the website of the Environmental Protection Authority in your region and search for information about environmental or sustainability accounting. Now perform a similar search on the website of Japan's Ministry of the Environment (www.env.go.jp/en). Skim through the information that you find on each website.

In its Environmental Accounting Guidelines, Japan's Ministry of the Environment identified the following environmental conservation cost categories:

Content	Category
Business area cost	• Environmental conservation cost to control environmental impacts resulting from key business operations within the business area
Upstream/downstream cost	• Environmental conservation cost to control environmental impacts resulting from key business operations upstream or downstream
Administration cost	• Environmental conservation cost stemming from administrative activities
R&D cost	• Environmental conservation cost stemming from R&D activities
Social activity cost	• Environmental conservation cost stemming from social activities
Environmental remediation cost	• Cost incurred for dealing with environmental degradation
Other costs	• Other costs related to environmental conservation

Required

(a) Is environmental accounting an ethical issue? Why?

(b) Which company provides the easiest-to-find and most understandable information about environmental policies and procedures? Explain.

(c) Discuss a company's responsibilities for reporting environmental information to various stakeholders including shareholders, managers, employees, other companies, government regulators, product customers and the general public.

(d) If one company provides better reporting than a competitor of its environmental behaviour, policies and procedures, does this mean that the company is more environmentally responsible than its competitor? Why?

(e) What factors are likely to affect an entity's willingness to publish an environmental accounting report?

(f) Discuss possible reasons why the governments of different countries place different degrees of emphasis on environmental accounting reports.

(g) Discuss ways in which ABC systems could be used to capture information for environmental accounting reports.

(h) Discuss ways in which the process of preparing and publishing an environmental accounting report is likely to help a company reduce its environmental costs.

(i) Should all governments require companies to publish environmental accounting reports? What values did you use to arrive at your conclusion?

21.33 Ethical decision making: the right thing to do[70]   **LO2**

In the past, drug makers have been reluctant to invest in cures for diseases in developing countries such as Africa and South America. Most people in these countries cannot afford to pay for treatments, and managers have typically invested in other long-term projects having higher returns. However, a few pharmaceutical companies have chosen to invest in neglected diseases, including tuberculosis, malaria and other tropical diseases. As an example, GlaxoSmithKline formed a joint venture with the World Health Organization to develop a malaria drug that costs less than 50 cents for a three-day treatment.

This type of investment has several goals. From a reputation perspective, managers accused of keeping drug prices artificially high may believe that providing low-cost cures will alleviate pressure from regulators and consumers to lower prices for drugs sold in the United States and other developed countries. Furthermore, people from some less-developed countries will eventually have the ability to pay for cures. Finally, 'it is the right thing to do,' according to journalist Robert Langreth. Novartis chairman Daniel Vasella says, 'If you only look at maximizing short-term profit, you may not survive in the long term'.

Required

Using figure 21.7, address the following question for this ethical dilemma to improve your skills in making ethical decisions. Think about your answers to these questions and discuss them with others: Does an ethical problem arise if pharmaceutical companies charge lower prices for drugs in developing countries than in developed countries? Why?

ENDNOTES

1. United Nations Division for Sustainable Development, www.un.org/esa/sustdev.
2. United Nations Sustainable Development Goals, https://www.un.org/sustainabledevelopment/sustainable-development-goals/.
3. UK Office of Climate Change 2006, *The Stern Review on the Economics of Climate Change*, www.sternreview.org.uk.
4. International Carbon Action Partnership (ICAP), *Emissions Trading Worldwide Status Report 2018*, https://icapcarbonaction.com/en/?option=com_attach&task=download&id=547.
5. Murray, C, Newell, R & Pizer, W 2009, 'Balancing cost and emissions certainty: an allowance reserve for cap-and-trade', *Review of Environmental Economics and Policy*, vol. 3, iss. 1, Winter, pp. 84–103.
6. Adapted from Murray, C, Newell, R & Pizer, W 2009, pp. 84–5.
7. International Carbon Action Partnership (ICAP), *Emissions Trading Worldwide Status Report 2018*, https://icapcarbonaction.com/en/?option=com_attach&task=download&id=547.
8. See Renewable Energy Group 2007, *Renewable energy country attractiveness indices, Q2 2007*, Ernst & Young, www.ey.com.
9. Australian Nuclear Science and Technology Organisation 2010, www.ansto.gov.au.
10. Accounting for Sustainability, www.accountingforsustainability.org.
11. International Integrated Reporting Council, http://integratedreporting.org.
12. Figge, F, Hahn, T, Schaltegger, S & Wagner, M 2002, 'The sustainability balanced scorecard — linking sustainability management to business strategy', *Business Strategy and the Environment*, Wiley InterScience, www.interscience.wiley.com.
13. Australian Government Department of Climate Change and Energy Efficiency 2010, National carbon offset standard (NCOS), p. iii, www.climatechange.gov.au.
14. Australian Government Department of the Environment 2015, 'Tracking Australia's greenhouse gas emissions', www.environment.gov.au.
15. The FullCAM accounting model is not discussed in detail here. For further details refer to the NCOS standard.
16. Australian Government Department of Climate Change and Energy Efficiency 2010, p. iii.
17. Alcoa 2015, 'Alcoa in Australia', www.alcoa.com/australia.
18. Australian Aluminium Council Ltd 2015, 'Aluminium smelting greenhouse performance', aluminium.org.au.
19. Alumina Limited, Sustainability update 2017, http://www.aluminalimited.com/emissions/.
20. International Organization for Standardization (ISO) is an international body of technical standards for various industries. The precise guidelines of ISO provide a long-term economic benefit for businesses that chose to implement them. In manufacturing, ISO 9000 quality standards are universally accepted and the newer ISO 14000 standards for the environment are now catching on (www.isostandardsguide.com). ISO 14001 was first released in 1996 and specifies the actual requirements for an entity's environmental management system in which it can be expected to have an influence.
21. Chua, WF 2006, 'Extended performance reporting: a review of empirical studies', Institute of Chartered Accountants in Australia.
22. We will use the term 'sustainability management accounting' to refer to both social and environmental management accounting. Many earlier texts refer only to 'environmental accounting' concepts. While these terms tend to be used interchangeably by some authors, note that in this book we consider the scope of sustainability management accounting to include both the 'private' as well as the 'societal' impact. Earlier environmental management accounting books tend to consider only the 'private' costs and benefits — those that are traditionally accounted for within the entity's accounting system. More recent trends (driven in part by external reporting requirements) are towards including social and environmental, private and societal sustainability management.
23. Chartered Institute of Management Accountants (CIMA) 2009, 'Enterprise Governance and Climate Change', European Network for Research on Accounting Change (ENROAC) conference, Dundee.
24. Adapted from Pohjola, T 2005, 'Application of an environmental modelling system', in PM Rikhardsson et al. (eds), *Implementing management accounting*, pp. 169–92.
25. These companies are just a few of the growing number of entities that produce special social, environmental, sustainability or triple bottom line reports to promote their activities to their shareholders and the wider community.
26. See Gray, RH 2000, 'Current development and trends in social and environmental auditing, reporting and attestation: a review and comment', *International Journal of Auditing*, vol 4, pp. 247–68; Deegan, C 2002, 'The legitimising effect of social and environmental disclosures — a theoretical foundation', *Accounting, Auditing & Accountability Journal*, vol. 15,

no. 3, pp. 282–311; O'Donovan, G 2002, 'Environmental disclosures in the annual report: extending the applicability and predictive power of legitimacy theory', *Accounting, Auditing & Accountability Journal*, vol. 15, no. 3, pp. 344–71; Nue, D, Warsame, H & Pedwell, K 1998, 'Managing public impressions: environmental disclosures in annual reports', *Accounting, Organisations and Society*, vol. 23, no 3, pp. 265–82.

27. Chua, WF 2006, p. 10.
28. For example, refer to publications from the Environmental and Sustainability Management Accounting Network, www.eman-eu.net.
29. International Integrated Reporting Council 2013, *The international <IR> framework*, www.theiirc.org, pp. 12–13.
30. International Federation of Accountants 2004, *Enterprise governance: getting the balance right*, February, www.ifac.org; Adapted from CIMA (2009) 'Embedding sustainability into Strategy', European Network for Research in Organisational & Accounting Change (ENROAC) Conference, Dundee.
31. Adapted from International Federation of Accountants 2004.
32. Figge et al. (2002), p. 278.
33. For further discussion on the definitions of strategic risk, refer to Simons, R 2000, *Performance measurement and control systems for implementing strategy*, 1st edition, Prentice Hall, chapters 12–13.
34. Hotten, R 2015, 'Volkswagen: the scandal explained', *BBC News*, 4 November, www.bbc.com.
35. ABC News 2015, 'Brazil dam burst: mine owners BHP, Vale tour devastation as new evacuations ordered over fears for third dam', ABC News, 12 November, www.abc.net.au.
36. Rush, D 2015, 'Deepwater Horizon: BP got "punishment it deserved" Loretta Lynch says', *The Guardian*, 6 October, www.theguardian.com.
37. Information from Mellish, M 2007, 'Santos clean up bill higher than feared', *The Australian Financial Review*, 8 February, p. 19.
38. Information from the United States Environmental Protection Agency 1995, *An introduction to environmental accounting as a business management tool: key concepts and terms*, Washington, June.
39. Information from United States Environmental Protection Agency 1995, p. 6.
40. Schategger, S & Burritt, R 2000, *Contemporary environmental accounting: issues, concepts and practice*, Greenleaf Publications, Sheffield, UK.
41. Environmental Protection Authority (EPA Victoria), www.epa.vic.gov.au.
42. Adapted from Jasch, C 2003, 'The use of environmental management accounting (EMA) for identifying environmental costs', *Journal of Cleaner Production*, vol. 11, p. 674.
43. This information has been adapted from United Nations Division for Sustainable Development 2001.
44. United Nations Division for Sustainable Development 2001, 'Environmental management accounting procedures and principles', prepared for the Expert Working Group on 'Improving the role of government in the promotion of environmental management accounting', New York, p. 108.
45. Refer to the introduction of Kaplan and Norton's 1996 text, Kaplan, R & Norton, D 1996, *The balanced scorecard*, Harvard Business School Press; also Kaplan & Norton 2001, *The strategy-focused organisation*, Harvard Business School Press.
46. See Figge et al. 2002 for further discussion on the sustainability balanced scorecard.
47. Lipe, M & Salterio, S 2000, 'The balanced scorecard: judgemental effects of common and unique performance measures', *The Accounting Review*, vol. 75, no. 3, pp. 283–98.
48. Figge et al. 2002.
49. ibid.
50. ibid.
51. Figge et al. 2002, p. 279.
52. Information from Hunting, SA & Tilbury, D 2006, 'Shifting towards sustainability: six insights into successful organisational change for sustainability', Australian Research Institute in Education for Sustainability (ARIES) for the Australian Government Department of the Environment, Water, Heritage and the Arts, Sydney, www.aries.mq.edu.au and www.environment.gov.au.
53. In the past, successful implementation of management accounting innovations has been commonly divided into 'technical' and 'behavioural' issues (see Chenhall & Langfield-Smith 1998; Young 1998; Shields 1998). This book takes a similar approach when considering the change towards sustainability practices within entities.
54. See Figge et al. 2002, p. 273.
55. Accounting for Sustainability 2013, '10 main steps to integrated thinking', www.accountingforsustainability.org.
56. Vesty, G, Brooks, A & Oliver, J 2015, 'Contemporary capital investment appraisal from a management accounting and integrated thinking perspective: case study evidence', *Sustainability and capital investment case studies*, CPA Australia, cpaaustralia.com.au, p. 59.
57. AMR 2015, 'Australia's most reputable company is Toyota again', media release, www.amr-australia.com.
58. See www.wci-coal.com.
59. Henty, J 2007, *Supermarket bag packing: a comparative time trial*, Environment Victoria, February, www.envict.org.au.
60. ibid.
61. New Zealand Government 2015, 'Environment Aotearoa 2015 report welcomed', media release, 21 October, Hon Dr Nick Smith, Minister for the Environment & Hon Craig Foss, Minister of Statistics.
62. ibid.
63. Sharpe, M 2012, 'Dirty dairying laid bare', *The Dominion Post*, 5 June.
64. Connor, T 2001, 'Still waiting for Nike to respect the right to organize,' *Global Exchange*, 28 June, available at www.corpwatch.org; 'Just stop it,' the NikeWatch Campaign, available at the Oxfam Australia website, www.caa.org.au/campaigns/nike.
65. ibid.
66. 'Sweatshop wars,' *Economist.com*, 25 February 1999.

67. Pownall, G 1986, 'An empirical analysis of the regulation of the defense contracting industry: the Cost Accounting Standards Board,' *Journal of Accounting Research*, vol. 24, no. 2, pp. 291–316.

68. Noreen E & Soderstrom, N 1994, 'Are overhead costs strictly proportional to activity? Evidence from hospital service departments,' *Journal of Accounting & Economics*, January, pp. 255–279.

69. Adapted from Pownall 1986.

70. Based on Langreth R 2002, 'A cure for neglect', *Forbes*, 18 March.

ACKNOWLEDGEMENTS

Photo 21A: © Jacob_09 / Shutterstock.com

Photo 21B: © acilo / Getty Images

Photo 21C: © Yulia Grigoryeva / Shutterstock.com

Photo 21D: © John Panella / Shutterstock.com

Photo 21E: © Marcin Balcerzak / Shutterstock.com

Figure 21.1: From 'United Nations Sustainable Development Goals', by United Nations, © 2019 United Nations. Reprinted with the permission of the United Nations.

Figure 21.12: © EPA Victoria

Figure 21.14: From 'Sustainability capital budgeting sheet', by United Nations, © 2019 United Nations. Reprinted with the permission of the United Nations.

Figure 21.17: © The Prince's Accounting for Sustainability Project A4S

Figure 21.18: © CPA Australia

Figure 21.4: © KPMG

Figure 21.8: © Elsevier

Extract 21A: © Environment Victoria

INDEX